MOZART

Also by Robert W. Gutman

Richard Wagner: The Man, His Mind, and His Music

ROBERT W. GUTMAN

MOZART

A CULTURAL BIOGRAPHY

Harcourt Brace & Company
New York   San Diego   London

Requests for permission to make copies of any part of the work should
be mailed to the following address: Permissions Department,
Harcourt, Inc., 6277 Sea Harbor Drive, Orlando, Florida 32887-6777.

Frontispiece: Saverio dalla Rosa's portrait of Mozart
in Verona at almost fourteen. *Courtesy of Corbis/Bettman.*

Library of Congress Cataloging-in-Publication Data
Gutman, Robert W.
Mozart: a cultural biography/Robert W. Gutman.
p.   cm.
Includes bibliographical references (p. 758) and index.
ISBN 0-15-100482-X
1. Mozart, Wolfgang Amadeus, 1756–1791.   2. Composers—Austria
Biography.   I. Title.
ML410.M9G96   1999
780′.92—dc21   99-31953

Designed by Lori McThomas Buley
Text set in Centaur MT
Printed in the United States of America
First edition
A C E D B

To the memory of Ted Hart

Frühling, Sommer und Herbst genoss der glückliche Dichter;
Vor dem Winter hat ihn endlich der Hügel geschützt.

—Goethe, "Anakreon's Grab"

Ich schreite kaum,
doch wähn' ich mich schon weit.

—Wagner, *Parsifal*

This is no mortal business, nor no sound
That the earth owes.

—Shakespeare, *The Tempest*

CONTENTS

CONTENTS

PREFACE

F ROM THE TIME of Mozart's death, the public became rooted in prejudices and misapprehensions concerning his life. Only in recent
decades did earnest efforts begin to eradicate from his biography the large
and seductive stock of supposititious and distorting legends, both devotional and defaming, that had achieved the authority repetition bestows:
most of the anecdotes about him have this kind of promiscuous pedigree.
Moreover, not unlike attitudes of mind that long surrounded Shelley and
reduced this "greatest radical voice in poetry since Lucretius" to the status
of Matthew Arnold's "beautiful and ineffectual angel, beating in the void
his luminous wings in vain," the prevailing view of Mozart's works, though
it seldom failed in tributes to his lyric gifts—his own "luminous wings"—
long continued unmindful of the spiritual depth and moral dimension of
his art. If today this aesthetic undervaluation has given way to clearer perceptions—in fact, his artistic reputation now carries all before it—biographical myths, quite otherwise, take an unconscionable time dying.

The temptation to equate the art of a genius with the life well lived
must for the most part be resisted as vain; however, when the parallel does,
as here, show forth triumphantly, it should be celebrated. The decades I
have passed studying Mozart have rich recompense in both acquaintance
with and loving admiration for this affectionate and generous man, an austere moralist of vital force, incisiveness, and strength of purpose who,

though—like all—bearing the blame of faults and lapses, yet played his role in the human comedy with honor, engaging with grace the frustrations of his complicated existence: his goodness of heart, unaffected charm, winning ways, and self-humor run like gorgeous threads through its web.

His biography and his creations receive my simultaneous attention, for Mozart's career took shape and meaning from the preoccupations of the mind with the works even as he responded to the spirit of his times. This full-scale study thus places him against the flow of his era's intellectual, political, and artistic currents as well as its daily routines, its domestic ways. However, the name of Mozart informs these excursions into cultural, musical, and traditional history: during their course, the reader will seldom lose sight of him. Though the nonspecialist may pass over these chapters without loss of biographical continuity, yet, inasmuch as they either eschew or explain technical terms, I hope that few will make such a jump carrying the cost of wider perceptions. My ambition has been to provide a comprehensive one-volume biography of Mozart combined with historical-critical discussions of his works, the essential purpose being to present him to both layman and connoisseur in terms of ideas, of cultural history.

By nature biography, like memory, is selective: it sets apart a corpus of facts and plausible conjectures and chooses a structure in which to house them, one calling to mind the workings of a kaleidoscope, its essential element the instability of a store of data that, though constant, yet can undergo instant transformation; but rotate the instrument and the same pieces of colored glass, turn by turn, will vary themselves into new patterns, the angled mirrors in the tube, moreover, providing images of reassuring symmetry and defining contours. For biographers—most of them hold such elements of design dear—the realigning of materials into fresh and balanced configurations offers rich possibilities (and, indeed, temptations). The discovery of new material, however, calls, not for a twist, but for reconstructing the very stock of data; thus, even while manipulating his elected paradigms and inflections, the biographer must remain ever aware of the protean nature of his craft, the precariousness of his efforts: his worktable rests upon a shaky floor; no one writes the last word.

Two schedules appear toward the end of these pages, one providing the sources of the quotations, the other a bibliography selected from the body of scholarship upon which this volume rests and to which it hopes to contribute. Though its debt to a host of distinguished Mozarteans will be obvious to those acquainted with this vast literature, the reader will nonetheless discover more than one unaccustomed interpretation of familiar documents and incidents. (After years of immersion in a subject, uncertainty can arise as to whether an idea or turn of phrase is original or has emerged from a corner of the memory.) Sensible of the biographer's responsibility to be more than a chronicler, more than a marshal of ascertainable facts, I nonetheless have guarded against permitting conjecture to cross into romance, in particular when gaps open in the record and one must cast an ever finer net: the text makes clear when supposition comes into play.

I shy from overuse of Christian names in biography. However, here "Wolfgang" seems appropriate to the child and adolescent, the unadorned "Mozart" becoming more frequent as he evolves into the master. This approach, which cannot be outright consistent, leaves his father, alas, answering too often to "Leopold," for which I would like to ask the distinguished gentleman's pardon. (Genial Mama Mozart, I imagine, would take no offense at the persistent "Anna Maria.") All in all, a tasteful resolution of the problem has been the goal.

When rendering foreign proper names and titles pertaining to a work, a rank, or an office, I set consistency aside; ear and custom guide my choice of a particular form: on the one hand, King Frederick, Emperor Francis, Elector Karl Theodore, *The Abduction from the Seraglio,* and *The Marriage of Figaro;* on the other, Kapellmeister Bonno, Titularkapellmeister Fischietti, Francesco Galli da Bibbiena, *Così fan tutte,* and *La clemenza di Tito.* With the few exceptions that add force to the rule, quotations from German, French, Italian, and Latin appear in the author's English, as do all foreign phrases but the most obvious, which remain untranslated. Since scores, recordings, and discs of Mozart's works abound, this book forgoes musical illustrations. Its body stands whole without the numerous footnotes; yet I trust that they enrich the points and arguments they amplify. I assume a general familiarity with the librettos of Mozart's operas from *The Abduction* to *La clemenza.*

Money Matters

THE UNITS OF currency most common in Mozart's world (the Holy Roman Empire) were the pfennig, kreuzer, groschen, gulden or florin (interchangeable terms), thaler (two varieties: reichs and spezies, the last also called konventions), and ducat. Four pfennig made a kreuzer and sixteen groschen a gulden, as did sixty kreuzer; a gulden equaled half a speziesthaler and two-thirds of a reichsthaler; four and a half gulden constituted a ducat (which in Austrian lands came in three varieties slightly less in value: ordinary, imperial, and kremnitz, all on the average worth about four gulden, sixteen kreuzer); the Prussian friedrich d'or amounted to eight gulden, the Austrian souverain d'or to thirteen and a half, the Bavarian max d'or to six and a half, and the south German carolin to nine. As to foreign currency, the French louis d'or (or pistole) stood at seven and a half gulden (twenty-four livres constituted one louis d'or), the Venetian zecchino at five, the doppio (double zecchino) at ten, the English pound sterling and guinea at eight to nine and eleven, respectively. The Italian gigliato converted to a ducat. Values fluctuated—in Germany even from one principality to another: Mozart, for example, insisted that his legacy from his father's estate be discharged in Viennese gulden, at the time (1787) valued at some twenty percent above the rate of exchange for the same coin in Salzburg, where the court of probate sat (see 672).

I hesitate to offer a key to values over against contemporary monies, for to attempt to calculate purchasing power in terms of today is to grasp at nettles. A most general view alone suggests the picture: in a provincial capital like the Salzburg of Mozart's day, an annual income of five hundred gulden could provide a small family with a decent life; in Vienna such a yearly sum could sustain only one person in comfort.

Identification and Dating of Works

IN THIS VOLUME, two numbers most often identify Mozart's compositions, the first taken from Ludwig von Köchel's *Chronological-Thematic Catalogue of the Complete Works of Wolfgang Amadé Mozart* of 1862 (K.^{1}), the second from its sixth and latest completed revision, that of 1964 (K.^{6}). A work bears one number if it is the same in K.^{1} and K.^{6} or if the number in K.^{6} represents an entry not in the first listing (for example, a composition unknown to Herr Köchel). If K.^{6} shifts a work from the appendix (*Anhang*, abbreviated as Anh.) of a preceding edition (for instance, a schedule of compositions at the time believed doubtful or spurious) and into the body of the catalogue, the earlier supplementary number appears first and then that of K.^{6}. Context makes clear why, on occasion, more than two numbers prove necessary. K. *deest* represents a work without, as yet, any Köchel entry but in all likelihood to appear in the latest revision of the catalogue, which, at the moment, moves forward. Since the appearance of K.^{6}, musicological investigation has altered the dates of many of Mozart's compositions, changes this book for the most part reflects. Thus, at times the reader will find its pages at odds with the chronology of K.^{6}. The catalogue in preparation faces Herculean tasks in accommodating such recent scholarship in the course of re-ordering the oeuvre in a system bespeaking, one hopes, simplicity.

THIS BOOK GREW out of a suggestion of William B. Goodman, an editor at Harcourt Brace Jovanovich at the time it published my *Richard Wagner: The Man, His Mind, and His Music* (1968). Through the following years, Bill and his successor, Drenka Willen, encouraged and advised perseverance. Much is owed them as well as other generous spirits: my nephew, David Ferris; my brother, Jeremiah S. Gutman; and Erna Schwerin, a gracious friend and sage colleague in matters Mozartean. Thanks must also go to Richard Burger, Arthur Ganz, Kenneth L. Geist, Wendy Hilton, David Kaufman, Ruth Milberg Kaye, Rita Mathsen, Michael von der Linn, and, in cherished remembrance, Alexander Seldin. Thomas Stowe began the transformation of the author's penciled daubs into computer copy, a task Teresa A. Odden then assumed. That both share an informed love of the English language gave their spontaneous criticisms particular value. Thanks must be expressed to Roberta Leighton, under whose fine editorial eye the preparation of the typescript for printing became an instructive and pleasurable task. I acknowledge my gratitude to the John Simon Guggenheim Memorial Foundation for a Fellowship (1978) freeing me to work in Europe and, moreover, lie under deep obligation to my niece Rebecca Menon and to Kenneth Cooper, the distinguished keyboard master, conductor, and scholar: both read the entire manuscript and offered invaluable comments.

INTRODUCTION

W

HO DOES SHE think she is, not wanting to kiss me? Why, the Empress herself kissed me!" Thus did Wolfgang Mozart, not yet seven and visiting the French court as a keyboard virtuoso, vent his pique upon another accomplished harpsichordist—Madame de Pompadour; after helpfully lifting him, she had drawn back from his effusive embrace. With him in Pompadour's apartments was his pious father, Leopold, who evidently enjoyed his presence in the tents of the ungodly. Critically examining Louis XV's blonde favorite, he found her "handsome" and "well proportioned" but "extremely haughty." Obviously her reserve upset his pampered son, eager for the "excessive praise" (Johann Adolph Hasse's phrase) in which the father smothered him.

Oddly enough, in his outburst Wolfgang pronounced one of the few names with power to awaken a deferential response in the formidable friend of the King. Although the Empress—Maria Theresa of the House of Habsburg—never wrote Pompadour directly, intermediaries kept them in touch. His pride injured, Wolfgang had innocently compared the royal mistress with the Holy Roman Empress, that unlikely pair joined by the expedience of statecraft. The title of Maria Theresa now sounded with unwonted authority in the halls of Versailles, where, not long before, the very word "Habsburg" had been anathema, a new diplomatic attitude that would one day make her daughter Archduchess Maria Antonia Dauphine and then Queen of France.

Less than a year before Mozart's arrival in Paris (November 1763), Maria Antonia had gathered him up after he slipped on the polished floor of her mother's Schönbrunn palace on the edge of Vienna. "You are very kind; I will marry you," tradition alleges he solemnly announced to the musical and pretty girl some three months his senior. (She seems not to have remembered him in later years: not Mozart, but her former singing master, Gluck, for a time became her protégé in Paris.) Two children growing up during the dying age of *galanterie,* they personified the ease, the graceful intimacy of mid-eighteenth-century art, that sensuous and often melancholy world of Boucher and the Van Loos.

At Versailles, Queen Marie Leczinska, the Polish wife of Louis XV, showed no less kindness to Wolfgang. He chattered to her in German, which she, born in Breslau, spoke as a native. At the *Grand' Couvert* (the sovereign's grand repast), Her Majesty translated Master Wolfgang's observations to the sullen King as she passed delicacies from the royal platters to the Mozarts, who stood nearby in a crowd of valets and flunkies.

Amid golden chambers fetid with the stench rising from improvised latrines; amid long corridors rank with the odor of splendidly arrayed, powdered, and unwashed courtiers and servants; amid the fusty magnificence of Versailles, the tiny child in his black suit and three-cornered hat cut a captivating figure. He "bewitched almost everyone," Leopold observed. Louis XV's daughters—that brood of princesses known as *Mesdames*—and the Saxon-born Dauphine made up to him the kisses withheld by Pompadour; so did the good-hearted Queen. Discarding court custom, royal personages paused on their way through galleries and apartments to embrace him; the English and Russian Ambassadors sought him out.

Gifts from the nobility rained down on him, and the high receipts realized at his Parisian concerts would take by surprise even his perspicacious, calculating father. In his *Correspondance littéraire* Friedrich Melchior Grimm declared Wolfgang to be "such an extraordinary phenomenon that one has difficulty believing what one sees with one's eyes and hears with one's ears." By February of 1764 Leopold could write home: "At the moment four sonatas of Mr. Wolfgang Mozart are being engraved. Imagine the furor they will make in the world when people read on the title page that they are the work of a seven-year-old child. . . ." Madame Victoire, the shyest and prettiest of *Mesdames,* accepted the dedication of the first set of these sonatas for harpsichord with violin accompaniment (K. 6 and 7); the second set (K. 8 and 9) bore the name of the Dauphine's lady-in-waiting, the daughter of the influential Duke d'Ayen: Adrienne-Catherine, Countess de Tessé.

Such women "do everything in Paris. . . ." "These are the people who can help you . . . ," Leopold pointed out nearly a decade and a half later as he advised his son—out of work, listless, and idling in Mannheim—to attempt a new series of Parisian triumphs, not too convincingly suggesting that the Countess and Madame Victoire would recognize in the homely, awkward young man the winsome prodigy of former years. But the Mozart who had reached his majority possessed neither the address nor the demeanor requisite to maneuvering at the French court. Grimm, who saw much of Wolfgang during this later visit to Paris, now wondered whether the youth—"unenterprising, too easily taken in, too little concerned with those means that lead to good fortune"—even had the capacity to earn a bare living. Wolfgang could not manage to alter the Parisians' first image of him: "What annoys me most of all here is that the stupid French believe that I am still seven years old. . . . Thus they treat me here as a beginner. . . ." He returned to Germany defeated.

His failure had been all the more bitter because Paris, despite the military and economic disasters of Louis XV's reign, remained *the* cultural arena of Europe, *the* tiltyard in which to win one's spurs as an artist. (Edward Gibbon exulted in having "in a fortnight passed at Paris . . . heard more conversation worth remembering, and seen more men of letters amongst the people of fashion, than . . . in two or three winters in London.") A success in Paris, father and son realized, could establish the adult Wolfgang as a composer and performer of substance. "*Off with you to Paris!*" had been Leopold's cry early in 1778: "Take your place at the side of the great people—*aut Caesar aut nihil* [either Caesar or nothing]. . . . *From Paris the fame and name of a man of great talent travel through the whole world; there the aristocrat treats men of genius with the greatest affability, high esteem, and politeness; there one observes a fine way of life that contrasts most astonishingly with the coarseness of our German cavaliers and ladies. . . .*"

This estimate epitomizes with particular intensity a complication common to father and son: a recurring dissatisfaction with their German homeland. From time to time both lamented what they held to be the crudity of much in German life and expressed an alienation from and an aversion to their origins. At calmer moments Wolfgang realized that his German heritage constituted the elemental medium through which his genius functioned and proudly credited himself with the stoic virtues associated with the nation's middle class. But animosity toward his native city and despair over the social and financial plight of German artists in their own German-speaking regions often overwhelmed him, and then rancor poured forth: "If Germany, my beloved fatherland, of which . . . I am proud, does not wish to hold on to me, then, in God's name, to the disgrace of the German nation, once again let France or England become richer by another able German. In nearly all the arts . . . it is the Germans who have always excelled. But where have they found fortune and reputation? Certainly not in Germany!"

If the psychology of genius correctly cites ambivalence as a stimulus to creation, then posterity gained much from this Mozartean quandary, which calls to mind Goethe's occasional uncertainties about the German language. He called it "barbaric German," "unhappy German," and for a time considered his tongue a poor instrument for poetry, envying the Italians their mellifluous language as Mozart envied them their unaffectedly graceful music.

Though the mature Mozart had set his heart upon a career in Paris, he would gladly have accepted a position at one of the great Gallicized German courts, despite their stuffy, straightlaced ways. His essential need, Leopold observed, was of "a big city where people of society gather, where merit has the hope and opportunity of reward. . . ." Such opportunities were particularly lacking in Wolfgang's relatively resourceless native district: its cultural institutions had fallen to a low level well before his birth. A thriving metropolis provides the most fertile soil for the performing musician. (Haydn's case was an anomaly.) Had either Austria or Bavaria, with their prosperous capitals, been his birthplace,[1] his way might have been less stony. But Mozart came from a moribund petty principality administered solely for the benefit of its administrators. Its court and populace had long evinced that passive mentality so destructive of artistic development. Decaying and increasingly absurd, immobility its principle of life, this odd bureaucracy of preposterous regulations exhibited the brooding tenacity and truculence of some curious armored Mesozoic creature awaiting extinction.

Though Mozart did not demand the undue of life—in fact, only the opportunity to function in comfort as composer and performer (*"wenn ich nur etwas bin"*)—his difficult personality did play its part in creating mutual antagonism between himself and the city of his birth. It came to show what seemed a vindictive reluctance to find any real use for his genius, and an official hostility ultimately contributed to driving him forth to take up residence in Vienna, the city of his death. He could never think of his compatriots with composure, finding even their language, their behavior, completely unbearable (see XXIV, n. 2). The populace, he became convinced, swarmed with idiots. To Abbé Bullinger, an intimate of the Mozart family, he summed up his bitterness toward home: "You know, best of friends, how I loathe Salzburg!"

---

1 His homeland did not come under Austrian control until the nineteenth century (see I, n. 14).

MOZART

CHAPTER I

Salzburg and Empire;
Prince and Burgher;
Leopold Mozart

MOZART WAS BORN on 27 January 1756 in Salzburg. Battlemented and domed, the Salt Town (more strictly, salt castle) straddles a bend in the river Salzach at a point where the last limestone foothills of the Austrian Alps meet the Bavarian tableland. Having shot through a gorge, the Salzach moves quickly through the protected spot where Rupert, Apostle of the Bavarians, settled (c. 700) in the ruins of ancient Juvavum. The Romans had founded this outpost at the foot of a high plateau (today the Mönchsberg) sheltered by a neighboring and commanding hill of hard stone. Plateau, hill, and another residual butte, the lofty Kapuzinerberg across the river, form an amphitheater of calcareous cliffs securing the low-lying city. Within a century, Rupert's colony had become an archbishopric of expanding lands and riches, an agent for the dispersal of Christianity across southern Bavaria and into the Tyrol, and a center of the flourishing salt trade with northern Italy. In time the archbishops crowned the new metropolis with the citadel of Hohensalzburg, symbol and safeguard of a growing prosperity.

Throughout Mozart's century there remained a sharp division between the city and its surrounding countryside, a contrast accentuated by the compact mass of the monumental structures crowded between the river and the rocky faces of the guardian hills. A superb, tightly enclosed complex of ingeniously dovetailed architectural units, Salzburg was enveloped by an idyllic landscape of distant peaks touched with snow, of sloping meadowlands fringed with forests, and of gardens sprinkled with villas and agricultural buildings. Wealthy burghers who owned farms beyond the ramparts enjoyed places of relaxation that also filled the needs of their tables. Though Mozart frequently visited such country houses, he remained incurably urban, a child of the capital of marble, stone, and stucco. As a boy he knew little of its bucolic dependent terrains, which included not only the present-day province of Salzburg but also areas now belonging to Bavaria and Tyrol.

The German principalities survived within a bizarre, resilient, and almost mystic structure: *Das Heilige Römische Reich Deutscher Nation* (*sacrum imperium Romanum Nationis Teutonicae*, the Holy Roman Empire of the German Nation), presided over by an elected Holy Roman Emperor, often simply called German Emperor. In theory, the Empire was not exclusively German, but, rather, international. However, history reduced it to its German-speaking components; even though from time to time kings of France, England, Denmark, and Sweden strove for the Imperial crown, the electors (see p. VI, n. 1) invariably chose a German prince, and, since the accession of Albert II (1438), almost invariably from the Austrian House of Habsburg (exceptions: Charles VII and Francis I, see pp. 78 and 80). To the Habsburgs' eyes, their election to Charlemagne's chair came to seem a matter of regal divinity, no less holy than the Pope's to St. Peter's—and simpler, since God appeared always to choose the same family.

Exercising a formal predominance, the emperor had influence sufficient to protect the security of member states from interior and exterior threats but power insufficient to exceed the traditional limits of his authority by seizing full sovereignty over German states other than his own. This mechanism, sustained by the tensions of ever-changing alliances within the confederation, held its delicate balance with extraordinary and improbable success. Though Napoleon's machinations contributed to casting it down, the Congress of Vienna set it up again in different form: in spirit the Empire lasted until Prussia routed Austria at Königgrätz (1866) and expelled her from Germany, the triumphant Hohenzollern subsequently assuming the crown of a new or Second Reich that excluded the heartland of the first.

A buffer state between Bavaria and Austria, the Salzburg of Mozart's time was a sovereign ecclesiastical domain of two hundred thousand inhabitants. Since 1278, when Rudolph of Habsburg made its archbishops princes of the Holy Roman Empire, they had been overlords answerable only to Imperial and Papal authority and rarely on friendly terms with those they governed. In 1511 Archbishop Leonhard von Keutschach cruelly put down an attempt by citizens to loose themselves from his power and make Salzburg a free Imperial city[1] like Augsburg. One of the final gestures of defiance on the part of a generally terrorized populace found expression in making common cause with the German peasant revolt of 1525, a movement nourished by the Reformation and seeking economic and social change.

To their political autocracy and misrule the archbishops added the rigors of religious persecution. Enforcement of the lamentable prescription *cuius regio, eius religio*[2] came to prevail. But that crowning imposture of worldliness unashamedly parading as piety, that ill-tempered, outrageous, and obtuse baroque absolutism of the Salzburg court (against whose obduracy Wolfgang Mozart's career crashed) became the creation of Wolf Dietrich von Raitenau. He ascended the archiepiscopal throne in 1587 when not yet thirty. Educated in Rome, he modeled himself upon Sixtus V, the energetic Pope whose chief architect, Domenico Fontana, had begun to transform the Holy City. Young von Raitenau quickly tamed whatever independent spirit remained in the archbishopric, reducing it to a tribute-paying vassalage on the pattern of the Papal States. He gave Protestants the choice of either conversion or forfeiture of their property and exile, and many prominent citizens left to find new homes in Wels, Augsburg, and Nürnberg.

Squeezing money from his subjects with harsh new taxes, he started to reshape medieval Salzburg in the image of baroque Rome. Wolf Dietrich fell upon the city as if to remodel or build anew everything at once. A town palace for himself (the expanded Residenz) and imposing court stables started to rise, as did *Lustschloss* Altenau, a pleasure-palace later renamed Mirabell, to house his mistress, Salome Alt, and their offspring.[3] The Vincentine architect Vincenzo Scamozzi visited von Raitenau's court during the winter of 1603-1604 and inspired the arrangement of Salzburg's harmonious squares; they call to mind those of the ideal city engraved in his *Idea dell'architettura universale* (1615). Unable to mask his delight when Salzburg's Romanesque cathedral burned down, Wolf Dietrich found himself suspected of having kindled the flames so as to reconstruct it à la Scamozzi; indeed, much of what remained of its sculptures he ordered

---

1 The free Imperial towns, or *Reichsstädte*, had greater independence in that their allegiance bound them not to any territorial state and its prince but directly to the Empire and emperor, a politically tenuous link leaving them for the most part loose from authority.

2 This maxim, formulated at the religious settlement of Augsburg (1555), gave a German prince the right to impose his creed, either Catholic or Lutheran, upon the inhabitants of his territories, those refusing to conform being constrained to emigrate.

3 A patrician's daughter, she bore him fifteen children. In 1611 ten of them were alive; three sons and seven daughters. Two years earlier, Emperor Rudolph II had raised Salome and her issue to the nobility as "von Altenau."

smashed. Fate, however, denied him the pleasure of transforming the ruin. He foolishly attempted to wage an economic salt war[4] with his powerful neighbor Maximilian I of Bavaria, who deposed him. The task of rebuilding fell to his successors: his elegant nephew Markus Sitticus (Marx Sittich),[5] and Paris Lodron.

Santino Solari modified Scamozzi's original mammoth plans for a new cathedral, and Sitticus laid its foundation stone in 1614, the nave of the great church being inaugurated fourteen years later during the episcopate of Lodron. The entire structure did not stand complete until late in the century, and, most likely to celebrate this achievement, a local composer— perhaps Heinrich Ignaz Franz Biber—wrote (1682) a polychoral mass[6] in the Venetian tradition of the Gabrieli family and as monumental as the spacious, magnificently modeled Italianate structure itself. (Wolf Dietrich had already established a court chapel imitating transalpine models and, in fact, headed by an Italian kapellmeister.) The score, almost a yard high and two feet wide, required more than fifty staves to accommodate its choruses and instrumental ensembles. A colossal affair, in whose performance about four hundred singers and instrumentalists participated, this *Missa salisburgensis* gave token of the ambitious musical program of the cathedral in which Mozart was to serve.

For capricious Archbishop Markus Sitticus, who had summoned him to Salzburg, Solari also designed the gardens and hunting lodge of Hellbrunn. A *villa suburbana* in the manner of the Papal pleasure-palaces, it lies a few kilometers south of Salzburg at the foot of an isolated Alpine mound, the Waldemsberg, which punctuates the valley floor. Archbishop Sitticus, perhaps best known for the pleasure he took in drenching unsuspecting guests with jets of water from secreted fountains, also occupied himself with music. During his first year on the throne (1612), he received a visit from Francesco Rasi, a Tuscan poet, composer, and tenor associated with the Florentine *camerata*, indeed, a pupil of its most famous member, Giulio Caccini. At the turn of the century, this group of literati and musicians had preached against counterpoint and helped develop an oratorical speech-song of realistic pathos. This so-called monody or vocal solo accompanied by nonpolyphonic harmony had become the basis of opera,

---

4 Losing contact with reality, in 1611 he seized nearby Berchtesgaden, a salt town in the hands of an Augustinian priory under Imperial and Papal authority. Maximilian responded by invading Salzburg. Panic-stricken, Wolf Dietrich fled. Conveyed back to Salzburg a prisoner and delivered to a nuncio specially dispatched from Rome, he abdicated under pressure in 1612.

5 Sitticus kept his dethroned uncle locked in the citadel of Hohensalzburg until death released him in 1617.

6 It was long attributed to the Roman composer Orazio Benevoli.

lately born in Florence. Rasi dedicated a collection of this "new music" to Archbishop Sitticus, who by 1616 had in his service the Veronese monodist Camillo Orlandi.

Several of the earliest performances of opera north of the Alps took place at Hellbrunn, one of whose garden sculptures clearly drew inspiration from contemporary theatrical presentations: the group in the Orpheus and Eurydice grotto (the hero playing a viol to attentive animals as Eurydice sleeps) obviously perpetuates in marble some version of the myth staged with music. In 1618 the Archbishop's courtiers heard a work about Orpheus in the open-air, arenalike stone theater on the Waldemsberg;[7] two years earlier, during Carnival, they had attended an *Orfeo* given on a stage built in the Carabinieri Hall of the Salzburg Residenz. This presentation may well have been Monteverdi's *Orfeo*; if so, the increasingly Italianate archiepiscopal retinue heard it within a decade of its premiere at Mantua, a performance in which Rasi almost certainly had sung the title role. (Thus operas such as the adolescent Mozart's *Il sogno di Scipione*, written for the Residenz, simply continued a tradition whose local practice, to all appearance, went back almost to the very birth of the genre.) Sitticus, like his uncle von Raitenau before and Archbishop Colloredo after him, attended the Collegium Germanicum in Rome; all gave themselves up to Italian art, and, throughout the seventeenth and eighteenth centuries, not only Italian musicians but Italian architects, painters, and sculptors contributed weightily to the cultural life of Salzburg. It became a city not of German gables, pinnacles, and tracery, but, rather, of Mediterranean roofs, symmetrical towers, and domes. The wall decorations that the Tuscan Arsenio Mascagni painted for Markus Sitticus at Hellbrunn evidenced his new ideal—Florentine and Venetian mannerism.

Less alien than the court opera were the *ludi scenici*. Performed at the end of the semester or during festal time on the well-equipped stage set up next to the *aula* (great hall) of the Benedictine university founded by Lodron, they mixed native German and imported Italian elements. An ollapodrida with a strong folk flavor, an academic presentation of this kind might combine mythology, biblical tales, and farce, and call into play pantomime, declamation, dance, song, and elaborate scenery in the baroque operatic tradition. Salzburg's academic theater had a lively spirit, and, as in Italy, intermezzi—light and diverting theatricals—sometimes obtruded between the acts of serious works, a Latin intermezzo, *Apollo et Hyacinthus*, with music by the eleven-year-old Mozart being a late example of the type.

---

7 The architects had the building stone for the palace quarried from the hill so as to leave a picturesque cavernous space for the theater.

Even after Archbishop Colloredo closed Salzburg's palace and academic stages in the seventeen-seventies, the city's provincial but vigorous theatrical life continued in his Hoftheater (court theater), now open to all, made from a ballroom Lodron had constructed near the gardens of the Mirabell palace. The entrance to the new auditorium (now the site of the present Landestheater) opened diagonally across from the Tanzmeisterhaus, Mozart's Salzburg home from his seventeenth to his twenty-fifth year. Enthusiastically, he attended plays, ballets, and operas.

2

IN MOZART'S DAY, life in Salzburg continued to revolve about the Archbishop, the Primate of Germany.[8] Even though in matters of policy outside the Reich (the German equivalent of the Latin *Regnum* and a word enmeshed in the idea of German sovereignty), he waited upon his liege, the Holy Roman Emperor, and the Imperial Diet sitting at Regensburg (in which, however, he had an authoritative voice), within the archbishopric he reigned as absolute master, a monarch elected for his lifetime and from among their number by a consistory of the cathedral's canons. They alone determined the qualifications for entry into their company. Since for the most part they belonged to collateral branches of heraldic families with roots in Bavarian lands or in Habsburg hereditary domains, power in Salzburg remained in these foreign hands. Munich and Vienna vied to capture the archbishopric for their Royal Houses: historically, Bavaria had always held itself guardian of Salzburg because of its proximity and its founding by Rupert—indeed, a Bavarian duke had given him the ruins of Juvavum and its surrounding lands—but after the Thirty Years' War Austria's influence mounted. Even so, and despite political pressure, the canons wisely respected Wolf Dietrich's exhortation that both Bavarian princes and Austrian archdukes be barred from St. Rupert's throne.

Many an archbishop used his years of authority simply to exploit his subjects and to fill his and his family's pockets. "Every canon yearns for this tasty morsel," Maximilian of Bavaria observed. The canons, many of

8 During the eleventh century, the Archbishop of Salzburg began to wear the purple as a sign of his special position as *legatus natus* or permanent legate of the Holy See. (After cardinals had assumed the legates' color, Salzburg's Prince-Archbishop, even if not a cardinal, continued, and continues, to dress so.) By the end of the next century, the Pope had made him *legatus natus* to the entire Reich. Step by step he became *primas germaniae* (Primate of Germany), a hegemony long a fact of German political life when Archbishop Guidobald Thun (1654–1668) first officially assumed the title. Until 1750, the resentful emperors in Vienna refused to recognize Salzburg's ecclesiastical precedence.

them related to ruling or departed archbishops, made up an oligarchy of clerical princes drawing splendid prebends and living in splendid state, the regal apparatus of Salzburg's ecclesiastical nobility being of a luxury out of proportion to the resources of a small principality. (Since 1612 the canons of Salzburg arrayed themselves in the great robes with trains worn by the canons of St. Peter's in Rome.)

A member of the chapter had excellent opportunities of becoming a bishop. Suffragan bishoprics subject to the metropolitan see of Salzburg—Regensburg, Freising, Brixin, Gurk, Seckau, Lavant, Chiemsee, and, until 1727, Passau—required its canons as their overlords. Thus the Salzburg chapter included bishops and, at times, cardinals, but, until a canon rose to a higher position, he had no need to take priestly vows. By Mozart's time, the regulation that a Salzburg canon lead a monastic life had long vanished: to become one of the canons—thirty-seven in number during Mozart's childhood—he had only to prove his noble German lineage and enter the subdiaconate, a minor order demanding bachelorhood. If a bishopric did not come his way, a young cavalier-canon might resign and seek his fortune through marriage. Most canons had relatives eager to spring at any opening in the ranks of the chapter. It permitted a single family a maximum of three canons of whom only two could be brothers, a prohibition that helped keep all but a pair of families from capturing the throne more than once: the Kuenburgs three times, the Thuns twice. (No stipulations existed as to age; children rarely gained admittance, though adolescents did: Archbishop Colloredo became a Salzburg canon at fifteen, Wolf Dietrich at sixteen.) An elaborate system assured each member a chance of nominating the successor to a deceased colleague: if a canon died during a month with an odd number of days, the Pope, through the Archbishop, filled the empty seat; the canons divided the even months among themselves, every few years each member having an assigned month during which the privilege of offering a name became his. Old and ailing canons were carefully watched during the final hours of every month, for the precise moment of death determined the future occupants of their places. However, a canon could resign *in favorem* and thus gain the authority to nominate his own successor. Over the niceties of this system floated the Emperor's right of *preces primariae* by which, during any month, he might suggest candidates to the Archbishop. Members could increase their wealth by becoming canons of more than one cathedral: Count Leopold Anton von Postatsky—who helped save Mozart's life at Olmütz in 1767—functioned as a canon there and at Salzburg; Colloredo at Salzburg and Passau; the Mozarts' friend and patron the Bishop of Chiemsee (Ferdinand Christoph, Count Waldburg-Zeil) at Augsburg as well as Salzburg.

Especially at the highest level, the appetite for benefices became insatiable: for example, Cardinal Guidobald Thun, who held sway simultaneously as Prince-Archbishop of Salzburg and Bishop of Regensburg, strove to be Bishop of Trient, too. That Mozart grew up an acute observer of this ecclesiastical culture trading in offices and concerning itself not with God's things but Caesar's helps explain a growing estrangement from the clergy.

Though concern for the prosperity of the bourgeois or the peasant proved rare, Salzburg's unwholesome political structure possessed one merit: an elective monarchy at least precluded a succession of congenital defectives such as defiled so many of Europe's inherited thrones.

The archbishop, the canons, and a throng of predictably venal kinsmen made up Salzburg's higher aristocracy. Beneath them labored the homebred "aristocrats"—the *Briefadel* with titles of paper. (Leopold Mozart irreverently called them "*Wildenadl.*"9) Underpaid struggling government officials, pen pushers whose cringing submissiveness had earned their advancement in the subordinate ranks of the Archbishop's highly centralized civil service, these parasitic class-conscious placemen completely identified themselves with their masters and, by untiringly extolling a system that gave their existence its only reality, glorified their own stagnation. Compared with an almost feudal Salzburg, the Paris of Louis XV appeared free and progressive. Citizens of petty German principalities lived uncomfortably close to the sources of authority and supervision and thus led more harried, regimented existences than their counterparts in France. The English traveler Mrs. Piozzi observed in Germany "a spirit of subordination beyond what I have yet been witness to . . . and . . . carried . . . as high as I think it can be carried." The Wetzlar Goethe revealed in *Werther* comes to mind, in particular the mortifications the superiors of such a society could inflict. Too often an oppressed functionary reacted by harassing those beneath him. Both Mozart and his father suffered from this singularly vulgar kind of bullying.

Access to the stiff, parochial courts became the ultimate reward of these embittered bourgeois bureaucrats, who bickered endlessly about questions of precedence and status and attempted to preserve solemnities and forms of etiquette long abandoned in Paris and even in Vienna. Ironically, the

---

9 *Briefadel* (paper nobility) and *Beamtenadel* (civil-service nobility) were gentler words for Leopold's *Wildenadl*, the first referring to the charter with which the ruler elevated the bourgeois, the second to the condition from which the charter plucked him. *Wildenadel* had a darker shade of meaning—another synonym, *Schwartzer Adel* (black nobility), being closer to it—and should be construed in a horticultural sense, this "wild nobility" having the character of those unruly flowers and weeds that invade cultivated gardens.

doors of provincial German palaces rarely opened to the craftsmen and businessmen to whom the nation owed whatever survived of its prosperity, although nobility occasionally came to merchants like Mozart's patrons the Haffners of Salzburg, whose wealth had grown to a point that could no longer be ignored and, that, in fact, permitted purchase of the appropriate letters patent.

Salzburg had declined steadily since the Middle Ages. Centers of world commerce had shifted with changes in the great highways of trade, and though, thanks to Archbishop Lodron's diplomatic talent, the archbishopric had escaped physical destruction during the Thirty Years' War, its disasters had completed the ruin of German mercantilism. As Salzburg's economic foundations increasingly sagged, the Archbishops had ever more energetically propped and embellished its lovely façade, employing the two greatest designers of the German Baroque: Johann Bernhard Fischer von Erlach and Johann Lukas von Hildebrant, whose styles, derived from the Italian Baroque, speak its language fluently and powerfully, but with a Teutonic intonation. Richly decorated elevations, geometric gardens, and altars choked with gilded saints and stucco angels gave an impression of municipal vigor;[10] but the state had fallen mortally ill, its death rattle audible by the time of Mozart's adolescence. For their salaries most of the sixteen thousand inhabitants of the capital either directly or indirectly depended upon a court treasury nearing exhaustion, about a fifth of the archbishopric's population upon pensions and allowances from the same ebbing source. Most alarming had been reports of more than two hundred thousand gulden discovered scattered in drawers, cupboards, and chests in the private apartments of Colloredo's deceased predecessor, a case, if not of brigandage, then irresponsibility—most rulers looked upon state revenue as their pocket money—and fiscal chaos. Total collapse of the machinery of government seemed at hand.

Yet, despite its grasping princes and commercial decay, the archbishopric did retain some measure of prosperity, particularly as a hub for the forwarding of merchandise to and from Italy, above all Venice, where Salzburgers enjoyed high respect at the Fondaco dei Tedeschi (the German merchants' warehouse); firms of packers and dispatchers dealing in groceries, silks, and metal wares prospered in Salzburg, as did a number of manufacturers. In his native city, not the courtier, but, rather, the bourgeois involved in trade and the professions gave Mozart consistent support: Johann Lorenz Hagenauer, wholesale grocer and owner of the house in

---

10 Not surprisingly, Salzburg's churches and palaces achieve their effects with modest materials.

which the composer had been born; Ignaz Anton Weiser (a half-brother of Frau Hagenauer), originally a textile marketer and later Mayor of Salzburg; Georg Josef Robinig, a dealer in hardware whose family owned real estate, a scythe factory, and an arsenic works; the court physician, Dr. Silvester Barisani; and the family of Siegmund Haffner, the wealthy merchant and Mayor of Salzburg for the ennoblement of whose son (to Edler von Imbachhausen) Mozart wrote the Haffner Symphony, having already composed a serenade for the wedding of young Haffner's sister. The Haffners had become rich enough to imitate the ways of the Residenz, the pride and aspirations of such a family symbolizing the passing of cultural leadership from one layer of society to another. The bourgeois financiers had begun to develop into the spenders and benefactors of the new era: the younger Haffner was to leave a princely sum for charitable works.

Mozart came to manhood as erosion wore away the boundaries between the roles the middle class and the nobility played in patronage. (Pondering, in 1777, the composition of a board of sponsors who might provide his son a monthly subvention, Leopold unreservedly indicated a bias toward merchants rather than aristocrats, whom he judged unpredictable.) The often close relationship between musician and private patron, whatever his social standing, would, in fact, soon give way to the impersonal mechanism of the bourgeois subscription concert (in which many a noble enrolled). Mozart suffered the worst of both new and old, not only living through the awkward displacement in Europe's courtly civilization but also, in his earlier years, experiencing that particularly unpleasant eighteenth-century phenomenon—the all-powerful and often irascible master, in this case His Grace the Archbishop of Salzburg. Its government too often functioned with few thoughts for the well-being of those on less than commanding levels of service.

3

MOZART'S MOTHER OWED her childhood poverty to the shabbiness of the archiepiscopal civil service. Her father, Wolfgang Nikolaus Pertl, came from a modest background: his father had been a clothmaker, his grandfather a coachman at the Residenz. Young Pertl forced his way up the social ladder through law studies at the university of Salzburg. This schooling, along with experience in Graz as secretary to Seyfried, Duke of Krumau and Prince of Eggenberg, enabled him to enter the Archbishop's employ on a decent level, and he eventually rose through the tax office to be Secretary of the Exchequer. Four years after his marriage in November 1712 to the widow Puxbaumer (born Eva Rosina Barbara Altmann), he became deputy prefect (*Pflegekommissar*) of the prefecture of Hüttenstein–St. Gilgen. On Christmas Day of 1720, Mozart's mother, Anna Maria Pertl, received baptism at St. Gilgen on its idyllic lake, the Abersee (today the Wolfgangsee).

Although the highest administrative and judicial authority of the prefecture (*Pfleg*), Pertl had miserable pay, which had to be produced by the fees, fines, and duties he collected. They proved inadequate, and he found himself borrowing from the Exchequer against his mythical wages in order to keep up the appearances his office demanded. When he died in 1724 (at the age of fifty-seven) owing more than four years' salary, the wretched system that had ruined him seized his estate. The four-year-old Anna Maria had to leave the comfortable house her father had built in St. Gilgen[11] to be raised in Salzburg on the miserly pension awarded her mother. Anna Maria's letters, their orthography individual even for eighteenth-century Germany, reveal her scant education. But they are warm, loving, and acute in perception. Penury and what appears to have been an extended illness during adolescence did not impair her cheerful disposition. Fate fashioned a shrewd housekeeper and a sagacious, amiable mate for Mozart's father.

Unlike his wife, whose entire family had its roots in the soil of Salzburg, he came from Swabia. Johann Georg Leopold Mozart was born on 14 November 1719 in Augsburg, on the river Lech. The university drew him to Salzburg, where he married and settled.[12] Nonetheless, he took care to petition and pay the required fee to the municipal council of his native city for permission to wed and live abroad while at the same time retaining his civic rights: Leopold clung to the security of Augsburg citizenship. As a native of a free Imperial city, he must have become alarmed by the implacable absolutism of the Salzburg Residenz.[13] (He would develop a code for letter-writing, a naïve, futile device meant to outmaneuver the Archbishop's censors.) Moreover, he wished to protect his inheritance rights. The university

---

11 Pertl had prevailed upon the Archbishop (Franz Anton von Harrach) to pay for constructing a building accommodating both administrative offices and apartments for the *Pfleger's* family and his clerks. In 1784 Mozart's sister, Nannerl, married one of her maternal grandfather's successors in office and took up residence in this same house. It still stands.

12 Handel, for example, had followed the opposite and more usual course, migrating from Halle, a provincial town of Empire, to Hamburg, one of its great free cities.

13 Beneath a gilded surface, the state of culture in Salzburg remained in many respects primitive: the execution of poor wretches found guilty of witchcraft, for example, continued, to public approval. Witches constituted a reality for the world in which Mozart (and Goethe, too, even in Enlightened Frankfurt) grew up: only five years before Mozart's birth, Salzburg put a sixteen-year-old laundress's assistant to death for having had relations with the devil. Such barbarous legalized insanity must have shocked and frightened moderates like Leopold. Though Salzburg burned a "witch" for the last time in 1762—"at present, there are no longer witches," Wolfgang wryly wrote sixteen years later—unfortunates in its prisons remained subject to torture until almost the end of the century.

of Salzburg registered him as a *Suevus* (Swabian), and he legally remained one until 1755. In time he came to consider himself not a Swabian, not a Salzburger, certainly not an Austrian or a Bavarian,[14] but, rather, a child of the Holy Roman Empire, a member of the *deutsche Nation*—a German. His son took this attitude for granted and looked upon Vienna (in Leopold's words) as "the capital of his German fatherland."

Leopold descended from lower-middle-class artisans. His father, Johann Georg Mozart—spelled in many ways, among them: Mozarth, Mozhard, and Mozer—had been a bookbinder of Augsburg, a publishing center; his mother, Maria Anna Sulzer, also from Augsburg, was a weaver's daughter whom Johann Georg had married a month and a half after the death of his first wife. Leopold, born in the Frauentorstrasse in Augsburg's St. George's parish, grew up on the Jesuitengasse midst the cluster of educational buildings at the heart of the Jesuit quarter, and attended its Jesuit institutions: the Principia or preparatory school of the Gymnasium of St. Salvator (1724–1729), the Gymnasium itself (1729–1735), and the Lyceum of St. Salvator, a theological-philosophical seminary (1735–1736). With its schools and colonies of printers, engravers, and painters, Augsburg boasted an academy of art; however, the city had no university, and Leopold broke off his studies at the Lyceum and quit home to seek elsewhere the privileges of higher learning and the degree of doctor. After a propitious opening year (1737) at the university of Salzburg, where he enrolled under the faculty of logic, he became a truant. Choosing not to explain his excessive absences when summoned by the dean, he found himself declared "unworthy of the name of student" and expelled in 1739. He had discovered a career outside the university's doors: by 1740 Johann Baptist, Count Thurn-Valsassina und Taxis, a canon of Salzburg cathedral and president of its consistory, had taken him into service as a musician. That year Leopold dedicated to this young prelate six trio sonatas for two violins and continuo etched on copper by the composer himself—his first printed work.

What had occasioned his apparently impetuous decision to become a musician, and how had he prepared himself for so specialized a calling?

---

14 Austria did not annex Salzburg until almost three decades after Leopold's death (two and a half after his son's). During his life, federal nomenclature placed the Archbishopric within that geographic sphere of the Reich known as the Bavarian Circle. Leopold addressed letters from Paris to "*Salzburg en Baviere*" for the convenience of the postal service; similarly, in order to identify the area clearly on the map, Daines Barrington (in his report on Mozart to the Royal Society of London) described the prodigy's birthplace as "Salzbourg in Bavaria"; and for the same reason, the church record of Anna Maria Mozart's death, signed by her son in Paris, referred to her husband's service in "*Salzbourg, en Bavierre.*"

4

LEOPOLD HAD FIRST turned toward music during his school days at Augsburg, learning to play the violin and organ and singing soprano for the Benedictines at the monastery of SS. Ulrich and Afra and also for the Augustines at the church of the Holy Cross. He remained essentially an autodidact in music; his instructors here were dilettantes: at the Gymnasium, Pater Balthasar Siberer, a Tirolese from Schwaz im Unterinntal, whose real disciplines embraced grammar and philosophy; at the Lyceum, Pater Georg Francklin of Hüfingen, a grammarian and natural scientist. His first violin teacher may have been Heinrich Sebastian Awerth, from Öttingen im Ries, a theologian and Prefect of St. Joseph's seminary (the Mozart family moved to quarters in one of its wings during Leopold's third year). From the fathers, Leopold learned less about music than about German speech and literary style (his exhortative letters to his son should be ranked with Chesterfield's); from them he also acquired workable Latin; a bit of Greek, French, and Italian; some science; and, most important, ordered argument and proper work habits. Augsburg's Jesuit schools formed the basis of his considerable culture. In turn, he passed on the best of their scholastic traditions to Wolfgang, who, other than in music,[15] had no preceptor but his father.

Until his voice broke, Leopold regularly acted and sang in those Latin plays and ambitious spectacles traditional at the end of the school term. (At the age of five, his son would make his first appearance on a stage in just such a work, *Sigismundus Hungariae Rex*, little Wolfgang figuring among the dancers [*salii*].) In Salzburg, Leopold would gain a reputation for dramatic creations: cantatas for Easter Week and music for a student play, *Antiquitas personata* (1742), performed in the small *aula* of the university.

His adolescent enthusiasm for music at first remained subordinate to an ambition to enter the Church. Johann Georg Grabherr, a canon in the chapter of Augsburg's St. Peter's am Perlach and a witness at the marriage of Leopold's parents, had godfathered him. But his early resolve to be ordained—no doubt born when Canon Grabherr showed interest in his education—began to weaken and then shattered with father Mozart's death in 1736. Franziskus Erasmus Freisinger, a fellow student of Leopold's at St. Salvator's, later recalled the growth of his musical ability[16] and the guile with which he kept from the Jesuits his uncertainties about becoming a

---

15 The boy did have a brief but intense period of training in counterpoint under Padre Martini in Bologna and took singing lessons in London from Giovanni Manzuoli.

16 Freisinger described how excellently Leopold had played the organ during their visit to the abbey of Wessobrunn, a short excursion from Augsburg. The error persists that they first studied together and became friends at Salzburg.

priest. He had to hoodwink them as long as possible: his father dead, Leopold depended upon them for support. They became his parents and, in respect to not only education but also character, molded the boy; their mark remained upon the man: with his inveterate tendency to teach, preach, and indulge in exegetics, he retained the manner of a classic Jesuit throughout his life—intellectual, ambitious, suave, and frequently cunning, his personality dominated by a brooding melancholy relieved by sallies of sardonic humor.

He determined to cut a grand figure. Whatever his doubts about a future calling, clearly study at a university would offer the increasingly cultured youth an opportunity to rise above the artisan family he was coming to despise. Despite sharp social distinctions, the sons of patricians, merchants, and civil servants mixed freely with poor boys on scholarship at German universities, which, fostering careers in administration and law, opened the only reliable route by which a young man of insecure social caste might break loose from the condition of his birth. Leopold saw the university as his only means of deliverance, especially as his widowed mother, preoccupied with her younger children, neglected his needs.

Forced to survive on Jesuit stipends, Leopold felt abandoned and learned to loathe her. (He always maintained that she had cheated him of his inheritance, and, shortly before Wolfgang's birth, made a final and ineffectual attempt to get his share.) She may have felt justified in leaving him to the obliging Jesuits and devoting the funds from her husband's bookbindery to the youngsters who might eventually follow their father's profession. Leopold's two brothers did in fact become bookbinders: Joseph Ignaz Mozart (1725–1796) and Franz Aloys Mozart (1727–1791), the first establishing his own business, the second maintaining his father's shop in the Jesuitengasse. (In addition, the year of his son's birth, Leopold still had two sisters. It would appear that the entire family opposed his receiving any legatary settlement.)[17]

Neither affection nor understanding linked the quarrelsome, pugnacious Maria Anna and her eldest son. She distrusted him and "little by little," so he charged, allowed "the other children to gain control of her

---

17 Wolfgang's friendship with the daughter of Franz Aloys would keep him and the Salzburg Mozarts in contact, but further discord over money evidently broke their ties with Joseph Ignaz. Clearly he was the brother Leopold discussed with his wife in two letters from Milan (8 December 1770 and 2 February 1771). During his absence in Italy, he learned that Joseph Ignaz had applied to him for a loan; from afar he did not censure Anna Maria's desire to help—she had already sent a small sum to Augsburg—but felt it more appropriate that Ignaz turn to fellow businessmen. Leopold made clear his low opinion of a brother who had yet to repay a previous loan: "Don't imagine," he advised Anna Maria, "that we will ever see a kreuzer of this money."

substance." As she approached her sixtieth birthday, signs of senility appeared; in 1755 Leopold wrote his publisher, Johann Jakob Lotter of Augsburg: "That she is both pitiful and not entirely rational is, alas, all too true, were she 1,000 times my mother." Inflating Hamlet's "ten times," he identified Maria Anna with Queen Gertrude, an accessory to making her son, the heir apparent, into an outsider. Yet Leopold seemed content to leave his mother to heaven. She died on 11 December 1766, having lived into the era of her prodigy grandson's success. Intractable, she had held aloof from his performances in Augsburg, her declining faculties no doubt reinforcing her hostility; the rift between her and Leopold had been unbridgeable since his young manhood.

5

WHEN THE JESUIT fathers learned of his intent to shun the priesthood, they ceased to bother themselves about his future. With their patronage he might have gone on to a Jesuit university in Swabia or Bavaria—to Dillingen or Ingolstadt. The Mozart family had associations with the lovely town of Dillingen, where Leopold's great-grandfather, the master mason David Mozart (1620–1685), had worked on the parish church of SS. Peter and Paul. But the resourceful Leopold, who had learned to survive by his wits, revived ties with the Benedictines of St. Ulrich's. One of them, Rupert Sembler, was about to join the faculty of the university of Salzburg. He prepared the way for Leopold's matriculation and had the pleasure of conferring the baccalaureate upon him in the summer of 1738. Leopold furnished the information for his biographical sketch published by Marpurg in 1757; it tells of university studies in philosophy (*Weltweisheit*) and law.

How Leopold supported himself as a student in Salzburg remains obscure.[18] In all likelihood he turned his musical talent into money, at the same time taking further musical training. He must have found arduous the scramble for a living, studies in music, and pursuit of the doctoral curriculum. Moreover, the period of "youthful dalliance" (*jugendlichen Narrenspossen*), to which he vaguely and ruefully alluded in maturer years—"the devil prompted evil thoughts in me"—no doubt ran its course at this time. He gave up work on the doctorate.

---

18 In the beginning he must have received help from the Benedictines of Ulrich and Afra. Like the Jesuits, they had to have ended disappointed in a protégé not only cashiered from the university but also averse to embracing any aspect of the religious life. During a visit to Augsburg in later years, he shrank from renewing contact with them, even for a trifling favor, embarrassment probably holding him back. His reluctance "had its reasons," he cryptically admitted.

Upon his arrival in Salzburg he had called upon Johann Ernst Eberlin, an organist at the cathedral. Of Swabian descent, he presumably became the adviser of this young compatriot whose situation must have awakened his sympathy: indigence likewise had impelled him to quit his studies at the university of Salzburg; like Leopold, he had been a student at Augsburg's Gymnasium of St. Salvator and participated in its dramatic productions. In time Leopold came to honor Eberlin's musical mastery and held up his compositions to Wolfgang as models.

That financial want drove Leopold from the lecture hall and turned him into a professional musician he intimated in his preface (in Italian) to his trio sonatas. He did not simply turn to account the fawning characteristic of inscriptions to princely patrons when describing how the Swabian Count Thurn-Valsassina, in all probability prompted by Eberlin, had torn him "suddenly from the cruel darkness of need." Nonetheless, Leopold resented his situation as a *valet de chambre (Kammerdiener)*, a household domestic serving the Count's needs on the same anonymous level as the menials tending his toilette. Nor was Leopold less a lackey when, in 1743, with the help of Eberlin and the Count, he secured a provisional place as fourth violinist in the Archbishop's orchestra, a position that became permanent only in 1747, with an annual salary of two hundred forty florins, along with an allowance for bread and wine of four florins and thirty kreuzer a month.

He yearned to climb above the low social status to which he found himself restricted. Always striving to become part of that amorphous middle class of university teachers, lawyers, and lower court officials, he would attempt to clothe himself in the dignity of a scholar, his treatise on the violin of 1756 being, in a sense, his academic apologia. He began to call himself "Dr." Mozart. (His socially pretentious family for a brief while even attempted to assume the titular "de Mozart"!) The condescending tone rings false in his letter of 18 October 1777 wherein he discusses the education of Jakob Wilhelm Benedikt Langenmantel, his contemporary at both St. Salvator's and the university of Salzburg. Langenmantel had gone on to earn his doctorate at Innsbruck and then advanced through the civil service of Augsburg, eventually becoming its Chief Prefect. (Although the doctorate did not command the prestige of such a title, it had some pretension to privilege; and Langenmantel held both degree and position.) At one time Leopold must have hoped for his kind of administrative career and rank.[19]

---

19 Not only envy lay at the root of Leopold's resentment of him: the young patrician had witnessed his dismissal from the university. In 1737, the prospective freshmen had journeyed together from Augsburg to Salzburg.

When the musical precocity of his son—whom he dragged across Europe and exhibited like a dancing bear—opened the palaces of the great to them both, he relished those delicious moments when he could play the man of quality. Leopold's voice sounds through his son's later observation that "a courtier cannot make himself into a kapellmeister, but a kapellmeister can certainly be a courtier." In Rome, during April of 1770, Leopold thrust himself before the Pope in a bold maneuver "all the more amazing," he exulted, "in that we [he and Wolfgang] had to pass through two doors watched over by Swiss Guards in armor and push through many hundreds of people. . . . But fine clothes, the German language, and the practiced freedom with which I had my servant call out in German to the Swiss Guards to make way, helped us through everywhere. They took Wolfgang for a German cavalier; others even believed him a prince—an idea the servant did not discourage—and I was presumed his tutor" (see p. 270).

He enjoyed such adventures. How he delighted in the fluid, even promiscuous social atmosphere of great cities—London, Paris, even staid Vienna—where bourgeois, artist, and aristocrat mixed in drawing room and theater, where pedigree saluted talent. But upon his return to Salzburg he again had to pull on the livery of a musical lackey. When the better-known Michael Haydn became part of the Archbishop's musical household, he received permission to dine at the officers' table, a privilege never accorded the Mozarts. Much that his peers accepted as custom, Leopold felt as indignity. He had the self-consciousness of a new age: although uncertain what his place in society should be, he rejected the one it forced him to occupy.

This tendency came to the surface with histrionic directness in his petition (December 1747) to dwell as a married man in Salzburg while retaining Augsburg citizenship. Here he not only drew a picture of his father as a still vital worthy to whom he owed thanks for sponsoring his well-spent university career in Salzburg, but also described his bride as the daughter of a prosperous family. The document may be viewed as a fantasy substituting a resurrected, generous father for an unsympathetic, stingy mother and transforming both a failed student into an accomplished scholar and a penniless country girl into an heiress; or the petition may appear, in plainer words, as a parade of shameless lies, all the more foolish in that the simplest inquiries could have unmasked them. The intriguing exercise has at its heart the germ of that delight in pretense and self-aggrandizement that would become a lifelong trait.

If Goethe could manage to pose successfully as a patrician and even to reject without compunction the fact that his grandfather had been a ladies' tailor, these airs on his and his father's part came off well because the clever tailor had become a successful innkeeper and wine merchant and left behind a fortune of ninety thousand florins. Leopold lacked such an advantage, and his final attempt to get a portion of his father's estate appears to have been born of desperation. Having failed, he placed the burden of his hopes upon his son's tiny shoulders.

Leopold's resentment continued deep, and, despite an authoritarian Jesuit background and devotion to the rituals of Catholicism, he became increasingly critical of the inequities in contemporary social, political, and religious institutions, of infamy and corruption conveniently symbolized for him by the despotic ecclesiastical government of Salzburg. His extended tours with Wolfgang opened his mind to the influence of the Enlightenment. But, to an extent, his days at the university had prepared him for the new ideas. Winds of change had long been blustering through the great capitals of Europe, and even in sleepy, provincial Salzburg occasional gusts had freshened the air.

CHAPTER II

Sapere aude;
Liberal Sensibilities
and Irreconcilable Tendencies

KANT CHOSE THE Horatian motto *Sapere aude* (Dare to know) for the cultural ferment called the Enlightenment. It started late in the reign of Louis XIV and ended with the overthrow of his great-great-great-grandson Louis XVI. The French called this decisive period in the history of ideas the *siècle des lumières* (the century of luminaries) and with Gallic assurance looked upon themselves as *the* illuminants. Doubtless the most spectacular of the new lights did shine in France, though the geographical extension of the movement—Moses Mendelssohn and Lessing in Germany, Filangieri and Beccaria[1] in Italy, Smith and Hume in Scotland, Franklin and Jefferson in America—reached as wide as its spectrum of ideas. For the philosophes, the word "philosophy" had to do with freedom of inquiry. Academics, men of letters, journalists, and scientific amateurs, they constituted a select international company of urbane, articulate, and polemic intellectuals. At times ostentatiously eulogizing one another, at times sharply differing and indulging in public disagreements, they nonetheless found their commonality in a characteristic way of thinking: through books and pamphlets, varying in style from self-conscious and bellicose pretentiousness to graceful wit, they held a paper conversation

---

1 In the course of their first visit to Milan (early in 1770), Mozart and his father appear to have met Beccaria.

from which grew a community of ideas united not by a coherent body of doctrine but by a similar outlook.

Many of the seminal ideas first came from England and Holland, and these exciting thoughts energized in French heads would erupt into violence. Prudently, Maria Theresa forbade the establishment of a chair of English literature at any university within her Habsburg domains; she knew London to be the home of Freemasonry,[2] a movement sharing the philosophes' social perceptions and sense of humanity, attitudes that shaped the Mozartean age; the conservative Empress would become perhaps its most formidable royal hunter of Masons.

Reputedly, Voltaire became a Mason during the English sojourn that made him a Newtonian.[3] His *Éléments de la philosophie de Newton* appeared in 1738—the year of Leopold Mozart's baccalaureate and of *In eminenti*, Pope Clement XII's condemnation of Freemasonry—and had to be published in liberal Amsterdam, French authorities having refused to license its printing. Here a thinker and stylist addressed not the specialist but the cultivated reader, with whom he lucidly discussed the new scientific theories transforming philosophy. Men like Voltaire and Lessing (the author of *Gespräche für Freymaurer* [Conversations for Freemasons]) saw themselves as educators with the task of bringing difficult and obscure matters within the mental compass of the lettered public. As a result, the new hypotheses advanced in physics and psychology, disturbing to long-held moral concepts, became widely broadcast. Not surprisingly, the work most closely associated with the philosophes and their desire to disseminate the new theories, the massive *Encyclopédie*, truly their ultimate exemplar, had a Mason among its publishers.[4] By questioning the credibility of evidence accepted for centuries, the *Encyclopédie*, whose very name denoted interrelationships, helped unsettle the religious and political convictions of intellectual Europe and transmute its values.

"Let your reason furnish the answer . . . ," the second priest in Mozart's *The Magic Flute* advises the questioning birdman, Papageno. The philosophe believed that through rational analysis the world could be under-

---

2 The London Grand Lodge was founded in 1717.

3 During his final, triumphant visit to Paris, its Masons feted him. If he had been initiated in England decades before, they seemed unaware of the fact, for they hailed him as a brother simply because of his love of humanity and his hatred of cruelty and fanaticism: Thus, "you have fulfilled the obligations of a Freemason before you promised us to keep them."

4 Ephraim Chambers, editor of the English *Cyclopaedia* (1728), the stimulus for the *Encyclopédie*, had also been a Mason. In 1737, Andrew Michael Ramsay called upon his fellow Masons to create a universal dictionary of the arts and sciences, an appeal underscoring those cognate attitudes uniting Freemason and philosophe.

stood, explained, and regulated. Its good was to be cherished, its evil conquered. European thought became permeated by the idea that society had the means to construct a better civilization, that through the exercise of reason, the human lot might be ennobled. Enlightened man did not limit his glance to heaven, accepting whatever came his way. If, in his *Essay on Man* (1733), Alexander Pope, advising submission "Safe in the hand of one disposing Power," could proclaim that "Whatever is, is right," the true philosophe did not accede to such vindications of divine patience with evil; instead, he gazed about, beheld misery and abuse, and determined to join battle against them. He saw much of the prevailing system as his enemy, especially traditional Christian doctrine, which he felt to be deception and an obstacle to freedom and compassion. "I shall not say with Pope that all is good," Diderot observed. "Evil exists; and it is . . . not the effect of a ridiculous apple."

Progressive minds assigned the Bible's revelations and miracles as well as the Church's sacraments to superstition and looked upon ideas like God and the soul at best as ideals, at worst as illusions. The three boy-messengers in *The Magic Flute* would assuringly proclaim: "Soon superstition will die, soon the wise will prevail. . . . Then the earth will be a paradise, and men will be like gods." Indeed, Kant looked upon the *Aufklärung* (Enlightenment) essentially as a revolt against superstition, and Voltaire had urged: "Let us . . . reject all superstition in order to become more human," the very quality enabling Tamino, hero of *The Magic Flute*, to rise above his mere royal condition and gain a place in the temple of the elect.

Throughout the eighteenth century, as acquiescence and uncritical assent to traditional wisdom withered, the cultural climate of Europe inexorably changed. "I will not obey this inhuman order," sings Gluck's Agamemnon, appalled by the cruel will of the gods. No less horrified by their "barbarous" iniquities and "abominable altars," Mozart's Idomeneo struggles to deny Olympus the blood of an innocent, his son Idamante: "You are unjust; you cannot lay claim to it"; his lover, Ilia, in turn expounds to Idomeneo the heretical view that the cure lies within oneself, for "the gods are no tyrants; all of you misinterpret the divine will." The glittering surface of Mozart's *Così* envelops a no less profound work about the undermining of comfortable assumptions and the pain of putting them aside: by the final curtain, the philosophe Don Alfonso opens the two young couples' eyes to their vanity in clinging to unexamined received ideas and in attempting to flee self-knowledge; now aware that their happiness can proceed only from actions guided by reason, the soldiers and their fiancées determine to make a new beginning by espousing what he has demonstrated concerning the reality of the human condition and their own temperaments. Of the four lovers, the passionate Fiordiligi and the perplexed Ferrando will have the greater difficulties in adjusting to the lesson that neither virtue nor truth but accommodation is all.

The ground beneath social, political, and religious structures was giving way. Leopold Mozart numbered himself among those "many good Catholics . . . of the opinion that His Holiness the Pope cannot command except in matters of faith. . . ." Increasingly, fewer vouchsafed him even this authority. Ferdinando Galiani remarked: "Even excommunication, the sole thundering weapon left to this old empire, is no longer respected. . . ." Pondering the growing incredulity concerning the Papal claim to infallibility,[5] Leopold Mozart commented: "We live in a century during which—if we but live a bit longer—we will hear many new things." (He died two years before the storming of the Bastille.) Sympathetic to the temper and energy in the fresh currents of the age, Leopold respected the power of the critical intelligence. Above all, he came to believe that deference did not constitute a pattern man must inexorably trace.

Only two years before Wolfgang Mozart's birth, Rousseau, in his *Discourse on . . . Inequality . . .*, had wondered how anyone could doubt that it is against natural law "that a child should rule over an old man, that an imbecile should lead a wise man, and that a handful of people should fatten itself with superfluities while the hungry multitude goes without the essentials of life." Rousseau had recently written *Le Devin du village* (*The Village Soothsayer*), first presented at Fontainebleau in the presence of their Majesties (1752) and then performed at the Opéra during the following carnival season. Certainly Louis XV, his Queen, and the general public did not sense danger in the social innuendos of the seemingly innocent pastoral operetta, an adaptation of which Mozart would set to music as *Bastien und Bastienne*. (Indeed, the King soon took to going about singing the shepherdess's opening air, "with the vilest voice in his whole kingdom."[6]) At the gentle climax of the action, Rousseau's shepherd disdainfully threw away the luxurious and corrupting ribbon given him by a lady of rank, happily receiving in its place the simpler band of his shepherdess; but truly daring had been the operetta's pantomime, in which a courtier at-

---

5 Only in 1870 would a Vatican council define Papal infallibility as a dogma settled and incontrovertible since the Church's first days, when Christ gave the privilege to Peter.

6 Thus wrote the tenor Pierre Jelyotte, who impersonated the country gallant, a role essayed by Pompadour herself in man's attire when she had the work done at Bellevue, her house overlooking the Seine. At the premiere, Marie Fel sang the role of the shepherdess. Concerning Fel's and Jelyotte's later acquaintance with the Mozarts, see pp. 173–74.

tempted to seduce a village girl with money and jewelry and threatened her protective rustic lover—prefigurations of Mozart's Zerlina, Masetto, and Don Giovanni. Though the aristocrat, moved by entreaties, relented and united the pair, the implications of the explicit dumb show must nonetheless have excited astonishment.

Alexis de Tocqueville observed that the "propensities natural to democratic nations, in respect to literature, will . . . first be discernible in the drama, and it may be foreseen that they will break out there with vehemence." During the seventeen-fifties, Diderot began to write intense, realistic plays treating the austere values, the *sensibilité*, and the ideals of the middle class as edifying, the virtue, for example, of his chivalrous young bourgeois, Dorval (*Le fils naturel*), insinuating the unworthiness and corruption of the great. On the whole, such political audacities could be ventured only in a great cosmopolitan center like Paris. In German lands a complaint like Leporello's exasperated *"non voglio più servir"* (I no longer wish to serve) remained unspoken, though it could be sung if in a foreign tongue. It was in the Habsburgs' Bohemian capital that this unwilling domestic of Mozart's Don Giovanni first voiced his dissatisfaction, followed by an insistent, reiterated "no." Mozart must have been aware of the political overtones of this contumacy, recalling a comment he had made to his father relative to their Prince-Archbishop: "Even if I had to go begging, I would never again serve such a lord."[7] In Vienna, Mozart's Figaro, more courageous than Leporello, had already made known, though in Italian, his intention to call the tune to which his highborn master would have to dance.

Five years before the beginning of the French Revolution, this resourceful servant-hero of Beaumarchais's *Marriage of Figaro* and his sweetheart had made their first appearance (at the Comédie-Française), audaciously and irrepressibly defying the base and ignorant ways of the *ancien régime* and holding them up to ridicule. (Vienna heard Mozart's musical version of the comedy two years later.) "Detestable," cried Louis XVI, who clearly saw what the Figaros of his realm were up to as his courtiers flocked to the theater to laugh at their own caricatures. As the path toward skepticism, agnosticism, and egalitarianism broadened, the liberal concepts of the Enlightenment gained momentum and then hurtled forward with revolutionary force.

---

7 Having left Esterházy service upon the death of Prince Nikolaus, Joseph Haydn relished the sweetness of a new freedom. "I often sighed for release," he wrote from England in 1791. "The realization that I am no bond-servant makes ample amends for all my toil."

2

THE LISBON EARTHQUAKE'S effect upon Voltaire hastened the triumph of the Enlightenment: he communicated his reaction of anger and compassion to intellectual Europe and stirred it to thought. The catastrophe occurred on All Saints' Day (1 November) 1755. Within moments the city tottered to rubble as a tidal wave (more properly, a tsunami) broke over it. Thousands perished under debris, vanished into the earth, or were washed into the estuary of the Tagus. Vibrations migrated far beyond the epicenter. By December, Leopold Mozart was speculating about the safety of Salzburg. Munich, Ingolstadt, and Augsburg had already trembled, and he humorously ascribed to the oscillation of his native city the uncomplicated accouchement of Christina Sabina Lotter, his publisher's wife. But for Anna Maria—within a month of delivering Wolfgang—Leopold desired no such drastic inducement. "God be praised!" he wrote Lotter, "as yet there has been no earthquake here." Mozart entered the world in a calm, unshaken Salzburg, but at a moment of intellectual convulsion. Europe, in awe, followed the dreadful news from Lisbon. A flood of commentary poured forth, and disturbing questions posed by Voltaire soon found widespread response.

Pope had regarded chance as "Direction, which thou canst not see"; Leibniz, the great German philosopher of the Baroque, whose ideas still suffused German learning, had postulated a universe so perfectly arranged that all things were for the best.[8] But Voltaire, hearing of the Portuguese calamity, asked: "What will the preachers say, especially if the palace of the Inquisition is still standing?" In his impassioned *Poeme sur le désastre de Lisbonne* he arraigned Leibniz for failing to tell "why the innocent as well as the guilty equally endure this inevitable evil" and in *Candide* composed a set of brilliant satirical variations upon the theme of Leibnizian optimism. The shipwrecked hero, spewed ashore just in time to witness the destruction of Lisbon, finds himself seized by Inquisitors who believe "the spectacle of people being burnt to death by a slow fire . . . an infallible antidote for earthquakes." Whipped and bloody, Candide asks, "If this is the best of possible worlds, what then are the rest?"

As the earth trembled and Lisbon fell to ruin, Candide's companion and mentor, Dr. Pangloss, had calmly analyzed the geological basis of the

---

8 Many German civic authorities of the time believed the state to partake of Leibnizian metaphysics. If, as they had learned at the university, the world's phenomena coalesce in an implicit harmony that only error, accident, or abuse can temporarily disturb, then the state, being perfect, required not reform but, rather, suppression of occasional random and superficial distortions of the natural order. Administrative solutions thus appeared quite simple: not change, but restoration.

phenomenon. He assured the survivors: "All this must necessarily be for the best. As this volcano is at Lisbon, it could not be elsewhere." In Dr. Pangloss, Voltaire savagely caricatured Leibniz. But the target must have been even wider, the parody also embracing Leibniz's disciple and apologist Christian Wolff (1679–1754), a timid father of the *Aufklärung*. His writings played a significant part in German thought until the emergence of Kant. Indeed, Leopold Mozart's correspondence from time to time echoes Wolff's voice, especially on matters concerning moderation in religion (see p. 192).

Science, though in its infancy, particularly threatened the credibility of the Bible. As early as 1712, the Marquise de Lambert observed that in the salon the Christian Mysteries had become a laughingstock: "Anyone but venturing to express a belief in God was thought to belong to the lower orders." Cardinal de Bernis remarked in his *Mémoires* that by 1720 people of quality for the most part ignored the Gospels. They gave the Old Testament even less attention. (After listing the assassinations recorded in Kings and Chronicles, Voltaire, while expressing admiration for the Holy Spirit's literary style, lamented that it had been lavished upon so unedifying a subject.) Pretending to allay skepticism, many articles in the *Encyclopédie*, in fact, indulged in sowing and augmenting doubts concerning revealed theology, delighting in chronological calculations meant to perplex believers. Shells encountered far from the sea no longer found an adequate explanation in Noah's flood, which, moreover, seemed not to have interrupted the activities of the Chinese. Had their great achievements continued under water? Such questions, born of the new science and history, put religion on the defensive.

Wolff countered by constructing a philosophy in which supernaturally revealed religion might survive the claims of modern research. Miracles, he said, did not deny but, rather, transcended reason. His new "Christian rationalism" enfolded the irrational by rearranging and attenuating Leibniz's complex thought, reducing it to formula: falling back upon a dualism of sense-experience and intellectual knowledge, he transformed the contingent into the necessary, his popularization reconciling revelation with the claims of cogitation, the precarious with the teleological, miracles with the divinely regulated order of nature.

However shallow Wolff's system, it served as a welcome stopgap to cautious Germans like Leopold Mozart, clinging to their past and offended by the insensitivity and destructiveness with which the Enlightenment treated the mysteries of redemption. A philosophy advancing the idea that all knowledge might be encompassed left no room for the intuitive. Voltaire's scientific approach to scripture offended worthies like

Leopold, who, moreover, could not concur with those musicians and theorists rushing to accommodate the new and fashionable rationalism.

They construed the so-called *Affetto* or *Affekt* (the expressive manner in which to perform a musical work) in terms of mathematical or chemical formulae, interpreting words like "cantabile" or "vivace" as exact and infallible measurements permitting no latitude. With Wolffian moderation Leopold advised performers to seek within themselves the inherent character and pace of a composition, qualities good musicians, he felt certain, grasped instinctively. He was hardly alone in appreciating many of the reformative tendencies and achievements of the Enlightenment while, at the same time, finding it, on certain levels, obtrusive, limiting, undermining, and not without its own array of prejudices. Horace Walpole, visiting Paris, sighed: "There is God and the King to be pulled down first; and men and women, one and all, are devoutly employed in the demolition." Rousseau lamented: "We have all become doctors and ceased to be Christians."9

It should not surprise that, when the full French Enlightenment arrived in Germany, Rousseau, with his belief in a benevolent providence, had stronger influence than the dry, cynical Voltaire. Even so, though Wolfgang Mozart, thinking to please his father, affected disdain for Voltaire, this philosophe's perceptive, curious, and informed ideal man—not Rousseau's intuitive, unread, and contented innocent—became the Mozartean model for the ultimate legislators of society: Prince Tamino and his beloved, not the birdman and his sweetheart. Mozart's visionary world became Voltairean, that is to say, intellectually aristocratic and hierarchical. However, he ended his days comforted by a God still clothed in traditional vestments, by a concept more material than Voltaire's universal intelligence, for him little more than an expedient social and moral postulate. Leopold Mozart, for his part, had considered it a joyous victory to hear a Voltairean, Friedrich Melchior Grimm, cry in amazement: "Now for once in my life I have seen a miracle; it is the first!" The miracle was the child Wolfgang, the victory more Wolffian than Catholic.

Wolff's religious metaphysics, "vague and slender," in Grimm's words, but also reassuring and disarming, had that element of delusion often attractive to the German mind. From the refuge of unruffled Faith, Wolff's adherents could calmly contemplate the progress of the natural sciences while declining to face the implications of the scientific method. Leopold Mozart, contentedly harmonizing the providential and reasoned, sustained a lifelong interest in the new discoveries: he recommended expanded in-

---

9 The Swiss-German philosopher Isaak Iselin (1728–1782) similarly observed: "There is no need to heap insults upon throne and altar in order to be a friend of truth and a defender of humanity."

stallation of lightning rods despite ecclesiastical condemnation of their use as insupportable presumption on the part of those who would meddle in decisions belonging to heaven alone. Leopold knew of Benjamin Franklin's "Philadelphian experiments," discussed widely in Europe—he had a high opinion of "Dr. Francklin"—and disdained the usual practice of ringing church bells at the approach of a storm in order to drive away evil spirits.

On his Grand Tour he observed with delight the exhibits in Bologna's Instituto delle Scienze and the British Museum; enthusiastically examining whatever natural-history collections presented themselves on his route, he judged those at Brussels the finest. His effects auctioned after his death included two microscopes and a telescope three feet long with a double lens. Leopold's friend Dr. Franz Anton Mesmer, active Freemason, founder of psychotherapy, and apostle of "animal magnetism" (whose method of treatment at his *magnetisches Hospital* Mozart made merry with in the first finale of *Così fan tutte*), guided himself by a precept of his professor at Ingolstadt, the Wolffian jurist Adam Ickstatt: "Science does not damage faith, which is endangered only by superstition and ignorance." This maxim became Leopold's.

The Wolffian movement gained strength: by the thirties, a proselytizing Society of Alethophiles had formed at Berlin, its purpose the dissemination of Wolff's teaching, its motto *Sapere aude*;[10] by the middle of the century, Wolffians formed a fashionable philosophic school at German universities, and, in time, established themselves at religious houses like Kremsmunster, the influential Benedictine monastery near Steyr. Even in conservative Bavaria, at the time still medieval in many ways, a group of Augustinians—Eusebius Amort in their number—had instituted (1722) *Parnassus Boicus,* a journal encouraging the arts and sciences, monasteries like the Augustinian priory of Pölling (near Wessobrunn) and the famed Benedictine cloister of St. Emmeram at Regensburg supporting such Wolffian endeavors. Though a teacher like Ickstatt might furnish his pupils with French Enlightenment literature, Wolff's system helped sustain faith: among literate Germans it dwindled relatively slowly; while the French "leaped into unbelief, their German brethren were seduced into it, step by reluctant step."[11]

---

10 The heads of Leibniz and Wolff, disposed in the manner of a two-faced Janus and ornamenting the helmet of an armed Minerva, adorned the society's medal, as did the motto.

11 The young Georg Christoph Lichtenberg charmingly exemplified the combination of scientific curiosity and traditional faith of many Germans of the time (he would become a famed professor of physics at Göttingen and commentator on Hogarth): while a schoolboy, he wrote down the question "What is the Aurora Borealis?," addressed the inquiry to an angel, and placed it in the attic (see XII, n. 29).

The year of Wolfgang Mozart's birth and three years before the appearance of Voltaire's Dr. Pangloss, a thirty-two-year-old physicist and mathematician in Königsberg, Immanual Kant, wrote a paper on the scientific aspects of the Lisbon earthquake. Though reared in the emotional anti-intellectualism of pietism, he found the anchorage of his mighty development in the philosophes—Voltaire, Rousseau, and especially Hume—and became a religious freethinker. He, however, first took the path followed by his contemporary Leopold Mozart: the untroubled, middle road opened by Wolff. While for the mature Kant and his followers the assuming of God and immortality—albeit acknowledged a philosophic convenience—became an open question, Wolff's cautious religious metaphysics sufficed Leopold. Though Wolff's doctrines had crested at Salzburg in the forties, that is, subsequent to Leopold's departure from the university, they had begun circulating during his student days and had the power to kindle into flame the ethical ideas often smoldering in youthful minds: Wolff tinged many of his best pages with the loftiness of Spinoza, whom Novalis celebrated as *"der Gottvertrunkene Mann"* (the man intoxicated with God). Wolff's thought breached the confines of Leopold's Jesuit education.

"On the Practical Philosophy of the Chinese," one of Wolff's most famous lectures—infamous in the eyes of his sectarian pietistic colleagues at the university of Halle—bears spiritual affinity with the generous impulses that often swept Leopold and Wolfgang Mozart relative to religious toleration. The essay holds cultural communion with the Masonic humanitarianism of four of the son's stage works, the themes of which assert the idea of reconciliation among men and their subdual of national hatreds: *Zaide,* a musical torso with many of the paradoxical, provocative, but no less noble characteristics of Lessing's contemporary *Nathan der Weise* (*Nathan the Wise*);[12] *Idomeneo,* whose young hero removes his captives' bonds and whose heroine, through love for him, heals the enmity between Trojan and Greek; *The Abduction from the Seraglio,* rich in Voltairean irony as a renegade, Pasha Selim, gives a Spanish Catholic a lesson in magnanimity; and *The Magic Flute,* Mozart's ultimate essay on reconciliation among those equal to moving toward love, forgiveness, and Enlightenment.

---

12 Lessing wrote *Nathan* and his *Gespräche für Freymaurer* concurrently. Nothing remains of the Melodrama *Semiramis* Mozart began in Mannheim during 1778; but Enlightened ideas must also have colored this work Otto von Gemmingen-Hornberg adapted from Voltaire's tragedy: both von Gemmingen and Wolfgang Heribert von Dalberg, Intendant of the Mannheim theater, belonged to the Freemasons. Indeed, von Gemmingen became master of the lodge Mozart would join in Vienna (see p. 645).

Wolff extolled the philosophy of Confucius as demonstrating that reason alone can construct an admirable ethical system, that high moral values do exist outside of Christianity, that Christianity, in any case, has no monopoly of nobility of thought. Without divine revelation and Grace, Confucius, solely through the power of human reason, attained moral truth. (Though the virtue of Mozart's Pasha Selim appears less reasoned than inherent, it, too, has its origins beyond the pages of the Gospels, as does that of the lovers in *Idomeneo* and the *The Magic Flute*.) Clearly, Wolffian teachings helped dispose Wolfgang and his father toward a liberal sensibility—if Mozart had no direct interest in speculative philosophy, he could not have been divorced from its influence—and point them toward Kant's moral imperatives and, above all, Freemasonry. It had first taken root in German cities during Leopold's stay at the university.

German Masonic lodges often became elite groups—including nobles and artists as well as bourgeois—devoted to the orderly and progressive renovation of society. At liberty to follow or dismiss Christian dogma, members united in adherence to tolerant, egalitarian ideals. Freemasonry's not rare obscurantism formed but its popular image; though many poked fun at the idea of townsfolk decked with exotic paraphernalia evoking ancient and gothic mysteries,[13] the Order had the profound goal of going beyond particular religions, many of them, at the time, devoid of humanitarian substance, and offering a compensatory overarching morality based upon belief in God and confidence in the eventual construction of a virtuous and therefore just society. Mozart foresaw it in *Idomeneo* as the Prince and his beloved win the blessing of Olympus, enter upon their rule, and thereby undo the furious, irrational, unenlightened Elettra. *The Magic Flute*, Freemasonry's spiritual manifesto, set forth with even more authority its composer's faith in the coming of this golden age, which, in fact, arrives just before the final curtain: "Our power is shattered and destroyed," cry Elettra's successor, the Queen of the Night, and her vassals; "we plunge into eternal night!" They vanish. Enthroned in his temple, Sarastro, the High Priest, expounds the victory: "The sun's rays have banished the night and undone the dominion hypocrites had gained by stealth." The darkness of fanaticism has fled before the light of reason.

---

13 Freemasonry at times revealed startling irreconcilable tendencies: devotion to the liberal exercise of reason and the scientific method did not exclude—in particular among those following the rituals and mysteries of the German sects known as the Strict Observance and the Rosicrucians—pursuit of the secrets of the universe through the arcane and hermetic, a search for primordial transcendental wisdom and revelation once received but since lost (see pp. 654–56).

3

DID MOZART DIE a Catholic? In his final months he honored the Holy Sacrifice of the Altar in his unfinished Requiem; yet, at the same time, in *La clemenza di Tito* he, with complete musical conviction, celebrated aristocratic justice, a concept with little regard in his eyes. Both were commissioned works, and at the height of his powers Mozart could not do otherwise than create masterpieces. Even so, the Requiem breathes an intense, personal piety, its most moving moments those extraordinary proddings of God to fulfill His promise to Abraham.

Though the members of the Masonic lodge Mozart chose to join were Catholic, they rejected Papal pretensions to absolute authority and showed indifference to Rome's denunciations of their Order; they embraced it as in every way Christian, indeed, Catholic, viewing its teachings in the light of Father Muratori's (see p. 40 and n. 15), which centered upon devotion to acts of beneficence, the word forming the very name of Mozart's lodge (*Wohltätigkeit*). The Masonic funeral oration celebrating Mozart's death observed that he had "learned the great art of living in virtue so that he might die as a Mason and a Christian." He had remained a religious man, a Catholic (if of the Enlightened or Muratorian variety), though one much at odds with the Church.

He did not end the kind of son Rome held most dear: *The Magic Flute* and *The Abduction from the Seraglio* had shot more than one volley at the Church. A reader of Enlightened books,[14] he had become devoutly anticlerical and favored the judicious secularization of more than one of its institutions and rituals, burial among them. His own interment respected in spirit the reforming Joseph II's directives for simple procedure, despite their having been repealed; at the same time, Mozart's funeral, accordant with Masonic instruction, and doubtless answering his desires, in no way violated the propriety and usage of the time (see pp. 745–46).

His final surviving letter to his father and brother Mason (4 April 1781) echoed with resonances of *Phädon or Concerning the Immortality of the Soul* by the "German Plato," the Jewish philosophe Moses Mendelssohn, and meditated upon life and death in Masonic terms. "You understand what I mean," Mozart had insisted as he touched upon the mysteries of the lodge

14 In Salzburg during 1829, Mary and Vincent Novello visited Mozart's widow (then Frau Nissen) and her son, Wolfgang Amadeus (born Franz Xaver Wolfgang). Mary reported to her diary: "One of his [Mozart's] favourite authors is at present in her possession, and which she most frequently peruses, it is in 9 volumes but being a forbidden fruit in the Austrian states [Austria had absorbed Salzburg thirteen years earlier] she did not name it—I suspect some of the French revolutionary works."

and his joy in its revelations.[15] His alienation had become that of a modern man: a child of the Enlightenment, he looked upon happiness, especially his right to the joy of fulfilling his talent, as something to be pursued and communicated. "On no occasion do I go to bed without reflecting that, young as I am, I may perhaps never see another day. And yet none of all those who know me can say that in company I am morose or sad." In contrast, Leopold, a product of Wolff's temporizing generation, remained distressed and uncertain about his devotion and attachments.

15 His library contained not only Mendelssohn's *Phädon* but also another text of import in his moral development: John Kirkby's *Automathes or the Capacity and Extent of the Human Understanding* (London, 1745), which set store upon the exercise of charity: a Jew and a Protestant helped Mozart travel the Catholic, indeed Muratorian, path toward the mystery of Grace.

CHAPTER III

The Mask and the Face: Ambivalence without Resolution

SUDDEN SHIFTS FROM Jesuitical orthodoxy to Enlightened liberalism characterized Leopold throughout his life. A collection of music he compiled for Wolfgang included a scattering of hymns so that the child might praise God in the course of his studies: a Jesuitical exercise with Protestant texts! Yet, his son's communing with his Maker in pietistic verse notwithstanding, he could not dismiss the idea that, in the course of traveling, a prolonged stay in too Protestant an area might somehow damage Catholic children. When the family visited the Palatinate in 1763, it swarmed with not only Lutherans and Calvinists but Jews, too, and he became alarmed by the absence of holy-water stoups, crucifixes, and dishes for fast days in hotels open to all.[1] But the pragmatic Leopold soon asserted himself: "Basta! It is not our fault." All was for the best: had not Wolff's Determinism proclaimed purpose to be all-pervading? And, indeed, with the years, friendships with men like the Lutheran Counselors Hopfgarten and von Bose and with a Dutch Jew, the cellist Emanuel Sipurtini, would strengthen, in Leopold, Wolff's belief that no single religion

---

1 Catholic and Lutheran churches stood side by side in his native Augsburg, but communicants of the two faiths remained culturally and socially apart, even to the point of dressing in distinct ways.

had spirituality to itself: "How can one be a Persian?" Montesquieu had asked; Leopold sought the answer.

Von Bose presented Wolfgang, whom he called the "little seven-year-old Orpheus," with a copy of Gellert's *Geistliche Oden und Lieder* (Sacred Odes and Songs). Leopold admired the sentimental, didactic Gellert. He, too, embraced Wolffian optimism while retaining a measure of pious melancholy, in his case of the pietistic variety. Leopold corresponded with this famous Protestant writer, whose works he encouraged his friends to read. Broad-mindedness stood forth as, perhaps, Leopold's greatest moral gift to his son, to whom, however, the father's vigilant Jesuitical distrust of men and their motives remained foreign. "Take this as a universal rule: all men lie and add or subtract as suits their purposes. One must for certain not believe any assertions that, if bruited about, would add to the speaker's reputation or wheedle some advantage for him. Without doubt these would be lies!" Late in life he addressed this advice to his daughter; his son no longer listened. To little purpose had the father striven to inject into him a preceptive pragmatism both Jesuitical and Wolffian: "No reasonable person—I need scarcely say Christian—will deny that all things will and must come to pass according to God's will. But does it follow from this that we should act blindly, live carelessly, plan nothing, and simply wait for something to drop from heaven of its own accord? Does not God Himself and do not all reasonable people require us to weigh the consequences and results of all our actions according to the compass of our human reason and to take pains to look as far ahead as we possibly can?"

After visiting London and Paris, Leopold spiced Wolff's pallid rationalism with dashes of fashionable English Deism and French Cynicism. (In Paris he had met Friedrich Melchior Grimm, the ex officio tattler of the philosophes, a dedicated skeptic whom he described in a newly acquired Enlightened vocabulary as "a man of learning and a friend of humanity"; even Frau Mozart took to using this jargon.) However, true skepticism never gnawed at Leopold: he remained vacillating between the doctrines of Christian Wolff and those of the Roman Church.

In sympathy with the new scientific temper, he ridiculed the miracle mongers of a corrupt priesthood—nevertheless, in Italy he could not resist purchasing a piece of the True Cross—and he passed on to Wolfgang a mocking, insolent attitude toward those who held power in the religious (and social) structures of his time. Yet he did not question the value of these structures and continued zealously to fulfill the formal duties of the Faithful. Indeed, he wrote his wife from Italy (14 April 1770) of the miraculously preserved bodies of Santa Rosa, exhibited in her great church at

Viterbo, and of Saint Catherine Vigri, Abbess of the Poor Clares, in the church of Corpus Domini at Bologna. He and Wolfgang took away souvenirs, "from the first . . . relics and a powder against fever, from the second a belt. . . ." But piety did not blind him, and he found sickening the "detestable" and "malicious" on both sides of the altar who hid "under the cloak of sanctity," especially those girls who "confess so long to cunning, clever priests . . . that they strike up closer acquaintance and become priests' whores." Of such scandals "I can furnish examples and proofs," he informed his daughter in the voice of a caustic, Enlightened Frenchman—a Diderot forensically documenting society's ills. The angry allusion touched upon his Augsburg niece, Maria Anna, so precious to his son. Leopold but feigned to joke when chiding her for having "too great an acquaintance with priests"; quite early he had recognized her as *"ein Pfaffenhuer."*[2]

Leopold's bitterness toward clerics increased with age. But he never lessened his devotion to the divine truths, personified for him in the wonder-working Madonna who still presides over the high altar of Maria Plain, a pilgrimage church crowning a bluff a few kilometers from Salzburg. This sacred portrait remained his lodestone of faith, and he appealed to it for big and small favors.[3] His first crossing of the English Channel cost him so much vomiting that he took the precaution of having masses said at Maria Plain to prepare smooth waters for his return. Yet he scolded his daughter for exposing herself to drafts by hearing mass daily in a chilly church; Sunday and feast-day masses sufficed: "Man must answer before God for his health. . . ."[4] Leopold sprouted contradictions, to which his son fell heir. But while Wolfgang sought to confront his ambivalence and attempt its resolution, as a rule Leopold dared not try his strength. Evidence does survive of an incident in which his usual restraint burst: three years before Wolfgang's birth, he put out a lampoon against a priest named Egglstainer and one of the counts of Thurn und Taxis; this foolhardy act led to his being hauled before the syndics of the cathedral chapter, who "tore his text to pieces . . . scattered it at his feet," and gave him the choice of apologizing to those he had insulted or of going to prison "for a fully well-merited punishment."

2 In 1784 she gave birth to a daughter fathered by Abbé Theodor von Reibeld, a canon of Augsburg cathedral.

3 The Mozarts also petitioned and returned thanks to a second sacred image in Salzburg: the tiny, elaborately attired ivory figure of the Infant Christ in the church of St. Maria Loreto, the so-called *Loreto-Kindl.*

4 Here he calls to mind Diderot's advice to his sister Denise (25 November 1778): "Whatever harm you do your health is not guiltless. . . . Often it is better to remain warm in bed than to get numb in church."

What he considered fraudulence and abuse in the Church continued to make him, on occasion, cast away all tact: in 1766 he inveighed against encouraging postulants to take the vows of any religious order before their twenty-fifth year, a practice suggesting to him the methods of the recruiting sergeant: "Why not determine upon [entry] in the twenty-fifth year?" "Perhaps," he, with ill grace, observed to a wealthy friend whose eighteen-year-old son had recently become a Benedictine novice, "because in the meantime many a rich candidate might examine and apprehend his calling better. . . ."5 Leopold came to despise the clergy (as did his son), at times disdainfully looking back at his old teachers as "crack-brained." Yet he mixed compassion for the ordinary Jesuit with contempt for their affluent leaders (he called them "the Rabbis" in his observations on Pope Clement XIV's suppression of the Order).

As if to mock their purpose, Jesuit schools of the eighteenth century bred many a freethinker, Diderot, Helvetius, and Voltaire among the most celebrated. Leopold listed Diderot as one of his Parisian acquaintances and, despite Helvetius's reputation as author of the radical *De l'Esprit* (1758) and the Papacy's condemnation of it, visited him in Paris. (In 1764 Helvetius recommended Wolfgang, "one of the most singular beings in existence . . . a little German prodigy," to the English aristocracy.) Moreover, through Madame d'Épinay and Damilaville, the confidant of Voltaire, Leopold made efforts to have Wolfgang play at Ferney before this poet-philosophe whose works civil and religious authorities repeatedly damned. Opportunism determined Leopold's course: he clapped on an appropriate mask—smiling and liberal or dour and orthodox—to please a particular host or patron and probably dared not ponder which role he found more comfortable. Such impersonations had become modish at court and in the Church and put the less practiced at risk of mistaking disguise for reality, a misstep most dangerous when the mighty assumed borrowed feathers.

2

SOME RULERS DID interest themselves heart and soul in Freemasonry and the writings of the philosophes, an inclination heightened by the disposition of the Enlightened not to undermine, but, rather, in tranquillity to contemplate building afresh social and political hierarchies already in

---

5 In 1770 Maria Theresa would decree that in her German hereditary lands no novice might take final vows before completing his twenty-fourth year. She also limited the "dowry" a novice brought to a monastery.

place. Mozart's supporter Elector Maximilian III Joseph of Bavaria, for example, had, like Mesmer, studied with Ickstatt. Clerics, too, embraced the modish humanitarianism and freely changed or multiplied their affiliations as their speculations entered new phases;[6] and more than one (as had Jean Meslier) ended by excoriating Christianity or aspects of it: at the monastery of Kremsmünster, Placidus Fixelmillner, head of its educational work, impugned the Middle Ages as a time of darkness and lectured on the philosophy of Wolff and the gifts of the Enlightenment. But, for the most part, princes and ecclesiastics merely toyed with Enlightened ideas[7] as little more than a fashionable diversion; a congenital belief in imperturbable absolutism remained. (Mozart's leading patron, Emperor Joseph II, became the definitive example of the reformer-autocrat.) A slender veneer of sensibility, philosophy, and manners concealed this hard pith of eighteenth-century society, this unmodifiable, fixed core discerned, however, by many a worldly-wise philosophe.

Inveighing against tyranny, they often derived stipends from the very kind of prince their pamphlets denounced: well dressed, they delivered onslaughts upon privilege in the drawing rooms of the exquisite; but as he freely lauded the libertarian ideals of the ancients while stuffing his stomach at a powerful, iron-handed aristocrat's table, the philosophe took care to stop short of citing less venerable models of arbitrary power lest he lose his napkin. Giuseppe Parini, poet of liberty, enemy of servility, and author of *Il Giorno,* perhaps the century's most annihilating attack upon a degraded artistocracy's abuse of prerogatives, found himself cobbling for Mozart the cloying, sycophantic verses of *Ascanio in Alba,* a pastoral celebrating Empress Maria Theresa's dominion over the poet's helpless native land. But, then, his income derived from Vienna.

The hand that feeds may at most be tapped, never bitten: the beholden had to study the emotional climate of each court in order to discern those limits not to be overstepped. Hénault remarked of the essays dealing with princely personages in Voltaire's *Century of Louis XIV:* "Such things may be told confidentially in one's chimney corner, but one does not write them

---

6 For a time, Vienna-born Karl Leonhard Reinhold belonged simultaneously to the Barnabites (he had been a Jesuit novice but turned to this teaching Order), the Freemasons, and the related society of the Illuminati. The Hungarian Ignatius Aurelius Fessler remained a Capuchin even as he became a Jansenist in Vienna and then a Mason at the university of Lemberg, where his writings thrust at the concept of absolute monarchy. Subsequently, he decamped to Russia and rose to be a Lutheran bishop, by which time he had—can it be hoped?—shed some of his earlier identities.

7 Absolutism played the game of harnessing such views to its own cause: the Bavarian Academy of Sciences, with its emphasis upon educational work, came into being (1759) for the purpose of weakening the Church to the advantage of the palace.

down." Even at liberal Weimar the satiric wit of Jakob Reinhold Lenz proved too outspoken, and he received a mortifying ducal order to quit the capital within twenty-four hours. It was an Enlightened archbishop, Hieronymus Colloredo, perhaps a Mason and for certain an enthusiastic admirer of Voltaire, who found Mozart's sense of independence insupportable.

With the passing years, Mozart more and more recoiled from training himself to dissimulate, from practicing the toadying necessary to success at the palace. He could not endure his colleagues, "always fawning," day to day changing identities. "Only don't crawl, for I can't bear it," he admonished his father. ("Tell me," elegant, fine-spoken Prince Tamino asks the rustic, rough-hewn bird-catcher Papageno, ". . . who are you?" "A man like you," he replies.) But, subdued by time, Leopold became ever more cautious, for the venturesome paid a heavy price: a chamberlain's boot would evict his son from the Archbishop's anteroom.

Voltaire had suffered a public thrashing by lackeys of Chevalier Gui Auguste de Rohan-Chabot,[8] a humiliation of no matter to the aristocratic "friends" of the young poet who had naïvely assumed their Enlightenment to extend beyond the dining room and opera box. At the time of the assault, the Prince de Conti mockingly asked: "What should become of the rest of us if poets had no backs?" How ironic that in a letter to Paris (6 April 1778) castigating the contemptuous attitude of the Archbishop of Salzburg toward the Mozarts, Leopold intimated that the solution to the problem perhaps lay in Wolfgang's entering the service of the Rohan family.

The well-born played at Enlightenment most enthusiastically in Germany. After his accession, Frederick the Great, rescinding the ban instituted by his father, recalled Christian Wolff, whose essay on Confucius had led to his banishment.[9] But he lectured to empty halls. The Wolffian compromise had run its course, the full Enlightenment stood forth, and Frederick intensified his efforts to lure its most dazzling representative, Voltaire, to Berlin. In the early days of their correspondence, Frederick (who soon became a Freemason) had urged Voltaire to write to him "only as a man" and to despise his "titles, names, and external glamour." Later, infuriated by the very candor he had invited, he let fly with imperious brutality: "Learn in what

---

8 He should not be confused with a hero of the Seven Years' War, Louis-Antoine-Auguste de Rohan, Duke de Chabot, for whom Mozart performed in Paris. (He did not assume the title of Duke de Rohan until 1791.)

9 The Pietists had, to boot, persuaded Frederick's father, Frederick William I, that Wolff's Determinism, once sanctioned, would cause wholesale and unpunishable desertions from the Prussian army, each culprit excusing himself on the ground of an inevitable chain of causation!

wise it is fitting that you write me. Understand that some liberties are permitted, and some impertinences are intolerable. . . ."

If this outburst betrayed in a thoroughly heavy-handed manner the true limits of monarchy's Enlightened ways, another no less arrogant tyrant understood how to show grace in managing a *philosophe-confident.* At St. Petersburg, Catherine of Russia—whom Vittorio Alfieri called the "philosophizing Clytemnestra"—listened with courtesy to the social reforms proposed by her guest, Diderot; declared him "extraordinary"; sent him home heaped with favors; and continued a rule unaffected by his conversations or memoranda: sufficient that a philosophe in residence provide the powerful with prestige and distraction. Guillaume du Tillot, the Frenchman who administered Parma for Philip of Bourbon—and who delighted in the visiting Wolfgang Mozart's conversation—imported Condillac to educate the heir to the duchy. But neither the Bourbons nor Tillot had any use for the philosopher-king of Condillac's dreams, and it should not surprise that Prince Ferdinand proved unsullied by any taint of liberalism—indeed, of intelligence. At the court of Parma, only Condillac himself looked in earnest upon his *Cours d'études,* though it nonetheless issued from Parmesan presses with a flourish of trumpets and in a grand edition of thirteen volumes.

The behavior of Count Almaviva in Mozart's *The Marriage of Figaro* lays emphasis upon the prudence required at rococo courts not to confuse the mask with the face. Though Almaviva had abolished the *jus primae noctis* (the right of the first night: the noble's privilege of deflowering a retainer's bride),[10] the opening act finds him vexed to discover his servants making a show of taking as noble and substantive what he had intended—as they well know—only as an Enlightened gesture. These peasants and domestics are not Dresden china figures with Roman profiles and swirling, immaculate linen, but practical delegates seeking to manipulate him into a line of conduct he has no intention of pursuing. The chorus of retainers plays a role more than peripheral to the main intrigue: obsessed, they feed Almaviva's bursts of anger.

---

10 History preserves scant records of such a custom. A myth drawing together the worst features of aristocratic licentiousness, it gained renewed vitality in Mozart's day through Voltaire's play *Droit du seigneur,* produced in Paris (1762) in the wake of the commotion surrounding the Calas trial (see p. 88 and XI, n. 30). Beaumarchais's *Figaro* put to use the invidious elements of Voltaire's drama, making them even more acute; but what today's public regards as historical fact, eighteenth-century audiences knew to be a fiction turned to dramatic account. The "*droit*" motif also sounds, even if as a distorted echo, in the graveyard scene of Mozart's *Don Giovanni:* the hero tells his servant Leporello about a recent adventure with a pretty girl who had welcomed his advances, thinking him Leporello. Not amused, he in turn asks: "Could she not have been my wife?" "All the better," Don Giovanni retorts, laughing.

The surly Almaviva's settled convictions of the immunity of pedigree accorded with those of Emperor Joseph II, whose name usually follows some liberal sobriquet, too often earned by his mastery of Enlightened mummery and masking. Joseph forbade performances of a German translation of Beaumarchais's politically controversial *Marriage of Figaro*, finding in it "much that is objectionable." However, he encouraged Mozart to create a less flammable musical version of the play, to be, moreover, performed in Italian, a language that most less-than-aristocratic Viennese theatergoers, despite their pretensions, did not command, the singing, into the bargain, clouding the words for those who did. Like Almaviva, Joseph had no desire to set aside his precedence. He, too, looked upon servants as furniture: while visiting the Neapolitan court, he did not hesitate to beat a flunky before the eyes of his host and brother-in-law, King Ferdinand; but with him he had no need to play the liberal. Joseph, the Great Reformer, revived the public burning of books offensive to his government: "Those who oppose us with ridicule or threats must be arrested, whipped, and kept in jail." Though his own orthodoxy lay under suspicion, he ordered proven Deists rewarded with twenty-four strokes on the backside. Government, Joseph believed, must be directed by reason; this he learned from the philosophes. A monarchical perception of what constitutes reason must always be sound; this he learned from his Imperial mother, whom Parini and the adolescent Mozart thus celebrated in their *Ascanio in Alba*: "You control all hearts with so gentle a rein that liberty is no longer desired." Here is the very relationship that in Mozart's *Magic Flute* binds Pamina to her jailer, the emperor-like wizard-philosophe Sarastro. Caught in an attempt to escape, she confesses to him: "I am truly a criminal; I wanted to flee your power."

Sarastro acts much like an Enlightened and absolute German ruler of the time;[11] the potentate who orders Monastatos punished with seventy-seven lashes on the soles can, close upon, declare—and at the moment with moving sincerity: "In these holy halls revenge is unknown; love guides the transgressor back to duty." The harsh sentence, extravagantly praised by Sarastro's courtiers, falls strangely upon the ear. His initial mock-graciousness toward the Moor followed by the severity of the sentence calls to mind Maria Theresa's more ill-humored days and Joseph's intemperate sarcasm, his self-righteousness, and the barbarities of the Josephine

---

11 In the face of *The Magic Flute, The Abduction from the Seraglio, The Marriage of Figaro,* and *Don Giovanni,* to say nothing of many passages in the Mozarts' letters, it becomes difficult to account for Alfred Einstein's contention that Mozart did not interest himself in politics. During Mozart's era, one's choice of literature became tantamount to a political decision.

penal code, its enforcement often preceding from the strange bypaths and crooked ways of his ill-disguised sadism. Like Emperor Joseph, Sarastro did not hesitate to call upon the services of an *agent provocateur*, here Monastatos, whom he then denounced. Not surprisingly, when he met Frederick the Great, the Habsburgs' legendary enemy, Joseph cried out: "That man is a genius . . ."; the double-tongued Frederick had become the Great Reformer's model.[12]

3

WHEN FREDERICK THE Great mounted the Prussian throne, Leopold Anton, Count von Firmian, reigned as prince-archbishop of Salzburg (1727–1744). Like Frederick, he sought to play the philosophe and toward this end sponsored a learned society modeled upon the Italian academies. It concerned itself with the researches of Lodovico Antonio Muratori, who had put down the foundations of medieval Italian studies. Father Muratori colored his appraisal of the past with a contemporary Enlightened liberalism and the ideal of a Christian life as shaped by acts of charity. (In the face of rumors of his heresy—indeed, atheism—he had to appeal to Pope Benedict XIV for support.) Inevitably, Firmian's modish Muratori Society, which examined theological and ecclesiological problems in a tone far too cosmopolitan for Salzburg, came into conflict with the more provincial, parochial professors at the university, who opposed giving the reins to progressive studies.[13] Predictably, Firmian (who puttered with the fashionable and Enlightened hobby of astronomy) in public took the part of his "modern" protégés; unpredictably, he found himself suspected of Masonic proclivities. (That, as chance would have it, the Italian word for Masons is *muratori*, had helped create a strange conflation in many minds.) Again, the true nature of the game had been misunderstood, the mask mistaken for the face.

How preposterous to suppose that a movement encouraging men of varying confessions to live and work together as brothers could have ef-

---

12 They met at Neisse (August 1769) and again in Mährisch-Neustadt (September 1770), for which conference Florian Leopold Gassmann wrote *La contessina*, his most successful opera. Leopold Mozart saw the Emperor's attitude toward the King in the light of an attempt to wile him into conciliation.

13 A liberalizing reform of the university's curricula in time followed the unavailing complaints and then departure of a number of aristocratic students to take up their studies at Protestant universities. In contrast, even though Empress Maria Theresa supported the Muratorians, the ecclesiastical authorities cowed into submission the young nobles with similar protests at Vienna's Savoy Academy.

fected a change in this fanatic shepherd of souls who wrote the darkest page in Salzburg's annals. In power when Leopold Mozart arrived in Salzburg, he had forced some twenty thousand Protestants to sacrifice their possessions and flee his see (1731–1732), many to seek the hospitality of Frederick the Great's father in East Prussia, some to voyage as far as Savannah, Georgia, in the New World. Despite harsh decrees, Protestant teachings had not died in the archbishopric, especially in its remote mountain districts. At first Firmian neglected public education in these areas, believing that a populace unable to read would be immune to the contagion of Protestant literature. But it proved too late for this curious approach. The Jesuits triumphed when the Archbishop issued the mandate to emigrate on 31 October (Reformation Day!) of 1731. In enforcing the principle of *cuius regio, eius religio* drawn up almost two centuries earlier, Firmian set in motion a train of personal distress, national upheaval, and economic disturbance few of his fellow German rulers would have countenanced, whatever their prejudices.[14]

The twelve-year-old Leopold Mozart must have witnessed a first contingent of weary *Salzburger Exulanten* (Salzburg exiles) draw up before the great Red Gate of Augsburg on New Year's Eve.[15] They found relief. Augsburgers could comprehend the tragedy: a century before (1629), Emperor Ferdinand II had forbidden their city the exercise of any religion save that of Rome, and eight thousand Protestants had departed to follow their banished clergymen. Long since protected from such invidiousness by the ecclesiastical settlement of the Peace of Westphalia (1648), Augsburg's citizenry—made up of a Lutheran fellowship living at peace within a Catholic bishopric—would, during the coming months, watch the arrival of almost six thousand homeless. Some of the hymns Leopold was to

---

14 Ever since the Electors of Saxony embraced Roman Catholicism in order to gain and retain the Polish crown (1697), the Prussian House of Brandenburg had taken upon itself the protection of German Protestants: Frederick William of Prussia attempted to stay Firmian's hand by threatening reprisals against Catholics in Prussian lands. Emperor Charles VI, busy negotiating the delicate question of the Pragmatic Sanction (see p. 73), found himself in an awkward position: the Habsburgs presided over both Catholic and Protestant princes; Imperial authority rested upon a personal mysticism proceeding not from doctrine but from dynasty. (In an ironic outcome of events, some decades later, the Jesuits, cast adrift by the Pope and Europe's Catholic monarchs, were to be welcomed in Protestant Prussia by Frederick William's son, Frederick the Great.) In the end, little could be done in Salzburg save arranging financial reimbursement to Protestants for homes and farms left behind. The principality became exclusively Catholic, Archbishop von Keutschach having expelled its Jews in 1498 "for ever and eternity."

15 Goethe's *Hermann und Dorothea* derived from an incident related in a narrative (1732) touching upon the passage of the Salzburg exiles.

teach his son sounded from the throats of these victims of Firmian as they massed before a city sacred to them through the Augsburg Confession.[16]

Firmian did contribute a few things of value to Salzburg. Along with his sense of history and scholarship he had a feeling for architecture and sculpture, an enthusiasm still visible in the palace of Leopoldskron and the Kapitelplatz horse pond with its majestic Neptune by Joseph Pfaffinger. Firmian also completed and embellished Lustschloss Klesheim, his favorite residence.[17] Moreover, his rapacious rule proved not without benefit to Leopold Mozart and his family: enriched by their uncle and ennobled by the Emperor, Firmian's nephews[18] were to become patrons of music, an art to which the dour Archbishop remained indifferent.

---

16 It would be misleading to suggest that intolerance became foreign to Augsburg. When in 1730 its Lutherans celebrated the bicentennial of the Augsburg Confession, the headstrong, inflammable Jesuit pater Franz Xaver Pfyffer thundered against this statement of faith; and two years later, from the same pulpit in the cathedral, he attempted to justify Firmian's persecutions. Yet, despite animosities and bickering, Augsburg respected the parity between Catholics and Lutherans guaranteed by the Peace of Westphalia, and the two faiths achieved a reasonable understanding and modus vivendi.

17 Early in the century, Fischer von Erlach had begun this palace (northeast of the city) for Archbishop Johann Ernst Thun.

18 Salzburg imitated Rome even as to nepotism's patterns of abuse: the greed of favored Papal nephews seizing as much treasure as quickly as possible, impelled by the realization that such opportunities came to an end with the uncle's death.

CHAPTER IV

Salzburg's Handsomest Pair;
Strategic Blunders and Patrician Ways

WHEN LEOPOLD MOVED to Firmian's court orchestra in 1743, he improved his expectations; but the new archiepiscopal fourth violinist continued in a weak financial position. He and his fiancée, the impoverished Anna Maria Pertl, had to endure a long engagement about which Leopold later observed: "Good things take time."

Just when they met remains unknown, but the beginning of their courtship coincided with the early days of the War of the Austrian Succession (1740–1748). Charles Albert, Elector of Bavaria, his heart set on the Imperial crown, contested young Archduchess Maria Theresa's title to her late father's Austrian possessions and sent an army down the Danube valley toward Vienna. The Archbishopric, geographically between the warring powers, suffered economically and feared for its independence. To coax the Virgin to extend her protection, the canons vowed to adorn her miraculous image at Maria Plain with a double crown blessed by the Pope, should the principality survive. Every house in Salzburg readied a caldron of pitch to provide light in case of a night attack. This proved an unsettling time in which to plan a marriage. It became clear, moreover, that Anna Maria's mother would have to join whatever household the couple might set up. But despite poverty, war, and the prospect of supporting and living with an indigent mother-in-law, Leopold wed Anna Maria in the cathedral on 21 November 1747, an occasion he later described as his entry into "the order of patched pants."

The opening years of the marriage must have been a financial ordeal surmounted by love, her domestic ingenuity, and a common bond in music. She came from a musical family: her mother was a musician's daughter; and Anna Maria's father, while a student at the university of Salzburg, had not only performed solo bass parts in the end-term presentations, appearing in Heinrich Biber's *Ladislaus und Matthias Corvinus* in 1688,[1] but also sung at the monastery school of St. Peter's.

Leopold and Anna Maria became known as "Salzburg's handsomest pair." Time treated Leopold kindly; he remained imposingly attractive. But his wife soon lost her beauty: her likeness shows the jowled, beaked, but intelligent and pleasant face that also looks out at posterity in portraits of her son. Leopold knew the dealer in textiles Ignaz Anton Weiser.[2] He doubtless urged his brother-in-law the merchant Lorenz Hagenauer to rent an apartment to the Mozarts in his house on the city's main street. At 9 Getreidegasse, between 1748 and 1756, Anna Maria brought into the world three boys and four girls; of the seven there survived beyond infancy only two: the fourth-born (30 July 1751), Maria Anna Walburga Ignatia, called Nannerl, and the last.

Leopold served five archbishops. After the death of Firmian in October 1744, the canons raised the hunchbacked and sickly Count Jakob Ernst von Liechtenstein to St. Rupert's chair. During his short reign he took pleasure in music and masked balls and, imitating Versailles, maintained a *grande bande* of twenty-four strings. In 1747 he died, leaving an ailing exchequer to be nursed by his successor, Count Andreas Jacob von Dietrichstein. Sociable, he delighted in music, masquerades, and, in particular, the gaming table, though the popular whirling dances troubled him. He saw them as a dangerous phenomenon—a gyrating harbinger of dreadful things to come.

The *Ländler*, the *deutscher Tanz* (the Teutscher or German dance), the allemande, and the contredanse—all had contributed to the development of the incipient waltz, which, despite the disapproval of French dancing masters, had become popular among the less than princely. (Montaigne, visiting the house of the Fuggers in Augsburg, had stared in astonishment at couples turning as they danced in close embrace.) By the middle of the

1 Biber had begun his musical association with Salzburg, probably as court composer, during the winter of 1670–1671.

2 A man of literary ambitions, Weiser had written the texts of two oratorios set by Leopold: *Christus begraben* (Christ Entombed, 1741; revised 1755) and *Christus verurtheilt* (Christ Sentenced, 1743). He was to be the poet of Wolfgang's *Die Schuldigkeit des ersten Gebots* (The Duty Imposed by the First Commandment).

eighteenth century, this exuberant, sensuous kind of movement had invaded Germany's palaces, in which, however, the elder generation still danced in the strict ceremonial patterns of Versailles: the father of Maria Theresa, Emperor Charles VI, permitted his daughters to participate in the spinning German dances, but he and his Empress refrained from joining, and only looked on. In 1752 Archbishop Dietrichstein, less broadminded, banned turning dances in Salzburg.[3]

Such prohibitions proved vain. Along with the decline of the minuet began the weakening of court ritual, that superb *cortezia*, for centuries Europe's fine-grained touchstone of comportment: the spontaneous new dances sent a free social spirit sweeping through the ballrooms. Waltzing together, Goethe's Werther and Lotte expressed their passion, he holding her in his arms "and flying around like the wind." Men like Dietrichstein not only worried about the sexual improprieties of dances that no longer formalized love play and the erotic, but also sensed a greater peril: social dancing had become a breeding ground for Enlightened ways.

"The public dance floors are visited by all classes," a traveler to Bavaria reported; "these are the places where ancestors and rank seem to be forgotten and aristocratic pride laid aside. Here we see artisans, artists, merchants, councilors, barons, counts, and excellencies dancing together with waitresses, women of the middle class, and ladies." In Salzburg, Lorenz Hübner, a priest and writer devoted to the history of the city, could be seen dancing with his cook at the gatherings in the city hall. By 1778 matters reached such a state that Archbishop Christoph Bartholomäus Migazzi of Vienna and his council found it deplorable that "Jews, indistinguishable from others by their dress, now frequent inns, ballrooms, and theaters, and mix with the Christians who are there." Like his father, Wolfgang Mozart delighted in these entertainments. As a boy in Salzburg he reveled in dancing at the Stern with Maria Ottilie Feyerl, the court baker's daughter. Later, the still virginal young man—or so he claimed to Leopold—commented with more than a touch of pride upon the lady "of ill repute" he had partnered at a public ball in Munich, an assemblage at which any Don Giovanni might meet every kind of woman on Leporello's celebrated list.

Toward the end of the first act of *Don Giovanni*, Mozart summons echoes of just such a concourse. The illuminated hall of the grandee's palace stands open to all. Here that staid, indeed almost baroque, couple

---

3 The Queen of Prussia averted her eyes when she beheld the waltz at its introduction to the court in 1794. The Hohenzollern would have nothing to do with the dangerous dance: as late as the reign of the last German Emperor (1888–1918), etiquette forbade it in the royal palaces.

Don Ottavio and Donna Anna perform the minuet; the host and Zerlina join in the bourgeois *contradanza,* more recent in origin, improvisatorial in spirit, and symbolic of her desire to better herself; and the clever Leporello pulls Masetto into the plebeian *Balla la Teitsch* (a *Deutscher*) in order to hold him fast and make him dizzy with its turns. ("A *Deutscher,* a *Deutscher!*" the public cried out to the orchestras of Viennese ballrooms.) All levels of society crowd the dance floor, and, if not for Zerlina's outcry, which makes an end of things, a general mixing of classes and much changing of partners, rooms, and dances would ensue, the *Balla la Teitsch* sooner or later predominating.

This whirling, intoxicating dance embodies the motto of the evening; first announced by Don Giovanni, seconded by Leporello, and taken up by the three masked guests, it rings out boldly: *"Viva la libertà,"*[4] words Mozart gives a musical weight evidencing an unmistakable bias. In Prague, the city of this opera's premiere, the practice arose, even in Mozart's days, of having the chorus join the proclamation, which the score, in fact, limits to the soloists. Archbishop Dietrichstein had had every reason to fret: De la Cuisse wrote his dance manual of 1762 *"pour tout le monde,"* and, indeed, during his closing years, Mozart turned out remarkable and varied sets of dances for ballrooms crowded by every layer of Viennese society.

2

HOW IRONIC THAT elaborate machinery ground out waltzes in the miniature theater Archbishop Dietrichstein built in the park of Hellbrunn, diminutive wooden figures, activated by water, performing to compositions that must have been among Wolfgang Mozart's earliest artistic impressions. Dietrichstein loved musical wheelworks. In 1753, the year of his death, he ordered the court organ builder, Johann Rochus Egedacher,[5] who, along with Lorenz Rosenegger, had worked on the apparatus of the theater, to refashion the *Hornwerk.* For generations this mechanical organ, projecting from a wall of the fortress overlooking Salzburg, had played only a single piece (based upon a tune by Augustin Ebler). Egedacher increased the instrument's capacity to the point of accommodating twelve selections—one for each month—five of the new compositions being by

---

4 At a ball Garrick organized in Stratford to honor Shakespeare's memory, James Boswell appeared masked as a Corsican war chief wearing a headband with gold letters reading: *"Viva la libertà."* The motto had become international.

5 In a letter of 12 December 1765 written from The Hague, Leopold, concerned about the condition of a harpsichord in his Salzburg apartment, requested that "Herr Egedacher" (either Johann Rochus or his brother, Johann Joseph) make repairs if the strings had sprung.

Eberlin (who had supplied music for the Hellbrunn contrivance), six by Leopold Mozart.[6]

Dietrichstein's successor, Count Siegmund Christoph von Schrattenbach, proved distinguished by a quality rare among Salzburg's archbishops: piety. Addicted to prayer, he stoutly believed in the divine origin of all ideas that came to him while in this attitude. His election had been the accidental result of fierce divisions within the conclave of canons.[7] (I think of a similar impasse that brought a religious Fleming, Adrian VI, to the pontificate, 1522.) Though his devoutness and his devotion to stray dogs contrasted with the epicurean tradition of many of his predecessors, Archbishop Schrattenbach did have a taste for music and the stage. During his reign Leopold improved his position in the orchestra. But the highest prize remained beyond his reach.

He found rapid advancement barred by the seniority of colleagues. Achieving the shadowy designation of court composer (*Hofmusicus*; 1757) must have buttressed his vanity; but the post of kapellmeister alone battened the purse, and this distinction never came to him (nor, except as an honorary title, to his son). Leopold desperately wanted precedence, at times not only styling himself "Dr." but also, despite unconvincing denials, taking on the identity of kapellmeister of Salzburg when sufficiently far from home. He did not become second violinist until 1758, and only following Eberlin's death moved on to be vice-kapellmeister (1763).

Blunder played its part in hampering Leopold's progress: his courting of Count Waldburg-Zeil, Dean of the Cathedral, former rival of Schrattenbach for the throne, and, in his eyes, an agitator. (Schrattenbach remained well disposed toward Wolfgang despite his father's maneuvering.[8]) Like many in Salzburg, Leopold surmised that the feeble Schrattenbach could not live long—he would, in fact, sit in St. Rupert's chair for almost nineteen years—and that before long Zeil would be his successor. To crown Leopold's miscalculations, in the consistory (again deadlocked) that sat after Schrattenbach's death, Zeil, Munich's candidate, found himself forced

---

6 The original *Hornwerk* went back to the time of Archbishop Leonhard von Keutschach (elected in 1495). In 1759 Lotter published the new compositions for the renovated *Hornwerk*, along with variations on the Ebler melody by Leopold Mozart.

7 Schrattenbach became archbishop with the forty-ninth ballot, a desperate point in the proceedings: had a fiftieth failed to elect, the Pope would then have filled the vacancy. The election involved thirteen days of balloting falling between 12 March and 5 April 1753.

8 Leopold tried to ingratiate himself with Archbishop von Schrattenbach by turning Wolfgang's confirmation into a diplomatic occasion; as part of the ceremony, the candidate took a new name, here—Sigismundus. Though no record of the conferment survives, it probably took place in 1769, perhaps in the Archbishop's presence. In his letters Mozart availed himself of the name only twice, both times for comic effect.

to withdraw in the face of the irresistible force Vienna brought to bear; on 14 March 1772 the choice fell upon the Habsburgs' protégé, Count Hieronymus Joseph Franz de Paula Colloredo, the formidable Bishop of Gurk.[9] The Mozarts' devotion to Zeil appeared as little commendable to him as it had to Schrattenbach. Leopold, who imagined himself an adroit strategist, had once again become tangled in the web of his own intrigue: like the old, the new Archbishop proved content to see him a subordinate.

Those long, and often unauthorized, absences from court, during which he toured with his prodigy son, contributed heavily to his failure to become kapellmeister. In 1768 the Residenz ordered the first suspension of his salary for his unilateral extension of a leave; moveover, from time to time he foolishly endeavored to beguile the pay office into remunerating him for such periods. To Hagenauer he admitted: "I am not performing my services in Salzburg, as most of the courtiers . . . are certainly saying." In 1769 he publicly acknowledged: "Of course, I have been at home little since 1762 [the date of the first tour]."[10] Even so, factors other than his truancy, the etiquette of seniority, and the favor of Count Zeil also held him back.

The old affair of the lampoon, with its threat of prison, could have done his career little good. Moreover, Daines Barrington's report to the Royal Society (see p. 199) invites questions concerning Leopold as executant. In London, Barrington witnessed his uncertainties while sight-singing a score with the nine-year-old Wolfgang, who "looked back with some anger, pointing out to him his mistakes and setting him right." A huffy Master Wolfgang staring not in surprise but in anger perhaps indicates that such mishaps were not exceptions. One example does not build a case; however, there survive few facts to establish Leopold as a superior performing musician.

He appears to have been a dependable colleague in a court orchestra of not very demanding standards[11] and gained a reputation for unassuming,

---

9 Thirteen ballots, consuming five election days, resolved the issue.

10 In 1766, while the Mozart family tarried in the Lowlands, Beda Hübner, the librarian of St. Peter's in Salzburg, felt it necessary to remind his fellow townsmen that Leopold remained "de facto vice-kapellmeister."

11 Salzburg had few natives among its court musicians, most of whom came from other areas of the Reich and from Italy. The slovenliness of the archiepiscopal orchestra may be ascertained in Wolfgang's letter of 9 July 1778. Though contempt for his native city may have led him to exaggerate when he called into play the adjectives "rough, ragged, and careless," Charles Burney confirmed their essential pertinence: the Archbishop's "band," he reported, "has been accused of being more remarkable for coarseness and noise, than delicacy and high-finishing." Leopold, too, deplored the situation. Yet, as a performer, he had no reputation for a technical distinction that might have improved it; indeed, the documents of his tours preserve no instance of his ever scheduling himself as a soloist. In Salzburg he in all probability worked with efficiency, directing rehearsals or conducting performances when so deputized.

well-manufactured compositions at times using popular programmatic devices. In 1757 Marpurg listed among Leopold's scores (in addition to those for church): symphonies, serenades with instrumental solos, concertos, trios, divertimentos, oratorios, music for plays and pantomimes, descriptive pieces, marches, notturnos, minuets, and opera dances. Leopold assembled the musical clichés of his time in a respectable, orderly manner: that various of these efforts have, until recently, passed for the young Wolfgang's argues a level of invention sufficient to hammer into suitable form whatever the sentiment and fashion of the moment demanded. The puzzle of sorting out the authorship of such works derives from the skill with which the boy imitated the techniques and handwriting of his teacher-father, whose habit of correcting, touching up, and copying the prodigy's creations compounds the confusion.

Only one work from Leopold's hand has a place in today's repertory: the so-called Toy or Berchtesgaden Symphony, once ascribed to Joseph Haydn and in all probability Leopold's reworking of movements from an anonymous cassation.[12] The symphony represents the homely style and jejune material that brought Leopold his greatest successes as a composer. He knew where his strength lay, how to capitalize essentially pallid musical ideas, and cherished no chimeras about his creative gifts. His schooling, inclination, and temperament declared the scholar and pedagogue, endowments his superiors had quickly recognized: they made him violin instructor of the choirboys. It was as an educator that he built his reputation.

The year of Wolfgang's birth, he brought out in Augsburg his *Versuch einer gründlichen Violinschule* (Essay on a Fundamental Violin Method). By the turn of the century it had become the most influential violin treatise of the time and achieved several German editions and translation into French and Dutch. Although publishers issued these versions only after Wolfgang had made the Mozart name internationally known, from the beginning critics recognized the *Versuch's* excellence. Marpurg's *Historisch-kritische Beyträge* (Historical-Critical Articles) compared it favorably with Francesco Geminiani's influential thesis and complimented a "pure" German rarely encountered among musicians: "Those who know how to direct the bow most adroitly do not always control the pen . . ."; and Daniel Schubart, in his *Ideen zu einer Ästhetik der Tonkunst* (Ideas for an Aesthetic of Music), had high praise for a work in which he recognized both an indebtedness to the Italian school of Tartini and a German of true quality. Whole sections of Leopold's correspondence with his publisher, Lotter, concerned questions of diction. The example of Gellert and Gottsched helped Leopold

---

12 This musical form is related to the divertimento and serenade (see XVIII, n. 18).

form a style that strove to avoid anything "forced." His fame as a distinguished theorist with a talent for the clear, facile, if often sarcastic phrase[13] came quickly, and in 1759 Marpurg, author of the monumental *Abhandlung von der Fuge* (Treatise on the Fugue), invited him to join a newly forming musical society in Berlin.

Even before the appearance of his *Versuch*, Leopold had received an invitation to become a member of the *Korrespondierende Sozietät der musikalischen Wissenschaften* (Corresponding Society of the Musical Sciences), founded in Leipzig by Christoph Lorenz Mizler, a pupil of Sebastian Bach and disciple of Christian Wolff. (News of the book's excellence had traveled to Leipzig from Lotter's printing house.) The Society's journal embraced the Pythagorean tradition associating music with mathematics, a point of view in the spirit of Wolff's desire to base truth upon evidence of mathematical certainty. Though flattered by the invitation—"I'll be damned! That makes you feel like something!"—Leopold, no longer a young and eager student of philosophy but a harassed, middle-aged music teacher struggling with pupils who had to start "from A B C," looked upon the Society's goals with uncertainty. In the preface to the *Versuch* he advised Mizler's organization to renounce its theoretical pursuits and turn instead to practical research: a study of ways to build better violins seemed to him a valuable project. As might be expected, his *Versuch* proved an eminently pragmatic professional guide, its intention the building of technique and with it the "foundation of good style."

3

AN URBANE LEOPOLD, holding what was probably his beloved Jacob Stainer instrument, stares from the engraved frontispiece of his book. The portrait, he felt, had its faults: "Everyone says that I am depicted as somewhat too fat and much too old." His neck, he complained, appeared too thick, his face swollen. Yet, for all that, the general impression gave him satisfaction: "This picture represents a truly important person." It was this vanity and striving for elegance and station that alienated him from the average Salzburger—he avoided his wife's plebeian relatives—and kept him in some degree a stranger in his adopted city. A letter to Lotter in Augsburg (4 October 1755) rings with both a cry for friendship and a lament about Salzburg: "Why cannot people who love one another always be to-

---

13 Johann Adam Hiller feared that Leopold's often prickly bent of expression might discourage readers from taking up his book—a minority opinion.

gether? And why must one seek one's best friends in distant places rather than nearby?"

Leopold's demeanor could hardly have smoothed his way among his musical colleagues, many of whom found their recreation in the bottle;[14] he held himself aloof, his condescension increasing with each journey abroad. His patrician ways and cultured German doubtless irritated in a locale renowned for its provincialism, boorishness, and earthy vernacular. (When the buffoonlike comic figure Hanswurst made his entrance upon the Viennese stage, as a rule he spoke the homespun, spongy dialect of Salzburg.) Though, when necessary, he could turn an uninhibited south-German folk idiom to account, this saturnine Swabian from the Lech never felt at home on the Salzach and came to loathe his Salzburger son's broad, coarse clowning, suspecting that his failure to achieve a position at some great court lay partly in his frequent attempts to raise a smile by assuming Salzburg rural speech and comportment.[15] "Clown [*Flegel*]" would, in fact, be the word hurled at Mozart as a noble literally kicked him out of Colloredo's retinue.

The few Salzburg musicians with whom Leopold became friendly included Johann Andreas Schachtner, a court trumpeter who also played violin and cello. He, along with Hagenauer and Placidus Scharl, a Benedictine and professor at the Gymnasium, formed the core of a small circle that gathered at the Mozarts' apartment to discuss literature and music. A product of the Jesuits at Ingolstadt, Schachtner gained applause (including that of the influential littérateur Gottsched) for his translation of a Latin play. He provided Leopold with the text of *Der gute Hirt* (The Good Shepherd), a religious singspiel, and would serve Wolfgang as translator of *Idomeneo* and librettist of *Zaide*. But music history's true debt to him concerns a letter he wrote to Nannerl soon after her brother died: it relates those amusing, moving anecdotes describing the awakening of one of the most extraordinary musical talents the world has known.

This phenomenon gave Leopold his true direction. Wolfgang's musical education engaged all his efforts: he gave up composing and sought to live

---

14 Leopold reported the social finale of a private concert the court musicians gave at the Eizenbergerhof, a casino outside the gates of Salzburg: "By the end, everyone was drunk. They shouldered one another in procession and collided with the large chandelier ... smashing the center bowl and other pieces. Replacements will have to be had from Venice. . . ." Archbishop Colloredo even permitted himself a public joke about the alcoholism of his court musician Michael Haydn. "That's a fine way to talk!" Leopold remonstrated.

15 Sometime during 1786, Mozart would begin a farce, *Der Salzburger Lump in Wien* (The Scamp from Salzburg in Vienna), no doubt written for an amateur performance in his house. Herr Stachelschwein (Porcupine) from Salzburg would seem to be the hero of the fragment, a part Mozart probably intended to play.

through the boy; to form him in his own image became the unique occupation of his existence. Lord Chesterfield's words to his son might well have been written by Leopold to his: ". . . the dearest object of my own [life] has been to render you as perfect as the weakness of human nature will allow." Young Chesterfield had the advantage of living far from his exacting parent; but despite love and solicitude, Leopold, everpresent, made relentless demands. What must have been the martinet spirit of Papa's tutoring sessions colors the *Versuch*: "Here are the pieces for practice; the more distasteful they are the more I am pleased, for that is what I intended to make them." His household functioned with Jesuitical rigor, certain hours being allotted to work, others to self-examination. Unfinished tasks were not tolerated. He never recovered from the shock of Wolfgang's revolt against life built upon a monastic *regula*.

4

AN ATMOSPHERE OF disquietude enveloped the Mozart apartment early in 1756. During January, while correcting proofs of his *Versuch*, Leopold diplomatically concealed his annoyance with the many errors as he corresponded with Lotter, whose less than secure grasp of diction and grammar tried a temper already frayed: harassed by his duties at court, the drudgery of giving lessons, and his time-consuming compulsion to produce a perfect book, Leopold found himself further irritated by the receipt of an anonymous note (signed "*Herzensfreund* [bosom friend]") criticizing his facile program music; above all, he felt qualms about the imminent confinement of his wife. (In August 1750, her declining health had necessitated his somehow financing a cure at Bad Gastein.) On 26 January Leopold wrote Lotter that her confinement impended. At eight o'clock in the evening of the following day she gave birth to a boy. "However, the *placenta* had to be removed," Leopold reported to Augsburg. "As a result, she was astonishingly weak. [She had, in fact, been near death.] But now, God be praised, child and mother are well. . . . The boy is called *Joannes Chrisostomus, Wolfgang, Gottlieb.*"

In the register of births the scribe entered "*Joannes Chrysostomus Wolfgangus Theophilus.*" The infant received baptism in the cathedral at ten-thirty in the morning of the twenty-eighth. The day of his birth had been the Feast of St. John Chrysostom (John Golden Mouth), whose name and sobriquet thus fell to him.[16] The final name, a Latinized-Greek version of

<hr>

16 Following a variant of the church calendar, Salzburg celebrated 27 January as the Feast of John Chrysostom. Today the Church universally honors him on 13 September, reserving 27 January for Angela Merici, foundress of the Ursulines.

Gottlieb (beloved of God), descended from his godfather, Johann Gottlieb Pergmayr, city councilor and merchant.[17] Though, with the years, Amadeo, Amadè, and Amadé, variations of Amadeus,[18] the Latin translation of Gottlieb, had the best of it (no doubt thanks to Mozart's hobby of playing variations upon names), from the beginning the child most often responded to Wolfgang, which honored his maternal grandfather, or to its diminutive, "Wolferl." (St. Wolfgang, whose shrine stands by the Abersee at no great distance from Anna Maria Mozart's birthplace, became the boy's patron.) The infant born some twelve weeks after the Lisbon earthquake and in the sixth year of the *Encyclopédie* had entered a momentously changing world. But few in Salzburg could imagine that the *ancien régime* was slipping to ruin, that the Archbishopric and the Holy Roman Empire itself had entered their final years.

17 More than a decade after Wolfgang's christening, Leopold observed with searing irony that Pergmayr had yet to send the godfather's traditional baptismal gift of silver.

18 With Pergmayr standing sponsor, the Mozarts' fifth child—born in November 1752, he lived only three months—had been baptized Joannes Carolus AmaDeus (*sic*), the parish register of deaths enrolling Theophilus for his third name. (Though manufacturing Latin and Greek versions of names had an especially secure tradition in a church-state modeling itself upon the Vatican, the practice permeated record offices throughout the Holy Roman Empire.) In his surviving correspondence, Mozart styled himself "Amadeus" on only three occasions, each time, as in his use of his confirmation name, to be funny (see n. 8).

CHAPTER V

The Prodigy's Earliest Years

LEOPOLD HOPED TO write a biography of his son, and from the beginning of his career the Mozarts preserved letters and documents to serve this plan. The book remained unwritten: only toward the end of his father's life did Wolfgang move toward notable success; moreover, time had brought increasing antagonism between them. In the absence of any systematic account of his earliest years, the reminiscences of Nannerl, Schachtner, Scharl, and Hübner (see IV, n. 10), though slender and not always reliable, have marked importance, as do the vignettes of times past in Leopold's letters.

When Leopold started to teach Nannerl the clavier, Wolfgang was three. He listened attentively and soon made a beginning by picking out thirds at the keyboard; she recalled the pleasure he took in their sound. To provide her with a repertory of exercises, Leopold had compiled (1759) a volume of music—much of it minuets—arranged to be progressively difficult, the student gradually encountering more complex rhythms, wider skips, ornamentation, and hand-crossing. Composers represented in the collection included Johann Nikolaus Tischer (1707–1774), Johann Joachim Agrell (1701–1765), and Georg Christoph Wagenseil (1715–1777); and Leopold must be credited with not a few of the anonymous pieces.

Soon after turning four, Wolfgang started to use Nannerl's book. He made extraordinary progress. Within the year, his father introduced him to the organ. In addition, he took up the violin,[1] beginning with a historic demonstration of musical precocity: he vehemently insisted upon playing second violin during a reading of some new string trios at the Getreidegasse apartment. (Someone had given him a miniature violin, and he wanted to use it.[2]) Leopold told him to stop nagging; after all, he had as yet received no instruction on the instrument. Insisting that he needed none to handle second violin, he started to toddle off in tears. Leopold relented, but only with the understanding that Wolfgang play extremely softly along with Schachtner. "With astonishment I soon noticed that I was completely superfluous," Schachtner recalled. Quietly, he put down his violin, and the youngster, on his own, successfully navigated the set of six trios. Emboldened, he then declared himself capable of doing justice to the first-violin part as well. The company agreed to the experiment, and though Wolfgang had to resort to "wrong and irregular positions, yet he played in such a manner that he never really broke down."

Like most composers, Mozart began to learn his craft by imitating. At four he could master assigned pieces within an hour—a minuet within half this time—playing them "faultlessly, with utmost neatness, and in exact time," Nannerl recalled. Using as model what he had learned, he would then improvise at the keyboard. According to Scharl, "playing fantasias became his greatest passion." He extemporized on the violin, too, and Schachtner has left an endearing picture of him "fiddling away at his fantasia." Yet, though capable of reading music and of assembling his own syntactic musical sentences, he could not write them down, a frustration not long endured.

One Thursday after church, Schachtner and Leopold returned to the apartment to find him scribbling what he claimed to be a clavier concerto. He disclosed a smudge of notes written over ink blots, not only his first concerto but also his first adventure with an inkwell. Schachtner observed "tears of wonder and joy" in Leopold's eyes as he stared at the sheet and called attention to the "correct and proper" notation. Probably to mask his emotion, he teased the boy: "It can't be used because it is so extraordinarily difficult that no one could cope with playing it." Wolfgang protested: "That's why it's a concerto: you must practice it until you get it right; look, here's how it goes." He played and, Schachtner remembered, "succeeded in wringing just enough from it to enable us to grasp what he had in mind.

---

1 Just when he began to play the violin cannot be established; on this point Schachtner fell into error (see p. 71).

2 This instrument must have been the *Geigerl* he played when first entering Vienna (see pp. 64–65).

At that time he had the idea that playing concertos and working miracles must be one and the same."

Considering the infantile level of Mozart's earliest compositions,[3] the musical value of his maiden clavier concerto cannot have been high. (Taking Leopold's banter seriously, some conjure a vision of the lost smears as a lost masterpiece.) What made the child exceptional were not the parodies he "composed" or extemporized, but, rather, his fine sense of pitch and his dexterity at the keyboard and with the bow. On one occasion, some days after playing Schachtner's violin, he remembered it as tuned an eighth of a tone lower than his own. Leopold asked Schachtner to fetch his instrument and compare it with Wolfgang's. "I did so," wrote Schachtner, "and he proved to be right."

He had so delicate an ear that until almost his tenth year he could not stand the sound of a solo trumpet. Wishing to cure what he feared might become a phobia, Leopold persuaded Schachtner to take the boy by surprise with trumpet blasts. Almost three decades later Schachtner still recalled with shock what had followed: "Scarcely had Wolfgang heard the blaring tones than he turned pale and began to sink down; had I continued any longer, he would certainly have suffered a convulsion."

Professor Samuel Tissot, a student of child prodigies and their nervous systems, observed Wolfgang and in 1766 wrote an article about him for the Lausanne weekly *Aristide ou le citoyen*.[4] Tissot noticed that "wrong, harsh, or excessively loud sounds bring tears to his eyes." Any unaccustomed and loud noise disturbed him. (During a visit to the Tower of London, the roaring of the lions "frightened our Master Wolfgang,"[5] in all likelihood a memory still vivid when the eleven-year-old wrote the menacing music to the second aria of his *Die Schuldigkeit des ersten Gebots: "Ein ergrimmter Löwe brüllet"* [An Angry Lion Roars].) The unsteady pitch of trumpeters distressed him no less than their shrillness. On 30 December 1767 Prior Aurelius Augustinus of Sternberg (near Olmütz) traveled to Brünn to attend a concert in which the Mozart children took part, assisted by local instrumentalists; he especially remarked Wolfgang's inability "to abide the trumpets because they lacked the capacity to play in tune with one another."

---

3 The temptation to descry impending greatness in the simplicities of these compositions should be resisted; moreover, Leopold's role as inspirer, corrector, and even creator of his son's juvenilia appears to have been extensive. More than one of their contemporary detractors suspected no less.

4 Duke Louis Eugene of Württemberg worked with Professor Tissot on this small treatise (see p. 217).

5 Goethe, too, abhorred loud sounds and all his life had an especial horror of barking dogs.

From the beginning an astounding digital adroitness served his exquisite ear. His ability to manage violin parts by manipulating in irregular positions he matched by a no less ingenious legerdemain at the clavier. He developed devices enabling his doll-sized hand to cope with formidable keyboard passages. Daines Barrington marveled at his execution—"amazing, considering that his little fingers could scarcely reach a fifth on the harpsichord." Placidus Scharl remembered how "at proper speed and with wonderful accuracy," Wolfgang "skimmed the octave his short little fingers could not span." When the Mozarts came back to Salzburg from their Grand Tour, he was close to his eleventh birthday but had scarcely grown since his departure almost three and a half years earlier. In his *Diarium*, Beda Hübner hailed the tiny virtuoso's return; that he still could not bridge the octave made his performances "all the more exceptional and admirable."

Leopold began writing down Wolfgang's compositions at the beginning of his sixth year, putting to use blank pages in Nannerl's exercise book. It thus sheltered Mozart's earliest surviving work, an Andante for piano (K. 1a) in C of 1761.[6] With these six measures began the suite of creations that would end thirty-one years later with the transcendent D-minor Requiem.

2

LEOPOLD CULTIVATED HIS son's gifts assiduously and trumpeted them aggressively as he transformed himself from preceptor into showman. He planned concert tours, confident of astounding the great courts of Europe by what he called "a story such as probably comes to light but once a century and which in the realm of music has perhaps never yet appeared to quite *this degree of the miraculous.*" He had come to see Wolfgang's gifts in terms of Wolff's exegesis of miracles: they might be accepted if recognizable as part of the divinely regulated order. *"Moreover, if it is ever to be my duty to convince the world of this miracle,"* wrote Leopold, *"it is at this very time when people ridicule whatever bears the name of miracle and deny all miracles."* Struck with wonder, Europe's potentates would, he felt certain, thrust princely fees and donations upon Wolfgang and help raise the Mozarts to a new social position. Leopold easily justified to himself what to others appeared raw opportunism: to develop a talent that came from God clearly constituted a duty to God; to profit from this duty became, in

---

6 In her late and clouded years, Nannerl took to tearing leaves out of the book and giving them to visitors as souvenirs. The sheet preserving K. 1a had this fate. The remains of the book rest in the Salzburg Mozarteum, random pages surviving elsewhere.

turn, an obligation to the family. A kind of Wolffian-Jesuitical dialectic determined Wolfgang's future.

But a fear nagged at Leopold: he dreaded his son's reaching an "age and physical growth that would no longer attract admiration for his achievements." As Hübner observed, nature aided this contest with time: Wolfgang remained so small that to lie about his date of birth continued an easy matter.

Leopold wished it known that he did not act the usual parent of a prodigy, that he never pressed Wolfgang, but, rather, as Professor Tissot reported, "has always been careful to moderate his fire and prevent him from surrendering himself to it." Nannerl, too, described him as "certainly never forced to compose or perform." She sent forth this pointed statement—written for Schichtegroll's late obituary of Wolfgang (1793)—as a defense of Leopold's tutelage of the child; it had known criticism from the earliest days of the family's tours. Though the rancor with which her memoirs assail Mozart's widow suggests that, on occasion, Nannerl could be a biased witness,[7] one has, nonetheless, every reason to believe her remembrances of her brother's being pulled from his work lest he exhaust himself by spending night and day at the clavier or with his compositions.[8] Leopold told Barrington of a Wolfgang "often visited with musical ideas, to which, even in the midst of night, he would give utterance on his harpsichord." He became an object not of coercion but of uninterrupted attention and artful inducement, the father pointing the way. "He let himself be led," Schachtner recalled: "It remained a matter of indifference to him what he was given to learn; he simply wanted to learn and left the choice to his deeply beloved Papa. . . ."

---

7 Through a late marriage, Nannerl climbed to the lowest rung of the paper nobility to become the haughty Reichsfreiin (bordering upon baroness) Maria Anna von Berchtold zu Sonnenburg. (Her husband inherited the "von" given his grandfather by Archbishop Firmian and received the Imperial title of Freiherr in 1792; see p. 640.) Like her father, she considered Wolfgang's wife, Constanze, a social inferior and regarded her entrance into the family as an intrusion. Further, it would seem that in later years the veneration the widow Mozart inspired grew to be more than the sister could bear. (Joseph Mainzer described the awe and excitement Constanze's very presence awakened during her trip to Munich early in 1827.) Nannerl's memoirs have given posterity the picture of a slovenly, improvident Constanze (see XXIX, n. 4), whose correspondence, however, reveals a woman managing with foresight the complicated affairs of her husband's estate and guiding the careers of their children.

8 His habits in this respect changed little with the years. Doris Stock has left an anecdote of his visit to Dresden in 1789: as he improvised before dinner, "the soup was allowed to grow cold and the roast to burn, simply so that we might continue to listen to the magic sounds the master, totally absorbed in what he was doing and insensible to the rest of the world, drew from the instrument."

Nannerl wondered whether, apart from music, her brother had ever had any real pastimes as a child. He did show a talent for arithmetic. For a while "he talked of nothing, thought of nothing but figures and turned into slates the walls of the staircase and of every room in the house— indeed, the walls of our neighbors' houses, too; and many a threat and many a chastising did he receive before his zeal was checked." Even so, soon he had little time for anything but music, which, after his first clavier lessons, began to pervade even his play. Schachtner observed that "no sooner did he begin to devote himself to music than his taste for all other pursuits as good as died, and even games and toys, if they were to interest him, had to be accompanied by music. When we—he and I—carried his toys from one room to another, one of us always had to carry them all so that the other might sing and fiddle an accompanying march."

He cut the figure, Nannerl recalled, of "a small but well-proportioned child" and continued "quite handsome" until 1767, when smallpox disfigured his face; "even worse, when he returned from Italy [December 1771], he had the yellow color of the Latins, which made him quite unrecognizable."[9] (Wolfgang longed to look well tanned and had probably overexposed his skin to the Italian sun.) Somewhat later, when she had grown to be a "regular beauty," his sallowness passed, but so did whatever remained of his good looks. He took on a most modest appearance: "thin, pale in color, and completely devoid of pretensions as to physiognomy and physique."

Between fits of temper, the child often showed himself oversweet, forever demanding affection, compliments, and the reassurance of endless hugs and kisses. Ten times a day he would ask Schachtner whether he loved him. Sometimes, "just for fun," Schachtner would say "no." Then, he recalled, "bright tears" appeared in Wolfgang's eyes, "so tender and kind was his good heart." (The adult Mozart wrote: ". . . as soon as people lose confidence in me, I lose confidence in myself.")

"Right after God comes Papa": the boy worshiped Leopold, who would later recognize that their relationship rested less upon friendship than etiquette. Nannerl described their good-night ceremony: every evening Leopold had him stand on a chair and sing a tune[10] with a mock-Italian

---

9 Seldom did the Mozarts have anything good to say about Italians: with the exception of such patriarchal luminaries as Padre Martini and Sammartini, the Italian musician remained, in their dictionary, a bad musician and of tainted character. Mozart described Clementi as *"a ciarlatano, like all Italians"* (*Wälsche*). This family bias grew from jealousy of the favored positions Italians held at German courts.

10 It mimicked the melody of "Willem van Nassau" (see p. 208).

text beginning, "*Oragna fiagata fa.*" Next came Papa's turn to render the song. Then they kissed, and Wolfgang went to bed. The anecdote seems less charming after reading in Nannerl's memoirs that until his tenth year they reenacted the ritual every night: it became a performance "on no occasion omitted." When he was twenty-two and struggling for independence, he testily informed his father: "The days are indeed gone when, standing on a chair, I used to sing to you *Oragna fiagata fa* and finished by kissing you on the end of your nose." Thus he answered Leopold's bewailing what seemed to him a change in Wolfgang from a retiring and modest prodigy into a waggish, hot-tempered young man hungry for praise. But the self-effacing Wolfgang upon whom the father now looked back had sprung in large part from his imagination.

"Examine yourself, learn to know yourself, my dear Wolfgang," Leopold crossly wrote early in 1778, "and you will discover . . . a bit too much *arrogance* and *self-love.*" How he longed for the mite of a creature who again and again had recited his own bizarre plan for being forever united with Papa: the child contemplated one day enclosing his aged father in a glass case to protect him from the air, a reverie whose darker side Leopold did not apprehend. (In southern Germany, churches expose under glass the partially clothed and elaborately bejeweled skeletons and cadavers of saints; here, probably, lay the impulse for the notion.) A recital of this engrossing, grisly fantasy of the parent's death became part of the bedtime *Oragna* ceremony. To Leopold this idea of enshrinement seemed endearing, and he never tired of hearing the innocent voice repeat what must have been, at bottom, a vision of the father rendered supine and harmless.

Leopold's remembrance differed from Schachtner's concerning the essentials of Wolfgang's temperament: Leopold reminisced about a boy so shy that he wept when overpraised, Schachtner about a little friend with "a fiery disposition" who "revealed nothing less than pride or ambition. . . . If he had not had the advantage of the good education he enjoyed, he might have become the most infamous villain, so receptive was he to every attraction, the goodness or badness of which he was not yet able to examine." At receptions he put to use a set of observations on his demureness culled from Leopold's pious utterances and, on special occasions, no doubt prepared by Papa himself. In 1766 Professor Tissot ascribed to Wolfgang "a modesty such as is rare at his age, and rare combined with such superiority. It is truly edifying to hear him attribute his talents to the author of all gifts and to hear him conclude from this, with amiable candor and an air of the most intimate conviction, that it would be unpardonable to pride himself on them."

This little speech reflected rehearsal, indeed drill, for he was, in fact, quite—and justifiably—vain. At times, lest he refuse to play, Leopold had to delude him into believing his audiences to be composed of musical connoisseurs. The famed arrogance of the mature Mozart stemmed from the narcissistic gratifications in which parents and sister indulged him: his position as star of the family's traveling company made him think the world a playground designed to exhibit his accomplishments. Hasse expressed his disquiet about the extravagant eulogies Leopold directed toward his son who, it should not surprise, proved unprepared for the changes adolescence brought.

Unpredictable, he could be winning—the diary of Johann Karl, Count von Zinzendorf, spoke of a "child of spirit, lively, charming"—or he could treat with people *de haut en bas*: when a German prince, meaning well, soothingly invited him to forget the presence of his august auditors and put aside all nervousness, Wolfgang reacted by confidently settling himself at the harpsichord and announcing that he had already played before the German Empress. Indeed, at the Imperial court, just before starting a concerto by Wagenseil, he had called out to this famous composer to come forward to turn the pages.

Admirers often found themselves at a loss to know how to behave toward him. How, for example, was one to address this *Wunderkind*? The "*du*" seemed too familiar for the virtuoso, the "*Sie*" too formal for the child. A gentleman, caught in this dilemma, felt it wise to use the "*wir.*" He began: "We have been traveling, then, and earned much honor for ourselves." (The Mozarts had just returned from their Grand Tour.) He went on in this manner until Wolfgang protested: "But I have never seen or met you anywhere but at Salzburg." Not yet eleven, he was highly articulate, terribly arch, and outrageously bright.

His poise and haughtiness notwithstanding, the artist could, in an instant, revert to the child. "He would sometimes run about the room with a stick between his legs by way of a horse," wrote Barrington, who in London (June 1765) had the opportunity to be "alone with him for a considerable time." One day, as he performed for a dazzled Barrington, "a favorite cat came in, upon which he immediately left his harpsichord, nor could we bring him back for a considerable time."

On the other hand, the child could unpredictably and with lightning speed become the master: in the course of one of his meetings in London with Johann Christian Bach, Wolfgang spent part of the time rolling to and fro on a table. As he tumbled about, his eye fell upon the open score of an aria from Bach's *Zanaida*. Although the music lay upside down, he pointed out a note as wrong. William Jackson, a witness, recorded: "It was so, whether of the composer or copyist I cannot now recollect. . . ." Presumably the boy returned to his gyrations. Perhaps he needed to relax; sitting between Bach's knees, he had just finished competing with him in developing a fugal subject at the clavier. Jackson recalled: ". . . each led the other into very abstruse harmonies and extraneous modulations, in which the child beat the man. More than once they presented this affecting picture of the elder musician enveloping the younger (see XII, n. 27).

CHAPTER VI

The First Visit to Vienna

LITTLE IS KNOWN about Leopold's first concert tour with Wolfgang and Nannerl (12 January to early February 1762), a visit to Munich, capital of Maximilian III Joseph, Elector of Bavaria.[1] In all probability, the Mozarts succeeded in presenting themselves at the court of this serious musical amateur, a composer and instrumentalist who, in Burney's opinion, rivaled London's renowned Karl Friedrich Abel on the viola da gamba.

Over half a year passed before the next journey: on 18 September, Leopold, Anna Maria, and the children set out for Passau, most likely by river. A music copyist and bassoonist, Joseph Richard Estlinger, attended them as factotum: "our Estlinger" looked after the family's clothing, baggage, and errands. He must also have kept the music in order, during an extended trip whose expenses Leopold met through letters of credit arranged by his landlord, Herr Hagenauer.

The preceding May, a canon of Salzburg and Bishop of Gurk, Count Joseph Maria Thun-Hohenstein, had become prince-bishop of Passau, the

---

1 The right to choose the Holy Roman Emperor belonged to an electoral college of German princes, each bearing the title of elector. Before the Thirty Years' War (1618-1648) they numbered seven: the three Prince-Archbishops of Mainz, Cologne, and Trier and the four secular rulers of Bohemia (inevitably the Habsburg Emperor), Brandenburg, Saxony, and the Rhenish Palatinate. For its support of the Habsburgs, Bavaria emerged from the war as an electorate, and in 1692 Vienna conferred this status upon Braunschweig-Lüneburg.

espicopate superbly commanding the confluence of the Danube, Inn, and Ilz. He kept the Mozarts waiting several days before granting Wolfgang—but not Nannerl—the opportunity to perform. (From the beginning, like Leopold, she functioned as a supporting player, adding her hands to her brother's at the keyboard when the ensemble so required and, if time permitted, venturing a solo.) His reward took the form of "one whole ducat." Aware of Thun-Hohenstein's ambition one day to succeed to the throne of Salzburg, Leopold wryly noted: ". . . we pray that our Archbishop may live long."[2] Thun-Hohenstein's parsimony (the result of huge outlays for his investiture) did not lower Leopold's optimism: downstream lay Linz, the bustling capital of Upper Austria, and, farther on, the ultimate goal—Vienna.

During the subsequent Danube journey, the family had as fellow passenger Count Ernst Johann Herberstein, a canon of Passau and later first Bishop of Linz. Leopold sought his company. He made recommendations, and they had immediate and happy effect: at Linz, under the sponsorship of Count Leopold Schlick, an administrator of the region, Wolfgang and Nannerl made their first documented concert appearance in public. A short time before the music began, young Count Karl Palffy-Erdöd, son of Maria Theresa's Hungarian Court Chancellor, stopped in the city to pay his respects to Countess Schlick. She urged him to come with her to hear the children.

Returned to Vienna, he told Archduke Joseph (the future Emperor Joseph II) about the extraordinary musical experience, and he, in turn, told the Empress. The news traveled quickly. When Leopold attended Gluck's *Orfeo* only four days after arriving in Vienna, he heard Joseph's brother, Archduke Leopold (the future Emperor Leopold II), spreading the word from his opera box about "a boy who is in Vienna and plays the clavier admirably." In addition, the Schlicks had come to town and been in touch with the court intendant, Count Giacomo Durazzo, concerning Wolfgang's gifts; and Canon Herberstein, who had preceded the Mozarts to the capital, added his nod of approbation. Leopold wrote the Hagenauers: "As soon as it became known that we were in Vienna, the order that we go to court arrived," a triumphant justification of his faith in the aristocracy's network of kindred tastes.

After stops in Mauthausen, Ybbs, and Stein, the post-boat (*Wasserordinaire*) had brought the Mozarts to Vienna on 6 October 1762. Leopold had Wolfgang strike up a minuet on his little fiddle as the luggage, sealed in preparation for inspection, arrived at the landing stages and customs barriers near the Danube canal. The officer in charge, enchanted by the

2 Upon receiving news of Thun-Hohenstein's death the following year, Leopold wrote: "God can cancel many a debt."

diminutive figure sawing away before him, let the Mozarts' baggage pass unchallenged. They made their way to temporary quarters on the Fleishmarkt and then settled into a room on the Tiefer Graben, a long, narrow chamber "a thousand feet long and one foot wide."

2

AT COUNT THOMAS Vinciguerra Collalto's palace next to the Church am Hof, Wolfgang, at the harpsichord, had his Viennese debut on 9 October. Thereafter, he visited other great houses of the city. The Viennese aristocracy welcomed him as the most delectable dessert of the season, Pállfys, Harrachs, Choteks, Waldsteins, Kaunitzes, Kinskys, Colloredos, and Esterházys indulging a child who not only performed phenomenal musical parlor tricks, but also showed a remarkable manner—bantering, brisk, self-assured, and, at times, deliciously impertinent.

Leopold feared no one would believe what had occurred when Wolfgang came before Maria Theresa at Schönbrunn. "When I tell it," he wrote Hagenauer, "people will think it a fable; suffice it to say that Wolferl jumped into the Empress's lap, caught her around the neck, and vigorously kissed her." Such conduct would have been objectionable at any great court save her's, where ceremony and informality blended. (Sir William Wraxall observed among Vienna's upper orders "a sort of patriarchal simplicity": they seemed to him "one large family," Maria Theresa the "common parent.") Her husband, Francis I, their daughter Archduchess Maria Antonia, and Georg Christoph Wagenseil,[3] music teacher to the Habsburg archduchesses, looked on at this singular meeting.

Things went marvelously well at the great summer palace beyond the city walls. The Imperial family appreciated and indulged Wolfgang: Emperor Francis delighted in the performances of the "little wizard" (*Hexenmeister*) and teased him affectionately; other royal children appeared and took to him at once, guiding him on a tour of the Empress's private apartments.[4]

---

3 Leopold had keyboard concertos by Wagenseil copied in Vienna. In all likelihood they entered the children's repertory in arrangements for four hands (see XII, n. 11).

4 Archduchess Johanna Gabriele, who was to die of typhus within weeks, insisted upon showing the fascinating little visitor her own rooms, leading him by the hand. On 16 October at the Hofburg (the Habsburgs' palace within the city and the symbolic seat of their authority), he gave a special concert for Archdukes Ferdinand and Maximilian Francis. The first would one day be Governor of Austrian Lombardy, the second (Maria Theresa's youngest son and the same age as Wolfgang) Prince-Archbishop-Elector of Cologne and patron of the young Beethoven. In Maximilian's honor Mozart would write *Il rè pastore*; for Ferdinand's court at Milan, *Mitridate, Ascanio in Alba,* and *Lucio Silla.*

Leopold luxuriated in finding himself welcomed as a distinguished pedagogue, the Emperor insisting that his daughter-in-law, Archduke Joseph's
wife, Isabella of Parma, perform on the violin for the author of the *Versuch*.
(This must have been one of his proudest moments.) The Mozarts spent
three enchanted hours at Schönbrunn and then drove straightway to the imposing palace (formerly Rofrano, now Auersperg) of Joseph Maria, Prince
of Sachsen-Hildburghausen, Vienna's foremost musical amateur.

Leopold's letter to Hagenauer of 19 October 1762 provokes wonder as
to how the boy of six bore the schedule his father arranged: "Today we
were at the French Ambassador's. Tomorrow Count Harrach has invited us
from four to six. However, which Harrach he is I do not know; I shall see
where the carriage leads. . . . A certain rich nobleman has hired us to play
for six ducats (from six or half past six until nine) as part of a big concert
at which the greatest virtuosos now in Vienna are to perform. The nobles
book us four, five, six to eight days in advance in order not to lose the opportunity and miss us. For example, the Chief Postmaster, Count Paar, has
already engaged us for next Monday. Wolferl now gets enough driving—
at least twice a day. Once we traveled at half past two to a place where we
stayed until quarter to four; Count Hardegg then had us picked up in his
carriage, which drove us at full gallop to a lady with whom we remained
until half past five. Count Kaunitz had us fetched from there, and we tarried with him until about nine." During these "visits," Wolfgang sat at the
clavier playing, improvising, sight-reading, singing, and fitting a bass to a
given melody; he also did tricks such as playing on a keyboard covered with
a cloth and proving his absolute pitch by naming the notes of bells, clocks,
and pocket watches. Though he adored performing and receiving praise,
strain would soon tell its tale.

For the moment, the effulgence of court life made Leopold blink at
caution. The Empress had sent Wolfgang a gold-trimmed lilac suit made
for Archduke Maximilian; Nannerl received a gala dress from the wardrobe
of an archduchess; and further visits with the Imperial family followed.
Most to the point had been the one hundred ducats presented by the privy
paymaster along with a royal request that the Mozarts prolong their stay.
Moreover, after Wolfgang played before the French Ambassador, he extended an invitation to Versailles. All bade fair beyond Leopold's most optimistic expectations.

Even so, he could not persist in ignoring the shadows moving toward
him. He continued on in Vienna, extending his leave at the very time he
should have been in Salzburg. Kapellmeister Eberlin had died the preceding June. An agreement of long standing dictated that Giuseppe Francesco
Lolli move up to the kapellmeister's post, a preferment leaving the vice-

kapellmeister's chair vacant. Leopold, who coveted it, felt frustrated to be far from the political jostling now in full play and soon to determine its new occupant. "Have you any notion," he asked Hagenauer from Vienna, "how advantageous to me it would be were I to become [vice-kapellmeister] while I am here?" Immediate advancement might to some degree have extricated him from an embarrassment of his own creation.

Vienna had come "to regard" the Archbishop's subordinate violinist— he felt forced to admit to Hagenauer—as "the Kapellmeister of Salzburg"; the Emperor, himself, harbored this impression: "Where is the Kapellmeister of Salzburg?" he cried at Schönbrunn, eager to lead Leopold to Isabella of Parma. If not openly misrepresenting himself, he did nothing to clear up a misunderstanding. News of what had developed into an ill-considered masquerade must have reached Salzburg: in a letter to Hagenauer (6 November 1762) an uneasy Leopold none too convincingly declared himself "aloof from all lies and bragging" (*Wind-machereyen*).[5] Repeatedly he urged Hagenauer to act as his agent in the matter of the promotion by soliciting the intervention of Count Franz Lactanz von Firmian, the Archbishop's High Steward: "You might, for example, find a quite natural opportunity to speak to him in the cathedral after ten o'clock mass, although it would be even better were you to go to see him."

At the same time, resolved to call the Salzburg court's attention to his superiority, Leopold essayed a reverse strategy of turning his absence to advantage: he claimed to be moving toward a new independence, letters to the Hagenauers outlining tales to be circulated at home. (At this moment he probably did not regret the archiepiscopal censor's opening and perus-ing mail as a matter of routine.) All manner of prospects, he declared, stood before him: ". . . I now find myself in circumstances that permit me to earn a living here [Vienna]"; and he spoke with a touch of mystery of "addresses in Holland and France" to be put to use were the position of vice-kapellmeister denied him. He let fall that he remained no less loyal— "I still prefer Salzburg to all other advantages"—but warned: "I must not be held back."

This pose rested upon outright bravado: Wolfgang had little chance of sustaining the interest of the Viennese beyond several months; and though

---

5 A few months later he defended a colleague caught playing the same game: Joseph Nikolaus Meissner, bass at the Salzburg court, had signed himself "*Capello Magister*" (Kapellmeister) in a letter brought to Leopold's attention. In order to mask what he later acknowledged to have been the singer's "foolishness," Leopold explained that Meissner had simply meant to describe him-self as "a *magister* [master] in singing." Leopold admired Meissner, whose tours of European courts had set him an example.

Leopold had received an invitation to Versailles and, perhaps, one to The Hague, such gestures, he well knew, implied nothing permanent. He recognized the dilemma: today's sensation becomes tomorrow's tedium; a *Wunderkind* must earn quickly and move on. There floated before Leopold not the fantasy of settling in France or the Lowlands but the concept of a Grand Tour. Wolfgang had to be relentlessly pushed through Europe were the maximum number of florins to be pulled in before the awkward age overtook him. But an ominous cloud, threatening to set this plan at hazard, would not disperse.

3

THE HEALTH OF the child, who most often operated with a machinelike precision, had become a matter of concern; there had been more than one alarm: he had caught cold in the rain and wind of the Danube journey and on 21 October, after a second appearance at Schönbrunn, came down with a rash and lesions diagnosed as "a kind of scarlet fever"; moreover, the teeth he had started to cut added to his misery. A crabbed Leopold complained to Hagenauer: "Hypothetically calculated, this adventure [Wolfgang's illness] has cost me fifty ducats." Many opportunities had fallen forfeit while the child kept to his bed. Not until 4 November did Dr. Johann Baptist Anton von Bernhard permit him to leave the house.[6]

On this day, the festival of St. Charles Borromeo, Leopold took him to the Karlskirche, the masterpiece Fischer von Erlach had designed for Maria Theresa's father, Emperor Charles VI, in the fields beside the river Wien.[7] The Mozarts then appeared on the glacis, the cleared area (once occupied by moats) just beyond the walls of the inner city, and walked in the Josef-

---

6 A notebook of musical examples, ostensibly assembled by Leopold as a gift for his son on his name day (31 October, the Feast of St. Wolfgang) and put forth as presented to him during this illness, has proved to be an anonymous omnibus collection, its inscription to Wolfgang a forgery.

7 The twin columns flanking the church's portico, like those in the great hall of von Erlach's Imperial Library, symbolized the Pillars of Hercules—the rocks the demigod set up on either side of the Strait of Gibraltar—and thus Charles VI's chimerical claim to the throne of Spain. The device derived from that of his forefather Emperor Charles V. (However, his heraldic bearing, the two columns along with the motto "Plus Ultra" [Still Further], had implied authority not only over Iberia, but also beyond this boundary of the ancient Roman Empire.) Upon the death of his cousin Charles II, the sickly, dim-witted, and childless Habsburg King of Spain, and while still heir presumptive to Habsburg headship, Charles VI had installed himself in Barcelona as a *soi-disant* Charles III of Spain. But Louis XIV had moved with speed to establish his grandson Philip d'Anjou in Madrid as Philip V. If in time and by treaty the Habsburgs had to renounce Spain to the Bourbons (see XV, n. 10), in his inmost heart Charles VI continued to consider himself its king.

stadt suburb. By exhibiting his son in these gathering places and promenades, Leopold indicated to society that Master Wolfgang, again in health,
felt ready for new engagements. But the aristocracy, fearing smallpox,
avoided anyone showing signs of fresh marks or rashes. Even to utter the
word "smallpox" to Maria Theresa's Chancellor, Count Kaunitz, was to
destroy his day; similarly, smallpox could not be mentioned in the presence
of the Imperial Court Poet, Metastasio ("and whoever *did* name that disorder," Mrs. Piozzi discovered, "though unconscious of the offense he had
given, Metastasio would see him no more"). Thus Wolfgang's schedule
filled by slow degrees. "If he had not been at home for almost two weeks,"
Leopold lamented, "he would have come in for some presents. Enough!
Now we must see whether things will start moving again. Before this business everything was going so very well."

To express their thanks to Dr. Bernhard, the Mozarts made music at his
home on 5 November. Four days later Wolfgang gave a concert at the
Windischgrätz house, an occasion when Count Collalto handed Leopold
a poem by "a certain Pufendorff." The melancholy, stilted verse expressed
hope that Wolfgang's "body brook the exactions of the soul," that he escape the fate of the *Wunderkind* of Lübeck, who suffered an early death.
(He had been a prodigy of science and language.) The pace Leopold set
his son had awakened discussion, in particular at court: Maria Theresa
looked askance at what she regarded as the exploitation of a child in an aggressive hunt for ducats. Count von Zinzendorf described Wolfgang as "*le
pauvre petit*": there seemed something disquieting about the sight of the
little fellow, so serious when at the keyboard, his tiny body propped up by
cushions, his feet barely on a level with the stretcher of his chair. The
poem embodied wide concern, heightened when Wolfgang, having gone
out too soon, again had to take to his bed. When, on 19 November,
Leopold stood in attendance, probably in the Hofburg, at the gala banquet
honoring Saint Elizabeth (the patron of Maria Theresa's mother), the Empress called to him from the Imperial table to ask about his son's health.

It could not have been improved by his series of December concerts for
the Hungarian nobility in nearby Pressburg. The weather had turned raw,
and Wolfgang and Leopold journeyed back to Vienna in the terrible cold,
rocking along over those vague trails of ruts the Hungarians called roads.
They would "have returned [to Vienna] with fewer ribs," Leopold wrote,
had he not purchased a fine coach in Pressburg. Engaging a carriage had
proved expensive—even when an aristocrat placed his own at their disposition, the tips to drivers and lackeys could equal the cost of a hire—
and Leopold had invested an impressive twenty-three ducats in a private
vehicle for future travel.

The first of Mozart's Viennese tours came to a close on 27 December, when he entertained at a dinner given by Countess Kinsky in honor of Field Marshal Count Leopold von Daun, hero of the battle of Kolin (see p. 83). Four days later the Mozarts departed the Habsburg capital for Salzburg, which the new coach entered on the evening of 5 January 1763.

4

WOLFGANG HAD NEVER fully recovered; the Hungarian campaign had cost him much strength. Once more he fell ill, and with signs so alarming that fears of smallpox ceased only when the pain finally settled in his feet. As in a similar attack some four years later (November 1766), fever and insomnia seized him, and he lay paralyzed from his knees to his toes; most likely he had rheumatic fever. A week passed before he could leave his bed.

Fearful of the worst, Leopold also had professional worries, his main business at court being to mend fences. He had stretched Archbishop Schrattenbach's complaisance to breaking: with the visiting Prince-Bishop of Eichstätt to entertain at the very time the Mozarts prolonged their stay in Vienna, he had become "very angry." To justify his ever-lengthening absence, Leopold had resorted to transparent inventions. The same letter describing the family's schedule at the gallop had also served up the most ironic of the fabrications he wished Salzburg friends to broadcast—the leisurely manner of journeying necessity imposed upon him: ". . . for the children's sake I must travel slowly so that from time to time they may rest for a few days and not fall ill." A bit later he blamed his delayed return upon "the unusually cold weather." Nor had he scrupled to pen the tale of a severe toothache that had disfigured his face, documenting his account with the less than subtle device of a convenient witness: "Lieutenant Winkler, the [Salzburg] court drummer's brother, who visited us [in Pressburg], did not recognize me when he entered the room and thought he had come to the wrong place." Leopold had also tried to turn to account the news of smallpox in Salzburg to declare to Hagenauer, whose daughters Maria Ursula and Maria Franziska had become infected: "Now you know the reason why we do not wish to go home." But that opportunities in Vienna and the invitation to Pressburg had directed his course drew the true picture. The Archbishop could not have been deceived.

Having experienced the rich life and splendor of Maria Theresa's capital, Leopold chafed against the necessity of returning to a backwater of Empire and had no intention of remaining: he had come back simply to pause for breath and maneuver himself into a promotion bringing with it a more seemly title. His letter to Lotter of 17 February indicates that he had already plunged deep into designs for a new tour: "We only await the arrival of the swallows. . . ." These preparations could not have remained secret as he gathered letters of introduction. That the orchestra could no longer expect regular service from him must have confirmed the court in its decision to bring to Salzburg Johann Michael Haydn, Joseph's younger brother, since 1757 Kapellmeister of Schrattenbach's nephew, the Bishop of Grosswardein (Nagyvárad) in Hungary.[8] By midsummer, Haydn would be established in Salzburg as court composer and *Konzertmeister.*[9]

After mass on 28 February 1763, his birthday, the Archbishop announced changes in his musical household: Lolli became kapellmeister and Leopold Mozart vice-kapellmeister. Schrattenbach's pique had vanished, and he granted the title, no doubt because it would be of advantage to the Mozarts at foreign courts. As yet, Leopold inspired less animosity than irritation at the Residenz, which remained proud of the children. Indeed, that very evening they performed in the council chamber of the palace. Both played the clavier, and, in addition, Wolfgang stepped forward as a violinist "with a solo and a concerto." In later years Schachtner told Nannerl that his anecdotes of Wolfgang's first efforts with the violin pertained to "the days right after you returned from Vienna." Here Schachtner's memory failed: Leopold would never have permitted even this astounding prodigy to appear bow in hand before the Archbishop with what could have been, at most, considering the latest illness, only a month and a half of experience. Wolfgang had taken up the instrument before the journey to Vienna—had he not fiddled his way through the customs barrier?— and, once back in Salzburg, devoted the weeks following his recovery to practice. Moreover, by this time he could write down his compositions himself: he had come to terms with staff and clefs, and with the inkwell itself.

---

8 At the moment, Grosswardein/Nagyvárad, under the name Oradea Mare, belongs to Romania.
9 For *Konzertmeister*, see pp. 253–55.

CHAPTER VII

Stratagems and Treacheries:
A Glance Back

O N 9 JUNE 1763 the Mozarts left Salzburg. Accompanied by Sebastian Winter serving as general domestic and hairdresser, they entered upon a journey that would last three and a half years, the palace of Versailles its ultimate goal. (Leopold did have in mind a possible excursion to London.) The family's route to France took the shape of a lazy S curve plotted on the capitals and main towns of Bavaria, Swabia, Württemberg, the Palatinate, the Rhineland, and Flanders, the moment being opportune for an extended tour through the network of kingdoms, duchies, electorates, principalities, and dependencies that made up the Germanic body. Four months earlier, in the Saxon Elector's superb shooting lodge of Hubertusburg, an agreement ending the Seven Years' War received the endorsement of Austria, Prussia, and Saxony; England and France concluded a separate treaty at Paris, an event celebrated by opening the Place Louis XV (today the Place de la Concorde). Europe was at peace. By spring, Salzburg's contingent of troops, weary and decimated, had come home.

Here is the point at which to consider the background of the dynastic and political alignments in place at the end of the war, a diversion that will help locate in history the prodigy who performed at Europe's courts, both brilliant and modest, many of them confronted by dramatic changes.

2

THE HUBERTUSBURG COVENANT formed the final act of an intricate drama. It had begun almost a half century earlier with an apprehensive conjecture of Emperor Charles VI: the growing tendency of the Habsburgs to bring into the world many fewer males (and these sickly) than females, made him fear that his wife would never bear a healthy son (within the year of his birth, their son lay dead), that the successor to his hereditary rights would be a woman. With the years the fear turned into obsession and then ineluctably into reality. Not even the miracle-working Styrian Madonna of Mariazell, whose aid Charles invoked, seemed able to stave off this danger to the House of Habsburg. He envisioned the chaos his death might bring: his territories dismembered by contentious relatives and rapacious neighbors, his proud titles scattered, his dynasty extinguished—anxieties that led him to strange concessions and political reshufflings. He clutched at remedies.

In the end, reconciled to being the last successory male of the Habsburg line, he strove to assure the accession of his elder daughter, Archduchess Maria Theresa, to all his hereditary possessions. Since not even Habsburg authority and prestige could gain for her the elective Imperial crown of Charlemagne—Salic law excluded women from wearing it—through bribes, negotiations, political gyrations, and accommodating treaties, he attempted to buy his brother rulers' agreement at least to respect an arrangement he had imposed upon his own family: the Pragmatic Sanction. In effect, it bequeathed to her, should he leave no male heir, the Habsburg territories under strict entail as an indivisible whole and thus set aside the rights of the daughters of Joseph I, his departed elder brother and Imperial predecessor (see n. 5). Upon this decree reregulating the succession and proclaiming the integrity of the Habsburg estate rested Maria Theresa's precedence in inheriting its patrimony in Germany, Hungary, Transylvania, Croatia, Bohemia, and Moravia.

Music formed one of the strongest links between the Emperor and his handsome heiress. A vocal student of Hasse and Wagenseil, she delighted in describing herself as Europe's oldest virtuoso, for Charles had encouraged her to sing in court operas from the age of five. Self-assured, she gained his confidence, and her intelligence and dignified bearing helped palliate his anxieties, ever deepened by his foolish and unsuccessful military adventures. *"Biancheggia in mar,"* sung by the personification of Constancy in Mozart's *Il sogno di Scipione,* praised Charles's tenacity of purpose in a sea of troubles (see p. 300). It is understandable why he insisted that any opera he might attend conclude happily.

He found solace anticipating the election of his son-in-law, Francis of Lothringen, as Holy Roman emperor: through him Maria Theresa would be empress in name, through her inheritance empress in fact. The talismanic Imperial title, since 1437 uninterruptedly a possession of the Habsburgs, had through the centuries bestowed a certain quasi-religious magnificence upon them, helping to bind together the citizens of their ramshackle territories, that strange and rather unhappy synthesis of peoples of divergent origins, traditions, and needs. Herder's famous image likening the Holy Roman Empire to an absurd monster—"a lion's head with a dragon's tail, an eagle's wing, a bear's paw . . ."—might have painted with equal appropriateness the disparate character of the Habsburgs' private possessions, many of which lay without the boundaries of the Reich.

France, long coveting Lothringen (Lorraine), had exploited the betrothal of Maria Theresa and Duke Francis as an opportunity of securing his rich duchy, the remnants of the ancient Frankish kingdom linking middle and western Europe and lying between German- and French-speaking spheres. The marriage would make Lothringen a household property of Austria, an idea unthinkable to Versailles. Lothringen became the price of its recognition of the Pragmatic Sanction: for personal dynastic ends, the Habsburgs agreed to sever from the Empire a part of the Germanic world. (By the end of the century Johann Gottlieb Fichte would sarcastically inquire whether Germans from Lothringen or Elsass [Alsace] really cared whether or not a geography listed their home towns as part of the German Empire.) At Paris's behest, Vienna threatened Francis with forfeit of his Imperial bride should he refuse to surrender his native land to French hegemony. But he was not to go empty-handed: in exchange for signing away Lothringen, Tuscany was to fall to him upon the eagerly awaited death of the childless Medicean Grand Duke, Gian Gastone. Exhausted by debauches and in the power of his favorite, the infamous Giuliano Dami, he seldom quit his bed in the Pitti Palace. He obligingly died in 1737, the year after the marriage of Maria Theresa and Francis. With Gian Gastone at rest in his family's unfinished mausoleum, the young couple took possession of their new territory—in Mozart's *Ascanio in Alba*, Maria Theresa, through the voice of Venus, lovingly recalls her days in Florence with Francis—the birthplace of opera becoming a Habsburg domain during the generation preceding Mozart's. (In the next century, the see of Salzburg would be secularized and its territory transferred to the Habsburgs as compensation for their loss of Tuscany.) Its identity as Lothringen dissolved, Lorraine at first passed to Louis XV's genial father-in-law, Stanislaus Leczinski—a king of Poland twice deposed by Saxony—as a consolation prize with the remainder to France upon his death. (Mozart paid tribute to Stanislaus's handsome rebuilding of his new capital of Nancy [Nanzig in Lothringen days].) The Polish and Tuscan successions thus found mutual resolution as part of a general settlement between Versailles and the Hofburg—Sebastian Bach's secular cantata *Preise dein Glücke* (1734) alludes to the War of the Polish Succession (1733–1735), a time of "lighning and din," when ". . . French power also threatened our Fatherland [Saxony] with sword and fire"—the protocols constituting a diplomatic work of art, rococo in its refined invention, subtle artifice, and fragility.

Emperor Charles died on 20 October 1740, and Maria Theresa entered upon her reign. Less than half a year earlier, the crown of Prussia had passed to Prince Frederick, one day to be called "the Great." He repudiated his late father's recognition of the Pragmatic Sanction and on 16 December 1740 ordered his army to seize the wealthy and largely Protestant province of Silesia from the inexperienced Maria Theresa.[1] The dismemberment feared by her father began as the third of the upstart Hohenzollern to style himself king drew the sword against Germany's ancient, foremost, and guardian dynasty. History, Maria Theresa observed, could hardly show a crowned head who started under circumstances more grievous.

Frederick came to body forth the shameless standards of honor obtaining among the mighty, that severance of personal and political responsibility so often depicted upon the operatic stage. The hallowed ordinance of social distinctions commanded an increasingly less universal awe:[2] Germans like the Mozarts became more and more conscious of the moral squalor and rapaciousness of princes and reluctant in any way to trust them. If Gottsched had thought it unfitting to put aristocrats on stage in comic situations, seeing impropriety in their being laughed at, Mozart, in his operas, leaped at exploring their faults and foolishness: the pompous Count Belfiore (*La finta giardiniera*) reciting the glories of his ancestral tree to the tittering of his auditors ("Why, for God's sake, are you laughing?"

---

1 Though engrossed in his Silesian adventure—which some at first naïvely looked upon as a Protestant crusade—he did not permit it to interfere with his plans to give Berlin a splendid new opera house: even in the field, he concerned himself with the progress of construction on that difficult site facing the Linden Allee and sent instructions concerning the hiring of artists and questions of scenic design and stage machinery.

2 For his father's amusement Mozart ticked off names among "the crowd of nobles" at one of his Augsburg concerts (1777): "Duchess Smack-Bottom, Countess Piss-with-Pleasure, and then Princess Smell-of-Shit with her two daughters. . . ." This assembly calls to mind the cast of characters Goethe and Johann Heinrich Merck, with Rabelaisian humor, drew up for *Hanswurst's Wedding* (1774), a dramatic project that remained a fragment.

he desperately asks, even his simple mind suddenly aware of some kind of cultural crisis); or the young nobleman Belmonte, bargaining for his and his beloved Constanze's freedom—he had briefly halted the venture to rescue her until set at rest concerning her fidelity!—but making no gesture to ransom their faithful servants; or Don Giovanni and Count Almaviva, both studies in the depravity and mendacities of aristocratic predators.[3] (Rousseau opined: "I look upon any poor man as totally undone should he have the misfortune to have an honest heart, a fine daughter, and a powerful neighbor.") If Mozart could aver that "the heart ennobles the man" and that, "though no count," he "might well incorporate more honor than many a count," royal Frederick argued in a quite different mold: "If anything is to be gained by honesty, then we shall be honest; if, on the other hand, deceit is called for, let us be knaves." This is the voice of Basilio, whose aria in the closing act of Mozart's *Figaro* advises that a camouflage sufficiently shameless and, if necessary, abhorrent, can win many a day. The "insane day," whose unfolding constitutes the plot of Mozart's *Figaro*, pictures the dilapidation of aristocratic ambition, the grossness of aristocratic privilege, all the while presuming their inevitable demolition. Frederick could not have suspected that his scenario of war would, through many a long and exhausting scene, lead toward the same end: Berlin's challenge to Vienna would hasten the dissolution of Central Europe's old order.

With remote England her main ally, Maria Theresa had no immediate remedy against the Prussian King's marauding excursion. Russia, in turmoil—Tsarina Anna had died three days before Charles VI—at first could provide no aid. Frederick's escapade grew into the War of the Austrian Succession, the extended, tumultuous prelude to the Seven Years'

---

3 The libretto of *The Abduction from the Seraglio* does not make clear whether Belmonte without heed abandons Blondchen and Pedrillo to their own ingenuity (which they at once exercise) or, worse, turns from a couple become useless to him and whom, as subordinates, he counts for less than completely human. Upon glimpsing Constanze after their long separation, he had remarked to his valet: "Pedrillo, if you but knew what love is!" "As if it were nothing to the likes of me," came the smart retort, anticipating the accents of the hero of *The Marriage of Figaro*. Not by chance do its plot and that of *Don Giovanni* turn upon attempts to deflower the betrothed of a social inferior, though the verb hardly suits Zerlina, the knowing peasant girl, whose safety Giovanni mockingly pledges "in the hands of a nobleman" even as he forces her lover, that not unintelligent bumpkin Masetto, to depart. He flashes back: "Yes, I understand, my lord; I'll bow my head . . . I won't answer back. You are, after all, a nobleman; upon my faith, I can't doubt it," Mozart casting this riposte in relief by using it not for a swiftly passing recitative but for an aria. However, it is in Figaro's master, the petty and petulant Count Almaviva, that Mozart left his ultimate portrait of the aristocrat as feckless sexual purloiner: "Shall I behold my servant happy while I sigh in longing?" he demands, furious to be outwitted in his attempts to seduce Figaro's bride-to-be, outraged to discover the contempt in which the retainers of the castle hold their lord, astonished to observe them asserting their dignity and worth.

War. Louis XV of France, indolent and reluctant, but encouraged to anticipate tearing the Austrian Lowlands and Luxemburg from the House of Habsburg, let himself be prodded into putting aside his pledge to support the Pragmatic Sanction.[4] He joined the Prussian adventure, the Duchess de Châteauroux, Louis's *maîtresse en titre* of the moment, receiving her reward for helping forge the ruinous alliance: a charming letter from her "very fond friend, Frederick."

Maurice de Saxe, a soldier of fortune and bastard of the house of Wettin (one of the more than fifteen-score illegitimate children sired by Augustus the Strong of Saxony-Poland), rapidly emerged the ablest officer in the French army invading Germany. In the vanguard of the expeditionary force preparing to plunder Maria Theresa, he elatedly wrote: "Here is the general muddle, and I have a part to play in it." The way to the Imperial city remained unprotected. By October 1741, the French had reached St. Pölten, a short march from Vienna. It lay frozen in panic.

For the Danubian monarchy the struggle had become one of life and death. Joined by Maurice's half-brother, Augustus the Weak, since 1733 ruler of Saxony-Poland (he, too, betrayed an earlier acceptance of the Pragmatic Sanction; see n. 5), the coalition planned to reduce Maria Theresa solely to the throne of Hungary. France had been opposing her husband's candidacy for the Imperial crown, championing, instead, the Wittelsbach prince, Charles Albert, Elector of Bavaria. Having invaded Upper Austria and moved on Linz, he appeared at St. Pölten in the camp of the French, the Franco-Bavarian campaign occasioning those uneasy days in Salzburg during the courtship of Leopold Mozart and Anna Maria.

But the invaders did not strike at Vienna, where a peace could have been dictated. The French hesitated, all at once reluctant to hand the heart of the Empire to their subsidized puppet, Charles Albert. He had come to

---

4 England and Holland did not desert the Pragmatic Sanction. In August 1742 an English squadron appeared in the Bay of Naples and, under threat of bombardment, extracted an agreement from the King of the Two Sicilies, Charles of Bourbon, to cease threatening Maria Theresa's Italian dominions. (They included Lombardy and her husband's recently acquired Grand Duchy of Tuscany.) Believing that the navy should continue to furnish the main contribution to the expanding war, many in England opposed any wholesale employment of troops on the Continent. But King George II committed the nation to land operations and rushed to the defense of his native principality of Hannover. (He considered his island kingdom his lesser realm.) Flushed, bellowing, and waving his sword, this ludicrous figure somehow led the so-called Pragmatic Army to victory over the French near the village of Dettingen am Main on 27 June 1743, an event Handel celebrated in London by composing the *Dettingen Te Deum*. Elements of its closing chorus would reappear transformed in the Kyrie fugue of Mozart's Requiem (see p. 755). He did honor to more than one English triumph.

look upon most of the Habsburg crown lands as his own,[5] his claim resting upon the almost two-hundred-year-old testament of Emperor Ferdinand I. ("Clumsy the historian," Mozart was to observe, "unable on the spot to concoct some kind of lie. . . .") Charles Albert coveted not only Austria but also Tyrol and Bohemia. Would a Bavaria thus enlarged and a strengthened Prussia serve the real aim of France—the perpetuation of German factionalism? Versailles, which had beguiled itself with thoughts of a non-Habsburg German emperor loyal to its interests, now paused to ponder the question anew.

Suddenly an urgent problem presented itself: to prevent their suspect Saxon allies, eager for spoils, from installing themselves too comfortably and perhaps permanently in Bohemia, the French and Charles Albert turned northward in double quick time. They spared Vienna—an error in strategy—but Prague fell to Maurice de Saxe. The crown of Wenceslas now in her hands, France made Charles Albert King of Bohemia in December 1741 and, early the following year, contrived with the electors that he be crowned Charles VII of the Holy Roman Empire. The German Emperor had become a surrogate of the French King.

"The bold Bavarian, in a luckless hour, / Tries the dread summits of Caesarean power." Samuel Johnson thus described the gamble of the new Emperor, who at once became entangled in a train of disasters operatic in their larger-than-life drama, sudden and calamitous shifts in fortune, and occasional farcical episodes. As an operatic character Charles Albert might appropriately have sung the kind of simile aria in which the hero, bewailing his plight, compares himself to a mariner adrift in a tempest. In Mozart's *Idomeneo*, Arbace, the King's confidant, advises anyone with ambitions for a throne to stifle them or come to terms with tribulation. Mozart wrote this work for the court of Munich, where Arbace's counsel must have evoked thoughts of the unfortunate Emperor-Elector, still remembered and beloved. Indeed, the Wittelsbachs may well have looked upon *Idomeneo* in the light of an allegory of their vicissitudes during the war.

---

5 Charles Albert had married Maria Amalia of Austria, a daughter of Emperor Charles VI's brother and predecessor, Joseph I. Since the Pragmatic Sanction had cut off from their Habsburg legacy both Maria Amalia and her sister, Maria Josepha, wife of Augustus the Weak of Saxony-Poland, not surprisingly the Wittelsbach of Bavaria and the Wettin of Saxony-Poland sought to wreck Charles VI's grand design once he had entered his tomb. Even in the Austrian heartlands Charles Albert did not lack adherents, who not only acknowledged his legal pretensions but, in any case, preferred a dashing prince to a chit of a girl. The handsome Charles Albert drew strong emotional responses. Some twenty years after her husband's death, Goethe's mother told Bettina von Arnim that Charles Albert had been the only man for whom she had felt passionate love, even though she had beheld him only a few times and from afar. Goethe enjoyed the fantasy of imagining himself his son.

For Maria Theresa the Pragmatic Sanction had begun to provide a legal foothold, an almost sacred rallying cry. The very day of Charles Albert's coronation at Frankfurt, a force fiercely loyal to her, the famed Hungarian cavalry, stormed into his hereditary Bavarian lands, into his very capital, Munich. He found himself cut off from those gilded chambers he had commissioned from such masters of rococo decoration as the elder Cuvilliés, John Baptist Zimmermann, and Joseph Effner in the Munich Residenz, Nymphenburg, and Schleissheim. *Et Caesar et nihil* (Both Caesar and nothing) went the quip about this homeless, pathetic figurehead defeated by his enemies and despised by his new allies. Marshal de Noailles described him to Louis XV as a "phantom," a nuisance wearing the crown of Charlemagne.

Even so, at his ill-fated coronations, tradition chronicles events important in the history of music: the violinist Johann Wenzel Stamitz offered concerts that heralded the beginning of an illustrious school of German music destined to have a powerful influence upon Mozart's instrumental style. But for Versailles the investitures of Charles VII had no happy issue. Having patched together with Maria Theresa a secret temporary peace leaving most of Silesia in his hands, Frederick of Prussia abandoned the French, now shut up in Prague by an Austrian army, to what would become a calamitous retreat (1742).[6] The day they broke out of the starving and damaged capital found him in Berlin, celebrating the opening of his new opera house.

After Emperor Charles VII's death in 1745,[7] his son took the Bavarian throne as Elector Maximilian III Joseph. (His was the first capital visited by Mozart [see p. 63], the unassuming and musical Elector, who bore the epithet of *der Vielgeliebte* [the much loved], and his sister, Maria Antonia Walpurgis, developing into his admirers and patrons.) He deferred to Maria Theresa, renouncing all claims to her paternal domains. If Mozart's *Idomeneo* held up to Munich the example of this noble son redeeming the nation from the reckless course of his father, Mozart's *Ascanio in Alba* and *Il rè pastore* glorified the ultimate prerogative Vienna felt confined to itself: that of presiding over the German world as God's deputy. Munich's reconciliation with Vienna seemed like the characteristic finale to this kind of dynastic opera, of which Mozart provided the Habsburgs four examples (*Mitridate* and *Lucio Silla* in addition to *Ascanio* and *Il rè pastore*). They all

---

6 In Prague during May of the following year, Maria Theresa would assume the crown of Wenceslas and become queen of Bohemia.

7 "His foes' derision and his subjects' blame, / ... [He] steals to death from anguish and from shame" (Johnson).

ended with reason triumphing over reckless passion or misguided resolve and bringing the joys of reunion, renewal, and restoration. Indeed, the seat of the Holy Roman Empire returned to Vienna: the Imperial title came to Maria Theresa's handsome, adored, and inept Francis, the conjunction spawning the House of Habsburg-Lothringen.

Recognizing his limitations, he would leave political matters to his increasingly formidable Empress and thus bear the privileges of his station and few of its responsibilities. At his coronation in Frankfurt during October 1746, the spectators included Christoph Willibald Gluck; en route from Milan to London in the company of Prince Ferdinand Philipp von Lobkowitz, he had made a halt to observe the ceremonies. Frankfurt would celebrate the next coronation with a performance of his as yet unwritten *Orfeo*, a musical harbinger of a new age (see p. 147).

3

MIDST THE STRATAGEMS, bickerings, and treacheries of the War of the Austrian Succession, Maria Theresa firmly established her position. She had begun to command an admiration bordering upon reverence. When he asked Gluck to compose Metastasio's nineteen-year-old *La Semiramide riconosciuta* to open the newly renovated Burgtheater in the spring of 1748, Nikolaus Esterházy no doubt intended the Viennese to see in this tale of the heroic Babylonian Queen a tribute to Maria Theresa's pluck. Five years earlier, at her coronation in Prague as queen of Bohemia, performances of a drama about Semiramis had served to predict the ultimate acceptance of the Pragmatic Sanction with its bestowal of authority upon a woman. Now Gluck's opera confirmed and glorified Maria Theresa's victory. (At the summit of his powers he would, in her widowhood, pay her yet deeper veneration: his *Alceste* (1767) celebrated a virtuous, magnanimous Queen, noble in mourning and heroic in resolve.) She had survived, preserved most of her inheritance, and truly become German empress. Even as the war approached its dying hours, Vienna began to formulate new designs with distant goals that envisaged attack—to repossess Silesia became an obsession—and the treaty signed in the autumn at Aix-la-Chapelle (Aachen) proved to be but a truce between rounds of bloodletting: the wags of Paris spoke of the peace that passeth all understanding. In London a crew raised a templelike "machine" designed by the Florence-born Jean-Nicolas Servandoni to accommodate a display of fireworks, while George Frideric Handel worked on music to accompany this salute in Green Park to the dubious achievement of Aix. (Some twelve thousand people attended the public dress rehearsal at Vauxhall.) The celebration seemed oddly out of scale with England's limited role in the war and the meager gains it had brought her. London, however, became the strategic center of an imaginative initiative with which Vienna contemplated permanently checkmating Berlin.

Wenzel Anton von Kaunitz-Rietberg, the Empress's chief adviser (and to be among Mozart's first and most helpful Viennese patrons), resolved to rearrange the pieces on the board before resuming the game. He had long planned to use the Marquise de Pompadour to help undermine the cornerstone of French foreign policy—hostility toward the Habsburgs. It had, Kaunitz argued, diminishing pertinence in the age of a rising Prussia: détente, rapprochement, and an ensuing French alliance appeared to him the Empress's most promising means of recovering Silesia from Frederick. When Vienna learned that, coincident with the fraying of his ties to Versailles, he had begun flirting with its traditional enemy, England, Kaunitz counseled Maria Theresa to warn King Louis of the perfidy and then turn his gratitude to profit.

As early as 1750 Kaunitz, while ambassador to Paris, had sounded Pompadour, rare among the mistresses of the French kings as the possessor of a mind as well as beauty. (His fine hand may be traced in her receiving the dedication of the Parisian edition of Metastasio's works, a compliment to her discerning cultivation of the arts.) Leopold Mozart was to laud her "unusual intelligence," though contempt for her as Europe's foremost courtesan doubtless lay behind his pungent observation that in France "the most money is lavished upon Lucretias who do not stab themselves." She could not remain unflattered by the role in which the Empress had cast her. With the support of her protégé, the Abbé de Bernis, she encouraged the King to execute a political about-face, and, to the end of her days as *maîtresse en titre*, a reign that closed only with her death, continued devoted to the House of Austria and Maria Theresa. Leopold Mozart observed that Pompadour even adopted an Imperial manner of her own.

Toward the middle of the fifties, a series of bellicose acts and retaliations on the seas embroiled England and France. By September 1755, Leopold Mozart, dryly commenting on their "corsairlike" conduct, recognized that they, in fact, had once again come to "open war." Already standing to arms, Europe would soon catch fire. On 16 January 1756, eleven days before Mozart's birth, Maria Theresa's warning proved true: Prussia and England, reversing alliances, signed the Convention of Westminster. Deserted by Frederick and incited by Pompadour, Louis XV found himself enrolled in the Empress's personal crusade against Prussia, his army becoming her convenience, an instrument of her vendetta, his folly a triumph for Kaunitz: "We owe her everything," the Hofburg's Ambassador wrote of Pompadour, who received from Vienna a miniature of Maria Theresa framed in diamonds.

4

IF PARIS SUBMISSIVELY followed her former foe into the catastrophes of the coming conflict, Vienna, seeking to imitate the French capital, for a while became its cultural suburb, a development underlined by Count Durazzo's engagement of Charles-Simon Favart to function as *agent littéraire* to the Habsburg court. He sent Vienna fortnightly reports on theatrical matters of importance in Paris (and even in the provinces)—on actors, composers, singers, musicians, choreographers, dancers, stage designers, and theater machinists—and forwarded copies of current French books, plays, reviews, and epigrams; still more, he retailed the latest scandal.[8]

In contrast to this essentially frothy Viennese partiality to French mode, more intense, indeed all-embracing Francophile tendencies infused the capital of a King who believed the substance of civilization to reside in French letters: Berlin, since the accession of King Frederick, had increasingly modeled its social conventions, values, and tastes on the standards of Paris, the energy and pertinacity of his ambitions for Prussian intellectual and artistic prestige systematically building, even in the face of his ossifying musical and literary inclinations, a cultural ambience of enormous promise.

The French disdained Berlin as the sort of capital Paris had been at the time of the Dark Ages of Hugh Capet. But during the fifties the eyes of Europe turned toward Frederick's court, where Voltaire's glittering wit ornamented intimate royal suppers, where Maupertius presided over an academy founded by Leibniz, where the King's musical household included Emanuel Bach, where the Royal Opera gave meticulous performances before a monarch who took his seat in the first row of the pit, the better to keep watch over every detail. The premiere on 27 March 1756 of Carl Heinrich Graun's *Merope*, its libretto adapted for the most part by the King from Voltaire's tragedy,[9] symbolized the height of Berlin's great days, soon to be interrupted by mounting international tensions.

---

8 Favart dispatched his reports religiously from the beginning of 1760 to the end of 1764 and thereafter sporadically until 1770. Karl Eugene of Württemberg, too, had a consultant in Paris to keep him abreast with developments in French art and society.

9 The court poet, Tagliazucchi, turned into Italian poetry the King's preliminary prose sketch in French. Apropos of Graun's *Montezuma* of the preceding season, Tagliazucchi's Italian verse also derived from Frederick's French prose, in this case an original creation. New librettos commissioned for Frederick's theater came, at the least, under his review.

Voltaire remarked that political alliances resembled a quadrille, partners changing every moment. But by summer Frederick could no longer freely step and skip forward and backward, right and left *en quadrille*: he had become the central figure in a menacing round dance. Anticipating an attack by a new encircling coalition of France, Austria, Saxony, Russia, and Sweden, he took to the field, striking at Saxony, whose boundaries thrust so close to Berlin itself: on 26 August 1756 he set his troops in motion; on 9 September they entered the Saxon capital of Dresden. The Seven Years' War had begun.

The allies did have skilled commanders, among them the cultivated Count Leopold von Daun (for whom Mozart performed in Vienna). But, as in the War of the Austrian Succession, French and Austrian military leaders too often distinguished themselves by their vanity. The King of Prussia, challenging heavy odds, found himself aided, on the one hand, by the self-seeking and ineptitude of these courtier-generals in patches and powder and imbued with petty illusions of fame—he celebrated their "divine stupidity"—and, on the other, by the adroitness of his own officers, in particular his in-laws of the House of Braunschweig: Duke Ferdinand and his nephew (the King's, too) Hereditary Prince Karl Wilhelm Ferdinand, the "German Achilles" (soon to extol Mozart and his father).

Frederick accomplished miracles with an outnumbered but highly trained, nimble-footed army that time and again adroitly eluded destruction. His efficiency and imagination at first puzzled and then shook Versailles and the Hofburg.[10] As Berlin thrust her way into their company, the Continental balance began to shift; France's and Austria's unwieldy baroque military machines sputtered and stalled, the formal patterns of warfare they inscribed having ever less effect during this new age of rococo volatility and lightness of touch. In an acerbic image Leopold Mozart used the Empire's coalition army as an example of swiftness—but with the agile Prussian forces at its heels! He had the battle of Rossbach in mind.

Voltaire recognized Rossbach (1757) as one of the century's decisive events. Outmaneuvered by Frederick, a French army, together with the Army of Empire led by the Prince of Sachsen-Hildburghausen, fled the field, panic fastening upon all ranks from commander to common soldier. Dread of Frederick's extemporaneous, mobile way of warfare persisted for years: in 1778 Leopold Mozart wrote an amusing vignette of an Imperial officer who had ensconced himself in peaceful Salzburg "in an attempt to

---

10 Luck also played its part: at the very time her forces had begun to move toward Brandenburg, Empress Elizabeth of Russia died (5 January 1762); her nephew and successor, German-born Peter III, idolized Frederick and commanded the troops to disengage.

recover from his fear of Prussian powder and shot." Rossbach set the pulse of German nationalism beating: in all the states of Germany, Frederick started to arouse begrudging admiration. It can be sensed in the letters of the Mozarts, at bottom loyal children of Empire but blinded from time to time by the transforming, idealistic light in which he could bathe his disreputable gambles,[11] his brilliance throwing into shadow the sluggish Habsburgs trailing their ancient Imperial prerogatives. (Near the end of his career, Mozart would turn his gaze from an atrophying Vienna toward the vital Berlin Frederick had fostered.) Humiliated, Hildburghausen laid down his command after Rossbach, henceforth devoting himself to administering his family's duchy. This arbiter of musical taste soon dissolved his private orchestra, perhaps the finest in Vienna: Gluck, Bonno, and Dittersdorf had left his employ when, five years after Rossbach, the Mozarts rushed from Schönbrunn to his palace.

That autumn, when the Imperial family first received the Mozarts, the exhausted combatants pressed for another breathing space they called a peace. Bernis had plaintively asked: "How can we hope for military success? We shall always have the same generals [Saxe had died], and the King of Prussia will always beat us at the game of war." From Vienna, Leopold Mozart wrote Hagenauer in October 1762: "I have absolutely no news to write you, for here they talk as little about the war as if there were no war." It was petering out, its significant action unfolding as a succession of piratical enterprises far from Europe. Maria Theresa had awakened to the futility of continuing in a struggle whose focus had shifted, France to the cunning of England's game: entangling her on the Continent while destroying her navy, ruining her maritime shipping, and seizing her colonies. The contest had resolved into one between the Channel powers. "We shall win America on the continent of Europe," William Pitt predicted.

For meddling in the German imbroglio Louis XV paid with the loss of Canada and India. Leopold Mozart dated his return to Paris in 1766 as "the day after the beheading of M. de Lally, former Viceroy in Pondicherry." Come home to France after capitulating to the English, he found himself sentenced to death on a trumped-up charge of treachery and dragged to the scaffold with a gag in his mouth lest he assert his innocence. Thus did Louis XV reward a devoted officer whom no more than

---

11 Conflicting opinions concerning Frederick shattered the tranquillity of many a German family. In Goethe's, for example, he and his father took the King's part, while the poet's maternal grandfather, Frankfort's chief magistrate, supported the Empress. At his death, Mozart's library included four volumes of *Frederick II's Posthumous Works*, published in fifteen parts in Berlin (1788).

a lack of men, money, and supplies had forced to yield the Coromandel coast.[12] The miscalculations and incapacities of the French King and his government had begun to help lay the foundations of the British Empire and Bismarck's Reich. "Our bells are worn threadbare with ringing for victories," Horace Walpole had trumpeted as early as October 1759.

If Maria Theresa had to suffer the permanent loss of Silesia and failed in her attempt to re-establish Austria as the supreme and dominating German state,[13] she must have luxuriated in the enfeeblement—indeed, the ruin—of France, hers a royal *Schadenfreude.* Ironically, the Bourbon-Habsburg alliance continued, and as a pledge of its endurance the Empress would hand over her beautiful, high-spirited, empty-headed daughter Maria Antonia to the court of Louis XV.

The Seven Years' War left Prussia spent but intact. Though in July 1760 Frederick had allowed himself the outrageous pleasure of bombarding Dresden (the allies had wrested it from him the preceding September) and bringing down the Kreuzkirche, he must have contemplated with heavy heart the holes Russian artillery had opened in his Berlin opera house and the mess a contingent of Saxon soldiers had left in the Charlottenburg palace during a brief Allied occupation. But restorers soon set to work,[14] and in the chapel of a king whose distaste for the rituals of Christianity approached the obsessive,[15] a Te Deum solemnized the Peace of Hubertusburg and Prussia's emergence as a great power. Sebastian Bach had composed his *Musical Offering* for Frederick, furnishing two of its canons with

---

12 In 1757 the English had put Admiral John Byng to death for his failure to prevent the French conquest of Minorca. He, however, had proved bungling and irresolute, his execution being held a necessary proof that the revised Articles of War applied to all ranks.

13 The Westminster protocols joining Berlin and London in league first identified Germany as an entity distinct from the Habsburgs' hereditary heartlands. With mounting Prussian influence, this would become the accustomed usage.

14 Dresden, on the other hand, required more than restorers: the ruins stood for years. Frederick's malevolent assault horrified the courts of Europe, aware of how much he envied the beautiful capital. (Not only did great buildings fall to dust under his shells but also the collected manuscripts, some of them uncopied, of Hasse, a composer he revered.) Such vicious destruction, akin to the devastation and ruin Louis XIV had visited upon those opposing him, no longer found applause, even among military men. Although the conscience of the age still encompassed pillage and in time of war many a city had to pay ransom to escape this fate—during its four-day occupation, Berlin gave two million thalers to Austrian and Russian raiders lest it be sacked—a commander like Maurice de Saxe had made every effort to spare "great capitals, the adornments of their countries," urging that such places be declared "open."

15 In his *Montezuma* (see n. 9), Frederick made the conqueror, Cortez, a symbol of "the barbarousness of the Christian religion." Something of this spirit shows itself in Mozart's *Abduction from the Seraglio* when a renegade brands a grandee of Spain with the same mark: "barbarian."

prognosticative mottoes now realized, augmentation and ascending modulation symbolizing the King's "good fortune" and "glory."

Paris marked the end of the fighting with Favart's *L'Anglois à Bordeaux*—the English Ambassador requested that its original title, *L'Antipathie vaincue* (Repugnance Overcome), be changed!—written at the command of a king with little to celebrate. When Leopold Mozart arrived in Paris late in 1763 he observed "everywhere the wretched fruits of the recent war." The magnificence and delicious follies of Versailles could not hide from him the miserable condition of the nation: "If God is not especially gracious," he wrote, "France will go the way of the former Persian Empire." Louis XV, Madame de Tencin observed, "preferred knowing nothing to knowing anything disagreeable." Things as they are will last my time" became his consolatory observation; he admonished Choiseul, his leading minister: "Calm yourself, for the evil is incurable."

In Potsdam, across the park from Sanssouci, built by Knobelsdorff in the *bon goût* of prewar days, Frederick began to raise perhaps the ugliest royal residence in Europe, the Neues Palais,[16] symbol of what had been lost and of what was to come.

5

WHEN THE MOZARTS' Pressburg coach departed Salzburg late in the spring of 1763, many German courts had turned to indulging an almost desperate prodigality in attempts to recover their prewar grandeur. In Vienna, however, Maria Theresa realized that nothing would ever again be the same. During the war, the magnificent operatic establishment founded by her grandfather Leopold I had dissolved. (Lady Mary Wortley Montagu had much admired it.) The sumptuous theater designed by Francesco Galli da Bibbiena had already fallen to demolition in 1747-1748, to be replaced by a ballroom, the Redoutensaal. At the time of the Aix Treaty, the court had so reduced its expenditures on opera that Gluck, who would have preferred to settle permanently in Vienna, felt it wiser to rejoin Pietro Mingotti's traveling opera troupe as its conductor. The scenic magnificence of Gluck's *Tetide*, given in Vienna to honor the nuptials of Maria Theresa's heir apparent, Archduke Joseph, and Infanta Isabella of Bourbon-Parma (1760), merely responded to the requirements of a Habsburg-Bourbon dynastic union; retrenchment continued on less exalted operatic occasions as the Empress devoted herself to the kind of social reform more often asso-

---

16 An amazing finial surmounts its awkward dome: a crown supported by three almost nude female figures bearing the features of Maria Theresa, Catherine of Russia—and Pompadour.

ciated with this son and successor, who built his finest achievements upon groundwork she had set.[17]

In Berlin, her bane, Frederick—at fifty-one fast becoming the desiccated, crabbed *der alter Fritz* (old Fred)—also directed his energies along practical paths: the rebuilding of Prussia's agriculture, army, trade, and coinage.[18] If he did follow the whim of erecting the Neues Palais (1763–1769), even so, his milieu became more and more shabby: Goethe was to comment upon the tattered curtains in Sanssouci. The theatrical productions for which Frederick's theater had become renowned now interested him little. Determined to keep their costs within limits, he descended to a sometimes ludicrous parsimony, even, on one occasion—to the delight of Berlin's wits—forcing the castrato Coli to sing the title role in Graun's *Ifigenia in Aulide* in order to pare down operatic personnel. (The oft-repeated tale of Coli's plight no doubt inspired Mozart's impish proposal that the Salzburg court manage the heavy costs of mounting operas by having its castrato, Francesco Ceccarelli, "at one moment be the female character, at another the male . . . in operas in which the primo uomo and the prima donna never meet.")[19] Frederick not only practiced thrift in casting but also ordered scenery reused until it fell to pieces. He confessed: "For seven uninterrupted years the Austrians, Russians, and French led me such a dance that I have somewhat lost my taste for it in the theater. . . ." Indeed, he had lost his taste for the stage in general,[20] the Maecenas of former years begrudging his performers their every thaler.

In contrast to Berlin and Vienna, a more familiar spirit overspread capitals such as Paris, Stuttgart, Mannheim, and Dresden, whose rulers consumed their states' resources in extravagant display. Only weeks before the Mozarts began their Grand Tour, Augustus the Weak had returned to Dresden after seven years of refuge in his eastern capital, Warsaw. Ignoring

---

17 However, she remained aware of ceremony's importance to a monarch and regarded opera as part of this apparatus. For the celebration of Joseph's wedding, see pp. 86 and 146.

18 Claude-Adrien Helvétius, who would befriend the Mozarts in Paris, accepted a royal invitation to Berlin, where, amid controversy, he reorganized Prussia's excise system.

19 Mozart elaborated his point, giving play to his marvelous sarcasm: "In this way the castrato can play both lover and beloved and thereby make the piece more interesting; one would admire in the pair of lovers a virtue so enormous that they most diligently avoid the opportunity of speaking to one another in public." Doubtless Mozart also had in mind a case much in the spirit of Coli's: in Munich during 1774, the castrato Tommaso Consoli sang the role of the heroine, Elisa, in Pietro Guglielmi's setting of *Il rè pastore*; the next year in Salzburg, Consoli undertook the part of Elisa's lover, Aminta, in Mozart's version of the same Metastasian text.

20 His interest in music waned in concert with his declining ability to play the flute as his breath control diminished, his fingers stiffened, and his teeth rotted.

the misery in Saxony's abused countryside and damaged towns, he immediately addressed what to his eyes appeared the major task before the nation: re-establishing the Dresden opera as Europe's finest.[21] He sumptuously refurbished the theater, used as a storehouse during the Prussian occupation; the doors opened again during the summer with Hasse's *Siroe*, mounted with an opulence that seemed to defy the distress in the streets.

Rousseau asked: ". . . in a country where music has become an affair of state, what will affairs of state be other than songs?" This most musical of the philosophes recognized matters more pressing than opera as requiring attention: it had become increasingly difficult to ignore the squalor growing in the shadow of luxury; the callousness to human suffering of absolute rulers who reduced the multitude to an instrument of their fantasies. During the autumn of 1762, Diderot wrote to Sophie Volland of the poverty surrounding the exquisite royal estate of Marly—"peasants without roofs, without bread, and on straw." At the very time the Mozarts set out for Versailles, Voltaire published his *Traité sur la tolérance*, the ghastly execution of Jean Calas, an innocent victim of a conspiracy of Church and state, having evoked this passionate protest and plea.[22] Voltaire cried out against the whole *ancien régime* when he thundered (letter of 5 July 1762 to d'Argental) about the secret judgment in the Calas trial: "Is there any more awful tyranny than to be able to shed blood without having to account to anybody for it? . . . Well, you monsters, from now on it must be done. You do owe an account for the blood you shed!"

Mozart would address kindred monsters in *Zaide*, and with no less resonance. Allazim's aria *"Ihr Mächtigen"* (You, the powerful) appeals for a new sense of justice, for an end to the oppressive sway of rulers unacquainted with suffering, for a concept of aristocracy based not upon blood but upon fortitude and virtue: "Wrapped in fortune and authority, you, the powerful, look down unmoved upon your slaves and fail to recognize your brothers. He alone comprehends pity, kindness, and mercy who, before his elevation to high rank, has been tested in the dust by the vagaries of fate."[23] Early in 1778, in a diatribe upon the excesses of aristocratic

---

21 Augustus died as he had lived—a zealot of opera: a stroke felled him (5 October 1763) as he prepared to attend a rehearsal of Hasse's *Leucippo*. Frederick the Great remarked: "The conquest of ten countries would not make him leave the first act of an opera."

22 The Mozart and Calas families had in common both a portraitist and a champion; see XI, n. 30.

23 The libretto of *Zaide* owes a significant debt to Rousseau, whose powerful and widespread ideas had brought into European life an unrest impossible to evade. The aria calls to mind certain Rousseau-inspired radical lines by Mozart's future librettist Lorenzo Da Ponte (which his *Memoirs* outline but do not quote). That his students at the seminary of Treviso went about quoting them helped provoke the Venetian Senate to prohibit this professor of literature from ever again teaching in its domains.

privilege and materialism, Mozart flared up to the point of making an un-characteristic identification of himself with the "lowly, wretched, and poor"; he insisted: ". . . our wealth dies with us, for it is our brains—and these no one can take from us unless he chops off our heads. . . ."[24]

Though Rousseau's *Émile* (1762) had warned that the century inclined toward revolutionary upheaval, the courts the Mozarts would visit the following year showed little awareness of this drift. The disasters of war generally struck the prince's subjects, not the prince himself—the assumption about which the dramaturgy of many an opera turned. (In Mozart's *Idomeneo* the royal adviser, though mouthing a commendable, if unusual, concern for the suffering populace, nonetheless seems content to see the entire nation go down if only the very author of the catastrophe, King Idomeneo, survive.) After Hubertusburg it seemed a matter of course once again to piece together the old fabric of lavish royal entertainments. But the perspicacious Leopold Mozart became aware that its pattern could no longer be adjusted with ease to a changing world, that the design, in fact, now showed strange discontinuities and sudden breaks. His letters offer frequent and penetrating observations about this social and political phenomenon.

---

24 Goethe, whose associations with the nobility remained in their way almost as problematic as Mozart's, fell into a similar mood in Book V of *Wilhelm Meister* (1783-1784); here, as spokesman for those in poverty, he observed: "Only to us poor, who possess little or nothing, is granted in rich measure the enjoyment of friendship's happiness. . . . We have nothing but ourselves. This whole self is, of necessity, our offering and . . . assures the friend an eternal benison." Wilhelm proclaimed: "A noble may have friends but cannot be a friend." Moralizing at the end of his tale *The Two Friends from Bourbonne* (see p. 155), Diderot remarked that "as a rule, total and solid friendship can occur only between men who have no worldly goods, for in such a case a man is his friend's entire fortune as he is likewise his friend's."

CHAPTER VIII

The Mozarts' Grand Tour. The First Phase: Bavaria, Swabia, Württemberg, the Palatinate, and the Rhineland

ERR HAGENAUER MUST have been startled by the first news from the travelers; the letter came from Wasserburg, a charming town set on a narrow peninsula formed by a loop of the Inn, but only sixty-five kilometers northwest of Salzburg. "This is a snail's pace," Leopold wrote on 11 June 1763, "but we are not at fault." He had, in fact, been negligent in blinking at the delicate condition of the Pressburg carriage. Two hours outside Wasserburg a wheel had broken into pieces. "We were stranded. Fortunately, the weather was bright and beautiful, and, even more fortunately, a mill was close at hand." With temporary repairs made and Leopold and Sebastian accompanying the coach on foot to lighten the load, the company made a bizarre entry into Wasserburg just after midnight in search of a cartwright, a smith, and an inn-keeper.

The mishap consumed much time and money, for a second wheel also required attention. In the end Leopold bought two new wheels and had to bear the expense of quartering the driver and feeding the four post horses.[1] To while away the hours he and Wolfgang examined the organ of St.

---

1 Like the public vehicles (the stagecoach and the mail coach, the latter more compact and lighter, hence faster, shakier, and less comfortable), the private carriage made a series of stops at stages,

James's church. (Its choirmaster, Johann Sebastian Diez, also had Lotter of Augsburg as his publisher.) Some eight months earlier, during a luncheon stop at Ybbs on the Danube, Wolfgang had astounded those in the parish church with his extemporizing at the organ. On that occasion he had used only his hands; but at Wasserburg Leopold taught him how to turn the pedal board to account: "Thereupon, pushing away the stool, he experimented while standing [*stante pede*];[2] remaining upright, he preluded as he worked the pedal and gave the impression of having practiced in this manner for several months."

Its carriage in order, the family reached Munich on the evening of 12 June. Though Elector Maximilian III Joseph of Bavaria had charged Johann Baptist Zimmermann with creating the Great Hall at Nymphenburg, the court's suburban palace to the west of the city, and had ordered François Cuvilliés both to complete the Amalienburg pavilion in the palace gardens and to build a theater for the Munich Residenz, he thereafter avoided the extravagance of his father and stopped building. The Bavarian palatial rococo ended as the Elector found all-absorbing relaxation in the saddle, at French plays, and in making music with his courtiers and visitors. Music became his principal artistic diversion and, in fact, had inspired his two major architectural projects: the Great Hall functioned no less than the theater as a glorious space in which to perform. This enthusiast, Leopold felt certain, would welcome the prodigy who had appeared in the capital a year and a half before.

On the thirteenth, the Mozarts drove to Nymphenburg. They walked in the park, contriving to remain clearly in view from the windows, for Leopold knew that Prince Frederick Michael of Birkenfeld-Zweibrücken-Rappoltstein would be within; catching sight of the family he had met in Vienna, on the spot he arranged the children's appearance for that very evening. Wolfgang had his usual success. Performing on the violin and clavier, he consumed the allotted time, and the concert came to a close without Nannerl's having touched the keyboard.

The next two evenings the Mozarts appeared at the palace of the Elector's cousin Duke Clemens Franz de Paula, and on the eighteenth stood in attendance while Maximilian Joseph dined at the Munich Residenz with

where, if the journey was to continue without a substantial break, grooms led the exhausted horses away and immediately readied a fresh team. (Four horses, a pair of leaders in front, a pair of wheelers behind them, usually drew the heavier coaches.) The drivers, too, worked in relays, and the stopping places provided the services of an inn. The Mozarts' coachman stayed with them until Munich, where, no doubt, he hired himself out to a party traveling toward Salzburg.
2 Leopold loved to sprinkle his letters with Latin phrases.

his sister Maria Antonia[3] and Prince Frederick Michael. Leopold's main problem lay in controlling expenses: "The charming custom here is to keep people waiting a long while for the royal recompense, so that one has to be happy to receive the equivalent of what one spends." He encountered Aloisio Luigi Tomasini,[4] a young man who had studied—perhaps with him—in Salzburg and become the Esterházy orchestra's first violinist. Leopold delighted to find the twenty-two-year-old virtuoso "grown tall, strong, and handsome." He took less pleasure in Tomasini's report that after performing at court he had cooled his heels for three weeks and in the end received an inadequate emolument. (It included the inevitable gold watch.) In any case, the family had to linger: the Elector wished to hear Nannerl play, and the Mozarts awaited an opening in his schedule of hunting by day and French comedy and concerts at night.

The Munich sojourn ended well: Nannerl won applause, and both Maximilian and Clemens sent generous payment. Moreover, at their inn, the Zum goldenen Hirschen, the Mozarts had made the acquaintance of two amiable Saxon patricians traveling together, Friedrich Karl von Bose and Georg Wilhelm von Hopfgarten. The new friends agreed to meet en route. Above all, favorable comments upon the Mozarts were afloat at the highest level: Prince Frederick Michael, soon to visit the Elector Palatine, Karl Theodore, at Mannheim, promised to tell him of the family's impending arrival; and Duke Clemens not only provided a letter of introduction to Karl Theodore but also, as an afterthought, had one to the Electress delivered to the Mozarts' hotel in Augsburg, their next stop.

Alighting at Augsburg on 22 June, they remained two weeks. Time had

---

3 In the famous Bavarian-Saxon double wedding of 1747, Maria Antonia had married the Electoral Prince of Saxony, Frederick Christian (the son of Augustus the Weak), his sister, Princess Maria Anna Sophie, marrying Maximilian Joseph. To avoid expenditure, he had seen to it that the festivities took place not in Munich but at the Saxon Court. Unfolding for nearly a month at Dresden and Pillnitz, they included performances of operas by Hasse and Gluck. The closing months of 1763 were to be painful for Maria Antonia: upon the death of Augustus the Weak in October, her husband became elector; but before Christmas he succumbed to smallpox, and their son took the throne as Frederick Augustus III under the regency of his uncle Prince Frederick August Xavier. (Leopold and Wolfgang would be in the royal gallery of Versailles when Louis XV returned from reporting the news of Frederick Christian's death to another of his sisters, Maria Josepha, Dauphine of France.) A jill of all artistic trades, the redoubtable Maria Antonia had received coaching in musical composition from Hasse, in singing from Porpora, and in painting from Mengs; Metastasio criticized and corrected her poetry. She had painstakingly prepared to take her place as the muse of European royalty only to suffer the irony of being electress only a matter of weeks. Upon receiving the crown, her son recommended her retirement to private life. A frequent visitor to her brother's court, she was to attend the premiere in Munich of Mozart's *La finta giardiniera*.

4 When Joseph Haydn became assistant kapellmeister of the Esterházy orchestra in 1761, Tomasini already occupied its first violinist's desk.

not mitigated Leopold's dislike of his native city, and the unproductive outcome of the stay did not improve his humor: "I was detained in Augsburg for a long time and profited little or nothing." He had put up at the princely Zu den drei Mohren on the Maximilianstrasse and should not have been surprised to find everything "uncommonly expensive." Though a newspaper report eulogized his "2 wonderful children" and "the extraordinary gifts a magnanimous God has bestowed in so abundant a measure upon these two dear little ones," Leopold's terse and testy description of the Augsburg sojourn bespoke the failure of their three performances (28, 30 June and 4 July) to attract wide interest.[5] Leopold observed "those who came to the concerts to be almost all Lutherans." Perhaps influenced by his hostile mother, the Catholics withheld support. Leopold's letters, his lists of individuals encountered, and Nannerl's journal[6]—none contains the name of any Augsburg relative, even though his mother and brothers lived in the city.

But Augsburg did provide agreeable moments: the family visited both Elias Holl's city hall with its Golden Chamber and the church of Ulrich and Afra, where Leopold had sung as a child. And the Mozarts suddenly found themselves welcoming friends: on the twenty-fourth, the Ignaz Weisers stopped at the Drei Mohren, to be followed four days later by the pair of Saxons, Bose and Hopfgarten. There were hours with the Lotters and with new acquaintances: Pietro Nardini, the Livornese pupil of Tartini and since 1762 first violinist of Duke Karl Eugene of Württemberg; and Johann Andreas Stein, the instrument-maker. Wolfgang and Leopold visited his residence-workshop "on the Lech, outside the town" and left Augsburg with a "pretty little clavier," one of Stein's portable instruments, which, Leopold wrote, did "good service for practicing during our travels."

Furnished by local business friends of Hagenauer with "the finest letters of credit to different places,"[7] the Mozarts quit Augsburg on 6 July and, by way of Günzburg, reached Ulm the same evening. The following morning they visited the minster and examined its three-manual organ, a celebrated instrument completed almost thirty years earlier by Georg Friedrich Schmahl. By afternoon they were again on the road. Leopold hastened from a city he found "dreadful, old-fashioned, and tastelessly built. . . ." A son of Augsburg and resident of Salzburg, cities transformed

---

5 Wolfgang and Nannerl often gave their public concerts in the main room of a local inn. The Augsburg appearances probably took place at the Zu den drei Königen.

6 She had begun to jot down her impressions, for the most part of buildings and their interiors.

7 The letters included one to Strassburg: for a time Leopold toyed with the idea of approaching Paris via Alsace.

by the Renaissance and the Baroque, he loathed Ulm's crooked streets and half-timbered houses: the mystery and capricious fantasy of the Gothic offended this modern man with his Enlightened yearning for order, balance, and a vocabulary of ornament speaking the architectural language of ancient Rome. He would feel most at home in a city like Mannheim, axially arranged with a symmetric array of squares, their matching pavilions sporting pediments and pilasters, a concept expressing that *"Regularität"* (just proportion and harmony of elements) toward which his sensibilities inclined.[8] His son came to share this taste mirroring an Enlightenment prejudice no less pervasive in Germany than in France: individuals as varied in awareness as Winckelmann and Lessing could not endure the Gothic.

The coach moved through the enchanting scenery of the Schwäbische Alb and then into the fertile Neckar valley. "One sees . . . to the right and left nothing but water, forests, fields, meadows, gardens, and vineyards," Leopold wrote, "and these at the same time and mixed in the most beautiful way." Though ill-disposed toward any town in half-timbered style, he, and especially his wife,[9] took "the greatest pleasure in the countryside of Württemberg." The Mozarts' destination was its capital, Stuttgart, seat of Duke Karl Eugene, known for his lavish patronage of the arts. Leopold carried a letter of recommendation to him from Salzburg's Canon Anton Willibald, Count Waldburg zu Wolfegg und Waldsee. However, at Plochingen, a station for changing horses, Leopold learned that Karl Eugene had left Stuttgart for Ludwigsburg, his palace in the countryside to the north, and intended to travel on to his hunting lodge of Grafeneck (near Reutlingen) on the tenth. Shifting course,the Mozarts' coach arrived at Ludwigsburg late in the evening of 9 July. A town had sprung up to ac-

---

8 Enchantment with *Regulärität* suffused Leopold's interest in a project to create another entrance to the city of Salzburg by tunneling the rock of the Mönchsberg. Opened by Archbishop Schrattenbach in 1766 and inaugurated the following year, this New Gate—soon called Siegmund's Gate in his honor—did not receive general traffic until 1774. Leopold realized that a suburb would come into being at the outer opening of the passage: "I only hope that a design will be made to which the new houses will have to conform in order to insure a beautiful uniformity, at least in respect to the height of the houses and the alignment of their stories." He wished matters arranged so as to permit the horse pond of the court stables to dominate the attention of travelers as they emerged from the portal into the city, and he imagined a road parting to the right and left of this monument enclosing Michael Bernhard Mandl's commanding sculpture of a horse and trainer. To achieve this balanced effect, Leopold recommended pulling down the false wall (decorated in 1732 by Franz Anton Ebner with painted horses) masking the site of a quarry become depot. Here, Leopold thought, might be created the space needed to accommodate this plan sharing the spirit and disposition of Archbishop von Raitenau's grandest, if unrealized, architectural vision: a *via triumphalis* leading to the palace and the cathedral.
9 The reader of his letters easily forgets Anna Maria's presence on the tour, so little did he write about her.

commodate the needs of the court, and the family took lodging at the Zum goldenen Waldhorn, opposite the palace. In the hope of making contact with officials, Leopold rushed to attend a French comedy at the Duke's theater.

The following morning he called upon Karl Eugene's kapellmeister, the Neapolitan opera composer Niccolò Jommelli, and Baron von Pöllnitz, Master of the Hounds. The letter of recommendation proved of no use: nothing could be done. His Highness, occupied with the imminent progress of his court, had not a moment to spare as he went to all lengths to commandeer every horse and coachman in the area; when he moved, so did an army of almost two thousand attendants, and he feared that the eight hundred horses at the moment in his stables would be insufficient. The Pressburg carriage could not roll; Leopold found himself marooned; attempting to outflank the Duke, he had made an expensive, embarrassing miscalculation.

Thwarted, he let his resentment fly; it struck a familiar target—the Italians. Their machinations, he declared, had barred the palace doors: "I regard the whole affair as the work of Herr Jommelli, who goes to no end of travail to root out Germans from this court and put in Italians exclusively." Jommelli's high salary and comfortable life fed Leopold's pique. It mounted to high pitch when he heard that the court's Italian clique had expressed astonishment at "a child of German birth" possessing "such musical genius, so much comprehension [*Geist*] and fire." Clearly, Wolfgang had performed somewhere at Ludwigsburg, perhaps at the hotel.

Leopold frequently charged windmills of imagined affronts, carrying on feuds of his own invention. (He would later burden his son with ill-founded suspicions of Gluck's integrity.) Jommelli stood at the peak of his fame: only five months earlier (11 February 1763), the premiere of the Stuttgart version of *Didone abbandonata*[10] had shed luster upon Württemberg. The idea of his intriguing against an unknown seven-year-old touched the ludicrous. For Leopold, visions of conspiracy would remain the easiest way to account for adversity.

At Ludwigsburg the family again met Bose and Hopfgarten and heard Nardini perform—"rather lightly," Leopold observed, at the same time declaring it impossible to experience anything finer "in respect to beauty, purity, evenness of tone, and singing quality." However, Leopold's most discerning remarks concerned not music but civic and economic aspects of

---

10 Stuttgart witnessed Jommelli's third version of the opera (to Metastasio's text) given its premiere in 1747 at Rome's Teatro Argentina. He had made the first revision in 1749 for Vienna's Burgtheater.

this small state whose revenues its Duke appropriated in extravagant proportion as subventions for opera, concerts, and dance. Once a harpsichord pupil of Emanuel Bach,[11] he had a love of music that developed into a passion Burney described as almost Neronic. Moreover, the Duke's zeal for building turned no less intense: he contemplated devoting over a million gulden to constructing Schloss Solitude, a retreat to rise on a wooded plateau west of Stuttgart. Both the name and remote site of this new palace gave the measure of his distaste for his capital.

Stuttgart had become the scene of a struggle between this despotic, capricious ruler eager to heighten his autocracy and the parliamentary Estates, no less eager to delimit it. Not his fellow German princes but Louis XV provided the standards of authority and magnificence with which he identified himself. Enraged by demands to restrain his spending, he even toyed with the idea of abandoning Stuttgart and restricting his court to Ludwigsburg; the mandate, he thought, would not only keep the contumacious Estates at a distance but also ruin the merchants and purveyors of a city whose citizens dared remonstrate against him: they directed cries of outrage to the Reichstag in Regensburg and to the Imperial sovereignty in Vienna and had even brazenly vandalized the exterior of Stuttgart's sumptuous opera house; it had become the very symbol of Karl Eugene's plundering of the national exchequer.

With Jommelli's arrival from Rome in 1753, Stuttgart had begun its rapid change into a brilliant artistic center whose upkeep would in the end utterly strain the duchy's financial resources. Not only did Jommelli's services as composer-conductor-administrator command lavish reward but highly paid musicians worthy of his efforts had to be hired as well: among the violinists, Nardini and Antonio Lolli, who by the mid-sixties would be earning a salary of two thousand florins each;[12] among the vocalists, the soprano Maria Masi-Giura, and Giuseppe Aprile (Scirolino), a castrato whose formidable high E enabled him to lay claim to six thousand florins a season. In 1760 Karl Eugene induced Gaetano Vestris (*le Dieu de la Danse*) to join the ducal ballet, and that same year Jean Georges Noverre began his career in Stuttgart as dancer-choreographer, his aesthetic influencing the

11 Bach dedicated his Württemberg sonatas (1744) to Karl Eugene.
12 The Austrian violinist Florian Johann Deller joined the Stuttgart orchestra two years before Jommelli began his tenure. Deller never achieved the high position or remuneration of Nardini or Antonio Lolli (the last often confused with Giuseppe Francesco Lolli of Bologna, a tenor who joined the Archbishop of Salzburg's musical household in 1741 and became its vice-kapellmeister eleven years later).

direction of Jommelli's operatic style. Only a month before the Mozarts' arrival in Württemberg, Servandoni had come from Paris at a huge fee to design scenery. The Mozarts glimpsed Karl Eugene's artistic household at its most flourishing: in quality of personnel and magnificence his theater for dance and opera had few rivals. Nor did he neglect the spoken word, but supported the company of French actors Leopold had applauded.

A strange business helped finance these enterprises: mercenaries, many of them barbarously forced into service. Karl Eugene provided Württemberg peasants for hire as soldiers to foreign states.[13] In raids on villages, farms, rustic taverns, and country churches, his agents abducted healthy males for impressment, while, at the ducal residence, a large and fantastically uniformed household guard and officer corps composed a glamorous façade masking Württemberg's shabby military dealings and strengthening Karl Eugene's wild fancy of his stature in European affairs. Chimera, indeed: even among fellow sovereigns his name had become scandal.

Educated in Berlin early in the reign of Frederick the Great, Karl Eugene shared the Prussian taste for tall and magnificently, if impractically, uniformed young troopers.[14] (Frederick called him his "ape.") From Ludwigsburg, Leopold observed: "You see only men of the grenadier type. . . ." "A handsomer body of men . . . cannot possibly be found." On the streets he heard "nothing but: 'Halt! March! About face!'" and the view from his window brought to his mind a picture of supernumeraries costumed as "soldiers getting ready to play their parts in a comedy or opera." (Nannerl enjoyed the drilling and parades.) "Because I wrote from Ludwigsburg," Leopold later commented in the safety of the Palatinate, "I did not dare add that soldiering is driven to excess there; indeed, twelve to fifteen thousand soldiers swaggering about every day incredibly and dashingly attired—actually, they can hardly walk in their identical gaiters and

---

13 Schiller's *Kabale und Liebe* reflects the hostile environment of Karl Eugene's Württemberg. The young Schiller, drafted into the Duke's military academy, in the sequel endured painful service as doctor to a ducal regiment. Lorenz Leopold Haschka (the Viennese poet who wrote the text of Joseph Haydn's "Hymn to the Emperor" and of Mozart's unfinished cantata K. 429/468a), unaware of Karl Eugene's love of opera, thus attacked his practice of selling his subjects: "Shrill fifes, the rumble of kettledrum and tambour / The din of chains and tympany, / The cries of the scourged— / This alone is music for this prince."

14 Johann Christoph Gottsched's impressive stature had obliged him to flee Königsberg (1724) lest he be forcibly enrolled in the Prussian Royal Grenadiers. Frederick the Great, soon after his accession, disbanded the Potsdam Guard of six- to seven-foot soldiers, the regiment then becoming more famous for the beauty of its men than for their height. Frederick's homoeroticism appears to have been foreign to Karl Eugene, who recruited bed companions from the coryphées of his ballet.

breeches of the finest linen—are too few to take seriously and too expensive to joke about. In short, there are too many."

Its walls, to all seeming, formed "more of soldiers than of hedges and garden trellises," Ludwigsburg appeared to Leopold "a very peculiar place"; perhaps by the time of his departure he felt relieved that Karl Eugene had remained inaccessible.

On the morning of 12 July Leopold at last secured coach horses and left for the Palatinate.[15] Karl Theodore, the Elector Palatine, did not summer at his sprawling palace in Mannheim but some nine miles to the south at Schwetzingen, where Voltaire had written *Candide* while his guest. Leopold and Anna Maria again delighted in the landscape as the carriage moved toward the Rhine valley by way of Vaihingen an der Enz and Bruchsal. The first, a picturesque gothic town set in the widening Enzthal, Leopold found to be "a wretched Lutheran place"; Bruchsal proved more to his liking, especially its baroque palace, a residence of the prince-bishops of Speyer. After a night at the Zum Riesen, the Mozarts inspected the episcopal state rooms. "In the very best taste," wrote Leopold, "... nothing more pleasant can be seen." It surprises that he made no mention of a famed stairway designed by Balthasar Neumann (as he would at Brühl; see n. 29).

In Bruchsal, Leopold attended to financial matters. His Bavarian money did not convert favorably, and attempts to get a better rate may explain the family's two-day stay in the tiny town. During the evening of the thirteenth, a storm of a violence unequaled in Leopold's experience lashed the Zum Riesen, but "crash on crash through the night" did not disturb Nannerl's and Wolfgang's sleep.

The following day, the family entered Schwetzingen and put up at the Zum roten Haus. The recommendations of Prince Friedrich Michael and Duke Clemens smoothed the way: late in the afternoon of the eighteenth, Wolfgang and Nannerl appeared at the palace to take part in a gala concert lasting from five until nine. The Mannheim orchestra, which had accompanied Elector Karl Theodore to his summer seat, overwhelmed the Mozarts: "Incontestably Germany's best," Leopold wrote of an ensemble whose beginnings went back to events surrounding Johann Stamitz's performances at the two coronations of the unfortunate Charles Albert.

---

15 Also called the Pfalz, Rheinpfalz, Untere Pfalz or, in its Electoral status, Kurpfalz, the Rhenish Palatinate must be distinguished from Oberpfalz, the Upper Palatinate; it has Regensburg as its main city and lies above the Danube, extending from Amberg in the west to the Bohemian Forest in the east.

2

DURING THESE FESTIVITIES, the impassioned music-making of this violinist from Deutschbrod in Bohemia had aroused excitement. The following June, Stamitz again appeared in Frankfurt (at Johann Philipp Scharff's handsome hall near the Liebfrauenkirche) not only as a now "celebrated virtuoso" but also in the role of composer. The increasingly well-known musician must have received Charles Albert's recommendation to Elector Palatine Karl Philipp. When, as newly crowned King of Bohemia, Charles Albert visited Mannheim to attend the wedding (17 January 1742) of Karl Philipp's nephew and heir, Karl Theodore—an event the Elector celebrated by opening an opera house designed by Alessandro Bibbiena—Stamitz had already entered Mannheim service, no doubt quickly becoming a significant element in the court's musical life. With Karl Philipp's death and the accession (the last day of 1742) of that enthusiastic amateur upon the flute and cello Karl Theodore, he and Stamitz embarked upon enriching and refining Mannheim's orchestra and building a major musical establishment, an ambition advanced by the muddle and confusion spreading throughout the Holy Roman Empire and its dependencies.

The close of Karl Philipp's reign and the opening years of Karl Theodore's coincided with the most tumultuous period in the War of the Austrian Succession, when a legion of performers, quitting areas likely to become battlegrounds—in particular Bavaria, Austria, Bohemia, and Moravia—began, as did Stamitz, to gravitate westward. ("Music," Burney observed, "is one of the arts of peace, leisure and abundance. . . .") In tranquil Mannheim, between the Neckar and the Rhine, two generous, appreciative rulers successively welcomed not a few of the emigrants.[16] It cannot surprise that Mozart and Joseph Haydn felt at home with the Mannheimers' musical idiom: it, like theirs, had roots in the southeastern lands of the Empire. Both masters experienced the influence of the precise, intense orchestral style developed under composer-conductor Stamitz (by 1750 the Elector's Director of Instrumental Music), his colleagues, and his students.

The Mannheimers played with the fervor their leader had shown before Charles Albert. As composers, they adopted a conglomerate of emotional

---

16 Born (1724) the son of Pfalzgraf Johann Christian in Drogenbos, near Brussels, and educated at the universities of Leyden and Leuven, Karl Theodore pursued Karl Philipp's new pattern of turning to the German world rather than to Italy alone when filling important musical positions. Emperor Charles VI's choice of an Austrian, Johann Joseph Fux, as principal kappellmeister—a position he occupied from 1715 to his death in 1741—had been an exception presaging Frederick the Great's taste for German conductor-composers (see p. 110).

techniques including quick alternations of forte and piano and, in particular, the Italian crescendo and decrescendo. In vogue in Rome during the
early years of the century, this device involved the swelling and then
diminution in volume of long notes, phrases, or entire passages. When
Jommelli first introduced the effect at Stuttgart, the initial wave of mounting orchestral sound cast a spell upon his listeners: agape, they "gradually
rose from their seats; not until the following diminuendo did they realize
that they had almost ceased to breathe." Especially in its first or crescendo
phase (the so-called rocket), this coloristic excitation became the principal
charge on the appropriative Mannheimers' musical escutcheon[17] and entered Mozart's musical vocabulary as early as the opening movement of his
Hague Symphony in B flat, K. 22 of 1765.

"Nowhere in performance," Christian Friedrich Daniel Schubart wrote
of the Mannheim ensemble, "were light and shade better marked, nowhere
the half and whole tints of the orchestral palette more clearly expressed."
Using a generous proportion of winds to strings, turning to account the
sensuous quality of the clarinet, yet reserving melodic prominence for the
violin, the Mannheimers explored a new protoromantic world of sound. In
their search for the soulful, the Electoral musicians so exploited the ap-
poggiatura that this expressive ornamental note became known in Germany as the "Mannheim sigh." Here, in the realm of tonal color and
performance practice, lay the Mannheimers' significance, for, as composers, Stamitz and his school too often produced a mediocre patchwork
of short-breathed phrases disposed in bland harmonic patterns. "To tell
the truth, I never liked Mannheim compositions," Leopold Mozart confessed, aware that an effective application of Mannheim devices often disguised a paucity of inspiration. His son, he felt, should scorn such
methods, but from time to time even he fell back upon them.[18]

Under Stamitz's (and Jommelli's) pupil Johann Christian Cannabich,
the Electoral orchestra reached a virtuosity that, if at times mannered—

---

17 From his headquarters in Stuttgart, Jommelli enjoyed a productive relationship with nearby
Mannheim, whose musicians had become acquainted with his works even before his arrival in
Germany.

18 In the overture to *Il rè pastore*, for example, the Mannheim crescendo and forte/piano in brisk
dialogue manufacture a driving vigor that suggests, but comes short of, a true musical idea.
Mozart from time to time wrote such filler, that is, music with neither melodic profile nor
contrapuntal movement, but, rather, made up of instrumental mechanics: scales, figurations,
arpeggios, military and hunting fanfares, alternations of textures and timbres (often an enthusiastic tossing back and forth of such elements), and repeated notes and chords (along
with dramatic pauses), all seeming to punctuate nonexistent sentences. This kind of writing
without content, rare in Mozart, constitutes the essence of more than one of his contemporaries' works.

Leopold Mozart's opinion—long remained without peer. By the time of the Mozarts' Grand Tour, not Paris nor London, not Vienna nor Berlin possessed Europe's foremost orchestra: it flourished in tiny Mannheim. A saying ran: "Prussian tactics and Mannheim music place the Germans in the van of all nations." Coveting Mannheim's pre-eminent position in orchestral music, Karl Eugene of Württemberg had attempted (1748) to entice Stamitz into his service, for not even Stuttgart's accomplished band approached the level of Mannheim's in respect to the compliant give-and-take essential to the finest ensemble playing. At Stuttgart, Daniel Schubart observed "an orchestra of virtuosos" constituting "an army of kings who know no master"; in contrast, Mannheim's more pliant musicians looked upon their conductor as a musical emperor and yielded to his wishes. Blending the expressive effects of their German and Italian contemporaries into a disciplined, unified, finely shaded, carefully notated style characterized by changing and emotional dynamics, the Mannheimers anticipated the eclecticism of Haydn and Mozart and pointed the way toward a German hegemony in instrumental music that would last almost two centuries.

3

THE GERMAN LANDS, connected only by the federative thread of the Empire, offered no uniform social landscape, and the variety within the Palatinate's civic structure astounded Leopold Mozart no less than the quality of the Elector's orchestra. After years in a tedious, insular church-state, he relished the richness of a cosmopolitan community in which Catholics rubbed shoulders not only with Protestants but with Jews, too, and produced little friction. Whatever comparisons he made revealed Salzburg wanting. Its besotted musicians in mind, he observed that the Mannheim orchestra included "young people of thoroughly good character—neither drunkards, gamblers, nor dissipated fellows; thus their conduct, like their performances, is held in high esteem."

His children "set all Schwetzingen astir." In addition to performances at the palace, they must have played privately for the court musicians listed in Leopold's journal. The most important of them for Wolfgang's future would be Cannabich and members of the Wendling family: the violinist Franz Anton; his brother, the flutist Johann Baptist; and the latter's wife, Dorothea. The journal also mentions Franz Anton's bride-to-be, the tenor Sarselli's daughter, Elizabeth Augusta, "who sings very well." Under Cannabich's baton, she and Dorothea would appear in Mozart's *Idomeneo* as the first Elettra and Ilia, respectively. In coming years he would produce a group of "Wendling" works: an aria for Dorothea, the orchestration of a flute concerto (K. 284e; it has not survived) composed by Johann Baptist, and two songs for their daughter Gustl (see pp. 402–04).

Bent upon forming new friendships helpful in shaping this and future tours, Leopold took the family later in July on a three-day excursion to Mannheim. Electoral *Hofkapellmeister* Ignaz Jakob Holzbauer, abstaining from the summer rituals at Schwetzingen, had remained in the capital. Doubtless the opportunity to meet this respected Viennese with valuable connections in Italy inspired the Mozarts' visit, during which they also encountered the Bohemian violinist Georg Tzarth. To Leopold, Mannheim seemed "a city in miniature," its low, handsome buildings and wide perspectives evoking his admiration, particularly at night: "Nothing more beautiful can be seen than one of these illuminated prospects . . . ." The family visited Alessandro Bibbiena's opera house, his Jesuit church, and the treasure-filled palace, its right wing also to his design.

Another excursion from Schwetzingen, this time to Heidelberg, ended as almost pure sight-seeing, for Leopold found no musician worthy of his time in this former capital, which the Electoral court had abandoned for Mannheim some four decades earlier. "Very much like Salzburg," Leopold observed, "that is, in respect to its situation": built at the point where the Neckar, swiftly emerging from the Odenwald, flows through a gorge and into the plain of the Rhine, Heidelberg, like Salzburg, huddled between hill and river, the site guarded by a stronghold set on a height. But, unlike the Archbishops' fortress, Heidelberg's had suffered ruin from military action. Leopold commented upon the incendiary invasions of Louis XIV as he contemplated "the fallen-in doors and walls," the "sad fruits of the late French wars."[19]

In the castle's cellar the Mozarts beheld the giant *Fass*, a beer cask of enormous capacity (more than two-hundred-thousand liters; Heine would refer to it in his *Dichterliebe* as the measure of the coffin to contain his love and pain); they also looked in on the silk and embroidery workshops housed in a still-usable eastern portion of the structure. Leopold's journal mentions the "waistcoats" (*Vestien*) manufactured there; perhaps father and son, both lovers of finery, made purchases. The Heidelberg visit did have one professional moment: Wolfgang tried the organ of the gothic church of the Holy Spirit, his playing provoking such astonish-

---

19 Early in 1689, in a maneuver to seize the right bank of the Rhine, Louis XIV's War Minister, Louvois, commanded French troops to lay waste the Palatinate: they devastated Heidelberg, Mannheim, Speyer, Oppenheim, and Worms. During the year following the Mozarts' visit, a bolt of lightning completed the ruin of Heidelberg castle.

ment that the town magistrate ordered an inscription commemorating the event.[20]

The arrival of a generous fee from the Elector signaled the Mozarts' departure from Schwetzingen. To turn their backs to its pleasures could not have been easy: Leopold and Wolfgang relished its orchestra; the father, no less, its "unsurpassed" troupe of French actors; Nannerl its "most beautiful" ballet; and, over and above, the terraces, waterways, and fountains of its wide-spaced gardens offered a succession of delights. Daniel Schubart called Schwetzingen a magic place where *"alles sang und klang"* (everything sounded with song and instruments). Many musicians figured among its fifteen hundred Electoral retainers in residence. Burney described hearing music from every window: "at one house a fine player on the violin; at another, a German flute; here an excellent oboe; there a bassoon, a clarionet [*sic*], a violoncello, or a concert of several instruments together." In late October of his penultimate year, Mozart devoted a day to revisiting this enchanting summer seat. By evening he had returned to Mannheim and professional matters. He claimed to have made the excursion simply "to see the garden"; clearly his object had been to recapture images of a happy time.

The Mozarts set out for Mainz via the ancient city of Worms. In contrast to the liveliness and rococo charm of Schwetzingen, dour, medieval Worms with its brooding Romanesque cathedral oppressed Leopold, who nonetheless reflected upon the great events in the town's history, in particular the Imperial diet at which Luther had appeared before Charles V. After an evening at the Zum Schwan, a miserable way, more path than road, brought the family to Oppenheim, which, like Worms, still bore scars of the French invasion. From Oppenheim to Mainz the carriage made its way "right along one side of the Rhine, while passing fields, villages, gardens, and vineyards on the other." Once again Leopold called attention to the beauties of landscape, a discernment foreign to his son, whose letters would show scant awareness of nature.[21]

On 3 August the Mozarts beheld the bulk of Mainz cathedral. It dominated the ecclesiastical city-state (Kurmainz) situated on the Rhine's left bank at the influx of the Main. The handsome city pleased Leopold, especially the Favorite, a summer palace from which the Archbishop-Elector

---

20 The inscription vanished with the removal of the organ to the Jesuit church.

21 Mozart admired the park of Schwetzingen. Designed in the Lenôtre tradition, an example of nature tamed and ennobled by man, it displayed pure artifice. If less self-consciously, so, too, as the perceptive Leopold remarked, did the manicured German countryside, its farms and hamlets set within grass and woodlands. Related to this kind of controlled informality, the English garden, as varied by the Viennese, would in time inspire Mozart's praise (see p. 568).

might contemplate the meeting of the rivers without quitting his bed. At the moment he could not enjoy the panorama: Archbishop Emmerich Joseph, Count Breidbach-Bürresheim had fallen ill and seemed near death.[22] The circumstance, Leopold feared, might hobble the family's opportunities, but he bounded into Mainz's musical life, seeking out enthusiasts and performers. Even without an appearance at court and the recommendations and gifts it could generate, the children gave three concerts and earned two hundred florins.

Leaving the heavier luggage behind at the Zum König von England, the Mozarts took the daily market boat up the Main to the free Imperial city of Frankfurt. In this commercial and cultural capital of the area the children triumphed. Leopold's public announcement of a concert on 18 August appealed "to all those who take pleasure in extraordinary things . . . ," for "with incredible skill a girl of 12 and a boy of 7 will play concertos, trios [the father, of course, took part], and sonatas." The boy, the advertisement promised, would perform on both violin and clavier. "Further, be it known that this will be the only concert inasmuch as immediately afterwards they are to continue their journey to France and England."

Leopold's ploy pictured Paris and London impatiently expecting the youngsters, who, to all seeming, would rush from the hall to a waiting carriage. Twelve days later a second notice observed that the "general admiration awakened by the . . . skill of the two children of the kapellmeister to the court of Salzburg"[23] had "already entailed a threefold repetition of the concert planned as a single occasion." Even so, at the request of "several great connoisseurs and amateurs," a fifth concert—"quite definitely the last"—would be heard on 30 August and, like the first, take place in Scharff's hall (the scene of Stamitz's triumph some two decades earlier). The puff promised the usual tricks: Wolfgang would name notes sounded for him singly or in chords on every imaginable instrument and by bells, glasses, and clocks; he would also play the clavier with its keys covered by a cloth and improvise "in all keys, even the most difficult, not only on the harpsichord but also on an organ. . . ." The fourteen-year-old Goethe, with his family, had attended the first concert of the series. Almost seven decades later he still remembered "the little fellow with his powdered hair [Frisur] and his sword." The household accounts of the poet's methodical father list in Latin "4 gulden, 7 kreutzer for the concert of two children."

22 He would recover and earn the distinction of being the prince who in 1769 summoned the poet Wieland to a professorship at Erfurt.
23 Without shame Leopold continued to use the title whenever the misrepresentation had a chance of convincing.

Frankfurt's architecture disappointed Leopold: he found rather mean both the Römer, the venerable town hall in which the Electors officially chose the German emperor, and the modest medieval square it faced: he had "imagined something very different"—no doubt with the monumental Viennese structures of Fischer von Erlach in mind. But for him the old quarter did hold a fascinating curiosity: the Jews bustling through the narrow streets. Leopold associated their comings and goings with an epidemic of banking-house failures that had spread from Amsterdam to German cities. (Ruin faced financiers who had linked their speculations to a continuing war.) He kept an eye on currencies and their conversion rates. But though devaluations and a suspicious mood among Frankfurt money dealers disquieted, he refused to contemplate any retreat from his new patrician ways.

Hagenauer may have questioned them—his share in their correspondence has not survived—for in a long letter to him of 26 September 1763 Leopold took the defensive: "We must travel nobly or worthily in order to preserve our health and the reputation of my court. Our intercourse is restricted to the aristocracy or other distinguished persons, and, even if I don't exactly like to say so myself, it is nonetheless true that by such comportment I do great honor to my court and receive exceptional courtesies and special respect." He lamented the high cost of hotels, laundry, dining, and tips, but made clear that the children's earnings kept pace with an ever higher style of living. How he relished this turn in fortune.

It is easy to imagine Hagenauer, in addition to pressing Leopold to put up at less expensive hotels, urging him to sell his carriage and make use of, if not the general transportation system (see n. 1), then of the private post chaise. It did not depend upon relays of horses and drivers but restricted its journeys to points within a limited radius of its owner's stables: after reaching its halting place, it turned back. Passengers wishing to go farther had to await or make arrangements for a post chaise proceeding in their direction; thus traveling a considerable distance by post chaise, though more comfortable than the crowded public vehicles, involved the highest number of changes and, in accordance, more breaks at inns. Leopold clung to his own carriage not only because he enjoyed playing the aristocrat but also to spare his family the fatigue of an array of chaises, the attendant transfer of luggage, the expense of additional inns, and the shabbiness of the public conveyances.

Each day brought new sights and experiences. If the meager cuisine of the Rhineland (and the poor quality of its well water) appalled Leopold, the absence of meal or flour dishes (*Mehlspeisen*) being particularly vexing to a south German, he found redress in Rhine salmon and the variety of fine wines; and, into the bargain, the curious and titillating customs and costumes encountered on the way improved his humor. "Oh, how much I could write!" he chortled while giving Hagenauer an account of an Englishman with whom the family had taken its meals in Mainz: "At least every other day he bathed in the Main just before the dining hour and would then come to table looking like a baptized mouse." Though one expected *bizarrerie* from the English, their manner of dress—emulated in Europe's great salons—verged on the altogether fantastic to Salzburg eyes, Leopold being especially taken aback by the men's outfits: waists "high up under the shoulders so that the coat hangs down to the middle of the calf; add to this old-fashioned narrow boot sleeves—a detestable sight but in truth their latest mode."

Delightedly outraged, Leopold mocked even as he himself became increasingly elegant. He doted on his new pair of Mannheim boots, which though expensive, he purred to Hagenauer, "would please you no end . . . you can't find more beautiful leather or more comfortable, beautiful boots." For her part, Nannerl, beginning to blossom, now took her evening walk boldly wearing a broad-brimmed English hat. Were she to appear so attired in the streets of Salzburg, Leopold declared, "people would come running as if a rhinoceros were passing through."[24]

With gratitude he observed his daughter gaining ground as a performer: "Nannerl no longer suffers under comparison with the boy, for she plays in such a way that everyone speaks of her and admires her fluency." An exaggeration: though she made music with refinement, her technique remained fragile (see p. 302). Leopold worried about the effect of Wolfgang's success upon her pride; he, too, felt concern, for his hands led in applauding her solos. Such anxieties proved groundless: she had no jealousy of the little brother who would soon become her teacher; in her eyes his only hostile act would be his marriage, and she never forgave him for betraying what she looked upon as a family pact: to remain together forever.[25]

Set against the quick-witted Wolfgang, she appears insipid: the jottings in her travel journal have a tone curiously childish for someone on the threshold of adolescence. It seems a reasonable supposition that, once

24 In 1749 Parisians had beheld a live rhinoceros for the first time. Abbé Guillaume-Thomas-François Raynal's fortnightly newsletter informed his subscribers of the twenty horses required to transport the creature's wagon and its daily diet of sixty pounds of hay, twenty pounds of bread, and fourteen pails of water. "It appears that so far rhinoceroses have not been very useful," he remarked, and, indeed, the rhinoceros became a symbol in Europe of the amazing combined with the wasteful.
25 Their clash over the settlement of Leopold's estate would complete the unraveling of a relationship under mounting stress from the time he settled in Vienna on his own in 1781.

Wolfgang's genius showed itself, Leopold poured limited energy into awakening and training her mind. But she did show a persistent interest in architecture and decoration and on an excursion to Biebrich—across the Rhine from Mainz (and today part of Wiesbaden)—in particular appreciated the fine palace on the river.

It cannot be determined whether the Mozarts' visit to Biebrich (and excursions to Wiesbaden and Kostheim) took place before or after their return to Mainz on the last day of August 1763. Whatever the case, by early September Leopold had exploited Kurmainz and its environs to the full in respect to concerts and tourism. The time had come to move down the Rhine to Koblenz, a favorite residence of the Archbishop-Elector of Trier.

4

ON THE EVENING of 13 September the family took ship. The Mozartean Rhine journey opened well: a Mainz admirer sent six bottles of Hochheimer to the quay. But strong winds and heavy rains pursued the travelers; forced to pause in untidy river towns, in which Leopold found even the churches intolerably dirty, the boat made its way in fits and starts. The spasmodic voyage put Wolfgang out of sorts. He caught cold, a reminder of that episode on the Danube when a similar minor complaint had heralded illness. In a letter to Hagenauer, Leopold felt compelled to justify the expensive trip by river: the drenched road along the Rhine, he alleged, threatened to give way; a carriage—theirs had been stowed on board[26]—might plunge into the river.

On the seventeenth the Mozarts disembarked at Koblenz, tucked into the triangle formed by the Moselle's confluence with the Rhine, the fortress of Ehrenbreitstein towering above. They settled into the Zu den drei Reichskronen, and the next day Wolfgang emptied his bag of musical tricks before Archbishop Johann Philipp, Reichsgraf von Walderdorff. Another concert, on the twenty-first, before a small group of nobles proved a stumble: the drab provincial court's interests centered in eating and drinking. Yet Leopold lingered ten days: "Above all else, I must look after the health of my children." It had become essential that Wolfgang's *Schnupfen* (the sniffles) abate before the tour proceeded.

Despite his exertions, he continued happy and mischievous, though one morning he did awaken weeping for home, an unusual display. As a rule, this remarkable hothouse creature showed himself poised and precious, his

---

26 The riverboats transported passengers (with and without carriages) as well as freight and produce.

tongue sharp. With a combination of childish honesty and professional dudgeon, he had recently (in Mainz) informed the violin virtuoso Karl Michael Esser that he played well but did "too much" and "would do better to play what is written." (For Wolfgang's taste Esser had added an excess of ornamental notes.[27]) Such imperious comments on the shortcomings of fellow artists would become more devastating with the years, and Mozart would pay for an acerbic candor difficult to forgive when the precocious child became a man.

For all the poor weather, Wolfgang must have felt fit by 27 September, when the family, the carriage aboard, proceeded by private boat to Bonn, since the thirteenth century seat of the Archbishop-Elector of Cologne. Alas, Elector Maximilian Friedrich, Count Königsegg-Rothenfels, also Prince-Bishop of Münster, had left for Westphalia to visit this second see, and the travelers found little to detain them in the sleepy town. (Leopold failed to meet Ludwig van Beethoven, the Elector's kapellmeister, who seven years later would become grandfather to a more famous Ludwig.[28]) They spent the night at the Zum goldenen Karpfen and, having enjoyed the sweeping views of the Rhine flowing beneath the gentle range of the Siebengebirge and inspected the palace, left for Cologne in their coach the next day. Journeying via Brühl, they visited the palace of Augustusburg (the Archbishop of Cologne's summer residence),[29] its park, and, folded into the landscape, the sumptuous hunting lodge of Falkenlust.

The chambers decorated with mirror, lacquer, shell, and marble; the jewels, paintings, tapestries, and sculptures; the porcelains and clocks; the gardens with their French parterres, waterworks, aviaries, and menageries— all the outspread riches of the Elector enchanted the Mozarts but could not compensate for his absence, to them a financial blow. The stay at Cologne (29/30 September) simply continued their sight-seeing, and Leopold's comments about the city reveal increasing ill humor. He found

---

27 "Too much," defines the complaint: the boy felt that those with few skills in ornamentation had best use it with moderation. Esser and the Mozarts would meet again more than seventeen years later. Leopold attended a concert he gave in Salzburg on 9 December 1780. By this time he had become something of a charlatan, specializing both in playing "a complete concerto of his composition on only a tuned-up G string" and in whistling recitatives and arias to his own accompaniment. From Salzburg he went on to Munich and dined with Mozart, then at work on *Idomeneo*. Esser attended rehearsals of its first two acts and praised them.

28 Leopold's journal indicates an encounter in Koblenz with a certain "Novandini," probably Johann Konrad Rovantini, a court violinist, whose son, Franz Georg, became Beethoven's violin and viola teacher.

29 Built from plans by Cuvilliés in 1728, the palace received its superb stairway (designed by Neumann) some twenty years later. Leopold made note of it.

fault with everything, the slovenliness of the easygoing, Frenchified Rhinelanders his refrain.

He thought Cologne big and sad, its famed cathedral filthy, "like a stable." The historic pulpit from which, tradition said, Luther had preached, had come to a pitiful state, a brick serving to even out its broken legs; indeed, most of the furniture appeared near collapse, moldings ripped off. The choir had been closed to visitors, and, to cap matters, a drunken clergyman emerged from vespers to unlock and display the cathedral's treasure. "Would it not be more edifying," Leopold bitingly wrote, "to set the house of God into capital and clean condition rather than to have jewels, gold, and silver—with which numerous saints' bones are especially thickly encased—lying in iron chests and shown for money?" The psalmody infuriated him: "more synagogue than church chant." "Boys who sing antiphons in such a manner should have their mouths stopped up; it is impossible to believe; this is not singing—it is shrieking."

The angry mood persisted. Circumstances had worked against him in the three ecclesiastical electorates of the Rhine: the illness of the Archbishop of Mainz (which had thwarted the bestowal of a princely gift); the provincialism of the Archbishop of Trier's court at Koblenz (though he did treat Leopold with generosity); and the absence of the Archbishop of Cologne, the richest of these princes. Between the Lower Rhine and Paris lay but one major court: that of Brussels.

On the last day of September 1763, the Mozarts' coach left Cologne's hotel Zum heiligen Geist and turned westward along a wretched road leading through Jülich to the Maas and Brabant. That evening they put up at Aachen in the Zum goldenen Drachen, intending to pause only long enough for Leopold to put his money affairs in order. The bewildering variety of German currencies afloat throughout the Empire—even the smallest principality might mint its own coins—had been problem enough: "One prefers not to think of what one loses [in exchange] here and there." But now, at the French border, the increasingly evident sou heightened the confusion. Leopold had to sort it out.

Hot sulphur springs had made Aachen a frequented watering place since Roman days. (In 1737, after suffering a stroke, Handel had taken its baths.) Leopold's expectations suddenly mounted when he discovered a famous royal amateur of music undergoing the cure—Anna Amalia of Prussia, sister of King Frederick. Aachen turned out to be "the most expensive place encountered so far on the trip," moaned Leopold, who at first intended only an overnight stay. Yet he remained until 2 October. True, an attack of sciatica had put him out of sorts, and he wanted a brief respite from travel. But clearly he also needed time to meet a Princess known for her appreciative friendships with her brother's cembalist, Emanuel Bach, and her music teacher, the theorist, Johann Philipp Kirnberger. Kreutzer or marks, reichsthaler or schilling, louis d'or or sous—some kind of money might be coaxed from such a patron; it appears that she heard Wolfgang and Nannerl perform.[30]

"Had the kisses she gave my children, especially Master Wolfgang, been money [*lauter neue Louis d'or*], we would be happy enough, but kisses can pay for neither the inn nor the post horses." Grown used to the extravagance of great rococo courts, Leopold despised the austere ways of this daughter of King Frederick William I (whose deathbed concern had been to plan a thrifty funeral). Prussian pietistic hostility to magnificence remained a mystery to Leopold. Moreover, he misjudged the authority of the sober Princess, who, in fact, had been at her brother's side in transforming the cultural desert Berlin had been during their father's reign into a musical capital threatening to overshadow Vienna itself: "Her whole equipage and court retinue resemble a doctor's suite as closely as one drop of water another," Leopold scoffed, refusing to take seriously her suggestion that he proceed not to Paris but to Berlin. He would not even reveal her proposals: "No one would believe me, for I don't believe them myself. . . ."

She may well have recommended his seeking the post of Berlin kapellmeister made vacant four years earlier by the death of Karl Heinrich Graun. The conductor of Frederick of Prussia's court orchestra, Johann Friedrich Agricola (he also held the directorship of the opera), had fallen into royal disfavor: the King viewed the Saxon musician with frightening contempt, withholding from him the title of kapellmeister; and though esteeming the virtuosity of his chamber-harpsichordist, Carl Philipp Emanuel Bach, Frederick had emphatically less enthusiasm for his compositions. Leopold, who doubtless assumed in Amalia's presence the name and manner of the kapellmeister of Salzburg, may well have appeared to her a possible candidate for the still-unassigned Berlin post: Frederick decreed that only a German might occupy it (he preferred French dancers and actors, Italian singers, and German conductors and composers); furthermore, the writings of the critic Marpurg had made Leopold's name and book known in Berlin, Europe's new center of musical theorists. Here the spoken and written word about music threatened to take precedence of music itself.

Less of a composer than the harassed Agricola (a pupil of Sebastian Bach and Johann Joachim Quantz), Leopold never could have filled the de-

---

30 Nannerl's reminiscences, written almost three decades later, mention a concert she and her brother gave in Aachen.

manding job. Yet, had he settled in Brandenburg, some position would in all likelihood have opened for him, perhaps among the theorists, and Berlin might have offered Wolfgang several years under the eyes of Emanuel Bach, who remained in Frederick's service until 1768. (He then left for Hamburg as an honorary Hohenzollern kapellmeister, a title Amalia bestowed.) But Fate was to lead Wolfgang not to the flat, sandy plain of the Spree and the household of Emanuel Bach but westward to the Thames and friendship with his younger brother and pupil, Johann Christian.

5

IN TIME MOZART came under the influence of both. For forming a musical style the era of his boyhood offered rich and sometimes contradictory possibilities, their very breadth symbolized by the divergent musical personalities of Christian and Emanuel Bach. The art of music now thread its course between two major dispensations: composers and performers, the child Mozart among them, found themselves in passage, fabricating new tonal languages from impressions gained along the route. On the one hand, it revealed glimpses of the massive, portentous baroque monuments of the recent past and, on the other, it opened to closer view a new and more modest tonal architecture admitting both graceful, brittle musical structures in the spirit of Christian Bach and dramatic, soul-stirring creations more characteristic of Emanuel.

The musical predilections of Frederick of Prussia and Princess Amalia underscore the confusing variety of stylistic choice peculiar to the era and throw light upon the windings of the aesthetic maze through which Mozart would find his way. More adventuresome than her brother, Amalia valued Emanuel's passionate style,[31] yet, oddly enough, failed to appreciate the same spirit in Gluck's reform opera (see pp. 142–43), which at first she made much of and then, like Frederick, disparaged: "It all sounds alike." Even so, despite such bias, Amalia did open her ears to the new and warm musical sounds of the time, while the splenetic Frederick, his captiousness increasing with age, shut the doors of his salon tight against them.

An amateur flutist, he maneuvered best in less rapid passages, and his sycophants in chorus declared him supreme in the expressive rendition of

---

31 She also admired the baroque masters. In her Berlin circle, Gottfried van Swieten cultivated acquaintance with Handel's and Sebastian Bach's works. Later, in Vienna, this musical amateur gave his own Bach-Handel concerts, in which Mozart participated (see pp. 634–35). Thus, by an indirect course, Amalia had a hand in helping to reveal to him in wide perspective the repertory that so impressed itself upon the style of his closing years.

slow movements: he gave them, wrote the composer-littérateur Johann Friedrich Reichardt, an intimacy of feeling that brought politic tears to his eyes. (The no less politic castrato Senesino found it impossible not to weep over the beauty of Maria Theresa's singing.) To the King, "adagio" signified either repose or the seductive melancholy of a Watteau *fête champêtre*, never piercing grief or lamentation. Frederick took pleasure in the elegiac and introspective but turned from a *cri de coeur*; thus his limited patience with Emanuel Bach's more emotional compositions and with Gluck's and the Mannheimers', too. Their fervid spirit and abruptly changing moods jarred the royal sensibilities, and, until age claimed his front teeth, the great warrior continued to pipe away at the feathery, facile sonatas and concertos of his adored flute teacher, Johann Joachim Quantz.

Born during the closing days of the heroic Baroque,[32] nurtured on the elegance of the *régence,* this *prince philosophe* (Voltaire's phrase) could not come to terms with the new striving for expression, a propensity by its nature violating the canon of courtly forms, those graceful patterns so dear to him and now shattering in the rising clamor. Speaking their final exquisite words, masters of the decorous like Quantz and Christian Bach had grown increasingly inaudible against the hubbub of an intense, highly colored, spontaneous musical language.

Tradition disintegrated as propriety yielded to importunity; artistic boundaries eroded and gave way, and what remained of the old began to appear strangely dislocated. The "new music," King Frederick complained to Maria Antonia of Saxony, "has degenerated into a babel of sound, bludgeoning the ears instead of caressing them . . ."; and she, quite agreeing, replied that modern composers but turned out "a lot of noise." Leopold Mozart had recourse to the same catchwords when deprecating a vogue in Salzburg for Stamitz's symphonies: "A lot of noise," he declared.

I seize upon the interval between the Mozarts' departure from Aachen and their arrival in Brussels to consider the general state of contemporary European music, instrumental and operatic, only at first glance a mixture of irreconcilable tendencies:[33] the perceptive not only recognized in them a net of mutual influences and characteristics permitting reconciliation, but they also descried the aesthetic direction in which most composers would bend their steps as the concept of a cultivated, schematic style held in

---

32 The *Thema regium,* the subject he gave Sebastian Bach and from which the *Musical Offering* grew, suggests the King's grasp of baroque music, in particular its mechanics.
33 So they appeared in the work of contemporary designers, in particular those buildings whose carefully balanced, somber, classic façades masked asymmetrically disposed, light, and sparkling interiors alive with painted cupids, ribbons, and rococo wriggles.

common continued to dissolve in the warmth of that new plebeian in-wardness and individuality enveloping all the arts. The immediate back-ground of this extraordinary period, outwardly perplexing but inwardly orderly and inevitable, must be explored. It was a season of fermentation and redress.

CHAPTER IX

A Season of Fermentation and Redress

WHEN THE MOZARTS embarked upon their Grand Tour, German music had recently lost its two towering masters of that weighty and noble style known as the Baroque. In London during April 1759, a great "Concourse of People of all Ranks" had assembled in Westminster Abbey to attend Handel's burial at the foot of the Duke of Argyll's monument; only nine years earlier, a more modest gathering in Leipzig had followed Johann Sebastian Bach's oaken coffin to St. John's churchyard. True, Telemann, born before both masters, still labored in Hamburg during the Mozarts' journey; he, however, had assumed a new manner and spirit of composition.

The death of Louis XIV in 1715 had betokened the Baroque's imminent passing. With the regency of his nephew, its dissolution quickened, and this solemn aesthetic gave way to two fragile heirs: *le style galant* and *le style bourgeois.* The first was the sensual, frothy, aristocratic art also known as the rococo; the second—it, too, characterized by an avoidance of baroque heaviness—represented a serious, emotional, middle-class taste, its determined striving for sensibility (*Empfindsamkeit*)[1] at times lapsing into sentimentality.

---

1 *Empfindsamkeit* has the sense of *sensibilité,* the French noun Otis Fellows defined as "exaltation in excess of the circumstances."

Though the erotic, cool courtier contrasted in marked degree with the upright, warm burgher, the border between the pair of artistic styles taking their names from these stereotypes often became blurred: painters, sculptors, and musicians frequently mixed the *galant* and *empfindsam*. The antitheses and tensions between courtly and bourgeois art might exist side by side in single works, sometimes in uneasy acquiescence, sometimes reconciled: the statuary of Falconet, the canvases of Fragonard and Greuze, and the sonatas of Friedemann Bach and Georg Benda come to mind. The final works of the clavier virtuoso Ernst Wilhelm Wolf represent a particularly successful musical composite of this kind. Wolf underwent, the critic Johann Friedrich Reichardt remarked, a "happy change in his style" by adding to his "serious and . . . meaningful" *bourgeois* manner "the variety and charm" of the *galant*. Proceeding in the opposite direction, musicians like the organist Franz Vollrath Buttstett and the pianist Johann Schobert (the latter a strong influence upon the young Mozart; see pp. 170–72) deepened their, at bottom, *galant* idiom with *empfindsam* elements.

Mozart showed himself adept at darting from one of these manners to the other, at mingling them to create a rich *stylus mixtus* (occasionally interlarding it with fragments of the Baroque, by his time known as the "learned style"). The union of *galant* and *bourgeois* could be easily accomplished, their antagonisms easily conciliated, for, in addition to a common reaction against baroque grandeur, both shared a contempt for baroque tectonics. In this abhorrence of strict counterpoint, they had recourse either to melody accompanied by a simple, incidental chordal substructure or to the free (actually, disintegrating) polyphony espoused by composers like the Neapolitan Domenico Scarlatti; here independent part-writing vanished, voices capriciously entering and dropping out at will, the loose texture—spiced with arpeggios, trills, tremolos, and scales—providing only at times the semblance of the older discipline. The very backbone of baroque musical structure had fatally weakened; its striding, ceremonious, and often melodic bass lines lay broken at best into smaller spans.

The old continued for the most part to be increasingly disparaged. Like Johann Friedrich Doles, Sebastian Bach's pupil and his second successor at St. Thomas's in Leipzig, Leopold Mozart had little patience, beyond lip service, with contrapuntal traditions other than as an instructive discipline; his treatise on violin playing did not give time-honored central importance to the baroque polyphonic technique of the multiple stop, but, rather, focused upon expositions of ornamental devices and nuances more pertinent to his son and his coevals. Leopold repeatedly urged him to write popular music, to shun both overbold experimentation and the convolutions of the learned style. Had not Georg Christoph Wagenseil, though lauded by his teacher, Fux, as a young man who would remain true to contrapuntal ways, lost little time setting out on the primrose path to *galanterie?*

Thus the generation that followed Sebastian Bach showed its back to the solemn complexities of his works, much as the art historian and critic Johann Joachim Winckelmann at this very time rejected Bernini and his school. Even Bach's two most famous sons turned against his manner of composition, in which, as Johann Adolph Scheibe complained, all the parts "must operate with each other and be of equal difficulty and none of them can be recognized as the principal voice." A writer and theorist more sympathetic to Bach, Christoph Lorenz Mizler (one day to be an admirer of Leopold Mozart), observed in 1738 that although "Mr. Bach at times writes the inner lines more fully than other composers," his model being "the music of twenty or twenty-five years ago," on occasion he could "write otherwise": "Anyone who heard the music performed by the students at the Easter Fair in Leipzig last year [1737] . . . , which Kapellmeister Bach composed, must admit that it was entirely in accordance with the latest taste and approved by everyone. So well does the Kapellmeister know how to suit himself to his listeners."

But even if the new mode of expression did at times invade Sebastian Bach's music, he remained a thoroughly baroque artist and no less fearful of the crisis being prepared by the rise of the *galant, bourgeois,* and mixed styles. His contemporary Telemann had turned toward the fashionable *style galant*: increasingly, he espoused inner voices devoid of vigorous counterpoint, ornament, and dissonant notes, though imitative and fugato passages continued in the work of this master whose contrapuntal wizardry dazzled even Handel. Telemann was seeking a midcourse, hardly the path for the dogged Sebastian Bach, who, in his dramatic cantata *The Strife between Phoebus and Pan* (c. 1732), confronted the fact of baroque art in dissolution and took an unequivocal—indeed, combative—position.

Phoebus defeats Pan in a singing contest and bestows ass's ears upon Pan's advocate, the Phrygian King Midas. Pan symbolizes composers of the new *galant* and *empfindsam* music—agreeable and simple, immediate in its appeal, and easily comprehended. Bach, speaking through Phoebus, chides Pan: "For nymphs [and, assumedly, for students at the Leipzig Easter Fair!] you may suffice, but the Gods cannot take pleasure in your inglorious piping." (Somewhat more circumspect, Leopold Mozart reminded his son: "The grand, elevated style belongs to grand subjects: everything has its place.") Bach-Phoebus will tolerate neither Pan's presumption in deriding the solemnity of Olympian song nor the fatuity of

Midas, who had cried out to Pan in adulation: "You alone . . . sang lightly and without affectation." "The Midas of Salzburg": thus did Mozart characterize his Archbishop.

Musical means other than the simplest appeared affected to the new generation, an attitude Leopold Mozart emphasized to his son, though here expedience played its part. Aware that the long ears visited upon the Midases of this world in no way impaired their golden touch, he urged Wolfgang to come to terms with them, not by combining various levels of music within a single context but by writing compositions of every coloring and spirit: "I recommend that in your work you remember not the musical public alone but also the *unmusical.* You know that there are 100 of the uneducated to every 10 real connoisseurs. Therefore, don't disregard the so-called popular style, which tickles long ears, too." (Joseph Haydn faced the difficult matter of mixing music diverse in quality when canceling several measures of his Symphony No. 42 [1771]: he regretted having written them "for far too learned ears.")

Mozart's reply indicated that "so-called popular taste" did not, to his mind, exclude excellence: his music, he affirmed, offered something to "every kind of person except the long-eared," an aesthetic of balance underlying his discussion of the piano concertos K. 413/387a and 415/387b. He looked upon them as representing a "mean between the too difficult and the too easy"; as "very brilliant and agreeable to the ear without, of course, descending into bloodlessness. Here and there only connoisseurs will be able to experience a gratifying discernment, but at the same time those who are not connoisseurs will end deriving pleasure without knowing why." He would doubtless have been at one with the allegory and polemic of Bach's *Phoebus.*

The cantata, moreover, concerned what Bach held to be superficial critics as well as superficial music, Midas representing Johann Adolph Scheibe. He had castigated Bach's works for their "turgidity," lack of "charm," and "excess of art"—in short, for their want of *galant* and *empfindsam* traits[2]—reproaches calling to mind Ernst Ludwig Gerber's difficulties with Mozart's music: ". . . an unpracticed ear finds it difficult to follow his works; even more experienced ears must hear his things several times."

Bach's *Coffee Cantata* (c. 1732) outdid his *Phoebus* as satire. Calling into play the imposing machinery of the baroque church cantata and opera to set a text depicting a middle-class domestic squabble, he slyly turned the tables,

2 Scheibe's condemnation of Bach appeared in 1737, but his animosity toward the older musician had arisen as early as 1729.

by implication ridiculing the relatively primitive musical implements of the new style when used for lofty themes. That the coming line of composers exploiting the latest musical speech would be led by two of his sons affords a certain irony.[3]

2

IN IMPORTANT CENTERS across Europe—Johann Christian in London, Carl Philip Emanuel in Berlin and Hamburg—these sons of Bach held sway during a respectable interregnum separating the collapse of one mighty musical dynasty and the rise of another. Christian's open Italianate style, his genial cantabile melodies cast in rounded phrases, and his impeccable taste and craft represented the best of the coquettish, brittle *galant*. (Even so, he had his musical moods of private, deeply felt sentiment.) In contrast, Emanuel's idiom favored *bourgeois* emotionalism. (His fine workmanship, however, at times mirrored the ornamental and often rattling *galant*.) While Christian showed the colors of the *galant*, Emanuel, epitomizing the *bürgerlich, empfindsam* (middle-class, sensitive) soul, at times indulged an intensity of expression presaging the romantics.[4] He became a force in that tempestuous aesthetic and political movement known as Storm and Stress (*Sturm und Drang*; see pp. 320–27), and Beethoven was to take pleasure in his works. They at times give the impression of being improvisations, tearful, sentimental sections alternating with turbulent, freely modulating fantasias.

Taken together, Christian and Emanuel embodied a hybrid musical generation of crisis and experiment. Via *le style galant* and *le style bourgeois*, they linked the baroque art of their father with the classical Viennese school of Haydn, Mozart, and Beethoven. (In the Rondo for piano, K. 485, in D,

---

3 Handel's alleged observation to Mrs. Cibber that "Gluck knows as much about counterpoint as my cook Waltz" exemplified the contempt with which baroque composers regarded practitioners of "easy melody-making," Marpurg's derisive phrase. Gustavus Waltz, who may have functioned as Handel's factotum, sang bass parts for him, among them the title role at the premiere of *Saul*. The sarcasm on Handel's part rings with authenticity. In Diderot's *Rameau's Nephew* (begun in 1761 and revised in 1765, 1772, and 1776), the eponymous protagonist of the satire explains that, in respect to musical instruction, his "dear uncle's treatise [*Traité de l'harmonie* of 1722, here identified in terms of its basic principle, "*la basse fondamentale*"] has much simplified matters [*la leçon*]."

4 Wilhelm Friedemann, the eccentric and indolent eldest of Bach's sons, not only commanded baroque counterpoint but also wrote intense *empfindsam* works. A superb improviser, he composed much less than his two famous brothers, had little influence, and died in want. Ernst Ludwig Gerber maintained that the "playful" Viennese Rococo provided Mozart a safeguard against his inclination to the temptations of the abstruse and delivered him from "the fate of the great Friedemann Bach, whose flight the eyes of but few other mortals could follow."

Mozart, full of play, would symbolically bring the brothers together by taking a theme derived from Christian and manipulating it in the manner of Emanuel:[5] celebrating their styles, he re-created and transformed them.) Linked tandem, the Mannheimers and this pair of Bach brothers decisively shifted the balance of power in European music toward the Germans.

At the time of Mozart's first journey to Paris, the old and new stylistic elements had begun to coalesce into an incipient musical constellation destined to shine with most brilliance in Habsburg lands. Joseph Haydn had recently left his post with Count Morzin to enter the service of the Esterházy court, the famous contract making him vice-kapellmeister to his Serene Highness Prince Paul Anton having been concluded at Vienna in 1761. About a year and a half earlier, the Prince, visiting Morzin, had applauded the premiere of Haydn's first symphony. A Mannheim crescendo opens this prognosticating work, which crowned a struggle begun over a decade earlier with a neophyte's groping attempts at composition. One influence had particularly contributed to his development.

During the seventeen-fifties, exciting musical vistas had opened before him as he played sonatas by Emanuel Bach on a worm-eaten clavier in a garret of Vienna's Michaelerhaus; Haydn later observed: "Who knows me well must have found out that I owe a great deal to Emanuel Bach, that I have understood and diligently studied him." He emphasized this debt during his late years, looking back upon his career in sharp perspective. Though the compositions of Haydn's first period remained in the *galant* manner (Porpora, Wagenseil, and Matthias Georg Monn his models) and betrayed but occasional signs of Emanuel's *Empfindsamkeit*, with the years it showed itself a puissant influence as the younger musician's work grew in agitation and dramatic tension and ultimately achieved that resourceful composite of *galant* and *empfindsam* traits associated with the Viennese classical school. What were these elements?

The ideal of the *style galant* had been to entertain and to do so with grace—perhaps to touch the heart but not to draw tears. Having renounced the involute, rhetorical polyphony of the Baroque and turned to accompanied melody, the *galant* composer too often overembellished it with light ornaments. The texture remained unruffled and thin, triplets tended to dominate the mincing rhythms, and the fragmentary melodic ideas fell into diminutive cadenced units.

Though accompanied melody, too, constituted a major component of the *empfindsam* style, it, in contrast, made use of sharp accents and abrupt

---

5 Emanuel thought his younger brother's music too simple and exhorted him: "Don't be a child"; Christian replied: "I must speak syllable by syllable [*stammeln*] so that children will understand me."

changes of tempo, dynamics, and mood: the music opened doors upon heightened expressive power by means of varied rhythms (including syncopations), rich harmonies, bold modulations into distant keys, quick alternations of major and minor, an abundance of melodic leaps to notes outside the harmony, deceptive cadences blurring the contours of phrases, and abrupt pauses.

Haydn triumphantly amalgamated the two styles and at the same time gave his composite a fluency near in spirit to that of the baroque masters. While they had achieved flow by subjecting passages to repetition and sequential treatment,[6] Haydn animated the neglected, vitiated inner voices of *galant* and *empfindsam* structures: he revitalized all their layers with a unifying, driving thematic activity that gave the impression of counterpoint and organic growth as musical figures and fragments traveled from part to part, sometimes in thoughtful *empfindsam* colloquy, sometimes in a sprightly *galant* game of hide-and-seek. Here is what Leopold Mozart described as *il filo*, the thread binding a movement into a whole as if by magic.

Haydn spread the material of this instrumental seeming-polyphony throughout the tonal fabric, the play of musical ideas engendering a variegated texture. (As the inner voices became busier, the need to fill out the sound with a keyboard instrument declined, ensembles increasingly dispensing with it; see p. 142.) He achieved this baroquelike sense of continuous unfolding despite the recurrent sectional character of his compositions: though their periodicity and plurality of meter and melody were inherently foreign to late baroque music (whose persistent homogeneous pulse set in motion a unified body of thematic material), their variety and flexibility of rhythms, one dissolving imperceptibly into the other, nonetheless provided the locomotion driving the larger design onward.

Emanuel and Friedemann Bach had also inclined toward vital textures, motivic writing, and, at times, the latter's correlate—development. Their volatile styles, however, had constant changes of direction, while Haydn endowed his movements with a sense of overall alignment and succession. Moreover, in turning the segmentary, patchwork court divertissement into a fluid but integrated whole tinged with *bourgeois* subjectivity, he simultaneously transformed the lively charm of the German Rococo and the sentimental theatrics of *Empfindsamkeit* into the elevated drama of the Viennese classical school: Haydn forged that superb musical argument to which Mozart subjoined his own.

---

6 It consists in the repetition of a phrase at another pitch, often a tone or semitone above or below.

3

BY THE SPRING of 1763, when Leopold Mozart doffed his court livery to journey to Paris and play the gentleman, Haydn had worn for some two years the dark crimson-and-gold uniform (green coats appear to have been added by the eighties) of the Esterházys' musical household. Living on those vast, remote Ostmark estates, where the family ruled as princes of the Holy Roman Empire, indeed, as the Palatines of Hungary, he would quietly, sedulously develop a rugged artistic individuality. Not only passages of pathos but also humorous touches and, as in the case of the Mannheimers, hints of folk melody began to color his compositions. A hobnailed peasant *Ländler* had taken the place of the highbred minuet as early as his fifth symphony (c. 1762), a rustic touch inspired by that yearning for warmheartedness and the simple charms of nature characteristic of the age of Chardin, Goldsmith, and, above all, Rousseau, whose epistolary novel, *Julie, ou la Nouvelle Héloïse* (1760), had opened a decade of epochally changing artistic currents long quietly flowing.

The following year, the Viennese witnessed a powerful projection of these new ideals: the premiere of Gluck's ballet-pantomime *Don Juan*, a repudiation of the princely and cold ballet divertissement. The pulsating, trenchant score, well known to Mozart,[7] and its scenario and steps by the Imperial ballet master, Gasparo Angiolini (who also performed the title role), pertained to the aesthetic of danced drama Noverre had recently set forth in his *Lettres sur la danse et sur les ballets* (1760):[8] the treatise advocated abandonment of the stiff, stylized conventions of the "number" ballet in favor of choreographed dramas in which heartrending plots might be realized by means of natural movement.[9] (Had not Scheibe, after admiring with condescending air "the onerous labor and uncommon effort" of Sebastian Bach's contrapuntal intricacies, declared them "vainly employed" since they "conflict with nature"?) Mozart's future friend and collaborator, Noverre, had answered Rousseau's momentous call for soulful naturalness in life and art.

---

7 It contributed to Pedrillo's serenade in *The Abduction*, to the theme for variations in the string quartet in D minor (K. 421/417b), and to the fandango in the third act of *Figaro*.

8 The *Lettres* appeared late in 1759 but bore the publication date of 1760. Noverre's future antagonism toward Angiolini would rest upon the latter's insistence that his mentor, the Viennese Franz Hilverding, rather than Noverre, had invented the *ballet d'action*, in particular the *tragédie en ballet*. Though they, separately but simultaneously, worked along similar lines, in point of model productions, Angiolini in justice claimed Hilverding's priority and thus primacy (*Lettere . . . à Monsieur Noverre*, 1773).

9 Noverre, like Diderot in his *Entretiens sur le Fils naturel*, may have had in mind something not unlike animated representations of scenes in the manner of Greuze.

An entreaty for a renewal of humanity through the forsaking of deluding appearances and therewith a return to the true essence of man had resounded through the salons and theaters of Paris since the days of the *régence.*[10] More than a manifestation of the *style bourgeois*, this summons had a political—indeed, corrosive—force that accelerated the process of crisis, change, and, in time, rebellion. Rousseau had become the leading expositor of this tendency.

The vital organs of intellectual Europe, he claimed, had been poisoned; an urbane, polished, but almost substanceless surface concealed the decay beneath, and, among the institutions of civilization, the arts, he charged, bore heavy guilt for this conspiracy to mask reality; instead of improving the lot of man, the arts, subservient to a debased established social order that encouraged inequality, had made his condition worse: "Before art had molded our manners and taught our passions to speak a contrived language, our customs were rustic and natural, and differences of behavior at once announced differences of character." Declaring that "for a long time, the society of man has offered only false appearance without reality, without truth," Rousseau came to see Europe's task as learning "to distinguish reality from appearance and the man of nature from the fictitious and fantastic man who is the fruit of our institutions and prejudices." This, in spirit, would be the lesson set by Don Alfonso in Mozart's *Così fan tutte* and no less an exercise in *Figaro* and *Don Giovanni.*

The young became intoxicated with these concepts permeating Rousseau's thinking and treated systematically in his *Discourse on the Arts and Sciences* (1750). Lorenzo Da Ponte, the future librettist of *Così*, used the *Discourse* as the basis of his pupils' recitations closing the academic year at the seminary of Treviso. During the ensuing outcry, he found himself dismissed: the theme, in his words, "appeared—or, at least, was made to appear—scandalous, unwise, and contrary to the good order and peace of society." In Venice he became known as a "ridiculer of pigtailed aristocrats"; in Salzburg, Mozart in mockery signed himself "Lord Pigtail (Elder von Sauschwantz)." Their mutual liberalism helped seal their professional friendship.

In their first major collaboration, *The Marriage of Figaro*, Rousseau's principle of the general will or common good hovers over the luminous conciliation achieved in the final moments: Count Almaviva's contrition restores harmony to the domain of Aguasfrescas, the characters' sense of

---

10 Fénelon, who died but months before the coming of the *régence*, had urged warmer, more simple diction in the pulpit. In Germany, even the tedious classicist Johann Christoph Gottsched insisted that poetry be an imitation of nature.

well-being deriving from the new social contract guiding their relationships one to the other. But Mozart and Da Ponte could not have expected the Count to persevere in the virtue thrust upon him by a household united in defiant intrigue: bringing about and then maintaining a rational and moral community, Rousseau had warned, required the mounting of perpetual guard against the particular hypocritically disguising itself as the general and, under the semblance of propriety, pursuing its narrow, unworthy, and often vicious purposes—a special talent of Almaviva and the very modus operandi of the Queen of the Night during her manifestation before Prince Tamino in *The Magic Flute.* In the end she casts away all disguise and in two nightmarish visions reveals her pitiless drive toward power. Only upon his arrival at the borderland before Sarastro's kingdom and its triple temple gates of Wisdom, Reason, and Nature does Tamino at last recognize her guile and his inability as yet to distinguish at first glance bad faith from good, appearance from reality.

To end the dissembling and deceit that jumbled being and appearing became a revolutionary goal. The proposition at the heart of Da Ponte and Mozart's *Così fan tutte* would assert that society for the most part contents itself with taking illusion for actuality: that Mozart's music renders equally convincing the suitors' declarations of love as both Neapolitan officers and Albanian interlopers becomes the ultimate paradox. "Happiness," Mozart, with condescension, assured a worried father, "consists solely in the imagination"; he did not count Leopold among those strong enough to rid their minds of accepted notions and rhetoric and to explore the conscious and unconscious discrepancies between pretense and reality. If the son investigated the problem with telling incisiveness in his late operas, he had, in fact, begun this exploration very early.

The opening tableau of the almost nineteen-year-old Mozart's *La finta giardiniera* (see p. 334) had already given notice of fatigue with the masquerades and hollow nostalgia of the aristocratic world. The curtain rises upon a seeming Edenic haven of security, a garden in which five protagonists sing together of bucolic contentment. Then, one by one, they reveal their true feelings, dissecting their emotions in a series of short solos telling of hidden sorrow, furious jealousy, and both unrequited and unwelcome love. Having disclosed the pain and eroticism beneath the idyllic surface, they reassume their public postures in a repetition of the beginning ensemble, now revealed to be a fiction. The ironic elegance of Mozart's music for this *introduzione* sharpens the libretto's prosaic words into instruments of dramatic edge as he sets a discrete nursing of wounds within a public refrain: "What a happy day"; the scene becomes a travesty of the affected and already old-fashioned pastoral opera, a comment upon the nature of so-called reality, and an indication of the growing stress between directness and reserve, between the spontaneous and the formal. At the same time, the dilemma is marvelously funny and irreverent, an anticipation of the Mozartean theater of restiveness and paradox.

4

MOST OF THE writers, actors, musicians, and dancers who first created in the new spirit could hardly have realized that their efforts acknowledged the implications of Rousseau's antithesis, what he viewed as the primary tension between man and society; nevertheless, by instinct they exalted liberating, democratic ideas at the expense of privilege and, however ingenuously, helped create the necessary conditions under which Rousseau's concept of nonalienated man might flourish. If the central portal, marked "Wisdom," provided Mozart's Prince Tamino entrance into this regenerated world, that inscribed "Nature" opened before them.

There can be adduced few more striking examples of early searchers eager to decode the laws of nature and find reality than the leading mistresses of Maurice de Saxe, that lusty German mercenary who triumphantly led French troops into Maria Theresa's lands. Before the War of the Austrian Succession provided him this opportunity, he had demonstrated prowess in only two areas: the drill yard and the boudoir. Two of his mistresses had been among the most gifted stage performers of the century: Adrienne Lecouvreur, till her death in 1730 the first actress of France, and Marie Sallé, a dancer whose fame grew even greater in London than in Paris, where she had made her debut at the Opéra in 1727.

Seeming to live their roles rather than play them, both placed emotion above ceremony and decoration: Lecouvreur by setting aside the traditional heavy wig and costume, relics of the Baroque, as unsuited to that simpler style of recitation she substituted for the customary singsong declamation; Sallé by discarding the cumbersome ritual *panier* and headdress of the court dancer as inimical to the free movement of her fledgling pantomimed dance dramas. (She influenced David Garrick and Noverre.) Maurepas described her voluptuous but economical gestures and movements as sentiments made visible. The London correspondent of the *Mercure de France* declared her dramatic gift to rival that of Lecouvreur, whom Voltaire celebrated as having "all but invented the art of speaking from the heart . . ."; Adrienne, he said, put sentiment and truth where before there had been pomposity and rhetoric: she "knew the language of nature. . . ."

In a letter to another actress, Marie Ange Dangeville (who had just created the role of Tullie in his tragedy *Brutus*), Voltaire exhorted her "not to hurry anything, to animate everything, to mingle sighs with your declamation, to pause much. Above all, perform . . . with much soul and energy. Put terror, sobs, and long pauses into the finale. Appear desperate in it, and you will make your rivals despair." He imparted this advice some nine months after the death of the divine Adrienne, her art fixed in his mind.

Both she and Sallé, as harbingers of the new aesthetic, anticipated in spirit both Diderot's theory of naturalistic drama (see n. 9 and p. 613) and the ardent eloquence particular to the most famous violin virtuosos of the coming decades: Stamitz, founder of the soul-stirring Mannheimers; Nardini, whom Mozart heard play at Ludwigsburg and would again at Florence, a musician renowned for his heartfelt adagios and known to weep as he fiddled; and Friedrich Schwindel, that high priest of musical *Empfindsamkeit*, whom the Mozarts would encounter at Brussels. In his *Versuch*, Leopold Mozart had declared the violinist's highest goal to be a simple, unaffected expression: the instrumentalist must, by judicious bowing, make the strings sing and thus communicate "the pathos of the music. . . ." "An inability to play anything without artifice" formed his principal criticism of Esser, who clung to those baroque ways of performing and composing both Mozarts characterized as the sliced-noodle school.

Leopold's son grew up in a world in which nature, warmth, and soul became the shibboleths, artists increasingly subordinating technique to expression. Emanuel Bach implored performers on the keyboard to strive in their execution for a "freedom ruling out everything slavish and mechanical. Play from the soul, not like a trained bird!" Voltaire's charge to Dangeville sounds at one with Mozart's advice to Aloisia Weber at the time she set to work on his recitative and aria for Andromeda (K. 272): she was to think about "expression; to reflect carefully upon the sense and force of the words"; to put herself, "in all seriousness, in the position and situation of Andromeda"; to imagine herself "to be this very person." Above all, Mozart admired the artist who sang "to the heart." "We must not merely practice steps, we ought to study the passions," Noverre exhorted, and Diderot advised opera composers to construct their arias by having the singer "imitate in cadence the inarticulate accents of passion. . . ." Even conservative Emperor Charles VI had urged the castrato Farinelli to temper the complexity of ornament overwhelming his baroque bravura style and to add pathos to it.[11]

Keyboard performers, too, had begun to sound these same plangent accents that denied the baroque ideal of rigidly contrasting intensities: a

---

11 Farinelli would press on to develop the poignant art with which, not without irony, he won the favor of Emperor Charles's archrival, Philip V of Spain.

completely different concept of dynamic effects had come into being—
impassioned and volatile. Early in Mozart's career, the sounds of the harpsichord had begun to yield in popularity to the warmer, more pliant tones
of a new instrument: the *gravicembalo col pian e forte* (the cembalo, capable of
playing loud and soft). Designed with hammers to strike the strings—the
harpsichord had, instead, quills that plucked them—this contrivance
(nicknamed fortepiano, pianoforte, or piano) permitted the performer a
new flexibility in determining the amount of sound: finger pressure upon
the keys regulated the force with which the hammers hit, a freedom and individuality of touch unachievable on the harpsichord; its jack-and-quill action and inflexible mechanism of stops, as well as the time needed to set
them, foreclosed quick changes in volume and color, restricting them in
general to contrasts between whole sections of a composition. Of course,
baroque keyboard literature with its breadth and power had not lacked
heartfelt expression, passion, and, indeed, theatricality; the mechanical innovations of the piano, however, added to the dynamic range qualities of
spontaneity and intimacy and with them those sudden changes of mood
belonging to the new aesthetic. (In London, the boy Mozart played on a
strange composite: a harpsichord with a swell box controlled by pedal and
providing the graduated tonal hues of the piano; see p. 197.)

An Italian, Bartolomeo Cristofori, built the first pianoforte, c. 1710 in
Florence, while in service to the Medici. In 1713, when still an electoral
prince, Augustus the Weak of Saxony visited Florence, where he must have
examined the invention; his capital would lose little time taking over its development: Christoph Gottlieb Schröter exhibited to the Dresden court
his own model of the hammer-lever action as early as 1717, and for almost
half a century the Germans dominated piano-building. Their instruments,
in the service of the new *Empfindsamkeit*, admitted many shades of tonal intensity and myriad and smooth transitions between.[12] As early as 1763, in
the preface to his Opus I, Johann Gottfried Eckart, a keyboard virtuoso
from Augsburg, made clear that growing German predisposition to the
piano he would help mold in Mozart (see XI, n. 16): "I have attempted to
make this work equally useful on the harpsichord, clavichord, and fortepiano. For this reason I felt obliged to indicate both the loud and soft [pas-

---

12 Frederick the Great purchased several pianos from the famous instrument builder Gottfried Silbermann. On one of them Sebastian Bach improvised a fugue exploiting the so-called royal
theme—Frederick proposed it—that became the basis of the *Musical Offering* (see pp. 85–86 and
VIII, n. 32). This famous encounter (Potsdam, 1747) revealed Frederick marshaling an open-
mindedness not in his grain: the upholder of the aesthetic of the *régence* not only reconciled himself to the *empfindsam* sounds of the piano but also spoke with admiration of baroque improvisations
he at heart must have considered outmoded, their intellectual power notwithstanding.

sages], which would have been of no purpose had I taken only the harpsichord into consideration." The rise of the German pianoforte paralleled that of the Mannheim orchestra. In their capacity for communicating a wide range of emotion, both epitomized the protoromanticism of the age.[13] Bringing their sonorities together in the piano concerto, Mozart attained a fullness of expression he never surpassed.

The emotional needs of the time also inspired a revival of interest in the soft tones of the clavichord, whose sound, like the piano's, the performer could color: tangents attached to the keys agitated the strings, and a vibrating finger produced a vibrato or *Bebung*. (In private moments Mozart resorted to the clavichord; during Salzburg days he chose to keep one within reach of his desk.) A delight in such immaterial and graded effects also led to enthusiasm for musical glasses (whose mechanism Benjamin Franklin improved in London in 1761). Moistened fingers passing around the brims of cups, containing more or less water as each note required, produced sweet and intimate strains—plaintive, disembodied, melancholy. They, too, yielded to modification through an oscillating touch: notes might be swelled, softened, and prolonged. Leopold Mozart commented upon the "mournful impressions" the instrument awakened in him. Though Gluck performed on it (London, 1746), an Englishwoman, Marianne Davies, became its most famous exponent. (She may have acquired her "armonica" from Franklin.) Mozart first met her in London during his visit of 1764–1765 and again in Milan in 1771. Two years later he tried his own hand at playing musical glasses in Vienna. During his final year, he wrote for another celebrated mistress of the instrument, the blind Maria Anna Kirchgassner, the ethereal Adagio and Rondo, K. 617 (the glassharmonica quintet; see XXXIV, n. 16) and the solo Adagio, K. 356/617a.

---

13 Diderot saw Enlightened man as a keyboard instrument endowed with feeling, the philosophe being both instrument and musician, his senses "so many keys that are struck by nature . . . and that often strike themselves." If this metaphor proves elusive, it does testify to Diderot's interest in the art of the instrument builder. In 1771 he determined to possess a piano and acquired one made by Johann Zumpe (see XII, n. 9), having first sought the advice of Grimm, Christian Bach, and Dr. Burney. Zumpe had built the instrument Christian Bach played in 1768 at London's earliest public solo performance on a piano, the very year Paris's Concert spirituel (see XI, n. 10) first used the instrument. Diderot's image of the keyboard supposes a nexus of sensations to be awakened as chords of simultaneously sounding senses. The philosophes concerned themselves with such interactions: they explored relationships uniting ear and eye, sound and color, and fixed their scrutiny upon the *clavecin oculaire*, an invention of a Jesuit, Father Louis-Bertrand Castel. It superficially resembled a harpsichord, save that the keyboard manipulated not quills but multicolored ribbons. They moved to form so-called ocular sonatas, a work of art associated with one sense being represented in terms of another—a faint and amusing adumbration of Scriabin's *clavier à lumière*.

5

AS TASTE MOVED toward an ideal combining color and pathos, the fragile *galant* little by little dissolved into the more robust *style bourgeois,* and a
warm spirit dominated an altered artistic climate. Ever more the times
prized the joy of seeking out simple truths in harmony with perceived phenomena, new animating principles that made devotion to the natural a
consuming drawing-room pursuit. In the salons and on the promenades of
Vienna, Johann Pezzl observed women dressing in a way "so very much
more natural, tasteful, buoyant, and pleasing than hitherto." He applauded
the demise of the hoop skirt, to his eyes an obstruction concealing the natural attractiveness of even the most slender girl, making her look like "a
herring barrel"; and he no less commended the passing of the stiff headdress, its place taken by the English country hat with its pastoral embellishments of ribbons and flowers. Nannerl Mozart had appropriated it
early in her travels.

Men of fashion, too, adopted English headgear, an outgrowth of their
recent practice of laying aside their wigs. By the mid-eighties, Mozart, who
had appeared at professional and important social functions wearing the
statutory white rococo *perruque* and ceremonial sword, began on occasion
to abandon both and publicly to exhibit his magnificent growth of blond-
chestnut hair in which he took such pride: Joseph Lange's unfinished oil
portrait (1789–1790)[14] shows it simply dressed and pulled back, as does
Doris Stock's drawing of the same months. "I am a chameleon," Goethe
conceded, and Mozart became no less one, forever drawing energy from
the latest currents. Eager to identify himself as up to date, he followed the
mode in vocabulary (as had his father in younger years); recoiling from
Anton Schweitzer's opera *Rosemunde,* he cried in fashionable excess:
". . . there is nothing natural about it, all of it being exaggerated," a rever-
beration of Gluck's dedication to *Alceste.*

Here Gluck had proclaimed "simplicity, truth, and lack of affectation . . . the sole principles of beauty in all artistic creations." He remarked
in a letter to the *Mercure de France* (February 1773): "To imitate nature is the
acknowledged aim . . . which I seek to attain; always as simple and natural
as possible, my music merely strives to achieve the fullest expression and to
reinforce the poetic declamation." Gluck's music dramas became the most
complete manifestation of the Encyclopedists', in particular Diderot's,
doctrines of operatic dramaturgy before the mature Mozart's creations for

---

14 In artistic quality the finest of all Mozart likenesses, it, moreover, so his wife attested, exhibits
a close resemblance.

the stage. His first big operatic success, *The Abduction from the Seraglio*, awakened praise for a music "uncommonly eloquent, the language of the heart and of nature. . . ." Even the very young Mozart, so Guiseppe Parini declared after hearing the opera *Mitridate*, had studied "the beauty of nature" and represented it "adorned with the rarest of musical graces." Philosophes like Parini prepared the way: lifting up the book of nature they invited the sensitive to read and only then to write.

In 1755—the year Noverre, in London, first experienced Garrick's pliant dumb show—Mademoiselle Clairon, appearing at the Comédie-Française in Voltaire's *L'Orphelin de la Chine*, made her famous entrance arrayed in the Chinese manner.[15] Here she followed the example of his "*petite fée*," Justine Favart, another of Maurice de Saxe's mistresses. When performing in "*Les Amours de Bastien et Bastienne*" (1753), a parody of Rousseau's operetta *Le Devin du Village* (see pp. 22–23), Justine[16] had appeared at the Théâtre Italien turned out as a village girl—arms bare, hair matted, and in woolen dress and wooden shoes. At a time when actresses playing peasant maids wore *paniers*, pinned diamonds to their tresses, and pulled on gloves reaching to the elbow, the vivacious Justine not only sought authenticity of costume but also adopted an appropriate regional accent. Here she embraced the spirit of Haydn's stylized *Ländler*, an attitude not unrelated to the cottage in which Mozart's royal Aminta and his love (*Il rè pastore*) hoped to live midst innocent Trianon-like simplicities recalling Marie Antoinette's farm in the park of Versailles.[17]

Mozart even coquetted with a new genre of drama that put aside singing as unnatural, substituting for it the spoken word recited above and between orchestral utterances. ("One should treat most operatic recitatives in this way," he declared, arguing that sung recitatives disavowed any connection with nature and ought to be used "only occasionally, when *music can express the words well.*") The creation of a generation eager to renounce anything too mannered in representing the soul and its passions, this so-called Melodrama entered the lists against those grandiloquent musico-dramatic forms struggling to maintain authority.

---

15 At this time, voices raised in the name of the new naturalism exhorted the Comédie-Française to remove from its stage the seats favored spectators occupied by tradition.

16 She, her playwright husband, Charles Simon Favart, and Harny de Guerville collaborated on the parody, which converted *Le Devin*'s mood of Arcadian innocence into one of rustic realism. Mozart's *Bastien* rests upon a German translation of *Les Amours*.

17 The sculptor Louis François Roubillac had already helped set this tone in England: with his life-sized statue of Handel—created in 1738 for London's Vauxhall Gardens (see p. 188) and now in the Victoria and Albert Museum—he created a public monument exceptional for its time in representing in stone a famous personality informally dressed and seated at his ease.

CHAPTER X

Courtly Opera and Its Decline; a New Aesthetic and Decorum

THE FORCES TRANSFORMING instrumental music, drama, and ballet compromised the hegemony of that pair of splendid if timeworn manifestations of aristocratic ideals, *opera seria* in its late and crowning expression and the *tragédie lyrique*, both long sacrosanct. To grasp Mozart's dimension as a dramatic composer, their origins, characteristics, and decline must be examined, as well as the traits of their immediate heir, the reform opera of Gluck; and that robust survivor, the comic opera, must also be considered. The *tragédie* excepted, all flourished with particular brilliance in the city associated with Mozart's greatness.

Opera seria culminated in the labors of two Italian literati whom Emperor Charles VI summoned in turn to Vienna and made his Caesarean poets: Apostolo Zeno (1668–1750) and Metastasio (Pietro Trapassi, 1698–1782), who ultimately refined and codified the genre. Inspired by Corneille's and Racine's elevated plays with their stern moral dialectic, Zeno and Metastasio repudiated the often sprawling and anarchic opera books of their immediate precursors and determined to create simplified musical dramas of noble pathos.[1] They raised the quality of operatic Italian, eschewed distracting and irrelevant comic scenes so dear to late

---

1 In the same spirit, Gottsched embarked upon a reform of the German theater and its diction by holding up the example of French classicism.

seventeenth-century librettists, and circumscribed such abused expedients as ballets, supernatural manifestations, and effects requiring the overuse of stage machinery.[2] Though their school of *opera seria* developed its own tiresome sub-intrigues and seldom attained the integrity of its French models, to an extent, Zeno and Metastasio did achieve something of the grave elegance they sought.

For his part Metastasio displayed within an austere framework such felicity and suppleness of language and so appealing a variety of verse forms that few opera composers of his era could resist taking in hand his increasingly revered texts. His stoic, graceful poetry at times showed an Arcadian, Watteau-like quality of remote and courtly melancholy. But, unlike the painter, he enjoyed munificent patronage and became one of Europe's monuments: visitors stared in awe at the windows of his rooms in Vienna's Michaelerhaus;[3] comparing him to Homer and Dante, admirers found solace in his ambivalent art depicting insecure, menaced, erotic worlds that contingency time and again rescued from disaster.

As the heroic mold showed widening clefts and courtly pretensions crumbled, to set to music Metastasio's librettos became a more and more tedious ritual. Vittorio Alfieri's aversion to meeting the conservative old poet symbolized his decline in the eyes of the Enlightened generation. (Had he not refused to contribute to the *Encyclopédie*? Had not Alfieri sickened to observe him genuflecting before Maria Theresa?) Near the close of the century, Mozart found himself coping with the *impedimenta* Metastasio's dramas had become for musicians accustomed to less idealized verse. Metastasio's *La clemenza di Tito* had passed the half-century when Mozart, like many before him,[4] clothed a version of it in music, this time for the coronation in Prague of Emperor Leopold II as King of Bohemia. Despite its furbishing up with modern touches, the work tendered a futile, almost pathetic reassertion of ceremonial etiquette in an age without belief in its purposes. Royalty inspired an ever declining residuum of reverence: a

---

2 Dancing and grandiose spectacle did at times invade *opera seria*, in particular the subspecies *festa teatrale* (see p. 137): in the entr'acte of Mozart's *Ascanio in Alba*, for example, at Venus's command the city of Alba Longa rises full-built from the earth to the accompaniment of ballet music. Handel had excelled in a variant of *opera seria* in which supernatural scenic effects became a major element—the magic opera.

3 Metastasio maintained private quarters within the apartment of his close friends and heirs, the family of Nicolò Martinez. His daughter, Marianne, who became a respected composer, took lessons in voice and clavier from the young Joseph Haydn. He, in fact, lived under the beams of the same great house: Viennese garrets, lighted by dormers in the sloping roofs, often became home to tailors, gilders, music copyists, wood-carvers, and painters, artisans whose work required a great deal of regular light.

4 Among them Gluck, Hasse, Caldara, Jommelli, Galuppi, and Anfossi.

monarch could no longer persuasively present himself as an extension of Metastasio's world; an audience could discover little relationship with these aloof proceedings, their moments of rococo sentiment notwithstanding.

It seems out of keeping that the master of ironic realism, creator of Papageno and Monastatos, of Figaro and Don Giovanni, of Susanna and Despina took nurture from the Metastasian drama; yet, no contemporary musician could have had closer acquaintance than Mozart with its texts: during childhood they had formed his course in operatic training, his father rummaging in them for passages the boy might set to music as practice pieces. The words of his earliest preserved vocal exercise, the angry "*Va, dal furor portata*" (K. 21/19c), written at the age of nine, came from Metastasio's *Ezio*; the music may have been related to the "rage" aria he improvised for Daines Barrington (see p. 199), Wolfgang working himself up "to such a pitch that he beat his harpsichord like a person possessed, sometimes rising in his chair."[5]

Three years later, during a sojourn in Vienna, he visited Metastasio in the Michaelerhaus and at the keyboard improvised arias the laureate himself chose haphazardly from his librettos. Early in 1770 in Milan, Count Karl Joseph Firmian gave the Turin edition of Metastasio's works to Mozart, now fourteen, and before twenty he had drawn upon them to compose *La Betulia liberata*, *Il sogno di Scipione*, and *Il rè pastore*. To boot, the poets of another two of his boyhood operas, *Mitridate* and *Ascanio in Alba*, counterfeited Metastasio's manner. It seemed befitting that the book of Mozart's *Lucio Silla* found its way to Metastasio's desk for emendation. Even at the height of his powers, pursuit of material for concert arias led Mozart back to the poet—to *L'Olimpiade* and *L'eroe cinese*, (K. 512, 1787, and K. 538, 1788)—for, well beyond the era of such fossilized texts' aesthetic or political pertinence, Mozart could feel at one with any number of Metastasio's characters by reason of their fitful but thereby no less astonishing truth to nature in many details of their sufferings. Communicated through music often so powerful that it outstrips the occasion, Mozart's insight into such protagonists' litanies of perplexity and distress accomplishes the ultimate miracle of animating the inanimate.

Though with the completion of *Idomeneo* Mozart wrote no more *opera seria* (excepting the anomalous *La clemenza di Tito*), many of its idiosyncrasies remained part of him. In *Don Giovanni* he cut the aristocratic Donna Anna and Don Ottavio from fine, if somewhat refractory, blocks of Metastasian marble. Intruders from a distant, Imperial world, they ap-

---

5 Perhaps he contributed this material to a London performance that patched together a score for *Ezio* by assembling its arias as composed by a variety of hands, a so-called *pasticcio.*

pear suggestive of those fragments of antique sculpture Renaissance carvers at times embedded in their reliefs. From the moment of their creation there must have been something atavistic about these musical portraits, for *opera seria's* statutory conventions had already begun to ring false even as Mozart first took them up.

2

ITS SUBJECT MATTER taken from history, myth, and heroic legend, the plot of a Metastasian *opera seria* unfolded through the medium of recitativo secco, rapid and dry musical speech supported, punctuated, and embellished by the harpsichord. In moments of heightened emotional tension the singer might abandon this neutral secco for arioso, a flowing, broadly phrased style of recitative midway between secco and song. An instrumental ensemble at times joined the singer during arioso passages, the resulting recitativo accompagnato often becoming a spacious, noble declamation.

Metastasian arias were lyric outpourings in which the characters made known their reactions to the turns in the plot as revealed by the various kinds of recitative, attitudes ranging from the contemplative to the impassioned, from gentle melancholy to fury. It became the librettist's task to provide texts of generalized and thus predictable emotions, the principals being as a rule posturing puppets, counterfeit papier-mâché heroes and heroines incapable of shaping situations and maneuvered through a methodically, indeed, geometrically constructed, scenario. It exploited the contrast between the thrust and flux of the recitative and, however agitated the atmosphere, the relative abeyance of the aria.

Since *opera-seria* librettos led their players into similar circumstances and crises, a typical situation bringing about a typical reaction—the summing up or preceptive response—arias, say, of duty, sacrifice, friendship, love, anger, or repentance could be transplanted from one part of an opera to another, indeed, from one opera to another.[6] The question of the cogitative integrity of the plot seldom posed a hindrance to strategic seamanship in *opera seria's* rolling seas of generalities: in 1783, when intrigue forestalled

---

6 Even in Mozart's *Don Giovanni*, a work tempering the *seria* with the *buffa*, it matters little in which scene Don Ottavio sings *"Dalla sua pace."* "My peace depends upon hers" forms the modest burden of this aria Mozart interpolated right after Donna Anna's *"Or sai chi l'onore"* on the occasion of the opera's Viennese premiere. Directors tend to shift Ottavio's lovely lyric solo from here to there, often to good effect. In contrast, his *"Il mio tesoro"* has particularity and should remain where Mozart placed it, although a textual reference to the "friends" (Elvira, Zerlina, and Masetto) being addressed in no way inhibits many a tenor from singing the demanding aria alone on stage.

the performance of an aria Mozart had composed for the tenor Johann Valentin Adamberger (itself an interpolation into Pasquale Anfossi's *Il curioso indiscreto*), the composer remained stoic: "I can easily turn it [*Per pietà, non ricercate*, K. 420], to use in one of my own operas." In adapting an aria to new circumstances, a composer might embrace it as a whole, bend the music to new words, or even make off with the text alone, the course recommended by Anton Raaff when, cast in the title role of Mozart's *Idomeneo*, he found one of his arias filled with tongue-twisting words: in their place he asked Mozart to compose verses taken from Metastasio's *Il natale di Giove*, written some four decades earlier. "No one knows it, and we can keep quiet," Raaff argued, aware that Varesco, the poet of *Idomeneo*, would not attend the premiere. For a while Mozart considered acquiescing, for the suggested text filled the dramatic stasis well.

His genius (and that of Handel) could transcend even *opera-seria* mechanics of this kind and create commanding characters of psychological truth, figures revealing themselves step by step—that is, solo by solo—each aria presenting a single "*Affekt*" or typical emotion: *opera seria* at its fullest and best offered a kind of cumulative dramaturgy. The ability to sketch such shifting mental dispositions with dizzying celerity and economy must count among Mozart's most powerful gifts.

Da capo (ABA) in its musical form, the Metastasian aria demanded overwhelming virtuosity (above all of the wildly appreciated castrati): the singers had to embellish the vocal line and improvise variations on it, in particular in the course of the final section or reprise. The clatter of dishes, the clink of glasses, the noise of card parties in the boxes, and the hum of gossip—the sounds with which the audience, for its part, accompanied the recitative[7]—would suddenly stop. (Both Mozart and his librettist Da Ponte lamented "the boredom and monotony of the long recitatives.") An expectant hush fell over the hall as the soloist embarked upon the aria and sooner or later let loose a surplusage of ornaments engulfing the written notes and exploiting the distinctive qualities of the

---

7 Most often in Italy, all manner of diversions kept the singers bizarre company and helped save the boxholders from boredom: they played at faro, chess, or cards and could slake their hunger with baked goods hawked from box to box or with complete dinners brought and served to them. No matter how serious the opera, they felt themselves at Carnival and, as Samuel Sharp observed of the Neapolitans, liked to "laugh and talk through the whole performance, without any restraint." The babble in the Verona opera house made it difficult, Mozart complained, to hear the singers; at Naples, Charles Burney found the audience so noisy that he could make out distinctly neither voices nor instruments. When Goldoni visited the court of Parma, he marveled at the silence in the theater at Colorno, where French etiquette prevailed. It did not in the cities of the Empire; even Mozart had to admit that during a performance in Prague of Paisiello's *Le gare generose*, "contrary to" his "usual habit," he "chattered away."

voice. At times the aria assumed the architectonic proportions of a vocal concerto, the so-called *aria di bravura*: cadenzas might even be injected between the divisions of the tripartite form.

It should not surprise that such vocal fireworks more often obscured than advanced dramatic issues. Charles de Brosses, a friend of the young Mozart and translator of Metastasio (see p. 214), felt that though the "exquisite" arias "pinned to the end of every scene" might well "enchant the ears," they nevertheless permitted interest in the libretto "to cool off." At the conclusion of their solos the performers strode toward the wings with a flourish and, so they hoped, to applause, *opera seria* being a succession of recitative entrances and aria exits,[8] an arrangement Mozart, by the time of his *Idomeneo*, came to deplore as artificial in the extreme. He found downright painful the dramatic paralysis suffered by the singers the libretto doomed to stay on stage and listen to the long arias: "actors who must simply stand by."

At times the protagonists of *opera seria* indulged in duets, seldom in an ambitious ensemble like the flowing finale for the five principals of Mozart's *Il rè pastore.* As a rule more than two soloists joined voices only at the end of a work, as in the quintet in block harmony concluding his *Mitridate,* the kind of perfunctory *coro finale* meant to accompany the audience's departure from the boxes. A chorus in the modern sense constituted an anomaly, such as the welcome sung by the shades, so marvelous and Handel-like, in Mozart's *Il sogno di Scipione.* In the closing decades of the century, the addition of varied and vital ensembles became an expedient composers like Mozart—to splendid purpose in *La clemenza di Tito*—turned to account as a means of modernizing old-fashioned *opera seria* (see pp. 148 and 728–29).

Didactic in tone and elevated in style, *opera seria* offered a stateliness answering that of the halls through which it sounded. The plots served as yet another mechanism of court flattery: *opera seria* became dynastic opera reaffirming the values of those who paid for it, the hero's virtues—courage, benevolence, probity—purporting to characterize the occupant of the

---

8 *Opera seria* can be viewed as a parade of closed and varied musical compartments: arias often differed in sentiment from those preceding and following. Moreover, the middle part of an aria as a rule contrasted in mood with its flanking sections. In thus pitting broad areas one against the other, the composer of *opera seria* called to mind a harpsichordist setting stops between sections or movements. *Opera seria's* giving way to the playful metamorphoses and tumbling energy of *opera buffa* paralleled the harpsichord's decline upon the ascendancy of the piano: in both cases a structure capable of subtle and bold transitions supplanted a static one no longer answering the emotional needs of the age. (The harpsichord did survive into the age of Rossini as a continuo instrument [see X, n. 23] for *opera buffa.*)

royal loge; the Metastasian hero became a prince of the Enlightenment strutting in costume.[9] Nonetheless, even on stage the benevolent tyrant could not always mask an inherent nastiness and cruelty. Though the chorus at the end of Mozart's *Lucio Silla* hails the dictator's "triumph over his own heart," this reformation comes rather late to efface the impression of him as fatuous, repugnant, brutish; and modern ears find most bizarre that moment in Mozart's *La clemenza di Tito* when the emperor famed for his mercy arrives in the arena impatient for what he calls a "joyous entertainment": the spectacle of his political prisoners being thrown to wild animals.

Politics suffused *opera seria*, which featured as subject conflicts between affairs of the heart and affairs of state, in particular disruptions opened by the caprices of aristocratic protagonists torn by love or lust, jealousy or avidity: Farnace in Mozart's *Mitridate*, a traitor to his royal father, whose bride he covets; or Vitellia and Sesto in Mozart's *La clemenza di Tito*, driven by their passions—the one by greed for power, the other by lovesickness—to plot the murder of their emperor. It appears a paradox that Metastasio's stage, on which he aspired to offer panegyrics to princes, repeatedly laid bare their corruption and the moral degradation and futility of an entire society, revelations hardly obscured by the inevitable reform of the despot during the closing moments of the drama.

The childlike ease with which such a character passed from one extreme sentiment to its very opposite reflected the erratic personality of many a prince.[10] (Vittorio Alfieri believed the tyrant to be at his most dangerous during these sudden benevolent moods.) In Mozart's *Lucio Silla* the repair of the dictator's character proceeds at a leisurely pace compared to the lightning change that renders dutiful the hitherto treacherous Farnace, eldest son of Mozart's King Mitridate. "Vile impulses, I abandon you and listen only to the dictates of my heart"; and even less persuasive is the abrupt repentance of the hitherto vicious, arrogant Vitellia of Mozart's *La*

---

9 The Enlightenment embraced autocratic as well as parliamentary political systems: in theory the autocrat evinced high personal morality as well as devotion to the well-being of a realm resting upon an even-handed dealing out of justice and a rational system of individual responsibility. The citizen's contribution to the state functioned as a privilege to be measured by his place in society, his service being but part of the whole. Over it hovered the autocrat, the nation's first servant, whose exalted position thrust upon him the burden of the most demanding and widespread privileges of dedication. Only in terms of such an argument can Joseph II's or Frederick the Great's claims to Enlightenment be grasped.

10 Pasha Selim in Mozart's *The Abduction from the Seraglio* does not belong to this species. His innate nobility and the example of Constanze's heroic love prepare this despot's grand act of benevolent accommodation.

clemenza di Tito, who, conscience-smitten, confesses her transgressions; one might as well imagine Wagner's Ortrud suffering a Pauline conversion.

For their part, the great accepted and applauded these pantomime-like transformations as evidence of their own capacity for amendment and clemency, as testimony to the Enlightenment of those born to bear the responsibilities of governing. *Opera seria* became one of their most grandiose vehicles of self-deception; they luxuriated in settling back to hear exegeses of the perils of majesty; in Mozart's *Idomeneo* Arbace expounds: he who "aspires to it must . . . not complain should it prove nothing but martyrdom." (Yet, his master, the king, does not suffer death for his trespasses against Olympus; this, rather, becomes the fate of the "thousands" of his subjects who fall victim to the monster created by his impetuosity and irresponsibility.) It must be stressed that to courtly audiences *opera seria* offered a stageworthy, gripping theatrical experience whose values and implications illuminated their ideology.

Mozart had first pursued *opera seria* in *Mitridate,* a work of generalized sycophancy construing the vagaries of aristocratic honor, and then in *Ascanio in Alba* and *Il sogno di Scipione.*[11] The last two, however, belonged to the category of short *opera seria* called *festa teatrale* or *serenata teatrale,* works that served more particular complimentary purposes. (Celebrative programs inevitably coupled an *opera seria* of this kind with a ballet.) Mozart's *Ascanio* honored the marriage of Maria Theresa's son Archduke Ferdinand to Maria Ricciarda Beatrice of Modena, the hero, Ascanio, and the shepherdess, Silvia, representing the groom and bride; Mozart's *Sogno* paid homage to the Archbishop of Salzburg, symbolized by Scipio the Younger, the relationship underscored by recourse to a *licenza.*

An epilogue or prologue, a *licenza* linked the *opera seria* directly to a person or persons, that is, to an event like a royal birthday, wedding, or coronation. Since the courts reused *opera-seria* texts[12]—more than two decades before Mozart's birth, Metastasio had brought *Sogno* into being to celebrate Emperor Charles VI's name day—the *licenza* served to transform a

---

11 Mozart began *Sogno* before *Ascanio,* but tradition lists it as the earlier (see pp. 292 and 300).

12 On the other hand, the musical setting of a *festa teatrale* seldom outlived the occasion inspiring it, though Sebastian Bach provided a famous exception in his *Christmas Oratorio* (1734–1735), which drew upon secular cantatas he had written for the Saxon court: he joined to new texts music not only from his *Hercules auf dem Scheidewege* (a homage that had celebrated the birthday, 5 September 1733, of Prince Friedrick Christian) but also from both *Tönet, ihr Pauken!* composed for the birthday of Electress Maria Josepha (8 December 1733) and *Preise dein Glücke* (5 October 1734), a commemoration of Augustus the Weak's election as king of Poland (see p. 77). However, even in this case of the mighty Sebastian revising his own music, at moments it sounds alien to the new words, the effect an uncomfortable accommodation. Such adaptations would appear to have come off better when an old text acquired a new setting.

generalized poem of flattery into a specific hymn of praise.[13] Mozart's first commission from the Salzburg court took the form of a *licenza* honoring the anniversary of the Archbishop's ordination (see n. 17).

The identification of the hero of the action with the lord and patron or his family imposed upon *opera seria* a prevalence of happy endings: Charles VI demanded them, and only on rare occasions did Metastasio permit a leading protagonist a tragic fate. Operas "must end happily... no matter how absurdly things are brought about," John Gay scoffed in his *Beggar's Opera*. Gluck could not allow his Orfeo to be torn to pieces by the Thracian women: *Orfeo* celebrated the name day of Emperor Francis, and matters had to conclude with festive mirth.

A trace of this tradition survives in Mozart's *Don Giovanni*: its final curtain does not fall upon the scene of the great libertine's descent into hell midst flame, smoke, and earthquake; rather, the action proceeds from this catastrophe to a bright final sextet, which sorts out the characters' immediate futures and, reiterating a platitude indicating the fate awaiting the dissolute, sends the self-righteous home, strengthened and encouraged.[14]

3

PARIS AND VERSAILLES in their high days of courtly *gloire* had also demanded operas with joyful finales; but, while a protagonist's sudden conversion to virtue or magnanimity disentangled the strands of a Metastasian plot, French opera ended crises and undid disasters by a device beloved of the earliest Italian librettists: a literal, palpable *deus ex machina*. This figure flourished in the magical environment of Parisian *opera seria*, the *tragédie lyrique*, for it celebrated stagecraft, in particular the *merveilleux*.

---

13 A *licenza*'s tribute tended toward the fulsome. "Scipio, my lord ... is not the subject of my verse; when I speak of him I think of you. His illustrious name is a veil with which to cover my properly respectful timidity. My tongue exalts Scipio, my heart Girolamo [Hieronymus]": so sings the epilogist in *Il sogno di Scipione*. Mozart began it to honor the fiftieth anniversary of Archbishop Schrattenbach's ordination. He cut the ground from under the premiere by dying. Mozart then turned the work into one appropriate to the installation of Colloredo as successor to the prelacy by substituting his first name for Schrattenbach's—Girolamo for Sigismondo—in the *licenza* and making similar adjustments in the body of the work. *Sogno*, with music by Luca Antonio Predieri, had first come into being (in 1735) to celebrate a Carlo (Charles VI).

14 Here, the mechanical convention of the happy ending (*lieto fine*) achieves inspired purpose: Don Giovanni's downfall, harrowing but neither tragic nor transfiguring, requires the resolution provided by this musically miraculous ensemble which, despite its feeble adage, somehow consoles. For Mozart's ambiguous attitude toward the opera's finale, see XXXII, n. 7.

The term embraced spellbinding metamorphoses and the no less ingeniously engineered arrivals of celestial visitors traveling in winged chariots
or on clouds. To its traditional taste for recurring entrées of dancers in extravagant and fantastic costumes,[15] the French court added a special delight
in the busy machinery by which the gods descended and rose to disseminate the gospel of the Bourbons' enduring fame.[16]

This espousal of scenic panoply formed the hub of the matter in which
the *tragédie lyrique* differed from the Metastasian reform opera: the latter
suppressed the bravura feats of the stage mechanic only to replace them
with those of the vocalist; on its side the *tragédie lyrique*, outlawing extemporaneous vocal embellishments, counterbalanced what it lacked in rapid
repeated notes, trills, skips, and runs with wonders achieved by slides,
traps, tackles, and winches. The Italian dramatist Carlo Goldoni, no friend
to undecorated music, described the Opéra as "heaven for the eyes, hell for
the ears."

Mozart found himself no less appalled than Goldoni by the sounds he
heard from French throats: "The singing—ohimè!" he exclaimed during
a visit to Paris in 1778; "I shall thank Almighty God if I escape with my
taste intact." But, flying in the face of the *tragédie lyrique*, a Parisian taste
for Italian light opera had persisted. Pondering its robust health in so
alien an atmosphere, Mozart asked: "Why, then, despite their wretched librettos, do Italian comic operas please everywhere?" "Because," he concluded, "in them music remains master and makes one forget the rest."
He felt the need to flee France for Italy so that his musical taste might
"revive." The frigid formalism of the French vocal line, so distressing to
Goldoni,[17] the Italian, and Mozart, the Italianized German, had, in fact,
been born of a distaste for things not indigenous, a consuming antipathy
spurring the French on to invent their own singular musical speech for the
theater.

---

15 Under Louis XIV the Académie Royale de Musique (the Opéra) did not have the arsenal of
dancers it would build under his successor, and in the beginning made do with about a half-
dozen males; *danseuses*—they had long performed at court presentations—first appeared on its
stage in 1681.

16 The spirit of the *tragédie lyrique* survived well into the nineteenth century, as Berlioz's *Les Troyens*
attests.

17 Mozart wrote his first *licenza* (K. 36/33i; 1766) for an intermezzo adapted from Goldoni, also
the voice behind the text of an aria (K. 217; 1775) Mozart composed for insertion in the
Galuppi/Goldoni opera *Le nozze* (1755). The libretto of Mozart's *La finta semplice* likewise derived
from Goldoni, a setting of whose *Il servitore di due padrone* (in German translation) Mozart began
during the early months of 1783. The score remained unfinished, only vestiges surviving (see p.
617). The two never met.

Traditional Gallic hostility toward any foreign tongue had baffled the efforts of Louis XIV's chief minister, the Italian-born Cardinal Mazarin, to establish Roman opera in Paris from the time of his first attempt (1647). (Not the music, not the performers, but Giacomo Torelli's stage machinery excited the public.) A nation drawing near its era of glory rejected aesthetic subservience. The King, who had put aside Bernini's plans for reconstructing and expanding the Louvre and handed the commission to native architects, proved no less determined in respect to the national stage: after some indecisive experiments, a highly self-conscious Parisian species of opera came into being when Jean-Baptiste Lully, born in Florence but educated in France, and his librettist, Philippe Quinault, created *Cadmus et Hermione*, the first *tragédie lyrique* (1673). They fabricated the new genre from components of both Mazarin's imported opera and the Lully-Molière native *comédie-ballet*, the first contributing the marvels of Torelli's mobile décor (against which Metastasio would react), the second furnishing diversions of dance, interludes of orchestral music and rhythmically declaimed choral ensembles, and those passages of flexible musical speech, the *récit* (recitative), which would give Lully's vocal compositions their characteristic stamp.

Hinging on the conflict between duty and love, Quinault's mythological plots aped the weighty manner of such playwrights as Alexandre Hardy, Pierre Corneille,[18] and Jean Racine. The *tragédie lyrique* thus shared with *opera seria* a line of descent from the French classical theater, a heritage that endured in Mozart. (His first *opera seria*, *Mitridate*, rested upon Racine's drama, his *Idomeneo* upon Crébillon's *Idoménée*, his *La clemenza di Tito* upon Metastasio's reworking of elements in Corneille's *Cinna* and Racine's *Andromaque*.) In addition, reciprocal influences flowing between Quinault and Metastasio's major model, Racine, suggest the *tragédie lyrique* itself as a vital secondary root of the full-blown *opera seria*. For all that, in aesthetic the two remained far apart, their essential dissimilarities lying not only in their approach to stage techniques but also in vocal style: in Paris it spurned Italian exuberance to develop, as Goldoni and Mozart ruefully noted, along austere lines.

Stately, cool in contour, of the subtlest turns, its rhetoric governed by the inflections of verse, in particular Racine's, as declaimed at the *Comédie-*

---

18 Quinault had direct acquaintance with the same Spanish sources Corneille tapped. The French, Saint-Évremond complained, infused these Spanish plays with a plethora of love scenes, which became the mainstay of the opera. He voiced fears that "the present stubborn fad for the opera ... will soon ruin the tragedy, which is the most beautiful thing we have." Charles de Brosses observed that "by wanting to unite too many pleasures, opera weakens their enjoyment" and thus had "moments of tediousness, something good French tragedy does not know."

Française (the touchstone for French diction), Lully's refined *récit* dominated Quinault's texts.[19] But even though the arias proceeded in freer meters, they remained stark for Italian taste; anticipating them patiently at the Opéra, Goldoni discovered with stupefaction that they had passed him by: "I took the whole for recitative," he complained in amazement. A more abundant sound, on the other hand, characterized the ambitious choral ensembles, of which Mozart took special cognizance. His father had observed of even the church music at Versailles: "Everything for individual voices and intended to resemble an aria was empty, frozen, and miserable—in a word, French; the choruses, in contrast, were all good and even superior." Mozart observed: "I am, indeed, glad that the French esteem choruses," in his eyes the populace's only sign of musical acumen.[20]

Seeking to make his name in Paris, Mozart anticipated setting Jean François Marmontel's French translation of Metastasio's *Demofoonte*. It was to be converted into a *tragédie lyrique* and "on the whole," in Mozart's words, "adapted to the French stage" by adding choruses and dances. Leopold advised his being guided by the taste of the Parisians: "I implore you; listen to their operas before you write . . . and [observe] what in particular pleases them." He had confidence in Wolfgang's ability to soak up influences: "I know you; you can imitate anything." The father wanted a success at any artistic price: "If only you can be applauded and well paid, let the devil take the rest!" (In a less opportunistic mood, Leopold held French music "not meet for the devil.")

Leopold did not understand that his son absorbed into his musical tissue solely those elements he sensed to be salutary: Mozart's *Demofoonte* remained unwritten;[21] even more mannered than *opera seria*, the icy *tragédie lyrique* chilled him. One day he would draw upon its silvery riches, as witnessed by the choral scenes and *merveilleux* of his most grandiose opera, *Idomeneo*. Not a small portion of this Gallic influence, however, descended

---

19 Quinault's *récit* retained the Alexandrian couplets of French classical tragedy. At first Lully called upon the basso continuo (see n. 23) to sustain the *récit*, but, from the time of *Bellérophon* (1679), he had increasing recourse to the accompagnato.

20 Mozart found French performances of foreign vocal music offensive: "If only French women would not sing Italian arias," he implored in April 1778, having heard Antoinette-Cécile Clavel Saint-Huberty perform an aria by Gluck at the Concert spirituel and no doubt judging her guilty of violating the Italian language and German style. The preceding year the soprano—in fact, Strassburg-born—had appeared at the Opéra in Gluck's *Armide*.

21 For a time Mozart continued to contemplate composing a *tragédie lyrique*. He never did, perhaps for the better: his two French Wendling chansons (see p. 404), their musical enchantments notwithstanding, reveal a lack of sympathy with a language, so Leopold indicated, he could never master.

to him through his compatriot Gluck, who, like Metastasio before him, had turned to French models for inspiration in the never-ending business of reforming Italian opera.

4

IN VIENNA, GLUCK had transformed the Metastasian *opera seria*, based upon the aristocracy's narrow ethical code, into psychological drama universal in theme. His librettist, Raniero de Calzabigi, yet another reformer patterning his work after Racine, simplified diction, purified the action of superfluous accessory plots, which had come to plague *opera seria*, and strove to construct a unified, taut drama. Unlike Metastasio, Calzabigi concerned himself not with dynastic quarrels but with the lofty affairs of the timeless archetypical figures of the ancient world. Gluck, in turn, translated their elevated emotions into music. Schiller-like, he sought a new grand style by casting out what he held to be contingent and fortuitous, his goal: achieving the purest and most idealized expression of the human situation. With no little help from the example of Jean Philippe Rameau, the eccentric genius who became Lully's embattled successor in Paris, Gluck developed into a symphonic dramatist, establishing a musical line that would stretch through Mozart to Berlioz, Wagner, and Richard Strauss.

Gluck's reform operas discarded the secco: the orchestra accompanied all of the recitative.[22] With this change vanished his primary need for the basso continuo, that baroque practice of anchoring vocal and instrumental compositions with a harpsichord reinforced by a bass string or wind instrument.[23] In place of the secco cum continuo (Mozart satirized the latter as archaic in his song *"Die Alte,"* K. 517, the refrain being "the good old days"), Gluck brought into being a noble orchestrally inflected speech-song no less varied and supple than Lully's, the instruments even more thoroughly investing the words. This at times rhapsodic accompagnato—"the unaffected language of emotion"—became the major asset in

---

22 Gluck's occasional, indeed, casual recourse to secco in the first version of *Alceste* represents a perplexing relapse proving the rule.

23 The basso continuo (also called figured bass, thorough bass, and through bass) constituted a kind of musical stenography: the clavier player translated a code of figures—written above or below the lowest line of the composition—into a chordal accompaniment and often enriched it with improvised ornamentation giving the illusion of polyphonic texture. The Viennese classical era put an end to this kind of extemporized filler: not only did the orchestral fabric become more active (see p. 120), but also composers drew back from this impromptu padding and, excepting embellishment, stabilized the instrumentation through more detailed notation.

Mozart's legacy from Gluck, in whose hands the French *tragédie declamée* re-solved itself into a kind of German *tragédie chantée.*

At climactic moments Gluck's plaintive recitative flowered into arias; but, like Lully, he did not permit vocal ornamentation to distend these lyric moments; often they seem closer to song than aria: for Herder the arias of *Orfeo* had the simplicity of folk ballads. Gluck's reform cut the vo-calists down to a size fitting within the dramatic structure, which he re-solved to protect "from all the abuses that have crept in, either through ill-advised vanity on the part of singers or through excessive complaisance on the part of composers. . . ." At the outset this sobriety proved difficult for both public and performers to comprehend: when Millico, a castrato engaged by Parma for the title role in *Orfeo*, began to read through the part, it at first glance appeared to him so plain that he started to sob, fear-ing that antagonists desiring his ruin had tricked him into the contract.

Showing the fullness of his debt not only to the lean anatomy of Lully's vocal style but also to his histrionism, Gluck gave weight to the chorus (which he used as an agent of the drama), orchestral interludes, and tableaux reflecting a Parisian sense of stage-picture, the genre born in Vi-enna assuming the Opéra's choreographic displays. He transfigured *opera seria* by means of French *goût*, Winckelmann's new vision of the ancient world (see p. 519), and the humanity of the philosophes.[24] Zeno and Metastasio had tidied up late seventeenth-century *opera seria*, turning it into a well-crafted if inflated genre of concession and expedience. Gluck and Calzabigi in turn recaptured the spiritual grandeur of the *seria's* early days in Florence and Mantua, turning it into *tragedia per musica*—so they called *Alceste* (1767)—a realization of pathos through the medium of tone.

The overture to *Don Giovanni* affirms how deep the breadth and emo-tional engagement of the *intrada* in D minor opening *Alceste* dwelled in Mozart's memory. Earlier, in an act of homage to Gluck—and as a gift to his betrothed—he had composed a recitative and aria text taken from the opera.[25] However, he remained ever so selective in his borrowings from the elder master. The protagonists of his most Gluck-like work, *Idomeneo,* for example, do not come upon the stage as austere heroic archetypes, but as

---

24 It might seem odd that the philosophe Diderot advised French composers to "see the light" not only by studying the operas of Italians like Hasse and Traetta—of course, Pergolesi, too—but also by reading Metastasio; however, to Diderot the idiom of *opera seria* seemed warm and natural in comparison to that of the Lully-Quinault school.

25 He intended the aria, K. 316/300b of 1778–1779, to be his engagement offering to Aloisia Weber (see p. 469).

complex, changing humans,[26] whose music retains the florid style of the Metastasian *opera seria*—as does the aria for his beloved.

A Metastasian opera text, intended from the first for a limitless line of composers, of necessity passed through various remodelings. That Calzabigi, in contrast, fashioned *Orfeo, Alceste,* and *Paride ed Elena* for Gluck alone anticipated an individuality of expression to be prized by the coming age, an attitude growing by slow degrees and thrust into relief when Ferdinando Bertoni apologized for having applied his modest musical talent (1776) to the libretto of the Gluck-Calzabigi *Orfeo.* But even as Bertoni prescribed a new dignity for serious opera,[27] it continued to lose credit; the impious, in fact, had already cast its fate: armed with the weapon of laughter, they forced the doors of Europe's court theaters; not a coup d'état, but infiltration won the day.

5

BY THE BEGINNING of the War of the Austrian Succession, Lully's operas, having held the stage for over half a century, had begun to play before smaller audiences. His solemn *récits* and mythological plots now appeared tedious—singers added rococo ornament to the vocal parts to make them seem more modern—and the works of his followers André Campra and André Cardinal Destouches showed no less wear.

In 1752 Eustache Bambini's gadabout troupe, performing an *opera-buffa* (Italian comic-opera) repertory including Pergolesi's *La serva padrona,* gained the favor of Paris, of the philosophes in particular. (The city named Bambini's nine or ten players the *Bouffons* or Comedians.) The same year, a company of French actors captivated the Viennese with comedies interspersed with songs: even as Bambini's simple offerings undermined the school of Lully in its own capital—indeed, on its own stage—these refreshing French actor-singers, presenting a kind of inceptive *opéra comique,*[28] subverted *opera seria* in its great eastern bastion, the citadel of the Caesarean poets. Though, thanks to the insistent and sclerotic conser-

---

26 Beethoven felt ill at ease with Mozart's all-too-human operatic characters and in *Fidelio* attempted to recapture the spirit of Gluck's abstract and monumental figures and their transcendental overtones.

27 Antonio Tozzi had offered no excuse for setting before the Munich public (9 January 1775) his own musical version of Calzabigi's *Orfeo* as reworked by Coltellini. (For this same carnival season Mozart provided Munich with *La finta giardiniera.*) Gluck's and Calzabigi's wishes had no legal force: in the absence of copyright laws, pirating continued unobstructed (see p. 626).

28 Like *opera buffa,* it interspersed airs and simple ensembles; but while recitative carried the plot of *opera buffa,* spoken dialogue answered this service in *opéra comique.*

vatism of Maria Theresa's father, Vienna had prolonged baroque rituals and traditions in music,[29] painting, and architecture, with his death a change in taste and sensibility had started to show itself with confidence, a desire for a less ponderous lyric theater preparing the warm welcome the French visitors found.

But three years after this success, the Hofburg suffered a brazen attack upon Maria Theresa's cherished Metastasian ideals: the onset took the form of Gluck's *L'innocenza giustificata*, created for her husband's birthday. Count Durazzo, intendant of the Viennese theaters, had begun the work by culling a number of aria texts from various librettos by Metastasio. Gluck then set these solos to music, and Durazzo bound them together with freshly written recitative forming a story similar to that used half a century later by Gluck's disciple Spontini in his *Vestale*. (When in 1768 Gluck revised *L'innocenza*, he retitled it *La vestale*.) Pretending to honor Metastasio by building a pasticcio from his verses, Durazzo manipulated them to construct a simple, moving action devoid of Metastasian conventions: under the cloak of homage, he appropriated the poet's words only to turn them against him. Durazzo helped prepare the soil from which Gluck's reform sprang. Close upon four years later Durazzo would ask Favart to supply Vienna with operetta books, a move betokening Metastasio's fading from the center of Vienna's operatic life.

The year 1752 had begun to set the new tone not only in Vienna and Paris but also in Schwetzingen, where Karl Theodore added to his palace park a playhouse intended only for light opera. Moreover, that very year Leipzig, too, embraced the new mood with the Koch theatrical troupe's presentation of the first singspiel, or German comic opera, *Der Teufel ist los, oder Die verwandelten Weiber*, its music by J. C. Standfuss, its text a translation and remodeling of an English ballad farce. The door had opened upon a development Mozart would crown with *The Abduction from the Seraglio* and *The Magic Flute*.

During the fifties, Gluck, who had taken up residence in Vienna at the turn of the decade, began to cultivate the *opéra comique*, his masterpiece in

29 A favorite of Emperor Charles VI, Johann Joseph Fux continued to interlard his stage works with rich and learned counterpoint at a time when most composers of opera had taken up the simpler, chordal idiom. To the end of his life, Charles's retrograde aesthetic beaconed its message across Europe, luring Vivaldi, in the twilight of his career, to Vienna. From his native Venice, where he found his high-baroque style compared with disparagement to the lighter manner of younger composers, he made his way by the end of June 1741 to the capital of his old admirer (Vivaldi called himself the Emperor's *Maestro in Italia*). In the meanwhile Charles had breathed his last: nine months after his death (and five and a half after Fux's), Vivaldi, too, found his grave in Vienna (28 July 1741), young Joseph Haydn and five fellow choristers singing his requiem.

this genre, *La rencontre imprévue,* appearing in 1764 between those lofty reform operas *Orfeo* and *Alceste.* Leopold Mozart put credence in rumors
that Gluck would swerve from his mythologizing in the high tragic style,
so unfashionable and old school to many, and return to comic opera, if
only for practical reasons: Vienna, Leopold observed, had a bounty of "excellent" singers for light works but "none for serious opera."

Not even magnificent Dresden could escape the times: Augustus the
Weak must have stirred in his coffin as his grandson Frederick Augustus
III struck the capital's *opera-seria* company from the list of royal expenditures (1764) and put in its place Giuseppe Bustelli's *opera-buffa* troupe
giving performances at the Zwinger palace in a hall open to the public.
Frederick Augustus commissioned only one *opera seria,* a gesture toward his
mother, Maria Antonia: to solemnize his wedding (1769), Johann Gottlieb
Naumann's *La clemenza di Tito* filled the stage of Dresden's neglected but
still magnificent theater. At the same time, the fortune the splendid cast
and production consumed but confirmed the young ruler's belief that such
pretentiousness belonged to the past.[30]

Joseph of Austria's reluctance to indulge the pastime of *opera seria* derived no less from a sense of fiscal responsibility and fatigue with things
baroque. (A renowned intermittent stinginess also played its part; Leopold
Mozart lamented: "This gentleman absolutely abhors anything that might
give rise to expense. . . .") Even so, Joseph maintained a lively curiosity
about new music. The imaginative fusion of Rameau-like and Italian elements in Tommaso Traetta's *Le feste d'Imeneo* (1760), a bewitching *opéra-ballet,*
performed at Joseph's marriage by proxy in Parma to its Duke's daughter,
Isabella (see p. 66), no doubt led Prince Joseph Wenzel von Liechtenstein,
Joseph's representative at the Parmesan nuptials,[31] to recommend the work
to the Hofburg. Indeed, Isabella herself dispatched a copy of it to Joseph,
whereupon a summons flew from Vienna to Parma that Traetta furnish the
Burgtheater with a new opera.

It in no way provided the Emperor a refreshing entertainment with the
tender sensibilities of the wedding divertissement: instead, an *Armide* studded with elevated moments made its way across the boards (January 1761,
with, in all likelihood, Traetta conducting from the harpsichord). Com-

---

30 Under Napoleon he would become King Frederick Augustus I. He took the Electoral throne
    after the brief reign of his father, Frederick Christian, whose widow, Maria Antonia, had she
    remained in power, would doubtless have made certain of *opera seria*'s survival at the Saxon
    court, at least to the end of her days. She died in 1780 (see VIII, n. 3).

31 The festivities concluded, von Liechtenstein escorted the bride to Vienna. His famous golden
    carriage, which had already provided his spectacular entry into Parma, carried him through the
    gates of the Imperial capital.

posed to favor not Joseph's but his mother's taste, it retained much of *opera seria*'s traditional apparatus while turning chorus, ballet, and spectacle into impressive elements evolving from the action. Traetta's *Armide* proved to be neither a precious Parmesan diversion nor just another canonical *opera seria*, but, rather, a passionate musical drama: in fact, a harbinger of Gluck's *Orfeo*, which followed within months.[32] It, in turn, overwhelmed the Empress, who attended fourteen performances, Calzibigi reported. But one weighty opera after another could hardly have pleased Joseph: he must have shown at best a restrained, even tepid, response to both, although in time he did take a more friendly stance in respect to *Orfeo*.

Its powerful constituent of German instrumental music had small chance of gratifiying his Italianate taste.[33] Yet he did remain heedful of this innovative and affecting opera's significance as a symbol of Germany's musical ascendancy and Vienna's role in it. If he himself did, in fact, elect *Orfeo* to celebrate his coronation as King of the Romans[34] (Frankfurt-on-Main, 1764; the entertainment included Traetta's *Ifigenia in Tauride*), the choice entailed determinations less personal than political, for in his heart he delighted in the shot-silk elegance of a rococo *opera-ballet*, the energy of the singspiel, the liveliness of *opera buffa*: that is, in canvases proportionate to small-scale characters caught in the coils not of high-flown disaster but of simple misunderstanding. He would commission and take enormous pleasure in Mozart's *The Abduction* and *Figaro*, works in which much that he loved found reconciliation.

Leopold Mozart put the matter succinctly when he wrote from Vienna in 1768: "At present no *opera seria* is given; people simply don't like it. . . ." Hasse, the Habsburgs' favorite composer of Metastasian texts—Burney

---

32 The libretto of Traetta's *Armide* derived from a sketch by Durazzo (after Quinault) as developed and versified by Gianambrosio Migliavacca. Durazzo appears to have used Traetta as a bridge by which to lead Vienna to Gluck's reform. The artistic relationship between the two composers became close. Traetta's *Il cavaliere errante*, an *opera buffa* of 1778, would pay humorous tribute to Gluck's by then extraordinary fame: one of the characters goes mad, imagines himself Orpheus, and sings a deadly parody of *Che farò*, the aria Gluck gave Orpheus to sing his grief over his wife's second death.

33 Some two decades after the premiere of *Orfeo*, in the course of escorting Grand Duke Paul of Russia and his party on the first stage of their journey from Vienna to Venice (for their visit to Vienna, see pp. 579–91), Joseph tarried with them in Wiener Neustadt. There he and Paul, a passionate admirer of Gluck, diverted themselves by singing arias from his *Orfeo* and *Alceste*. The long stretches of weighty accompagnato—the heart of these operas—not the lyric moments, tried Joseph's patience.

34 The German Emperor had the right to procure the election of his heir apparent as King of the Romans (*Romanorum rex*). Upon the Emperor's death, he succeeded immediately as Emperor Elect. As sponsor, Emperor Francis accompanied Joseph to his election and coronation in Frankfurt.

saw him yoked to the poet "like Plato's *androgyne*"—now shunned the theater, where, aghast, he had beheld "strange things [comic operas] holding
sway." Though Metastasio regarded Gluck as the mad author of his ills,
the modern barbarian pounding at the gates of the sanctuary, in time
Gluck's reform opera came to be recognized as, in effect, *opera seria's* brief
and noble Viennese peroration.

Yet until the turn of the century, *opera seria* did continue in Italy, at a
number of German courts, and in a few pockets of tradition in London,
the genre's survival seeming at first glance to have been at defiance with the
spirit of the times. Nevertheless, as early as Baldassare Galuppi's setting of
Metastasio's *Artaserse* (1749), *opera seria*, in a Darwinian process of natural
selection, had begun to transform itself, as in Mozart's *La clemenza di Tito*,
by making free with *opera-buffa* components: ambitious finale ensembles
(for soloists, choristers, and at times both combined) and short songful
passages (perhaps an air or duet) contrasting with the grand arias. They,
moreover, no longer clung to the baroque da capo formula, but, often taking on a less static binary disposition (two tempos: slow and then faster),
grew into the so-called vocal rondo, a form Mozart first turned to brilliant
account in the revised *Idomeneo* (see XXXIII, n. 42). However, even when
light of texture and mood, the elements appropriated by *opera seria* partook
of the lyric rather than the humorous colors of *opera buffa*: while this genre
did not hesitate to fasten upon the serious, *opera seria* held back from, contrariwise, absorbing the antic, as it pursued a path of retreat from the
Metastasian aesthetic (see p. 338).

Its decline had evidenced less the effects of war, economic stringency, or
royal taste or whim than the intellectual revolution stimulated by the
philosophes, who lost no opportunity to transmute the values of society
even in the face of those who wished to reverse or, at the least, to stop
time.

6

LIKE JOSEPH OF Austria, Frederick the Great looked upon himself as a
modern man possessed by the doctrines of the philosophes. But, unlike
Joseph, who, whatever his preferences, forced himself to experience the
modern in art, Frederick preserved no less conservative an attitude toward
opera than toward instrumental music. His noble Corinthian opera house
in Berlin nursed those stunted German offshoots of the Metastasian tradition, the operas of Hasse—admired no less by the Hohenzollern than the
Habsburgs—and of Carl Heinrich Graun, works in turn shaping the taste

of Christian Bach, one of the finest operatic talents of the time and a signal influence upon Mozart.

With the death of their father in 1750, Friedemann Bach had taken the adolescent Christian from Leipzig to Berlin to live with their brother Emanuel. The idiosyncratic musical aesthetic of the King of Prussia became Christian's: an enthusiasm for both airy *galant* instrumental music, of which he would become a polished exemplar, and late-baroque *opera seria*.[35] To it he brought his gifts of melodic elegance and effluence, a rare and ravishing orchestral color, and a distinctive lyricism. These very qualities also distinguished his purely instrumental idiom—in ironic unfitness it derived in no small part from *opera buffa* itself—and counted among the gifts he bequeathed to Mozart, who cherished as his "favorite piece" Christian's setting of *Non sò d'onde viene* from Metastasio's *Olimpiade*. Mozart composed this text twice: K. 294 and then 512, the first for soprano, the second for bass.

After an apprenticeship in Italy, Christian passed the prime of his career in London, where he befriended the boy Mozart. (The dedication of Mozart's harpsichord sonatas for Queen Charlotte of England places Christian Bach, alongside Handel and Hasse, among Germany's musical illustrious.) In London, as Leopold Mozart had also observed of German cities, more and more patrons gathered at performances of *opera buffa*. (Despite his indebtedness to it, Christian could never bring himself to write one.[36]) The Mozarts heard all kinds of opera during their stay in London (1764–1765), but by the 1768–1769 season the King's Theater, which had employed both a "serious" and a "comic" troop, engaged only the comedians.

Christian Bach must have confronted the changing fortunes of *opera seria* in 1774 with the failure of his *Lucio Silla*[37] at the court of Elector Karl Theodore of Mannheim, a sophisticated capital weary of baroque operatic clichés: the stilted plots and rhetoric fell heavily upon the ears of a public that ruminated Rousseau's exhortations to renounce the mannered and the artificial. The following year, Leopold Mozart, who pored over the barometer of public taste, wrote his son, then resident in Mannheim: "Should

---

35 Tastes not as inconsistent as might first appear: *bourgeois* and *galant* came into the world as successors of the Baroque (see p. 114), the first as a parvenu foster child, but the second as a true blood descendant who, albeit delicate, frivolous, and given to slumming, nonetheless continued to evince the aristocratic spirit of his lineage.

36 At any rate, he did contribute individual numbers to musical comedies in English: an aria adapted from his *Orione* for *The Maid of the Mill* of 1765 and an aria based upon Michele Mortellari for *The Flitch of Bacon* of 1778.

37 Bach set to music a revision of the text Mozart had composed four years earlier.

you succeed [in getting a commission to compose an opera] . . . it would be superfluous for me to recommend your imitating the natural and popular style, which everyone easily understands."

Father and son observed the clearest sign of *opera seria*'s giving way: Italy now manufactured fewer of those most contrived ornaments of the century, the castrati. In Mannheim, Wolfgang found "only two . . . they are already old and will, I think, be allowed to die off." Throughout Europe, a decrease in the number and quality of every variety of *opera-seria* singer had become conspicuous, and, his swelling distaste for the lofty genres notwithstanding, Leopold did bridle at a corrective expedient the Viennese had hit upon: casting *buffa* performers in Gluck's *Alceste.* He had lost sight of the fact that in his reform operas Gluck prized singers, whatever their background, eager to explore the musical capabilities of language. Performances of *Alceste,* in fact, had to be cut because the delicate *buffa* voice of Antonia Bernasconi, his choice for the title role, could not cope with the strain. Moreover, vocal categories had grown more and more fuzzy: in 1772 the Baglioni sisters, Constanza and Rosa, contracted with Vienna to sing whatever serious or comic parts the management might designate.

At times, coincident with the arrival of a major singer, the invalid *opera seria* revived. In Berlin during the seventies, the prima donna Gertrude Schmehling (Mara) restored life to the operas of Hasse and Graun and for the moment arrested a decline inevitable in the face of the Berliners' delight in the singspiel. (Her technique had fallen off by the time Mozart heard her in Munich in 1780.) But even Frederick the Great proved unequal to shoring up what would collapse under the blows of Berlin's critics. By the end of the decade the *opere serie* at his opera house, whose pit stood free to anyone decently dressed, drew audiences so small that the King commanded companies of soldiers to attend and thus help warm the great auditorium. Out of patience, he absented himself more and more from it, and, ignoring the trends in his capital's musical life, devoted his leisure to cultivating his garden at Sanssouci.

The evening of his reign had begun. Without fear of punishment, his Kapellmeister, Johann Friedrich Reichardt, an admirer of Gluck, described the *Orfeo* of Graun, whose style Frederick himself had molded, as "an old Italian hotchpotch." The failure of Duke Karl Eugene's appeal for subscribers to a proposed edition of Jommelli's Württemberg operas (1783) epitomized the growing number of musical recusants refusing to attend the *opera-seria* rites of the *ancien régime:* Karl Eugene received not a single response.

Had he heard of the Duke's solicitation, Mozart would have shown little interest: quite early a curiosity about *opera seria* and Jommelli in particular had spent itself in a prodigy prematurely encouraged to plow the nearly exhausted Metastasian field, to set texts foreign to his generation, temperament, and, often, comprehension. Could a fourteen-year-old, whatever his genius, grasp the cool Racinian artifice of *Mitridate, rè di Ponto*?

Only a few months before beginning its composition, he had indicated his assessment of *opera seria* in a terse comment on Jommelli. His letter of 5 June 1770 to his sister parroted a fashionable scorn of the genre: "The opera here [Naples] is one of Jommelli's [*Armida abbandonata*; see p. 279]. It is beautiful but much too elevated [*gescheid*] and too old-fashioned for the theater." The score's sheer craft had excited his lively approval during rehearsals, but then second thoughts intruded. Had what initially attracted him been the very quality Jommelli's countrymen rejected? His *Armida*, they complained, had "too German" an accent, his years at Stuttgart in the service of Karl Eugene having enriched his harmonic vocabulary and instrumentation with traits of the weightier Central European style.[38] He, in fact, showed signs of transcending the collective emotions of *opera seria* by intensifying the pathos of his accompagnati and by the mid-fifties had begun to dare venture upon the journey Gluck would triumphantly complete. Attempting, like the maturing Traetta, to pierce the boundaries of *opera seria*, to loosen and expand it, Jommelli earned from learned and conservative Padre Martini the title *"musicien philosophe"*—bestowed not without a touch of the caustic.

Even in Jommelli's hands the structure of *opera seria* remained too little changed to satisfy young Mozart. When, at the end of his career, circumstances led him to return to it and set to music *La clemenza di Tito*, he observed with satisfaction that his and Caterino Mazzola's free and updated remodeling of Metastasio's libretto, by interfusions of *opera-buffa* traits, had "made [it] into a real opera" (*ridotta a vera opera*). For Mozart, traditional *opera seria* never had reality.

7

METASTASIAN *OPERA SERIA* proved to be not only an epilogue to the monumental Baroque but also, in one guise, a prologue to the intimate refinements of the rococo: the ceremonial appurtenances of this ambivalent form notwithstanding, it, as in *feste teatrale* like Mozart's *Ascanio in Alba* and *Il rè pastore*, could contract to the proportions of an idyll. As the century unfolded, deflation overtook much that presented itself on the stage along

---

38 The Kyrie of his requiem in E flat, written at Stuttgart during the year of Mozart's birth, long passed as a work of Joseph Haydn.

with its decline as an exclusive pastime of the monarch: the theater now served the public, too. Mozart described hissing, abusive members of a Munich audience that answered a demand for order from the Electoral box with cries that the price they had paid for admission exempted them from compliance; in Mannheim he witnessed and admired the beginnings of a national theater whose administration had passed from the Prince to a group of councils, one of which admitted performers.

Such tendencies found bitter foes. During the decade of Mozart's *The Magic Flute*, Goethe, then director of the rebuilt Weimar theater, showed undisguised contempt for popular taste, in particular the naturalistic acting style it favored, and showed those on both sides of the footlights a despotic hand. He made his actors return to intoning their lines in a life-less baroque manner so they might symbolize rather than impersonate their roles. No less imperious with his audience, he thundered: ". . . the public must be controlled." "No one can serve two masters, and of all mas-ters the last I would select is the public that sits in a German theater." For its part, this public refused to be abused and elected not to attend his the-ater: despite ungrudging funds from the court, it failed. Goethe did offer performances of Mozart's *The Magic Flute*, and the elocutionary stilts upon which he had Sarastro and his attendants stalk must have towered on high.

Even in Salzburg, yet more provincial than Weimar, the Archbishop had to give way before the townsfolk's demand to express its taste in repertory and have access to seats. The doors of Europe's court theaters now stood open to an Enlightened ticket-buying and book-buying bourgeoisie, whose new heroes were small-scaled naturalistic creatures—flawed, extravagantly conscious of their defects, often defenseless before them, but nonetheless striving for dignity. Prévost's Des Grieux, though wallowing in his humilia-tions, struggled to free his beloved—not an enchained princess but the pros-titute Manon Lescaut—and no God descended to set his miserable affairs aright.[39] Not far in the future would be the even more wretched Werther.

Christian Fürchtegott Gellert took Prévost, and Richardson, too, as models for *Das Leben der schwedischen Gräfin von G. . . .* (1747–1748). This emotional tale of the return of a prisoner of war long believed dead re-vealed a comprehension of many layers of society. Gellert, with diffidence, recommended his novel to an admirer who well represented the new read-ing public—Leopold Mozart. One of the many Germans hungrily assim-ilating new books, in particular those from England, Leopold would

39 Antoine François Prévost's *Les Aventures du chevalier des Grieux et de Manon Lescaut . . .*, part VII of the *Mémoires et aventures d'un homme de qualité . . .*, had appeared as a separate volume as early as 1731.

present Nannerl with the seven volumes, in German translation, of Richardson's *Sir Charles Grandison.*

Literary Anglomania held sway: the 1780 catalogue of Wolfgang Mozart's friend the Viennese publisher and reprinter Johann Thomas Trattner, comprised over sixteen hundred entries, many of them English in either origin or inspiration.[40] Johann Timotheus Hermes could evade the suggestion of plagiarism and at the same time turn to account the vogue for the novels of authors like Fielding and Richardson by putting on the title page of his *Geschichte der Miss Fanny Wilkes* (1766): "For all practical purposes translated from the English."

Hermes's popular *Sophiens Reise von Memel nach Sachsen* (1769–1773) once more drew upon a variety of English sources. The novel remains forgotten today except for three poems inserted into its prose; they provided Mozart the texts for the songs "*Verdankt sei es dem Glanz*" (K. 392/340a), "*Sei du mein Trost*" ("*An die Einsamkeit,*" K. 391/340b), and "*Ich würd' auf meinen Pfad*" ("*An die Hoffnung,*" K. 390/340c). Commentators have suggested that a commission occasioned these Mozartean excursions into an unvarnished bourgeois emotionalism epitomizing the English-derived, moralizing romance: that, in pursuit of a fee, Mozart, in effect, stumbled into an alien world. But these songs—K. 390 and 391 with their almost Schubertean moments, K. 392 celebrating the small and the modest along with patient endurance—exploited modes of thinking about domestic life and love by this time fashionable in literary Vienna and already part of Mozart's sensibility, perceptions approaching the Biedermeier in spirit and of a piece with much in his contemporary *Abduction from the Seraglio*; and though Mozart would soon break this pattern to explore different kinds of erotic dilemmas and sexual fantasies, at the end of his days it would come together again in *The Magic Flute.*

A public thriving on sentimental verse in the English manner no longer had a taste for those imposing baroque visions of the universe subscribed to during Leopold Mozart's youth; nor did philosophers: they had done with penning giant bodies of credenda and now, at their most felicitous, expressed themselves in short forms—pamphlets, poems, epigrams. The extent to which their decorative aphorisms did, in fact, embellish larger philosophic designs remains a question.

Their writings showed kinship with the new instrumental music, which did not, as in baroque times, extend in unbroken lines of polyphony stretching over pages. If Goethe could hear eternal harmony conversing

---

40 A rage to read (*Lesewut*) seized Vienna. In the Trattnerhof, his publishing house with apartments to let, he opened a special room in which, for a monthly fee, the curious might peruse the firm's offerings. Literature engrossed Leopold as it did his son.

with itself in the works of Sebastian Bach, the compositions of his sons, of Joseph Haydn, and of the young Mozart provoked no such metaphysical thoughts suggesting the music of the spheres:[41] their music conversed not with eternity but with the listener—and in short, repeated, conversational phrases that not only appealed to the mind but went to the heart in a straighter, easier course.

In the comic opera, composers took possession of the cavatina, a songlike aria restricting repetitions of words and verbal phrases and thus opportunities for vocal improvisations and decorations—Mozart would use it to exceptional purpose in *Figaro*—this conciseness contrasting with the redundance of the baroque da capo form. Weary of the latter, Mozart had set out on his new course by the time of *Idomeneo* (1781), most of whose arias he cast in binary designs.[42]

Sharing this tendency toward diminution, painters entered the age of the easel picture and began to cultivate the *petits genres* so admired by Diderot. (He became besotted in the presence of Greuze's feigned naïve young girls, "those little hypocrites who have always broken their pitchers, cracked their mirrors, or lost their pets"; think of Mozart's Barbarina and Zerlina.) Critic and patron, dismissing not only historical/mythological paintings in the *grand goût* of the Baroque, the so-called *machines,* but also Watteau's elegant, amorous dream landscapes and Boucher's worldly-wise erotic art, now sighed before Chardin's and Greuze's more simple canvases. Didactic, filled with pathetic expression, but, as with Greuze, not without a strong element of sexual excitement, they depicted with realism and sympathy the affairs of contemporary men and women of the middle and even lower classes, holding them out as moral paragons.

A turning point in taste had been Largillière's preference for painting his sitters not in the artificial poses dear to the grand tradition but, rather, in

---

41 A basic entente connects Sebastian Bach's music with Leibniz's theories. (In his final years Bach turned to introspective, abstract musical problems.) Both men bear the seal of the same baroque spirit that, by strictly organizing and integrating parts within a consistent whole, brought into being vast disciplined structures. Pre-established harmony characterizes Leibniz's concept of a universe in which a single cause directs individual centers of force he called Monads. They constantly change, both according to their own principles and, simultaneously, in accord with one another, each Monad reflecting the whole universe, the universe being made up of Monads. Bach's counterpoint offers an image in the same mold: motivic Monads of tone interacting in a resonant Leibnizean world.

42 In Germany, the da capo aria had begun to give way by the seventeen-thirties. Frederick the Great considered it an abuse, and not only because it spun out words beyond their literary substance: few of his singers had sufficient skill in the art of improvisation to vary the repetition felicitously. In the musical setting of his *Montezuma* (1755) he insisted that Graun avail himself of the compact form.

attitudes and with a mien of unaffected graciousness, an inclination awakening thoughts of the intimate kind of portraiture Rosalba Carriera took to Paris early in the 1720s. There comes to mind, *mutatis mutandis*, Sesto's and Annio's delicious *duettino* (*"Deh prendi"*), which Mozart could not resist inserting midst the torrents of elevated sentiments and noble music flooding *La clemenza di Tito*; *Idomeneo*'s third-act love duet (*"S' io non moro"*), whose high-flown course suddenly veers toward the frolicsome in a concluding allegretto (*"Ah il gioir"*) of enticing rococo charm; and the allegretto duet for sopranos (*"Su conca d'oro"*), an episode approaching folk song and embedded within *Idomeneo*'s imposing first-act finale. With such felicitous digressions Mozart tempered what Niemetschek, the first important biographer of Mozart, called "the austere beauties" of the heroic opera, lighter idioms suddenly invading it. The third example, moreover, makes the dramatic point of giving a homely idiom to the lowborn: two women of Crete, drawn, in fact, from the chorus.

The printed word exceeded music in the power to transfigure the non-privileged and the submerged: the man of letters gave the times their defining temperament of challenge and quickened this leaning in other forms of artistic expression. Diderot's mettlesome and virtuous lawbreakers, Felix and Olivier (*Les Deux amis de Bourbonne*), roused the reading public, especially the Germans, with a new concept of morality: Goethe relished the adventures of these "brave poachers and smugglers," from whom came Schiller's band of noble robbers. With heroism so reduced in scale, what claims could the exertions of a Rinaldo, an Orlando, or Mozart's rather foolish Lucio Silla exercise? The royals and demigods of Metastasio, Quinault, and their disciples appeared quite ridiculous.

Entering a Salzburg ballroom in which the maskers danced arrayed as "a company of gods," Mozart and four of his companions delighted in the incongruity of their being costumed as members of the lower orders: a lackey, a courier, a hairdresser, his apprentice (Mozart), and a porter (Leopold). Such antimaskers had a long tradition in the *bal masqué*, but by this time (1776) their appearance could take on provoking implications of social criticism. Whatever the case, this particular apprentice's playful mischief, as he frolicked among the Olympians, can well be imagined.

La finta semplice, Mozart's first Italian comic opera, poked fun at *opera seria*, as did his last, *Così fan tutte*. (His second, *La finta giardiniera*, failed because it enunciated with excessive gravity too many vestiges of the old high style.) Comic opera took on the special task of parodying the serious, and it became a German specialty to provide a Sancho Panza–like commentator upon whatever remained of heroic action. Under such names as Hanswurst, Kasperle, Bernardon, Anton, and, in one famous case, Papageno, this yokel, by turns clownish, earthy, mischievous, and touching, functioned as critic of his social betters, parrying with his ironic wit and thrusting with his down-to-earth common sense at codes of conduct as humorous, for the most part incomprehensible, suspicious, and ridiculous to him as to the new audience. It particularly relished the way he used his outrageous folk dialect as a weapon against those spouting refined *Hochdeutsch*; to news that he "will never experience the heavenly pleasures of the ordained," Mozart's Papageno replies with relief: "So what [*Je nun*]! There are more people like me!"

The aristocracy, itself, had become fatigued with the heroic mold. Maria Theresa built handsomely at Schönbrunn, but not the stupendous terraced palace her uncle and father had envisioned: compared to the Roman-like colossus Fischer von Erlach had conceived for them, the building Nicolaus Pacassi in the end reared to her taste proved a modest suburban home. The Queen-Empress had turned from the grandeur of the Baroque. (Her impatience with Spanish court ceremonial, regarded by her chamberlains as preordained, disconcerted them.) Designers put aside planning monumental palaces and, instead, turned to redecorating in less forbidding style: lightening colors, lowering ceilings, bringing asymmetry into grandiose axially conceived chambers, arranging the new smaller-scale *en cabriole* furniture in informal, intimate groups so as to make gossiping more comfortable. "If it is natural, flowing, and light . . . the slight can be great," Leopold Mozart advised his son, whose song *"Verdankt sei es dem Glanz"* (see p. 153) concludes with: "It is no disgrace to be small." In this new age of psychological and intuitive observation, the *opera seria* could not survive its stilted stereotypes. Audiences rushed to the delights of *opera buffa*.

Its characters, though eccentrics, rested upon a base of keen observation. The middle class sensed humanity beneath the disguises and, though looking through a distorting lens, could see itself mirrored in the bizarre shapes. Though existing within a frame no less stylized than that enclosing *opera seria*, the creatures of *opera buffa*, even the endless succession of duped dotards and counterfeit soubrettes, remained accessible, and its heroes, unlike *opera seria*'s frigid demigods, driven to sacrifice passion to duty, contrived that love bear away the victory. In contrast to the lethargic pace of *opera seria*, ever a statuesque drama of character, *opera buffa* took its rise from situation, the intrigue unfolding in brisk rhythms.

With time, *opera buffa* inclined not only to amuse but also to touch. It was Mozart who most felicitously transformed the genre's schematic commedia dell'arte figures into individuals of flesh and blood—Arlecchino, for example, becoming his Figaro, Columbina his Susanna. In *Figaro* the sextet pleased him most, those moments when Marcellina, without abandoning the elements of farce and caricature at her roots, melts into a loving parent upon discovering Figaro to be her son: even when turning the grotesque to account, Mozart ennobled.

Much as Richardson exalted the destinies of the unpretentious,[43] so Mozart romanticized the personages of *opera buffa*: at his command, the *commedia per musica* issued from the *opera buffa* as he gave it psychological direction, moral earnestness, and ethical purpose. Making the drama of character part of the comedy of situation, he, like Shakespeare, set tragedy and comedy side by side. As he shifted from plane to plane, the moribund *opera seria* became subsumed under the vital *opera buffa* by means of a brilliant exploitation of their complicated interrelationships, that mingling of emulation and rebuff, admiration and irreverence (see p. 338).

8

THE GENIUS SO accomplished in manipulating and coming to terms with the disparate dramatic and musical materials of the times had to grapple with those related and volatile social factors that were at the very moment overturning the artist's base of regular—that is, aristocratic—patronage. Yet he succeeded: venturing upon a freelance career in Vienna, he discovered only a weak foundation to support his ambitions; but with extraordinary energy he reinforced it, going beyond the nobility to draw support from the high middle class and, as had been his experience in Salzburg, those in the professions: he raised the structure Beethoven would strengthen and enlarge.

The decaying courts provided musicians, artists, and writers decreasing opportunities, and Enlightened aristocrats themselves turned things keel upwards by seeking entry into the drawing rooms of the cultured high bourgeois; here the most creative minds assembled. In Paris, where this tendency showed itself first and at its most sparkling, princes came as private individuals to such gatherings (Madame Geoffrin's biweekly dinners, for example) to sup to the conversation of habitual guests like Boucher, Marmontel, d'Alembert, Marivaux, D'Holbach, Helvétius, and Grimm, or of foreign visitors, perhaps Galiani, Hume, or Gibbon. In Vienna, Emperor Joseph II delighted in visiting the salons of the intelligentsia. Though its

---

43 An unparalleled international success accrued to a sentimental *opera buffa* based upon Richardson's novel *Pamela*: Nicolò Piccinni's *La Cecchina, ossia La buona figliuola* (1760), its libretto by Goldoni. The opera's power to sell tickets recoiled upon the young Mozart: the premiere in Vienna of his *La finta semplice* fell victim to fears of box-office failure, the impresario putting the work aside and in its place giving *La Cecchina* and its sequel, *La buona figliuola maritata* (1761).

patronage was to remain sporadic when compared to that of the nobles in their halcyon days, the bourgeoisie would become the leading inspirer and consumer of the arts and little by little take hold of the machinery of culture.

By the time of Mozart's birth, Riche de la Pouplinière, a bourgeois financial magnate and a patron and pupil of Rameau, already possessed a private theater in his Parisian mansion and a musical establishment that would rival the Prince de Conti's: at various times Rameau, Gossec, and Johann Stamitz formed part of La Pouplinière's musical household. The Mozarts came to know as dedicated, if less glittering, a benefactor: Karl Ernst, Freiherr von Bagge,[44] an eccentric Baltic German who, having augmented a depleted fortune by marrying a banker's daughter, indulged his passion for music. Settling in Paris in 1750, he put a small group of instrumentalists on salary and reinforced them, so Leopold Mozart recalled, with "visiting virtuosos, many of whom came to him for advice," and in order to "make further acquaintances in a foreign city." Leopold and Wolfgang had the opportunity to meet the newcomers as well as the Parisian musicians who flocked to Bagge's, "some," Leopold observed, "to play through their latest compositions, others to hear music from other countries . . . and the recently arrived virtuosos from abroad."

The Mozarts acknowledged an obligation to this salon supported by a Swiss financier's fortune and in Vienna attended performances likewise given by a connoisseur who used his wife's means to indulge his musical pleasures: Dr. Franz Anton Mesmer. For a stage in his mansion, he ordered the adolescent Mozart to compose *Bastien und Bastienne.*

Bourgeois patrons did not deny themselves the satisfaction of the fine arts: in London, Richard Mead, like Mesmer a physician, commissioned paintings for his imposing collection, to which he admitted students; in France, Pierre Crozat, born of a commercial family, emerged as a major collector; and Pompadour, openly called a grisette by her enemies among the aristocracy, encouraged the arts, amassing impressive treasures. (At Versailles she built a special hôtel to house the overflow.) Indeed, the accession of this bourgeois charmer born with the name Poisson (fish) to the powerful position of *maîtresse en titre*—to say nothing of her keeping hold upon it—in itself constituted a revolution in decorum. There had devel-

---

44 Freiherr did not of necessity indicate an aristocrat. Many bourgeois Germans acquired this subordinate rank of nobility: Mozart's sister, for example, through marriage. She ended her days grandly signing her letters "*Maria Anna Freyfrau von Berchtold zu Sonnenburg Raths und Pflegers-wittbe* [sic] *v. St. Gilgin*" (see p. 640).

oped a delight in cultural leveling, in a mixing of social strata.[45] Leporello's catalogue aria in Mozart's *Don Giovanni* saucily argued this phenomenon epitomized for the courts of Europe by Stanislaus Poniatowski's[46] message to Madame Geoffrin upon his ascending the Polish throne: "Mama, your son is King." The spirit of the times cried out for *opera buffa*.

---

45 Maria Theresa knew how to draw profit from this state of affairs: her many domestic pieties made the Empress appear to her subjects as a paragon of bourgeois patterns, a perception she encouraged.

46 Mozart played for Poniatowski in Vienna during either 1762 or 1768.

CHAPTER XI

The Grand Tour Continues:
Brussels and Paris

OPERA BUFFA MIGHT well describe the atmosphere at the court of Brussels, where Emperor Francis's brother, Prince Charles Alexander of Lothringen, ruled as governor-general of the Austrian Lowlands, western outpost of the Holy Roman Empire. Maria Theresa had long doted on this good-natured incompetent who had married her sister, her beloved Marianne. A widower since 1744,[1] he passed much of his time hunting, gorging, and swilling. His raucous laughter echoed through his palace (the rebuilt Hôtel de Nassau), which he crammed with paintings, tapestries, and Chinese porcelains. He devoted his sober hours to collecting (he also tried his hand at the brushes and worked in lacquer) and to music. Thus the Mozarts drew near his capital on 4 October 1763 with reasonable hopes. By way of Liège, Tirlemont, and Leuven (Louvain), they had made their way from Aachen—and their encounter with Amalia of Prussia—crossing Limburg and entering Brabant, but not without obstacles: the iron hoops on the carriage wheels had burst, and there had been stops for repairs.

---

1 The dying Marianne had been under the care of the Dutch physician Gerhard van Swieten. Having heard of his extraordinary efforts to save her sister, Maria Theresa summoned him to Vienna in 1745 to serve as her personal doctor. His son, Gottfried, accompanied his father and became one of Mozart's important patrons.

Charles indicated a desire to hear the children play "within a few days." But weeks passed without word from him, and Leopold began to champ the bit: under command to await the Prince's pleasure, he had to idle and watch his bill at the Hôtel d'Angleterre mount. Even so, gifts from the nobility kept him in good humor: "We might soon set up a shop for snuffboxes, needle cases, and such things." Wolfgang filled time with work on a sonata for harpsichord and violin (K. 6) begun in Salzburg; and they discovered much to see, Leopold revealing a growing interest in the fine arts.

In St. Peter's church at Leuven, a Last Supper by Dirk Bouts had rooted him to the spot; in Brussels he admired works by the Van Eycks, Rubens, Honthorst, Jordaens, Brill, Mostaert, Mierevelt, Van Dyck, Spranger, and Rembrandt. He breathed in that special atmosphere of Flemish churches, with their altars of black and white marble, their fittings of polished brass. The commercial activity of Brussels amazed the Mozarts. Coming from the landlocked heart of the Empire, they enjoyed the sight of oceangoing ships sailing through the center of the city, gliding through the paved banks of the canal that led to Antwerp and the sea. (Such ships had to fly the Dutch flag; see XIII, n. 5.)

Excellent tourists, they entered into the spirit of whatever came their way. On the road in Limburg and Brabant they had eaten before open fires at rustic inns, absorbed to watch a meal of meat and turnips being ladled from a cauldron suspended above the hearth; laughing as a troop of pigs invaded the dining room to waddle and grunt beneath the tables (Leopold imagined himself part of a peasant genre scene); staring inquisitively at the ubiquitous wooden shoes or at the women in hooded cloaks.

If Leopold found the locals and travelers a graceless but interesting lot, the proprietors of Limburg's and Brabant's public houses had stirred his ire with their penchant for presenting the foreigner with an inflated bill. At such moments of linguistic trial, the Mozarts had to adjust to the fact that their native tongue no longer sufficed: they were in an outland of the Reich and about to leave its sheltering arms. But at least German ruled at the court of Brussels, where, on 7 November, at "a big concert" in the presence of Prince Charles, Leopold realized "a rich booty of fat thalers and louis d'or." Eight days later he packed his family into the battered Pressburg coach and set out for Paris via Mons, birthplace of Orlando di Lasso.

2

THE FELLIES, AXLES, and springing of the carriage were light. Leopold's praise of the highway through Picardy notwithstanding—"paved like the streets of a city and planted on either side with trees like a park"—the stone cobbles took their toll, and all the more when the drivers lashed the horses to the gallop. The exhausted teams of men and animals changed every two hours at closely spaced stages. (Leopold had availed himself of the express relays to Paris.) Accustomed to the methodical conformity of German coachmen and postilions, he found diversion in the ever-so-individual outfits of the succeeding teams of personnel climbing aboard: "Sometimes I took them for a pair of peddlers; sometimes for a pair of rogues from a farce; sometimes for a pair of Italian donkey drivers; sometimes for a pair of vagabond hairdressers or dismissed, jobless lackeys or even valets; sometimes for a pair of discharged sergeant majors." The battle of Rossbach flitted across his mind as the tempo of the wheels surged: he felt like a soldier in the "Army of Empire pursued by two divisions of Prussians." As the coach whirred through L'Île-de-France, the landscape opened to views of châteaux set within parks. On 18 November 1763 the Mozarts beheld Paris lying before them, a sight astounding to central European eyes: a great capital without ramparts and fortified gates.

Maria Anna Rosalia Joly ("Sallerl" to the Mozarts), Nannerl's friend and a servant in the household of Count Georg Anton Felix Arco, High Treasurer of Salzburg, had arranged that they put up at the Hôtel de Beauvais on the Rue St. Antoine (today, 68 Rue François Miron), the town house of his son-in-law, Count van Eyck. His Countess, Maria Anna Felicitas, a Salzburg acquaintance of the Mozarts, placed at their disposal a comfortable room containing her own two-manual harpsichord. Leopold observed that "all, even the tiniest corners [of the Hôtel de Beauvais] serve some purpose," an allusion to his surprising discovery: the Count, Maximilian Emanuel Franz, Bavarian Minister to Paris, ran a gambling casino in this residence shielded by extraterritoriality.

Leopold accepted the situation with unwonted tolerance as just one more example of modish eccentricity. At least his own house continued in order—his children spirited, in good health, and ready to conquer Versailles. But news arrived compelling a delay: the French court had put on black; Joseph of Austria's wife, Isabella of Parma (the violinist who had performed for Leopold at Schönbrunn) had succumbed to smallpox in Vienna on 23 November, and in tribute to this grandchild of King Louis,[2] Versailles suspended entertainments.

---

2 Isabella descended from the Bourbons through both her father (Infante Philip, second son of Philip V of Spain and thus a great-grandson of Louis XIV) and her mother (Louise Elizabeth, Louis XV's eldest daughter, hence a great-great-granddaughter of Louis XIV). The Treaty of Aix had awarded the duchy of Parma to Infante Philip, making it into a Bourbon bastion between the Habsburg presence in Lombardy and in Tuscany.

The period of mourning over, the Mozarts, who had obtained a recommendation from Louis de Noailles, Duke d'Ayen (see p. 441), drove to Versailles. They lodged at the Au Cormier from 24 December to 8 January. If newcomers made a strong impression at Madame de Pompadour's receptions, they stood fair for success at court. Wolfgang's petulance at their first meeting (see p. xix) did not prejudice her, for the Mozarts visited not only her apartments in the palace—"a paradise," Leopold declared—but her private Parisian mansion (today, the Élysée). There, in a room dominated by Boucher's portrait of her (1758) and Charles André Van Loo and Charles Parrocel's of the King (1724), the children played on a harpsichord "all in gold leaf and lacquered and painted with utmost art."

A less enchanting atmosphere pervaded the chambers of the Queen; her daughters (*Mesdames*); her awkward son, the Dauphin; and his virtuous Dauphine, Maria Josepha of Saxony. Above all scandal, they made up what most considered the dullest circle at court. Leopold, who played all parties, standing ever ready to switch the weights on his scale, saw his fortune at Versailles as more easily decided by this stolid element than by Pompadour and her partisans: he inclined toward retracing the pattern proved so effective in Vienna— a homey success within the royal family and an ensuing avalanche of invitations from those eager to flatter by imitation. Hence the dedications of Wolfgang's two sets of keyboard sonatas with optional violin (1764), one to the Queen's daughter Madame Victoire, the other to the Dauphine's lady-in-waiting and d'Ayen's daughter, the Countess de Tessé. Although the Hofburg boasted a more informed devotion to music than that of Versailles, the Bourbons limping behind the Habsburgs in such matters, Leopold did feel emboldened to hope for some kind of patronage from the Queen of France and her children, and with it wider advantage.

Queen Marie (*la bonne reine*), having long played a minor role in Louis XV's life, which revolved about hunting and extramarital sex, had withdrawn into the consolations of Catholicism, gluttony, and music. She occupied herself with good works and the Jesuits, was rumored to have washed down at a single sitting one hundred eighty oysters with two quarts of beer, and, according to Hénault, the superintendent of her household, played the guitar and harpsichord with enthusiasm, deaf to the wrong notes she struck. Hers was not a refined musical taste. However, this woman, by nature dispassionate, had opposed her husband on a musical matter and, in consequence, found her name linked to a barbed aesthetic controversy: to her astonishment, she had come to be a symbolic, almost doctrinal presence in the musical life of Paris.

3

LITTLE MORE THAN a decade before Mozart's visit, the performances of Bambini's itinerant *opera-buffa* company, the so-called *Bouffons*, had led Paris into a celebrated wrangle. The Queen, as did Enlightened society, preferred the visitors' informal Italian offerings to the stately *tragédies* of Lully and his school, defended by the King and Pompadour in the name of national tradition. Opposing factions, the King's Corner and the Queen's sprang up—advocates of Bambini assembled in the pit near the Queen's box, the Lullians near the King's[3]—and engaged in the War (*Querelle*) of the *Bouffons*, fought with pamphlets, many of them abusive.

The King's Corner countered Pergolesi with Rameau, hailing as Lully's heir the crotchety old master, who, in fact, received no less praise from the opposition. (It viewed him in a revolutionary light: the philosophes strove not to alienate France's greatest living composer.[4]) The Queen's, the innovative faction, had first joined issue and proved more effective than its conservative and, from the beginning, defensive antagonists. Even so, the paper quarrel resolved nothing: in spirit it still raged in full fray when, early in 1764, Leopold Mozart wrote from Paris of the "perpetual war between Italian and French music," a continuing manifestation of that larger struggle between champions of the new emotionalism in art and those holding to the past—in effect, yet another fomentation inspired by Enlightened thought. In the course of this "war," an astonishing irony continued to mock the fitness of things: pious Queen Marie Leczinska, friend of the Jesuits, had entered musical history as the nominal head of a vituperative polemic instigated by the enemies of autocracy and clericalism.

Her favorite child, the prudish Dauphin, had many of his mother's predilections—he, too, developed a formidable embonpoint; with acrimony Louis XV asked: "Have I not a well-nourished son?"—and, like his German wife, took inordinate pleasure in music. (The court at Dresden had celebrated their union with Hasse's revised version of his *Semiramide riconosciuta*.) "Nothing interested them," complained the Duke de Luynes, "not hunting, not cards, not plays, only music," a taste shared by *Mesdames*. They showed skill at the violin, viola da gamba, and clavier (Madame Adelaide[5] even

---

3 The *Bouffons* performed in Paris from 1 August 1752 to 7 March 1754, holding forth, sometimes three times a week, at the Opéra itself, their short pieces functioning as curtain-raisers or postludes to regular French repertory works. "The comparison between the two idioms, which could be heard on the same day and in the same theater," Rousseau observed, "opened French ears."

4 Not an impudent d'Alembert: he announced that Rameau gave the French not the best music within his power to write but, rather, the best within their's to comprehend.

5 K. Anh. 294a/C14.05, once accounted a violin concerto Mozart dedicated to Princess Adelaide, has long been revealed a hoax.

played the horn), and all of them delighted in their harp lessons from a dashing young watchmaker making his way at court: handsome and roguish Pierre Augustin Caron, better known as Caron de Beaumarchais. He had first attracted attention by inventing a new escapement for watches and soon devised an improved pedal mechanism for the harp. Mozart's visit found the future creator of *The Marriage of Figaro* in Madrid;[6] thus he failed to meet the musical genius with whom his name would be joined.

4

THE ROYAL ACCOUNTS of mid-February 1764 list twelve hundred livres paid to "Sieur Mozart for his children's musical performances in the presence of the royal family." In addition, to much acclaim, Wolfgang had played the organ for an hour and a half in the royal chapel. Behind such recognition stood neither the Queen and her children, nor Pompadour; but, quite out of reckoning, a German matron and one of her German acquaintances active in the affairs of Versailles.

Leopold had arrived armed with letters of introduction, the most helpful of which came from the wife of a Frankfurt merchant (probably Johann Georg Wahler). She had recommended the Mozarts to Friedrich Melchior Grimm, a Bavarian man of letters become secretary to Louis Philippe, Duke d'Orléans, grandson of the once regent. A master manipulator with exceptional connections, Grimm stepped forward as the Mozarts' champion and indicated the smoothest avenues leading to court. With the help of Orléans's son, the Duke de Chartres, Leopold secured permission to give public concerts. (Since they infringed upon the performing privileges of established musical organizations, such events had to be set in motion with delicacy.) Grimm took over the sale of tickets and even arranged for the wax to light the hall. He coached Leopold in court etiquette, in particular those turns of phrase current at the palace, and put into proper sycophantic style the elaborate dedications in French prefaced to Wolfgang's first two sets of sonatas, even, it cannot be doubted, choosing the dedicatees. Grimm boldly took the reins, making the Mozarts' concerns his own. With a flourish he had described to readers of his fortnightly newsletter, the *Correspondance Littéraire, Philosophique et Critique*, Wolfgang's success in Paris.

"A kapellmeister from Salzburg named Mozart has just arrived here with two of the most delightful children in the world." After praising the

---

6 Beaumarchais maintained that he made this journey in order to confront José Clavijo, who had jilted his sister. Goethe's drama *Clavigo* rests upon this incident, which he drew from Beaumarchais's memoirs.

"daughter, aged eleven," who "plays the harpsichord brilliantly," Grimm proclaimed "a phenomenon": the "incredible" talent of her brother, "who will be seven next February." (Leopold had dropped a year from the age of both.) Grimm's seeming hyperbole rested upon an occurrence that, he asserted, had quite unhinged him.

In his presence a woman had asked the boy "if he would accompany by ear . . . an Italian cavatina she knew by heart. She proceeded to sing," and he "tried a bass that proved to be not completely correct because it is impossible to prepare in advance the accompaniment of a song one does not know. However, when the air came to an end, he entreated the woman to begin again, and with this repetition not only played the entire melody with his right hand but with the left added the correct bass. Thereafter, ten times in succession he pressed her to begin again and with each recapitulation changed the character of the accompaniment. He would have gone on twenty times had he not been deterred." Witnessing this exhibition, the agnostic Grimm claimed to understand why "St. Paul had fallen into a trance after his strange vision."

The son of a Regensburg pastor, Grimm had imposed a stylish Gallic surface upon his somber German core. A student at Leipzig of both Johann August Ernesti and Gottsched, this gifted linguist and ruthless climber had made his way in Paris and from his base in the Orléans household cemented relationships with the prominent. An international reputation came to him with his editorship of the *Correspondance*. Founded by the Abbé Raynal and sponsored by Princess Dorothea von Sachsen-Gotha, this journal of literature, art, and Enlightened chitchat had as subscribers a tiny but most select group—some twenty crowned heads, princes, and overlords of Europe, who looked upon it as essential to their efforts to keep up with things Parisian. (Appearing in handwritten copies made by scribes across the border in Zweibrücken in order to elude French censors, it at times traveled in diplomatic pouches; the panegyric to Wolfgang must have rested upon more than one princely breakfast tray.) The German Grimm became a symbol of Paris's undimmed power not only to draw to itself talent from every quarter, but also to prescribe standards from afar.

A diplomat and a courtier, Grimm strove to ally himself with success.[7] In a moment of exasperation, Diderot, who wrote book and art reviews for the *Correspondance*, observed that this exploitative Bavarian had the soul of a Hyrcanian tiger: "They are said to be the worst of all. . . ." Half-

[7] He took as mistress the wealthy and brilliant Louise d'Épinay, famed for having—the year of Mozart's birth—installed Jean Jacques Rousseau in the Hermitage, a cottage on her estate near Montmorency. During Mozart's third stay in Paris (1778), she would prove a sympathetic friend.

humorous and random, Diderot's observation nonetheless helps explain the poisonous relationship that later developed between Grimm and an older Mozart whose career appeared to have run aground. Yet, if Grimm would judge the Mozart of 1778 as doomed to miss the mark, it must have seemed a wise speculation in 1763 to shine as sponsor of an enchanting young countryman full of promise. Throughout his career, the scent of the Machiavellian hung about Grimm.

Not only he, but another German, Baron Paul Heinrich Dietrich d'Holbach, figured among the *beaux esprits* of France. His library, prints, paintings, natural-history specimens, and, above all, superb kitchen made his house a gathering place for men of letters. (Ferdinando Galiani dubbed him "*maître d'hôtel de la philosophie.*") Such a salon served to forge strong links between German and French intellectuals; the Grimm-d'Holbach circle, the Parisian fellowship Leopold Mozart came to know best, reciprocated and intensified his sympathies and confirmed his judgments upon the French: exhaling an acid irreverence peculiar to Paris, above all concerning French music, it evinced a preoccupation with musical theory echoing his own. (The subject occupied a disproportionately large space in the *Encyclopédie.*) Indeed, from the enthusiasm both shared for music grew the turbulent friendship of those *frères ennemis,* Rousseau and Diderot, beside whom had stood the Germans, d'Holbach and Grimm, at the ready with their paper cannonballs, eager to do battle in the War of the *Bouffons.*

There Grimm had shone at his most brilliant. If d'Holbach had taken to the field first with a satire on Parisian singers and instrumentalists, Grimm produced that annihilating volley entitled *The Little Prophet of Böhmischbroda* (January 1753).[8] In this delicious satire, a Bohemian violinist, transported by magic to the Opéra, experiences its artistic insufficiencies. Grimm of Regensburg and d'Holbach of Edesheim played powerful roles in weakening the foundations of Louis XIV's proud academy, in shaking Lully from his pedestal.

In the close league of Gallic and Germanic philosophes, Diderot and Grimm demonstrated uncommon personal and aesthetic affinities. (Sainte-Beuve would look upon the first as "the most German of Frenchmen," the second as "the most French of the Germans.") Voltaire demanded: "What is this Bohemian [Grimm's little prophet] thinking about, to have more wit than we?" (Such comments delighted the Germans; Leopold Mozart's copy of Grimm's polemic would pass from hand to hand in his Salzburg

---

8 D'Holbach called his attack (November 1752) "*Lettre à une dame d'un certain âge sur l'état présent de l'opéra en Arcadie; aux dépens de l'académie royale de musique.*" Grimm's piece constituted a riposte to *Titon et l'Aurore,* Jean-Joseph Cassanéa de Mondonville's *tragédie lyrique* produced on 9 January 1753.

circle.) Diderot, though he did attempt a temperate examination of the fracas, had his fun by proposing a devastating motto for the curtain of the Opéra: "*Hic Marsyas Apollinem*" (Here Marsyas [flays] Apollo). No less crushing had been Rousseau's observation (*Lettre sur la musique française*, 1753) that "the French do not and cannot have music, and, if they ever do, it will be a pity."[9]

Contrary to such obloquy, Paris possessed musical resources much envied: the Opéra, a formidable institution despite its detractors; the public instrumental performances of the Concert spirituel[10] at the Tuileries (the Concert des Amateurs at the Hôtel de Soubise would not begin until 1769); the musicales of private orchestras in the mansions of the nobility and the high bourgeoisie; and a number of enterprising music publishers. It was because so many of these exceptional amenities flourished under the aegis of the privileged that the Germans and their French allies enjoyed twitting official Paris about a stunted, dilettantish musical life further arrested by swagger and chauvinism, censure that in the larger sense went counter to fact: for years Parisian institutions had opened their doors to German musicians, whose local advocates, in fact, looked upon them as leading the way.

5

"IT IS A pity that people in this country know so little about music," Grimm wrote toward the end of his puff on the Mozarts in the *Correspondance*. Eager to turn their visit into ammunition for the war against French music, he recounted Wolfgang's triumphs in Vienna, Munich, and Schwetzingen, implying that the child could hardly fare as well in France, a land lacking Germany's musical taste. Here was hauteur—and satisfaction, too.

The ascendancy of Grimm and d'Holbach in those aesthetic deliberations so dear to Paris paralleled the growing authority of German composers and performers in its concert rooms. As early as 1737 Telemann had arrived in Paris and enjoyed success at the Concert spirituel, and during 1751, within the decade of Stamitz's appearance at the coronation of Charles VII, the Concert spirituel performed one of his symphonies; in

---

9 On the other hand, he avowed having written his *Devin* to demonstrate the possibility of French opera in the vein of *opera buffa*.

10 Church precept at first restricted this society, founded in 1725 by Anne Danican Philidor, to performances on those feast days when the doors of the Opéra had to remain closed: hence the perplexing name of an organization in time devoted to playing instrumental and vocal music of all genres, except compositions with French words; on the last point, the Opéra remained jealous of its privilege.

1754 he took a year's leave from Mannheim to visit Paris, and his work again found a receptive audience. (Many believed the career of this violinist, born in Deutschbrod in Bohemia [Böhmen], to have inspired Grimm to create the fiddler hero of *The Little Prophet of Böhmischbroda*.) Five years later, a "Symphonie-concert" by Wagenseil appeared on a program of the Concert spirituel.

As by slow degrees the issue of French versus Italian music exhausted itself in literary combat, the German musician as visitor or resident established himself in Paris as a model.[11] With Emanuel Bach, Hasse, Stamitz, and Joseph Haydn in mind, Nicolas Étienne Framéry could predict (1770) Germany's musical predominance. It was to assert itself powerfully with the arrival in Paris of Gluck bearing his reform opera.

Though in his *Armide* (1777) he would humor the Parisians by doing obeisance before Quinault and Lully's treatment of the myth—by using much of the old text and a bit of the music—Parisian accretions notwithstanding, Gluck's Italian heritage remained an essential of his vocabulary; he produced, as Marmontel observed, "composite" works "implying, even in the face of their prevailing German taste, a reconciliation of the outstanding characteristics of French and Italian opera." Accommodation, absorption, in particular the smoothing out of antithesis, identified Germany's new and cosmopolitan musical art. Anton Raphael Mengs, born in Aussig, resident of Rome, and apotheosis of the eighteenth-century international painter—a Gluck of the palette—urged a style combining Raphael's line, Correggio's chiaroscuro, and Titian's color. In the same spirit, Quantz, flute master of Frederick the Great, observed that, by combining the musical styles of various nations, "a mixed style obtained . . . one that might be called the German style." It had become a particularly German gift to see the possibilities of creating a strong metal through an amalgam. Had not Handel and Sebastian Bach made their own syntheses of Italian, French, and German elements?

Mozart (like Goethe) would raise German eclecticism to commanding heights: he blended the Baroque and Rococo with Storm and Stress (that tumultuous German movement doting on eccentricity, surprise, and exaggerated individualism; see pp. 320–27) and partook of Italian songfulness, Gallic wit, and German melancholy. At the time of his first journey to France, a number of German composers living in Paris had begun to

---

11 During his frequent visits to Paris, Duke Christian IV of Zweibrücken brought along musicians from his own household and from Mannheim, among them Johann Baptist Wendling in 1762 and Christian Cannabich two years later. When Mozart returned to Paris in 1778, he found a group of German musicians in the service of the Duke d'Ayen.

anticipate this kind of fusion, albeit in a modest way, in their sonatas and concertos. However, these musical genres, though popular, remained less than intellectually fashionable: philosophes, in particular d'Alembert and Cahusac, disparaged them.

Ruled by their literary orientation, they esteemed sung music, in particular Italian opera, as the highest form of an art whose task, so they believed, was to imitate nature, "to paint the sentiments." Though the tonal investiture of a text seemed to them the most efficient way of accomplishing this end, they did value music without words if it represented natural phenomena (storms, earthquakes, and the like) or one of the affections (gaiety, melancholy, sanguineness, for example), the sounds summoning up in the listener's mind either particular images or states of mind. "Music that does not paint is but noise," d'Alembert insisted, insinuating that natural phenomena and human sentiments had musical equivalents.

Not all philosophes had such narrow musical horizons. Diderot, for example, could find few rewards in this predilection for programmatic allusion—most of all he decried the *pittoresque* and *caractéristique* (which he adored in painting)—and, though it might seem odd that a man who rejected the tradition of Lully as too learned should turn toward the Germans, Diderot, in fact, welcomed their erudition and, yet more, their surges of emotional audacity and pain—their *Empfindsamkeit.* Encouraging his daughter, Angélique, to take up the clavier, he selected for her a repertory weighted toward the Germans. It included works of Emanuel Bach[12] (perhaps even some by his father) and the two leading masters of the German school of Paris: Johann Gottfried Eckard from Augsburg and the Silesian Johann Schobert, in the employ of the Prince de Conti. For the most part self-taught through studies of Emanuel Bach, whose intense style he adopted, Eckard gave Angélique music lessons. Diderot looked upon him as "divine, marvelous, sublime" and spent the three hours of one of his clavier concerts "no longer aware of the world's existence, the only real thing" being "those marvelous sounds and I."[13]

In condemning the "fad" of absolute music (under "*Sonate*" in the *Encyclopédie*), Rousseau underscored the breadth of its cultivation in the Paris

---

12 Returning from the court of Catherine the Great, Diderot passed through Hamburg; pausing there to buy music for Angélique, he solicited from Emanuel Bach a promise to forward to Paris some of his unpublished sonatas.

13 The Augsburg instrument builder Johann Andreas Stein had taken Eckard to Paris in 1758. Educated as a painter and etcher, he remained undecided as to his true calling until his highly praised Parisian appearances as a pianist decided the issue. No doubt Stein provided Leopold Mozart with an introduction to him. As observed above (see p. 126), his preferring the piano to the harpsichord set Mozart an example.

of his time. Instrumental music had a distinguished tradition in France,[14] and the public continued to take refreshment in the Concert spirituel and to give German virtuosos and German music ready hearing. (However, Jean-Baptiste-Antoine Suard's memory deceived him when he recalled having heard Mozart "play the harpsichord at the Concert spirituel.") Furthermore, Eckard and Schobert (and Leontzi Honauer from Strassburg), so Leopold reported, "were taking the lead [from the Parisians] in the publication of clavier compositions." They presented copies of them to the Mozarts. For long stretches these sonatas do not reach beyond the commonplace, but their imaginative sections, in particular Eckard's developments, impressed Wolfgang. Even so, his Victoire and Tessé sonatas reveal less Eckard's and Schobert's influence than Wagenseil's,[15] although Mozart's first attempts three years later to confront the keyboard concerto would be much indebted to the German Parisians.[16]

Leopold thought Eckard "honest," hardly his opinion of Schobert: ". . . not at all the man his reputation sets forth: he flatters to one's face and is utterly false." He envied Nannerl, Leopold maintained: "My little girl plays the most difficult pieces . . . with unbelievable precision and in such a manner that the *mean Schobert* cannot conceal *his jealousy*. . . ." Leopold's propensity to rail at imagined enemies had reappeared. Perhaps Schobert had not praised her sufficiently to satisfy a protective father, who then put up his back; or he might have taken this bizarre stand in order further to ingratiate himself with Grimm, who preferred Eckard to Schobert, rivals at the keyboard and as composers. Whatever the case, Nannerl could hardly have stirred up the envy of so famous a virtuoso.

His compositions, at bottom facile and *galant*—the quality that enabled him to keep hold of his fashionable salon audience—also explored an *empfindsam* idiom that attempted to realize on the keyboard those orches-

---

14 Two notable masters of French instrumental music, Jean-Marie Leclair and Rameau, had reached their final months during this first of Mozart's Parisian *séjours*. Still active during his second stay (1766) would be Louis-Gabriel Guillemain (1705–1770) and Jean-Joseph Cassanéa de Mondonville (1711–1772). The symphonies of the former and sonatas of the latter helped prepare the achievements of the Walloon and then French symphonist François-Joseph Gossec (1734–1829), who, in turn, became indebted to German models: the Mannheimers and Haydn. Gossec would meet Mozart in 1778, during his final Parisian stay.

15 With their infusion of infantile stuff taken from Wolfgang's pieces in Nannerl's exercise book, these concoctions remain difficult to assess, all the more because they betray Leopold's hand (see p. 195).

16 In these earliest of his keyboard concertos (K. 37, 39, 40, 41) he adapted sonata movements not only by Eckard, Schobert, and Honauer but also by the Pomeranian Hermann Friedrich Raupach, another of the German school of Paris, and Emanuel Bach. In 1771 Mozart would create three amiable clavier concertos (K. 107/21b) out of keyboard sonatas by Christian Bach.

tral devices of dramatic contrast favored by the Mannheimers. Burney wrote of Schobert's "light and shade, alternate agitation and tranquility, imitating the effects of an orchestra," an achievement all the more remarkable in that he did not share Eckard's preference for the piano but remained faithful to the harpsichord. However, like Eckard, the element of wild fantasy in his works—"spirit and fire, especially in the allegros"—marked him as an early exponent of Storm and Stress, his reputation resting upon driving performances of astonishing technical address.

Surrounded in Paris by these gifted Germans, Leopold lost perspective. Echoing with sententiousness Grimm's musical polemics, he anticipated that "within ten to fifteen years the present French taste . . . will have thoroughly died out."[17] (Jean-Pierre Legrand, organist at St. Germain-des-Prés, has "completely abandoned his [former] idiom"; "his sonatas are [now] in our style," Leopold trumpeted.) But the thin-textured works of even the best German composers of Paris provided weak nourishment for so proud an expectation: to be sure, during the reign of Louis XV, the strict national character of French art did erode; that these Germans played a part in this cultural phenomenon diversifying the musical taste of Europe's mightiest metropolis lent them, in their own and their countrymen's eyes, a prominence hardly commensurate to their modest authority and accomplishment: whatever historical position Eckard and Schobert occupy today derives at most points from their encounters with a visiting eight-year-old.[18]

Royalty, too, gave him music from its own pen: Louise-Marie-Thérèse d'Orléans, daughter of the Duke d'Orléans (she would become Duchess de Bourbon), "took the liberty" of dedicating and presenting to him her rondeau for clavier. Her brother, the Duke de Chartres (later, the regicide Philippe Égalité), twice bore father and son company in calls upon this princess, then resident in a cloister on the Rue de Charonne. As in Vienna, the great houses opened to the Salzburgers: they paid their respects to the Duke d'Ayen at St. Germain, and the Prince de Conti summoned them to the Hôtel du Temple.

Louis François de Bourbon, Prince de Conti has a secure place among France's princes of the blood who, during the War of the Austrian Succession, distinguished themselves by their remarkable military incompetence. Versailles forced him to resign his command when, in an ill-contrived

---

17 For his part, the German theorist Marpurg expressed respect for the French tradition, placing Jean-Marie Leclair (*l'aîné*) in the company of Handel, Telemann, the Grauns, and the Bachs.
18 Eckard lived into the Napoleonic era, but Schobert, his wife, and one of their children died in 1767 after making a meal of toadstools mistaken for mushrooms.

strategem, he attempted to undermine the position of Maurice de Saxe. With the outbreak of the Seven Years' War, Conti found his request to lead the Army of the Rhine rejected, a clear signal that he renounce soldiering.[19] However, he did have a turn for other things: if his true talents did not reveal themselves in war, they did in society.

During the sixties, his orchestra, along with guest artists like the singers Marie Fel and Pierre de Jelyotte, appeared in the Temple's famed *salon des quatre glaces.* Only the expense of maintaining some dozen or so dancers from the Opéra's *corps de ballet* finally compelled the Prince to dispense with his musical establishment, a less basic need. But this sacrifice would not be made until the seventies. In November or December of 1763, Leopold noted in his journal: "Prince Conti at the Temple." Wolfgang became a familiar in the lofty salon, with its green walls, rose hangings, white woodwork touched with gold, and glittering mirrors and sconces—exquisite surroundings in which his patroness and Conti's mistress, the Countess de Tessé, did the honors. For certain Leopold was looking back with nostalgic appreciation upon the Temple and its high musical standards when, in later years, he advised his son to seek "a monthly salary from some prince in Paris."

In the spring of 1766, the Mozarts, having visited England and the Lowlands, would return to Paris and remain until early July. During this second stay, Michel Barthélemy Ollivier, Conti's *premier peintre,* executed an interior (now in the Louvre) depicting a musical party in the salon of the Temple: Wolfgang, a doll-like figure, sits at an elegant clavier, his tiny body lost in the flowered brocade of a *régence* chair too large for him; to his left, Jelyotte tunes his guitar;[20] the Prince, his back to the viewer, engages in conversation as guests help themselves to a lavishly bestowed buffet, a

---

19 Even so, Louis XV retained affection and high hopes for this favorite cousin. The idea of controlling Poland, weak and vulnerable, engrossed the King, whose tortuous secret diplomacy sought to capture its elective throne for France by purchasing it for Conti upon the death of Augustus the Weak. Louis never openly espoused the plan, for his family already included two icons of rival Polish factions: one, his daughter-in-law, the Dauphine, granddaughter of Augustus the Strong and daughter of Augustus the Weak, Saxon monarchs who, each in turn, had pulled Stanislaus Leczinski from the throne of Poland; and the other, Queen Marie, Stanislaus's daughter! The scheme to elevate Conti did not go beyond reason; driven by the winds of money and the gales of power, deputies to the Polish Diet made and unmade kings with practiced ease, selling their votes to the highest bidder. In this case, power had the better of the struggle: the presence of Russian troops in Poland rendered the King's and Conti's ambitions and bribes futile. With Frederick the Great's approval, Catherine of Russia in 1764 bestowed the Polish crown upon her former lover Stanislaus Poniatowski (see p. 159). Castoff King Stanislaus Leczinski had long before received the duchy of Lothringen as a lifelong palliative (see pp. 74–75).

20 Not only France's most famous *haute-contre* (high tenor), he had also been royal guitar-master.

so-called English tea; the concert seems about to begin, for some of the company have already settled themselves to await the first sounds. If the diminutive size of the figure representing Mozart limits its iconographic importance, the painting does evoke the refinement of an assembly chez Conti.[21]

6

PARIS OFFERED THE Mozarts not only the pleasures of rococo elegance but also the wear and tear of an often less than refined or even comfortable everyday life. Their struggle with French food on the whole concerned the difficulty of observing fast days in a Catholic city indifferent to the Church's prohibitions. "I only wish I had a dispensation, for, when all is said and done, I want to have a clear conscience," Leopold wrote home, adding that the indulgences he granted himself might one day raise obstacles to his canonization. Moreover, used to the abundance of Germany's fresh lake fish, he looked with "disgust" upon the "dead fish" to be had in Paris and started at the cost. Only wine seemed a good buy, and, though the Mozarts boiled the filthy cooking and drinking water pulled from the Seine and hawked in the streets, they all fought the traveler's traditional battle with diarrhea. The city the Mozarts visited must be distinguished from the Paris of today. Leopold's contemporary, the Neapolitan bon vivant Ferdinando Galiani, suffered no less from its "poisonous water" and lamented: ". . . no fruit, no cheese, no good seafood."[22]

In the middle of February 1764, Wolfgang suddenly came down with a high fever, a severe inflammation of the throat, and accumulations of phlegm so massive that he appeared to be in danger of choking. He remained in bed four days. Nannerl, too, fell ill, but less severely. "One must take all things as they come," Leopold reasoned, with his next breath lamenting some twelve louis d'or lost to canceled appearances. He besought the help of the Madonna of Maria Plain and the ivory Holy Child in Salzburg's Loreto church; his prayers answered, he requested the Hagenauers to express thanks with appropriate masses. He had taken fright: extreme fever awakened fears of smallpox. Yet he had rejected suggestions

---

21 Conti would have a further, if indirect, link to Mozart's career: a champion of Beaumarchais and aware that the playwright contemplated a sequel to his *Barber of Seville,* the Prince challenged him to put his ideas to paper; Conti's enthusiasm inspired the first draft of *The Marriage of Figaro.*

22 Be that as it may, he reveled in the intellectual, social, and artistic resources of the city (see pp. 277–78).

that Wolfgang be inoculated—a "general fashion" in Paris—leaving it to God to decide "whether He wishes to keep this wonder of nature in the world in which He has placed it or to take it to Himself."[23]

Early in March, the Mozarts' servant, Sebastian Winter, returned to the city of his birth, Donaueschingen, to become hairdresser to its Prince, Joseph Wenzeslaus von Fürstenberg. The parting must have wrenched Wolfgang: Nannerl's memoirs reveal his closeness to Sebastian, "our servant," who used his talent for drawing to make a map of the boy's fantasy Kingdom of *Rücken* (Back), labeling its cities, market towns, and villages from its young monarch's dictation. As he traveled from court to court, his lively imagination had created a domain of good and happy children over whom he ruled, and Sebastian had played an important part in the game. (They must have raced into one another's arms when the Mozarts visited Donaueschingen in 1766.[24]) Winter's place fell to an Alsatian, Jean Pierre Potivin, for whom Leopold, with ill humor, had to purchase new livery.

The Mozarts found Paris prodigal in new experiences. Most likely, Wolfgang accompanied his father to the Place de Grève (today the Place de l'Hôtel-de-Ville) to watch the public executions.[25] "Amateurs of the extreme penalty have something to see practically every day," observed Salzburg's as a rule compassionate Vice-Kapellmeister, who witnessed the dispatch of a chambermaid, a cook, and a coachman, "hanged in company, side by side" for embezzling their blind mistress of three thousand louis d'or.

It is difficult to imagine Leopold and his son callous to human suffering; yet, all levels of eighteenth-century society became educated to cruelty in acts of punishing: the poor jostled one another for a view of the tortures inflicted at public chastisements; the rich, lifting their opera glasses and nibbling bonbons, looked on from window seats. Not only the lure of

---

23 The year of Mozart's birth, the Genevese Dr. Théodore Tronchin had successfully inoculated the children of the Duke d'Orléans against smallpox. However, Leopold knew the procedure, albeit widespread by the sixties, to be not altogether safe. Confronted some years later with an epidemic of smallpox in Vienna, he would prove less willing to leave his son's fate to Heaven alone, though he sought safety not in immunization but in flight.

24 Twenty years later, on 30 September 1786, Mozart wrote him: "Dearest friend! — companion of my youth! Though, of course, I have been often enough in Rücken through these many years, yet I never had the pleasure of meeting you there. . . ." Nannerl could not recall the origin of the kingdom's name; the historian Michael Levey suggested that it might have had to do with the landscape seeming to unfold "backward" through the coach window.

25 The boy would see the gibbet in use during a visit to Lyon (1766), an experience recalled more than five years later in Milan, where he looked on at the hanging of "four rascals in the Cathedral square." He observed: "They hang them here as they do in Lyon."

brutality and sadism but sheer curiosity, too, as both Diderot and Voltaire observed, drew many to witness these agonies.[26] The barbaric inhumanity of the Place de Grève, whose mechanisms could make a single conviction into half a dozen deaths, rarely awakened compassion in the mob. (It did protest if it thought a sentence too severe in proportion to the crime.) Decent people, Voltaire remarked, had their coachmen drive quickly through the square—the half-rotten dead (or even the dying) might be left on the scaffold or wheel indefinitely—and, by attending the opera, sought to forget what they had seen.

Leopold observed that requital for crimes had to be exacted or no one would be safe. Acquainted with the mortifications and hardships of life, he took them in his stride. His letters show a man eager to learn from or take delight in whatever might afford instruction or amusement, his pen yielding a kaleidoscopic record of a unique Grand Tour: the colors change from bright to somber and then back again as he leaps from descriptions of snuffboxes, ribbons, armlets, and fichus to pungent observations on the French economy; from comments on the latest collars to a trenchant account of the army of cripples that made up a disquieting proportion of Paris's population: "You will not soon come upon a place filled with so many miserable and mutilated people. You can neither be in a church more than a moment nor walk more than a few streets without meeting the blind, the lame, the limping, some half-putrefied beggar . . . a host of such people from whom disgust makes me avert my eyes." Like Mrs. Piozzi, he jumps "from the ugly to the charming," from his repugnance in the presence of the wretched (whom he describes with insouciance) to a celebration of Pompadour's beauty.[27]

Horror and enchantment kept close company in Paris. Through stinking streets lined with the slime of decaying offal and foul drainage and

26 The clearheaded Christian Bach chastised his friend Carl Friedrich Abel when he arrived in tears, having watched the hanging (1777) of the English divine Dr. William Dodd, condemned for forgery. Bach remonstrated: "I cannot admire the man who shall take a front seat in the Tyburn boxes to behold a human being die like a dog in a string."

27 From 1784 to 1787, Hester Lynch Piozzi, the former Mrs. Thrale and friend of Dr. Johnson, kept a journal of her Grand Tour. Of Paris she wrote: "I will tell nothing that I did not *see*; and among the objects one would certainly avoid seeing if it were possible, is the deformity of the poor. — Such various modes of warping the human figure could hardly be observed in England by a surgeon in high practice, as meet me about this country incessantly. — I have seen them in the galleries and outer-courts even of the palace itself, and am glad to turn my eyes for relief on the Duke of Orléans's pictures; a glorious collection!" Though they came from very different cultural climates, Leopold and Mrs. Piozzi offered many observations of the same mind on European life.

crowded with the destitute and despairing,[28] rumbled coaches whose beauty amazed Leopold, many of them japanned, like harpsichords, with the glossy hard polish of vernis Martin. If he found "very few beautiful churches"—the gothic Notre Dame could hardly have pleased him—recompense abounded in the "large number of beautiful hôtels or palaces on whose interior decoration no expense has been spared, each of them containing extraordinary things: all in all everything a person can but ever imagine as necessary to the comfort of his body and delight of his senses."

In these mansions he beheld with awe an English creation combining elements of the flush toilet and the bidet: "On both sides are handles [*Wasserpippen*] that can be turned after the business has been done [*nach der Execution*]; one handle causes water to spurt downwards; the other sends the water—*which can also be warm*—spurting upwards. I don't know how to explain it to you more fully in polite and respectable language," he wrote Hagenauer; "you must imagine the rest or ask me in good time. These cabinets are, moreover, the most beautiful one might imagine, their walls and floors as a rule of tile in the Dutch manner; on various pedestals—lacquered or of white marble or even alabaster—rest chamber pots of the most exquisitely painted porcelain, gilded at the borders; on similar pedestals stand glasses of perfumed water and large porcelain pots filled with aromatic plants. Usually one finds a handsome sofa nearby—for a sudden fainting spell, I believe."

From England, too, had come the Parisian custom to carry silk parasols: a practical mechanism, observed Leopold, in the past astonished and delighted by the wild extravagance of English fashion. Now it became the turn of French mode with its "astounding follies" to titillate, the rage for heavy makeup proving ever so bewitching; he played the scandalized burgher: "Whether Parisian women are in truth beautiful, I cannot tell you," he wrote Frau Hagenauer, "for they are so unnaturally painted—like the dolls made in Berchtesgaden—that this horrid embellishment makes even a naturally comely woman unbearable to the eyes of an honest German." This "idiotic mode in all things" affected men's dress, too, Leopold

---

28 The caveat already entered concerning cuisine must be extended to include architecture: readers must guard against picturing the Paris Mozart visited in terms of its contemporary appearance or, indeed, of French building styles of the seventeen-sixties. At the time, many medieval quarters survived as filthy slums to be swept away only in the following century in the course of Baron Haussmann's drastic demolitions; in their wake arose those tree-lined boulevards and promenades flanked with monumental structures, whose extended, homogenous façades (crowned with high roofs of leaden green) flirted with a proud pomposity—an image that for most still identifies a capital Mozart did not know.

being struck, in particular, by sword bands "bound round and round with fine fur; a good idea, for the sword will not catch cold."

The murk beneath this transparent world of fashion, the ill health beneath the brilliant surface, did not escape his glance: he could discern few signs of recovery from the Seven Years' War, "for the French have determined to continue their external magnificence. As a result, only the tax collectors are rich, the nobles sink deep into debt, and most of the wealth ends in the pockets of about a hundred people—a few big bankers and *fermiers-généraux* [excisemen]."[29]

7

SUFFERING INSOMNIA, POOR digestion, congestion of the lungs, and shortness of breath—she had tuberculosis from earliest youth—Madame de Pompadour, like Leopold, beheld the deplorable state of France, its economic ruin wrought by the war she had encouraged: the defeats and misfortunes could scarcely be numbered. By spring only two matters seemed to engross Parisians: her declining health and an eclipse of the sun (disappointing to Leopold, for it fell on a rainy day, 1 April, "as dark as the usual drawing on of evening"). Favart paired the topics: "The sun is sick/ Pompadour, too." The Marquise would never emerge from the shadows: with courage she awaited death. How unfortunate that her long reign had reached its twilight when the Mozarts came to Versailles; had she lived, there might well have been place for them in the entourage of a remarkable woman Voltaire described as "one of us."

Early in the new year of 1764, Hopfgarten and Bose, at intervals the Mozarts' traveling companions, had said a final farewell before departing for Italy, whence they planned to push on to Vienna. Leopold advised breaking their journey in Salzburg, recommending the hospitality of the Hagenauers. He saw these departing Lutheran friends as "possessed of everything an honest man should have in this world."

During the spring, the Mozarts likewise thought of moving along. The proceeds from the first of Wolfgang's two public concerts (10 March and 9 April at the little theater of M. Felix near the Porte St. Honoré) exceeded expectations: Leopold took in over one hundred louis d'or and in fine spirits contemplated the best means of sending money back to

---

29 They paid Versailles fees representing prescribed revenues from assigned districts and, in turn, sent agents into them to wring whatever possible from the populace, the difference between the fixed and the collected monies being the profit or loss realized by such a farmer-general of enforced duties.

Salzburg. But interest in the prodigy had reached and then quickly passed its crest: despite the participation of Baron Bagge's orchestra (with generous heart put at the Mozarts' disposition) and of the celebrated virtuoso violinist Pierre Gaviniès (who refused a fee) along with the singer Clementine Picinelli, the April appearance attracted a thin crowd. Leopold could not have been surprised: the family's trunks were already packed.

Soon after their arrival in Paris, Louis Carrogis de Carmontelle, a gifted amateur artist in the Duke d'Orléan's circle, had, at Grimm's request, made several watercolors of the children and their father, one of which he had engraved by the Swiss-born Christian von Mechel.[30] Leopold described the charming scene, set in a gallery opening on a park: "Wolfgang plays the harpsichord; I stand behind his chair playing the violin,[31] while Nannerl leans one arm upon the harpsichord and with the other holds music, as if she were singing." (Carmontelle represented her as altogether subaltern.) Early in April, Mechel rushed to complete what would be the Mozarts' publicity portrait; their departure for England impended.

---

30 He worked in conjunction with his master, Jean Baptiste Delafosse, who signed the copperplate of the engraving. On 9 October 1766 the *Donnstags-Nachrichten* of Zurich advertised it: a "well-arranged representation . . . by the very same artist who made the drawing of the Calas family" (see p. 88). Early in 1765, while Jean Calas's widow and children still remained prisoners in the conciergerie, Caramontelle had made their portrait: Grimm then commissioned Delafosse to engrave it in the hope of selling copies for the family's benefit.

31 Did Leopold protest Carmontelle's representing him in a graceful but impracticable pose: playing the violin while standing with legs crossed, the very attitude he gave Grimm in the double portrait with Diderot?

CHAPTER XII

England

WITH THE SEVEN Years' War concluded, travelers once again crossed the Channel, restoring business, social, and artistic exchanges. John Russell, fourth Duke of Bedford, who had played a significant part in the peace negotiations in Paris, had yet to return home. At Versailles he and his son, Francis Russell, Marquis of Tavistock, both much taken with Wolfgang, encouraged the visit to England Leopold had long contemplated. Thanks to Grimm, the court fell in with the plans, recommending the Mozarts to its ambassador in England and arranging that they depart unencumbered, the Pressburg carriage to be stored with an officer of the Admiralty at Calais and part of their luggage with the Parisian banker Hummel. Leopold felt the need for a second servant and hired an Italian named Porta, who, it developed, did not lack traits of an adventurer. His immediately apparent talents combined a command of some kind of English with an ability to deal with those vociferous, roguish porters famed for intimidating the traveler as they snatched up baggage, hauled it off to a hotel, and then demanded exorbitant fees. "Whoever has too much money need only undertake a journey from Paris to London," Leopold counseled; "his purse will certainly be lightened."

At Calais the family first beheld, Nannerl recorded in her journal, "how the ocean ebbs and waxes." In a private boat Leopold hired for his party of six—he sold the remaining four places to other voyagers—they set sail for

Dover on 22 April 1764, only a week after the final ebbing of one of the strongest currents in French art and politics.

The outer walls of the small and elegant new palace she had begun to build in the Trianon gardens had barely risen when the Marquise de Pompadour made her hasty final departure from the palace of Versailles, her lifeless body lightly covered with a sheet and borne on a stretcher. It was said that the dreadful weather must have made her less sad to leave: the spring howled with freezing storms. Winds no less bitter than those buffeting her cortege on its way to Paris at the same time propelled the Mozarts toward Calais, where they arrived on Maundy Thursday (19 April). Strong contrary winds prevented boats from putting out, and a visit to the Capuchins helped fill the Mozarts' hours even as it offered an opportunity for Easter confession. After a wait of three days, they made the Channel crossing, all of them suffering seasickness but nonetheless diverted by dolphins piercing the surface of the water to disappear again into its depths.

"Perhaps even to England . . . ?" Frau Hagenauer had ventured at the time of Leopold's departure from Salzburg; he had voiced to friends the ambition to visit George III's island kingdom. Now approaching it, he experienced a sense of triumph: to Salzburgers the crossing would seem an almost unimaginable journey, and he searched his memory in vain for the name of a single citizen of the archbishopric who might have cast anchor at this realm of more than six and one half million souls.

He decided to learn English: "It will do no harm to have someone at the Salzburg court who speaks English; one never knows how handy it might be."[1] Perhaps the old dream of an administrative position stirred again. (Soon he would attempt to set up contacts for the exportation of English goods to the archbishopric, especially watches whose "balance and wheels function on diamonds.") He had taken as his own the motto ascribed to Cesare Borgia: "*Aut Caesar, aut nihil*" and buoyantly looked forward to learning a new tongue, to undertaking new projects. At the same time, he had the security of knowing that in London many of the powerful spoke the language of the Empire: the Mozarts were about to disembark at what remained, to an amazing extent, a German court, and, for the

---

1 Many an intense Anglophile (the young Handel's mentor, Johann Mattheson, for example) did flourish in Germany early in the century, but only after 1750, and thanks to Voltaire's influence, did English thought and culture begin to flow across the Channel with transforming force. Although translations into French, German, and Latin had served the Germans' taste for English literature, they now desired to read the originals, even in provincial Salzburg. In 1775 Leopold Mozart would note a Silesian named Schwarz teaching English in Munich; by 1778 Schwarz would be in Salzburg, instructing some fifteen pupils.

benefit of Hagenauer, Leopold would attempt to unriddle the mysteries of the Act of Settlement and the Hanoverian Succession.

2

THE MARRIAGE IN 1613 of James I's daughter, Elizabeth, to Frederick V, the Elector Palatine, began that devious path of events that would bring a line of petty German princes from the expanse of marsh called the Lüneburger Heide to the tidal meanders of the Thames and the throne of England. The third of the Georges, like his grandfather and great-grandfather before him, wore two crowns: that of his ancestral land, the Electorate of Hanover (it had subsumed Lüneburg, among other principalities) and that of the family's relatively newly acquired possession, the Kingdom of Great Britain and Ireland. Natives of Hanover, the first two Georges had preferred the electorate as their residence, German as their language. If their sojourns in England often had given the impression of squalid foreign encampments in Whitehall and St. James's, matters did change with the accession of a prince who declared: "Born and bred in this country, I glory in the name of Briton."

At the outset, George III's future seemed auspicious. Considerate in nature and unaffected in air, he and his German Queen, Sophia Charlotte of Mecklenburg-Strelitz, devoted themselves to a regimen of domestic simplicity more German middle class than royal and in sharp contrast with the bawdy ways of the King's immediate predecessors. His skies still unclouded—not until the following year would the first symptoms of mental unbalance appear—he was approaching his twenty-sixth birthday and in the fourth year of his reign when he met the Mozarts.

After spending their first night in London (23 April) at the White Bear in Piccadilly, they had moved into three small rooms let by a hairdresser named John Cousins in Cecil Court opening on St. Martin's Lane. The Duke of Bedford's recommendation and the friendship of the French Ambassador to London carried weight: within four days the Mozarts stood before the royal couple at Buckingham House.[2]

Music had an important place in the lives of the new German line of English monarchs:[3] if one virtue seasoned the vulgarity and loutishness of

2 Finding St. James's Palace cramped and decrepit, George III purchased the mansion of the Dukes of Buckingham (1763) as a dower house for Queen Charlotte; he called it the Queen's House. Transformed through the years, it has, with brief interruptions, remained the royal family's private London residence.

3 Music, for example, had been the only strong emotional link between George II and his accomplished wife, Caroline of Ansbach.

the first two Hanoverians to rule England and the atmosphere of hatred and feud that hung over them, it was their particularly German love of fine music.[4] Enchanted in Venice by Handel's opera *Agrippina* (first performed on 26 December 1709), Prince Ernst, younger brother of Elector Georg Ludwig of Hanover, advised the composer to visit its music-loving court. Shortly after arriving there (1710), Handel succeeded Agostino Steffani as Electoral kapellmeister. But the ambitious musician, eager to reconnoiter lucrative opportunities, soon slighted his duties to slip away to London on overextended leaves. For all that, Georg Ludwig forgave the delinquent not long after his own arrival on English soil: in 1714, as George I, he ascended the throne made vacant by the death of Queen Anne, last of the reigning Stuarts. Soon reconciled with the House of Hanover, Handel became the glory of its patrimony, the lion of contemporary composers. His example inspired Leopold Mozart, who had brought Wolfgang to England—so the father announced in the *Public Advertiser*—"not doubting but that he will meet with Success in a Kingdom, where his Countryman, that late famous Vertuoso Handel, received during his Life-time such Particular Protection [*sic*]." That English society had suffered this son of a provincial Saxon barber-surgeon to escape his class and become a "gentleman" must have stirred Leopold. Handel had been dead only five years when the Mozarts entered Buckingham House.

Music had its part in the royal household's daily business. Even when cavorting with his children, George III had his band perform in an adjoining room, he himself calling out his choice of pieces, most of them Handelian. He played violin and flute and managed at the harpsichord, an instrument Charlotte "played quite well, for a Queen," as Joseph Haydn observed during a stay in London. She also sang. Before such musically alert—but, to the world of fashion, dull—nobility Leopold and his children performed at their best. In Paris, serious music-making too often became a tiresome accompaniment to the true art of the salon—conversation. Conjecture conjures up the scene of Wolfgang playing at the Prince de Conti's to rattling dishes and to muffled chitchat growing into a chorus of praise at the final cadences. (Mozart's devastating, if less than altogether informed impression of the Duchess de Rohan-Chabot's salon, at which he assisted in 1778, survives; see p. 415.) In contrast, Buckingham House, with its attentive, courteous listeners, must have reminded the Mozarts of Schönbrunn. Their Britannic Majesties permitted few irregularities in the pattern of their daily

---

4 Further, one must remember George II's founding of the University of Göttingen (an institution that helped bring English political ideas to Germany) and of King's College (later Columbia College) in New York.

schedule, and, no doubt, the Mozarts appeared at the usual evening concert between dinner and backgammon, occasions when the Queen's music master, Christian Bach, took his place at the keyboard to accompany King George's flute.[5]

By the time Charlotte became queen (1761), she must already have had Christian in mind for her household.[6] (During her childhood, Emanuel Bach had come from Berlin to Strelitz to give her music lessons, no doubt at times in the company of his younger brother and ward, Christian.) His feeble ode welcoming her to England, its insipid text by John Lockman, probably and fortunately never reached performance. How and when the text arrived at his desk in Italy remains unknown, though one suspects Charlotte's hand. At all events, in the spring of 1762, he received a commission for two operas from the King's Theatre, Haymarket, took leave of his post as an organist at the cathedral of Milan, and that summer made his way to London. He captured its applause, and that of the palace, with his operas *Orione* (February 1763) and *Zanaida* (May 1763), their idiom, Italian in melodic grace and German in instrumental richness, suiting the royal taste. That same spring he published a first set of harpsichord concertos, which he dedicated to the Queen. By the time of Wolfgang's appearance at court, Christian had become Handel's successor as music master to the royal family and a dominant figure in London's musical life. But two months before, he had inaugurated what would prove a historical musical partnership with a fellow wanderer from Saxony, the gambist, Carl Friedrich Abel:[7] the Bach-Abel concerts would remain high points of London's musical calendar for almost twenty years.

A versatile performer and composer, Abel (whom Burney believed to have been a disciple of Sebastian Bach) had remained in the service of Augustus the Weak of Saxony until its cultural institutions dissolved under Prussian occupation at the beginning of the Seven Years' War. King Frederick had turned Dresden's main buildings—the opera house itself—into depots and infirmaries, and the death of Maria Josepha, the Electress-Queen, completed the dislocation of the capital's artistic life.[8] When the

---

5 At the very same time, Christian in London and his half brother Emanuel at Potsdam attended to the pipings of their royal masters.

6 A recommendation from Bach's teacher, Padre Martini, must have decided the matter.

7 Abel had substantial influence upon Mozart, who, while in London, made a copy of a symphony by the elder musician (Opus VII, No. 6) long accepted as an original work of the younger (K. 18/Anh. A51).

8 With her daughter-in-law—another Maria Antonia—she had remained behind in order to give some show of independence in the face of the foreign intruders, Frederick having permitted her husband, Augustus, to escape to Warsaw.

Austrians liberated Dresden in September 1759, Abel had already made his way to London, the new center of wealth and opportunity.[9]

England had triumphed in her struggle for naval and therewith commercial supremacy. Having gained the better of Spain in the sixteenth century and of Holland in the seventeenth, she now mocked a France swept from the seas. The tides not only of England's prosperity but also of her cultural prestige were running high: the nation from which the Enlightenment had received impetus seized the intellectual leadership of Europe. Even so, as foreign artists thronged to London, its citizens, like those of many dominant cities before and after, observed their musical life become the monopoly of foreigners:[10] as in Paris, the Germans and the Italians had control. "London is good pasture-land for talent," Helvétius wrote the year the Mozarts presented themselves at the Queen's door. Yet, their influential recommendations notwithstanding, it would not have opened so quickly without the help of their compatriot Christian Bach, whose new office included the arranging of such visits. Leopold Mozart entered Buckingham House with high expectations: "I didn't travel to England for the sake of a few thousand gulden," he announced to friends.

The graciousness of the King and Queen continued to overwhelm him. Though Maria Theresa received and bore herself informally, guests remained aware of an Empress's presence. Quite otherwise, George and Charlotte, young and attractive and with easy and amiable ways, at times almost made the Salzburg visitors forget their hosts' exalted rank. A week after the first visit to Buckingham House, the royal carriage passed the Mozart family in St. James's Park. The King opened the window and leaned out; waving his hand and nodding his head in enthusiastic greeting, he sent a special salute toward Master Wolfgang.

On 19 May he again appeared at court, the King's brothers, the Dukes of York and Gloucester (Edward Augustus and William Henry; see XXXII, n. 33), forming part of the royal circle, as did the Queen's brother.

---

9 The Seven Years' War made short work of the instrument-makers' profession on the Continent, and a number of clavier builders emigrated to London, among them Johann Christoph Zumpe, who had been trained in the circle of the famed Silbermann family. The Swiss Burkhardt Tschudi (the name appears in a variety of spellings), founder of the English firm that became Broadwood and Sons, had, however, come to London as early as 1718, Zumpe briefly working for him before setting up on his own. The Mozarts met both and developed a close tie to Tschudi (see p. 197).

10 A situation of a piece with those practicing the decorative arts: as wall and ceiling painting and plasterwork grew ever more fashionable in England, an army of European masters and artisans arrived to offer their services; and though the native-born James Thornhill might receive the commission to embellish the inside of St. Paul's dome, he could not command the fees paid to foreigners.

At these gatherings King George asked Wolfgang to seat himself at the harpsichord or organ and read at sight—pieces by such masters as Wagenseil, Christian Bach, Abel, and Handel—or to accompany the Queen's singing (the Duke of York might even step up to do that service for the prodigy); most of all the boy relished being asked to pick up a volume of Handel, select some bass lines at random, and spin out new melodies above them. Leopold did not have to wait for his quid pro quo: upon leaving the royal apartment, twenty-four guineas were handed him. "If such a thing happens every three or four weeks, one can put up with it," he exclaimed.

In technique and musicality Wolfgang had begun to develop at a formidable rate, his performances by this time resting upon not only showmanship but artistry, too. "What he knew when we departed Salzburg but foreshadowed what he knows now," Leopold wrote Hagenauer. "You yourself and all of Salzburg have no idea [of Wolfgang's progress], for he has become at all points different." More and more he immersed himself in the scores of Christian Bach; as Leopold sat writing to Hagenauer, Wolfgang greeted this Salzburg friend "from the clavier, where at the moment he is . . . playing through Kapellmeister Bach's trio"—perhaps one of the six trio sonatas dedicated to Augusta of Braunschweig-Lüneburg (1763).

Leopold had committed Wolfgang to play a harpsichord concerto at a benefit on 17 May for the violoncellist and composer Carlo Graziani. Too late Leopold learned that during the warmer months, the royal family apart, "nobody who has leisure or means remains in London." Few potential patrons would attend this local public debut. The concert was postponed to 22 May, ostensibly because of difficulties in scheduling an orchestra. On 21 May, two days after Wolfgang's second demonstration at court, Graziani announced in the *Public Advertiser* that the boy had fallen ill, and, as a result, the benefit might not include the scheduled concerto. In the end, Wolfgang did not perform for Graziani at Hickford's Great Room in Brewer Street. The indisposition had probably been strategic: ignorance of London's social ways had led Leopold to miscalculate. He would soon put things right.

The nobility had to be in town on 4 June, the King's birthday. Leopold decided to set the debut on the following day. Wolfgang had an enormous success at the Great Room in Spring-Garden (near St. James's Park), where the Society of Artists held its exhibitions. Members of the diplomatic corps and many aristocrats appeared and applauded. (The Bedfords and the French Ambassador, Claude-Francois Regnier, Count de Guerchy, had been at work.) Leopold, enjoying the "shock . . . of taking in one hundred guineas within three hours," realized a fine profit despite the costs of renting the hall, the music stands, two harpsichords—the children performed a double concerto—and of paying for accessory musicians[11] and candles. He had put his best foot forward, and the capital took the Mozarts to its heart. And they returned the compliment: London fascinated them.

3

THE MOZARTS COULD not turn their heads fast enough to take in the spectacle surging about them. The city seemed "nothing but a masquerade" to Leopold, who lost little time joining what seemed to him a kind of game: father and son paraded in English wardrobes, mother and daughter in the indispensable English hat. "No woman crosses an alley without a hat on her head," Leopold observed, his eye always cocked to the absurd. But more than a delight in new costumes and a sense of whimsy had inspired the transformation: the Mozarts' Parisian clothes had aroused the ire of street urchins, who hurled cries of "Bugger the French" at them. "The best thing to do is to keep quiet and act as if you don't hear anything," advised Leopold, who, rudely reminded that the Seven Years' War had just ended, hastened to give his family an English look.[12]

The wealth of England's aristocracy and, in particular, the relative prosperity of its lower classes astonished him. He determined to reap a rich harvest as quickly as possible: "Once out of England I will see no more guineas; one must profit from the occasion." To make the Mozart name known forthwith, he volunteered Wolfgang's services as harpsichord and organ virtuoso at a benefit for the new Lying-in Hospital. The boy would perform "an act of an English patriot," he wrote Hagenauer, "a way of wooing the love of this in all respects extraordinary nation."

The concert took place on 29 June[13] in the rotunda of Ranelagh

---

11 They included Signora Cremonini, a singer at the Drury Lane Theatre, the tenor Gaetano Quilici, the violinist François-Hippolyte Barthélémon, and the cellist Giovanni Battista Cirri. Programs of the Mozarts' London concerts have yet to come to light. Perhaps Wolfgang and Nannerl offered something by Wagenseil: either a concerto for two harpsichords or one for soloist as rewritten by Leopold for a pair of instruments. Whatever the children performed on 5 June, it doubtless constituted the substance of the work for four hands they would play almost a year later (13 May 1765) in Brewer Street (see VI, n. 3 and p. 197).

12 Some four decades earlier, Voltaire, on the point of being attacked by toughs on a London street, cried out to them: "Brave Englishmen! Am I not unfortunate enough in not having been born among you?" Utterly thrown off balance, they offered to carry the strange-looking Frenchman to his lodgings. Leopold tidied up his translation of "Bugger."

13 It had been postponed from the twenty-seventh, a porter having lost a packet of eight hundred tickets.

Gardens, one of London's celebrated public pleasure-grounds. In these landscaped parks decorated with fountains and sculpture, people of all ranks mixed: promenading, listening to music, taking tea and coffee or dining, and, at times, indulging their licentiousness. Vauxhall, the most elaborate of the gardens, left Leopold spellbound:[14] strolling there at night, he fancied himself in the Elysian Fields and, for the sake of his Salzburg friends, attempted to write about an experience he at first thought "impossible to describe."

"Imagine an uncommonly large garden that has every kind of prome-nade, each illuminated like daylight by a thousand lights enclosed in the most beautiful glass lanterns. In the middle is a kind of high open sum-merhouse in which is to be heard an organ and music on trumpets, drums, and all instruments." On every side Leopold observed tables for refresh-ments and special dining pavilions arranged like opera boxes. Of the many wonders of Vauxhall, the illuminations spanning the promenades—"some like arches, some like pyramids of light"—most enchanted him and Frau Mozart. He realized what a shrewd business venture Vauxhall represented: "Here each person pays only *one shilling* and for this shilling has the delight of seeing many thousands of people and the most beautifully illuminated garden; and of hearing beautiful music. More than six thousand people were present when I attended. *A single shilling* is not much. But one is only certain that it takes a shilling to get in; how many it will take to get out one doesn't know. You resolve firmly not to waste money. How mistaken! You go here and there; you become tired; you sit down. In the end, you permit yourself a bottle of wine, perhaps a few biscuits with it; that costs about four or five shillings. Finally, you see a few baked chickens being car-ried past. You beckon; they arrive. You see, thus are guineas lured from one's purse."[15]

The democratic spirit at these pleasure parks gladdened him: "Here everyone is equal, and no lord allows any person to uncover before him; having paid their money, all are upon equal terms." He even rationalized in terms of English liberalism—and in almost Panglossian tones—the cost of Vauxhall's massive illuminations: "This is something that can exist nowhere in the world but here: since neither *the private citizen alone* nor *the noble alone* is in the position *to maintain such expenses daily,* and since nowhere

---

14 The site of Ranelagh Gardens now forms part of Chelsea Hospital Garden; Vauxhall Gardens lay in Kennington, across the Thames.
15 Boswell found Vauxhall "a mixture of curious show, gay exhibition, musick, vocal and instru-mental, not too refined for the general ear; for all which only a shilling is paid; and, though last, not least, good eating and drinking for those who choose to purchase that regale [*sic*]."

else are the noble and the common man as united as here, so costly an undertaking can therefore be supported nowhere but in England."

How different London's atmosphere from that of the courts he had hitherto known: the sovereign's residences appeared to him "rather middle-class; for certain not royal." The Continent's palaces proclaimed opulence; London's had an unobtrusive, anonymous air, the rabbit warren of buildings constituting St. James's (and the Parliament) offering a lamentable and makeshift spectacle. The populace, too, at first confused him: he found it difficult "to distinguish a tailor's or a shoemaker's wife from a Mylady, save that the first two are most times better turned out than the last, who, if there is no special reason, does not display herself."[16] Even the beggars—forbidden to solicit openly—showed an independent spirit violating his concept of their proper role. "They have another way of asking alms . . . one holds out a pot of flowers, another toothpicks of quill, another copper engravings, another sulphur matches, another sewing thread, another ribbons of various colors, etc.; others sing in the streets and offer you the commonest printed songs, which one hears with disgust from hour to hour." He appears to have met more than one Autolycus.

For all its size, London seemed to him less overwhelming than Paris. He felt at home and became a kind of flâneur. Avoiding the hole-riddled roadways through which quaking carriages made their way, he used the sidewalks, as a rule in better state: "One prefers to walk rather than to run the danger of breaking a couple of ribs. . . ." On foot he sought out those "most beautiful shops" hidden away in charming courts or reconnoitered curious neighborhoods where lower-class women went about their affairs with tobacco pipes in their mouths. Fascinated by the social and economic structure of the capital, he devoured the two volumes of William Maitland's *The Hystory and Survey of London from its foundation to the present time* (1760) and various guidebooks. (English had come to him quickly, and he continued to study it in Salzburg.) He accumulated a considerable knowledge of the city, ever marveling at its giant scale;[17] at the variety and sheer tonnage of what it consumed in food and beverages; at the profligacy with which it burned fuel; at the very magnitude of what it raised in houses and public works; at its elaborate system of public charities. With admiration

16 Here Leopold sounds much like Defoe: commenting (*Everybody's Business, Nobody's Business*) on the difficulty in England of telling mistress from maid on certain social occasions, he concluded that with consistence the maid dressed better. During a visit to the Greenwich Fair in 1726, Voltaire did not believe his eyes when the girls in elegant attire he had taken for people of fashion proved to be servants on holiday.
17 "When one stands on London Bridge and contemplates the host of ships always lying in the Thames, the amazing multitude of masts makes one seem to behold a thick forest ahead."

he observed the government force a drop in the price of bread: concern for the stomachs of the poor and uneasiness over their discontent rarely manifested themselves in that Holy Empire from which he came.

Though London became his standard against which to measure the shortcomings of other cities, he nonetheless recognized English institutions as not all praiseworthy, the great metropolis as not without blemishes. (A breakfast of tea with milk or cream and a pile of buttered bread and toast constituted a native institution this German did not esteem![18]) He could admire the fresh, sweeping English political landscape and yet perceive ugly patches, having witnessed the severity with which the authorities moved against the disorders in the streets committed by the hungry and unemployed during the weaver riots of 1765. The Bloomsbury Square mansion of his patron, the Duke of Bedford, besieged by an angry mob, had to be protected by royal infantrymen.[19]

If such rough-and-tumble upset him, he did make clear his good opinion of orderly protest, something quite new to him. Having witnessed more than four thousand protesting marchers, some bearing black flags and all wearing the weaver's green apron, surge past his doorstep, he applauded the courage with which English workingmen asserted their demands: "How good that here the folk and so many thousand honest people who earn their bread by the sweat of their brows, who really constitute the state and who utterly sustain the coherence of civil life, are not forced (by the few hundred who live their lives in abundance) to languish and suffer, but have the right to demonstrate, have a way to discover the truth and to force a change for either better or worse. This is quite something!" This servant of a minor tyrant who ruled by whim found himself deeply moved by a spontaneous expression of popular power. He had yet to encounter elsewhere the degree of liberty, security, and happiness England enjoyed and, like Voltaire before him, came to see the nation as a symbol of freedom.

Admiration of the English as egalitarians remained a tradition in the Mozart family:[20] the sprightly Blonde in *The Abduction from the Seraglio* re-

---

18 In his opinion, the English middle class "in the main ate like the Slavic and Hungarian regiments of the Imperial Army (*Mit einem Worte sie essen wie die Panduren*)"—not a compliment. For a while the family ordered its meals from caterers, but Frau Mozart soon returned to the stove.

19 The workers held Bedford, a member of the ministry, responsible for the import policies, vis-à-vis France, that had caused the crisis.

20 During the Mozarts' residence in London, George Grenville formulated his plan to raise revenue by extending to America England's system of duties on legal documents. In the colonies this Stamp Act excited antagonism and unrest, in London discussion and debate, of which the Mozarts had to have been aware. Though partisans of the English, Leopold, Frau Anna Maria, and Wolfgang were to let slip an almost breathless admiration for the Americans.

veals herself a freeborn Englishwoman determined to defy bullying, her dumbfounded overseer, the Turk Osmin, wondering how her countrymen could tolerate such independence, above all in a woman;[21] and in the cavatina "*Se vuol ballare*" from *The Marriage of Figaro*, a musical line patterned on the traditional minuet gives way to one inspired by an English dance tune and rhythm, the courtly dance disintegrating as, in a forceful, aggressive musical idiom borrowed from the land of liberalism and equality, the servant Figaro expands a rebellious plan to outwit his master. "I am a thoroughgoing Englishman," a joyful Mozart announced in 1782 upon learning of the British successes at Gibraltar and Trincomalee.

4

ALL AT ONCE, during the summer of 1764, the London stay, indeed the entire tour, seemed near disaster: Leopold fell gravely ill. Recovering in the salubrious air of the small village of Chelsea—"an hour outside the city" (Leopold had been borne there in a sedan chair) and with "one of the most beautiful views in the world"—he attempted to explain to Hagenauer the strange history of his malady: "I must tell you that here they have a kind of native complaint called a 'cold.'"

On 8 July, while preparing to set out with the children for a six o'clock concert at the Earl of Thanet's, Leopold had sent for a coach. None was to be had, and, summoning a sedan chair, he placed Nannerl and Wolfgang in it and decided to follow them to Grosvenor Square on foot. Aware only of the beautiful weather, he for a moment forgot how swiftly London porters whisked along.[22] The afternoon had remained warm. "To cut a long story short, before we arrived at Lord Thanet's, I often thought it would be impossible for me to continue on any longer, for London is not Salzburg. Accordingly, I arrived sweating as profusely as one can." He buttoned up, but to no avail. Cool evening air began moving through the open windows. The entertainment lasted until eleven, when, already affected, he followed the children home in a second sedan chair.

For several days it appeared that he had escaped serious indisposition. But soon his tonsils became inflamed; he underwent bleeding and purging;

---

21 This pert soubrette descends from the lofty Roxane of Montesquieu's *Lettres persanes.* The favorite in Usbek's harem, she writes him: "How could you have thought me naïve enough to imagine that I was put into the world only to adorn your whims? . . . No! I might have lived in servitude, but I have always been free."

22 The speed of English transportation astounded him, in particular of those "most beautiful English [carriage] horses . . . that run in such a manner that the attendants on their perches can all but breathe because of the force of the air."

he could no longer digest, the pains in his stomach growing unbearable. The doctor could bring no relief: to the contrary, his prescriptions for opium further injured the patient's nervous system.[23] Providently, Leopold had made friends with the cellist and composer Emanuel Sipurtini, a Dutch Jew who had settled in London some six years earlier. He sent for a second doctor, his cousin, a Portuguese Jew. His treatment eased a crisis that for a time had appeared to be approaching the fatal: Leopold had already discussed with Frau Anna Maria possible surrogates to act as Wolfgang's teachers and mentors.

Leopold spoke of his Jewish doctor (*"des ... Hebräischen Medici"*) with enormous respect and for a while imagined he might best tender thanks to his new Jewish friends by converting Sipurtini, who had become dear to him. (Of the two, Sipurtini must have seemed the more likely prospect: he had turned from Judaism to embrace a kind of Masonic universalism.) And though with returning good humor Leopold expressed hopes to become "missionary to England," he did have second thoughts and with discernment remarked: "One must proceed most gently in these matters."

Experiences with London ways time and again confirmed his inherent sense of decency. His lines on the diversity of nations at the Royal Exchange call to mind Voltaire's famous description of it (in the *Lettres philosophiques*, first published in English in 1733) as "a place more venerable than many courts of justice, where the representatives of all nations meet for the benefit of mankind. There the Jew, the Mahometan, and the Christian transact together as tho' they all profess'd the same religion, and give the name of Infidel to none but bankrupts."

In London, which had three synagogues, the Mozarts often found themselves in the company of Jews, many of whom, in particular the Portuguese, dressed with Parisian elegance: ". . . nothing about them resembles a Jew," Leopold marveled, looking in vain for beards, velvet gowns, and traditional headdress.[24] But Leopold lamented that many Jews, like Christians, neglected their faith, a matter he had perhaps discussed with the "Mr. Frenck" (Frank), listed under "Jews" in his London notes, a member of the family associated with London's Great Synagogue. (With Charles Burney present, Wolfgang performed in the drawing room of one of the

---

23 Throughout his correspondence Leopold showed deep knowledge of the chemist's art, analyzing the compounding of medicines and describing the procedures in Latin.

24 In 1762 Isaac de Pinto observed of Portuguese Jews that they "do not wear a beard and are in no way different in their clothing; their rich engage in scholarship, in elegant ways, and in ostentation to as great a degree as the other people of Europe, from whom they differ only in religion."

Franks.) More and more pews stood empty in England's houses of worship. Yet, though decrying a general decline in orthodoxy, from time to time Leopold enjoyed feeling part of the new and freer spirit.

"Wasn't it a shame that there wasn't also at least a Jew in the company?" he joked after describing to Hagenauer a bizarre baptism in a London home. The child's father, from Hesse and a dealer in music and instruments, held the fashionable views of an Enlightened agnostic; the mother, a Swiss Calvinist, to an extent remained devout. Their guests included the godfather, a Lutheran from Braunschweig; the first godmother, a German Calvinist; and a second godmother—*mirabile dictu,* "a good Catholic woman from Salzburg," one Anna Maria Mozart! If Leopold's desired Jew was lacking to season this extraordinary mixture, the minister did add another touch: he belonged to the Church of England. Both Leopold's presence at this ceremony and Frau Anna Maria's direct part in it underscore London's role in unchaining their minds. It should not surprise to discover a born Jew as godfather to their son's first child.

How thwarting that Leopold's letters from London vouchsafe only few and fugitive glimpses of Anna Maria: enchanted by the lights of Vauxhall; worn out ministering to a sick husband; full of play and dissolving into laughter while communicating in pantomime with her English maid. ("Good morrow, sir," just about exhausted Frau Mozart's English vocabulary, and the only Londoner she could understand was the night watchman calling the hours.) But Leopold's most winning vignette of Anna Maria shows her standing godmother at that strange christening.

The Mozarts spent some seven weeks (6 August to c. 25 September) on the border of Chelsea at the house of the Randal family in Five Fields Row (today 180 Ebury Street) and then returned to London to take up quarters rented from a corset-maker, Thomas Williamson, in Thrift Street (now 20 Frith Street), Soho. Leopold decided to stay in England for some time. If his financial reserves had suffered, at least illness had overtaken him in the world's richest city: opportunities to recoup remained, and he determined to spare no effort "galloping around" in order to win back the nobility. Yet his old fears grew with each passing month, and he maintained with ever more insistence: ". . . my children are still young." He felt that should he return home without having made the most of as yet unexplored opportunities he would merit being "led to the madhouse [*nach dem St. Sebastians spithal*] straightway upon re-entering the city of Salzburg." Regaining his strength during the autumn of 1764, he declared: "If the benevolent Lord but sends us good health, we need not worry about guineas."

5

IN PARIS, GRIMM analyzed the Mozarts' problems at the close of 1764: "Although they arrived much too late, they did well at the beginning. . . . But the entire summer is an absolutely dead season in London; the father, moreover, has had a serious illness, thought himself dying, and required three months to recover. It is therefore a question of making good this winter the losses of the summer. . . ."

In all likelihood Grimm prompted Leopold to contemplate giving sub-scription concerts at Carlisle House, the establishment on Soho Square of the Venetian-born singer-hostess-procuress Teresa Cornelys. Her opulently appointed chambers, hung with blue and yellow satin, had hitherto been the scene of masked balls with suppers, music, card playing, flirtation, and prostitution. For a while she possessed the field, accommodating as many as six hundred maskers at supper; indeed, if desired, four hundred at one enor-mous horseshoe-shaped table. But she feared becoming démodé and was seeking to add to her enterprise a cultural lure in the form of exclusive sub-scription concerts. She and Leopold met and no doubt discussed music-making by his children as a possible addition to her regular "assemblies."

From afar Grimm made an artful if unsuccessful attempt to set the seal upon the matter by winning it the patronage of one of the most eminent visitors to Mrs. Cornelys's entertainments: the Duke of York. Grimm well knew what lay at the heart of her profitable undertakings, and therefore it remains difficult to believe the inquisitive Leopold Mozart ignorant of her reputation. Yet, she had assumed the respectable exterior of a Shavian Mrs. Warren—an impersonation galling to Casanova, the father of her daugh-ter, Sophie—and thus may have taken Leopold in; and others, too: her disguise and enterprises flourished until the decade turned.[25]

Whatever Leopold's suspicions, the children would experience nothing giving offense in the elegant public rooms of Carlisle House, where they might brandish their wares before the highest aristocrat and richest bour-geois and earn a fee into the bargain. The public, however, for the most part found it sufficient to see Wolfgang and Nannerl once. If Leopold showed himself blind to their limitations in respect to the repertory and artistic breadth necessary to sustain a series, Teresa Cornelys foresaw how rapidly their novelty would wear thin. She had appeared under the name Pompeati in Gluck's *La caduta de' giganti* and, with the transparent alias of Signora Cor-

---

25 Indicted in 1771 for keeping "a common disorderly house," for a while she kept herself afloat, but ended her days in prison. Burney, who heard her in the theater, found her singing "mascu-line and violent" and with "few female symptoms . . . perceptible."

neli, in Thomas Augustine Arne's *Judith*. Knowledgeable in the ways of performers and audiences, she turned a deaf ear to Leopold. (He must have discussed his hopes concerning Carlisle House with Bach and Abel, who, in
their kindness, perhaps for a time indulged his illusions.) Gioacchino Cocchi
became director of her new concerts, soon taken over by Bach and Abel as
managers and performers; their programs in all probability included music
from Wolfgang's pen.[26]

The London expedition never regained an earlier momentum: for a while
it moved along tolerably and then lost ground. Late in 1764 Leopold ordered
the engraving of Wolfgang's six sonatas for harpsichord with the accompaniment of violin or flute and with violoncello ad libitum (K. 10–15). Composed during the autumn of 1764, this set shows the influence of Christian
Bach. Like the Versailles sonatas and those soon to be written in the Hague,
K. 10–15 are in essence keyboard works: unlike the figured bass accompaniment of an earlier generation, the clavier part contains the substance of the
piece, the accompanying parts being expendable, the few touches of violin
cantilena improving the occasion (as in K. 13 and 15) notwithstanding. The
edition displayed a dedication in French to Queen Charlotte, who acknowledged with a handsome gift of fifty guineas this awkward attempt at
whimsy. Whom did Leopold induce to compose this sequence of pitiful
paragraphs all at once changing tone to end with a salvo celebrating the
English and their liberties?

Wolfgang had again appeared at court on 25 October, the fourth anniversary of King George's accession and the boy's third and final audience
with the royal couple, perhaps the occasion on which (according to
Grimm) Christian Bach "took him between his knees, and they played al-
ternately on the same harpsichord, extemporizing for two hours in a row
in the presence of the King and Queen."[27] Yet without warning they

---

26 Their Wednesday "Soho Concert," at Carlisle House, for which the resourceful Mrs. Cornelys, ever mindful of the amenities, would provide "tea below stairs and ventilators above,"
descended from the London tradition of musical entertainments scheduled at regular intervals
in taverns and public chambers of a higher class. In this area Mrs. Cornelys's best-known predecessor had been Thomas Britton: the sixteen-seventies had not passed when he organized
weekly concerts over his Aylesbury Street (Clerkenwell) shop, a charcoal storehouse where he
offered not only music but coffee at a penny a dish. His gatherings lasted into Handel's day.
By 1731, Francesco Geminiani had begun to arrange subscription concerts in Hickford's Room,
Felice de Giardini succeeding him in 1751. The individual entrepreneur—Leopold Mozart had
come to be one—dominated the concert life of eighteenth-century London.

27 With Bach and others, Mozart more than once indulged in this charming game. Grimm's anecdote, corroborated in Nannerl's memoirs, parallels William Jackson's (see p. 62); and Burney,
who had "frequent opportunities of witnessing" Mozart's "extraordinary talents and profound
knowledge in every branch of music," recalled how he "played on my knee, on subjects I gave
him. . . ."

ceased their patronage. Some five months later, Leopold hinted at his having turned down a proposition requiring his settling in England: the offer may have originated in Buckingham House, which, spurned, looked in other directions.

His admiration for England apart, Leopold longed for Germany, especially the warmth of its homes. An English fire did little to relieve the aches and chills of someone accustomed to the more even heat of tile stoves. The capriciousness of the weather, the dampness, the fog, and the air befouled by dust and the smoke of thousands of chimneys made the great metropolis at times seem to him nothing more than a "vent hole." "As soon as good weather arrives, one must go out of the city or travel and breathe in the air if one wants in any wise to remain healthy." (A desire to escape London's grime had doubtless played a part in his plan to visit the fashionable watering-place of Tunbridge Wells during the summer of 1764.)[28] Besides, too often he found a frightening harshness in Hogarth's London:[29] as in Paris, shocking contrasts between the elegance of the great houses and the coarseness and brutality in the streets; weird juxtapositions of magnificence and filth, sagacity and folly, charity and avarice. This was not a place in which he wished to raise his children. And, despite his fellowship with Protestants and Jews, he could not imagine a permanent household anywhere but in a Catholic country. (The family attended mass in the chapel of the French embassy.) But, whatever the nature and source of the important offer, he could not have set it aside easily: he wrestled with a decision that cost him "several sleepless nights." Perhaps similar uncertainties perplexed him when he declined an invitation young Prince Dmitrij Alekseević Golicyn, the Russian ambassador to Versailles, had extended in Paris: to journey to the court of Catherine the Great, where Galuppi, Traetta, and Paisiello were to make careers.

The English visit ended with a flurry of activities—some sad, some desperate—designed to remind London of the prodigy's presence. Engraving the sonatas for the Queen in part served this purpose. Leopold supervised the work intently, for a mishap had attended the appearance of the Tessé sonatas: though he had corrected and improved the manuscript, his too-hurried proofreading had overlooked a triple musical solecism: three parallel fifths in the second minuet of K. 9; to Leopold's mortifica-

28 Leopold's illness, Nannerl recalled, put an end to the idea.
29 William Hogarth died in his house at Leicester Square the day after Mozart's final visit to Buckingham House. Leopold's comments upon Hogarth's London have much in common with those of the great German interpreter of this artist's work, Georg Christoph Lichtenberg, who would visit England in 1770–1771 and again in 1774–1775 (see II, n. 11).

tion, they appeared in the printed edition. But he would come to look upon the slip as beneficial: too many thought him the composer, and it helped strengthen faith in the name on the title page.

6

SPARSE ATTENDANCE AT the children's concert at the Little Theatre in the Haymarket on 21 February 1765 confirmed the falling-off of public interest. "Not as strong as I hoped," complained Leopold, who, by March declared himself financially so hobbled as to be unable to buy those English "curiosities" the family longed to take home.[30] On 13 May in Hickford's Great Room in Brewer Street, "the little Composer and his Sister" made their last appearance in a London hall, playing, so the *Public Advertiser* had promised, a "Concerto on the Harpsichord," in all likelihood a work for two claviers from the pen of Wagenseil (see n. 11 and VI, n. 3) but arranged by Leopold for four hands on one instrument and to be played on the remarkable mechanism Burkhardt Tschudi had recently completed and put at the Mozarts' disposition: the two-manual clavier he had built for Frederick the Great. Perhaps on this occasion the children also used it for a sonata, which commentators often venture to identify as K. 19d: an understandable temptation, for Leopold reported his son's having written such a work in London and, moreover, claimed precedence for him in this still out-of-the-common genre of one instrument, four hands. But the rather rudimentary K. 19d may be thought Mozart's work only at the longest odds: although its closing movement opens with the theme that would begin the finale of the serenade K. 361/370a of 1781 and contains a quotation from Christian Bach to be used in the piano concerto K. 414/385p of 1782, K. 19d, which did not come to light until late in the same decade, may well be a counterfeit (see XXX, n. 20).

The registration of the new Tschudi harpsichord could be changed by an innovative pedal that controlled the stops and thus the color, and, by shifting the keyboard, also the volume: ". . . the decrease and increase of tone can thereby be accomplished at will, which crescendo and decrescendo have long been wished for by clavier players." So advised Salzburg's *Europaeische Zeitung* (6 August 1765), its observer in London applauding Tschudi's decision to have "his extraordinary instrument [*Flügel*]

---

30 Leopold not only suffered fits of parsimony but quite early formed a policy of decrying to family and friends the obvious financial success of the tour. To ignore its mishaps and formidable expenses would be unfair to him; yet, a single concert in London could yield a profit exceeding his annual salary.

played for the first time by the most extraordinary clavier player of this world, namely by the very celebrated nine-year-old master of music, Wolfg. Mozart, the wonderful son of Mozart, the Salzburg Kapellmeister. It was quite enchanting to hear the fourteen-year-old sister of this little virtuoso play the most difficult sonatas on the clavier with the most astonishing dexterity. . . . Both perform wonders!" Alas, despite a reduced price of admission, few witnessed these wonders described by the appreciative London reporter—in all likelihood Leopold Mozart himself.[31]

Successive announcements in the *Public Advertiser* of the children's final concert had laid bare the family's melancholy situation. The first notice had advised that tickets for "the Benefit of Master Mozart . . . and Miss Mozart" were to be had at half a guinea each "of Mr. Mozart, at Mr. Williamson's in Thrift-street, Soho; where those Ladies and Gentlemen, who will honour him with their Company from Twelve to Three in the Afternoon, any Day in the Week, except Tuesday and Friday, may, by taking each a Ticket, gratify their Curiosity, and not only hear this young Music Master and his Sister perform in private; but likewise try his surprising musical capacity, by giving him any Thing to play at Sight, or any Music without Bass, which he will write upon the Spot, without recurring to his Harpsichord." Publication on 20 March of the sonatas dedicated to the Queen had provided yet another expedient: "by taking each a Book of Sonatas,[32] or a Ticket," the curious could hear the children play in private and also observe Wolfgang go through his repertory of musical legerdemain. There must have been but a trickle of callers: by 9 April the price of tickets had dropped to five shillings.

Even after the last concert, Leopold continued to solicit visitors: they could "find the Family at Home . . . every Day in the Week from One to Three o'Clock" and for a fee of "5s each Person" might put Wolfgang's "Talents to a more particular Proof, by giving him any Thing to play at Sight." Leopold decked his advertisements with admonitions concerning the family's impending departure, but the public remained indifferent. By summer, sorely pressed, he parted with appearances in order to scrape together the last guineas. During July he hired "the Great Room in the Swan and Harp Tavern in Cornhill," where tickets of admission (now two shillings sixpence) gave "an Opportunity to all the Curious to hear these

---

31 It appears that at first he intended the puff for the *Postzeitung* of Augsburg: hence the free use of his superior's title.

32 At the apartment Leopold also offered for sale the Versailles sonatas along with the engraving after Carmontelle's watercolor.

two young Prodigies perform every Day from Twelve to Three." The Swan and Harp doubtless preserved taproom tradition, drinking, smoking, and homely sociality accompanying the music.[33] The taxing schedule in an unaccustomed atmosphere must have taken a toll in pride and mettle: if the children had often played in public rooms, their concerts had always been special occasions in dignified surroundings and with nothing of the drudgery of daily repetition.

During June, when the family had put itself on exhibit every day at home, Daines Barrington, a respected jurist, amateur scientist, antiquarian, and enthusiastic connoisseur of music, arrived at Thrift Street to subject Wolfgang's talent to the test. A member of the Royal Society, he planned to submit to it the results of his investigation. The prodigy's concerts had impressed him, and, above all, he hoped to scotch suspicion, widespread in London, of Leopold's duplicity concerning his son's age[34] and to provide "irrefragable proof" of the boy's genius. The report, which he did not submit until 1769,[35] would declare, without prejudice to Handel's memory, "that the scale most clearly preponderates on the side of Mozart" in any comparison of the two as prodigies.

Another member of the Royal Society befriended the Mozarts, the Reverend Andrew Planta, Assistant Keeper of Printed Books in the British Museum. It had to have been Barrington who brought Mozart to the attention of the German-speaking Planta and the trustees of this recently founded institution, and at their request Leopold made it a gift: copies of his son's published sonatas (K. 6–15) and the engraving of the three Mozarts. Moreover, the museum received the manuscript of an anthem the boy had composed without doubt for the occasion of his visit to its collections, so haphazardly exhibited in Montagu House on Great Russell Street. In its attempt to capture the flavor of a catch in "old English" style, the anthem, "God is our Refuge" (K.20; the words from Psalm 46, verse 1 of the King James Bible)[36] constituted a touching gesture of farewell to the capital in which he had learned so much.

---

33 An assembly room formed an ingredient of an inn or hotel with even modest pretensions. But the Swan and Harp was a tavern and its "Great Room" in all probability a large barroom.

34 Some three weeks after Mozart's ninth birthday, notices in the *London Evening Post* and *Lloyd's Evening Post* described him as "a German boy, of about eight years old. . . ." Such information came from Leopold, and that he did not lie consistently made matters worse. Through the Bavarian Ambassador to the Court of St. James's, certification of Wolfgang's date of birth in time reached Barrington from Salzburg.

35 It was read to the society in 1770 and published the following year.

36 The anthem represents Mozart's unique recourse to a text in English, save a few phrases in Nardo's wooing aria in *La finta giardiniera*.

7

HE HAD COME to London a precocious performer; he left as a promising composer. While Leopold had kept to his bed in Chelsea, Wolfgang filled the days sketching pieces (K. 15a–ss/Anh. 109b) in a new notebook, the so-called London Album. Almost four decades later, Nannerl recalled that when "our father lay close to death, we were not allowed to touch the keyboard. And so, in order to occupy himself, Mozart composed his first symphony; [he used] all the instruments—especially trumpets and kettle-drums.[37] Seated at his side, I had to copy the symphony down. While he composed and I copied, he said to me: 'Remind me to give the horn something worthwhile to do!'" (His archness had not diminished; Barrington more than once remarked upon it.) This ambitious effort cannot be identified among Mozart's surviving works, but an ingenious symphony in E-flat major (K. 16) bears witness to a style showing the *galant* influence of Christian Bach and Abel along with Schobertian moments in the Andante. It, moreover, harbors Mozart's first use of his so-called motto, a sequence of four notes (do-re-fa-mi) that would appear here and there throughout his oeuvre, to crown all in the final movement of the Jupiter Symphony.

He continued to work on symphonies, which at this time did not represent a more elevated kind of instrumental music but, rather, a ready-to-hand genre often bearing the name of overture and for the most part functioning as prelude or postlude to a stage work or concert and even serving to mark the intermissions. While preparing for the performance of 21 February 1765, Leopold had written: "Oh, I have so much to do! All the symphonies . . . will be by Wolf. Mozart. I must copy them myself, unless I want to pay 1 schilling for every sheet." K. 16 and the more assured symphony K. Anh. 223/19a may have had their first hearing in the course of this evening.

If these symphonies indicate the extent to which Christian Bach's works provided a staple of Wolfgang's musical diet in London, he did also feast upon Handel. Late in February and throughout March of 1765 a Lenten season of his oratorios unfolded at Covent Garden (*Judas Maccabaeus, Alexander's Feast, Samson, Israel in Egypt*, and *Messiah*). Though no document reveals the immediate effect of these masterpieces upon the child, the final entry in his London Album attempts a four-voice fugue (K. 15ss/109b), and, in K. 20, the "sacred madrigal" deposited in the British Museum, the imitative treatment of voices ends as less "old English" than Handelian. Barrington told of Christian Bach's beginning a fugue and then leaving off

---

37 This equivocal description could also be interpreted as a reference not to the first symphony he composed but, rather, to his first with "all the instruments."

abruptly, whereupon Wolfgang took it up "and worked it after a most masterly manner."

London also gave impetus to his love of opera. He must have attended many performances, for his father wished him to succeed, above all, in this lucrative field. Writing to Hagenauer on 8 February 1765, Leopold touched upon London productions of "5 or 6 operas: the first was *Ezio*, the 2nd *Berenice*, both pasticci [see X, n. 5] by various [unidentified] masters; the 3rd *Adriano in Syria* [sic] recently composed by Sgr. Bach. . . . A newly composed *Demofoonte* by Vento is coming," Leopold continued, "and then yet another few pasticci."[38] At this point, he cut matters short: "About all these things—in their time and by word," his haste depriving posterity of his and Wolfgang's reactions to London's lyric stage. But the operatic devil already possessed the boy: the previous summer Leopold had reported his son's "continual absorption in an opera he wishes to perform in Salzburg with nothing but young people." London quickened such ambitions by exposing him to the art of one of the most admired singers of the day.

If the elegance of Italian operatic music first decisively reached Wolfgang through the works of the Italianized German Christian Bach, another major Italian influence upon him arrived in the person of Giovanni Manzuoli, the Florentine castrato who reaped a harvest of applause and guineas during the Mozarts' English stay: "No one makes much money this winter [1764–1765] except Manzuoli and a few others in the opera," moaned Leopold Mozart; "Manzuoli is receiving 1500 pounds sterling for this winter, and the money had to be guaranteed in Italy . . . otherwise he would not have come to London." Leopold estimated the castrato's earnings for the season at more than twenty thousand German gulden. Burney saw him as Farinelli's successor (see pp. 125 and 267), "his manner of singing . . . grand and full of taste and dignity." His art fixed in Mozart's mind the technical principles of Italian singing. Quick to notice the change in his vocal style, Grimm would write in the *Correspondance* of 15 July 1766, soon after Wolfgang's return to France: "Having heard Manzuoli in London for a whole winter, he profited so well from this [experience] that, though he has an excessively weak voice, he sings with as much taste as soul." What he learned from Manzuoli both in the opera house and in private instruction remained a permanent part of his musical being; the secrets of Italy's pellucid cantilena first came to him in London's wet and fumes.

---

38 Bach contributed music to both *Ezio* and *Berenice*, as did Mattia Vento, a Neapolitan who had settled in London in 1763. Perhaps the Mozarts attended Thomas Arne's *L'olimpiade* (after Metastasio's text), produced during April of 1765: in his journal Leopold recorded in English a meeting with "Doctor Arne and his Son. Composers."

That Bach's *Adriano in Siria*, even with Manzuoli as Farnaspe, disappointed Londoners pleased the city's colony of Italian musicians: for all the science and finish of his Italianate style, Bach in their eyes remained a German, a rival, an intruder, and for a time Manzuoli had kept his vow never to sing anything Bach composed. That a German child patronized by the Bach-Abel circle found a friend and advocate in a leader of the Italian camp gave token of a talent so extraordinary that it eclipsed partisanship.

The imperious sway of the Italians over musical London made a strong impression upon Leopold. Despite the Teutonic bias of Buckingham House, their primacy had only begun to fade in the face of the ever more confident Germans. The superior musician's ties to Italy remained his main credentials: the public still expected the non-Italian to have drunk deep from Italian wells. Leopold could not close his eyes to the debt the artistic and material success of Handel in the immediate past and of Christian Bach in the present owed to their tutelage in Italy: it alone bestowed ultimate authority and prestige; and, most important, there the student could learn the art of the opera as nowhere else. In an advertisement for the benefit at Ranelagh Gardens, Leopold had implied that Wolfgang had already been to Italy and won its approval. To turn this deception into truth as soon as possible, the father resolved to return home by way of Milan and Venice.

His spirits sank as he faced the task of removal. "Time is needed just to get away from here and make arrangements for all our baggage; to look at it makes the perspiration run down my face. Just think! We have lived in one place for a whole year and are at home here! More preparations are needed than when we left Salzburg, for we cannot leave anything here and yet cannot take everything with us." At about ten in the morning of 1 August 1765, the Mozarts, accompanied by their servant, Potivin,[39] at last quit English soil. To prepare their smooth way over the Channel, the Hagenauers in Salzburg had invoked the Madonna of Maria Plain. The weather proved glorious, the wind favorable. At not yet two o'clock, the travelers disembarked at Calais, eager for the luncheon table.

---

39 In the course of the Mozarts' journey home, Leopold wrote from Paris (9–13 June 1766) of the "one servant" still in his employ, a young man, "certainly not a child," but vulnerable enough to require guidance lest he "fall into bad company . . . temptation allied with opportunity can transform even angels into devils." This endangered angel could only have been Potivin: the artful Porta, whose trustworthiness Leopold had come to doubt ever more, had gone his way in London. By early November, with the family's re-entry into Salzburg imminent, Potivin would quit the Mozarts' service to take up an offer about which Leopold had misgivings: as valet to a Parisian gentleman.

CHAPTER XIII

The Lowlands, Paris, Burgundy, and Switzerland

O N 19 SEPTEMBER 1765, Leopold Mozart sent Lorenz Hagenauer
a letter "from The Hague; but not from The Hague near Munich
[on the Inn, north of Wasserburg] nor from The Hague which lies near
Lambach in Austria [in the district of Wels]: No! Rather from The Hague
in Holland. To be sure, this will appear very odd to you. . . ." But Hagenauer could not have been altogether surprised: his wife had suspected that
Leopold would visit the capital of the House of Orange. At all events,
from London Leopold could still announce to Salzburg: "We . . . are not
going to Holland; of that I can assure you." He had unflattering notions
about the Dutch, viewing them in the light of those Flemish innkeepers he
had encountered ("a bit uncouth"). For him the adjective "Dutch" ("Hol-
ländisch") embraced everything in the Lowlands apart from the Habsburg
court at Brussels.[1]

He had quit London on 24 July with the intention to return to Paris,
collect his possessions, and proceed to Italy. The Dutch envoy to London,

---

1 The frontier between the seven northern United Provinces (the Dutch or Protestant Lowlands)
and the southern provinces (the Flemish or Catholic [the Habsburg] Lowlands) corresponded
not to a decisive linguistic or religious division but to maintainable defensive lines: both Catholics
and Protestants resided above and below the border and, the Walloons apart, all spoke the same
language, if in different dialects. The ancient Countship of Holland, the richest of the United
Provinces, had become their political nucleus and given its name to the northern union.

Count Jan Walraad van Weldeeren, had extended an invitation to visit his prince, young William V, but Leopold turned it aside along with offers from Copenhagen, Hamburg, and St. Petersburg: he wanted no more winters in chill, damp, northern places, recently having shipped the family's furs to Paris in a trunk he did not wish to open soon again. He looked to Italy for warmth as well as musical nourishment.

The travelers had broken their journey toward the Channel to attend the races at Canterbury[2]—thanks to Leopold's enthusiasm for English-bred horses (see XII, n. 22): "What horses! What magnificent horses!"—and then tarried to the end of the month at nearby Bourne Place, a country estate for the moment occupied by the twenty-one-year-old Horace Mann, whom they had met in London. Leopold had seized upon the invitation of this nephew of Sir Horace Mann, the British Minister in Florence, as much to build bridges to the diplomatic community in Italy as to indulge an enthusiasm for the races.

Learning that the Mozarts were about to leave England, van Weldeeren had tracked them to Kent: Princess Caroline, sister of William V of Orange (and wife of Karl Christian of Nassau-Weilburg) insisted upon receiving the child about whom her royal English relatives[3] had sent news. The Ambassador strengthened her behest with financial promises so generous as to foreclose refusal. Nannerl, enthusiastic about seeing Holland, spurred the visit that was almost to cost her life. "I had to come to Holland against my inclination; though my poor daughter did not breathe her last, I have seen her near the agonies of death." So Leopold mused in The Hague on 5 November 1765, as he looked back upon months of family illness.

In Calais he had anticipated Princess Caroline's glittering fees by taking quarters in the luxurious Hôtel d'Angleterre. After repossessing the Pressburg carriage, the Mozarts made their way via Dunkirk and Bergues to Lille. Illness forced them to linger a month (until 4 September) in the handsome, bustling town—Flemish, though within the confines of France—first the son and soon afterward the father suffering severe colds. (During the stay in Lille, news came of Emperor Francis's death on 18 August.) With Leopold still not recovered in full, the coach rolled

---

2 Whether a concert planned for the children in Canterbury's Town Hall took place remains in question. *The Kentish Post or Canterbury News-Letter* of 20 July gave notice of a concert on the twenty-fifth by "the celebrated German Boy, Aged eight Years [he was moving toward ten], and his Sister," but none of the family's letters, diaries, or reminiscences mentions it.

3 She and her brother were children of the late William IV of Orange and his consort, Princess Anne, daughter of King George II of England and harpsichord pupil of Handel.

on to Ghent, where Wolfgang played the organ in the church of the Bernardines, and then to Antwerp. There he performed on the organ in the spacious seven-aisled cathedral.[4] If this masterwork of the Flemish late gothic did not answer Leopold's taste—he admired the Exchange, dating from the Renaissance—its treasures awed him, in particular Rubens's "Descent from the Cross." But for all its works of art and monuments, Antwerp showed a face discomposed by serious physical and emotional damage—scars left by the religious struggles as well as the deep and still-flowing wounds inflicted by the Peace of Westphalia, which had written an end to the port's prosperity: Holland had obtained the right to close the river Scheldt to ships from the southern Lowlands, Antwerp, its commercial artery thus severed, being sacrificed to Amsterdam;[5] and, into the bargain, the French had sacked and plundered Antwerp during the War of the Austrian Succession, giving a final touch to what Leopold Mozart described as "the present grievous state of the once great commercial city."

Though drawn into the War of the Austrian Succession, Holland had contrived to remain neutral during the Seven Years' War and, in spite of economic decline since the middle of the century, continued to benefit from the blocking of the Scheldt: Prince William presided over a prosperous nation and maintained a comfortable court at The Hague, Leopold's destination. Leaving the carriage behind in Antwerp—the region's network of waterways, provided with horse-drawn barges, furnished reliable transportation—the Mozarts journeyed by way of Rotterdam, arriving at The Hague on 10 or 11 September. Shifting his ground, Leopold admitted: "I should have been very sorry not to have seen Holland: all the towns of Europe I have visited for the most part resemble one another, whereas the Dutch villages and towns are completely different from all others in Europe."[6] The landscape, too, bore little similarity to any he knew. Not an inch of tillable soil remained uncultivated in a countryside intersected by small canals with rows of trees on either side, the lines of both canals and trees as straight as if drawn with a ruler. Leopold appreciated this orderliness, though even he came to think of it as a bit "excessive."

---

4 Despite the brevity of the stops in Calais, Dunkirk, and Bergues, Leopold had sought out their leading organists, Wolfgang no doubt playing on the local instruments.

5 Thus a substantial volume of Rhine trade moved only with Dutch sanction: ships had to fly the Dutch flag to enter or leave the harbor of Antwerp.

6 The adversities about to overwhelm him in Holland would prevent his setting down for Salzburg friends the detailed impressions of daily life he had provided from France and England.

Hastening to fulfill his responsibilities at court, on the twelfth he began a series of concerts: two for Princess Caroline[7] and "several" in the presence of Prince William—he put a carriage at the family's disposal—for whom music had a "principal interest." But Nannerl did not appear with her father and brother: she had felt it unwise to leave the quarters Leopold had taken at La Ville de Paris.[8]

All at once she had begun to exhibit symptoms of a chest cold. At first it seemed of little consequence: she showed every sign of coming to herself; indeed, Leopold made no move to postpone the "Grand Concert" scheduled for 30 September in the Oude Doelen, where an orchestra was to accompany brother and sister in clavier concertos and play at least two of Wolfgang's symphonies. On the evening of the twenty-sixth, however, a chill seized her, and high fever set in; an anxious Leopold scrutinized her inflamed throat. Her condition grew threatening, and Doctor Levie Heymans, recommended by the diplomatic corps, bled her. Day by day she became more emaciated, and a "priest found her condition so serious that he ... gave her the Holy Sacrament of Extreme Unction." The parents began to resign themselves to God's will: "Had anyone heard the several evenings of conversation among the three of us—my wife, myself, and my daughter—during which we persuaded her of the vanity of this world and of the blessedly happy death of children, he would not have listened with dry eyes. Meanwhile, in the next room, little Wolfgang entertained himself with his music."

During her hours of fitful slumber and delirium, Nannerl spoke in English, French, and German, and, in spite of their distress, the Mozarts found themselves laughing at her ramblings. Old Professor Thomas Schwenke, the royal physician dispatched by Princess Caroline, arrived in

---

7 Mozart accompanied her at the clavier and commended the "sweetness" of a voice for which he composed a group of arias, long vanished. (Though perhaps they included the string-accompanied K. 23 for soprano, its text from Metastasio's *Artaserse;* early in 1766 Wolfgang revised this work composed the previous October.) Two other soprano arias (with texts from *Artaserse*) survive from this Dutch period, but he could not have intended them for her: unlike K. 23, whose words set forth a loving woman, K. 78/73b and K. 79/73d treat of heroic matters—no doubt meant for castrato—and have a richer scoring.

8 Upon arriving at The Hague, Leopold lodged at this establishment frequented by artists. Later, he moved into the house, on the Hof-Spuy, of a clock-and-watch maker named Eskes. This change could not have taken place until after 27 September, for an advertisement in the *'s Gravenhaegse Vrijdagse Courant* of this date still gave Leopold's address as the hotel. Nannerl became seriously ill on the twenty-sixth, and the Mozarts must have remained at the Ville de Paris for some time. A later notice in the same newspaper makes clear that they were living with Eskes at least by 17 January 1766.

time to gain gratitude for a recovery to which his medical science contributed the *coup de maître*: a prescription for "good calves soup with well-boiled rice."

On 15 November, just when the patient had improved enough to get out of bed and attempt to walk, just when Leopold and Frau Anna Maria, who had divided the vigil at Nannerl's side, felt they had ridden the storm, Wolfgang came down with the very same kind of fever, possibly typhoid, that had attacked his sister. (He must have looked unhealthy for some time: as early as 1 October, the British Minister to The Hague, Joseph Yorke, Baron Dover, observed that members of the capital's medical fraternity didn't think he would "be long lived.") He endured a four-week struggle with death, lying for eight days in a near comatose state. His lips turned hard and black and peeled away three times; his tongue seemed to have turned to wood; he lost all power of speech. But, by degrees, his attempts to mutter succeeded and his faculties returned. When, around 7 December, Leopold first dared lift the "completely unrecognizable" child from his bed and carry him to a chair, he was "nothing but . . . tender skin and tiny bones. . . ." On 11 December, his parents began to lead him "across the room a few times so that little by little he may learn to move his feet again and also to stand upright unaided."

As Christmas approached, Leopold looked back upon almost three months during which his wife had not dared leave their rooms. But now Nannerl no longer bore traces of her ordeal, and Wolfgang showed every sign of regaining his strength. His children, Leopold realized, had "risen from the dead." The prayers of friends at the altars of Salzburg had helped the family through the long crisis as had the assistance of Prince William and his sister,[9] Wolfgang having captivated the House of Orange as he had the Hanoverians. ("Your generosity, your kindnesses . . . recalled me to life," a Mozartean inscription to Princess Caroline would acclaim.) Coyly, Leopold observed to Hagenauer: "At all events, who my friends are here I cannot tell you, because to do so might be considered boastful."

He rejected the idea of taking the children home: the risk of exposing them to the rigors of such a journey in midwinter would be, he insisted, too great. Instead, Leopold roused them to a flurry of professional activity: missed opportunities and lost fees were to be made good. Wolfgang

---

9 Leopold prided himself on his ability to get money posthaste in all emergencies. In The Hague he not only received generous gifts from the palace but also borrowed on his letters of credit. Before leaving England he had probably transferred to Salzburg a large part of his profits to date.

and Nannerl returned to the platform on 22 January 1766 at the Oude Doelen, her first appearance before a Dutch audience,[10] which may have also experienced the premieres of two Mozart symphonies: K. 22 (with an inspired, chromatic Andante) and K. 19, both in all likelihood written during his convalescence.

Leopold decided to break his residence in The Hague with a stay of some five weeks in Amsterdam at the Lion d'Or. He scheduled a performance in the beautiful Salle du Manège on 29 January and, most noteworthy, received permission to give a second concert on 26 February: it fell within Lent, when, as a rule, all entertainment had to be suspended. But in the case of the Mozarts the authorities made an exception: "To propagate miraculous gifts," they declared, "serves to praise God." The first program included "overtures [symphonies] from the hand of this little composer"; the second, too, featured "Wolfgang's own instrumental music:"[11] thus the pair of "Haag" symphonies may have figured on both occasions.

The court had asked him to provide music for the ceremonies and parties marking Prince William's formal accession as hereditary stadholder of the seven United Provinces; upon his eighteenth birthday on 8 March 1766, the guardianship of Duke Ludwig Ernst of Braunschweig-Wolfenbüttel would come to an end. For the festivities Wolfgang set to work on his "Seven Variations for Keyboard" on the Dutch national anthem, "Willem van Nassau" (K. 25), a tune with which he could not have been more familiar (see V, n. 10), and a quodlibet for orchestra, the so-called *Galimathias Musicum*, K. 32,[12] in whose finale he again used the anthem. In addition, manipulating a melody by Christian Ernst Graaf, Prince William's Kapellmeister,[13] he put together a set of "Eight Variations for Keyboard," K. 24. (They are quite artless.)

---

10 Had her illness compelled her father to cancel the Grand Concert scheduled for 30 September, or did he reshape it to exhibit Wolfgang alone?

11 The children also offered their usual mixture of concertos and solos.

12 A quodlibet is a suite in which popular tunes appear, often to incongruous and humorous effect. Here some rather heavy touches of jollity call to mind Leopold's "realistic," descriptive peasant compositions: indeed, references to Schwabian folk song reinforce the impression of his active participation in creating the score. He must also have devised the charming conceit inspiring the architecture of K. 25: one variation for each province of a nation represented collectively by the hymn being varied.

13 In The Hague the Mozarts met Graaf; Giovanni Battista Zingoni, Princess Caroline's music master; and Johann Christian Fischer, the oboist from Freiburg in Breisgau who would settle in England and marry Mary Gainsborough, the painter's daughter. A minuet by Fischer was to be the basis of Mozart's popular variations for keyboard, K. 179/189a, of 1774; in Holland, Wolfgang also set down compositions in a notebook (K. 32a) that became one of his widow's cherished possessions. It has vanished.

By the beginning of March the Mozarts had returned to The Hague, and the children performed on the eleventh at court, which heard the two sets of variations and maybe the quodlibet, too (though Mozart might not have had time to complete it). Since recent study places the composition of the "Lambach" Symphony (K. Anh. 221/45a)[14] alongside that of the quodlibet, this "third Hague Symphony," much in the spirit of K. 19 and 22, might also have played a part in the celebrative music.

Leopold now pondered a future for his son as a composer. His music had begun to mount beyond assemblages of clichés: no longer kindergarten creations, the six sonatas dedicated to Princess Caroline (K. 26–31 for clavier and accompanying violin composed during February 1766 and engraved in The Hague the following month) reveal well-defined subjects, well-turned phrases, a sense of continuity, and a growing fluency. It is possible that Leopold already had a plan under way to have him, upon their return home, startle the Archbishop's court with an ambitious composition: the *"Poesie"* Leopold complimented in his letter of 12 December 1765 may have been a reference to the oratorio *Die Schuldigkeit des ersten Gebots*; perhaps at his request, Weiser had written and forwarded it from Salzburg as a text for Wolfgang to take in hand.

His Salzburg apartment, Leopold suddenly realized, would be inadequate to the family's new circumstances; not only would the already marriageable Nannerl require her privacy—at home it would be impossible to continue the family's sleeping arrangements on tour, Nannerl often sharing her mother's bed, Wolfgang his father's[15]—but a more urgent need had to be met: "Where," Leopold wondered, "will Wolfgang set up? Where will I find a special place for him to study and work, of which he will have much?" The child, whom Leopold's public notices had hitherto described with phrases at times suitable to a circus performer, had become "our little composer," and the father foresaw for himself an ever-widening role as mentor.

His work, too, had its place in the House of Orange's celebration: he took pride in a Dutch translation of his *Versuch*, dedicated and presented to Prince William by its publisher, Joannes Enschede of Haarlem. Encouraged by the organist Henricus Radecker, Enschede invited the Mozarts to the lovely town; he wanted Wolfgang to perform on its Groote Kerk's

---

14 The sobriquet derives from a set of the symphony's orchestral parts surviving in the monastery of Lambach. In the copyist Estlinger's hand, they incorporate revisions Mozart made in Salzburg during 1767 (see pp. 250–51).

15 In August 1766 Leopold requested Hagenauer to have a bed enclosed by curtains built for Nannerl; by November he concluded that the family had to leave the Getreidegasse for larger quarters. However, more than six years passed before the move to the Hannibalplatz.

(St. Bavo's) famous three-manual organ, built in 1738 by Christian Müller. During this visit of early April, Leopold received from the hands of the admiring Enschede a copy of the Dutch *Versuch*, an edition better turned out than the original, brought into the world a decade earlier by an unsophisticated if well-meaning publisher and an overworked, fretful author. Those difficult days must have seemed distant to Leopold, warmed by the sun of his family's good fortune. Holland had honored the Mozart name with the kind of esteem he had long sought.

2

FOR ALL THAT, he ruminated upon home, his nostalgia intensified by a surprising meeting with P. Vincento Castiglione, a native of the archbishopric.[16] He had quit it, visited England, become a student of medicine, and settled in Holland. "Of great service" during Wolfgang's illness, this resident of Amsterdam appears to have taken quarters in The Hague in order to help care for him. That Castiglione had turned to the Calvinists pained Leopold; he urged a return to Rome, though aware of the resentments of someone thrust into a novitiate when still a child. For his part, Castiglione seems to have had much pleasure meeting fellow Salzburgers and to have taken with indulgence Leopold's attempts at reconversion. (He did, in fact, embrace Catholicism again within two years.)

The encounter provided Leopold a fine bit of news to pass on to the Hagenauers, modest recompense for the chronicles of local table talk sent him by their eldest son, Johann. Leopold affectionately dubbed him "Herr Novellista Joannes" and took to quoting items from his letters as if citing the Evangelist's chapter and verse. More and more Leopold's mind wandered to friends in Salzburg, his goal as he turned from Haarlem to journey first to Amsterdam (a final concert on 16 April[17]), then to Utrecht (an appearance with the local *Collegium musicum* on 21 April in the Music Room of the Vreeburg), Rotterdam, Moerdijk, Antwerp (to pick up the carriage), and Mechelen (performances before Archbishop Johann Heinrich, Count von Frankenberg and Schellendorf, who in Paris had been generous to the family). Then on to Brussels, where the Mozarts rested for a

---

16 Thus Leopold did discover an inhabitant of Salzburg who had crossed the Channel before him. Southern Germany had a substantial population of native-born citizens of Italian ancestry. Often they retained the Italian form of their first names.

17 A merchant named Kuhlman presented the children with a copy of Georg Benda's *Sei sonate per il Cembalo solo* (1757) on 18 April, the day of their departure from Amsterdam. Benda would have a brief but strong influence upon Mozart (see p. 458).

day before crossing into France to arrive at the citadel of Valenciennes on the evening of 9 May 1766.

Leopold had learned that Grimm's close friend Madame Marie Thérèse Geoffrin, that extraordinary power in Parisian salon life, was whiling time away in the border city before setting out for Warsaw and a reunion with her protégé of former years Stanislaus Poniatowski, who had become King of Poland in September 1764. She may well have offered Leopold suggestions for his second Parisian campaign, a service rendered for Grimm's sake. (Her letter of some two years later recommending Wolfgang and Nannerl to Prince Kaunitz indicated that she had never heard them play, her faith in their talent resting upon the opinion of friends, among them Grimm.) Leopold wanted her goodwill. He comprehended the extent to which she could both launch and ruin careers: she steered the streams of conversation flowing through her house, her "Kingdom of the Rue Saint-Honoré," whence she commanded a cohesive band of philosophes and their satellites, a network of admirers (whom she, in Marmontel's words, "held in leading strings") extending from London to St. Petersburg. Continuing south from Valenciennes to nearby Cambrai, Leopold made a gesture, word of which he without doubt hoped might reach her: in the cathedral he paused to contemplate the tomb of Fénelon, the gentle and elegant archbishop whom the philosophes hailed as one of their precursors (and whose works he did admire).

The Mozarts arrived in Paris on 10 May, taking rooms Grimm had reserved for them in a house on the Rue Traversière (now 8 Rue Molière) near the Palais Royal. Though appalled by the high rent, Leopold thought it unwise to return to his former quarters at Count Van Eyck's palace, now no longer a sub-rosa gaming house but a notorious haunt.[18] Relieved to find in secure state the baggage left with Hummel, Leopold faced the task of reorganizing and repacking his possessions for the journey to Salzburg. (He would not have returned to Paris had he not left so many things behind.)

Little is known about this second Parisian stay. It included a meeting with the famous composer of *opéra comique* (and also a chess champion), François André Philidor, and a reunion with Christian Cannabich, on leave from Mannheim. The Mozarts also made the acquaintance of a pianist from Wimpfen im Tal (Neckar) on his first visit to Paris: Notger Ignaz Franz von Beecke, a member of the Court of Öttingen-Wallerstein. Several days at Versailles toward the end of May and the Mozarts' presence at

---

18 Moreover, the Countess, who had shown strong friendship to the Mozarts, had died early in 1764.

the Prince de Conti's English tea in the salon of the Temple indicate continuing popularity with the nobility. Wolfgang must have very much pleased Louis-Joseph de Bourbon, Prince de Condé:[19] he extended an invitation that would give the family's homeward route an unforeseen direction.

Leopold remained of two minds about Salzburg. At times he flattered himself with thoughts of a promotion upon his return, for Hagenauer had kept the court informed of the family's successes and made certain that packets of Wolfgang's published works made their way to the Residenz; and the father had sent word that he very much wanted His Grace to hear them. Yet in less confident moments Leopold realized that against the new fame of the Mozart name the Archbishop might weigh the liabilities evolving day by day from an absence so prolonged as to have passed out of the court's reckoning. By the end of the Grand Tour, Leopold could no longer suppress his anxieties and anger as ever more disturbing rumors came to him: "The nearer I approach Salzburg the more childish the gossip reaching my ears. I wish to remain spared such things. For several years, thank God, I was peaceful and free of such vexations, and I want to remain far from them. In particular, very odd things are being said about our reception at court. I assure you [Hagenauer] that these things appear very strange to me and could have an effect many might not expect: after great honors, rudeness is not to be suffered and forgotten."

He could not predict his own attitude when passing through Salzburg's gates. Could someone who had traveled like an excellency, who had chatted with the Empress, the Emperor, the Queen of France, and Their Majesties of England once again unrepiningly don the livery of a court fiddler? Leopold did not know. On a visit to Paris, so famed a prince and warrior— and gifted violinist—as Karl Wilhelm Ferdinand of Braunschweig, had sought the Mozarts out on the Rue Traversière and greeted Leopold with eulogies as author of the *Versuch.*[20] How he luxuriated in such recognition, in intercourse with the great. Were these days now to end?

Once more he found reasons to defer a direct journey to Salzburg. Illness upon illness, so he claimed, had eaten into his reserve funds, and he made it sound quite reasonable to attempt to defray expenses on the eastward journey, and perhaps even turn a profit, by making any stop that might generate fees: "There will be many paying for this voyage who as yet

19 The title of Prince de Condé fell to the head of the cadet branch of the House of Bourbon, the title of Prince de Conti to the head of the House of Condé's cadet branch.
20 The Prince observed of Wolfgang's command of harmony: ". . . many a kapellmeister at the peak of his art dies without knowing what this child knows at nine years of age."

know nothing about it," he assured the Hagenauers. Solid judgment demanded his taking home as swiftly as possible a pair of children only yesterday near death, but he excluded the thought. Had he learned so little from that ordeal in The Hague? And how long could he ignore the fact, discussed in Paris and later in Salzburg, that Wolfgang had grown little more than not at all? He remained glaringly undersized, as if striving to accede to Papa's deepest desire. Defying reality, Leopold wrote home about "how my children have grown." In contrast to this kind of magic, Grimm set his own qualms to rest by celebrating the child's wit, spirit, grace, and sweetness, his gaiety providing reassurance "against the fear one has that so premature a fruit might fall before maturing."[21]

3

IN A LETTER begun in Paris on 9 June 1766, Leopold did not dare tell Hagenauer of his newly projected route home; he promised to reveal it in "the heading of the next letter." Dated over two months later (16 August), it began: "Do not be shocked that I am writing you from Lyon." He had quit Paris the evening of 9 July and turned southeast.

As Governor of Burgundy, the Prince de Condé had to attend the triennial meeting of its local *parlement*[22] at Dijon, capital of the province. There he had invited the Mozarts, who were to provide entertainment for this learned and cultured nobleman pulled by official duties from the pleasures of Versailles, Paris, and his domain of Chantilly. Around 12 July the family arrived in Dijon and remained some two weeks. On the eighteenth, Wolfgang and Nannerl made a public appearance, honored by the presence of Condé, at "a grand concert" in the Great Assembly Room of the Town Hall. They performed "concertos on two harpsichords and pieces for four hands on the same instrument." In addition, Wolfgang, sang "an aria of his own composition," and the audience heard several of his symphonies. He doubtless supervised their performance, perhaps as first violinist directing with his bow; or he may have followed a baroque tradition at the time still surviving in France: pounding the beat on the floor with a staff. What is certain is that the instrumentalists made a botch. In his journal Leopold called upon Italian, French, and English to describe them: the

---

21 In his *Correspondance* (15 July 1766), Grimm reported that, since Wolfgang's first appearance in Paris, no more than an infinitesimal physical growth had accompanied his musical progress. For Pater Beda Hübner's similar comment, see p. 57.

22 A French *parlement*, a multi-chambered law court charged with registering royal edicts, should not be confused with the legislative parliament the English enjoyed.

violinists as "*asini tutti*" (a pack of asses), one of them meriting "*trés mediorce*" [*sic*], another "*un miserable italien detestable*" [*sic*]; a violist as "*un racleur*" [a scraper]; a cellist as "miserable"; and a pair of brothers playing oboe as "rotten." A missing page deprives posterity of what adjectives in what language Leopold held in reserve for the horn players. Clearly the concert had its disasters, an official summary of the event ignoring the performances as it concentrated upon the etiquette observed, the costumes worn, the refreshments consumed, and the graciousness of Condé.

If Dijon had wretched musical resources, it did enjoy an enviable reputation for its literary salons and Academy.[23] At the center of the city's intellectual life labored the first president of the Burgundian *Parlement* and member of the Academy, Charles de Brosses—magistrate, philosophe, encyclopedist,[24] historian, linguist, archeologist, and geographer, whose voyage to Italy in 1739 resulted in both his monograph (the first) on the ruins of Herculaneum and his charming *Lettres familières écrites d'Italie.* Sarcastic and cranky,[25] this lively spirit (enclosed in a tiny body), musical enthusiast, and translator of Metastasio must have had much to discuss with the Mozarts, in particular *opera seria*, which seemed to him a faulty structure incapable of housing both drama and music in comfort. Possibly he prompted the young composer to sing that aria—likely enough to a text by Metastasio—at the concert on the eighteenth.

In addition to recompense from Condé, for whom they without doubt played in private, the Mozarts found yet another reward of their Burgundian visit in the region's wines; Leopold wrote Hagenauer: "Oh, how often I wished that the wine tended us with overflow was in the cellar of a good Salzburg friend." Vineyards excited Leopold's interest, and, since his route from Dijon to his next stop, Lyon, remains unknown, it seems not out of order to imagine a journey through Gevrey-Chambertin, Vosne-Romanée, Nuits-Saint-Georges, Beaune, Pommard, Volnay, Meursault, Puligny-Montrachet, and Mâcon. In Dijon he had made arrangements to ship Burgundies to Salzburg, and perhaps dreams of claret played a part in his

---

23 For its prize essay of 1750, the Academy of Dijon had proposed the question concerning the sciences and arts that provoked Rousseau's treatise on the corruption of society. During 1753–1754, Rousseau wrote the *Discourse on Inequality* in response to yet another theme set forth by the Dijon academicians. Their inquiries thus inspired two of the most famous works of the century.

24 De Brosses submitted to the *Encyclopédie* the entry under *Étymologie*, which Anne-Robert-Jacques Turgot reworked.

25 De Brosses sold a life tenure on the estate of Tournay to Voltaire, with whom he had an easy friendship until a foolish dispute (1761) over the price of a few cords of wood brought it to an end. The incident showed neither at his best.

sudden, fleeting, and wild idea of turning the carriage toward the Atlantic and Bordeaux.

A stay of about a month in Lyon (the family arrived about 26 July) betrayed his mounting indecision concerning Salzburg, Leopold again asking why he should return, and, indeed, at a "time when my children's youth still evokes astonishment." He toyed with various plans: to push on southward to Marseilles; or westward to Bordeaux; or, returning to the Italian project, eastward to Turin ("which lies under our noses"), thence to Venice—in time to witness and perhaps contribute to the festival of the *Ascensa*[26]—and then home by way of the Tyrol. Admitting his "inordinate appetite for travel," in the end he had to give in to cries from Salzburg to return for the sake of the children's health; he had to submit to the disappointment of renouncing the trip to Italy: "I have promised to go home and will keep my word." In this spirit of resignation he asked the Hagenauers to provide the Getreidegasse apartment with a glass show-cabinet in which he might display the gifts gathered during the tour, symbols of the family's triumphs.

Records survive of only one public appearance of the children in Lyon: on 13 August they took part in the series of weekly Wednesday concerts (with orchestra) given by the Académie des Beaux Arts in a hall on the Place des Cordeliers, opposite the church of St. Bonaventura and near the rushing Rhone. Johann Rudolf Forcart, a ribbon manufacturer of Basle, reported his sympathetic response to the "little virtuosos" and astonishment at the size of the audience of more than three hundred: "They say he [Wolfgang] earned close to 1,000 livres that day."[27]

Leopold at once put part of this money to use; "I have had new clothes made for my wife, my daughter, and Master Wolfgang, and have not forgotten myself," he wrote Hagenauer. "Material of silk is, to be sure, somewhat expensive at the moment, but, be that as it may, one should not have been in Lyon to no purpose." Here he supplied an indulgence meant to sweeten bitter medicine: that final resolve to return to Germany; he would proceed by way of Switzerland.

4

LATE IN AUGUST (perhaps on the twentieth), the Mozarts arrived in Geneva, probably via Pont d'Ain, and departed during the second week of

---

26 Music took the lead in these days of revelry, which rolled into one the Feast of Christ's Ascension and the celebration of the city's marriage to the sea (*Sposalizio del Mare*).

27 The public advertisement of the concert did not mention Nannerl; Forcart's comments, however, make her participation clear.

September,[28] an extended visit during which Leopold busied himself with calls on local watch manufacturers in the hope of negotiating trade with Salzburg. In London he had attempted, under Hagenauer's sponsorship, to arrange the shipment of English watches. Although Geneva, neighboring upon the Empire, offered the German importer less complicated opportunities,[29] Leopold did not pursue them without uncertainties: the city had been shaken by disturbances that continued to reverberate despite the conciliatory efforts of Voltaire, who lived nearby at his domain of Ferney-Tournay.[30] Yet, this so-called *guerre de Genève*, long seething between a patrician council and those it governed, hardly answered Leopold's description of "internal civil war in full flame": as the French representative to the city observed, the children found themselves "well-received and feted," the authorities permitting them "to give two concerts at the Town Hall" and then with good grace setting the light attendance down to "the season when the number of inhabitants in Geneva is much diminished. . . ." Moreover, the theater saw in the political quarrels no reason to interrupt performances, its impresario, it would seem, even entertaining a suggestion that Wolfgang appear on its boards as an entr'acte entertainer.

The Mozarts managed to see the sights and to visit "persons famous for their cleverness and unusual talents." With recommendations from Grimm, Étienne Noël Damilaville, and Madame d'Épinay, the family made music in private for the friends of Voltaire. His publisher, Gabriel Cramer (who had played an important role in luring him to Geneva after his break with Berlin, and whom Grimm had advised of the Mozarts' visit) declared that Wolfgang played the harpsichord "as it has never been played." But the sage of Ferney lamented Wolfgang's having chosen "a rather unfortunate time to bring harmony into the temple of Discord. You know," Voltaire continued to Madame d'Épinay, "that I live two leagues from Geneva; I never go out; I was very sick when this phenomenon blazed on the black horizon of Geneva: in short, to my very great regret he left without my having seen him."[31]

Such an encomium, however, seemed too high-flown to a young musi-

---

28 The precise dates of their stops in France and Switzerland must be inferred through conjecture: references in their letters and reminiscences do not always comport with other evidence.
29 Leopold bought pocket watches in London and Geneva for the purpose of private resale (see p. 222).
30 Under Voltaire its chief industry became the manufacture of watches.
31 The convalescing *grand seigneur* of the philosophes compensated himself for this loss by having various *operas comiques* played in his private theater at Ferney: "The entire troupe of Geneva to the number of fifty was kind enough to give me this pleasure."

cian who had just visited Voltaire, seeking his advice: André-Ernest-Modeste Grétry, but recently come from Rome. Leopold had asked him to compose "a very difficult sonata movement" that might test Wolfgang's ability "to play anything at sight." Although his performance of the resulting Allegro proceeded "without stopping," he met the challenge by "adhering to the modulations" but all the while "substituting a quantity of [simplified] passages for those I [Grétry] had written. . . ." Unaware of the subterfuge, those present thought themselves at "a miracle"; everyone "but myself," Grétry tartly recorded. Even Mozart had his sleight of hand.

Leopold's traversal of Switzerland continued at its leisurely pace. Bern his goal, he left Geneva with the intention of pausing in Lausanne for luncheon. However, news of the family's route had reached Duke Louis Eugene of Württemberg who, since his marriage to Reichsgräfin Sofie Albertine von Beichlingen, resided at Villa Monrion, near Lausanne. The Mozarts found his servants awaiting their coach. "I could do nothing other," Leopold wrote, "than let myself be persuaded . . . to stay in Lausanne for five days."

Louis Eugene collaborated with Dr. Samuel Tissot in a commentary on Wolfgang's genius in *Aristide ou le Citoyen* (11 October), a Lausanne periodical published under the Duke's auspices. Tissot declared: "I have seen much of our young musician; I have observed him attentively. . . ." And, indeed, the family spent many hours at Villa Monrion, Wolfgang composing in the presence of Tissot and the Duke,[32] who to all appearances wrote the lines printed a week later in the same magazine: "When I see the young Mozart with light heart creating those tender and sublime symphonies, which might be taken for the language of the immortals, every fiber of my being resounds, so to speak, with immortality. . . . I could almost imagine this child, precious to heaven . . . to be one of those pure spirits who inhabits the happy abode destined for me." Wolfgang composed some flute solos (the lost K. 33a) for this sentimental soldier-prince, whose dissimilarity to his egomaniacal brother, Karl Eugene, the reigning Duke of Württemberg, astonished Leopold. At the end of the visit, Louis Eugene found it difficult to let the Mozarts depart; seated in his carriage, Leopold shook his hand in farewell, probably on 19 September, and promised "to write often."

Leopold spent eight days in Bern (a stop whose particulars have yet to be uncovered) and then, via Baden in Aargau, went to Zurich at the end of

---

32 The Mozarts also gave two public concerts in Lausanne: the first on 15 September attracted an audience of seventy to the Town Hall; the second took place three days later.

September for a stay of about two weeks, probably at the Zum Schwert. Wolfgang and Nannerl performed in public on 7 and 9 October in the hall used by the local *collegium musicum* (*beim Kornhaus*, next to the Fraumünster), whose ledger records payment to "a Salzburger for symphonies and notturni."

Leopold had sought out Salomon Gessner, who doubtless helped open the *collegium's* doors to the children. In addition, his publishing firm of Orell, Gessner, and Co. took over distribution of the Mozarts' Parisian engraving. Poet, painter, and engraver, Gessner had a famous name: his *Idyllen* (1756) had become the most popular book in German, a position it would hold until the appearance of *Werther*; and in translation his epic poem *Der Tod Abels* (1758) had established his international reputation. This "Swiss Theocritus" had brought out his literary works in four volumes (with vignettes by his own hand), which he presented to the Mozarts during their visit on 3 October, his inscription hailing the children as "the glory of the nation[33] and the admiration of the world." (The first two volumes remained in Mozart's possession until his death.) As her gift, Frau Judith Gessner gave the family Christoph Martin Wieland's poetical works, her brother offering a German translation of Samuel Butler's *Hudibras* to Leopold. Zurich provided the kind of scholarly surroundings he held dear.

By the time of the War of the Austrian Succession, it had begun to challenge Leipzig's position as the literary heart of the German-speaking world: the Swiss scholars Johann Jakob Bodmer (probably the translator of Leopold's copy of *Hudibras*) and Johann Jakob Breitinger posited an aesthetic of poetry based upon imagination and feeling and therewith fomented a revolt against the rationalistic attitudes of Leipzig's Johann Christoph Gottsched and his disciples. For a while the new Swiss literary ideas drew men like Klopstock and Wieland to Zurich. But in the end neither felt at home with its own variety of academic coercion. The spiritual force and spaciousness of Klopstock's finest passages, the graceful fancy and ironic gaiety of Wieland at his best left the arid, tedious polemics of Zurich's (and Leipzig's) theoreticians far behind, and, by the time of the Mozarts' visit, the city's literary movement had lost some measure of confidence, tone, and spirit. Nonetheless, Zurich did retain a vigorous intel-

---

33 Gessner's inscription betrayed a romantic attachment to an all-embracing but long past German political unity. The Treaty of Westphalia had recognized Switzerland's severance from the Reich, an independence the League had already possessed de facto for almost a century and a half.

lectual life, and Leopold Mozart expressed delight in mixing with the "savants" of German Switzerland.[34]

This may have been the time he encouraged Wolfgang to set to music Gellert's *Geistliche Oden und Lieder* (Baron Bose's farewell gift to the boy),[35] a not unlikely consequence of breathing Zurich's literary atmosphere. (That this verse had a place among the most popular creations of the antagonistic Leipzig circle adds irony to the supposition.) Moreover, in Zurich the Mozarts probably learned to know the Anacreontic poets, the Halle partisans of Bodmer and Breitinger, in particular Johann Peter Uz, whose poem *"An die Freude"* Wolfgang would compose (K. 53/47e of 1768).

During the second week of October, the Mozarts left Zurich. After an overnight stop at Winterthur, they went on to Schaffhausen, most likely on the fourteenth, leaving two days later to cross into Germany. Though Salzburg lay directly to his east, Leopold showed it his back: the carriage turned northwest, rolling through that magical land (between the Upper Rhine and the infant Danube) where the edge of the Black Forest begins to merge with the Schwabian terrace lands. At Donaueschingen, near the source from which the Danube gains its first strength, stood the castle of Prince von Fürstenberg. He expected the family.

Sebastian Winter, the Mozarts' former servant, erstwhile cartographer of Wolfgang's Kingdom of Rücken, and now retainer of Prince Joseph Wenzel von Fürstenberg, had helped arrange the invitation. To the Mozarts' surprise, another old friend awaited them: as the carriage pulled up, Joseph Nikolaus Meissner stood by, ready to offer his welcome and to help with the baggage. On one of his many tours, Salzburg's famed bass had stopped at the residence of Joseph Wenzel, who, to judge by the marathon of concerts upon which the children embarked, revealed himself an indefatigable musical amateur: most of the twelve days of their stay, they performed at gatherings lasting from five until nine. With pride Leopold alluded to the children's growing ability to sustain a varied repertory over the course of these evenings, on one of which Wolfgang conducted his *Galimathias Musicum*. He composed several violoncello pieces (K. 33b, now lost) for

---

34 The spirit hospitable to the concept of a high cultural life revolving about letters dwelled less in Vienna, Munich, and Berlin than in centers with more assertive middle-class intelligentsias and elites: Leipzig, Hamburg, and Zurich. From these cities blew the winds that would lay low whatever remained of the German Rococo.

35 That von Bose's gift comprised this series of "divine songs" appears certain. A diffuse letter Leopold received from Gellert may have served in part to acknowledge receipt of music from Wolfgang's hand. The letter (undated) responded to one from Leopold written during the Grand Tour. No music by Mozart for the Gellert poems has come to light.

His Highness, who, having rewarded the children with louis d'or and jewels, burst into tears at their departure.

By way of Messkirch, another historic seat of the Fürstenbergs, and then following the Danube to Ulm and Günzburg, the carriage came to Dillingen,[36] a residence of Joseph I, Bishop of Augsburg[37] and Landgraf of Hessen-Darmstadt. The Mozarts remained two days (4–5 November), performing for him and admiring the town's architecture, to which the children's great-great-grandfather had contributed (see p. 15).

About midway between Dillingen and Augsburg, the family paused at the pilgrimage church of Markt Biberbach. Here Wolfgang met the twelve-year-old Joseph Sigmund Eugen Bachmann, Schwabia's *Wunderkind*. With enthusiasm the boys plunged into an organ competition, in all likelihood arranged by Bishop Joseph.

Leopold allotted Augsburg little time: he stayed one night at the Zu den drei Mohren[38] before pushing on to Munich, arriving there 8 November and again putting up at the Zum goldenen Hirschen. Almost three and a half years had passed since Maximilian III Joseph received his promise to return on the homeward journey, a commitment Leopold now regretted, remembering how long the Residenz kept artists waiting for money. On the ninth Wolfgang appeared before the Elector at table. Seated between him and Prince Clemens Wenzel of Saxony, he at once had to compose a piece for which His Electoral Highness sang the theme. Perhaps this applauded work was the short a cappella four-voice *Stabat mater* (K. 33c), now lost.

That night Leopold noticed Wolfgang's fitful slumber. The weather had turned cold and wet, and the delicate boy had not yet adjusted to German stove heating. Whatever its origin, a serious illness overwhelmed him: feverish and paralyzed from the knees down, he relived the terrible days that had followed his first trip to Vienna. Not until the middle of the month did he show signs of recovery, and only on the twenty-first could he venture out. The very next day he again performed before the Elector.

These final weeks of the Grand Tour did not show Leopold at his finest. He felt louis d'or slipping away and wanted to fasten upon them by any

---

36 Perhaps the Mozarts visited Alexander Ferdinand, Prince Thurn und Taxis, at nearby Dischingen, where, according to a plan formed in Paris, the Mozarts and the pianist von Beecke were to cross paths.

37 A free city, Augsburg had no temporal ties to its bishop, who often felt it politic to reside outside its territory, though he had a handsome episcopal palace on the Fronhof near the cathedral. Bishop Joseph gave Wolfgang the bejeweled golden ring to be seen in Salzburg's Mozart Museum.

38 It appears that the Mozarts said farewell to their servant, Potivin, in Augsburg (see XII, n. 39), where Leopold's mother would die the next month (11 December 1766).

means. He had hoped, once Maximilian Joseph's fee had arrived, to make a quick journey north to Regensburg: there stood the main palace of Alexander von Thurn und Taxis; there, in the city of the Reichstag, Louis Eugene of Württemberg and Joseph Wenzel von Fürstenberg would tarry during the coming weeks; all three would delight in having Mozart at their call.

Petulance and disappointment suffused Leopold's letters: Wolfgang's illness had put the journey to Regensburg out of the question. The family would now return home via Altötting and then follow the Salzach to Laufen, an autumn residence of the Salzburg court. Perhaps Leopold might still catch Archbishop Siegmund there, pay his compliments, and in the course of the audience sound the depth of his predicament. "But who knows what is in store for us upon our return to Salzburg? Perhaps we will be greeted in such a manner that we will happily put our knapsacks over our backs and leave. At least, God willing, I am bringing the children back to the Fatherland. If they are not wanted, it is not my fault. But they will never be had gratis." The court, he feared, might not pay for performances by its Vice-Kapellmeister's children; in any case, not the kind of fee to which he had become accustomed. (That the Archbishop's generous gift had set the tour in motion had dropped from his memory.) Time pressed upon him ever more heavily: "Every moment I lose is lost forever; and if I ever knew how precious time is for the young, I know it now."

"There is a strong rumor that once again this Mozart family will not remain here long," Beda Hübner reported in his Salzburg *"Diarium"* of 29 November, "but will soon travel through the whole of Scandinavia, the whole of Russia, and perhaps even travel to China. . . . De facto, I believe it certain that nobody in Europe is as famous as Herr Mozart with his two children; indeed, after God, he has his children to thank for his fame and his great wealth. The now completed journey is said to have cost them something near 20,000 florins; I can easily believe it; but how much money has he not presumably collected?" Such were the rumors and sniggering speculations flying through Salzburg on the very day of the family's return, the irony obvious in the words of even this kindly cleric, so well-disposed toward the Mozarts that he had framed his copy of their engraved portrait.

CHAPTER XIV

Back in Salzburg;
Vienna and Moravia

WHATEVER RESENTMENTS AND jealousies Salzburg harbored vanished with the return of the prodigals, who arrived "in good health," Hübner reported, "to the solace, joy, and pleasure of everyone of high and low station and to their own honor, fame, and praise." But Leopold flew his colors much too high, heaping up for inspection the hoard of watches, rings, snuffboxes, necklaces, and other gewgaws gathered during the tour. The Getreidegasse apartment, so Hübner thought, took on the look of "a church treasury." His published estimate put the collection's value at some twelve-thousand florins. By a display many found ostentatious, Leopold not only sought to stupefy the townsfolk; he also sold some of the articles, indulging a bit of legerdemain, so Hübner hinted: slipping purchased items into the category of gifts to the family from Europe's "great monarchs and princes" (see XIII, n. 29).

After a life of coaches and hotels, Wolfgang, almost eleven, settled into a routine of study. Using exercises from Fux's *Gradus ad Parnassum* (1725), Leopold, so tradition maintains, drilled him in the honorable and strenuous art of traditional German cantorial counterpoint known as the *strenger Satz*—Schubart, in his *Aesthetik der Tonkunst*, commended Leopold's knowledge of it—and together father and son read scores by Emanuel Bach, Hasse, Handel, and Johann Ernst Eberlin, Leopold's mentor of former days.

Thanks to Grimm's *Correspondance*, aristocratic Europe knew of the Mozarts' celebrity,[1] and the Archbishop, proud of the children, in no way sought requital for an absence that had continued beyond anything he had at first contemplated. Wolfgang's artistic and technical development astounded local musicians like Anton Cajetan Adlgasser, organist of the cathedral, and Michael Haydn. Both confessed "that they lacked the confidence to enter into competition on the clavier with this boy," whose gifts as a composer the Residenz at once appreciated and used.

For the anniversary celebration (December 1766) of Archbishop Schrattenbach's ordination, Wolfgang provided a *licenza*: a recitative and exuberant tenor aria (K. 36/33i) for *Il cavaliere di spirito*, an entertainment (inspired by Goldoni) performed at the palace by a troupe of Italian players from Linz. He also added a *licenza* for soprano (K. 70/61c), a recitative, and an aria rich in coloratura to Giuseppe Sarti's opera *Vologeso*, given the following March to honor the Archbishop's birthday. Here Mozart employed an idiom projecting the rhetorical gestures of the Baroque with astounding confidence.

His Serene Highness placed increasing trust in the young composer, who, about the same time, set to work on an offertory for the Feast of St. Benedict (K. 34).[2] On 8 December 1766 "at high mass in the cathedral," Beda Hübner heard "a symphony" by Mozart, which "found great acclamation among all the court musicians. . . ." On festive days, symphonies did have a place in the service,[3] and to its "astonishment" the congregation celebrating the Immaculate Conception heard what must have been part or even the whole of one of the works he had composed in England or Holland. The measure of the admiration Wolfgang had begun to command at

---

1 A muddled reference to Wolfgang had even appeared in a report of the Vienna Court Chancery (19 January 1765) concerning its efforts to fix upon the earliest age at which Jewish children might take baptism. In an effort to determine when a child's intellectual faculties become sufficiently developed to make a rational decision (*iudicium discretivum*), this body brought forward the example of "certain children born at Salzburg, led about the world during their seventh year, and so experienced in music as even to compose, which requires more than a *iudicium discretivum*." In February, Maria Theresa decided that Jewish children might not be baptized before completing their seventh year.

2 A faulty if persistent tradition assigns its composition to a stay at Kloster Seeon during the Mozarts' return journey to Salzburg; but their homeward route could not have taken them to this romantic Benedictine monastery: they traveled home not via Wasserburg but, rather, made their way through Altötting and Laufen.

3 Archbishop Schrattenbach's successor would oppose the use of wordless music in the service and went so far as to prohibit it, an injunction marked by consistency most often in parish churches. Scholars conjecture that the composition Hübner heard might have been, not a symphony, but Mozart's first Epistle sonata (see p. 302).

court may be taken from its decision that he share with Adlgasser and Haydn the composition of an ambitious oratorio, *Die Schuldigkeit des ersten Gebots* (The Obligation of the First Commandment, K. 35). Even if Leopold had already begun plans for this project through correspondence with its librettist, Ignaz Anton Weiser, it could not have been set in motion before the boy had proved himself at home.

Salzburg heard the first part of this theological allegory—Wolfgang's contribution and his first attempt to set his native language—in the Residenz on 12 March; parts two and three, by Haydn and Adlgasser, respectively (both lost), followed at intervals of a week. (On 2 April the authorities ordered Wolfgang's section performed again, this time in the *aula* of the university.) If distributing the composition of an extended piece among various composers in no way violated custom, entrusting a weighty Lenten commission to an eleven-year-old did. His work combined baroque recitative in the manner of Hasse, Handel, and Eberlin (whose Salzburg oratorios he had perused) with arias evidencing his kinship with the rococo *buffo* manner of Christian Bach[4] along with elements of the *strenger Satz*. He drew just what he required from the succession of musical impressions experienced on tour and at home. The first major work of the newest and youngest composer at the provincial court of Salzburg showed him to be anything but provincial. The future master made himself known in a music that wrings pathos from an uninspired text whenever it puts forth the slightest dramatic possibilities: then he pens passages of ardent, supple recitative and paints words in a manner recalling Sebastian Bach. The Archbishop's privy purse rewarded the score (a *sinfonia*, seven arias, and a closing trio) with a gold medallion having the weight of twelve ducats.

In his report to the Royal Society of London, Daines Barrington gave an account of Wolfgang's return to Salzburg, "where he . . . composed several oratorios, which were much admired." However, "the Prince of Salzburg, not crediting that such masterly compositions were really those of a child, shut him up for a week, during which he was not permitted to see anyone, and was left only with music paper, and the words of an oratorio. During this short time he composed a very capital oratorio, which was most highly approved of upon being performed."

If this tale, in great measure inaccurate, reflected any reality, it bore upon Archbishop Siegmund's desire to silence lingering suspicions concerning Leopold's long-questioned role in his son's compositions. Adl-

---

4 In 1768 Mozart turned the seventh number, "*Manches Übel*," to use in *La finta semplice*, his first *opera buffa*, music that had originally served as an aria for the Christian Spirit now underpropping the amorous Philidoro's descriptions of those sexual titillations he most enjoyed.

gasser and Haydn observed how much matters had changed: in quality and technique Wolfgang's works had passed beyond anything his father could have conceived or in any significant way improved; from the boy's pen now flowed an exuberance of musical invention, a quality of which Leopold's compositions had in large measure been innocent. Though he corrected Wolfgang's counterpoint exercises and pointed the way in matters of repertory, Leopold had come to function not as exemplar but as protector, manager, and amanuensis.[5]

Even so, the musical quality of *Die Schuldigkeit* once again raised cries of disbelief,[6] and, to discredit them, the Archbishop may have shut Wolfgang in while he produced a composition. This confinement, if it took place, brought forth, not the oratorio, but the Passion Cantata, K. 42/35a, the so-called *Grabmusik*, a moving dialogue (between an angel and a soul passing into eternity), in all likelihood performed in the cathedral on Good Friday of 1767 and again five years later, when Mozart added a concluding recitative and chorus.

The stream of commissions continued to flow. On the afternoon of 13 May 1767, syntaxians of the university's Gymnasium, as part of their end-of-term festivities, put on a work they had ordered from the child maestro: *Apollo et Hyacinthus seu Hyacinthi Metamorphosis* (K. 38), his musical setting (in the spirit of Eberlin) of a libretto in Latin[7] based freely upon Ovid and with hints from Pausanias. It came from the pen of Rufin Widl, a monk from Seeon and the boys' professor of syntax. An appreciative audience heard an overture, recitatives, choruses, arias, and ensembles disposed in the manner of an Italian *intermezzo*, that is, as a succession of additions to another work, here as prologue to, and entr'actes in, Widl's Latin play *Clementia Croesi* (The Clemency of Croesus). Both *Clementia* and *Apollo* concerned bereavement, forgiveness, and reconciliation, the intermezzo providing a gloss upon the play.

Its piecemeal presentation notwithstanding, *Apollo*, which made use of the ingenious baroque stage machinery of the *aula*, constituted Mozart's first opera. It gave much augury of his future greatness in the genre, in particular the final act, with its moving *accompagnati* framing the death of

---

5 In his letter to Wolfgang of 11–12 February 1778, Leopold was to remonstrate: "Consider whether I have not always treated you with kindness and served you as a servant his master. . . ."

6 Leopold did attempt to work changes on *Die Schuldigkeit*, but, as the manuscript reveals, they proved feeble.

7 When the mood of the music plays the words false, doubts arise about the eleven-year-old's command of Latin (see n. 10). Moreover, Leopold must have left certain passages unexplicated: the child could not have been conscious of the thinly disguised homosexuality pervading the text.

Hyacinthus, the exquisite duet of the regretful King of Sparta and his daughter, and the economy and magic of the instrumental means by which Apollo metamorphoses the beloved dead youth into a bed of flowers: once more, the most dramatic moments drew forth Mozart's best. The evening of the premiere he entertained the scholars and the public with a harpsichord concert: a triumphant day.

Though without official position, he had become a figure in the city's musical life, and, along with Nannerl, must have taken part in the musical entertainment arranged at court late in March for the Imperial Envoy to Spain, Franz de Paula Gundaccar I, Prince Colloredo. During this visit, the Prince had lodged with his brother, Hieronymus, Count Colloredo, a canon of the cathedral, Bishop of Gurk, and one day, as Archbishop of Salzburg, to become the chief object of the Mozarts' loathing. Count Colloredo probably heard the boy play during this period of good fortune in his native city. The question presents itself: who were those "enemies in Salzburg" Leopold evoked? Over and above a reserve bordering upon arrogance that from the beginning had set him apart from most Salzburgers, he had come to regard the city in the abstract as the real enemy.

The tour had revealed to him the indeed small scale of any success in Salzburg, where a composer's rare and modest opportunities made him appear like a jack-in-the-box springing up for a moment, only to fall. That the very kind of occasional provincial commission he had once filled now occupied his son weighed upon a father aware that, before long, the court would have nothing new with which to challenge so extraordinary a talent. By dint of Wolfgang's gifts and his own exertions, he had, for a while, torn loose from these petty surroundings and delivered them both from his old, embittering struggle with narrow circumstances. Home again, he could not stay his glance from peering deep beyond the mountains encircling the drowsy capital.

He had returned to feel his ground and, for a while, to remain in possession of his title and emolument; moreover, he had to permit Wolfgang a period of relative quiet. In the course of the tour, the veneer that made him appear a miniature adult had at times shown abrupt breaks revealing the child beneath: upon learning in London of Kajetan Hagenauer's entry upon a novitiate in Salzburg's St. Peter's monastery,[8] he had burst into tears, fearing to lose this closest friend (ten years his senior!), with whom he loved to catch insects and shoot air guns. Only when assured of Kaje-

---

8 The fourth son of Lorenz Hagenauer, as Father Dominicus he celebrated his first mass on 15 October 1769. For the occasion Mozart wrote his so-called Dominicus Mass (K. 66; see XXX, n. 5).

tan's freedom to receive visitors did he calm down: "As soon as he gets back to Salzburg," Leopold promised, Wolfgang "will go to St. Peter's, have Mr. Kajetan catch a fly for him, and then shoot with him."[9]

The boy permitted himself few such outbursts, but dutifully persevered in his father's strict program of musical study and composition. When contemplating moving to a new apartment, Leopold considered only silent streets so that no sounds might draw Wolfgang and Nannerl to the windows and away from their tasks. "You know," he observed to Hagenauer, "that my children are accustomed to work. Were they to become used to idle hours with the excuse that one thing interferes with another, my entire edifice would tumble down; habit is an iron shirt. And you yourself know how much my children, in particular little Wolfgang, have to learn."[10] As likely as not, he had the pleasure of few visits with Mr. Kajetan at St. Peter's.

As the *Versuch* makes clear, Leopold's ideal instrumentalists trained their intellect as well as their fingers; he provided Wolfgang a wide general culture. In language, history, and geography, the tour had been his school, Leopold lecturing all the way, the dimensions of this discourse to be gauged by the breadth of the topics touched upon in his correspondence: painting, architecture, literature, religion, economics, and, of course, music; his voice reverberates in letters at once elegant and conversational. At the same time, the tour helped stimulate in Wolfgang a freedom of outlook and expression that became fundamental to his character.

If, approaching adolescence, he was no longer that too often obnoxious prodigy known to have punctuated the less than accomplished musical performances of others with cries of "Pfui!" and "That is wrong!" an extraordinary outspokenness and self-assertion continued to prevail. "Don't be so candid!" Leopold was to caution: "Play the Englishman. . . ."

Along with his studies and composing, he worked at broadening his concert repertory. Adding instrumental introductions, interludes, and accompaniments to scattered movements taken from clavier sonatas by composers, mostly of the German School of Paris, father and son fabricated a convincing texture of alternating solo and tutti passages, patching together

---

9 Mozart enjoyed the Salzburgers' favorite entertainment of shooting air guns at homemade targets decorated with humorous and often vulgar designs and inscriptions, a game to which his entire family showed a passionate addiction.

10 At thirteen Wolfgang started serious study of Latin and, no doubt at his father's prompting, chose as a favorite model sentence to be parsed: "*Cuperem scire, de qua causa, a quam plurimis adolescentibus ottium adeo aestimatur, ut ipsi se nec verbis, nec verberibus, ab hoc sinant abduci*" (I should like to know for what reason idleness is so popular among most young people that it is impossible to draw them from it either by words or by punishments).

the semblance of four clavier concertos (K. 37, 39, 40, 41; April–July 1767; see p. 171). If Mozart could not yet cope on his own with the genre in which he would become sovereign, they had hit upon this handy way of providing the ambitious works he required for the platform, an urgent need in light of Leopold's hopes for a new tour. These rose with news of the approaching marriage of Maria Theresa's daughter Archduchess Maria Josepha. It offered him a legitimate excuse to ask for leave, a request impossible for the Archbishop to deny: he could hardly stand in the way of his famous young subject's attending upon the Imperial family during the festivities planned in Vienna, events preluded in Spain some years before.

2

WITH THE LAST breath (August 1759) of Ferdinand VI of Spain, who had lingered in a pitiful state of lunacy—Farinelli's singing could no longer calm him, as it had his predecessor, Philip V—the crown of the issueless monarch passed to his half brother Charles of Bourbon, King of the Two Sicilies. Assuming the title of His Catholic Majesty Charles III,[11] he exchanged his luminous capital of Naples for bleak Madrid, the Sicilies becoming the possession of his boisterous eight-year-old son, now King Ferdinand IV (see XV, n. 43). Charles left him protected by a compact with his northern neighbor, Maria Theresa's second son, Leopold of Austria, now Grand Duke of his departed father's Duchy of Tuscany. To celebrate and further strengthen the alliance between Bourbon and Habsburg, so often at loggerheads in the past, Ferdinand at his majority was to marry one of Maria Theresa's daughters.[12]

The Austrian Archduchess whom Vienna and Madrid first settled upon for King Ferdinand's bed—that gentle Johanna who had led Wolfgang through her apartment during his first visit to Schönbrunn—had died (see VI, n. 4); her sister Maria Josepha stepped up to become the royal betrothed. Empress Maria Theresa, though aware of Ferdinand's coarseness and ill-breeding, nonetheless required Josepha to offer herself as a political sacrifice: "If only she fulfill her duty to God and her husband and attend to the welfare of her soul," the Empress wrote, "I shall be content even if she is not happy." On 12 January 1767 King Ferdinand became sixteen and of age. He was to receive his bride in his kingdom during Octo-

---

11 Maria Theresa's father had once taken the same title (see VI, n. 7).
12 In 1765 Leopold of Austria had married Maria Luisa (Ludovica), daughter of Charles III of Spain and sister to Ferdinand. She became the German Empress whom myth maligns as having called Mozart's *La clemenza di Tito* "a swinish German mess" (see XXXIII, n. 51).

ber; it had been agreed that she would start her journey south after impressive ceremonies in Vienna.

The Mozarts, accompanied by a servant, a certain Bernhard, left Salzburg for Vienna in the Pressburg carriage on 11 September 1767. By way of Vöcklabruck, the monastery of Lambach (its abbot, Armand Schikmayr, a friend of Leopold's since their university days, invited them to lunch), Linz, Strengberg (via Enns), the abbey of Melk (its organist recognized Wolfgang as soon as his fingers touched the keyboard of the great Sonnholz instrument[13]), St. Pölten, and Purkersdorf in the Wienerwald, they arrived in the Imperial capital on the fifteenth, putting up at a goldsmith's in the Weihburggasse. They had met with a long wait at customs, their belongings searched "down to the marrow." The days had passed when Wolfgang could fiddle his way through such an inspection.

Disaster already hovered over the expedition: coincident with their arrival, their landlord's eldest son took to bed with smallpox, and his father felt it prudent to keep the guests ignorant of the matter even as the disease widened its grasp throughout the city. Unaware of the danger, Leopold rejoiced once again to experience music and theater "every day"; operas by Florian Gassmann, Hasse, and Galuppi paraded across the boards as well as plays adapted from Beaumarchais, Wycherly, and Gellert. Leopold singled out two new works: the *Amore e Psiche* of Gassmann and the *festa teatrale* commissioned in honor of Maria Josepha's engagement, Hasse's *Partenope* (a setting of Metastasio's libretto), in which Gaetano Appolino [*sic*] Vestris appeared as principal dancer and a promising twenty-one-year-old castrato, Venanzio Rauzzini, sang.

Though the *Kaiserstadt's* cultural life surged with vigor, a significant change had occurred since the Mozarts' last visit: shattered by the death of Emperor Francis, Maria Theresa had cut off her hair, renounced jewels and cosmetics, and restricted her wardrobe to black; this once munificent patron of the arts had gone into seclusion. Leopold reported with disappointment: "Her Majesty the Empress no longer holds concerts in her apartments; she goes neither to the opera nor to plays, and her manner of life is so divorced from the world as to be impossible adequately to describe."[14]

The crowned head of her House, she nonetheless had made her eldest son, now the German Emperor Joseph II, co-regent in Habsburg lands

---

13 The Mozarts had examined the monastery's baroque chambers designed by Jakob Prandtauer, dined, and then proceeded to the church. Many religious houses made a business of such tourist visits and provided the functions of an inn.

14 An exaggeration: at the theater on either 7 or 8 January 1767, Casanova had witnessed her first public appearance since Francis's death, but such excursions remained sporadic.

and, upon the death of Daun, commander of her armies. She had begun to return to affairs of state, bringing to them a determination to stupefy herself with work until she could neither think nor feel. Joseph, autocratic and tactless, lost few opportunities to cross her; years of conflict between the Dowager Empress and her Emperor son lay ahead, too often neither giving ground, now one, now the other threatening to abdicate as Habsburg Regent in weary quarrel after weary quarrel.

At the same time, Joseph maintained toward her a ceremonious show of filial devotion, which, in fact, rested upon deep affection. In contrast, he made malicious jokes about the inferior rank among Europe's princes of his late father's Lothringian family. Joseph had never respected Emperor Francis, a spoiled idler surrounded by flatterers, and swept away the army of huntsmen and gamekeepers he left behind. (Maria Theresa had indulged his every whim.) But, though the new Emperor, who despised outward show and for whom sobriety seemed the ultimate virtue, set about paring down expenditures, he did lavish money upon the celebrations surrounding his sister Josepha's wedding. No stranger to the opulence of courts, Leopold Mozart commented upon the prodigious public illuminations and fireworks.

He became uneasy about rumors that Emperor Joseph, traveling incognito, would follow Josepha to Naples to visit with his new brother-in-law: Joseph, so the whisper ran, might be gone from Vienna for half a year.[15] With the Emperor absent and the Empress inaccessible, what of Leopold's hopes for Wolfgang in Vienna? In addition, Viennese aristocrats had begun with diplomatic skill to demonstrate, at least for the moment, that they, too, could retrench. "Now you will ask me," Leopold wrote Hagenauer, "what the . . . nobles in Vienna are doing. — What are they doing? — They are cutting down expenses as much as possible in order to ingratiate themselves with the Emperor. When the head spends with prodigality, everyone cuts loose; when, to the contrary, the head is frugal, then everyone plays the good housekeeper."

To crown the Mozarts' problems, etiquette demanded their appearance at court before they set about making formal visits to the houses of the titled,[16] and, though news came of the Emperor's friendly remarks about the children, he did not summon them. Yet the situation could change in an instant, and, meanwhile, at less rigid gatherings money might be coaxed from the throng of foreign nobles assembling for the wedding; moreover,

---

15 He did not leave for Naples until March 1769.
16 When in 1762 the Mozarts made their debut before Viennese society, Schönbrunn had already welcomed them.

in light of the family's new fame, Leopold expected at least a few of them to hold out offers of permanent employment. The prospect of high patronage did open as the Empress emerged from her apartments to appear fleetingly at a series of gala receptions. But she did not neglect her perpetual mourning.

Since Emperor Francis's death, at fixed times she descended to the crypt of the Capuchin church, there to lament and pray before his tomb. She insisted that Maria Josepha, about to quit Vienna, perhaps forever, take formal leave of her father's remains. Near his sarcophagus lay the still-unsealed coffin of Emperor Joseph's second wife, a Bavarian princess and a recent victim of smallpox.[17] Maria Josepha, the Viennese were to contend, emerged from the royal vault carrying the virulent infection.

On 7 October 1767 Leopold informed Hagenauer "that on Saturday evening Her Royal Highness, the Princess-Bride, felt unwell, and yesterday smallpox broke out. You can well imagine the confusion. Indeed, the journey to Naples has already been postponed until early in the coming year." That the Empress had forced her reluctant daughter to share a three-hour subterranean vigil offended Leopold: "The terrible odor, etc., the impression, etc., provoked a high fever. . . ." On 15 October, in his words: "The Princess-Bride became a bride of the Heavenly Bridegroom." If the gorgeous retinue of thirty-four coaches made ready for her departure on the sixteenth disbanded, a no less splendid escort would assemble in the spring to accompany yet another sister; Leopold had correctly speculated: "Perhaps fate will now choose Archduchess Carolina, who is fifteen."[18]

The court turned to mourning, and the theaters closed for six weeks. Few understood better than Leopold what such circumstances could mean to performers: "One can easily imagine the confusion arising from this in all the places through which she [Maria Josepha] was to have journeyed. They have arranged festivities and testimonials of respect and have incurred great expenses. . . ." His bitter humor broke through as he thought of three famous singers awaiting Josepha's arrival: ". . . in Florence Signor Manzuoli, Signora de Amicis, and Signor Raaff have memorized their

---

17 Also a Maria Josepha, this daughter of the Wittelsbach Emperor Charles VII had married Joseph in 1765, an event the innermost circle of Schönbrunn celebrated with a short festival opera, *Il Parnasso confuso*, the text by Metastasio, the music by Gluck, the performers including four Austrian archduchesses (Maria Elizabeth, Maria Amalia, Maria Josepha, and Maria Carolina) accompanied at the cembalo by Joseph himself. He detested his pimply, unhappy bride, whose rights of inheritance, however, would provide him with a stratagem to claim Bavaria as his own.

18 The Empress gave Ferdinand a choice between Archduchesses Maria Amalia and Maria Carolina. He put the matter into the hands of his royal father, who, with the aid of portraits dispatched to Madrid, picked the latter.

parts to no purpose." Vienna, Leopold realized, would not return to normal until the beginning of the new year.

The epidemic continued to grow, and, he observed, the Viennese now "talked of little else but smallpox." But, strange to say, he clung to the expectation—absurd in this chaotic situation—of a summons to court; he lingered in the capital, delaying his departure even after discovering the truth about the goldsmith's house, for by this time his younger children had also become infected. Leopold searched for a new lodging. In the end, Frau Anna Maria, Nannerl, and the servant remained at the Weihburggasse, Leopold and Wolfgang moving to a quarter of the city believed free of contagion, possibly to the house of Franz Xaver Peisser, a business associate of Hagenauer. (The parents, of course, could not have been indifferent to Nannerl's fate: since she had developed a few pockmarks in childhood, they assumed her immune.) But no one could hide; by this time the outbreak ran through all of Vienna.

At court, the royal physicians disclosed to Archduchess Maria Elisabeth the nature of the fever of which she complained. Calling for a looking glass, this most beautiful of the Empress's daughters said farewell to a face she suspected would be greatly altered should she live.[19] News of her plight at last convinced Leopold that at this time the Imperial family did not desire a harpsichord recital. A hurried departure explains why Wolfgang's duet on the death of Maria Josepha (K. Anh. 24a/43a for two sopranos) remained incomplete.

Where to flee? Leopold required a place far enough from Vienna to provide "a change of air" while the epidemic and the mourning period ran their course; and he hoped to pass these weeks in a town where the children might give concerts. He headed north toward the Habsburg crown land of Moravia, whose two leading cities had influential people with close links to Salzburg: Countess von Herberstein, a niece of the Archbishop, had chosen this time to visit Brünn, where her father, Franz Anton, Count Schrattenbach, presided as governor of the province; in Brünn,[20] too, resided Countess Josepha Podstatsky-Liechtenstein, a daughter of Count Arco of Salzburg; and, in addition, her brother-in-law, Count Leopold Anton Podstatsky, a canon of Salzburg cathedral, once president of its consistory, and nephew of former Archbishop Liechtenstein of Salzburg, could be found at Olmütz, where he also functioned as a canon and, since 1764, as dean of the cathedral.

---

19 She survived, her beauty ruined, and would retire to the contemplative life (see p. 551).
20 Contemplating an excursion to Moravia at some time during this latest journey, on 29 September Leopold had written Hagenauer to ask whether the Countess had left for Brünn.

3

"Te Deum Laudamus!
Wolfgang has prevailed over smallpox!
And where? — in Olmütz!
And where? — in the palace
of his Excellency Count Podstatsky."
So began Leopold's letter to Hagenauer of 10 November 1767.

On 23 October the family had left Vienna and on the following day arrived in Brünn. Count Schrattenbach and his daughter immediately began to arrange a concert. But "a certain inner instinct" Leopold "could not banish" impelled him to push on northeast to Olmütz. (He promised a performance in Brünn on the return journey to Vienna.) Though the Pressburg carriage required the services of a smith in Wischkau, it rumbled into Olmütz on the twenty-sixth. The crowded hotel Zum schwarzen Adler could provide only a damp, smoky room. But soon Leopold had to worry about more than a faulty stove. Wolfgang's cheeks began to glow red and hot; his brow burned; his hands felt cold as ice; he passed a restless night. In the morning, the hotel found comfortable quarters to which he was carried, wrapped in furs. His fever continued to mount, and he fell into delirium.

Leopold sought out Count Podstatsky, to whom he confided his fear that Wolfgang had smallpox. Making light of any risk of infection, the Count ordered his servants to prepare rooms for the family and dispatched his own physician, Dr. Joseph Wolff[21] to the hotel to examine the boy and fetch him. Again swathed in furs, he was borne to the cathedral deanery, where, flecked and grotesquely swollen and waited on by the Count's staff, he endured nine days of blindness. Nannerl recalled visits of both Court Chaplain Johann Leopold Hay (later Bishop of Königgrätz), who taught Wolfgang card tricks during his long recuperation, and a local fencing master, from whom he took instruction once his strength returned.

By 29 November Leopold could report that Nannerl, too, had withstood the disease, neither child showing more than a few marks.[22] Leopold recognized the hand of God in that sudden impulse to travel on to Olmütz, there to meet with the compassionate Count: "This deed shall redound in no small way to the honor of his Excellency, Count von Podstatsky in the biography of our little one, which I one day intend to publish; in a certain sense, a new epoch in his life now begins."

---

21 While recuperating, Wolfgang composed an aria for Dr. Wolff's daughter. It may be "*Cara, se le mie pene*" (K. deest).

22 In later years Nannerl described her brother as much blemished by smallpox scars; perhaps they became more prominent with time, or the memory of them did.

The children's health restored, Leopold began the journey back to Vienna two days before Christmas. He stopped in Brünn to spend the holiday season (24 December–9 January) with the Schrattenbachs. Wolfgang gave that promised concert and found himself "accompanied on various instruments by locals of Brünn," proud to hear Leopold declare himself "completely satisfied" with their efforts. The program may have included the premiere of the Symphony in F, K. 43, in all likelihood begun in Vienna and completed in Olmütz during the days of recovery, its gentle Andante an orchestral arrangement of the duet for father and daughter in *Apollo et Hyacinthus*. With a minuet injected before the concluding Allegro, K. 43 constitutes Mozart's earliest four-movement symphony.

In icy temperatures and winds the family then traveled via Poysdorf to Vienna. On 10 January the carriage, requiring six horses to pull it through the snowdrifts, arrived at the Zum rotem Säbel on the Hohe Brücke, Mozart carrying with him a second, but unfinished, symphony in four movements, K. 45 in D. He hastened to complete it.

The Empress had only to learn of the Mozarts' ordeal in Olmütz and safe return than she summoned them. Like her daughter Elisabeth, she, too, had but recently recovered from smallpox. With fellow feeling she clutched Frau Mozart's hands and stroked her cheeks as Leopold in amazement beheld the Empress and his wife tête-à-tête, for a moment made equal by their children's struggle with death. This visit (19 January) lasted, a flattered Leopold related, "from half-past two until half-past four in the afternoon. His Majesty the Emperor came out into the anteroom, in which we were awaiting the end of the Royal Family's coffee collation, and brought us in himself. In addition to the Emperor and Her Majesty the Empress, Prince Albert of Saxony[23] and all of the Archduchesses were present; not a soul was there apart from this noble company." Maria Theresa posed questions about the family's Grand Tour. Then she chatted with Frau Anna Maria, Joseph with Leopold and Wolfgang, while Nannerl listened "and blushed very often." Of course, the Empress gave in and heard some music. Yet, for all this atmosphere of "astounding affability," Leopold foresaw no financial gain in the visit. Maria Theresa now left artistic and financial matters to Emperor Joseph, who, Leopold noted, "doubtless believes he has paid us with his most gracious conversation."

---

23 A son of Augustus the Weak of Saxony-Poland and his Electress-Queen, Emperor Joseph I's daughter Maria Josepha of Austria, Albert had married (1766) Maria Christina, the favorite daughter of his second cousin, Empress Maria Theresa (who created him Hungarian Palatine). Art history owes a particular debt to him as founder of the Albertina collection in Vienna.

Wolfgang's face still showed spots, now turning a threatening red in the cold. The demands of precedence answered by the royal visit, Prince Kaunitz, under different circumstances, would have helped the Mozarts assemble a group of aristocratic patrons, but, fearful of infection, he avoided Wolfgang. Searching for opportunities as he watched his funds diminish, Leopold yielded to delusions of persecution: "All the clavier-players and composers in Vienna—with the sole exception of Wagenseil, who, however, is sick . . . —opposed our advancement." Leopold saw them joined in a conspiracy of silence, leagued to avoid listening to Wolfgang! "And why? —so that on the many occasions when they might be asked whether they had heard the boy and what they thought of him, they could always say *that they had not heard him and that it could not possibly be true, that it was humbug and buffoonery, that it was prearranged, that he was given music he already knew, that it was ridiculous to believe that he composed, etc., etc.*"

Spinning out this foolishness, Leopold for the moment forgot the observation he had made at the time of Wolfgang's return to health: "a new epoch in his life" had, indeed, begun—adolescence. His salon tricks no longer charmed; the amusing and winsome imp of former years was no more. Yet, if he could no longer work this old allure, he now had so much more to offer: at twelve, he could put most of the capital's performers and composers into the shade. But how might Leopold demonstrate this fact, how force Vienna to look upon his son as a professional? Here was the fulcrum of their frustrations. Leopold struggled "to convince the public of the true situation. . . ." Then, the opportunity to make the point came upon them unawares: in an offhand, capricious mood, Joseph II asked Wolfgang whether he would like to compose an opera and also conduct it.

The Emperor must have thought the idea enchanting as he let it fly. He seldom suggested anything that might cost him money, and his blithe readiness to put the question to Wolfgang a second time derived from the court's complete freedom of financial responsibility toward its theaters: a concessionaire, Giuseppe Affligio, leased the Burgtheater and its branch, the Kärntnertor theater. Under the perfunctory surveyance of a court official, Durazzo's successor, Count Johann Wenzel Sporck, he assumed all financial risks, enjoying the profits, sustaining the losses. The mounting of a new opera did not cost the Emperor a single ducat, and, of course, Affligio had to provide the Imperial family free ingress.[24]

---

24 During Carnival, licensed concessionaires and the Emperor divided the profits from the many balls and dances taking place in all corners of Vienna. Whoever goes to these entertainments, Leopold Mozart noted, "does the court a good turn."

The Dutch Minister, Count Frederik Christoph von Degenfeld-Schomburg, who had heard Wolfgang in Holland, urged Affligio to act upon the Emperor's whim, and Leopold pressed for an agreement. As news of the bizarre plan traveled through Vienna, a troubling question arose: did it answer the fitness of etiquette that within the same Imperial institution a Gluck conduct one night, a twelve-year-old the next? Gluck, himself, seemed not to know, and Affligio, certain he was dealing in fiction, did not care. He promised to pay Leopold one hundred ducats for an opera he assumed could not be delivered. And should the father write a workable score in his son's name or an opera by some miracle come from the youngster's own hand, Affligio felt secure in his methods, had he need to apply them, of ridding himself of the complication; in the meantime he would play the game and humor the Emperor.

Affligio selected a libretto: *La finta semplice,* an *opera buffa* bearing the name of Marco Coltellini, a Tuscan scribbling for the Imperial theaters. Leopold did not know that Goldoni, in fact, had written the text, which, with music by Salvatore Perillo, had suffered shipwreck at Venice some four years earlier: Affligio had ordered Coltellini to pick an abandoned libretto and make in it only those few changes sufficient to warrant some claim to authorship. A minimum of effort was to be expended, just enough to maintain appearances.

Walking in the clouds, Leopold gave play to fantasy: *La finta semplice,* applauded in Imperial Vienna, would become a musical passport to Italy, its opera houses, in the sequel, demanding works from a now recognized young master; the second journey to Vienna, to date a disappointment, would become the foundation of an Italian triumph. Leopold began collecting letters of introduction to influential people in Italy and at the palace discussed a proposed Italian journey: the Emperor promised recommendations to his brother in Florence, his new brother-in-law in Naples, and the Habsburg Court at Milan.

Affligio continued his pretense of good faith by assigning the roles in *La finta semplice,* and no sooner had Wolfgang completed the music of the first act than his father invited the singers to judge it. They expressed glowing approval, at the same time asking for changes that might better exploit their talents. (At first unaware of Affligio's intentions, they lent themselves to the project.) A matter of course, requests of this kind continued as composition of the opera advanced. But often Wolfgang could not begin the alterations until Coltellini revised the words, and the poet worked, Leopold began to notice, at a most leisurely pace. It became clear that *La finta semplice* had little chance of reaching the stage until after Easter, and Leopold had to acquaint the Salzburg secretariat with the necessity of his remaining away yet longer, at the same time keeping back any suggestion of his plan to push on to Italy after the premiere. Even so, he did give Hagenauer the task of persuading a certain Rochus Alterdinger to translate the *Versuch* into Italian, for in the past the treatise had proved helpful in introducing its author to foreign musical circles. Since Alterdinger held an administrative post at the Salzburg Residenz, in no time it fathomed Leopold's intentions.

By spring the Emperor had departed for Hungary and the Turkish frontier; *La finta semplice* could not be performed until his return in June. Wolfgang completed the opera during July 1768, by which time Leopold had begun writing home about "all sorts of concocted intrigues and malicious persecutions." His funds had continued to sink; he let the servant, Bernhard, go; Vienna grew hot, the dust rising in clouds. The Mozarts, who had arrived carrying furs, now sweated in unsuitable clothing. Leopold begged the Hagenauers to send the family's summer wardrobe: he in particular wanted that marvelous silk suit from Lyon.

"Thy will be done," he intoned, his uneasiness increasing as one postponement followed the other. "Only our honor keeps us from leaving," he had to admit by late July, blaming himself for entangling his son in a skein of intrigue: "Had I known all that I know now and had I been able to foresee incidents that have taken place, Wolfgang would never have written a note but would have been home long ago." It had been years since he had felt so much the provincial, helpless in a great and indifferent city. Oddly enough, he still remained unaware of the enemy's face; his old delusions returned: "All the composers, among whom Gluck is a leader, undermined everything in order to prevent this opera's taking place." But Gluck and his colleagues had contributed nothing to the machinations Leopold, in high wrath, catalogued: "The singers had been instigated, the orchestra stirred up, and every means used to stop the performance. . . . Meanwhile, a few people spread the word that the music was worthless; others that it did not fit the words or violated the prosody because the boy did not sufficiently understand Italian."[25] Rumor also ran that *La finta semplice* was untheatrical, simply would not play, and that, in any case, Leopold had written the score. Frantic, he arranged a series of open tests of Wolfgang's abilities: in the houses of his main supporters—Prince Kaunitz, the Duke of Braganza, Court Composer Giuseppe Bonno, Hasse, and even Metastasio—the

---

25 Leopold's phonetic spelling of Italian betrayed a still unsettled appreciation of its pronunciation, while the at times debatable musical prosody of *La finta semplice* reveals the Mozart of 1768 as having but a fitful affinity with the language's niceties. These shortcomings would vanish with their travels in Italy.

young composer opened at random a volume of Metastasio and improvised music to the first aria text that met the eye.

He might have spared himself the exertion. Behind the war of words being waged against him lay a simple issue: money; Prince Kaunitz—though without premeditation—had provoked a financial crisis engulfing Affligio.

Eager to enjoy the pleasures of French drama, Kaunitz had cajoled him into importing a troupe of players from Paris. Affligio also hired a French ballet company under Noverre, who in 1767 had left the service of Karl Eugene in Stuttgart. The dancers drew admiring crowds, but audiences remained thin at the plays, only a few aristocrats and members of the diplomatic corps attending. Emergency subsidies from various nobles proved insufficient to offset the losses. When Wolfgang completed his score, an astonished Affligio, in no mood to consider further indulging the Hofburg by mounting the work of a twelve-year old, struck it down with calumny, and the court dared not protest lest he bring up the embarrassing matter of those expensive French actors performing before empty seats.

When Affligio's role in the imbroglio at last became clear to Leopold, he raged against a German composer being so treated "in the capital of his German fatherland"; he cited the agreement, at which point Affligio, bristling, revealed himself in full hostility: yes, if the father insisted, he would arrange a performance, but of a quality to discredit the son. Affligio guaranteed that, if produced, *La finta semplice* would be ridiculed and hissed.[26]

At this point Leopold should have retreated. With any real experience of court politics (or perhaps with just more common sense in the affair), he would have retired to lick his wounds and, in time, recover. Even in the face of malicious opposition, a rehearsal with orchestra of its first act had taken place and proved *La finta semplice* performable. Given the continuing good will of the palace and, in the course of things, an accommodation with Affligio, opportunities remained at the Burgtheater, if not one season, then the next.

At all events, an injured and furious Leopold pressed on to a foolish act, perhaps the basis of what eventually turned the Habsburgs, Maria Theresa in particular, against him. In 1771 she would oppose Wolfgang's receiving a permanent position in Habsburg service because hiring him would mean putting up with and sustaining his family, in her eyes "useless people" (that is, of no use to a court). This attitude may have been born of her displeasure to learn of the petition denouncing Affligio that the Emperor received

---

26 Involved once too often in shabby transactions, Affligio would be convicted of forgery by a Florentine tribunal in 1779 and end his life chained to a galley.

from Leopold's hand on 21 September 1768. Puffed up, he failed to realize that in condemning the management of an important adjunct to the Imperial Household—an adjunct in whose affairs the highest nobles and court officials meddled with much freedom—the liveried Vice-Kapellmeister of Salzburg, on illegal protracted leave from his post and in danger of dismissal,[27] had taken a step inappropriate to his station. The complaint presumed his right to the honorarium for the unperformed opera and the costs run up in Vienna while to no purpose awaiting its premiere, claims he enunciated with much presumption when submitting the document to the Emperor.

Leopold's tone hardly commended itself to absolute monarchs. The affable ways and courtesy of the Imperial family had led him into that fatal error of mistaking the mask for the face: as a matter of fact, the Empress had come to believe that by "running about the world like beggars," the Mozarts, "people of that sort [*ces sortes des gens*]," demeaned the very concept of princely service. She doubted they would change their ways were the Habsburgs to take them into their employ and resented Leopold's attempt to be both salaried and independent. Further, in the hope of inducing diplomatic pressure from home, he had gone so far as to suggest in public that the Burgtheater's temporizing in the matter of *La finta semplice* reflected Vienna's contempt for provincial Salzburg and its Archbishop. The Hofburg could not have failed to learn of this ill-advised, unfounded talk.

When His Imperial Majesty accepted Leopold's petition, he promised justice: Count Sporck would investigate. Leopold never heard another word on the matter. Yet, for all his agitation, he had kept some of his wits about him: even though the petition had taken the form of a resentful, tactless memoir rehearsing at length his struggles with Affligio, it made no mention of Emperor Joseph's having set the affair in motion or of fictitious conspiracies in Vienna's musical world. Even as his anger mounted Leopold had forced himself to perceive a part of reality in its true shape: Joseph would not appear like a genie out of a bottle; a production of *La finta semplice* would not take place; and, at best, the petition might persuade

27 In March 1768 the Archbishop had ordered Leopold's salary suspended unless he report to Salzburg the following month; by May, the Chief Steward had informed him that he might remain away as long as he liked, provided he did not expect remuneration. This new arrangement appealed to Leopold, for it gave him, so he thought, freedom to embark upon the Italian tour at his pleasure. But his having used Archduchess Josepha's impending wedding as a pretext to quit his duties for an indeterminate time had awakened resentment at home, and by autumn rumors concerning the tenuousness of his position had begun to circulate. As the months rolled by without his return, the Salzburg court contemplated sending him packing should he reappear.

the court of Vienna to issue a statement of faith in the boy's abilities. Toward this end Leopold organized a schedule to accompany the complaint: *Register of All this Twelve-Year-Old Boy has Composed since his Seventh Year, which* [list] *can be Verified by Original Manuscripts.* Leopold dreaded the smiles of contempt awaiting him in Salzburg.

Today, it pains to follow Affligio's pragmatic course that ended in driving on the rocks the first *opera buffa* by the composer of *The Marriage of Figaro* and *Così fan tutte.* But in 1768 Affligio had to do with a less awesome victim: the overbearing father of an aging child prodigy, and that some of the criticism bruited about *La finta semplice* did not lack foundation aided Affligio's campaign.

For the libretto, outmoded when he cobbled it up, Goldoni had nailed together a number of worn-out comic situations derived from the commedia dell'arte. They required little more than music appropriate to stock intrigues, certainly nothing in the way of psychological realization of character or interrelationships. In view of the work's miscarriage, so distressing to the Mozarts, it would seem the return of an injury to sing its praises. Alas, *La finta semplice* (K. 51/46a) evokes feelings of discomfort: neither amusing nor expressive of sentiment, but foolish, awkward, and patchwork, the opera fails to hold together because its music does not convince; it runs too high an account with the Neopolitan opera's fund of clichés. Though at times Mozart revealed a sense of continuity and drive, and attained the animation, flow, and varied texture demanded by the *buffa* style with its rapid give-and-take and its ever-busy, changing effects, yet, too often, the nimble pace he could by this time maintain without effort in symphonic movements eluded him on the stage.[28] Moreover, several of the arias have little connection with the characters singing them.[29] (Did he understand the burlesque dialogue?) Some scenes are adroitly manufactured, most quite wooden. Only here and there do moments of musical charm and wit give promise of what was to come; too many a time the tired formulas of the farce evoke the stock musical response: the twelve-year-old lacked the resources to surmount them. Affligio does not stand accountable as sole offender in this sad business: Leopold had pushed his son beyond his depth.

---

28 He deftly converted his symphony K. 45 into the overture to *La finta semplice*, suppressing the minuet, reworking the orchestration (and now and then the meter), refining the proportions, and providing a new ending running on without a break into the opening scene.

29 The Mozarts showed themselves too responsive to the singers' demands for set pieces flattering to their voices but not always reconcilable with the pertinent dramatic situations (see n. 4).

Losing control and feeling himself adrift between reefs, Leopold had sought a way out by means of the petition. But what he had intended to be a white flag and an entreaty for honorable terms succeeded only in antagonizing by dint of a diction both whining and overproud. Yet, despite this tactical error and the abandonment of the opera, Wolfgang had turned the months in Vienna to musical advantage, even managing a few minor successes. These had begun some two and a half months after the return from Moravia.

4

TOWARD THE END of March 1768, the children had given a "grand concert" at the home of the Russian Ambassador, Prince Golicyn,[30] and most likely also contributed to the "excellent dinner music" heard at court on 6 April, the eve of Archduchess Carolina's marriage by proxy to Ferdinand of The Two Sicilies, his homonymous new brother-in-law acting in his stead. (She was to meet her groom at Portella.) Leopold tendered a copy of his *Versuch* as a wedding offering. During these days his optimism still soared: even as Wolfgang worked on his opera for the Burgtheater, a private commission had come his way.

In the course of the summer, a musical enthusiast, wise in the ways of intrigue and no doubt quick to foresee the fate of *La finta semplice*, contrived to furnish Mozart with what would prove a solace for its demise: Dr. Franz Anton Mesmer called upon him to compose the operetta *Bastien und Bastienne* (K. 50/46b), completed immediately after *La finta semplice* and first heard during the autumn in Mesmer's mansion in the Landstrasse suburb.

This singspiel's libretto for the most part rests upon *Les Amours*, the parody of Rousseau's *Devin* (see IX, n. 16) as put into German by Friedrich Wilhelm Weiskern and Johann Heinrich Friedrich Müller. In addition to this version, Mozart used a revision of it from the hand of the family's old friend Schachtner. It would seem that just before the departure for Vienna, Wolfgang began composition of a pastiche he and his father pasted together from all these sources. In all likelihood they carried from Salzburg this project in gestation as stock-in-trade for one or another theater and brought *Bastien* forward when Mesmer indicated a desire to order an

---

30 He was Prince Dmitrij Michajlovič Golicyn, the Russian Ambassador in Vienna from 1762 to 1792, and not, often the case, to be confused with Prince Dmitrij Alekseevič Golicyn, the Russian representative in Paris from 1763 to 1768.

entertainment. He must have found in the text fortuitous allusions both personal and amusing.[31]

Tempting though it may be to espy in Mozart's frustrations at the court of Vienna a parallel to *Le devin*'s proto-revolutionary theme of rustic innocence beset by aristocratic obliquity, this political message hardly makes itself felt in his ingenuous treatment of the tale. (How Mesmer and Leopold looked upon this element in the plot is another matter.) "The noblewoman of the castle" offers no serious threat to the happiness of the bucolic lovers, whose simple crisis drew a far more convincing musical treatment from the adolescent composer than had the complicated and ofttimes vulgar situations in *La finta semplice*. The charming, melodious score of *Bastien und Bastienne*[32] derives in the main from the example of such Gallic composers of *opéra comique* as Monsigny and Philidor[33] (see p. 211), from German imitators of the genre (Gluck, for example), perhaps from Johann Adam Hiller's recently produced (Leipzig) new *Singspiele*, and from German song. Though here and there echoes of Leopold's "peasant music" reach the ear, all is light, open, and clear[34]—the deft, economical orchestration betrays a debt to Pergolesi; Mozart had to have heard his music in Paris—as the pastoral lovers quarrel and then reunite under the guidance of the shepherd Colas, that unmistakable adumbration of Sarastro in *The Magic Flute*. Both Colas and Sarastro made use of magic and Dr. Mesmer, too—indeed, in his case, of wizardry boasting astonishing necromantic paraphernalia. "Magic" interconnections link *Bastien und Bastienne*, *The Magic Flute*, and *Così fan tutte*, and also this trio of Mozart operas with the most bizarre aspect of Dr. Mesmer's career.

Two years before the creation of *Bastien und Bastienne*, Mesmer had published a thesis concerning the influence of the planets and stars upon

---

31 Vienna had heard *Les Amours* four years before Mesmer's arrival in 1759. No direct evidence links him to *Bastien*, but the tradition of his ordering it and housing its premiere, strengthened in Otto Jahn's magisterial *W. A. Mozart* of the last century, remains convincing. Thanks to his wife's wealth, Mesmer lived in baronial style. *Bastien* had its first performance indoors, in his Viennese house (or—a slender possibility—in his country home, the Rothmühle at Schwechat) and not, as long believed, in his Landstrasse garden: the Mesmers did not build their famous illuminated park with its outdoor theater until some years later (see p. 312).
32 The operetta begins with an *intrada*, or prelude. The coincidental similarity of its opening theme to that of Beethoven's *Eroica* startles.
33 During the winter of 1763–1764, the Mozarts had the opportunity of hearing French opera in Paris, not only grand *tragédies lyriques*—the Opéra had reopened on 23 January with Rameau's *Castor et Pollux*—but also lighter fare such as François-André-Danican Philidor's *Le sorcier*, which that same season had so marked a success that for the first time Parisians summoned an opera composer before the curtain of the Comédie-Italienne.
34 Perhaps not all: alien to this general lyricism is the grandiose, Handelian Adagio maestoso motif that binds together the sections of the aria *"Geh' hin!"* (No. 13).

human disease, and therewith set in place the preliminary stone of a theory soon to grow into a significant movement and cause. Mesmerism maintained that through the medium of an impalpable astral fluid—a subtle, all-pervading magnetic substance coursing through and bathing the universe—the movements of heavenly bodies affected human bodies, the fluid insinuating itself into the hollows of brains and nerves. It followed, Mesmer argued, that both formed repositories of the magnetic force, illness arising from disturbances in their store of it. Since there was but a single illness, so he promulgated, there could be but a single cure: by stroking the sick with magnets or by "mesmerizing" or massaging the body itself, he sought to set faulty magnetic reservoirs aright and thus restore health. Defining the fluid as admitting no vacuum, he went on to deduce that the same imponderable essence and panacea linking the brain with muscle, sinew, and bone must also link mind with mind. Thus from a kind of astrological therapy Mesmer proceeded to reconnoiter the unconscious, mysticism, and the occult.

The animosity of Viennese doctors and the strong urging of the police would in 1778 force him to remove (by way of Munich and Switzerland) to Paris,[35] where his séances became a haunt of the fashionable. Midst an exotic decor and to the accompaniment of music, his followers plunged iron bars into a special bucket in which, so Mesmer proclaimed, the Universal Fluid gathered. Hysteria, fits, convulsions, and ecstasy followed, many of the faithful being cured in a state of trance under the eyes of Mesmer, who presided over these rites in a lilac magician's costume and brandishing a "mesmerized" wand.

The antics of Mesmer and his cult provide much to smile at; but he did discover—really rediscover—not a little about the influence of the imagination upon healing (that powerful expectations often beget powerful results) and about musical therapy; moreover, in the area of psychotherapeutic treatment, he and his followers stumbled upon "magnetic sleep," or induced hypnosis. Though by the end of the century Mesmer had faded from prominence, Mesmeric Salons run by Mesmeric Fluidists had spread over Europe and England. Indeed, Mesmerism had provided so great a stir in Paris that in 1784 Louis XVI asked Benjamin Franklin, among other scientists, to investigate it. Franklin and his colleagues concluded that Mesmer's so-called Animal Magnetism was a delusion during which patients reacted to the contagion of group hysteria.

---

35 His unorthodox treatments to cure the blindness of the pianist Maria Theresia von Paradis— at first successful, they miscarried—raised the storm that compelled his departure. In 1784 Mozart would write a piano concerto for her, in all probability K. 456.

The mature Mozart followed the Parisian adventures of his onetime patron, and, some twenty-two years after the family's happy visits to the
Landstrasse mansion, called upon Mesmer's spirit to incite one of opera's
greatest *buffa* ensembles.

In *Così fan tutte*, Despina, the maid, disguised as a Mesmeric doctor and
speaking nonsense-Latin, "cures" a pair of rejected lovers (Ferrando and
Guglielmo masquerading as Albanians), who pretend to have swallowed
poison. "Dr." Despina produces a "Mesmeric stone" (a magnet), which,
she explains, "originated in Germany and later became famous in France."
The sham doctor and the sham patients join in a sham treatment: she runs
the magnet up and down their bodies, and they twitch, quiver, and wriggle
with convulsions as the magnetic fluid—satirized to delicious effect by
trilling woodwinds—ostensibly does its work. They counterfeit a trance
and demand love favors from their now sympathetic lady friends. Animal
Magnetism, Despina announces, will restore the sufferers to health within
an hour or two; meanwhile, they must—on medical grounds—be placated. Here Mozart made merry with one of the most detractory charges
brought against Mesmeric healing, namely, that "magnetic" stimulation
often became erotic excitement, sexual liberties playing their part, the doctor's hands wandering afield, his knees enfolding the patient's as his fingers
sought all over the body those "poles" on which to concentrate his ministering efforts.[36]

That Ferrando and Guglielmo lay writhing dressed in fantastic outfits
derived from a turn in the plot; yet the picture fell well within Mesmer's
scheme of things: as a Mason, he knew the appeal of ceremony and fantastic trappings to initiates yearning for purification and a faith bringing
with it bodily and psychic harmony, a state the lovers pretend to regain.
Indeed, Mesmerism grew from a para-Masonic circle into a schism within
the Masonic body. Resting, like Masonry, upon astrology, hermetic-
cabalist allusions, and upon the writings of Marsilio Ficino and Giordano
Bruno, Mesmerism developed into a pseudoscience with its own cosmic
theories and solemnities (and, in time, radical social and political dimensions, as well), though its Masonic origins always remained unmistakable.
Mesmer may have suggested the Masonic text of *"An die Freude"* (see
XVI, n. 50) to Mozart as a vehicle for a song, perhaps for use in some
mesmeric rite.

During his days in Vienna, Mesmer perhaps believed in the essential efficacy of the cure he had begun to evolve. Leopold found him honest and
a man of good cheer. A mutual interest in medical mysteries and apothe-

---

36 In *Bastien*, Colas hopes to collect his magician's fee in the form of embraces.

caries' brews might have been a point of contact between them, but Dr. Mesmer also possessed a pleasant tenor voice and performed on the violoncello, harpsichord, and glass harmonica. (He had recourse to the last to provide mysterious sounds during his séances.) Leopold celebrated his hospitality and with affection referred to the Mesmer family as "the whole gang." *Bastien und Bastienne* took form in a genial atmosphere drawing together artist, patron, and their families. In 1768 Mesmer had yet to develop the full ritual of his regimen and the personal eccentricities of his palmy days.[37] In the operetta's benevolent magician-shepherd he no doubt glimpsed something of himself: Colas may have provided him a few private chuckles.

Colas, whom the locals look upon as a prognosticator, reveals to the audience the source of his skill—a knowledge of psychology: "If a young person questions me about his future happiness, at once I read his fate in his lovesick glance." However, youth does not listen to reason but prefers to believe enchanters or magicians. He determines to help Bastien and Bastienne reconcile by making them believe in his power to perform wonders: a bit of humbug and hocus-pocus will bring them to reason. Proceeding to frighten Bastien with a portentous aria in C minor, he intones the kind of nonsense magic words found in Wolfgang's letters: "Diggi daggi, schurry murry, horum harum"; obviously "Dr." Despina studied her Latin with Colas. This reading from Colas's "Book of Magic" ends with a meaningful "quid pro quo."

A handsome quid pro quo from Dr. Mesmer doubtless rewarded Wolfgang's efforts, but in nowise could it have softened Leopold's disappointment: the singspiel, not the *opera buffa*, had achieved performance, and the first, as a genre, represented everything he hated about Vienna's musical taste. He had set down his thoughts on the subject late in January: "On the whole, it is well known and demonstrated every day in their theaters that the Viennese are not eager to see serious and sensible things and, to boot, have little or no comprehension of them and only want to look at foolish stuff: dances, devils, ghosts, magic, witches, apparitions, and [clowns like]

---

37 During this Parisian career, as Mesmerism spread over France like an epidemic, he not only took advantage of vulnerable adherents (they included Queen Marie Antoinette) and their bent toward the miraculous disguised as science, but also descended to the shadiest financial maneuvers in order to sustain and enhance his sumptuous way of life. A change in character did not overtake him on the Seine: less than lofty inclinations had shown themselves as early as his doctoral dissertation (*De planetarum influxu*), in modern times revealed a plagiarism. By the eighties Mozart recognized that imposture had always been a large part of Mesmer's constitution. Yet *Così* treats playfully an old patron for whom its composer preserved affection. His patients, too, may have looked back upon him with fondness: on the whole, he did less harm than most of the era's orthodox physicians with their merciless bleedings and enemas.

Hanswurst, Lipperl, and Bernadon."[38] Indeed, here and there Colas not only anticipates the magic of Sarastro but also suggests the buffoonery of Osmin, the Pasha's factotum in *The Abduction.* (Colas, however, does not color his diction with those vigorous colloquialisms the Viennese expected from their Hanswursts.) Part sage and part clown, the figure of Colas, the first significant creation of Mozart the musical dramatist, must have found favor with Dr. Mesmer, if not with Leopold, whose letters home remained silent about *Bastien und Bastienne.*

As conjectured above, he had regarded it as a safeguard: a plan under way, but held in reserve, to be trotted out in default of a substantial operatic contract. While the Burgtheater commission remained in place, he doubtless looked upon *Bastien* as a refreshing minor effort to contrast with a triumphant *La finta semplice*; but as its future clouded, he began, in light of his protracted leave, to fear the scorn of the Salzburg Residenz. It would consider the production of a short singspiel in a private mansion— as doubtless he did—meager recompense for humiliation at the Burgtheater. But at a stroke a splendid new commission arrived; at the top of his voice he proclaimed redress.

Whatever its opinion of Leopold, the Hofburg decided to make matters up to Wolfgang, to compensate him in public for his misadventure at the Burgtheater: with the Imperial family's encouragement, Pater Ignaz Parhamer, director of a famed orphanage on the Rennweg, asked him to provide music for a grand festivity.[39] The Mozarts already had Parhamer's goodwill and visited him often. In all likelihood Leopold had met this strange Jesuit a decade before in Salzburg, whither Archbishop Schrattenbach had summoned him to inspirit the faith of backsliding parishoners through his theatrical sermons. About the same time, he had become Emperor Francis's confessor, and soon thereafter the Empress confided the charitable installation to his care. Parhamer, famous during his missionary days for his flowing beard and pilgrim's staff and cape, retained his flair for the flamboyant. In his hands the Rennweg orphanage became one of Vienna's sights: he made the boy inmates of eight years and upwards into miniature soldiers, dividing them into battalions and insisting upon courtesy and drill of the utmost precision. His curriculum combined military

---

38 See XXIX, n. 12. In 1832 (when, had he survived, Wolfgang Mozart would have reached seventy-six) the youthful Richard Wagner experienced the Viennese magic theater. It was to contribute significantly to his dramatic vocabulary. Leopold did not live to see the genre he so despised crowned with *The Magic Flute.*

39 It remains possible that the Habsburgs had encouraged this commission before Leopold presented the petition to Joseph. At all events, even after its receipt they favored exhibiting the boy's talents at the Rennweg ceremonies.

discipline with musical studies, both instrumental and vocal; on festival days, "Kindergeneral" Parhamer's infantry paraded to "Turkish" music—imitating Janissary bands, it combined high-pitched woodwinds, drums, triangles, and cymbals, a manifestation of the *turquerie* stylish among the Viennese[40]—and, along with the choir, the boys' orchestra had its part in the Sunday service.

During the summer, the Mozarts had watched the Emperor lay the foundation stone of a new church for the Rennweg orphanage. On this occasion, he could still question Wolfgang about his work on *La finta semplice.* But by 7 December, when Archbishop Migazzi and Suffragan Bishop Franz Anton Marxer consecrated the as yet unfinished structure in the presence of the Empress and assorted archduchesses and archdukes, the opera had become a lost cause and the celebration the only opportunity for Wolfgang to demonstrate his abilities before a large and splendid Viennese assembly.

The *Wienerisches Diarium,* describing this divine service, observed: "All of the music for the orphans' choir at High Mass had been from first to last newly composed for this solemnity by Wolfgang Mozart, noted for his extraordinary talent; this twelve-year-old little son of Herr Leopold Mozart, Kapellmeister in the service of the Prince of Salzburg, performed himself and conducted with the greatest accuracy and to universal applause and admiration; in addition, he also sang in the motets."

The gathering heard three new works from his hand: a solemn high mass (K. 139/47a) scored for trumpets, trombones, and tympani; an offertory; and a trumpet concerto written for one of the boys.[41] Broad, noble—indeed, symphonic—in conception, the mass betrays the influence of Hasse, Eberlin, and contemporary Viennese church and operatic composers, the masses of Karl Georg Reutter providing their example of

---

40 Gluck, for example, had exploited an exotic Islamic atmosphere in his *Le cadi dupé* and *La rencontre imprévue.* (To swell his repertory of out-of-the-way compositions, Parhamer asked Leopold for his "Musical Sleigh-Ride," esoteric in Noverre's sense of the anomalous beauty to be found in foreign and rural customs and usages.) A most conspicuous example of the new taste for the eccentric expressed itself in Moslem livery: escorts dressed in Hungarian costume had become démodé; couriers in Turkish dress sprouting aigrettes and with boots curling at the tips now cleared the way for the most fashionable Viennese.

41 The last two compositions, K. 47b and 47c—his first documented concerto—have not survived (though some put K. 117/66a forward as K. 47b). The ambitious design of K. 139 identifies it as the Orphanage Mass: it cannot be the contemporary K. 49/47d, an economically scored *missa brevis,* a concise mass and hardly what Leopold described as a *"Solenne Mess"* (*sic*). From the same period comes a *Veni Sancte Spiritus* (K. 47), perhaps written for Parhamer's orphanage musicians and performed in von Allio's church of the Salesianerinnen on the Rennweg.

brilliant effects, the *Orfeo* and *Alceste* of Gluck lending at moments their unmistakable atmosphere.[42] The opening C-minor passages of the Kyrie offer astounding measures in which the young composer anticipates the profundity of his later years.

Of Wolfgang's ambitious contributions to the Rennweg ceremonies Leopold remarked: "Everything has its reasons." An authoritative hand—Maria Theresa's or Kaunitz's?—had sweetened a bitter cup. A sententious Leopold declared: "The mass little Wolfgang performed at Pater Parhamer's . . . has restored what enemies thought to destroy by obstructing the opera and has convinced the court and the public—the crowd was amazing—of the wickedness of our adversaries." Hagenauer, Leopold promised, would soon learn the details verbally: the Empress, having permitted herself the consolations of Wolfgang's religious music, had expressed her appreciation with generosity, and Leopold felt prepared to confront Salzburg.

During these months away, Wolfgang had ground out a great number and variety of compositions, his tiny frame, despite the recent near-fatal illness, somehow withstanding the strain. But the boy brought up to believe himself the center of the world must have suffered to watch his *opera buffa*'s production die its slow death, his first serious professional failure. It is difficult to imagine his being spared the father's distraught and occasional rehearsals of the calumnies in circulation or those cries of anguish and monologues he directed toward anyone sympathetic and within hearing. A poor courtier, he made no effort to mask his bitterness. Even the Samaritan-like Hasse began to weary of these "lamentations": "The father, as far as I can see, is equally discontented everywhere. . . ." Moreover, in his frustration Leopold had taken to speaking of his son in adulatory tones distasteful to those aware of their dangers. A "high opinion of the boy's natural good sense" alone gave Hasse hope that Wolfgang might "grow into an honest fellow." The extent to which he was experiencing, in addition to a particular disappointment, the insecurities and vulnerability of adolescence can only be guessed; but whatever the depth of his personal crisis during this period, his confidence in his musical abilities remained unshaken (as it would to his last breath), and 1768, its alarms, disillusionments, and miscalculations notwithstanding, had proved a year remarkable in his artistic evolution.

---

42 In the course of the Mozarts' Moravian stay, the premiere of Gluck's *Alceste* took place in Vienna (16 December 1767); during the following January they must have heard at least one of its several repetitions.

Facing the overall task Leopold had given him, that of proving himself a grown-up composer in the major genres, he had put forth an *opera buffa*, a singspiel, a grand mass, as well as purely instrumental music,[43] the long Viennese-Moravian sojourn proving decisive in his development as a symphonist. Another four-movement symphony, K. 48 dated 13 December, exhibits dramatic effects revealing not only Gluck's continuing hold upon him but acquaintance with musical ideas emanating from Eisenstadt and Esterháza, the twin centers of Joseph Haydn's activities.[44] In Vienna, Wolfgang also assimilated symphonic works by Dittersdorf, Hofmann, Wagenseil, Holzbauer, Gassman, and Vanhal. With freshness and ingenuity he could now turn traditional orchestral figures to his own purposes, with newfound craft—exceptional in his songful second movements— weave orchestral fabrics of startling invention, strengthening the warp here, lightening the weft there as he disposed his well-proportioned and finely colored patterns. He had begun to approach an individuality of manner; here were stirrings of genius.

---

43 A pair of lovely two-movement duos (K. 46d and 46e, dated 1 September 1768) for violin and continuo, here an unfigured bass, perhaps represent the beginnings of a set of sonatas abandoned when a Viennese commission became defunct.

44 Haydn traveled to Vienna from Eisenstadt during March of 1768, a rare and brief visit, during which he conducted his stirring *Stabat mater* (1767) at the Brothers of Mercy. That the Mozarts attended stands to reason, but no record survives: Leopold failed to keep his journal (see XXXI, n. 3).

CHAPTER XV

The First Sojourn in Italy

L EOPOLD'S PRUDENT CULTIVATION of Archbishop Schrattenbach's relatives in Moravia and Vienna helped sway the Salzburg court to take him back. (The prose of its decree stopping his salary had hinted at dismissal.) During April 1768, with foresight he had the children step forward to perform at the wedding in Vienna of Schrattenbach's nephew Count Otto Wolfgang von Schrattenbach, a district governor stationed in Graz. His father, the Archbishop's brother Franz Anton, journeyed from Brünn to attend what Leopold called "the Salzburg Wedding Festivities": "I volunteered my services, and we gave a concert and entertained the wedding guests for a whole evening to everyone's pleasure and satisfaction." The Schrattenbachs who had gathered in Vienna for the celebration doubtless wrote the Archbishop, urging him to look upon the Mozarts with sympathy, their efforts reinforced by his niece Countess von Herberstein, now back in Salzburg from Brünn.

Retracing their route of some sixteen months earlier, the Mozarts re-entered Salzburg on 5 January 1769. On the way, they had again stopped at the two Benedictine abbeys of Melk (Wolfgang regaled its Lord Abbot on the organ) and Lambach, to whose monks Leopold presented a gift: the orchestral parts of The Hague Symphony K. Anh. 221/45a, revised in Salzburg and taken to Vienna. An orchestra made up of the Lambach brothers doubtless played it during the visit, along with a symphony by Leopold, a copy of which he also left behind.

In Salzburg, the overconfident father attempted a ridiculous game. At the Residenz astonishment greeted his humbly couched request of early March 1769: the salary withheld during his absence ought to be restored, he maintained, because a miserable adventure had detained him in Vienna against his will and emptied his purse. But before long he threw off his ill-fitting disguise of submissive court servant and acknowledged what everyone had long recognized: his eagerness to quit Salzburg for the south. That Wolfgang's illnesses had frustrated hopes to crown the Grand Tour with a sojourn in Italy had but sharpened Leopold's determination to make the pilgrimage; he had come to look upon it in terms of the boy's destiny: "A journey which, all circumstances weighed, can no longer be postponed." His introduction to the second edition of his *Versuch* (September) would announce the plan. In the end, the Archbishop, who had already sent several of his musicians to Italy to perfect themselves,[1] would again help finance an experience he recognized as important to the education of a remarkable young subject. However fatigued the palace may have become with Leopold,[2] its goodwill toward Wolfgang remained. In recompense, Archbishop Siegmund expected him to return polished by Italian culture and ready to contribute to Salzburg's musical life. Leopold would accept the money and set out on a trip intended, in his eyes, to prepare his son for a position in some more important capital. But they could not leave until the end of the year: before an impatient Leopold lay months of waiting.

If he experienced awkwardness in picking up the threads of his professional life, his son suffered none. Commissions came, and he set to work. Were the enemies in Salzburg against whom Leopold continued to inveigh, in fact those who could not stomach him? Early in March, Johann Christoph von Zabuesnig, a young Augsburg merchant, visited Salzburg. He used his slender gift for verse to celebrate Wolfgang in a poem evoking a Europe envious of the land that had given him birth, a land that showed continuing eagerness for his creations.

His carefully wrought *Missa brevis* (K. 65/61a of January 1769),[3] written

---

1 For example, the soprano Maria Magdalena Lipp, recently become Michael Haydn's bride, had studied singing in Venice at the Archbishop's expense.

2 The Archiepiscopal exchequer did not permit itself to be cozened: despite his high-handed request—or perhaps because of it—Leopold had to rest content with payments dating from the time of his return from Vienna.

3 A *missa brevis* might telescope passages of text—here, in the Credo—successive sections being sung at the same time.

upon his return from Vienna and embodying a profound repose, may have been a peace offering to the court. This serious D-minor work must have occupied Leopold's thoughts when, in a gesture of conciliation, he asked the Archbishop to bear in mind the Mozart family's significant contribution to the music of the cathedral. The first performance, however, took place in Fischer von Erlach's Universitätskirche on 5 February and initiated forty hours of uninterrupted prayer before the exposed Blessed Sacrament, a spiritual exercise inaugurating Shrove Sunday and prefiguring Lent.[4]

Again the university called upon Wolfgang. Students of the philosophical faculty commissioned *Finalmusik,* special compositions for the post-examination period to be played before the Archbishop at his summer residence, Schloss Mirabell, and then in front of the university for the entertainment of the assembled students and professors. As a rule, the cassation and the serenade served such an occasion, suites closely related to the divertimento and, like it, made up of a series of pieces (see p. 353). When determined by the protocol of a related ceremony—often a torchlit defile—the time between movements varied; of necessity, a sense of cohesion could not always inform the whole, though an introductory march repeated as a finale not only answered the purposes of ritual but also formed a musical frame. Wolfgang's Cassations K. 63 and 99/63a as well as the Serenade K. 100/62a,[5] all composed during the summer of 1769, reveal the influence of Joseph Haydn, Michael Haydn, Christian Bach, Luigi Boccherini, and Giovanni Battista Sammartini. (It would appear that Leopold had his son study the two closely affined Italian masters in preparation for the journey south.) In addition, Wolfgang provided Salzburg with minuets for Carnival (K. 65a/61b) and during autumn wrote the Dominicus Mass for the ordination of Cajetan Hagenauer (see XIV, n. 8). His father's diary described as *"elegantissima"* this *Missa solemnis* in the magniloquent manner of Hasse. Such a composition reveals the silken ease with which Mozart could assimilate the styles of his models. Thus, it remains puzzling that he did not turn out even more during these tranquil months at home when, spared the exhaustion of travel, he suffered no serious illness and his relationship to the city of his birth seemed idyllic.

Indeed, the Archbishop went so far as to promise to place the musical resources of his household at Mozart's disposal in order to realize in Salzburg

---

4 Inventive explanations of why Mozart provided this mass with a Gloria, a section of the Ordinary suppressed during Lent, fall beside the point: though on the threshold, K. 65 is a pre-Lenten mass.

5 The following year he would put to use its march (K. 62) to accompany the king's entrance in *Mitridate.*

what had been denied him in Vienna: *La finta semplice* was to be produced at the Residenz during the spring with a cast including Meissner and Maria Magdalena Haydn. In addition, Mozart took steps to give *Bastien und Bastienne* a more dignified air by turning its spoken dialogue into recitative[6]—as in Rousseau's original version—for the court contemplated mounting the revised singspiel as well: a double boon, for a record of performed stage works could but strengthen Wolfgang's pursuit of opera commissions in Italy. Though conclusive documentation is lacking, in all probability the premiere of *La finta semplice* did take place in Salzburg during 1769. The *Bastien* project, however, came to nothing, perhaps because Mozart had no taste for bending German words to Italian secco style.

Leopold, who had hoped to depart during the autumn's mild weather, could not break away until almost winter. While the family waited its hour, a moving valediction took place: on 16 October "about fifty people" gathered to honor Pater Dominicus at the Hagenauers' country home in the Nonntal suburb; dinner over, Wolfgang and Nannerl performed. In this house the Mozarts dearly loved, brother and sister said farewell to their professional association. The pair of *Wunderkinder* touring side by side belonged to the past; only Wolfgang and Leopold were to set out for Italy; Nannerl would remain at home with Mother, practice, gather a few pupils, and hope for a suitable husband.[7]

In November 1769, Archbishop Siegmund bade father and son "*Wiedersehen*" with a magnificent gift of six hundred florins and, in addition, named Wolfgang, not quite fourteen, a *Konzertmeister* (unpaid), a title bestowed both to increase his prestige abroad and to bind him to Salzburg: an official letter promised, upon his return, "the remuneration due that office." What duties did the position imply?

When he left, his reputation rested upon his talent as a composer and at the clavier. Although he might on occasion, as in the cozy atmosphere of the Nonntal concert, pick up the violin, little indicates notable appreciation of his fiddling. His rank of Salzburg *Konzertmeister* should not be taken in the meaning of the word prevailing only since the early nineteenth century, that of first violinist of an orchestra. Indeed, Leopold's lamenting, in later years, his son's neglect of his bowing technique and the public's widespread ignorance of his even being a string player, argues the point (see p. 351 and XVIII, n. 22). More correctly, the title should be construed

---

6 For this never-completed renovation of *Bastien*, Mozart had in mind rewriting the bass part of Colas for a higher voice.

7 She had begun to receive the attentions of Franz, a son of Court Chancellor Franz Felix Anton von Mölk.

as designating a composer-conductor directing in the chamber either with the bow or from the clavier, the very context in which Milan's Regio Ducal Teatro introduced Mozart to its public in 1770: it styled him the Arch-bishop of Salzburg's *"Maestro de la Musica di Camera,"* the Italian phrase an-swering in spirit the Mozarts' concept of *Konzertmeister*; had they found fault with the Italian appellation, they would have had it changed.

Salzburg's second most famous *Konzertmeister*, Michael Haydn, though skilled on the strings, also made his reputation both at the keyboard and with his compositions, and neither he nor Mozart ever had any reason or right to intrude upon the prerogatives of Antonio Brunetti, who in 1776 advanced to become first violinist of the Salzburg orchestra, that is, *Kon-zertmeister* in today's usage. (The point can be made that Mozart wrote his violin concertos of 1775 not for himself but for Brunetti; see p. 351.) When Sebastian Bach, who came to Weimar as chamber musician and organist, rose to the post of *Konzertmeister*, a rank immediately below that of vice-kapellmeister, his additional duties concerned not the violin, with which he led the ensemble, but writing a fresh cantata every four weeks; this posi-tion, Weimar's court secretary recorded, "obliged" him "to perform new works every month." In like manner, Tomasini's progress in Esterházy ser-vice from First Violinist to *Konzertmeister* implied new tasks; and Gluck's responsibilities as Prince Hildburghausen's and Mingotti's *Konzertmeister* (see p. 86) embraced rehearsing and conducting with the bow or at the keyboard, although he had no particular virtuosity on any instrument other than musical glasses.

Insights concerning a *Konzertmeister*'s duties in eighteenth-century Salzburg may be gleaned from Leopold Mozart's responses to his son's comments from Paris (1778) concerning those days when he had carried the title at home: were he to return, Wolfgang insisted, he would refuse to play the violin along with the courtiers in their informal ensemble, a task he had, in fact, fulfilled with resentment and rather poorly; he would "no longer be a fiddler"; instead, he wanted to "conduct from the keyboard—accompany arias." Leopold countered by pointing out that, in truth, the young man had never functioned as *Konzertmeister*; in his case the title had been something of a sham: "Formerly you were an incidental *Konzertmeis-ter* [a reference to his having composed for the Salzburg Residenz only now and then], but in fact nothing more than a fiddler; now [Leopold had ne-gotiated the matter of a reappointment] you will be *Konzertmeister* and Court Organist with the main responsibility of accompanying at the key-board...." He "would preside," Leopold assured him, "with full author-ity, free of any coercion to pick up the violin." Thus, with his father's blessing, Mozart turned his back upon the instrument even as he prepared to reassume the official title and functions of *Konzertmeister.* In creating the adolescent an honorary *Konzertmeister* at the end of 1769, Archbishop Schrattenbach had simply executed the polished gesture of bestowing a theoretical title signifying a composer-conductor of a rank just below his father's.[8]

Carrying a stack of music—no doubt it included a symphony he had assembled by extracting four movements from the Serenade K. 100/62a—on 13 December 1769[9] the Mozarts had started their journey toward that land for which their countrymen have always longed with peculiar intensity.

2

LEOPOLD AND WOLFGANG relied upon Vienna's widespread control of Italian political and cultural life to smooth their way. Proceeding from one enclave of the Empire to another, they would seldom be without important German connections to exploit. Leopold of Austria governed Tuscany, and in Milan they would find Maria Theresa's lieutenants bending the knee to another of her sons, Archduke Ferdinand,[10] two years older than Mozart and filling a ceremonial role as governor and captain general of Austrian Lombardy. Effectual power resided in the Empress's viceroy and *de facto* plenipotentiary in northern Italy, Count Karl Joseph von Firmian,[11] a nephew of that archbishop of Salzburg under whom Leopold had first entered court service. Cognizant of the aid Firmian had once given Christian Bach, Leopold expected much of this patron of music through whose ancestral land the travelers would press south.

Firmian's family, like the Lodrons and Arcos of Salzburg, had its roots in the Tyrol, that strategic province in which the deep groove of the river Inn intersects with the Brenner route linking Teutonic and Mediterranean Europe, the rich valleys, inhabited in the north largely by populations German

---

8 At an informal quartet evening in Vienna (1784), an awestruck Michael Kelly beheld the players: Joseph Haydn and Dittersdorf the violinists, Vanhall the violoncellist, and Mozart on viola. While acknowledging with humorous reverence "a little science among them," he could not keep back his impression of only "tolerable" performances: "Not one of them excelled on the instrument he played. . . ."

9 Though Hagenauer entered this date in his calendar, they may have left on the twelfth.

10 From 1535 until the War of the Spanish Succession, Milan remained a Spanish dependency. The general Peace of Utrecht (1714) gave the duchy to Maria Theresa's father, Emperor Charles VI, who, in return, at least feigned to renounce his claim to the throne of Spain (see VI, n. 7).

11 Once a prominent member of Salzburg's Muratori Society (see p. 40), Firmian supported Enlightened causes, for a while helping the philosophe and first criminologist, Cesare Beccaria.

in origin, speech, and loyalty, becoming increasingly Italian in character as the traveler approaches Lombardy.[12] The Mozarts would have to pass through mountainous Tyrolese terrain, a not inconsiderable campaign in heavy snow and wind. Since the Pressburg coach could no longer ride such a storm, Leopold had decided to travel in rented carriages. The women remaining at home and Wolfgang now a grown-up, he saw no need even to take along a servant: a local could be hired whenever special assistance or a show of luxury might be needed. But Leopold did not look forward to managing the rituals of packing and unpacking: he had just celebrated his fiftieth birthday; become slow and stout on the cooking of Vienna—where a tailor had let out the bursting seams of his clothing—more than ever he required comfort.

He and his son delighted in the snugness of the fine carriage in which they went forth: "as warm as in a room," Wolfgang wrote his sister. Reassured by the skill of the driver, Leopold let himself doze; but Wolfgang remained alert and in high spirits, enjoying most the moments on those rare level stretches when the reins lay slack and the horses swept forward.

From Salzburg the Mozarts followed the Saalach, an affluent of the Salzach. Moving southwest to the village of Kaitl, they skirted Reichenhall and somewhat after seven reached the market center of Lofer and "a fine room and good bed" in the Prefect's house. After breakfast they veered toward the Inn and through "astonishingly deep snow" made their way via St. Johann in Tyrol to Wörgl, where they spent the night. Rising at five, they pressed on to Schwaz, nestling beneath towering peaks, and at half past five in the evening arrived at Innsbruck, capital of the Tyrol.

There, in 1765, during a celebration of his son Leopold's marriage (see XIV, n. 12), Emperor Francis had suffered a seizure and died in the passageway connecting the opera house with the palace. Favored by the Habsburgs through the centuries, the city had become, in Maria Theresa's eyes, a kind of cenotaph, and here she contemplated living out her years should she leave the throne. The Mozarts put up at the Zum weissen Kreuz on the fifteenth. Two days later, Wolfgang performed before the Vice President of the regional government, Count Leopold Franz Künigl, and received a fee of twelve ducats. The generosity and courtesy of the local aristocracy gratified the visitors, Count Johann Nepomuk Spaur, Burgrave of Tyrol and brother of a canon of Salzburg cathedral, showing them particular kindness.

Departing Innsbruck on the nineteenth, they turned south to drive between the Stubaier and the Tuxer Alps and take their rest at Steinach.

12 Mrs. Piozzi commented on "the sight of two nations, not naturally congenial, living happily together, as the Germans and Italians here do. . . ."

Then, passing through the great gate to Italy, the Brenner Pass, they descended to Sterzing (Vipiteno) and pursued the river Eisack (Isarco) to Brixen (Bressanone). There they paused before continuing further along the Eisack through Atzwang to Bozen (Bolzano), which furnished their resting place for two nights. They had to take breath and come to themselves: a proper carriage road over the Brenner would not be constructed until 1772, and they had suffered an ordeal as the horses struggled through the dangerous trails.

Below Bozen the Eisack meets the Etsch (Adige), which then twists toward Verona. The Mozarts' route lay through this still magnificent valley. After an evening in Neumarkt (Egna), they lunched in Trient (Trento) and by night had installed themselves at the inn known to its German guests as the Zur Rose (L'Albergo della Rosa d' Oro) in Rovereto (Rofreit).[13] It was Christmas Eve.

They found old friends, among them Her Imperial Majesty's District Commissioner Nicolò Cristani, who, during a residence in Salzburg, had studied the violin with Leopold; he remembered Frau Anna Maria and commented upon Wolfgang's resemblance to her. Into the bargain, the mayor of prosperous, comfortable Rovereto proved to be Baron Giovanni Battista Todeschi, whom the Mozarts had met in Vienna. He put his house at Wolfgang's disposal for a Christmas Day concert attended by the local aristocracy. But all of Rovereto wanted to hear him, and the next day he gave a public organ recital in the church of San Marco. On this occasion he first experienced the animation and ferment of Italian life. The eager throng, filling nearly every space, pushed forward and formed a human wall that for a while would not give way even to permit him an avenue to the instrument: "Several strong fellows had to go before us and clear a path to the choir...," Leopold related, "for everyone wanted to get close to us." Both Mozarts found the experience intoxicating. The next day (27 December) they departed. Through the hills of Valpolicella they came to the Lombard plain.

3

"GREEK AND ROMAN antiquities salute one at the gates," wrote Mrs. Piozzi about Verona, the birthplace of Catullus. Straying outside the bounds of Habsburg Lombardy, the Mozarts entered this handsome city of Venetia[14] and put up at the Due Torri. Viewing the sights—they found

---

13 Rovereto was the seat of a branch of the Lodrons, Bozen the city of the Firmians, though Count Karl Joseph had been born in Deutschmetz (Mezzotedesco) in the province of Trient.
14 Verona had been subject to Venice since the early fifteenth century.

the Roman amphitheater and archeological museum of exceptional inter-est—occupied a good part of their two-week stay, Leopold making use of Johann Georg Keyssler's guidebook (*Neueste Reisen . . .*), the Baedeker of its day. But, more important, in Verona Wolfgang first heard an Italian opera in the land of its creation—Pietro Alessandro Guglielmi's *Ruggiero*[15]—and experienced an Italian city in which most of the administrative aristoc-racy, unlike that of Lower Tyrol, spoke not German but Italian as a first language.

Wolfgang began to express himself in Italian, which he practiced in let-ters to his sister. Proceeding well enough for several sentences until the temptation to pun in two languages became too great, his writing then dis-solved into an Italo-Salzburgisch medley. He gave but brief reports, de-pending upon his father to chronicle the facts of the journey,[16] which Frau Mozart and Nannerl followed on maps and with their own copy of Keyssler. In these very earliest specimens of his correspondence, he demonstrated not only his father's ease with words but also a light humor manifesting touches of an insistent vulgarity, at its most winning in its pic-ture of the buffoon at the opera, whose art consisted in breaking wind at every jump.

In Verona he again performed in church before an excited audience, this time on the two organs (Epistle and Gospel) of the Carmelite monastery of San Tommaso Becket (7 January 1770). "Such a mob had assembled at the . . . church," Leopold wrote, "that upon our arrival we scarcely had room to step down from the coach. The throng was such that we were forced to go through the cloister where, in a moment, so many people came running toward us that we would not have been able to make our way through had not the fathers, who were already awaiting us at the portals, taken us into their midst." After the recital, "the tumult was even greater, for everyone wanted to see the little organist." Two days earlier, Wolfgang's appearance at the Accademia filarmonica, his first official public concert in Italy, had been no less a triumph.

"But you know how things are; journalists write . . . whatever comes into their heads," Leopold informed family and friends in an attempt to explain two mistakes appearing in the *Gazzetta di Mantova*'s account of the Verona concert: somehow, the reporter had believed Leopold to be Salzburg's "present *maestro di cappella*" and described "the little German boy, Sig. Amadeo Wolfgango Motzart" as "still under thirteen years."

---

15 The preceding May, Venice had heard the premiere of *Ruggiero*, whose librettist, Caterino Maz-zolà, would prepare the text of Mozart's *La clemenza di Tito.*

16 Wolfgang did help keep the travel journal.

Leopold's problems of pride in respect to title remained beyond his control and would in no degree diminish with the years; but, ironically, he chose to fall back upon his old and ever more foolish device of misrepresenting Wolfgang's age at the very time he had begun to show his audiences an increasing sophistication. The little boy identifying the pitches of bells and playing on covered keyboards had had his day; Wolfgang now offered himself as a serious composer and conductor of symphonies and as a dazzling sight-reader and improviser: after "a most beautiful introductory symphony of his own composition, which deserved all its applause," so the *Gazzetta* reported, he then, "extempore, played a clavier concerto splendidly and afterward diverse sonatas completely new to him." Next, upon being given four verses, he composed "an aria in the best taste and in the very act of singing it." More improvisations followed, and he also "played a trio by Boccherini very well at sight." An element of trial persisted in such an appearance, but the critic's description breathed admiration awakened by talent rather than astonishment provoked by a freakish child.

Verona's aristocrats desired a permanent reminder of this remarkable visit, and, at the urging of Pietro Lugiati, an official of the provincial exchequer, Wolfgang sat for his portrait, one of the finest in the brief canon of authentic Mozart iconology.[17] The painter, Saverio dalla Rosa, put on canvas those intense eyes that survey the viewer with a glance at a time serious and sensuous, the still taut and smooth face nonetheless suggesting the heavy jowls to come. Elegant in dress and posture, Mozart sits in a rococo chair before a harpsichord (made by Joannis Celestini), a Molto allegro (K. 72a) open on the music desk.[18] Still handsome, he appears disturbingly knowing and yet ageless some twenty days before his fourteenth birthday.

How he adored the life surging about him. Goethe would announce that travel to Italy should have its purpose not in enjoyment but in learning. For Wolfgang it was impossible not to take pleasure even as he learned. Verona's streets swarmed with maskers, as did the opera house, where the Mozarts had use of the Marchese Alessandro Carlotti's box. "What fun!" Wolfgang cried as he greeted the ladies, saluting them with the traditional: "*servitore umilissimo, Signora maschera.*" His eye for physical beauty already

---

17 Fewer than a dozen genuine likenesses of Mozart survive, many representations appearing in publications time and again being dubious or spurious. This last category bulges with fantasies eagerly accepted by those unwilling to acknowledge that a transcendent genius can be homely.

18 The painter's skill of detail preserves a fragment of a composition (inspired by Handel) Wolfgang had perhaps played at St. Tommaso's, for aught we know a movement from a lost keyboard sonata.

sharp, he commented to Nannerl, in his ollapodrida of Italian and German, on Italy's prima donnas, judging their figures as well as their voices with relentless humor. His spirit bubbled, and he made an enormous impression upon Verona: specializing in improvised rhymes and epigrams, its local poets, in turn, showered him with *ex abrupto* anacreontic verses of praise. The city did not soon forget him: on the first anniversary of his public concert, the Accademia filarmonica would name him an honorary *maestro di cappella*.

On 10 January in freezing weather, father and son traveled to Mantua, Virgil's city, set midst the swampy lagoons of the Mincio. Arriving in the early evening, they settled in the Croce verde and rushed off to hear Hasse's *Demetrio* at the opera.

Mantua had belonged to Vienna since 1708, when, with the exhaustion of the Gonzaga line, Maria Theresa's uncle, Emperor Joseph I, claimed the dukedom as a fief of Empire. Under Habsburg patronage, the city had recently established a Reale Accademia di scienze, lettere e arti, a public educational and artistic institute in which both aristocrat and bourgeois participated. It maintained an orchestra of eighteen and, but six weeks earlier, had opened a *teatrino* designed by Antonio Galli-Bibbiena, a chamber whose beauty overwhelmed Leopold. Here, on 16 January, Wolfgang played at a public concert[19] featuring three of his symphonies.

The acclaimed appearance notwithstanding, Count Karl Oktavian Colloredo, President of the Accademia, showed an unmistakable personal indifference to the Mozarts and withheld an invitation to perform at his home. Yet, though schooled to brook occasional coolness, they found themselves unprepared for the rebuff dealt them by another of Mantua's highest aristocrats, Prince Michael II von Thurn und Taxis, who maintained an estimable musical establishment headed by Giovanni Battista Pattoni. His Highness's servants had orders to close the doors to the Mozarts; the Prince, they were told, had no time to receive. Leopold stood openmouthed: he had expected hospitality and patronage, for Prince Michael had married a Lodron of Salzburg, and his household staff included several Salzburgers. He and Count Colloredo must have heard of the Affligio affair and the petition and wished no involvement with musicians who did not know their place. For a while Leopold refused to accept the snub; in a ludicrous move to gain an audience, he and Wolfgang trailed Prince

---

19 Luigi Gatti may have participated. A *vicemaestro* of the Accademia, he would become kapellmeister of Salzburg in 1783 and therewith destroy Leopold's hopes of attaining the post he so often pretended to occupy. In Mantua, Gatti made a copy of one of Wolfgang's masses, perhaps K. 66.

Michael's carriage from street to street, without shame following behind it through the gates of his palace in an attempt to thrust their presence upon him. They did not succeed.

In happy contrast, Count Francis Eugene Arco welcomed them. A cousin of Salzburg's Lord Chamberlain, he had passed part of his youth in the archbishopric. His friendliness helped soften the blow the pair's pride had suffered at Prince Michael's hands. Nonetheless, the discourtesy had for the moment unnerved Leopold; he began to complain: "Nothing but dressing and undressing, packing and unpacking, and, in addition, no warm room; freezing like a dog; everything you but touch is ice cold." He was, he informed Salzburg, "severely tried."

4

THEIR FEET ENVELOPED in muffs lined with wolf fur, the Mozarts on 19 January traveled in numbing weather to Bozzolo. No sooner had they alighted at the Albergo della Posta than Don Carlo Saragozzi, a priest and professor of music, took them to his house, where Mozart's playing gave "unspeakable pleasure" to a gathering of local dignitaries. Leopold questioned them about possible danger from highwaymen and the best routes to Milan. The next day the Mozarts' coach continued on to Cremona.[20]

Safely arrived, they heard Michele Angelo Valentini's *La clemenza di Tito* at the Teatro Nazzari and admired the orchestra—it used instruments from the workshops of Stradivari, Guarneri "del Gesù," and Bergonzi!—if not the famed but declining Maria Masi-Giura, once adored at the Stuttgart opera during the great days of Jommelli: "Prima donna not bad," Wolfgang noted, "already, I believe, as old as a dog; sings not as well as she acts. . . ."

On the twenty-third the Mozarts entered Milan, a major goal of the journey. Unwell, Count Firmian could not receive them, but Therese Germani, the Viennese wife of his steward, took the visitors in charge, often inviting them to her quarters for dinner. In addition, one of the Count's aides, Leopold Troger, who had a sister in Salzburg, also made much of them. They settled in three spacious chambers in the Augustinian monastery of San Marco,[21] not far from Firmian's palace near the ancient Porta Nuova. Wolfgang enjoyed the comfort of his new retreat. He had suffered

---

20 The icy weather and the inviting schedule of the Cremona opera appear to have decided the route. Though snow covered the road to Cremona, it could be negotiated when frozen.

21 Though Troger fathered the arrangements, no doubt Leopold presented the brothers of San Marco with a letter of recommendation from the Augustinian monastery of Mülln near Salzburg.

from the cold and showed the world a red and leathery face—"as if he had been on a military expedition," Leopold joked. The young virtuoso had a more serious problem: his frostbitten hands. His hotel rooms had been, for the most part, unheated; but now he could curl up on four mattresses to which Frater Alphonso applied a warmer every night.

While awaiting Firmian's summons, Wolfgang and Leopold kept themselves diverted and visible by attending performances of church music and opera. They heard Niccolò Piccinni's *Cesare in Egitto* and met its celebrated composer. But Wolfgang now sought sociality not just with the great: in Milan he became friendly with two adolescent castrati, whom he had probably first met in Cremona, and composed for them a couple of Latin motets (which have not survived).

At last Firmian received the Mozarts, on 7 February, when Wolfgang performed before an assemblage including Sammartini. On this occasion Firmian gave the young man the Turin Edition of Metastasio's dramas.[22] Eleven days later, Wolfgang reappeared at Firmian's apartment in the Melzi palace to play before Duke Francesco III of Modena and his granddaughter Maria Beatrice Ricciarda, the betrothed of Archduke Ferdinand.[23] And all the while, the spirit of Firmian's gift was bearing issue: with Piccinni, Hasse, and Christian Bach as models, Mozart busied himself during February and early March composing arias to Metastasian texts for another grand soiree at Firmian's; two of these exercises, both for soprano castrato, survive: the monumental K. 88/73c from *Artaserse* and K. 77/73e, its words from *Demofoonte* and remarkable for an accompagnato mercurial in its changes of mood.

On 23 February Wolfgang gave a public concert, followed on 12 March by Firmian's gala for more than one hundred and fifty guests; once again Duke Francesco and his granddaughter listened to the young musician. (Duke Francesco and his circle, it would seem, introduced him to Count Agostino Litta, once the Milanese Maecenas of Christian Bach.) Princess Beatrice had begun to contemplate taking Mozart into the household to be formed upon her marriage.

---

22 It did not reach its thirteenth and final volume until 1787. Wolfgang received the first nine volumes; they had come out in 1757.

23 Maria Theresa had chosen her to be Archduke Leopold's bride while the Hofburg still anticipated his presiding over Lombardy. But the death in 1761 of the Empress's second eldest son, Archduke Karl, had changed the succession: Leopold moved up to his late brother's position, which, according to Habsburg-Lothringen statutes, demanded the throne of Tuscany; Lombardy fell to the now third eldest brother, Ferdinand—and Maria Beatrice Ricciarda into the bargain. Vienna retained an urgent interest in securing a hold upon Modena (see p. 290). Firmian, a bachelor, knew what he was about when, to strengthen social connections, he set himself up in the Melzi palace, property of Princess Renata Melzi (born von Harrach), the morganatic wife of Duke Francesco III.

The Mozarts were sailing before the wind. The arias made a profound impression upon Firmian, for he put into their hands the yearned-for prize: a contract for the first opera of Milan's 1770–1771 season at the Regio Ducal Teatro,[24] an award contingent upon the approval, taken for granted, of the courts of Vienna and Salzburg. Before Leopold hovered a fee of one hundred gigliati and indemnity for expenses in Milan during the opera's composition. With letters of recommendation to the cities to the south and with rich recompense for the concerts chez Firmian, the pair left Milan on 15 March 1770. Once the libretto reached him in the course of his travels, Mozart could set to work on the recitatives and then return to Milan early in November with time enough to tailor the arias to the singers. Leopold's bold plan had worked. Though in Italy Wolfgang had often performed gratis,[25] the public's enthusiasm and Firmian's admiration had won the day.[26]

Proceeding southeast, the Mozarts put up at Lodi for the night. Before retiring, Wolfgang completed his first string quartet, K. 80/73f, a tentative, slender effort in three movements (between 1773 and 1775 he added a fourth), the lower instruments much of the time accompanying the violins, for the most part moving in thirds and sixths. The work betrays a touch of Salzburg folk melody and the more immediate influence of Boccherini and Sammartini. Refined models for the quartet style just emerging in Europe abounded in the chamber music of these northern Italian masters.

Even in the face of Italy's consuming interest in opera, both Lombardy and Tuscany had persevered in cultivating purely instrumental music, Austrian dominion over these areas no doubt strengthening this predilection. It had shown itself with particular emphasis during the years just before Mozart's visit: in 1765 when Sammartini, with Boccherini as first cellist, presided over a festival orchestra of sixty musicians giving concerts in both Cremona and Pavia; and again, about a year later in Florence, where Boccherini, Filippo Manfredi, Pietro Nardini, and Giuseppe Maria Cambini (so a tradition stemming from him contends) formed what may have been the first continuing string quartet.

---

24 Built with Vienna's blessing within the archducal palace and opened in 1717, it burned in 1776. That same year Empress Maria Theresa ordered the architect Giuseppe Piermarini to begin construction of its replacement on the site of the demolished church of Santa Maria alla Scala.

25 Since, for example, the nobles of Verona offered free access to the concerts they sponsored, as did Maria Theresa's institute in Mantua, in neither city did a visitor like Mozart receive a fee, a public appearance being held up as its own reward in opening opportunities to private concerts and commissions.

26 Winckelmann had described Firmian as "the finest and most learned of all the aristocrats I know."

At the time of Mozart's first visit to northern Italy, Boccherini had not long before established himself at Madrid (1769) in the service of the Spanish Bourbons, the hunger of European courts for Italian composers and performers persisting unappeased. Moreover, the foreign musicians who flocked to Italy served as supplementary grist helping satisfy this appetite: having studied in the conservatories that gave the peninsula its musical primacy, and thus properly Italianized, they swelled the exodus of musical emigrants to the centers of greater political influence and wealth. (Of course many Italian and Italian-trained musicians returned every now and then to refresh themselves.) But Sammartini, breasting the current with fixed resolve, had remained in Milan. The evening's labor in Lodi attests that his subtle instrumental style—light, gallant, and *buffo*, the first violin presiding—for a while had its effect upon Mozart's musical vocabulary and syntax.[27]

5

FROM LODI, BIRTHPLACE of the Mozart string quartet, the coach, following the line of the ancient Via Aemilia, proceeded through Piacenza to Parma, where Leopold, had he made this journey a few years earlier, might have contemplated a long stay. Although the city had been an important center of music, with the death in 1765 of Duke Philip of Bourbon and the departure for Venice of his *maestro di cappella*, Tommaso Traetta, its brief but extraordinary period of musical ebullience subsided. By 1769, when Philip's son, Duke Ferdinand,[28] married Empress Maria Theresa's

27 He had already absorbed much of the Italian manner from Christian Bach, who, during his residence in Milan, had been open to Sammartini's influence. Josef Mysliveček, a Bohemian composer with a high reputation in Italy, where he had studied, thought to have found in Sammartini's symphonies the origin of Joseph Haydn's style (an observation, the story ran, vexing to Haydn, who had described Sammartini as a *Schmierer* (scribbler). Mozart set no less store upon Mysliveček's scores than Sammartini's. In fact, at one time scholars attributed Mysliveček's oratorio *Isacco* to Mozart, so remarkably did the Bohemian's composite of German and Italian elements anticipate and help form Mozart's musical language.

28 Philip and Charles of Bourbon, Ferdinand's father and uncle, respectively, were sons of King Philip V of Spain (see VI, n. 7) and his wife, the termagant Elizabeth Farnese. After inheriting the Duchy of Parma through his mother's family, Charles became King of The Two Sicilies and later wore the crown of Spain as Charles III (see p. 228). The Treaty of Aix passed the Duchy of Parma on to his younger brother, Philip, who in 1739 had married Louis XV's favorite daughter, Louise Elizabeth. Her stupendous dowry sustained the ambitious artistic and musical projects of his reign. Their son Ferdinand's union with Archduchess Maria Amalia of Austria represented an attempt to reconstitute the alliance between the Habsburg and Bourbon-Parma families, a link that had been cut in 1763 by the death of Ferdinand's sister, Isabella, first wife of Emperor Joseph II (see XI, n. 2). By her marriage, Maria Amalia, whom Charles III of Spain had rejected as a daughter-in-law (see XIV, n. 18), became his niece.

An anonymous portrait of the six-year-old Wolfgang Amadeus Mozart. © *Archive Photos*

Salzburg seen from the Kapuzinerberg: dominating the background, the citadel of Hohensalzburg; to the right, the domed cathedral; farther right, the tower of St. Peter's.
© *Archive Photos*

Mozart's sister, Maria Anna (Nannerl) at eleven, a companion portrait to that of Mozart at six.
© *Archive Photos*

The almost eight-year-old
Mozart, his father, and
sister performing in Paris;
an engraving after a watercolor
of November 1763 by
Louis Carrogis, known as
Carmontelle.
© *Archive Photos*

Vienna's Michaelerplatz: left, the Hofburg; center, the protruding wing of the Burgtheater, the
Imperial theater and opera house. © *Archive Photos*

Michel Barthélemy Ollivier's painting of the ten-year-old Mozart performing in Paris at the Temple, the home of Louis François, Prince de Conti. *Corbis/Bettmann*

Mozart's parents: Johann Georg Leopold (above) in an anonymous portrait of 1765; Anna Maria (left) in one of a decade later. © *Archive Photos*

Within the engraving:

Sinfonia

di
Leop: Mozart

CONVENIT IGITUR---IN GESTU NEC
VENUSTATEM CONSPICUAM, NEC TUR-
=DINEM ESSE, NE AUT HISTRIONES,
AUT OPERARII VIDEAMUR ESSE.

Leopold Mozart at thirty-seven: a Salzburg court musician, author of a treatise on
the violin, and father of the composer. © *Archive Photos*

Mozart's first cousin,
Maria Anna Thekla Mozart,
the "Bäsle," a sketch c. 1777.
Corbis/Bettmann

Mozart's sketch of
the "Bäsle" in his letter
to her of 10 May 1780.
© *Archive Photos*

Anonymous portrait (1777) of Chevalier Mozart wearing the insignia of the Golden Order awarded to him in Rome by Pope Clement XIV. © *Archive Photos*

An engraving of the anonymous family portrait (1780-81): Nannerl, Wolfgang, and Leopold Mozart, with a portrait of the recently deceased mother in the background. © *Archive Photos*

daughter Maria Amalia, Parma had relapsed into a dreary parochiality: operatic entertainment for the wedding had to be brought from Vienna, Gluck providing a group of *feste teatrali* preceding his *Orfeo*, for the occasion cut and done in one act. The new Duchess of Parma, who knew the Mozarts—she had accompanied her mother to the performance of the Orphanage Mass—did not receive them, perhaps yet another reminder of the disfavor with which more than one pair of Habsburg eyes regarded Leopold subsequent to the Affligio petition. But Maria Amalia maintained a high opinion of his son: she would ask Milan for a copy of his new opera, perhaps her first step toward attempting to restore Parma to musical life.

In an ironic turn of fate, blame for Parma's precipitate musical decline lay in large part with the man who had put down the foundations of the capital's meteoric musical eminence: Guillaume du Tillot, the Bayonne-born, all-powerful Minister of State, who had governed for years while his Bourbon master hunted, adorned his palaces, and fussed with his Parisian wardrobe. Du Tillot had suddenly lost interest in music, a change of heart astounding on the part of this Enlightened Frenchman who, in the wake of the Bouffons' War (and with the counsel of Count Francesco Algarotti), had set Traetta and the poet Carlo Innocenzo Frugoni the task of reconciling Italian and Gallic operatic styles. Apparently still holding the reins of government with a strong hand at the time of the Mozarts' visit, in fact Du Tillot's career had begun its descent. Dominating the weak-willed Duke Ferdinand, in short time that energetic harridan Maria Amalia would rout the Francophiles at the court of Parma and, fulfilling her mother's bidding, turn the duchy into an appanage of Vienna: in 1771 du Tillot would be dismissed.

Though aware of Parma's languishing musical life, Leopold perhaps anticipated at least one performance at the great palace of the Pilotta when he paused in the capital to take quarters with a certain Pattone (or Paccone). A letter of introduction from Count Firmian opened the way to Du Tillot's study, but nothing came of the encounter: he satisfied himself with Wolfgang's lively conversation and indicated that if anything was to be done about a concert, the Imperial ambassador ought to do it. Though, in the end, no one did anything, Parma, even so, proved profitable to the Mozarts; it still possessed a musical resource worthy of their attention: the court's *virtuosa di camera*, Lucrezia Aguiari (Agujari).

She had appeared in Gluck's Parmesan wedding entertainment of the preceding year. A soprano whose vocal range extended to "C *sopra acuto*" (three octaves above middle C), as Leopold put it, this last of the city's musical lights still shed her remarkable luster.[29] She invited the Mozarts to dinner and sang for them, an astounded Wolfgang jotting down several of the passages she executed in the musical stratosphere. Years later in Munich he recalled her phenomenal technique.

Continuing through the Emilian landscape, Leopold and Wolfgang, by way of Modena, arrived in Bologna (24 March), that majestic, melancholy Papal[30] and university center, the city of masters and scholars, and the very capital of studies in musical composition and in the science and history of music: here resided Europe's unparalleled arbiter of such matters, Padre Martini.

Born in Bologna in 1706, Giovanni Battista Martini entered the Franciscan order and became *maestro di cappella* of his native city's church of St. Francis. His reputation as Europe's ultimate musical theorist rested upon his mastery of those rigorous polyphonic principles associated with the Roman school of the sixteenth century and Palestrina's name. Padre Martini demanded of his pupils clean, independent part-writing and a clear melodic-linear style. If his own compositions too often remained synthetic creations distilled from the past and of little vitality, his teaching, its pith not only the *stile antico* of the Renaissance but baroque counterpoint as well, inspired students and strengthened what they achieved in the *stile moderno*.

Swollen legs had rendered his step infirm by the time Mozart met him, and he suffered from a hacking cough. But, with that kindness shown Christian Bach years before, he welcomed the boy, who soon venerated the humble scholar. He possessed a kind of saintly goodness, his only perceptible weakness being a craving for chocolate. Had his schedule permitted, Leopold at once would have requested Martini to take Wolfgang for a sustained period of tutelage, even though he really had no need of it: formal if sporadic encounters with Fux's *Gradus* (see p. 222) had helped give him sufficient skill in baroque counterpoint; and acquaintance with the Renaissance style, in no way of practical use, would have bestowed little more than a certain distinction as a learned musician. But Leopold saw a series of lessons, whatever their matter, as a way to build intimacy with a master who might be induced to turn his formidable international connections to their account: his letters of recommendation commanded respect at Eu-

---

29 To her annoyance, playbills and newspapers—as did the Mozarts' letters—referred to this natural child (perhaps of the Marchese Bentivoglio) as *La Bastardina* or *Bastardella*. When Aguiari visited Charles Burney in England (1775), his daughter, the novelist Fanny Burney, informed her diary that the soprano's nickname derived "from some misfortune that preceded her birth, but of which none so innocent as herself."

30 Bologna had belonged to the Papacy since 1506.

rope's mightiest courts, where, moreover, Wolfgang would then have the right to announce himself as one of the great icon's disciples.

A few probing sessions revealed to Martini the youth's pragmatic if limited grasp of strict baroque counterpoint (a discipline he would embrace with open arms years later in Vienna, when the true greatness of Handel and Sebastian Bach burst upon him); of Renaissance polyphony he, of course, knew nothing. Leopold decided to bring him back to Martini for an extended term of studies during the summer. Indeed, the Mozarts' return would respond to a double enticement: long hours of intimate association with the good padre and the hope of a second stay at the Albergo del Pellegrino with its famed and noble kitchen.

Of immediate value to Wolfgang's future were the potential patrons he encountered in Bologna. At this very moment Count Joseph Clemens Kaunitz, a son of Maria Theresa's Chancellor, tarried as a guest in the palace of Count Giovanni Luca Pallavicini-Centurioni, an Imperial field marshal long in Austrian service. The Mozarts carried a letter of introduction from Count Firmian. The palace doors flew open. On the evening of 26 March, Mozart (along with the castrati Giuseppe Aprile and Giuseppe Cicognani) performed in the Pallavicini palace before an assembly astounded to find Padre Martini in its midst: he seldom attended concerts. It had probably been on the afternoon of the same day that Leopold and Wolfgang visited Carlo Broschi, once known as Farinelli. The famous castrato lived in retirement on his estate outside the city's gates (see IX, n. 11.)

The Italian expedition mounted in tempo. Mozart, as usual, had made his Bolognan debut as quickly as possible before those gatherings of the highborn to which his authoritative connections gave access. But, for the time being, Leopold renounced pursuing further engagements in salons of subaltern rank; once established with the nobles and local musicians of distinction, he hastened on, his immediate concern being to reach Rome during Easter week, a scene of perpetual gala, its streets, palaces, and holy places overflowing with aristocrats and princes of the Church. Thereafter he planned to push on to Naples, Italy's largest city—it approached half a million—and its metropolis of opera. Such centers offered rich opportunities for high fees, and he determined to garner many before returning to Milan in the autumn.

Handsomely rewarded by Pallavicini, the Mozarts left Bologna on 29 March. In wind and rain they made their way over the Apennines and into the valley of the Arno to arrive in Florence on the thirtieth. Wolfgang had caught cold, which Leopold cured in quick time at the Albergo dell' Aquila Nera with infusions of tea and extract of violets. On 1 April at ten in the morning they presented themselves in the anteroom of Grand Duke

Leopold's High Steward, Count Orsini-Rosenberg, a letter from Count Firmian giving them precedence[31] over some fifty, without question outraged, suppliants. Rosenberg at once arranged an audience at the Pitti Palace before the Grand Duke, who had known the Mozart children since their first Viennese tour. He looked about, missed Nannerl, and asked for her.

The next day Wolfgang performed at the ducal summer villa of Poggio Imperiale. Lorraine-born Marquis Eugenio (Eugène) Ligniville, a court director of music and a formidable contrapuntalist, set Wolfgang thorny problems in fugue, which he solved, so Leopold joked, as if "eating a piece of bread."[32] An old friend, the violinist Nardini, who had entered Habsburg service, performed with Wolfgang (Boccherini's six violin and clavier sonatas of Opus 5, published the preceding year) during what became a long evening of music in the handsome palace beyond the Porta Romana. The beauty of Tuscany moved Leopold: the wonderful prospects, the Arno rolling through the valley, the hills rising behind. He wrote his wife: "I wish you might see Florence, its surroundings and situation; you would say that one should live and die here."

The Mozarts enjoyed a reunion with the castrato Manzuoli, now become a Habsburg chamber singer. And, armed with a recommendation from Horace Mann of London (almost five years earlier their host at Bourne Place, near Canterbury), they looked up his namesake and uncle, England's envoy to the Pitti Palace; though the House of Hanover no longer gave serious thought to Stuart strategies to dispossess it of the English throne, this Horace Mann nevertheless had the task of keeping an eye on the Roman-born Young Pretender, Charles Edward Stuart,[33] again resident in Italy, his circle an inevitable hotbed of mischief. He would soon become one of Mozart's admirers.

A celebrated poet of the Tuscan court, the airy and witty Corilla Olympica (Maria Maddalena Morelli-Fernandez),[34] introduced Mozart

---

31 In addition, young Kaunitz had arrived from Bologna and announced the Mozarts' impending appearance to the High Steward.

32 Mozart copied down for study nine sections of a canonic *Stabat mater* by Ligniville (K. Anh. 238/A17), under whose influence he was to compose, in all likelihood during his subsequent stay in Rome, a canonic Kyrie for five sopranos (K. 89/73k). Ligniville helped whet the youth's enthusiasm for the canonic exercises he was later to pursue (K. Anh. 109d/73x), some perhaps under the eyes of Padre Martini in the course of the second visit to Bologna.

33 His father, the Old Pretender—James Francis Edward Stuart, a son of James II by Mary of Modena—had died in 1766. The Hanoverians bestowed the title "Pretender"; to the Stuart party, he had been James III.

34 The *Gazzetta di Mantova* (19 January 1770) had compared Mozart to her, calling him "a miracle of music and one of those freaks [*scherzi*] nature causes to be born . . . a Corilla to shame the poets." Lorenzo Da Ponte placed her among the best of Italy's "*improvvisatrici.*"

to Thomas Linley of Bath, an English prodigy studying the violin with Nardini, and the youths, the same age, formed a friendship: both yearned for the companionship of contemporaries. In addition, a musical congeniality grew between them. Wolfgang not only accompanied Thomas but turned again to the violin, alternating with him in solo display. They made music together, Leopold observed, "not as boys but as men!" A melancholy Thomas followed the Mozarts' coach to the gates of Florence as they departed for Rome on 6 April. In his name Corilla had hastily put together a panegyric honoring Wolfgang.[35]

6

THE WEATHER PROVED miserable, the food and accommodations vile, as Wolfgang and Leopold moved south through drenching rains, probably proceeding via Siena and Orvieto. Having subsisted, in the main, upon brussels sprouts and eggs, they at last found a decent table and a good night's sleep at Viterbo. Then, passing over the Sabatini mountains, they approached a Rome still embraced by its countryside: vineyards and pasturelands dotted with cypresses, castellated farmhouses, ruins drowned in foliage, the landscape extending right up to the Aurelian walls and spilling within the gates. At noon on 11 April, the Wednesday of Holy Week, lightning flashed and thunder rolled as the Mozarts' coach traversed the Piazza del Popolo;[36] father and son, exuberant and elated, beheld the grandiose panorama of the Eternal City—magnificent, overwhelming, bewildering, and crowded with pilgrims and functionaries. Leopold could find only an uncomfortable room in a lodging house. Wolfgang wrote home: "Oh I am having a hard time, for there is but one bed in our quarters, and Mama can well imagine that I get no sleep with Papa."

Without delay they set out for St. Peter's, first stopping at the Collegium Germanicum, just above the Piazza Navona, to announce their arrival to Rome's German community—and probably to look up one of the students, Albert Andreas von Mölk of Salzburg, a brother of Nannerl's suitor (see n. 7). At St. Peter's, they marveled at the harmoniousness of an architecture in which symmetry, order, and purity of detail prevailed in spite of the complexity, richness, and huge scale of the forms. In the great

---

35 In 1778 Linley died in a boating accident while on holiday at Grimsthorpe Castle in Lincolnshire. His father, Thomas Linley, Senior, a composer and impresario in Bath and London (and father-in-law of Richard Brinsley Sheridan), may have written the English words upon which the text of Haydn's *Creation* rests.

36 In 1786, Goethe would enter the citadel of Western culture through the same gate, a culminating moment of his life.

basilica Mozart suffered a moment awkward for an adolescent: too tiny to reach the foot of the venerated statue of the first Pope, he had to be lifted up to kiss that metal slipper worn smooth by the piety of generations.

In the Vatican on Holy Thursday they watched Pope Clement XIV wash the feet of a dozen poor priests and then serve them the traditional meal. Leopold boasted that Wolfgang's and his magnificent manner enabled them to pass unquestioned through the ranks of Swiss Guards and unimpeded reach the Papal apartment. But the pair, accompanied by a hired servant, formed a spectacle somewhat less overawing than Leopold imagined: the sentries, in fact, took them for part of the German retinue of Prince Xavier, the former Regent of Saxony (see VIII, n. 3), who had arrived in Rome some days before and enjoyed free access to the private chambers.

Wolfgang boldly approached the cardinals' table and planted himself between two seats. One of the cardinals next to him politely inquired who he might be. The name drew recognition, for Field Marshal Pallavicini-Centurioni of Bologna had written his cousin in Rome, Cardinal Lazaro Opizio Pallavicini, to expect the Mozarts. After an exchange of courtesies, Wolfgang kissed the Cardinal's ring, and he, in turn, doffed his biretta in salute. The Roman adventure had opened well. Pallavicini, head of the Vatican's State Secretariat, arranged the Mozarts' move within days to rooms forming part of the apartment of Steffano Uslenghi, Papal Courier to Portugal, in the Palazzo Scatizzi, a wing of the Collegium Clementinum.[37]

Leopold had planned a *coup de théâtre* that might at a stroke bring Wolfgang's name to the ears of the Roman aristocracy and of the Holy Father himself. After their tour of St. Peter's on the eleventh, the Mozarts had gone to the Sistine Chapel to hear the Tenebrae service. It ended with the singing of a Miserere by Gregorio Allegri (1582–1652). Custom restricted performances of this setting of Penitential Psalm 50 (Vulgate) to the Sistine Chapel and forbade its musicians to reveal to outsiders the admired ornamented passages (for a quartet of soloists) traditionally inserted into the score. The prohibition for the most part found respect: few copies of the complete work circulated without Papal sanction, for a vigorous legend insisted that excommunication would fall upon those who broke the ban.

After the service, Wolfgang returned to his room and did his best to write down from memory all nine voice parts of the composition. His copy hidden in his hat, he went back to the chapel on Maundy Thursday in the hope of filling in and making corrections during a second hearing; alas, the choir sang a different Miserere. However, on Good Friday the

---

37 Abbate Francesco Antonio Marcobruni, educated in Salzburg and Postal Director of Rome, handled the details of the change of abode.

singers repeated the Allegri, and he made the necessary additions and changes. One senses the Mozarts' astonishment at the poverty of the score taking shape on the staves, Leopold now attributing its effectiveness to the magnificence of the rites and the skill of the singers.

At any rate, the Mozarts now possessed the recondite Miserere and let the fact be known. In Salzburg, Frau Anna Maria and her friends feared the worst: Wolfgang might suffer proscription. Leopold, realizing that he had sent to Salzburg too dramatic an account of the adventure, wrote to allay her fears: the Pope knew of the feat and hurled no thunderbolts; in fact, it had but awakened new admiration for their son, who was soon playing and singing an arrangement of his musical trophy for Roman society as Cristofori, a castrato of the Sistine Chapel, looked on.

In heavy rain Leopold went about delivering his letters of recommendation to the nobles of Rome, a matter of importance in a city in which public concerts would be unlikely: apart from music in the churches and the festival concerts of the Congregation of Santa Cecilia, Rome offered little public entertainment; opera, once cultivated by the Barberini and Rospigliosi, had not recovered from Pope Innocent XII's puritanical order that razed the Tordinona opera house in 1697. Indeed, under his successor, Clement XI, a ban had still enjoined opera in Papal territories, a state of affairs that had led the young Handel to cultivate the chamber cantata (really miniature opera) during his sojourn in Italy. Only three years before the Mozarts came to Rome, Christian Traugott Weinlig, visiting from Saxony, described the debased state of the operatic performances permitted under Pope Clement XIII, castrati assuming the female roles, women having been forbidden the stage. The city's significant musical life unfolded not in public places but at the *conversazioni* in the salons of princes and cardinals.

On the twentieth the Mozarts went to the Corso, the long and splendid street on which people of society drove to and fro by way of showing their clothes and equipages. This elegant traffic made its turnabout by pouring into the square dominated by the column of Marcus Aurelius, facing which rose the imposing palace of Prince Chigi. Here, for certain in its Golden Chamber, Wolfgang appeared before a company including Cardinal Pallavicini and the Young Pretender. The following day, father and son promenaded in the gardens of the Villa Medici with members of Rome's English colony, one of whom, William Beckford of Somerley, they had met in London.[38]

---

38 The Mozart literature often confuses him with both William Beckford (1709–1770), twice Lord Mayor of London, and his son, another William Beckford (1760–1844), famous as the eccentric creator of *Vathek* and the crumbling sham towers of Fonthill; the confusion also embraces their nephew and cousin, respectively, Peter Beckford, the sponsor of Clementi (see p. 580).

Five days later, Wolfgang entered the Barberini palace to play for Princess Cornelia Barberini-Colonna's guest, Prince Xavier of Saxony; the assembly again numbered Cardinal Pallavicini and the Stuart Pretender—"the so-called King of England," Leopold observed. Perhaps Xavier, having heard his sister-in-law, Maria Antonia, Dowager Electress of Saxony, speak of Wolfgang, asked to hear him play at this gathering honoring the impending marriage of Xavier's great-nephew, Dauphin Louis of France, to Empress Maria Theresa's daughter, that Maria Antonia about to become Marie Antoinette.

Bearing a letter of recommendation from Field Marshal Pallavicini-Centurioni, Leopold and Wolfgang visited Prince Andrea Doria-Pamphili's palace on the Corso, the young man's "prodigious talent" exciting admiration. (However, it was in the house of a certain "bourgeoise Madame Doria" that Count Kraft Ernst zu Öttingen-Wallerstein, in Rome on his Grand Tour, heard Wolfgang "do astonishing things.") The Mozarts' journal also suggests a call at one of the Borghese residences. Day after day they made their way through chambers rich in porphyry, onyx, verde antique, and agate, no doubt, as usual, pleasing the company, no doubt, when necessary, indulging princely caprices and vagaries.

They encountered familiar and less exalted figures, too: Meissner, on his way back from Naples to Salzburg, joined Mozart in a concert on 2 May at the Collegium Germanicum, Wolfgang (so one of its administrators, Father Giovanni Biringucci, recorded) playing the harpsichord "*a stupore*," the audience then reassembling in a neighboring church, either S. Agostino or S. Apollinare, "where he played the organ";[39] and in the church of the Holy Apostles Leopold chanced upon Porta, the family's erstwhile domestic in England. His offer again to serve received a curt rejection. Leopold distrusted this man, whose fine dress and jewelry he glanced at with suspicion.

His critical eye also fell upon the clerical parasites clinging to the robes of the princes of the Church. To a degree, the Enlightened attitudes he had displayed in London and Paris stirred again; he wrote his wife: "You cannot possibly imagine the arrogance of the clergy here. Any one of them having the most minor position with a cardinal believes himself as good as the cardinal himself, and every cardinal drives to Papal functions with a cortege of three or four carriages, each filled with chaplains, secretaries, and valets." (Here was the baleful model many a Salzburg canon strove to imitate.)

---

39 Mozart earned substantial fees for his appearances at Roman gatherings; yet at the Collegium he performed gratis, perhaps no less out of friendship toward its Salzburg scholar, von Mölk, than by reason of Leopold's desire to tighten links with his family.

7

"THOUGH IT GROANED under . . . the tyranny of priests," eighteenth-century Rome, David Hume observed, "carried to perfection all the finer arts of sculpture, painting, and music. . . ." The Mozarts' journal contains the name of the Roman most influential in these matters, the man whose taste his fellow aristocrats acknowledged as matchless in the Eternal City: Cardinal Alessandro Albani, nephew of Pope Clement XI. Having encouraged the antiquarian research of his German protégé, Johann Joachim Winckelmann, the Cardinal had gathered in the dazzling Villa Albani, his museum-palace near the Porta Pia, one of the era's finest collections of ancient art. Moreover, the year of Mozart's birth, he had offered himself as Gluck's protector in Rome and decorated him with the Papal Order of the Golden Spur.

The Mozarts gained entry to what remained of the Albani-Winckelmann circle. Their arrival in Rome found the aging Cardinal still active. But, unlike Gluck, Mozart did not meet Winckelmann, the great aesthetician and father of historical art criticism, the spirit of whose Romantic Hellenism, through Gluck's example, was to color so many pages of *Idomeneo*:[40] in 1768, while on his way back from Vienna to Rome, Winckelmann had met a sordid death in Trieste at the hands of a good-looking adventurer he had befriended. Very likely, the Mozarts viewed the marvelous objects he and Albani had arranged at the villa, that very center of passionate intellectual life, where the Hellenic spirit had presided over a historic and transforming mixing of Italian and German cultural temperament and insight—halls most fit for Mozart to wander.

In Rome he again turned to the symphony: from this time dates K. 74 in G, its opening Allegro running into the following Andante in the manner of a theater overture, the closing movement containing his first use of tones vaguely Hungarian, gypsy, or Asiatic in hue—so-called Turkish music. Research has brought into question the credentials of other Mozart symphonies long identified as of this Italian period: their authenticity has foundered on the shifting ground of analysis embracing style, provenance, handwriting, and paper. Some no longer occupy their former chronological places, and more than one, their pedigrees prejudiced or tainted, have lost their homes within the Mozart canon.[41]

---

40 Concerning this undercurrent flowing from Winckelmann's aesthetic to Mozart's, see pp. 519–22.
41 Significant documentation, for example, suggests three possible composers for K. 84/73q: Leopold Mozart, Dittersdorf, or Mozart himself, who may have begun sketches for it during his first visit to Milan and carried them to completion at the time of the second stay in Bologna.

Between composing and appearances at *conversazioni*, the boy did find leisure hours in which to learn to play boccie, which he planned to teach to his sister. (At times Leopold even imagined him growing taller.) Yet little time for physical diversion could be fitted into an ever intensifying schedule. Leopold now contemplated his son's performing before Pope Clement XIV and leaned upon Cardinal Pallavicini to arrange the matter. He, however, reflecting upon the lack of precedent for a musical virtuoso performing in a pontiff's chambers, hit upon the idea of reminding the Holy Father of another way of honoring the young Salzburger. But to seize the expedient moment the good Cardinal required time: upon the Mozarts' return from the south he hoped to see his way to play Albani to Wolfgang's Gluck.

A religious man, an amateur of architecture, painting, and history, Leopold could not have left Rome without regret: in terms of the Faith, of the arts, and of tradition, it was the consummation of all Italy had to offer. Doubtless he had made time for the sweet and unremitting labor of sorting out its wealth; doubtless he experienced that special rapture of walking its streets and discovering its glories. But ahead lay the city of Vesuvius, which, fortune willing, could confer extraordinary financial rewards.

With the appearance of such composers as Francesco Provenzale (c. 1626–1704) and Alessandro Scarlatti (1660–1725), operatic hegemony had begun its passage to Naples; by the time of Mozart's birth, it had become an operatic center to which all Europe paid homage,[42] an eminence already in formation with Charles of Bourbon's building of the San Carlo theater (1737) and the sovereign ascendancy of the city's conservatories of music. Wolfgang contemplated revealing to Naples the scope of his talent for opera by duplicating his tour de force so effective in Milan: composing arias for some grand aristocratic salon, a plan assuming sufficient time to establish a strong presence. King Ferdinand and Queen Carolina's capital, the Mozarts assumed, would with good grace provide them opportunities to court an opera contract, and, with it, security against the possible collapse of previous arrangements with Milan: Leopold recognized what shifting, fragile things such agreements could prove.

Warm weather came to Rome, and Leopold grew eager to leave. Malaria often infected the area, and overnight the atmosphere might turn unwholesome. Yet he dared not move; a more palpable danger infected the

---

42 Joseph Jérôme de Lalande, a scientist who toured Italy during 1765 and 1766, called Naples "the principal source of Italian music, of great composers, and excellent operas," the Neapolitans possessing, he maintained, eardrums with membranes "more taut, more harmonious, more sonorous than elsewhere in Europe."

route to Naples: brigands. They had recently fought a series of fierce skirmishes with a patrol of Papal soldiers. Travelers dared take to the road
only in convoys.

Once again Leopold put to use his connections with the Augustinians.
On 30 April, he and Wolfgang dined with Padre Francisco Javier Vasquez,
General of the Order, in its headquarters near the Collegium Germanicum. He marked the course of their safe progress; they were to join a
group of his fathers traveling south via Terracina and would be welcome
to take their rest and meals at Augustinian hospices along the route: at
Marino near Lake Albano; and at Sessa, Capua, and Naples itself.

8

ON 8 MAY 1770 they set out, cheered by the prospect of good food and
clean beds, for Meissner had chilled them with tales of the terrible inns
that lay before them. After lingering at Capua in order to observe ceremonies accompanying a noblewoman's taking the veil at a nearby convent,
they entered Naples on the fourteenth and went directly to the Augustinian monastery of S. Giovanni a Carbonara. There they remained several
days before finding quarters in the house of a Signora Angiola.

Confounding scenes had opened before their eyes. The metropolis appeared to be one agitated, fearful, unending crowd: beggars and thieves in
terrifying number living in the open; footmen barking abuse as they ran
in front of their masters' coaches to shield the swarming populace from
the wheels; the shouts, the cries, the blasphemous oaths, the nakedness, the
filth, the fouled churches through which bawling children and dogs ran; the
fussing with heathen-like devotional superstitions. Leopold looked upon
the city's hysterical veneration of its patron, Saint Januarius (San Gennaro),
as pure paganism: Christ's value to most Neapolitans, it seemed to Leopold,
resided in His occasional power to sway Januarius's decisions as to when to
spare or visit upon the local inhabitants the wrath of the great volcano
under which they lived. Vesuvius slumbered when the Mozarts arrived, but,
to Wolfgang's delight, soon began to throw smoke and fire into the sky.

Their repugnance notwithstanding, the very abundance and coarse texture of Neapolitan life, its strange rhythms unpredictably contrasting
bustle and languor, fascinated the travelers from well-ordered southern
Germany. Not only did an animated world to all appearance in perpetual
carnival have its attractions, but so did the fine climate and situation of a
city with environs rich in lovely landscape and evocative reminders of the
ancient world. If not the holiday mood, then certainly the weather sent father and son to a tailor to order summer suits; they chose rose moiré and

cinnamon Florentine cloth trimmed with silver lace, and ended, so Wolfgang assured his sister, "as beautiful as angels." Splendidly fitted out, they attended and enjoyed the *opera buffa* at either the Teatro dei Fiorentini or the Teatro Nuovo and marveled at the magnificence of the San Carlo, with its gilded ornaments and fabled mirrors. Spending most of their time as tourists, they examined Pozzuoli, Baia, Pompeii, and Herculaneum; explored Vesuvius; took ship on what Wolfgang called the "*Merditeranischen*" (Excremental) Sea; lunched with the Carthusians in the Certosa of San Martino, just below the citadel of Sant' Elmo on the Vomero; and visited the royal palaces built by Charles of Bourbon, those of Capodimonte, Portici, and Caserta. Such pleasurable if unprofitable pursuits beguiled the Mozarts while they awaited a summons to appear before his bizarre son King Ferdinand.

In *The Merchant of Venice*, Portia observes of the Neapolitan prince: "Ay, that's a colt indeed, for he doth nothing but talk of his horse; and he makes it a great appropriation to his own good parts that he can shoe him himself." Here was the homely spirit of Ferdinand of The Two Sicilies: who fished and then set up in the marketplace to sell his catch for as much money as possible (if only to give it away); who competed in rowing against the local oarsmen; who had a passion for macaroni, gathering it into his mouth with his fingers; who, seated on his *chaise percé*, engaged his brother-in-law, the Holy Roman Emperor, in conversation, inviting Joseph of Austria—as he did his courtiers—to admire the royal faeces. The Habsburgs had their own prodigious coarseness, but Ferdinand's astounded even them.

At the time of the Mozarts' Neapolitan visit, Maria Carolina of Austria, fresh from Schönbrunn and the Hofburg, had but begun the work of adapting to the rude, rustic court her husband had organized within the gilded palaces of his father of Spain; of adjusting to a formidable sex life with someone who rarely washed or even changed his clothes (". . . at least he does not stink," Emperor Joseph, reported); of reconciling herself to slaughterous hunting parties that ended with His Majesty wallowing in the carnage, dressing the meat, and splashing himself head to foot with gore. Akin in personality to her sister Maria Amalia of Parma, the driving Maria Carolina forced herself to accommodate, sensing the power that could be hers—and Vienna's—once this young donkey grew to trust and depend upon his wife. A sense of duty strengthened her, and she acted the part her mother had assigned: "In your heart and in the uprightness of your mind be a German; in all that is unimportant . . . you must appear to be Neapolitan." (In spite of her accomplished deviousness, not until 1777 would Maria Carolina succeed in toppling from power Prime Minister

Bernardo Tanucci, Charles of Bourbon's agent and the real ruler of the Kingdom.) Above all, she was growing to love her little Ferdinand as slowly she shed her German ways and adopted a new tone. When, full of hope, Leopold and Wolfgang arrived at the court of Naples, Maria Carolina showed faint interest in harpsichord recitals à la Schönbrunn; her husband even less.[43]

The Mozarts' stay in Naples proved a financial failure somewhat repaired by the kindness of a few aristocrats. Tanucci received the pair at the palace of Portici (where they glimpsed the royal couple at mass) in deference to a recommendation from Leopold of Tuscany's Ambassador to Rome, Baron Matthäus Dominikus de Saint-Odile (who had heard Wolfgang play in Rome at Prince Chigi's). Tanucci's wife took the visitors to her heart and put at their disposal a steward instructed to take them where they would. And, a happy turn of affairs: Maria Theresa's representative to King Ferdinand's court proved to be Count Ernst Christoph Kaunitz (another son of the Prince; see p. 267). He offered his residence for one of Wolfgang's few concerts in Naples (28 May); the audience included Count zu Öttingen-Wallerstein, Catherine Hamilton—first wife of William Hamilton, George III's Minister to The Two Sicilies[44]—and the diminutive philosophe, Neapolitan diplomat, and economist, Abbé Ferdinando Galiani, only yesterday Tanucci's eyes and ears at Versailles.

In the front rank of telltales, Galiani had suffered an embarrassment disastrous to his diplomatic career: in the course of a casual conversation, he had disclosed Bourbon state secrets. Informed of this monumental indiscretion, Charles of Spain, with Versailles's assent, ordered Tanucci to

---

43 Ferdinand had a German mother: Maria Amalia, a child of Augustus the Weak of Saxony and Emperor Joseph I's daughter Maria Josepha (see VII, n. 5). Under thirteen at the time of her engagement to Charles of Bourbon and not yet fourteen at their marriage—a Papal dispensation had been necessary—Maria Amalia, though doubtless trained in music during her childhood in Dresden, had exercised little influence upon Ferdinand: indeed, she had found herself obliged to leave the eight-year-old behind in Naples as its king when she sailed off— unhappily—to become Queen of Spain (see p. 228). When the new Queen of Naples, Maria Carolina, felt her precedence well enough established, she reclaimed her Habsburg cultural background and ventured into the capital's intellectual and artistic circles. With Maria Carolina at his side, Ferdinand began to develop a love of German music, in time even a connoisseur's taste for it. In 1786 he would commission from Joseph Haydn a set of five double concertos for the *lira organizzata*, a bizarre instrument combining elements of the hurdy-gurdy and organ. Haydn later composed eight notturnos, again featuring two *lire organizzate*, for the delighted monarch, who urged him to visit Naples. Their meeting would take place years hence, when the King and Queen visited Vienna, a journey during which they at last heard Mozart perform (in Munich, November 1790; see p. 716).

44 The Mozarts had met the Hamiltons in London. The husband would be knighted in 1772. Ten years later, Catherine died, and the year of Mozart's death he married his mistress, Emma Lyon, who went on to fame as the paramour of Horatio Nelson.

recall him to Naples. For the Abbé, life stopped outside the gates of Paris ("save death itself, nothing could be worse than this blow"[45]), and the Mozarts' presence became a restorative for an exile in his own land who longed for the sophisticated joys he had taken for granted on the Seine. His letter to Madame d'Épinay of 7 July makes clear that he had heard Wolfgang play in former years. Though suggesting that adolescence now made "the little Mosar" (*sic*) appear somewhat less remarkable than heretofore, Galiani nevertheless recognized in him "the same miracle. . . . He will never be anything but a miracle, and that is that."

Wolfgang would seem to have performed at salons throughout the city whenever some *principessa*, wishing to hear a few pieces on the harpsichord, sent a carriage to fetch him. Few Neapolitan nobles, however, called upon professional musicians; rather, they exhausted their revenues on articles of display, in particular brilliant costumes and equipages. In the end only foreigners, the Imperial and British Ministers, troubled to invite the Mozarts for evenings of serious music-making, the concert at Firmian's having been preceded by one at the Hamiltons' villa on the bay (18 May). William Beckford of Somerley attended, and Mrs. Hamilton, a gifted performer, trembled when her turn came to play for Wolfgang on her beautiful Tschudi instrument.

As the days slipped by, Leopold found it difficult to bear the King and Queen's silence and determined to force the issue. He and Wolfgang joined the *passeggio*, a daily procession of vehicles that rolled along the harbor road and jetty. When Queen Carolina sped by, cannons from the fleet boomed in salute, and the carriages one by one came to a halt, their occupants bowing in obeisance. On several occasions Wolfgang observed her acknowledging his greeting, the evident marks of recognition and her warm smile raising hopes each time. (She must have heard him perform in Vienna; see p. 241.)

Expectations rose when he and his father wheedled an invitation to a Whitsunday reception (3 June) at the French Ambassador's.[46] It celebrated the marriage at Versailles (16 May) of the Dauphin to Maria Carolina's sister Maria Antonia. But the Mozarts gained nothing from the gala evening: they made no new acquaintances to advance their cause at court, and Maria

---

45 Though in name a secretary in the Neapolitan embassy, in reality Galiani had performed Tanucci's critical diplomatic maneuvers in Paris, bypassing Juan de Baeza y Vicentolo, Count of Cantillana, the Ambassador and a figurehead. Galiani tried every means of inducing the three Bourbon powers to rescind the decision, but Louis XV's minister, Choiseul, closed the matter with the ruinous observation: "*Il s'est noyé dans son crachat*" (He drowned in his own spit).

46 In all probability, Leopold secured the tickets through Simon Doncker, whose friendship the Mozarts had enjoyed in Holland. (They made much of his lean beauty.) Doncker now lived in Naples with an official of the French foreign service.

Carolina and Ferdinand remained distant, even, in Wolfgang's eyes, comic figures. At the San Carlo, when he and Leopold attended the premiere of Jommelli's *Armida abbandonata* (30 May 1770; see p. 151), they beheld the royal couple in the box of honor, Wolfgang relishing the futile attempt of the gaunt, wiry, and short Ferdinand to appear no less imposing than his heroically proportioned German wife: he climbed upon a stool.

The Mozarts consorted with the renowned composers resident in the city—Jommelli (who had returned from Württemberg the preceding year), Giovanni Paisiello, Gian Francesco (Ciccio) de Majo, and Pasquale Cafaro—and Wolfgang performed for students of one of its famous academies of music, the Conservatorio della Pietà dei Turchini. Suspicious, his young listeners soon divined his secret; they found him out: he wore a magic talisman. When, forced by their demands, he removed his ring and then played with no less brilliance, the general astonishment had no limits. How he must have enjoyed this adventure. Alas, it brought no money.

For Salzburg, Leopold put a good face upon his disappointments and wrote home of contracts under discussion with opera houses in Naples and other Italian cities. Conversations, in fact, did take place with the San Carlo, but, to reassure the Hannibalplatz, Leopold had to make much of little; and though his artful prose represented the weeks of waiting as filled with gainful activity, his impatience and unhappiness at times broke through: Queen Maria Carolina and King Ferdinand, whose "coarse Neapolitan upbringing" Wolfgang deplored, must have been the "certain people" Leopold looked upon as "so stupid" that "it does not for a-moment occur to them that they are stupid." "What kind of a creature the King is," he observed, "is perhaps wiser to speak of than to write about."

9

THOUGH LEOPOLD HAD planned to quit Naples by midsummer and spend the hot weeks in Tuscany, Emilia, the Marches, and Liguria, his decision to leave the Kingdom on 25 June seems to have been made in anger and haste.[47] Evidently the bandits had been cleared from the way, for the Mozarts departed in a *sedia* drawn by a single horse with a postilion riding alongside. Such a light two-wheeled chaise could traverse the road to Rome in twenty-four hours. As if in flight, Leopold hurled himself toward the Eternal City, for him a symbol of appreciation and safety.

---

47 He had been unable to realize his hope to leave for Rome in the retinue of Count Kaunitz, who had been summoned to Moravia.

Disaster almost overtook the party during the final stage. Stretches of deep sand and soil slowed the progress of the speeding vehicle. As the postilion lashed the struggling horse confined within the shafts, it reared and stumbled, pulling the carriage down.[48] With one hand Leopold held back Wolfgang—on the point of being hurled into the road—and at the same time plunged forward, colliding with the iron bar supporting the mudguard and gashing the shinbone of his right leg.

Both horse and carriage could still function, for the exhausted and frightened Mozarts entered Rome not far behind schedule. At the various post stages Leopold had announced himself as the Imperial Ambassador's (Kaunitz's) steward, and attendants doffed their caps, the Papal customsmen, for their part, bowing in respect and waving him on. At the Palazzo Scatizzi, Signora Uslenghi at once took her guests in charge. No sooner did Wolfgang sit down than he began to snore, his sleep so deep that Leopold undressed him and put him to bed without his awakening.

Leopold's leg swelled. But soon the wound ceased to suppurate and, though reduced to hobbling about, he somehow made his way to St. Peter's on the vigil and day of the Feast of Peter and Paul (29 June) to see the illumination of the dome and the ceremony of the Neapolitan Tribute.[49] Moreover, he visited Cardinal Pallavicini in his apartments in the Quirinal Palace. There, on 5 July, the Mozarts learned that the Holy Father had created Wolfgang a Knight of the Golden Order, a degree of the Golden Spur higher in rank than Gluck's. Pallavicini handed Wolfgang the insignia of cross-studded sash, sword, and spurs, a Papal patent (signed the day before) bestowing this extraordinary favor upon a musician who "excelled since . . . earliest youth in the sweetest sounding of the harpsichord." On 8 July, at the palace of S. Maria Maggiore, he appeared before Clement XIV, who, once outside Vatican walls, could "deign to hear him and applaud the merits of this young man." A German prelate, in all likelihood Hieronymus Colloredo, Bishop of Gurk, stood in attendance. (If, indeed, he looked on, his presence mocked the future.) Pallavicini had arranged matters tidily.

The young dignitary signed a note to his sister as "Chevalier de Mozart," but there could be no doubt that he remained—as on occasion he styled himself—her "Bruder Hans." (Johannes was Mozart's first bap-

---

48 "You realize that two horses and a postilion constitute three beasts," Leopold observed. The postilion or groom rode to the left, his mount yoked to the spring-frame of the *sedia*.

49 Every year, Naples sent the Pope a rich symbolic gift in acknowledgment of its ancient and abstruse theoretical status as a Papal fief. From the time of the Angevins, the offering took the form of a *chinea*, or white palfrey bearing seven thousand gold ducats.

tismal name.) "Shit in your bed and make a mess," the new Knight of the Golden Order advised her.

10

THE AIR GREW stifling, and Leopold's anxiety about malaria returned. On the evening of 10 July he and Wolfgang left Rome by the ancient Flaminian Way. (Signora Uslenghi had refused money for lodging them and gave the youth a marvelous farewell gift: *The Thousand and One Nights* in Italian.) They had embarked upon what would be an exhausting journey: fear of contagion from the hot air of day made Leopold choose to travel by night despite the inevitable disruption of eating and sleeping habits; even more upsetting would be the vermin-infested inns ahead.

Crossing the peninsula by way of Civita Castellana (where Wolfgang tried the cathedral organ after mass), Terni, Spoleto, and Foligno, they reached Loreto on the sixteenth and paused to make their devotions at the shrine of the Virgin in the Chiesa della Casa Santa. (In fine humor despite the discomforts, Wolfgang promised to bring his mother gifts from holy Loreto: "Little bells and candles and bonnets and fleas.") Traveling on along the Adriatic, they encountered mounted soldiers and police at close intervals, a guard against Barbary pirates, who often landed to prey on pilgrims making the journey to the sanctuary. Through Ancona, Senigallia, and Pesaro, they came to Rimini, joined the Via Aemilia, and by way of Forlì and Imola arrived again in Bologna on 20 July. Alas, the Pellegrino must have been full, for they had to put up across the street at the San Marco.

His exertions in Rome immediately after the accident and the rigors of the journey had told upon Leopold. The wound opened, and his leg and foot swelled; the ankle soon distended to the thickness of the calf; he could stand only with difficulty and suffered gnawing pain. The Pallavicini household dispatched doctors to his side, and they confined him to his room, indeed, his bed, while any infection remained.[50] Leopold, who usually tidied up after his son, lost heart to observe the chaos rising about them: "You can imagine what our household looks like," he wrote Mother Mozart, "now that I cannot get about. You know what Wolfgang is."

For the first time he could roam a foreign city alone, relishing a new sense of independence. Even so, one token of dawning adulthood for the moment dismayed him: his voice had broken, and he now had a shaky scale of

---

[50] He did receive visitors, among them the composer Joseph Mysliveček, and the Manfredini brothers: Giuseppe, a castrato, and Vincenzo, a composer, teacher, and theorist, just returned from St. Petersburg.

barely five notes, a short portion with which to vocalize the new opera he had already begun. Within days of his arrival in Bologna the post had brought the libretto from Milan: *Mitridate, Rè di Ponto* by Vittorio Amedeo (sic) Cigna-Santi of Turin, the projected cast—and thus the vocal category of each role—being indicated. Mozart could begin devising a tonal plan.

At the same time, everything would crash down if Leopold became a permanent invalid or died of the tenacious infection. His left foot, too, had begun to ache and soon he could at best hobble with difficulty. Field Marshal Pallavicini invited him and Wolfgang to be guests at his country estate, Alla Croce del Biacco, not far from Bologna. The Mozarts remained for more than seven weeks (10 August to 1 October), installed in palatial chambers and waited upon by footmen and valets. Leopold spent his days reclining, even forbidden to rise when his princely hosts approached; wherever he went in the house, servants followed with a comfortable chair and footstool. He and Wolfgang dined at the family's sumptuous table—the variety and quality of Italian fruit in particular delighted the Salzburgers, who luxuriated in their first encounter with watermelon—and Wolfgang made a friend his own age, the Field Marshal's son, Count Giuseppe Maria. From this paradise the pair (and, when he could manage, Leopold, too) went forth on carriage excursions through the enchanting countryside. Wolfgang, who longed for exercise, took to riding a donkey, and all the while Leopold regained the use of his legs.

On 30 August he felt well enough to visit the city with Wolfgang and the Field Marshal to attend the annual festival of the Bologna Philharmonic Society. Held in the church of S. Giovanni in Monte, this sacred concert in honor of Saint Anthony of Padua offered a liturgical pasticcio: it included vespers and high mass, their various sections composed and conducted by ten different members of the Society. About a hundred instrumentalists (including three organists) and choristers took part.[51] At the performance father and son once again met Charles Burney, touring Europe in search of material for his history of music. He recalled how the "celebrated little German" had "in 1766 astonished all hearers in London": "there is no musical excellence I do not expect from . . . [his] extraordinary quickness and talents. . . ."

During September, Leopold interested himself in church politics: the Bavarian Elector's resolve that Munich become a bishopric, the question of Papal infallibility, and Rome's impending suppression of the Jesuits. Their relentless amassing of power over Europe's political and intellectual life

---

51 The generous dimensions of Mozart's *Litaniae de venerabili altaris sacramento* (K. 125) of 1772 breathe memories of these impressive services.

had awakened a hostile response: Portugal had expelled them in 1759, France in 1764, Spain and The Two Sicilies three years later; and now these nations sought to constrain the Pope to put an end to the Society of Jesus. Europe watched Clement XIV edge toward this act of political expediency. The Brotherhood, however, had fostered harmonious relationships with the Germans, whose officialdom, clerical and lay, advised him to hold back. Leopold devoured tracts on both sides of the issue.

Sharing his father's interest in the limits of authority, Wolfgang read Fénelon's utopian novel, *Télémaque*, probably the Italian translation issued in Venice (1748). He also continued studying the text of *Mitridate* and framing its harmonic structure. On 29 September he began composing the recitatives (and no doubt profited from Padre Martini's counsel concerning questions of prosody); the arias would take form later, when, working with his singers, he might "measure the garment right on the body." He and his father, now eager to arrive in Milan earlier than expected, revised their travel plans: Leopold abandoned his hope to visit the Borromean Islands.

By the beginning of October, Wolfgang and Leopold had moved back from Alla Croce to Bologna and begun packing their array of trunks and boxes; books and music had been accumulating at a frightening rate, and they started to ship their acquisitions over the Alps to Salzburg. On the fourth, in the vast church of St. Petronio, patron of the city, they attended a musical service celebrating his feast. "Beautiful but long," Wolfgang remarked of an occasion marred by the dreadful playing of trumpeters imported from Lucca. Two days later, he performed on one of the organs in the basilica of St. Domenico. And every day he worked with Padre Martini; it had become imperative that the young musician confront the mysteries of strict Renaissance vocal polyphony: thanks to his teacher, an extraordinary opportunity had presented itself.

On 9 October he appeared for examination before members of the Philharmonic Society. Given an antiphon melody, he received instructions to use it as the *cantus firmus*, or basis, of a four-part setting in the old style. Ushers led Leopold away and locked him in the library, while Wolfgang found himself confined in a chamber opening on the other side of the hall. After about thirty minutes—candidates often required three hours— he had done what he could with an idiom and discipline he as yet could not govern.

What went on behind the scenes must be conjectured. Padre Martini had set in motion a strange affair he may have regretted but, it would seem, regulated to the end. In truth, Wolfgang's exercise (K. 86/73v) had little to do with the venerable *stile osservato* and, under ordinary circumstances, might not have found serious consideration. "His endeavor [*esperimento*]," the minutes of the examination evocatively read, "was judged to be sufficient considering the circumstances. . . ." But what had the eyes of the academicians perused? Wolfgang's floundering attempt? Or a corrected and improved rendering in Padre Martini's hand but bearing Wolfgang's name? Or both? (The manuscripts survive; in addition, Mozart made copies of Martini's version.) Had the Society taken the precaution to sequester the father but not the mentor? Or perhaps it had been understood that, whatever the result on the examination paper, the young man—famous, gifted, and a Papal Knight—would enter into membership but, at the same time, be obliged to see a master contrapuntalist's solution to the problem. Whatever the circumstances, each of the judges raised a white sphere signifying approval. The conditions that an applicant be at least twenty years old and have conservatory training having been waived, Wolfgang received the company's congratulations. Letters patent were prepared, and Padre Martini wrote a testimonial stressing the young man's brilliance as a practical musician and, it would seem, paid the initiation fee.

II

ON 18 OCTOBER the Mozarts reached Milan and the quarters Herr Troger had rented for them near the opera house. Passing through heavy storms, they had waited a full day in Parma for the high waters to subside. The rain, which continued in Milan as Wolfgang labored at his opera, restricted the period of exercise he and Leopold hoped to make a daily routine: after the midday meal, a walk to Firmian's palace. Yet the poor weather and the size of his task kept Wolfgang at his desk all hours. He excused himself to Mama: "I cannot write much for my fingers ache badly from composing no end of recitative." As his singers began to assemble, he showed the grave face, Leopold noted, of someone "concerned with solemn matters"—the passionate dynastic action of *Mitridate*, an *opera-seria* poem worthy of heroic efforts: using Giuseppe Parini's translation of Racine's drama as his source, Cigna-Santi had concocted a stirring libretto, which Quirino Gasparini, a major figure in Turin's musical life, had already set to music in 1767.

Leopold did not repeat the blunders that had contributed to the ruin of *La finta semplice* in Vienna. Perhaps letters from Frau Anna Maria helped him sustain this more reasonable course: he would, so he assured her, remain patient, attempt whatever extraordinary or outrageous things might be required of him ("shit oranges"), and help Wolfgang surmount the "inevitable annoyances every kapellmeister must endure from the rabble of virtuosos." Finding the Italian world of opera "completely crazy" and continuing to use turns of phrase Salzburg appreciated, he announced that, if need be, father and son, like the Hanswurst, would "nibble their way through the Mountain of Shit."

Vexations did not lack. Seeing an opportunity for mischief, Gasparini sent the prima donna, Antonia Bernasconi, arias from his own *Mitridate* with the intent of enticing her to insert them into the new score.[52] Having seen Mozart's versions, she refused to lend herself to the cabal. Of course, he had reports of the inevitable self-serving, backbiting comments on his age, talent, and nationality. Nor could he always please his singers: again and again, Gugliemo d' Ettore, exponent of the title role, demanded that his arias be rewritten.

For all that, success hovered in the air as the rehearsals unfolded. A reading of the recitatives revealed, no doubt thanks to Padre Martini, a firm grasp of Italian diction. Moreover, when sixteen instrumentalists played through the score in search of copyists' errors, its professionalism stopped the mouths of skeptics and detractors. (The copyists rejoiced in the well-turned phrases, for they had the right to sell excerpts to the public.) The rehearsals on stage aroused Leopold's highest hopes. But he let others praise; his ears, he feared, might be "too partisan." With pathos he wrote home: "A good hour after Ave Maria on the day of Saint Stephen, picture to yourself Maestro Amadeo at his clavier midst the orchestra and think of me observing and listening in a box or balcony; in your thoughts wish him a successful performance and say a few 'Our Fathers' for him." On the evening of 26 December, Wolfgang, dressed in a new scarlet suit with gold braid and blue lining, led some sixty instrumentalists and seven singers in a premiere that evoked cries of *"Viva il maestrino."*[53]

As a rule, the first opera of the Milan season drew weak houses; but not *Mitridate*: it triumphed. As local custom demanded, the composer played continuo and conducted from the clavier for the first three performances. Thereafter Wolfgang joined his father among the spectators, and Giovanni Battista Lampugnani, who had played second clavier, moved up to first as

---

52 To pique her special interest, he had rewritten them. This abbé, pupil of Martini, and *maestro di cappella* of Turin cathedral, commanded the Mozarts' respect as a musician: an *Adoramus te*, long attributed to Wolfgang (K. 327/Anh. A10) has proved to be a study copy in Leopold's hand of a work by Gasparini. He would meet the Mozarts in Turin early in 1771.

53 What with encores and three ballets (to music by Francesco Caselli and, in all likelihood, danced after the acts), the performance lasted six hours. The premiere past, the management ordered the ballets to be shortened.

Melchiorre Chiesa stepped in to fill his place. Lampugnani had known considerable success as a composer for the stage, while both formed part of the Milanese school of symphonists over whom Sammartini presided. Leopold wrote his wife: "If about fifteen or eighteen years ago, when Lampugnani had written so much in England and Melchior [*sic*] Chiesa so much in Italy . . . someone had told me that these men would take part in the music of your son and, when he left his clavier, would have to sit down and accompany his music, I would have referred such a person to an insane asylum."

By indulging his singers, Mozart had dedicated his work to success: through their dazzling vocal feats he won the audience. Fixed in the Metastasian mold, the basic plan of *Mitridate* (K. 87/74a) consists of a chain of recitative from which at intervals, like pendants on a necklace, hang arias, many of them studded with coloratura embracing leaps, runs, arpeggios, and all manner of taxing display. Among the twenty-five numbers following the concise overture only two are ensembles: the quintet closing the opera and the second-act finale for male and female sopranos. (During rehearsals, the *primo uomo*, Sartorino [Pietro Benedetti], assured his colleagues that, should it "fail to please," he "would let himself be castrated again.") But apart from this duet, two affecting arias in the minor (one for the heroine, the other for her gentle suitor), and some accomplished accompagnato, few places in the libretto offered Mozart's imagination points of penetration. By and large he appears self-conscious, only at moments awakening the protagonists to musical life: their self-examination and renunciation set sympathetic musical vibrations astir in him by fits and starts, and he brought into being a score less wrought by inspiration than hammered out by sheer energy.

Of course, no one could have expected a boy not yet fifteen—no matter what his gifts—to see with Racinian vision, to project the playwright's brilliant interaction between the active and the reflective, a dialectic the architecture of *opera seria*, as in so many of Handel's, accommodates with such felicity. Unable to exploit the structure of the genre or the psychological subtleties of his characters, Mozart failed to achieve dramatic continuity. For all his efforts he, in fact, could barely come to terms with the plot: there is little exploitation even of its externals, in particular the bold contrapositions and chiaroscuro of that pair of sons unlike in character but both in love with their father's betrothed. In Mozart's hands, the tragic dilemma does not energize; it disintegrates. And though brilliant instrumental obbligatos at moments excite the ear, yet his use of the orchestra seems somewhat timid: he must have feared inviting cries of "*troppo tedesco*" (the charge that had undone Jommelli in Naples), the malicious having warned Milan of young Mozart's "barbarous German music." But the sheer craftsmanship of the score, the challenges it offered the singers, and the youth of the composer, all combined to enrapture the public; it gave him the affectionate nickname of "Il Sigr: Cavaliere Filarmonico."

During the composition of *Mitridate,* Troger had invited the Mozarts to his country home in the vineyards outside Milan. Now his daughter, Frau Marianne d'Asti von Asteburg (Salzburg knew her as the "Trogermariandl"), asked them to a celebration (3 January). She prepared a dish for which Wolfgang had especial nostalgia—liver dumplings and sauerkraut—though the company also feasted upon capon and pheasant. It was time to relax, to rein in a bit, and on the fourteenth Wolfgang and Leopold left on an excursion to Turin, in hope of catching the premiere of Paisiello's *Annibale in Torino* two days later at the Teatro Regio.

Though Wolfgang may have given concerts in the beautiful capital of the kingdom of Sardinia,[54] the Mozarts had in mind simply enjoying the Shrovetide opera season, which also included the premiere of Gaetano Pugnani's *Issea* and, into the bargain, Ignazio Platania's *Berenice.* Leopold must have sought out those Piedmontese violinists who preserved the style of the founder of their school: Corelli's (and perhaps Vivaldi's) pupil Giovanni Battista Somis (1686–1763). By the last day of January the Mozarts had left their quarters at the Dogana Nova to return to Milan to hear the second opera of its season, Carlo Monza's *Nitteti* (its premiere had fallen on the twenty-second); to take farewell of Count Firmian; and to pack and be off to Venice.

12

IN WRETCHED WEATHER, by way of Canonica, Brescia (where they attended the *opera buffa*),[55] Verona, Vicenza, and Padua, the Mozarts made their way toward the island capital and on Shrove Monday (11 February 1771) crossed the shallow waters that kept it secure, a "continent" apart: the city of Tiepolo, Longhi, and Guardi, then in its golden decline.

---

54 The Treaty of London (1720) had compelled Duke Victor Amadeus II of Savoy and Piedmont to exchange the kingship of Sicily (which he had acquired only seven years earlier by terms of the Treaty of Utrecht) for that of Sardinia. In 1730 he abdicated in favor of his son, who, at the time of the Mozarts' visit, still ruled in Turin both as Charles Emanuel III in the Savoyard succession and as Charles Emanuel I, King of Sardinia.

55 They heard either Antonio Boroni's *Il carnovale di Venezia* or Nicolò Tassi and Alessandro Felici's *L'amor soldato.*

They stayed in the house of the Ceseletti family (whom the Hagenauers recommended) near the Ponte dei Barcaroli and spent much time with the wife and daughters of Johannes Wider, a business associate of Hagenauer and once a merchant of Salzburg.[56] Frau Wider and her brood of six, adopting the travelers, stuffed their stomachs and washed and mended their linen. The ladies attempted to turn Wolfgang into "a true Venetian" by making him submit to the "*attáca*," that is, forcing him down and spanking his bottom. With pride he wrote Nannerl, "all seven women joined forces and yet were unable to get me to the floor." He delighted in frolicking with them, his sensuality alert and keen.

All at once Leopold beheld Venice itself as a source of peril (even as he felt renewed anxiety about those close sleeping arrangements at home). His eyes, it would appear, saw an immediate threat to Wolfgang in the enchanting Wider girls and also Venice's ubiquitous courtesans—celebrated for both their sexual and musical accomplishments—who provided the city's most sought-after amusements. If the reflective judged Rome the culminating point of the Grand Tour, young men seeking pleasure found the Serene Republic no less memorable: "As for women, it is not in a city like Venice that a man abstains from them," Rousseau had declared. As to "what can profit or injure the young," Leopold considered himself most knowing: he suddenly recognized Venice as "the most dangerous place in all of Italy," thus ascribing to outside—and to him malevolent—forces his son's assertion of his sexual personality and with it his dawning sense of independence. Most likely Leopold held back from the belittling spirit and stratagems of ridicule and contempt he would later apply in such crises; but his stance must have seemed clumsy enough midst the physical openness and emotional freedom of Italian life. In Venice he once again showed himself an angry man.

Though his letters home drew a picture of its great families—the Corner, Bragadino, Dolfin, Maffei, Grimani, Mocenigo,[57] Venier, and Valier—vying for Wolfgang's visits, their gondolas ever at his disposal, Abbate Giovanni Maria Ortes, a writer active in Venice, penned Hasse a different tale: that of a surly Leopold piqued by the indifference of the Venetian nobles. Ortes's observations ring true: "I do not think . . . that they [the Mozarts] find themselves very much pleased with this city,

---

56 The lions' heads decorating the portals of many a house in Salzburg bore witness to the strong business connections linking it to the city of Saint Mark (see p. 9).

57 At the time, Alvise Mocenigo IV reigned as Doge of Venice.

where they probably expected others to seek after them, rather than they after others. . . ."[58]

Wolfgang gave at most four intimate recitals in the salons of the Venetian aristocracy: one before the Patriarch, Giovanni Bragadino, another in the palace of Giovanni Antonio Dolfin, and two for Caterina Corner, who presented the virtuoso with "a beautiful snuffbox and . . . exquisite lace cuffs." As expected, his benefactor of long standing, Count Jacopo di Durazzo, since 1764 Maria Theresa's ambassador to *La Serenissima*,[59] summoned him to perform (3 March), and two days later he gave his only "big concert" in the city, perhaps at the Maffei's.

He must have played at the four famed *ospedali* (dei Mendicanti, della Pietà, degli Incurabili, and dei Derelitti, the Ospedaletto). Originally hostels—whence the name—for pilgrims during the Crusades, through the centuries they had come to concern themselves for the most part with the care and schooling of foundling and orphaned girls. The *ospedali* had developed the role of music in their curricula and in time became true conservatories, such masters as Vivaldi, Galuppi, Hasse, Porpora, Jommelli, and Traetta serving on their faculties. By the time of Mozart's visit, children of the nobility, for a fee, could also attend the music classes.

The Mozarts had the opportunity to hear opera: Giovanni Battista Borghi's *Siroe* at the Teatro S. Benedetto and Boroni's *Le contadine furlane* at the Teatro di S. Moisé. Leopold came to an agreement with the S. Benedetto: Wolfgang was to write an opera for this "magnificent and noble theater,"[60] contractual discussions in all likelihood occasioning the Mozarts' otherwise inexplicable month-long stay in a city in the main loath to offer them patronage.

On 12 March they departed, journeying to Padua on the waters of the Brenta in a hired boat and accompanied by Herr and Frau Wider, two of their daughters, and Abbate Ortes. (The Widers had packed formidable picnic hampers.) Together they explored Padua's monuments,

---

58 Venetian patronage had a collective stamp: while offering little beyond household concerts and lessons as direct support to the professional musician, the nobles, along with Church and state, helped maintain those opera houses, confraternities, academies, and *ospedali* (orphanages dedicated to pedagogy) that provided musicians significant opportunities.

59 Count Johann Wenzel Sporck had taken his place as the Habsburgs' theater intendant (see p. 239). Posterity owes a debt to Durazzo's bibliophilic pursuits in Venice: from the Ospedale della Pietà he purchased a collection of Vivaldi's compositions; in time it came to rest in the Turin National Library and formed the material from which scholars of the twentieth century constructed the Vivaldi revival.

60 It burned in 1774; reborn in the Teatro La Fenice (1792), it returned to ashes in 1996, and, at the moment rises once more.

and Wolfgang seized the opportunity to play the organ of the "incomparable" church of Santa Giustina, so admired by Goethe. The Mozarts went their own way to call upon the local musical celebrities: the eminent contrapuntist Francesco Antonio Vallotti, the composer Giovanni Battista Ferrandini,[61] and Don Giuseppe Ximenes d'Aragona, a littérateur, vital force in Padua's musical life, and correspondent of Padre Martini. Doubtless on his recommendation, Ximenes gave Wolfgang a commission to compose and dispatch to Padua an oratorio to a text by Metastasio: *La Betulia liberata.* On the fourteenth, the Widers and Ortes turned back to Venice, and the Mozarts quit their quarters in the Palazzo Pesaro to proceed to Vicenza, whose Bishop—from the House of Cornaro—insisted upon a visit. They then continued westward.

Pietro Lugiati welcomed them in Verona on the sixteenth. During their stay of several days in his house, Wolfgang gave a concert, and Leopold received news realizing his most buoyant hopes; though holding back details until the proper confirming documents arrived, he wrote home to prepare the family for remarkable prospects. Wolfgang had completed but his first Italian sojourn, for Vienna would command him to make two return journeys to Milan: first, to create a festival opera celebrating the marriage of Ferdinand of Austria to Beatrice of Modena in the autumn of 1771 (certainly she and Firmian had urged the commission); and then to compose the principal opera of the carnival season of 1772. The ruling Austrians, not their Milanese subjects, were handing him this double prize. Vienna had reason to rejoice: by gathering Modena within their fold, the Habsburgs had enclasped a territory between their Lombard and Tuscan dependencies and thus of strategic importance; the Habsburg court of Milan wished to celebrate with music by the young German with whom it contemplated forging close bonds.

Much the same route that had brought the Mozarts to Italy led them home. By way of Rovereto and Innsbruck, they made their way through snow and high winds. Leopold had hoped to sing an Eastertide alleluia with his wife and daughter; and so he did: on Maundy Thursday (28 March 1771) he and Wolfgang re-entered Salzburg after an absence of fifteen and a half months.[62]

---

61 As part of Elector Charles Albert's musical household in Munich, he had taught the princely children: viola da gamba to the son who became Maximilian III Joseph and singing to his sister, Maria Antonia Walpurgis (as well as to the tenor Anton Raaff). Ferrandini's *Catone in Utica* had opened Munich's Cuvilliés theater in 1753. He and the Mozarts had friends and colleagues in common.

62 They had to stay at a local inn for a short time: Hagenauer had put renovations into work at the house on the Getreidegasse, and the Mozart apartment was topsy-turvy.

CHAPTER XVI

Two More Italian Visits
with German Respites

THE SALZBURG COURT had to make the best of Vienna's latest demands upon Wolfgang and regarded the Mozarts' presence as no more than a respite. Though the father returned to his duties, the exchequer did not, as at first planned, put the son on salary: there would be insufficient time for him to find his footing as a working *Konzertmeister.* In view of its contribution to the Italian journey, however, the Residenz did not hesitate to ask for new compositions. His five-movement *Litaniae Lauretanae* (K. 109/74e),[1] a supplication to the Virgin written during May and deriving from a litany by his father, offers deeply felt passages—the elegant Sancta Maria and the elegiac Agnus Dei—as does the Ora pro nobis of his four-movement *Regina coeli* (K. 108/74d), produced the same month. These compositions for chorus and soloists go directly to the heart. Powers he could summon only at moments during his complex interactions with *Mitridate's* high-flown rhetoric opened wide as he set the simple and tender religious poetry known to him since childhood.

During these months in Salzburg he composed the symphonies K. 75 in F and K. 110/75b in G, possibly for use at the Residenz but doubtless with Milan in mind. In the second and more spacious work, with its tendency

---

1 Lauretanae derives from Loreto. A series of orisons, a litany opens with a Kyrie and closes with an Agnus Dei, a sequence of devotional invocations and petitions unfolding between.

toward animated inner voices, Joseph Haydn's influence may be sensed. (While en route to Italy, Leopold would write home requesting Nannerl to send him one of Haydn's string trios.[2]) Aware of an inevitable late return from the impending journey, Mozart made time for work on a *serenata drammatica* the court had commanded for performance in January (to celebrate Archbishop Schrattenbach's fiftieth year as a priest). In addition, he devoted much of this spring and summer to fulfilling the commission from Don Giuseppe Ximenes: *La Betulia liberata* had to be completed by the middle of August, when father and son were to set out, since composing the wedding *serenata* would consume most of Wolfgang's time in Milan. They planned to pause in Verona en route, post the score of *Betulia* to Ximenes; and, late in autumn, return to Salzburg by way of Padua, there to hear the oratorio performed. Its subject, Judith's raising the siege of Betulia by slaying the Assyrian general, Holofernes, derived from the Apocrypha.

Metastasio's didactic treatment of the story[3] has not lacked depreciators; nonetheless, this strong and elegant verse, which attracted such composers as Reutter the Younger, Gassmann, Cafaro, Bernasconi, and Jommelli, served Mozart well. His *Betulia liberata* (K. 118/74c) has splendid moments: the agitated, introspective three-part overture in D minor with its reminiscences of Gluck's *Alceste* and premonitions of *Don Giovanni*; Judith's heroic "*Parto inerme,*" sung as she leaves the invested city; her dramatic accompagnato describing the murder; the first aria of Ozia, governor of Betulia, his gracefully turned phrases developing into extended bravura melismas;[4] his melodically captivating prayer alternating with the Israelites' pious exclamations (an affecting Gluck-like ensemble repeated as Judith prepares to visit the hostile camp); the contrite Amital's lyric and inspired "*Con troppo rea viltà*"; Judith's celebration of the Assyrians' flight, the chorus adding its praises by putting to use the Gregorian *tonus peregrinus*, the melody the Church employed for psalm 113 (Vulgate), "*In exitu Israel*",[5] an erudite touch Leopold might have suggested. Unlike the score of *Mitridate*, the oratorio issued from the emotions and motivations of the characters,

---

2 He also asked for works by Wagenseil, Adlgasser, and Giovanni Marco Rutini.

3 An oratorio had a structure similar to that of *opera seria*, save a division into two rather than three parts.

4 An oratorio's text eschewed the voluptuous extolling of amorous passions characteristic of most operas, but its vocal lines did not shun the sometimes shameless delights of florid embellishment. Many an oratorio aria, its text altered, could do service in the opera house (see XIV, n. 4).

5 Mozart would return to this psalm tone in the *Maurerische Trauermusik* (see p. 645) and in the Introit of the Requiem (see p. 755). *Betulia's* final number also includes material from a theater score by Michael Haydn, perhaps a gesture of homage.

not the technical possibilities and limitations of individual performers; indeed, Wolfgang had no idea what singers Ximenes had at his disposal.

Betulia did not come to performance: it seems clear that Padua rejected it because Mozart remained too German a composer, one of the reasons Milan would in time cast him aside.[6] Ximenes may have anticipated receiving an oratorio exhibiting signs of Padre Martini's laying on of hands; but of this ministration *Betulia* betrayed no trace—and little enough even of the more conventional Italian operatic manner. Though Hasse, the most Italian of German operatic masters, had provided Mozart's broad model, the sober cantorial spirit of Eberlin, of the German Baroque with its many notes, stirred beneath this setting of Metastasio's rococo text.

If Burney could condemn the orchestration of certain Italian operas (Piccinni's, for example) as too busy and dense, then how overwhelming to most ears must Mozart's scores have seemed, what with their bustling instrumental activity of detailed workmanship, the orchestra having no less a part than the voices in the effect of the whole. Burney praised Hasse's "genius" in "accompanying those sweet and tender [vocal] melodies," which he "never suffocates . . . by the learned jargon of a multiplicity of instruments." But from early days, Mozart stood condemned for overindulging his pleasure in this "learned jargon."

Burney would have a hard time of it with a Mozart scena of 1778 for castrato soprano and orchestra (see p. 441): though impressed by this "great master of harmony . . . possessed of a consummate knowledge of the genius of different instruments," he nonetheless decried a lack of melodic "invention" in both the vocal and orchestral parts. The richness of Mozart's harmonies and the variety of his instrumental subtleties confounded those with a taste for Italian opera's free-flowing, melodic spans supported by chords, and even a Burney could remain a stranger to the true nature of Mozart's melodic fertility, so luxuriantly palpable in line against line, the vocalist emerging like the soloist in a concerto. Many knitted their brows at this inclination to conceive of the voice as a heightened extension of a total harmonic-instrumental concept, a principle at odds with the southern ideal of accompanied melody.

The orchestral intricacies of Mozart's operas sat uncomfortably with Italians in particular: rich writing for the winds, divided viola parts, and cellos aspiring for independence (that is, refusing to follow along with the double basses) seemed to them excesses too often painful for the very good reason that, apart from performances at a Habsburg court, they seldom

---

6 *Lucio Silla*, written for Milan at the end of 1772, would be Mozart's last opera commissioned for Italy (see p. 303).

heard opera orchestras capable of going beyond approximations of such complicated German scores. When, for example, Gluck prepared the premiere of his *Il trionfo di Clelia* for the opening of Bologna's Teatro Communale (1763), seventeen full rehearsals failed to produce the orchestral precision he had come to expect in Vienna as a matter of course.

With second thoughts about Mozart's scena, Burney did concede that, "if well executed," it "would, doubtless, be masterly and pleasing." In much the same spirit, Leopold Mozart summed up the problem when he wrote his son: "Subject to a mediocre orchestra, your music will always fall short, for it is written with such discrimination for all instruments and is not as plain as Italian music generally is." Though Empress Maria Luisa's description of his *La clemenza di Tito* as a *porcheria tedesca* and Emperor Joseph's censure of the "too many notes" in *The Abduction from the Seraglio* have both proved apocryphal, the very vigor of these myths derived from the deep irritation of many with the thickness of German instrumental textures.[7]

Betulia's shadowy resonances and gravitas, the somber color of the minor mode streaking the harmonic texture, revealed yet further *empfindsam* German qualities less than endearing to Paduan taste. In Italy major keys found preference even for tragic moments, and in its tendency to follow a course in the near foreground of the score and to pursue brilliance and euphony, Italian operatic melody often did violence to dramatic relevance, a state of affairs unacceptable to the maturing Mozart. Moreover, into the bargain, Judith turned out to be a contralto rather than the bright soprano more traditional for a heroine.

A solemn and often melancholy masterpiece conceived in gray Salzburg, *La Betulia liberata* pointed the way toward Mozart's accumulating crisis with transalpine taste, a perplexity that would soon turn to dust his ambitions in Milan. There, in the end, true success depended upon the natives, not their German masters, who sang his praises all out and thereby misled him: he imagined he had conquered the Italians, for with good humor they applauded his talent, delighted in his youthful charm, and remained no less aware that his immediate advantage rested upon his being a German among ruling Germans.

Leopold's failure in Italy to take into account and perhaps alter (or, at least, disguise) Wolfgang's artistic bearing, as well as their ever more perplexing relationship with the House of Habsburg, would raise obstacles by

---

7 Only after Gluck's reform operas had received a Parisian imprimatur did the Italian public accord them grudging respect, in spite of their "thick" orchestration.

the end of the second Italian visit. At all events, as they prepared for it, father and son remained insensible of the ground sliding from under them.

2

FULL OF SPIRIT—"like two deer . . . but not in heat!" wrote Leopold[8]—father and son left Salzburg on 13 August to travel the now familiar route to Milan.[9] They arrived eight days later. Under a relentless summer sun the city stirred with preparations for the archducal wedding and its attendant spectacles, illuminations, banquets, masked balls, and receptions ("three hundred persons" were to "dine at court every day"): candlemakers poured some twenty thousand pounds of wax; painters and upholsterers freshened the opera house; wooden tribunes rose in the squares.[10] For a time, Wolfgang had to content himself with far from pointed activity—sketching random musical ideas to be shaped into he knew not what: the libretto of the *serenata teatrale*, sent to Vienna for approval, had not yet come back. He jested about the way musical thoughts for unknown words came to him in his room: "Above us is a violinist, below us another one, next to us a singing teacher who gives lessons, and in the room opposite ours an oboist.[11] It's fun when one composes! One picks up many ideas." When the book, *Ascanio in Alba*, did arrive, the librettist, the court poet, Abbate Giuseppe Parini,[12] needed time to make the emendations Vienna required in this tale of gods and demigods. Wolfgang did not lay eyes upon a stable text until the end of August, and Parini continued to fuss with it well into September; the wedding was to take place on 15 October, the *serenata* two days later.

First, Wolfgang wrote the three-part introductory music: a bustling Allegro assai, an Andante grazioso to be danced by the Graces, and an

---

8 On its face lighthearted, this strange remark may reflect Leopold's continuing apprehension concerning his son's sexual ripening and its possible expression and consequences in Italy. During this stay in Milan, Wolfgang, almost sixteen, did not have the freedom to go to the theater alone; when an indisposition confined Leopold to their quarters, he, too, remained indoors in the evening. He wished to attend Hasse's *Ruggiero* on 2 November 1771 but reported home: "Since Papa is not going out, I can't be there."

9 Familiar save one segment: instead of journeying from Verona to Milan via Mantua, Bozzolo, and Cremona, they followed the route through Brescia and Canonica. On the road between Rovereto and Verona they met the violin virtuoso Antonio Lolli (see VIII, n. 12).

10 During a street celebration in October, one of the stands collapsed. Some spectators fell to their deaths; others suffered injury. A late arrival spared the Mozarts: directed to the galleries on the opposite side, in horror they witnessed the accident.

11 The Mozarts stayed in a building lodging musicians, an accommodation the palace in all likelihood suggested and perhaps the very quarters in which *Mitridate* had come to completion.

12 Parini, who enjoyed the patronage of Count Firmian, had praised Mozart's *Mitridate* (see p. 129).

Allegro chorus of praise to Venus, also to serve as ballet music; this sung and choreographed ensemble, Viennese in tone, led into the goddess's opening recitative. (Soon after the premiere, he composed a Presto [K. 120/111a] so that Allegro, Andante, and the new Presto, replacing the chorus-ballet, might form an independent symphony.) In addition, he provided music for an entr'acte ballet[13] binding together the two sections of the *serenata*, the kind of task more often given, as in the case of *Mitridate*, to a second composer. Wolfgang followed his usual course of composing the arias as the cast assembled. Despite a severe cold, on 23 September he completed the score (K. 111), written much in the manner of a Gluck festival piece. So soon after the very personal *Betulia*, he found no difficulty grinding out this decorative, quite neutral work. Parini's allegorical pastoral inspired ornamental recitatives, arias, and choruses, all celebrating less the young couple than the formidable mistress of the Hofburg and her rule over Lombardy. She dominates what is in spirit an extended *licenza*.

Venus (Maria Theresa) descends to Latium from the clouds with her grandson Ascanio (Ferdinand), her purpose: to marry him to Silvia (Beatrice), a local judicious and virtuous nymph of the race of Hercules. (Beatrice was the daughter of the Hereditary Prince of Modena, Ercole [Hercules] Rainaldo d'Este; Parini found it necessary to stress her wisdom and integrity for, as Leopold noted, her homeliness could not be disguised.) While awaiting Ascanio, Silvia has fallen in love with the vision of a beautiful youth—here Cupid, who assumed Ascanio's likeness at Venus's bidding. Silvia hopes that this handsome apparition will materialize as the hero heaven has selected for her. But when he appears, Ascanio follows his grandmother's command to deny his identity and thus test the nymph's sense of duty. Torn by passion for this alluring figure of her vision, she remembers her responsibility to give herself to the bridegroom chosen by divine will: she collapses in anguish, recovers, and finds the strength to resist her love, her virtue victorious over her passion. Venus, witness of the edifying struggle, then reveals herself and sets matters right. The goddess, leaving the joyful pair as her deputy rulers in a land she much loves, returns to Olympus (Vienna!) in a cloud.

Parini had baked a rich pastry the court devoured with gusto. Mythology celebrated Venus's son Aeneas as the founder of Rome, his son Ascanio (Iulus) as engenderer of the Julian line. Parini's politically shrewd apologue suggested the groom's late father, Holy Roman Emperor Francis, as begetter of a new succession of latter-day Roman rulers embodied in

---

13 The bass line of these dances survives; perhaps elements of them may also be discovered in K. Anh. 207/Anh. C 27.06.

the House of Habsburg-Lothringen; indeed, on the stage of Milan's Regio Ducal Teatro, Venus's magic created Ascanio's new city of Alba Longa, birthplace of Romulus and Remus and cradle of ancient Rome (see X, n. 2). Such allusions could have been no less pleasing to Maria Theresa than her own marvelous role in the allegory: floating in the empyrean as goddess and eternal mother, whom Ascanio addresses as *"cara madre."* Such a work, a very private affair, resembled a mythology painted for the *studiolo* of a Renaissance prince, the allegory clear to an inner circle. The Austrian and Lombard aristocrats at the premiere of *Ascanio* followed its symbolic nuances; what the general public made of them in the repetitions open to it must be guessed.

Mozart's score mirrors the frigid intellectualism of Parini's text and at the same time suffuses it with a gentle melancholy, transparent orchestration transforming and welding weak joints much as a fine lacquer both burnishes and strengthens a fragile bibelot. Despite a prevalent vapidity, the music offers felicitous moments: Silvia's deeply felt *"Si, ma d'un altro amore"* sung as she ponders that vision of the gentle youth who changed all; her *"Spiega il desio,"* its glittering coloratura painting her anticipation of the bridegroom's arrival; Ascanio's spacious and Gluck-like *"Ah, di si nobil alma,"* a tribute to her virtues, and his *"Torna mio bene,"* a poignant plea for her love. And though the accompagnato of the recognition scene fails in effect, that depicting Sylvia's determination to resist delusion and temptation forms a dramatically and psychologically satisfying link to her touching *"Infelici affetti miei,"* in which she triumphs over herself in cadences at times anticipating those of Countess Almaviva. *"Ah caro sposo"* provides the lovers and the priest of Venus with an impressive trio giving way to the pedestrian closing chorus.

The success of *Ascanio* owed much to sympathetic singers, in particular the Mozarts' old friend Manzuoli as Ascanio and Antonia Maria Girelli-Aguilar as Silvia; gifted dancers and choreographers; and the designers (the Galliari brothers) and technicians who achieved the extravagant effects expected on such occasions.[14] The work drew the wedding couple back a second time—*Ascanio* had four repetitions—and Wolfgang had the pleasure of hearing *"Bravissimo maestro"* issue from the royal box. Indeed, the *serenata* awakened an enthusiasm denied the wedding festivities' grand *opera seria*, Hasse's *Ruggiero*.

The aging master, long eager to withdraw from composing operas, had given in to Maria Theresa's promptings that he write it. Yet, despite the

---

14 Noted for their canvas drops painted in ingenious perspective, Bernadino, Fabrizio, and Giovanni Antonio Galliari created the scenery for all three of Mozart's Milanese operas.

novelty of a libretto by Metastasio with medieval legend as its source, *Ruggiero* struck its audience as stale. Moreover, it suffered "all those mishaps that could possibly occur. . . ."[15] "I regret," an unconvincing Leopold wrote, "that Wolfgang's *serenata* has so overshadowed Hasse's opera, and to a point I cannot describe." Wolfgang had to acknowledge congratulations even as he and his father walked through the streets. Hasse took his eclipse in good part and continued to enjoy their company. Myth assigns to this period his observation that the boy would cause all other contemporary composers to be forgotten.

From the time of his first meeting with Princess Beatrice, now an Austrian archduchess, Leopold had surmised that she contemplated taking Wolfgang into her service. Early in this second Italian stay, the father had begun to document in his letters home a series of indispositions—constipation, vertigo, and, finally, rheumatism—invented to justify a late return to Salzburg should a successful unveiling of *Ascanio* lead the Habsburgs to discuss a permanent engagement. He determined to remain in Milan at least until the princely couple returned from their wedding trip. Then a summons to an audience would come: Ferdinand had indicated that much if no more. Wolfgang devoted these November days of waiting to new compositions: a symphony in F, K. 112, with a lovely cavatina-like Andante for strings as well as opening and closing Allegro movements bound together by related initial phrases; and a divertimento in E flat, K. 113[16] (here he first scored for clarinets), beginning with a theme in the manner of Christian Bach, indeed, kindred to the one he would use to open his own *Lucio Silla.*

To Nannerl and her mother, unhappy to have been left behind, Leopold offered hints about a future in Milan: "Perhaps you will not miss the opportunity of seeing opera in Italy." Unaware of Vienna's aversion to him—to be underscored by Maria Theresa's including in a letter (12 December) to Ferdinand an admonition that he close the doors to "*le jeune salzburgois (sic)*"—Leopold must have felt perplexed to sense the wind change direction and turn chill. "If it would give you pleasure [to hire Wolfgang], I do not want to stop you," the Empress wrote her son, at the same time indicating her assessment of the Mozarts as opportunists. Little

15 They included Manzuoli's boiling over: cast in both *Ruggiero* and *Ascanio,* he expected additional payment for participating in the *serenata.* Refused a supplement, he rejected any compensation and after the performances left Milan in a huff. He may well have vented his displeasure upon Hasse's rather than Mozart's rehearsals.

16 K. 112 and 113 appear to have had their first performances at the Milanese residence of Albert Michael von Mayr, son of the Imperial Paymaster and a member of Archduke Ferdinand's retinue. Since their earliest visit to Vienna in 1762, the Mozarts had known the von Mayr family.

partial to actors, she had come to look upon the ever-traveling family much as itinerant players and could not have kept from reflecting upon the father and son's perpetual readiness to cut loose from the accommodating and generous Archbishop, whom, in fact, they seldom served. She looked upon them as guilty of more than lapses of decorum: in her eyes they had broken a compact. Moreover, distressed to learn of the failure of Hasse's *Ruggiero* and regretting her honeyed words enticing him to compose it, she must have found inappropriate and galling the contrast between the young man's good strike and the elder's humiliation: "I am pained for old Hasse's sake," she informed Ferdinand on 6 November. Perhaps she also heard reports of Leopold's crowing.

As yet unacquainted with the depth of her displeasure and fatigue with the Mozarts, Ferdinand, back from the Este palace at Varese, received them on 30 November. Awaiting counsel from Vienna, he prevaricated. Archbishop Schrattenbach had ordered Leopold's salary stopped during his absence,[17] a goad to prod him home within a reasonable time. On 5 December he left for Salzburg.[18]

He strove to remain sanguine. Had not Count Firmian given Wolfgang, in addition to his fee, a watch set with diamonds, a gift from the Empress? "The matter is not over [*leer*]; I can say that much," Leopold wrote on 8 December from the town of Ala[19] during his journey toward a Salzburg about to be shaken by political change.

3

ON THE DAY after the Mozarts' return to Salzburg (15 December 1771), Archbishop Schrattenbach died (his obsequies celebrated by Michael Haydn's C-minor requiem, which would have significant influence upon Wolfgang). The interregnum proved long and bitter, Vienna meddling without shame in the work of the elective consistory. After three months of political maneuvering, it lifted Count Hieronymus Franz de Paula Joseph Colloredo, canon of Salzburg, Prince-Bishop of Gurk, and son of

---

17 In the end, Leopold received full payment, thanks to *Ascanio*'s success. However, it appears clear that the Residenz had resolved never again to tolerate the Mozarts' remaining away to attend all repetitions of a premiere even as their salaries accrued at home.

18 On 9 November he had still talked of visiting Padua on the way; thereafter, not a word about the plan. Perhaps he had tarried too long in Milan to fall in with the schedule of Padua's musical season; more likely he learned that Ximenes found *Betulia* unacceptable.

19 He had developed friendships with the Pizzini family, whose members lived in both Rovereto and Ala. Between 11 and 13 December father and son also paused in Brixen, performing for its bishop, Leopold Maria Joseph, Count Spaur.

the Imperial Vice-Chancellor,[20] to the throne of St. Rupert. Upon hearing Hieronymus's name proclaimed from the balcony of the palace, the assembled Salzburgers stood amazed, hushed by shock. He spent every second winter in their city, and they knew him well: aloof, hectoring, and haughty, he showed subordinates deep disdain, reserving courtesies for those of the highest rank. An Enlightened reader of the philosophes, a disciple of Joseph II, and partial to the English and English manners, he would, like the Emperor, manifest a reforming zeal unrelated to the traditions, happiness, and well-being of those he attempted to benefit:[21] he would labor to improve a populace he despised, nursing with hauteur that contempt for and rudeness toward others too often intrinsic to those who put forth theories exalting equality and humanity. As Colloredo and his attendants processed to the cathedral for the Te Deum celebrating his election, the crowd again looked on in silence.

His accession seemed promising to Mozart, who converted the *serenata* begun to commemorate the half-century of Schrattenbach's ordination—Metastasio's *Il sogno di Scipione*, its subject taken from Cicero—into a celebration of Colloredo's investiture (see X, n. 13). Though the allegory, despite editing, retained more pertinence to the military misadventures of Emperor Charles VI, whom its first version honored, than to the careers of either the departed or the new archbishop, the splendor of a theme imbued with so high a moral and classical tone recommended *Sogno* to occasions requiring praise of an upright, law-abiding life devoted to the practical virtues.

In his sleep, Scipio Africanus the Younger finds himself in heaven. Costanza (Steadfastness) and Fortuna (Chance) appear and demand that he select one of them as a guide through life. The spirits of his father and adoptive grandfather draw near and speak of duty, immortality, and the vanity of earthly things. When Scipio, wavering between two destinies, finally chooses Costanza, the furious Fortuna departs as a tempest breaks forth. It awakens the dreamer, who declares himself faithful to his decision.

Metastasio's verse drew uneven results from Mozart. Too often uninspired and, at times, downright plodding, the score (K. 126) even passes over one of the text's few obvious opportunities for expansive musical invention: those passages in which Fortuna calls calamities down upon Scipio

---

20 Vice-Chancellor Rudolph Joseph, Prince (since 1764) Colloredo-Mels and Wallsee, had welcomed the Mozarts to his palace during their first visit to Vienna. His son, Hieronymus, may have seen Wolfgang on at least two prior occasions (in Salzburg and Rome; see pp. 226 and 280).
21 Colloredo had become an adherent of Jansenism, an anti-Jesuitical reformed Catholicism teaching the ascendancy of national churches and monarchs (*Staatskirchentum*), over the Holy See, a movement he first encountered at the Collegium Germanicum in Rome.

and he, in turn, describes the din she has raised in the heavens; here Mozart provided only pedestrian accompagnato. Moreover, the work's modest frame bears with difficulty the weight of da capo arias. But there are Mozartean felicities: the brief but grandiose Handelian chorus of shades, Publius's eloquent "*Quercia annosa,*" and Costanza's spectacular "*Biancheggia in mar.*" Her heroic manner presaging Fiordiligi's, she warms to the Metastasian image: battered by the ocean, the rock, though for a while submerged, survives the waves, the waters, grown calm, then lapping its feet.

If the Residenz did present *Sagno,* it took the form of a cantata, that is, an unstaged performance in a revised and cut version as part of the festivities following the new Prince-Archbishop's official entry into the capital and his enthronement (29 April). At all events, he looked with favor upon the boy and in August would grant him a modest salary to accompany his title of *Konzertmeister,* even though the Mozarts could give no clear indication of just when he might assume regular duties and establish a firm foothold on the ground of Salzburg's musical life. Its reform and reorganization figured among Colloredo's earliest projects, and the symbolic salary enunciated his assumption that Mozart would soon play a vital and consistent role at the palace and the cathedral.

An almost inhuman schedule lay before him: writing both the first opera of the coming year for Milan and the second of the same carnival season for the Teatro San Benedetto in Venice. When Leopold entered into these arrangements, he had not asked himself just how his son would find his way to beget, put on paper, and rehearse two works, one right after the other and in two different cities. (Perhaps Leopold had looked upon each project as insurance against the dissolution of the other; see p. 274.) Almost half a century later, Nannerl recalled her brother's "very serious illness when he was just sixteen years old," that is, during January 1772, soon after the exertions of the second Italian journey. Did the sight of the sallow—"extremely yellow," Nannerl remembered—bedridden adolescent help lead Leopold to reality? In the end, the agreement with the San Benedetto, though the earlier, fell by the wayside, in all probability at his prompting; he dared not fail the Habsburgs.

During this second interim between Italian tours, when it became unmistakable that Archduke Ferdinand would not take Mozart into permanent employ, Leopold offered his son's services to the music publishers Breitkopf of Leipzig, advising on 7 February that he "will write any kind of work you may consider desirable, if you but let us know in time." Wolfgang began to turn out a mass of compositions in anticipation of entering the Breitkopf catalogue (the firm proved uninterested) and also to answer the needs of the coming stay in Milan and those of the Archbishop: an enthusiastic violinist, he enjoyed playing along with his orchestra, whose standards he had set about raising. As a matter of course, he would welcome additions to the repertoire.

Mozart devoted himself to the symphony; eight flowed from his pen: K. 114, 124, 128, 129, 130, 132, 133, and 134,[22] the last with an Andante whose Gluckean poetry anticipates those magical moments dotting the landscape of his maturest creations. A new spaciousness distinguishes this confident and varied suite of creations pregnant with his future achievement in the genre: the symphony as the vehicle of a personal and, at times, monumental statement. Its moods ranging from rough merriment, mockery, and wit to high-souled grandeur, the series, a consistently evolving body of work, offers a synoptic view in its juxtaposition of the Italian and German approaches to instrumental composition: on the one hand, the unfolding of either lyric cantabile or *buffa*-like melodic lines, on the other, the finely wrought interplay of thematic development.[23]

For the cathedral he wrote three church or epistle sonatas for strings and organ continuo (K. 67/41h; 68/41i; and 69/41k; see p. 359), to sound at high mass between the readings from Epistle and Gospel. As a new display piece for Nannerl and himself, he produced a rattling, knockabout sonata for four hands in D (K. 381/123a), which can be identified among the compositions Louis de Visme, a correspondent of Burney's, heard them perform in Salzburg during the summer of 1772. Nannerl had let her fingers grow stiff—Leopold had to urge her to practice—for Burney, via de Visme, reported with sarcasm: ". . . she is now at her summit, which is not marvellous."

De Visme also commented upon the poor state of the musical household Colloredo had inherited. As key to his program for its betterment, on 5 September he lightened the duties of Kapellmeister Giuseppe Francesco Lolli—over seventy and failing—by giving him a coequal colleague, Domenico Fischietti. A Neapolitan who had been active at Prague and Dresden, he carried the recommendation of Hasse and Wagenseil. Leopold took the appointment in bad part: even with his decade of prolonged absences and the consequent neglect of his responsibilities at court, he had somehow expected the prize and with it the title. To be passed over outraged him, and henceforth he and his son rarely referred to Fischietti

22 Between 1772 and 1774, by adding a closing Presto, he turned *Sogno*'s two-movement overture into a symphony (K. 161 and 163/141a).
23 The number of movements drew another line of distinction, the Italian variety having three (K. 128 and 129, for example), the German four, a minuet presenting itself before the finale. A contrapuntal flavor and a heavier component of winds also helped define the German style.

without acerbity; his preferment gave birth to the Mozarts' historic animosity toward Colloredo.

During October a cross and mortified Leopold made ready for the third
Italian journey as Wolfgang worked on the tonal plan and recitatives of the
libretto newly arrived from Milan: *Lucio Silla*. On 24 October 1772 they
departed. Their stop at Innsbruck provided an excursion eastward to lovely
Hall im Inntal (today Solbad Hall), where Wolfgang played the organ of
the convent church.[24] During an overnight stay in Bozen (which he described as a "pigsty"[25]) he started a string quartet (K. 155/134a).

If Leopold brooded over the Fischietti affair, Wolfgang happily surrendered to thoughts of home, to which a new tie drew his spirit. But three
days after their arrival in Milan (4 November) he urged Nannerl to visit a
certain young lady and give her his compliments (*"di farle un complimento da
parte mia"*).[26] Toward the end of the month he thanked his sister: "You
know for what."

At first he had little to do: he could give no concerts, for the fashionable did not return to Milan until late in December, when the Teatro
Regio Ducal opened its doors; and, once again, the composition of arias
and dramatic accompagnati had to await the arrival of the singers and an
appraisal of their vocal resources. The Mozarts, who had heard *opera buffa*
during their usual stop in Verona (Giuseppe Gazzaniga's *La locanda* and
Pietro Alessandro Guglielmi's *La sposa fedele* had been on the boards) now
whiled time away at Milanese *buffa* performances, though Wolfgang did
start to write *Silla's* overture and choruses. But soon the tempo quickened.
He had to set new dialogue to music and alter and, in places, compose
afresh secco recitatives already created in Salzburg: the librettist, Giovanni
de Gamerra, had sent his libretto to Vienna for approval, and Metastasio
had returned it with additions and changes.

By the third week of November, the *primo uomo*, the castrato Venanzio
Rauzzini, appeared; but not until late on 4 December did the prima donna,
Anna Lucia de Amicis,[27] make her way from Venice after an eight-day

---

24 This renowned *Damenstift* (a religious retreat for aristocratic women), famed for a rich musical
tradition, possessed an organ (1747–1748) built by Andreas Mitterreiter. Leopold may have
seized the opportunity to visit Hall in order to call upon Johann Michael Hochwanger, a mentor of his Augsburg student days and since 1739 the *Stift's* kapellmeister.
25 That this handsome city of the South Tyrol presented a picturesque gothic tableau—in particular, the medieval *Lauben* (vaulted arcades) repugnant to the Mozarts' taste—may explain
this extreme reaction.
26 She was probably Dr. Barisani's daughter, Maria Theresia, whom Nannerl later described as
her brother's "favorite mademoiselle."
27 The Mozarts had already met her: perhaps as she passed through Mainz in 1763, but without
doubt seven years later in Naples, when she sang in Jommelli's *Armida abbandonata* (see p. 279).

struggle through rain and mud. Though the premiere would be upon him in three weeks, Wolfgang remained calm, confident, even amused: "I still have fourteen numbers to write and then shall have finished," he wryly informed his sister.

For the moment, however, no amount of work could fill a huge hole in his score: the tenor engaged for the title role, a certain Cordoni, had fallen ill, and Mozart had to put the part aside during the search for a substitute. When he finally arrived in the person of Bassano Morgnoni, a mediocre church singer from Lodi with little experience on stage, only nine days remained before the premiere. At once Mozart realized that the part had to be both brief and a musical cipher and reduced from four to two the number of arias originally planned. Even so, he had to stay up nights to bridge the gaps.

Lucio Silla (K. 135), ambitious in scale and with three ballets,[28] would occupy six hours. The opera made challenging musical and technical demands upon the Teatro Regio Ducal, which functioned with astounding efficiency: manuscript, ink still wet, flew from the composer to the copyists as singers and instrumentalists read and rehearsed what they could and the Galliari family readied the scenery. Indeed, the curtain rose on the appointed day—26 December 1772—if not at the appointed hour.

The performance had been scheduled for one hour after the sounding of the Angelus, that is, six o'clock. But the Archduke lingered over his midday meal and left himself insufficient time to compose those personally written New Year's greetings the Empress expected to receive in Vienna. Writing did not come easily to His Highness, and for more than two hours an increasingly nervous cast and uncomfortable audience—it had assembled early and jammed every corner of the overheated opera house—awaited his arrival. Not until eight o'clock did the overture's opening Molto allegro begin its animated course; not until close upon two in the morning did the senators and the Roman populace exult in the Campidoglio over Silla's sudden transformation from fearsome tyrant into all-forgiving ruler and yield the stage to the final ballet. During the long performance, some *opera-buffa* incidents, unforeseen by librettist and composer, had jolted the progress of the stately *opera seria*.

Morgnoni overacted extravagantly, Leopold reported: "Though the prima donna expected a gesture of anger from him during her first aria, he so exaggerated this angry gesture that he appeared to want to box her ears

---

28 Sketches for one of them, an early example of Mozartean *turquerie*, survive as *Le gelosie del serraglio*, K. Anh. 109/135a. Mozart did not compose all of its dances: in several the hand of Joseph Starzer may be traced. Carlo de Picq (Pick and Le Picq) designed the choreography.

and strike her nose with his fist. He made the audience laugh. In the fervor of her singing, Signora de Amicis could not be altogether certain why the public laughed; taken aback and not knowing who was being laughed at, she did not sing well the entire evening, for jealousy, too, entered the picture: whenever the *primo uomo* [Rauzzini] came on stage, the Archduchess [Beatrice] clapped her hands, for he had arranged that the Archduchess be told that he would not be able to sing out of nervousness; thus he ensured the court's encouragement and applause—a castrato trick." On the following day, de Amicis required a personal audience of an hour with the royal couple to restore her vocal powers. Thereafter, the repetitions of *Silla* went well, twenty-six consecutive performances forcing a postponement of the season's second production, Paisiello's *Sismano nel Mongol.*[29]

4

SCHOLARLY COUNT FIRMIAN probably chose the subject of *Silla*, the third of Mozart's Milanese operas and in a sense a sequel to his first. The audience must have recognized the link, for the tyrant's adviser described him as "the proud terror of Asia, the conqueror of Pontus ... who has seen a humble Mithridates at his great feet." De Gamerra put together a deftly crafted series of dramatic confrontations: a few digressions in no way blunting its clarity of direction, the libretto progresses decisively toward the predictable finale. As in most *opere serie*, the protagonists, each an embodiment of a single *Affekt* or basic psychological motivation, move within close orbits clearly defining their issues and emotional allegiances; they remain as fixed in their paths as the "masks" of the commedia dell'arte. *Silla* involves a high-minded hero, his faithful wife, a cruel (and then suddenly magnanimous) dictator, his wicked adviser, and the inevitable confidant and confidante, members of the opposing factions whom love unites during a triumphal closing scene.

Though the libretto does not escape a certain portly and dry pretentiousness—an inherited infirmity of its species—Mozart's music imbues much of the text with youthful vigor. If, at its least felicitous, the score suffers from a monotony of texture (a disorder that too much unrelieved solo singing frequently inflicted upon *opera seria*), and if, when regurgitating the stiff formulas of Neapolitan opera, it at times fails to transcend the words and offers stretches of the commonplace, *Silla* does beguile with pages of melting cantilena spun forth with breathtaking ease. Over and above, at its most inspired, the work exhales the passion of a new age, especially in that

---

29 Mozart admired the opera, which, like *Silla*, had a text by de Gamerra.

scene in which Mozart, seizing upon the musical possibilities of a strong dramatic situation—the reunion of a husband and wife—threw himself into the sufferings of his characters and penetrated their souls.

A proscribed senator most believe dead, Cecilio returns in secret to Rome. He learns that his wife, Giunia, and her attendants gather in the underground chamber housing the tombs of her ancestors, there to decry Silla's tyranny. Cecilio hastens to surprise her in this devotion. Giunia arrives and apostrophizes her father's ghost and the husband she mourns. When he steps forth, she at first takes him for a spirit from Elysium. At last convinced that Cecilio lives, she falls into his arms.

In this first of his great operatic scenes—it invokes the stately eloquence of Gluck's *Orfeo* and *Alceste*[30]—Mozart reveals a new sense of structural development, of organic sequence: a stream of subtly inflected recitativo accompagnato gives way to a chorus punctuated by a solo lament; the expressive accompagnato then returns and shades into a blissful duet beginning with the alternating and concluding with the combined voices of the united couple, all of these elements interlinking. Mozart gives the lovers an extraordinary intensity (the chorus, too, for it has become a vital element of the action), and their humanity finds credence, a not insignificant achievement in *opera seria*. For a moment, he outstrips the genre, combining and merging loose and strict forms, a hint of the consummate craftsman to come. Further, here, as throughout *Silla*, that tonal eroticism, so often tingeing his later stage works, insinuates itself,[31] presumptive of a young man no longer portraying the passions through hearsay but, rather, drawing upon experiences that have passed beyond flirtations.

Of course, his virtuosity did not match that of the mature Handel, who had both exploited and camouflaged so many awkward conventions of *opera seria*. Mozart's *Silla* in the main offers the usual heavy-gaited parade of numbers, the finale being painfully feeble, Morgnoni's limitations no doubt in part the cause. Like many an *opera seria*, *Silla* does not end or even just stop: it collapses as the chorus tenders its platitudinous rejoicings over the tyrant's promise to mend his ways.

Silla may have pleased the Germans at the court of Milan but could hardly have set the Italians astir. Mozart had not, as in *Mitridate*, abstained from orchestral feasting, and *Silla's* most striking musical moments proved as German in concept as *Betulia's*, the moving Giunia-Cecilio encounter having the personal tone of Storm and Stress, that emotional aesthetic-political movement just beginning to shake the German soul

---

30 The example of Traetta and Jommelli also helped Mozart fabricate his *Silla.*
31 Cecilio's *"Pupille amate"* has a winning seductiveness in melodic line and tonal investiture.

(see pp. 320–27).[32] The Italians did not look upon cultural ferment as foreign, but among them it reached expression in the sober rhetoric of a Parini rather than in the emotionalism of the German brotherhood. Its importance as a center of the innovative spirit notwithstanding, the Lombard capital could not have found *Silla* to its taste. Wolfgang's resolute German aesthetic direction—it had been less conspicuous in the pastoral world of *Ascanio*—as well as Leopold's decline in Imperial favor determined *Silla's* place as the last of Mozart's Milanese operas.

To Salzburg, Leopold wrote of well-filled houses but made no reference to critical comments on the music. For certain, De Amicis (Giunia) and Rauzzini (Cecilio), more than the opera, drew the crowds. The Mozarts had long valued her refined art and virtuosity,[33] but the formidable musicianship and technique Rauzzini had developed since last they heard him (Vienna, 1767) had taken them by surprise. In gratitude to the handsome young castrato, Mozart wrote for him the brilliant motet *Exsultate, jubilate* (K. 165/158a), and he performed it during January of the new year in Milan's church of the Theatines.[34]

5

DURING REHEARSALS, WOLFGANG had found himself occupied with the seasonal reawakening of Milan's social life, this year more animated than usual, for Count Firmian had given the city over to celebrating the cardinalate of his brother, Count Leopold III Ernst, Prince-Bishop of Passau:[35] candles and torches bespangled the city's palaces; carillons sounded; trumpeters and drummers played in the streets; and in Firmian's apartments Their Royal Highnesses attended at least one of three gala concerts at which Wolfgang performed. In all likelihood the guests heard his set of three divertimentos for string quartet (K. 136/125a, 137/125b, and 138/125c); he had written them in Salzburg early in 1772 in anticipation of

---

32 Combining pathos and the eerie (much in the spirit of the painter Johann Heinrich Füssli [Fuseli], then engrossed in his Roman studies), the scene came into being at the very time of Goethe's experiments with the so-called operatic passages in his *Götz von Berlichingen.*

33 Writing to his father from Mannheim on 17 January 1778, Mozart would recall "the terrifying passages" he had created for her in *Silla.*

34 In 1774 Rauzzini went to England. Having become famous as singer, composer, teacher, and impresario, by 1787 he had settled both in Bath and at a country home in nearby Perrymead. There he entertained with grand hospitality. In 1794, one of his guests, Joseph Haydn, touched by the castrato's devotion to the memory of his dog, Turk, composed a four-part canon to a text taken from Turk's funerary monument. Rauzzini's pupil Nancy Storace had close professional and personal links to Mozart during his decade in Vienna.

35 He had succeeded Count Joseph Maria Thun-Hohenstein (see pp. 63–64).

just such Milanese gatherings. Filled with pulsating movement and orchestral in conception, they could be played by a quartet, a larger string ensemble, or be converted into symphonies by the addition of wind parts should the occasion demand a more abundant sound.

Archduke Ferdinand belonged to that exalted class that never had need to apologize or explain. He let not a word escape to the Mozarts concerning the matter of a post in his service, his relationship to them remaining friendly, if cool. Distressed, they now attempted to secure themselves against the possible loss of Ferdinand's favor by seeking an appointment at his brother's court of Tuscany. Leopold dispatched to Florence beseeching letters and the score of *Lucio Silla.* Desperation made him forget that chains of paper, no less than stands of arms, held the Habsburg world in place. Well after *Silla's* run, he lingered in Milan, awaiting word from either prince—for a moment hopes mounted with news that the matter had reached the Grand Duke's desk in the Pitti palace—and refusing to read the signs, long obvious, that the Habsburgs wanted no permanent arrangements with him. Any inclination of the Empress had its effect no less in Florence than in Milan.

For the benefit of Salzburg officialdom and its censor, Leopold justified his repeatedly postponed departure for home by reciting litanies of old and transparent excuses, detailing searing attacks of rheumatism that confined him to his room and made him dread traversing the Alps before a full recovery. He so warmed to this literary exercise that all at once he began to fear that family and friends might be taken in: using his "secret" code, based upon an obvious interchange of consonants with vowels, on 30 January 1773 he informed his wife: "So far no further reply has come from the Grand Duke in Florence. What I have written about my illness is all untrue. I was in bed for a few days, but I am now in health and am going to the opera today. However, you must spread the word that I am ill. You can cut off this small sheet [of the letter] so that it does not fall into the hands of others."[36] No doubt Leopold's childish cipher had long amused the censors; no doubt they acquainted the Archbishop with the contents of the "small sheet"; no doubt his opinion of both Mozarts continued to drop: in a note to his sister, Wolfgang appeared to lend himself to the deception.

As February slipped by, Leopold found his ability to dissimulate taxed: he had to fall back upon talk of his persisting and agonizing rheumatism until reports of deep snow in the Tyrol and impending milder weather inspired him to voice fears of "being overwhelmed by an avalanche" should

36 Perhaps Frau Mozart did not destroy it because she believed the code unbreakable; she may have permitted the complete letter to circulate among less than discreet friends.

he travel north. By the end of the month a different kind of debacle did overwhelm him: even as Milan maintained silence, word arrived from Florence. Leopold apprised his wife: "As to the affair in question, there is nothing to be done. I shall tell you everything when we meet. God intends something else for us." He remained unaware that a worldly hand—that of the Dowager German Empress—had ordained the affair.

He and Wolfgang passed through the Brenner for the last time. "I find it difficult to leave Italy," lamented the father who, like his son, would never again see this land of warmth, color, and youth. Mozart, the last of the great composers for whom the journey south seemed obligatory,[37] clung to the idea of Italy as an incurable nostalgia.

6

THE DELINQUENTS RE-ENTERED Salzburg on 13 March 1773, the eve of Archbishop Colloredo's election anniversary, a time of celebration with music. Certainly he would have dismissed them had they shown their faces even a day later.

Wolfgang must have been happy to be near his "favorite mademoiselle," and Leopold, without a new contract to brandish, yet striving to keep countenance, emerged from the wreckage talking of bold plans: perhaps another Grand Tour (the family, he warned, must put aside every available kreuzer); or perhaps one more attempt at a permanent position in Vienna. Vain fancies! Did he look upon the seventeen-year-old as a child prodigy? And that thoughts of Vienna could still feed his hopes reveals his blindness to just how wearying the disenchanted Habsburgs found his importuning; they would have continued to call upon his son as an occasional composer if only Leopold had stopped pressing for more.

Mozart lost little time seating himself at his desk: but eleven days after the arrival home, he completed K. 166/159d, a divertimento for winds commissioned by a Milanese patron (it includes clarinets and English horns, instruments the Salzburg ensemble lacked). He had composed in Milan, perhaps for the same client, the similarly scored divertimento K. 186/159b. In Salzburg he also put the seal to the last of six three-movement string quartets (K. 155/134a, 156/134b, 157–159, 160/159a) begun in Bozen and, for the most part, realized in Milan.[38] Here he no

---

37 Through the decades, Haydn's employer, Prince Nikolaus Esterházy, had evaded granting him an extended leave to fulfill his dream of going to Italy. Yet when, upon the Prince's death in 1790, he at last had the freedom to travel, he left for England.
38 Some maintain that he returned from Italy with the set complete.

longer restricted the viola and cello to providing accompaniments for the violins: the lower voices now and again offer their own melodic contributions, albeit timidly; and the second violin, also gaining independence, is no longer fated to travel forever in bondage to the first, but on occasion strikes out on its own. The contrapuntal writing shows growing ease, the various strands a keener interplay, the thematic material an increasing unity and intensity; and, throughout, he ventures audacious introspective touches in the minor.

In March he began a series of three-movement symphonies: K. 184/161a, concentrated, powerful, and charged with agitation and melancholy; the buoyant K. 199/161b, which came into being in April as did K. 162, celebrative and accentuated by trumpet flourishes; and K. 181/162b of May with its lovely oboe solo in the Andantino grazioso. The first and last of these symphonies proceed like an Italian overture, their movements (fast-slow-fast) flowing one into the other. His years of simple imitation and then of creative copying and assimilation past, he had begun consistently to transform his models into a personal idiom filled with a new poetry, subtle depths now visible beneath the accomplished surfaces.

If the symphonies provided stock for Salzburg's orchestra (as well as future tours), K. 207 of April furnished one of its violinists with a brilliant vehicle: Mozart's first surviving concerto (see p. 351). The occasional private commission did continue to come his way—the divertimento K. 205/167A of July (along with its march, K. 290/167AB), written for a celebration within the Antretter family[39]—but he concentrated upon the requirements of the Residenz and the cathedral. In June he completed a closely knit mass in honor of the Holy Trinity (K. 167), a composition for chorus and a festive orchestra reflecting Colloredo's taste for brass, here four trumpets, and kettledrums punctuating a concise setting of the text. He appears to have been placated by the industry of his young *Konzertmeister,* who, like his father, seemed to give the appearance of settling into the routine of Salzburg's musical life.

Soon after the return from Italy, Leopold had moved his family from the Getreidegasse to a spacious residence across the river: the Tanzmeisterhaus on the Hannibalplatz (today, Makartplatz). The Mozarts' financial situation had bettered: both men drew salaries, and Nannerl gave lessons. But despite his comfortable circumstances and apartment, Leopold surveyed the city and his professional surroundings with fierce contempt. He had returned from Italian sunlight to Salzburg's iron sky to bow before

---

39 Johann Ernst von Antretter, the head of the family, functioned as a district commissioner and member of the Archbishop's war cabinet.

courtiers outraged by his deceptions and fatigued by his attempts to move in worlds they considered outside his proper sphere. He saw his future as one of indignities at their hands. Time had nearly run out: time to gain at least some shadow of independence; time to flee provincial servility.

The Archbishop himself opened a way for the Mozarts to travel again. He had decided to visit the Imperial family in Vienna and his ailing father in nearby Sierndorf. Unaware of duplicity, he fell in with the Mozarts' request to make a simultaneous excursion to Vienna; the circumstances could not have been more opportune, as more than one Salzburger remarked.

On 14 July 1773 father and son departed and within two days had installed themselves in the house of the coppersmith Gottlieb Friedrich Fischer, on the Tiefer Graben. "Fools are fools, wherever they are!" wrote Leopold, piqued by a rumor flying through Salzburg; this latest trip, it was said, had to do with Wolfgang's candidacy for an important Viennese post soon to be vacant: Hofkapellmeister Florian Gassmann lay near death. The gossip hit the mark, and Leopold and Wolfgang feared being unmasked. When Anna Maria and Nannerl wrote, begging to join them, the response discouraged the idea, not only on grounds of expense: the gathering of the entire family in Vienna would fuel the chatter.

Leopold's letters home became little more than tattle about acquaintances: their marriages, their inheritances, their indiscretions. He could report no court chitchat, no concerts in Viennese palaces, though he did invoke the name of Maria Theresa: "Her Majesty the Empress was very gracious to us, but that was all. . . ." They had at last secured audience on 5 August, probably at Laxenburg, that favorite Habsburg hunting lodge in the game-rich Danube plain and linked to Schönbrunn by avenues of horse chestnut trees. She could not have been unaware of the motives that had brought the Mozarts from Salzburg; on her guard, she let fall not a word of encouragement.[40] Though doubtless Wolfgang performed, Leopold recorded only the awkwardness of the encounter: at last he recognized the grimace beneath her consummate courtesy. At best he might hope that she remain aloof from the reorganization of the Hofburg's musical forces inevitable upon Gassmann's death; for certain, she would not help provide the funds the Mozarts needed as they awaited the possibilities it would open up: immediate opportunities had to be sought elsewhere.

Father and son had signaled their presence in Vienna by strolling on the Bastei, the wall encircling the inner city and serving as a popular promenade; the nobility continued indifferent. True, many had left for the summer, but

---

40 Her steward had to have informed Archbishop Colloredo's household of the Mozarts' visit.

even so, excepting Laxenburg, Wolfgang did not perform at any of the many nearby country seats. Even his powers of self-deception at an end, Leopold had to confront the truth: his son's days as a virtuoso prodigy had run out. Leopold's willingness to dine with Porta—that onetime and distrusted servant had again crossed his path—bespoke many open hours on the Mozarts' calendar. They would have received little attention had not old allies opened their doors: fellow artists like Noverre, *Hofcomponist* Joseph Bonno,[41] and Marianne Martinez (see X, n. 3); good bourgeois like the Mesmers and the Imperial Paymaster, Johann Adam Mayr; and admirers among the clergy. Perhaps during an evening with such friends, Wolfgang improvised his exquisite six variations for keyboard (K. 180/173c) on a theme from *La fiera di Venezia*, an opera by Antonio Salieri, and at the moment on the boards in Vienna.

Mesmer had transformed his home by adding a park with statuary, an aviary, and a theater. In these charming surroundings, Wolfgang took part in a concert (18 August) that may have included the Antretter divertimento. He and Leopold also visited Mesmer at his country house near Schwechat and made an excursion to the watering place of Baden.

On Saint Cajetan's Day (7 August), they called at the Theatine fathers[42] in their monastery near the Hohe Brücke. Wolfgang entertained them with music, even, so Leopold wrote home, having "the impudence to [borrow a violin from a Herr Teyber and] play a violin concerto." (To his father's dismay, he no longer practiced the instrument.) If the Theatines enjoyed his talent *en famille*, the Jesuits invited him to step before the public. The following day in the Order's church am Hof, Leopold conducted his son's Pater Dominicus Mass. A great success,the performance may well have been the Jesuits' last festive event in their famed gothic edifice, remodeled more than a century before into one of the glories of the early Viennese Baroque.

"Now it is all over with the poor Jesuits!" Leopold exclaimed on 4 September. Pope Clement XIV had dissolved the Order on 21 July. But pontifical acts remained without effect until promulgated by the civil authority, and the Habsburgs refused to publish the Brief of Suppression; Rome, they insisted, had first to recognize their right to confiscate for their own purposes and convert into state property those Jesuit institutions and rev-

---

41 A Viennese of Italian descent with a decade of study and work in Naples, Bonno had become *Hofcomponist* in 1739.

42 The Theatines had come into being in 1524, through the labors of Cajetan (Gaetano) of Thiene, one day to be a saint, and Giovanni Pietro Caraffa, later Pope Paul IV but, at the time, Bishop of Theate (*Chieti*). His episocopal identification—Theatensis—gave the Order its name.

enues in their lands. Rome yielded. "By the sixteenth of this month [September]," Leopold wrote, "the Jesuits' monastery auf dem Hof must be cleared out. Their church treasure, their wine cellars—in short, all their property—have already been placed under seal." He mused "that the Jesuits would have been left in peace had they been as poor as the poor Capuchins, for in Rome they have already begun to appropriate their [the Jesuits'] property *ad pias causas*, an easy business, for even if the Pope helps himself, the matter is still *ad pias causas*."[43]

Maria Theresa and Kaunitz had won the diplomatic victory that wrenched the plunder from the Pope's hands. She, however, became appalled when faithful Kaunitz deserted her side to support her son's design to wrest spoils from a helpless Poland, "to extort," in her words, "advantages from the conflict between Russia and the Porte [Constantinople] and to extend our frontiers and secure gains we never dreamed of before this war. [Events in Poland had drawn Turkey into war with Russia in 1768, the French persuading the Turks to attack.] We have been behaving like Prussians while seeking at the same time to preserve the appearance of honesty. . . ."

Watching Empress Catherine proceed toward her goal of making the north shore of the Black Sea her own by absorbing the territory of a Turkey pitiably unprepared for combat, Joseph of Austria and Frederick of Prussia had long feared the political balance of power compromised. It might best be adjusted, they had concluded, were Vienna and Berlin—and St. Petersburg, too—to dismember Poland, each annexing whole stretches of it.[44] Despite Maria Theresa's lament over her son's "fishing for advantage in this whirlpool"—"She is always weeping, but always annexing" (*qui prenait en pleurant*), Frederick scoffed—each brigand nation's share of the booty had been mutually agreed upon in treaties framed during 1772: the first partition of Poland, Vienna's negotiations with Frederick resting in

---

43 Prince Kaunitz urged the quondam members of the Society to remain and put to use in orphanages, schools, and universities their talents as educators. Among his acquaintances Mozart numbered several Jesuits who had adjusted to new ways, among them Abbé Bullinger, who taught in Salzburg (see XVIII, n. 36), and his colleague Pater Philipp Gerbl, to whom fell the post of kapellmeister at Augsburg cathedral. However, many of the Fathers became drifters even in Habsburg territories, where, if unemployed, they might claim a modest compensatory pension.

44 Catherine had contemplated devouring Poland when she made one of her lovers its king (see pp. 159 and 211). Her ultimate aim was to swallow Turkey as well and place her second grandson, Constantine, on the throne in Constantinople as tsar of a new Russian Eastern Empire. Frederick of Prussia observed the Russo-Turkish encounters with sardonic amusement: they seemed to him like "a set of the purblind . . . constantly beating a set of the altogether blind. . . ." For the entanglement of Mozart's *Abduction* in the meshes of these political complexities, see p. 592.

the hands of its ambassador, Gottfried van Swieten, in the next decade to be one of Mozart's most helful patrons. Emperor Joseph looked upon his prizes, the greater part of Galicia and its neighboring principality of Lodomeria, as replacements for lost Silesia. During September 1773, when his capital believed him on a protracted visit to these newly acquired kingdoms, he startled the Viennese by reappearing without notice in their midst. Leopold Mozart associated this unexpected return with information passed on to him by, among others, his wife: the Turks, a false rumor ran, had turned the tide and would force the Russians to withdraw, Prussia then taking over their share of Polish White Russia. The Viennese— and the visiting Mozarts—reveled in these tales of the sordid struggle in the marshes of the Berezina and the Bug.

Speculating upon the dangerous political developments to the east— Wolfgang even injected a reference to Constantinople ("known to all") in nonsense verse he sent home—and observing with compassion the Jesuits' attempts to adapt to parochial or secular ways, the Mozarts tarried in Vienna until the third week of September. (Before returning to Salzburg, Archbishop Colloredo had given them permission to extend their leave; had he already begun to hope they might never return?) They shivered in summer clothing as the weather turned cool, and Leopold's waistline again thickened on Viennese cooking even as his purse grew thinner. He waited but dared not commit his expectations to paper: "The reason why I *must* remain here so long will be communicated at the proper time and will be found sound by everyone." The reason, which grew less valid as September advanced, melted away as Herr Gassmann's health returned.

Leopold had hoped to travel home by a new route: southwest to the pilgrimage church of Mariazell and then westward to the Abersee, where he wished to show his son the birthplace of his mother and the chapel "of his patron saint." In the end they again drove by way of Linz and greeted the Hannibalplatz on 26 September. In Vienna, Gassmann continued what appeared a substantial recovery. (He would die some four months later, 20 January 1774, his post of *Hofkapellmeister* falling to Bonno, Gassmann's protégé, Salieri,[45] receiving Bonno's former title of kapellmeister as well as the rank of conductor at the Burgtheater.) A disconcerted Leopold cried out: "Things will and must change."

---

45 Five and a half years Mozart's senior, the Legnago-born Salieri had studied in Venice. There he met Gassmann (1766), who took him to Vienna to complete his education. Within four years he appeared before the Burgtheater's public as an opera composer. He became part of Gluck's circle.

7

IN A BRIEF note from Vienna, Wolfgang had professed idleness, claiming to have "nothing to do," indeed, to be "going about the room like a
dog with fleas." But the frustrating sojourn had, in fact, been productive:
at the bridge of July and August he had completed a second commission
from the Antretters: the serenade K. 185/167a (and its march, K.
189/167b), perhaps begun at home and carried to Vienna. (Dispatched to
the Antretters, it had its premiere before the end of August in Salzburg
with Meissner conducting, Brunetti in all likelihood executing the violin
solos that embellish three of the movements and give them a concerto-like
texture.[46]) Most important, he had come back to Salzburg with a sheaf of
string quartets (K. 168–173) written from mid-July to late September.

He had studied Joseph Haydn's opus 17 of 1771 and opus 20 of the following year, each of these epochal series comprising six string quartets.
The intensity of expression in both sets reflected the so-called romantic or
Storm and Stress crisis coloring Haydn's recent symphonies. Opus 20,
however, brought into play not only their compelling dramatic effects but
also an innovation in Haydn's works: the pointed exploitation of the contrapuntal devices dear to an earlier generation.

Haydn's twelve latest quartets became Mozart's inspiration for his six of
1773.[47] He adopted the four-movement sequence favored by the senior
composer, on occasion appropriated his idiosyncrasies of phrase and
melody, and confronted the complexities of the older style in order to
achieve a similar "learned" texture. Since, for example, Haydn had given
three of the opus 20 quartets fugal finales, Mozart attempted the same
scholarly approach in the closing movements of K. 168 and 173. But
though he diligently cut and sewed the venerable costume, he used too
much buckram, decking them out with counterpoint more stiff and
dogged than inspired. His Viennese quartets lack Haydn's wit (a capacity
persisting even in the face of his ardor and darker moods). Above all, they
suffer from problems born of contradictory impulses: not only a dispro-
portion between a fully developed artistic ambition and a yet developing
technique but also an incompatibility—one he would in time reconcile to
the full—between the display of personal feelings and an impersonal self-
imposed polyphonic stringency. (Intricate syntax presupposes devices of
subordination he had not yet postulated.) But if the turbulent fullness of

---

46 Mozart made a symphony out of four of the serenade's eight movements.
47 They betray other influences, among them earlier Haydn quartets and works by Gassmann,
   Bonno, Vanhall, Gluck, and Handel.

the Italian quartets is lacking in the Viennese, they do at moments wear his own special hues of sentiment and melodic charm; and they did serve as proving ground for his development as a contrapuntist.

They must have come into existence at Leopold's bidding, the father wishing to throw him into direct rivalry with the master the Empress praised and rewarded at Esterháza even as Mozart brought his cycle to a close in Vienna.[48] Whatever the reason—perhaps his own fiercely competitive spirit and delight in battle as well as Leopold's high aspirations— he had, as in the matter of *La finta semplice*, striven beyond his limits. Still in his future—indeed, still in Haydn's—lay sovereign mastery of what posterity would call classical counterpoint, that superb art of ever-shifting precedence in which thematic material moves from one voice part to another, melodic phrases subsiding into accompaniments only to bloom again as melody, the entire organism of voice parts always alive with change and potential.

If his new quartets but hinted at the future, Wolfgang had closed the Viennese visit by beginning a prognosticative work. In all likelihood, Franz Reinhard Heufeld, the administrator of German drama at Vienna's Kärnt- nertortheater and a member of Mesmer's circle, arranged that he write choral pieces and possibly entr'actes for *Thamos, König in Ägypten*, a "heroic drama" by Tobias Philipp von Gebler. "Wolfgang is composing something most enthusiastically," Leopold had observed in Vienna on 18 September, the "something" the *Thamos* score, K. 345/336a, completed in Salzburg late in 1773, perhaps in time for performances of the play at Pressburg on 11 December and at Vienna's Kärntnertortheater during the following April. In all probability, Salzburg first heard the score when Karl Wahr's troupe gave *Thamos* in the course of its 1775–1776 season in the archbishopric. Mozart would take up this music twice again (1777 and 1779), revising and expanding it (see p. 489). Though the entr'acte pieces have an incisive concision recalling Gluck's *Don Juan*—commentators now tend to look upon them as products of the first reshaping of the score—the opening choral hymn, even the first version of 1773, reveals a Mozart hurrying on in advance of himself to enter that tonal cosmos over which Sarastro would one day rule, a universe no less prefigured in the first entr'acte by sustained chords set between strong upbeats and spacious rests.

A mason who in 1785 would be Mozart's "venerable" in the movement, von Gebler conceived his *Thamos* as a Masonic allegory. The play derived

---

48 During her fabled journey to Esterháza (September 1773), Maria Theresa heard Haydn's *L'in- fedeltà delusa*, his *Philemon und Baucis* (the last played by the marionette troupe) and, in the ex- quisite Chinese pavilion, his "Maria Theresa" symphony (No. 48).

from *Sethos* by Abbé Jean Terrasson, the French novel that would also contribute to the plot of *The Magic Flute*.[49] *Sethos*, which had appeared in 1731 (a German translation came out in 1777–1778), told of the education of an Egyptian prince, his initiation into the ancient mysteries, and his travels. *Thamos*, too, dealt with a prince entering a cult guarding those same secret rites Freemasons claimed as their heritage. As observed, the musical idiom Mozart devised in 1773 to represent the Isiac mysteries' noble moral and social principles would return in *The Magic Flute*: the years would refine, but not in essence change, his first musical correlative to Illumination, a musical image derived from the conflict between darkness and light depicted in von Gebler's text.[50]

Thamos, like *Sethos*, belonged to the literary genre of Fénelon's *Télémaque*, that guide to the education of a prince that Wolfgang had read during his stay in the Bolognese countryside. From childhood he had close views of the vagaries and inadequacies of those who sat on thrones, and the social virtues of rulers became one of his lasting concerns. He was to leave behind a profound tract on the subject, a parable of the initiation—or liberal education—of a prince cleansed of meaningless fears and thus made open to the workings of reason, to Enlightened ways, to the virtues of a diligently pursued benevolence,[51] to Fénelon's belief that "Kings exist for the sake of their subjects, not subjects for the sake of kings."

---

49 Masonic ritual itself owes a debt to the Abbé's novel, a hoax he pretended to have translated from the Greek. The title ran: *Sethos, histoire ou vie tirée des monuments, anecdotes de l'ancienne Égypte . . . traduit d'un manuscrit grec.*

50 Mozart had already shown curiosity about the mysteries and set to music two Masonic poems: in 1768 Johann Peter Uz's "*An die Freude*" (K. 53/47e; see p. 244) and, about four years later, Ludwig Friedrich Lenz's "*O heiliges Band*" (K. 148/125h). Since adolescence he had kept frequent company with Masons.

51 There can be no doubt that Mozart had a direct and strong hand in shaping the libretto of *The Magic Flute* (see pp. 724–25).

CHAPTER XVII

An Attempt to Breathe Freely; Munich

WITHIN A YEAR of his return to Salzburg, Mozart composed two
symphonies of remarkable emotional power: K. 183/173dB in G
minor (October 1773) and K. 201/186a in A (April 1774). Critics of the
past have related them to the Storm and Stress movement, an argument
underrated today, but one that still reaps benefits if its subjective nature
remains clear and present. True, the adjectives the Mozart literature has
loaded upon these symphonies might be applied with propriety to those
of the preceding spring, but—and most important—to a less compelling degree: the later works speak a language of heightened turmoil and
tenderness.

With Mozart's continuing residence in Salzburg, the paramount source
documenting his life, the family letters, dries up: gaps open in the narrative. The works, however, continue, and, though the pitfall-scarred path
joining the qualities of a work of art to puzzles in its creator's biography
must be tread with caution, here the effort seems worth the dangers. The
course of exploration will range through consideration of the position
Mozart had reached in his profession, speculation about his state of mind
and spirit following the retreat from Vienna, examination of the Storm
and Stress movement, and theorizing upon his relationship to it with the
new symphonies as a focus.

2

HIS DEVELOPMENT AS a composer had been in no way meteoric, but gradual and consistent: he seldom demonstrated immediate mastery of the untried; nothing had burst forth full grown. If Schubert found his way almost at once, writing *Gretchen am Spinnrade* at seventeen, Mozart at the same age still labored to assemble a style. Though drawing upon the concepts of others, he put into his service only elements suitable to his purpose; absorbed and distilled into his own substance, the patterns and prototypes he borrowed and assimilated then merged and in the process reappeared transformed and fresh, a development evident during his final visit to Milan; and with his recent stay in Vienna he had taken more complete hold of a technique the quartets had helped forge, a strengthened artistic will gaining confidence as it imposed order. What he produced upon his return to Salzburg showed itself above measure persuasive. He had entered upon his musical maturity: his compositions now belonged to him.

At moments their hitherto untroubled surfaces had begun to be ruffled by melancholy turns of phrase, and, much in the same spirit, a disquiet, all at once unbound, now agitated a personality until this time able to keep an iron check upon it. A disillusioned young man, converted to and sharing his father's distress, found it difficult to breathe in Salzburg's narrow artistic and social byways and looked back wistfully upon his days abroad. He indulged a continuing and painful effort to recover his past, to regain that delicious deferential respect he had once received, even from the mighty; an exorbitant and unrealistic hope: he now labored in an unfamiliar and embittering professional atmosphere.

The Habsburgs' choice of Bonno as Gassmann's successor, along with Salieri's growing prominence in Vienna, had forced Mozart into regular musical service at home: he could no longer look upon Salzburg as just a stopping-place. His duties, though far from arduous, included turning out *galant* pieces upon demand, the kind of bloodless routine his father had striven to spare him and for which his glamorous childhood had offered little psychological preparation. At times he must have felt the need to stand aloof and compose for himself or some imagined audience beyond Salzburg's gates, a perplexing estrangement for a court musician of the time; when in this mood, he wrote in the emotional vein associated with Storm and Stress, whose heady currents saturated the German world. Before discussing his contribution to this movement, its relationship to the wider area of European thought should be touched upon.

3

BY THE MIDDLE of the century—the time of Rousseau's *Discourse on the Arts and Sciences*—the engaging simplicities of rationalism's regulated and impersonal planning no longer sufficed: youth had become disillusioned with the dry mechanics of the philosophes, displeased with the fine-grained veneer of optimism they glued over a rotting core. In Germany an assemblage of forces impelled the rising generation to seek new potentialities and enthusiasms: an admiration, shared by Mozart, of Shakespeare's freely constructed dramas[1] and with it a rejection of French classicism; a related taste, which Mozart would applaud, for the informal English garden (see p. 568), whose fuzzy willows, serpentine paths, and meandering streams refuted Lenôtre's strict Gallic aesthetic of clipped shrubs, balanced walks, and symmetrical waterways; a reborn and concomitant appreciation of the picturesque qualities of the Gothic[2] along with a delight in ruins, inclinations Mozart came to share during his Vienna years; and an idealizing reverence for the ruggedness of the ancients, the Greeks in particular (yet another disposition toward the remote, in spirit consonant with that taste for the trumped-up ancestral and the pasteboard medieval—after all, Werther rejoiced in the robust athleticism of Homer as well as in the counterfeit lamentations of Ossian[3]). The Hellenic ideal became a particularly German obsession, a banner Mozart paraded in *Idomeneo* and a symbol of a dawning German nationalism. It, in turn, somehow appropriated both the Gothic and the Attic as its private heritage and gibed at the French, whose language, music, and sense of self Mozart could never endure. Above all, Storm and Stress showed zealous disdain for hierarchical values and bourgeois standards of courtship, the resounding cries for free love reaching their extreme in the *libertà* Mozart's Don

---

1 At times Mozart found harmony of proportion lacking in Shakespeare: "Were the ghost's speech in *Hamlet* not so long, it would have better effect." He became acquainted with Shakespeare at the theater and through Wieland's eight-volume prose translation of 1763–1766.
2 Even Metastasio had a fleeting infatuation with the fashion (for his *Ruggiero*, see p. 297).
3 On the Continent, not only the Germans appreciated these epic verses by James Macphersen, who had passed them off as his translations of a third-century Gaelic bard named Ossian, a figure he had, in fact, invented: Girodet's famous painting of 1801, destined for Malmaison, shows a classically robed Ossian receiving France's fallen generals in his cloud palace; Napoleon, who read Ossian in Italian translation, ranked him higher than Homer. The rhapsodic welcome the Continent gave the impostrous Ossian touched Mozart directly: he began to set what he called "a bardic song" (K. Anh. 25/386d). Celebrating the relief of the British garrison at Gibraltar by Admiral Richard Howe, it came from the pen of Johann Nepomuk Michael Denis, the translator of Ossian into German (1768). Mozart's composition remained a fragment, its progress arrested because, as he put it, his "fine ears" could not tolerate Denis's "pompous, extravagant" verbiage; it bore the influence of Macphersen's fraud.

Giovanni extolls: "Tomorrow morning my list will be longer by ten." Such passions helped carry a generation of young Germans away from rationalism and toward the introspective and subversive ideals of Storm and Stress.

An epochal spiritual revolt of warm emotion against cold intellect, the movement, even so, became more than an extension and intensification of *Empfindsamkeit*: Storm and Stress invoked perceptions concerning man's relation to society's constraints—insights comprehending language, culture, and custom. While *Empfindsamkeit* had appeared in divers strengths, modulations, and gradations as an expressive coloring within divers artistic currents, Storm and Stress, at its most aggressive, stood forth as an individualistic and antirationalistic phenomenon, often explosive and with a strong infusion of the political.

The intimidating and asphyxiating atmosphere of the typical petty German court—a stuffy, threadbare, anti-intellectual "little Versailles" such as the Salzburg of Mozart's day—outraged young bourgeois Germans. But lacking even the dream of achieving power—a dream that would become reality for young Frenchmen—and detesting their own middle-class world as much as the aristocratic world, which, in any case, remained closed to them, they turned in upon themselves to create those subjective concepts of inner freedom and power, that intuitive and, at times, even pathological mode of thinking called Storm and Stress. If young Frenchmen had revolutionary dreams, young Germans indulged in passionate fantasies. They had to ignore the hopeless reality of a homeland politically fractured and economically stagnating.

Mozart became one of these restive German youths; though playing no direct part in the literary and scholarly currents streaming around him, he proved susceptible to their flow. Pursuing the high social and financial position he felt just payment for his talent, from the beginning of his career he refused the place the society of his time most often allotted the accomplished musician—that of elevated domestic. Here lay the origin of much of his celebrated arrogance. Haydn submitted to constraints Mozart, and then Beethoven, loosened.

Storm and Stress took its name from *Der Wirrwarr* [The Whirligig] *oder Sturm und Drang* (1776), a drama by Friedrich Maximilian Klinger (von Klinger four years later).[4] Tall, lean, and handsome—rumor ran that he sustained his debaucheries by eating raw meat—this policeman's son, whom the poet Heinse called "the lion, the king of beasts," became the spokesman of lively young Germans like Goethe who, under Herder's

---

4 Today, its inchoate, delirious dialogue inspires embarrassment.

influence, had made a start at modernism by studying Rousseau. Klinger wrote: "The young man who has no guide should choose this one [Rousseau]. He will certainly lead him through life's labyrinth and equip him with power to endure the struggle with fate and with mortals." Goethe's friend and "shadow," Jakob Reinhold Lenz, wished to set up statues of Rousseau and Shakespeare side by side, and, had he lived longer, Mozart might have completed monuments to both: his version of *Le devin* continues to give it fitful life, and in his closing days he very likely held in reserve the idea of composing a *Tempest.*

Protesting against everything they regarded as hypocritical in German life, the *Stürmer und Dränger,* rebellious children of rationalism, heaped contempt upon the parent who had formed and nourished them: negating their legacy, they exalted the inexplicable, the metaphysical, the intuitive. Rousseau had disparaged wisdom gained from books, cautioning against the man of letters, of all men "the most sedentary, the most unhealthy, the most reflective, and therefore the most unhappy." Johann Georg Hamann of Königsberg, *"der Magus im Norden* (the Magician of the North),"⁵ whose sibylline utterances fired young Germany, hailed instinct as the truest teacher. "Think less and live more," he advised. Madame de Staël recognized the correspondence between such irrationalism and the German spirit. Its disposition to surrender the mind to the senses helped shape the two morally deformed but stupendous heroes who in Germany became twin symbols of the age: Goethe's Faust and Mozart's Don Giovanni.

If Faust balanced arrogance, unscrupulousness, and contempt for law with a poetic search for universal knowledge and experience, indeed, for the secrets of the cosmos—a profound and meditative quest that permitted Germans to look upon him as an ideal prototype—Mozart's Don Giovanni knew no such counterpoise: in him unchecked self-indulgence had spread to infect every fiber, his search, at all points strange to any examination of his own nature or ends, becoming a cynic's exclusive pursuit of uninterrupted sensual gratification. Despite his courage and charm, Don Giovanni, governed by Faust's most unhealthy tendencies as led to their ultimate point, suggested just where Rousseau's most extravagant disciples might lead his retreat from the institutions of civilization. (Mozart found antidotes to Don Giovanni's egoistic, provoking force in the persiflage and dialectic paradoxes of *Così fan tutte* and in the idealism of *The Magic Flute.*) Much like Faust turning from his scholarly tomes to embrace magic, German youth, too often inclined to confuse the dark with the deep, cast ra-

5 The oracular and mystic in his writings as well as his birth in Königsberg inspired Friedrich Karl von Moser to bestow this sobriquet.

tionalism aside: the *Stürmer und Dränger* took up Rousseau's challenge to his century and toppled the widespread, assuaging assumptions proclaiming the promise of unilinear, unending material and human progress, of well-being, and of the coming empire of virtue—the very ramparts of the *Aufklärung*. The young had come to look upon the alienated self as alone providing truth: they struggled not to better themselves, the utilitarian goal of the Enlightenment, but to realize their singularity.

Even so, Rousseau's inner self revealed a moralist in great degree concerned, like one of Faust's souls, with man, his potentialities, his responsibilities. D'Alembert recognized Rousseau's philosophy as proceeding not from his head but from his heart. (Goethe's mutilated Götz lamented: "They [his enemies] have left me only the poorest part of my being—my head. . . .") Yet, paradoxically, Rousseau gave voice to his passionate concern about the social inequalities of his age in rigorous prose of a cold, white fury and irresistible logic. He reflected upon the disparity of wealth and, the year of Mozart's birth, deplored the plight of "unhappy peoples groaning under an iron yoke, mankind crushed by a handful of oppressors, a famished crowd vanquished by sorrow and hunger—a multitude whose blood and tears the rich drink peacefully, and everywhere the mighty armed against the weak by the formidable power of the law."

In contrast, the attitude of the urbane, elite philosophe toward the masses resembled that of an aloof, cautious philanthropist. Moving with ease through the salons of despotic princes, he framed reforms meant to perfect a society in much of which he took immense pleasure. For his part, Rousseau viewed this society as soulless and monstrous and prescribed for it a drastic cure: the complete undoing of what he held to be its corrupting institutions, the abnegation of those conveniences, amenities, vanities, and over-refinements in whose pursuit man—ever more dependent upon them—renounced virtue. To Rousseau, Voltaire's seignorial manner and delight in luxury seemed an ultimate corruption worked by a pernicious, exhausted system. Society, Rousseau believed, had to be refounded to provide fewer temptations to such weaknesses. He saw mankind propelled by a greed consuming its natural innocence. His hopes fastened upon the possibility of regeneration, and over them hovered the concept of a present fallen from the heights upon which a nobler past had once stood. As the careers of Winckelmann, Piranesi, and Robert Adam bore witness, Storm and Stress proved to be a period of intense archaeological studies.

With its assaults upon privilege, its vision of a free society, and its desire to wipe out the present and start again, Storm and Stress had revolutionary implications that changed the thinking of a vital and courageous generation. The familiar, prejudiced, and unfair view of it discloses only the foolish, the reckless, and the maladjusted, the last typified by Goethe's Werther, forever in a state of crisis, wandering in a labyrinth of feeling, and torn by tensions and contradictions. However, many caught up in the ferment of the time remained at the helm of their emotions and intellect, even as they contemplated their own personalities and promise with obsessive fascination.

In his early twenties, a roguish Mozart analyzed himself in terms of extremes, using the fluctuations of his handwriting as the basis of a parallel: "... I can write as I wish; in a hand that is fine or unruly [*wild*], straight or crooked. Recently I was in poor humor; I therefore wrote in a fine, straight, and serious hand. Today I am in high spirits; I therefore am writing in an unruly, crooked, and happy hand. It comes down to what you prefer; you must choose between the two [extremes], for I have nothing between: fine or unruly, straight or crooked, serious or happy. ..." In the spirit of Storm and Stress Mozart equated the irregular with felicity.

An almost pathological *Weltschmerz* did seize someone like Goethe's acquaintance Plessing, a true neurotic tormented by hypochondriacal spells and depressions. And, in addition to such unbalanced personalities, Storm and Stress numbered young men who simply postured; there was much playacting: think of those unbridled male friendships with their wild oaths and rhetoric, tears and embraces, quick quarrels and effusive reconciliations, and toasting and drinking with volleys of crashing glasses, all of these exercises punctuated with histrionic sighs for ladies who had proved unaccommodating. The mature Mozart made marvelous fun of such behavior in *Così*. He knew the patterns well.

His own aggressive conceit as a youth had in part derived from his and his compeers' need to assert their individuality and animal spirits in the face of their seniors. (*Così*'s delicious reversal of roles in the war between youth and age, the four young lovers upholding the middle-class values the mature Don Alfonso refutes, in essence celebrated a Mozartean love of paradox.) The Stolberg brothers (Counts Christian and Friedrich Leopold zu Stolberg-Stolberg) set the bourgeois by the ears when in public they stripped off their Werther costumes of blue tailcoats, top boots, and buff waistcoats and breeches to plunge naked into lakes and streams. In the same manner, the young Goethe did not hold himself above playing the part of his own untamed Götz von Berlichingen: during his first months in Weimar he wildly proclaimed his freedom from his father's house by bellowing scandalous oaths in the ducal dining room—though Goethe revealed himself a profound student of scatology, here Mozart surpassed him[6]—and by galloping through the town, terrifying the inhabitants with the cracking of his large hunting whip. Jung-Stilling described the poet in Elberfeld: "He dances around the table, makes faces, and conducts himself in so odd and childish a manner that people in Elberfeld doubt whether he is quite sane," a description startlingly similar to the shocked Leopold Mozart's of his son's behavior at the sober court of Hohenaltheim: ". . . you [Wolfgang] entertained with a thousand jests, took up a violin, and danced about as you played, whereupon people took your measure . . . as a merry, high-spirited, mad fellow." On more than one occasion, Leopold remonstrated against what he held to be Wolfgang's unseemly tomfoolery.

In this world of pranks and poses, "genius" turned into a word tossed about to describe any young man who languished or pranced and then set down his thoughts in agitated cadences. For the *Stürmer und Dränger,* genius too often became synonymous with a forced originality. In Weimar, Goethe dismissed the clavier playing of Ernst Wilhelm Wolf as not "original." With reference to the poet's antics in the capital, Wolf struck back: ". . . since Goethe's arrival everything has become original with us."

When considering the broad and complicated phenomenon of Storm and Stress with its multifarious and contrary elements ranging from sophomoric to profound, it serves to bear in mind that here the irrational and the rational interpenetrated, that not a few of the pranksters had their serious sides: less exalted examples than Goethe and Mozart, the madcap brothers Stolberg achieved reputations as distinguished translators from the Greek. Moreover, what appears incongruous or naïve at the distance of two centuries may at the time have shown a different complexion, as, for instance, those mysterious secret societies that took vigorous rise in Germany during the period of Storm and Stress: with the aid of arcane texts and exotic props men approached Enlightened ideas through the emotions rather than the intellect and, like Mozart's Prince Tamino, first felt what they only later named.

Ceremonial manuals and formalities inspirited the initiates (though such ritual could offend the staunchly canonical: Joseph Haydn, drawn to Freemasonry's "humanitarian and wise principles"—and probably prodded by Mozart to join the fraternity—underwent induction, never to return to a second meeting). Truly earnest young poets figured in those who consecrated the Göttinger *Dichterbund* in September 1772 by dancing hand in hand around an oak while calling upon the moon and stars to witness their

---

6 They, in fact, practiced this minor art relatively seldom, the brilliant exceptions, however, establishing for both a particular renown.

union; the rite affirmed respect for their Fatherland's past and belief in virtue, freedom, and friendship.

Thus neither the occasional foolishness of the scholarly Counts Stolberg nor the lachrymose sufferings of the debilitated but often astute Werther of necessity characterized *in toto* the *Stürmer und Dränger* and their multi-faceted creations. The tenor of Johann Adam Hiller's comments upon the new musical style of the time, with its "strange mixture of the serious and the comical, the sublime and the lowly," might have been written about many a score by Joseph Haydn—"next to a serious thought you will find a cheerful one, as in Shakespeare's tragedies," he observed—or apply equally well to *Götz von Berlichingen*, the vigorous and often coarse revolutionary masterpiece of 1773 that made Goethe the spiritual leader of young Germans. The uncouth Götz pursues magnanimous, lofty ideals in opposition to society and its laws, here symbols of injustice, oppression, and baseness. (The cries punctuating the dinner scene of the drama's third act sound again in the ballroom of Mozart's *Don Giovanni*: "Long live liberty.")[7] In contrast with the overall roughness of *Götz*, Goethe's voice in his imposing hymn to rebellion, *Prometheus* (1773–1774), imparts—like Gluck's in his reform operas—gravity, profundity, and decorum. Though, as disciples of Rousseau, the *Stürmer und Dränger* looked upon art as confession, their works were not inevitably distempered and whimpering or extrovert and vociferous.

Werther of 1774, a work born in crisis and written at high speed almost in a state of somnambulism, emanated from Goethe's sudden need to liberate himself from his own psychopathic tendencies. However, not its young hero's sentimental excesses stamp it as a pivotal work of Storm and Stress but, rather, his incalculable moods, his love of nature, his collision with the social order, and the fact that the poet wrought the novel with the heat of inner experience. Goethe's Prometheus expressed the essence of Storm and Stress in his question "Have you alone not done it all, you holy, glowing heart?" as did both the outburst of Goethe's imprisoned Crugantino, "What do you know of the needs of a young heart like mine?"[8] and Faust's avowal, "Feeling is everything; names are but sound and smoke obscuring the glow of heaven." Here the cries of modern heroes sounded.

Though stage works, Gluck's *Don Juan* of 1761 and Mozart's *Don Giovanni* of 1787, marked the main musical boundaries of Storm and Stress,

---

7 Goethe recast the *Götz* of 1773, a closet play, from a first version of 1771–1772. Theater audiences know the work in yet another arrangement, that of 1804; here Goethe expunged such passages as the praise of liberty; in the interim he had become a high courtier, an *Exzellenz!*

8 He is the not-so-wicked highwayman in *Claudine von Villa Bella.*

the causal qualities and abstract tonal dialectics of sonata form with its modulatory dynamics and thematic conflicts also became a distinctive expression of the movement, as did the dramatic possibilities of the Melodrama, which, combining the spoken word with orchestral accompaniment and commentary, absorbed Mozart's interest. Emotionalism, subjectivism, an outpouring of soul—these are the tendencies in *Prometheus*; in the *Urfaust*; in Benda's Melodrama *Medea*; in Haydn's string quartets of Opus 17 and 20; and in Mozart's "Little" Symphony in G minor, K. 183/173dB.[9]

4

IF ITS OPENING Allegro con brio's rhythmic tension, motivic coherence, and emphatic diction owe much to Joseph Haydn, the movement's dark agitation summons recollections of Gluck's *Don Juan*, *Orfeo*, and *Alceste* and also Mozart's own overture to *Betulia*.[10] He even weighted the Menuetto and the closing Allegro with premonitions of disaster, the assuaging Andante thus contrasting all the more with the threat and defiance dominating the rest of a symphony lifted into the realm of drama. Imbued with the spirit of Hamann[11] and rising from a vital root of identity, K. 183 advanced to the borderland of the romantic symphony, a terrain Mozart would revisit in later years.

The ease with which he could put aside one musical personality to assume another,[12] Mozart demonstrated by composing, even while at work on the G minor (October 1773), a very different kind of Symphony, K. 182/173dA in B♭, to a certainty written for the Residenz: open, Italianate, and calling to mind Christian Bach, it has no hint of the tragic. Elements

---

9 The nickname helps distinguish it from Mozart's symphony in G minor of 1788. Haydn's symphonies numbered 44–47, contemporary with the quartets, share their Storm and Stress characteristics, as do two piano concertos by Salieri (in C and B flat, 1773).

10 He must already have put this D-minor overture to use as a symphony. A taste for minor-key symphonies had brought forth the three, each in G minor, by Joseph Haydn, Christian Bach, and Vanhal. Such works, rich in rhetorical gestures, in all likelihood had ties to both the theatrical moods of Storm and Stress and the spoken drama itself. Moreover, music in the major also interacted with the contemporary stage: for example, Joseph Haydn's conversion of his incidental music for *Der Zerstreute* into his Symphony No. 60 in C, assembled by 1774. (The play was a German version of Jean François Regnard's *Le distrait* of 1697.) Compositions in a variety of humors started life with their composers eyeing the possibility of performances in both concerts and the theater: perhaps Mozart's K. 184/161a (see p. 310) and K. 318 (see p. 484).

11 Hamann's *Aesthetica in Nuce* of 1762 became Storm and Stress's treatise on beauty: "Not a lyre! Not a brush! But a shovel for my muse, to sweep the threshing floor of sacred literature!"

12 No less remarkable than his turn for blending one style with another was his ability to achieve aesthetic détente when setting diverse elements side by side: antithetical elements did not refuse his call for sociability.

of Storm and Stress returned in the Symphony in A, K. 201/186a of April 1774 (the year of *Werther*). Its breadth of expression ranges from a pride of step evoking baroque stateliness to a soulful reverie of so personal and often breathless an effluence as to have been eschewed in a work tailored for Archbishop Colloredo. No doubt with him in mind, Mozart wrote the Symphony in D (K. 202/186b) of May 1774. *Galant* in idiom, anonymous in spirit, it to some degree offsets a piecemeal effect by binding together the first and last movements through related opening motifs.

Before the end of the year he composed a postlude to this sheaf of symphonies: K. 200/189k in C of November 1774, one of the finest creations of this period bridging his youth and early manhood. The Little G minor tells its tale of cutting despair, of the despondent if impetuous side of Storm and Stress; an anguish that does not exclude resolution invests the Symphony in A; while that in C, streaked with melancholy and exquisitely finished, resolves the moods, gestures, and mannerisms of Storm and Stress into poignant, intimate memories; they reverberate with its more delicate arguments, which recall rather than celebrate the passions and embody that superb equipoise to become the essence of Mozart's art. Both the opening Allegro spiritoso and the closing Presto again suggest a cyclic device, here their insistence upon the interval of a falling fourth as a motif in common. The Andante forms the heart of the work, gossamerlike passages for muted strings seeming to portray a reverie now and again threatened by the more material winds. No less poetic are those measures of the Menuetto wherein a forest horn call interrupts the dance. Perhaps revelatory of a youthful soul emerging from perplexities, K. 200, filled with felicitous nuance, vibrates with emotions still under strict restraint.

5

IF, SINCE HIS return from Vienna, Wolfgang had written in a degree to his own taste, yet he had to keep peace at court and for the most part did so by his performances at the keyboard. The Residenz, in fact, valued them more than his compositions: Colloredo had no need to be reminded that at his disposal stood a supreme virtuoso. But the Archbishop also expected a *Konzertmeister* consistently to produce suitable music, and Wolfgang could not long postpone confronting a bitter dilemma: though Salzburg offered a field too limited for his capacities, no other city had sought his permanent services. His career had been running down: he had repeatedly missed the mark—in Milan, in Vienna, and would now in Salzburg should he delay adjusting with more zeal to the court's musical preferences. He found the situation crippling: to look at his disconsolate father was to distinguish the outlines of his own future were he to continue long in Salzburg. But even if he dreamed of mapping an independent course, where could he go and how manage? He had yet to take a step without Papa, who, moreover, clapped hands on his salary. It seemed unmistakable that successful *Stürmer und Dränger* had, like Goethe and the Stolbergs, comfortable private incomes.

With hopes turned to debts (so he claimed), his bold plans unrealized, the pragmatic Leopold did not bridle his tongue. His aversion to Wolf-gang's Storm and Stress symphonies—which either found little praise in Salzburg or did not reach performance—betrayed an aging man's fears; he now longed only for what security might yet be wrested from fate, a secu-rity put at hazard by the inclination these symphonies symbolized. They sprang, he declared, from insufficient "discrimination" (*Man wird immer heickler*), did Wolfgang "no honor," and were best "not made known. . . . When, with the years, you have grown in judgment, you will be glad no one has them, though they pleased you at the time you created them."

Leopold wrote these words on 24 September 1778, close upon Mozart's return to the symphony in Paris after some three and a half years (follow-ing the completion of K. 200). It can be assumed that the sharp observa-tions rehashed objections Leopold had raised when K. 183, 201, and 200 came into being. The comments cannot bear upon Mozart's symphonic production up to this time, for, as late as the return from the second Ital-ian tour, the father found nothing troubling in his son's compositions: his letter of 7 February 1772 to Johann Gottlob Immanuel Breitkopf (see p. 301), in fact, attempted to open the way to publication of Wolfgang's works, including, of course, the symphonies. (When, in later years Leopold resumed the negotiation, he could not have had the intention of send-ing to Leipzig items not to his taste.) The letter of September 1778 re-ferred to scores Leopold believed the public should neither read nor hear. He informed Wolfgang: "I have released [*hergegeben*] none of your sym-phonies . . . ," evidence of the criticism's relevance to the Salzburg compo-sitions alone, for, throughout the tours, Leopold had called upon scribes; with his blessing, manuscript copies of earlier Mozart symphonies lay on the shelves of more than one princely, ecclesiastical, and municipal archive.[13] At all events, returned from Milan and *Silla*, Leopold felt the weight of his court's expectations that its composers on the whole conform to rococo

---

13 Did Leopold suffer a turn of mind when, sometime during the seventies, he bound the autographs of nine of his son's Salzburg symphonies (1773–1774)—K. 183, 200, and 201 among
them—in a single volume on whose cover he listed their keys, orchestration, and incipits
(opening themes)? Did this table of contents serve archival purposes alone, or did he intend to
send copies of it to publishers?

models. He now grasped just what tendencies had destroyed his son's career in Milan and recognized that miracle alone could change the Archbishop's musical preferences.

Subject to the pressures of a family that looked to him to help sustain a comfortable life—into the bargain, Nannerl, almost twenty-three and with expensive tastes, remained unmarried—Wolfgang had in all likelihood announced his impending capitulation to the muse of practicality in K. 202, that *galant* symphony in D. If in his eyes his father appeared ever more as among the enemy, he kept silent. In fact, he prided himself upon his ease and stoicism in adjusting to contingency. ("If necessary, I go in the direction circumstances demand; when I have diarrhea I run, and, when I can no longer contain myself, I shit in my pants.") Nevertheless, it must have cost him much to cut himself down to size—and in a genre in which his goals had come to be higher than the decorative. Following what must have appeared to him the least painful path, he fled the field: with the completion of the valedictory K. 200, he abandoned the symphony. (Were the court to require one, he could assemble it from a serenade.) Only years later and far from Salzburg would he reclaim this territory.

Like a prophecy, the final movement of the rococo symphony in D dissolves rather than ends: taking the form of a *Kehraus*, that is, the concluding dance of a ball, the closing Presto seems a symbolic link to those *divertissements* that would come from his pen during the following so-called years of slumber in Salzburg. Whatever his crisis of inner protest, he recovered and adjusted, assuming an opportunistic *stylus mixtus*: under a predominantly *galant* idiom, it stealthily subsumed *empfindsam* elements along with bits and pieces of the learned, even now and then indulging furtive touches of Storm and Stress: he proposed to diet, not to starve.

Storm and Stress's effect upon Mozart, as in the case of Joseph Haydn, had proved therapeutic: by infusing their hitherto largely ornamental styles with doses of emotions more deeply felt than those of *Empfindsamkeit*, it functioned as an antibody protecting their musical systems against *galanterie*'s nervous preciousness and capriciousness. Mozart mounted guard against these risks when constrained in Salzburg to keep the nostrum by and large out of reach: as if to compensate, a precautionary dryness at times impoverishes the rococo compositions he turned out during this period at home, a quality most evident in his compositions for clavier.

6

HE NEVER CEASED adding strength to his distinction as a keyboard virtuoso. Though the sonata for four hands, K. 358/186c, written for Nannerl and himself (late 1773 or early 1774)[14] outdid his previous attempt in the genre (K. 381/123a), his heart did not lie in playing duets with his sister. More persuasive had been his clavier concerto K. 175, created for his own use some two months after the Little G Minor. Breathing a wiry athleticism and confidence belonging to the more moderate aspects of Storm and Stress, sinewy K. 175 bustles with rhythmic vitality, overflows with exuberance, and—like the opening movement of his first extant concerto for a wind, that for bassoon (K. 191/186e of the following June[15])—frisks and leaps while exuding wit, whimsy, and a rough charm.[16]

Salzburgers may well have received this first of Mozart's keyboard concertos—it would become one of his warhorses—with the chill that in all likelihood greeted the Storm and Stress symphonies: he would not return to the keyboard concerto until January 1776, when he composed the *galant* and well-behaved K. 238 in B flat. He banked the fiery and kept distant from the shadows, exerting himself to appear impersonal, agreeable, and at times commonplace. Not until his permanent removal to Vienna would his instrumental music regain in full what he had felt forced to renounce by reason of the Archbishops's predilections.

Even so, they achieved but partial satisfaction in Mozart's second Litaniae Lauretanae, K. 195/186d of May 1774, apparently intended for the cathedral: the powerful Salus infirmorum could not have pleased Colloredo, though he might well have luxuriated in the silken line of the Agnus Dei and the prettiness of the Sancta Maria, which gives the impression of having been snatched from either an *opera buffa* or the less elevated pages of an *opera seria*.

Mozart did answer the Archbishop's demands from first to last in a pair of terse and frugally scored *missae breves*, K. 192/186f and K. 194/186h, both composed during the summer of 1774 and thus soon after the D-major symphony: they rush forward as if to fly from too subjective a statement and to confess Colloredo's belief in dispassion and concision. Mozart stitched contrapuntal diversions and shreds of the *empfindsam* into a *galant* homophonic idiom, the choral texture enlivened with a quartet of soloists (banished a year before in K. 167); and omnipresent flows a mellifluous but pithy Italianate singing line: Mozart's *stylus mixtus* at its most

---

14 Its Adagio's initial theme derived from the Allegro of the Milanese quartet K. 160, which, in fact, had borrowed the material from Joseph Haydn's first string quartet.

15 A court bassoonist may have commissioned this work, designed to exploit the instrument's technical possibilities.

16 In Vienna during 1782, Mozart wrote a set of variations (the Rondo K. 382) to take the place of the Allegro originally closing K. 175, a movement whose contrapuntal elements Mozart at the time believed inimical to Viennese taste.

agile. (In his earlier masses these elements had rubbed shoulders but had yet so sympathetically to embrace.) Though significant for presaging the reciprocal play of weave and pattern in his future liturgical production, these twin masterpieces of burnished concentration command attention for their own qualities.[17]

Of no less inventive craft were the twelve variations for keyboard based upon a minuet by Johann Christian Fischer (likewise composed during the summer of 1774; see XIII, n. 13) and also Mozart's earliest surviving solo clavier sonatas, K. 279–283/189d–h and 284/205b, each in three movements.[18] This series must be acknowledged at this point even though it would come into being early in 1775 during an excursion to Munich. Mozart hoped that the sonatas might attract a publisher and cultivate a patron, in all likelihood the Archbishop's sister, Princess Maria Theresia Colloredo,[19] who shared her brother's taste in music. Although at his concerts Mozart had to play on the instrument at hand, the question of choosing either harpsichord or piano for performing these works invites a brief review of his acquaintance with the two instruments.

He grew up with a two-manual harpsichord made by Christian Ernst Friederici of Gera; it came into Leopold's possession about 1760. His son's high opinion (1777) of pianos from the Regensburg workshop of Franz Jakob Späth sustains the assumption that earlier the family had acquired one of them. Although the first direct evidence of Mozart's performing on a piano concerned a "contest" in Munich at the hotel Zum schwarzen Adler in 1775 (see p. 344), in his boyhood he must have played the piano during visits to Vienna, where it had become fashionable; indeed, a royal portrait of 1769 depicts Archduchess Maria Antonia seated at a handsome example. Only in the next decade did the instrument begin to achieve social cachet in Salzburg: in 1777, its Archbishop's sister, Countess Schönborn, ordered a piano from Johann Andreas Stein of Augsburg. Mozart's praise of Späth's pianos had but preluded his announcement that he had discovered Stein's to be even finer. He would delight in availing himself of them when playing his Munich sonatas (see p. 377), which seem to have been, in fact, written with the piano in mind:

---

17 The Credo of K. 192 employs Mozart's four-tone motto (see p. 200).

18 Since childhood he had improvised clavier sonatas, often carrying several in his head and, no doubt, when under pressure, trotting out one or another of them as fresh inspirations. (After his death, Nannerl sent three of his solo keyboard sonatas, [K. Anh. 199-201/33d-f], which she identified as among his "first compositions," to the publishing firm of Brietkopf & Härtel, in whose keeping they went astray!)

19 In 1776 she would marry Count Eugen Franz Erwein Schönborn.

their quick changes of dynamics seem better managed on it than on the harpsichord.[20]

Betraying acquaintance with Joseph Haydn's latest keyboard sonatas (Opus 13, published in 1774), the first five of the set constitute a stylistic unit. It speaks a *galant* language infused with tinctures of the *empfindsam* (often taking the form of richly varied dynamic changes) and at the same time shuns too strong a challenge to the fingers, but not the musicality, of amateurs and their teachers.[21] Spare in texture, limpid, and discreet, the five sonatas flee the clouds and seek the open. For this they pay a price when in the hands of a less than sensitive performer: then they appear impoverished in character and inner life and drift toward either bustling or idling in passagework and figuration. Nothing of the kind, but abounding in substance, the sonatas bear the imprint of genius: the enduring misconception of their composer as a maker of tinkling, bloodless music may well rest upon the limitations of the many who have dutifully, if unthinkingly, rattled away at them down the centuries. Yet to know Mozart only through these works is to know only a very small part of him; here he pursues exquisite simplicity masking as anonymity, though now and then a modulation or even an entire movement lays open the depths: the soulful F-minor Adagio of K. 280, which Leopold and Nannerl so admired, or the Adagio of K. 282.

Big in scale and orchestral in aspiration, the sixth and last sonata of the set makes a full and open turn back to the world of bolder gestures and higher spirits. That he abandoned his original sketch of an opening movement in *galant* style and began again in a more impassioned manner underscores the reversal. He put aside the plan à la Colloredo: a new patron, Freiherr Thaddäus von Dürnitz, a major in the corps attached to the Munich Residenz, hovered over K. 284.[22]

---

20 In respect to the keyboard concerto—the pastiche works apart—he appears to have conceived his first, K. 175 of 1773, for the harpsichord, the piano becoming without question his favored instrument for the genre only with K. 271 (1777; see pp. 359–60). By this time the new instrument had the best of it: the Mozart family portrait of 1780–81 shows Wolfgang and Nannerl seated at a piano (see pp. 523–24).

21 When Mozart characterized the sonatas as difficult, he perhaps had in mind the demands made by their intricate dynamic markings.

22 Dürnitz would appear also to have ordered the sonata for bassoon and violoncello, K. 292/196c, as well as three bassoon concertos now lost. Mozart's letters report him as remiss in paying. Some suggest two bassoons as the original instrumentation of K. 292; others look upon the composition as spurious. Pointing to the cello's downright subsidiary role, characteristic less of a duetting chamber work than an orchestral part, Kenneth Cooper put the case (orally) that K. 292 might be a bare-bone reduction, for the purpose of practice, of one of the missing concertos.

This return to the mainstream of his artistic growth derived from Mozart's all at once pondering the prospect of a new career outside Salzburg, one giving promise of his resuming the spontaneous expansion of his expressive palette, a development that from his childhood had moved side by side with the evolution of his technique. The pendulum, at rest for months, had swung forward, propelled by the hand of an old admirer, Elector Max Joseph of Bavaria. Indeed, all the sonatas had come into being in his capital, and it would appear that by the time Mozart began the sixth, Salzburg had once again receded in his mind. Elated by propitious omens, he had journeyed to Munich late in 1774.

7

THE GOOD NEWS had come during the summer. Max Joseph, whom the Mozarts had last visited on their return journey from Paris, commissioned Wolfgang to provide Munich with an *opera buffa* for the coming carnival season. Archbishop Colloredo had no choice but to permit Mozart to complete the work there and oversee its premiere. By September he had received the libretto: Abbate Giuseppe Petrosellini's adaptation of Calzabigi's *La finta giardiniera*; with a score by Pasquale Anfossi, this version had recently been a success in Rome.

On 6 December 1774 father and son departed for Munich, layer upon layer of clothing and footwear, all prescribed in minute detail by Leopold, protecting them from the fierce cold. Ever more fussy concerning details of travel, he betrayed a growing need to write large what once had been understood: his indispensability at the helm. It must have appeared strange to both Salzburg and Munich that a man of almost nineteen dared not nor could not attend to his professional affairs without unremitting paternal supervision; but Leopold had long made his son think himself a cripple in respect to anything practical.

By way of Wasserburg, they arrived in Munich on the seventh and took up residence with Johann Nepomuk Pernat, a canon of the Liebfrauenkirche.[23] They met with the court's intendant of theaters, Count Joseph Anton von Seeau, and, once recovered from toothache and a swollen face, Mozart pressed forward with his score. He amused himself, too, at a performance of Franz von Heufeld's comedy *Die Haushaltung nach der Mode*.

At the first rehearsal of *La finta giardiniera*, a muddle, it became clear that knocking the score—of unexpected complexity and length—into shape

---

23 Only in 1821 did Munich become an archbishopric, the Bishop of Freising assuming the title of Archbishop of Munich-Freising. At this juncture, the Liebfrauenkirche became a cathedral.

demanded more than the allotted time. Rescheduling could not have been easy: the company, which kept some twenty works in repertory, had begun to prepare the season's new *opera seria*. The management, however, twice postponed Mozart's premiere so that singers and instrumentalists might get the parts into their heads. The auguries signaled goodwill.

He must have taken particular pleasure in anticipating his sister's arrival. She had seen only those few modest productions of his stage works in Salzburg, for Leopold had snapped his purse closed at any suggestion that she attend the premieres in Milan. But she could rest assured of hearing *La finta giardiniera* in a capital only a day's journey from home. In the house of a Frau von Durst, Leopold found her a "suitable" lodging, that is, free, comfortable, respectable, and with a harpsichord.

He made plans to draw her into Munich's musical life and dispatched precise injunctions to Salzburg: she must practice the clavier with diligence, "especially the sonatas of Paradisi [Pietro Domenico Paradisi, or Paradies, whom the Mozarts had met in London] and Bach etc. and the concerto of Lucchesi . . ."; moreover, she was to bring to Munich not only these compositions but also Wolfgang's sonatas and variations[24] and, indeed, whatever pieces remained in her fingers. Leopold succeeded in dismissing the fact that this spinster of twenty-three now lacked anything of the precocious or distinguished at the keyboard. His behest that, for use as publicity, she pack copies of the Grand Tour engraving (depicting the mite Wolfgang, herself, and Leopold) suggests a father suffering a regression precipitated by the thought of again being with his two children in a great capital: a sad attempt to resurrect the past.

Nannerl received his directions for shielding herself against the cold during her journey: how to wrap her head; how to wrap her feet; how and when to have a bundle of hay spread on the floor of the coach to help keep them warm. She truly needed such wearying instructions: like Wolfgang, she had been brought up to be almost helpless. Incapable of either dressing her hair or making up her face, she depended upon Mama, their maid, and friends willing to be suborned.[25] Realizing that she would have to

---

24 Leopold probably had in mind Paradisi's set of twelve clavier sonatas, Christian Bach's keyboard sonatas of opus 5, Andrea Lucchesi's clavier concerto in F, Wolfgang's sonatas from the Grand Tour—by no means those examples from childhood mentioned in n. 18—and his Salieri and Fischer variations. He had his concerto K. 175 with him.

25 In Salzburg, women of Nannerl's social rank and age pulled their hair back under a traditional cap (*Berghaube*), but she wore her hair "up" in the manner of the titled. (The demands of her coiffure seem to have devoured much of her day.) Leopold and Wolfgang, who used *"geschopfte"* (with hair piled high) as a word of contempt for the kind of court lady they despised, could not have been pleased with Nannerl's aping this fashion. She continued to array herself in a manner reflecting her days as a touring virtuosa (see XXVI, n. 35).

manage such procedures on her own at Frau von Durst's, Leopold urged her to practice them as well as the clavier!

Wolfgang sent her his own requests: to bring to Munich, along with the Fischer variations, Eckard's on a famous minuet by André-Joseph Exaudet[26] and to fulfill an urgent petition concerning a girlfriend. "I beseech you; before your departure, do not forget to keep your promise, that is to pay the visit in question, for I have my reasons. I beg you to deliver my compliments there, and in the most expressive and tenderest manner. Oh, I need not be so anxious, for, of course, I know my sister; she is tenderness itself. I am certain that she will do her utmost to do me a kindness, and to her own advantage—rather nasty; we shall kick up a row about this in Munich. . . ."

On 4 January 1775, Nannerl arrived in the company of Frau Maria Victoria Robinig with her daughter Luise, and Joseph Franz Xaver Gschwendtner. They carried news of a rumor making its way through Salzburg: that Wolfgang had received an appointment at the Electoral court and would not return. Johann Baptist Hagenauer, a distinguished sculptor[27] (a cousin of the Mozarts' benefactor), had recently quit Archbishop Colloredo's service to take up a position in Vienna, and Wolfgang's friends had been quick to draw and, in their imaginations, implement a parallel. But La finta giardiniera would not bring him the caress of reborn fame and with it a new post: the forceful, innovative score misfired; the egregious libretto, however, found acceptance as a matter of course.

8

THE MARCHIONESS VIOLANTE ONESTI, wounded and left apparently dead by her jealous lover, Count Belfiore, recovers and sets forth to his native district of Lagonero, whither he has fled, her purpose to find and pardon him. Disguised as Sandrina, a gardener, she enters the service of Don Anchise, Lagonero's chief magistrate. By chance, he is about to betroth his niece, Arminda, to the same Count Belfiore. He arrives at Don Anchise's villa to woo Arminda and is astounded to discover Violante alive. All at once wishing to punish him, she resists his ardent advances by denying her true identity and maintaining her role as simple gardener. A letter arrives revealing that authorities in Milan have linked Belfiore to the supposed murder and require Don Anchise to institute an inquest. To save Belfiore, Violante discloses her masquerade. A furious Arminda, recognizing that

---

26 They had appeared in Paris (1764) as *Menuet d'Exaudet avec des variations pour le Clavecin.*
27 In 1771, he and his brother Wolfgang created the monument celebrating the Virgin Mother (*die Mariensäule*) in the square onto which the cathedral of Salzburg opens.

her suitor's love for Violante has begun to rekindle, contrives that she be abducted and left in a wild and neighboring forest filled with ravenous beasts. Violante takes shelter in a cave to which, for varying reasons, the other characters make their way during the night.[28] Under the pressure of events, she gives way to madness, as does Belfiore. Led back to Don Anchise's estate, they enjoy a healing sleep in the garden and awaken restored. He questions and entreats; she forgives. With this reconciliation, the chain of love affairs surrounding them breaks into pairs: Violante's servant, Roberto (heretofore disguised as Nardo, her relative and fellow gardener), will marry Serpetta, Don Anchise's maid; Arminda returns to her former lover, the cavalier Ramiro, whom she had deserted for Belfiore. Only the magistrate, who had pursued his maid until he turned to woo his lady-gardener, remains alone, a situation well within the *buffa* tradition.

Upon this *reductio ad absurdum* of the Richardsonian theme of aggrieved virtue achieving the libertine's reformation, Mozart lavished some of the loveliest music he had yet conceived (K. 196); it surmounts the plot to delineate several unmistakable Mozartean presences: the heroine—graceful, *souffrante*, resourceful, and filled with delicate feeling;[29] her lover—manic, childish, and vain, but in the end showing signs of growing up; the maidservant—hard, prying, spiteful, but pert; her admirer—burly, bluff, and honest; and the infatuated addlepate—long in the tooth and pompous but saved from the spent routine of stereotype by his human qualities and also by his being a tenor rather than the bass usual in such roles.

Somewhat at a distance from this quintet of, in the main, *buffa* personalities stand Arminda and the high-bred Ramiro: portrayed by a castrato, he breathes the rarefied air of *opera seria*, his very presence bringing an exalted Metastasian atmosphere of higher purposes; Arminda—aristocratic, petulant, cruel, and quite insufferable—also expresses herself in the exalted style, though she does stray into *opera-buffa* vernacular. For their part, Violante and Belfiore without effort slip back and forth between the two worlds, living actively in both. At first, a delicious marzipan ingenue, in the wilderness she must execute a turbulent scene in which heroic aria, accompagnato, and cavatina merge to form an arc of anguished sound worthy of a less idiotic situation. Belfiore begins by presenting himself in a "portrait" aria cast in the noble tradition, and his role includes accompagnati of tragic

---

28 Groping about in the dark, they mistake the identity of those into whom they stumble, the confusion calling to mind that in Count Almaviva's garden during the closing act of *The Marriage of Figaro*.

29 The work shows indebtedness to the Richardson/Goldoni/Piccinni *Buona figliuola*. Violante, a kind of Pamela, already reveals Mozart's special and tender empathy for the subtleties of women.

intensity. Yet his *"Care pupille,"* which starts seriously, ends in low farce, and his "ancestor" aria calls to mind not Metastasio but W. S. Gilbert.

La finta giardiniera exemplifies that contemporary delight in mixing genres, here embedding *opera-seria* elements within the body of *opera buffa*,[30] to create the *dramma giocoso*, a process Goldoni began and which Mozart would one day refine into an unsurpassed musico-dramatic amalgam. The framework of the Metastasian *opera seria* proved too unyielding to accommodate the reverse: *opera-buffa* types found unmanageable any modus vivendi within its rigid confines; the walls of *opera buffa* proved more hospitable and enduring.

The *opera-buffa* protagonists of *La finta giardiniera* remain types, schematic figures engaged in conventional harlequinades. Yet they have put aside the thin puppet- and caricature-like masks of the commedia dell'arte, those often brutally fashioned silhouettes of eccentrics from whom the traditional *opera-buffa* cast derived, and, putting on flesh, have developed graded contours; reflecting the fashionable tendency to play at glossing over social divisions—another way of mixing genres—they prove at ease in treating with the *seria* figures who have appeared, indeed taken refuge, in their *buffa* domain.

They expect these grand visitors to be circumspect and passive, restricting themselves to arias nobly pathetic in style but not excessively so: such moments simply served to transform *opera buffa* into a kind of sentimental comedy—society escaped boredom by escaping into sentiment—and the public did not anticipate exposure to passages of edifying moral earnestness, to anything calling to mind that school of virtue so dear to Metastasio. Not homilies or profundity but entertainment had become the ideal, though a few pious conceits and even a bit of melancholy or high-souled rage, if not too extended, offered a change in mood all the more to be savored because of the inevitable and swift return of the *buffa* players.

The vocalists sustained the intrigue by means of recitative and through the medium of the ensemble, which had begun to be a vehicle for propelling the action toward a critical point, most characteristically at the end of an act. Mozart would play a singular role in this development (again, one of Goldoni's innovations), and in *La finta giardiniera* the profile of the multisectional Mozartean finale had begun to firm.

It would become a complex, many-voiced musical correlative to the action and dialogue, a literal mutual mirroring of tonal and dramatic tensions. Combining protagonists as the words demanded, the finale grew

---

30 Even the farcical *La finta semplice* includes moments in the manner of *opera seria*: vide Giacinta's *"Che scompiglio,"* Rosina's *"Amoretti,"* and Fracasso's *"Nelle guerre d'amore."*

steadily in animation and urgency. The individual singers voiced phrases incisive enough to define and, if necessary, differentiate particular points of view but not so sharp as to break the ensemble's overall integrity. Mozart further sustained unity by a brilliant exploitation of recurrent orchestral motifs taking the form of a rhythmic movement or a melodic figure—in Salieri's words, "an orchestral motion . . . capable of supporting and binding together vocal lines broken into segments as demanded by the text"—and, in addition, by a fluidity permitting the meter and the vocal and instrumental densities to shift in answer to the stage direction and the verses' ever-changing exigencies. These artful transitions enabled one unit to flow into the next in a stream of verbal and musical loquacity, a marvelous alacrity of pace, the consequence of control and measure, giving to the whole the impression of self-renewing impulses. Moreover, in the course of responding to the libretto's proprieties, the classic Mozart finale ensemble simultaneously met the claims of melodic balance and coherent relationships of key and all the while realized the miracle of rendering the sectional as continuous.

At moments *La finta giardiniera*'s finales to the first and second acts, approaching the level of his mature examples, have begun to adumbrate a spirited new operatic dramaturgy whose pervasive drive would, at its best, gather together the tissue of the plot and give it a new turn. Lorenzo Da Ponte looked upon such a finale as "a kind of little comedy or operetta all by itself."[31] Alas, those at the premiere of *La finta giardiniera* found Mozart's manipulation of the device excessive, as they did much else.

9

THE STYLISTIC ELEMENTS at war in *La finta giardiniera* betray a Mozart torn between inner and outer purposes. This disruption may have originated in the ambiguous origins and intent of the commission. Why had

---

31 Of a different stamp from the finale ensembles of *La finta giardiniera*, those of *La finta semplice*, though remarkable creations for a boy of twelve, are short-breathed and cliché-ridden and lack the extended tonal progressions that build dramatic urgency; but so do the *opera-buffa* finales of most composers of the time, who, to induce excitement, relied upon the piling up of characters rushing on stage in a state of agitation. Plunging into his career as a librettist, Da Ponte confronted the problem of writing texts for such ensembles, which, he observed, had as their chief effect "noise, noise, noise, for the finale almost always closes uproariously." At first he looked upon it as an amusing embarrassment: "Operatic doctrine decreed that the finale had to bring to the scene every singer in the cast, be there three hundred of them and whether by ones, twos, threes, sixes, tens, or sixties and, accordingly, in need of solos, duets, terzets, sextets, tenets, or sixtyets." In time he would struggle to provide the extended finale with words that did not offend reason.

he received it? Had Leopold enjoyed recourse to some powerful patron in Munich: Count Zeil, Bishop of Chiemsee,[32] or the Elector's sister, Maria Antonia, Dowager Electress of Saxony? Or perhaps Elector Max Joseph had concluded that a young German who had written operas in Milan for the Habsburgs be put to the test in a major capital of his homeland. That the opportunity also harbored the aim of judging his fitness to join the Elector's musical retinue seemed a certainty, if not to the court, then to the Mozarts, who expected a thoroughgoing success to force this passage. Since Vienna's gates remained shut to them, Munich had assumed signal importance in their eyes (though they did begin to reweave their ties to Vienna by visiting the Imperial Ambassador, Count Adam Franz von Hartig).

At all events, Wolfgang determined to impress Munich and went astray because at the same time he determined to impress himself no less. In a miscalculation born of divergent desires—on one hand, a desperation to carry the city by storm, on the other, a dizzying hunger to make the most of his freedom from the musical restrictions of Salzburg, so stifling to his inclinations—he fabricated an overambitious score rich in stylistic contrarieties and with finales of a complexity beyond anything a Galuppi, Piccinni, or Gassmann had attempted.[33]

Doubtless, the public found the *opera-seria* elements most troubling: they showed an inclination to seize the rein; moreover, the tone of Storm and Stress with its emotional exhibitionism often colored them, as in Arminda's G-minor aria, *"Vorrei punirti indegno,"* wherein she contemplates vengeance in an idiom suited to Elettra (*Idomeneo*) or Donna Anna; and Violante's scene in the forest must have irritated, not only for its depiction of terror but also because it ran on into the concerted finale of Act II to form a great vault of continuing tonal energy.[34] Mozart blinked at the fact that an audience looking forward to an *opera buffa* would regard such an outburst as unseemly and so great a span of uninterrupted music as tiresome. In addition, instead of the thin sounds usual in *opera buffa*, his

32 The Bishop preferred to reside in Munich, though he had a palace in Salzburg (the Chiemseehof) and a summer estate in nearby Anif. His long stays in Munich ruffled Colloredo, who suspected him of plotting.

33 Whether at this time Mozart possessed any knowledge of Haydn's operas remains uncertain. The Esterházy did permit their occasional performance outside the family's private theaters, but these works could hardly have been known to many beyond the world of the privileged. For *La fedeltà premiata* (1780) he would design finales of imposing dimension that left their mark upon Mozart's *Figaro.*

34 Concerning Mozart's resolving one scene into another in *Idomeneo, Don Giovanni,* and *La clemenza di Tito,* see pp. 306 and 515–16.

orchestra poured forth sensuous harmonies enveloped in resonant instrumentation. Next to *La finta giardiniera*, most contemporary *opera-buffa* scores—Joseph Haydn's the grand exceptions—strike modern ears as poverty-stricken.

How disturbing the audience must have thought these weighty sonorities; how perplexing the ensembles' eccentric proportions; how odd the overall atmospheric tone (born of the bold mixture of genres; Goldoni had warned of the difficulties of balancing one against the other). Mozart had overshot the mark by remaining true to himself: his genius was not a liquid that inevitably took the shape of the vessel into which it poured, even during his years of "slumber." His desire to please had, in fact, been an artful surface with which, from time to time, he fooled even himself. In any event, that beneath lay a resistant center spoke for itself in Munich, and it amazes to what extent Elector Max Joseph's company attempted to come to terms with a long, unconventional, and confusing work.

He, in fact, discovered in it moments to admire. However, repetitions and a place in the repertory depended upon the ticket-buying public, and, more immediately, fate intervened: illness struck the cast. Two widely spaced performances followed the premiere on 13 January 1775 in the Hoftheater am Salvatorplatz,[35] Electoral *Vizeconzertmeister* Johann Nepomuk von Croner conducting. (Contrasting with Milanese practice, the court of Munich frowned upon a composer presiding over the first representations of his own opera.) Thereafter, the work vanished from the Munich boards.[36]

A brief review of the premiere performances survives as quoted by Christian Daniel Schobart: "Flames of genius quiver here and there; but it is not yet that still, calm altar-fire that mounts toward heaven in clouds of incense—a scent beloved of the gods." Munich's critical perceptions no doubt resembled those of the *Dramaturgische Blätter* of Frankfurt am Main concerning the opera as given there and in Mainz during 1789: "A motley . . . business . . . more for the connoisseur who knows how to unravel its refinements than for the dilettante . . ."; despite its "majestic" and "humorous" moments and an "abundance of strong harmonies," the opera,

---

35 The three survivors of the famous double wedding (see VIII, n. 3) shared the royal box, Dowager Electress Maria Antonia of Saxony joining her brother and sister-in-law.

36 A composer received a fee for composing and preparing an opera; no royalties ensued, but benefit presentations served further to reward the creator of a successful work, as did the publication of excerpts and arrangements. Here he had to move with dispatch, for no copyright obtained and poachers abounded.

though "ingenious," stood condemned as "nearly always difficult" and "in the highest degree tasteless and tedious."[37]

Once its fate in Munich became clear, father and son faced the reality of another failure; and there had been embarrassment as to the visitors from Salzburg: because of the postponed premiere and repetitions, several of their friends returned home without having heard the opera. Had Mozart's days of glory as a prodigy carried within them the seed of retribution? Of course, straightway following the first performance, a letter to Mama had announced another triumph: the packed theater, the people turned away, the applause,[38] the gracious compliments of Max Joseph—all true enough.

Before the premiere, Leopold had entertained "every hope" of Wolfgang's composing the *opera seria* for Munich's next season. But almost six years would pass before another Wittelsbach commission came to him, on this occasion from Max Joseph's successor, a musical connoisseur sympathetic to the new emotionalism, Elector Palatine Karl Theodore; he had, in fact, come to Munich and attended the second performance of *La finta giardiniera*,[39] by which time (the end of February) Seeau had moved the production from the theater to a ballroom on the Prannergasse. To be sure, problems of scheduling played their part in the relocation, but he did hate the work and later, to Mozart's fury, insisted that the public "had hissed" it (see p. 468 and XXVI, n. 44).

The day after the opera's first night, Archbishop Colloredo appeared without notice: having toyed with the notion of spending part of the holiday in Munich, he had made up his mind on the spot and, upon arrival, went directly to the court theater, Antonio Tozzi's *Orfeo ed Euridice* (see X, n. 27) getting under way as the prelate took his place in the Electoral box. Deferment of the succeeding performances of *La finta giardiniera* precluded his hearing it—if, indeed, the idea occurred to him—for he de-

---

37 Despite critical disparagement, for a while the opera made its way in German translation: by the end of the seventies it had entered the repertory of Johann Böhm's touring company in a singspiel version using a text in all likelihood from the hand of Johann Franz Joseph Stierli the Elder, a member of the troupe. Salzburg heard Böhm's players in the transformed work during the season of 1779–1780 (see p. 485). In May 1780 they performed it in Augsburg as *Die verstellte Gärtnerin* and two years later brought it to Frankfurt am Main under the title *Sandrina oder Die verstellte Gräfin*. In 1789, the Electoral National Theater of Mainz took up the opera, now called *Das verstellte Gärtnermädchen*, a production the company took to Frankfurt later in the year.

38 In his diary, the secretary of the Saxon legation in Munich noted the "general applause" [*fut applaudie generalement; sic*]," a less than roseate observation.

39 For this first repetition Mozart had to abbreviate the score in the interest of a singer not fully recovered from an indisposition.

parted on the twenty-sixth. The center of ceremonies and receptions, the Primate of Germany could have given few, if any, thoughts to his two musicians on leave. They did not participate in a concert Seeau organized in his honor and appear to have had no contact with him. Leopold gave an account of Colloredo's embarrassment to receive compliments upon the "Salzburg" premiere he had missed: "He became so disconcerted that he could reply only with a bow of the head, a shrug of the shoulders." At best an embroidery upon hearsay—perhaps he had an awkward moment when reminded of the Mozarts, their leave, and its purpose—this tale may well have been an improvisation to help Frau Anna Maria take heart.

Even if Mozart did not stand in the highest opinion of Colloredo and his court, they bore him no ill will. During rehearsals of *La finta giardiniera*, he received a letter from the Salzburg Residenz ordering an opera, a *serenata teatrale*, to celebrate the impending arrival in the archbishopric of Maria Theresa's youngest son, Archduke Maximilian Franz. Very likely in contemplation of contributing even more to this festive visit (and of having, to boot, something new should Max Joseph's chapel call upon him), Mozart made time in Munich to begin K. 220/196b; known as the Sparrow Mass because of the reiterated chirping violin phrase punctuating the Sanctus, it breathes heartiness and vigor, if little poetry.

No record survives of Nannerl's receiving an invitation to perform during this Munich *séjour*, and even Wolfgang seems to have awakened little demand as a virtuoso, a blow to Leopold's fantasies. Still, through the efforts of Canon Pernat, the Liebfrauenkirche scheduled two Mozartean compositions: the faithful observing the Hours on New Year's Day heard both a *Litaniae de venerabili altaris sacramento* by Leopold and Wolfgang's setting of the same text (K. 125). Moreover, in the court chapel on Sunday, 12 February, Leopold conducted a *missa brevis* by his son and, a week later, "another one," in all likelihood K. 192 and 194 in turn.

During the first week of March, Max Joseph again attended *La finta giardiniera*, its third and final representation. And, even as the Mozarts prepared to leave Munich, he caught Wolfgang unawares by setting him an imposing task: to compose "some contrapuntal music" demonstrating his headway in cantorial style. The assignment, along with the Elector's harking back to the opera, suggested a persisting interest in Wolfgang; but those masses sung in the chapel had not answered questions about his grasp of the time-honored discipline, a tradition Max Joseph esteemed. At full speed Mozart wrote the D-minor *Misericordias Domini*, K. 222/205a, performed during the offertory at high mass on Sunday, 5 March, perhaps again in the court chapel. The antiphon leaned upon a subject taken from Eberlin and showed debts to Adlgasser and Michael Haydn. Mozart remained proud of this trial-piece, which, its remarkable technical address apart, communicated a quickened inspiration and profundity giving it a place among his finest creations for the church: in a composition designed to exhibit method, he went beyond its reach. (The modern listener starts at hearing, threading its way through the orchestra, a melody anticipating Beethoven's "Ode to Joy.")

If he gave no concerts in the great houses and palaces of the city, he did play at the Hotel Zum schwarzen Adler. Its proprietor, Franz Joseph Albert, had an excellent fortepiano on which Mozart engaged in a competition with an old acquaintance, Ignaz von Beecke. An observer (quoted by Christian Daniel Schobart) pronounced him the superior: acknowledging Mozart's ability to manage all digital difficulties and to "read anything at sight," this critique nonetheless asserted that he had "little more to offer," von Beecke, on his side, dispensing "winged velocity, grace, melting sweetness, and a quite individual self-formed taste. . . ."

Wolfgang found the contest less than agreeable and thereafter could not write von Beecke's name without adding some opprobrious comment upon his manner of performing. In Mozart's opinion, playing the clavier in strict time did not vitiate but, rather, enhanced expressiveness, the right hand's privilege of indulging the freedom of rubato having validity only if the left remained in tempo (an argument Leopold had pursued in his *Versuch*). Von Beecke's unrestrained, all-pervading rubatos—Schobart likened them to "fire" and "abundance"—which he accompanied by grimaces, sickened Mozart, outraged to see this kind of extravagance carry the field. Some two and a half years later, still nettled, he asserted that connoisseurs well knew that he could "wipe the floor with Beecke" (*dass ich den Becché im sack scheibe* [*sic*]).

The Munich season, Leopold observed, had "more entertainments than any other place known to me." Throughout the weeks of Carnival, the three Mozarts, in costume, danced their way through a taxing schedule of masquerades. (Nannerl made an excellent effect as an Amazon.) By the end of February, the forced conviviality of a weary Leopold had curdled. Though they kept themselves on view, no invitations to the gilded chambers of the Residenz came, no contract for the following season. With few professional activities to report, Leopold turned to chronicling the latest Munich scandal, in particular, the amorous exploits of Signor Tozzi; he urged Frau Anna Maria to broadcast them so that Germans might learn the simple truth that "Italians are knaves the world over," his target not only Tozzi and Munich's Andrea Bernasconi but also Salzburg's Fischietti and Brunetti.

As late as 1 March, Leopold still awaited remuneration for *La finta giar-diniera*. (With relief he learned that royalties accumulating from the *Versuch* had arrived in Salzburg.) On the sixth, the trio of Mozarts set out for Wasserburg, and the following day their carriage turned into the Hanni-balplatz. Leopold and Wolfgang had completed their final tour together.

CHAPTER XVIII

Salzburg Interlude; Cashiered

ELEVEN DAYS AFTER the Mozarts' departure from Munich, Arch-duke Maximilian arrived there on his way back from France. Follow-ing a visit to the Habsburg court at Brussels, he had journeyed to Paris to embrace his brother-in-law and sister, since the preceding May King Louis XVI and Queen Marie Antoinette; Maximilian then began to make his way eastward. Uncertainty concerning his schedule troubled the Mozarts: when he left Munich on 21 March 1775, His Highness would perhaps call at Salzburg; or, since he planned to make a southern tour some weeks later, he might go straightway home and salute Archbishop Colloredo in the se-quel, that is, while en route from Vienna to Italy. To the Mozarts' relief, he chose to return to the Hofburg, intending to set out again on 20 April and to arrive in Salzburg the following day.[1]

Wolfgang thus had a breathing space of several weeks in which to com-pose the libretto chosen to honor this Imperial guest—Metastasio's *Il rè pastore*. Written in 1751 for the Habsburg court[2] and first set to music by the Mozarts' friend Bonno, the text thereafter engaged the talents of many

---

1 This Vienna-Salzburg schedule required, in effect, unbroken relays of horses day and night.
2 On 27 February 1775, Marie Antoinette had crowned a reception at Versailles in honor of Max-imilian by presenting an adaptation of Gluck's *L'arbre enchanté*, also first created (1759) for Schönbrunn.

composers, including Felice Giardini, whose version Leopold and Wolf-gang must have heard, with Manzuoli in the cast, during their months in London. Mozart set to music this tale of Aminta the shepherd in a revision by Archbishop Colloredo's confessor, Giambattista Varesco: he compressed Metastasio's three acts into two, making both cuts and additions. Given the limitations imposed by the genre, the occasion, and the cleric's middling talent, the result proved respectable. This *festa teatrale* must be approached without recollections of Tasso's *Aminta*: they have in common only the hero's name and pastoral occupation; Metastasio's libretto takes its independent, didactic course.

Raised a shepherd and unaware of his true identity as the son of the last rightful king of Sidon, Aminta dwells in the idyllic countryside outside the city, happily tending his flocks and cherishing his love for Elisa. Alessandro of Macedon has just overthrown the usurper of Sidon's throne, who chose suicide rather than surrender. Learning of Aminta's lineage, Alessandro orders it revealed to the astonished youth and bestows upon him royal robes and his father's crown. Moreover, the clement conqueror proceeds with plans to calm opposing factions and assure peace in the land by marrying this new and legitimate monarch to the usurper's daughter, the worthy Tamiri. She, however, loves and is loved by Agenore, a Sidonian noble and Alessandro's friend and counselor. Tamiri throws herself at Alessandro's feet in despair that she must exchange love for rank; Elisa arrives to tell him of the ties between Aminta and herself; and he appears once again in shepherd's garb to return robes and crown to Alessandro and claim Elisa in their place. Alessandro, hitherto ignorant of these relationships and struck by the virtue of the lovers, unites them according to their desires. Aminta, with Elisa at his side, returns to the kingship, and Alessandro promises to conquer yet another realm and place Agenore and Tamiri on its throne.

Mozart could dominate the most varied material: within weeks he turned from the ostentatious Storm and Stress passions and *opera-buffa* volatility of *La finta giardiniera* to execute this *galant* exercise in frigid clarity. The score (K. 208)[3] remains limpid and the musical sentiments tender even during those crises of the heart—prepared by Metastasio with Cartesian rigor—when the skies briefly cloud: neither Metastasio nor Mozart could suffer any blemish to disfigure their Arcady, that counterfeit world unencumbered by depth of thought or passion—a landscape without weeds.

In this Eden, gilded as if by a Pinturicchio, all the personages express themselves in the same cloying poetry. Though, like Metastasio, Mozart

---

3 As proof of his accomplishments, in October 1777 he sent Joseph Mysliveček a copy of it.

fell back upon formulas, he revitalized them: combining technique and bravura to manufacture the illusion of inspiration, the music succeeds in bestowing felicitous nuances upon the platitudinous verse, even managing to sweeten its most disquieting moralities.

Of course, the *serenata* provides a measure of particular Mozartean enchantments: Aminta's *"Aer tranquillo"* with echoes of the *"Alleluja"* section of the motet, *"Exsultate, jubilate,"* the vigorous orchestral passages anticipating the violin concertos soon to come; Aminta and Elisa's lyrical love duet, *"Vanne a regnar,"* closing the first act; Alessandro's buoyant *"Se vincendo"*; Aminta's *"L'amero"* gently illuminated by silvery, haunting violin obbligatos; and the finale, a Rondo by turns spirited and melting in which the five protagonists mix their voices.

Like *Ascanio in Alba,* this pastoral fable panegyrized the Habsburgs' most parochial precept derived from their canon of eternal domestic truths: that they would forever benevolently hover over the affairs of the Deutsches Reich, whenever necessary adding branches to the laurels of the family by securing new kingdoms for its scions. "So much virtue must not lack a throne," Alessandro announces just before the finale, an observation most appropriate to Archduke Maximilian, his future as an anointed overlord already in preparation at the time of his visit to Salzburg: its court had to have consulted with Vienna when choosing and editing the text of the pastoral. Its message pointed toward the prospects of an amiable prince who, indeed, would not remain throneless.

The Hofburg underscored this signal by playing upon the coincidence of three events, all of 8 December 1756: the Archduke's birth, his father's forty-eighth birthday, and the premiere of Gluck's *Il rè pastore* (at the Burgtheater), which had celebrated it. For those who comprehended what lay hidden in the folds of its imagery, the Salzburg *Il rè pastore* became its own *licenza.*

In 1780, Maximilian would take the tonsure along with first vows and become coadjutor and then successor to the Prince-Archbishop of Cologne,[4] for whose death he had but four years to wait. When he mounted the throne of the Electorate (*Kurköln*), the Habsburgs gained a perch on the Rhine between the French and the Prussians and added a piece of Westphalia to the family's properties.[5] Such an accession proceeded from

---

4 He was that same Maximilian Friedrich whom the Mozarts had sought but failed to meet during their Grand Tour (see p. 108).

5 The Elector-Archbishop of Cologne, a *Reichsstadt,* kept court without the city at nearby Bonn (for a somewhat similar situation in Augsburg, see XIII, n. 37) and since 1719 also functioned as prince-bishop of the Westphalian city of Münster.

diplomatic negotiations in which, for certain, the Habsburgs' most distinguished ecclesiastical liegeman, Hieronymus Colloredo, played a major role.

Wolfgang and Maximilian had first met in Vienna as children (1762). Maximilian remained his admirer, and through the years Mozart found him witty, appealing, sensible, and pithy in conversation. But all these traits vanished—so the ever more anticlerical Mozart would claim—once the Prince became a priest.[6] At all events, as churchman and Electoral Highness, Maximilian would build at Bonn the cultural ambiance in which the young Beethoven flourished.

Maximilian attended *Il rè pastore* on 23 April 1775[7] at the Salzburg Residenz, where, the preceding evening, Fischietti had presided over his musical setting of a *serenata teatrale* by Metastasio: *Gli orti esperidi.* On the twenty-fourth, an informal gathering concluded the trio of musical festivities honoring the Archduke, the performers including Colloredo's niece and Leopold's clavier pupil, Countess Antonie Lützow, and the Archduke and Archbishop, each taking fiddle in hand and joining the orchestra. At the end came "the famous young Mozart," who at the clavier "played various things by heart with as much art as grace." For these days of celebration, the court had augmented its musical forces by summoning from Munich—no doubt through Leopold's offices—the flutist Johann Baptist Becke,[8] and the soprano castrato Tommaso Consoli (in all probability the Ramiro in *La finta giardiniera*). He took the title role in Mozart's *serenata,* which, like Fischietti's, unfolded as an unstaged presentation, what Archduke Maximilian described as a *"musique-concert."*

2

MOZART HAD BEGUN his longest stay in Salzburg since returning from his first journey at the age of six: two and a half years would separate his arrival home after the miscarriage of *La finta giardiniera* and his next departure,

---

6 "You should see him now [1781]! Stupidity peers out of his eyes. He talks and holds forth for an eternity, and all in falsetto. . . . In a word, it is as if this gentleman had undergone a complete transformation." (Mozart would remark of the Abbot of Kaisheim: "He is a truly amiable man, despite being a priest and prelate.") Mozart reflected little upon the possibility of becoming kapellmeister in Kurköln: he remembered it as no less provincial than Salzburg. In 1781 Maximilian would recommend him as teacher of clavier to Princess Elizabeth of Württemberg (see p. 578 and XXVIII, n. 35). Maximilian was to send money to Mozart's widow within the month of his death and be among the first to attempt to collect his manuscripts.

7 Lessing arrived in Salzburg four days later; no record exists of his having met Mozart.

8 Becke—not to be confused with the pianist Ignaz von Beecke—made a contribution to *Il rè pastore*: his impending presence among Salzburg's instrumentalists inspired Mozart to scatter brilliant flute passages in the score.

a span offering him opportunities to consider and consolidate. Leopold looked upon this period as one in which his son might grow intellectually: the quiet pace of Salzburg offered the "opportunity in some measure to explore useful fields of knowledge, to cultivate the mind by more intense reading of good books in various languages, and to practice languages." He developed an enthusiastic acquaintance with literary culture, in later times describing how he would often "pull a book out of his pocket and read" as had been his "habit in Salzburg."

Beneath his outward show of *galanterie* he continued to mature as a composer and, as the score of *La finta giardiniera* threw into relief, this deeper Mozart made use of every promising occasion to reveal himself. But on the whole he once again came to terms with Salzburg circumstances: the necessity at once to turn from the ashes of *La finta giardiniera* to the poetic conceits of *Il rè pastore* had provided a valuable transition back to the previous state of things. Moreover, free of the nervous and physical strain endemic to the touring musician, he seemed reinvigorated. These became months of resilience and fecundity, his talent called for by the Residenz, the cathedral, the university, the local theater, the nobility, the patricians, and his colleagues. Music poured from his pen: even while preparing the performance of *Il rè pastore*, he had started an ambitious cycle of concertos.

In the spring of 1774, about three weeks after writing the *galant* Symphony in D, Mozart had produced what he called a "*Concertone,*" a composition related to the concerto grosso and *sinfonia concertante* (see XXI, n. 9), all characterized by multiple soloists confronting the full orchestra. In his *Concertone* (K. 190/186E), the oboe's and cello's moments in the spotlight notwithstanding, a pair of violins share the principal solo roles.[9] Here Mozart returned to explore further the instrument that had engaged his attention in his concerto K. 207 and the Antretter serenade, an inclination fully realized in the sequence of four *galant* violin concertos (like K. 190 and 207, all in three movements) brought into being in Salzburg during 1775: K. 211 in D; K. 216 in G; K. 218 in D; and K. 219 in A, the first dated 14 June, the last 20 December.

He would not have written these works for himself: by this time he picked up the violin willingly only at rare moments, for the most part at exuberant private gatherings, when the wine glasses clinked, his spirits soared and, with them, his confidence in his technique. He took in ill part having to play the instrument as part of the ensemble at court concerts in which the Archbishop and courtiers joined, occasions when Mozart turned apathetic and prickly.

---

9 Perhaps their modest technical demands offered Colloredo the opportunity to shine.

He practiced enough to maintain his bowing arm, but, once away from home, let his violin rest: "I can well imagine that your violin is hanging on the wall," Leopold would chide his son during his tour of 1777–1778. (As early as Mozart's second visit to Bologna, his mother had fretted that his violin might well be lying untouched.) Leopold lamented this neglect: ". . . many do not even know that you play the violin"; "you yourself do not know how well you play; if only you would *do justice* to yourself and *play with assurance, courage, and spirit* —yes, in effect, *as if you were Europe's first violinist.*"[10]

Reminding him of his capacity for putting disagreeable experiences from his mind, Leopold issued an admonition: "Out of foolish conceit, you must never play [the violin] with negligence . . . ," the imputation being that he had done so. Indeed, his habit of fiddling cavalierly during evenings at the Residenz—he smarted for having to wear livery when seated with the orchestra—had led the Archbishop to grumble. Recognizing an astonishing endowment—"he can play anything"—court violinist Antonio Brunetti had sought to change Colloredo's condescending estimate of Wolfgang's abilities with the bow. However, praise of the young man's potential did not impress an employer irritated by his insouciance when in the company of his orchestral colleagues. This exchange strengthens grounds for belief that Mozart composed the violin concertos of 1775 for Brunetti (who became the court's first violinist the following year): that his unhappiness with K. 219's Adagio forced Mozart to replace it with another (see n. 15) even suggests Brunetti as patron of the cycle. Though passagework and smart bowing effects take subordinate roles, the concertos call for a refined sense of phrase and a pure, singing Italian tone.

Baroque masters had furnished Mozart with precedents for his first violin concerto, K. 207 of 1773: an archaic flavor invades it; turns of phrase call to mind Vivaldi and Corelli as the impersonal and imposing composition parades its arresting melodies, each unit proud and sure of itself but showing little concern for what has marched before or will tread behind, the orchestra all the while remaining discreet.[11] Its role continues circumspect in K. 211 of 1775, which assumes a French rococo tone in the Andante,

---

10 Leopold adapted the final phrase from Wolfgang's letter to him of 6 October 1777 (see n. 22).

11 K. 207 has been linked to Leopold's remark (3 August 1778) about "your [Wolfgang's] concerto for Kolb." However, the reference would appear to bear upon some divertimento or serenade movement in which Franz Xaver Kolb, an amateur violinist active in Salzburg's musical life, distinguished himself. Some insist that, in the light of more than one musical resemblance to *Il rè pastore*, K. 207 maintain its traditional place as the first of the violin concertos of 1775—and this despite evidence that someone unknown altered the year on the manuscript from 1773 to 1775 and that handwriting studies of the score suggest 1773 as its date. Furthermore, cannot the music anticipate rather than reflect?

an *opéra-comique* ariette: here the solo violin sings the kind of enchanting melody Mozart would turn to account in Zaide's address to the sleeping Gomatz (see p. 488).

The broad opening Allegro of K. 216 puts to use the *ritornello* of Aminta's aria *"Aer tranquillo,"* from *Il rè pastore*;[12] and Mozart prepares the closing Rondeau as a savory potpourri of quotations from favorite tunes.[13] Yet, throughout the concerto, touches of Storm and Stress's darker colors enrich the picture but do not burst its *galant* frame, a stylistic equilibrium anticipating that of the Haffner Serenade (see below). Moreover, the relationship between soloist and the other instrumentalists, prosaic, indeed, elementary in K. 207 and 211, has here given way to intimate interplay even as demands upon the violinist mount and the orchestra speaks a more variegated language. These tendencies, continuing in the rest of the set, render the three final concertos a group unto itself.

The second of this inner constellation, K. 218, proffers its variety of humors with new authority: vigor in the Allegro; the elegiac in the Andante cantabile, the soloist inscribing arcs of sensuous sound; trenchant wit in the Rondeau, a kind of celebration whose episodes, like those of K. 216, include popular melodies, among them a theme suggesting bagpipes.[14] In the opening Allegro aperto of K. 219, the solo violin's entry suggests a prima donna's meditative accompagnato leading to an aria. If the Adagio flows with a pathos Brunetti found "too mannered" (*zu studiert*),[15] caprice overruns the Rondeau, in particular its exotic "Turkish" interlude; Mozart

---

12 Like most composers, from the early days of his career, Mozart had plundered his completed compositions for material to rework (see XIV, n. 4). He continued to convert opera overtures into independent symphonies (for *Ascanio*, see p. 296), adding an Allegro (K. 121/207a) to the two-movement overture to *La finta giardiniera*, probably in the spring of 1775; the following year he built upon the one-movement (Molto allegro) overture to *Il rè pastore*, subjoining to it both the opera's opening *Andantino* aria in a purely instrumental version, an oboe assuming the vocal line, and also a freshly composed finale in the form of a Presto assai (K. 102/213c). Such practical utilization of operatic odds and ends cannot be looked upon as forming part of Mozart's true symphonic oeuvre, which, however, does embrace those symphonies he condensed from serenades designed with the double purpose in mind.

13 That they include an allusion to the Strassburg, a contredanse dear to Wolfgang, inspired the Mozarts to give its name to K. 216, which Brunetti played at least once in the Salzburg theater: after a performance of Voltaire's *Zaïre*, the Strassburg concerto filled the time the actors needed to change costumes for an epilogue. Thus Salzburg heard K. 216 along with Michael Haydn's incidental music to the play, a score both Mozarts admired.

14 The movement includes material also used in the contredanses for Count Czernin, K. 269b (see pp. 525–26).

15 In 1776 Mozart composed a substitute Adagio, K. 261, even though, after K. 219, he had washed his hands of the violin concerto as a separate genre. (He continued to render its elements useful in seranade and divertimento.) K. 268/Anh. C 14.04 in E flat and K. 271a/271i in D have proved spurious.

built it of material from the ballet *Le gelosie del serraglio,* composed three years earlier for performance with *Lucio Silla* (see XVI, n. 28), the final movement thus evoking golden days in Milan.[16]

Nostalgia apart, he appeared content and never at a loss to summon a practical and comfortable response to even the most arid ideals of *galanterie.* This facility found its epitome in his concerto for three keyboards in F, K. 242 of February 1776, tailored to the digital limitations of Countess Maria Antonia Lodron and her daughters Aloisia and Josepha (the last—known to intimates as Giuseppina or Pepperl—a pupil of Leopold's).[17] It avoids complicated interaction among the soloists and also between them and the orchestra, the principle being one of alternation not integration, dialogue rather than interdependence. The work impresses by running passage-work and meandering figuration, both offering a simulacrum of virtuosity. Moreover, the middle movement, an Adagio, if without deep emotion, does put forward an ingratiating substitute: a most graceful melancholy.

For Countess Lützow, a professional at the keyboard, Mozart wrote the Concerto in C, K. 246 of April 1776 (which he took into his own repertory). The score unfolds with casual amiability; too casual, perhaps, for, despite moments of charming sentiment and élan, the work lacks profile and direction, though it churns an agreeable froth. Contrasting in its sweep and vibrance, K. 365/316a (between 1775 and 1777), a double piano concerto often associated with Nannerl, may also have been a vehicle for Mozart and the Countess.

As if to counterbalance forsaking the symphony, Mozart set about composing a number of divertimentos and serenades. Collections of loosely assembled and often episodic movements (see p. 252) and thus without the sustaining, unifying, and controlling impulses of his most recent symphonic production,[18] they nevertheless provided a testing-ground for his

---

16 The theme Mozart put to use appears twice in the ballet, both in major (#8) and minor (#32).

17 Pepperl's part, so meager as to be superfluous, dissolved when Mozart arranged the work for two instruments.

18 If Mozart differentiated among serenade, divertimento, and cassation, the lines of distinction have become too faint to decipher: at times, he used cassation and serenade as interchangeable nouns; besides, he referred to his divertimento K. 287/271H also as a cassation, as did his father, who, aggravating the problem, wrote *"Concerto o sia Divertimento"* on the manuscript of the divertimento K. 113. In search of generalizing conclusions, commentators tend to regard "divertimento" as connoting a work to be realized by a smaller group (in particular, one instrument to a string part), "serenade" as implying a larger ensemble and synonymous with cassation. Leopold's note may have indicated his view of K. 113 as a divertimento in dimension but a concerto in spirit. Terminological confusion became further confounded by Mozart's practice of fabricating symphonies out of serenades by extracting, reworking, and stringing together appropriate movements; and, into the bargain, perplexity hedges questions as to what made certain of these related compositions more appropriate to performance indoors, others to outdoors, some peculiar to the day, others to the night; hybrids, they obviously fulfilled divers duties.

symphonies to come, a laboratory for research relative to sonata, rondo, menuetto, variation, and the polemics of the concerto. Under the patronage of the first-year scholars of the university's faculty of philosophy, he wrote the serenade K. 204/213a[19] (August 1775) celebrating the end of the academic term. Like the energetic K. 203/189b of the preceding summer, doubtless also commissioned by students, this vividly scored agglomerate sheltered movements for solo violin akin to segments of a concerto. (He manufactured symphonies out of both K. 203 and 204.)

During the summer of 1776, he created the most impressive of these sprawling serenades, all in D: K. 250/248b, commissioned for the festivities attending the marriage of Maria Elizabeth, sister of Siegmund Haffner the Younger.[20] Three of the movements call for a virtuoso at the solo violin: the first Andante, the first Menuetto, and the Rondeau constitute a "Haffner violin concerto."[21] Such a happy occasion among friends would have tempted Mozart to pick up the bow.

Answering this mood by being for the most part leisurely and insouciant—a kind of holiday misrule often prevails in the serenades—for all that, the Haffner Serenade does not draw back from shadow and at moments must have outsoared the convivial garden regale; even at his *galant* best, he found it difficult to remain detached. Kaleidoscopic in its humors, the Haffner transcends the *style galant* while respecting its canons. And if, reveling in his technical mastery, he lovingly manipulated his material to considerable length, yet the overall arrangement and proportion of the work derived from the needs of the entertainment: the nine-movement Haffner Serenade expanded to twice the dimensions of the Storm and Stress symphonies. But nowhere does its invention exhaust itself, Mozart strengthening interest by a variety of brilliant instrumental colors: two each of oboes (or flutes), bassoons, horns, and trumpets in addition to the solo violin and the rest of the string family.

---

19 K. 204 has material in common with the problematic Symphony in D, K. 95/73n: its Andante opens with a theme recalling Menuetto I in K. 9, second of Mozart's Tessé sonatas (1764); shifted from triple to duple time, the same idea, close in contour to its lineaments in the symphony, appears in the second Andante of K. 204. Although folk song may provide the origin of the theme, the close agreement of its manifestation in K. 204 and 95 would appear to weaken doubts about the authenticity of the symphony.

20 The byname clung to him although no longer appropriate: his father had died in 1772. On the eve (21 July 1776) of the wedding, the musical party took place in the garden of the family's summer residence near the Loreto church.

21 A first Haffner Symphony emerged from the serenade, Mozart touching up structure and orchestration in the course of transition. For the more famous Haffner Symphony, K. 385 of 1782, which derived from a second celebrative composition written for the same family, see p. 626.

Smaller in scale and with touches of hard and knowing parody, K. 239 of January 1776, the so-called *serenata notturna*, at first glance suggests the venerable concerto grosso with its principle of counteraction. But here Mozart's modest instrumental groups do not engage: instead, they confirm one another. On the face of it preparing to paint a canvas in the style of the past, he proceeded with wit and charm, in his use of the kettledrums in particular, to portray not the energetic gestures of the Baroque but the gentle acquiescence of the Rococo.

Though the occasion for which Mozart wrote K. 239 remains un-known—Carnival?—the divertimentos K. 247 and 287/271H of June 1776 and June 1777, respectively, had the patronage of Countess Lodron and honored her name day. (They must have inspired Leopold's observation that his son wrote "long" divertimentos!) Mozart scored both for string quartet and two horns. Boasting an exquisite Adagio conceived in terms of a violin concerto, K. 287[22] has claim to be the most poetic creation of his season of Salzburg *galanterie*, an aesthetic more characteristically represented by his lighthearted, elegant, and Gallic—even if with touches of the slapdash—divertimento K. 251 of July 1776, called forth, for certain, by Nannerl's name day; in fact, a septet, it has the instruments of the Lodron divertimentos with the addition of an oboe.

To heighten the Archbishop's pleasure at table—not unlike Don Giovanni's, the supper laid, his private band playing—Mozart, following the imperatives of supply and demand, turned out a series of delicately proportioned divertimentos in three and four movements, in effect wind sextets (paired oboes, horns, and bassoons): K. 213 of July 1775; K. 240, 252/240a, and 253, the first two composed early in 1776, the third in August; and K. 270 of January 1777. The stiffness of the Milanese divertimentos has given way to effortless mastery of the wind band. Their genial content at odds with the often rueful, astringent quality of the instrumental combinations—a delectable paradox—these Colloredo divertimentos yield a motley tone of humor, irony, and pathos, the artful mixing of timbres giving a very personal suggestiveness to many a conventionality.

---

22 In an informal reading of this divertimento at Albert's hotel in Munich on 4 October 1777, Mozart played first violin, the challenges of its part as daunting as those in any of his concertos. Reporting the event to his father two days later, he wrote in jest of having performed as if he "were the greatest fiddler in all of Europe" (see n. 10). Leopold, in turn, took up his son's comment, making it the basis of an injunction that he return to practicing the violin and in fact become what he joked about being. How odd and ironic that commentators, lifting Leopold's borrowed words from context, cite them as proof of Mozart's position as the greatest violinist of his age, a level both knew to be within reach had he wished to take the pains. At his death, the inventory of his household goods listed two musical instruments, neither a violin: a piano and a viola.

During the summer of 1777, Mozart's rising interest in the winds led him to compose a three-movement concerto, K. 271k, for Giuseppe Ferlendis, an oboist from Bergamo who had joined the Archbishop's orchestra two years earlier. The concerto runs an untroubled decorative course making capital of Mozart's adeptness in dealing, when necessary, with the Rococo in undiluted state.[23] The recurrent theme of the finale would reappear in *The Abduction* (Blondchen's "*Welche Wonne*").

About the time Mozart completed the Ferlendis concerto, the Bohemian composer Franz Xaver Duschek and Josepha (born Hambacher), his vocal pupil and now bride of less than a year, came to Salzburg to visit her widowed maternal grandfather, Ignaz Anton Weiser. The pair met the Mozarts, and on 15 August Josepha performed in the Tanzmeistersaal, the handsome reception chamber of their apartment, Wolfgang and Nannerl also contributing to the music-making. She and Leopold made light of Josepha's talent, but Schiedenhofen, a friend of the household,[24] judged her soprano "uncommonly clear and agreeable; she had taste and her singing gave much pleasure."

Josepha's strong dramatic instincts inspired Mozart to revisit that musical idiom of his larger ambitions. (During these years in Salzburg he suggested a Jonah resigned to his residence in the Leviathan's stomach, filling the hours resourcefully while awaiting the moment to emerge; but this Jonah did from time to time peer forth in search of dry ground.) During August he composed for her the scena "*Ah, lo previdi . . . Ah, t'invola*," K. 272, a spiritual ancestor of Beethoven's "*Ah perfido*," whose premiere she would, in fact, give almost twenty years in the future. Taken from an *Andromeda* by Cigna-Santi, librettist of Mozart's *Mitridate*, K. 272 portrays the daughter of Cepheus at first in turmoil imagining the suicide of her beloved Perseus and then sinking into repose and bliss before a vision of their crossing the Lethe together. Built of impassioned accompagnato, arioso, and cavatina, this concert aria evokes the expressiveness of Gluck, a noble vocal line, stripped of decorative coloratura, even calling upon phrases characteristic of the elder master.

No less Gluck-like, if less heroic, "*Ombra felice! . . . Io ti lascio*," K. 255, unrolls as a traditional recitative and aria of farewell (from de Gamerra's [?] *Arsace*, which Michele Mortellari had set). This grand valediction had come into being during September 1776 for the alto castrato Francesco

---

23 Concerning Mozart's reworking of the concerto, see pp. 401–02.
24 The diary of Johann Baptist Joseph Joachim Ferdinand von Schiedenhofen, a Salzburg court councilor and friend of the Mozarts, contains valuable entries concerning the family.

Fortini, a member of Pietro Rosa's operatic road company then resident in Salzburg. At the same time, Mozart provided the troupe with a scena in *buffa* style for the tenor Antonio Palmini: "*Clarice cara*," K. 256, to be interpolated into Piccinni's *L'astratto, ovvero Il giocatore fortunato.* Such compositions served as substitutes for the operatic commissions Mozart thirsted after: in this area Salzburg offered little.[25]

The Residenz no longer turned its presence chambers into opera halls, and the new theater abutting upon the Hannibalplatz sheltered only itinerant troupes like Rosa's. An extended visit by a dignitary of Archduke Maximilian's rank alone could inspire Colloredo to dip into his purse and command an opera; and from the courts of Vienna and Munich the Mozarts heard not a word. They endured hurt and anxiety, fearful that the tide had ebbed once and for all. Mozart, for whom opera constituted *the* loftiest genre, had tumbled into the situation of a painter longing to devote himself to imposing dramatic canvases, in the *grand goût,* but reduced to turning out picturesque scenes and landscapes. As the recurring dream of opera and Italy visited him anew, disappointment gnawed, and by the autumn of 1776 Salzburg once again soured his temper. Between the lines of his famous letter to Padre Martini (4 September 1776) runs the plea that somehow he contrive the means to lead him—and Leopold, too![26]— back across the Alps.

On its surface the letter reads as an appeal for the revered scholar's opinion of a humble student's progress as a contrapuntist: the Mozarts had enclosed that offertory antiphon written for the Bavarian Elector, as archaic a piece as they had in the cupboard. Replying from Bologna, Martini ignored the hints, devoting his words to the professed request: they expressed pleasure at finding in K. 222, an exercise cast in an ingenious homemade *strenge Satz,* "all that modern music requires"—to a man most at home in the tonal world of the Renaissance, perhaps the antiphon did seem modern—and complimented the young man's "great improvement in composition." Furthermore, Martini expressed a desire to possess likenesses of both him and his father.[27] The meaning could not have been clearer: the

---

25 During the spring of 1775, he had composed two arias for tenor, K. 209 and 210, to be inserted into *buffa* operas. The second, intended for Piccinni's *L'astratto,* has a surprising affinity to the music Rossini would give Count Almaviva playing the drunk in *The Barber of Seville.*

26 Leopold made a draft in German or Italian and then had an Italian colleague either translate or polish it.

27 Martini's answer survives only in a draft that does not include the matter of the portraits. As evinced by Leopold's response, the final version did.

portraits were to enter the padre's collection; the originals were to stay in place.

Though a ploy—Wolfgang knew that as critic and instructor Martini had little to offer him—the whining letter from Salzburg unfolded a true account of a musical provincialism that had reduced the father to lassitude and offered the son a future built upon the sands of the court's shallow taste. In particular he lamented the frustrations of writing church music for the Archbishop, complaining that "even a solemn mass said by the Prince [Archbishop] must not last longer than three quarters of an hour," a caveat at odds with the majesty and traditions of Salzburg's cathedral, where, in Archbishop Schrattenbach's day, an entire symphony might have been heard during high mass (see p. 223).

Mozart did not always hold the court-appointed aesthetic course. The "*Missa longa*," K. 262/246a of summer 1775 (the sobriquet appears on the manuscript), had departed from rule in respect to both duration and style: disregarding the Archbishop's aversion to ambitious counterpoint, Mozart permitted himself two proud fugues, one terminating the Gloria, the other the Credo. In contrast, the trio of richly tooled masses in C—K. 258 (December 1775), 259 (December of either 1775 or 1776), and 257 (late 1776 or early 1777)[28]—not only followed Colloredo's demand for brevity and the idiom of *galanterie* but accommodated his taste for a bit of pomp in the scoring, a fondness, as Mozart put it, for "trumpets [*trombe di guerra*], tympany, etc."

K. 259's epithet of "Organ-Solo" Mass derives from the organ obbligato in the Benedictus, a device with recent (1775) and distinguished precedent in Joseph Haydn's *missa brevis* in honor of Saint John of God. Hurtling onward in breathless fashion, K. 259 has the sleekest finish of the three C-major masses,[29] which, despite the refined chiaroscuro, flowing

---

28 On 28 May 1778, Leopold made mention of a mass the family nicknamed the Spaur. Inasmuch as Friedrich Franz Joseph Spaur became Dean of the Salzburg consistory in 1777, Mozart might have put to use either K. 257 or 258 (the context of Leopold's letter excludes K. 259) in a service celebrating the preferment. Or he may have dusted off an earlier mass: K. 262 cannot be ruled out; nor is K. 275/272b—a *missa brevis* written during 1777 before Mozart's departure for Munich in September—out of the running.

29 The rococo mass's propriety remains a question still argued: whether such music inspires or unsettles religious emotions. In truth, when of the highest quality, its gifts to the spirit betoken no less than those of great church scores of any other era; the occasional problems of suitability the *galant* liturgical style can still awaken in communicants or in spectators at divine service (or even in the concert hall) derive from personal and insular terms of cultural reference: the Holy Spirit appears as much at home in Ottobeuren, Die Wies, and Vierzehnheiligen as in Vienna's gothic St. Stephen's. That the artistic idiom of the Rococo served its secular as well as religious needs paralleled a phenomenon recurrent in previous periods, one reinforcing the doctrine

line, and inspired detail in their interplay of orchestral and vocal forces, somehow do not take a firm hold on the memory. Yet, even in the face of limitations from without confining Mozart's response to the incomparable text, he did not coquet with it: the score gave answer not in musical poetry but in musical prose of a crispness and eloquence that turned the Residenz's aesthetic coercions to admirable account. In respect to idiom and dimension, composing the three masses in C bespoke a confrontation not with a dilemma but with what had become a challenge; their composition could not have involved exhilarating wanderings on the heights or searchings in the recesses of the soul, yet they honor God by exuding a tone of high courtesy even as they enthrall the ear.

He must have intended for the Organ-Solo Mass the spirited epistle sonata (see p. 302), K. 263 of December 1776. With its pair of trumpets, it stands outside the series of epistle sonatas he had composed between the summer of 1775 and the spring of 1776 (K. 212, 241, 244, and 245), all scored only for violins and basso continuo. Like K. 263, the last two have organ obbligatos, embellishments that augment the engaging contrast between the texture of the sonatas and the thinner, more neutral surface of the masses they enrich, the touch of restless turbulence in K. 245, for example, lending to its mass (K. 194) a spasm of emotional color. Like tympany and *trombe di guerra*, such a fleeting show of impasto delighted Colloredo's fancy for flourishes in moderation.

He was easily pleased: one simply gave him what he wanted. However, by this time Mozart may well have dared ask himself the famous query Rousseau put to Voltaire: "Tell us . . . how many works of virile beauty have you sacrificed to your finesse, how many great masterpieces has that spirit of gallantry of yours cost you, who are so fertile in producing pretty trifles?" Mozart's scores of the period often reveal ennui: it lurks in the lean tissue of much of his *galant* music, and beneath lay the sensitive pith of the matter: the quandary of maintaining a satisfactory professional and personal relationship with the Archbishop. It had started to totter toward dangerous imbalance, on his side a kind of choleric quarrelsomeness, on the Mozarts' an astonishing lack of tact and judgment.

The arrival in Salzburg during the winter of 1776–1777 of a French pianist named Jeunehomme lifted Mozart's spirits and, in the sequel, excited the imagination of more than one Mozartean. Little is known of the visit

---

that God took on human shape as He went about His task of redeeming mankind. For the general populace, a church looking at first glance like a gilded opera house offered anything but an obstacle to worship. Ironically, an elite of the Enlightened irreligious led the attack upon the rococo aesthetic in the sanctuary.

or the visitor other than his associating the concerto K. 271 of January 1777 with her. Legend asserts that she awakened his passion and inspired the composition. He did refer to the concerto as "the one for the Jeune-homme woman" (*das für die jenomy* [*sic*]; his phonetic spelling of French lays open how wretchedly he pronounced it). The standard English translation of his letters adds a touch of romance by making her into a mademoiselle, the gratuitous affix at variance with the fact that both Mozarts called her "Madame."[30] Among commentators restricted to English, the "Mlle" helped inspire the myth of a love affair, although a knowledge of German has not always impeded the same leap. At all events, Mozart must have had his future tours no less than Madame in mind when creating this first of his major piano concertos,[31] a touchstone work in which the soloist at once insists upon center stage.

The opening Allegro bespeaks powerful resolve as, returning to the freshness and urgency of K. 175, Mozart shed the expedient livery of *galanterie*: the piano will not wait for the instruments to complete their initial statement but interrupts, orchestra and soloist each enunciating friendly, if emphatic, determination to have the best of it. They conclude a truce in a plaintive Andantino in the minor, contours and coloration calling to mind an operatic arioso with the pathos of Storm and Stress. The closing Rondeau: Presto—Mozart would adapt its refrain for Monostatos's *"Alles fühlt der Liebe Freuden"* in *The Magic Flute*—chatters with an abundance of detail, the movement woven like the finest linen. It seems of a piece that K. 271 proclaimed its composer's self-possession and awareness of artistic purpose close upon the moment the structure of his Salzburg life began to fall about his ears.

3

DURING AUGUST 1777 the Archbishop hurled cruel advice at him—"that he betake himself to Naples and enroll in one of its conservatories." Not a fool, but carried away by fury, Colloredo thrust at what he thought the tenderest spot in Mozart's musical equipment: his still very German style. At bottom, however, the outburst sprang from very different, indeed conflicting, grounds: outrage to observe Mozart's undisguised disinclination to devote his future to the Residenz. Aesthetic preferences apart, Col-

---

30 Mozart on 5 April 1778; his father fifteen days later.
31 On more than one occasion Mozart pretended to have created for patrons works he had, in fact, slipped from his portfolio.

loredo appreciated and rewarded him with commendable consistency, but by the summer of 1777, he and his father no longer masked, even from the palace, their perception of Salzburg as a torpid place of exile.

Neither could find a good word for the city despite an archiepiscopal beneficence that for fifteen years had accommodated their requests for leave. This generosity they had, in turn, abused by overstaying and, as Colloredo well knew, by unashamed soliciting of positions in foreign places. Yet both he and his predecessor, in deference to Wolfgang's talent, had stomached Leopold's dilatory maneuvering abroad and permitted the pair to slip once again into their old places whenever they crept back.

At home their superior manner gave offense precisely because it declared their disdain for Salzburg: it was not Vienna, not London, not Paris, not Munich—unarguable insufficiencies but without remedy. Before 1777 and their collision with Colloredo, they would have found difficulty setting forth any defensible rationale for their loathing of Salzburg, unless they reasoned that from their paper obligation to the Archbishop grew the seeds of that recurring failure to secure permanent employment elsewhere: those to whom they applied looked upon their readiness to play Colloredo false as anything but a recommendation of prospective moral engagement. Leopold and Wolfgang may have come to think themselves victims who could not win.

Yet, in defiance of Wolfgang's fading fame, their demands for special treatment continued. In truth, the Residenz would have been pleased to be done with them as early as 1774: at that time Leopold and Wolfgang had sought furlough for yet another trip to Vienna even though they had been there only the preceding year on a leave their ingenuity had prolonged to over two months. Colloredo had turned the request of 1774 into an opportunity to advise Wolfgang to quit Salzburg for good inasmuch as, in his terms, it could offer no future. At once the Mozarts dropped the petition, horrified by the plain speaking it had provoked and the loss of regular income it threatened; they had become too long accustomed to the Residenz's drawing in its horns. The father, moreover, could not imagine Wolfgang going his way alone. Yet, in spite of raps from the archiepiscopal rod, Leopold refused to confront reality: the days of indulgence had passed; at the Residenz the conviction grew that he would be wise to treat his son like a grown man who, once and for all, had either to come to terms with the facts of Salzburg life or make his exit; something between would no longer do.

If at the time of *La finta giardiniera* Colloredo had discovered no politically expedient way to turn aside Elector Max Joseph's request that

Mozart travel to Munich to produce the opera and, into the bargain, had honored the tradition, by this time ridiculed in chorus, of Papa's accompanying him everywhere, the court did have the recompense of seeing them return chastened. For two years they kept their peace. Then, putting aside the limits connoted, if not defined, Leopold precipitated the crisis prompting the Archbishop's acrimony, and then an anger threatening the family with ruin.

On 14 March 1777 Leopold presented him with a petition, now lost. Subsequent documentation suggests that it contained a plea for an increase in salary. But, locked into the strict hierarchy of the orchestra with its graded titles and corresponding emoluments, Leopold could not have hoped for a significant change in his situation; the entreaty must have concerned his son, whose relationship to the court had been, from the beginning, looser, indeed what he himself called "only half-time service." Whatever the appeal, it found no favor, and in June father and son again planned to hazard a request for liberty to tour during the summer. A miscalculation: an impending but still unscheduled visit of the Emperor required all servants of the court to remain on duty; not until 31 July did Joseph II, returning from Paris, arrive in Salzburg, confer with Colloredo, hurry on to Vienna, and thus free the Mozarts to sue for leave.

Colloredo would not hear of Leopold's going but again wondered why Wolfgang did not set out without Papa. Leopold, in fact, had begun to weigh this idea—the bizarre thought of his wife's substituting for him on the journey perhaps already flitting across his mind—when the Archbishop demurred: for the moment, everyone was to stay in place. His musical household had begun to plunge toward crisis, animosities hardening between its German and Italian members: a new kapellmeister, Giacomo Rust, an Italian, his surname notwithstanding,[32] had been striving, and with mounting despair, to assert authority over Michael Haydn. (Rust would soon succumb to a mysterious and expedient illness he blamed on the weather and return to Venice early in 1778.) Besides, squabbling also broke out within the national factions: Haydn and Leopold clashed. Passing over sober reflection on the wisdom of Wolfgang's putting forward yet another petition to tour at a time when the Archbishop desired everyone at his task until the dissensions had run their course—and also misjudging the family's prestige in the court's eyes—Leopold fastened upon what he thought to be the tactical moment: early in August he had Wolfgang submit the request.

---

32 He had received the appointment in June 1777, Fischietti becoming a titular kapellmeister.

Leopold's voice leaps from its every sentence. Adopting an ironic, scholarly tone foreign to the mocking banter of his son and calculated to put the Archbishop in his place, Leopold alias Wolfgang (Colloredo could not have been fooled) set about reading the Primate of Germany a lecture on the Gospels. The heart of the communication offers a mixture of pretended subservience and outright cheek.[33]

"Most gracious Sovereign, Prince, and Lord! By taking pains to put their children into the position of earning their own bread, parents fulfill an obligation both to themselves and to the state. The more talent the children have received from God, the greater their obligation to make use of it in order to improve their own and their parents' circumstances ... and to provide for their own fortune and future. The Gospels teach us to profit from our talents.[34] Accordingly, before God and my conscience I owe it to my father (who indefatigably devotes all his hours to my upbringing) to be grateful to him and, with all the strength I can summon, to lighten his burden and to take care of myself at the present time and later of my sister, too. . . . May Your Serene Highness therefore graciously permit me to beg most submissively to be released from service [*Dienstentlassung*] as I am obliged to make use of the coming September lest I be exposed to the bad weather of the quickly ensuing cold months."

At once grandly written, theologically sophisticated, punning, and insolent, this passage no doubt kindled the wrath Colloredo emptied upon Wolfgang. Some three years earlier, when he received the Archbishop's advice to quit Salzburg, the disintegration of its musical establishment had not yet threatened. But now the mounting disarray provided the Mozarts a situation they thought to turn to their advantage: it appears plain that Leopold composed the suit for Wolfgang's discharge in the belief that a disheartened Colloredo—not even a salary of one thousand gulden could keep Rust in Salzburg—by this time eager to hold on to him, would feel intimidated and deny the request for a release only in order to grant in its stead both an increase in salary and a leave. But in his own hand the Archbishop penciled on the quittance of the petition:

---

33 In light of the recipient's temperament, the petition exhibited even less tact than the *species facti* Leopold had submitted to Joseph II in 1768.

34 Luke 19:11ff and Matthew 25:14ff have relevance to Leopold's purport only in the Vulgate, where, in both cases, Saint Jerome used *talentum* for the word Luther rendered in the first passage as *Zentner*, in the second as *Pfund* (in the King James Version, pound and talent, respectively). Recourse to biblical allusions had a tradition in official Salzburg documents, and Leopold's play upon the twofold meaning in German of *Talent*, if not original, came off well. The Archbishop, however, was not amused.

"Father and son herewith granted permission to seek their fortune else-where according to the Gospel."[35] With this ironic injunction, he cashiered *both* Mozarts.

Learning of his dismissal from a *decretum* directed to his son on 1 September, Leopold suffered shock. Only then did he glimpse the depth of Colloredo's displeasure. A superior education, not insignificant culture, experience in the great world, and mordant wit had made it difficult for Leopold to assume the servant's role with persuasive conviction. Nevertheless, he made the attempt to observe the court's formalities, though the obsequiousness and infinite deference Colloredo's savage egoism demanded had remained in large measure beyond him (and altogether beyond Wolfgang); now the high-handed petition left Colloredo in no error as to the level of both Mozarts' true and intolerable impertinence. Few had the right to address him in tones implying equality of dignity. Leopold had set the stage for his own fall.

The Archbishop determined to make the father swallow the leek and, at the same time, his patience at an end, pounced upon the opportunity to rid Salzburg of the son, so filled with himself. (In Michael Haydn the court would continue to have an admirable composer—if unreliable organist.) His diction parroting Maria Theresa's, Colloredo, railing against the Mozarts, refused any longer to "put up with their traveling about begging." He hurled his thunderbolt, and only after a prostrate Leopold suffered weeks of anguish and public disgrace was he restored to his former position. A *decretum* of the Archbishop (26 September 1777) rehabilitated him. Having petitioned for revocation of his dismissal, he found himself returned to "the position formerly occupied," but with the understanding that "he conduct himself calmly and peacefully with the kapellmeister and other persons employed in the court's musical establishment," an allusion to the controversy with Michael Haydn. (Leopold pretended to find the reference incomprehensible.) The directive closed with the enjoinment that he "take pains to render good service to the Church as well as to His Grace's Person," demeaning turns of phrase. Yet, although Col-

---

35 The case of Johann Sebastian Bach's petition for release from service in Weimar (1717) comes to mind: Duke Wilhelm Ernst, angered by what he held to be the request's peremptory tone, kept him under arrest for almost a month. Bach left Weimar in disgrace. By Mozart's day, Enlightened thought had changed the atmosphere, and though instances of coercion and tyranny did obtain, artists, musicians, scholars, and writers could, on the whole and with ease, loosen the ties binding them to a particular court: their unimpeded movement from state to state prevailed throughout the Reich and contributed to the remarkable efflorescence of the German spirit during this period.

loredo saw to Leopold's degradation, at no time did he order him struck from the payroll.

With the news of his removal, he had taken to bed, and, even after reinstatement, remained shattered. Excepting sporadic bursts of desperate determination, he never fully recovered his audacity, indeed his self-confidence. In the autumn of 1777 and almost in his fifty-ninth year, Leopold Mozart passed from middle age to become a broken and often hysterical old man, guile now his only weapon.

It is an exercise in the unhistorical to denigrate Colloredo as incorrigible or philistine. He was neither, but, rather, an absolute monarch. That he did not hand the Mozart affair to subordinates to regulate but gave it his personal and retributive attention evidenced a visceral antipathy: impatience with Leopold and Wolfgang had yielded to pique; pique to contempt; contempt to aversion.

Even when hopes for Leopold's rehabilitation had begun to materialize, the household on the Hannibalplatz continued humiliated and in despair. After almost three and a half decades in service and many a proud climb, the distinguished and clever Leopold Mozart had completely missed his footing. To cover his embarrassment and preserve something of his reputation he found no course but to lie about his and Wolfgang's roles in what he called "the story." Schiedenhofen recorded in his diary: "In the afternoon [6 September 1777] . . . I visited the Mozarts, where I found the father ill because he and his son have been dismissed from service thanks to the latter's having presented an application to the highest authority for permission to travel." The Mozarts had given Schiedenhofen their version of "the story." The request had, of course, been for Wolfgang's release from service in order to travel. Leopold strove to suppress a complete account and to paint Wolfgang and himself as baffled innocents, Colloredo as an unpredictable tyrant. (In fact, the Archbishop had not only granted the petition but, in addition—a humiliating piece of mischief—given Wolfgang his father as an unencumbered, that is, unemployed, companion, perhaps an ironic reversal of Leopold's having kept a grown man on leading strings.) Misrepresentation persisted as the only expedient by which the Mozarts could explain their recent ordeal. They proved foolish enough to play this game in apartments in which the truth had become known.

4

HAVING RECEIVED HIS release with the Archbishop's devastating recommendation that he seek Italian schooling still in his ears, Mozart, surrounded by illness and confusion, prepared to turn his steps toward Munich; it still floated before his mind's eye as his golden city. Well before the crisis, he had wrung from Leopold a nebulous agreement, no more than a sop, as to his one day leaving the Tanzmeisterhaus; he yearned to break loose: "You could hardly wait for the moment . . . ," recalled Leopold, who did not long stick at using the meaningless understanding to lay responsibility for the family's broken fortunes at Wolfgang's door, alleging that his too eager impatience had quickened the crisis. In a state of uncertainty, for a time he shouldered the guilt. Perhaps at first he posited a link between his waxing hostility against his father and the calamity that had overtaken him and then went on to imagine the thought as bringing on the event; weeks after his departure, in the course of reflecting upon Leopold's humiliation, he could still blurt out: "I was the sole cause."

Yet even if he had been high-handed at court, his father, alone, prepared the march of events; moreover, his abased and agitated condition upon beholding the dimensions of his blunder had thrown his son into perplexity: the once Zeus-like parent lost all capacity and aroused in him a pity that resolved itself into embarrassment. "This was, you see, the . . . most important reason for my quitting Salzburg in such a hurry." But at least the muddle had opened a path out of the labyrinth.

When he framed his plan and composed the fatal petition, Leopold had felt able to force a leave for himself, too: never did he "imagine having to experience that sad day [of separation from Wolfgang]." Not until his reinstatement did he take firm hold of the at-first-glance unaccountable idea of splitting the family in two, Nannerl remaining with him in Salzburg, Anna Maria going off with Wolfgang on his travels. Newly risen from his own ashes, he now had to stay behind and rebuild his career, if only for his wife's security. "I solemnly swear to you," he subsequently wrote Wolfgang, "that . . . I bound myself to Salzburg in order, come what may, to assure your . . . mother a pension." For his own peace of mind he leaned upon the matter of the pension as dramatic and conclusive evidence that during those difficult September days, not he but fate had cast the die: to Mama had fallen the role of companion on the journey.

Leopold viewed her main task as guarding against that susceptibility he counted the most dangerous threat to the young man's fulfilling himself: his intense responsiveness to women. Perhaps Mozart attempted to stand up against the idea of his requiring a governess-duenna: Leopold felt it politic to speak only of the need of someone to attend to the business of housekeeping. In the circumstances, for the first time the Mozarts had to improvise an important undertaking:[36] their prestige had fallen off and with it the confidence and connections to shape a well-considered course. How the court must have laughed as the almost-twenty-two-year-old master set out to conquer the world, not Papa, but Mama, now at his side.[37]

Before their departure, Leopold had commissioned a local artist to paint Wolfgang wearing the insignia of the Golden Order, and, early in December 1777, Hagenauer's forwarders would dispatch the portrait to Padre Martini in Bologna.[38] It had "no great value as art," Leopold acknowledged, though assuring Martini of its "most excellent likeness: that is what he looks like." ("A unique likeness," Leopold again emphatically observed at the time it left the Tanzmeisterhaus.) He stares forth, a homely young man seeming somewhat older than his years and with a troubled expression. This gloomy Wolfgang remained behind on canvas; his own mien altered as soon as the family carriage started to roll.

Carrying him and his mother, early in the morning of 23 September 1777, it pierced the Klausentor and took the road to Munich; Anna Maria had beheld Salzburg's panorama for the last time. In the apartment on the Hannibalplatz, Leopold and Nannerl verged toward emotional collapse as Wolfgang, moving through the lovely landscape, began to shed the burdens long afflicting him: the court, the Archbishop—Papa. "My heart," he would write home, "has been as light as a feather since I got away . . . !" The sparkling creature of earlier years reappeared. (With two Salzburgers alone in the carriage, could the mood have remained serious?) His father's anguished retrospection had always been foreign to him. Free of authority—Mama was easily managed—he passed from his usual passivity in practical matters to become what he called (ironically?) "a second Papa," who, "attentive to everything," knew how to deal with postilions, porters, and the like (*Kerls*), mastering difficult situations, so he charmingly claimed, by putting on the solemn look of his new portrait.

---

36 Letters of credit arranged by Hagenauer and loans from Ignaz Anton Weiser, Johann Franz Kerschbaumer (a Salzburg merchant), and Abbé Bullinger helped make the journey possible. A Jesuit, Franz Joseph Johann Nepomuk Bullinger had, upon the suppression of the Order in Bavaria, made his way from Ingolstadt to Salzburg (c. 1774), where he worked as tutor in the palaces of various noble families. Like Leopold a born Swabian, he soon became an intimate of the Mozart household. Wolfgang called him "my best friend of all."

37 At eighteen and alone, Handel had quit his native Halle to seek his fortune in Hamburg, a circumstance in no way unusual.

38 It hangs in Bologna's Conservatorio di Musica G. B. Martini; the Mozart Museum in Salzburg possesses a copy made in 1926. Leopold did not act upon Martini's tactful suggestion that he, too, send his portrait: ". . . I do not think my snout merits being put in the company of men of talent."

Leopold's influence receded with every league. Recent weeks had re-vealed him stripped of his magic power—indeed, naked: the authoritarian himself degraded by authority. As Wolfgang's letters little by little dis-closed to him his new and shadowy position, he would become reduced to almost Lear-like apoplectic rages, post after post laying bare his new, fallen, and helpless condition. Wolfgang had suddenly spun out of his orbit and beyond his control.[39]

39 Within two months, Leopold committed an error revealing his deep inward recognition of the degree to which his relationship with Wolfgang had turned around. The complimentary close of his letter to Anna Maria and Wolfgang of 10 November ran: "I am your old husband and son." Saucy Wolfgang ended his letter of the seventeenth to Nannerl and Leopold with "I am your young brother and father" and pointed out Leopold's slip. He, in turn, closed his answer of a week later: "I am your old husband and father, N.B., not your son."

CHAPTER XIX

The Tour with Mama: Prelude

BY WAY OF Wasserburg, Wolfgang and his mother arrived in Munich on 24 September and put up at Franz Joseph Albert's Hotel (Zum schwarzen Adler) in the Kaufingerstrasse. Their plan of action followed a familiar pattern; fees, profits, and gifts earned by concerts and special commissions were to cover the expenses of traveling through the ecclesiastical and secular courts of the Reich;[1] the ultimate purpose: inciting some prince or municipality to offer Wolfgang a permanent post.

He seemed a colt galloping in a field, a new resourcefulness evident in his visits both to Count Seeau—that he had knowledge of "the story" should have sounded a warning about spinning fantasies—and to the family's patron, Count Zeil, Bishop of Chiemsee. To them he indicated his hopes for serving Munich and its Elector. The Mozarts continued to bustle about, meeting friends and going to the theater.[2] "We lead a most charming life," Anna Maria wrote her husband, "up early, late to bed, and visitors all day long." "Everything will come out right," she assured him,

---

1 Wolfgang had in mind a journey extending beyond Germany; not so Leopold (see n. 29).

2 They attended Gustav Grossmann's *Henriette oder Sie ist schon verheiratet*, an adaptation of Rousseau's *Julie, ou la nouvelle Héloïse*, and took exceptional pleasure in *Das Fischermädchen*, a German version of Piccinni's *La pescatrice*. This performance made Wolfgang long to write a German opera, an inclination, so his father would insist, born less of his infatuation with the genre than with the leading lady, Margarethe Kaiser.

"when the hooks and eyes (*Hafftel* [*sic*]) have been put on." Was Thresel, the housemaid, "punctual in taking Bimperl [the fox terrier] to piss?" Anna Maria also asked about the pet birds, sent her prayers, and greeted her old companion: "Adio ben mio [*sic*]. Keep well. Shove your ass into your mouth; I wish you good night; shit in your bed. . . ."

Wolfgang felt much in command and wrote home with regularity and in naughty high spirits. Barely out of Salzburg, he advised Leopold—and not even in the family cipher—to "take care of his health . . . not to vex himself, but to laugh heartily, to be merry, and always to bear in mind with gratitude, as we do, that although Mufti H. C. is a prick, God is merciful, compassionate, and full of love." A horrified Leopold in turn begged him to commit to paper no more quips about H. C.: "Remember that I am here [in Salzburg]; such a letter may go astray or find its way into other hands." Wolfgang's psychological independence seemed to have dawned at a stroke; Leopold's power to arouse his fears appeared to have vanished overnight. Yet in spite of good-humored fooling and jokes, he showed filial duty and ceremonial courtesy in his letters,[3] handling the remnants of parental authority with ease.

Advice, of course, continued to flow from Papa: Wolfgang was to avoid "strong wines and too much wine"; he must be "inordinately polite to courtiers"; perhaps he might give a concert in Seeau's garden or compose a piece for the viola da gamba, the Elector's favorite instrument; if questioned concerning his former salary, Wolfgang was to speak of the Salzburg Residenz's parsimony toward its German retainers and at the same time throw a few bricks at its well-paid Italian musicians. He had little time to digest this counsel before Zeil apprised him of a message from the Elector: "At present, it is still too early." In words that might have been Colloredo's, he recommended that the young man "travel to Italy. . . . I am not refusing him, but it is still too early."[4]

To Italy! Had Max Joseph remembered those long Storm and Stress passages in *La finta giardiniera*; or had he been in touch with the court of Salzburg and felt it politic to echo its Archbishop? Outraged by the "flagrant infatuation of so many German princes with Italy and the Italians" (*entsezlichen* [*sic*] *Welschlands-Paroxismus*), Wolfgang continued to pull strings

---

3 He conformed to custom in addressing his father with the formal *Sie* and not the informal *du*, a pronoun symbolizing equality and thus reserved in the eighteenth century for relationships less hierarchical than those between children and parents.
4 At their second meeting, he found Seeau "not so natural as at the first": in no time a policy of caution in respect to the visitor had formed.

so that he might present his case in person and countervail by stressing his Italian credentials.

On the morning of 30 September he entered the Munich Residenz with permission to station himself in a narrow chamber through which Max Joseph would pass on his way to chapel. An informal encounter had been arranged: His Highness, progressing to mass and then to the hunt, would pause. For his father's benefit, Wolfgang wrote an account of the meeting.

"Count Seeau went by and greeted me in a most friendly way.... When the Elector came up to me, I said: 'Your Electoral Highness, allow me to dare lay myself most humbly at your feet and offer you my services?' 'So, you have left Salzburg for good?' 'Yes, Your Electoral Highness, for good.' 'But why? Did you have a quarrel with him?' 'Why, in faith, Your Highness, I only requested permission to travel [*nur um eine Reise gebeten*]; he refused it. I was therefore compelled to take this step, though I had long contemplated leaving, for Salzburg is most certainly no place for me.' 'Good God! There's a young man for you! But certainly your father is still in Salzburg?' 'Yes, Your Electoral Highness. He most humbly throws himself [at your feet] etc. I have already been to Italy three times; I have written three operas;[5] I am a member of the Academy of Bologna, where I had to pass an examination at which many maestros have labored and sweated for four to five hours; I completed it within an hour. May that witness my ability to serve at any court. My sole wish, however, is to serve Your Highness, who himself is a great———.' 'Yes, my dear child, but there is no vacancy here. I am sorry. If only there were a vacancy here.'[6] 'I assure Your Highness that I should certainly do honor to Munich.' 'But it is of no use; there is no vacancy here.' He said this as he walked away."

Wolfgang had properly argued that he had already taken from Italy what he required and, indeed, had awakened its notice: following Leopold's suggestion, he had emphasized the honor won in Bologna. Less wise had been to fall in with his father's example of distorting the circumstances surrounding the departure from Salzburg: Mozart failed to perceive the Elector's acquaintance with the facts. As he questioned, Max Joseph had sounded a series of caveats from which the young man neglected to draw the proper inferences. He did not hear the implications behind Max Joseph's words and disparaged Salzburg and misrepresented

---

5 That is, the three Vienna commissioned for Milan: *Mitridate, Ascanio in Alba,* and *Lucio Silla.*

6 A transparent excuse: even if, as a rule, the departure or death of a court musician created a vacancy or *Vacatur* by freeing a corresponding budgeted salary, supplementary funds might have been tapped; or the Elector could have provided the means from his *Kabinettskasse.*

its Archbishop.[7] The Elector of Bavaria must have wished to spare himself any embroilment: probing lightly, he found a situation with which he did not wish to deal. Leopold had made his son a figure of controversy. Perhaps he had begun to appear an eccentric.

2

WOLFGANG HAD RELEASED an aggressive bombardment; the Elector, in turn, raised a shield emblazoned with "No vacancy." From Salzburg, Leopold indicated that it would be wise to quit the field at this point and seek another fortress to storm. But Mozart lingered, delighting in Munich, in the company of friends, and in making music for them at Albert's hotel.

Albert put forward a plan to keep his young friend nearby: to set up a group of ten sponsors, each contributing a modest monthly stipend, the aggregate providing Wolfgang a decent income. He clutched at the suggestion, which Leopold, from afar, viewed with skepticism. Would the scheme be like "fires of straw that kindle quickly and end in smoke?" Who would these patrons be—reliable merchants or flighty, unpredictable aristocrats? What would be expected in return? If, as seemed likely, the less than straightforward Seeau furnished the most substantial donation, would Wolfgang then become his hostage, a musical factotum drudging away in the Munich court theaters? Though infuriated by his son's failure to see the perils of the scheme, Leopold managed to veil his irritability and impatience. Within weeks, this control would wear away.

Unknown to Wolfgang, another and more practical proposal to assist him had emanated from Munich: Joseph Mysliveček had written to Leopold with an offer to help his son secure an operatic commission from Naples. A patient in a Munich hospital and as yet unaware of Wolfgang's presence in the city, Mysliveček lay recovering from the effects of a barbarous and disfiguring treatment to halt the advancing calamities of venereal disease, a predicament Leopold exploited as a warning to Wolfgang: "Surely, *propria culpa haec acciderunt* [this happened through his own fault]. Whom can he blame but himself and his detestable life? What a disgrace before the whole world! Everybody must flee and abhor him; truly a self-created misery." Once informed of the plan, Wolfgang had to announce himself to Mysliveček; but Leopold did not want them to meet: Wolfgang was to communicate by post, exculpating his neglect to visit with the ex-

---

7 A foolish course for someone still so weak in the strategies of self-protection that time and again his natural candor betrayed his attempts to misreport; but perhaps this lie had proved so imperative and irresistible that Leopold and Wolfgang had come to believe it.

cuse—at twenty-two!—that his mother forbade his going to the hospital ("*dass die Mamma es dir verbiethet* [*sic*]").

He nevertheless went, perhaps as a challenge to Leopold, although it took all his courage to look upon the colleague whose nose the Munich doctors had all but burned away. Despite assurances that no danger of infection existed, Wolfgang, even so, arranged to see him, not in his room, but during his daily walk in the hospital garden. "Half in tears" and "shaking from head to foot," Mozart took his hand. They exchanged affectionate words, and Mysliveček proceeded to business; though confident of being well enough to travel south the next year, he told Wolfgang: "Because I have already composed six times for Naples, I do not mind undertaking the less important work and relinquishing to you the better opera, namely the one for Carnival. . . ." He offered to draft a letter to the Naples impresario. Mozart was to return the following day and copy it.

He could not bring himself to reappear; to his father he related the dilemma: "I found it impossible to persuade myself to go to him in his room; and yet I should have to if I wanted to write, for I could not do so in the garden. Therefore, I promised him to arrive without fail. But the following day I sent him a letter in Italian saying in plain words that 'I thought it beyond my powers to come to him,' that 'I had eaten close to nothing and been able to sleep but three hours,' that 'in the morning I was like a man who had lost his reason,' that 'he was always before my eyes. . . .'" Mysliveček replied (also in Italian): "You are too sensitive to my pain. I thank you for your good heart. . . ." He sent Wolfgang the rough.

A pity that nothing came of it (see XX, n. 24), for at this time Mozart felt "an inordinate desire once again to write an opera." "I need only hear an opera discussed; I need only be in a theater and hear the orchestra tune—oh! I am at once quite beside myself." Not performing but "composing" had become his "only joy and passion," and along with this fervor returned that vision of Italy and its limitless charms and opportunities: "When I ponder the matter, it seems to me that in no other country have I received so many honors or been so appreciated. . . ." He made himself forget that Mozart the *Wunderkind* had awakened the applause of Verona, Milan, and Rome.

Though Wolfgang had begun to grow up with rapid strides, some of the dependencies of childhood now and then roused themselves: a brief regressive process set in when, memories of covered keyboards and chiming watches stirring, he pictured himself triumphing at a musical "test" before the Elector and a host of famous musicians. No less childish had been his decision to take Mama with him on that visit to the hospital (though she showed her wisdom by disappearing into the chapel); and that he revealed himself baffled as to the origin of Mysliveček's troubles surprised even

Leopold, who had moralized on the subject with such priggish ostentation: "I will explain some other time and in more detail what the whole story of his illness involves," he lamely answered.[8]

Even so, that a thoroughgoing reorganization of Wolfgang's personality had begun, the processes of detachment and maturation arriving with remarkable rapidity, must have become clear to Leopold when he read the description of the encounter with Mysliveček, so moving in its concern with human values. Wolfgang had begun to speak in a new voice. He had discovered that the basic structure of his personality had little to do with Leopold's and that he no longer needed his father's strength. In his early twenties, almost a decade late, Mozart underwent his psychological puberty: he embarked upon the road to internal freedom, and his personality began to achieve its own outlines. (The change might have come even later had not miscalculation and accident loosened Leopold's grip.) Not only had his identification with his father's ambitions and purposes weakened, but soon he would be carting his mother along with him like a piece of dearly familiar but outworn luggage.[9]

Anna Maria, of course, still had her very practical role; she wrote to Leopold: "Tomorrow, that is the 11th [October], we will leave here.... I am busy packing, which tires me no end, for I am doing it all myself; Wolfgang cannot help me in the slightest way." Sweating and cursing—"I could shove my feet into my snout for exhaustion"—she had relaxed by polishing off two bottles of Tyrolese wine[10] at the Freysingers (Franziscus, once Leopold's fellow student at Augsburg, his wife, and their two daughters) while her son paid visits and attended the pantomime theater.

At home, Leopold had long fumed about the protracted stay in Munich, "where there is no hope of taking in a single kreuzer." Resentful of Wolfgang's holding court and courting compliments ("You cannot loll about [at Albert's], consuming money and losing time"), he would, in the course of the tour, more than once testily remind his son that "pretty words, epigrams of praise, and cries of 'bravissimo' pay neither coachmen nor innkeepers."

---

8 Having discovered Wolfgang's surprising innocence concerning venereal diseases, Mysliveček, in an attempt to shelter it, only further confused him by maintaining (in a note) that the disfigurement had proceeded from injuries sustained in "a capsized carriage" and treatment "at the hands of ignorant doctors."

9 He had long arrogated a parental function in his relationship to Nannerl. The ties between them would little by little fall away.

10 Anna Maria and Leopold drank heartily, as did their son. At Albert's table he limited himself to "a small glass of wine with the final course of fruit"—or so he reported to a father concerned about possible "excess" and harboring the fear of Wolfgang's succumbing to the alcoholism common among Salzburg musicians.

For all that, Leopold continued the struggle to dam his aggressions, once again falling back upon vague hints about the machinations of those perennial "secret enemies." He, in fact, executed a smart about-face upon learning that Wolfgang (again with Anna Maria) had been to the hospital a second time, to bid Mysliveček farewell: "When all is said and done, he is, no mistake, to be pitied! Your terror, your anguish, etc. when you saw him are more than comprehensible to me. I would have felt the same; you know my heart!"

When, on 4 October, the Elector, the Electress, and their court left Munich for a journey of several weeks through the Bavarian upland, Mozart had to renounce the pretense to any real purpose in remaining. In the hope of at last pulling him from the spell of the city, Leopold outlined the possibilities before the travelers—the courts, the princes, the routes: he advised their proceeding toward the Main, the Neckar, the Rhine, and the Mosel, areas in which they would encounter fewer Italian musicians in positions of influence; he pointed out that Protestant princes, in fact, now tended to favor Germans. But Wolfgang paid little attention to Leopold, who could never reconcile himself to his son's ignoring proposals not to his taste: "Many of the points I raise remain unanswered; you will notice that I reply to all of yours." The two, however, agreed that the next stop would be the Lech and Leopold's native city.

3

WITH A LONG pause to permit the coachman to feed the horses, Wolfgang and Anna Maria's journey to Augsburg consumed almost an entire day (11 October 1777). At Leopold's insistence, they avoided the expensive Zu den drei Mohren and put up at the Zum weissen Lamm,[11] a few steps around the corner from his brother's house on the Jesuitengasse. Wolfgang found Uncle Franz Alois "a most upright, dear man" and, among the Augsburg relatives, appears to have met only him, his wife, and their daughter, Maria Anna Thekla, known to history as the "Bäsle" (darling little female cousin).

Mozart hastened to introduce himself to Jakob Wilhelm Benedikt Langenmantel von Westheim und Ottmarshausen, chief prefect of Augsburg. Knowledge of their initial encounter derives from Wolfgang's amusing description, in which he painted him as exemplifying Leopold's opinion of the city's chief prefects, renowned, so he maintained, as boorish buffoons. He could not put aside his old resentment of this childhood schoolmate.

---

11 Thirteen years later, Goethe would lodge there en route to his second stay in Italy.

Prejudiced by his father's antipathy, Wolfgang in no time discarded any effort to foster the patrician's friendship. Looking upon him as a kind of Don Anchise (*La finta giardiniera*), he made his own ill-mannered contributions to a first meeting that set the disagreeable tone of much of the Augsburg visit.

He had expected a welcome with honors. Instead, von Langenmantel comported himself (in Leopold's image) like "a reigning King of Diamonds ... speaking down from the height of ... his niggardly throne." In a mischievous shot, Wolfgang addressed him as "Your Grace."[12] Not the fool Mozart's account would portray and recognizing the Archbishop of Salzburg and himself as the butt of this game, von Langenmantel responded in archiepiscopal fashion by directing a condescending pronoun toward the impertinent visitor. The blow struck home: Wolfgang became infuriated. For a while they skirmished in this absurd manner until each thought he had the better of it. A truce emerged: von Langenmantel changed to the "*Sie,*" and Wolfgang felt it wise to accept his invitation to play the clavier in the quarters of his son, Jakob Alois; he presided over the patricians' private music society,[13] which, Wolfgang hoped, might sponsor one of his concerts. The mannerly respite proved short: during a subsequent encounter at Jakob Alois's dining table, acrimony broke forth anew.

Leopold had advised Wolfgang to wear his Papal cross in Augsburg. Jakob Alois and his brother-in-law went too far in teasing him about the decoration. Finding himself mocked for affectation by a family whose pretentiousness he despised, he exploded in anger, his humor having already been upset by young von Langenmantel's declaration that he could not arrange the concert because the music society's funds were "in a bad way." Gathering up hat and sword, Wolfgang exited exclaiming: "What a tawdry lot."

"Let the whole company of patricians lick my ass," he wrote home. Furious, he announced his impending departure, pointing out to more than one Augsburger that, thanks to the beggarliness of the patricians, the city would face disgrace and scandal once it became known that the famous son of Leopold Mozart had passed through its gates without having had the opportunity to perform in public. He was coming to appreciate the importance of a court as a focus of patronage. Like his father, he saw Augsburg as the quintessence of the German philistinism Wieland satirized in *Die Abderiten* (see XXVI, n. 32).

---

12 In letters, Wolfgang referred to Chief Prefect (*Stadtpfleger*) Langenmantel—literally, long mantel—in Italian as Longotabarro, or added the prefix "arch" to his title, thereby turning it into Mozartean insult as *Erzstadtpfleger.*

13 He took Mozart to the theater, where they saw *Der Teufel ist los oder Die zweyfache Verwandlung,* a singspiel with a text after Michel-Jean Sedaine, the music most likely by Philidor. The company, Franz Joseph Moser's, which came from Nürnberg, included Emanuel Schikaneder.

Johann Andreas Stein hastened to patch things up, appealing in particular to his fellow Protestants among the patricians. Since he had last seen Wolfgang (1763), this renowned instrument builder had moved (1774) from the banks of the Lech to a mansion on the Maximilianstrasse. Certain that Stein could not possibly recognize him, Mozart decided to play a part upon first presenting himself and, in the sequel, to let his playing at the keyboard betray his identity: he saluted Stein in the person of Herr Trazom, a student from Munich eager to test the instruments. (How he delighted in this *cancrizans* [crablike] spelling of Mozart—"*arschling*" [ass-backwards] as he described it.) But Jakob Alois's smirk raised suspicion and spoiled the sport.

At Stein's, Wolfgang spent rewarding hours examining the pianofortes,[14] marveling at their "escape" action (*Auslösung*). He explained it to Leopold: "When one presses the keys, the hammers fall down again the very moment they bounce against the strings, whether one holds down or releases the levers." He rejoiced in a mechanism capable of providing a "balanced" tone, in this respect finding Stein's instruments superior even to those of Franz Jakob Späth of Regensburg. Wolfgang played his six clavier sonatas on one of these house pianofortes; it bestowed, he declared, an "incomparable" effect, in particular upon the Dürnitz (see p. 332).

Stein gained his end: Mozart found the Russian Hall in the palace of the Counts Fugger (next to the drei Mohren) at his disposal for a public recital. "I wanted to be begged," he later admitted, and the von Langenmantels, in fact, treated for peace: "I really thought you would slip away from us," Jakob Alois said to him in apology; "I actually supposed you might have taken offense at our recent joke." "By no means," Wolfgang replied: "You are, I believe, still young [Jakob was Wolfgang's age!], but be more careful; I am not used to that kind of joke."

As a gesture of conciliation, on 16 October he performed at a meeting of the patricians' music society in the Geschlechterstube (genealogical room) opposite the city hall. ("The orchestra," he wrote home, "can bring on cramps."[15]) His own concert in the Fugger palace took place six days later. The audience included Friedrich Melchior Grimm, since 1775 a baron.[16] On his way to Paris, he had tarried in Augsburg just to attend but remained

---

14 He took the opportunity to perform on the instruments Stein had built for the churches of Augsburg: the organ of 1755–1757 (a masterwork of Stein and his brother, Johann Georg) in the Barfüsserkirche and that of 1766 in the Augustinian church of the Holy Cross. Mozart also played Eusebius Ammerbach's venerable organ (1581) in St. Ulrich's.

15 He did find the orchestra of the Holy Cross monastery to his liking. For the brothers, he played his Strassburg violin concerto, which, he boasted, "went like oil."

16 He had received the barony in preparation for becoming Minister of Saxe-Gotha to the French court.

unnoticed by either Wolfgang or Anna Maria—the kind of mistake Leopold would not have made.[17]

Mozart delighted his audience with a program built around the Lodron triple concerto[18] played on Stein pianofortes, Johann Michael Demmler, organist of the cathedral, performing the first part, Mozart the second, and Stein the third. Upon reading the announcement of the concert in the Augsburg newspapers, Leopold had expected Wolfgang to call upon Stein's eight-year-old prodigy daughter, Maria Anna (Nanette),[19] to take part in the concerto. But Mozart had knit his brows at the child's mannerisms at the keyboard, inspired, he felt certain, by the example of his bête noire, von Beecke, a friend of the Stein family.

The concert brought in the tour's first significant receipts. At home, Leopold felt somewhat encouraged[20] and relished the notice—he had inspired Wolfgang to solicit it—written by that steadfast Mozart admirer Zabuesnig; he hailed "Chevalier [Herr Ritter] Mozart, son of the famous Salzburg musician and native Augsburger. . . ." Young Mozart "may place himself at the side of the nation's greatest masters and, indeed, is at least half our own. . . ."

Though gratified by his success and Stein's friendship, Mozart passed his happiest moments in Augsburg in the company of cousin Maria Anna. Two years his junior, slender, pert, flirtatious, and with a sense of fun and a kindred delight in obscenity, she captivated him. Aware that a mutual infatuation had begun, Leopold treated it cannily, his touch light, even phrasing with humor a hint that he knew of her reputation for indecorum, especially with the clergy (see p. 34); he fenced with her artfully.

The most arresting biographical aspect of the letters Mozart wrote her following his departure from Augsburg does not concern the famous

---

17 Though shortsighted, Mozart never wore eyeglasses. Grimm had to rush away after the concert and thus did not make himself known (see n. 29).

18 The clavier concerto K. 238 and the Dürnitz sonata appeared on the program, too. (He had played the less intense sonata K. 283/189h for the patricians.) Mozart also improvised, among other offerings, "a splendid sonata in C," perhaps an early version of what would become K. 309/284b (see pp. 383–84).

19 During a recent stay in Vienna, where he demonstrated his pianoforte to the court, Stein had arranged that Nanette perform for the Habsburgs. In 1794, two years after her father's death, she was to marry the pianist Johann Andreas Streicher, and they, along with her brother, Matthäus Andreas, would transfer the Stein workshop to Vienna. After Matthäus set up on his own, the firm functioned under the name "Nanette Streicher, née Stein." She would become a particular friend of Beethoven, her husband of Schiller.

20 Wolfgang's susceptibility to praise and his practice of giving free, impromptu recitals for flatterers incensed his father: "All the compliments, visits, etc. are but accessory and to be taken as frippery as you keep an eye upon your main purpose—to bring in money. All your endeavors must be directed toward earning, all prudence exercised toward spending as little as possible. . . ."

coarseness of many a turn of phrase—perhaps a touch excessive, even for a southern German of his time, in an unlimited delight in the ritual of the privy and the functions of bowels and sphincter[21]—but, rather, a timbre, new to his voice: the tone of a man of sexual experience. Without question the Bäsle instructed him in its delights and dangers.

In the eighteenth century, the awful specter of venereal disease loomed as unassailable. "Whom love does not deter, apprehension does," moaned Goethe: "Nowhere does one in security lay one's head in a woman's lap. Neither the marriage bed nor adultery is safe any longer; husband, wife, and friend, one is injured in the other." This fear of infection would haunt Mozart no less. It seems clear that in the autumn of 1777 and his friendship with the Bäsle he began to indulge the variety of pregenital pleasures. He sought release in this safer kind of love play, holding back from complete genital consummation until his marriage;[22] he indicated as much to

---

21 It has been argued that this predilection must be understood in terms of an era preceding the Victorian with its prudery and inhibitions. But why, then, did his widow, confronted by what she held to be a problem in Mozartean biography, advise: "The truly tasteless—if very witty—letters to his cousin indeed merit mention, but for certain should not be published in full." Even though Mozart reached manhood in the decade of Goethe's *Götz*, whose language for a while inspired a fashionable flow of foul speech in German drawing rooms—in an amusing paradox, it for a while became part of the cult of sentiment—others, no less representative of the age, approached nasty subjects via circumlocutions. Even today, when unconstrained obscenities thrive in print, on the stage, and in films, the sheer exuberance of Mozart's preoccupation with the anal cavity startles. At times he seems a naughty baby at stool; at times an adolescent striving to shock; at times a man morbosely coprophilous; at times, an utterly amusing wag as, for example, when he declaims to his cousin in the manner of an *opera-seria* recitative: "Ah, my *ass* burns like fire! What does this signify? Perhaps some *muck* wishes to come forth? Yes, yes, *muck*; I know you, see you, taste you—and—what is this? Is it possible? Ye Gods! My ears—do you deceive me? No—it is so. What a long melancholy tone!" Beneath the heroic cadence of the text seem to sound those majestic chordal formulae that might preface an aria on the subject.

22 He closed a letter (13 November 1777) to the Bäsle: "*Je vous baise vos mains, votre visage, vos genoux et votre———, afin, tout ce que vous me permettes de baiser*" [*sic*] (I kiss your hands, your face, your knees, and your———, in a word, whatever you permit me to kiss). Eight days earlier he had requested her to get in touch with Josepha, the younger of the Freysinger sisters (see p. 374), and beg forgiveness on his part for his failure to send her a promised sonata. "Why should I not send it?" (*Warum soll ich sie nicht schicken?*), he asked the Bäsle, playing upon the similar sounds of the verbs to send (*schicken*) and to f—k (*ficken*) and upon the fact that the *sie*, ostensibly standing for the sonata (feminine in German), might also connote Josepha. In his punning, symbolic way he was pondering: "Why should I not f—k her?" He thereupon asked his cousin: "Would you do me this kindness?"—on the surface, "Will you communicate with Josepha," in reality, "May I f—k you?" "Curious," he continued, "I would certainly do it for you if you wished it. Why not? Why shouldn't I do it for you? Curious! Why not? I don't know why not." He really knew: the reputation of the Bäsle—who may well have been eager to enjoy this kindness—for promiscuity. The so-called nonsense in the Bäsle letters veiled much: doubtless their code words "spuni cuni" referred to their genitals.

his father when the latter questioned his familiarity with a Munich prostitute, and the confidence may well have been true (see p. 526).

Maria Anna expected to marry him. (She would lay bare the tenacity of her fantasies about and identification with him when registering the birth in 1784 of her illegitimate daughter by Abbé von Reibelt [see p. 34]: she assumed the name of "Trazin," a feminine counterpart to "Trazom" [his "arschling" version of Mozart] and meaning, literally, the wife of Mr. Sweet [zart], but spelled backward.) They arranged to exchange portraits,[23] and she attempted to open a correspondence with the family in Salzburg, the brave effort beginning and ending with the same semiliterate letter.[24] Their parting (26 October), which she thought temporary, proved difficult.[25] Leopold and Nannerl elected to represent this "sad farewell of two persons dissolving in tears" as a vignette on a target they and their Salzburg friends used for one of their shooting matches: the choice spoke of antipathy disguised as good-natured sport. Members of this fellowship devoted to air-gun marksmanship—the "company of shitters," in Wolfgang's phrase—each in turn provided targets painted with topical scenes decked with explanatory verses (see XIV, n. 9). The target used on 16 November depicted the Bäsle, who, drying her eyes with a cloth that dragged on the ground, lamented to a booted Wolfgang ready to leave: "Accursed fate! Alas! It seems you did but come and now are on your way. Who would not weep?"

Leopold described the illustration to Wolfgang, who declared it "capital," the verses "incomparable." He, however, had suggested a quite different motif for the November meeting: "A small fair-haired man bending over and displaying his bare ass; out of his mouth come the words: 'Good appetite for the feast'; the other man to be represented as booted and spurred and with a red cloak and a beautiful, fashionable wig; he must be

---

23 To please him she dressed in the French manner, and he requested a portrait of her so attired. The well-known pencil sketch preserved in Salzburg's Mozart Museum, however, shows her in traditional Augsburg Catholic costume. It stands within the bounds of possibility that the portrait of Mozart he himself commissioned for her survives as the miniature in Augsburg's Mozarthaus. Yet, the physiognomy troubles: if it is Mozart's, the artist has much refined the cast of the features; but Mozart may have insisted upon an idealized image. At all events, this painted ivory did come from the estate of the Bäsle, who died in Bayreuth during the eighteen-forties.

24 A distinction must be drawn between such plodding semiliteracy and the capricious orthography and grammar adopted by many Stürmer und Dränger—including, for a time, the young Goethe—as a sign of their uniqueness.

25 His letter to her from Mannheim of 3 December 1777 contains a gross affirmation of fidelity: "Apropos, since I left Augsburg I haven't taken my pants off—except at night before going to bed."

of medium size and shown in the position of licking the other man right in the ass; from his mouth come the words: 'Oh, in truth, there is no end to it.'" Here was Mozart's picture of how his business with the patricians—and, in particular, Jakob Alois—had concluded. (He, in fact, referred to Jakob Alois as "the young [ass] licker von Langenmantel.") He felt triumphant.

4

ON 26 OCTOBER mother and son left Augsburg, lunched at Donauwörth, passed beneath the towers of Harburg Castle, and went on to Nördlingen; by seven o'clock they had set up in "a miserable inn" in Hohenaltheim, a country seat of Prince Kraft Ernst zu Öttingen-Wallerstein. (Mozart had met him in Rome and Naples.[26]) To Leopold's annoyance, the protracted stays in Munich and Augsburg had caused Wolfgang to miss Prince Taxis at Dischingen—he had already dispatched his musicians to his Regensburg palace—and Kraft Ernst's country estate provided the only opportunity for music-making between Augsburg and Mannheim,[27] the Mozarts' next important stop. Alas, Kraft Ernst, still mourning his wife, a princess of Thurn und Taxis who had died over a year and a half earlier, had no desire for music; indeed, he had even put his orchestra on holiday. The Mozarts might have suspected his *Hofmusikintendant*, Ignaz von Beecke, of inventing tales to shut a rival out, had not Wolfgang met with the Prince and observed his distracted state.

The Mozarts did not leave Hohenaltheim until the twenty-eighth, for Anna Maria had caught a heavy cold. Wolfgang filled the hours with visits to both the Prince, who kept bursting into tears, and von Beecke, who received the visitor "with much courtesy."[28] Using a recapitulation of their conversation as a device to inform the Tanzmeisterhaus of what he had

---

26 A count when they first met (see p. 272), he became ruler of Wallerstein in 1773: Vienna created him prince the following year. The Mozarts had links of long standing to his family: not long before Wolfgang's birth, Leopold contemplated sending a pastoral symphony, among other compositions from his hand, to Kraft Ernst's father, Count Philipp Karl. Kraft Ernst would turn into an enthusiastic patron of Joseph Haydn.

27 A northern detour to Würzburg would have been purposeless: its bishop and his court had already taken up autumn residence at Bamberg, his eastern seat. Wolfgang's haphazard progress exasperated Leopold, who, had he held command, would have informed himself of pertinent court calendars. Arranging for coachmen and horses to the next destination as yet strained Mozart's talent for such matters to its limits.

28 Von Beecke, who held the rank of captain, invited Mozart to the officers' table where—so the violinist Anton Janitsch and the cellist Joseph Reicha reported to Leopold—he behaved antically (see p. 325).

planned in secret as the tour's end, Mozart wrote: "He [von Beecke] asked me where I was going. I said, 'In all probability to Paris.'" A shocked Leopold replied: "To Paris? . . . Taking your course toward Paris without letters of introduction? What route will you follow so as to be able to earn something on the way? . . . And when you finally get there, to whom will you turn?"[29] For the moment Leopold masked the full depth of his alarm lest Wolfgang's composure be undermined: he had arrived (30 October 1777) at the court of Mannheim, whose "rays," Leopold declared, "like the sun's, spread through the whole of Germany, indeed, through the whole of Europe."

---

29 On the same day (13 November), their letters crossing, both Leopold and Wolfgang found the courage to write the word "Paris" to one another, the father daring voice what he had suspected, the son at last sounding the note long stifled. However, Wolfgang had talked in public of visiting Paris at least as early as the visit to Augsburg, for Grimm invoked Paris to explain why he could dash from Mozart's Augsburg concert of 22 October without compunction: ". . . since I was hard pressed for time and continuing my journey that very night . . . I did not introduce myself; having learned that our Amadeo was going to Paris, I put off speaking with him until that time."

CHAPTER XX

Mannheim

MOZART DID NOT introduce himself to Mannheim's musical life: he confronted it, forthwith taking umbrage at musicians ignorant of his reputation; did they not know that once he had "set all Schwetzingen astir"? The conductor Cannabich, veteran tenor Anton Raaff, and Kapellmeister Holzbauer[1] greeted him with courteous regard, as did the violinist Christian Franz Danner. But others stared with indifference at the puffed-up little man who confused lack of recognition with ill will: "They seem to think that because of my small size and youth I possess no importance or maturity. They will soon learn."[2] It was a poor beginning.

Aware of the necessity to build a cadre of allies, he at once reaffirmed ties with Cannabich and his family and, as seal to an alliance in which each hoped to turn the other to account, began to give clavier lessons to the daughter of the house—Rosa (Rosina Theresia), with whom he enjoyed flirting. (He believed the thirteen-year-old to be at least two years older.) As their study piece he composed a clavier sonata (K. 309/284b; see XIX,

---

1 Mozart had met Cannabich and Holzbauer in 1763, Cannabich again during the second visit to Paris three years later.
2 Leopold lamented this attitude: "Your pride and egotism . . . are only affronted when you are not at once accorded befitting high esteem. [You expect] even people who do not know you to read genius in your brow."

n. 18), its middle movement representing, so he announced, a tonal picture of her character. He strengthened growing fellowship with the oboist Friedrich Ramm by presenting him with a concerto given out to be only now written for his talents but, in fact, the old vehicle for Giuseppe Ferlendis. It quickly became Ramm's warhorse, and its popularity in Mannheim would soon prove embarrassing and costly to its composer (see pp. 401–02). He also renewed acquaintance with the Wendling family, adding them to his advocates and, abetted by Holzbauer, besought the court's director of music, Count Louis Aurel Savioli, to arrange an audience for him with Elector Karl Theodore.

Socializing and making music in sympathetic households, Mozart, as a rule, ate with his new companions. But the cost of both the attic room he and his mother shared at the Pfälzer Hof and her meals continued to erode a capital already alarmingly depleted: only his concert in Augsburg's Fugger palace had brought in a sum worthy of notice; he had to achieve some kind of remunerated relationship with the Mannheim court.

The palace had invited him to play the clavier at a concert on 6 November, the third of four galas celebrating the Elector's name day (4 November, the Feast of Saint Carlo Borromeo). He and his Electress, Elizabeth Maria, applauded the visitor. "I believe it has been fifteen [really fourteen] years since you were here," His Highness observed; ". . . *on ne peut pas jouer mieux*" (one cannot play better), his daughter, Countess Karoline Luise, added. For all that, the polite atmosphere[3] had a chill, and Mozart should have discerned its source. A major figure in the city's musical life, Abbé Vogler, had begun his self-protective and retaliative work; from the start, Mozart had adopted a course of offending him.

Among Mannheim musicians, Georg Joseph Vogler, a pupil of Padre Martini and the Elector's Chaplain and Vice-Kapellmeister, stood closest to his ear. Embracing Cannabich and his clique, a misguided Mozart also embraced their biases, in particular an aversion to Vogler. Putting faith in their belief that the Abbé's influence at court had entered steep decline, Mozart began to indulge the fantasy of a soon-to-be-empty vice-kapellmeister's chair, Cannabich encouraging the newcomer to see himself in the role of a Hotspur whose sword would rout the enemy. Though with good reason scorning Vogler as performer and composer ("a miserable

---

3 Polite and noisy, too! The public made no less a racket at concerts than at the opera. The gala, Raaff hoped, might give him an opportunity to adjudge Mozart's art, but he could "hear nothing because of the bustle and din." The Electoral couple took the precaution to sit "right next to" the instrument.

musical jester, an exceedingly conceited fellow who can't do very much"[4]), Mozart showed little mother wit in broadcasting this disdain.

Only just settled in Mannheim, he attended what the court prospectus put forward as a rehearsal under Vogler of Handel's *Messiah.* Against expectation, Vogler opened by leading the musicians through a magnificat from his own hand. Holding out for a while, Mozart, in an ill-judged gesture, quit the hall—in all likelihood ostentatiously. He gave second public notice of his contempt by marching out of a rehearsal of one of Vogler's masses right after the Kyrie and crowned his folly by refusing to leave his card at the Vice-Kapellmeister's home; first Vogler had to come to him (a self-destructive decision and perhaps a reaction against his father's admonition that "through surpassing politeness," he "make friends of everyone," Leopold having in the same breath invoked the name of Vogler, "a clever man much respected by the Elector"). Vogler displayed skill in handling the matter; with naïveté Wolfgang recorded that the Abbé did "conquer his pride" and pay the courtesy visit (14 January 1778); but, of course, by this time he had undermined the interloper in the eyes of the palace. "I believe that I stand in his favor," a credulous Mozart observed after Vogler had smothered him in flattery and cordiality.

When it became clear that a private meeting with the Elector would not materialize through official channels—from afar Leopold guessed why—Mozart, at one jump again foxlike, glimpsed an inviting indirect route: it led via the Palais Heydeck, residence of the Elector's four natural children.[5] Savioli introduced Mozart to their household, where he enchanted at the clavier as he besought the governess to help him become their musical mentor.[6] He hoped to seize the opportunities provided by the Elector's informal visits: from time to time he dropped in during the music hour; with luck, Mozart might meet and chat with him outside the impositions of court etiquette.

---

4 Something of the charlatan did cling to Vogler; though posterity remembers him as the teacher of Weber and Meyerbeer, his contemporary reputation rested upon his musical theorizing, much of it factious. Leopold Mozart became a jealous admirer of Vogler's pragmatic ways: his political influence made his *Kuhrpfälzische* [*sic*] *Tonschule* (1778) the official text in the Palatinate for teaching clavier, singing, and composition; since Leopold contemplated writing a general musical method by condensing material from famous theorists (among them, Agricola, Fux, Marpurg, Mattheson, d'Alembert, and Rameau), he felt envious disappointment to discover Vogler working along the same lines.

5 Two of them played the clavier: nine-year-old Countess Karoline Luise and Count Karl August, one year her junior. Their mother, the dancer Josepha Seyffert, whom the Elector had raised to the nobility as Countess Heydeck, had died in 1771.

6 The music he represented as composed for them included the easiest of his Fischer variations.

The strategem worked: more than once in the course of his appearances at the Palais Heydeck, Mozart found himself in the presence of Karl Theodore, who proved cordial, cautious, and, now and then, probing. On one occasion he remarked: "I have heard that you have written an opera for Munich." He was trying the young man's temper, for, as Mozart well remembered, His Highness had attended the second performance of *La finta giardiniera*. Ignoring the provocative remark, Mozart replied: "Yes, your Highness, I commend myself to your Highness's good graces. I could wish for nothing more than to write an opera here." He then movingly said: "I ask that you do not altogether forget me." That misbegotten Italian *buffa* score enclosed splendid "German" pages, and, trusting to Karl Theodore's recollection of them, Mozart deftly turned to the musical issue nearest the Elector's heart by adding a confident "Thank and praise God, I also know German."

For some time, Karl Theodore had been standing sponsor to the development of German *opera seria*,[7] an attempt to further the enterprise composer Anton Schweitzer and poet Christoph Martin Wieland had set on foot in Weimar in 1773 with the production of their *Alceste*. Two years later, this lofty five-act drama sung in German found its way to Karl Theodore's Schwetzingen stage. The premiere in Mannheim on 5 January 1777 of *Günther von Schwarzburg*, its music by Holzbauer to a text by Anton Klein, had reinforced hopes that, despite occasional infelicities of style, a new kind of German opera, transplanted from Weimar, had begun to take root at Karl Theodore's court. Mozart, who attended a performance of *Günther* (5 November 1777) found the music "very beautiful," if the libretto "not worthy of such music." During his stay in Mannheim, the opera house pushed forward with its preparation of Schweitzer and Wieland's latest serious German work, *Rosemunde*, and Mozart lent a hand at one of the rehearsals. (His opinion of the score declined with every hearing.) The court of Mannheim, he politicly indicated to Karl Theodore, had embarked upon cultivating a new German musical genre to which he wished to devote himself. "That might easily turn out," the Elector rejoined as he terminated the conversation in his children's music room.

The weeks passed. From the palace came contradictory signals concerning Mozart's prospects. Embarrassment now made Savioli avoid him. Karl Theodore found it difficult to make up his mind (*"Ich bin noch nicht resolvirt"*). Vogler had become master of the game, and Mozart began the slide into a pit of his own digging.

---

7 Musical nationalists like Karl Theodore regarded Gluck's reform operas as foreign works.

2

"THE MOST BEAUTIFUL autumn within living memory" had passed, chill had turned to frost, frost to piercing cold and heavy snow. At first included from time to time in the invitations extended to Wolfgang, Frau Mozart found herself forgotten. Isolated in her garret room, she let slip a rare reproach: "I am at home alone, as is the case most of the time." Alarmed by her shrinking funds, she ate and drank sparingly[8] and ordered a fire only when dressing or undressing. She suffered, and a decline in her health began. At fifty-seven, she could not sustain the rigors of further travel in such weather: mother and son had to await the thaw.

Leopold became furious. Why had Wolfgang not followed his counsel, opportunities in Mannheim failing, to proceed at full speed to the ecclesiastical courts of the Rhine-Mosel,[9] where concerts might well have yielded enough to cover expenses and get the pair at least within striking distance of Brussels or Paris? Dallying in Munich, dallying in Augsburg, dallying and now marooned in Mannheim, Wolfgang—so Leopold thundered—had pursued pleasure and phantoms as his money melted away; if, from the beginning, Paris had been his goal, why, he should already be there, earning money rather than trifling away time, snowbound in a city with little interest in him. As an immediate remedy, Leopold suggested an appeal to Elector Karl Theodore's good nature: Wolfgang might point to the strain a winter journey would impose upon his mother and ask for support until spring in return for his participating in Mannheim's musical life. Leopold also urged that he prod Zeil and Seeau in Munich to get him at the least some kind of informal affiliation with the Bavarian court.

Not gold but the proverbial gold watch expressed the Elector's appreciation of Mozart's performance at the gala. He observed: "I am in earnest considering having an additional watch-pocket put on all my trousers; when I go to some great lord, I shall wear both watches—moreover, now the fashion—so that it will not occur to him to present me with another." Humor masked his anxiety: to get through the coming months he would be dependent upon the help and hospitality of new friends, few of them without self-interest. In exchange for domestic courtesies, he, besides teaching Rosa, made keyboard arrangements of Cannabich's ballet music (perhaps his *Ulisse et Orphée*) and provided the Wendlings with several compositions (see pp. 101–02). His faction remained small; not a few

---

8 "I never drank wine at the inn except when Wolfgang took a meal there, and then we shared a glass."

9 Prince Clemens Wenzel of Saxony, whom the Mozarts had met in Munich on the Grand Tour, had become Prince-Elector of Trier in 1768.

Mannheimers found him presumptuous,[10] a judgment strengthened by a heavy-handed prank he played during mass in the court chapel.

With Holzbauer's connivance, he commandeered the organ and disconcerted celebrant and congregation by a display of improvisational virtuosity utterly foreign to local liturgical practice.[11] He claimed to have given the show just "for fun," but clearly his purpose had been to provoke recognition of his dazzling mastery of the instrument. He lost the day, though consoled by the appreciative guffaws of friends who encouraged the romping of someone at moments still half man/half boy: the grand *Meister* demanding deference, the adolescent outraging his elders. At home, Leopold found himself plagued by a thousand fears and driven to think him thoughtless, at times almost indifferent to his predicament: his letters made light of everything. Papa's hopes were hanging by ever more frayed threads when he received from Mannheim an astounding self-reproach:

"I, Johannes Chrisostomus Amadeus Wolfgangus Sigismundus Mozart, confess that yesterday and the day before (and also on other occasions) I did not get home until midnight; and that at Cannabich's from ten o'clock until the aforesaid hour . . . I frequently without difficulty, indeed, with downright facility, did make rhymes—in truth, sheer filth: to wit, about muck, shitting, and ass-licking, albeit, strictly speaking, in thought and word but not in deed. . . . Moreover, I must admit that I out-and-out enjoyed myself. I confess all these my sins and offenses from the depth of my heart. . . . Wherefore, I beg holy dispensation if it can be easily provided; if not, it is of no matter, for the game will go on all the same."

That this avowal parodied church formulae offended Leopold and Abbé Bullinger; moreover, in view of the troubled situation, the family did not relish any kind of jest. In reply, Leopold fired a barrage of acrimony, hitting every target: "You must have other, more important thoughts in your head than tomfoolery: you must be busy anticipating a hundred things, otherwise you will suddenly be without money and sitting in muck; and when there is no money there are no longer friends, even if, without fee, you give a hundred lessons, compose sonatas, and, instead of attending to more important matters, concern yourself with smut every night from ten o'clock until midnight. Then ask for credit! Why, at once all jokes will cease, and in an instant the most smiling face will to a certainty

---

10 His arrogant public posture appeared odd in a professional traveling with his mother.

11 Thus he made a point of ignoring his father's admonition: "You must not neglect going to the chapel [in Mannheim] to observe the style in use—length, shortness, etc., for such lords always consider best that style to which they are accustomed. *Consuetudo est altera natura*" [Custom is second nature]!

turn serious." "Good God! Solely on your account I am . . . in debt, and you think that perhaps you can coax me into good humor with a hundred stupid jokes."

Wolfgang reported little of substance to Salzburg: his letters, Leopold complained, added up to little more than a "mishmash." He could not even begin to fathom the travelers' intentions. Peevishness and scolding had become his routine: "Of course, your journey is not my business! Is this not so?" Consumed by indignation, he demanded particulars, for, "in the end, upon whom but your poor old father will everything fall?" He had no answers to basic questions: "What?—Why?—Whither?" he shouted from Salzburg.

Wolfgang seemed to enjoy being evasive, even deceptive, and, when challenged or found out, defended himself by righteous declarations that his aim in withholding information had been to spare the family any solicitude; if Leopold ascribed this restraint to "carelessness, thoughtlessness, and laziness," then "I can only thank you for your good opinion and with all my heart regret that you do not know me—your son." He found the reproaches "undeserved," though aware that they sprang from love: "Nothing can lie more upon my heart or throw me into a more deadly agitation," Leopold cried, "than *ignorance* and *doubt* and with them inevitable anxiety concerning those I hold dearer than my life." But Wolfgang had ceased to care about his father's needs.

Karl Theodore continued to delay any decision concerning Mozart, who by early December, upon the advice of friends and perhaps in the end influenced by Leopold's jeremiads, roarings, and groanings in the distance, settled upon a new course; it reflected his state of wavering between dashed hopes and lingering expectations. Toward spring, in the company of Johann Baptist Wendling, Ramm, and court ballet master Étienne Lauchéry, he would journey to Paris; if, by this time, Karl Theodore had invited him into service,[12] the trip would be a Lenten excursion; in the absence of such a proposal, he would remain on the Seine and seek his fortune there. In either case, Frau Anna Maria was to return to Salzburg once mild weather set in; both recognized the futility of her role.

She had no authority over him, played no part in his affairs, and found her situation painful. Nor could she communicate to Salzburg her true estimate of her son's capacity to run his life. He read her appendages to his letters just before they went to the post, and she feared his anger should

---

12 Entreated by Leopold to sing Wolfgang's praises to Karl Theodore, Padre Martini would do no more than write a commendation and address it to Raaff, who was to pursue the matter with the Elector. Martini consistently distanced himself from the Mozarts and their problems.

she unburden herself: his supposed monitor had become his prisoner. Under cover of a commonplace, she did succeed in sending a signal of distress to Leopold—"I often just wish I could be with you for at least one day in order to relate to you all the things we are not able to write about"—and once she managed to outwit her keeper. Adding a postscript to his letter of 4 February "in greatest secrecy and haste while he is at table so that I am not caught," she lamented to Leopold: "In a word, he prefers being with others to being with me. I take exception to one and another thing not to my taste, and that annoys him. You yourself must ponder what is to be done."

Wolfgang had arranged that she live in comfort during her remaining months in Mannheim. In return for his giving clavier lessons to Privy Court Councilor Serrarius's fifteen-year-old stepdaughter, Therese Pierron, both Mozarts were to have quarters in his home. These arrangements worked well. Serrarius and his family made much of Anna Maria and insisted that she share their evening meal and amusements. She felt in good hands as Mozart rushed about, dining with friends and teaching. In addition to working at the clavier with Therese and Rosa, he instructed Danner and a Dutch officer, Ferdinand de la Pottrie, in figured bass and techniques of composing unpretentious rococo pieces, so-called *Galanterien.* Most important, through Johann Baptist Wendling he received a commission from another Dutchman: a certain De Jean[13] offered two hundred florins for, so Wolfgang reported to Leopold, "three modest, simple, and short concertos and a couple of quartets for the flute." Leopold could breathe again: the generous fee would take Anna Maria and Wolfgang through the winter in Mannheim and also get her home and him to Paris. Leopold wrote that, to extend credit sufficient to pay their hotel bill, he would have to make a new loan.[14] Only with a new infusion of gulden had they been free to move to the Serrarius house somewhat before mid-December.

Leopold advised Wolfgang to complete the works for De Jean quickly, collect his florins, and thus have the additional means and therewith the confidence to work out details of Mama's safe homeward journey and to concoct a strategy for Paris. In Mannheim his hopes never had a true foundation: from the beginning, Vogler latched the doors of the palace

13 Perhaps, Willem van Britten Dejong, a patron of Dittersdorf; or Ferdinand de Jean, a surgeon with the Dutch East India Company.
14 He should not have been astonished to discover his son ignorant of how to manage letters of credit, those documents empowering extensions of funds from one firm or money dealer to another. Wolfgang seemed to think a passing visit to one of Hagenauer's business associates sufficient to open a new flow of florins. In such matters he cultivated incomprehension.

against a hotheaded, dangerous rival.[15] At all events, few could guess that by the beginning of the new year its audience chambers would stand abandoned, that with such swiftness the sun would set upon the Palatinate's golden days.

3

WHEN ON 30 December 1777, Elector Max Joseph of Bavaria succumbed to smallpox, apprehension stirred throughout the Holy Roman Empire. With him the main line of the House of Wittelsbach died, and the throne in Munich passed to his cousin Karl Theodore of Mannheim, head of the second or Pfalz (see VIII, n. 15) branch of the family. With reunion of the two great Wittelsbach domains—Bavaria and the Palatinate—at hand after centuries of separation, the German Emperor moved to temper the full effect of a development at odds with his ambitions.

Joseph II had always looked upon Bavaria as a vexing geographic obstruction to the amalgamation of Habsburg territories. The death of Max Joseph gave him an opportunity to narrow the impediment by expanding the power and holdings of his House westward. With recourse to the inheritance rights of his dead second wife (Max Joseph's sister; see XIV, n. 17), Emperor Joseph dusted off a genealogical claim to the greater part of Lower Bavaria and started to mobilize. Leopold sent detailed accounts of this course of events to Mannheim (his informant, the Munich flutist Johann Baptist Becke), where Anna Maria and Wolfgang became sought-after sources of information; its palace silent, the Palatinate capital had to make do with rumor and speculation: "Here one hears nothing at all," Anna Maria wrote; "everything is so quiet—as if one were not in the world. People only sigh and wish to have the Elector back again."

Karl Theodore had sped from Mannheim to Munich[16] (the courier who brought him the news of his accession, Mozart reported, received three thousands florins) and claimed the allegiance of the Bavarians as their legitimate Duke. But the might of Joseph II, his troops on the frontier, could not be ignored, the Emperor, moreover, adding another expedient of persuasion: the promise to create Karl Theodore's natural children legitimate

---

15 Reluctance to see a composer-conductor of Mozart's caliber installed in Mannheim may also have led Cannabich to think twice.

16 The departure of the Elector disconcerted the poet many considered Germany's greatest: Wieland. He had come to Mannheim in the company of Kapellmeister Schweitzer for the final rehearsals and premiere of their *Rosemunde.* (Wieland met Mozart and heard him at the clavier.) The premiere postponed with indefinite promises, Wieland returned to Weimar. The opera finally reached the Mannheim stage on 20 January 1780.

nobles of Empire should he peacefully relinquish the eastern territories. To the mortification of his new subjects, on 3 January 1778 he agreed to the partition of Bavaria. Within two weeks, the Emperor's soldiers marched across the border at Braunau and Schärding and advanced to Straubing, Kelheim, and Cham. A new Austrian province, Straubing its capital, came into being. (The Munich operatic troupe that had planned a spring season in Salzburg, a disappointed Leopold apprised his wife and son, decided to play, instead, for the openhanded Austrian officers stationed in Straubing.) For the moment, Joseph had achieved his ends: he had made up the loss of Silesia a second time, but now with lands fortifying the Germanic character of his dynasty's holdings; and he had scotched deep the tissue of Bavarian ambitions.

This triumph of Joseph's aspirations roused Frederick of Prussia. Though in truth seeking to prevent the Austrians from reaping a full harvest by making all of southern Germany a Habsburg sphere, the master hypocrite stepped forth as defender of Bavaria and the Reich against an Emperor placing his own interests above those of greater Germany. The King did not lack allies: Frederick Augustus III, Elector of Saxony, who claimed a portion of Bavarian territory or treasure—either would do—on behalf of his mother, Maria Antonia, sister of the deceased Max Joseph ("just too much," observed Anna Maria Mozart); and the brother Dukes of Zweibrücken, Karl August Christian and Maximilian Joseph, next and successively in line to the Bavarian throne should cousin Karl Theodore's children remain illegitimate.[17] Once again, Vienna and Berlin, the major and rival German powers, menacingly raised their banners. Its sovereignty and soldiery notwithstanding, Bavaria lacked the strength to defend its ground, but the hoary mechanisms of restraint and checkmate embedded in the structure of the Holy Roman Empire began to move toward preserving traditional forms of balanced power.

From the first, every detail of what began as a war of negotiations and threats, of words and attitudes, held the Mozarts' interest;[18] much of the conflict "would be fought with the pen," Leopold anticipated, and to him Wolfgang recounted with precision whatever he might learn of the expanding crisis: "The Duke of Zweibrücken [Karl August] has, in a publicly printed document, protested to the Reichstag against the arrangement be-

17 Maximilian Joseph succeeded Karl August as Pfalzgraf von Zweibrücken-Birkenfeld in 1795 and four years later followed Karl Theodore on the Bavarian throne as Maximilian IV Joseph. Thanks to the electorate's ever closer ties to France, Napoleon raised it to a kingdom, and, on 1 January 1806, Maximilian Joseph assumed the title of King Maximilian I of Bavaria.
18 Leopold had even related in numbing detail the agonies of Maximilian III Joseph from his first headaches to a description of his corpse covered with purplish pustules.

tween the House of Austria and the Elector of the Pfalz; has appealed to the Roman Empire for support; and has even journeyed to the King of Prussia, who thereupon declared in an open communication that he would never suffer the division of the Bavarian electorate. The Reichstag is now exploring the legitimacy of the Austrian claims."

At first the Mozarts supported Frederick:[19] they had yet to find the Emperor sympathetic; moreover, in this affair the King's no less selfish motives still remained shrouded. From the earliest days of the emergency, Anna Maria had been apprehensive: "God grant that everything turn out well and that nothing disagreeable arise." She could not shake off worrying whether a safe route back to Salzburg could be found through areas on the edge of upheaval: "My journey home would not be at all entertaining were soldiers all over the countryside. God protect me from such a thing; I would die of fright."

At all events, for months the main action remained the scurrying of diplomats and messengers from capital to capital; not until July would Frederick send armies into Bohemia and the War of the Bavarian Succession begin in earnest. By that time Mozart would be in Paris, accompanied not by his Mannheim friends but by his mother.

4

MOZART HIMSELF WRECKED the plans he and his friends had forged. Early in February 1778, he abruptly announced to Leopold that he had been deceived in Wendling and Ramm and could not bring himself to travel to Paris in their society: let them be off on their pleasure trip; he would remain in Mannheim and somehow keep afloat. He had come to see them in their true light; his eyes had opened overnight to recognize Wendling and his family as, "sad to say, altogether without religion" and Ramm as "a libertine," observations parroting Anna Maria's: she had "never liked his associating with Wendling and Ramm . . . bad company in which he might even be led astray."

That Mannheim included many with Enlightened ideas could hardly have burst upon him. He, in fact, associated with two of the city's most liberal-minded literary men: von Dalberg and von Gemmingen-Hornberg. The Mozarts, moreover, had trumpeted with pride their own and Wendling's

---

19 Wolfgang sent Leopold a satiric poem on the Austrian presence in Bavaria, the Emperor declaring: "Bavaria be calm. I come as protector, and what I protect I hold fast." The Mozarts did not hesitate to write of political matters without resort to their code; rather, they turned to it when speaking ill of their own court, in particular the Archbishop.

knowledge of Paris and his familiarity with their "bosom friend" Grimm, who without reserve advertised his hostility toward conventional morality and religion. Leopold sensed deception. He did not know what to make of his son's capricious declaration that Wendling's companionship might do him moral damage. How bizarre and unconvincing the horror he voiced over the fact, well known among German musicians, that Johann Baptist Wendling's daughter, Elisabeth Augusta (Gustl), had been Elector Karl Theodore's mistress; how peculiar the young man's precipitate announcement that he must avoid those with whom he had but yesterday passed happy hours.

Matters became clear to Leopold when Wolfgang described his particular consolation in giving up the journey to Paris. In a letter home (17 January 1778), he had spoken in an offhand manner of someone copying music for him, "a certain Herr Weber," whose daughter "—I don't know whether or not I have already written about his daughter—in my opinion sings truly admirably and has a beautiful, pure voice." By 4 February he informed Salzburg that the Webers mirrored the Mozarts: in the father he beheld a second Leopold; in the daughter, Aloisia, another Nannerl. The Webers sustained his spirits, the Tanzmeisterhaus learned, as he tarried in Mannheim, continuing his labors on the commission from De Jean.

That Wolfgang had found a consuming love for Aloisia,[20] Leopold grasped immediately. At last he could place in perspective his son's hitherto puzzling letter of 22 November; here he had written with ambiguity ("oracularly," as he put it) of "something . . . very good, precious, and valuable for me"—but, he warned Leopold, something that might prove "very bad in your eyes." From the father's point of view the situation could not have become more threatening: to remain at Aloisia's side Wolfgang stood ready to have done with his tour and render his family's sacrifices vain.

He had brought into play two devices to call off his removal to Paris: for Leopold's ears he cried down his Mannheim friends; to them, on the other hand, he told a story of unexpected and important letters (from Vienna) compelling him to change plans and await further communications:[21] per-

---

20 During December, as Aloisia began to absorb him, the Bäsle retreated to the background of his mind. A gap of almost three months (3 December 1777 to 28 February 1778) appeared in his correspondence with her, and there followed a silence of over nine months, broken only when he feared his courtship of Aloisia might founder. His perception of Rosa Cannabich also changed: all of a sudden he saw her as "a girl of fourteen and a dilettante" who "is still too childish and frivolous."

21 An idea inspired by his having asked Leopold to secure from the Mesmer circle in Vienna a letter of recommendation to Queen Marie Antoinette of France; moreover, at Wolfgang's instigation, Leopold had initiated a correspondence with Vienna in an effort to put him forward as composer to Emperor Joseph's nascent German National Singspiel.

haps he would follow to Paris, he gave them to understand, perhaps go else-where. Of course, he in no way altered his relationship to the Wendlings and Ramm, and, since gossip traveled quickly in a small *Residenzstadt,* they knew all, sympathized with the lovesick young man, and pretended to believe him.²²

He felt divorced from his old self, from his own imperatives, and imagined a new responsibility fallen to him: to mold Aloisia into Europe's greatest soprano. ("When Wolfgang makes a new acquaintance," Anna Maria observed, "for such a person he is ready to give his life and all he holds dear.") He tutored her in vocal technique and interpretation, using as exercises arias from his *Lucio Silla* and *Il rè pastore.* The less-than-sympathetic Mama Mozart acknowledged Aloisia's voice to be "incomparable."

She came from a musical family. Her father, Franz Fridolin Weber (from Zell im Wiesental), worked at the Mannheim theater as copyist, bass singer, and prompter. (He was the elder brother of Franz Anton Weber, within the decade to be father to Carl Maria.) Fridolin's household consisted of his Mannheim-born wife, Maria Caecilia, and their daughters: Josepha, Aloisia, Constanze, and Sophie.²³ All of the sisters sang.

Mozart's talent overwhelmed the Webers. Further, they looked upon him as a charming cavalier of means. At first they had no idea that his financial resources did not approach even the lamentable level of their own, a situation he strove to becloud. Poor and eager for help, their dazzled eyes beheld in him a well-dressed, elegant young man who possessed the resources to stand godfather and patron to Aloisia's career. That within a short time it would flourish as his own faltered prepared her later estrangement from him, its roots, it seems likely, nourished by resentment at having been duped during those idyllic days in Mannheim: he had insisted that the power of the Mozart name would in no time carry her to Europe's great stages. Why, Papa would set the affair in motion.

Losing his head, Mozart wrote home of his new sense of mission, to devote himself to Aloisia and her professional future: chaperoned by her father, he and she would tour Europe: "I think we will go to Switzerland, perhaps also to Holland"; and in the course of escorting her to Italy, he planned to stop at Salzburg to introduce her to the family! He conjured the vision of Josepha, the eldest of Weber's daughters, accompanying the travelers as housekeeper and cook.

---

22 Leopold observed of this romance: ". . . everyone in Mannheim knows about it."
23 To his father Mozart described a family of "five girls" and "a son"; of a fifth daughter nothing is known; of the son only his name: Joseph Nepomuk.

Reading these fantasies, Leopold felt he must explode or lose his reason. How could Wolfgang permit himself to be bewitched by such ideas? The impresarios of Italy remained silent when Leopold wrote them concerning his not unknown son;[24] now this son was requesting him to treat with Verona and Venice on behalf of a girl still in her teens who had yet to walk the boards of even a provincial German theater.[25] Could Wolfgang be serious about trailing over the face of Europe with her and, into the bargain, at a time when the armies of Austria and Prussia stood under marching orders? Would this aberration last and his story culminate in so ludicrous a finale? And if he did vanish with the Webers, who would satisfy the debts of the aborted tour? Fearful of a future in penury as a hireling, Nannerl, Leopold reported, collapsed, weeping (see p. 405).

Leopold felt it wise to set before Wolfgang the grimmest picture imaginable of the family's financial position: "As you are aware . . . I am now about 700 florins in debt and do not know how I am going to support myself, Mama, and your sister on my monthly salary. . . . [True, the comfortable life at the Hannibalplatz required Wolfgang's income.] Thus you must perceive as bright as the day at noon that the future and fate of your old parents, and, of course, your good sister, who loves you with all her heart, are alone in your power. . . ." Leopold drew a picture of himself as stripped of both the dream of a comfortable old age and of meeting death in peace. Once again, he had to take on "the *bitter task* of giving lessons. . . . I do not wish to reproach you. I know that you love me, not only as your father but as your most undoubted and surest friend; that you realize that, apart from God, our happiness and unhappiness, indeed, my continuing life or my early death are—if I may say so—in your hands." Had the resources of family and friends been devoted to an unreliable youth who would end roaming about gypsy fashion? These days must be numbered among Leopold's most desperate. "Afflict me thus if you can be so cruel," he called to the son, struggling to spur him on: "Win fame and wealth in Paris. Then, when you have money, go to Italy and get operatic commissions."

Leopold's "amazement and horror" at the plans for a knockabout existence with the Webers compelled retreat; Wolfgang brushed the matter away lightly, if clumsily: the "intoxication" of the moment had led him to consider a course urged upon him by Aloisia and her father; ". . . *considering present circumstances,* it goes without saying, I never entertained the idea,

---

24 Mysliveček's offer to help Mozart secure an operatic commission from Naples had proved a device to insure Leopold's doing him favors.

25 She had sung at court concerts. Maria Aloisia Louise Antonia Weber's conjectural date of birth ranges from 1759 to 1761.

though I gave my word of honor that I would write you about it." He asked for an end to caviling, having been hurt in particular by cutting remarks concerning his preoccupation with women; acid had spilled from Leopold's pen: "You were infatuated out of all proportion with the little singer . . . in Munich [Margarethe Kaiser; see XIX, n. 2] and wished nothing more than to aid the German theater [the singspiel]. Now you announce that you do not even want to write a comic opera.[26] . . . In Augsburg, too, you played a bit of theater by amusing yourself merrily with my brother's daughter. . . . Then Herr Cannabich's daughter found herself overwhelmed by exalted praise, the portrait of her temperament expressed in the Adagio of the sonata: in short, she now became the favorite. . . . Suddenly you strike up a new acquaintance with Herr Weber . . . and the daughter becomes the leading lady in a tragedy unfolding between this family and your own."

Fearing that Wolfgang would entangle himself in a disastrous relationship—"My son, in all your doings you are hotheaded and rash!"—he urged utmost caution in respect to women: "The greatest reserve and highest acumen are needed, nature herself being the enemy; and he who, in an effort to maintain the necessary reserve, does not call upon his entire and keenest judgment will later on exert it in vain to extricate himself from the labyrinth, a *misfortune most often with no end but death.*"

In addition to the infection risked in random amorous gratifications, Leopold also foresaw danger were Wolfgang to marry at this time: "It depends upon nothing else but your common sense and your way of life whether you become an ordinary musician forgotten by the world or a famous kapellmeister of whom posterity will continue to read in books; whether, herded into captivity by some female, you die on a sack of straw in a room full of needy children; or whether, having passed a Christian life, you die fulfilled, with honor and reputation, esteemed by all the world, and with your family prospering."

Leopold had good reason to dwell upon the perils and responsibilities of matrimony. Wolfgang had begun to send signals of his intention to wed Aloisia. Upon hearing of Schiedenhofen's marriage he had observed: "This is, I believe, but one more money match and nothing else. I should not like to marry in this way; I want to make my wife happy, not make my fortune

---

26 Once he had taken up with Aloisia, whose vocal ability, embracing both cantilena and coloratura, suited her to *opera seria*, he condescended to the singspiel, the genre in which Margarethe had so delighted him. "Do not forget," he now wrote Leopold, "about my desire to write operas . . . but Italian, not German; *seria*, not *buffa*." It angered Leopold to observe not artistic or practical but sexual considerations bending his son's professional ambitions.

through her." Above all, he did not want Leopold to imagine that he had seduced Aloisia: "There are people who believe it impossible to love a poor girl without having evil designs; and that pretty word *maîtresse*, wh—e in German, is really much too charming. I am no Brunetti, no Mysliveček! I am a Mozart, and a young and clean-minded Mozart. . . . I would have much to say on the subject, but I cannot: I find it impossible. Among so many faults I also have this one—that I persist in believing that my friends who know me, do, in fact, know me. . . . It is bad enough that one needs words—and letters to boot. I am not writing all of this about you, my dear Papa." He could have had in mind no one else.

5

AT THE TIME when he still took for granted traveling to Paris with Wolfgang, Wendling had assured Anna Maria that he would "care for" and "truly be a father" to a young man as dear to him as "a son." When Wolfgang slipped from his arrangement with Wendling, Anna Maria moved to resume an all-but-abandoned parental role: Wolfgang had to be conveyed from Mannheim and its dangers. Realizing that he would never pull himself from Aloisia, she resolved to take steps: upon his completion of the De Jean commission and receipt of the fee, she would not return to Salzburg but, instead, pack his bags, drag him into the carriage, and be gone to Paris. Leopold conveyed a reciprocal understanding despite the piercing intensity of his desire soon again to fold his wife in his arms. ("Often I cannot get you out of my head the whole day long.") Anna Maria was to lead the hero to the arena and at the same time extricate him from an involvement both parents perceived as preparing the family's ruin.

His description of his journey to Kirchheimbolanden with Aloisia and her father had aggravated the Hannibalplatz beyond endurance. On 26 November 1777, he first raised to Leopold the possibility of performing for Princess Caroline of Nassau-Weilburg, "whom we knew so well at the Hague." Her estate at Kirchheimbolanden, on the edge of the Pfälzer Wald, lay but a short journey northwest of Mannheim. During his stay (he arrived on 23 January 1778 and gave his last performance for her five days later), Mozart played the man of quality and means, insisting upon paying a disproportionate share of the trio's expenses and with a free heart pushing Aloisia forward at the concerts. In the end, a furious Leopold learned that the Princess had divided the fee between them. En route back to Mannheim, the travelers idled away five days in Worms, entertained by Frau Weber's brother, Dagobert Stamm, Dean of the monastery of Saint Andrew. The scatological rhyming verse Wolfgang sent Mama from

Worms on 31 January (he returned to her about 2 February) revealed his utter reluctance to carry the De Jean commission through;[27] it was to provide the funds needed to get him to Paris, and he blocked this path even as Anna Maria resolved that he travel it: he dawdled over a project whose completion would separate him from Aloisia.

If Paris no longer allured his ambitions, he did continue to look back wistfully at Munich: of all capitals, he now wanted it as the axis of his activities; and if a quirk of history had at a stroke transformed the court of Mannheim into the new court of Munich, it remained guesswork as to just what this new political configuration might mean to Germany's, let alone his, future.[28] In any event, the imminent fall of proud Mannheim had become more than conjecture: overnight, it had turned into a second Residenz, a backwater, its citizens stoically awaiting the official proclamation of the court's permanent removal to Munich. They well knew that most of their best musicians and actors would then join the ministers of state streaming toward Bavaria. Mozart wooed Aloisia in a stunned, stricken city, the De Jean commission lying neglected. He would have been hard put to advance any professional reason for staying.

Catastrophe came: De Jean announced his impending move to Paris and paid Wolfgang only ninety-six of the agreed-upon two hundred florins "because," he had to confess to Salzburg, "I have completed for him not more than two concertos and three quartets. . . . It is not surprising that I have been unable to finish. I never have a quiet hour here. I can only compose at night and consequently can't rise early, too. Moreover, I am not always disposed to work. To be sure, I could scribble away the whole day long, but such compositions [*so eine Sach (sic)*] go out into the world, and, in truth, I do not want to be ashamed to have my name on them. Besides, as you know, I immediately become laggard when obliged to write for an instrument I persist in finding unbearable."

That the problematical intonation of wind instruments disturbed Wolfgang's ears came as no new story to Leopold, who well knew that in the past such considerations had never hindered his son's powers to create. Rather much has been made of a bias Mozart indulged to camouflage the real reason for his failure to finish the De Jean commission—his complete absorption in Aloisia with that intensity youth alone knows.

---

27 "Herr Wendling [Johann Baptist, who had recommended Mozart to De Jean] will doubtless be angry / that I have hardly written anything. / But I will come across the Rhine-bridge, / for I am certainly returning / to write the four quartets / so that he doesn't call me a prick. / I'll postpone the concerto until Paris, / where I'll scribble it straightway as I take my first shit."

28 A Salzburg rumor announced Wolfgang as successor in Munich to Kapellmeister Andrea Bernasconi.

If permitting the full fee to slip through his fingers held out expectation of prolonging his stay, it also put at augmented hazard his ability to sustain a comfortable day-to-day existence. He tried to shut his mind to this consequence, but reality intruded. (As De Jean prepared to leave Mannheim, Mozart must have wondered how long his only paying pupil, de la Pottrie,[29] would stay.) His disordered intentions and thinking coming to the fore as he reviewed the De Jean imbroglio, Mozart childishly insisted to Leopold: "But he must pay me the whole, for I have arranged . . . to send on the rest [of the compositions] later," an idea the Dutchman cannot have looked upon but as more bad faith. Leopold let fly: "Why did you write a *lie* to me?" In order to make the fee appear more imposing, Wolfgang had informed Salzburg that he was to provide two quartets. But now, in a careless moment, he unmasked himself, mentioning a third (in work?); and, in cold fact, was not a fourth yet due (see n. 27)?

Leopold warmed to his exprobratory task: "Have I not now, as before, guessed everything? It is my responsibility at a distance to see more and make sounder judgments than you who have these people right under your nose. . . . In truth . . . you have bought experience at considerable cost to us." To an extraordinary degree he took in ill part Mozart's refusal to teach for money: "I will gladly give lessons as a favor, in particular to someone in whom I observe talent, joy, and a delight in learning; but to be obliged to go to a house at a certain hour or to wait for someone at home is what I cannot do, no matter how much it might bring in; that is impossible for me."

"You prefer to give lessons as a favor, do you?" Leopold shot back. "And you likewise prefer to leave your old father mired fast in hardship. This exertion is too great for a young fellow like you, even when it is well paid. It is better that your old father of fifty-eight run about with effort and sweat for a wretched fee in order to furnish himself and his daughter with the necessities and to be able, in case of need, to send the little that remains to you *instead of paying his debts*; and, all the while, you amuse yourself by giving a girl lessons for nothing. My son, do reflect and summon your powers of discernment! Ponder whether you are not treating me with more cruelty than does our Prince. From him I of course have no expectations; from you I expect everything. From him I must await the bestowal of favor; from you I can hope for everything by virtue of your filial duty. He is, after all, a stranger to me; you, however, are my son. You know what I have endured for more than five years—indeed, how much has weighed upon me on your account. The Prince's conduct could but bend me; you,

---

29 In exchange for lessons, Danner had his kitchen provide Frau Anna Maria her midday meal.

however, can crush me. He could only make me ill; you, however, can kill me." Leopold feared that the whole family would never again assemble at the Hannibalplatz: "I have neither my wife nor my son, and God knows whether or when we will see one another again! My utter joy hearing you play and to hear your compositions is gone; everything around me is dead! Your sister alone sustains me."

This combination of pain, alarm, self-pity, and abuse continued from Salzburg. When, in response to Wolfgang's less than tactful request for compositions to add to Aloisia's repertory, Leopold sent to Mannheim various arias (by Monza, Gasparini, Grétry, Ferdinando Bertoni, and Giuseppe Colla), he opened his diapason of lamentation to full compass; the burst answered, in particular, his son's misguided request that the music be sent "gratis": "I have the honor of dispatching five arias and of paying for copying three of them and for postage . . . though, in God's name, I myself am penniless. I look like poor Lazarus. My dressing gown is in such tatters that if someone rings in the morning, I must make myself scarce. . . . Had someone told me a few years ago that I would have to wear woolen stockings; that in frosty, dry weather I would be happy to pull your old felt shoes over my old ones; that in order to protect myself from the cold I would have to put on two or three old waistcoats, one over the other—would I really have believed it? We cannot give a thought to going to the theater or to balls. Such is our life: cares within and cares without."

A "horrified" Wolfgang found it difficult to grasp what, since his departure but months earlier, had worked so swift and complete a deterioration upon his father's wardrobe; he etched his retort with irony: "Tears came to my eyes as I . . . read that you had to go about so badly dressed. My very dearest Papa! Certainly this is not my fault—you know it!" For the first time Leopold received his son's strong reproval.

Though he had begun to realize that for dramatic effect his father could sacrifice veracity, by degrees he gave ground to parental pressure to consider departing for Paris—but only because he set his mind upon coming back to Aloisia at the first possible moment. Ever on the lookout, Leopold advised: "It would be ill-considered to leave anything behind in Mannheim"; he sought to exclude at least this excuse for a return. The decision to move on, however, remained theoretical: money alone could set the carriage wheels in motion, and not only had Leopold announced his indisposition toward further borrowing from friends, but De Jean, standing firm, sent not a florin beyond the ninety-six. In fact, he may well have regarded them as an overpayment; in respect to the second flute concerto (K. 314/285d), Mozart had played him false: it proved to be not a new creation but a close version—transposed from C to D and modified ever so little—of the oboe concerto composed for Ferlendis and then presented to Ramm, who piped it all over Mannheim, De Jean doubtless among the auditors. Yet, whatever his disappointment with Mozart, he did receive him later in Paris.[30]

6

AT THE TIME he at last departed Mannheim for Paris, Mozart had completed for De Jean not three quartets, as he represented to Leopold, but two (for flute, violin, viola, and violoncello): K. 285, famous for its poetic middle movement, the flute set in the foreground against pizzicato strings; and 285a, cast in two movements perhaps to save time and effort (though Mozart might well have invoked Christian Bach's precedent). As to the first of the flute concertos, K. 313/285c in G could hardly have answered De Jean's expectations: not "modest, simple, and short," it had the spaciousness of the violin concertos. Over and above the authority of the opening Allegro maestoso, the heart of K. 313 lies in the cantilena of its exquisitely colored and detailed Adagio ma non troppo. The closing Rondeau must have left De Jean breathless. Doubtless he felt more at ease with the Ferlendis concerto, neither technically nor musically as demanding, though decked out with filigree. Ferlendis, Joseph Haydn observed, had his limitations, and Mozart respected them.[31] Nevertheless, once again a tripping final movement must have tried an amateur's dexterity.

In his letter to Salzburg announcing the arrangements with De Jean, Mozart had also spoken of finding a "diversion" from his labors on the commission: composing a mass for the Mannheim court chapel and a set of piano/violin duets. Upon the departure of Karl Theodore for Munich, Mozart abandoned the mass, a step he regretted: "Alas, if only the Elector of Bavaria had not died, I would have completed the mass and brought it to performance. It would have made a great sensation here [Mannheim]. I was in just the right mood for it when the devil trotted out the accursed Doctor Sanfftel." (Popular wisdom ascribed Max Joseph's end to the incompetence of Sanfftel, the physician at his deathbed.)

Only a fragment of the mass survives (see pp. 468–69). Indeed, the Mannheim period shows a meager harvest—a few works, most of them less than imposing: the compositions for the Wendlings, an aria for Aloisia,

---

30 De Jean arrived in Paris without his Mozart scores. He had packed them in a trunk left behind in Mannheim by error.

31 An entry in Schiedenhofen's diary for 25 July 1777 bears upon a Mozart flute concerto rehearsed and performed that day in Salzburg. Perhaps, soon after composing the Ferlendis concerto, Mozart reworked it for flute; or the reference may be to a lost concerto. K. 315/285e, a meditative Andante for solo flute and orchestra may have formed part of the De Jean commission.

one for Raaff, a sonata apiece for Rosa and Therese, the De Jean commission, and the duets. Of all, the last have greatest weight and owed their existence to a fortuitous inspiration.

During his recent visit to Munich, Mozart had come across six piano/violin duets characterized by a tight, integrated ensemble (each instrument, in fact, claiming equal importance), the work of Joseph Schuster, a composer in the service of the Saxon court. Posting them to his sister, Wolfgang had written: "They are not bad. If I stay on [in Munich] I, too, shall write six in this style, as they have had much success here." However, not until his stay in Mannheim did he begin work on the set—by this time envisaging it as a gift for Electress Maria Elizabeth— completing the first half (K. 301/293a, 302/293b, and 303/293c) before departing for Paris, where he would bring the undertaking to completion (with K. 304/300c, 305/293d, and 306/300l). Mozart's masterworks for piano and violin begin with this cycle of "Kurfürstin" or "Palatine" sonatas.

In his unfledged, innocuous Versailles, London, and Hague examples (see pp. 171 and 195) the dispensable accompanying violin (or flute in the English sonatas) for the most part serves to thicken and color the texture by filling in harmonies here and there and paralleling or imitating melodic lines and figurations in the clavier part. In contrast, the Palatine sonatas give each instrument opportunities to sing the melody, accompany it, join in colloquy, or offer independent interjections. (Ideas conceived for the De Jean commission found their way into K. 301 and 303: some of their melodic contours betray an origin in the special qualities of the flute.) Rococo works of great urbanity, the first three Palatine sonatas (all in two movements) show that accomplished invention and technique long part of Mozart's craft, and the question must be put as to why he required Schuster's modest example as a stimulus to apply to this genre his full science.[32]

It permeates K. 296 (March 1778), the three-movement piano and violin sonata he dedicated to Therese Pierron. His last musical word before he left Mannheim, the sonata conjures up the possibility of personal allusions, its Andante sostenuto, calling to mind an aria in the tenderest manner of Christian Bach, perhaps a farewell to Aloisia. At all events, few would dispute that subjective emotions color the recitative and aria "*Alcandro, lo confesso / Non sò d'onde viene,*" K. 294, the poetry from Metastasio's *Olimpiade.* This solo portrays a king's perplexity to experience a flood of tenderness toward a young man he has condemned to execution. (The youth proves to

---

32 Perhaps because here Joseph Haydn offered no model (although his keyboard sonata in D of 1773 acquired a violin part from Charles Burney's hand). Mozart's Palatine sonatas do invite a choice between harpsichord and piano (*Clavecin ou Forte Piano*).

be his son, long thought dead.) With Raaff in mind, Mozart attempted to give the verse—dear to him in Christian Bach's setting[33]—a melodic line appropriate to a tenor voice still magisterial, if frayed. Yet, as he worked, thoughts of Aloisia pressed upon him, and he turned to composing the words for her, wrenching them from all connection with the libretto to become the confused reflections of a maiden troubled by the first stirrings of love. "I do not know whence this tender inclination comes, this strange agitation new to me and arising in my breast," she sings to music recalling the Andante of the piano concerto K. 175. By thus transforming Metastasio's lines, Mozart could force Aloisia's lips to form the longed-for avowal. K. 294 exploits sustained cantilena and embellishments including runs that touch the E flat in alt. He had strengthened Aloisia in the bravura facet of her art, having pressed into service during their lessons his group of cadenzas composed for arias by Christian Bach (K. 293e).

Turning to propitiate Raaff, Mozart wrote "*Se al labbro/Il cor dolente*," K. 295, its text by Antonio Salvi. The aria looks back to the more mechanical and sober aspects of the baroque tradition in which Raaff had received his schooling; cantabile elements dominate, vigorous virtuoso passages being eschewed. In contrast, the still compelling voice of Dorothea Wendling, a mistress of the lyric line and tragic tone, kindled Mozart's imagination as he composed the short scena, "*Basta, vincesti/Ah, non lasciarmi*," K. 486a/295a. She had selected this passage from Metastasio's *Didone abbandonata*.

"Something so excellent": thus had Leopold recorded his admiration of his son's first gift to Gustl Wendling, the ariette "*Oiseaux, si tous les ans*," K. 307/284d, written soon after his arrival in Mannheim. Not long before his departure he presented her with a second and no less exquisite ariette, "*Dans un bois solitaire*," K. 308/295b,[34] whose poetry evokes the antique world of the pastoral, the miniature drama having the spirit of a rococo vignette by Adam Friedrich Oeser. This was the Gustl whose liaison with Karl Theodore offended Mozart—or so he wrote home.

7

IN SUCH MATTERS he had succeeded in misleading his parents: for a while they believed his protestations of disenchantment with the godless

33 "Although I know the Bach setting and admire it so much that it is always in my ears, I nonetheless wished to attempt to see whether I might write a version totally unlike Bach's. Mine is not at all similar—not in the least."
34 She chose both texts, the first by Antoine Ferrand, the second by Antoine Houdart de la Motte, from a French anthology of 1765.

Wendlings and their coterie; he hammered at the idea.[35] Leopold nodded approval, and, too long out of touch with the great world he once had known, proceeded to a major blunder: he wrote Grimm a letter identifying Wolfgang's moral fastidiousness as the reason for his not journeying to Paris in the company of his Mannheim friends. (Leopold had perhaps forgotten that Grimm and Wendling knew one another.) To the cosmopolite he relied upon to be Wolfgang's mentor in France, he painted himself and his son as utter provincials. Grimm could hardly have looked forward to greeting a young man who, it seemed, had developed into a prim philistine. In this matter Frau Anna Maria proved wiser. "No one [in Mannheim] knows that this is the reason why Wolfgang has not traveled with them [Wendling and Ramm], for we would only be ridiculed," she informed Leopold, who more and more felt alien, cut adrift, and disconsolate. Not only did his son's uncertain situation weigh upon him: a painful circumstance also forced him to face the precariousness of Nannerl's future.

On 21 December, Adlgasser had suffered a stroke while playing the organ at vespers, and worshipers carried him from Salzburg cathedral to his deathbed.[36] The Archbishop allotted the wife and children of his organist a pittance. Their dilemma made Leopold confront the certainty that, were he to die the next day, his family would receive even less from the hostile court: Anna Maria might scrape through, but Nannerl would have to enter domestic service, the course the Residenz prescribed for women left without sufficient pension or inheritance. Her willingness to surrender her savings to help finance the continuation of her brother's faltering tour betokened not only affection but the concern of an unmarried woman approaching twenty-seven without prospects. Once more, she roused herself and began to practice the clavier in preparation for taking pupils. A promissory note backed by her funds[37] made it possible to

---

35 The poem he sent Anna Maria from Worms included: "To tell the truth, I would much prefer / to go out into the world, to great distant parts / with these people [the Webers] / rather than with these nobodies who / surround me. . . . / I value Weber's ass more than Ramm's head; and a sliver of this ass is worth more to me / than all of Monsieur Wendling."

36 The incident had elements of tragi-farce: even after the seizure, he continued to play, the effect being, to Leopold's ears, "of a dog running over the keys." Like many Salzburg musicians, Adlgasser drank too much, and, at first, his colleagues and the congregation assumed that, hidden behind the instrument, he once again had raised too many cups.

37 Leopold permitted her to put money aside, a privilege never given Mozart, who, the father insisted, botched practical matters. Perhaps he feared that money might lead the young man to begin shifting according to his own purposes. The idea suggests itself that Leopold feigned drawing upon his daughter's account in order to embarrass and cow his son (see XXIII, n. 9 and p. 503).

arrange new letters of credit, and the travelers could set their date of departure from Mannheim: 14 March 1778.

Two days earlier, friends bade them farewell at an afternoon concert at the Cannabichs'. Aloisia not only joined Mozart's two clavier scholars, Rosa and Therese, and the Electoral orchestra in his concerto for three claviers but also sang *"Aer tranquillo"* from *Il rè pastore* and *"Non sò d'onde viene"* in its first performance with instrumental accompaniment. The compliments and the warmth of the gathering for a moment made him forget Mannheim's bitter predicament and rekindled his yearning for a future in Aloisia's city: "Who knows, perhaps it will happen. I hope so; I still have the feeling; I still persist in the hope." The Webers sped him on his way with gifts: from Aloisia two pairs of lace cuffs she had worked; from her father Friedrich Samuel Bierling's translation (1752; in four volumes) of Molière's comedies.

Perhaps they helped distract him during a journey to Paris of nine and a half days. He and Anna Maria had chosen the shortest route: via Metz.[38] They traveled in their own coach, which the driver had bought from them and could claim upon the journey's end. (He had already placed the body on a new chassis.) As they neared Paris, the weather turned stormy. "The wind and rain almost choked and drowned us," Anna Maria wrote; "we both got soaking wet in the carriage and could scarcely breathe. We passed through the customs examination [at the French border] well enough except for Wolfgang's having to pay a duty of thirty-eight sous on his small music paper; in Paris we had no customs inspection at all."

They arrived on 23 March and took up residence with a Herr Mayer. A dealer in secondhand goods who acted as the Parisian agent of the Augsburg firm of Arbauer, he also rented rooms. His house in the Rue Bourg l'Abbé had been recommended to Leopold for its comfortable German atmosphere; here Anna Maria could feel at home.

---

38 Excepting Metz and Clermont-en-Argonne, the towns through which they made their way can only be conjectured; Leopold absent, no journal was kept.

CHAPTER XXI

Paris I:
The Whirlwind Dies Down

SOME FIVE WEEKS before Mozart's departure from Mannheim, Voltaire had left his estate at Ferney, he, too, bending his course toward Paris. Returning home to die after an absence of almost thirty years, he arrived on 10 February.

Admirers waited upon the eighty-three-year-old patriarch whose presence overshadowed all else, even court gossip and the hostilities attendant upon the Bavarian succession. Despite the reproaches of his physician, the ailing object of the city's attention made himself accessible to crowds of the devoted and curious. In the streets his carriage attracted mobs insistent upon escorting it, the most feverish even kissing the horses. The Académie held an unprecedented public session in his honor, and delirium greeted his visit to the Comédie-Française. Throughout these ovations he retained his fabled fire, eloquence, vivacity, and wit, even as his body bent with strain and he moved toward death.

Its evident imminence provoked his final duel with the Church, a contest that engrossed Paris: would the great freethinker be forced to refute his writings and thus save his remains from the lime-filled carrion pit, the fate priests would assign them should he die unconfessed and unrepentant; or would he resolve the dilemma into some mutual accommodation?[1]

---

1 It was as a corpse that he won the contest: friends placed his embalmed body upright in a coach; propped by a servant who made it simulate a man asleep, the cadaver escaped Paris and indignities at the hands of its clergy to find peaceful burial at Scellières, in the province of Champagne.

Until almost the hour he took to his deathbed, adoring visitors thronged his drawing room to chorus homage. They included the great: among them Marmontel, La Harpe, the blind and ancient Madame du Deffand, and Benjamin Franklin (whom the sage addressed in English). Gluck, too, made his call, his unwilling rival, Piccinni, taking care to arrive the same day—if some two hours later. What energy Parisians could spare from the spectacle of Voltaire's apotheosis, they devoted to the foolish rumpus involving the adherents of these two masters, a domestic war of pamphlets flaring in the salons and cafés. Neither had a hand in inciting it.

With the premiere of his *Iphigénie en Aulide* (a setting of Du Roullet's text, itself a remodeling of Racine's tragedy) at the Opéra in the spring of 1774, Gluck had become a force in French musical life. The success stirred the management to implement an agreement that he provide the house with a series of scores, and he set about contriving French adaptations of his Viennese reform operas. During the summer of 1774 Paris heard his gallicized version of *Orfeo* (he had created it during the mourning period following Louis XV's death in May) and in 1776 that of his *Alceste*. He also began two new works for Paris: a *Roland* to Marmontel's rewriting of Quinault's text and an *Armide* to the latter poet's revered libretto.

In a move to ignite and fan the flames of rivalry, the Opéra also invited Piccinni to put the Quinault/Marmontel *Roland* to music. Piccinni had arrived from Naples on the last day of 1776 in response to an invitation extended by the Opéra and endorsed by Marie Antoinette. At all events, neither he nor Gluck had any idea of the Opéra's premeditated game to set them one against the other; nor did the Queen.[2] When he learned of it, an indignant Gluck quit the arena into which the management had decoyed him, breaking off work on *Roland* and devoting his energies to *Armide*. It reached the Opéra in September 1777, Piccinni's *Roland* following four months later.

Despite the endeavors of Gluck and the dignified, if often perplexed, Piccinni to elude even the suggestion of contest, the Opéra, the critics, and the public would not be denied the pleasures of a new ordeal of words: they fomented a simulacrum of the Bouffons' War by setting up a polemic opposing the economic and sober dramatic values of the German to the sensuous aesthetic of the Italian.[3] At the height of this contrived and deftly exploited polemic; in the midst of Voltaire's much debated last carousel

---

2 She had lent her patronage upon the recommendation of both Marchese Domenico Caraccioli, Naples's Ambassador to Versailles, and his correspondent, Abbé Galiani.

3 Attempts to create a scandal centering about Gluck had begun at the premiere of *Alceste* in its French version, when a group hired by the Opéra's management hissed it.

with the clergy; in the thick of the public apostrophes in his honor and the commotion surrounding the premiere of his tragedy *Irène*, at the Théâtre Français, the well-nigh unknown composer from Salzburg began his siege of Paris. He could not have chosen a worse time.

2

MOZART BEGAN, AS was his way of beginning, in a whirlwind of energy. All hopes rested upon Grimm, and the Mozarts lost no time leaving a card at the recently built dwelling he shared with its owner, Madame d'Épinay, on the Rue Chaussée d'Antin. The rented fiacre then lumbered on in quest of Ramm and Wendling,[4] the former's libertinage and the latter's impiety no longer matters of concern.

Mother and son found a changed Paris of old neighborhoods transformed and new and extended districts. They recognized the necessity of moving to a central location "nearer the aristocracy and the theaters." By 11 April 1778, Madame d'Épinay had found them a comfortable apartment on the Rue du Gros Chênet—"very clean . . . and with healthy air." But, even then, Wolfgang could not cope with the sprawling metropolis.

Leopold had sent him a list of "our Parisian acquaintances, all of whom will be delighted to see you."[5] But almost at once Mozart renounced the ritual of leaving cards, complaining to his father: "You write me that I should set about paying calls in order to make new friendships and renew old ones. But that is impossible: on every side distances are too great for walking; or it is too muddy, for Paris is filthy beyond belief." To screen a lassitude—no doubt born of apprehension—that had in no time overtaken him, he emphasized the vast scale of a changing Paris and the need to control expenses: "Travel by carriage involves the honor of laying out from 4 to 5 livres a day. . . ." Since walking proved hazardous and transportation costly, he had no choice, he declared, but to limit his activities. The whirlwind died down even as it spiraled upward; what had been meant to be a flight to the clouds—*aut Caesar, aut nihil*—did not even achieve the dignity of a resolute, plucky Icarian disaster: he barely cleared the shrub. Grimm had to set in place Wolfgang's few important Parisian connections.

---

4 They had set out from Mannheim on 15 February.
5 Leopold failed to realize his hope of arranging a meeting between his son and Diderot, known for his generosity and a devotion to German music; Leopold also contemplated Wolfgang's informing Voltaire of the opportunity at hand to make good his having missed him in Geneva. "Monsieur de Voltaire is in Paris," Leopold observed in March—a signal ignored.

The Baron had received that impolitic letter from Leopold, which, he boasted, included "nothing less than a complete description of my life" and detailed the "harassment, persecution, and tyranny" the Salzburg Residenz, in his belief, had visited upon Wolfgang and himself. This tale, he hoped, would awaken Grimm's "pity and move his heart to help us." The cold, undemonstrative philosophe received a different impression: Leopold but confirmed an image of the family's parochialism, inferior social position, and inability to effect its betterment. Grimm saw himself as part of an elite whose culture and worldliness placed it above the nobility: he would not long interest himself in the affairs of someone fated, it would appear, to remain a "little Hans."

Yet, whatever his impression of the grown-up Wolfgang, whatever his impatience with Leopold's importuning, in the beginning Grimm did lend his support; more: he held out his hand in active co-operation, taking Wolfgang to musical performances, sharing his enthusiasms and aversions. Above all, Grimm saw to it that his protégé became a regular guest at the table of the director of the Concert spirituel, the distinguished tenor of the Opéra Joseph Legros,[6] to whose apartment important musicians made their way. In addition, Mozart from time to time lunched with Noverre, now ballet master of the Opéra; and, thanks to Raaff's recommendation and to letters from Cannabich and Otto von Gemmingen, Mozart also received the hospitality of the Minister of the Palatinate, Karl Heinrich Joseph, Count von Sickengen. If this sensitive amateur of music could offer little more than encouragement, Noverre did attempt to interest the Opéra in commissioning Mozart to compose a ballet and also an opera based upon the story of Alexander and Roxanne. In letters home he made the mistake of representing these hopes as certainties.

Legros alone provided immediate and remunerative help; he asked Mozart to make additions to a miserere by Holzbauer: a trio, a tenor aria with chorus, a couple of recitatives, and four choral numbers, the thus expanded miserere to be performed at the Concert spirituel during Holy Week.[7] Wolfgang had to compose at Legros's, the commission having

---

6 He sang Achilles at the premiere of Gluck's *Iphigénie en Aulide*. His performance had inspired the composer to rewrite for him the castrato role of Orfeo in his *Orfeo ed Euridice*, the work—revised throughout—becoming *Orphée et Eurydice*.

7 In the end, the enlarged score had to be cut; an unenthusiastic audience heard only two of Mozart's choruses, and, it would seem, his name did not appear on the program. His contributions to the miserere, K. Anh.1/297a, applauded at rehearsal, have not come to light. Only one of the two influential societies serving Paris's public concert life commanded the resources to perform a composition of this kind: the Concert spirituel had a chorus; the rival Concert des amateurs did not. Founded in 1769 by François-Joseph Gossec and from 1773 to 1781 directed

come while he still lived at Herr Mayer's house, whose narrow stairway did not permit passage of a harpsichord.[8] Gossec, visiting Legros, let his eyes fall upon the manuscript in work, and he praised what he saw.

Legros must have been no less admiring: the presence in Paris of a quartet of famous Mannheim wind players—Wendling (flute), Ramm (oboe), Jan Vaclav Stich, who called himself Giovanni Punto (horn), and Georg Wenzel Ritter (bassoon)—inspired him to ask Mozart to write a sinfonia concertante[9] exploiting their talents. He completed it during April.[10] Raaff, too, had arrived in Paris—he had, in fact, been a soloist in the miserere—putting up at the same building in which Legros resided. All at once, Mozart's situation appeared promising: overnight an intimate of the Director of the Concert spirituel and surrounded by colleagues from Mannheim eager to help a young countryman make his way in the great capital sympathetic to German instrumental music.

For all that, he, to a regrettable extent, vitiated much sympathy by dwelling upon what he felt to be the indigenous limitations of Parisian musical intellect: "The French have at present improved their taste only just enough to listen to good music," he observed to Leopold; "but for them to perceive that their own is bad or, at least, to notice a difference—on no

---

by his disciple Joseph Boulogne, Chevalier de Saint-Georges, it enjoyed the reputation of having the finer orchestra. Grimm's connections led Mozart to Legros, not to the fascinating Saint-Georges. This Guadeloupe-born son of a plantation owner from Lorraine and a black became one of the most handsome and exotic figures in Parisian society, a master of fencing, riding, dancing, and music, as both violinist and composer.

8 Mozart, of course, composed in his head with ease. Perhaps on this occasion he required an instrument at hand in order to demonstrate his progress to Legros.

9 With its multiple soloists who, unlike the homogenous soloists of the baroque concerto grosso, disengage from the general orchestral fabric, the sinfonia concertante (Mozart used the French appellation, *symphonie concertante*) had grown fashionable in Paris in company with a rage for virtuosity (see XXV, n. 9). A bit past the middle of the century, a taste for the genre had appeared in Vienna.

10 The autograph (K. 297B) went astray, and Mozart never made good his intention to reconstruct it from memory. Thus the composition does not survive, at least not as he set down the notes. Yet its shadow may well have determined the outlines of the problematical sinfonia concertante for oboe, clarinet, horn, and bassoon (K. 297b/Anh.C14.01), in all probability a very corrupt derivative, its sources surrounded by mystification. Be that as it may, Mozart's expressive force makes itself felt, even though the change in instrumentation—an oboe replacing the flute, a clarinet the oboe—occasioned much rewriting as did, doubtless, a desire to improve upon Mozart. Even so, his diction remains recognizable, if not always his syntax. This sinfonia concertante may be considered relative to an old master painting that, despite the mutilation of its panel—sawed off on one side, extended on the other—and a surface so overpainted as to cloud a clear assessment of the original, nonetheless permits glimpses of the quality and authority of the forms beneath the alterations. On the other hand, it has been proposed that the two symphonie-concertante movements embedded within the Posthorn Serenade (K. 320; see p. 483) derive from the Legros commission.

account!" It is not difficult to imagine his venting these echoes of Rousseau at gatherings in Legros's chambers and with intention to jar the company. Borrowing the spirit of Gluck's example would have been a shrewder course in respect to these almost obsessive anti-French predilections.

Gluck detested the French, their capital, and its Opéra no less than he; yet Gluck knew (as did the Mozarts) that Paris alone defined an international career: it remained the gleaming fork to which European art still tuned. Gluck, however, possessed a formidable barrage with which to force his way. Of Leopold's generation, he had the bearing of a maestro who enjoyed the patronage of the Dowager German Empress and her daughter, the Queen of France[11]; and he excelled in the arts of intimidation and dissembling. Reichardt, paraphrasing Gluck, described how he made short work of the French ("as changeable as fire" with "their narrow-mindedness and presumption") by "treating and using them in his own grand manner." Though it would have been impossible for Wolfgang to emulate such seigneurial condescension, he might well have attempted that subtler diplomacy Gluck could also summon: throwing opponents off guard through sheer blandishment proved as helpful to his career as his imposing comportment. In particular, he knew how to flatter the French in an area without measure dear to them: he praised the beauty of their language, declaring it a handmaiden to music no less felicitous than Italian; and with the very breath that denied the validity of Rousseau's operatic dogma, he cajoled Rousseau and his followers into friendship.[12] Unlike Mozart, who had no taste for those aesthetic disputes so dear to Paris, Gluck reveled in them and called attention to himself through publications.

Mozart, for his part, lost few opportunities to deride the French, their disputations, and their speech: "In truth, the devil invented the language." "If only accursed French were not so contemptible for music; that is the misery of it; by comparison even German is divine." He saw himself an "honest German" struggling "among downright cattle and beasts," his terms for French musicians. He longed to do what Gluck had done—to astound Paris with imposing operas. For a time he came to regard this goal

---

11 Addressed as Chevalier, Gluck wore his Papal order with gusto; Mozart had long hidden his away.

12 He praised Rousseau's modest musical gifts with implausible excess: a wicked ambiguity tinged his declaration that *Le devin du village* remained "a model no one has yet imitated," a cutting disingenuousness his declaration that Rousseau, had he dedicated his chief creative energies to music rather than letters, might himself have first achieved the Gluckean reform. For his part, Rousseau expressed his pleasure in *Iphigénie en Aulide* with a no less marvelous equivocality: "You have realized what I held to be impossible up to this day." Neither fooled the other, and both enjoyed indulging this reciprocal diplomatic extravagance and fraudulence touched with venom, a sport to which Mozart could never lend himself.

in the light of a national mission "to teach the French more and more to know, esteem, and fear the Germans." (He became furious to overhear Parisians refer to him as a "dumb German.") Paris with its pretensions and snobbism aroused his patriotism, and he came to look upon his responsibility there in terms of doing "honor to . . . the whole German nation." He harbored a Gallophobia no less intense than Goethe's.

But five years had passed since the appearance of Goethe's prodigious *Götz*, so startling to Germans, its diction, structure, and the blunt vivaciousness of its hero setting at defiance all that French literature and criticism had long imposed upon their taste. Buckling himself into German armor and flaunting its sharp angles in Parisian salons, Mozart—in later years he nicknamed himself "porcupine" (see IV, n. 15)—became a kind of Götz, carrying on vigorous "honorable feuds" and striking not only for German glory but for pleasure's sake, too. His plainspokenness calls to mind Goethe's when he addressed the Italians and French in his panegyric to Strassburg cathedral ("What have you done that you dare scoff . . . you dagos [*Wälscher*]! . . . This is German architecture, our architecture; for the Italian has none he can call his own, still less the Frenchman[!]") Though the young and well-traveled Mozart never showed the degree of clannishness of the young and insular Goethe, both saw in German art the workings, in the poet's words, of "the strong, rugged German soul."

Patriotic sententiousness assailed Mozart only by fits and starts, his sense of humor never far off ("I can do as well as . . . Piccinni although I am only a German"); but, to his misfortune, he clung to his father's view of their disappointments not as functions of chance or blunder but, rather, of enemy conspiracy and perversity. Mozart found it impossible to face the fact that he, not the French, had changed: "On the whole, Paris is much altered; the French are very short of being as polite as they were fifteen years ago; they now border on rudeness and are arrogant to a disgusting degree." His Francophobia admitted neither self-analysis nor external reality: in this area he could not measure with sober mind either himself or the Parisians and excoriated those who still looked upon him as a seven-year-old even as he longed for the indulgence once accorded the prodigy. His daimon manipulated him to strange contradictions and destructive confrontations.

3

"I THINK THAT once again some intrigue is afoot; doubtless here, too, I again have my enemies. However, where have I not had them? . . . I believe that *Cambini*, an Italian maestro here, is the prime mover." Thus Mozart explained to Salzburg why the performance of the sinfonia concertante had fallen through. But in this affair, as often before, he had fathered his predicament.

Legros had the score in keeping and intended to hire copyists to extract the parts. For days Mozart noticed it lying set aside. Then it vanished. He searched, found it hidden in a pile of music, but did not mention the discovery; rather, with seeming unconcern he asked Legros whether he had given the work to be copied. He replied, no less casually, that he "had forgotten" about the matter. With no effort to fabricate an excuse, he made clear his displeasure with Mozart and sent a signal that there would be no performance. Mozart had, so he bragged, "cut to pieces" (*die Augen* . . . *ausgelöscht*) the Livorno-born violinist and composer, Giuseppe Maria Cambini, during a meeting in Legros's quarters. Legros felt no less offended than his guest, a respected figure in Paris, where he had established himself early in the decade.[13]

Mozart had heard one of Cambini's "very pretty" quartets in Mannheim. Meeting him at Legros's, he complimented the work and launched into it at the keyboard. No sooner begun, he mischievously indicated that the quartet had quite gone from his head even as he played on, jauntily turning excess into insult as his fingers reshaped the material. Hearing his effort transformed by genius made Cambini less than happy, though he succeeded in stammering: "What a marvelous head." Seeking to impress, Wolfgang had managed only to evince deplorable taste and diminish himself. There had been no intrigue about the sinfonia concertante; nothing had gone on behind the scenes; not Cambini but Mozart had been the "enemy": his prank much offended. When he at last measured the damage it had done[14]—for a time he found himself unwelcome at Legros's—and realized the extent to which Cambini "did not enjoy it," Mozart put the blame upon Ritter, Ramm, and Stich: they, he insisted, had urged him on (*"liessen mir keinen Fried"*), and he had responded "in all innocence."

His behavior at Legros's had been of a piece with his declaration that his pursuit of patrons in Paris had become "impossible." This defiant passivity,

---

13 Gluck felt it wise to praise him. Cambini had composed a passage from Quinault's *Armide* two years before Gluck took up the libretto. With the appearance of this new musical setting, Cambini asked that performances of his excerpt cease. In response Gluck stated (January 1778) that he would "take great pleasure in hearing the *Armide* scene by M. Cambini" and would always delight in listening to music better than his own. "One must have but a single aim: the advancement of art."

14 See XXII, n. 11. On 12 and 19 April, the Concert spirituel performed a sinfonia concertante, not by Mozart, but by Cambini, who turned this genre to extraordinary account, writing not far from one hundred examples.

often expressed in playful malice and hauteur, deepened after his visit to the Duchess de Chabot. Grimm had provided a letter of introduction in the hope that she would reintroduce him to the Duchess de Bourbon (who, when still Mlle. d'Orléans, had so adored the prodigy of days past (see p. 172). In a famous passage of Mozartean prose, he described his encounter at the end of April 1778 with Madame de Chabot (born Elisabeth-Louise de la Rochefoucault) at the Hôtel de la Rochefoucault in the Faubourg Saint-Germain.

"I had to wait half an hour in a large ice-cold, unheated room, which hadn't a fireplace. At last, the Duchess de Chabot made an appearance. Most courteous, she asked me to make allowances for the clavier inasmuch as she had none in good order. She invited me to try it. I said that with all my heart I would be delighted to play, but at the moment found it impossible since the cold had taken all feeling from my fingers. I asked to be shown to a room at least with hearth and fire. '*Oh, oui, Monsieur, vous avez raison*' was her only reply, whereupon she sat down and began to draw and continued to do so for a whole hour in the company of some gentlemen, all seated in a circle at a big table. I had the honor to wait a full hour. The windows and doors stood open, and not only my hands but my whole body and my feet became frigid even as my head began to ache. There was *altum silentium*, and during this long wait I did not know what to do for cold, headache, and boredom. I kept thinking: Were it not for M. Grimm, I would leave on the spot. To be brief, I at last played on that miserable, wretched pianoforte. But most vexing was that Madame and all the gentlemen did not for a moment interrupt their drawing but kept at it, and thus I had to play for the chairs, table, and walls. Under these annoying circumstances I lost my patience. I began the Fischer variations, played half, and stood up. No end of praise followed. Even so, I said what had to be said: namely, that I could not do myself justice on that clavier and would like to choose another day when a better instrument might be available. But she would not comply; I had to wait another half hour until her husband arrived. He [Louis-Antoine-Auguste de Rohan Chabot], for his part, settled down beside me and listened with all attention, and I—I at once forgot the cold and my headache and, in spite of the wretched clavier, played as I play when in good spirits. Give me Europe's best clavier with an audience that understands nothing or doesn't want to understand or does not feel with me when I play, and I lose all pleasure."[15]

---

15 That Mozart most likely composed the introspective piano sonata in A minor (K. 310/300d) in expectation of performances in Paris would seem to speak for the presence there of not a few connoisseurs like the Duke; such serious enthusiasts had made up a significant part of Schobert's public. The middle movement of K. 310, in fact, includes a quotation from him.

He did not grasp that the Duchess had expected him to provide back-ground music for a session of her well-known drawing academy. She and other amateurs met in her family's hôtel to sketch under the eyes of teach-ers as distinguished as Jean Baptiste Marie Pierre and Fragonard. She took the young musician's engaging cheekiness in stride, perhaps in the end comprehending his distress and attempting to save his day from going al-together sour: his self-assertion could not have concealed his helplessness from her or himself. Grimm must have stood aghast at the poverty of Mozart's social perceptions as he related, no doubt triumphantly, his ad-venture in one of the capital's great houses. No second summons to it came to him; nor did he find the way opened to the Duchess of Bourbon. To Madame de Chabot his sense of himself must have seemed to verge upon impudence, and one amusing exposure sufficed.

At this juncture Grimm began to be censorious of him. So sovereign an attitude toward the ways of the aristocracy signaled the inevitable fall of someone dependent upon patronage. Indeed, he would soon assume a sim-ilar posture in respect to the most promising connection Grimm made for him—an introduction, on a personal level, to the important de Guines family.

4

"WOLFGANG HAS LIGHTED upon a good household," Anna Maria wrote her husband on 14 May. "He has to teach composition for two hours every day to a mademoiselle, the daughter of the Duke de [Guines][16]; he pays handsomely and is the Queen's favorite." The father had some reputation as an amateur on the flute, and the daughter played the harp. He wanted an instructor to guide her in writing sonatas combin-ing both instruments. Mozart praised her as a performer but echoed to Leopold her own doubts "as to whether she also has talent for composi-tion, in particular regarding ideas ... Well, we shall see. If she doesn't come up with any ... for at the moment she, in truth, has none at all, then it is to no purpose, for, God knows, I can't give her any."

Aware of de Guines's "great influence" at Versailles and inspirited by Anna Maria's account of his affection for Wolfgang (*liebt den Wolfgang über alles*: a bit of hyperbole to lift spirits in Salzburg), Leopold could not un-

---

16 Anna Maria neglected to write out his name. Moreover, thanks to her error as to his station, Adrien-Louis Bonnières de Souastre—in fact, not Duke but Count de Guines—appears mis-titled in much of the Mozart literature. He had been a representative of Versailles in Berlin and London.

derstand how his son could contemplate abandoning fine fees and finer possibilities over the matter of the daughter's creative insufficiencies. Leopold summoned his most reasonable tone.

"My dear son! I beg you: try to preserve the friendship of the Duke de Guines and to establish yourself in his eyes. . . . Since the Queen is pregnant, as a matter of course there will *be great festivities at the birth*; you might receive something to do that can make your fortune, for on such occasions *what the Queen but demands* is carried out. You write: 'Today I have given the Duke's daughter her 4th lesson'; and you already expect her to write down her own ideas? Do you think that everyone has your genius? With time she will find her way! She has a good memory. Eh bien! Let her steal or—put with more polish—adapt what she has learned [*applicieren*]. It does no harm in the beginning—until one gathers courage. By giving her variations, you have started on the right path. Now, carry on! If Monsieur le Duc but hears some little piece by his daughter, he will be beside himself. This is indeed a fortunate acquaintance!"

Mozart accepted the counsel. He needed income and continued, though with little enthusiasm, to instruct her until summer, when her betrothal made an end to the lessons. De Guines immortalized his musical relationship with his daughter—to whom he had, Mozart observed, an unhealthy emotional attachment—by commissioning the concerto for flute and harp in C (K. 299/297c, completed during April), in fact, a modish sinfonia concertante.

At the height of his activity as a teacher in Paris, Mozart had, including Mlle. de Guines, only three pupils. Even so, he found them a burden. "It is no joke to give lessons here: you have to wear yourself out to the full; and unless you take *many pupils*, you don't earn much.[17] You must not think this laziness on my part. No! Rather, it is in every respect against my spirit and my way of life. You know that I am, so to speak, out and out involved in music, that my whole day revolves around it, that I love to reflect, study, and consider. Well, my present way of life [teaching] impedes all this. Of course, I have some free hours, but these I need for rest rather than work." Baron Grimm recognized that Wolfgang resented every teaching hour as an hour lost to creative endeavor, and, at the same time, lacked the stamina to support a heavy load of pupils.

He ended on less than cordial terms with de Guines, who showed himself by no means punctilious in paying for services. This indifference to the needs of inferiors and his stewardess's slippery haggling when Mozart

---

17 "He could have more [than three pupils]," Anna Maria wrote, "but cannot take them because everything is so out of the way."

demanded payment followed practices all too usual.[18] Against them the victim had as weapons firmness, patience, and courtesy, a trio of qualities Mozart did not always command in the same breath: he could not mask his outrage in confrontations with her.

During sunnier days of his association with de Guines a proposal sprang up (from a source never identified) that Mozart become the King's organist. The idea may have originated with de Guines: perhaps he empowered Jean Joseph Rodolphe, a horn player in the royal chapel, to broach the idea. Mozart wrote home: "He has offered me the post of organist at Versailles, if I wish to accept it. The salary is 2000 livres a year. Under the conditions, I should have to live at Versailles for six months but might spend the remaining six in Paris or wherever I might choose. I do not think I shall accept. I must hear the advice of good friends on the matter. When all is said and done, 2000 livres is not so large a sum: it would certainly be, were it in German coin, but not here." The cost of living in Paris, however, did not form the sticking point; rather, the vision of a career at the organ keyboard wounded his pride: "But really! To be an organist! I should very much like a good post; but even so, nothing less than kapellmeister—and well paid."

That the appointment was not Rodolphe's to bestow; that at best he played the part of intermediary, at worst of well-meaning admirer expressing no more than "a pious wish"—all this seemed clear to Leopold. However, for his son's sake, he assumed the reality of the offer and rehearsed its advantages, astonished that Wolfgang showed no sign of doubting its substance and, at the same time, appeared disposed to throw it away.

"You should consider . . . that *you would have half the year for other profitable pursuits; that, whether you are ill or well, it is presumably a permanent appointment; that you can give it up when you like; that you would be at court,* therefore always under the eyes of the King and Queen and thereby so much nearer good fortune; that *when a vacancy occurs, you can obtain one of the two positions as kapellmeister; that, should there be royal offspring, you would in due course teach clavier to the young children, which would be very lucrative; that no one could prevent you from writing for the theater and the Concert spirituel, etc., etc. or from having music engraved with dedications to wealthy, prominent acquaintances, for, in particular during summer, many ministers frequent Versailles; that Versailles is a town in itself, or at all events, has many distinguished residents, among whom you would, in any case, find one or two men or women as pupils; and, to conclude, that* [the appointment]

---

18 Leopold Mozart, for example, struggled to persuade the Salzburg exchequer to settle a long overdue account with Mysliveček.

is the most certain way to assure yourself the protection of the Queen[19] and make yourself popular. Read this to Baron von Grimm and ask his opinion."

It must have jolted Leopold to learn that Grimm's opinion accorded with Wolfgang's, though the Baron saw the matter from a different point of view: the young man who could not maintain his footing in Legros's reception room would stumble badly at court. "To gain the day in Paris one must be cunning, enterprising, and bold," observed Grimm, who expressed the wish for a Wolfgang with "one half the talent and double the amount of address (*entregent*) in the salon." Mozart's reluctance in any way to turn the Parisian *matinée* and *soirée* to account—"you do not go about enough," Grimm remonstrated—foreclosed opportunities of making him a topic at the proper gatherings. He remained too private, reluctant either to develop social connections or to seek the company of fellow musicians, the last a disinclination encouraged by Leopold. His nature required enemies, and he persuaded his son to feel the same need: both unflaggingly scanned the horizon for them.

Leopold imagined Piccinni and Gluck "doing everything to prevent" Wolfgang's securing a commission from the Opéra; "and will not Grétry be jealous?" the father asked. In truth, these composers could not have been concerned about or even aware of Mozart and his ambitions. He remained aloof when encountering Piccinni, a stance hostile and foolish in view of Grimm's support of him: "He is most courteous to me, and I to him. . . . Be that as it may, I seek acquaintance neither with him nor with other composers. I understand my concerns, and they theirs; that suffices." But did Piccinni recall who Mozart was? Did Gluck remember the child-composer of *La finta semplice*? As for Grétry, he kept his eyes not upon an insignificant Salzburger but upon Gluck, the reef against which his hopes to prove himself as a composer of serious opera had run aground. Mozart's presence did not even ripple the tides of Paris's artistic life: he came and departed all but unnoticed. During the tempestuous season of 1778, Gluck's and Piccinni's musical hold on the city would have taxed the capacity of any newcomer, even one adroit in the ways of society, to arouse interest. Grimm admitted as much.[20]

By the end of July he had washed his hands of Wolfgang—"I hardly think you will make a success here [Paris]"—aware that the young man's

---

19 Breaking with de Guines, Mozart shattered his only link to Marie Antoinette. He carried no letter of recommendation to her. Heufeld, now von Heufeld, to whom Leopold had appealed for one on 16 January 1778, had artfully refused (doubtless he had learned of the Habsburgs' displeasure with the Mozarts); nor had the Mesmers been of aid in the matter.

20 François Joseph Gossec wrote: "I cannot even hope to produce a work on the stage so long as M. Gluck continues to hold it."

mind was fixed upon the Webers and Mannheim. He seemed disjointed from his surroundings, his apathy deepening: ". . . I often scarcely know or care about anything." He missed Aloisia and thought of little else. "Are you off to Mannheim?" Grimm asked, eager to see the last of him. With obsessive frequency Mozart had been writing to Fridolin Weber, who barely stirred to reply, no doubt less than impressed, and certainly not taken in, by the verbiage flowing from Paris.

In his letters Mozart postured as a matter of course: disguise became reflex as he presented that particular ideal of himself he wished his correspondent to entertain. To varying degrees, most indulge this technique. Mozart, however, developed an astonishing ability to create ever new paper Wolfgangs functioning in ever new psychic environments.

Poor at the outright lie, he always retained a talent for the half-truth. The costume he pulled on was frequently outré: indeed, his epistolary style could grow overdone, on occasion to a point disparaging credibility—Leopold had come to pay little attention to those simulations of heavy seriousness, still less to those flights of mawkish piety and moralizing—the case in his only letter to Weber that has come down to posterity. Here Mozart assumed the role of statesman, taking on Leopold's lecturing tone, including the expletory "*basta*," banalities accumulating as a pompous, long-winded Wolfgang proffered the fruits of his practical wisdom.

His single surviving letter (in Italian) to Aloisia, in contrast, overflowed with an apologetic meekness—even in the passages that gave the *carissima amica* a singing lesson through the post—a submissiveness, it would appear, mirroring his manner in her presence. Under her eyes he departed from the frivolous, lighthearted, rough-and-tumble sexuality with which he assailed the Bäsle: hungry for Aloisia, he nonetheless felt it wise to evince to her, not impetuousness, but tender, generous concern and the honorable intensity of his love. Never again did he repeat this exercise in self-effacement.[21]

Legros had, of course, been deaf to his naïve entreaties to hire the untried Aloisia for the Concert spirituel, and Mozart fell back upon cobbling up other impossible schemes for her, promising the Webers to "arrange something . . . with the Concert des amateurs" (see n. 7); to "search out an opera for her in Italy"; to receive father and daughter as his guests in Paris—"the journey, food, lodging, wood, and light would cost you nothing." (He did come to his senses about the invitation, and beat a quick retreat: "I hope you will not doubt my preferring to see you today rather

---

21 "I never have done talking about you," he confessed to Aloisia; nor did he take less pleasure in encouraging mutual friends to speak of her.

than tomorrow; yet, as a true friend, I must dissuade you from coming here this winter. . . .")

He continued to ring changes upon his persistent and irresistible dream of making common cause with the Webers, of living with them "in the same place, happy and satisfied." On no reasonable grounds, he hinted that, thanks to von Sickingen's family connections, both young people would soon have engagements in Mainz. In the meantime, so Mozart advised, Weber was to give symbolic warning that he would remove his daughter from Mannheim if its court (or what remained of it at the palace) continued to pay her only for individual appearances: when summoned to sing she was to plead illness; to inevitable questions about her health, Fridolin was to answer that she "suffered from melancholia, hardly to be cured here." According to this Mozartean libretto, Mannheim officialdom would thereupon recognize how indispensable she had become and grant her a regular and handsome salary: "Indeed, he [the Elector] must have her—he needs must have her. In truth, whom does he have in Mannheim? . . . in Munich?"

In Aloisia's situation Mozart perhaps recognized some ingredient of the crisis into which he himself had fallen the previous September; at that time, some compartment of his mind may have wished a firm hand to show itself, bring the Residenz around, halt his departure, and thus shield him from the unknown. In any case, events already in march would soon lead him back to Salzburg.

CHAPTER XXII

Paris II:
The Plan to Bring Mozart Home

WOLFGANG'S CAVALIER ATTITUDE toward the widespread advantages incidental to serving the French royal family had persuaded Leopold that, whatever the validity of Rodolphe's offer, his son's
Parisian adventure had run its course. As Mozart later admitted, not for a
moment did he consider service at Versailles: his disdain for the post of
organist apart, he could not imagine a life devoted to the French court, the
French language, and French musical taste. Seizing the moment, Leopold
designed a plan to bring him home without loss of honor: the Versailles
proposal, cleverly put to use at the Salzburg Residenz, would provide the
incitement, the decline of the Archbishop's musical establishment the
rationale.

Mozart's departure; Lolli's debility; Fischietti's mediocrity; Adlgasser's
death; Meissner's retirement; Michael Haydn's deepening alcoholism and
befogged laziness (his head and hands less and less capable of agreement);
his father-in-law Lipp's equal aptness for the bottle along with his incompetence as second organist;[1] his daughter Maria Magdalena's impending
withdrawal from service; and Brunetti's scandalous begetting of illegiti-

---

1 The drunken antics of Haydn and Franz Ignaz Lipp kept Salzburgers amused. Haydn drank
  even during services—a *Viertel* of wine after each litany, according to Leopold—and, when stu-
  pefied, called for Lipp, himself in a state little better, to take over.

mate children—all had taken their toll of whatever morale the Archbishop's musical household once possessed. In need, above all, of a sober
organist, a cembalist, and a kapellmeister, Colloredo had begun firing off
letters to Italy, Bohemia, and Austria—in particular, he sought as head either Ferdinando Gasparo Bertoni of Venice or Luigi Gatti of Mantua (see
XV, n. 19)—but could put nothing in place.

At this juncture Leopold received Wolfgang's account of his conversation with Rodolphe. When Countess Maria Franziska Wallis, the Archbishop's sister, as a matter of courtesy asked news of Wolfgang, Leopold
reported offhand that the route to the post of royal organist to Louis XVI
had opened before his son; he had but to choose to travel it. As Leopold
expected, within hours the Countess reported this development to her
brother. She had taken the bait, and he followed suit. Colloredo moved to
steal a march upon Versailles: a verbal protocol took form. Countess Wallis communicated it to an intermediary, Abbé Henri—for reasons of etiquette she spoke of it as her own—who passed it on to Bullinger, he, in
turn, advising Leopold. Thus did the high word from the Residenz make
its way to the Tanzmeisterhaus. The proposition proved simple and direct.

If Leopold desired to reunite his family, wish could become reality were
his son to agree to a proposal comprising two phases: a period of probation would precede his being named kapellmeister. (After Lolli's approaching death, by this time in plain sight, an agreement of long standing
would permit Fischietti to continue in service for an unspecified time.)
But, even for the interim, Salzburg had leaped to outdo what it believed to
be a genuine overture from Versailles; Mozart would at once assume two
posts: *Konzertmeister* with the sole obligation to perform at the clavier for
the Archbishop's pleasure (see pp. 253–55); and organist with duties limited
to playing the great instrument in the cathedral, a condition exempting
him from everyday services employing the auxiliary organs. The agreement's first stage, compensated at fifty gulden a month—a sum one-third
higher than his former salary—would provide opportunities to observe
the temper of the young musician who had so high-handedly quit the
court. Despite the shortcoming, from Mozart's point of view, of no stipulation as to just when he would become kapellmeister, the proposal took
cognizance of the Prince's dignity and the artist's pride.

Via Abbés Bullinger and Henri, Leopold, in turn, communicated to the
palace utter astonishment: why, he would never have mentioned the opportunity at Versailles had he imagined his words being interpreted as a
call for a counteroffer; he pretended bewilderment and withdrew from any
discussion of the affair. As he expected, the court followed him in full cry.
"I have been watching this fun for quite a while," he reported to Paris.

With the professed purpose of conferring about a Herr Mandl, an organist recommended to the Residenz, Count Franz Joseph Starhemberg, a canon of the cathedral, summoned Leopold. He at once realized that the court's interest in Mandl might well be a fiction: in no time the discussion turned to Wolfgang. Abandoning any pretense of the Archbishop's ignorance of the proposal, Starhemberg asked Leopold to communicate it to his son. The salary, Leopold in turn made clear, had to be commensurate to Wolfgang's abilities, otherwise, there would be no purpose in writing to Paris. Indeed, his response to those fifty gulden would be laughter, a sum all the more laughable, Leopold pointed out, because any maestro accepting a post in Salzburg would be at a loss to augment his salary in the traditional way of giving lessons: a musician of reputation already instructed most of the city's good pupils—one Leopold Mozart! How he relished his bizarre and protected position as counselor to his enemies.

From afar Wolfgang followed his father's wily campaign: "In truth, in this entire matter you have performed masterfully—like Ulysses." Leopold held back from insisting upon his deciding forthwith: "I am not writing all this, my dear Wolfgang, with the intention of inducing you to return to Salzburg, for I place not the slightest reliance upon the Archbishop's words." The court, he insisted, "shall have to propose very favorable and advantageous conditions if anything is to be done—which is hardly to be expected. We will wait and see."

On the surface granting Wolfgang a free hand, Leopold had, in fact, announced a *fait accompli*: there remained only the business of extracting the most from the bargain. Having squandered his opportunities, Wolfgang had no choice. But Leopold did not strip him of the dignity of pretending to one. The accomplished manipulation of the court and of his son showed Leopold calling forth a new subtlety born of desperation: Wolfgang had to begin to earn rather than consume. And how much Leopold missed his son and his wife, who, assailed by fear of the darkening political landscape, wondered when she would see Salzburg again. "Most of all, I would like to know how matters stand with the war," Anna Maria had inquired of Leopold on 14 May 1778, adding, as if to persuade herself: "Here people talk of peace between the Emperor and the Prussians."[2]

---

2 She took as much interest in politics as Leopold and Wolfgang. If the military stratagems occasioned by the Bavarian succession posed personal problems and even dangers for her, even so, she showed no less curiosity about the Americans' war for independence, so avidly discussed in France, which, spurning England, had adopted their cause. On 18 December 1777, Anna Maria had informed her husband: ". . . the English have suffered a terrible defeat at the hands of the Americans [General Burgoyne's catastrophe at Saratoga on 17 October]." Leopold noted its political consequences: "France recognizes the independence of the thirteen American colonies

2

FIVE DAYS LATER, Goethe wrote from the court of Frederick the Great, whither he and his master, the Duke of Weimar, had journeyed to confer on means to contain the ramifications of the Bavarian succession: "I can say this much—the greater the world, the more detestable the farce; I swear that no obscenity or asininity in a Hanswurst show is as disgusting as the behavior, one with another, of the great, the lesser, and the small." Experiencing a nonetheless "agreeable feeling to sit by the springs of war at the moment they threaten to overflow," he paid particular attention to "the great music box turning and ringing before us. From the movement of the puppets one can infer the hidden wheels, especially the old master-cylinder which emits these consecutive melodies: [it is] inscribed Fr[idericus] R[ex] and has a thousand pegs and pins." The Mozarts found this Frederician music no less fascinating.

With animation Leopold had written to Paris of the dangerous propinquity of King Frederick and Emperor Joseph, their forces drawn up either side of the border separating Silesia and Bohemia: "The main Prussian army and the King himself lie close to Silberberg and Glatz; the Emperor is with his main army, which stretches from Gitschin to Königgrätz. Thus their advanced posts are very close."

The cleverness with which Frederick "had spun dissension" between the Emperor and Elector Karl Theodore did not escape Leopold: regretting the surrender of Mindelheim and Burghausen to Austria, the Elector, thanks to Frederick's incitement, moved to take the matter to the Reichstag. Tension grew. "In Prussia and Austria," Leopold learned, "people are being hauled off the streets and out of their beds and made into soldiers," as, all the while, the great music box continued to turn and ring, setting into motion whatever figures its axis could regulate. While Frederick, with satirical sparring and unctuous assurances, indulged in cabal, a perplexed Frau Mozart speculated in Paris upon his unclear intentions and uncharacteristic hesitation: "He has always been the one to strike straightway," she observed. "One awaits a Prussian attack any day," Leopold assured her on 29 June 1778, four days before Frederick began to cross the Adlergebirge.

Vienna had wrongly guessed his military days to be over. ("The Emperor makes a tremendous mistake,"the poet Klopstock wrote Gluck, "if he thinks that the old man in Potsdam has grown too old.") When all

---

and has concluded treaties with them." He became excited by the possibility of his wife and son seeing Benjamin Franklin in Paris and asked them to confirm whether France "has really declared war against England."

signs confirmed that diplomatic juggling could not reverse the Hofburg's annexation of Lower Bavaria and Frederick descended into Bohemia, he discovered an Imperial army of two hundred fifty thousand extending some fifty miles along the Elbe. Far from burned out but ever the realist, he husbanded the flame of his aggressive spirit and, imitating the Austrians, chose to intimidate and bluff. His massive force, like Joseph's, roosted week after week, neither commander daring combat, both content to beat the tattoo, to skirmish, to maneuver. ("Marches and countermarches," Leopold reported.) Both feared that some casual movement might take charge and blunder lead to battle. Just in time, weakening supply lines provided the rescue.

Frederick's military operations became little more than forays ravaging the countryside either to find food (by digging potatoes) or to deny it the other side by destroying the fields. The country folk repaid the invader in kind: "The Bohemian peasants," Mozart announced from Paris, "are . . . inflicting prodigious damage upon the Prussians." (Even "being in Salzburg," he bantered, must be "better than being in Bohemia.") The so-called Potato War dragged on until downpours gave Frederick the excuse to withdraw by easy stages. At any rate, he had appeared, grim visaged, and made a show. At cross-purposes with his brother, Prince Henry,[3] and not of a mind to press further, he began to ponder less costly means of imposing his will.

From Paris, Mozart could view Frederick in lengthened perspective and found the sight unengaging: the King's personality, ever more sour, no longer lent romance to his brigandage. By the end of July an incredulous Wolfgang wrote Leopold: "Now something about the war! . . . All I have heard is that the King of Prussia has had to retire some twenty miles. . . . [Paris, wide of the mark, thought his choreographic disengagement the consequence of Austrian action.] However, I don't believe it, although with all my heart I wish the Prussian to be beaten over head and ears."

If this Mozartean desire remained unrealized, with Frederick's orderly departure those loyal to Vienna toasted outright victory: "There is not a single Prussian left in Bohemia," Gluck exulted at the end of September. "We have completed, thank God, one of the most glorious defensive campaigns without giving battle." He drew a parallel between his operas and

---

3 Prince Henry commanded a second corps, a unit of combined Prussian and Saxon troops that issued from Dresden and forced its way over the mountains into Bohemia with the object—unrealized—of marching on Prague, effecting a junction with Frederick, and moving toward the Danube. Leopold breathed admiration for the skill with which Henry pushed through terrain considered impassable.

Emperor Joseph's campaigners: "First they are abused; then people find them not so bad after all."

Though early in the conflict the Emperor, in one of his more preposterous moments, had contemplated summoning the King of Prussia to combat in the chivalric manner, he soon put wild whims aside and by degrees lost all spirit for the Bohemian enterprise. Perhaps he glimpsed the depths of his military incapacity; perhaps news of Russian troops on his Gallician border unnerved him. But without question an initiative on the part of his mother sent him into a near apoplectic rage: taking it upon herself to separate the bullies, the Empress in secret had proposed peace to Berlin in the name of common sense. ("What a war this is!" she lamented; "here nothing can be won and everything lost.") What with Mama's prodding, the royal generals' reluctance to join battle, the drenching rain, and the men and equipment mired in bog, the perilous situation resolved itself into farce as Frederick's soldiers in slow time retraced their steps. Lower Bavaria remained in Habsburg hands.[4]

On the very day Frederick moved to invade Bohemia, Wolfgang had hastened to give his father "news that, perhaps, you have heard by this time: to wit, that the godless arch rascal, Voltaire,[5] has—how shall I put it?—died [*crepirt (sic)*[6]] like a dog, like a beast. That is his reward!" Leopold opined that though Voltaire had "died [*gestorben*] in character [*wie er war*], he ought to have managed things somewhat better [if only] for the sake of his posthumous fame," an assertion breathing a measure of admiration for the sage who had given Europe a supreme gift—a vision of individual freedom governed by social morality. Leopold had learned of the philosophe's death without recantation and of the smuggling away of his corpse (see XXI, n. 1). Wolfgang, on the other hand, alluded to the account of Voltaire's final fate as broadcast by Parisian priests, in its classic version an operatic, indeed, Don Giovanni-like finale: tricked of the opportunity to affront his remains, they fell back upon the tale of a lost sinner in his final moments cringing and crying out in horror as he glimpsed

---

4 But not for long: what Frederick failed to win in the Bohemian mud he would achieve at the conference table; mediated by the French and the Russians, the Peace of Teschen (May 1779; see pp. 567 and 618) reduced Habsburg territorial gains in Bavaria to the modest area of the Innviertel. At Teschen the King of Prussia emerged the hero, the German Emperor the villain, his attempts to aggrandize his power held repugnant to the Treaty of Westphalia, which, functioning as a charter of German constitutionalism, both affirmed its purposes and served as a mechanism for their defense.

5 "*Erz-spizbub* voltaire" (*sic*); a slap at Archbishop Colloredo, who admired Voltaire.

6 *Krepieren* does service for animals; although the simile might justify the verb, the sentence adds up to a vulgarity Mozart thought might please his father.

the depths of hell.⁷ If Voltaire's death had been long expected, another caught father and son unawares.

3

TOOTHACHE, EARACHE, AND sore throat had plagued Anna Maria Mozart throughout April. To her alarm, her supply of black powder, the nostrum with which Leopold ministered to most maladies, ran out. Since he also recommended bloodletting as a universal preventive and cure, she decided to undergo the procedure. However, it had become unfashionable among Parisians, and for some time she could not locate a barber-surgeon. At last, on 11 June she submitted to bleeding and responded well for several days. Nevertheless, headaches soon engulfed her. She took to bed on 19 June, by which time chills, fever, and diarrhea had set in and with them extreme enfeeblement. She deteriorated rapidly but refused to admit a French doctor. Wolfgang lost time looking for a suitable German. He dosed her with "rhubarb powder mixed with wine," at first held out hope, but then bluntly warned that she might expire at any moment.

Through an old friend, the Bohemian musician Franz Joseph Haina,⁸ Mozart summoned a German priest, and on 1 July she made her confession, received extreme unction, and partook of the viaticum. Before long she could at most mutter and lost her hearing. By the time Wolfgang resolved to go against her wishes and opened the door to Grimm's French doctor, nothing could be done. She fell into delirium and then into unconsciousness. Wolfgang remained at her side: "I pressed her hand, spoke to her—but she did not see me, did not hear me, and was without faculties. Thus she lay until she expired. . . ." "She . . . burned out like a candle." On the evening of 3 July 1778, he for the first time witnessed the death of a loved one.⁹ Anna Maria's final agony had begun at 5:21 P.M. on 3 July and ended exactly five hours later.

---

7 Perhaps Mozart only made a show of believing this clerical version, a posture permitting him to humor, so he thought, his father and to outrage Grimm, one of Voltaire's lieutenants.

8 Also known as François-Joseph Heina, he had first met the Mozarts in Paris in 1763, at which time he played horn for the Prince de Conti and Baron Bagge and served as a trumpeter in the light cavalry of the royal guard. In 1775 he began a career as a music publisher specializing in Mannheim chamber works. He and his wife showed many courtesies to Anna Maria, inviting her to dine and keeping her company during Wolfgang's absences. Anna Maria left an account of promenading with Haina in the Luxembourg gardens and of their visiting the palace's "beautiful picture gallery."

9 Haina and a nurse also stood by; her remuneration took the form of a ring Madame d'Épinay had given Anna Maria during the Grand Tour. She was buried in one of the three cemeteries belonging to the church of St. Eustache, Haina handling the details.

He found himself altogether collected and turned to ponder how best to prepare Salzburg for the news; how to cushion a shock that might otherwise kill his father forthwith. Anna Maria's body lay nearby as, in the first hours of 4 July, he wrote Leopold:[10] "I have very unpleasant and tragic information to communicate. . . . My dear mother is very ill." He described her symptoms and her decline, letting fall that Grimm's doctor still harbored some optimism. "But I haven't much . . . and have resigned myself without reservation to God's will and hope that you and my dear sister will do the same. . . . I do not say that my mother will die or must die or that all hope is lost: she can yet regain vigor and health, but only if God wills it." With subtlety he identified his observations as facile consolations and then, at a stroke, closed this chapter to turn "to something else" in a different tempo and mood: "Let us abandon these mournful thoughts; let us hope, but not too much." He then hurled himself into a discussion of the single success of his months in Paris. This book follows Mozart's dramatic literary leap that no doubt astounded a prostrate Leopold, wrenching him from his wife's deathbed on the Rue du Gros Chênet to the Salle des Suisses in the Tuileries and a performance of his son's Paris Symphony. It had been the product of his renewed ties with Legros.[11]

4

AFTER THE ESTRANGEMENT over Cambini, Mozart had continued to visit Raaff and thus to cross the threshold of Legros's residence. The spectacle of the proud young man marching past his quarters had come to an end only when Legros followed to Raaff's, made peace, and on the spot ordered from Mozart a "grand symphony" to open the Concert spirituel on Corpus Christi. Though the score of his sinfonia concertante had made a strong impression, Legros, despite the reconciliation, found it impossible to present a work tailored to the talents of the four prodigious Mannheimers, by this time no longer together in Paris. "It is, indeed, a pity,"

---

10 Mozart headed his letter 3 July. While it traveled to Salzburg, Leopold had begun to compose (12 July) his congratulations to his wife on her living "to see her name day [26 July; St. Anne's Day] once again." Voicing hope that their separation, "which troubles my heart," would soon end, he had just begun to rehearse the latest news from the Bohemian front when Wolfgang's communication announcing her "illness" arrived (13 July).

11 Concerning Mozart and Legros, this and the preceding chapter represent a sorting, reconstruction, and reordering of events Mozart recorded but dislocated with much cunning. The wholesale confusion Mozart sowed in his letters right after Anna Maria's death appears the product less of a mind discomposed by shock than of a desire to cover his traces, in particular regarding his sinfonia concertante's running aground. Leopold became maddened as he attempted to cut his way through a trail his son's masterful pen had from first to last tangled.

Mozart observed on 9 July, "that he did not have it performed: it would have been well received. But now he no longer has the opportunity to do so; where are four such people available at the same time?" (In the light of the exodus of musicians from Mannheim, the answer might well have been: Munich.) Mozart recognized the commission for the symphony as his final opportunity to awaken the notice of Parisians. He set himself the task of writing a work with the promise of winning the admiration of "the *few* intelligent French who might be there" and, in addition, of interesting the greater number—the "asses" who would perhaps "also find something in it to give them pleasure."

He had completed the symphony, K. 297/300a, by 12 June, when he ran through it on the clavier at von Sickingen's and won compliments. But the full rehearsal gave him "an anxious heart"; the orchestra "bungled and scratched its way through," and he conjured the fantasy of taking strong measures during the performance: advancing upon the conductor and first violin, Pierre La Houssaye, snatching instrument and bow from his hands, and leading the work himself. But things went well at the premiere (18 June), described with enthusiasm in the letter written but hours after Anna Maria's death.

"Right in the middle of the first Allegro came a section I felt certain had to please. It carried the entire audience away, and great applause followed. Because I knew, as I wrote the passage, what kind of an effect it would make, I introduced it once again at the end, and calls came for a da capo. [Identifying these measures remains conjectural.] The Andante also won favor, but in particular the last Allegro: aware that every concluding as well as opening Allegro here [Paris] begins with all the instruments playing together and generally *unisono*,[12] I began with two violins [the first and second sections] playing alone and *piano*—but only for eight bars—followed immediately by a *forte*. The audience, as I anticipated, murmured 'Shhh' during the *piano* and, directly the *forte* came and they heard it, all hands clapped." Sporting with his listeners, he won the game, his vivid prose turning an honorable success into a major triumph.[13]

---

12 Mozart ridiculed the ponderous pride the French took in what they supposed to be a particular skill in achieving utmost precision at "the first stroke": "How the oxen here carry on over it! The devil take me if I can see any difference; they all begin together just as in other places. It is laughable."

13 Only one critique appeared: the *Courrier de L'Europe* (26 June 1778) declared that Mozart, "who from the tenderest age made a reputation for himself among performers on the harpsichord, may be placed among today's most skillful composers."

5

EVEN THOUGH MIDNIGHT had passed, he must have broken off several times in the course of writing this singular letter in order to concern himself with visitors and funeral plans. Whatever the interruptions, it proceeded, the thread of continuity twisting with much art. Having sent a covert message about his mother's death and trumpeted the story of his symphony's reception, he turned to what he considered his most important communication: his intention to ask a paternal blessing upon his engagement to Aloisia. He proceeded by way of a mawkish paean to the virtues of German bourgeois life.

"Immediately after the concert, I went in high spirits to the Palais Royal, had a good ice cream, said the Rosary as I had promised, and went home. I do and will always prefer being home or in the company of a good, true, honest German who, if unmarried, lives alone with decorum and like a good Christian or, if married, loves his wife and raises his children properly." Mozart persisted in believing that such paper-flower platitudes took his father in; yet the image of Wolfgang saying the Rosary over the remains of his ice cream at the Palais Royal—of all places—could not have but struck Leopold as preposterous.[14]

The reference to the glories of German connubiality served not only to connote, for Leopold's benefit, the state Wolfgang wished to enter but also to impugn Baron Grimm and his relationship with Madame d'Épinay. In Mozart's book he had revealed himself as anything but a "good, true, honest German." After pausing to hurl brickbats at Grimm's late comrade-in-philosophic-arms, Voltaire, and at the congenitally uncomprehending citizens of Paris (and then vowing to do his "utmost" in spite of them), Mozart arrived at his goal: "I have something in mind for which I pray to God every day. If it is His divine purpose it will come to pass; if not, then I am no less content: at least I will have done my part. If all goes well and turns out as I wish, then [my plans] will have reached the point at which they will remain unrealized unless you [Leopold] do your part [give your blessing], which I trust to your kindness to do without fail. Only at this moment don't indulge in unprofitable speculation, for I want to beg an

---

14 He did fall into the trap of taking seriously his son's allusions to having composed a second Paris symphony. Wolfgang's imagination had hatched this work as a device to persuade Salzburg of his industry and improved fortunes. He must have inwardly blushed for having written so little since leaving home. On 8 September, the Concert spirituel did perform "a new symphony" by Mozart, a score no doubt pulled from his luggage and fobbed off on Legros as just created. It could have offered little to indulge Parisian taste.

immediate favor of you: that I [be permitted to] hold back from stating my thoughts explicitly until the right time."

Thus he paralleled mixed signals concerning his mother's death with wooly intimations of his desire to share his destiny with Aloisia. He harbored some dim, archaic, and intuitive identification between dead mother and prospective bride and, though a conscious motive could not have been involved, tendered to Leopold an instinctual synthesis that no doubt shocked him.

When, at 2:00 A.M. of 4 July 1778, Mozart completed his letter to Leopold, he did not put his pen down but pressed on to unfold the true story to Abbé Bullinger: "Mourn with me, my friend! . . . I have to tell you that my mother, my dear mother, has ceased to be! . . . I ask no more of you at the moment but . . . that you prepare my poor father most gently for this sad news. I have written him by this same post, but only to say that she is seriously ill. . . . Therefore, I beg you, best of friends: watch over my father for me; speak words of courage to him so that, when he hears the worst, he may not take it with excessive grief and pain. I also commend my sister to you with all my heart."

Five days later he wrote to his father and confessed "the small and very necessary deception." "Indeed, when I wrote to you, she was even then delighting in the joys of Heaven." He could not bring himself to discuss details of the loss; its full force had not reached him: "Therefore, let us say a devout Paternoster for her soul and move on to other matters; all things at the appropriate time."[15]

By 9 July, he had given up the apartment on the Rue du Gros Chênet to join the household of Baron Grimm and Madame d'Épinay, where he had a room and a place at table. (Grimm's generosity rested upon his taking for granted the unwelcome guest's speedy departure.) Mozart wrote Leopold: "I am as contented as my situation permits. It would be a great aid to my regaining peace of mind were I to hear that my dear father and sister are submitting with utter resignation and resoluteness to the will of God. . . ." But he could not forgo once again bringing up the subject of Aloisia: "Keep in view that you have a son and brother who employs all his strength to make you happy, well knowing that one day you will not deny

---

15 Perhaps to counterbalance his dispassionate mind and temper in the wake of Anna Maria's death, commentators concocted the tale of his channeling a sorrowing son's grief into the piano sonata in A minor. Yet he might well have composed this masterpiece, which can be dated no more precisely than between spring and midsummer of 1778, before she showed a sign of serious illness. Somehow the no less profound Palatine sonata in E minor of the same period escaped mythologizing.

him his desire and its fulfillment—which certainly do him honor – and will do everything to see him happy."

Even in the face of the applause for his Paris Symphony, he continued to rail at the public—"the French are and always will be asses"—and did not know how to turn success to advantage: he remained, in Grimm's words, "almost as little ahead [in Paris] as on the day of his arrival, having, moreover, consumed close to a thousand livres." His thoughts turned back to Salzburg. Its proximity to Munich, toward which the Webers, along with so many Mannheim musicians, would inevitably travel, for the moment made him think of home with unaccustomed tractability, even enthusiasm, especially in light of those negotiations in respect to his projected return. He began to indulge fantasies about how Archiepiscopal Kapellmeister Wolfgang Mozart might reorganize Salzburg's musical forces.

CHAPTER XXIII

Paris III:
Kapellmeister Presumptive

W ERE HE TO become kapellmeister, he would reshape the Archbishop's musical forces on the model of Elector Karl Theodore's.
Presiding with the authority of a Cannabich—"the best conductor I have
ever seen," a leader "loved and feared by his subordinates"—he would
bring discipline to Salzburg's drunken band. "Loathsome!" he remarked
when Leopold wrote of Michael Haydn's ever more frequent fits of ine-
briation. "This is one of the main reasons for my finding Salzburg odi-
ous—these uncouth, shabby, and dissolute court musicians. Indeed, an
honest, well-bred man cannot live with them; why, instead of wanting to
seek their association, he feels compelled to be ashamed of them!"
Salzburg's orchestral players, Mozart insisted, must, like Mannheim's,
"have good manners," be "well dressed," and "refrain from going to public houses to swill.[1] This can never be the case with them unless the Prince
trusts you [Leopold] and me and gives us full authority in all matters requisite to music; otherwise all would be without purpose, for in Salzburg
everyone—or, rather, no one—troubles about the music. Were I to take

---

[1] For all that, in Paris he had discovered two former Mannheim musicians to be less than
paragons. The brothers Carl and Anton Stamitz, who settled there early in the decade, had become, Mozart asserted, "a pair of wretched music scribblers, gamblers, carousers, and fornica-
tors." He avoided Anton's company; at the time Carl was on tour in England.

up the challenge, I should have to possess complete freedom of action. The Chief Steward must have nothing to say to me about musical matters or anything concerning music." His proposals, he acknowledged, envisioned "a great deal. But it is not impossible. Were everything arranged in good order, I would not hesitate. . . ."

God Himself appeared to favor Mozart's swift return to Salzburg: on 11 August 1778 Hofkapellmeister Lolli went to his grave. As a reminder of mutual understanding, Leopold recommended himself to the Archbishop in a memorandum suggesting a family claim to the vacant post, many of whose duties had, in fact, long been his and Fischietti's. His responsibilities diminishing year by year, Lolli had ended drawing a vice-kapellmeister's salary while Fischietti continued to carry the title *Titularkapellmeister*; and, worthy of notice, the court calendar named no new kapellmeister. Leopold picked up the few tasks that had been left the ailing Lolli, assumed supervision of the archiepiscopal music library and music school (the *Kapellhaus*), and, in return, received an increased stipend. The master plan had begun to unfold with remarkable neatness. There remained only the matter of arranging the arrival of the kapellmeister presumptive.

"Thanks to my courageous endurance . . . I have succeeded," Leopold announced to Wolfgang on 31 August. That morning, by word of mouth, the Archbishop had agreed to his recall and appointment as *Konzertmeister* and organist. "Now," Leopold continued, "all hinges upon whether you believe that I still have my head on my shoulders; whether you believe that I am pursuing your best interests; and whether you want to see me dead or alive. I have thought everything through. The Archbishop has declared that, in respect to operatic commissions, he will permit you to travel anywhere," though it was understood that should Leopold suffer fatigue or indisposition, his son would stand as his deputy. Having gained the day, Leopold dropped any pretense to Wolfgang's having a choice: "My next letter will inform you that you are to leave." Expecting to have the certificate of appointment in hand within days, Leopold declared the reign of Italian musicians in Salzburg at an end.

Colloredo had even nodded assent to that proviso of such moment to Wolfgang; Leopold sent assurances to Paris: "As your father and friend I swear to you that you will not have to play the violin at court. . . ."[2] But Leopold in no way embraced his son's "fine ideas [*Delicatessen*], which are

---

2 In his informal discussion with Countess Wallis concerning Wolfgang and Versailles, Leopold made it understood that this point had to be the basis of any rapprochement with the Archbishop. Since Leopold's duties for the most part had to do with teaching and preparation, Mozart ran little risk of having to stand in for his father as a performer.

extravagant in respect to our Salzburg orchestra." Wolfgang seemed unaffected when this castle tumbled down but remained uneasy that the Residenz offered no "written guarantee for the kapellmeister's position." Aware that such a commitment could hardly precede the period of probation, an obligation he did not wish to dwell upon, Leopold smoothed away this anxiety: stipulations on paper, he contended, might prove an impediment should some court more important than Salzburg beckon. Munich, he felt certain, would flash across Wolfgang's mind.

Munich became the bait with which Leopold lured him back. Elector Karl Theodore's *séjour* in Mannheim (he had returned there in July) was but strengthening his resolve to hold permanent state in his Bavarian capital: Mannheim's efforts to salvage its own wreck had failed. "Mannheim has been superseded," Leopold observed, sending Wolfgang the official list of Karl Theodore's musicians moving to Munich: it included Cannabich, Raaff, the Wendlings, Danner—and Fridolin Weber. Trotting out every ploy, Leopold argued the advantages of Salzburg "as a center between Munich, Vienna, and Italy," names calculated to set Wolfgang afire.

With skillful contrivance Leopold dwelled upon his readiness to scuttle the arrangement with Salzburg at any time a firm and better offer might materialize; he continued to excite particular hopes about Munich: that list of transplanted musicians, he pointed out, contained the names of "neither clavier player nor organist and also no kapellmeister." In safe harbor, he fell back into his deceptive ways: from the beginning of his bargaining with Colloredo, he (and, later, Wolfgang) determined to sail without compunction to a deeper port should the winds prove favorable; and somehow Leopold made himself believe that they might pull anchor under such conditions "without prejudice" to the name of Mozart.[3]

At the same time Leopold enjoyed new latitude in Salzburg; Anna Maria's death had freed him from having to submit evermore to the whims of the court; he no longer had to preserve her widow's pension: "That is now over; I no longer need it; therefore, rather than suffer vexation, we will depart [Salzburg],"the pronoun enunciating a continuing partnership with

3 At the height of his negotiations with Colloredo, Leopold requested (21 August) Padre Martini in Bologna to write a second letter recommending Wolfgang to Karl Theodore, Martini's first on the subject (to Raaff) having gone astray. With the accession of Karl Theodore, Munich, all at once commanding Mannheim's resources in addition to its own, gave promise of eclipsing Vienna as Germany's musical capital. Leopold clutched at every means to force a place for Wolfgang at the new court as an occasional composer of German opera, the hope being to maneuver him next into the position of *Hofcomponist* and, in the end, kapellmeister. By autumn, Leopold had to acknowledge that, for the time being, a position for Wolfgang in Munich remained out of the question.

his son, its extent indeterminate. But, whatever the future, the moment demanded Wolfgang's presence at home: Leopold demanded that he pay off the family's debt.

In Paris the time to pack approached, and Mozart took stock, facing the fact that he could live "in comfort" but not "content" in Salzburg, a provincial capital without its own dramatic or operatic troupe; indeed, without singers of consequence. And, after months of freedom, he could not have looked forward to returning to his room in the house of a father whose letters betrayed a goodwill far from consistent: once again hostility had begun to bend Leopold's words.

He held his son in substantial measure responsible for Anna Maria's death and could not stop himself from tracing this terrible accusation. By 3 August he had created his own version of events: "You had your affairs to attend to and were away from home all day; and, since she did not fuss, you took matters with light heart as, all the while, the deadly and clear peril advanced; only then did the doctor come—and it was far too late." Further, and clearly with malevolent intent, Leopold told Wolfgang about the secret postscript she had sent to Salzburg: "At a time when I hoped to see her already back from Mannheim and in Salzburg . . . a letter from you threw me into amazement, perplexity, and distress. In this very letter, and without your knowledge, she explained that with good reason and out of love for you she wished to accompany you to Paris." She had "sacrificed herself for her son."

Not content with this slash, Leopold then sent him (27 August) the actual wording of the postscript, save editorial changes and two omissions; the pretext: that the appended message demonstrated the depth of a mother's concern and love. Friendship with the Webers and the "calamitous" journey with them to Kirchheimbolanden had, Leopold insisted, set in motion the events dooming Anna Maria: "Had your mother returned from Mannheim to Salzburg, she would not have died."

How unjust, and all the more so in light of what Leopold censored in the postscript: absent was Anna Maria's appeal that he ponder and chart a course to lead Wolfgang out of entanglement with the Webers; absent, too, her caution concerning the secrecy of her communication and her expression of anxiety that Wolfgang might surprise her while she wrote. Leopold outright betrayed her: he had, of course, fallen in with her plan to continue on to Paris but now thought it wise to suppress anything that might call attention to his own part in the matter. He appears strangely moving, however, in the role of editor, straightening out his wife's punctuation, spelling, and grammar.

For a moment Leopold's kinder side did assert itself, and he sought to soften his recklessness by invoking "Divine Providence," which, whatever the concatenation of circumstances, had "appointed 3 July as the day of your mother's death."[4] But again he lost control and predicted a second sacrifice—his own life—on the altar of his son's folly should he fail straightway to appear in Salzburg; exploiting the young man's vacillation of mind, time and again he turned to devices meant to sow guilt and excite pity: "You will have difficulty recognizing your poor father. On two occasions when the Archbishop summoned me, my appearance so shocked him that he told everyone about it. . . . My constitution is made of iron, otherwise I would already be dead. . . . No one but you can save me from death." With Wolfgang at his side, he "would live many years longer."

He soon realized that emotional outbursts and harsh attacks left but surface wounds: that Wolfgang's thoughts turned not upon his dead mother; not upon his father's state of mind or health; not upon either virulent imputations or insults pouring from Salzburg; but upon Aloisia. From the beginning Leopold had identified her as the subject about which he was not to "speculate . . . until the right time." This absurd caveat had placed him at a disadvantage: his artillery could not sight a target as yet undefined.

He tried cajolery and urged openness: "You should look upon me more as best friend than father." The father/friend wished only to "reflect upon the matter and devise the means." But all at once the tone darkened with his invitation that Wolfgang choose between two courses: "to consult with me, your father and friend," or, in the pursuit of "whimsical impossibilities . . . to kill the father." He reminded his son "how often the hastily formed notions you get into your head have misled you." But Wolfgang would not be taken in: to disclose his ideas before their time had come, he assured Leopold, would "do more harm than good to your peace of mind; the matter concerns me alone and will affect your situation neither for the better nor the worse. . . . Be certain that in all matters I know to be linked to your happiness and contentment I will always put my complete confidence in you, my best of fathers and truest friend, and will inform you in detail." Leopold had met his equal in elegant sarcasm.

---

4 In an astounding letter (31 July 1778) to Count Ignaz Joseph Spaur—a canon of Salzburg cathedral, he had succeeded his uncle as bishop of Brixen that very year—Leopold traced Anna Maria's death to Archbishop Colloredo, "the fatal instrument" that caused "the most honorable of wives and finest mother . . . to find her grave in Paris." Leopold must have deeply trusted the new Bishop to dare write this preposterous indictment (even if hedged with talk, like the sop thrown Wolfgang, of "the unbreakable chain of Divine Providence") and to speak of "the loathsome, tyrannical circumstances that finally drove my son to leave his fatherland." Concerning other members of the Spaur family, see XVI, n. 19 and XVIII, n. 28.

He would not be deterred. Pounding at his theme, he summoned theology to his aid: "Experience . . . has sufficiently convinced me that there is no true friend—*construed in its widest sense*—but a father. Even children are not in the *same degree* friends of their parents. Reflect; ponder the facts: you will find examples enough in the world to convince you of my proposition's truth. For this reason, too, God found it necessary to impose upon children the commandment that they honor their parents (and even added a punishment) but did not think it necessary to impose a commandment upon parents." Leopold's voice reassumed its distinctive quality as he redefined the struggle in terms of a traditional, threatening paterfamilias, father/friend and son no longer suggesting an equation but, rather, a scale in uneven balance: on the father's side stood the angels, tipping the pan precipitately. But Leopold soon put homilies aside to follow a no less Jesuitical path of enticement.

Without allusion to that plan of Wolfgang's upon which speculation had been enjoined, Leopold, with studied innocence, began to draw Aloisia's name into his stratagems. Aware of his son's hope, should he return to Salzburg, of making a place for her there—"if the Archbishop wants a new female singer, by God, I could not direct him to a better one"—Leopold assured him that the court had become "absolutely determined to hear her": why, when she comes for an audition, Leopold bubbled, "she must stay with us."

Determined to appear reasonable, he succeeded only in making a botch of his new impersonation: "Concerning Mlle. Weber, you must in no way imagine that I have anything against this friendship. All young people must go through this kind of foolishness." He urged Wolfgang to continue to exchange letters with her even after he came home(!): "I will certainly not ask you about it." Moreover, as proof against his curiosity, Leopold suggested that Aloisia write not to the Hannibalplatz but to one of Wolfgang's local friends. Endeavoring to appear co-operative and cordial, the father, instead, revealed himself condescending and worse: his overtures breathed contempt. He awaited the return of a child to whom to give the law: in Salzburg the past stood poised to seize Wolfgang.

Suddenly, his relationship with Aloisia wheeled about: the pupil outsped the teacher, and by mid-September she needed neither Salzburg nor Mozart. Ironically, she had arrived at the goal long his own: an auspicious engagement at the court of Munich. Count Seeau wanted her to devote her voice, honed by Mozart with so much love, to the new German repertory. Raaff had played a part in Aloisia's good fortune, Mozart having secured his promise in Paris "to give her lessons as soon as he arrived back in

Mannheim" and "to take up her cause." But he could do nothing for
Mozart, whose interests he had also undertaken to further: at the court of
Karl Theodore the current continued to flow counter to the Salzburger,
and not even the respected tenor could make head against it.

2

MOZART'S LETTERS HOME let pass few opportunities either to hint at
the strength of his desire to wed Aloisia[5] or to indicate the extent to which
marriage had become a physiological necessity for him. He could find no
"solace" (*soulagement*) with Parisian women: "Most of them are whores,
and the few who are not have no breeding." It therefore followed, he
sweepingly insisted, that "most young men" in Paris suffer "a shameful
death in bed. One speaks to no one here who has not already had one of
these lovely diseases bestowed upon him three or four times or who at the
moment is not endowed with one of them. Here they accompany children
into the world. But I am not writing you [Leopold] anything new; you have
long known this; but you may for certain believe me: things have grown
worse."

What was the "clean-minded" Wolfgang Mozart to do? Limits to even
this splendid young German's control were in sight. Why, when it gave
way, he might be forced to protect himself against infection by seducing
innocents, an idea he ominously put forward by the simple device of declaring it far from his mind: "In my view, nothing is more shameful than
to lead an honest girl astray and copulate with her." He had begun to define the case his letters had over the months offered piecemeal, symbolically, and not without sanctimoniousness: if he did not marry soon, he
might have to abandon principles and lay himself open to disease. Ignoring the adolescent threat of self-immolation through lust, Leopold answered forcefully: that matter upon which he was not to speculate required
"a position with a good salary"; "building castles in the air" had rendered
Wolfgang's mind "unfit to cope with all the realities at hand."

In any case, his days in France were running out, and he would not long
remain imperiled by either enchanting *demoiselles* or those "unnaturally
painted" women of Paris once not unnoticed by his father. With enthusiasm
Grimm reinforced the summons to Salzburg. Weary of Mozart—whose
borrowing from him kept mounting—he did not disguise an eagerness to

5 A commonplace observation on Leopold's part may have led Wolfgang at first to mistake the
 mood in Salzburg as sympathetic to his resolve: "It is inexplicably grievous," Leopold had written, "when death severs a solid, blissful marriage; to understand this, one must experience it."

shut the door behind a guest who, on his side, did not spare his host sting-ing sarcasm; here he seems to have hacked when a thrust would have sufficed: Grimm became a very angry man. (Wolfgang, however, remained on friendly terms with Madame d'Épinay and lunched with her: "Were it not for Madame d'Épinay, I would not be in this house.") Informed of the changed atmosphere on the Rue Chaussée d'Antin—"M. Grimm has the capacity to help *children*, but not adults . . . do not imagine that this man is as he was"— Leopold warned his son against rudeness: a belated precaution.

Thrown off balance and unsure whether to struggle on free, if debt-encumbered, in hated Paris or to return to the security of a child in no less hated Salzburg, he continued perplexed. But his attempt to exploit an un-expected opportunity revealed his predisposition: he looked upon Salzburg as the more bitter cup. Despite his denunciations of the French, whose pride insulted his own sense of superiority, part of him longed to find firm ground and strike root in their soil.

3

WITH HELP THAT seemed to have dropped from the clouds, he threw off his lethargy in an attempt to reawaken the patronage of Louis de Noailles, Duke d'Ayen, who, some fifteen years earlier, had opened the doors of Ver-sailles to him. An old acquaintance from London days reforged the link: the castrato Giusto Ferdinando Tenducci. A notorious spendthrift, early in his career he had been detained eight months in debtors' prison and more recently (1776) had evaded his creditors by fleeing England for the Conti-nent. By the middle of August 1778 he had made his way to Paris to enjoy the favor of the same Louis de Noailles and the company of Christian Bach, lately arrived from London to settle preliminaries to a production of his opera *Amadis de Gaule*. Bach and Tenducci showed themselves delighted to find Wolfgang in Paris, and Tenducci took him along on a visit to Noailles's palace at St Germain-en-Laye.[6]

A desire to be away from Grimm no doubt influenced Mozart's pro-longing to ten days (19–28 August) a stay during which, in all likelihood at his host's behest, he turned out a scena, K. Anh. 3/315b, for Tenducci. The flavor of this St Germain "commission"—it has not survived—may be apprehended in Charles Burney's description of it as a "very elaborate and masterly composition, discovering a great practice and facility of writ-ing in many Parts." Though admiring the "learned and recherchée [*sic*]" modulations, he nonetheless found the work deficient in melody (see p. 293).

---

6 Wolfgang could not recall having performed there as a child.

Christian Bach had already composed a scena for Tenducci, and Mozart's harmonically strong and richly orchestrated effort may well have been a homage to both.

Alarm gripped Leopold when he learned that Bach had offered to help Wolfgang make his way to England. London, Leopold warned, must "absolutely not be considered"; its authorities "arrest people for debts of three or four guineas," a situation perilous to anyone with a cavalier attitude toward borrowing. And, no less frightening, the idea of Wolfgang's passing hours with the prodigal Tenducci must have shaken the father.[7] In his eyes, still keen for men and situations, the arrival on the scene of this ungovernable coxcomb provided the climactic point of the Parisian drama; Leopold determined to propel it to its finale before what he feared to be a tide of indolence became a flood.

Early in September he began to marshal arguments—a veritable catalogue raisonné—for Wolfgang's return to Salzburg. He hated Paris; why, then, did he stay, especially in the light of a propitious alternative? Had he none, he would, indeed, *have* to stay, endangering his health, draining himself by giving lessons, and, overtired, composing in the little time left over—"a dangerous business and against your spirit."[8] His life would become a burdensome day-to-day affair that would not exclude the business of dirty laundry and missing buttons. And who would make good his inevitably growing debts? Was there any sense in his hesitating to seize the security and opportunities of Salzburg, where he could live and work in comfort and, at the same time and at first hand, pursue his interests in other German cities? Were he to fail to return and, instead, continue to borrow in pursuit of "empty hopes," he would ruin his father and sister as he, himself, went down in indigence or worse.

Only the absence of the wherewithal to leave Paris could justify his remaining. Since Leopold undertook to provide such resources, he declared the matter settled. Indeed, to preserve "credit and honor" he had somehow begun to repay his loans.[9] On 17 September he gave final warning: if

---

7 Mozart's letters did not touch upon the possibility of his going to London; nor, at the time Leopold wrote the above warning (3 September), had he received Wolfgang's account (27 August) of his meeting Bach and consorting with Tenducci. Leopold had heard of these developments earlier, in all likelihood from Grimm.

8 Here Leopold shot Wolfgang's ammunition back at him.

9 Questions already raised (see XX, n. 37) point to the family's finances as a tangled skein. Despite inklings of deception on Leopold's part, this book follows Mozart's example up to and including this stage of his life and, if only for the moment, holds back from any direct attack upon the credibility of Leopold's protestations concerning his indebtedness. Not until later would Mozart permit himself the open suspicions and then deductions to be explored in later chapters (see pp. 503 and 545).

Wolfgang, ignoring arguments to return and help in this responsibility, decided "to remain and live a fortuitous life in Paris," then he had to meet a difficult truth head on: he would no longer have a lifeline to Salzburg. Deliverance for Wolfgang lay not in closing his eyes, but, rather, in opening them wide to see that little, confining Salzburg alone could rescue him and, at the same time, set him free to sound broader opportunities. Here Leopold performed at his Jesuitical best, threatening the lake of fire as he held forth hope of salvation. He issued his command: Return at once or "I might have to abandon you completely," a phrase that must have cost him much.

He ordered Wolfgang to prepare to travel home by way of Munich, where Elector Karl Theodore and his newly reorganized and aggrandized court expected to take up permanent residence by the end of September.[10] There Mozart was to seek audience and explain his return to Salzburg as an act of affection: his answer to the pleas of a recently widowed father longing to embrace his son, whom, moreover, the Archbishop had invited back into his musical household at a handsome salary. At first Leopold wanted Wolfgang to let drop an inflated figure and then to suggest that, even so, his father would prefer to see him in Karl Theodore's service. But almost in the same breath Leopold changed strategy, recommending that Wolfgang remain silent in Munich about his reinstatement, thus preserving the illusion of success in Paris: he was to account for his journey in terms of filial duty alone. Yet, no matter how inventively the Mozarts danced around the facts or hyperbolized, associations of failure hung about Wolfgang. For all that, Leopold continued to predict his son's good fortune in Munich: in time Count Seeau would have to commission a German opera from him, for Schweitzer and Holzbauer could not fill every need in this area and *Hofcomponist* Joseph Christian Michl, just dismissed, did not, whatever his status, merit discussion.[11]

Again Leopold underlined that his son need have no qualms about the nature of his new career in Salzburg: its center would be the keyboard; he need never touch bow to string. Yet, Leopold hoped Wolfgang might deign to do so on occasion, if only as an act of diplomacy: "Like the Archbishop himself and all the courtiers who join in, you, too, will not account it degrading to play the violin [in the orchestra], for example, in the first symphony [of the evening], your role being that of a connoisseur (*wohl*

---

10 They did not arrive until 9 October.

11 Munich had heard Michl's *Il trionfo di Clelia* in 1776. A figure in the capital's musical life since the sixties, Michl found himself among the many driven from their court positions upon the advent of Karl Theodore (see pp. 467–68).

auch als Liebhaber)." The encoded phrase indicated that such occasions would not require Wolfgang to wear livery: he must have found dressing in uniform, even if only now and then, a trial.

Leopold saw the family's financial future as promising: debts were heavy, he maintained, but the creditors, sympathetic locals, had no heart to press their claims. The incomes of father and son would provide a yearly sum toward repayment and yet leave enough for an easy life: even at the outset, the Mozarts would be drawing the equivalent of Adlgasser's and Lolli's salaries combined, and this apart from fees for lessons and commissions. Only one of Leopold's points could be countered—his attempt to paint Salzburg's social life in bright colors: accounts of traveling companies giving comedies and operettas, dances at the city hall, and evenings with the air-gun company hardly read well in Paris.

4

MOZART'S RECENT ENCOUNTER with Christian Bach helped him face his insignificance in Parisian life and throw aside his illusions concerning the Opéra: here Noverre had gone back on his promises and now made clear a reluctance to smooth the path; Grimm, to Mozart's wrath, had expressed doubts that he "possessed the qualities to write a French opera" and must have discussed the question with Noverre. Mozart watched Bach enter the great portal closed to him. "Bach," he reported home, "is going to write a French opera; he is here only to hear the singers; then he will go back to London, write the opera, and return to put it on the stage." Paris had invited him to play the role in which Leopold—all at once making a desperate final effort to bestow upon the faltering Parisian campaign the dignity of direction, indeed, some raison d'être—encouraged Wolfgang to envision himself: that of creating the work, in Grimm's words, "so long looked for to reopen or end the war between the Piccinnists and the Gluckists." (Leopold, of course, saw his son as setting about this enterprise after his tour of duty at home.) The very day of Bach's arrival in Paris, Leopold wrote Wolfgang to suggest that he might be the champion to end the struggle: "Just because there are two parties, a third may hope for more approbation. . . ."

First given in the presence of Marie Antoinette on 14 December 1779, Bach's *Amadis de Gaule,* a hapless mixture of French and Italian elements, would barely achieve a *succès d'estime,* punning wags declaring that the aesthetic schism at the Opéra "required a bridge, not a ferry [*bac*]." Grimm had been led astray by Mozart's difficult personality: he might well have begun to build this bridge and realize the reconciling work Grimm himself had postulated—an opera of "warmth and effectiveness" combining "Gluck's originality and sublime élan" with "the charm and variety of Piccinni." Mozart embodied the neutral force equipped to realize this design, not through polemics but by accommodation: in Mozart's near future lay *Idomeneo*, a masterpiece answering Grimm's desires. His *Correspondence* of 1 March 1764 had, in fact, recommended the subject of Idomeneo as particularly "suited to musical setting," and, during friendly days, he and Mozart perhaps exchanged ideas on the matter.

The Opéra did offer music by Mozart during the 1778 season: in May and June he composed, so he stated, twelve sections, including an overture, of *Les petits riens* (K. Anh. 10/299b), a ballet-pantomime choreographed by Noverre. A decade earlier he had created it for Vienna's Burgtheater, the score probably by Franz Aspelmayr. For Paris, Noverre decided to adapt this entertainment to music by Mozart and other composers (Gossec doubtless among them), the mimed and danced doings of Cupid and various shepherdesses now to serve as an entr'acte during performances of comic operas by Piccinni and Anfossi. As "a labor of friendship for Noverre," Mozart found himself writing "half a ballet." For it he received no fee; no critic—Grimm skipped over the matter—made mention of his elegant dances; nor did his name appear in connection with the work.[12]

His contribution to *Les petits riens* breathes a sensitive appreciation of the French manner. In Paris, he had the opportunity to hear music by Gossec (it dominated the repertory of the Concert spirituel), Rameau, Grétry, Philidor, Nicolas Dezède, and even Rousseau, as well as Frenchified operas—or excerpts from them—by Gluck (*Armide, Orphée, Alceste,* and *Iphigénie en Aulide*) and Piccinni (*Roland*). But Mozart left no record of such experiences:[13] at the time, he resented the Gallic spirit too deeply to credit it with anything worth his attention. Yet, though it availed him nothing in respect to professional goals, his sojourn in Paris, like that in Mannheim, enriched him: while declaring (in September) that he played the clavier "as well as I ever shall," he admitted to Leopold that "this journey has not been unprofitable to me in respect to composition. . . ." Momentous consequences of his Parisian musical impressions would appear in *Idomeneo*, a work drenched in the aesthetic of the Opéra; immediate effects stood forth in the Paris Symphony: it flaunted the Mannheim school's tricks and traits as transformed by Parisian pomp and magnificence of scale.

---

12 K. 299c may be a draft of the ambitious "new ballet" Mozart had hoped to create with Noverre at the Opéra.

13 Even after Grimm discontinued his invitations, Mozart could attend performances: he had sufficient funds.

His months in the Palatinate capital had permitted a leisurely study of the resources and methods of Europe's finest orchestra. He had become aware of richer potentialities in respect to orchestral color: more varied instrumental hues (in particular touching the winds); more varied effects in the combination of light and shade through sharper contrasts and subtler dynamic gradations; and additional means to increase dramatic intensity. He paraded many of these devices, reinforced by infusions of elevated French baroque gesture, in the Paris Symphony, created for a public hospitable to Mannheim composers and for an orchestra at home with their ways. Mozart wrote the Mannheim school's finest work, not in Mannheim—Cannabich had not encouraged the attempt—but in Paris, where his ambition aspired less to display mastery of the Mannheim vocabulary than to satirize the stately French frame in which he placed it: to concoct a wicked travesty of French musical tradition along with a better intentioned parody of Mannheim mannerisms; to proffer them in terms of French proportion, breeding, and solemnity and, at the same time, to make a personal game of these very qualities. In consequence the Paris Symphony disquiets: it becomes uncomfortably unclear just where the mock-heroic and the mock-pathetic delimit themselves.

The symphony, moreover, lacks that different kind of Mozartean equivocality—the soulful ambiguity vibrating through so much of his music. His disguise as a Franco-Mannheimer fits so famously and he buttons his costume down so tightly that at first glance he is hardly to be recognized. His other Parisian commission, the concerto for harp and flute, shares the symphony's striving for weight and the grand manner and perplexes no less as to the true nature of this striving: although it rolls on convincingly in a broad, unified stream and offers enchantments in its gorgeousness of detail, the concerto, combining in style discreet baroque and inflated *galant* elements, proves just as insecure and variable in artistic direction. Further, both compositions communicate an uncharacteristic detachment on the part of a composer who favored neither with his usual verve, that marvelous Mozartean sense of spontaneous play.

The public's warm response to the symphony delighted Legros, though in his judgment the Andante suffered from excessive length and "too many modulations" (perhaps an allusion to the sheer wealth of the material). This opinion derived, Mozart insisted, "from the fact that those in attendance forgot[!] to make as long and sustained a din with their applause as for the first and last movements. The Andante, which has *my* highest approval as well as that of all arbiters, connoisseurs, and most of the audience, is just the contrary of what Legros says: it is thoroughly unaffected and short. But to satisfy him and, as he claims, others, I have composed another."

With the Paris Symphony, Mozart had for the first time sought the approval of the amorphous, unpredictable public at large, its taste an amalgam of contradictions foreign to both the aristocratic and high-bourgeois patronage he had hitherto alone known. Possessed of scant experience in coping with the temper of this heterogeneous spirit, a perplexed Mozart did little more than turn out a second Andante that appeared to be the first wearing different apparel.[14] However, he felt the need to declare them distinct. "Each is valid in its own way, for each has a different character. For my part, I prefer the second," he surprisingly proclaimed. It bewilders to attempt to connect the threads of his argument, to find the key to the psychological and artistic processes at work; but his disquiet betrays itself and with it a desire to please.

Perhaps a reaction to his labors to propitiate the French helped lead him back to the *Kurfürstin* violin/clavier sonatas. Nostalgia seems to dissipate itself into K. 304/300c in E minor, which resonates with Germanic introspection and, moreover, prefigures the following century in its bold and organic manipulation of themes so expansive and assured as to have provided materials for a grand concerto. In its gravity, K. 304 finds kinship with the piano sonata in A minor (see XXI, n. 15 and XXII, n. 15), these works of high seriousness forming the proudest monuments of the, for the most part, unproductive stay in Paris.

Both manifest a transformation of the dramatic and melancholy elements of Storm and Stress into a seamless musical expression embodying pain, strife, and even violence, while never being less than exquisitely consolatory. The third and final movement of the piano sonata pursues its mysterious course with overwrought persistence, a tone poem of lacerating cries heard midst a spectral chase of almost unabating intensity, yet a concentration of emotions not without touches of elegiac resignation and serenity. This brief Presto's breadth of structure and intensity of content bespeak a new Mozartean language of controlled passion, a disciplined dialectic of reason and glowing instinct—the imprint of his greatest works.

The pair of masterpieces in the minor completed, this cast of mind had, for the moment, exhausted itself. Turning to write the two final sonatas of the *Kurfürstin* cycle, he seemed suddenly to remember its original purpose of piquing Electress Maria Elizabeth's interest. The weathercock swerved:

---

14 Specialists remain at odds over which of the two versions was the earlier; Parisians heard the new Andante at the second performance of the symphony (15 August: Assumption Day).

the opening Allegro molto of K. 305/293d in A exploits the Mannheim crescendo, while 306/300l in D (in three movements; the other sonatas in the set have two) exhibits symphonic yearnings; assuming the amplitude of the violin concertos, including a cadenza in the final movement, it partakes in their emotional world of concertante animation. Yet too often the contrived and striking obtrude, thrusting forward with an eagerness to impress by brilliance and to be done with the job.

The two sets of clavier variations Mozart composed at this time courted applause in much the same spirit. Scholars have tended to look upon them as oblations to a Parisian taste for virtuosity. Yet, he had improvised and written such pieces before and would do so again in Vienna. They took the form of a simple tune (frequently folklike) subjected to a series of alterations and transformations, individual variations often presenting the challenge of specific technical difficulties such as arpeggios, hand-crossing, broken octaves, and ever-changing figurations. Though, as vehicles for the display of technique, such Mozartean variations come short of the organic unity of those he created as movements within an encompassing genre like the sonata, the Parisian examples compensate with their dazzling variety of texture and cumulative force. The powerful nine variations for clavier (K. 264/315d) on a well-known air by Nicolas Dezède (*"Lison dormait"* from his operetta *Julie*) are harmonically rich, heroic in scope, and finger-breaking in their rhythmic complexities and trills. More lyric and conventionally didactic, the twelve variations for clavier, K. 354/299a, built upon a setting of *"Je suis Lindor"* (probably composed by Antoine-Laurent Baudron) from Beaumarchais's already famous *Barber of Seville*, may have provided Mozart's first literary acquaintance with the playwright, at the time completing his *Marriage of Figaro*.

5

IF MOZART PLEASED himself with the Lindor variations—they joined his stable of battle horses—and Legros with the Paris symphony, his flirtation with Noailles at St Germain ended in smoke, the most recent example of how the doors to the kind of future he craved slammed closed one after the other, a state of affairs all the more frustrating because his ambitions did not reach beyond the reasonable. Packing his baggage, he must have wondered why things went well for him only to a certain point. Though he attempted to rein in any temptation to bring to the surface the full measure of the unhappiness a close reading of his letters betrays, his growing despair would approach an emotional breakdown once he started back to Salzburg: to return, he blurted out, was "truly to commit the greatest folly in the world."

It had been his hard-won habit to be at once patient and physician: not to discharge the anger appropriate to a crisis, but to subsume and thus transcend disappointment and bitterness under a grinning disposition in which frolicking and mockery alternated. But as his days in Paris shortened, he could not even call this counterbalancing mechanism to his aid: amid violent fluctuations of feeling, he became acrimonious; out of countenance with all but his ideal vision of Aloisia, he treated Grimm with the open, raw discourtesy he longed to—but dared not—visit upon his father.

He had forged the first link in the chain of current misery and in Wolfgang's mind had now merged with Grimm to form a single enemy bent upon robbing him of his conquest of Paris. Midst broken hopes and ambitions, this irrational, aggressive idea sprouted suddenly and grew luxuriantly: that he had to leave Paris just at the time when "honor, reputation, and money" neared his grasp—and with them the means to pay the family's debts—he charged to the account of this double-visaged villain.

"Of course," Wolfgang wrote Leopold, "when people learned of my resolve to depart, they countered it with facts I could dispute and overcome with but one weapon: my true and tender love for my best of fathers, for which, naturally, they felt obliged to praise me; they added, however, that if my father only knew of my present circumstances and good prospects— and had not received different and outright false information from a good friend—he would certainly not have written to me in such a vein that I find myself without any foothold from which to resist." He determined to pass to the offensive, for if he harbored guilt about his failure and anxiety about the future, he had no doubts as to his capacities, a conviction Leopold also held, but now as a sad burden.

It weighed upon the father to observe accumulating indignities and disappointments plague a son he knew to be singled out for greatness. Yet, though Leopold saw no alternative but to reassert authority, he need not have so baldly betrayed his lack of sympathy with Wolfgang's struggle to force a passage to adulthood. Aware that he must, in any case, one day relinquish something so precious, Leopold clutched it all the more passionately. His grip left bruises that never healed.

Nor did he himself escape disfiguring marks: the once beloved mentor had become an alien and even hated intruder as the ancient tragedy of ambivalence inherent in the father-son relationship played itself out, pulling both down into an abyss of conflict. But if Wolfgang pondered breaking loose for good and all, he did not yet have the strength.

6

WHEN, AT THE close of August, he put into Grimm's hands the arrangements for Wolfgang's departure, Leopold remained as yet unaware of how strong their mutual hostility had grown. He fixed the general route: by way of Strassburg. There Wolfgang had to collect letters of credit to enable him to continue on; and there he was to inquire about Prince Fürstenberg: were he in residence at Donaueschingen, a slight dip south to his castle could bring several days of well-paid music-making. This possible roundabout apart, Wolfgang's direction was to be eastward to Augsburg, where money from Uncle Alois would carry the journey forward to Munich and Salzburg. But Wolfgang had a different itinerary in mind: at Strassburg he planned to veer sharply north toward Mannheim. ("I might be going out of my way, but not much; at least it would not seem much to me.") He did not know when the Webers planned to leave Mannheim for Munich, and this detour guaranteed his seeing Aloisia.

Dashing to Mannheim had no purpose, Leopold, in turn, insisted, for the Munich opera expected Aloisia by the end of the month: "I would not at all like your misusing me by making a silly trip augmenting my debts; this would be the dumbest prank." Moreover, having just learned of the House of Fürstenberg's recent financial distress, Leopold struck Donaueschingen from the list of visits and recommended that Wolfgang, instead, proceed to the territories of Margraf Karl Friedrich of Baden-Durlach and then travel on to Württemberg to seek out Karl Eugene in Stuttgart or Ludwigsburg: "You should do everything within your means to speak with His Highness, the Duke." Subduing disagreeable memories of the Grand Tour, Leopold extolled him as "a noted and amazing musical amateur" who "has established an important music school for the young, which even the Emperor has visited [1777];[15] it deserves to be seen."[16] Should Carl Anselm, Prince (since 1777) of Thurn und Taxis, be sojourning at Dischingen, it might be the next stopping place; then the Cistercian monastery of Kaisheim, followed by Eichstätt, whose bishop owed his throne to his relative the late Archbishop Schrattenbach of Salzburg. From Eichstätt, Augsburg was an easy journey.

---

15 On this occasion, Karl Eugene had Jommelli's *Didone abbandonata* performed for his Imperial guest and presented him with its original manuscript.

16 The military academy created in 1770 at Schloss Solitude and moved to Stuttgart five years later had evolved into an institution embracing the arts and sciences. (Had Mozart made the visit, he might have met Johann Christoph Friedrich Schiller, one of the medical students.) It became the distinguished humanistic college known as the Hohe Karlsschule.

Leopold sowed these seeds, taking for granted their finding inhospitable ground; but of one thing he declared himself certain: "Were I with you, I would at least fully cover the cost of the journey; indeed, I would probably have a profit. . . . But whether you are in the mood to follow such a path, I do not know." He now at all points mistrusted his son's ability to arrange anything. Leopold went on to sound an alarm: "At the moment, the Roman Empire swarms with deserters from the Prussian army who have become criminals and turned to highway robbery. . . ." "One must know the exact distance between one place and another so that now, when the days are short, one doesn't run the danger of travel by night."

So eager had Grimm become to rid himself of a guest whom he now looked upon as an affliction that, despite monies already loaned, he volunteered to lay out yet more for Wolfgang's passage to Strassburg, assuring Leopold that he could repay all at his convenience. He assumed that the Baron would work matters out expeditiously and at a good price, but with regard for comfort. Grimm, however, chose the cheapest convoy departing at the earliest moment. On 11 September Mozart complained of Grimm's insistence that he "depart within a week." He gained a respite only until the twenty-sixth: Grimm drummed him out of Paris.

Leopold as well as Grimm prodded him to move at the double, both fearing he might act upon some impulsive idea in an attempt to protract his stay. In the end, he came up with only one proposal, quite madcap, in respect to his journey home: "Since I shall not have a lot of extra luggage with me—when the opportunity presents itself, I shall dispatch in advance what I do not require—I could, were it possible, get myself the kind of pretty cabriolet [a sort of chaise drawn by one horse] now in vogue here. That is what Wendling did. . . . The cabriolets here are . . . no longer open as they used to be: they are enclosed and have windows; but they still have two wheels and accommodate two persons who are not too stout."

Wolfgang, who doubtless threw this caprice on paper for the sport of aggravating his father and earning a response of fuming fireworks, must have been disappointed when Leopold replied in the patient, placating tones with which one might address a simpleton: his son, he felt certain, could select a "pretty cabriolet"; but would it be mechanically sound? And who would drive it, who change the horses, and who pay for driver and horses, to say nothing of the conveyance itself? The two had begun to play destructive games.

His days in Paris vanishing one by one, Mozart bestirred himself to pursue matters long neglected: to collect his full fees from Legros and de Guines and settle matters with De Jean. Further, he hawked his Palatine sonatas, and the publisher Jean Georges Sieber took the gamble of issuing them. Mozart hoped to carry presentation examples to Munich, but the engravers foresaw insufficient time to complete their work before his departure. To his disquietude, he had to abandon proofreading to surrogates and could only hope that reasonably accurate copies overtake him during his journey toward Bavaria.

It occurred to him to prepare shortened versions of his violin concertos for Paris. ("We Germans," he acknowledged, "have a taste for length;[17] however, when all is said and done, it is better to be short and good.") But for this project time had run out, as it had for selling several of his piano concertos and piano sonatas to Sieber.[18] His early symphonies, Mozart realized, would hardly succeed in Paris—that so-called second Paris Symphony could not have fulfilled the public's expectations excited by the first—and he talked of rousing himself to compose "six trios . . . for which I shall be well paid." Again, the hour had passed. He had miscalculated on almost all points.

Longing for more time in Paris to tidy things up, he contemplated putting off his journey: he wanted to move from Grimm's residence to von Sickingen's and remain there until he had proofread his sonatas. But Grimm threatened him with a high price for such a maneuver—undying enmity: for appearance's sake Grimm demanded that the break be quick and clean. Wolfgang could not stifle his anger and told him off; Grimm maintained his composure, eager to close the chapter with some seemliness.[19]

On 26 September Mozart set out for Strassburg, where, so Grimm assured him, he would arrive within five days. He found himself in a wretched diligence: "It goes inch by inch, doesn't change horses, and takes ten days." (The driver's schedule indicated twelve!) In the crowded compartment he worked himself into a "rage" but soon realized that the presence of a fellow voyager with "the French disease"—"he did not even deny it"—might provide a sound excuse, in Leopold's eyes, to break the journey. All perturbations seemed minor compared to being awakened in the early hours of the morning at inns where the passengers had time for only the briefest repose; yet, after eight days of such misery, they had only

17 Called *der lange Geschmack*, this predilection contrasted with Archbishop Colloredo's Italianate taste for conciseness.
18 Wolfgang and Leopold felt at ease about turning into money any composition of which either retained the original or a copy. Composers often resold their works, adding ever new dedications.
19 To counteract any account of the incident Grimm might send to Salzburg, Mozart would take the childish step of writing home from Strassburg about the esteem in which its citizens held him for his "stylish demeanor," "sedateness," "courtesy," and "good manners."

reached Nancy. At the end of his physical resources, Mozart alighted to rest and seek a more endurable conveyance. The city's "handsome houses, fine broad streets, and superb squares" charmed him.

He lingered about a week to refresh his shaken, exhausted body and must also have used these days to contemplate his situation in peace. The rush of activities at the end of his stay in Paris had left him few hours in which to ponder the painful process that had caught him up: "One thunderclap after the other," he observed, had deprived him of "time in which to think things through accurately and coolly." King Stanislaus's architectural wonders alone cannot explain so long a stay in a city that had lost its court and therewith any substantial means of patronage:[20] nor does Mozart's later account of his difficulties in finding transportation from Nancy convince. Most likely, he needed time to put himself above the immediacy of his situation, time to acquire insight into it, time to seek self-direction, even if only to assimilate his plight as a necessary part of going on with his life. His mind must have given way to the simultaneous and relentless intrusion of childhood memories; he may have sunk into paralysis and despair. There was reason enough.

His passage to independence and maturity—long, hazardous, and, until recently, buried beneath the needs of others—had been forced back into its subterranean bed. The freedom of the past months: his waning anxiety concerning his father; his intimations of shared power with his father; his appropriation of his father's role; his feeling of excelling over his father and thus defeating him—all had proved illusion and delusion, a sequence of fantasies. He found himself renouncing the challenge and returning to a pathetic vulnerability: circumstances, manipulated by Leopold, were delivering him back to Salzburg as an eternal child taking his dead mother's place. Though a fragment of its former self, Leopold's presence, still formidable even from the distance, again threw its threatening dark over him. Wolfgang sensed the danger: the old yoke stood ready to couple him to a father who had always confused his own identity and destiny with his son's.[21] But Wolfgang continued powerless to impose his will, to come to terms with himself and thus end his protracted adolescence. His advance toward manhood once again made a halt in Leopold's re-emerging shadow.

---

20 Upon Stanislaus's death in 1766, Lothringen had passed to France (see pp. 74–75).

21 Leopold had distanced himself from any connection with Wolfgang's resignation and departure from Salzburg; but, now reclaiming the nominative plural, he wrote of "the step we took" and of Bullinger's readiness, once the family's finances returned to order, of providing funds "should we have need of money for a journey to Italy."

In Salzburg, Nannerl had bought Wolfgang a pair of beautiful lace cuffs; Tresel, the Mozarts' housemaid and cook, had started to lay away the capons upon which the family would feast his return; and Bimperl was saving up "many thousands of licks. Can you want for more?" Leopold asked. But there hovered about the whole the feeling, not of a hero's, but of a prodigal's return. Wolfgang sensed the mood.

CHAPTER XXIV

Slow Progress Toward Salzburg

O N 14 OCTOBER 1778, he reached Strassburg, drew upon the credit awaiting him, and collected his mail. A letter from Leopold conveyed deep anxiety: ignorant of Wolfgang's prolonged stay in Nancy—he had written home of his intention to remain only one night—and informed that he had yet to appear in Strassburg, the father feared that either illness or thieves had overtaken him. Weber, too, had written and with even more cause for alarm: without a word from Wolfgang for weeks, he thought him in all likelihood dead, for a rumor in Mannheim ascribed Anna Maria's quick decline to a contagious disease. Weber's account of Aloisia's daily visits to the Capuchin church to pray for Wolfgang's soul moved and de-lighted him.

Leopold had advised his leaving Strassburg posthaste if it held out only trifling opportunities for music-making. The presence and goodwill of Maximilian Joseph von Pfalz-Zweibrücken-Birkenfeld (see XX, n. 17) em-boldened him to hire a hall and give a recital on the seventeenth. Even with the Prince attending, the room was nearly empty. Still, Mozart heard shouts of "bravo and bravissimo" and, receptive to assurances that a larger public would come, stayed on to give a costly concert with orchestra ("which is very bad but demands generous payment") a week later in the theater. Again, vacant chairs; he regarded the Strassburgers' indifference with good humor: "Nothing is more dismal than a great T-shaped table laid for 80 with only three at the repast."

The weather had turned cold, and heavy rains brought high flooding that closed the roads. He seemed happy to be stranded on the Rhine, enjoying the company of a little group of admirers: the organ builders and brothers Johann Andreas and Johann Heinrich Silbermann;[1] Franz Xaver Richter, a Moravian composer formerly in the service of Karl Theodore and now the heavy-drinking kapellmeister of Strassburg cathedral; the organist Sixtus Hepp; and the bankers through whom Leopold had arranged credit. To amuse himself and his new coterie, on his name day (31 October) Mozart gave another concert at the theater, this time clearing a small profit.

By early November the waters had receded. He left on the third, not in the diligence to Stuttgart—the course Leopold urged—but in the one to Mannheim, which he reached within three days. He made the preposterous assertion that locals recommended this extended indirection as the best route to Stuttgart, thanks to its superior roadway; he informed Leopold, and not without provocation: "In foreign regions one must follow the advice of people whom experience has taught." So much for instructions from Salzburg: he had refound some degree of independence. His wild humor returned, and he looked upon his failure at Strassburg with proud disdain. During the preceding months, he had cast off skin after skin in an effort to find himself. For the moment he seemed reconciled to the fact that the same Wolfgang always reappeared.

In view of his defiant stand, he felt it wise to propitiate Leopold by an extravagant compliment on his coming name day (15 November): the son, declaring it his desire not to outlive the father, implored heaven "that throughout my entire life—all the years, and I intend to live many—I may be able to congratulate you. However strange and perhaps ridiculous you may consider this wish, I assure you that it is genuine and heartfelt [wohlmeinend]." The tribute seems a countercharm meant to neutralize thoughts wandering in a quite different direction.

Though by this time aware that Aloisia had already made her way to Munich, even so, he felt an overmastering need once more to contemplate "dear Mannheim": to walk its streets; to embrace the city in which he had known such joy. But this was to be more than a sentimental journey and a device to postpone his return to Salzburg—a pattern already well set. He also harbored the absurd hope that Elector Karl Theodore would soon be-

---

1 Mozart played on Silbermann organs in two of Strassburg's Protestant churches: the New Church (Neue Kirche or Temple Neuf) and St. Thomas's.

come so affronted by the accents and manners of the Bavarians—Mozart held the rough and hardy ways of his fellow south Germans in unrelenting contempt—that he would return to his northern capital.[2] Wolfgang imagined him trooping back to Mannheim, his court and artists—including, of course, Aloisia—following close behind. As the climax of this fantasy, he would invite Mozart into princely service, thus joining his and Aloisia's professional and personal lives.

Determined to stay in Mannheim as long as he could hold out, he even started to take pupils. Frau Cannabich provided immediate help. Her husband had already left for Munich, where he was to share the musical directorship with Carlo Giuseppe Toeschi. She had remained behind with the children to complete the removal of the household and invited Mozart to be a guest in her home. He accepted, finding in her much of the coarse charm and lively temperament of his mother.

Like the Bäsle, Marie Elizabeth Cannabich delighted in anal humor, throwing herself with Rabelaisian abandon into the high jinks of filthy rhyming. Mozart no longer mentioned the name of her daughter Rosa: Elizabeth now counted among his "best and truest friends. . . . When we are alone together, alas, a very infrequent occurence, we speak most confidentially. Of all the good friends who frequent her house I am the only one who has her entire trust, who knows all her domestic and family vexations, anxieties, secrets, and circumstances. I assure you [Leopold] that we did not get to know one another so well the first time [his preceding stay in Mannheim]; in this we concur; we did not truly understand each other. But living in the same house affords greater opportunities to get to know another person."

There hangs about this unnecessary explanation a certain defensiveness along with the whiff of erotic attachment—for certain sublimated, though he sought to insinuate to Salzburg a mutual seductiveness. He enjoyed

---

2 Goethe, too, suffered with difficulty the peculiarities of southern German speech: "One would scarcely believe the B, P, D, and T to be . . . *four* different letters." If the failure to differentiate among consonants disturbed the poet, the southern German's reduction of the language's open, clean vowels to messy diphthongs plagued the musician. Mozart contrasted the tidy Mannheim accent with what could be heard on the streets of Munich: "What a language! How common!—as is the whole way of life! It will pain me once again to hear *hoben* [*haben*] and *olles met einonder* [*alles mit einander*]. . . ." He found Salzburg's dialect, uses, and simple citizens even more exasperating: indeed, beyond hope. Almost without exception, he experienced an assault upon his ears and sensibilities when meeting Salzburgers on his travels. Of Maria Viktoria von Robinig, with whom he had to be sociable in Munich during January 1779, he wrote: "You cannot believe what I suffered during the visit of Madame Robinig here, for it has been a long time since I have spoken with such a fool." She personified everything he could "not bear" about "Salzburg and its [native-born] inhabitants. . . . To me their speech and their manners are thoroughly intolerable."

Elizabeth's conversation, zest for living, and reassuring, earthy humor; and since his love for Aloisia did not nourish itself in silence and grow strong in secret, no doubt talk often turned to her. (She owed her new position in Munich not only to Raaff but to Herr Cannabich, too.) The practical Elizabeth no doubt provided a realistic reaction to the idealization with which Mozart invoked the name of his goddess.

Basking in Frau Cannabich's hospitality, Wolfgang continued to rebuild hopes for a position in Mannheim. They rested, so he believed, upon his composing a Melodrama. It called upon an actor or a pair of actors[3] to recite a poetic text, sometimes with and sometimes without orchestral accompaniment, the instruments, in addition, often providing comments between the spoken phrases.

During his previous stay in Mannheim, he had "with the greatest delight" attended two performances of such a work—Georg Benda's *Medea.* Recalling the experience, Wolfgang wrote his father: "Indeed, nothing has ever so surprised me, for I always imagined this kind of thing as making no impression! Of course, you know that what is involved here has to do not with singing but declamation," the effect, in his mind, seeming to produce a reversed image of opera: "The music is like an *ad libitum* recitative," the synthesis of "spoken word and music creating the finest result." Benda, Mozart continued, "has composed another [Melodrama], *Ariadne auf Naxos,* and both are truly admirable. You know that Benda has always been my favorite among Lutheran kapellmeisters. I love these two works so much that I carry them about with me. Now imagine my joy at the prospect of composing in total harmony with my inclinations." Within days of arriving in Mannheim, he had convinced himself that it would commission him to write a Melodrama for its recently reborn "German National Theater."

This expression signified little more than a theater in which German works occupied a continuing place in a repertory built upon the pursuit of pedagogic and morally uplifting ideals. Such institutions had varying sponsorships and structures: the one established in Hamburg during 1766–1767 (with Konrad Ekhof among the actors) had been a short-lived private endeavor; that organized a decade later by Joseph II in Vienna's Burgtheater became an enterprise over which the ruler hovered intrusively, a state of affairs also prevailing at Munich's Nationale Schaubühne (National Stage), which opened in 1778. But the National theater built 1775–1777 in Mannheim, for its part, grew into an anomalous and fertile variant: there princely subsidies supported not a court, but a corporate aesthetic.

---

3 Hence the genre fell into subdivisions of Monodrama and Duodrama.

During this theater's first years, its horizons and resources awakened scorn: Lessing scoffed that the Mannheimers' concept of a German national theater "excluded all players but those born in the Pfalz," and Mozart deplored the company's "miserable" singers. However, matters changed in 1778 when Karl Theodore, about to leave permanently for Munich, gave his former capital a parting gift that might ensure its continuing artistic distinction: he bestowed upon Mannheim's National theater a historic franchise granting it funds from the Wittelsbach court and independence from its whims; the administration of the theater passed into the hands of the city's new intellectual leaders, a productive, bourgeois elite; yet, at the same time, governance also included changing councils on which the players had voice.[4] Heribert von Dalberg, who had tried in vain to persuade the Elector to remove his university from Heidelberg to Mannheim, had succeeded in swaying him in respect to this new concept of a national theater. As first director of the transformed institution, von Dalberg moved quickly to fasten upon a fortuitous opportunity: at the very time he set about putting his stamp upon the reorganized company, members of Abel Seyler's renowned traveling troupe became available for service.

Boasting Ekhof as star and Schweitzer as musical leader, the Seyler performers had in 1771 made their headquarters in Weimar. Three years later its palace, which contained the theater, burned to the ground.[5] The players moved from Weimar to Gotha, became the mainstay of Duke Ernst II's court theater, and prospered until the death of Ekhof during the summer of 1778. The ensemble then threatened to break up, and von Dalberg took steps to bring it to Mannheim with the view of incorporating it into his own organization.[6] By autumn Seyler's actors had begun performing singspiele in Mannheim, and an excited Mozart wrote his father in November: "The Seyler troupe, whose fine reputation you know, has arrived here; Herr von Dalberg is its director." If not quite accurate, Mozart's statement did anticipate events: within the year the new establishment

---

4 This structure derived in part from the open-minded conventions of Joseph II's National theater, where, alas, his meddling rendered them ineffective.

5 The auditorium in ruins and the troupe of actors gone, local amateurs held forth in a ballroom-playhouse hammered together by the end of 1775, the time of Goethe's arrival at the court of Weimar. He became a kind of master of the revels in charge of the homemade theatricals, pressing into service members of the ducal family, courtiers, officials, townsfolk, occasional guest professionals, and, above all, himself. European courts had long taken pleasure in dilettante entertainments, but at Weimar the fire made them a favorite sport. Creating for the Duke's retinue a series of playlets, librettos (for singspiele), pantomimes, masquerades, and mummeries, Goethe underwent a process of discovery in respect to verse and dramatic forms.

6 Schweitzer, who had been with the Seyler troupe since 1769, remained in Gotha and in 1778 became Benda's successor as ducal *Kapelldirektor.*

would absorb the best of the Seyler/Gotha performers (including August Wilhelm Iffland), Seyler thereafter functioning under von Dalberg.

During his stay in Paris, Mozart had expressed himself with less enthusiasm about Seyler, in particular disparaging his manipulation of the repertory. Writing to Fridolin Weber in fear that Aloisia might join the company, he had painted it in unattractive colors, condemning what he alleged to be Seyler's custom of regarding musical presentations simply as stopgaps: "... as with all troupes, the play [die Comoedie] is always the main thing. Now and then they turn the singspiel to account to provide rest for the actors; very often to give them time and opportunity to change [costume]; and, on the whole, to offer diversity."[7]

Now Mozart saw the Seyler ensemble within a different frame: as enfolded in a new and vital institution with von Dalberg at its helm, an innovator who sought to work with playwrights and those few prominent musicians who had not followed Karl Theodore to Munich—the composer Holzbauer, the young cellist Peter Ritter, and the violinist Ignaz Fränzl. Mozart strove to force a place for himself among them. Doubtless he also dreamed of becoming von Dalberg's long arm in transforming the workaday German theatrical aesthetic, in emancipating the German stage from the jumble of French plays and Italian operas crowding it and leaving small room for native works.

Von Dalberg's theatrical mission sharpened Mozart's Germanism: a true national theater—something Lessing, not long before, had regarded as an indulgence being prepared for a people unprepared for it—seemed on the point of materializing. (Von Dalberg brought his company into being at the very time Lessing toiled at the final version of Nathan der Weise.) Both Mozart and von Dalberg shared a vision of the German theater embracing all aspects of the nation's dramatic art: plays, singspiele, German serious operas, and those ever more popular Melodramas toward which von Dal-

---

7 In his eagerness to forestall Aloisia's joining the Seyler company, Mozart overdrew and confused the case. Although the singspiel used singers, more often it called upon actors. Since for the most part they had little or no vocal training, the music tended toward the simple and folklike. The text defined the singspiel, as Leopold Mozart well knew: he, for example, praised the famous acting couple the Heigels as singspiel performers; their acting, he maintained, more than made good their singing. His son lent himself to such views: to his ears, polished vocalism helped the singspiel little if the performers spoke the dialogue wretchedly. In Vienna he voiced dismay at the attempt of Antonia Bernasconi (who had sung Aspasia in his Mitridate and the title role at the premiere of Gluck's Alceste) to make a success in the singspiel. Her struggle with the spoken lines upset him, her native (despite her name) street German destroying all illusion: "Just imagine her! When, from time to time, she makes the effort to force herself [to improve her accent], it is as if one were listening to a princess in a puppet show." Aloisia's main value to Seyler would have been in the few vocally demanding works he might mount.

berg favorably inclined. What made the Seyler players attractive to him included their command of this new genre, whose idiom they had imbibed from Schweitzer and Benda. The latter had, in fact, written the *Medea* Mozart so admired for Abel Seyler's wife, the actress Sophie Friedericke Seyler-Hensel.

Perhaps Mozart knew of his own city's putative role in the rise of the Melodrama. Salzburg's Johann Ernst Eberlin appears to have composed the earliest in 1753 as part of his music to a Latin play, *Sigismund.* Yet, most often Rousseau's *Pygmalion* receives recognition as the first of the genre. Begun about a decade later, this *scène lyrique* remained incomplete until, during a stay in Lyon, Rousseau prevailed upon the amateur composer Horace Coignet to join him in adding music to the action. In the end, Rousseau reserved for his own talents only two of the twenty-six instrumental sections, his passage depicting the blows of the sculptor-hero's hammer giving him particular pride. The premiere took place under private auspices in Lyon during 1770. *Pygmalion* achieved publication the following year and began to circulate. In France the music awakened such enthusiasm that Rousseau pretended to be its sole composer: it required a published clarification on the part of Coignet to make known just how modest the philosophe's musical contribution had been. Abroad, however, not the score, but Rousseau's words commanded attention and almost at a stroke appeared in German. Franz Aspelmayr launched into setting to music Joseph Gottwill Laudes's German translation, and their *Pygmalion* had its premiere in Vienna during January 1772. Four months later, Weimar followed with another German version; here music by Schweitzer underlay J. F. Schmidt's rendering of Rousseau's French.

That same year, Schweitzer received a commission from the actor and writer Johannes Christian Brandes for a Melodrama about the forsaken Ariadne. He envisaged it as a vehicle for his wife, the actress Esther Charlotte Brandes, and, as a first step, put together a libretto inspired by Heinrich Wilhelm von Gerstenberg. In the end, Schweitzer, taken up with his *Alceste,* had no time to keep on with the Melodrama and, in fact, began incorporating whatever he had written of it into his opera. Brandes's project seemed to have lost all ground. However, after the Weimar theater went up in flames, he and his wife moved to Gotha, where Benda took on the commission. Given its first performance during January 1775, Benda's *Ariadne* provided Madame Brandes with a success her rival, Madame Seyler-Hensel, found difficult to bear: Benda had also to write a Melodrama for her. His *"mit Musik vermischtes Drama"* concerning Medea, its text by Friedrich Wilhelm Gotter, first came to the stage in May 1775 and provided Seyler-Hensel with a no less triumphant signature role. This pair of

Melodramas, created for an extraordinary pair of actresses, were the scores
Mozart so spiritedly discussed with his father.

The prominence of famous tragediennes, including Corona Schröter,[8] in
the rise of the Melodrama but underscores the problem Mozart would have
to face when inserting it into an opera: the Melodrama succeeds best in the
throats of actors, not singers, a predicament repeatedly asserted in performances of the most famous extended Melodrama still in the repertory, that
in the dungeon scene of Beethoven's *Fidelio.*[9] Not only Benda's music for
Medea and *Ariadne,* but also the vigor of Brandes's and Gotter's words[10] and
the skill of the actors reciting them at first fired Mozart's enthusiasm; it
would cool when he realized that such texts, as projected by singers, inevitably emerged overacted. By the time of *The Abduction from the Seraglio,* he
would look upon the Melodrama as defying consolidation within the opera.
But during those autumn days in Mannheim, having long admitted reservations about the effectiveness of recitative as a medium for communicating a
text, he saw in the new genre a possible heaven-sent corrective.

He did not limit his interests to matters of the stage, but sought entry
into what remained of Mannheim's concert life. To fill the gaps opened by
the departure of so many court musicians from Mannheim to Munich,
Fränzl had begun to organize a series of *Liebhaberkonzerte* (music-lovers'
concerts). Mozart set to work on a composition they might perform together at the new society: a double concerto or sinfonia concertante for
clavier and violin, K. Anh. 56/315f. Over and above the stratagem of ingratiating himself, Mozart did prize his playing—its "very beautiful
round tone . . . beautiful staccato . . . and a double trill such as I have never
heard but from him."

Beginning the concerto symbolized Mozart's resolve to establish footing in the new Mannheim, a determination powerfully strengthened when

---

8 The Melodrama also caught Goethe's interest: in response to Wieland's urging that he commemorate in poetry the death of Gluck's young niece Marianne, he composed the monologue
Proserpina (derived from Ovid), in which the daughter of Ceres and Jove recites her woes before the gates of the nether world. But *Proserpina,* conceived by Goethe as a Melodrama, first
came before the public (Weimar, 1778) as an unaccompanied spoken piece: Corona Schröter—
the following year she would take the title role at the premiere of his *Iphigenie*—declaimed
Proserpina's words without the interplay of the musical commentary by courtier-composer
Karl Siegmund Seckendorff.

9 Violetta's reciting the letter in the closing act of *La Traviata* has both beauty—and brevity.

10 Best known for his dramas incorporating French literary ideals, Gotter had a role in transforming Shakespeare's *Tempest* into *Die Geisterinsel,* and would invite Mozart—alas, to no effect—to compose music for it. He, in fact, never made use of any text by Gotter, the setting
of whose *Wiegenlied* (K. 350/Anh. C 8.48), long accounted Mozart's, has proved to be from the
pen of Bernhard Flies.

von Dalberg held up to him von Gemmingen's *Semiramis* as prototypal material for a Melodrama. Without a formal agreement (though he implied otherwise to Leopold), Mozart took upon himself to underlay the text of *Semiramis* with music. The decision involved opportunism—and still more: clearly his enchantment with the Melodrama had already ignited the idea of one day setting it within the architecture of opera; he wanted to try his hand at supporting the spoken word by a finely shaded score mirroring its pathos and psychological implications.

The intensity of von Dalberg's interest in *Semiramis* had given rise to a solacing fantasy: for Mozart the position awaiting him in Salzburg became suspended in time as he envisioned himself passing two months in Mannheim composing and then rehearsing what he called "the declaimed opera"; its success at the National Theater, he felt certain, would lead to a permanent engagement, and, somehow, the disturbing image of Salzburg would shatter and fade.

Von Dalberg did not share these reveries: he had done little more than suggest and reconnoiter; and Mozart's local reputation for neglecting commissions, a consequence of the De Jean imbroglio, must have flashed across von Dalberg's mind. As he began to beat a retreat, Mozart, in a most injudicious way, importuned him for a written arrangement, grandly threatening to leave for Munich were his "final conditions" (*mein letztes Wort*) not met. In the end, von Dalberg made himself altogether unavailable, refusing to respond to Mozart's ill-tempered remonstrances: "I have called upon you twice to pay my respects, but did not have the good fortune to meet with you. Indeed, although you were at home yesterday, I, nevertheless, could not speak with you!" Another door had closed.[11] But Mozart lingered in Mannheim in hopes that von Gemmingen—or some miracle—might put things right.

2

AWAITING HIS SON'S return, Leopold felt driven to the wall: "I really don't know what it behooves me to write. I shall go mad or consume myself and die. I find it impossible, without losing my mind, to recollect all the projects you have thought up and communicated to me since your departure from Salzburg. They have all added up to proposals, empty words,

---

11 Mozart made little effort to conceal his contempt for *Cora*, a drama by von Dalberg, who had approached him to set it to music. Yet, in his painful situation he might have taken on the task at a proper fee had their relationship not abruptly ended. Von Dalberg also opened discussions about *Cora* with Gluck and Schweitzer, but they stood aloof.

and, in the end, to *nothing whatever*. . . . Your stay in Nancy amounted to throwing money out the window for, instead of spending money unnecessarily there, you should have used it to find some means of your own to make your way to Strassburg more quickly. Then you sat down in Strassburg until the downpours burst forth, although I had previously written that if things didn't look promising, you should immediately leave. . . . But *people praised you,* and *that is enough for you!* . . . The crazy idea that you might put up in Mannheim, from which the court has departed, could not have possibly occurred to me. . . . Did you cunningly draw eight louis d'or in Strassburg simply for the purpose of sitting about in Mannheim? You hope to get an appointment in Mannheim? An appointment? What are you talking about? At this time you must take an appointment neither in Mannheim nor in any other place in the world. I will not hear the word *appointment*. . . . The main thing now is that you return to Salzburg. . . . Your whole purpose is to undo me simply to pursue your airy, futile plans. . . . To sum up! I am determined not to die in shame and debt for your sake— and still less to leave your poor sister in penury. You know no better than I how long God will permit you to live."

Anxiety brought forth Leopold's least admirable traits: he threatened to strip Wolfgang of all dignity in the eyes of his Mannheim friends, in particular Frau Cannabich, by sending her a letter revealing that "in fourteen months" he had plunged his father "into 863 florins of debt." He saw her the villainess of the piece, the main factor in Wolfgang's dalliance: "Were I to say to her *that she should give this information to all who are advising you to stay in Mannheim and tell them that I require you to return to service in Salzburg for a couple of years, since by this means I have the prospect of paying off these debts,* none of them would utter another word to hold you back; rather, they would make quite different faces. In short, up to now I have written my letters not only as a father but also as a friend. After receiving this letter, I hope that you will hasten your journey and behave in such a manner that I may welcome you with joy and not greet you with reproaches. Indeed, considering that your mother had to die an untimely death in Paris, I hope that you will not also wish to have on your conscience being an accessory to your father's death." Leopold bristled with suspicion and animosity as he repeated the terrible charge. He knew but one way to revenge himself: to treat Wolfgang like a phenomenal matricidal baby who had to be slapped. Their relationship had reached its nadir.

Regressing to a condition of tension and insecurity and possessed by the idea of the Mannheim National Theater as his agent of rescue, Wolfgang could not think coherently. His letters reveal a flow of images depicting reality in rapidly changing frames: in a composed moment, facing the fact that his path would inevitably lead home, he asked Leopold to make much in Salzburg of the *Semiramis* "commission," to cry the news at court "so extravagantly and with such intensity" that the Archbishop, apprehensive of competition, will "decide to offer me a better salary"; that said, he announced that Colloredo "cannot pay me enough for that slavery in Salzburg!"; thereupon a grandiose and defiant fantasy floated before him as he experienced "the greatest pleasure in contemplating . . . a visit [to Leopold!] but sheer disgust and anxiety in picturing . . . [himself] at that beggarly court!" He blustered: "The Archbishop had certainly better not begin to play the high and mighty with me as was his custom; it is not altogether impossible that I will turn up my nose at him!"

These rapidly changing arguments, dismantling themselves as he made them, betokened a convulsive, dichotomous process: both a flight from reality's impositions and an attempt to substitute action for anxiety by reducing his conflicts to some well-defined situation. In any case, by early December he had returned to stubborn facts. Acknowledging to Salzburg that his efforts on *Semiramis* involved neither assurances nor fees, he broke off work on it[12]—the unfinished score has vanished—and put aside the double concerto for Fränzl and himself, which had grown to one hundred twenty measures of exquisite promise.

Only on 3 December did he find the spirit to reply to Leopold's terrible words about Anna Maria's death: "Truly, I never would have imagined that— But peace! I don't want to say more about it, for it is all over now: next Wednesday, that is the 9th, I will leave [Mannheim]." The question of who, over the years, had lived upon whose labors could not have been far beneath the surface of his mind as he contemplated his departure and that balance sheet his father had drawn up and threatened to send Frau Cannabich, the accusatory eight hundred sixty-three florins its ugly coda. Blind to his son's psychological struggles, the depth of the humiliation his retreat from Paris entailed, and the widening complications of the guilt oppressing him, Leopold saw only foolishness and mulish resistance. Always quick to grasp the trunk and shake the branches, he did not know what to make of a son who could barely recognize the tree.

For the moment regretting his brutal comments and accusations, Leopold had written on 23 November in as conciliatory a tone as he could manage. His Wolfgang was "not wicked" but "simply inconsiderate." He "would be all right in time" but for the moment remained incapable of "thinking things through in a rational way." Not his fear of the Archbishop

---

12 Within the year he would be planning a singspiel with elements of Melodrama for Vienna's National Theater (see p. 486).

but his love for Aloisia and his desire to marry her had brought him to this critical state; confronting the forbidden subject, Leopold declared himself in no way opposed to their union: "I was not when her father was poor; why should I be so now when *she can make your success* rather than your making hers?" Leopold went on to paint the good-fellowship that would grow between the Mozarts in Salzburg and the Webers in not-too-distant Munich: at this point, to have his son at his side he would have proposed keeping company with the devil.

3

COELESTIN II ANGELSPRUGGER, Imperial Abbot of Kaisheim[13]—whom Leopold had recommended to his son as "a great admirer of virtuosos"—was in Mannheim and about to journey home. Wolfgang succeeded in attaching himself to the prelate's retinue, receiving permission to share the advanced carriage with his cellarer and secretary. They traveled southeast in the direction of Heilbronn, not south to Stuttgart. But Mozart rested assured that by this time the Tanzmeisterhaus cared little about the route if only it led toward Salzburg. If Leopold had not been able to resist reviving his threat to write to Frau Cannabich should Wolfgang tarry longer in Mannheim, he could not resist forcing upon his father a suggestive description of her distress at her young friend's departure: "We believed that it would be impossible for us to separate. I left at half past eight in the morning, but Madame did not get up: she would and could not say farewell; I did not want to burden her heart and set out without having seen her."

The Imperial Abbot's suite left Mannheim on 9 December and made its way home to Kaisheim (just north of Donauwörth)[14] four days later. Mozart's impressions of this venerable Cistercian establishment, where Swabian infantry and cavalry had a permanent presence in barracks, recall Leopold's comments upon Ludwigsburg. Wolfgang found the "fierce soldiery" (*grausame Militaire*) both puzzling ("to what end . . . ?") and amusing ("During the night at fixed intervals I hear shouts of 'Who goes there?' to which I in turn answer, 'Now wouldn't you like to know?'"). He enjoyed the Order's hospitality and prolonged his stay until the twenty-fourth so that he

---

13 An *unmittelbares freies Reichsstift* (an unencumbered, free Imperial monastery), it resembled a free city in being answerable, anent its political powers, only and directly to the Emperor.

14 Mozart made uncharacteristic reference to the beauty of the route ("*eine der angenehmsten*") that led him through Heidelberg, Heilbronn, Schwäbisch Hall, Crailsheim, Dinkelsbühl, and Nördlingen to Donauwörth.

might again fall in with the traveling plans of the Abbot, who intended to celebrate part of the holidays in Munich. On the evening of Christmas day, Mozart made his way through its streets to the Webers' new home.

His having remained more than a month in Mannheim implied no lessening of ardor to possess Aloisia Weber, but, rather, argued the intensity of his desire to establish himself somewhere other than Salzburg before asking her hand. Munich now provided the last hope: close to despair, he came to indulge the idea that the sonatas written for Electress Maria Elizabeth might serve as a starting point for negotiating an appointment. With post after post arriving without them in Mannheim and then Kaisheim, he had fretted, certain that the Parisian engravers must have long since finished their work. Ascribing the hitch to Grimm's unwillingness to follow the matter through, he predicted disgrace should he appear at the Munich Residenz with empty hands.

Leopold, chiding him for making too much of a commitment that in all likelihood had long faded from the Electress's memory, suspected this harping upon the sonatas to be but another device to delay: "Let the devil wait for them. This is ridiculous. Who knows what lies hidden beneath these pretty civilities!" (He had to have wondered whether there had even been a formal promise of the gift.) With or without the sonatas, Wolfgang had no immediate future with the Wittelsbach court, Leopold now insisted. In October his letters had begun to raise questions about Munich; he had let them hang fire until the safe and appropriate moment.

Well into summer's end, he, at his most Machiavellian, had continued to coax Wolfgang back with optimistic talk of Munich: "If you remain in Paris, then all your hopes concerning Munich will prove unavailing" had been the expedient message as late as 10 September. But by this time Leopold knew such expectations to be groundless in view of the crisis about to overwhelm the Bavarian civil service: few seasoned professionals could have been unaware of the chaos in matters of precedence and dignities about to engulf it. That same September, Joseph Fiala, a Bohemian oboist whom Elector Maximilian Joseph had hired for his Munich orchestra the preceding year (spring 1777), began negotiations to enter Archbishop Colloredo's service. Fiala had caught sight of the darkening clouds accompanying the Mannheimers to Munich, as had the no less perceptive agent arranging his move to Salzburg—Leopold Mozart. But only in November, when Wolfgang had crossed the Rhine on his way home, did Leopold start to sing to him a more accurate tune about Munich and ended by ringing a clanging tocsin.

The gathering of Karl Theodore's Mannheim household in his new capital had given rise to so great a number of court musicians that the Residenz undertook to force veteran instrumentalists into retirement even as it closed the lists to Bavarians; Karl Theodore gave preferment to his own: overnight, the Bavarian accent became less pervasive in the Electoral waiting rooms. Further, Leopold espied a second army of usurpers mustering in the wings: the House of Zweibrücken, the new and immediate heir to the throne in Munich, maintained musical forces that would seek privilege there and, upon the death of Karl Theodore, already in his fifty-fourth year, march upon the city. Leopold advised his son to open his eyes to these facts and pass through it as quickly as possible.

Mozart had no such intention; he had serious, time-consuming business in the capital: to talk with Aloisia about their future and to appear before the Electress. The engraved pages of the sonatas had finally reached him, but only hours before his departure from Kaisheim, and now he had to dart to and fro having them bound and securing an audience with her; moreover, he planned to see Munich's production of Schweitzer's *Alceste* (to be unveiled on 11 January) and, into the bargain, had arranged to meet the Bäsle. He had resumed their correspondence and set this Munich rendezvous. She was, he instructed, to put on a good face and share his joy in Aloisia; contemplating some kind of prefatory betrothal celebration, he suggested with remarkable swagger: "Perhaps you will have a great role to play." He indicated that their days of sharing sexual play had passed; that they could not even lie together since he would lodge not at an inn but with the Webers. But he wrote no less flirtatiously than in former times: with the Bäsle he appreciated just how seductive he could be and flaunted an aggressive sexuality.

A formidable presence continued to block his gaining any advantage at the Residenz—Count Seeau. Like Baron Grimm, he had a strong aversion to Mozart and racked up public remembrance of *La finta giardiniera*, exaggerating its failure. Though Mozart hoped that Raaff's eulogies might provide a counterpoise, the Munich court, in fact, needed no reminders of the composer's talent; here lay the deep irony of his situation: at the very first Monday concert of the former Mannheim—now Munich—orchestra in the Kaisersaal of the Residenz, all the music, save a symphony by Cannabich, had been Mozart's, including *"Non so d'onde viene"* enchantingly sung by Aloisia. Yet even though—Cannabich excepted—court officials held back from tendering the visitor any courtesies, he sought to turn to account the capital's interest in traditional settings of the liturgy (the case at least during the reign of Maximilian Joseph) and decided "to compose a mass," no doubt returning to the one begun in Mannheim. The measures of the Kyrie that remain (K. 322/296a, close to identical with K. Anh.

12/296b) reveal glimpses of an imposing landscape of the spirit; the appeals for God's mercy seem in a high degree personal and awaken a powerful response and with it regret that once again he found himself putting the project aside; Munich gave him no encouragement to continue.

The Electress did receive him and his sonatas (7 January 1779) in her simple, elegant chambers. They charmed him: "She is lodged . . . just like a private person" in surroundings "very handsome and decorous . . . exactly as I intend to live one day." He voiced this buoyant notion only two weeks after having suffered the rebuff of Aloisia Weber.

4

LEOPOLD HAD ALWAYS doubted the sincerity of the Webers' affection for his son, suspicions first openly set forth in November in an effort to prepare him for disappointment: "My dear Wolfgang! I persist in thinking Herr Weber a man like most of his kind: they make the most out of their poverty and, when their situation improves, no longer know you. He flattered you when he needed you. Now he would perhaps not even admit your having shown or taught her [Aloisia] anything. On the whole, those who have been poor become very arrogant when their affairs turn prosperous."

Wolfgang realized that this indictment touched the daughter as well. Perhaps he, too, had apprehended some reverse when summoning to his side the Bäsle with her balm to heal wounds. She arrived the day after his audience at the Residenz. By this time he had somewhat recovered from the trick fate had played upon him, and, under the changed circumstances, no doubt his cousin ministered to his emotional and sexual needs. Posterity has only indirect knowledge of their friendship at this time and knows little more of the crisis that had refreshed this mutual sympathy—Aloisia's dismissal of his suit.

On 29 December he had laid bare to Leopold: ". . . today I can only weep. I have much too sensitive a heart. . . . I really cannot [write]—my heart is far more disposed to cry! I hope you will write soon and console me." He had come to Munich bearing Aloisia glorious tribute: the bravura scena "*Popoli di Tessaglia/Io non chiedo,*" K. 316/300b, a recitative and aria of compass and volubility begun the previous summer in Paris. At that time he had declared to her: "Because I have created it for you *alone*—hence I desire no commendation but yours—I can only say, indeed, must confess, that of all my compositions of this kind, this scena is the best I have ever written." He wished to hear her sing it before applying the final touches.

Although for a year she had been the center of his existence, he had been only on the margin of hers. As far as can be judged, Munich's new prima donna now saw little wisdom in entangling her life with a Salzburg court musician who seemed powerless to shape his own course. Though perhaps still harboring umbrage at the young man who had first presented himself as well set up, she cut the tie delicately. That he continued to live in the Weber apartment while polishing the aria, presenting it to her on 8 January, indicates that the relationship dissolved in a civilized manner, their continuing cordiality in no way at odds with the cherished anecdote of his immediate response to her refusal: taking his place at the keyboard to sing "Let the one who doesn't want me kiss my ass"; it would have been in character for him to veneer his misery with boisterousness. Decades later, when he was dead and famous and she dilapidated in fortune and forgotten, she regretted having set him aside and insisted that he continued to love her to his last day—no doubt a bit of mischief aimed at her sister, the wife Mozart had adored to distraction. Even so, for a while after the break, Aloisia's presence troubled him—"I am not uninterested in her"— and he admitted finding it "providential" that in the months ahead their paths seldom crossed.

No less than Aloisia's having done with him, fear of facing Leopold taxed his spirit. The Bäsle had quickly dried his eyes and helped close a sad chapter. At the same time, he hit upon the idea of turning her presence to further advantage. Leopold's antagonism gained strength each day Wolfgang remained in Munich; setting his face against squalls of censure, he asked his father's permission to bring her along to Salzburg, the request in itself a hint that assent might well direct the wanderer home all the sooner. But Leopold saw through the scheme of using her as a buffer: he wanted no niceties of hospitality to interfere with his first and frank meetings with his son. Aware that, through the good offices of a friend working for the Munich mail coach, she had free entry, Leopold advised her to avail herself of this perquisite when she came to Salzburg in the vague future: maybe in January, but, more to his convenience, some months later; he especially recommended Salzburg's summer weather!

His sarcasm apart, perhaps he now allowed himself to ponder the possibility of marriage between the cousins. The day of her arrival in Munich, Wolfgang had insinuated to Leopold the idea of taking her *faute de mieux*: "My Bäsle is here. Why? To please her cousin? This is, indeed, the ostensible motive! But we shall talk about the matter in Salzburg." Yet, in defiance of his father's signals of reluctance at the moment either to enter such a discussion or to receive her, Mozart persisted in plans to lead the Bäsle to the Hannibalplatz.

5

STILL, HE HELD back from traveling those final miles. His journey from Paris had entered its third month; at any moment the Salzburg Residenz might revoke the agreement so painstakingly negotiated for him; every passing day his refractoriness appeared more scandalous: his letter to Leopold from Kaisheim had even offered the outrageous suggestion that the Archbishop hire the Augsburg organist, Demmler—"also good at the clavier"—to fill in "until I myself arrive."

Scorning even to mention Demmler's name, Leopold warned against sitting about in Munich and against any attempt to enlist Cannabich's support for the idea, his skill in tapping Wolfgang's energies for private ends a clear memory. Should Cannabich open the matter with Salzburg, the post would quickly bring him a financial account of the ruinous tour: running out of threats, Leopold banged the same dreary gong with its tone of frustration, anger, and exhaustion. He feared his son could no longer distinguish between manipulation and self-deception.

"I am heartily sick of writing so much; during the past fifteen months I have, and to no purpose, almost written my eyes out of my head. Your head refuses to give up the idea of establishing yourself in Munich. Don't you understand that it doesn't accord with our interests?" At the same time Leopold pointed out that even if some miracle brought an appointment at six or seven hundred florins, they would not go far in view of the inflation in unstable Bavaria. Alluding to the political maneuvering in play at the major courts of Europe, he warned that no one knew how long Karl Theodore would survive on his new throne: "I wager my soul that Munich musicians would take a reduction of a third in their salaries to get a job with a future. I say this not out of a desire to have you keep your position at home for a lifetime. In no way; absolutely not! I only want to know with certainty that our debts will be paid. . . . I am old; I cannot know when God will summon me to eternity. I do not want to die in debt; nor do I want it known that you were the cause of this indebtedness. [Once again Leopold removed himself from any role in the matter.] At the moment none but Herr Bullinger knows about this.[15] I do not want these obligations to occasion a wretched sale of our possessions upon my death, with half of the value tossed away."

Mozart took for granted that, no matter where he settled, his energies had to be applied to discharging the liabilities Leopold bewailed. He did

---

15 Delicate qualms from someone who ten days earlier had threatened to reveal all to Cannabich! Moreover, the Hagenauers, too, had a complete picture of the Mozarts' liabilities, if not of Leopold's assets.

not doubt his son's good intentions in the matter but, rather, his power to realize them and wanted him working under paternal eyes. As a final spur to force his return, Leopold painted the political situation in dramatic colors.

6

GOBBLING DOWN LOWER Bavaria had but whetted Emperor Joseph's appetite for the entire dish, and European diplomatic pouches now carried the outlines of his latest designs upon the electorate: a plan to absorb it outright. In exchange for the throne in Munich he offered Elector Karl Theodore much money, the Austrian Lowlands and, with them, the title of Burgundian King.[16] On the surface Joseph put forward an imaginative proposal to simplify German political geography, for Bavaria neighbored upon his hereditary domains just as the Lowlands did upon Karl Theodore's (the Pfalz). By 1785 Vienna would maneuver him into agreeing to this consolidation of territories, and only the bellicose reaction of his heirs and their allies, prodded by Frederick of Prussia, would put an end to the scheme.

At all events, in the closing months of Mozart's tour the proposed barter appeared on the way to becoming an astounding fact attended by perilous consequences. "If you [Wolfgang] have common sense, you will perceive at first glance that Salzburg is the best corner in which tranquilly, safely, and contentedly to await the dénouement," Leopold wrote at the end of 1778, as he began to elucidate "the dangerous prospect before Europe." He had deciphered the Emperor's grand ambitions with penetrating accuracy.

"Russia," Leopold observed, "has already declared her opposition to the Austrian occupation of [Lower] Bavaria. At the moment over 30,000 men stand ready to strengthen Prussia: all Lutheran or Protestant princes— [of] Sweden, Hanover, Hesse, Braunschweig, etc. . . . —some in private, some in public, have come to an understanding with Prussia. . . . If Russia lets loose, so will Turkey against the Russians; if Sweden and Hanover reinforce Prussia, then France will have to . . . call up auxiliaries for Austria. War will envelop the Reich . . . and, if he can, Prince Henry, will attempt with his Prussian army to invade Bavaria by way of Straubing. . . . In short, a terrible general war will break out."

---

16 As a youth, Emperor Charles V (like his father) had presided in Brussels as Duke of Burgundy, a title inherited through his grandmother, Mary of Burgundy. With refined cunning, Joseph held up before the House of Wittelsbach the allurement of this storied scepter, which he, as Emperor, had power to elevate to the kingship.

Leopold looked upon the "great plan to exchange territories" as a way to "maintain the balance in Europe" by reorganizing the Reich as an entity more "secure" not only "against attack by France" but also from within: he pictured Bohemia and Franconia "safe from Prussia," and—the master-stroke—the House of Wittelsbach "protected against onsets by Austria. . . . Perhaps this can be brought about if *Austria gets all of Bavaria* and in return *relinquishes* to the Elector *as much of the Lowlands* as equals the whole of Bavaria. The Elector would in consequence have territories closer to one another. . . ."

Wolfgang, his father, insisted, "must wait out this great epoch in a quiet corner, in particular because Prussia and Austria are summoning, one against the other, the whole of the Roman Empire. . . . Thus you [Wolfgang] see that there is imminent nothing less than a complete turning over and exchange of lands or a terrible war in which all of the powers will become entangled; and then the great will have things to think about quite remote from music and composers. . . . In short, a reasonable man must reflect upon eventualities, and there are a hundred other reasons, impossible to enumerate at the moment, that make it necessary for you to decide to spend a couple of years here."

The lesson in politics over, Leopold turned from instruction to censure, with lightning speed calling Wolfgang to account: "You departed Paris on 26 September. Had you traveled directly to Salzburg, I . . . *could have* paid off 100 florins of our debts. . . . I think that I have now made myself clear—or must I take the mail coach and fetch you myself? Certainly my son will not let things come to this pass!" They almost did.

Mozart thought himself "guilty of no fault . . . incompatible with being a Christian and a man of honor." But, for months, fear of again seeing his father had brought him close to despair. To find a way out of his quandary, he asked an old friend of Leopold's to play the mediator: the Munich flutist Becke was to arrange a truce between father and son. Becke's New Year's letter to Leopold struck the perfect tone, this vivid recital betraying the hand of a certain great dramatist to be.[17]

"I count this day [29 December] among my most satisfying. . . . I have had the good fortune to have your delightful son at my home almost the entire day. . . . He burns with desire to embrace his dearest and most cherished father, which will come to pass as soon as circumstances permit. Yet he quite lowered my spirits, too, for during the course of an hour I hardly succeeded

---

17 Mozart permitted his authorship to come into sight toward the end of the letter: the first person plural takes the place of what, in all consistency, should have been the first person singular.

in halting his tears. He has so good a heart; I have never seen a child whose bosom carries more feeling and love for his father than your son's.

"He has a gnawing [*kleine*] fear that your reception of him may not be as tender as he wishes. I, however, hope for something completely different of your paternal heart. Surely he deserves to have all love and pleasure at his father's side. His heart is so pure, so childlike, so candid toward me; how much more so will and must it be toward his father.

"Only to hear him speak vindicates him as the best of characters, the most honest and upright of men. And how many like this are there in the world? . . . Please write to us soon and assure us of your true fatherly love. . . . Make his stay in Salzburg truly agreeable and friendly. All his pleasure and delight have his father and sister as focus: apart from them he no longer recognizes anything in the world. [In short, Aloisia has set him aside.] Such things I write to you alone. . . ." The German reads like a translation of Richardson, and, indeed, Mozart knew his Richardson well.

"Such things," put forth as from the pen of a third party, astonished and embarrassed Leopold. "Taken aback," he replied to Wolfgang[18] gently and nobly: "If your tears, sadness, and deep anxiety have no other cause but that you doubt my love and tenderness for you, then you may sleep peacefully, eat and drink peacefully, and journey here still more peacefully. I now truly see that you do not fully know your father. It would appear from our friend's letter that this is the main reason for your sadness. Oh! I hope there is no other! [Leopold, of course, had learned why his son could "only weep."] You have no grounds to fear a chilly reception or disagreeable days with your sister and myself."

Herr Gschwendtner, the family friend[19] who had escorted Nannerl to the premiere of *La finta giardiniera*, regularly traveled from Salzburg to Munich on business. During his January visit he found himself entrusted with a delicate service: to realize Leopold's recent suggestion to Wolfgang that he return to the Hannibalplatz in Gschwendtner's "very comfortable carriage." "You could not find a more convenient opportunity and one more beneficial to your purse," Leopold had coaxed, moreover promising the young man, who so loved to dance, that he would be home in time for the first ball of the season. The mission succeeded: on either 14 or 15 January, Gschwendtner's carriage took the road to Salzburg carrying Mozart and, in all likelihood, the Bäsle, too.[20]

---

18 Leopold's reply to Becke has not survived.

19 Through his brother, Vital, who lived in Paris, he had advanced monies to Mozart and his mother.

20 Just when she went to Salzburg—at this time or somewhat later—remains uncertain. She spent several weeks with the Mozarts.

CHAPTER XXV

At Home:
Bucolic Salzburg

H E COULD HAVE been only just out of the coach when Leopold
had him sign a petition begging the Archbishop for reinstatement.
(Either Colloredo had rescinded the earlier understanding or this request
in Leopold's hand served to formalize it.) The document must have flown
to the Residenz: on 17 January 1779 Colloredo "graciously retained and
admitted the suppliant" with the understanding that he "irreproachably
and with unremitting diligence acquit himself of his required duties in the
cathedral as well as at court and in the music school [the *Kapellhaus*, where
he was to take on the keyboard lessons] and as far as possible serve the
court and the church with new works of his own composition."

At this point well nigh all important traces of Mozart's daily existence
vanish for the almost two years he again lived in his father's house. No occasion arose for their exchange of letters, and neither kept a journal,
though now and then Wolfgang did make entries, some of them impudent
and outrageous, in his sister's. Its blandness and complacency give a picture
of quotidian bourgeois life in bucolic Salzburg: in her hobbling German
she wrote of, to all seeming, perpetual confessions and mass-going; of
card-playing, meetings of the shooting society, exchanges of visits with
friends and neighbors, walks with Bimperl, and afternoon coffee and
chocolate. She also touched upon the round of music lessons (all three
Mozarts gave them); the goings and comings of father and son to and

from their duties at court; her excursions to the theater; music-making at home (social gatherings in the large salon of the Tanzmeisterhaus included old regulars like Bullinger and Schactner, now joined by the court castrato, Francesco Ceccarelli, and the oboist Fiala); and visits by her women friends, who time and again labored with the by now historic task of erecting her hair in the aristocratic manner. Her accounts, like Da Ponte's *Memoirs*, disappoint in their few significant references to her brother.

The family strove to regain something of the old spirit. Leopold had provided for his son's comfort, rearranging his room to accommodate a new press designed to house his wardrobe—he had long practiced dandyism, still cautious but on the increase—and stowing a clavichord beneath his writing table. There must have been good days. Wolfgang has left a charming glimpse of a quartet of young people taking chocolate in the oriel of Ignaz Joseph Hagenauer's chambers: the host (the landlord's son), Nannerl, the Bäsle, and himself. The three Mozarts no doubt enjoyed no less cozy hours together, and Leopold did show awareness that the Wolfgang who had returned was not the Wolfgang who had left. But in the long run father and son could only destroy one another's happiness.

The Bäsle remained Wolfgang's confidante and playmate; nothing more came of their camaraderie. She must have recognized the lethargic tempo of Salzburg as adverse to her temperament. That, for her ears, he began to call his sister "Zizibe," a sobriquet for a prudish, affected girl, suggests friction between Nannerl and the exuberant, unbuttoned visitor, who, it appears, departed Salzburg early in the spring. His letter to her of 24 April 1780, the first extant after this final separation, lays aside the boisterous private diction of his usual *Bäsle* manner: he opens with a moving expression of gratitude for one of her letters, "so beautiful that I do not know where to find words sufficient to attest my thanks to you for it," a clear reference to her having put a graceful end to the idea of their making a life together: he must have been grateful for a seemly coda to their play.

Some two weeks later, he wrote her again.[1] Beginning in his raucous and capricious manner, he ended with a tender tribute, an adaptation of Klopstock's *"Ode an Edone "*(1771), the changes making it into a hymn of appreciation for her visit to Salzburg and a celebration of their friendship. He sees her when "the evening darkens, when the moon shines. . . . Spirit, appear and transform thyself," he conjures, "and be my own little cousin."

---

1 In jest or error he headed this letter "10 May 1709." Long assigned to 10 May 1779, it dates, as internal references confirm, from just one year later. The third page contains Mozart's humorous drawing of his Bäsle, her hair piled high in the manner Nannerl affected (a joke at her expense?) and with firm bare breasts, the nipples prominent and erect.

The tone of lament and loss is unmistakable; but soon she would once more fade from his concerns.

2

THE DEEP CHANGE Mozart's personality underwent in the course of this final residence in Salzburg speaks for itself in the letters he wrote immediately afterward from Munich during the weeks (November 1780–January 1781) leading to the premiere of *Idomeneo.* His reports, observations, and queries to Leopold impart both a newly won quasi-domination that keeps watch against any intrusion, and a benevolent tolerance. The threat had become a stimulant: a good-natured, earnest Mozart seeks his father's professional advice, their exchanges being between equals. The young man who on his tour had gone from crisis to crisis, each time righting himself with more difficulty, had somehow found a clarification of self, redefined his position, and achieved emotional equilibrium and psychological independence, developments all the more remarkable in that no love affair had lent him support in turning aside Leopold's bitter moods. The contest proved less strenuous than Mozart had feared; perhaps he had even found it sportive. Pride and detachment suffuse the inspired nonsense he scribbled at home in Nannerl's diary and the dispatches he sent from Munich. In the late morning of his brief life he had learned how to play a different kind of amiable lunatic and, at the same time, the man of affairs. Time had whetted the edge of his satire, paradox becoming one with axiom. An assured Wolfgang Mozart sat down to write *Idomeneo,* a composer bemused by his own brilliance and ready to face a challenge equal to it. Somehow, during those twenty-two months at home he had hustled himself into man's estate and emerged from his torn condition with his sense of self protected. What had brought about this transformation?

Biography abhors a vacuum, and the absence of substantial material encourages the temptation to carry a few facts further than justifiable. Aware that conjecture and psychological speculation are not history, for all that, it goes against the grain to resist theorizing upon the nature of the relationship between father and son right after Wolfgang crawled back to Salzburg.

Since they had to live and work together, Leopold no doubt felt it expedient to sum up Wolfgang's account of moral conduct so as to produce a supportable balance, though, beneath whatever accommodation and conviviality they managed, something dark lurked. It would seem that the main factor in Wolfgang's swift personal recovery, indeed, victory, lay in what he found in the Tanzmeisterhaus: not what had terrified him from afar—the fulminating Leopold of the letters, his pen as a sword in hand—but an aging, defeated father who, away from his inkwell, lacked the spirit to take command and excited in his son not trepidation and aggression but pity and something of the old affection. Never again would Leopold gather even the traces of control.

No doubt he continued to look upon Wolfgang as a tangled garden that from time to time had to be weeded and trimmed. But the Munich letters make clear that by the end of 1780 the father's position in the household had become less than the son's. When the canker of resentment now and then discharged its venom—"If I had been with your mother [during her illness] I am confident she would still be alive"—he let the unpleasantness pass, realizing that in this ritual Leopold but flailed himself. He had sent her on a mission she could not fulfill, on a journey from which she could not return.

If Wolfgang had found sufficient distance to pardon his father's explosions of impotence and guilt and moved to break through the embarrassment hedging their relationship, the barrier to what he himself felt about his mother's death remains impenetrable. He may have felt very little: he appears to have preserved not a remnant of identification with her; or perhaps his composure after her death and his quick erasure of remembrance helped open routes of escape from the hardship of mourning. One searches his post-Paris letters in vain for any sense of loss regarding this prop of devotion and affection who had so feared for his journey through life (though the absence of evidence does not constitute evidence of absence). Upon his return from Paris, his difficult personal situation occupied him to the full, and sentiment found little part in his new inventory of purposes and problems.

To be back must have seemed to him a penance all the more wretched for not having been self-imposed. More than ever he beheld in the ecclesiastics and courtiers of Salzburg only men of narrow hearts and little minds, blusterers of petty grandeur, ineffectual pawns on Europe's political chessboard. The archbishopric seemed to him oppressive in its monotony and bovine dreariness, boggy ground on which to build: a climate unpropitious to harmonizing aspirations with reality.

Though painful reflection had made him acknowledge his *Wunderkind* days of golden glory as irrecoverable and nostalgia about them as unprofitable, throughout his life he continued to nurture expectations of privilege; even as he hung about his neck the albatross of Salzburg service, he did not undercut these expectations, resolving to reconcile himself only for a while to thwarted fulfillment and a submissive manner. But how long could he persevere in soldiering on disguised in a mask that covered his face badly? Capable of measuring himself, he never measured too small; aware of possessing musical gifts no one had possessed to greater degree, Wolfgang Mozart could not have long resisted flaunting defiance and contempt in his cap like Fluellen's leek. It must be assumed that his return to court began with a show of well-bred disaffection and distaste: in the habit of playing Thomas to anyone who presented himself as godlike, he could hardly have greeted the Archbishop with a *Pater peccavi.*

He produced little more than what his new position and patrons demanded; but despite his retrospective description of his life at this time as insular and leaden, his work as burdensome, and his spirit as depressed, the passivity and listlessness that had overwhelmed him in Paris had, in fact, dissipated almost at once: even in the face of a court and a public content to have him grind grists from the same old sacks, he created a series of masterpieces implicit with new directions. (Salzburg's calm did have its blessings.) His musical development, from childhood gradual and without crisis—apart from the dislocated temper of more than one of the Parisian creations—continued without effort. This process, implausibly orderly and homogeneous, led to a phase of further refinement, to works of a quality he was to equal but never surpass. Scrutinizing the past not in a single mirror but in many and manipulating in full-blooded mastery his inherited and accumulated polyglot vocabulary, he now commanded a style deceptively simple on the surface but filled with intricacies and elegances, a style of cultured grace that did not exclude a distilled sensuality so complex, penetrating, and compelling as to ennoble as it seduces.

3

DURING THIS FINAL Salzburg period, his church music reached a new eloquence in two masses in C (K. 317 of March 1779, the so-called Coronation Mass, and K. 337 of exactly one year later)[2] and two settings, likewise in C, of the vesper service (K. 321 and K. 339, also of 1779 and 1780, respectively).

2 The tradition linking K. 317 to the crowned icon in the church of Maria Plain has proved apocryphal; indeed, practical musicians have wondered how its cramped spaces could have accommodated the forces the score demands. The mass's nickname derives from Salieri's having conducted it at three Habsburg coronations: Leopold II's crowning as both German Emperor (Frankfurt, 1790) and King of Bohemia (Prague, 1791), as well as Francis II's as German Emperor (Frankfurt, 1792), the First Reich's last Imperial investiture. The Hofburg began to refer to the work as a coronation mass. K. 337, which Salieri also performed during these ceremonies, for a while bore the same sobriquet.

The full chorus dominates both masses despite the vocal solos it gener-
ates and the formal "arias" in the Agnus Dei movements[3] (composed for
the soprano voice of Maria Magdalena Lipp-Haydn). Though, as if to
placate a Colloredo listening with watch in hand, Mozart often enough
propelled the music headlong in the manner of his earlier Salzburg masses,
the two works, in particular the second, offer greater inner substance and,
further, an outward glamour the imaginative use of a rich orchestra bestows. Along with strings, organ, and tympani, K. 317 has pairs of oboes,
horns, and trumpets and also three trombones, K. 337 using the same instruments except that bassoons replace the horns. Moreover, the organ
contributes auxiliary flourishes: in K. 317 to an ambitious epistle sonata (K.
329/317a); in K. 337 to both the Agnus Dei and another epistle sonata (K.
336/336d) taking the form of a diminutive concerto. These showy moments for keyboard gave Mozart the pleasure of exhibiting himself at the
cathedral's great organ.

Festive and celebrative, K. 317 has a golden texture; with its lively surface
effects and light-filled, softly brushed technique, this mass partakes of the
Rococo, preserving that *grazia* and decorum inherent in its finest productions. Although K. 317 does have introspective sections when, for example,
the words implore God's mercy or speak of the Incarnation and Crucifix-
ion, most of the score hurls itself forward, aglow with excitement. In contrast, K. 337, grayish and silvery in tone, a somber, twilight Missa solemnis
and the last mass Mozart would complete, has a sacramental earnestness
and doctrinal conviction proclaiming purposes higher than racing, however
gleamingly, through the text; K. 337 pauses and with weight affirms its lofty
ambitions: in the magical hush with which the Dona nobis pacem ends and
in the somber Benedictus cast in a severe, almost Handelian fugal style.
With its expressive power and profound intent, K. 337 points toward the
two great mass torsos to come.

For the two vespers or evensong services—*Vesperae de Dominica* (Sunday
vespers, K. 321) and *Vesperae solennes de confessore* (solemn vespers for a saint's
day, K. 339)—liturgical use called for six movements: psalms 110–113 and
117 (King James numbering) with the Magnificat (Luke 1:46–55) as
postlude.[4] The pair of vespers has more than words in common: in each,
an idiom homophonic in essence but of remarkable fluidity governs; in

---

3 The Countess's arias in *The Marriage of Figaro* derive from these liturgical solos: "*Dove sono*" from the
  aria in K. 317, "*Porgi amor*" from that in K. 337, poignant melodic ideas first conceived in connection with the Lamb of God's sufferings becoming points of departure for depicting Countess
  Almaviva's. The Kyrie of K. 317, moreover, anticipates Fiordiligi's "*Come scoglio*" in *Così fan tutte.*
4 K. 321a, a seven-measure fragment, may be what survives of an earlier attempt at the Magnificat
  of K. 321.

each, as in Mozart's contemporary masses, a four-part chorus at times yields to soloists, the *Laudate Dominum* taking the form of an extended soprano aria; in each, the orchestra (though it lacks the variety of winds in the masses) quickens the high pathos and drama Mozart drew from the vigor of the psalms and the ecstasy of Mary's canticle. Devotional in function, for all that, the settings dispense a theatrical aura; unlike the tonally unified masses, they explore a wide variety of key, a bold course held in tension by balanced opening and closing sections in C. Moreover, as in the masses, the web of sound pulsates with the subtlest cross references to the melodic contours of Gregorian incipits associated with the texts.

The conduct of the worship imposes its own cohesiveness through the stubborn repetition of the lesser doxology (the Gloria Patri) after each section. In an inspired musical game, Mozart turned to advantage a necessity that might otherwise have proved wearying: the musical variety of the verbally inviolate and recurring formula provides one of his vespers' delights. (Is it irreverent to find a parallel in the prodigal harmonic and coloristic changes he would ring upon Osmin's refrain of "Trallalera" in *The Abduction*?) No less impressive is the learned counterpoint in the *Laudate pueri* movements, doubtless a calculated indecorum signaling both his difficulty in consistently wearing the professional disguise Colloredo required of him and his lack of concern always to maintain it.[5]

With the weight and commanding voice of grand oratorios, the vespers pursue a musical articulation of feeling that takes on magisterial dimension as they assume the epic stride of the Handelian baroque, here reawakened to vigorous life and filled with thunderous scoldings and exultant hosannas. Mozart had begun to reap the Handelian harvest,[6] whose full measure would come to him later in Vienna. His sense of the significant word and phrase drives these scores forward in a flow combining tension and ease, fluctuations at once quicksilver and inevitable, his inspiration burning intensely throughout as he dissolves the drama of the words into music. With their great presence and their coherence of meaning and method, the vespers stand as major landmarks of the Mozartean canon. With good reason he thought highly of them.

---

5 Here Mozart could invoke tradition as justification: composers often fell into a contrapuntal style when setting the *Laudate pueri.*

6 K. 276/321b of 1779, Mozart's final setting of the Regina Coeli, one of the Church's four great antiphons invoking the Virgin, also dates from these Salzburg years. While he cast two previous versions (K. 108/74d of May 1771 and K. 127 of one year later) as a series of movements, he housed K. 276 within a single energetic and highly concentrated Allegro in baroque style. A jubilant creation for four-voiced chorus (with soloists) and orchestra, it time and again unashamedly recalls Handel's Hallelujah chorus.

The desire to create works with deep perspective, evident in the vespers, informs the celebrated sinfonia concertante for violin and viola (K. 364/320d in E flat) of summer 1779. Perhaps he intended it for Leopold and himself as a second step toward building a new family repertory[7]—he played the viola with fluency and bore it, unlike the violin, no resentment—for earlier that year he had composed a two-piano concerto, K. 365/316a,[8] to perform with Nannerl; or, perhaps, as in Paris and Mannheim, a local taste for concertos with more than one soloist had grown. During the same summer or the following autumn, he started work on a triple concerto or sinfonia concertante[9] for violin, viola, and violoncello (K. Anh. 104/320e), whose surviving fragment, like that of the Mannheim double concerto, augurs greatness.[10] That he almost always worked ad hoc resulted in serious losses.

Casting off every vestige of formula, the three-movement K. 364 has not a superfluous note to distract from the clarity of its graceful musical thought; nothing of the virtuoso's delight in difficulties for the purpose of vanquishing them; all is spaciousness, poise, and noble reserve: even the Mannheim rocket launched in the opening Allegro maestoso takes its place as an unobtrusive organic element in the movement's construction. Intimacy binds the soloists one to the other and to the orchestra: all converse as equals in a powerful, rhetorical but economical style whose riches are this very economy. The path to the piano concertos and symphonies of Mozart's final years opens with this sovereign composition.

If K. 364 brings together elements of the concerto grosso and the concerto, the components coalescing into a bewitching accommodation offering no suggestion of competition, the smiling, extrovert concerto for two pianos, also in E flat, presents quite another face—one of joyous rivalry. Though, with its histrionic pronouncements, the orchestra does take an ac-

---

7 Musicians who balance a less than virtuoso technique with superior taste can succeed in the soloists' parts, which thus lay within the capabilities of both Mozarts.

8 This traditional dating has been challenged.

9 Some would maintain that a delight in virtuosity along with a limited enthusiasm for development set the sinfonia concertante apart from the usual concerto for multiple soloists. However, neither characteristic bears upon K. 364. The suspicion obtains that no proper distinction existed and that Mozart, having taken up the more fashionable synonym in Paris, simply continued to use it in Salzburg.

10 Both the unfinished triple concerto and the violin/viola concerto employ the device of the scordatura, a purposeful mistuning: in K. 364 the viola soloist's part is written and played a half tone lower than it sounds, the soloist, in compensation, having pitched the instrument a semitone higher than the norm. In consequence, a brighter tone (especially if the strings are fine) shines above the orchestral sound and places the violist on the same level of intensity as the violinist. At the same time, the scordatura permitted positions (on the fingerboard) affording the violist an easier task, especially in the case of a small hand. (Mozart's?).

tive role,[11] the heart of K. 365 lies in the spirited interplay between the soloists: their good-humored repartee carries all before them as they spar and reconcile. The concerto avails itself of devices more massive than subtle: the opening Allegro sets the mood with a pompous flourish (a family joke concerning the Parisians?), and, introspective moments notwithstanding, an amiable bantering prevails, broad contrasts of loud and soft creating a monochromatic but strong color scheme. If the refinements of K. 364 are not to be sought here, the rollicking athleticism amply rewards.

Another big work, K. 320, a seven-movement serenade of August 1779, must have embellished one of the city's private (the university?) or court functions. It begins with an Adagio maestoso ushering in an Allegro con spirito sensuous in sound and replete with those Mannheim mannerisms and baroque musical gestures Mozart delighted in parodying. With a somewhat heavy tread, an ensuing Menuetto leads to the twofold ornament of the serenade: an Andante grazioso and a Rondeau that together constitute a discrete sinfonia concertante, pairs of flutes and oboes forming a solo ensemble of exquisite conversationalists. (In Vienna, Mozart would press these movements into service as an independent composition.) In the succeeding D-minor Andantino, foreboding intrudes upon a hitherto confident, at times swaggering, world. Its assertive spirit returns in a Menuetto whose second trio displays the *cor di posta* (post horn) giving the serenade its nickname. Mozart's resort to this street instrument (Salzburgers heard it announce the mail diligence) has inspired the fable that it signaled his longings once again to quit Salzburg;[12] more likely, it attempted a touch of folk humor in the tradition of Leopold's sleigh bells and toy instruments. A hurtling Presto concludes a serenade Mozart studded with touches of mocking humor and framed with a pair of marches (K. 335/320a, 1 & 2). They, the minuets, and the concertante movements fell away when, during the next decade, he turned K. 320 into a three-movement symphony.

Less imposing in scale than K. 320 but with no fewer felicities, K. 334/320b, a divertimento in six movements (not including the march enveloping it, K. 445/320c) written for the Robinigs and scored for string quartet and a pair of obbligato horns, figures among Mozart's most subtle accomplishments of these Salzburg years. Its Andante in particular proffers measures of surpassing beauty; this D-minor theme and its six variations

---

11 In Vienna, Mozart would augment the winds in the outer movements, adding clarinets and trumpets (along with drums) to the original pairs of oboes, bassoons, and horns.

12 This myth spawned another: the opening movement as depicting an argument between the composer and the Archbishop.

exude a despair foreshadowing the finale of his string quartet in the same key, K. 421/417b. Yet, from the Andante's tragic evocation, Mozart could at one bound leap into the humorous strut of the first Menuetto (except for *Don Giovanni's* his most famous), eerie horn sonorities adding touches of the menacing. Even a summary appreciation cannot keep from extolling both the elegiac mystery suffusing the two trios contained in the second of the pair of minuets and also the penetrating rhetoric of the Adagio separating them. In its high pathos this divertimento, like K. 364, presages *Idomeneo*.

Mozart composed three symphonies during this stay in Salzburg, all, it would appear, for performance at court. He cast the first, K. 318 in G of April 1779, as a single tripartite movement: an Allegro spiritoso enclosing an Andante. Instinct with energy and calling for two pairs of horns, the work has theatrical qualities that have inspired attempts to relate it (as an overture or sinfonia teatrale) to one or another drama. More lightly scored, thematically integrated, and courtly, the second of the symphonies, K. 319 in B flat of the following July, seems at heart a chamber work.[13] The third of this trio takes pride of place: the three-movement K. 338 of August 1780. In C major, Olympian in tone, and of concentrated vigor, it may have been the Mozart symphony Bonno conducted in Vienna (1781) with an orchestra that included forty violins, ten violas, eight violoncellos, ten double basses, six bassoons, and with the remaining winds doubled (see p. 534). Mozart rejoiced in this luxuriant rendition of what he identified simply as "my symphony."[14]

4

BY SPRING OF 1779 Salzburg could provide Mozart a consoling diversion: attending performances of Johann Heinrich Böhm's troupe at the new theater. (Before it opened, itinerant companies seeking a stage in the city had to solicit an invitation to appear at the Residenz or else make do with the cramped facilities of either the City Hall or the tavern on the Waagplatz.) Böhm offered a schedule of tragedies, comedies, farces, singspiele, ballets, and mixed genres. The following year Emanuel Schikaneder's players succeeded Böhm's[15] and presented a no less varied repertory.

---

13 Originally in three movements, K. 319 acquired a minuet early in the Vienna years. In it Mozart exploited his motto (see p. 200) as he had in the opening Allegro and the Andante.

14 Some believe the Paris Symphony the recipient of Bonno's grand treatment.

15 Having contracted with the Residenz to bring his company back to Salzburg for the 1779–1780 winter season, Böhm reappeared in September. However, soon tempted by more promising opportunities in Mainz and Frankfurt, he sought to terminate the agreement obliging him to

Wolfgang and Leopold established ties with both companies, and their personnel became familiars at the Tanzmeisterhaus. The Mozarts received the privilege of free seats at any performance, and, in return, Wolfgang provided each ensemble with music: for Schikaneder's an aria (K. Anh. 11a/365a)[16] for a play indebted to Gozzi (see XXVI, n. 42); for Böhm's the revised and expanded incidental music to *Thamos*; and it stands to reason that Mozart put his hand to the singspiel version of his *La finta giardiniera* that Böhm presented in Salzburg during the 1779–1780 season;[17] further, Mozart had such touring troups in mind—as well as Emperor Joseph and his newly founded *Nationaloperette*[18]—when beginning work on the singspiel known as *Zaide* (K. 344/336b) during the summer of 1780.

Though the new theater enhanced Salzburg's theatrical life, those acquainted with great cities recognized its provincial level. Despite his pleasure in the visiting actors, Mozart complained: "If only [Salzburg] had a dramatic troupe worthy of the name," and with pain Schikaneder learned that what succeeded with more sophisticated audiences might easily fall to the ground in Salzburg. So naïve that it could confuse art and life, the Salzburg public had been known to intervene in the action to keep a villain from a foul deed and then pursue the offending actor to his inn to upbraid and even threaten him. Nannerl Mozart, despite her wide travels not untypical of the town's theatergoers, enjoyed dramas that made her sick with weeping: "I cried so much at the play that I came home with a headache," she proudly recorded.

Mozart's failure to complete *Zaide* may be set down to a quandary: on the one hand, to create a singspiel responsive to the high-flown suffering in which the public of Germany's lesser towns took mawkish delight (such a work would be all the more useful to traveling companies); on the other, to satisfy Vienna's inclination toward comedy lightly seasoned with the serious—tomfoolery touched with tears. Only later would he comprehend

---

remain until Ash Wednesday. In turn, the Archbishop made known (October 1779) his intention to seize the troupe's wardrobe and perhaps Böhm himself should he betray the slightest disposition to slip the players out of town. Schikaneder's actors would seem to have had a couple of short runs in Salzburg during the summer of 1780. They took over the theater in September, remaining until February 1781.

16 He had already composed arias for visiting troupes during the mid-seventies: K. 209, 209a (a fragment), 210, 255, and 256.

17 An entry Mozart made in Nannerl's diary during March 1780 details a concert probably given in the salon of their home, the items including a performance by Johann Georg Murschhauser, one of Böhm's tenors, of what must have been Don Anchise's first aria in *La finta giardiniera*.

18 On 17 December 1777, Emperor Joseph had authorized the establishment of a national singspiel troupe (*Nationaloperette*) to be allied with his theater of spoken drama at Vienna's Burgtheater. Under the directorship of Ignaz Umlauf, the new company began life just two months later (with his *Die Bergknappen*) and would survive until March 1783.

and embrace this Viennese formula and hit the mark with *The Abduction from the Seraglio*. In Salzburg, however, even as he clung to hopes of *Zaide's* production in the Habsburg capital, he gave way to propitiating a less than metropolitan taste; if his aesthetic dilemma did not impale his capacities, it did impede them: *Zaide* remained unfinished. What survives of it comprises a series of fifteen numbers: a chorus, arias, ensembles, and Melodramas in the manner of Benda. The connective spoken text is lacking, as are overture (Mozart usually wrote it last), denouement, and title, the last a gap tradition has filled with the heroine's name.

The avuncular Schachtner, it appears certain, produced the libretto, and Mozart, lifelong a declared enemy of literary excess, the "outlandish," and the "unusual," set about composing a text whose noble literary course could at moments bend toward sentimental claptrap. Perhaps he found compensation in making two of the stronger scenes into Melodramas. To plant such Benda-like passages within the body of a singspiel revealed a Mozart venturing beyond ready-made models in an effort to deepen his colors as a dramatist, an unusual boldness on his part: as a rule he practiced an adventurous conservatism, his work testifying to an invigorated and transformed continuity, not to sweeping change.

Yet he did stamp the Melodramas in *Zaide* with the imprint of the new: they, in fact, approach the following century's romantic naturalism. Sprinkled with expressive instrumental phrases, they have compelling effect, though these recitations amplified by music could not have mixed comfortably with *Zaide's* purely spoken dialogue (conversations Mozart would in time recognize as too drawn out). Only new concepts of transition or connection could make this innovative synthesis hold, and the young composer, whose art would one day become the very measure of subtle coherence, could perhaps not yet discover them. At all events, his cutting off work on *Zaide* constituted his abandonment of the Melodrama. In *The Abduction* he would lay his work out in a more conventional design, outline with a sharper edge, harden his forms, and rigorously separate their functions. Pasha Selim speaks without music.

In all likelihood, Mozart called his drama *Das Serail* (*The Seraglio*), the title of a contemporary (1777) singspiel whose text by Franz Josef Sebastiani (it had music by Johann Joseph Friebert) Schachtner ransacked for his libretto. Sebastiani's *Serail* rests in considerable part upon Voltaire's drama *Zaïre*.[19] It

---

19 In 1777 Leopold Mozart attended a performance of *Zaïre* in the Salzburg theater. Here Michael Haydn's incidental music (see XVIII, n. 13) provided a due measure of so-called Turkish noise (as a rule, piccolo, triangle, cymbals, and drums). In *The Abduction* Mozart would give the Viennese a generous allotment of it; what survives of his more doleful *Zaide* has none of these strident, colorful sounds.

tells of three Christians of noble birth languishing in slavery to a sultan. At first glance reminiscent of *The Abduction*, the situation takes a different turn in Voltaire's and Sebastiani's hands: the prisoners discover themselves to be father, son, and daughter, relationships continuing—a logical assumption—among Allazim, Gomatz, and Zaide in Schactner's scenario for Mozart.

Voltaire's *Zaïre* permits a tentative reconstruction of *Zaide*: unlike Sebastiani's *Serail*, which ends in accommodation, it may have culminated in an act of violence, as did Voltaire's tragedy, wherein the heroine sinks down under the blade of the Sultan, ignorant of the family relationships and carried away by jealousy of the brother he perceives as a rival. With vividness Mozart's score develops two strong characters moving toward catastrophe: Sultan Soliman displays his towering capacity for violence and Zaide her no less vehement rage as she defies his threats—the Mozart biographer Otto Jahn wondered how a happy denouement could possibly issue from this situation!—the fury of both born of the passionate attachment growing between the younger captives. If the general line of Schachtner's plot followed Voltaire's, the bloody act provided the solution to this Wagnerian crisis.[20] But there can be no certainty: Mozart suspended work on *Zaide* before reaching the finale.

Beneath the surface of *Zaide's* extravagant pathos and modish, picturesque *turquerie* lies a serious fantasy of an old culture breaking up; of escape from the inequities of absolutism to freedom, fulfillment, and the promise of life; of mankind, with its propensities toward good and evil, in the end following the nobler instinct. In Voltaire's *Zaïre*, the Sultan emerges from his dark emotions: aghast at his butchery, he frees the hero and his father and then kills himself. Whatever turns the plot of *Zaide* may have taken, clearly Mozart strung its music on the same or a similar moral thread: the singspiel unfolds in the earnest world of Lessing; the main protagonists embody moral concepts no less elevated than Metastasio's, the mold still heroic, but agitated and German rather than measured and Roman; criticizing the inegalitarian tendencies at work in society and speaking in the voice of *wahre Menchlichkeit* (true humanity) for the oppressed and the outlawed, this bizarre, *larmoyant* German "operetta seria" put forward in clear focus the humanizing inwardness that would be a permanent element in Mozart's mature works for the stage.

---

20 The heroine's ardor for her brother does not form part of Voltaire's drama: here she falls in love with the Sultan. In Christoph Friedrich Bretzner's *Belmonte und Constanze* the hero proves to be the Sultan's son, a motif Mozart and his librettist discarded when they turned Bretzner's book into *The Abduction* (see p. 595).

Yet, from the first, the enslaved Gomatz holds himself aloof from his less well-born fellow prisoners; for him freedom and equality do not constitute an equation: as in *The Magic Flute*, the hero labors in a stratified Voltairean world, not midst the simplicities of collectivism. Release can bring him only physical freedom: he has always been inwardly free. Mozart may well have found something of himself in Gomatz—youthful, magnanimous, but remote, and, at times, gauche.[21]

Not only Gomatz but Zaide and the Sultan, too, harbor ambiguities Mozart exploited: her rash, almost mad defiance—in her aria "*Tiger! Wetze nur die Klauen,*" anticipating Constanze's audacious, if more stately, heroism in "*Martern aller Arten*"—little comports with the young harem-favorite's earlier and diffident presentation of herself in an exquisite lullaby of soothing symmetries (*Ruhe sanft*), filled with niceties of phrase and recalling Christian Bach and Grétry; and the Sultan's fierce fluctuations of humor in two striking arias, "*Der stolze Löw'*" and "*Ich bin so bös als gut,*" reveal the volatile and often demonic forces loose within him. (In contrast, Allazim continues rocklike and unequivocal throughout, his aria on equality, "*Ihr Mächtigen,*" gaining its effect from a steady but impassioned rhetorical drive.)

Zaide drew not only from Melodrama, *opera seria*, and *opéra comique*, but also turned to account a specialty of the singspiel tradition: the comic bass aria, here Osmin's "*Wer hungrig.*" (He figured in the action not as the Sultan's housemaster, the role another Osmin would play in *The Abduction*, but as a slave dealer supplying the harem.) In contrast to Osmin's singspiel ways, Zaide and Gomatz, in their exaggerated solemnity, belong in spirit to the world of the *seria*, though his aria of thanks to Allazim ("*Herr und Freund*"), inspired by Gluck's lighter vein, has comic touches of an engaging confusion.

The commonplace opening chorus in the manner of Johann Adam Hiller apart, *Zaide*'s ensembles felicitously depict the flow and fluctuation of the passions: the lovers' delectable duet ("*Meine Seele hüpft*"); the trio ("*O selige Wonne!*") sung by the three Christians, a spiritual outpouring that darkens as Zaide descries in the heavens an omen of calamity; and the quartet in which the Sultan joins them ("*Freundin, stille deine Tränen*"). In trio and quartet Mozart's alchemy transmutes leaden words into gleaming gold; these are moments both human and transcendent, prodigies of his expanding genius.

---

21 Perhaps Mozart heard other personal echoes in this tale of father and son in forced service to an overlord: behind his back Salzburgers called Colloredo *Grossultan*.

No less transcendent, the final version of the incidental music to *Thamos*[22] dates from this period of his fitful attempts somehow to turn Benda's Melodrama to his own advantage. In all likelihood, Böhm's Salzburg performances of the play included the premiere of the complete enlarged score. Its fourth number, a curiosity, would seem to be the orchestral component of a Melodrama. How this music underlined or alternated and intertwined with the heroine's declaimed vow dedicating her virginity to the sun god remains conjectural, for only a succession of key words as superscriptions, rather than the full text, appears in Mozart's manuscript, which, moreover, does not indicate the pauses for recitation.[23]

In this last reworking of his *Thamos* music, he dropped the concluding orchestral piece, substituting for it an extended vocal composition for bass soloist, chorus, and orchestra. He charged this grand elegiac utterance in D minor, the words probably by Schachtner, with intimations of *Don Giovanni* and *The Magic Flute*. In respect to the entr'actes (see p. 316), Mozart had ventured to quit the treadmill of inherited ideas: if tradition demanded that such interludes reflect the mood of the preceding and not prefigure the following stage action, he looked upon them as free both to ruminate and to anticipate. Here he followed the thinking of his father and the example of Michael Haydn.

Mozart's affection for the scores of *Thamos* and *Zaide* had to do not only with their quality but also with his joy in writing for the stage. He much regretted their miscarriage. *Zaide*, fallen between two aesthetic categories, had never come to term, while the *Thamos* music, he was to learn, had no future in the city once again most in his mind: though the play had suffered shipwreck in Vienna (1774), he had hopes that one of its stages might undertake a revival, and he would be crushed to discover that the city's pundits had fixed *Thamos* in the category of "discarded works." He

---

22 Mozart's undimmed enthusiasm for *Thamos* gives notice of what would become an increasing and abiding attraction to dramas concerning a father's abdication before a son. Thamos's father, Rameses, has deposed Menes, King of Egypt, and seized the scepter. However, contrary to general belief, Menes did not succumb to assassins but, disguised under the name of Sethos, has become high priest of the temple of the sun. Thamos is to assume power upon the death of his ruthless, usurping father. Menes, who, in the role of Sethos, has witnessed the virtue of this young prince, steps forward and reassumes the crown long enough to see his enemies dispersed, bless the union of his daughter, Sais, with Thamos, and leave him the throne of Egypt: the idealized father gives way before the idealized son.

23 Some look upon the words as cues Mozart inserted to jog his memory of the text as he composed an exclusively instrumental interlude representing Sais's frame of mind. Alfred Einstein, finding the music "scarcely comprehensible in itself," believed it to be the accompaniment to a pantomime.

would write from Vienna early in 1783: "I am truly sorry that I shall not be able to use the music to *Thamos*... it should be given for the sake of the music alone—but this is scarcely to be. What a terrible shame!"

The only chance for salvage lay in finding another drama to which the incidental music might be fitted. Around 1785 Böhm would succeed in incorporating a simplified version of it into the closing act of Karl Martin Plümicke's *Lanassa* (derived from Antoine-Marin Lemierre's *La Veuve de Malabar*), at the same time pressing the moody symphony K. 184 into service as an overture. During Mozart's last visit to Frankfurt (1790), Böhm's company, resident in the city, had *Lanassa* on the boards, and thus the composer had the opportunity to hear his beloved score once again, even if in a debased version.[24]

It cannot be doubted that Mozart intervened to assure that the libretto of *The Magic Flute* incorporated elements of *Thamos* and *Zaide*. Under new names, his last singspiel perpetuates several of the play's protagonists: Pamina derives from Thamos's love, Sais, as does Prince Tamino from Thamos; the Queen of the Night owes much to the figure of the treacherous priestess Mirza, and Sarastro has no less a debt to the priest-king, Sethos-Menes. Along with these characters from the drama, *The Magic Flute* took on its Masonic Egyptian trappings and its symbolic struggle between sun and shadow, while also drawing upon the playwright's main source, Terrasson's *Sethos*. Above all, by way of Constanze in *The Abduction*, *Zaide*'s courage as well as her moral refinement and belief in the human capacity for benevolence descended to the heroine of *The Magic Flute*.[25] As its official librettist, Schikaneder had the difficult task of weaving comic episodes into this heavy fabric.

---

24 Only after the choruses of *Thamos* had acquired religious texts in Latin and German did some of this incidental music take on a wide public life. In its masquerade as the Latin motet *Splendente te Deus* (K. Anh. 121/Anh. B [zu K. 345/336a]), the opening chorus praising the sun formed the offertory of a service Antonio Salieri conducted as part of the ceremonies in Prague celebrating Leopold II's coronation as King of Bohemia (1791; see p. 731).

25 The temptation beckons to see a formal link between Gomatz and Tamino in that both use the portrait aria; but it counted as an operatic commonplace: Belfiore in Mozart's *La finta giardiniera*, for example, sings praises to the likeness of Arminda.

CHAPTER XXVI

The Second Bavarian Miracle

L ATE SUMMER OF 1780 brought Mozart his second Bavarian miracle: five years earlier, Elector Maximilian III Joseph had called him to Munich to write *La finta giardiniera*; now he received a summons from Karl Theodore, again to compose an opera for Carnival. Documentation of this work begins with Mozart's arrival in Munich on 6 November 1780, in his luggage those sections of the score already in progress: he had begun choruses and recitatives as well as arias for those in the cast with voices familiar to him and had marked out the opera's broad masses and tonal course. His letters from Munich, though they concentrate upon both his relationships with his artists and revisions in the libretto, have, in addition, detail sufficiently rich and widespread to support reasonable inferences about the opera's origins and the circumstances hedging its development.

That earlier conversation in Mannheim's Palais Heydeck (see p. 386) had helped determine the bestowal of the commission. ("Slow and steady wins the race," the Elector now remarked to Mozart in Italian, clapping him on the shoulder.) And, most vital, Cannabich's recommendation had been strong; if he once harbored ambivalence about the young Salzburger as a rival, it had vanished, for he asked his patroness, Countess Maria Josepha Paumgarten, the Elector's favorite of the moment, to lend her support; with generosity she stood forth as midwife to the enterprise. Of her and her family Mozart observed: "This is the best and most useful house for me here. It enabled my project to get going and . . . to move along."

For the Countess, a student of singing, he wrote the concert aria "*Misera, dove son! / Ah! non son' io*" (K. 369, scored for pairs of flutes and horns in addition to the quartet of strings), the words from Metastasio's *Ezio*. The Elector's *chère amie* as Fulvia, lamenting the loss of her "innocent husband" and imploring the gods to strike her down with a thunderbolt, must have raised eyebrows. Here Mozart appears to have been having fun: proposing a game in which she agreed to join. The aria posits a quick and uncommon intimacy with the highborn family.[1]

Even with the Paumgartens' goodwill, he could not have made a beginning without the nod of Count Seeau, who, for the moment, found wisdom in following the course indicated by his Prince's mistress. Further, the orchestra and singers, in particular Raaff and the Wendlings, contributed toward encouraging an atmosphere sympathetic to a composer whose gifts they knew at first hand. If Leopold's role had become that of bystander, at least he could bask in vindication of his insistence that Wolfgang return from Paris, of his contention that in time Munich would open its doors. A measure of content returned to the house on the Hannibalplatz.

Karl Theodore had not fallen in with all of Mozart's entreaties at the Palais Heydeck: Munich did not order the serious opera in German he longed to write, but, rather, an *opera seria* in Metastasian-style Italian verse, which was to tell the story of King Idomeneus of Crete. As its point of departure, the new text was to use a French libretto dating from the reign of Louis XIV: an *Idoménée* by Antoine Danchet. André Campra had set it to music in 1712. Considering that as recently as 1774 Christian Bach's *Lucio Silla* had failed at Karl Theodore's Mannheim theater for the very reason that it was an *opera seria* (see p. 149), questions arise as to why he and his circle, sympathetic to innovation, chose this timeworn form for the vital young composer. The hand of Seeau would seem to reveal itself: perhaps he believed that a less orthodox book might open the door to the *mezzo carattere* (a part at once serious and comic) and tempt Mozart to excess; that the stiff, traditional structure, but smartened up with Parisian touches—a Munich tradition—would best contain this prodigal talent. Seeau remembered *La finta giardiniera*—and not with pleasure.

---

1 Although Mozart filled 7–10 March with an excursion to Augsburg, he inscribed: "Monaco [the Italian for Munich] li 8 di Marzo 1781" on the manuscript. He must have completed the aria (perhaps a farewell gift to the Countess) in Augsburg and, preoccupied, wrote "Monaco," whither he returned by the eleventh.

Mozart pressed into service as librettist of the new opera the cleric who, some five years earlier, had edited for him Metastasio's *Il rè pastore*. Nannerl's diary of 22 August 1780 reads—in Mozart's hand: "Abbé Varesco at our house in the afternoon." This meeting no doubt had led to a series of discussions intensifying when the memo of understanding and material to be adapted arrived from Munich. (Prompted by Grimm's recommending the story of Idomeneus as the stuff of an opera, Mozart, while in Paris, may have got hold of Danchet's book.) Mozart played a leading role in framing the texts of his major operas, a practice by this time under way.

At first the proximity of composer and poet had proved an advantage. But their collaboration did not end well: Varesco received Mozart's most searching demands for changes after he had left for Munich; Leopold became his son's representative in Salzburg, prodding—often with clumsy hand—a more and more disenchanted Varesco to make the alterations, cuts, and additions Mozart's letters demanded. Into the bargain, the Abbé found himself consulting with Schachtner, whom Seeau, at Mozart's suggestion, had hired to turn the Italian verse into German (the translation disappointed Mozart) for a bilingual program-book. The Mozart-Varesco *Idomeneo, Rè di Creta*, ossia: *Ilia ed Idamante* (K. 366) came into being in two cities; even so, it emerged imposing and graceful, betraying little of the travail surrounding its creation.

The roots of the simple plot intertwine not only with the story of Agamemnon and Iphigenia but also with the biblical narratives of Jephthah and his daughter and of Abraham and his son. A storm raised by the god of the sea, Nettuno, threatens to overwhelm the fleet of King Idomeneo as he sails home to Crete from the Trojan War. He vows a sacrifice to the god in exchange for safe harbor. Nettuno demands human flesh on the altar of his temple, the victim to be the first person the King encounters upon arrival. Reaching the coast of Crete safely, almost in the same moment he meets Idamante, his son. Horror-stricken, Idomeneo flees. His attempts to evade fulfilling his vow enrage Nettuno, who sends a monster to begin annihilating the people of Crete. Idamante discovers his own continuing existence to be the cause of their suffering and, having slain the monster, presents himself for sacrifice at the god's altar. Idamante's beloved, Princess Ilia of Troy (a prisoner whom the King had sent on to Crete under escort with other captives), offers her life in place of the Prince's. Nettuno relents on condition that Idomeneo step down so that Idamante may mount the throne with Ilia as his queen.

Critics enjoy shooting arrows at Varesco; the letters of the Mozarts invite the sport. Yet their harsh judgment of him as a professional—they had worked with him before, and the modest level of his talent should not have surprised them—has to be tempered with their even harsher comments about his being an Italian. Indeed, they despised this child of Trent in the Tridentina as a "half-Italian," in their eyes a creature even "worse than a pure Italian." Since this warped prepossession had no logic, little reliable about him can be discerned through the mists of their prejudice. (When coping "with Italians . . . ," Mozart declared, "one must be a bit crude.") If they finally showed a begrudging appreciation of his workmanlike effort, he had nothing but grief in dealing with them. In the end, even though they required so much new versifying that he had to redo the clean copy for the printer four times, Mozart opposed his receiving extra money: "He ought to be obliged to me all the more: regard for his own reputation [*Ehre*] compelled the changes"—Mozart at his most foolish.[2]

The libretto, evolving under his guidance, proved a well-crafted structure offering a challenge worthy of his genius. His call for concise, unaffected, and flowing verse had been unrealistic given the portentous conceits of *opera-seria* poetry and Varesco's limitations, though in the closing act he rose to a noble level: even Metastasio at his most lyric seldom achieved the continuity of felicitous phrase Mozart demanded. This desire for a new naturalism also led him to request aria texts setting forth their arguments in one section rather than the accustomed two; the second implied a dacapo return of the first, and the repetition now struck him as artificial and boring. He had already begun to seek a Da Ponte.

Mozart continued to put forward brilliant prescriptions for furbishing up the libretto; his goals: clarity and brevity. (Not a few of the revised verses came from his own pen.) His new aesthetic course provoked his dissatisfaction, above all, with the unmotivated exits *opera seria* engineered in order to leave characters alone on stage for their arias. ("It seems so simpleminded to me that everyone rushes away so that Madame Elettra [Princess Elettra, Ilia's rival] may be by herself.") Varesco, however, hardly showed himself unique in this abuse: the exit conventions of *opera seria* had come to be more casual than causal. Mozart's impatience with them reveals an impatience with the genre as a whole.

---

2 Considering himself quit of *Idomeneo*, Varesco had just requested a supplement from Seeau when Leopold, at his imperious worst, pressed for new verses: Idomeneo's final aria, he insisted, had to be done afresh. The Abbé flew into a rage; "*Torna la pace al core*" (Peace returns to my heart) came from the pen of an incensed librettist. Somewhat later Mozart came but a step from owning up to the discourtesies he and his father had descended to in the entire affair: in the spring of 1783 they held council as to sounding Varesco about writing a new libretto, an awkward measure in the light of their suspicion that he might "still be angry about the Munich opera."

2

AT FIRST, HARMONY hovered over the preparation of *Idomeneo*. Mozart reported meeting a changed Count Seeau; the hard edges seemed to have vanished as if he were "molded wax": "You wouldn't recognize him." But their politeness soon soured: had Seeau begun to discover how elaborate and expensive an affair he had slid into—and not without his own complicity; and did Mozart, having built too large, resist compromise?

If it faithfully reflected the provisions of the commission—no record of it or of its negotiation survives—Mozart's *Idomeneo* revealed the Munich opera contemplating an ambitious synthesis of *opera seria* and *tragédie lyrique*: a work embracing the extended arias of the first rather than the concise airs of the second but at the same time seizing upon its choruses, dances, tableaux, and wonders of décor—a composite demanding imposing proportions. In Munich, to refashion a *tragédie lyrique* into an *opera seria* did not leave the beaten path, the usual assumption, at all events, being the dominance of the Italian aesthetic. But Mozart did not make Danchet's five-act drama into an *opera seria* simply somewhat less circumspect than tradition imposed in respect to choral, choreographic, and scenic effects: he had Varesco follow the latest manifestation of the genre as expanded by Piccinni at the Opéra. Seeau had no doubt pointed in a Parisian direction, but just how far he wished Mozart to travel so spacious a highway can only be surmised.

Despite simplification of the plot (Danchet had both the King and his son in love with the heroine and, following French taste, required much coming and going of intervening divinities), compression of this pared-down scheme into *opera seria*'s requisite three acts, a happy ending adroitly designed by Varesco, and the poetry à la Metastasio, Mozart's *Idomeneo* remained a *tragédie lyrique* in soul and scale. He and Varesco laid hand upon every opportunity for the choreographed interludes and *merveilleux* of the Opéra. (In Paris, Grimm had stressed the opportunities for spectacle the tale enclosed.) *Idomeneo* incorporates religious processions and ceremonies; military marches; pantomime (including a coronation) and dance woven into the action; a shipwreck; a fleet preparing to depart; two violent storms (the winds racing to their caves after the first, bolts of lightning setting ships afire during the second); a monster issuing from the sea; a grand dumb show in which Nettuno, rising from the wild waves, calms them, fixes Idomeneo with a terrible glance, and disappears into the depths; and the materialization of the god to animate his statue. Much of what *opera seria* reported in narrative here filled the stage. *Idomeneo* became the sumptuous opera Mozart did not write for Paris; if the verse strives to be

Metastasian, much of the opera's architecture and decoration is French and Piccinniste as seen through a scrim of Gluckean facture.

Had Seeau expected a work of such dimensions? He began to apprehend its full scope only when, by 13 November, he received the first version of the libretto concocted in Salzburg, "whereby," Leopold Mozart advised, "His Excellency Count Seeau may see that everything has been carried out as prescribed." Mozart and Varesco had observed the letter; but the spirit proved an intrusion from some region of Mozart's aspirations. Seeau beheld a work so heroic in its pride of state that it befitted some great celebratory, monarchical circumstance quite wanting in the Munich of 1781. Mozart, in fact, called *Idomeneo* his "*grosse Oper*," and it would become known as his "*dramma eroico*" (borrowed from Gluck's description of his *Armide* as a *drame héroïque*). Once again, as in the case of *La finta giardiniera*, he gave Munich an opera inflated as to occasion. The exchequer stuck at paying its highest fee for the grandiose affair and remained with the figure first agreed upon, about two hundred fifty gulden. ("For pay such as this you cannot leave your score behind,"[3] a disappointed Leopold advised.) In time a supplementary payment would set things right, but wider expectations missed the mark: *Idomeneo*'s exceptional vocal, orchestral, and stage demands (as well as an old-fashioned atmosphere) would hinder its going the round of German theaters.

Once Mozart had installed himself in rooms on the Burggasse (in Herr Fiat's house, the "Sonneck"), Seeau arranged conferences including him, Cannabich (who was to conduct),[4] and those responsible for the staging: the court's ballet master, Jean-Pierre Legrand, and its director of scenic design, *Hofkammerrat* Lorenzo Quaglio.[5] If Seeau held to the hope that new

---

3 Mozart did not follow the customary practice of surrendering his autograph score or a copy of it to the theater; Munich retained a working or performing copy.

4 As in the case of *La finta giardiniera*, Munich protocol took exception to a composer's conducting the premiere performances of his opera. Since his arrival from Mannheim, Cannabich had in no time outclassed Toeschi at all points: "When Cannabich is present," Mozart observed, "old Toeschi . . . has no authority."

5 Though appraising Quaglio as "skillful and experienced," Leopold pothered over the nature of the King's first entrance: "whether Idomeneo remains on the ship [and then descends from it with his entourage]" or flees it "to seek safety on the rocks." Acknowledging that the answer lay with Quaglio, he nonetheless insisted that, in any case, the "shattered boats" Idamante observes "must be lying about." Earlier Leopold held to only one solution when countering an observation "that thunderstorms and the sea take no cognizance of etiquette" (perhaps a reference, on his son's part, to *The Tempest*). "Idomeneo," Leopold insisted, "must withdraw from the vessel with his retinue," his vow having persuaded Nettuno to spare the flagship and that part of the fleet not yet consumed by the whirlwind. Such an interpretation of the text rendered certain that "this landing will have a brilliant effect." Wolfgang, however, showed willingness to cut the spectacle if the King "could be convincingly shown in the dreadful storm, forsaken by every-

expository recitative might dispose of more than one of the scenic challenges, he erred: flying the colors of retrenchment, he rode with fixed lance at *Idomeneo*, but its very amplitude turned him aside; at best he could chip away here and there. Perhaps Mozart's excising the apparition of the sea god at the height of the tempest represented a conciliatory gesture. Whatever the case, comity did not remain the rule.

Patience ran out when Mozart insisted upon hiring three trombonists to play, along with two horns, the short solemn passage preparing and accompanying Nettuno's proclamation. Mozart took as model Gluck's *Alceste*, in which trombones underline priestly and oracular doings. But while Gluck put the trombones, not yet part of the normal opera orchestra, to work at various points in his score, Mozart wished to reserve their penetrating timbre for the supernatural voice—as he would in *Don Giovanni*—the singer to be placed offstage with the five instrumentalists so that the mysterious sound and its no less mysterious source might strike the audience with wonder. Since opera composers called upon trombones for special effects, theaters now and then did meet with a demand like Mozart's.[6] But the Count looked upon it as a poor bargain: the wax melted, the hard edges showed, and the old Seeau reappeared. A vigorous exchange ensued. The Count stood his ground: at the premiere it would seem that clarinets and bassoons did the trombones' work.

Another of Seeau's successful strokes concerned the scenery for the final act, whose action was supposed to move, by means of Quaglio's quickly rolled drops and shifting wings, from the gardens of the royal palace, to the square upon which it opened, and then to the hall of Nettuno's temple. In the end, all three scenes unfolded before a single stage picture, doubtless realized with much ingenuity—Quaglio's décor for *Idomeneo* gained high praise—but not what Mozart had in mind.

He took annoyance in stride. From *La finta semplice* to *Il rè pastore* he had perfected the technique, prevalent at the time, of ad hoc operatic composition: working within the feasible and wringing the best from resources at hand. With the cast before him, he proceeded to paint his portraits from life, perfecting those in work and creating new ones. As, piece by piece, soloists, choristers, and instrumentalists received and learned their parts and began to fit the segments together, news traveled among connoisseurs that something exceptional had begun to take form in Munich. But

one . . . swimming all alone in the greatest danger." Today directors tend toward this approach, a solitary King Idomeneo scrambling onto the stage, Alberich-like, from the rocks or the sea.
6 Trombones figured as a matter of course in church music: each of Mozart's recently composed masses and litanies (K. 317, 321, 337, and 339) called for three.

Leopold sensed danger: from Becke he had learned that comments in the practice rooms included not only *"beautiful"* but also *"new and strange"*; he feared the old pattern might repeat itself, the opera proving too German an affair and, after the premiere, suffering neglect. To no avail he besought his son to include a few simple numbers for those unable to find their bearings in his German orchestral style.

As growing praise of *Idomeneo* continued to reach Leopold, he put his fears aside: "You know that you can't have everyone as a friend; an undercurrent of doubt and objection always flows." Indeed, as Mozart brought into being his German *tragédie lyrique* in *opera-seria* Italian, what he called "a minor cabal" arose, calling into question an essential of this conflation: a rumor censured his Italian prosody. The charge incensed him. He prided himself upon his mastery of the language; and if, here and there, his *opere serie* did have irregular accents in sections wherein very few words had to be portioned out over many bars, did there exist an Italian-born opera composer guiltless of similar occasional anomalies? When Leopold heard this tale of metrical irregularities, he assumed that Mozart had indulged in the kind of extended baroque coloratura he dismissed, even while writing it, as "chopped noodles," passages that came off best when the singer suppressed the full word and sang only on the vowels.

Rehearsals took place first at Seeau's, then at the palace, Karl Theodore dropping in "incognito" (that is, he listened from an adjoining room). He marveled at what he heard—*"no music has ever had such an effect upon me; it is magnificent music"*—and assured Mozart: *"This opera will be charming and certainly do you honor."* And after hearing the terrifying storm music of the second act, the astounded Elector asked: *"Who would have imagined something so great lodged in so small a head?"*[7] During rehearsals, at his levee, and at table he expressed delight in *Idomeneo* and predicted a splendid success. But not even his exalted word could assure it: though the throne still determined the choice of a work, by now the taste of the parterre, not of the loges, determined its future.

Apart from dissonance with Count Seeau, everything in Munich gave Mozart pleasure. Why, he was even meeting those practical demands of daily life to which Leopold held him unequal. Enjoying princely praise and that of his singers and an orchestra without peer, he hurried to complete his opera for the city many now considered Europe's musical center. He would call this period the happiest he could remember.

---

7 Hearing these passages, Becke experienced an effect "so powerful that it would make anyone feel cold as ice even in the heat of midsummer."

From the beginning he had the orchestra's goodwill, and Leopold recommended that by a barrage of compliments he preserve it through the difficult period of rehearsals; the success of *Idomeneo* turned as much upon the instrumentalists as the singers: "I know your style of composing; it calls for constant and prodigious attention on the part of the entire orchestra, and the necessity of maintaining such a pitch of industry and vigilance for at least three hours becomes no laughing matter. Down to the worst violist, all react with eagerness to tête-à–tête praise and thereafter function with more zeal and attention. Such courtesy costs not more than a word or two. However, you yourself know this."

Mozart had no anxieties about sustaining the enthusiasm of old friends like Cannabich and Ramm. Cannabich announced himself eager "to rehearse like the devil" and emerged from conducting "bathed in sweat"; for his part Ramm, with praise much like the Elector's, declared after the first orchestral rehearsal: "I must candidly confess . . . that until this time no music has made such an impression upon me." Mozart savored these words of a "true German," who "tells you to your face everything just as he sees it." During this stay in Munich, Mozart furnished him with a three-movement composition whose engaging and inventive outer Allegros offered opportunities to display the technical dexterity upon which his reputation rested, the intervening brief Adagio (here the oboe sings of some quiet sorrow) giving scope to the spiritual qualities he could draw from slow tempos: the oboe quartet K. 370/368b.[8]

Of Mozart's traditional *opera-seria* cast of six (not including the bass singing Nettuno's small solo), two of the three stars praised their music: the Wendlings—Elisabeth (Elettra) and Dorothea (Ilia), the last declaring herself *"Arci-Contentissima."*[9] Raaff (Idomeneo), however, harbored reservations reflecting his sixty-six years. Mozart treated Germany's most celebrated tenor with ceremonial courtesy, rewriting and tailoring his arias to favor a noble cantabile surviving in the still intact middle section of his voice and at moments rewarding him with the *retardataire* "chopped-noodle" bravura that had made his fame. This relic of a seeming ancient time had become a somber reality with which Mozart had to cope: a sympathetic friend, but an artist with little to bring to the figure of the tortured king. Mozart would have preferred writing the part for the bass

---

8 K. 370 continues the line of the flute quartets, though its string trio has greater felicity of thematic manipulation and expression.

9 Aloisia's departure from Munich (1779) to take a position in Vienna spared Mozart a dilemma: *Idomeneo* had roles for only two female sopranos.

Giovanni Battista Zoncha (he had come to Munich from Mannheim) and clung to the hope of one day recasting it for a darker voice, an idea unusual in respect to the title role of an *opera seria*.[10]

That Domenico de Panzachi, the veteran (though only forty-seven) tenor singing King Idomeneo's counselor (Arbace), retained his range, determined the brilliance of this secondary character's vocal lines; and that Panzachi turned out withal to be "a good actor" led a grateful Mozart to make Arbace bulk larger than his dramatic purpose: he has two impressive arias of state and a forceful accompagnato heavy with nuance.

Unlike Panzachi, the two singers impersonating the chief male characters cut miserable figures on stage: his years of experience notwithstanding, Raaff remained a primitive player—"like a statue," Mozart commented—while Vincenzo dal Prato, the castrato playing the prince-hero (Idamante), had little dramatic skill and no presence. When Mozart heard them read the recitatives of the father and son's first encounter, he almost despaired. He could shape arias to exploit his singers' capabilities or mask their deficiencies, but cuts alone could assist those without the subtlety of elocution and gesture needed to project dramatic recitative. By the premiere—encouraged by Seeau—he had reduced the scene to a few exchanges communicating its essentials. He never hesitated to pare down in the service of necessity.

Mozart had experienced Raaff's almost comic faults as an actor during Mannheim days, observing him at the opera performing a death scene: ". . . a very, very, very long aria in slow time," after which "he died with a smile on his face." But his singing did command regard,[11] hardly the rumor flying about dal Prato when Mozart arrived in Munich.

He could have had little time to unpack when an attempt got under way to convince him of the young (Mozart's age) castrato's ineptitude. He betrayed, the chatter ran, a total innocence of proper training and professional experience. Actually, Munich had summoned him from Stuttgart, where he had worked after singing on Italian stages. In his first and often quoted observations to his father about dal Prato, damning his technical deficiencies, in particular a shortness of breath, Mozart was retailing at second hand: he had yet to lay eyes on, much less hear him. In all likelihood some faction had its preferred castrato ready to step in when its calumny had routed the newcomer. Ceccarelli as substitute suggested itself to Mozart, who wrote home of a possible future for him in Munich. Yet, dal Prato endured.

---

10 In his oratorio *Betulia*, Mozart had written the pivotal part for a female alto.
11 The premiere performances of *Idomeneo* would be Raaff's final professional appearances.

By late November Mozart started to refer to him in that Wolfgangian diction of disparagement and disdain so often spelling special personal affection ("The fellow is rotten to the core"). His *"molto amato castrato"* had come to be just that, and by the new year Mozart began to turn about in his appraisal of his voice: dal Prato, Leopold now learned, tended to sing "like the best of the boys auditioning for the choir school [Salzburg's]," hardly a rousing assessment; however, his voice, though "ill produced" (*keine Methode*) might, after all, be "not so bad," although it required abundant coaching. Mozart had taken him in hand, teaching him Idamante's notes as they traveled from head to hand to paper. Mozart revealed Idamante's torment and character through a taxing vocal part of long, elegant phrases exhibiting dal Prato's technical strengths. Its demands remain unassailable arguments for the castrato's abilities. He worked hard and came off well: Idamante has a dogged quality he shared; he struck Raaff as "learned," "diligent," and "with the most honest character and the best morals." His singing must have impressed (his princely bearing, no doubt, proved another matter). Munich had hired him only for the *Idomeneo* season but kept him on for the next twenty-five years.

3

MOZART'S LETTERS HOME reflect complete self-possession. Refusing to let Leopold get on his nerves, he assigns him tasks, mainly as liaison to Varesco and as procurer of horn and trumpet mutes unavailable in Munich and needed for the march sounding in the distance as Elettra hastens to the port.[12] The father's advice is sought with respect but not often followed. Still eager to give tutorials, Leopold trots out his classical learning to warn that Varesco has erred by having Ilia refer to Idomeneo's fleet and his kingdom as Argive (*Argiva*), an adjective restricted to the Greeks of Argos, when she should use Achean (*Achiva*), which includes the Cretans. Mozart shows no interest.[13]

When a whining wind begins to blow across Leopold's pages, Mozart makes clear that he will tolerate none of the old tricks; his reply has a keen edge: from morning until evening he composes, rehearses, and attends to social necessities; his eyes have wearied, his fingers grown stiff from writing,

---

12 The chorus "O voto tremendo" in the final act also features, to telling effect, mutes and covered drums.
13 Mozart added Swabian, Leopold's native dialect, to the list of exotic languages—Greek, Arabic, Turkish, Vandal, and Tartar—the pompous doctor (Despina in disguise) in *Così* boasts of speaking, a thrust at the scholarly airs of a father long dead.

and he has a cold; he wants to hear nothing unpleasant. "If you please, do not write me any more melancholy letters; at this time I require a cheerful spirit, a clear head, and an inclination to work—and one cannot have these when one is depressed!" He will not permit his father to retrace the old obsessive patterns.

But Leopold lived with a wound that shrank from healing; he attempted to force even the smallest opening through which to imply what he no longer dared pronounce:[14] "I will not be fortunate enough to live out my life in this world—at least my final days—in peace and ease of mind; and yet, I have earned [both]." Mozart cut this moaning short, his answer terse but moving: "God knows I understand and am sensitive to how much you deserve quiet hours; but, am I in truth the stumbling block? I would not be so, yet, alas, that is what I truly am." He thus defined their dilemma: if Leopold could no longer oppress, neither could he nourish and reassure.

Incapable of cruelty, Mozart fell back upon improvised reassurances, some of them crossing into fantasy: the success of *Idomeneo* would bring him a permanent position at Munich and free Leopold and Nannerl to take up residence there. He felt obliged to provide confirmation—certainly disingenuous—of their continuing as a unit, an acknowledgment Leopold now required to be ever renewed, for in his eyes the Munich commission, so long dreamed of and cultivated, had come to have dark implications.

It has become impossible to turn away from compelling evidence that Leopold retained a cache of funds made up of profits from the tours (see p. 503). His tales of a continuing need to borrow had been fabrications serving further to screen this fact from his son—he must have taken Nannerl into his confidence—and to build a reserve of guilt with which to intimidate and control him. For the past two years Mozart's salary had flowed into the coffers of the Tanzmeisterhaus, and now Leopold looked forward to receiving the remuneration for *Idomeneo.* Yet good sense suggested that his myth of a family in debt had run its course: he would have to admit—at the least—to solvency. The end of the father and son's long pull together lay in prospect, and should Wolfgang depart the Tanzmeisterhaus, Leopold foresaw not only emotional but also financial deprivation. In a letter to Munich he dared touch upon what seemed to him his enduring right to a share of his son's future income, wherever he might be,

---

14 Even with his son's call for restraint, he suffered at least one deplorable loss of control: after entreating Wolfgang to inform the Tanzmeisterhaus should he fall ill—in the event the father would "come at once"—Leopold discharged a broadside of familiar imputations concerning the negligence he imagined at the root of Anna Maria's death in Paris.

but, shying from confronting the claim directly, he called upon allegory; its subject: a recent communication he had received concerning the Residenz's castrato, Ceccarelli.

His father had written seeking information about his whereabouts, for Ceccarelli had led his family to believe that he had quit the archbishopric for good. He had, in fact, been on tour and, once back in Salzburg, persisted in the imposture "because," Leopold insisted, "he does not want to lend his father a helping hand and, as you know, prefers to spend money on all kinds of unnecessary clothes and trifles." (Leopold had given up dandyism; Wolfgang had not.) Mozart, in the habit of pouncing upon Salzburg gossip, remained silent about this morsel. Some weeks later, Leopold took it up once more; again, silence.

By this time Mozart harbored ripening conjectures about his father's hidden treasure[15] (see XX, n. 37, p. 545, and pp. 671–72); from their tours Leopold had sent substantial sums to factors with instructions to invest at high interest. His spinster daughter now his principal concern,[16] he brooded over securing her future and had made her brother an unwitting contributor to building up this secret reserve and with it her inheritance. More and more Leopold tended to look upon Wolfgang as a source of financial tribute, a process in plain sight by the period of *Idomeneo*. The domineering father—a popular figure on the stage of the time—wife and offspring subject to his law, bullied many a German household. The Tanzmeisterhaus, however, sheltered the anomaly of an of-age son who, having while a child created the father's fortune, found himself treated like a boy on an allowance. Irrespective of the young man's emotional independence, Leopold continued in charge of the family's money, the last frontier on which he contrived to maintain advantage: there he stood fierce and uninterrupted guard.

It is instructive to observe his less than evenhanded monetary policy toward son and daughter, when, early in January 1781, she declared her wardrobe unequal to the social events to surround the *Idomeneo* premiere and ordered a new gown of French silk. Leopold seemed almost amused at its cost: "somewhat over seventy florins"; and this a week after Mozart had felt obliged to apologize for having drawn an extra fifteen, on a letter of credit, to help him through days devoted to composing his opera: "There

---

15 Leopold's commissioning a family portrait (see pp. 523–24), a sign of robust financial health, perhaps indicated resignation to let the mask of make-believe penury fall.
16 Almost thirty, Nannerl had long entered spinsterhood. Yet she did have a serious suitor: fifty-year-old Franz Armand d'Ippold, director of the Collegium Virgilianum and a member of the Archbishop's council of war. Mozart supported a courtship Leopold opposed. The couple's hopes to marry collapsed in 1781.

are a hundred trifles that melt money away, and I, to be sure, do not spend without purpose."[17] (He applied about half the sum to emergency repairs to his own wardrobe.) Leopold made clear to him that the fee for *Idomeneo* had to cover the seventy florins.[18] As if in extenuation, Nannerl informed her brother that the local dances would go on without her: these she would "leave to the Salzburgers" in order to "save for Munich." In any case, she bristled at the *Wildenadel's* (see p. 8) having the privilege of "receiving passes" to these festivities.

Mozart had as yet to find himself on short rations: it goes beyond imagining that Leopold held back whatever his son required. Even so, the pecuniary arrangements at the Hannibalplatz worked so little to his advantage that he would find himself without a gulden of capital when at last he got loose from home—at which juncture Leopold renewed his cries of straitened circumstances, without shame continuing to demand a portion of what Wolfgang earned. Though muddy, the picture of Leopold's finances communicates some basic shapes; they are not attractive. Mozart's refusal to comment upon the Ceccarelli affair may have reflected reluctance to confront an ever more painful issue; here any challenge would have led to crisis.

Save for money matters, Mozart had become impervious to Leopold's strategies. Eager to underline this independence, he moved to reverse their epistolary roles. (*Idomeneo*, the tale of a rash and then vacillating king and his circumspect, resolute heir, turns the usual father-son parts about.) He complained of Leopold's letters, of their gloom and brevity. When one of them lacked a date—Leopold had often scolded him for such failings— he professorially grumbled, his sense of humor, however, undermining this new tone: why, the letter had no date "because," he cackled, "my sister began it." He asked for long and animated communications to which responses should not be expected. He teased Leopold: since social kissing had become a drawing-room ritual in Munich, he must, by the time of his arrival for the premiere, be practiced in kissing the ladies; but "on the chin so as not to turn their rouge blue."

The letters have many such passages of familial friendship. United in anxieties and hopes, the three Mozarts recognized the production of

---

17 Often enough he managed to get invitations for dinner (the midday and chief repast) and supper and had "no [regular] outlays excepting hairdresser, barber, and laundress." The court must have paid his rent at the "Sonneck," for he contemplated applying for additional funds to cover the few meals he took there.

18 The price of the dress consumed close to a third of the fee! Fine clothing figured among the most expensive components of comfortable living in eighteenth-century Germany; in comparison, the services of domestics cost little.

Idomeneo as decisive in Wolfgang's career. "All that will follow turns upon this," Leopold presaged; their letters paraded the old slogan: "Honor and glory." It seemed a happy coincidence that Archduke Maximilian, but recently become Grand Master of the Teutonic Order of Knights, had chosen to visit Munich on his way home to Vienna from Mergentheim, where his installation had taken place. (On 8 November Mozart saw him in the Munich Residenz at a concert in which the soprano Mara and the oboist Ramm took part.) The Habsburgs, who had withdrawn favor from the young Salzburger, might be stirred to second thoughts.[19] Ironically, it was the head of the Imperial family who put the premiere of *Idomeneo* at risk.

4

WORD OF MARIA THERESA'S sharply declining health troubled Nannerl. On 30 November 1780 she wrote her brother: "You probably already know that the Empress is so ill that at any moment she may play a pretty joke upon us. If she dies now, the opera [*Idomeneo*] may still be performed; but if she dies later, all my pleasure may come to nothing. . . . I hope to see you in Munich if it is God's will."

Even as Nannerl wrote, Maria Theresa lay dead. Sitting upright in a chair, she had declared: "I must not be taken unawares. I wish to see death coming." Death had obliged her on the evening of the twenty-ninth. Etiquette demanded that courts throughout the Holy Roman Empire mourn the Dowager German Empress. In Vienna official expressions of sorrow threatened to become insupportably protracted and intense. Emperor Joseph began to feign illness, so whisper ran, in order to escape their rigors. This gossip amused the Mozarts, who retained little affection or respect for the Habsburgs. Witticisms hedged their references to the departure of the formidable ruler: "I beg you," Mozart wrote his father, "to have my *black suit* thoroughly brushed, shaken out, repaired as well as possible, and sent to me by the next mail coach, for during the coming week everybody will don mourning, and I, who must always be darting about here and there, must also join the *weeping*."

---

19 The Mozarts had hopes that two members of the von Lehrbach family might play the intermediaries and help them rekindle Habsburg interest: Franz Christoph von Lehrbach, associated with the Salzburg Residenz, and his uncle, Count Franz Siegmund von Lehrbach. Formerly Vienna's ambassador at Mannheim, Franz Siegmund had moved to Munich to take up the same position at the new Electoral court. Mozart had met him in Mannheim (1778) thanks to a letter of introduction from the nephew. Just now come to Munich to visit his uncle, he attended the rehearsals of *Idomeneo* and hastened to write to Salzburg about the admiration the work excited. The Mozarts trusted that such words would reach Habsburg ears.

But how long would protocol demand that Wolfgang weep? Were Karl Theodore to ape Vienna as to the length of the commemorative rituals and shut the theaters, the premiere of *Idomeneo* would be deferred, and any prolonged postponement carried the germ of cancellation. But the danger passed: he kept the solemnities within bounds, his composure hardly unsettled by the thought of one less Habsburg. On 5 December Mozart reported that not only was "the entire mourning to last no longer than six weeks" but also "no theater" had "been closed, the plays continuing as usual." He expected his opera to reach the stage by 20 January. In any case, the date of the premiere shifted as day by day Seeau found it necessary to add rehearsals of the complicated production; his forces prepared *Idomeneo* with the professionalism of a great theater.

As his leave ran its course, thoughts of Salzburg disquieted Mozart. Not beneficence, but custom and political common sense had led the Archbishop to indulge Munich's request for the composer, whom he had granted six weeks away from his post: both knew that he would postpone his return—such had always been the Mozarts' way—just as both remembered that the conditions of his return to service included furloughs to fulfill operatic commissions; but, as a caveat, Colloredo, who contemplated taking his leading musicians with him on an excursion of his own, had authorized a particularly short stay.

Wavering as to whether to request an extension or simply help himself to it, Mozart asked his father: "By the way, what about the Archbishop?" Leopold offered to ride out whatever storm might break: "Concerning the six weeks, I have decided not to make any move or say anything. However, should the subject be mentioned to me, I have resolved to answer that our understanding was that *you would be allowed to remain in Munich for six weeks after composing the opera in order to attend the rehearsals and the performance inasmuch as I cannot imagine His Grace, the Prince, entertaining the belief that such an opera can be composed, copied, performed, etc., within six weeks.*" The creation of an opera kept on almost to the rise of the curtain; Leopold's sophistical message would be clear: his son would not return before the end of February. But would there be a court in Salzburg to welcome him back?

5

THE SALZBURG RESIDENZ had started to ready plans for the temporary transfer of the Archbishop's household to Vienna. His father, Prince Rudolph Joseph, long out of health, had become seriously ill—by late December, Leopold noted, "very dangerously" so—and Colloredo projected a sojourn of indefinite length in the *Kaiserstadt* both to be near him and to hold state. Uncertainties following Maria Theresa's death interrupted preparations only for the moment. The week chosen for Colloredo's departure from Salzburg coincided with the final rehearsals of *Idomeneo* in Munich. He left for Vienna on 20 January 1781.

An eccentric procession would precede him: relatives, courtiers, secretaries, valets, cooks, servants of every level—in fact, all Salzburgers necessary to the archiepiscopal well-being—were to make their way to the capacious House of the Teutonic Order of Knights (das *Deutschordenshaus des Deutschen Ritter-Ordens* on the Singerstrasse, near St. Stephen's cathedral), there to take up quarters and await their master's arrival. The musicians he ordered to be in attendance included his first violinist, Brunetti; his castrato, Ceccarelli; and his cembalist, Wolfgang Mozart. The court expected him to join his colleagues soon after the premiere in Munich. His leave would expire on 18 December. What with the inevitable extensions, it had not appeared unreasonable to expect him in Vienna by the end of January.

December moved toward the new year, and, "over neck and head," he pushed forward with *Idomeneo*'s third act; and, it concluded, a final task would remain: in the interest of curbing the length of a relentlessly growing score, the drama would not conclude with a "separate ballet"—by tradition assigned to a second composer—but, rather, have as its crowning finale a divertissement set "within the opera itself" (*zur Opera gehöriges*). Mozart assumed "the honor" of writing the addition, K. 367, so that "[all] the music will be by one master." But his long-sustained equanimity now showed signs of giving way: his fidgetiness while composing the "confounded dances" no doubt expressed anxieties concerning the vast dimensions of the opera. At the last moment he would yield to panic and, just before the premiere, cut to the quick the magnificent last act.

As *Idomeneo* took final form, Raaff added his share to Mozart's cares. The tenor, who, in response to his grumbling, had received new verses for his last aria, proceeded to object to their many "*i*"s as obstacles to effective articulation and vocalizing. (Varesco replaced this second text with yet a third: *Torna la pace*;[20] "Signor Raaff is too pernickety," Leopold commented.) Raaff also voiced unhappiness over the quartet, that early and never surpassed example of a ruminative ensemble, the main characters weaving its miraculous skein from the threads of their individual perplexities: Prince Idamante, about to engage the monster, reveals death as his goal; Ilia declares her readiness to share this fate; her fierce rival for his love,

---

20 At the premiere, this aria, the product of so much wrangling among composer, poet, and singer, went down before Mozart's pruning knife.

Princess Elettra of Argos, calls for vengeance; and guilt-ridden Idomeneo, execrating Nettuno, longs to breathe his last. These expressions of acquiescence, love, fury, and despondency combine in one great musical utterance (its parent: the quartet in *Zaide*).

Raaff could not grasp the point of it all, of stopping short and letting the progress of the opera hang fire while the four principals joined their voices; nor did he want to devote rehearsals to mastering an ensemble when, it seemed clear to him, this point of crisis in the drama really called for a simpler resolution: an aria by the leading tenor. The quartet, he complained, offered him "no opportunities" (*es ist zu eng*).

Mozart countered with a bold front: "So far nothing in this opera pleases me as much as this quartet; and once you hear it with all the voices, you will for certain talk in a different way. I have made every effort to serve you well in your two arias, will do the same in the third, and hope it will hit the mark. But as to trios and quartets, the composer must be free." Raaff retreated and later acknowledged the quartet's purpose and beauty.[21]

6

IN WHAT BECAME a struggle to complete *Idomeneo*, Mozart ended doing battle with himself. The opera's conclusion in sight, he, like the King of Crete, observed the sky turn angry, and for a short and disturbing period he, too, had reason to question his safe arrival in port. The episode embodied the first documented indication of tension between the cohesive forces of Mozart's creativity and the opposing stress of a personal crisis.

The inner quarter from which an artistic process takes direction defies detection: the psychological roots of art can at best be guessed at; their development remains a process most often unconscious for the artist and unfathomable to others. Although, like most musicians of his time, Mozart composed by the yard and with concern for the implicit requirements of occasion and expectation, his art must nevertheless have expressed his internal processes: he cannot have failed to discharge tensions and submerge crises in his works. Yet, until the time of *Idomeneo*, there appears to have been no special psychological constellation under which they came forth;

---

21 Raaff had to sacrifice yet another "opportunity" to the composer's sense of dramatic plausibility. His original design contemplated an aria "or, rather, a kind of cavatina," midst the storm choruses closing the second act. However, he concluded that a gale would "hardly subside to accommodate Herr Raaff's singing an aria" and, instead, provided an accompagnato in which the instruments "show what they can do." Mozart, moreover, only appeared to indulge Raaff by suppressing a second quartet (planned for the end of the last act) and putting in its place the grand final tenor aria: the change, Mozart realized, would be "much more effective."

in the face of emotional problems, he appears to have experienced neither artistic inhibition nor release: even during periods of procrastination and torpor his muse, if from time to time dilatory, did visit when summoned. Then in Munich she all at once declined to appear.

At work on the third act, the premiere almost upon him, he found his pen blocked when it touched the final, so-called clean copy. All along Leopold had suspected him of squandering his Munich days in playing the fool with friends. He did admit to having adopted new, easygoing attitudes toward work upon his return from Paris, and his father had become apprehensive lest they become habit. As early as 18 November he had sent him a homily on preparedness; the moralizing began with a certain timidity, Leopold, so it seems, clearing his throat: "A request on my part remains—do not postpone. When haste becomes a necessity you will *no longer have a choice* and will have to write down whatever comes to you; then you put at hazard honor, good fortune, fame—everything. And why? Because of time wasted in trifling, jokes, and merriment. . . ."[22] Passed hours cannot be recovered; whether good, mediocre, or poor, [the score of *Idomeneo*] must be ready on the day agreed upon, at which point there will be no remedies. Finish the task; then you can laugh from a happy heart."

Mozart had justice in his observation that his father did not know him. When had he ever failed to carry through? Months passed before he offered a quiet exculpation (26 May 1781): "Trust my word when I say that work, not idleness, suits my liking. Without doubt it is true that in Salzburg work became such an effort for me that I could seldom surrender myself to it. And why? Because my spirit did not find contentment." But in Munich his spirit had soared: admirers made a lion of him, and, a few annoyances apart, the score of *Idomeneo* moved forward. Then, as he approached the denouement, he found himself paralyzed to put into finished form a concluding act already shaped in his mind and sketched on paper. He acknowledged having "left to the last the composition of the greater and most intense [part of the third act]; but not from laziness or negligence; quite otherwise: I passed 14 days without writing a note because I found it impossible to do so. To be sure I did write something down, but not in clean copy." He concluded his recital of this strange experience allusively: "Of course as a result much time was lost; yet I do not regret it." He felt the two weeks well spent.

During this period of dislocation, in all likelihood he, even if at an unconscious level, caught sight of *Idomeneo*'s vast and profound perspectives

---

22 The letter recalls in tone and turn of phrase Leopold's reply to his son's "Mannheim confession" (see pp. 388–89).

reaching back to the immemorial taboo, recognized the drama's motif of oedipal will as the force holding him back, and discovered that he had but to find the strength to acknowledge it in order to emerge relocated and liberated. At its deepest level, *Idomeneo* tells a tale of patricide: the monster is King Idomeneo in his most frightening aspect. After a fortnight, a conflict, so acutely activated that Mozart could not proceed, resolved itself into a component of artistic creation: he came to terms with the oedipal deed and let Idamante's sword slay the monster-father.

Transcribed into symbols much reduced in power, Mozart's opera confronts the myth as transformed into less menacing form and transported to a more seemly social level. This first of his great works for the stage concerns itself with humans struggling with their passionate and erotic natures, their encounters circling around a problem central to him: the passing of authority from a waning generation. It has become customary to look upon the subject as having dropped to him from heaven and to regard the opera's psychologically profound score as a rich dividend of coincidence: the remarkable coming together, on the one hand, of a libretto concerning a tormented relationship between a father and son and, on the other, of a young composer able to identify himself with their dilemma.

Chance provides too simple an explanation. The theme of succession had long lodged in him: he had met with the motif in *Thamos* and, much earlier, during Bologna days, when the tale of King Idomeneus came into his hands: it lay embedded in Fénelon's *Télémaque* (see p. 283), that political manifesto in the form of a *roman à clef*. Here Idomeneus (Louis XIV) must be counseled to suppress in himself both his royal love of conquest and a monumental disdain no less for his own subjects than for the foreigners he has vanquished.[23] Mozart's opera makes passing reference to this arrogance, which his Idomeneo comes to recognize as one of the reasons for Nettuno's wrath against him. Still, in respect to moral constitution, Mozart's king contrasts in many commendable characteristics with Fénelon's autocrat, inured to honeyed words and innocent of any true awareness: counter to his serious flaws, the Idomeneo of the opera presents himself in

---

23 Fénelon looked upon his *Télémaque* as both sermon and warning to Louis XIV's grandson, the Duke of Burgundy, the book's purpose being to open his mind to political immorality, in particular unrelenting absolutism's arbitrary exercise of power. The hero, Odysseus's son, Telemachus, represents Burgundy. Spotted fever shattered Enlightened hopes in 1712 by carrying off this heir presumptive to the crown of France; his son would succeed his great-grandfather as Louis XV, whose reign, Leopold Mozart perceived, shadowed forth a cataclysm (see pp. 86 and 178). *Télémaque* sounded one of its early rumblings. In a note of 10 September 1770 from Bologna, Mozart informed Nannerl that he had reached the book's second section.

an aria (*"Vedrommi intorno"*) expressing torment at having to sacrifice an innocent victim.

Even so, Prince Idamante exists on an altogether higher ethical level. He knows what his father has but begun to learn. This young exemplar embodies the virtues of Fénelon's ideal philosopher-king. (Paul, the hero of Bernardin de St. Pierre's pastoral idyll, *Paul et Virginie* [1789], would declare *Télémaque* his favorite book.) In Fénelon's eyes, the prince must be the state's mainspring of duty and compassion, his mission and achievements to be measured by the welfare and contentment of his people and his charity for the defeated. "Only too well . . . have my own misfortunes taught me sympathy for the misfortunes of others," Mozart's Idamante tells the father he does not yet recognize,[24] the father who in short time will wrap himself in these sentiments and urge upon his son this very lesson learned from him: "If you would master the art of ruling, begin now by becoming the support of the unfortunate." Idamante's imperturbable patience with his father's fustian parallels Mozart's still remarkable forbearance toward Leopold's. Wolfgang must have heard familiar familial echoes in Idomeneo's declaration that his abdication gave Crete "another myself" in the person of his noble son!

Mozart's role in Munich's settling upon the Idomeneus legend for its Carnival opera seems no less clear than his strong hand in shaping the libretto from its earliest phases. As already conjectured, the project got under way with Count Seeau's determining its musical category—*opera seria* with Parisian embellishments; next, his opening a discussion of possible subjects (Gluck alone among composers had the prestige to define his own themes), the affairs of Idomeneus, in all likelihood Mozart's preference; then, his influencing the choice of this figure known to him since adolescence, the tale's resonances of steadfast Elector Maximilian III Joseph's succession to his heedless father (Emperor Charles VII) no doubt playing a role in the final selection (see p. 78);[25] and, last, Mozart's work with Varesco, whose bitterness no doubt took root in growing awareness of just how junior a partner the composer esteemed him.

What the new libretto used of Danchet's text and the changes worked upon it came in large part from Mozart. He drew upon incidents associated

---

24 Fénelon might have written this line for his *Télémaque*: in it the gods impose afflictions upon the hero in order to awaken in him the fellow feeling indispensable to a future king. True nobility, he learns, proceeds from adversity and suffering.

25 As did Franz Paul Grua's opera *Telemaco*, staged in Munich during 1780 with a libretto based in part upon Fénelon, the adventures of Telemachus helping turn the court's interest toward those of Idomeneus. Mozart's eagerness to show the court how a master, as opposed to Grua, would treat so elevated a subject cannot be left out of account.

with two islands over which Idomeneus (grandson of King Minos) ruled: Crete, scene of his tribulations upon his return from Troy—the material Munich expected—and Salentum, the city-state he had but recently founded when the eponymous hero of *Télémaque* landed upon its shores. Telemachus's *séjour* at Salentum provided his instructor-companion, Mentor (Minerva in human shape and representing Fénelon), opportunities to counsel Idomeneus concerning the political and economic organization of his new realm and, in particular, to attempt its moral transformation; toward this end Mentor lectured with eloquence upon the relationship of ethics to both the well-being of the state and principles of kingship. These questions in turn permeated the *Idomeneo* of Mozart, who transferred the spirit of new Salentum to Crete and, what with his German score, created in Idamante-Telemachus a kind of princely, Mediterranean Wilhelm Meister.

The figure of Goethe's Wilhelm Meister inherited much from the protagonist of Wieland's *Agathon*, (1766–1767; revised 1773), a spiritual odyssey, itself a descendant of *Télémaque* and combining the *Bildungsroman* and *Reiseroman* (the novel of psychological development and the travel novel). Such traditions inform Mozart's *Idomeneo*, its juxtaposition of the real and the supernatural, its multiplicity of perspectives, and its substructure of *Lebensphilosophie* cum German Hellenism subsisting within a brittle shell of Metastasian lacquer-work. The last constituted Varesco's elegant contribution,[26] in particular the courtly, delicately shaded character of Ilia, her joyful surrender to love menaced by the irrational emotionalism of Elettra.

These women who love Idamante evoked responses deep within Mozart: he gave them some of the opera's finest music. They offered contrasting opportunities to express in tone the ethereal nobility of the one, the frenzied self-assertion of the other. Elettra in particular engaged him.

---

26 This rococo component calls into question the parallels at times implied as existing between *Idomeneo* and Schiller's *Die Räuber*, written 1777–1778, published in 1781, and given its first performance one year later by von Dalberg's Mannheim company. A relationship does unfold, but it tells a tale of contrasts rather than of similarities. The cities that gave these works their premieres underline the divergence: Mannheim, in the eighties fast becoming a vital center of German theater, explored the new proto-romantic realism, while Munich continued to follow the conservative and less tumultuous fortunes of a court stage. The heavy weather of Schiller's play and its hero's inclination toward the exaggerated and even bombast find no correspondence in the opera's complete control of means and in Idamante's Metastasian eloquence; and, if both young men have in common their Storm and Stress opposition to iron despotism, the one embraces rebellion, the other Mozart's still persisting Voltairean belief in a humane and ameliorative continuity.

(Had the libretto come to Gluck's desk, his aesthetic of laconic austerity would have made him lop this fury of a princess from the plot—and Arbace, too, whom Mozart himself discarded upon revising the score in 1786.) A self-flagellating neurotic enclosed in combat with her own demons of jealousy and passion, she for the most part communicates only with herself during her step-by-step descent into madness. Pursuing a way peripheral to the dramatic flow, she provides an antithesis to the rigorous unfolding of the work's main business and high moral argument: the loftiness of human worth.

At the center of this disquisition stands Mozart's ideal self-image: Idamante. His exalted accompagnato in the temple scene and his arias, so persuasive in their heroic power and of an astonishing refinement and complexity of invention, hover in a rare plane between ardor and melancholia. No more noble or touching male portrait hangs in the Mozartean operatic gallery.

From the time of *Idomeneo*, Mozart molded more than one of his operatic characters in the likeness of his potential self, projective images proceeding from his aspirations and appetites of the moment and therefore no less real, if more intense, than his everyday self. These idealized self-presentations range in propensity from the concupiscence of Don Giovanni and the artful seductive techniques of Guglielmo and Ferrando to Idamante's greatness of heart. In him, Mozart celebrated not hierarchical and dynastic but universal values: not the imperatives of *opera seria* but the conscience of the Gluckean tragedy. *Idomeneo* does not use the operatic apparatus to reinforce authority: Metastasio's rulers survive the plots woven against them and then with magnanimity forgive the plotters, but in *Idomeneo* the figure of authority finds himself forced to give way to youth—one of the most persistent reveries of the *Stürmer und Dränger*.[27] Prince Idamante's invincible weapon is not his royal sword but the virtue directing it. The flawed father must step aside before this twofold embodiment of continuity and wisdom.

Continuity was his birthright, wisdom a gift of the gods. Not only his father, but also Prince Tamino—at the cost of taxing adventures a decade in the future—would struggle to attain something of his sagacity and acumen: a descendant of Idamante, but much less self-possessed, if no less

---

27 The court could have found little in the opera to reinforce a sense of its own image, above all, not in Ilia's reference to the populace in revolt and the high priest's plain-speaking demand (really a command) to the pusillanimous King: "And you still delay? Render unto Neptune that which is his." In *Idomeneo* the political affectations and ambitions of *opera seria* dissolve.

unremittingly earnest, Tamino comes on stage painfully short of the steel in his ancestor's spirit; instead of "furiously hurling himself" at the serpent-monster, he flees it. In contrast, from his very first appearance, Idamante is whole: Mozart in the prime of his young manhood and ready to do battle.

7

COURTING THE REWARDS of a German ruler whose musical taste he respected and the applause of a German capital he adored, Mozart, even so, must have found one aspect of his situation absurd: setting to music Italian words in a score he had determined to make into an affair of German weight and consequence, a creation he perceived as defining and shaping his identity as a German composer. Winckelmann's ambition as a young art critic and historian had been "to produce a work in German, the like of which has never seen the light of day, in order to show foreigners what we can do." Mozart had a not unrelated goal: to show how a German composer could write a serious opera international in style but German in sensibility, carry all before him in his native land, and—an ultimate hope—retain possession of the field. With *Idomeneo* he sought to carve out for himself in Munich a place such as Christian Bach had striven to occupy in Mannheim.

Determined to realize his long-held ambition to give Karl Theodore a German work, Mozart had the last and ironic word by clothing the Italian text of *Idomeneo* in unremittingly German sound: he reveled in weaving a limpid and subtle instrumental web of detailed workmanship and bewitching timbres. In opera never again would he so give himself up to the sheer gorgeousness of instrumental sonorities. (But, then, never again would he have the Mannheim/Munich orchestra at his disposal.) From this time on, each of his works for the stage would have its own musical language, but none so rich and varied as *Idomeneo*'s. The stretches of persistent, undifferentiated texture so often plaguing his earlier serious operas had vanished for good and all; in *Idomeneo* the orchestra's wealth of tonal color became a factor without precedent in its power to help convey the changing emotions and dramatic purpose of the protagonists.

They speak with a rhetorical refinement derived not in idiom but in spirit from the tradition of the *tragédie lyrique* and Gluck's reform operas. But while these genres most often offered personages resembling *trompe l'oeil* figures in grisaille, an all-purpose stately, if leaden, elegance washing over them, Mozart here sculpted a series of deep-cut individual images, a feat all the more remarkable in that the work for the most part retains the granitic building blocks, the additive dramatic structure, and the vocal athletics, heroics, and magniloquence of *opera seria*. But he bestowed spontaneity upon these conventions; in *Idomeneo* his creative energy never slackens, his invention never fails, and nothing seems superfluous, not even the *secco* recitative, its transient moods shaped by pliable bass lines and volatile harmonies. The score to which Mozart, alarmed at its length, dealt hacking cuts just before the premiere, could not have submitted to them on easy terms: in respect to arias and *accompagnati*, what went by the board represented a musico-dramatic loss; and the axe laid to the *secco* struck at narrative clarity.

These last-minute excisions[28] must have done mischief to the organic operatic architecture he had evolved in his desire to realize in full *Idomeneo*'s dramatic tensions. In the course of composing, once again he had reshaped the libretto, transforming, wherever possible, a static, incremental conception into a developing continuum, turning the successive into the progressive, sequence into flow, segments into a whole: tautly drawing together the lines of the action through a device he had used in the tomb scene of *Silla* and the wilderness episode of *La finta giardiniera*, he propelled the narrative forward, the dramatic circumstances permitting, by binding together contiguous numbers. In *Idomeneo* he followed this course straightway, thrusting the auditor into the argument: the final chord of the overture also serves as the first chord of Ilia's opening recitative, which introduces her first aria, "*Padre, germani*," it, in turn, leading without pause into her ensuing scene with Idamanate. In like way, the postlude to Elettra's first aria, "*Tutte nel cor*," both accompanies the change of scene to the storm-swept seacoast and forms a bridge to the chorus "*Pietà! Numi*"; the waters then quiet at Neptune's command, Idomeneo appears on land, and only then do more than two hundred uninterrupted measures come to an end.

The music extending from Elettra's "*Idol mio*" to the conclusion of the second-act finale provides a no less majestic span: the end of the aria abuts on the beginning of a march heard from afar as the stage picture shifts from the palace to the harbor, where she and Idamante are to embark for

---

28 They should not be emulated in the name of following the master: the effect of each omission must be measured. (The recensions and additions he later made in Vienna present yet another set of problems [see pp. 653–54].) His continuing alterations in Munich necessitated the printing of a new libretto (without a German translation), but it could not have kept pace with what the audience heard on opening night.

Argos. With scene folding into scene, she arrives before the assembled fleet and bids farewell to Crete; in spacious verse flanking her ravishing solo "*Soavi Zeffiri,*" the chorus apostrophizes the tranquil sea, inviting it to remain hospitable to the travelers; the trio of farewell ensues; in an instant a tempest boils up; the monster ascends from the depths; and the populace looks on in helpless horror and then scatters much in the manner of the Thessalians' flight from the temple of Apollo in Gluck's *Alceste.*

In this most spectacular scene in the Mozart canon, Nettuno raises the tempest to prevent the departure of the fleet and with it Idamante, the victim the King had sworn to sacrifice on the god's altar stone. Mozart did not write marvelous descriptive music simply to accompany a scenic wonder, dear as he found such displays. Like Shakespeare he used the storm to symbolize the discord tearing at his characters. But while Shakespeare manipulates the storm as a device setting in motion rushing and purging tides pulling his characters asunder or bringing them together in those great arcs of parting and reunion so often part of his dramaturgy, Mozart's buffeting torrent descends as an awesome curtain of chaotic waters only Nettuno's monster can penetrate. Before this barrier the characters must stay in place and ponder the solutions they will reveal in the quartet.

Such powerful overarching passages of Mozartean music drama anticipate the turbulence and urgency of the romantic century's operatic dramaturgy as well as its striving for musical continuity and seem to testify to *opera seria*'s undoing itself: ingenious transitions, in particular the evasion of firm cadences, enable the music to ebb and flow in unbroken currents as chorus, recitative, aria, and ensemble glide one into the other.

Here Mozart went beyond the tendencies toward integration to be observed in Gluck, Traetta, and even Holzbauer. In *Idomeneo* Mozart's fusing of scenes into linked sequences of incident parallels Wieland's use of like poetic devices in his almost contemporary verse epic *Oberon* (1780). After *Idomeneo,* Mozart returned to this kind of telescopic dramatic architecture only now and then and on a limited scale: for example, in the opening of *Don Giovanni,* whose overture filters into a solo, it into a trio in turn linked with the exchange between father and seducer, which then runs on into another trio; and in the close of *La clemenza di Tito,* the orchestral accompaniment to Vitellia's final aria holding its course during the scenic change revealing the chorus in the amphitheater.

That Mozart, a master of the sonata, also exploited the atmosphere of key as a unifying and histrionic element in his operas stares from their scores. He resorted to individual keys to express specific moods: what appears on the page, for example, in C minor, D minor, or E-flat major often represents sensations allied, respectively, to pain, disquietude, and dignity, the particular key embracing diverse aspects of the same quality.

Although, on receiving a libretto, he designed its tonal pattern, if need be it underwent adjustment: overriding the composer's personal considerations, the practical many a time determined the key: since, for example, certain instruments could play best or only in certain keys, the composer might find himself restricted to choosing among hospitable tonalities: in the case of *Idomeneo*, inasmuch as D major handily accommodated trumpets and drums, it helped answer the opera's needs in respect to moments of panoply. Moreover, the keys of the arias had to be a function of the singers' most secure top and lowest tones and their vocal comfort in respect to tessitura, that is, the overall pitch level of the part.[29]

The rub in discussions of Mozart and key concerns the rise in pitch since his time. European pitch in the second half of the eighteenth century varied from a third of a whole tone to a minor third beneath today's level. A fork Stein of Augsburg used to tune a piano for Mozart reveals an instrument set at half a tone under the modern standard. Whatever the refinements of the case, Mozart's C minor sounded closer to B minor of the present time, his D minor not far from its C-sharp minor, and the hieratic Masonic triad opening *The Magic Flute* and written as E-flat major verged upon what the modern listener would recognize as D major. But, since the absolute pitches of Mozart's tonics remain guesswork, transposition cannot help; his entangling of key and idea tells its tale at best on paper, where key may be construed as concept as well as sound. *Idomeneo* has D major (more or less the current C-sharp major to Mozart's ears) exerting throughout the work the tonic pull it would exercise to even stronger effect in *Figaro*.

Another binding force pervades *Idomeneo*: repeated melodies and harmonies—along with transformations of these elements—accompanying subjects or situations with histrionic concepts, images, or emotions in common. Several examples suggesting such connections can be isolated and at first would seem to yield extramusical connotations in terms of reminiscence or anticipation. Yet, as the opera progresses and the allusive

---

29 A comparison of "*Il mio tesoro*" (*Don Giovanni*; 1787) with "*Se all' impero*" (*La clemenza di Tito*; 1791) provides an instructive example of the singer's influence upon the choice of key: Mozart wrote both arias for the lyric tenor Antonio Baglioni and the earlier furnished the model for the latter as to key, range, and tessitura. Mozart cast both in B flat, which showed the singer to fullest advantage by throwing into relief his ability to sustain a high F (the dominant of B flat) and exhibit an occasional higher note, an A in the first, two B flats in the second. Baglioni's throat determined the key (and character) of these exhibition pieces.

themes accumulate, they show limited consistency and in the end add up to ambiguous, unpersuasive arguments and insights.

Mozart continued, here and there, to weave into his operatic scores evocative patterns of this kind, those in *Così fan tutte*, for example, calling up, to marvelous effect, prior concepts and, in turn, illuminating new and related twists in the plot. Such musical phrases even traveled from one Mozart work to another: the motif uniting *Idomeneo*'s final chorus with that of *The Magic Flute* also forms the melody Countess Almaviva sings in *Figaro* as she pardons her husband; and, again in *The Magic Flute*, Pamina and Tamino, preparing to conquer the terrors of fire and flood through the power of their love, hear a version (in the minor) of this same reassuring theme, set like a song of praise and twice sounding after threefold trombone-colored Masonic chords. And does not the quivering music of Tamino's companion, Papageno, as he expresses the wish to change into a mouse and creep away from the coming trials, find echo in the *"Quantus tremor est futurus"* (What quaking there will be) of the Requiem?

Yet none of Mozart's recurring musical/literary operatic ideas achieves sufficient dramatic profile to give the cumulative impression of a clear-cut leitmotif; in his hands, rather, they offer subtler affinities and correspondences, their expository function in all likelihood reflecting the workings of his subconscious, not a calculated system.

He turned his back upon system and methodological pretensions: he propounded no operatic thesis and found nothing in any degree salutary in the reform opera's self-imposed restrictions, looking upon them as Draconian and in the end obtrusive: during his Vienna days he would emphatically reject its aesthetic (see p. 594). He followed not doctrine but instinct, seizing upon every occasion the libretto gave for realizing drama through music, whatever its caste, whatever its means—a marvelous grab-bag approach.[30] The tonal vocabularies and techniques of the High Baroque, Rococo, *Empfindsam*, and Storm and Stress styles in all their variants provided the freely spun threads of *Idomeneo*'s musical fabric. Significant individual strands of it came from Gluck, whose librettist Calzabigi had pointed to his own declamations of his texts as the ordering principle behind the long-breathed lyricism of Gluck's accompagnati, inflections that in turn invaded *Idomeneo*. Its accompagnati, of unique presence and

---

30 This indifference to aesthetic speculation paralleled that of the young Goethe, who gloried in never having "thought about thinking" and reproached those who "measured too much and felt too little." He and Mozart shared the Storm and Stress heritage of Hamann (see p. 322 and XVII, n. 11), who, rejecting Enlightenment method and rule, along with their offspring, the contrived and constructed, embraced the liberating, spontaneous, and instinctive.

psychological insight, look back through Mozart's own fledgling *opere serie* to Gluck's *Alceste* and forward to *The Magic Flute*. Directly from Gluck, too, came the elegant and remarkable conceit of the choral ensemble enclosing a vocal solo; used by Mozart as early as the *Apollo* of his childhood and as late as the "*Ah grazie si rendano*" of *La clemenza di Tito*, this structure gives Elettra's farewell to Crete its extraordinary amplitude.

If, as to type, the arias of *Idomeneo* recall those in his *Mitridate* and *Lucio Silla*, they display more richly burnished surfaces and, as a legacy of the most recent Parisian *séjour*, command a Rameau-like power to realize dramatic gesture through tone. Even so, their varied and athletic *opera-seria* cadence sounded quite old school to Gluck's adherents. Yet they must have remarked with approval his particular influence upon *Idomeneo* in respect to its high moral earnestness; and with it might be perceived traces of Winckelmann's romantic Hellenism, a cultural undercurrent stimulating both composers, the elder pervasively, the younger less so.[31]

Winckelmann's static, Pentelic Greece can be discovered but fitfully in Mozart's turbulent Crete, where torrents bring stark terror and tumult; where a gruesome monster materializes; where, chaos threatening, an outraged citizenry takes matters into its own hands; where Princess Elettra roams palace and yard, singing her mad roulades. (This creature of primitive, elemental power would seem more at home in a painting of Fuseli or in some Aeschylean nightmare.) *Idomeneo* no more partakes of a Spartan literary than of a sedate musical decorum. Abundant, impassioned, and voluptuously abandoning itself to music, the opera runs a course counter to the Gluck-Calzabigi reform, despite its protoromanticism a thing of distillation and abstraction; indeed, even when dark forces hold the reform opera's stage—be they Furies before the gates of hell or spirits from this nether world—Gluck's presences remain contained and majestic, communicating the severity of what Fuseli came to call Winckelmann's "frigid reveries."[32] (*Pace*, Dr. Burney, who claimed to have discovered a Michelangelo-like terribilità in

---

31 The Calzabigi-Gluck dedicatory preface to *Alceste* (1769), the manifesto of the reform opera, at moments paraphrases Winckelmann's essay *Thoughts on the Imitation of the Painting and Sculpture of the Greeks* (1755). Mozart's acquaintance with the manifesto cannot be questioned (see p. 594), and evidence bespeaks his also having read the essay (see n. 34); perhaps Winckelmann's name reawakened his memories of Rome's Villa Albani (see p. 273).

32 Uneasy about the expanding and stultifying influence of Winckelmann's theories, Sir Joshua Reynolds pointed out that the ancients offered "something beside mere simplicity." No less critical, Wieland, in both the *Komische Erzählungen* and the *Geschichte des Agathon*, set before his reader ancient Greeks not heroic and idealized but flawed, frail, and vulnerable, the very mold in which Mozart cast them in *Idomeneo*. Wieland offered the ultimate corrective to Winckelmann's pellucid Greece in a work both Wolfgang and Leopold Mozart relished, the comic novel set in classical time *Die Abderiten* (1774 and enlarged in 1781, the year of *Idomeneo*'s premiere).

Gluck.) The fearsome and bizarre link relating *Idomeneo* to Winckelmann must be sought not in this antiquarianism, but, rather, in the Blakean incubus Nettuno summons from mythological depths.

Rising from the sea to ravage the coast, Nettuno's monster calls to mind those immense serpents that appeared over the waters washing the plain of Troy, advanced upon land, and with their suffocating folds and pestilential breath destroyed Laocoön and his sons. Through the writings of Winckelmann, and, later, of Lessing and Herder, the famed Hellenistic marble representing this moment of calamity became a frequented point of departure for Germans discussing classical art. In a strange irony, those characteristics of repose, serenity, and stoical restraint Winckelmann extolled as the essence of Greek sculpture do not turn the scale in this example, which he nonetheless celebrated as embodying their ideal: though contained within a strict and complex geometric design, the figures, baroque in their histrionics and with their limbs contorted, writhe and grimace in the reptile coils. Winckelmann's epochal aesthetic rested upon an epochal self-deception.

The inverse of Dr. Burney's sweeping appraisal of Gluck's staid reform operas as "calculated for exciting terror" by representing "the tempestuous fury of unbridled passions," Winckelmann's lapse prompts remembrance of an episode in Goethe's *Götter, Helden, und Wieland* (1774), a farce satirizing Wieland's use of classical material. Goethe has him dream of meeting the demigod whom he celebrated as both hero of his singspiel libretto *Die Wahl des Herkules* and benefactor in his opera *Alceste.* Stepping back in terror before this colossus, Wieland cries: "If you are Hercules, you are not the person I had in mind."

In Wieland's place, Lessing would have recognized the Olympian superman on the spot: unlearned in the fine arts but deeply read in the classics, he, even while beholding the Laocoön through Winckelmann's eyes, had pointed out his error in viewing "the best and maturest" literature of the ancients as bound by the same laws he put forth as governing their sculpture: the personages in their writings, Lessing insisted in his *Laocoön, or the Boundaries between Painting and Poetry* (1766), did not limit themselves to a narrow range of restrained emotion but, to the contrary, without trammels expressed the passions that shook their souls.

Winckelmann never conceded that art might express intense emotion to the full and at the same time achieve a heightened beauty innocent of excess. Yet, though his disciples continued to keep their gaze averted from the paroxysms of the Laocoön, instinct did prevail and induce a fortuitous outcome to an aesthetic game: the Laocoön became linked to German neoclassicism as its icon of high pathos; transformed by Lessing's explication, the sculpture turned into a symbol of a movement all too often seething beneath its staid, accustomed façades, its turbulence preparing the intellectual and emotional climate in which might grow a work such as Mozart's *Idomeneo,* a creation of German Hellenism in the spirit of the Laocoön as the chisel had formed it, not as Winckelmann claimed it to be.[33] Along with the vipers of the Eumenides, the Laocoön rushes to mind as Mozart's Elettra, in her final aria, calls upon eviscerating serpents to tear her open.

Mozart fully partook of the artistic ideal the Laocoön, in fact, represented, that of high passion held in leash. While at work on *The Abduction* he lay hands upon the substance, indeed, took up the very tone of Winckelmann's argument and adapted it to indulge in an exercise rare for him, that of legislating aesthetics, Osmin's aria of rage his point of departure: "Whether violent or not, the passions must never reach any degree of revulsion in their expression; music, even in the most ghastly situations, must never offend the ear but, despite such circumstances, must give pleasure and thus remain music." Here he put forward Winckelmann-like doctrine[34] in Gluck-like prose: a dignified defense of art against the pride of exaggeration, against undiscerning imitation of nature's peculiarities, especially in the course of representing the purging of overpowering emotions. Acknowledging Leibnizian individuality, Mozart nonetheless here fell back into the protective arms of moderation, thus announcing that in his scores, even at moments of painful dramatic crisis, pleasure and beauty would never become accessory, would never fall forfeit: he would not risk the ideal in an undiscriminating pursuit of the real. Against the background of Lessing's revisionary writings, Mozart espoused a pragmatic approach to Winckelmann's higher truths. In *Idomeneo* the disciplined beauties of the storm scene and of Elettra's arias uphold a commitment to the control the Laocoön, itself, displays in its *Idomeneo*-like balance of the ecstatic and the quiet, the eruptive and the dignified.

Idomeneo was the powerful pivot upon which Mozart's art turned into its

---

33 When Winckelmann wrote his impressions of the Laocoön, he knew it only from plaster-cast copies. Even after arriving in Rome and contemplating the original (Rhodian of the first century B.C.), he did not depart from the aesthetic interpretation and principles enunciated in his famous essay; they continued critical for his subsequent studies. Here was a politic wheeling around of the Terentian adage: "*tu si hic esses, aliter sentias*" (were you here, you would think otherwise). Yet, an instinctive recognition of delusion betrayed itself from time to time: his extolling Raphael's "active tranquillity," for example, approached the oxymoronic.

34 A striking resemblance claims notice: the similarity of Mozart's comments upon Osmin's aria to Winckelmann's discussion of the face—in particular, the mouth—and gesture of the father in the Laocoön group. The sculptor, Winckelmann maintained, eschewed depicting the excessive violence and intense suffering of the desperate scene and represented it as stamped with an ennobling "sage dignity."

final decade. Only one cavil might be raised about this masterpiece: the very extravagance of the musical feast and the listener's incapacity to do it justice at one sitting.

8

"ALL'S WELL THAT ends well!" Leopold trumpeted to Wolfgang: signs pointed toward triumph as friends gathered in Munich for the premiere. Victoria Robinig and her two daughters (she and the elder of the pair, Maria Elisabeth, always a trial for him) arrived on 8 January, the son even earlier, and all of them waited through the successive postponements; Dr. Barisani and his wife came on the twentieth, and Mozart looked forward to greeting Schikaneder. The final dress rehearsal was to take place on the composer's twenty-fifth birthday, the first performance two days later: 29 January 1781 in the new opera house to be known as the Residenz or Cuvilliés theater.

For a moment a cloud cast its shadow as Leopold painted a picture of strange scenes in the streets of Salzburg: the Archbishop's magnificent piebald horses set into traces and hitched to carriages that then moved toward Vienna, the seats packed with servants decked out in Hungarian uniform, the racks piled high with trunks and with chests of table linen and kitchen utensils. Leopold and Nannerl watched with apprehension: they intended to travel in the opposite direction, toward Munich and the premiere, and to the last moment Leopold feared receiving orders directing him eastward. He warned his son: "Should a completely extraordinary *chance occurrence* prevent our leaving, you will have a letter in Munich. . . ." But his duties at court had become for the most part administrative and educational; though members of the orchestra journeyed to Vienna, he had no place among them.

On 26 January Leopold and Nannerl arrived in Munich, in all likelihood with scores for impromptu music-making in their baggage. They had already sent Mozart the unfinished *Zaide* and the masses K. 275, 317, and 337 along with Leopold's suggestion that he enrich the last two with additional winds. *Zaide*, Mozart hoped, would interest Cannabich and his circle, while the church music might be performed and serve once again to remind Karl Theodore of the varied talents of *Idomeneo*'s composer. He had warned Nannerl: "My sister must not be lazy but must practice hard, for people have high expectations." As recently as 3 September 1780 at Salzburg's Mirabell palace they had performed both the concerto for three pianos in an arrangement for two instruments and the sonata for four hands, K. 381. In all probability they planned to repeat this program in Munich. If the concert took place, it provided the final public appearance together of the whilom *Wunderkinder.*

A sense of valedictory hung over the premiere and the days leading to it. At his son's insistence, Leopold had packed his braided suit: the father was to appear his former elegant self at the balls and masked gatherings of Carnival. (Nannerl needed no prodding to fit herself out in fine style.) Throughout these fulfilling if anxious days, the Mozarts communed with their past. The emotional ritual of experiencing *Idomeneo* side by side solemnized the final dissolution of whatever bonds still held together these three once so tightly intertwined lives. A painting in work at the time lays open their subliminal awareness of this imminent unraveling: a peroration in pigment not of the three but of the four Mozarts—the family of the Grand Tour. Within days of his arrival in Munich, Mozart had written Leopold: "What about the family portrait?" And a month later: "Certainly your likeness has already been begun, and my sister's, too? How have things turned out?"

The unknown artist—in error long identified as Johann Nepomuk della Croce—had begun the commission late that autumn, when Mozart sat for him. During the following weeks both the painter and Leopold found difficulties arranging sittings, and then father and daughter had minor illnesses. Once recovered, she persuaded the housemaid of friends to erect her hair à la Marie Antoinette[35] and, thus coifed, began to pose on the last day of the year, Leopold after the return from Munich. To depict the head of the dead mother, the artist had to await the delivery to Salzburg of Rosa Hagenauer-Barducci's portrait (1775) of Anna Maria, which would arrive from Vienna, where Rosa resided, during the summer of 1781; the painting reached completion soon thereafter. The product of a provincial dauber, it nonetheless holds in its spell those acquainted with its subjects' triumphs and defeats.

To the left, Mozart and Nannerl, elegantly clad (he in soft red, she in dark violet), sit at the keyboard of a one-manual *Flügel* (wing, that is, grand) piano. His right hand has crossed over her left, a maneuver connoting virtuosity and the precedence they claimed in duetting on one instrument. Their hands attend to the music on the stand before them, but their serious eyes have turned toward the viewer. Lost in melancholy and looking, it would seem, within himself (and stooping, so as not to be higher than his children), Leopold stands to the right, behind the piano. His left hand

---

35 The Emperor provided a rare specimen of his humor when explaining his royal sister's towering and much imitated way of dressing her hair as derived from her Viennese origins, the high-pitched roofs of St. Stephen's inspiring the style Nannerl had long indulged (see XVII, n. 25) and now followed in its latest Parisian variant.

exhibits his violin (in proportion much too large), angling it upright on the top of the piano, on which the bow also rests, his right hand caressing it. Twenty-five years earlier the title page of his *Versuch* had shown him as a performer, bow on strings; now, behind him and to the right, an inkstand with quill pen indicates his status as scholar and author, a statue of Apollo playing his lyre, set to the right within a small niche high in the back wall, symbolizing the art to which the Vice-Kapellmeister's literary efforts redound. In the center of the wall and on a level with Apollo hangs a portrait of Anna Maria within a gilded, beribboned oval frame. She appears to float as mediator between Leopold and the children.

He no doubt authored the symbolism of a design calculated to portray a father in no way subordinate to his son. If it fails to balance the shape formed by Leopold and his emblematic appurtenances, on the one side, with the heavier mass of the children, on the other,[36] in the realm of reality this equilibrium had become even more uncertain. Epitome of a distinguished past, tableau of a bittersweet present, the painting encloses an element of presentiment, too: Mozart's vital and resolute face, his jaw determinedly set—the composer of *Idomeneo*. A glance back at the "Golden Spur" portrait of 1777 helps discover the extent of his mental and psychological ripening during the final Salzburg years. He had grown up and discovered, if rather late, that he did not need the family, but that it needed him. After the high days of *Idomeneo* in Munich, he would see his father again on only two visits, his sister on only one: the tale of the Mozarts of Salzburg had ended, the premiere of *Idomeneo* its brilliant coda, the painting its moving icon.

9

PERHAPS MORE INFORMATION about the premiere performances of *Idomeneo* will come to light. The family together, no letters passed between father and son; no newspaper or journal offered comments other than the *Münchner Stats-gelehrten, und vermischten Nachrichten's* praise of Quaglio's scenery (1 February 1781), in particular "the view of the port and of the temple,"[37] a notice reprinted four days later in Augsburg's *Ordinari-*

---

36 The artist may not have gone altogether amiss: time or damage appear to have effaced a detail preserved in engravings and lithographs of the canvas: a niche containing two figures, no doubt allegorical, set into the wall to the left, between Nannerl's coiffure and a swag of drapery, both of which obscure parts of the recess.

37 No trace of the production remains. Possibly Gluckean classicizing found expression in the scenery, costumes, and the performers' poses, togaed protagonists striking sculptural attitudes before backdrops and flats in the manner of Piranesi; or the designs might well have availed themselves of only a few *all'antica* traits accenting a rococo fantasy of the ancient world, the singers appearing periwigged, furbelowed, and in paniers, high-heeled shoes, and with facial patches.

Postzeitung; and no critical observations in contemporary diaries or correspondence have revealed themselves. The vacuum is almost complete.

The opera must have found a reception confirming the high praise the Elector had bestowed during rehearsals, for, after the first night, the Residenz resolved to send Mozart a special "present" in addition to his fee. Moreover, some twenty cognoscenti stepped forward to subscribe to a prospective printed edition of the score, among them Prince Max von Zweibrücken. (The project faltered upon Mozart's departure from Munich.)[38] Some must have found *Idomeneo* too German—"unduly stuffed with accompaniments"[39]—yet, had it won less than general acclaim, he could hardly have looked back upon this period with such a deep sense of joy.

Still, for all his satisfaction and pride, he feared that the prize he grasped at, some kind of permanent association with Karl Theodore's court, might slip through his fingers, that he would relive those former days in Munich: "No vacancy." All at once, he no longer had a hold on affairs. Perhaps the Electress had become less than enchanted with a composer who, upon his return from Paris, his sonatas in hand, had bestirred himself to gain access to her chambers, only, since his more recent arrival, to dance exclusive attendance upon her husband's mistress; Her Highness now showed herself, at best, indifferent to his remaining. Cannabich had overestimated the breadth of Countess Paumgarten's influence and led Mozart to look upon "the great patronage" he enjoyed (that is, hers and that of her Lerchenfeld-Siessbach relatives) as links in "a chain" of social power ensuring his "present and future position." In December he had still felt secure in the support of "the most eminent and powerful houses of the nobility"; by February he discovered a wall thrown up against his aspirations.

Disappointment cannot have stolen upon him unawares. Time had taught him much about the precariousness of expectations, and, even while putting the final pieces of *Idomeneo* in place, he had toyed with reawakening a plan formulated in Munich years before: to assemble a consortium of enthusiasts providing him an annual subvention in exchange for specially composed music.

There had been a beginning in 1776, when the Archbishop's brother-in-law, Count Prokop Adalbert Czernin of Prague, the father of Countess

---

38 On 1 May 1795, Mozart's widow would announce a plan (it, too, foundered) to gather a number of subscribers to underwrite the publication of *Idomeneo* in piano score. Mozart left such reductions to others (see XXXI, n. 61).

39 From the periodical *Pfeffer und Salz* of 5 April 1786 come the only surviving relatively contemporary words of musical criticism touching upon *Idomeneo*. They concern its performance in Vienna during the preceding month (see p. 653). After the above-quoted censure, the reviewer added: "Do not construe this opinion in the wrong. . . . I am not speaking here of Mozart's art in general, but only of his opera."

Antonie Lützow, settled an annuity of ninety florins upon *"le petit Mozart."*[40] He could not have received it more than once, for Czernin died early the following year. (K. 269b, contredanses of late 1776 or early 1777, may represent Mozart's requital.[41]) As the date of the *Idomeneo* premiere neared, Mozart had written his father: "I would like to have a few gentlemen like old Czernin—this would provide a bit of yearly help— but at no less than a hundred florins per annum; in such wise they might have whatever kind of music they desired." Inquietude alone could have revived this idea. There must have been moments when he wondered whether his life was to be all overture and no play.

After the premiere he gave himself over to the pleasures of Carnival. For weeks he had confined his socializing to diplomatic visits with the Cannabichs and the Paumgartens. Now Leopold censured what seemed to him high indulgence—doubtless much wine, endless dancing, and ambitious flirting. Seeking a partner at one of the balls with whom to turn and wind through the contredanse, Mozart picked up a prostitute and luxuriated in both the exhilaration of the dance and the opportunity to offend his father. In response to his churlish reproaches, he later claimed not to have straightway recognized her for what she was and, once having comprended the situation, even so felt it only polite to continue in her company: "I could not simply walk away without saying why; and who would let fall such a thing to someone's face? In the end did I not often enough settle her down and dance with others? . . . Moreover, no one can say that I saw her at any other time or was in her house. . . ."

Looking back upon these days he admitted: "In all truth, I amused myself too much. . . ." His state of suspense concerning Munich and his ill will against Salzburg had disposed him to this countervailing revelry, as had a reaction to his exertions of the preceding months: not only composing his heroic opera but also four occasional works, the richest of them the piano and violin sonata K. 378/317d.[42]

Its passages evoking the vanished world of the Mannheim sonatas add

---

40 The adjective served to distinguish him from his father.
41 K. 269b, which survives incomplete in a reduction for keyboard, duplicates two numbers of K. 101/250a, a set of dances of the same period.
42 To the compositions for Ramm and Countess Paumgarten, both touched upon above, must be added "Die neugeborne Ros' entzückt," K. Anh. 11a/365a, its text adapted from Gozzi and scored for soprano, strings, and a pair of horns. Mozart wrote this aria for Schikaneder's Salzburg production of *Peter der Grausame, oder Die zwey schlaflosen Nächte,* a comedy Friedrich August Werthes based upon Gozzi. Only after Leopold's angry prodding—perhaps he feared losing his free seats in the theater—did Mozart make time during his labors on *Idomeneo* to keep his promise to Schikaneder and provide the work. It arrived at the Tanzmeisterhaus in time to be sung at the performance of 1 December 1780. A leaf of the long-vanished aria came to light in 1996.

to the difficulties of dating a creation in all likelihood conceived in Salzburg and completed in Munich. Yet, in addition to a retrospective, carefully weighed manner, K. 378 offers his latest rhetoric, its fresh variety of nuance in its morning stage. Further, a tendency to grow toward bigger structures and more brilliant sonorities shows itself: both the middle movement, an Andantino of emotional exaltation, and the insistent, pointed closing Rondeau suggest the breadth of the piano concertos soon to follow. New musical perspectives opened before him as in high if apprehensive expectancy he waited, so near the center but not quite at it.

10

"I SHALL HAVE another bed put into the room where the alcove is, for one must manage as best one can," he had announced to his father and sister while preparing to receive them on the Burggasse. Sharing the small apartment and living "like gypsies or soldiers," the Mozarts stayed on to attend the repetitions of *Idomeneo* and to await evidence of the Elector's favor: their proudest hopes, his naming Mozart a *Hofcomponist* (a title implying periodic commissions and not liable to embroil those on the civil-service lists) and, of course, the special present.

It was hurling defiance to dally in Munich in anticipation of perquisites as, all the while, the Archbishop of Salzburg gave receptions with music in Vienna, his famous cembalist conspicuously absent. Father and son had come to perceive Colloredo's begrudging Mozart permission to work at another court as reflecting both jealous awareness of his contribution to the archbishopric's reputation and a no less equivocal possessiveness. "What you wrote me about the Archbishop—my gratifying (*kitzelt*) his ambitions—to a point rings true," Mozart opined in reply to a letter of Leopold's now lost. Whether this argument hit near or wide of the mark remains in question, but of undoubted substance and capacity was Colloredo's simmering anger: having let himself be prodded into taking the errant musician back, he now felt betrayed.

His ire—and the Electress's pique—doubtless lay at the root of Mozart's failure to secure a relationship with Karl Theodore's court. To all appearances, the Salzburg Residenz again warned Munich against a musician at best indifferent, at worst hostile, to traditional attitudes toward service, a recalcitrant the Archbishop planned to cashier as soon as expedient[43]

43 At no time during Mozart's unilateral prolongation of his leave did the Archbishop hold back his salary. It, as a matter of course, made its way into Leopold's pocket as would the compensation for *Idomeneo* and the Elector's gift.

and whom Seeau now held in wrathful enmity. From the time of the battle of the trombones, Mozart had used incivility as his weapon to hold the Count in check, and there had been "many skirmishes"; Mozart admitted: "I had to be coarse with him, or I would have got nowhere." That in the end Seeau scheduled fewer repetitions of *Idomeneo* than at first foreseen suggests a return of injury:[44] a collision of the calendars for the theaters and the princely regales did disrupt these projections, but it might well have been avoided had a will to do so prevailed. No more than three representations of *Idomeneo* took place.

Ash Wednesday (28 February) ended the season: the theaters closed until after Easter. Yet, Karl Theodore could have excepted Mozart from the Lenten rule and permitted further performances of his opera, perhaps the reason for his continuing to linger in Munich:[45] by the first week of March, without a word to the Salzburg court, he had extended his official leave of six weeks by another eight. With nonchalance he then joined father and sister on an excursion to Augsburg (7–10 March), where he wished to have a watch repaired and hoped to see his cousin. The Mozarts visited and, it appears, lodged at the monastery of the Holy Cross, he and Nannerl rewarding their Augustinian hosts with some informal music-making. ("Delightful beyond description," commented their treasurer, one David Bartolomäus Strobl.) An order from the Archbishop—no doubt vehemently worded—cut the sojourn short; Mozart was to proceed to Vienna at once.[46]

Though his attitude toward Salzburg had coalesced into a combination of apathy and defiance, he hastened to comply. He would turn Colloredo's behest to his own purposes: it provided a way of parting from Leopold and Nannerl without a farewell and its inevitable pain and confusion, for they expected him to return home with the court; by joining it now he could, without exciting mistrust, start scouting opportunities in Vienna for building a new life. The family retreated from Augsburg to Munich on the eleventh, Mozart leaving for Vienna the following day, Leopold and Nannerl for Salzburg on the thirteenth.

"*Andrò ramingo, e solo* "(I shall wander forth alone), Idamante sings, the words beginning and concluding *Idomeneo*'s quartet. (Mozart may have

44 His ill will against Mozart did not subside with time: four years later, even in the face of *The Abduction*'s triumph in other German cities, Seeau sought to frustrate its production in Munich and, in the end, only gave way to Karl Theodore's countermand (see XXX, n. 2).

45 Mozart made note of Emperor Joseph's hint that he might permit the Viennese theatrical season of 1781 to "continue throughout Lent," a license not granted until 1786.

46 The order, which must have been sent on to Augsburg from Munich, does not survive. For certain, it also bore upon Leopold's absence from his own duties, for he scampered home.

looked upon its opening and closing phrases as congruent, the ensemble unfolding between them being but an instant in the minds of the characters.) The quartet held a unique place in Mozart's heart. In later years his wife told of his breaking down as they and two friends began to sing it: he fled the room in tears, she following and attempting to console and calm him. In the opera, Idamante, as he approaches the end of the quartet, also proves unequal to completing the lines: overmastered by emotion, he stops short, and the orchestra finishes his part for him—but haltingly, it, too, broken by despondency.

Whatever its emotional cost, Mozart struck a blow for his own sanity by severing himself from his family. Leopold could no longer represent bankruptcy as a believable threat, and Mozart would no longer permit himself to be exploited for purposes become alien to his own: over the last years he had overinvested his energies in his father and sister. He now gazed upon a gorgonizing decision and survived: he shook off his filial chains and departed, single-minded in his resolve to remain in Vienna. "I was aware of it as I set out from Munich," he admitted later; no precipitate whim led him to this move: "You know that I had it in mind, even without any particular cause," he reminded Leopold. The journey to Vienna became a headlong flight from his past. He had no intention to return to two establishments that grated upon his spirit in the extreme: the Salzburg Residenz and the Tanzmeisterhaus.

At home he had closed in upon himself, his manner toward the family compounding whim, waggery, and benign tolerance, all masking a numbing feeling of remoteness. He had made no new friendships: ". . . I meet with not a kreutzer's worth of social intercourse in Salzburg; *I decline to associate* with many people there, and in the eyes of most others I am not good enough.[47] My talent has no stimulus! When I perform or when one of my compositions is played it is as if to an audience of tables and chairs." For him to enter the Residenz had become to take up his cross. "I would consider it a delightful prospect to receive in writing that [Colloredo] no longer requires my services," he had written home from Munich as his official leave approached its end; his only regret: not having celebrated his departure from Salzburg with the ceremony of "wiping my

---

47 These observations would find a parallel in Leopold's remarks to Nannerl upon his return home from a holiday in Austria and Bavaria in 1785: "And where shall I turn? Have I anyone [in Salzburg] with whom to exchange a sensible word? I don't know if I am too clever in the eyes of many or whether they are too dumb! In short, I am experiencing a very sad contrast to the company I kept in Vienna, Linz, and Munich." The Mozarts' permanent status at Salzburg closed the doors against those intimacies with high aristocrats they had enjoyed when visiting foreign courts.

behind with my last contract." This vivid diction bespoke finality, an attitude Leopold had not discouraged as long as his faith held in *Idomeneo's* power to cut a passage to a new financial security.

Idomeneo was to have been the charm. But, if the charm had failed, the sky of Mozart's world did not cave in: even if he now had a sense of himself as someone at home only in a no-man's-land—no sentiment of belonging to Salzburg remained in him—he did not suffer any loss of nerve but rushed forward with firm belief in Vienna's mythic pretensions; for too long he had time and again glimpsed the promised land only to find himself, to all seeming, fated to wander in the wilderness; Vienna beckoned like the Sirens. Traveling by way of Altötting, Braunau, and Linz,[48] an assertive, unapologetic Mozart appeared on 16 March at the Deutsches Haus. His strategy: to pretend to be eager to buckle to at the keyboard, and, enjoying without cost both lodging and meals, to use every free hour to reconnoiter and then maneuver himself into some kind of position in Vienna. He anticipated forcing an opportunity to play the score of *Idomeneo* before the Emperor. With Maria Theresa at rest in the vaults of the Capuchin church, Joseph II, too, would perhaps become his own man.

---

48 Mozart's description of this uncomfortable journey supplied a final touch to the father's and son's recent intermittent, and embarrassing, attempts at man-to-man humorous exchanges. By intuition each realized that his manhood and its predominance had long been the issue. To Mozart's earlier complaint about the injury done his posterior by the mail coach during the drive from Salzburg to Munich—"From Wasserburg on I really believed I should never bring my behind to Munich in one piece"—Leopold had responded that, for his part, he would avoid the mail coach if only to spare his privates: "I prefer my two plum stones." After taking the mail coach on the first stage of his journey from Munich to Vienna, Mozart pursued both images, to a certainty with the purpose of outdoing (17 March 1780); not only his behind but "what lies around it (*mein Arsh und dasJenige* [sic] *woran er henkt*) burned severely," he announced, calling attention to his own generative potential and thus emphasizing his maturity. Between these remarks, Leopold again, and quite out of character, sought his imagery in the groin, remarking of his vexations with the court chaplain: "*Varesco mi a seccato i Cuglioni*" [sic] (Varesco has withered my balls). Without knowing it, Leopold had acknowledged his impuissance.

CHAPTER XXVII

Vienna:

Enchanted Ground

F OUR O'CLOCK ON the day of his arrival in Vienna, Mozart seated himself at the keyboard to begin his duties of providing the archiepiscopal receptions with clavier music. Just as he regarded this household in the light of a convenience to be abandoned when no longer of advantage, so Colloredo now saw him as a personal vexation to be turned to account for a time and eliminated at the practical moment. At first a modus vivendi held its course despite mutual and deep resentments. At this point in their relationship, neither took the other in; all the more surprising that Mozart seemed to have stolen a march upon his father, who expected him home, salary intact, in the wake of the Archbishop's retinue.

But had not Leopold suppressed his cunning and willed not to see? Did not the unconscious, recognizing what had been suppressed, find outlet in an extraordinary gesture that served as both symbol and shield? He and Nannerl had not returned to Salzburg alone; they took with them the not quite twelve-year-old Heinrich Wilhelm Marchand, elder son of Theobald Hilarius Marchand, director of Karl Theodore's company of German actors.[1] Lodging with Leopold in the Tanzmeisterhaus as his student of

---

1 Wolfgang had met Theobald in Mannheim and recommended that Aloisia Weber seek his guidance about studies in acting. An administrator of Mannheim's national theater during its earliest years, he, along with a contingent of players, had followed Elector Karl Theodore to Munich.

clavier, violin, singing, and composition, Heinrich would become a surrogate Wolfgang, in time even traveling with Leopold and playing concerts en route. Heinrich helped sustain him through the major crisis of his life: Wolfgang's defection. With remarkable prescience Leopold had improvised a proxy to replace a son whose image, in the father's eyes, would soon lie shattered upon the rock of treachery.[2]

Though his letters now and then included greetings from Vienna to Heinrich, Mozart reacted oddly to his presence in the Tanzmeisterhaus, putting it on guard against what he held to be the boy's questionable character and sexual precocity: he and his brother had made "infamous" comments in public about their father's extramarital gallantry (here Mozart seemed to warn of disloyalty); moreover, at the age of eight, Heinrich (Hennerle) had already begun to pay court. "I would certainly rather sleep in your arms," he told a young lady, "than awaken to find myself embracing a pillow." He offered her a voluptuous present and a carefree future: ". . . when my father dies, I shall have money . . . and then we shall live together in great comfort. Meanwhile, let us love one another and savor our love to the full, for what you allow me now you will not permit yourself to allow me later on."

Little Heinrich's grand scenes must have gone the rounds and set the theater world laughing; how else had Mozart learned these texts he passed on with glee? Both parents on the stage (Frau Marchand was the actress Magdalena Brochard), the child's mind had become a storehouse of dialogue heard in rehearsals and performances, and bits and pieces of it stitched together formed the roles he played in public. Since in the end Mozart had to admit the histrionic source of Hennerle's extravagance ("all day long" the Marchand boys "hear nothing but [elocutions on] love, despair, murder, and death"), he veered to sail on another tack and to identify Hennerle as dangerous in a different and very real way—to young men; he and his brother had been discovered in mutual masturbation: "I know that in Mannheim no one ever allowed his sons to go where the Marchands were. . . . Well, it is a great shame for the lad, but you, my father, will be able to turn him completely around." The heart of a criticism remarkable for its lack of any comment upon Heinrich's musical abilities, this sarcastic touch identifies the exercise as sheer mischief, a mockery of Leopold for having brought home a double who mirrored a quite different

2 When it became evident that Nannerl might yet marry and depart Salzburg, Leopold also took Heinrich's sister, Maria Margarethe, a singer (and, like Nannerl, older than the brother), into his home (1782) as a scholar. Both of these Marchand children made respectable careers, she in opera, he as violinist and at the keyboard.

Wolfgangean capacity: his strong sexual endowment. Wolfgang ended amused.

In Vienna, Colloredo kept him under watchful eyes: colleagues like Ceccarelli and Brunetti enjoyed housing subventions permitting them to lodge where they would, but he found himself assigned a room—a "charming one," he had to concede—in the more and more overcrowded Deutsches Haus itself; here the Archbishop, his personal staff, and his domestic servants resided, and here at midday (for Mozart "a bit too early") the entire court gathered for dinner. As to supper, each retainer received a sum toward providing his own. "What liberality!" Mozart scoffed.

His wry comments upon life in the Deutsches Haus sounded out of tune and touch with the realities of the Salzburg court. He grumbled about being seated at table with retainers of subaltern degree: considering himself worthy of a place in the company of Count Karl Joseph Arco,[3] he, instead, found himself beneath the valets but "above the cooks." He should not have been surprised that the arrangements in the refectory of the Deutsches Haus echoed those at home, the kind of ranking that through the years had led him to avoid dining at the Salzburg Residenz. The Mozarts prided themselves upon being "*in every respect* altogether unlike the other . . . musicians." Alas, neither they nor the court concurred.

His sense of affront turned to fury and then to obsession when he saw ensconced above him at dinner the very valets who stood in attendance outside the grand salons in which he performed and felt at home. When taking a meal with them he adopted "an air of utmost seriousness" and then rushed from the hall with his last mouthful. Directing his hauteur no less toward servants than officials, he infuriated all. Appalled to hear what Colloredo required of his musicians when he visited the palaces of Viennese society—they had to gather before the portals to await lackeys who then marched them in as a group—he murmured: "Just wait 'till I come along."

Immediately before his first such appearance—at Prince Golicyn's—he told his colleagues to go ahead without him: "I went alone on purpose because I feel ashamed to accompany them anywhere. When I got upstairs . . . I paid no attention to either valet or lackey but walked straight on through the chambers, into the music room—for all the doors stood open—and straight up to the Prince; I paid my respects and stood there conversing with him." Ceccarelli and Brunetti, having already been marched in, stood against the wall "not daring to move forward." Here

---

3 A court chamberlain and son of Count Georg Anton, he presided at the very center of the Archbishop's household.

Wolfgang painted a familiar Mozartean scene (recalling that of Leopold beguiling the Papal Guard); but the contours and colors had a new boldness; Mozart was declaring himself no part of Colloredo's service. He had his own plans.

2

IN VIENNA COLLOREDO forbade his musicians to give public concerts, a restriction that crossed purpose with these plans. With high drama Mozart portrayed himself as kept from earning a living (true in the sense that his salary went to Leopold): "The Archbishop . . . has made me suffer the loss of at least a hundred ducats, which I for certain could have made by giving a concert in the theater. . . ." To put him in mind of his duties, Colloredo had, moreover, at first refused to let him take part in the Viennese Society of Musicians' benefit concert for the widows and orphans of departed members. But, having made his point, Colloredo in short order permitted, perhaps even encouraged, the association's president, Joseph Starzer, to reopen the question in terms of public charity and thus turn things about: on 3 April in the Kärntnertortheater, the Viennese, the Emperor among them, heard both a symphony by Mozart played by a giant orchestra under Bonno (see p. 484; the Society alone could assemble such forces[4]) and the variations on *"Je suis Lindors,"* the composer at the keyboard of a "beautiful Stein pianoforte" lent him for the occasion by Countess Maria Wilhelmine Thun-Hohenstein, a new admirer. With this appearance, Vienna at last put aside its tenacious image of him as a child prodigy, recognizing a commanding composer and pianist: "I had to begin all over again because the applause had no end."

For a concert on 8 April at the palace of the Archbishop's convalescing father, Prince Rudolph, Mozart provided three new works: Ceccarelli performed the aria K. 374 (*"A questo seno/Or che il cielo"*) and Brunetti the

---

4 Such a benefit concert offering the much appreciated speciality of an orchestra huge for its time, here comprised eighty-five to ninety participants. That Mozart enjoyed the sonorous experience attests to their clean ensemble. At all events, he had already worked with large forces: more than fifty-three players (as of 1773) at the San Carlo theater of Naples; fifty-seven (as of 1770) in Milan's ducal opera house; and the same number at the Concert spirituel of Paris (as of 1778). During his Salzburg days, his complaints about the Archbishop's band in the main concerned its lack of clarinets and its musicians' deficiencies, not its size, in fact, more than reasonable for a provincial capital: an average of twenty-nine during the decade of 1767–1777. Indeed, early in the seventies, Vienna's opera houses had much the same total of forces: the Burgtheater thirty-three, the Kärntnertortheater twenty-nine. Haydn's Salomon concerts in London early in the nineties used some forty instrumentalists.

rondo for violin, K. 373;[5] he then joined the composer in the violin/piano sonata K. 379/373a, completed the previous night. Brunetti had the notes before him, but Mozart, without time to write down his part, played from memory[6]—at moments the piano suggests the sweep of an improvisation. When he realized that the exchequer would send no special fee for the compositions, he became furious, refusing to see the matter in the light of his failure over the past months to provide the court with anything in return for his salary; nor did he care to remember the "five ducats" "old Prince Colloredo" had given each of the three soloists. (Besides, the Archbishop had presented Mozart with four ducats after his first appearance at one of the "grand" concerts in the Deutsches Haus.) A distressing coincidence had made him lose his sense of proportion: he "had been invited to Countess Thun's the very evening . . . [of] the shit concert [his reference to his performances before Prince Rudolph] and, of course, couldn't go; and who was there? *The Emperor* . . . what an opportunity!" At the Countess's, what with Joseph in attendance, a soloist might receive as many as fifty ducats.

Provided that his musicians met their obligations to him, Colloredo did not take exception to their appearing in the private salons of the city. Mozart began to lunch with Countess Thun and other aristocratic amateurs of the clavier, the high point of these gatherings: Mozart at the keyboard. Soon only bad weather found him at table in the Deutsches Haus. He became a familiar figure at the residence of Court Councilor Johann Gottlieb von Braun, "Vienna's greatest enthusiast for the clavier"; at Johann Philipp, Count Cobenzl's; and in the apartments of Countess Schönborn, the Archbishop's sister and an old ally. For musicales so informal that he could not expect a gift for his efforts, Mozart developed techniques for "stealing away" when he had "played enough *for nothing.*" But he did not hold back when visiting old friends: the Mesmer, Bonno, Leutgeb,[7] and Weber families. Now and then he called upon the Fischers (see p. 311)

---

5 De Gamerra's *Sismano nel Mogol* provided the text of the aria, which, like the rondo, had an accompaniment of two oboes, two horns, and strings.

6 Three years later a similar circumstance would arise in the presence of the Emperor at the first performance of the violin sonata, K. 454, which Mozart composed for the Italian virtuosa Regina Strinasacchi. Joseph observed him pretending to read the piano part from what appeared in the royal opera glasses as blank pages (though in both cases Mozart perhaps made use of some kind of musical stenography).

7 A hornist in archiepiscopal service, Joseph Leutgeb had left Salzburg for Vienna (1777), where he purchased, or perhaps had inherited, a small cheese shop, in Leopold's words, "the size of a snail's shell." That a loan he had made to the Leutgebs in 1773 still remained unsatisfied proved no obstacle to his son's renewing an old friendship. Into the bargain, cheesemonger Leutgeb still commanded his instrument.

in the Tiefer Graben, but stayed as briefly as possible. To Nannerl he admitted that they awakened his snobbishness: he could not "endure the warm little room and the wine on the table. I am well aware that such people consider this the greatest courtesy, but I am no admirer of this courtesy, much less of such people." This fleeting impulse to look upon coppersmith Fischer's threadbare lower-class milieu with disdain must have been a consequence of the driving energy poured into scaling the upper levels of Viennese society.

Cobenzl's cousin Marie Karoline, Countess Thiennes de Rumbeke, became his pupil, as did the daughter of Councilor Johann Michael Auernhammer, whom the Mozarts had met during their visit to Vienna some fourteen years earlier. After hearing Mozart perform at the benefit concert, she burned to become no less his lover than his pupil and began to spread tales of their artistic and personal affinities, her chatter hinting at sexual intimacy. Outraged—he had yet to lay eyes upon her but had heard of her homeliness and corpulence—for a while he resisted his father's advice to make her acquaintance and recruit her as a student (With no inkling of her passion for Wolfgang, Leopold looked upon the Auernhammers as an alternative to the Webers, with whom, he feared, his son might again become too close.) "I'll go to Herr von Auernhammer and his fat daughter as soon as the weather improves," Mozart promised Salzburg at the end of March, dismissing her as a conceited liar. But he did need money, and by June they had become master and pupil.

Running from one end of Vienna to the other, he had as his "main objective" to excite comment about *Idomeneo* and thus bring it to the Emperor's attention. He read the score at the keyboard in Countess Thun's salon, where the company included Gottfried van Swieten; Franz Xaver, Count Rosenberg-Orsini, Joseph II's director of theatrical productions, whom Mozart had met in Florence; and Joseph von Sonnenfels, the jurist and educator (see XXVIII, n. 5). Evidently Mozart also played *Idomeneo* in the rooms of a transplanted Salzburger, Ludwig Gottfried von Moll. But the goal proved elusive, and Mozart continued to ponder how "in some becoming manner" to make his way to the Emperor, to whom he now wished to reintroduce himself as an adult and a serious composer. "I am *absolument* determined that he *needs must get to know me.* I should love to whip through my opera for him and then soldier on with some fugues, for that is what he likes." Not having "a short oratorio" to be presented "in the theater for [his] benefit, as everyone does here," became Mozart's particular regret, for he felt certain of his power to draw an audience. His claim to have the support of "all the [Viennese] nobility" puffed a bit, but with remarkable efficiency he had established his presence almost at a stroke. (In his prime

Leopold could not have done better.) Yet, to achieve his ends, he had passed over an important duty—and one onerous to him beyond endurance.

Colloredo bristled at his failure every day to hover about in the outer corridors of the Archbishop's apartments (*Antichambrieren*), a gesture symbolizing eagerness to fulfill the Prince's will.[8] With disingenuity Mozart insisted: "I did not know I was a valet. . . . I ought to have wasted a couple of hours every morning in the antechamber." But he had to retreat from the pretense: "True, I was often told that I ought to be seen there, but could never remember that this was part of my duty[!] and turned up faithfully only when the Archbishop summoned me."[9] He could not both "antechamber" and dart from salon to salon.

As week after week Mozart hunted patrons, Prince Colloredo regained full health; however, according to Mozart, the Archbishop's sudden decision to return to Salzburg rested less upon his father's recovery than upon a social injury the prelate himself had suffered: it had become clear that Joseph II would not summon him to Laxenburg, the Habsburgs' country retreat for the chase and intimate entertaining; long a sign of Imperial favor, such an invitation had become an even more propitious token under Joseph.[10] "The Emperor hates him," Mozart reported in authoritative tones that must be weighed with caution along with his other caustic remarks about Colloredo. Whatever the case, by early April his servants had begun one by one to receive instructions to prepare to journey home.

3

THUS THE ARCHIEPISCOPAL encampment in the Deutsches Haus dissolved piecemeal. Once notified to go, retainers might petition to remain somewhat longer with the understanding that, the request granted, they

---

8 Methods of *Antichambrieren* became part of the curricula at academies for nobles (*Ritterakademien*) like Vienna's Theresianum.

9 More than one of Mozart's letters represent his remissness and stumbles by means of capricious and baffling inconsistencies and suppressions (see XXII, n. 11).

10 Twice a widower and childless, Emperor Joseph lived a mean life within his dynasty's gilded palaces. He had ordered many of their rooms hammered closed, abolished much traditional Imperial ceremony, and reduced his staff of domestics and his household guard to the point of hazard. Only at the demands of protocol and for visiting relatives would he entertain on a royal scale at the Hofburg and Schönbrunn, and, when not on one of his many journeys, for the most part found his pleasure in dropping in upon the salons of Vienna's nobility and high bourgeois, in particular those who cultivated music. (For this reason Mozart had expectations of meeting him in informal circumstances.) To make up for an almost nonexistent court, the great families of the capital provided the elaborate social functions it required, thus pleasing a ruler happy to pay for as little as possible. Among his own residences, he felt most comfortable in his simple domicile in the Augarten or at the small castle of Laxenburg.

would then have to provide for their own food and lodging. (The exchequer did agree to cover their coach fares back to Salzburg.) Orders to pack and depart went the rounds, but Mozart received none: "As yet I do not know that I have to leave, for until Count Arco tells me so himself, I shall not believe it [a proud fantasy that the Count and not a lackey would inform him]. When he does, I shall disclose my plans to him." They, of course, would be a fabrication designed to secure permission to stay on a while; he intended to keep his salary flowing up to the very moment the court would discover that he had settled for good and all in Vienna and then dismiss him. He saw the city in deep perspective and golden light: "A glorious place—and for *my métier* the best in the world. I like being here and therefore am exploiting [opportunities] to my utmost."

Aware of the nature of his father's fears as his consciousness grasped that his son had broken away, Mozart sought to soothe: "Be assured, my sole intention is to make as much money as possible, for, after good health, it is one's best possession." His object in Vienna was not, as Leopold suspected, to dance, drink, and whore: "Think no more of my follies [those Carnival days in Munich]." He held up before his father's eyes the probable Viennese musical succession: "When Bonno dies, Salieri will become kapellmeister; and then Starzer will step into Salieri's place; and for Starzer's position no one has yet been mentioned."[11] Insisting that even without an official position he could more than double his Salzburg salary by taking a few pupils and giving freelance concerts, he derogated the archbishopric: "How sad and what a loss to waste one's youthful years vegetating in such a beggarly place"; "You must have a bit of patience, and I shall soon be able to show you how useful Vienna will be for us all."

That he pretended to ask for "friendly and fatherly advice" about a *fait accompli* exasperated Leopold; his part of the correspondence has not survived, but Mozart's tenacious expositions of his position and patient (at times, even humorous) responses testify to the accusations, rage, and demands that must have filled the prose from Salzburg. To assert his adulthood and right to chart his own course, he had begun his first letter to Leopold from Vienna with a new salutation: "*Mon trés cher amy!* "[*sic*]. "Amy" was not ventured a second time.

The days passed, and, among the Archbishop's servitors, Mozart alone remained without a scheduled date of departure, a strange limbo that

---

11 By all odds, Mozart here referred to Starzer's title of *Compositeur des Airs pour les Ballets*; he had received it during Durazzo's days. A founder of the Viennese Society of Musicians and a member of van Swieten's circle investigating the music of Sebastian Bach and Handel, Starzer wrote dance scores for Hilverding, Noverre, and Angiolini and also produced a body of respected chamber and orchestral works.

should have alerted him to danger. By the second week of April, rumor ran of an impending directive requiring him to make his way home, but not until its arrival could he petition to stay. Yet the peculiar delay did not put him on guard; he anticipated no difficulties: with confidence he looked forward to receiving his orders and then requesting and, as a matter of course, securing that leave with full salary he looked upon as providing a period of financial transition for his father and sister. It did not occur to him that his superiors might have withheld the instructions as part of a strategy that would point him toward shipwreck.[12]

From the beginning they had expected him, in the family tradition, to prolong to the utmost any leave he might be granted. But a new element had entered with their strong suspicion and then its corroboration that he stood at the point of irrevocably cutting his links to Salzburg. Misled by the Mozarts' old presumption of a slack archiepiscopal exchequer careless in its routine, ensconced behind an arras of passivity, and, excepting a few bluffing gestures for the sake of form, on the whole indifferent and unequal to enforcing threats, he had taken for granted an unchanging tradition dictating flexibility and generosity in the matter of furloughs. Overconfident, he had shown his hand.

Colloredo's secretary-censors, and from time to time, without question, he, too, perused the father's and son's correspondence, their "secret" code which they still fell back upon, most likely over the years a source of office jokes. In an excess of bravura (28 April 1781), Mozart, throwing aside the cipher, boldly invited the Archbishop to read of the disdain in which his cembalist held him: "Oh, if he would only read this," he taunted, "I should be delighted." Assistants for certain brought such a passage to Colloredo's desk, and indecision as to how to cope with Mozart ended: to play this audacious game of baiting one's ruler was to challenge the lightning, and, within two weeks of this provocation, Colloredo, in a sentence combining high aristocratic tone with colloquial directness, confronted him with: "If you will not serve me properly, clear out" (*Scherr er sich weiter, wenn er mir nicht recht dienen will*). And, close upon, during a general audience, the Archbishop made occasion to repeat the caveat, whose acerbity again took

---

12 On 11 April 1781 Mozart announced his departure as scheduled for the twenty-second. But he had responded to hearsay; no directive to this effect had arrived; by 18 April he admitted: "At this moment I have yet to hear a word about when I am to leave." On 28 April: "I cannot yet write . . . when or how I shall leave. It is all truly deplorable." Intended more for the censors' eyes than Leopold's, these observations sought to preserve the appearance that he still looked upon Salzburg as his home. Though by this time he knew that his father could have no doubts about his strategy, Wolfgang trifled with him, now playing the child eager to be obedient and return, now—and most often—the unfettered adult. Cruelty did not lack on either side.

Mozart aback; he had bargained for apathy. Yet he continued to assume that the squall would die down and the matter of the leave run a wonted route.

At the beginning of May, a footman informed him not of the date on which to journey to Salzburg but of a command to vacate his room in the Deutsches Haus: "to move out that very moment." He threw his belongings into his trunk and went to the Webers' apartment, in the house called Zum Auge Gottes on the square (Petersplatz) enveloping St. Peter's church. Fridolin Weber had died soon after the family's removal from Munich to Vienna; Aloisia had married the actor Josef Lange; and Caecilia Weber with three daughters still at home—Josepha, Constanze, and Sophie—now made ends meet by renting rooms. Comfortably installed, Mozart delighted in their attentions, in particular Constanze's.

On 9 May he reappeared at the Deutsches Haus hoping to learn the date chosen for his departure. Valets armed with instructions awaited him. Colloredo had left his cembalist no time to request a leave: to his astonishment, his orders enjoined him to prepare to set out the moment he presented himself; the Archbishop wished to put into his charge an important parcel, which he was to pick up and carry to Salzburg at once. The valets handed him fifteen gulden, forty kreutzer with which to purchase a place on the diligence and two ducats more for expenses on the journey.

He thought in double time, explaining that he could not settle his rent at the Zum Auge Gottes—an obligation contracted, he pointed out, by reason of his expulsion from the Deutsches Haus—until he had collected fees due him for clavier lessons; in short, he required time: "Surely no one will insist upon doing me injury." His spontaneous ingenuity found a prepared response: a plea for postponement had been expected. Schlauka, one of the valets, advised him to put aside an excuse that would not weigh with Colloredo and, instead, to show himself in a better light, indeed, as co-operative, by seeking audience—at all events unavoidable, for he had to collect the parcel—and telling a more palatable tale: that once apprised of his orders, he had sought to purchase a coach ticket, found all the seats engaged, and, for the moment, could do little more than await an opening. He failed to recognize the parcel as a ruse and Schlauka's recommendation as a snare.

Only just arrived in Colloredo's audience chamber, Mozart heard him call out: "Well, young fellow (Bursch),[13] when are you going?" He responded with Schlauka's tale, court officials no doubt standing at the ready to give it the lie. He had been lured into some kind of judicatory proceeding, for the encounter continued with the leveling of accusations, the

---

13 In such a context and delivered in a disapproving voice, Bursch takes on a disparaging meaning combining boy, menial, and knave.

Archbishop's most serious complaint (*Hauptvorwurf*): the failure to "antechamber." But an unexpected outburst interrupted what may well have been the prelude to formal charges leading toward disciplinary action: the Archbishop fell into a terrible rage.

"He did not pause for breath," upbraiding Mozart for serving the Residenz "so badly," calling him "the most negligent[14] knave he knew," and advising him to depart that very day for Salzburg lest his salary be stopped. Even in his fury Colloredo signaled clearly: at the most Mozart might cling to his job (the court had yet to locate another virtuoso cembalist); but a paid leave in Vienna—downright unthinkable; he was, in fact, being marched home carrying an absurd parcel as a symbol of submission. "Unable to get a word in," Mozart observed Colloredo "burning like fire." He added "scoundrel," "rascal," and "miserable fool" (*Lumpen, Lausbub* and *Fexen*[15]) to the invective, striking back at the insulting descriptions of himself in the Mozarts' letters.[16] As the abuse rolled forth, Mozart's "blood began to boil too furiously" to prevent his throwing fresh kindling on the flames: "So Your Grace is not satisfied with me?" The bold sarcasm brought a final explosion: "What, you dare threaten me? You miserable fool! Oh, you miserable fool! Look, there is the door. I will have nothing more to do with such a rogue" (*elenden Buben*). "Nor I any longer with you," Mozart countered. "Get out!" Colloredo shouted at a now no less enraged Mozart, who, from the threshold, hurled back: "This is final; tomorrow you shall have it in writing."[17] "I banish you," Coriolanus hurled at the Rome that had banished him: "Despising . . . the city, thus I turn my back. / There is a world elsewhere." For one glorious moment Mozart must have felt no less heroic and godlike. He wrote his father: "I hate the Archbishop to madness."

Colloredo could not have foreseen the audience closing with confrontation; least of all exhibiting him in a shouting match with an underling, both for the moment appearing passionate equals. At all events, each had achieved something: Colloredo, though at the cost of losing self-command, had sent his *bête noire* packing under circumstances to which no charge of arbitrary power could be attached; Mozart found himself done

---

14 Here "*liederlichste*" bears upon slovenliness in respect to professional obligations and has nothing to do with character. Misinterpretations of Colloredo's use of this adjective have helped reinforce the myth of Mozart's licentiousness.

15 Colloredo harped upon this last word, which Salzburg usage associated with the cretinism endemic in divers Alpine districts.

16 Some five weeks earlier, for example, Mozart had described the Archbishop as "our Archboor" (*Erzlimmel* [*sic*]) and without recourse to the cipher.

17 Mozart reported this dialogue to Salzburg. He would not have falsified it: courtiers his father knew had either witnessed the scene or received firsthand accounts of it.

with this second father, but, at the same time, debarred from the salary with which to placate the first. He, for his part, could have found little consolation in his son's attempt to assuage: "Be in no way anxious about me. I am so sure of my affairs that I would have quit without the slightest reason." He rejoiced to find himself "no longer so unfortunate as to be in Salzburg service" and began to compose his resignation; according to protocol, it had to take the form of a request for discharge.

On 10 May Mozart returned to the Deutsches Haus to hand Count Arco the petition for dismissal and return the monies advanced for the journey to Salzburg. He would accept neither, telling this twenty-five-year-old that his resignation had no value without his father's consent! Long sympathetic to the Mozart family, the Count wished to protect its financial position by forestalling the inception of any official paperwork on the affair: having just written his own father in Salzburg, asking him to sound Leopold as to his view of the dilemma, the Count sought to buy time. He felt obliged to inform Mozart of the letter, and he, in turn, poured out to Leopold a newborn and unreasonable distrust of both Arcos, whom he now labeled "snakes and vipers": "The Count has also had the kindness to write very pretty things about me to his father, all of which you [Leopold], I presume, have had to swallow by now. There will, indeed, be some incredible passages, but, when you write a comedy and want applause, you must exaggerate somewhat and not adhere with too much fidelity to the reality of things." The reference touched upon not only supposed misrepresentations but also the trick—the parcel—that had tripped up the otherwise so clever young man, for he now saw Arco as part of a conspiracy: "You must . . . consider the readiness with which these gentlemen [the Arcos] wish to serve [the Archbishop]." For their part, the "gentlemen" and Leopold agreed that young Arco would best hang back until Colloredo's temper had cooled and then review the matter with him.

The imbroglio could not have stoked Colloredo's resentments or engrossed his thoughts for long; but, in contrast, it possessed Mozart. The Archbishop, he wrote home, had impugned the family's name: "To please you, my dearest father, I would offer up my happiness, my good fortune, my health, and my life; but not my honor, which I value, and you, too, must value, above all else." If, with no little irony, this fanfare disclosed honor as the force leading the son out of the family, such abstractions formed the least part of Leopold's disquiet. Though aware that the name of Mozart would suffer decline in certain circles—it had, in any case, long exuded a strong scent of rebelliousness—Leopold's concern centered in the immediate: the loss of the salary. Again Mozart sought to calm him by declaring his "obligation to restore and replace by my care and industry . . . what you believe you have lost by the incident," for the moment coming up with the obvious medicine: "By the next post I shall send you a little money to convince you that I am not going to ruin here. As to the rest, I ask you to be cheerful, for my run of luck is just beginning, and I hope that my fortune will also be yours. Write to me in cipher [*heimlich*] that you are pleased . . . but in public round on me so thoroughly that no one may blame you," the last phrase permitting him, so he hoped, to ignore Leopold's cries of distress and anger as clever dissembling for the sake of the censor. To grand theatrical effect, Mozart warned that in his wrath Colloredo might strike at the house on the Hannibalplatz; but not for a moment could either he or Leopold in good earnest have thought him capable of such vindictiveness; this was not his way.

4

THAT, IN ORDER to delay matters, Arco had not scrupled to assert Mozart's complete dependence upon a paternal fiat, betrayed on attitude in fact summing up Salzburg's unchanging view of him as a child; the Count's letter seeking direction from Leopold but underlined this sad reckoning. Forcing Arco to admit the foolishness of his claim, Mozart did have the pleasure of reducing him to double-talk: "If he [Leopold] is satisfied, then you can ask for your discharge; if not, you can ask for it all the same." "A pretty distinction!" Mozart observed. But Arco persisted in turning aside his petition and the money advanced him for the diligence to Salzburg. Arco hoped for Colloredo's putting the incident behind him and permitting Mozart to return home.

More than the clash in the audience chamber (which, it seems unmistakable, he, in retrospect, came rather to enjoy), the conversation with Arco for a time unnerved him: this rejection of his maturity touched the very nerve center of his difficulties. The evening of their war of words he fell ill at the opera: ". . . in the middle of the first act I had to go home and lie down, for I was flushed, my entire body trembling. I reeled about the street like a drunkard." He became fearful of the far-reaching effects of the crisis upon his well-being and ever more resented Colloredo, "this fine servant of God" who had forced him to show his anger, now breaking through in new and persistent rhythms: the reorganization of his personality continued.

Over the years he had developed the self-destructive habit of keeping his fury within, a holding back he looked upon as a virtue, a feat of overcoming. If certain artists find rage energizing, for Mozart the giving way of his carefully contrived inhibitions and with it the discharge of bile cost him much. He regretted occasions when agitation got the best of him: "I am nothing short of distressed when forced to become perturbed."[18] Now but to think of Colloredo provoked a draining choler along with anxieties, dejection, and interference with the creative processes. He worried about his health: "Were I offered a salary of 2000 florins by the Archbishop of Salzburg and only 1000 elsewhere, I would take the second offer, for, instead of the extra 1000 florins, I should enjoy good health and peace of mind. . . . If you [Leopold] wish to see your son well and content, you will write me nothing about this affair and bury it in deepest oblivion."

Leopold, of course, did nothing of the kind and made short work of Mozart's new and ingenious defense against him—the pretense that all was well between them, the imprecations from Salzburg being for the benefit of the censors. On 16 May Mozart protested: "I could only suppose that the heat of the moment made you write me a letter such as I have been obliged to read . . ."; and three days later: ". . . I have yet to recover from my astonishment and shall never be able to do so if you continue to think and write as you do. I must confess to you that not a single element in your letter permits me to recognize my father!" In quiet desperation he would remark: "You cannot possibly be serious." He asked Leopold to come to his senses: "I beg you . . . to strengthen me in this resolution instead of trying to dissuade me from it; you are making me unproductive." Here was the new dread he had first experienced while composing the closing act of *Idomeneo*. Had the young prince only wounded and not slain the monster?

Refusing to check his explosions of outrage and injury, Leopold went so far as to send Mozart a catalogue of his shortcomings, a vicious gesture he took in stride. "I know and understand all my faults; but cannot a man change for the better?" he asked with good humor, then adding with playful mischief: "Indeed, might he not have already changed for the better?"—the gentle byplay advising his father that he no longer knew with whom he dealt. Among the most poignant moments of the letters are those when, without warning, some residue of Mozart's love for him wells up: "Have undoubted confidence in me; I am no longer a fool; and certainly still less will you believe me a godless, ungrateful son.[19] So rely upon my brain and my good heart, and you will never regret it." But Leopold refused all confidence.

---

18 Whatever his inner state, in public, and even with family and friends, he sustained self-control to a remarkable degree; his sister-in-law Sophie Haibel remarked after his death: "Never in all my life did I see Mozart flare up in rage, much less be angry." He did, however, enjoy a reputation for combining firmness, civility, and a certain edginess into a compound with which to voice high and sharp displeasure.

19 Leopold charged him with having boasted of eating meat on fast days. Mozart replied that he did not consider the practice "a sin, since for me fasting means holding back: eating less than

By this time neither had legitimacy in the eyes of the other. As Leopold intensified the crudeness of his tactics, Mozart all the more played the understanding victim, a role he enjoyed for at the same time he laced his letters with hostile asides and ill-disguised suspicions, what seemed his most innocent remarks often being his most deadly. Whatever Leopold's imagined injuries or grievances, Mozart, with terrible calm, identified himself as the more sinned against and as unwilling to continue to camouflage meanings, especially in respect to a once fear-arousing subject: money.

From his earliest days in the Deutsches Haus he had suggested that the mysteries enfolding the family's finances could no longer remain impenetrable. "Meanwhile, you are drawing two salaries, and I am not at your table" (*aus dem Brod*)—an audacious sally;[20] and: "What about the Elector's present [the supplement to the fee for *Idomeneo*]? Has anything yet been sent?" If he never saw a gulden of it, at least he had begun to look behind the scenes, a prelude to making known his need of some minimum capital to establish himself in Vienna.

Leopold's response to even the suggestion of such a challenge was to accuse him of lacking any understanding of money. Mozart bristled: "And where might I have learned the value of money since to this day I have had so little of it in my hands." Outraged by his father's demand that funds flow from east to west and turning the tables in a game of retribution, he tantalized with capricious paper promises and serpentine evasions, keeping a mirage of ducats floating before Leopold's eyes. Early in June: "I cannot send you more than thirty ducats." Two weeks later: "I shall remit the money as you have directed." With this assurance came regrets that he could not spare more: "Be assured that if only I had something, I would certainly strip myself bare. But things will get better." Then with trenchant irony: "You must never let people know how you stand." He lunged—and toward the throat: he had glimpsed the depth of Leopold's deceptions. Not a ducat traveled to Salzburg until a first and last gift in 1783, offered as a symbolic gesture (see p. 625). Talking in many tongues with that verbal

---

usual." Wheeling the matter around with lively wit, he extended a mocking absolution to the father who also accused him of avoiding attendance at mass and consorting with prostitutes: "... should I ever have the misfortune—which God will prevent—to stray from the straight and narrow, I shall absolve you, best of fathers, of all guilt, for I alone would be the villain. ..." Leopold could not grant that they had become very different men.

20 He may have had in mind a story about one of the Marchand boys. Once, when Marchand corrected Heinrich's younger brother, Daniel Ernst, at table, he "took hold of a knife," so Mozart had heard, "and said: 'Look here, Papa, but another word and I will cut off my finger at the joint, and then you will have a cripple on your hands, whom you'll have to feed.'" Perhaps there occurred to Mozart the contrast between Daniel's insolence and his own filial subservience in having over the decades used his ten miraculous fingers to provide the comforts of the Mozart household.

virtuosity and in that gallimaufry of moods and styles he had mastered, he kept Leopold floundering.

The brother courted his sister's continuing sympathy by shipping to Salzburg the fabrics, painted ribbons, and fichus only Vienna could provide and, in addition, threw himself into the task of prying loose the portrait of their mother from its painter and having it transported to Salzburg (see p. 523).[21] Discovering trust in one paragraph and challenge in the next, the Tanzmeisterhaus found it difficult to read even on the margins of his discourse from Vienna: to determine what was true, what implicit, what latent, what mendacious. But, after all, this had become his very view of his father's communications.

Even as Count Arco worked toward restoring peace, Mozart defied his efforts, once again abandoning the family cipher in letters underlining a strengthened purpose: never would he take on the blame and pretend to have been wrong; never would he follow Leopold's exhortations to apologize: "Am I to make myself out a cur and the Archbishop a worthy prince? No one can do the first, and I least of all; and the second God alone can accomplish if He desires to enlighten him. . . . I have been forced to take this step and cannot deviate from it by a hair's breadth—impossible." He regretted not having seized the initiative during the confrontation by stalking out of the audience chamber instead of giving Colloredo the opportunity to show him the door. His letters had a long history of comments bordering upon defamation of a ruler. If the censor did pass copies of them on to the judicial authorities in Salzburg and had he returned there according to the court's plan, they might well have summoned him; the affair of the parcel might have been a device to deliver him into their hands; on his only subsequent visit home (some two years later), he could not banish fears that they might yet take action.

5

BY JUNE THE Salzburg court, unsure of what to make of Mozart's status, had begun negotiations to hire the Bohemian composer and cembalist Leopold Anton Koželuch,[22] to fill his place. Midst preparations for his re-

---

21 The artist, Maria Rosa Hagenauer (born Barducci) of Salzburg, had married the sculptor Johann Baptist Hagenauer (1764), a distant relative of the Mozarts' friend and first landlord (see XVII, n. 27).

22 Koželuch declined the offer, observing, according to Mozart: "What deters me most is the Mozart affair. If he [Colloredo] lets such a man go, would he not do worse to me?" The quotation appears a Mozartean embroidery: established in Vienna and with ties to the Imperial family, Koželuch would have had no incentive to settle in Salzburg.

turn to his Residenz, Colloredo could not have given the problem of Mozart much thought. He, however, imagined quite otherwise: "The Archbishop speaks ill of me to everyone here [Vienna] and is not clever enough to see that it does him no credit, for I am the more esteemed: he is regarded as an arrogant conceited priest who looks down upon everyone . . . I as an engaging fellow." On this point, Mozart and his friends sang in chorus, but the matter bulked no larger among Vienna's concerns than among Colloredo's. He, in fact, had no idea that Mozart had acted upon his angry threat to request discharge, for Arco continued to rebuff the petition and thus prevent its arrival at the Archbishop's desk.

Though he would end a prime monster in the Mozart bestiary, the Count, until the lamentable last moments of the affair, followed an honorable course in his attempts to serve what he saw as the family's interests—the Arcos had always treated mannerly with the Mozarts—even to taking on a confiding tone when he met with Mozart on 24 May. They conversed, he reported, "with all possible calm" and "courtesy." Encouraged to speak without reserve, he identified his salary as the heart of his discontent: "What purpose would be served were I to go home now? Within a few months even without [any new] insult, I would desire my discharge, for I cannot and will not work any longer for such a salary."

Arco responded with an estimate of Mozart's financial future as a freelance musician in Vienna: "Believe me, you allow yourself to be dazzled out of all proportion. Here a man's reputation lasts a very short time. In the beginning, it is true, you receive all kinds of praise and make a good deal of money—but for how long? After a few months, once again the Viennese want something new." In reality, Mozart disagreed, believing that their love of change made itself felt in the theater, but that they maintained a steady inclination toward his "specialty"—his "métier" ("this is the land of the clavier"). For the moment he chose to be politic and concurred ("You are right, Count") in order to indulge in a mystification: "But do you suppose I will remain in Vienna? On no account; I know where I shall go." He sought to scotch the belief, by now widespread and, indeed, true, that he had rejoined the court only to get a footing in the capital: "That this affair occurred in Vienna must be laid at the Archbishop's door, not mine. If he knew how to treat people of talent, it would not have happened. Count, I am the best fellow in the world if only people act toward me in the same way."

With agility Arco pursued the drift of this flimflam: "Well, the Archbishop considers you a most arrogant (*Erz hofartigen*) person" (the *Erz* signaling his awareness of how Mozart's letters played with this prefix to mock Colloredo; see n. 16). "I know it," Mozart rejoined, "and, indeed, I am so toward him; I treat people as they treat me. When I observe some-one holding me in contempt and as of little consequence, I can be as proud as a peacock."[23] In an attempt to draw Mozart's confidence, Arco asked whether it did not seem evident that "he, too, often had to swallow Col-loredo's abusive words." But Mozart drew back: "You have your reasons for putting up with it, and I have mine for refusing to do so." Perhaps resent-ing the personal disclosure as factitious, he took the hand offered in friendship and used it to swing to what seemed to him a higher moral level. At this juncture Arco may have had done with the clever but difficult young man: the Count showed a different temper when next they met to play out their closing scene.

It unfolded on 8 June in the antechamber of Colloredo's apartment. Mozart had already handed in his petition of resignation four times (he had revised it twice) and on each occasion found it thrown back at him. With this fifth rehearsal of the ceremony, he became beside himself with rage, above all because the Archbishop was to leave Vienna for Salzburg the following day: "I could not let him depart thus, for I understood from Arco . . . that the Archbishop knew nothing about [the petitions]; conse-quently, how angry he might be with me for having stayed on so long only to arrive at the very last moment with a document of this kind. I therefore composed another memorandum in which I informed him that I had pre-pared a petition four weeks earlier; found myself, I know not why, sent running in circles for so long a time; and now had no choice but to present it to him in person and at the very last moment."

Mozart's fierce determination to secure a discharge reflected more than a desire to end things in good order: without formal papers of separation, he might have difficulties associating himself with another court. By turning away his applications, Arco not only closed the door upon the Residenz's taking action; he also—and, perhaps, with Leopold's complic-ity—week by week heightened Mozart's fears of being left without proper credentials, a significant pressure to force his return to Salzburg. At last seeing through the strategy, he attempted a countermove: his special mem-orandum to Colloredo. However, it read as an ill-disguised indictment of Arco. Had he forgotten that such communications had to pass under the Count's eyes? When they met in the antechamber on 8 June, at first Mozart could not account for the way he "snapped at me with such acer-

---

23 He wrote "proud as a baboon (Pavian)," an amusing slip, *paon* (peacock) doubtless the French word he had been seeking in place of its German equivalent, *Pfau*. He had adopted the Vien-nese affectation of infusing French words with liberal hand into correspondence and conversation.

bity and treated me as if I were a rogue": Arco must have just read the supplementary memorandum. After his efforts to appease and reconcile, he
looked upon Mozart as incorrigible and, like Colloredo, now wished to
send him flying. Barring his way to the Archbishop's presence and calling
out "clown" and "knave," the Count hurled him out of the room with one
of history's most famous kicks on the behind, "by order of the Prince-
Archbishop," Mozart, quite mistaken, maintained.

Indignation had carried away an aristocrat brought up in the traditions
of those who governed the civil service and of undisputed loyalty to the
power it served. Under no circumstances would he have permitted Mozart
to present to the throne a memorandum disparaging administrative procedures and, by implication, himself. He had but indulged in a certain latitude in order to oblige the Tanzmeisterhaus. His aggressive and primitive
impulses now erupted and struck at a young man who all at once seemed
to him a personification of ingratitude. Mozart now saw him in an equally
loathsome light as no less Leopold's than Colloredo's coercive deputy.
These figures of paternal authority for the moment formed one body: taking the shape of the Count, the monster of *Idomeneo* had risen from the
depths to boot Mozart from the room.

6

THE KICK WOULD prove salutary, dispersing whatever shreds of leading
strings still clung to him, casting out and unburdening him of the last
traces of *Salzburgisch* beliefs and convictions. Yet in the days following the
incident he felt soiled, judging himself with severity for not having
straightway answered the assault. But it had come without warning, and
oedipal fears, abruptly surging, had for the instant thrown him back into
childish helplessness. (A fortunate reaction: an attack upon the Archbishop's chamberlain would have been regarded as an attack upon the
Archbishop himself.) Later he claimed to have left without remonstrating
in a desire "to avoid showing disrespect to the Prince's apartments[!]"; but
clearly he had taken to his heels in shock. He could not get over the humiliation. "The affair is at an end . . ." he declared: "I sent word to Count
Arco that *I have nothing to say to him.*" "To hoof someone out of the door
with a kick on the ass"; "I am so sick of the whole thing that I don't want
to hear anything more about it."

There followed a brief period of inner turmoil relieved by self-
administered medicines: he compounded these intense emotions into re-
tributory, healing fantasies shared with the Tanzmeisterhaus. He imagined
the Archbishop attempting yet further wickedness only to find himself

revealed and undone: first, avenging himself upon Leopold and Nannerl ("Let him try! I almost wish he would"); then, news of this tyrannical vindictiveness arriving in a Vienna averse to Colloredo ("The Emperor not only cannot stand him, he hates him"); and, in the final scene, Joseph stepping forth as champion ("Were you [Leopold] . . . to come to Vienna and tell the story to the Emperor, you would receive from him at the least your present salary, for in such cases the Emperor acts admirably").

What must have been an even more satisfying daydream centered around scenes in which Count Arco received requital: "He hurls me out of the door and gives me a kick on my behind. Well, in German that means that Salzburg is no longer the place for me, except to provide a good opportunity of giving the Count a kick on his ass in return, even if it should occur in the public street. . . . In the near future . . . I shall write to the Count of what he may feel assured of expecting from me as soon as fortune wills that I meet him, wherever it may be—provided that it is not in a place I must respect"—the last reflecting a continuing preoccupation with his failure to have been upon his mettle at the moment of the assault.

Such fantasies helped him recover. But if from without his spirits appeared to rebound at a good pace, the deep trauma, dissipating by slow degrees, lingered beneath the surface of an elegant young man who, in an exquisite new wardrobe[24] (Clementi would be taken aback by his magnificence) cut so fine and, it would seem, relaxed a figure in Vienna's great salons: tensions remained, threatening to rupture the shell. In what other terms can one understand his excessive absorption in what he called "the Tyrolese tale"; it fascinated, frightened, but, most of all, elated him, inspiriting his ultimate Arco fantasy; he devoted the best part of a letter (8 August 1781) to a ghastly experience endured by a certain Herr von Wibmer.

Nothing is known about Mozart's acquaintance with him other than their having met in Munich. Wibmer, who had become associated with a touring theatrical troupe,[25] accompanied it to Innsbruck. There, on a Sun-

---

24 In his haste, Mozart had departed for Vienna with only one outfit, what he had on: "I had nothing . . . but my black suit, and the mourning [for Maria Theresa] had passed." He counted upon the Tanzmeisterhaus to forward the rest of his clothes by mail coach. For Leopold the task must have appeared a painful symbol of permanent separation. He dispatched the garments piece by piece, in truth, an inexpensive way of managing the matter, for drivers often delivered a small parcel as a favor. However, that a Mozart in possession of his complete wardrobe stood a fairer chance of putting down roots could not have failed to suggest itself to the father. Mozart found himself embarrassed: "The clothes did not arrive; I had to have some made; I would not go about Vienna looking like a ragpicker. . . . My linen had become pitiful to behold."

25 Mozart in error identified Wibmer as its founder and misunderstood his name to be Wiedmer.

day morning, a certain Baron Buffa accosted him in the street, castigating him for the inadequacies of the company's female dancer. The abuse mounted; Wibmer protested; Buffa boxed his ear; Wibmer returned the blow. The matter seemed over, and Wibmer made his way to his rooms to regain his composure and with the intention of taking the matter to the governor (*Präsident*) of the district, Count Paris Ignaz Wolkenstein und Trostburg.

Wibmer found members of Innsbruck's militia waiting for him. They marched him to the guardhouse, where he received a sentence of twenty-five lashes on his behind for having laid hands on the Baron, "for in Inns-bruck," Mozart observed, "the stupid Tyrolese custom evidently dictates that no one may strike a nobleman, even when justified to do so." Wibmer protested the illegality of the punishment in view of his own rank as a "von." In no way impressed, the soldiers next hauled him to the prison and there, in answer to his remonstrations and what they held to be his preten-sions, inflicted double the number of lashes. He fell into unconsciousness and had to remain in bed for three weeks before finding the strength to travel to Vienna to lay a complaint before the Emperor. Wibmer carried to him a letter of support from Archduchess Elisabeth (see XIV, n. 19), now Abbess of the Imperial *Damenstift* in Innsbruck.

Reports of capricious methods of dispensing justice in the Tyrol had reached Vienna, and Mozart adjudged von Wolkenstein the spirit behind the savage act. Certain that Wibmer could never obtain commensurate amends—"the lashes will always remain"—Mozart delivered his ultimate fantasy of the retribution he wished visited upon Count Arco: "Were I Wiedmer [*sic*], I would insist upon the following satisfaction—[Buffa] must be forced to endure fifty lashes in the same place and in my presence and, in addition, pay me 6000 ducats." If Vienna did not command this compensation, Mozart, in Wibmer's place, would accept no other from the culprit, but, "at the earliest and best opportunity" extract his own: "run-ning my sword through his [Buffa's] heart."

Not only fantasies but also, another of his traditional remedies, a good dose of persiflage, helped him calm the storm within. His had never been a frail equilibrium: throughout his many crises, a strong, balanced core for-tified by humor always reasserted itself. He had lost little time in again tak-ing up dealings with the world and wrestling with the often farcical realities of Viennese musical life. His genius had little capacity for routine, and he had long possessed an ability the Viennese admired: to appear playful, en-gaging, and combative, all the while switching mechanisms as circum-stances required; he showed ease in rearranging his façade, and Vienna respected a practiced dissembler. But he did not invest all his energies in the intrigues of professional matters: that special kind of self-exploration called courtship provided him the most helpful physic.

Though the Arco affair had a part in precipitating him into the consoling and pampering arms of the Webers, a more powerful force hurled him headlong: his sexual impulses, vital and demanding. He had decided no longer to postpone marriage and with it complete genital gratification. His move to the Petersplatz could not have been a sudden idea inspired by the order to quit the Deutsches Haus: for certain he had made arrangements quite early to join the Webers once his expected leave began. His migration to Frau Maria Caecilia and her three daughters represented a return and, over and above, a beginning—a setting out afresh, unsullied and unburdened. A flirtatious, seductive tone enveloped his doings. Leopold sensed it from afar and chose a broad, exposed front facing the formidable battalion of Weber women as the terrain for his final, pathetic and, at times, comical battle in a war long lost.

7

WITH HIS SON'S arrival as a boarder at Caecilia Weber's home, all of Leopold's fears converged into a single focus. The anger with which he addressed his letters to the Zum Auge Gottes may be imagined. His cannons shot a desperate warning; Mozart returned a measured reply: "I can assure you that what you wrote about the Webers is untrue. What is true is that I was a fool about Frau Lange [Aloisia], but, when in love, what is one not liable to do . . . ? Rest certain that old Madame Weber is a very obliging woman and that I cannot do enough for her in return for her helpfulness. . . ." Mozart found her *Dreimädelhaus* a place of gentle domesticity: fine food and wine—in later years even Leopold would celebrate her table—two claviers (one with a mechanism reminding him of the Tschudi instrument he had known in London), and the trio of charming young ladies eager to launder, mend, and console.

In an outrageous moment, Leopold drew a parallel between Wolfgang's treatment of him and the shabby—so they both at the time believed—behavior of Aloisia toward her mother. Mozart boiled over: "That you set me and Madame Lange in comparison utterly astonished me and upset my entire day. That girl was a burden to her parents inasmuch as she could not earn anything. Hardly did the time arrive when she might have shown her parents gratitude—bear in mind that the father died before she earned a kreutzer here [Vienna]—than she forsook her poor mother, attached herself to an actor, and married him; and her mother never received a pittance from her. God!" (The expletive sounded the cry of a son every day more resentful of the terrible truth that he himself did not have a florin of the thousands he had reaped.) Caecilia Weber had, in fact, haggled over and received a generous settlement and annual allowance from the Langes as the price of blessing their union, a fact she kept from Mozart: for his ears she constructed the fable of benefits forgot so that she might appear vulnerable and impoverished when the day arrived to negotiate with him.

There were few evils in which Leopold believed Caecilia unschooled, though he had yet to meet her or, indeed, any of the Webers. That the letters he wrote to Vienna during this period do not survive can, in all likelihood, be ascribed to Constanze: she must have destroyed them in order to spare her husband's memory and the Weber name those acid accusations hurled broadside by an old man become covetous and cruel, their flavor of wormwood growing fuller and more tart—so Mozart's responses reveal—with the son's removal to the Zum Auge Gottes. No longer did Leopold look upon him as a magnification of his own image; he raged as if wanting to smash a foe.

The more vehement Leopold's invective, the more dispassionate and pratical Mozart's replies; to one of the most distressing of his father's imputations he answered: "[You write that] I have yet to show you love and should now show it for the first time (Can you really say this?); that I never sacrificed my pleasure for your sake! What kind of pleasure do I have here? The care and toil of concentrating on making my way! You believe, it seems to me, that I am swimming in pleasures and entertainments [the Webers]. Oh, how you deceive yourself!" Mozart indicated that Leopold's denunciatory tactics would not succeed in forcing open a purse filled by such effort: "For the moment I have only just enough money for my needs." In fact, fees from lessons and salon appearances provided a comfortable bachelor's life.

The new Wolfgang Mozart, mantled in self-sufficiency, affronted Leopold beyond measure. Unwilling to cede tomorrow to the young, he wished the bygone to repeat itself indefinitely: the war he had for years waged against time had been a war against his son. At first glance Mozart, too, might be suspected of hoping to see the past overtake the future as he returned to the environment that had harbored his first attempt to establish a mature relationship: the Weber household with its resonances of Aloisia. But here he put the symbolic force of former days to constructive use: that of opening a passage to complete adulthood. During the last two years he had reaffirmed his sense of self and broken out of the family; now, in the process of further redefining his personality, he would find lover and wife, an ersatz Aloisia, in the less handsome but more agreeable Constanze. At the same time, he could neatly dispose of that final and intolerable outward link to Leopold, the consuming matter of money: in view of a new Mozart household and family to be sustained, Leopold would have to cease his financial demands. Whatever the cost to his psyche, Mozart permitted his image of Leopold to dissolve; indeed, it had begun to melt away in the heat of the father's greed. Mozart would enter maturity with Constanze at his side: *Mann und Weib.*

8

WITH LITTLE JUSTICE, tradition looks upon the Webers as a gaggle of unsavory women of whom Constanze proved—at most—the best. With no husband and three unbetrothed daughters, Caecelia Weber promoted the idea of Mozart's becoming her son-in-law: put to her shifts in expensive Vienna, she encouraged this suitor with no fixed financial resources and an ill-defined future, a strategy derived from either desperation or a belief that in time he would find his way; perhaps both. At least twenty-one, Maria Josepha seemed rather too old; Sophie at eighteen a bit too young; the nineteen-year-old Maria Constanze emerged the candidate. Even so, without his co-operation no intrigue could have succeeded: he wanted to get married and had set up chez Weber with the idea in mind. At Frau Caecilia's coquettish prompting he fell in love with Constanze and went along with the family's plan that they wed; it rested on firm ground.

Constanze had established a sympathetic alliance with him during that troubled visit to Munich, when Aloisia set him aside. Touched by his shock and misery, she had offered her friendship, and they developed an easy confidence. He welcomed her company and gave her music lessons, which they resumed in Vienna. Her fine ear, facility at the keyboard, excellent soprano[26], and appreciation of his sensitivity no less than his talent helped deepen a relationship "born," he recalled, "of her tender care and solicitude." In beauty she stood no comparison to Aloisia of the magnificent carriage, superbly defined cheekbones, and classic profile; but he came to prize Constanze's more modest charms, summed up for him "in two little black eyes and a pretty figure."

Leopold feared for his son's ensnarement even as the young victim surrendered to it in bliss. But a strange ritual journey lay before him: he would

---

26 It appears beyond question that Mozart measured the soprano solo lines of the mass in C minor to her vocal resources and that she sang at its premiere in Salzburg. Unlike her sisters, she held back from a professional career, though after Mozart's death she did appear in public at benefit concerts for the family. Here she favored selections from *La Clemenza* and, in particular, *Idomeneo*, which she sought to make better known. At home Mozart had delighted in her performances of Ilia's *"Se il padre perdei."*

be constrained to quit the Weber residence not only at his father's demand but also at Caecilia's. She suddenly announced her distress to hear horrid stories all at once going about Vienna—rumors her own nimble tongue had sent forth. They told of Mozart's preoccupation with Constanze having reached an intensity precluding his continuing to sleep in a room within steps of hers; of the peril to her reputation he had become; of damage to it that perhaps not even marriage could undo. How wrought up Caecelia appeared: why, the unfairness of it all!

Another topic of the day had doubtless shaped her machination: news that the Hofburg had all but fixed upon Mozart to compose the opera for the impending visit to Vienna of Catherine the Great's son and heir, Grand Duke Paul. (Mozart had much impressed the Emperor at the charity concert.) The fee, Caecelia realized, could get a young couple going in style: Mozart would be on his way. But the Hofburg held back from announcing a decision: it remained a matter of discussion among Count Rosenberg-Orsini, the actor and playwright Johann Gottlieb Stephanie the Younger, and the Emperor. Count Rosenberg encouraged Mozart's hopes; and when, at the end of July, even though final approval had yet to come, Stephanie sent him a libretto, he started to compose it, his head bursting with music. Signs of good fortune multiplied: by chance the opera's heroine bore the divine name of Constanze.

Though Mozart called for secrecy even as he wrote to Salzburg about the project, the personnel of the Burgtheater had word of it; moreover, Constanze could not have been a stranger to how her suitor filled his days; and her mother not only heard the buzzing but also had excellent means to make inquiries through Constanze's guardian, Johann Franz Joseph Thorwart, auditor of Joseph II's theaters. Mama Weber now saw Mozart in a new light: as a truly good catch. She determined to construct and cast a strong but fine, indeed, almost invisible net through which he could not slip and in this tactic had Thorwart as accomplice.

In the immediate future, Caecilia well knew, Mozart would have no desire to wriggle free, but she comprehended the ease with which a young man might change course. Sowing rumors impugning Mozart's moral integrity, she would propel him to proclaim it by signing a marriage contract. Caecilia did not have the advantage she had pressed in respect to the vulnerable Lange, who had led a pregnant Aloisia to the altar; thus, in Mozart's case, Caecilia sailed nearer the wind than most would have ventured and lay herself open to the possibility of legal counterblasts.

For a while she kept her mask from falling, and he believed her lies. He, too, lied without shame, his letters to Salzburg altogether misrepresenting his intentions. Advising his father, who had heard of the stories afloat in

Vienna, to "believe and trust him more than certain individuals who have nothing better to do than to slander the honest," he deplored having to "take another lodging, and that only because of idle talk. I regret being forced to this on account of tittle-tattle without a true word. . . . Because I am living with [the Webers], I am therefore to marry the daughter. The chatter . . . makes absolutely no mention of our being in love; rather, I lodge in the house and *marry*. If ever in my life marriage lies far from my thoughts, certainly [the time] is now. . . ." As if to strengthen himself in imposing this fraud, he then put himself through the exercise of paraphrasing Leopold's rehearsal of the calamities attendant upon early marriage: "God did not give me talent so that I might sacrifice it to a wife and thereby pass an unproductive youth. I am just beginning to live my life; should I myself make it bitter? I have nothing against matrimony, but at the moment it would be a calamity for me."

Turning back to the idea of moving, he found "no other course." He had to avoid any appearance of compromising Constanze, "though, in truth . . . those who do not frequent the house cannot even tell whether I enjoy her company more or less than that of the rest of God's creatures, for the children [the three daughters!] seldom venture out except to the theater, and I never go with them since I am, as a rule, not at home at performance time. On occasion we did visit the Prater [a pleasure garden in the Leopoldstadt; see XXVIII, n. 33], but then the mother came along, and, as I was in the house, I could not refuse to accompany them. Nor at that time had I yet heard any of this twaddle and nonsense. I must also relate that I was allowed to pay only *my share*. [Leopold's vexation about expenses on the trip to Kirchheimbolanden must have flashed across his mind; see p. 398]. Further, when the mother heard this talk and also learned about it from me, I must say that she herself did not want us [Wolfgang and Constanze] to go anywhere together and advised me to move somewhere else in order to avoid further unpleasantness. She said that she would not want to be the innocent cause of my misfortune [a marriage forced by circumstances]. This is the only reason why for some time, that is, since people began to gossip, I have contemplated moving." Caecilia must have had an extraordinary talent for acting.

Were it not for those "malicious tongues," Mozart sighed, he would not budge; nowhere else would he find such "comfort and such friendly, accommodating people. I will not say that being in the same house with the Mademoiselle, to whom rumor has but just now married me, makes me ill-humored or that I do not speak to her. But I am not in love with her: I play the fool and have fun with her when time permits (only on those evenings when I take supper at home, for in the morning I write in my room, and during the afternoon am rarely home); and that is the whole story. If I had to marry all with whom I have jested, I would at the least have two hundred wives."

Though at moments his wit rises to mock Leopold's fears, this letter of 25 July 1781 for the most part negotiates a sea of loose prose uncharacteristic of him: he seems, with eyes closed, to be laboring through the tide of deceptions. His father must have recognized the effort as altogether trumped up. Moreover, by implying that he gave Caecilia's urgings to depart the Webers more weight than Leopold's, Mozart canceled any hope that the letter's general tone might calm Salzburg. On the other hand, as to where to set up anew, circumstances constrained his following paternal advice; but perhaps he did so relishing an anticipated contretemps to be placed at Leopold's door.

9

AT FIRST MOZART had in mind moving to the home of "young [Joseph Conrad] Mesmer," the doctor's cousin and director of the school at St. Stephen's, but discovered that he and his wife had become patrons of the composer Vincenzo Righini,[27] who, in fact, resided with them. Whereupon, pursuing his father's recommendation, supported, Leopold stressed, by Karl Joseph Daun, a Salzburg canon, Mozart took quarters in the household of Leopold's and Daun's friends Johann Michael and Elisabeth Auernhammer. It included their daughter, Josepha Barbara, by now the young master's pupil, and so taken with him. By invoking the canon's name, Leopold had sought to disguise his purpose: that she succeed in distracting his son from Constanze. Daun must have made the arrangements, and, in all likelihood, the well-to-do Auernhammers did not ask for rent, but, rather, an adjustment in the fees for Josepha's lessons. Whatever the arrangement, early in August Mozart moved in, having hired a clavier for his new room.

A measure of skepticism must accompany enjoyment of his delicious, impudent, and, at times, brutal descriptions of life with the Auernhammers; he could not resist paying Leopold back in hard coin for his hostility toward the Webers. Mozart paints a picture of an eccentric domicile out of *opera buffa*, an establishment, the lively prose suggests, much more dangerous to the virtue of a young bachelor than the apartment he had just been forced to quit.

---

27 A year earlier, the Emperor had summoned the Bolognese Righini to Vienna. He became singing teacher to Princess Elizabeth of Württemberg.

Actors, musicians, dancers, and designers had always been part of the Webers' surroundings. They appreciated the free rhythms of an artist's life and knew how to bend to them. At their home Mozart had been able to compose until a craving for food forced him to put down his pen. (". . . as a rule, I write myself into a state of hunger.") "Whenever it became indispensable for me to keep on writing," he remembered with appreciation, "they delayed the meal as long as I wished." Most often he did not begin his toilet until afternoon, enjoying the luxury of laboring at his desk "without being dressed" and of slipping into an adjoining room in which he would find his midday meal and, if he chose to work longer, also take his supper. In the evening, however, he often made time to join the women, for they "did not go to table before ten o'clock."

A different spirit and regimen prevailed at the Auernhammers: they had their evening meal "as early as eight or at half past eight at the latest," and the routine of their kitchen often did not respond to his needs. When its schedule and his were at odds, he had either to resign himself to the expense of a caterer bringing a dish to his room or to the "waste of at least an hour" while he dressed before going to a restaurant. But if he found little comfort and contentment with the Auernhammers, they did afford him amusement: when he did appear in their dining room, he had to make efforts to "hold back laughter" at the ways of the hulking lady of the house, whom he called "this *meuble.*"[28]

His portraits of Elisabeth and Johann Michael offer close-ups of a Viennese couple with more than a few touches of Goldoni about them: she, "the most stupid and ridiculous gossip . . . wears the trousers; when she speaks he dares not utter a word"; he, so henpecked that his every outlay in the tavern or for a fiacre had to remain secret from her, in contrast, showed generous impulses—"the finest fellow in the world." To describe their daughter—"a holy fright"—Mozart opened a vein of coarser texture. The young man whose correspondence in the main shows gentle breeding—excepting a few rough passages, the most famous of them his complimentary closes and the faecal and sexual humor of the Bäsle letters—here descended to a vulgarity almost unique in his writing;[29] his purpose: to sneer at, agitate, and shock Leopold by maintaining that his

28 A piece of movable household furniture; in time Mozart came to terms with Frau Auernhammer.
29 An extravagant blending of pornography and scatology, the allusions to Countess Paumgarten's sexual favors to Elector Karl Theodore (letter of 13 November 1780; see p. 559) rank, on the ladder of Mozartean baudiness, side by side with his descriptions of Josepha and with certain of his riddles, canons, and entries in Nannerl's diary.

bumbling efforts to separate his son from the gentle Constanze had, with the complicity of Canon Daun, in fact led him to the very cave of Venus.

"As to the daughter: if an artist wanted to paint the exact image of the devil, he would have to use her face. She is as fat as a peasant wench, perspires so much that you feel like vomiting, and walks about in such skimpy attire that you can read clear as day: '*Please look here.*' True, there is enough to see to strike you blind: if you are unfortunate enough to turn your eyes that way, you are punished in appropriate measure the entire day—only tartar [a popular purgative] can help! So disgusting, dirty, and horrible! Ugh, the devil!"

There must have been much compulsive looking: she stimulated his voyeurism and eroticism. That this upsurge of sexual impulse had also awakened a disparaging spirit, that the female organ could so provoke resentful and angry remarks filled with abhorrence and fears of chastisement, revealed a young lover not free of anxieties as he looked forward to taking full possession of his genital function in the arms of his Constanze. He had already expressed such apprehensions at the end of his comments on Countess Paumgarten, painting a forlorn picture of himself as an unhappy man ("*ich unglücklicher Mann*") thinking of her privates ("*einen schönen Ring*"), but desperate ("*soll der Tod über mich kommen*") to have an erection ("*ohne Nase*").

Mozart's boorish thrusts at Josepha Auernhammer (begun late in summer) constituted an epistolary mechanism for Leopold's sake and also reflected a process deep within himself, one made up of an interplay of contrarieties: the central action of Mozart and Josepha's drama had a different reality, for, in fact, they worked well together at the piano and enjoyed a good-humored friendship. The possibility of erotic games cannot be excluded, though his aversion to her person appears to have been genuine. Whatever the case, he had forgiven her those foolish fabrications, for he held a high opinion of her talent and testified to the solid keyboard technique she had received from her former teacher, in all likelihood Georg Friedrich Richter.

"The young lady . . . plays with charm," Mozart had granted at the end of June, "though in cantabile she lacks the true, graceful singing style: she performs everything *détaché* [*verzupft*].[30] In secret she has revealed to me her plan, which is to work with diligence for two or three years more and then to go to Paris and make a career. She said: '*I am not pretty*; o [sic] contraire

---

30 Mozart prided himself upon a smooth and singing tone, which Josepha, schooled in the *détaché* manner, had yet to acquire. Beethoven, in turn, found Mozart's touch "delicate but choppy, with no legato."

ugly. I do not want to marry some chancery creature earning three or four hundred gulden, and I will not get anyone else. Thus I prefer to remain as I am and want to live by my talent.'" She contemplated in horror the prospect of being handed to a nonentity together with a dowry and approached her young teacher as a friend and co-conspirator, begging his help in realizing her goal of independence, an ambition he well understood.

By August he observed with satisfaction that "everyone who heard her [play] before [her studies with him]" remarked about how "entirely she has changed." But the inevitable had come to pass: "She is not satisfied if I spend two hours with her every day," Mozart moaned. "She wants me to sit there the whole day and, what is more, tries to make herself enticing! To crown all, she has fallen *sérieusement* in love with me, which I thought a joke, but now know to be a certainty. When I grasped it—for she took liberties such as making tender reproaches to me if I came somewhat later than usual or could not stay long, and more of the same—I felt compelled, so as not to make a fool of her, with good grace to tell her the truth. But it in no way helped; she fell ever more in love. I always remained very polite to her except when she started her antics, and then I became very rude. Whereupon she took my hand and said: '*Dear Mozart, please don't be so angry. You may say what you like. I am really very fond of you.*' Throughout the city, people, astonished that I have of my own accord chosen such a face, are saying that we are to be married. She told me that when she heard anything of the kind she always laughed at it; however, I knew from a certain person that she confirmed it, adding that we would then travel together. This incensed me, so the other day I spoke my mind in plain words. She ought not abuse my kindness. Now I no longer go to her every day, but only every other day and shall go more and more seldom. She is nothing but a lovesick fool."

A Mozart intent upon reducing the frequency of his visits to the Auernhammers' obviously no longer lived with them. His residence there had been brief: little over two weeks. Not only had he chafed under Josepha's attentions and the inflexible ways of the household, but crisis had overtaken it: the parents must have discovered the intensity of their daughter's attachment to him, for they determined upon his departing as soon as possible. With no thought for his needs, they left him insufficient time to find suitable new quarters; he wryly observed: "The good man [Herr Auernhammer], of course, had in mind only himself and his daughter." By the third week in August, desperation had driven Mozart to take a room he described as fit "for rats and mice, but not humans. [The landlady, herself, called her home the "rats' nest."] At midday you had to look for the stairs with a lantern. My room could be called a little closet. To get into it you had to pass through the kitchen. The door of my room had a little window. They [the landlords] promised to hang a curtain over it, at the same time asking me to open it as soon as I had dressed, for otherwise they would be unable to see anything, either in the kitchen or the rooms adjoining it."

He immediately recognized a blunder especially foolish owing to the impossibility of ever inviting guests to such a lodging. "Ah, that would have been a noble address at which to receive visits from various distinguished people." During the fourth week of August he sought refuge back at the Auernhammers',[31] who took him in, but only for as long as he required to locate a decent accommodation. He set out on the hunt (doubtless with the aid of the Webers) and from the Auernhammers' wrote Leopold about "bargaining" over the price of two rooms, "one of which I shall for certain take, since I cannot live here. . . . It appears that Herr von Auernhammer wrote you and reported that I actually had quarters! In truth I did, but what a place!" Embarrassed by having forced the young man's hasty exit, Auernhammer must have felt the need to communicate with Salzburg and set some kind of gloss upon a situation even more awkward than he knew: he had yet to learn of the squalor into which Mozart had stumbled. The dilemma dissolved by the close of the month: September 1781 opened with him installed in a house on the Graben, the great oblong open space that had become the bustling center of Vienna's commercial and social life.

---

31 When not skipping over or obfuscating the matter, Mozart studies tend to confuse the Rats' Nest with the Auernhammer home, thus making the landlady of the first into the mistress of the second!

CHAPTER XXVIII

Vienna:

Putting Down Roots

T HE TWO ROOMS between which he chose were on the highest floor of the mansion (today No. 17 occupies its site) across the Graben from St. Peter's and the Webers' residence. To escape the noise rising from the square, he took the space opening upon the courtyard. Perhaps the gilded lions embellishing the façade of the imposing dwelling alluded to Saint Mark and Venetian commercial affairs (see XV, n. 56), for in Mozart's time it had as main tenant a businessman: the purveyor Adam Isaac Arnstein, factor to the Habsburgs and Vienna's most notable Jew. He leased most of the structure—Jews could not yet purchase real estate in Vienna—as living quarters for his family, its domestics, and the personnel attached to his wholesale enterprises. Madame Theresia Contrini, who with Jacob Joseph Keesenberg owned the property, restricted herself to a chamber in the utmost story, where Arnstein doubtless housed his clerks. It seems a reasonable surmise that his son, Nathan Adam, arranged that one of these upper apartments be made available to Mozart: Nathan's wife, Fanny, knew the Webers; in fact, to much good opinion she had accompanied "a Mlle. Weber," perhaps Constanze, on the clavier in the salon of Baron Gottfried Adam von Hochstetter (January 1780), probably not an isolated occasion, considering women's growing participation in cultural life, in particular, musical

Gesellschaften (social gatherings).[1] What with the ties between the Webers and the Arnsteins, it would appear that Constanze persuaded them to install Mozart within a one-minute walk of her home. He entered into friendship with the Arnsteins—they would figure among the subscribers to his concerts—a relationship presaging the sympathetic links he and Constanze would forge with the Jews and converted Jews of Vienna. In their world he would meet Lorenzo Da Ponte, born Emmanuele Conegliano in the ghetto of Ceneda.

Like his father's place in society, Mozart's had been uncertain. In recent years he had felt even more the outsider, at times not unlike an exile seeking refuge. Yet he had learned to draw strength from being different, and showed sympathy for those who imparted something, even if only a whit, of his own image: the unconventional, the special, the rejected. As one who knew and endured society's distinctions and their expedient distortions, he must have recognized familiar and sympathetic qualities in his new Jewish acquaintances.

Vienna did not have many Jews: about forty families, five hundred souls at most, had permission to reside within the city. Because of his singular importance to its economy, Arnstein alone among them had license to set himself up conspicuously, impressively, and where he would. That he retained the patriarchal beard and caftan of tradition, while his son dressed in high fashion, indicated the social changes under way. The encroachments Cardinal Migazzi had deplored (see p. 45) were now becoming the rule; but if the fierce coercions, exacerbated by his and Maria Theresa's horror of the Jews (see n. 5) had passed, even so, they still had to endure a variety of humiliations and prohibitions,[2] though by law these vanished upon baptism.

A Jew like the younger Arnstein had much in common with those bourgeois at the time forming with rapid strides a new level of noble throughout the Reich. In the spirit of middle-class enterprise, Emperor Joseph had taken to selling titles wholesale, if not on the cheap (for a countship, for

---

1 "But let us be fair," Johann Pezzl protested in his *Sketch of Vienna* (1786–1790): "Intelligence, wit, and knowledge are not intrinsic to men." He held out the example of more than one hostess as "doubly engaging" for combining "a male intellect with feminine grace." Until the Josephinian era women had taken a minor role in Vienna's cultural life, and Fanny Arnstein's rise bore witness to the beginnings of a triple emancipation: female, bourgeois, and Jewish. By Napoleonic days she would preside over one of Vienna's most intellectual salons.

2 And not only in Theresan Vienna: in Frederick the Great's Berlin, for example, even though Moses Mendelssohn, with Kant among his competitors, won a prize (for an essay on metaphysics) offered by the Prussian Academy and also gained the status of "protected Jew," the King denied him entrance into the Academy by reason of his religion alone.

example, he demanded a tidy twenty thousand gulden).[3] Still, unlike Salzburg's *Briefadel*, mired in their consuming struggle between modest beginnings and high aspirations, many of Vienna's recently ennobled, in particular those with university training, became the focus of their capital's cultural and business life. It mattered little that most of Vienna's families of high descent, perplexed to see the distinction of means superseding that of birth, held aloof from the freshly titled: they remained content to league with the wealthy tradesmen, burghers, and financiers from whose ranks they had come and also with the Jews now taking advantage of the opportunities for integration the Emperor put forward with hopes of harnessing their ingenuity in matters of commerce.[4]

Bolstered by the rich and complex vigor of its origins, this omnium-gatherum of high bourgeois groups and newborn aristocrats began to coalesce into a kind of patriciate whose common meeting ground went beyond class. An elite of the mind, a reservoir of ideas, the brains and ethics of a new Vienna, this spontaneously evolving body, by its diversity and amorphous nature, threatened the integrity of the immemorial concept of proper and defined social orders, the more and more familiar figure of the converted Jew[5] most dramatically announcing the passing of the ancient certainties. For those starting their climb from lower levels, ascent could be effortful as they labored to assimilate new patterns of culture and behavior. More fluid boundaries ringed the top: through marriages offering ducats in exchange for lofty connections, many a rich bourgeois slipped into the company of the old order; and not a few of its members moved in the opposite direction to appear at the doors of the new salons.

Most of the ancient families of lineage nevertheless continued a moral slide into frivolity and ignorance, breaching faith with the only responsibility time had left them to justify their pretensions: an inherited code of propriety and with it devotion to the state—to its security, well-being, and culture. Throughout the Reich they in great measure became accounted laughingstocks, simpletons, and boors concerned only with the trifles of

---

3 "I despise men who purchase nobility," he told Casanova. "Your Majesty is right," he replied, "but what are we to think of those who sell it?" The Emperor never addressed another word to the witty and audacious Venetian.

4 A series of decrees culminating in the Toleranzpatent of 2 January 1782 opened to Jews certain economic areas hitherto closed to their participation and also gave them restricted access to the universities. Nonetheless, controls remained upon the number of Jews permitted in Vienna and just where they might live.

5 One such had entry to that Holy of Holies, Maria Theresa's apartments: her close adviser, Joseph von Sonnenfels, grandson of the chief rabbi of Brandenburg and son of the converted Jewish scholar Alois Wiener (born Lipman Perlin). Her loathing of Jews rested upon their being Christ's primal deniers; once they received baptism, she, in fact, favored them.

position—coats of arms, costume, and hunting prerogatives. Such attitudes, Vienna's chronicler Johann Pezzl observed, became typical of the Viennese dandy, for whom the deadly sins constituted "a sensible discussion, a useful book, hard work, and a bad meal." (Reformers put forward pleas somehow to educate the highborn so as to render them one way or another useful to society, and Vienna's Collegium Theresianum, an academy for young nobles, attempted an organized response.) In propitious contrast, Vienna drew profit from those serious and insightful high aristocrats who, eager to lead productive lives, withdrew from the sterile world of their birth to assume the values of the refined bourgeoisie and contribute to a reinvigorated society entering upon cultural transformation.[6]

From his first days in Vienna, Mozart began to shape a course touching the full gamut of this world in flux: the comfortable middle class; monied Jews; the elite bourgeoisie, in particular with purchased titles; those *Briefadel* having histories of distinguished service to the Hofburg; the loftiest nobility;[7] and the Imperial family itself. All of these parties, in fact, formed an affiliation of privilege, for overnight the old aristocracy's exclusive claims had become myth: there seemed to be only two entities—the unwashed multitude and those above it.

Unlike France, this was not a society in disintegration, but, rather, in metamorphosis. Though it pursued broad political discussion, the Viennese salon lacked the fierce originality, mental power, and the bitter, frustrated tone and sense of incendiary menace so often part of its Parisian models, which scorned, if not despised, the monarch. In Vienna raucous revolutionary politics found few forums; there change came in slow time and without perceptible struggle as, by degrees, systems of values and codes of manners, long accepted as predestined, proved too weak to keep new ideas at a distance. In this variegated and polyglot capital, with its shifting sense of decorum and its atmosphere of deracination, Mozart, as if in ironic mockery, at last put down roots.

---

6 This is the Vienna of Strauss and von Hofmannsthal's *Rosenkavalier* (though set in Maria Theresa's reign, the libretto sends forth Josephinian echoes), wherein the daughter of a newly titled "von" finds her hand sought by both a vulgar baron of the degenerating aristocracy and an as yet unformed but *empfindsam* young count, also of high birth. He wins her, and in all likelihood they become part of the new mixed society.

7 The wealthiest of the country nobility, living on revenues from their ancestral estates—most of them in Hungary, Bohemia, Moravia, and the Tyrol—resided in their Viennese palaces at least during the social season and in some instances year round. (Those aristocrats dwelling at or near the remote Habsburg courts of Milan, Florence, and Brussels only on occasion made the journey to the capital.) The landed gentry, in great measure without the resources to sustain urban establishments, tended to remain in their provincial homes.

2

FROM THE GRAY area between the well-established *Briefadel* and the aristocracy of birth came the most helpful of Mozart's early Viennese patrons, among them Countess Maria Wilhelmine Thun and Count Johann Philipp Cobenzl.[8]

The patriarch of the Thun-Hohensteins of Bohemia, Johann Joseph Anton, "Old Count Thun" in Mozart's parlance, divided his year between his palaces in Linz and Prague, while his son, Count Franz Joseph Anton Thun, lived in Vienna. A Freemason, he also embraced mesmerism and dabbled in alchemy and the occult, believing his touch to have curative power. Mozart held him "a peculiar but well-meaning and upright gentleman." His captivating countess, Maria Wilhelmine, made their drawing room a center of belletristic, scientific, and, in particular, musical discussions, pursuits that did not keep the company from chat, jokes, games, and dancing. Unpretentiousness prevailed at the best of Vienna's salons, and Mozart made himself marvelously at home in this world of free spirits where, if the mood seized him, he could play the fool and set the table in a roar. When at the keyboard, however, he demanded utmost seriousness; the slightest restlessness, noise, or talk and he broke off and might quit the instrument. "On such occasions," his first biographer Niemetschek, recorded, "the almost always gently courteous man quite lost patience and expressed his annoyance without reserve."

Poor musical manners had to have been rare among the guests of Countess Thun, in all probability once a pupil of Joseph Haydn. She played the piano, Charles Burney remembered, with "that grace, lightness, and delicatesse to which no fingers but a woman's can aspire." Wilhelmine captivated him outright, as she did Mozart,[9] Joseph II, Archduke Maximilian, and Count Johann Philipp Cobenzl (now an Imperial vice-chancellor), all of them sensible to the force of her beauty and intellect. Yet, no hint of scandal or even of amorous trifling or possessiveness touched her many friendships of this kind. Her salon interlocked with Cobenzl's: afternoons at one might dovetail with soirees at the other to form a harmonious social whole Mozart in particular savored; he felt to a remarkable degree at ease with Cobenzl, an old friend.

---

8 Mozart felt bound to cut his ties to a high aristocrat long helpful to him, Archbishop Colloredo's sister, Countess Schönborn: "She would for certain say something to me, which in all likelihood I would not swallow without answering; it is always better to avoid such things."

9 They may have met as early as 1762, when he performed at the palace of her father, Count Anton Corfiz Ulfeld.

Leopold Mozart placed the Cobenzls among those families involved "in the most important matters," and, indeed, Johann Philipp, as Habsburg representative, had played a principal role in negotiating the Peace of Teschen (see XXII, n. 4). He had studied at Salzburg, at which time Leopold must have met him. Their paths crossed in 1763 during the Mozarts' stay in Brussels, where the twenty-two-year-old Cobenzl formed part of the Habsburg court: his name appears in Leopold's journal; no doubt he heard the Wunderkind perform.

At the time of Mozart's arrival from Munich at the Deutsches Haus, Cobenzl's cousin Franz (also a Count Cobenzl) had begun his final days at Salzburg's school for pages. Mozart, who had made his acquaintance at home, proceeded to turn this link to advantage in Vienna by seeking the friendship of Franz's sister, Marie Karoline, wife of Count Chrétien Charles Thiennes et Rumbeke, a chamberlain at the Hofburg. She and Mozart forthwith reached a footing of intimacy, and it had been the Countess who reintroduced him to Johann Philipp. The cousins counted among Mozart's most devoted admirers, Marie Karoline preceding Josepha Auernhammer as his first Viennese student, Johann Philipp becoming both friend and protector. Mozart spoke of writing variations for Countess Rumbeke, most probably K. 352/374c, the eight keyboard variations on a chorus from Grétry's *Les mariages samnites*, a handsome set anticipating the opening movement of the piano sonata K. 331/300i (see p. 630).[10]

Mozart became a regular at Cobenzl's home in Vienna and more than once visited his country estate on the Reisenberg, a ridge of the Kahlengebirge overlooking the city. "The little house is not much," Mozart commented—Cobenzl had yet to enlarge and transform this villa taken over from the Jesuits upon the dissolution of their Order—"but the surroundings: the forest in which he has built a grotto as if made by nature!" Cobenzl had begun to create a park in the picturesque English manner. Mozart had beheld its like in many a princely domain, and his praise

---

10 The Rumbeke variations may be one of another two sets Mozart turned out during June of 1781, both based upon chansons: either K. 359/374a, the twelve variations for keyboard and violin upon *La bergère Célimène*, or K. 360/374b, the six variations for keyboard and violin upon "*Hélas, j'ai perdu mon amant.*" Any of the three sets might have derived from variations he had improvised before the court (". . . when everything [the concert] was over, I went on playing variations for an hour . . . for the Archbishop gave me the theme"). Of course, he might have written all three sets for the Countess. There remains the possibility that K. 265/300e, the twelve keyboard variations based upon the French air "*Ah, vous dirai je, Maman,*" once thought to date from the 1778 stay in Paris but now ascribed to 1781–1782, may have been associated with either the Countess or Josepha Auernhammer. Whatever the case, he himself needed a new stock of display pieces for Viennese drawing rooms.

("splendid and very agreeable") of a style not to his father's taste, and, therefore, hitherto not to his own, might have been another way of underlining his independence.

Yet he had been swallowing with pleasure those large and for him refreshing doses of Anglomania dispensed in many a Viennese drawing room, in particular Countess Thun's, and perhaps had begun to reconsider aesthetic matters in response to a new kind of salon celebrity all at once thrust upon him: it took rise from his being a source of informed admiration of things English by dint of those many months in London, during which he had enjoyed the patronage of Buckingham House and acquired the ability to read English and speak it after a fashion. He started taking lessons to broaden his command of the language and would befriend British musicians resident in Vienna: Nancy and Stephen Storace, Thomas Attwood, and Dublin-born Michael Kelly. Mozart could not have failed to encounter the Anglophile Baltic German Georg Forster at the Countess's during his stop in Vienna (1784). This natural scientist—he had accompanied Captain Cook on his second voyage to the South Seas—and, later, political revolutionary relished his every moment in her company and recalled reciting "English poems to her the entire evening": Gray, Pope, and Shenstone,[11] the latter also famous as a landscape designer.

No less fierce than the passion for English writers, a delight in parks and gardens in the English manner, indeed, a rage for English picnics on English-like lawns enclosed by English flower beds, had seized Viennese society; "the Viennese dandy," Johann Pezzl scoffed, "... thinks himself English when he picnics, drinks punch, and wears a round hat." Women of rank pursued male visitors, "young or ancient, handsome or ill-made," as long as they came from "somewhere between the Isle of Wight and the Orkneys."

However, as Foster's journal denotes, the aura not only of English ways but also of Enlightened English politics enveloped serious Viennese circles like Countess Thun's, which, mixing with the dedicated elite led by the charismatic doyen of Viennese Freemasonry, Ignaz von Born, kindled fertile intellectual exchanges that struck flame: does not Mozart's Mme. Pfeil (*The Impresario*), in choosing as her audition piece a passionate scene from

---

11 The Viennese salon knew English lyric poetry—Young, Gray, and Ossian—before it discovered the early romantics of its own tongue, in particular, Goethe. He, too, had followed the English route, Goldsmith's ballad *Edwin and Angelina*, for example, providing the inspiration for his *Erwin und Elmire* (1773). He acknowledged the potent influence of English sentiment upon himself and his contemporaries, especially its tone of disenchantment and melancholy. After acquainting himself with the first English translation (1783) of his *Werther*, he commented upon his pleasure in reading "my thoughts in the language of my instructors."

Sir John Vanbrugh and Colley Cibber's *The Provoked Husband*, invoke the stimulating spirit in which Mozart set to work composing Johann Nepomuk Denis's ode celebrating the English repulse of the Spaniards at Gibraltar (see XVII, n. 3)?

Mozart and Denis probably met at the salon of Court Councilor Franz Sales von Greiner, where the regulars included not only the literary figures Johann Baptist Alxinger and Lorenz Leopold Haschka (the first perhaps the best of the mediocre—and worse—Josephinian poets), but also *Hofcomponist* Salieri. Greiner's daughter, one day to be the writer Caroline Pichler, would recall: "My father wished our home to be filled with music. The great Mozart, though not my teacher, often gave me lessons free of charge, and I had ample opportunity to hear him perform and to perfect my playing under his tutelage." To a certainty Mozart could not resist guiding Caroline's talented fingers, thus pleasing her influential father (if not her regular music instructor, Josef Antonin Štěpán). Mozart's own pupils, however, paid and paid well.

Bold, he set his price for a lesson at half a ducat, an arrangement he described with more elegance as six ducats for a suite of twelve; but once aware of how often his ladies announced themselves unavailable, he demanded (as early as 1782) payment by the month for the dozen lessons, independent of cancellations. (When a young musician of exceptional talent came under his musical wing, as would Johann Nepomuk Hummel, the fee accommodated the pupil's means.) He decided to take no more than four students at a time lest he neglect composing. In any case, teaching did not occupy him all the months round: summer put a temporary halt to it, for then Viennese society went to the country; and he himself assumed the privilege of breaking off should commissions demand his full attention.

Though pomposity remained foreign to his personality, he prepared his appearances before his students with scrupulous care: "Every morning my hairdresser arrives at six o'clock and awakens me. I finish dressing by seven and then compose until ten, when I give a lesson to Frau von Trattner [Maria Theresia, wife of the publisher] and at eleven to Countess Rumbeke." They, Countess Thun, and Josepha Auernhammer constituted his roster of pupils during his early years in Vienna, and, as a rule three times a week in season, each saw her music master, always turned out with studied elegance. The sensual pleasure he took in this exercise induced his rhapsody about "a handsome red coat"—kapellmeisters often wore the color, as he did in more than one of his portraits—which he hoped to embellish with special buttons: "mother-of-pearl, a few white stones forming the surround, and, in the center, a beautiful yellow gem." (Was this the "crimson pelisse" Michael Kelly beheld him wearing—along with a "gold-laced

cocked hat"—at the first full orchestral rehearsal of *The Marriage of Figaro?*)
His wardrobe functioned as a kind of incognito, which, going beyond a literal expression of dandyism, became metaphor: a euphemistic representation of his campaign to conquer Vienna—his battle array.

3

HE THUS ADAPTED marvelously well to Vienna and its environment of
appearances, to a city in which fashion ruled. Fine dress had once defined
the old nobility, but the pendulum of privilege no longer unerringly regulated society: all at once, anyone with a proper wardrobe, self-confidence,
and creative energy might pass for anything—an Arnstein for a cavalier, a
Leporello for a Don Giovanni, a Mozart (as Clementi first thought him)
for a high chamberlain. It was at a Viennese dinner party that Casanova's
newfound friends created him "baron": "You have to be something," they
told him, "and you cannot be less than baron. You must confess yourself
to be at least that if you wish to be received anywhere in Vienna."

The social realignments in its salons offered conditions favorable to an
assortment of disguised opportunists and adventurers ranging from the
hopeful, through the unprincipled and unhinged, to the criminal.[12] With
few exceptions—Countess Thun's palace among them—anything but

---

12 During 1786, Paris witnessed the climax of a machination at the highest level—the Affair of the
Diamond Necklace. The unfolding of its underlying facts form a parallel to the change from the
bittersweet rococo tricks of Mozart's *Figaro* to the sinister and cruel conspiracies of his *Don Giovanni.* Though Cagliostro lurked behind the scenes, the chief architect of the French adventure
appears to have been a self-created Countess, the mistress of Cardinal Louis de Rohan. She persuaded him that Queen Marie Antoinette desired that he act as her agent in acquiring a necklace
once assembled for Madame du Barry. Having met at Versailles with a prostitute impersonating
the Queen, he came to terms with the jewelers and turned the treasure over to a second impostor, masquerading as her valet. By the time the jewelers discovered that she had neither ordered
nor received the necklace, the husband of the "countess" had disassembled it and absconded to
London with the stones. Though taken prisoner, whipped, and branded, she managed to escape
(with official connivance, many believed) and from London accused the Queen, whose attitude
toward the conspiracy proved mystifying. She had received word of the Cardinal's negotiation
but had done nothing to halt it. Had her purpose been to let the dunderhead, whom she despised, dig his own grave; or did she harbor hope of the fabled necklace's somehow coming into
her possession? On one issue Europe felt as one: she had let herself be made a fool. Because it
so compromised the Habsburg Queen of France, the incident in particular shocked the Germans. In Weimar, Goethe quite lost his balance over her involvement: to his mind, it "opened
up the immoral abyss of city, court, and state." His perturbation took artistic form in a
singspiel libretto, *Die Mystifizierten* (*The Hoodwinked*), a satire on impostors and those they impose
upon, which he revised as a play, *Der Gross-Cophta* (1791), a free dramatization of the conspiracy.
Though there survives no reference on Mozart's part to the scandal so hotly discussed in the salons and coffeehouses of Vienna, it takes little effort to imagine him measuring with a professional eye and expatiating upon this *dramma giocoso* with a royal prima donna of his acquaintance

courts of the muses, such gatherings, at which most of the guests jumped at any opportunity to exhibit at least the simulacrum of an Enlightened identity, became major axes of Mozart's activities. In his gorgeous apparel and with his polished manners and charm, he presented a liberated personality—blooming, in fact, dazzling, and yet with that redolence of equivocal identity not a few of his operatic characters would insinuate. For Mozart the Viennese drawing room and the Viennese stage became mutually reflecting mirrors, their chiaroscuro at its most powerful and revealing in *Don Giovanni.*

Mozart and Da Ponte shaped its libretto in Vienna, where, the premiere in Prague notwithstanding, the lion's share of the score came into being. The opera unfolds not in the "city in Spain" the libretto indicates, but in the *Kaiserstadt.* Other than place names, only a single touch of color in effect suggesting Spain appears on *Don Giovanni's* wide canvas: the hero's instructions that the folia be on the menu of dances at his ball. (*Figaro* at least has that marvelous fandango, its theme borrowed from Gluck.) Vienna makes itself felt as the scene of *Don Giovanni* in an emanation pervading both acts, that of the noted rendezvous for all manner of fornication—the Graben, Mozart's first permanent address in the capital. (The practice of extending the limits of the décor to include vast gardens and a bucolic hamlet beyond the fortifications arose after Mozart's death: designers placed in the country the peasants Da Ponte and Mozart had sent to the city on a rompish holiday.) *Don Giovanni* permitted the Viennese to observe themselves in images aping the parade of varied, paradoxical, and enigmatic characters who roamed this promenade; they ranged from its famous wenches (the *Grabennymphen* or *Grabenschnepfen,* the select of Vienna's three thousand prostitutes) to frequenters of the most fashionable salons. To embellish his party, Don Giovanni instructs Leporello to pick up at least one such nymph: "Go look for any girl standing in the square and bring her along, too."[13]

Vienna's favorite opera tunes, played for Giovanni as he sups, underscore just where his palace stands. With driving insistence the opera affirms the

---

in the leading *seria* role. At this time he wrote few letters: he met friends and colleagues in the course of the day; and by the close of 1786, yet another serious falling out with his father had reduced their correspondence to perfunctory exchanges.

13 Georg Emanuel Opitz's etching of a nocturnal serenade on the Graben pictures the inhabitants of a mansion bordering the square as they glance down from high windows upon a cluster of musicians performing in the shadows by candlelight and surrounded by a bevy of nymphs at work: several have their clients in hand; one finds herself between two lechers pawing her; and a lady of quality, no doubt pausing on her way to the mansion, looks on with curiosity. The etching exudes the very air of the dark Graben, its purlieus, and those skulking about them.

diversity of Mozart's Vienna and its capacity on every level and at every moment to transform itself: with equal ease to love and then betray, to entreat
and then coerce, to appease and then threaten, to comfort and then terrorize,
all of these contradictions as a rule exploiting—under the ethical banner of
jumbling and overturning hierarchies—the rich dialectic of disguise as a
leaven for altering identity. The opera's dark glass captures an assemblage of
for the most part self-fabricated personalities winding through a world in
which the precincts of city palaces, inns, squares, and alleys all shadow forth
the menace of the Graben after nightfall.

If no ambiguity of condition surrounds Donna Anna, her father, and
Don Ottavio, all of exalted background, Don Giovanni, born one of them,
has severed himself from his own to become a classless, disguised, undiscriminating libertine exploiting the darkest opportunities opened by the
new social interchanges and freedoms: a predator outside every community
and a danger to all; a man not unlike two famous adventurers from a lower
caste—Da Ponte's friend Casanova and Casanova's compeer "Count"
Cagliostro. Self-metamorphosed into noblemen, these charlatans, pursuing
their fortunes in palace and salon, rivaled Don Giovanni at his own high
level of spontaneous invention, and it seems a pity that a popular presumption of Casanova's hand in giving final form to *Don Giovanni's* text
cannot be substantiated.[14]

Not a scoundrel, but a decent enough lad, Don Giovanni's servant, Leporello, if from the country, has sharpened his wits in the squalor of the
town, having about him more than a touch of a pimp who has learned his
trade on the Hof, the Kohlmarkt, and the Graben. Moreover, like Zerlina,
who enjoys the brief illusion of quitting her low estate and marrying a
lord, Leporello, too, shows a strong appetite to hurtle over the barriers separating the hierarchy of class and its claims; he, in fact, has no lasting allegiances—a good beginning for his ambitions. He might well make a go of
it: discovering him not only dressed as his master but putting the impersonation over, an outraged Don Ottavio views the success as a dangerous
"betrayal." But he derives from the world of the *seria* and has no idea of
opera buffa's promise that one can make one's way, whatever one's origins.[15]

---

14 A member of Count Waldstein's household since 1785, Casanova resided at the Château of Dux, in
the Eber Valley, northwest of Prague. He did sketch words (unused) for a most troublesome spot
in the libretto: Leporello's attempt to escape from the dark courtyard of Donna Anna's house. Why
Casanova tried his hand at the scene remains a matter of speculation alone (see XXXI, n. 62).

15 Although lacking the confidence, aggression, and full measure of callousness, treachery, and deception Don Giovanni commanded, Leporello, with the final curtain, will perhaps not look about
for a new employer, as he asserts, but instead try his fortune in the salon. He is clever and no less
handsome than was his former master, whose wardrobe he might yet retrieve from the ruins.

Pezzl found amusement in Vienna's great salons thronged with "many a lady's maid blazing with her mistress's diamonds."

Donna Elvira appears a child of the merchant class become new nobility, a high bourgeoise whose convent background, even in the face of her frantic sexual passion, holds her unfadingly in possession. When Don Giovanni pairs the tormented Elvira, unrelenting in her earnestness, with Leporello, the mocking but gentle reverse image of his master—Leporello does pity her—they at moments make an affecting couple: their classes fleetingly meet, embrace, and therewith give a lesson as she casts off the tone of morbid parody for the most part coloring her vocal lines; for an instant Mozart sets the social melting pot at the boil.[16]

Elvira is not alone in undergoing crisis: *Don Giovanni* projects the dark inner struggles Rousseau had laid open, many of its protagonists denying their nature and thus their common humanity. Lying to themselves no less than to others, they betray their very essence by assuming roles either of their own infliction or imposed by society; caught in critical moments of change and powerless to seize control of them, they, with ever more desperation, cling to the false as all the while Mozart's music mocks their pretenses. In *Così fan tutte* he would mock his public as well: sowing confusion as to the measure of the characters' strengths and weaknesses; kindling perplexities as to whether he is attacking or acclaiming their solutions; offering a challenge—kindred to the games he played in his letters—to sort out the playacting from the real.

Figaro, Don Giovanni and *Così,* his trio of Vienna-born Italian operas, constitute essays on the give-and-take between self and society. The librettos turn upon masking,[17] that merry-go-round of illusion—in *Figaro* a sporting chase, but a cruel hunt by the time of *Così*—that swirl of delusive

---

16 In the sextet concluding *Don Giovanni,* Elvira announces her intention to go into seclusion—"*in un ritiro.*" She does not specify *sacro ritiro,* but one assumes an allusion to the cloister, especially in the light of a major source of the libretto, Molière's play *Dom Juan*: here the hero has abducted Elvira from a nunnery. Even though Mozart's opera relocates the scene of her seduction to her home in Burgos, it seems reasonable to assume the conventual in his Elvira's background.

17 Mozart delighted in pulling on the masks and costumes of the roguish Harlequin and the melancholy Pierrot, not only at public and salon balls but in private theatricals, too. His talent for mime doubtless equaled his skill on the ballroom floor, where he awakened admiration in the minuet. Constanze related that no less than a member of the Vestris family (in all likelihood Gaetano Appolino [*sic*]) gave him lessons in dancing and, assumedly, gesture, too; he must have attended many ballets in Paris. Music he composed for a Viennese pantomime to his own scenario survives, the fragmentary K. 446/416d of February 1783, one of several such works he created and performed in; here he cast himself as Harlequin, playing against the Columbine and Pierrot of Aloisia and her husband. The plot thus permitted Mozart to win in the game of taking his first love's fancy.

images he observed in Vienna's salons, with their sexual and psychological confrontations; their succession of humors, tragedies, and ironies; their decorous, brittle conflicts so often screening crises moving toward fulfillment or destruction and time and again tinged with improbity. In the drawing room he studied Vienna's adults at play, even their slightest shifts in attitude revealing ambiguities, camouflages, out-and-out incognito or travesty (how pathetic the Don Ottavios of this world, who, no matter what mask they pull on, remain incapable of alteration), not a few endearing caricatures, and ever and anon a sincere response and enduring relationship: the world he put on the stage.

The salon became his high academy of studies in the human comedy—Vienna's animated streets, life shooting off in all directions, provided a more basic school—and therewith the incubator of his ideological development and potency as a dramatist: here he observed the thinness of the boundaries separating artifice and reality and learned to plot his mature operas' moral perspectives extending from the more easily construed one-point views of *The Abduction* and *Figaro* to the bizarre, sometimes bleak, but penetrating multipoint vistas of *Don Giovanni, Così,* and *The Magic Flute.* Moreover, he discovered that to have import an action in the theater had to communicate both its narrative significance and its human dimension; and perhaps the salon helped stimulate his genius for the ensemble.

4

THE JOSEPHINE SALON had risen during the eclipse of what had once seemed the Hofburg's ever-enduring luster. In former years the center of Vienna's receptions, entertainments, and gala and feast days, the court had faded near to lifelessness. Though Joseph, dutiful in religion, did resign himself to processing in state on Corpus Christi and Saint Stephen's Day, he refused to exploit pomp as a device to provide ideological support either of an Imperial magnificence he disdained or of an enfeebled aristocracy he detested. (Joseph, in whom so many warring forces converged, tried to awaken this in great measure degraded class to the fact, long known to its French counterpart, that ideas had the power to sweep it away.) He saw in himself the capacity of becoming the focus of German culture even as he divested himself of the outward semblances of Imperial power and dissolved the symbolic and emotional bonds holding the Holy Roman dynasty in place: he erred memorably.

No less an autocrat than his late mother, he no less delighted in acting—and, in his case, often in the most public settings—the role of parent of the nation: playing the diffident Habsburg paterfamilias, this strange unaccountable creature mingled with his "children" in the streets and parks of the capital (going his rounds in an open green landau, the whip in his hands, a spectacle quite ragged around the edges) and appeared without ceremony as guest in the drawing rooms of the bourgeois elite. No dramatic act of self-emancipation had freed this group to assert its new social authority: it had moved to fill an empty space.

So long as conversation did not lead beyond the rhetoric of the slogan, the close-knit network of Viennese salons exhibited trends of thought with an affinity to Joseph's: moral philosophizing tinged with aesthetics along with discussions circling around fashionable ideas of the general welfare and an aristocracy of achievement à la Montesquieu. Joseph, however, had the luxury of quitting the world of theory: of progressing from the premise to its conclusion, from the vision to its realization; drawing upon Enlightenment theory, he had embarked upon an imposing repertory of social reforms (many of them amplifications of Theresan attitudes) that made Mozart and his father committed Josephinians.

Identifying as abuses much that the nobles and clerics defined as their rights, the changes touched the essence of life in Habsburg lands: instituting uniform taxation and with it an incipient redistribution of wealth; insisting upon equality before the law, especially in respect to ending the status of immunity and exception the aristocrat assumed as his privilege (as had Baron Buffa in Mozart's account of the Tyrolean affair); wiping out remnants of serfdom with their obligations of labor in the fields; easing the ecclesiastical grip upon a disproportionate part of the nation's real property (an outrage burdening all Catholic lands and an object of Leopold Mozart's anger); forcing the Church both to contribute to the secular weal a share compatible with Her enormous revenues and to reduce Her army of monks idling in monasteries, in particular those in the contemplative and mendicant Orders (they made Leopold boil with indignation), the monies generated by these new religious policies to be shifted to the endowments of parish churches, schools, foundling houses, and hospitals; establishing a universal and comprehensive primary educational system; and tolerating the permanent presence of Jews, Lutherans, Calvinists, and members of the Eastern confessions, along with sanctioning private religious observances on the part of these heterodox faiths, concessions meant to encourage the immigration of many who might stimulate economic growth.

When news of the Holy Roman Emperor's proposals reached Rome, the Pope, touched at many sore spots, raised a cry; to persuade Joseph to abandon or modify the program, he would plan a step almost unthinkable: a Papal journey to Vienna. Mozart refused to believe reports of it; the Emperor, he felt certain, would never permit such meddling. When Pius VI did appear (spring 1782), Mozart made light of the event as a kind of entertainment; the Viennese, Pezzl observed, viewed the visit as "wished upon them" but accepted it "with cheerful insouciance."

Joseph envisaged his grand design prospering within the tight framework of his arbitrary and disdainful power. He saw the Habsburg lands as best governed by a benevolent despot quite like himself. He knew that the world into which his mother had been born had died long before her death and wished to shape and control the new Europe forming around him. His desire to reduce the sum of human discontent cannot be gainsaid, but that his reforms stimulated curiosity and, above all, speculation—in short, public opinion—he found repellent. By the end of the decade he would combat it with his secret agents, whose infiltration of Viennese salon life would in time stifle even conjectural political discussion. The failure of Joseph's reign and his personal tragedy lay in a giant inconsistency: his simultaneously giving and taking back. "Both parts of a contradiction," Hobbes had written large, "cannot possibly be true."[18]

At the time Mozart settled in Vienna, Joseph had begun to acquaint his subjects with his formidable vision of the state. Quite in character, his manner resembled that of an authoritarian schoolmaster ever quickening the pace and insensitive to the shortsightedness of teaching too much too quickly to disparate, conservative, and reluctant scholars. Theory was comfortable, reality less so: despite the modish talk, whose play with catchwords disguised apprehensions and hostility, not a few members of the salons he visited saw in him a potential author of their ruin and would be among the most effective forces laboring to unravel his programs even as he wove them. (His disastrous foreign policy would also cripple his efforts.) Joseph had succeeded in awakening the dissatisfaction of all except the powerless: an almost universal diapason of protest would soon sound to the full, and reaction turn back much he believed steadfast in place. Casanova observed that, having sallied forth like a hero, the Emperor could never quite grasp why, for every hydra head he severed, the bleeding neck grew two more: "No one ever denied his claim to great courage, but he had not the slightest idea of the art of governing, for he had not the slightest knowledge of the human heart. . . ." Yet, in the end, the spirit of his at-

---

18 Two examples of the discords clashing within Joseph may help draw his picture: he abolished the death penalty only to substitute for it punishments so humiliating and cruel—indeed, savage—as at times to make execution seem preferable; and when, in the wake of his decrees of toleration, a group of Bohemian peasants insisted upon registering as Deists and stood their ground, he ordered them caned daily on the buttocks until they chose one of the traditional religions, a not untypical illustration of his concept of responsible Enlightened absolutism regulating and thus improving human affairs.

tempted reforms did remain irreversible. In a paradox, a phenomenon he with such perplexity embodied, this father of the Viennese salon became its enemy and then its issue.

The drawing room provided Mozart an immediate practical advantage: a base of patronage. Further, he soon learned that a Masonic lodge offered the same opportunity, let alone mixing as a "brother" with the nobility as well as many an influential bourgeois: lodge meetings constituted another kind of salon,[19] and at both he wooed sponsors. As one by one the nobles vanished as benefactors, collective support in the shape of the subscription concert bridged the gap, bourgeois and aristocratic names jostling one another on the subscribers' lists (see pp. 10 and 638). Mozart foresaw inhabiting a snug nest in Vienna by exploiting this phenomenon along with securing pupils, a publisher, and operatic commissions, the often awesome praise he received from the public and fellow musicians feeding his sanguinity. (When Ignaz Umlauf, ten years his senior and Kapellmeister of Emperor Joseph's singspiel troupe, invited him to hear a reading at the clavier of his new opera, probably *Das Irrlicht*, he began with an apology: "You ought not give your time to hearing it; I have not come as far [as you]. I do as well as I can."[20]) Above all Mozart wanted to compose opera and hoped with the passing years to fall back upon it alone, for a composer thus employed might reach a social and financial position as imposing as Gluck's. For the moment, Mozart, overflowing with vitality and in the splendor of his youthful genius, drew weapons from his entire armory, celebrating, not limitations, but all possibilities.

As a rule, a musician seeking to escape regular employment in a princely establishment had to be either a traveling virtuoso or an international opera composer, that is, someone willing to cut personal ties so as to be free to move from court to court, from theater to theater: Vincente Martin y Soler, for example, chased operatic contracts from London to St. Petersburg. But Mozart had come to look upon travel as an affliction: by the

---

19 Mozart's zeal for Freemasonry rested, above all, upon his devotion to its teachings and his yearning "to belong." Yet, in addition to moral improvement and professional advantage, the lodge provided the opportunity to indulge his delight in dressing up, and not only in ritual trappings; in contrast to England, where the aristocrat appeared at meetings in simple attire so as not to eclipse his middle-class brother, in German lands the reverse had become the custom: the bourgeois decked himself in no less elegant style than the noble, even the most modest burgher girding on a ceremonial sword. Mozart in his gorgeous best, his sword at his side, commands the lower right-hand corner of an anonymous painting (in the Historisches Museum der Stadt Wien) depicting a meeting of Viennese Freemasons.

20 This scene took place in Umlauf's home. He proved unable to read his messy manuscript, and Mozart sat down to it, playing, in Umlauf's words, "as if he had composed it himself." In private he disdained Umlauf's abilities.

time of his return from Paris he had already had enough of a life that "from youth on" had accustomed him "to depart from people, countries, and cities with no great hope of ever again seeing . . . good friends left behind." His vision of himself as an outright freelance and at the same time a resident of a great capital constituted a bold conceit for the Germany of his time,[21] in particular because independent musicians who fell ill could find themselves penniless, a contingency often enough worrisome to him. ("If I could have in writing from dear God that I shall . . . not become sick". . .) But he strove to put this fear aside: Vienna appeared to him a haven of bliss, a place to secure a firm footing, to marry, and to settle down. Though, during his first months there, he would have leaped at a reasonable court appointment, once success began to bear him forward he gave up thoughts of any position requiring the regular rehearsal and performance of other composers' music, *antichambrieren*, or debilitating ritual duties of any kind.[22]

When the post of music master to Princess Elizabeth of Württemberg, fiancée of the Emperor's nephew Francis, went to the insignificant Georg Summer,[23] a member of the court's musical establishment, and Righini became her singing teacher, Mozart at first suffered disappointment. But he soon realized that positions of this kind would have made demands upon his time out of proportion to the fee: in Summer's case, it augmented the salary of someone paid to dedicate himself to the humdrum of Habsburg service; for Mozart, Elizabeth might well have become a burden—"one cannot deal with a pupil who is a princess as toward other ladies, for, if a princess does not feel in the mood [to take a lesson], why, you have the honor of waiting. . . . I would be . . . neglecting other pupils or other work (by which I could easily make more . . .)." A sinecure from the Habsburgs

---

21 German writers with similar ambitions had to travel a no less difficult road. Lessing, for example, having for a time enjoyed the illusion of independence by taking in hackwork, had to face its toll of poverty upon his body and spirit: in 1770 he yielded to the Hereditary Prince of Braunschweig's (see p. 83) invitation to become librarian at Wolfenbüttel. In eighteenth-century Germany, an impecunious man of letters had to become a librarian, a schoolmaster, a household tutor, a clergyman, or—even like the tolerably well-off Goethe before he inherited—a government official. In France and England, however, writers often enough did find an independent livelihood possible, some, like Voltaire and Pope, accumulating fortunes by their pens.

22 Handel, the commanding, international figure who sprang from a humble, provincial family, had been Leopold's ideal for his son's future as early as their stay in London (see p. 183), and the great Saxon, along with Gluck, also became the mature Mozart's model: the hardened, brilliant freelance musician-entrepreneur, impatient with routine, jealous of his personal and artistic freedom, yet secure in support from the highest places.

23 The Hofburg acknowledged Salieri's right to regulate the appointment, which he, in turn, bestowed upon Summer.

such as Gluck enjoyed became his goal. Of course, Gluck had accumulated sixty years along with international and, above all, Parisian renown when, in 1774, he received the title of Imperial Court Composer, a benefice yielding an annual two thousand florins (in addition to the pension of six thousand livres Queen Marie Antoinette had bestowed upon him). But the warmth of Mozart's new relationship with the Hofburg stirred his hopes: events continued to play into his hands, in particular an extraordinary encounter in the presence of the Emperor, the consequence of a bizarre decision by the German-born Empress of Russia.

5

CATHERINE THE GREAT had dispatched her son, Grand Duke Paul, on a European tour, its apparent aim the furthering of those sympathetic links with the Habsburgs born during her recent (1780) meetings with Joseph II at Mogilev and her palace of Tsarskoye-Selo. She viewed him as a confederate in her plans (inspired by her favorite, Grigori Aleksandrovich Potemkin) for moving against the Turks and creating a Russian Byzantium to be called after the ancient kingdom of Dacia; for his part, Joseph saw in her an ally against Constantinople and a ruler at one with his resolve to settle accounts with Prussia. Grand Duke Paul was to make state visits to Louis XVI and his Habsburg Queen at Versailles, the Habsburg enclaves in Italy, and the Habsburg capital of Vienna. Yet many suspected another and sinister purpose in Catherine's sending her son out of Russia. Their relationship had long hung by a thread.

When her coup d'état deposed her husband, Peter III,[24] she had proclaimed herself, not regent for Paul, but empress and autocrat of all the Russias, thereby usurping his immediate inheritance, though she did recognize him as crown prince and heir. But with the years she grew to dislike him with a vengeance as he came to resemble Peter. (Even so, whisper continued to identify Paul as the son of her first lover, Sergei Saltykov.) She took the deepest offence when Paul received the adulation of crowds, Muscovites, in particular, hailing him as the true sovereign. He feared that one day some mysterious and fatal accident or illness, like the

---

24 This Karl Peter Ulrich, Duke of Holstein, had a Russian mother, who died soon after his birth: Anne of Holstein-Gottorp, sister of Empress Elizabeth. Upon the death of his father, Elizabeth had him brought from Kiel to St. Petersburg (1742), adopting the adolescent, confirming him in the Russian church as Peter Fedorovich, and proclaiming him her heir. He insisted upon keeping his German identity: even during his brief reign as Tsar Peter III, he preferred to uniform himself as a Holstein officer and stood firm against speaking, indeed, learning Russian.

bizarre hemorrhoidal hemorrhage that had felled his father, might remove him, too. Did not Frederick of Prussia call Catherine "the Messalina of the North"? Even as Paul and his consort, German-born Maria Fedorovna (see n. 25), prepared to depart, rumor ran that during their travels his mother would disinherit or make away with him and name his elder son, her adored Alexander, next in line to the succession. She refused to permit the child to accompany his parents (whom she mocked as *"die schwere Bagage"* [heavy luggage]), and they set out in gloom and uncertainty. Paul drew breath on his mother's sufferance: would he return to St. Petersburg in a coffin?

Once away from Catherine's nagging and sarcasm, he and Maria Fedorovna came into their own, all along receiving the honors appropriate to the heir of the Russian crown and, through his paternal inheritance, to a prince of the Empire. When they approached Vienna, Emperor Joseph drove out to escort them into his capital. (He had met the couple during his Russian journey.) Overcoming his father's and his own fierce Prussian sympathies, Paul fell in love with Vienna and under the spell of Joseph, who, in his good moments and for advantage, could summon up the art of conquering hearts.

To Joseph it seemed a happy turn of events that the grand-ducal visit[25] coincided with the presence in Vienna of both Mozart and the Roman-born clavier player Muzio Clementi. The Emperor invited them to appear at the Hofburg the day before Christmas (1781) to entertain Maria Fedorovna with a keyboard competition. Four years older than Mozart and once also a glittering child prodigy, Clementi, as the fourteen-year-old organist of Rome's S. Lorenzo in Damaso, had attracted the attention of the traveling Peter Beckford (see XV, n. 38), who "bought Clementi of his father for seven years" and took him to England, there to continue his studies. Having won a reputation in London at the clavier and as a composer, he returned to the Continent in 1780 for a concert tour, which had already

---

25 The Imperial couple arrived in Vienna during November 1781 and returned the following October on their way back to St. Petersburg. She, born Princess Sophie Dorothea Auguste of Württemberg and in 1776 baptized in the Orthodox faith as Maria Fedorovna, had become the second wife of Grand Duke Paul, one day to be Tsar Paul I. Her father, Duke Frederick Eugene, was the brother of Dukes Karl Eugene and Louis Eugene, the first the reigning Duke of Württemberg, whom the Mozarts had sought to meet at Ludwigsburg (July 1763), the second the musical enthusiast they performed before at Villa Monrion near Lausanne (September 1766). Her sister, Princess Elizabeth Wilhelmine, would wed Francis, eldest son of Grand Duke Leopold of Tuscany, himself the eldest of childless Emperor Joseph's brothers. Thus Francis of Tuscany stood right after his father as successor to the Habsburg scepter and, in consequence, the Holy Roman crown and would reign in Vienna as the last of Germany's Roman emperors.

taken him to Paris and appearances before Queen Marie Antoinette. He heard of the Imperial Russian couple's impending arrival in Vienna and, by way of Strassburg and Munich, made his way to the palace of her dour brother, who would count the holiday music-making of the two famous young virtuosos among his few cheering memories. An enthusiastic admirer of Mozart's "*talent décidé*" (a measured phrase, but from Joseph an encomium), he expected him to outdo the Anglo-Italian, and, in fact, made a wager to this effect with the Grand Duchess. Clementi knew of Mozart; he, however, professed not to have heard of the newly arrived "clavier player, an Italian," whom he met for the first time in the Emperor's music room just before the contest. They "had hardly started up a conversation when it immediately turned to musical matters," Clementi recalled, "and we soon recognized and in a most friendly way greeted one another as brother artists. . . ." Mozart described what followed the entrance of Joseph and Maria Fedorovna.

"After we had done with the business of formal compliments, the Emperor proposed that he [Clementi] begin: '*La santa chiesa Catholica* [sic],' he said, because Clementi was a native Roman. He extemporized and next performed a sonata.[26] Then the Emperor said to me: '*Allons*, fire away.' I, too, improvised and played variations. Then the Grand Duchess fetched forth some sonatas by Paisiello [her music master], wretchedly scribbled in his own hand;[27] of these I had to execute the Allegros and he [Clementi] the Andantes and Rondos. We then selected a theme from them and developed it on two pianofortes." The Emperor, too, came up with a theme, Clementi recalled, which he and Mozart varied in alternation.

Mozart had again borrowed Countess Thun's Stein piano, an instrument he loved. The Emperor, however, permitted him to avail himself of it only for his solos; for the variation rivalry on two pianos, Joseph insisted upon Mozart's using an instrument he discovered to be out of tune and with sticking dampers. "Such was the wish of the Emperor," who, in response to Mozart's remonstrations, airily called out: "Of no importance!" Experienced at the keyboard and on the strings, Joseph practiced every day and several times a week participated in private concerts with members of his musical household. Notorious for poking his nose into every detail, he

---

26 Its opening bears a striking resemblance to the subject of the quasi-fugato section in the overture to *The Magic Flute*. Though it might be held part of the common tonal vocabulary of the period, the theme, Clementi insisted, came from him, and he asserted his proprietary right by adding the following legend to the sonata upon its publication: "The composer played this sonata, along with the toccata following it, before His Majesty Joseph II, Mozart being present."

27 Maria Fedorovna used Paisiello's autographs rather than a scribe's copies.

could not have been unaware of the instrument's condition; he imposed a handicap upon Mozart, provoking him, but all the while enjoying the certainty of his power to skate around the hazards. A mosaic of aggressive moods, Joseph found particular pleasure in placing performers on trial without warning. In Casanova's view, "he had so little control over his own countenance that he could not even conceal the pleasure he felt in punishing. . . ." Mozart must have sensed a measure of malevolence in the atmosphere, for it took him much effort to put the best construction (*auf der besten Seite*) on the bizarre incident: to perceive in this typical and sadistic Josephine game not only mischief but confidence, too.

The demonstration over, both musicians doubtless exchanged all manner of praise in which the royals joined. No question of victor or vanquished intruded. Only later did the Emperor make known his opinion that in musicality and refinement Mozart had carried the day. (In agreement or out of tact, the Grand Duchess paid the wager.) But in terms of technique Clementi had traveled the course with brilliance: in fact, the cascades of thirds, sixths, and octaves pouring from his right hand had dazzled and disconcerted Mozart; in this area of virtuosity he had for the first time met his master, an experience he did not enjoy. Perhaps it festered in him and smarted because the core of his virtuosity, as Michael Kelly observed, lay, above all, in the "great execution and strength of his left hand."

In the concert's aftermath, he protested too much, summoning up remembrance of his father's *Versuch* and its passages decrying shallow virtuosity: "Clementi performs well as far as dexterity with the right hand goes. His strength lies in his passages in thirds. Otherwise, he has not a kreutzer's worth of feeling or taste—in a word simply a technician" (*mechanicus*). In particular those rippling thirds vexed: "He worked at them day in and day out in London, but can do nothing else." Advising Nannerl not to play Clementi's "valueless" sonatas, Mozart warned that all those sixths and octaves would spoil her touch, depriving it of lightness. Taken unawares and stunned by Clementi's facility, Mozart, at his most ungenerous, bristled. A quarter of a century later, when he had become renowned for a "nobler" and "more songful and legato [keyboard] style," Clementi recalled the concert at the Hofburg and his youthful "delight in a big and brilliant technique." Of Mozart's playing on that occasion he said: "Until then I had never heard anyone perform with such grace and elegance."

Surmounting a chronic parsimony, Emperor Joseph sent Mozart telling expression of favor: fifty ducats, more than half his erstwhile annual salary in Salzburg. Moreover, during conversation right after the music contest, Joseph had taken him aside to give a nod of support for his marriage hopes, an affectionate gesture implying much. In the afterglow of the

Mozart-Clementi encounter, so Count Zinzendorf noted with a certain weariness, the Emperor spoke "endlessly" of it. He had become proprietary about Mozart, who had reason to contemplate a firm future in Vienna, what with an opera for the court in work (see p. 555), and in light of his friendship with Johann Kilian Strack, one of Joseph's gentlemen of the chamber and, as cellist of his inner circle of chamber players, with considerable influence upon the Hofburg's musical life. (While cultivating him, Mozart did suspect his sincerity.) In addition, Franz Kreibich, director and first violinist of Joseph's ensemble, appeared a strong admirer.

While Mozart could have no doubt of the Emperor's favor—this testy authoritarian proved accessible and sympathetic—yet he did not possess the variety and depth of taste to utilize Mozart's genius at all points. In respect to instrumental music, no less than opera, Joseph's heart inclined toward the Italians. He had an emphatic distaste for much of what he had heard by Gluck and Joseph Haydn, though he did grasp their importance to the national culture and, more and more, Mozart's too. For the public's ear the Hofburg sounded the trumpet of German art while, in the privacy of his apartments, Joseph for the most part played and listened to undistinguished Italian fare. He, in fact, maintained a vantage point in his intimate musical sessions by hiring mediocrities to devote themselves to the mediocre: only thus could he shine at the head of his personal musical troops, indeed, play their teacher. "He delighted in talking with those who did not know how to answer him," Casanova recalled, "whether because they were amazed at his arguments or because they pretended to be so."

Despite his developing social vigilance, Mozart could not have long survived in such company: in no time he would have fired off his opinion of its capacities and repertory; among Strachs and Kreibichs, to say nothing of the royal counterfeit maestro, even the new Mozart could not have contained himself. Now and then Salieri did participate in the weekly round of musicales, but, no less accomplished a courtier than a practical musician, this elegant Italian, whose word had great weight with Joseph, commanded a renowned and monumental tact. He could not have failed to foresee awkward consequences were Mozart to enter into a world of music-making in which the Emperor assumed the role of kapellmeister. Any patronizing observation, however vague, could inflame this eccentric and prickly amateur, even at his best caustic and cutting, but many a time a humorless crank. He, too, must have viewed the matter with a clear eye, what with his old experience of the Mozarts' sense and unrestrained expression of their superiority: had not the lamentable business of *La finta semplice* begun and ended on his desk? And he had to have made inquiries of the Salzburg Residenz, where Mozart's antagonistic participation in the courtiers' chamber music had done him discredit; nor could Joseph have ignored the diplomatic courtesy of sounding Salzburg as to its view of the deserter's civic standing. At all events, Vienna's consorting with someone the arch-bishopric's officialdom now looked upon as nonexistent raised no stir.[28]

Embracing a tactical necessity, the Hofburg showed wisdom in exclud-ing Mozart from its intimate musical affairs and in looking upon his fu-ture relationship with it in terms of concerts and compositions for special occasions. That he would provide it with a new singspiel had been an early and high sign of Imperial appreciation and expectations. Yet, within the private chambers of the palace one small corner of music-making did show signs of growing into a professional undertaking, and Mozart la-bored to insinuate himself into it.

6

JOSEPH TOOK A German delight in the timbres of wind instruments, a taste he determined to bring to bear upon what so pleased him at the opera and ballet: tunes. From the ranks of the Burgtheater's orchestra he planned to gather a special wind band (*Harmonie*) and have it regale him at meal-time with highlights from the repertory. (Wind ensembles played during dinner at the better Viennese inns.) How Mozart had misjudged in pursu-ing Joseph with *Idomeneo*: the German Emperor took as little joy in high Gluckean rhetoric as did the King of Prussia, nay, rather basked in genial arias and hoped to have double pleasure in hearing them rescored for his new band.

Once aware of the plans for it and assuming that they included the commissioning of original works, Mozart composed the serenade K. 375 (for pairs of clarinets, horns, and bassoons) to demonstrate his mastery of wind combinations. The serenade became popular—indeed, literally—overnight: "I had written this music celebrating Saint Theresa's Day [15

---

28 On at least one occasion the Salzburg court's disowning any connection with him gave rise to difficulties: when he wanted to become a member of the Viennese Society of Musicians, he could not provide a copy or confirmation of his birth certificate, a *sine qua non*; either the Salzburg registry ignored his request or, anticipating a rebuff of silence, he did not petition. Unwilling to admit that the rupture with Salzburg did, in fact, have consequences in Vienna, he turned to his father for help under cover of wanting to use the document as a means to nullify gossip calling Leopold's probity into question: that he had lied to the Hofburg in 1762 about the age of his prodigy son who, the story ran, "had to have been ten, at the very least," when he first visited Vienna. He found himself teased and provoked by "the Emperor him-self," who "contradicted me to my face.... By exhibiting my baptismal certificate, I could at a stroke shut all those mouths." "Would it be at all possible to procure a copy...?" he asked Leopold, who could not or would not.

Mozart's wife, Constanze, painted by her brother-in-law, Joseph Lange, in 1782, the year of her marriage. © *Archive Photos*

Mozart's surviving children: Franz Xaver Wolfgang (left) and Carl Thomas; a painting c. 1798 by Hans Hansen. © *Archive Photos*

Mozart without his wig; a drawing by Doris Stock, 1789. © *Archive Photos*

An unfinished oil portrait of Mozart, again without a wig, by his brother-in-law Joseph Lange, c. 1789-90. © *Archive Photos*

Below: The Holy Roman Emperor, Joseph II, Mozart's major patron; right: his brother and successor, Leopold II, for whose coronation in Prague Mozart wrote *La Clemenza di Tito*.
© *Corbis/Archivo Iconografico, S.A.*

Hieronymus Joseph
Franz de Paula,
Count Colloredo,
Prince-Archbishop of
Salzburg (1772-1803),
the bête noire of
the Mozarts.
© *Archive Photos*

Thomas Gainsborough's portrait
of Johann Christian Bach, youngest
son of Johann Sebastian Bach and
an early and major influence upon
the young Mozart.
© *Archive Photos*

Christoph Willibald Gluck,
an operatic composer of
international fame with an
early and continuing
influence upon Mozart.
© *Corbis*

Padre Giovanni Battista (Giambattista) Martini
(1706-1784), famed music theorist who instructed Mozart
in counterpoint during 1770 in Bologna. © *Archive Photos*

Michael Haydn (1737-1806),
younger brother of
Franz Joseph Haydn;
a composer and colleague of
Mozart in Salzburg.
© *Archive Photos*

Franz Joseph Haydn (1732-1809),
Esterházy Kapellmeister and composer;
a major musical influence upon Mozart.
© *Archive Photos*

Lorenzo da Ponte (1749-1838), librettist
of Mozart's *The Marriage of Figaro, Don Giovanni*,
and *Così fan tutte*. *Culver Pictures*

Antonio Salieri (1750-1825),
opera composer, disciple of
Gluck, and Habsburg
Kapellmeister. © *Corbis*

The Holy Roman Empress,
Maria Theresa, one
of Mozart's first patrons.
© *Corbis*

October] for the ... sister-in-law [a Theresa] of Herr [Joseph] von Hickel, the court painter, at whose house it was first performed ... ; my chief reason for composing it was to let Herr von Strack, who goes there every day, hear something of mine [Strack, Mozart hoped, would commend K. 375 to the Emperor], and so I took meticulous pains; well applauded, it was played in three different places [to three other Theresas] on Saint Theresa's Night, for as soon as the musicians had finished it at one site, they were led away and paid to play it at another." When Emperor Joseph's *Harmonie* came into being during the spring of 1782, it took the form of an octet (pairs of oboes, clarinets, bassoons, and horns). In the course of the summer Mozart would rework K. 375 to fit this ensemble.

The serenade must have struck Herr von Strack as too serious in tone, in particular the opening Allegro and the Adagio, creations worlds from the artful and charming wind arrangements (for example, those by Johann Nepomuk Vent [Went]) that would undemandingly take their place as proper background for Emperor Joseph's dining and digesting. Mozart could force no entrance as composer to the Imperial *Harmonie*, though for a while he did have hopes of providing scores on a permanent basis to a wind band in the process of creation, that of Prince Alois Joseph Liechtenstein, recent heir to his father's prerogatives and fortune and busily rearranging the princely household. Mozart may have intended the serenade K. 388/384a of 1782 to attract this connoisseur's ear. The Menuetto and its Trio, furbished with canonic ingenuities (the minuet of Joseph Haydn's Trauersinfonie [No. 44, 1772] their model), and the variations of the finale have the air of the showpiece,[29] as does the ambitious serenade K. 361/370a, often given the predicate "grand." In all probability an offering to Constanze, still more, its spacious proportions, rich scoring, and sense of special occasion suggest its use at the Mozarts' wedding festivities.[30]

Sovereign in the repertory of *Harmoniemusik*, the grand serenade calls for an unusual selection of instruments: the octet of the Imperial *Harmonie*, an extra pair of horns,[31] two alto clarinets (Mozart's first use of these so-called basset horns), and, to help sustain the weight of this round

---

29 During 1787–1788, Mozart arranged K. 388 for string quintet (K. 406/516b; see XXXI, n. 45).

30 "Gran" (written in a hand not Mozart's) appears on the autograph. Although some believe K. 361 to have come into being close upon the first documented performance of at least sections of it—23 March 1784 at a benefit in the Burgtheater for the clarinet virtuoso Anton Stadler—the manuscript's paper suggests an origin as early as 1781–1782 and thus a strong link to the marriage celebration (4 August 1782).

31 The four horns, two in F and two in B flat, opened the door to the serenade's harmonic richness.

dozen of winds, a double bass, today often replaced by a double bassoon. The opening Largo announces an important work. Its seven movements sustain a succession of ever-shifting timbres as soloists rise out of the group to alternate and combine in varied sonorities balanced with brilliance and grace against the other instrumentalists. At times the world of opera obtrudes (its parts consolidated and words added, the Adagio might serve as a poignant vocal ensemble, the Romance as a soulful aria) as does a crisp military idiom inevitable with a large group of winds. If a plaintive mood at moments stamps the reedy trios of the rustic minuets and also certain of the handsomely argued variations of the penultimate movement,[32] the spirit of the Finale: Molto Allegro—cheerful and not without a touch of the rough and ready—impinges upon the happiest moments of his coming Viennese triumph, *The Abduction from the Seraglio*.

He had not seen the last of the wind players who had performed K. 375 throughout Vienna on Saint Theresa's Day and Night. At eleven o'clock in the evening of his name day (31 October), they "had the front door [of the Arnstein House] opened and, when they had drawn themselves up in the courtyard," he reported, "gave me, just as I was about to undress, the most delightful surprise in the world with the opening E-flat chord [of K. 375]. . . . I was serenaded (*eine Nachtmusik*) by 2 clarinets, 2 horns, and 2 bassoons, and, I'll have you know, playing my own composition." The "poor devils," whom Mozart with affection observed "tooting together very prettily," were celebrating a young man with rapid strides becoming a presence in Vienna. The Arnsteins and Madame Contrini must have had a share in the surprise and may well have paid for it.[33]

Mozart had made himself very much part of the solemn Arnstein household, to which he brought his sparkling light. (One of his letters discloses a charming scene: his calling upon Madame Contrini to borrow a

---

32 The second and final movement of the flute quartet K. Anh. 171/285b unfolds in almost complete musical agreement with this sixth movement of K. 361 and constitutes a reworking by Mozart's or another's hand. These rearranged variations, appended later in the decade to an Allegro of 1781, served to make a complete piece out of a flute quartet left a torso.

33 Mozart spent his name day in the Leopoldstadt at the house of a new patroness, Baroness Martha Elizabeth von Waldstätten (see XXIX, n. 7). His letter of 3 November 1781 may be construed as indicating an overnight stay; however, nothing in the text rules out his having taken the short carriage ride or leisurely walk back to the Graben in the evening. (The Leopoldstadt suburb lay to the northeast, across the subsidiary stream, which, once it acquired paved banks, became known as the Danube Canal.) In the first case, Mozart would have heard the serenade at her expense in her courtyard. Yet, in the light of his devotion to Constanze and the Baroness's reputation for promiscuity, which he dwelled upon more than once, it seems unlikely that he would have risked complicating his life by sleeping under her roof. (She had separated from her husband.) He even warned his father that her inviting him to visit Vienna and stay at her home harbored a sexual *arrière-pensée*.

hooded cloak for a masquerade, two visiting Salzburgers chasing playfully after him across her threshold.) But, Constanze apart, of all the friends who strengthened his new sense of belonging to Vienna, Josepha Auernhammer remained his staunchest anchor: the ugly summer crisis had yielded to common sense; in big matters Mozart remained free of littleness; from shaky beginnings had grown a relationship of generosity and trust.

If she had to renounce hopes of having him as lover—to make his commitment to Constanze unmistakable, from time to time he took her along to the Auernhammers—Josepha had requital in his energetic advocacy of her making a career. He showed pride in her accomplishments by dedicating to her his first Viennese publication—six violin and clavier sonatas (in order of printing: K. 376/374d, 296, 377/374e, 378/317d, 379/373a, and 380/374f), announced by the firm of Artaria at the end of 1781, subscribers having been gathered. He had composed the second in Mannheim for Therese Pierron (but chose not to include it in the Kurfürstin group engraved in Paris) and had begun the fourth during his final stay in Salzburg; he had hastily written the fifth for the concert at Prince Colloredo's, and, like it, the remaining three had come into being in Vienna, but later, during the summer of 1781. The sonatas added to his growing fame: "Unique of their type" and "rich in new ideas and marks of their author's great musical genius," Cramer's *Musical Magazine* would observe (Hamburg, 4 April 1783), the critic praising the intertwining of the two instruments "with such art that both sustain interest." The middle movement of K. 377/374e constitutes the ornament of the group, a soul-stirring theme and variations presaging the finale of the D-minor quartet, K. 421.

Josepha must have exulted to see her name united with Mozart's on the title page of the set and, in addition, to receive a composition for them to play together: the sonata for two claviers in D, K. 448/375a. If she had taken on the role of sisterly apprentice once Nannerl's, Josepha proved the better technician. When she and Mozart gave the sonata its premiere at a private concert at the Auernhammers on 23 November 1781, the audience, which included Countess Thun, Gottfried van Swieten, and one of the Counts von Firmian, heard a three-movement creation in which Mozart treated the pianists with digital equality. The program also contained the concerto for two claviers, K. 365, in a revised orchestration (the addition to its flanking movements of drums as well as pairs of clarinets and trumpets). Josepha's parents had come to terms with her professional ambitions: they sustained the costs of an orchestra in their drawing room, an element of their recompense no doubt the opportunity to play host to Mozart's aristocratic friends, the Auernhammer home being transformed for a few hours into a veritable salon. The event took place two days before a gala gathering at Schönbrunn in honor of the visitors from St. Petersburg, the bizarre climax of Emperor Joseph's struggle to entertain them, one in which Mozart more than once bestirred himself at the Hofburg's bidding.

7

JOSEPH HAD PERMITTED the social structure of the court so to crumble that the chamberlains still in place had prepared no comprehensive menu of activities for Grand Duke Paul and Maria Fedorovna. Furthermore, at this very time Duke Frederick Eugene of Württemberg and his Duchess, Fredericka, arrived with their children, Prince Ferdinand and Princess Elizabeth. Matters, the Emperor feared, would soon reach crisis: he felt at his wit's end to fill his guests' days. But they enjoyed the improvised schedule: Vienna provided its own rewards, and, in fact, Paul and his wife kept delaying their departure. After all, at the root of the gathering lay family affairs: the Württemberg couple had come to discuss the preliminaries for Elizabeth's marriage to the Emperor's nephew Francis of Tuscany, and to see their other daughter, the Russian Grand Duchess (see n. 25). At this German royal reunion, the unexpected informality proved a boon.

Drawn into seeking diversions for Joseph's guests, Mozart had begun "to look about for Russian popular songs in order to play variations on them," for certain a response to a request from the Hofburg. He had already heard a cry for help from Joseph's youngest brother, Archduke Maximillian,[34] to whom, without notice, fell the task of entertaining the Württembergers in his apartments. The very afternoon of the visit he timidly asked his old friend Mozart to come to the rescue by performing solos and accompanying arias. If he found the Duke, the Duchess, and Elizabeth "charming," Ferdinand seemed to him "an eighteen-year-old stick and truly silly" (*ein wahres Kalb*): a great irony for he must have been the "Prince of Würtemberg [*sic*]" Mozart listed in the 1784 inventory of subscribers to his concerts.

Even if, for reasons to be rehearsed, the Burgtheater decided not to prepare the premiere of Mozart's opera for the visiting royals, he sensed nothing adverse to his interests; confident of Habsburg support, he reined in a jot, taking enormous pleasure in observing the social panorama. In addition to plays, operas, ballets, and concerts, an extended sojourn by princes called for at least one grand festivity. But here Joseph's staff made a muddle: scheduling a ball on 25 November to honor the name day of Empress

---

34 He had yet to become prince-archbishop of Cologne and take up permanent residence in Bonn (see p. 348).

Catherine of Russia revealed a mortifying ignorance of the Roman and Russian Churches' divergence in respect to the calendar: in Russia the feast of her patron, Saint Catherine of Alexandria, fell on 6 December. Mozart found the Hofburg's embarrassment deliciously amusing; he loved to see aristocrats set down and looking foolish: "As yet no one knows what will happen," he reported with glee on 10 November. In the end, an evening in two parts did take place at Schönbrunn on the twenty-fifth: first, in the opera house, a revival of Gluck's *Alceste* (a week later it came to the Burgtheater); and then the ball, which Mozart kept from, for he foresaw disaster—the Hofburg had decided to open the festivity to all (a *freie Redoute*). His description of the fiasco and the events leading to it, though secondhand, has extraordinary immediacy.

"No lover of crowds, digs in the ribs, and blows, even of the Imperial variety, Herr Ego [Mozart] did not attend. It became the task of Strobel, the court's sergeant at arms, to distribute the tickets to the number of three thousand, and a public announcement made known that anyone could be put on the list by applying to the aforesaid Strobel. All the world jumped at the chance, Strobel took down the names, and all that had to be done was to send for the tickets. He did, however, dispatch them to the homes of the very well-known, and any lad by chance dawdling about got the job of making such deliveries. It happened that such a messenger asked someone passing on a stairway whether his name was So-and-So; as a joke he replied, 'Yes,' and got the ticket. I know of two families that did not receive their tickets because of this untidy way of doing things. They had been placed on the list, sent for their tickets, and learned from Strobel that they had been sent off long beforehand. Thus friseurs and chambermaids crowded into the ball.

"But now the best part, which has much irritated the nobility," Mozart recounted with chortling gusto as he went on to draw a picture of the disorder that had spread across the dance floor: "All the while, the Emperor led the Grand Duchess about on his arm. The nobility had two sets of contredanses: Romans and Tartars. In the course of one of them, the Viennese mob, even at best never noteworthy for its gentility, pressed forward to the point of pushing the Grand Duchess free of the Emperor's arm and into the middle of the dancers. The Emperor began to stamp, cursed like a lazzarone, pushed back a crowd of people, and vented his rage right and left. Some of the Hungarian Guard wanted to help him clear a space, but he sent them away. All in all it serves him right: such things don't work; rabble remains rabble."

Midst the absurdities surrounding the exalted visitors, an astounding rumor took the lead: the Emperor had become infatuated with both the

Grand Duchess and her sister. The report delighted the wits and gossips of Vienna, in particular Wolfgang Mozart, more than a bit of both. As to Joseph's inclination toward the lovely young Elizabeth, it had, Mozart wrote, become an open secret: "It hangs in the balance whether this morsel is to be for himself or for a Tuscan prince; more likely the latter. All the same, in my eyes the Emperor shows himself entirely too affectionate with her, without cease kissing her hands, first one, then the other, and often both at once. I am really astonished because she is, you might say, still a child. But if what people allege is true and does happen, I shall, in respect to this affair, return to the belief that charity begins at home. At all events, she is to remain here in a convent for two years. . . ."[35]

The shaky state of Emperor Joseph's nerves—undermined, Mozart implied, by his attempts to cope with the visitors—had opened a door upon a side of his personality as a rule hidden from others and, probably, himself. His flirtation with the Grand Duchess, even more unbecoming than his attentions to her sister, elicited acid from Mozart's pen: "To spare himself from cracking his brains to excess," the Emperor "holds back from entertaining [the Grand Duke] at all, feeling it sufficient to look after his wife, in his view a task for which he alone suffices." Having won Paul's affection, Joseph had then stopped short, perhaps all at once seeing in him a distorted image of himself: the child of a weak father and a mother of steel. In the spirit of popular comedy and its delight in topical comment, the Viennese gave Paul—dependent, despondent, introverted, and striving to maintain his claim to a throne by right his own[36]—the nickname Prince Hamlet,[37] whose relationship to Württemberg but added to a jest Joseph relished.

Often on his own in Vienna but not without resources, Paul joined forces with his father-in-law to take a moving enterprise in hand—their famous visit to the indisposed Gluck, an event that, in his words, "created a great sensation"; the surrounding streets became a sea of spectators

---

35 Early in 1782 Elizabeth settled in Vienna, living, pending her marriage to Francis of Tuscany, in the apartments once occupied by Dowager Empress Amalie (widow of Joseph I) in the Salesian cloister on the Rennweg.

36 The Viennese delighted in letting the parallels between Paul and Joseph speak for themselves: German emperor de jure after his father's death, Joseph did not in effect become emperor de facto until his mother's; and though, unlike Catherine, who forbade Paul any role in governing, Maria Theresa did share authority in Habsburg matters with her son and made a show of leaving the affairs of the Reich to his prerogatives, yet, until her last breath, that is, throughout her husband's reign and much of Joseph's, in the eyes of the Germanic and wider European world, she remained *The Empress*.

37 Mozart called Paul "*Grosthier*" (*sic*) or Big Shot for the sake of a double pun: on *Grossfürst* or Crown Prince ("*Nun ist das Grosthier der Grossfürst hier* [*sic*]") and *Grosstuer* or Braggart, random shots fired at aristocrats in general rather than the retiring Paul, whom he did not yet know.

straining to glimpse the astounding sight of two princes arriving to sing a musician's praises in his own drawing room. The Grand Duke, Gluck reported, "paid me the compliment of saying that, while he had heard much music, none had so touched his heart as mine."

Having suffered a series of apoplectic seizures in Paris, Gluck had returned home at the end of October 1779. His woeful plight had constrained the Hofburg against its will to put off the production of Mozart's new opera. Its fortune, Gluck's fame, and his languishing health became entwined, a convolution to be explained by turning back ever so little in chronology to scrutinize the evolution of this first of Mozart's enormous successes.

8

MOZART HAD BROUGHT the score of *Zaide* with him from Munich. He played it for the administrators of the National theater, among them the playwright-manager-actor Johann Gottlieb Stephanie (called Stephanie the Younger to distinguish him from an elder brother also on the stage) and Friedrich Ludwig Schröder, the renowned actor and translator of Shakespeare, whose Germanized *Hamlet* Mozart had seen performed by Schikaneder's troupe in Salzburg. Stephanie had met the Mozarts during their trips to Vienna and retained warm feelings for the former *Wunderkind.* Though dismissing the libretto of *Zaide* as unsuited to the Burgtheater, on the spot Stephanie promised to provide him with an appropriate text in its place. He had hardly bargained for such enthusiasm from someone famous for a difficult personality, in particular a talent for double-dealing remarkable even in Vienna. But their renewed acquaintance would continue an untroubled course: Stephanie's engaging ruthlessness appears to have hit Mozart's fancy, as would Da Ponte's roguery. For Stephanie's part, not only had the music of *Zaide* made a deep impression but, above all, the Emperor's interest in the composer gave notice of the path to follow: "I shall be delighted somehow to be of service to you," the impresario assured a grateful if at first incredulous young man.

The opportunity came in no time: through Count Rosenberg, the Hofburg commissioned Stephanie and Schröder to find and adapt a text for Mozart's use, and by summer Stephanie's editorial pen had begun to remodel *Belmont und Constanze oder Die Entführung aus dem Serail* by the popular Christoph Friedrich Bretzner. With music by Johann André, it had received its premiere in Berlin only weeks earlier (May 1781): the Burgtheater had gone about the usual practice of unashamed purloining, but, in this case, with unusual dispatch.

"Well, the day before yesterday," Mozart wrote on 1 August 1781, "young Stephanie gave me a libretto. . . . [It] is very good, has a Turkish subject, and is called *Bellmont and Konstanze* or *The Enticement from the Seraglio* (*sic*).[38] I shall use a Turkish style when composing the overture, the chorus in the first act, and the concluding chorus." He had already finished two arias and the trio closing the first act. "The time is truly short, for the performance is to be in the middle of September; but the circumstances connected with the date of the performance and, indeed, all my other prospects so raise my spirits that with ever so much eagerness I hasten to my desk and remain seated there with the greatest joy."

The attendant circumstances that so animated Mozart concerned the visit of the Grand Duke and Duchess of Russia. Stephanie wanted *The Abduction from the Seraglio* well in progress by the time Count Rosenberg would ask his advice as to what new opera to set before them. *The Abduction* would not only please the Emperor, now so partial to Mozart, but also be to the German taste of the royal couple. Into the bargain, the opera's setting in Turkey provided a reference to Empress Catherine's design to absorb this nation and send her younger grandson to Constantinople as its emperor. (In anticipation, she had directed that he be baptized Constantine.) No doubt the Turkish motif had prompted Schröder and Stephanie to pirate Bretzner's book so scandalously close upon its Berlin premiere.

Mozart had begun *The Abduction* while lodging with the Auernhammers and continued work on it in the Rats' Nest. Proceeding with astonishing speed, even in the midst of his crisis with Josepha—"at the moment I have to devote myself to composing, and not a moment is to be lost"—by 22 August he had finished the first act. Nevertheless, even though music flowed from him in torrents, when the Hofburg announced that St. Petersburg had put off the grand ducal visit until November, he had a sense of reprieve: he wanted to complete the opera "with greater deliberation" and at once asked Stephanie to recast the last two acts—to rearrange, rewrite, and, above all, to introduce a certain "fresh turn to the plot." Though over his head in work, Stephanie gave assurances that all would be done according to the wishes of a composer who had taken clear measure of his librettist: "He may write his plays by himself or with help; he may plagiarize or create; what matters is that he understands the stage and that his plays always please."[39]

---

38 Did Mozart mistake the title, reading *Entführung* (abduction) as *Verführung* (enticement or seduction); or did he suffer an amusing slip of the pen?

39 If a text answered with professionalism the company's capacities and the public's taste, few cared about how crooked the path that brought it to the stage. Lauding Johann André's accomplishments as librettist and composer, Goethe added: "One cannot reproach him for copying or pilfering."

Of a sudden, new influences began to push the premiere of *The Abduction* yet further into the future: Mozart observed Gluck's admirers, Chancellor Kaunitz among them, seeking "with great effort," to turn the Russian visit into an opportunity to pay tribute to Vienna's most famous and now ailing composer, a campaign advanced by Grand Duke Paul's veneration of him. Emperor Joseph "permitted himself," in Mozart's words, "to be prevailed upon": *Iphigénie en Tauride* was to be put into German— Mozart attested to Gluck's having set his heart upon hearing all his French operas in his native language[40]— and, along with *Alceste* in its original Italian, would replace *The Abduction* as the operatic salute to Paul and Maria Fedorovna. The translator, Johann Baptist von Alxinger, set to work, and some of the singers assigned to *The Abduction* plunged into study of these taxing scores: though members of Emperor Joseph's German company, they commanded Italian vocal technique, for, indeed, translations and adaptations of Italian and French works made up no small part of the repertory of the Burgtheater; its singspiel wing now housed some of the Reich's most accomplished singers.

Mozart attempted to hold his ground, for a brief time playing with the idea of asking Alxinger, whose poetry he valued, also to provide a German translation of *Idomeneo*. (From the beginning he had found Schachtner's wanting.) He planned to rewrite the title role for Raaff's pupil the bass Johann Ignaz Ludwig Fischer (scheduled to sing Osmin in *The Abduction*), to touch up the score here and there in the French manner, and to persuade the Hofburg to add this transformed *Idomeneo* to the works celebrating the Imperial visitors. (No doubt he envisaged Aloisia Lange as Ilia.) Before long, however, he had to put the idea aside, acknowledging that the singers would have difficulties enough mastering Gluck's two intense dramas in so short a time, to say nothing of the strain upon an Emperor pretending to enjoy them. "All in all, a third opera would be too much," Mozart concluded. But a third did appear on the schedule: Gluck's *Orfeo ed Euridice* (as a composite of the Italian and French versions); it completed a trio of works that would turn the close of 1781 into a Viennese Gluck festival.

---

40 Gluck, who arraigned himself for having "squandered" his "best powers upon the French nation," felt "an inward impulse" yet to write a significant opera in German "for my own nation." (Born in the Franconian Jura, where the Upper Palatinate and Bohemia lie close, he identified himself as a German.) Though he had begun work on musical settings of the lyrical interludes scattered throughout Klopstock's *Hermanns Schlacht*, Gluck had in fact never settled upon this tragedy, more suited to the study than the stage, as material for his operatic gift to Germany. His failure to put these "bardic songs" to paper—he kept them in his head, on occasion performing them for friends—bespoke artistic indecision and then enfeeblement: by the time he made the attempt to dictate them to Salieri, they had faded from his memory.

Mozart failed to force his way into it, and many Viennese no doubt looked upon his effort to tilt with the paralyzed master on his old terrain as rather forward.

Mozart watched the elaborate preliminaries for the Gluck productions: "supernumeraries recruited throughout Vienna and in all the suburbs" and a ballet master brought from Munich to work with the "sorry remnants" of a company of dancers over which Noverre had once presided; "they haven't moved a leg in full eight years," Mozart scoffed. He attended the rehearsals and studied the voices for which he had begun writing *The Abduction* but left no direct comment upon the music dramas themselves. His *Idomeneo* had revealed both respect for Gluck's powerful overall vision and also important, if limited, debts to his methods; but Gluck's musical economy (indeed, occasional poverty) could not have been to the taste of a young composer who, with fluency and a hundred charms along the way, expressed the poetic, the dramatic, and the rhetorical by means of traditional and decorous forms the elder master had dismissed as outmoded. Experiencing the Gluck works day after day sharpened Mozart's own sense of operatic mission: at this very time he set down those few and famous words challenging and forever placing himself apart from the Gluck-Calzabigi aesthetic: "In an opera the poetry must be on all accounts the obedient daughter of the music," a tightly drawn refutation of the dedication to *Alceste.*

What he had already composed of *The Abduction* pleased him; and, no less gladdening, the music "had earned applause on all sides," in particular Countess Thun's. He looked forward to a widening reputation in Vienna, to becoming "no less popular here as a composer than at the keyboard": a successful opera would once and for all set him on his legs. Reconciling himself to patience, he reflected that, even if at this moment "all [of *The Abduction*] were complete, nothing would be gained, for it would have to lie around" until the Gluck operas had crossed the stage.

In the interim, Stephanie, in consultation with Mozart, hammered at *The Abduction*: adding arias for Caterina Cavalieri, the Constanze, so that Mozart might turn to account her "flexible throat"; providing like service for Johann Valentin Adamberger, the stolid tenor singing Belmonte; and, most important, expanding the role of Osmin, the steward-overseer of Pasha Selim's household, in order to exploit the luxuriant bass of the popular Fischer; Mozart wanted to let those "beautiful deep tones shine forth."

As usual, he did not always wait for his poet to offer solutions but tampered with the libretto himself, even writing the text (polished by Stephanie) of Osmin's "*Solche hergelaufene Laffen,*" sketching the aria's words and music simultaneously. But unlike the revisions worked upon *Idomeneo,* which, other than cutting, had suffered no compromise for the sake of success, those he and Stephanie devised for Bretzner's text followed a pragmatic course with one striking exception: the "fresh turn to the plot" Mozart held necessary. He had, in fact, at first contemplated it in practical terms: inventing some new intrigue to fill a gap his reordering of Bretzner's scenario had opened, the result of his desire to provide the middle act with an ensemble finale (the remarkable quartet); but step by step the "fresh turn" took the shape of a new denouement, a change springing from personal concerns involving his new situation in Vienna and old attachments in Salzburg.

9

BRETZNER'S LIBRETTO CONCLUDES with Constanze's suitor, Pasha Selim, revealed as the father of her lover. In *The Abduction* no such relationship pertains: the Pasha's forgiveness does not represent a parent's benignity, but a philosophe's Enlightened triumph.[41] Psychological currents long set in motion had helped inspire this ennobling transformation: the motif of father and son in love with the same woman had long troubled Mozart, perhaps as early as *Mitridate*, but at fourteen he possessed no authority to demand revisions in its text. But by the time of *Idomeneo* and *The Abduction*, he could bend librettists to his will: it appears more than plausible that Varesco and Stephanie, in weeding out this complication, an important component of their sources, responded to his promptings; not a trace of such rivalry remains in either opera. Stephanie likewise freed Selim from Bretzner's traditional, indeed, Shakespearean expedient for unraveling a plot—relatives long separated or supposedly dead reappearing and recognizing one another (a convention Mozart would turn to marvelous parody in the *Figaro* sextet): extricated from any peremptory fatherly

---

41 At first glance, it perplexes that Mozart and Stephanie did not jettison the identification of the Pasha as a renegade Spanish nobleman, a device Bretzner took up in order to give conviction to the discovery of Selim as Belmonte's father. That *The Abduction* expunged the paternal but not the Spanish motif struck the critic Johann Friedrich Schink as artless (1782). Yet a Belmonte brought to light as the son of Selim's whilom persecutor provides a solution, if no less forced than Bretzner's, yet setting the stage for the Pasha's selfless utterances. Here Stephanie found a cadence smoldering with power, and Mozart restricted the lines to an actor's tongue, fine diction being indispensable. Though every singspiel actor's talents included at least simple vocalism (see XXIV, n. 7), a Selim expressing himself in ditties would have offered a strange complement to Constanze's elevated outpourings. Nor does it seem credible that the Melodrama ever presented itself as an alternative in the form of either a Monodrama for Selim or a Duodrama for him and Constanze: by this time Mozart had lost his enthusiasm for the genre; and, more important, so had the Viennese.

obligations, Mozart's Selim, without compulsion, rises above his passions and the potential for cruelty within himself;[42] Mozartean familial resonances enveloping the conclusion of *The Abduction* vibrate with all the more nobility as he stands forth, not an actual, but a symbolic parent—yet much like a Leopold moralizing at full spate—whose forbearing reversal, his *clemenza*, derives from an *opera-seria* tradition with which Mozart had long been at home. Fate had given him a book he could reshape to reflect his own yearning for reconciliation with Leopold. That enriching moment when Pasha Selim blesses Belmonte's union with Constanze speaks of Mozart's love for his own Constanze, his joy in contemplating their marriage, and his hope again to find the supportive, tender father of old.

A work combining such moments of emotional intensity with farcical comedy, the whole entangled in erotic and philosophic themes, *The Abduction* does not lack dramatic problems, in particular the doubts it awakens as to the strength of the spring regulating the scenario's main point of tension: the terrible things Pasha Selim threatens at the point his patience fails. In *Zaide* the heroine's commanding aria responds to a clear danger from Sultan Soliman; in contrast, it appears hard to take in good earnest Pasha Selim's capacity for barbarousness: the abundance and grandiose dimensions of Constanze's defiance of him (*"Martern aller Arten"*) and the mysterious profundities of her duet with Belmonte (*"Welch ein Geschick! / Meinetwegen soll't du sterben!"*), in which they face and overcome the very fact of death, square ill with the listener's perception of the actual peril in which they find themselves, for, whatever its dislocations, something of the enclosed paradise hovers about Selim's country estate. In Count Almaviva's world of obsessions, major disruptions rend the garden, wherein pain impends, then stings, and the mood turns bitter; Don Giovanni's true garden is the graveyard; Sarastro's realm often enough seems no less menacing; and Fiordiligi and Dorabella's green arbors on the Bay of Naples witness utter deceit, the confounding of lies and reality. But within the grounds of the Pasha's palace overlooking the sea, catastrophe seems out of the question: his dark moods do not convince.

On the other hand, *"Martern aller Arten"* does convince, soliciting admiration for its high purposes. The aria constitutes an amply scaled portrait in which Mozart draws with strong outlines, brushes on brilliant color, and, through gestures of power and dignity, transforms the hitherto subdued and enduring Constanze into a true daughter of Ilia, the Trojan princess who stepped forward to die in her beloved's place. In *"Martern aller*

---

42 Much as the worst within King Idomeneo rises from the depths in the shape of a monster, so Selim's destructive qualities form the essence of Osmin. At the end of the opera the Pasha's calming observations, to all seeming directed to Osmin, in effect address himself.

Arten," Constanze finds a new voice and achieves a new presence, a discovery of self and potential no less startling to her than to Pasha Selim. (At moments in the aria, she slips back into her former identity, to recover apace.) The majestic outburst prepares her role in the duet, wherein she raises Belmonte to the level of her metamorphosed personality, provokes Selim's *clemenza,* and opens the way for her descendant, Pamina, to guide her prince through fire and flood. The aria represents a salient juncture in the evolution of Constanze's character and of Mozart's dramatic ideology, and to work the drastic change he required space: the canvas had to be the right size—an earlier version runs even longer—no matter what the problems in light of the Pasha's transparent generosity.

The aria displays traits of character and, no less, a musical architecture underscoring Constanze's descent from Ilia, whose *"Se il padre perdei"* opens with a fourteen-bar instrumental introduction imbued with her gentle determination; enlarging upon the device, Mozart prefaced Constanze's *aria di bravura* with a grand orchestral prelude: sixty bars of enormous musical thrust (they might pass for a concerto's exposition) that constitute a tonal précis of the growth in presence and assertiveness the Pasha would witness. When she has completed the aria and swept out, he, since neither threats nor appeals have worked his ends, resolves to fall back upon guile. Mozart and Stephanie intended to weave this thread into the plot, but unable to puzzle out a strategy in the end left it dangling: a trace of their struggle to strengthen the core and substance of the opera's central argument, the clash of Constanze and Selim.

Having with Stephanie's guidance measured to Viennese taste *The Abduction'*s overall balance between laughter and tears and no doubt persuading himself that few would descry the heroic dimensions of *"Martern aller Arten"* as resting upon flimsy dramatic foundations, Mozart had done with the matter: he permitted mock-menace and mock-danger to dissolve into a healing affirmation of life and love as, their unreal fears allayed, Constanze and Belmonte enter into possession of a cloudless promise of renewal no less bright for the audience's having suffered little anxiety on their behalf. *The Abduction* ends with the father-figure at ease with a Belmonte absolved, in full degree an adult, and about to leave with his bride. The symbolic son will become a father. He begins a concluding "vaudeville"[43] resounding as a hymn of thanks for recovered benevolence.

Within the slight convention of the vaudeville, Mozart reassures and persuades that life has meaning. So much of his greatness as a musical

---

43 In a vaudeville, each of the characters, one after the other, sings a stanza to the same melody, often folklike, every stanza ending with a refrain in which all join.

dramatist lies in this gift to put to rest the terror that the individual functions within chaos and must endure as isolated: life threatens, Mozart offers security, and, like Shakespeare, makes us "precious winners all."
Whatever the failures of the libretto, by its end Mozart has refashioned
the father into the greathearted hero of old, and audiences experience a
sense of repair, reconciliation, and community as the finale moves in
bubbling playfulness toward the curtain. It closes upon a world without
ambivalence and troubling undercurrents, even though the brutish Osmin
interrupts to dispute the general praise of Pasha Selim's wisdom. But his
rage will subside: he represents no demonic force, no formidable evil (as
does the Sultan in *Zaide*); rather, a marvelous grotesque, he serves as a
warning of the tragedy that might have been (see n. 42); this "most ridiculous monster," so Trinculo observes of Caliban, is to be savored, his vulgarity a foil for the Pasha's resonant dignity, his stupidity throwing into
relief Pedrillo's address.

In a broader conceptual sense, a pure and joyful celebration, a wonder
and a frolic promising that May will forever reign in whatever garden Constanze and Belmonte choose to wander, the finale shapes a golden moment,
its sounds reverberating hauntingly in the minds of those aware of how
short a time such felicity holds. For Mozart it lasted his brief lifetime; *The
Abduction* had grown into a hymn to his great love; within a month of the
premiere, he would wed his own Constanze. The interplay of forces leading to this fulfilling day forms a most peculiar history.

CHAPTER XXIX

Vienna:
Defining His Rubicon

HE HAD EMERGED from under the mountain of psychological distress his family had piled upon him. In his eyes everything in Vienna, a city known to him since childhood, now bore marks of the bright
and new. Elation set his powers to work. His Constanze and his growing
fame filled his heart; he felt healed; in Vienna he tread enchanted ground.

He appeared a marvelous but consistent mixture: the image of a polished
man of the world filled with external graces (if not without a certain sanc-
timony) and reserving for friends his overflowing spirits, madcap humors,
and cynical banter (by this time illness alone could chill and numb this exuberance). Like Goethe, he learned to enact, when necessary, the chameleon,
a part helpful in conserving energy; but, unlike Goethe's, his character did
not spring from contradictions and show itself elusive at every turn; rather,
his quicksilver temperament, variable humors, and spontaneous play apart,
in essence he remained of a piece, an intense fusion under control and without Goethe's morbid strain. If, as Felix Mendelssohn observed, there were
many Goethes, there was only one Mozart, steadfast in his central bent.

As dower to this creator unique in the history of the human spirit, Vienna provided the framework within which he found ultimate expression:
Vienna gave him what Salzburg could not. At once, he caught the tone of
the metropolis: invigorated by an air he felt to be fresher than any he had
yet breathed, healthy in body, composed in mind, at ease and master of

himself, and with an exhilarating confidence in his gifts, he had found his way. Only one vexation cast its shadow: Leopold.

With his move to the Graben, Mozart had set new bounds to his correspondence with Salzburg, limiting himself to writing once a week; moreover, he refused any longer to tolerate Leopold's rebukes to his conduct and conscience in letters that had taken on an ever uglier tone, "as if I were an arch-scoundrel or a simpleton, or both at the same time." To a father who placed "trust in the idle talk and scribbling of others," he summed matters up: "When all is said and done, you have not the slightest confidence in me." He had learned that over the months three acquaintances had been feeding Salzburg stories about his private life, telling tales for the most part defamatory—and Leopold believed them.

The most vicious of the trio, Peter Winter, two years Mozart's senior and a violinist in the Mannheim orchestra, had migrated with it to Munich; in 1780 he went on tour to Vienna and remained to study composition with Salieri. For Leopold's benefit, either by letter or in conversation—perhaps during a journey to Munich via Salzburg—he painted Mozart's relationship with Constanze in colors lewd to the point of describing her as "a slut" (*Luder*). When he got word of this outrage, Mozart identified Winter as his "worst enemy": his hostility, perhaps born of a loyal affection for his old teacher, Vogler, whom Mozart had offended in Mannheim, had grown even more intense in Vienna. The second informant, Franz Xaver Wenzel Gilowsky von Urazowa, brother of Nannerl's friend Katherl, and Mozart's chum since childhood, sent the Tanzmeisterhaus a communication Leopold saw in its true colors only much later, when he made reference to Gilowsky's "shabby prank," that "stupid letter about [Wolfgang's] being in love." That Gilowsky had taken upon himself to forward gossip about Mozart to the Tanzmeisterhaus, Leopold came to realize, demonstrated both foolishness and treachery. A protégé of the Firmian family, Franz Xaver had settled in Vienna to study surgery. Word of his clumsy disclosure came too late to obviate Mozart's choosing him as his best man.[1]

Leopold had the richest source of mean-spirited tales in Herr von Moll, who, to Mozart's surprise, had turned on him, decrying his relationship with the Webers and insisting that he pursued fewer musical than sexual

---

1 Aware that the Mozarts had come to see through him, Franz Xaver avoided Leopold during his visit to Vienna in 1785. By this time Leopold recognized in him the paltry jealousy of the prodigiously talented on the part of a mediocrity lacking any real gifts. In time, Franz Xaver and Mozart reconciled, though he never regained his old warmth for "Gilowsky the braggart" (*Windmacher*).

opportunities among the ladies of Vienna. Josepha Auernhammer, who no doubt enjoyed imagining herself among these sirens, heard this accusation from von Moll himself and repeated it to Mozart. (Her loyalty to Mozart apart, the innuendos she at one time had let fall helped spread his reputation as a Don Giovanni.) To Leopold he dismissed von Moll as having put his "slanderous tongue" in the service of his favorite, Leopold Kozeluch, whom Vienna viewed as Mozart's rival cembalist. With pride Mozart claimed that his playing had excited Kozeluch's admiration: it had—along with a destructive envy. Eager to do Mozart any kind of injury, to a certainty von Moll was the mischievous meddler who maintained to Leopold that his son had awakened nothing but antipathy in Vienna, "at court and on the part of the old and new nobility," that his "boasting and criticizing" had made enemies of the professors of music. "How can there be such monstrous people?" a shocked Mozart asked his father.

Even if his sowing wild oats had some basis in fact and success had stimulated his arrogance, why did busybodies like Winter and von Moll harass him? Though the first wished to even a score and the second to defend his protégé, this strange business attests more to both the animosities Mozart's personality could awaken and the extent to which Leopold's possessiveness still made many look upon the twenty-six-year-old as a juvenile to be passed under his father's review. What grated most upon Mozart had been Leopold's readiness to believe any malignant hearsay that came his way.

Contemplating the tangled route that had turned back on its course to end all but where it had begun, at the upper end of the Graben and a stone's throw from the Zum Auge Gottes, Mozart let fly at his father: not Caecilia Weber's expostulations, he blurted out, but, at the last, Leopold's hectoring had forced him to resign the conveniences of the Weber household—to abandon "a comfortable carriage for a mail coach." "The foolishness God knows who puts into your head always outweighs my arguments." He demanded that Leopold cease discussing their disagreements with third parties. "People may write themselves blind—and you may agree with them as you wish—but, by God, I shall not on this account alter by a hair's breadth. . . . I will not give to others the smallest account of what I do or do not do. . . ."

That Leopold thought him idle he in particular took ill: "From all your letters I see that you believe I do nothing here but amuse myself. Well, you downright deceive yourself. I can truly say that I enjoy no pleasure [he, of course, delighted in Viennese life] except that of not being in Salzburg." He would never forget his father—that he might seems to have become Leopold's chief obsession—but would determine his own way. For the while he would remain in Vienna. If, however, things did not work to his advantage, he had in mind "going straight to Paris." On this point he did, not without malice, ask Leopold's thoughts.

Astounding that this letter of 5 September 1781 did not outright undo Leopold (soon thereafter he had his first "fit of vertigo"[2]): it clearly indicated the geography of Mozart's new independent territories, their defining Rubicon, and the price of any attempt to ford it. At all events, not Leopold but Nannerl took to bed: she fell into a quandary over d'Yppold's persistent courtship, and Mozart realized that she had to put aside her hesitations and enter the struggle on his side were she to have any hand in shaping her own life. "In all seriousness believe me, dear sister: the best cure for you would be a husband; just because [marriage] would have an effect upon your health, with all my heart I want you to wed soon." He feared she would retreat from confrontation and, as Leopold hoped, lose d'Yppold. Using her predicament as the foundation of a grand design in which many forces interwove—some tender, some aggressive, and many ambiguous, deeply disguised, and difficult to penetrate—Mozart with bold strokes brushed in a canvas he dominated as the central figure: the conqueror of Leopold; the new head of the family.

"I feel certain that you and d'Yppold have little, in fact, no future in Salzburg. But could not d'Yppold do something *here* [Vienna]? At all events, he cannot be altogether without resources.[3] Ask him about this; if he thinks there might be value in the idea, he need but indicate to me what route to follow; beyond question I will do my utmost, for I have great sympathy with your situation. Were things thus arranged, you would no doubt marry, inasmuch as, believe me, you could earn money enough here, for example, by giving private concerts and lessons. You would be much in demand and well paid."

The sister appropriated and made into his daughter and her fiancé reduced to a supporting role, Mozart proceeded to turn Leopold into a pale, inert, and childlike dependent, an exhausted patriarch installed in the son's nursery: "But my father would have to resign and come, too, and we could live together again with much contentment; I see no other solution. Even before I knew you had become serious about d'Yppold, I had something

---

2 Mozart proposed to his father two remedies for dizziness: "Take axle grease wrapped in paper and wear it on your chest; take the big bone of a leg of veal, wrap it in paper along with a kreutzer's worth of leopard's bane [a species of doronicum] and carry it in your pocket." It tempts to look upon these recommendations as pure Mozartean caprice, but they might have had their origins in home nostrums or, alas, even in professional medical prescriptions.

3 D'Yppold had a modest civil-service salary, no personal fortune, and little chance of finding a niche in Vienna, even with the help Mozart might ask of Count Cobenzl.

like this [leaving Salzburg for Vienna] in mind for you [an out-and-out paternal locution]. Only our dear father had become the stumbling block, for I wanted the man to be untroubled and not torment and vex himself. Pursuing this path [to Vienna] might bring the desired end, for with your husband's income, yours, and mine, we could get along and provide him with a tranquil and comfortable life." If in Munich Mozart had seen himself as a stumbling block checking his father's peace of mind, by this time he looked upon Leopold as the impediment to his children's self-fulfillment.

At first glance, this proposal might be thought a rare attempt to exchange a serious idea with Nannerl: Mozart went as far as to imply a line of demarcation within the family, the two of them on one side, their father on the other. But here a pure rescue fantasy paraded as substance: the scene depicted the hero-brother alleviating the sister's plight, an illusion constructed of ironies and duplicities. Yet such Mozartean inventions had nothing of the delusional: serving to smooth inner turmoil and liberate creative impulses, they subsided even as he wrote them down. Least of all did he wish this chivalric romance to become reality: Leopold's was the last face he wished to see in Vienna. The Tanzmeisterhaus recognized the proposal as yet another literary exercise and gave it no heed. For her part, Nannerl, who would refuse Constanze even pretended acceptance within the family, took her place across the line with her father. The future was to be estrangement, ranging from the hostile to, at best, the frigidly polite; and, in the end, Nannerl would reconcile herself to a pathetic ambiguity in respect to her brother's memory.[4]

At times provoked, at times bored by Leopold's tirades, why did Mozart not break with him, if only for a while, and give both a space in which to breathe, adjust, and then reconcile? A residue of sentiment and love helped maintain the links, whatever the strains; and a most practical

4 The information Nannerl sent to Friedrich Adolph Schlichtegroll for his extended obituary of Mozart (1793) concluded with a deplorable postscript added by the amanuensis conducting the communication, the family friend Albert von Mölk; here he no doubt echoed old prejudicial observations stemming from her and Leopold but which she scrupled at including in her own hand. (Schlichtegroll made use of the chafing remarks about her brother but not those touching the still very much alive Constanze.) Even if Nannerl remained ignorant of von Mölk's passing on the acrimony, the postscript's bile betrayed the father's and sister's view of the couple and helped form an important component of the Mozart myth, in particular the dismissal of Constanze: "Against the will of his father, [Mozart] married a girl quite unsuited to him; thus the great domestic confusion at and after his death." In truth, Mozart could not have found a companion more responsive than Constanze to his volatile and loving ways. No doubt to her sister-in-law's astonishment, Constanze emerged from mourning to become a most competent administrator of her husband's estate, making it into the basis of her and their children's lifelong prosperity.

consideration played its important part: the Tanzmeisterhaus sheltered Mozart's compositions. From this archive Leopold sent out scores, or copies of them, in response to his son's requests. In Vienna he would become ever more dependent upon this service: his concerts devoured material, and at times he even obliterated the dates on works received from home so that the Viennese copyists would be no wiser than the public in believing them new. (A practice he regretted: Nannerl recalled that "the stronger he grew as a composer, the less he could tolerate works from earlier days.") Although his moments of exasperation and wrath did not abate, Leopold continued as dispatcher even after recognizing that he no longer had an essential part in his son's life; the duty endured—a token of solicitude and concern and, perhaps, a vestige of control.[5]

While working on *The Abduction*, Mozart did attempt to rebuild his epistolary relationship with Leopold, espying, so he thought, a promising route winding through their common professional interests: he wrote descriptions of his approach to composing the text, a boon for posterity but viewed with less appreciation by Leopold, who had to read about his son's first opera composed without fatherly advice or even comments; the discussion concerned what he had done and would do; questions about what he might do did not arise.[6] Mozart thought he had made this disposition clear to Salzburg in his assessment of Countess Thun's reaction to those sections of *The Abduction* he had played for her on the piano: ". . . I credit *no one's praise or blame*, that is, before such a person has seen or heard everything *as a whole*; rather, I simply follow *my own instincts*." Furthermore, in the face of Leopold's criticism of infelicities in what he had read of the text, Mozart spoke up for it: "I am well aware that the verses are not of the best; but since they so fitted in and agreed with a musical conception al-

---

5 The following may be taken as typical of Mozart's instructions to Leopold (27 June 1781): "I shall send you the opera [*Idomeneo*] as soon as possible [for deposit in the archives]. Countess Thun still has it and at present is in the country. Have the sonata in B flat à quatre mains [K. 358] and the two concertos for two claviers [K. 365 and 242 in its arrangement for two instruments] copied and send them to me without delay. I should like to receive my masses one by one." Then, in respect to a double mishap concerning *Idomeneo* (30 January 1782): "With your next letter please send me a copy of the libretto of *Idomeneo* (with or without the German translation). I lent a copy to Countess Thun, but she has moved, cannot find it, and one assumes it has gone astray. Fraulein Auernhammer had another, has searched, but as yet cannot locate it. Perhaps she will; should she not, I will be in a predicament, for I require it now. To be on the safe side, please dispatch it straightway, cost what it may, for I need it at once in order to arrange my concert, which will take place on the third Sunday of Lent."
6 Three years earlier, Leopold, even then clutching at the past, called upon a commanding example in an effort to recover those days when his opinion carried weight with his son; to him he observed of Voltaire, less than three weeks before the philosophe's death: "Voltaire reads his poems to his friends, listens to their opinions, and makes changes."

ready in my head, they, as a matter of course, pleased me; and I would wager that in performance all will come off well."

More and more, *The Abduction* offended Leopold, who felt neglected and misprized: four days after its premiere Mozart posted the complete score to Salzburg in the hope of a congratulatory word, but none came. Did Leopold, sensing the parabolic flickerings at the end of the opera, resent it even more, in particular, the references to the hero's father, shaded in dark and threatening colors? Whatever the case, Mozart would succeed in forcing him to bestow a paternal benediction, if not upon his opera, then upon his marriage: to become a kind of Pasha Selim, though with reluctance and after the event.

2

ON 10 NOVEMBER 1781 Mozart had begun sending to Salzburg convoluted signals about Constanze, much in the spirit of those messages he had once posted from Paris announcing his resolve to marry Aloisia: "Beyond question," his father learned, "whatever is conducive to your son's happiness must be agreeable to you"; a week later, in answer to a suggestion on Leopold's part that he share his bed with Ceccarelli during his proposed fleeting visit to Vienna: ". . . as to sleeping [with someone] in one bed, I intend to do that with no one but my future wife"; and early in December Leopold received his son's mysterious acknowledgment of failure "to fulfill all your wishes in the way you contemplated." As Mozart must have hoped, this allusiveness led Leopold to insist upon plainer speaking. The reply breathed a tone at one with the demand for frankness; the words poured out: "You require an explanation. . . . Oh, with what willingness would I have opened my heart to you long ago, but for the reproaches you might have made."

He then set forth his reasons for planning to take a wife, recapitulating familiar arguments: "Nature speaks as loud in me as in any other, and perhaps louder than in many a big strong lout." Yet, even in the face of this vigorous sexuality, his sense of honor prevented him from seducing innocents, and "fear of diseases" barred his "playing around with whores." Without embarrassment he fell back upon the old threat of surrendering himself to them—"I would not venture to promise that, should I once err in this respect, I would rest satisfied with a single experience"—and then went on to advance a point Leopold would have to admit: a wife had become a clear-cut necessity to someone "from youth onward unaccustomed to attend to things like laundry, clothing, etc. . . . I am outright convinced that with a wife I should get on better—and on the same income I have as a bachelor." He then discharged the thunderclap: "Now, who is the object of my love? Do not take fright, I entreat you. At all events, certainly not a Weber? Yes, a Weber—but neither Josepha nor Sophie, but Constanze, the middle one."

He sought a parental blessing even while making clear that the marriage would take place whatever Leopold's disposition: "Without my dearest Constanze I cannot be happy and satisfied, and, lacking your assent, would be only half so." To bring him around as fast as possible he held out the bribe-like inducement of one half of any fixed income he might enjoy— pure word painting, as Leopold well knew—and also descended to a yet cruder stratagem: an unworthy letter to Salzburg pulled the Weber women down to the base level they occupied in his father's eyes—all except So-phie ("as yet too young to be anything but a good-hearted if irresponsible creature") and, of course, Constanze, who was to gain stature through an-tithesis. Mozart described her as "the martyr" of the family, a delicate spirit encompassed by the wicked: the "lazy, coarse, two-faced" Josepha; the "perfidious, malicious" Aloisia, still "a coquette"; and a mother ill-disposed toward his beloved and reserving her few favors for the other daughters. He pictured Constanze as in a fairy tale: foreign to the extrava-gance of her sisters, her hair dressed by her own art (a disparagement of Nannerl?), and clothed out of fashion but neatly in garments her fingers had sewn, she shouldered the responsibilities of running the household, re-ceiving only abuse in return—the Cinderella of the Petersplatz.

Gratuitous and out of proportion, undermining the characters of the two sisters and the mother had the air of betrayal: it becomes unsettling to witness Mozart's methods hardening into crudity; here little counts to his fair name, for, despite some ugly moments, the play unfolding on either side of the Graben partook less of serious high drama with its treacheries than of a domestic comedy—an intricate action with Caecilia Weber as star and director.

Mozart credited an enemy like Peter Winter with provoking the pres-sures forcing him into a marriage contract—someone who "must have shouted into the ears" of Constanze's guardian, Thorwart, "that I was a danger; that I had no settled income; that I enjoyed an intense intimacy with her; that I well might jilt her; and that I would leave the girl despon-dent etc." No belief can be given this histrionic hypothesis of an outsider's interference: in brief, the time had come for Caecilia and Thorwart to gather in what her rumors had grown, to go through the final scene for which Mozart's still uninterrupted daily visits to the Auge Gottes helped set the stage. (He even persisted in directing his mail to the Webers.) Even as she continued her fabrications, Caecilia protested faith in his honest intentions, asking him to confer and come to terms with a Thorwart she now pictured as bursting with angry insistence upon satisfaction: the young man's possessive attentions, he argued, had compromised a tender ward of the state.

A meeting at the Auge Gottes ended with Thorwart's ultimatum: Mozart had either to enter into a written agreement or find the doors of the apartment closed to him. "Can anyone who loves with sincerity and without alteration abandon his sweetheart?" this gallant asked as he himself drew up the document. It bound him to marry Constanze within three years or pay her a lifelong indemnity of three hundred florins. "Nothing . . . could have been easier for me to write, for I knew that . . . I should never forsake her and, should I be so unfortunate as to arrive at a change of mind [a playful non sequitur?], I would indeed be happy to free myself for 300 florins. . . . But what did the heavenly girl do when the guardian had left? She asked her mother for the document and said to me: '*Dear Mozart! I so trust your word that I need no written assurance from you*'; and she tore the paper to pieces. This act made my dear Constanze yet more precious to me."

She had followed her mother's script to this dramatic point, but would league with her no further: henceforth her loyalties, to Caecilia's shock, would attend Mozart's interests alone. With him bound by the honor he considered sacred, Caecilia in turn dropped all pretense to gentility and lay open her unsavory and alcoholic ways. She nagged him and Constanze to reside as rent-paying tenants in her apartment, an idea they ignored: "She is certainly very much mistaken in expecting us, when married, to take rooms with her because she has them to let. This is out of the question, for never would I do it and still less my Constanze. *Au contraire*, she intends to see very little of her mother, and I will do my utmost to put a complete end [to their intercourse]. We know her." The relationship between mother and daughter became ever more grinding.

When Leopold received word of how deftly Frau Weber had led the dance of the marriage contract, his outrage mounted like a Mannheim rocket, and no decrescendo followed. He realized how at all points she had hoodwinked Wolfgang, who soon had to agree; Constanze revealed all to him: "For a long time both [Constanze] and I have observed her mother's purposes." With näive trust and a willingness to be duped, he had closed his eyes to them and only now did he look hard at her. Leopold announced that the circumstances invited an official investigation of Caecilia and Thorwalt, for they had followed a path of brazen self-interest and ensnarement extending from her giving the young man the freedom of her apartment—she had lured him there, Leopold felt certain—to closing the trap of the contract. Leopold contemplated the pair's condemnation on charges of moral corruption and reveled in the thought of their being "put into chains and made to sweep the streets, all the while wearing placards about their necks with the inscription '*perverter of the young*' [the kind of humiliation the Emperor enjoyed inflicting]." Mozart, however, wanted the wounds to heal; after all, he had laid himself open to Caecilia's plotting, which, in the end, had left him beatific.

Even in the light of the puritanism and hypocrisy of Josephinian justice, Leopold could have found a way to stir up legal difficulties for Frau Weber only had his son been the child he still thought him. Yet, within eleven days of his father's vision of Caecilia and Thorwart in irons for leading a youth astray, Mozart celebrated his twenty-sixth birthday! If for the moment Leopold had lost touch with the real, so, too, had Caecilia.

More and more, she gave herself to the bottle. (Caecilia drank "very much more than a woman should," Mozart observed.) Threats of prosecution rumbling from Salzburg reached her ears even as she contemplated a daughter turned adversary. No longer equal to enduring the tensions and abuse at the Auge Gottes, Constanze, during July 1782, fled to Baroness von Waldstätten.[7] Unhinged, Caecilia responded by giving notice that she would call upon the authorities to return Constanze to the Petersplatz, for she, it seems clear, lost little time exchanging the Baroness's home for Mozart's new quarters on the Hohe Brücke (see p. 624). "Do the police here really have the right to enter any house?" Mozart asked, his anxieties multiplying as Constanze fell ill. Circumstances had decided their beginning life together even before Mozart edged the Tanzmeisterhaus toward a concessive view of their formal union. Nonetheless, it took him months to clean the slate of "all the evil" Caecilia "inflicted upon her daughter *before her marriage.*" (Constanze's first confinement would give Caecilia the opportunity to end the estrangement.)

If the mother's latest scenario had drawn upon *opera buffa*, Mozart's embraced the *seria*: since early in 1782, he had come to look upon his impending marriage in terms of a heroic labor of deliverance—"I must rescue her as soon as possible"—the fantasy of setting his sister free having blossomed into a vision of liberating his beloved. He saw himself as

7 The preceding November and April, Constanze had enjoyed visits with the Baroness. An excellent pianist, she made her home a place of music and permissive hospitality (see XXVIII, n. 33). Mozart and Constanze suffered a brief falling-out over a game of forfeits she had joined at the Countess's. Having lost a round, Constanze paid the penalty of permitting a young man to measure her calves with a ribbon. When he learned of the incident, an outraged Mozart protested that she should have demurred. From Leopold he had inherited a puritanical streak that nourished intermittent jealousy; with the years she would soften both (see p. 708).

Belmonte: indeed, for months the young Spaniard's stratagems to abduct his sweetheart from Turkish captivity had been at the very center of Mozart's artistic concerns.

3

BY MID-NOVEMBER 1781 he had received the first of Stephanie's revisions of *The Abduction from the Seraglio.* Additions, suppressions, and tinkering continued into the new year. Not until May could Countess Thun hear the composer play the completed second and third acts. On 3 June 1782 the opera went into rehearsal at the Burgtheater, and the premiere took place on 16 July. The playbill did not mention Stephanie, but identified the book as "freely reworked after Bretzner's," a politic nod toward the writer whose authorization had never been sought and a no less politic use of his well-known name. *The Abduction,* K. 384, carried all before it, and Mozart, his position now secure, moved to claim his bride.

On 27 July he wrote to Salzburg asking with good grace that his marriage with Constanze receive a father's favor. Four days later Mozart's words had turned insistent, even angry: "You cannot have any possible objection ... for she is a decent, honest girl of good parents. I am in a position to earn her *bread*; we love and want one another. All that you have written or might in any wise write me ... has no point for a man who has gone so far with a girl." He would no longer mince the truth: he revealed his alliance with Constanze as a physical *fait accompli.* The depth of his commitment to her admits no question, and, at at all events, Caecilia had done her work well. He felt obliged to resolve a matter touching both love and honor, though from his point of view one apprehension had persisted: the ground beneath a freelance might slide away should he fall ill. But he now reasoned this dread out of his mind: ". . . the highest nobility would extend powerful protection to me, especially as a married man."

On 2 August 1782, a priest of the Theatinerkirche heard Constanze and Mozart make confessions so soul-searching as to obviate the posting of banns, for, in almost the same breath, they pressed on with arrangements for the wedding: two days later, in the intoxicating aftermath of *The Abduction*'s triumph, Mozart, without paternal benediction, took Constanze to wife in St. Stephen's cathedral.[8] Leopold's show of indifference to *The Abduction*, in particular his reluctance even to open the full score of it

---

8 The wedding party, which included Caecilia, Sophie, Thorwart, and Gilowsky, proceeded from St. Stephen's to Baroness Waldstätten's, where she presided over a nuptial feast "more princely than baronial."

Mozart had sent to Salzburg, augured ill (as would the startling letter he sent to Baroness Waldstätten before the month's end[9]). However, by 7 August, the blessing did arrive, and, in return, Mozart sent moving words of thanks.

His happiness did not make him stifle thoughts of conditions Leopold had attached to accepting a daughter-in-law not to his taste. It appears that at the moment Constanze became Frau Mozart, her husband sacrificed all or most of his inheritance: "Long ago I made her aware of my circumstances and of just what my expectations consist in respect to you," he had written Leopold on the very day that tardy benison reached Vienna, but she did not hesitate "to give over her whole future to my fate." He must have believed his father would change course and that their relationship could be rebuilt upon the foundation of *The Abduction*'s success.

Most striking remained its breadth—the opera's attraction to all layers of Viennese life, not least the salons. "The sensation is such that no one wants to hear anything else, and the theater always swarms with people," Mozart crowed. To crown all, the Emperor appeared pleased: every turn of the plot revealed Josephinian precepts.

4

IN PART ENLIGHTENMENT essay, *The Abduction* celebrated virtue as a source of happiness, and, as a fillip, exploited the conceit and seeming paradox of a virtuous non-Christian: that Pasha Selim, a renegade, had retained God's mercies, uncovenanted in his new status, underlined that Grace might descend to those without Faith.[10] Informed with Wolffian

---

9 Here Leopold suggested to her that his failure to become Salzburg's kapellmeister had been the direct consequence of Mozart's "behavior" in Vienna; in this view, the contretemps involving Count Arco brought to pass the father's being "offered up as a sacrificial victim" expiating the son's "impatience" and "quick temper." This obsession grew from Leopold's refusal to admit that Gatti's impending appointment as kapellmeister (February 1783; see XV, n. 19) had its beginnings in negotiations under way since 1778. The court had long closed the door to any advancement in Leopold's career and, in fact, felt itself generous in simply keeping him on; that he could have thought otherwise must have dumbfounded Mozart. His father's disappointment in not even having been considered for the post turned to fury. It expressed itself in his complaints to the Baroness and more than two years later still burned in him as, with uncharacteristic vulgarity, he described to Nannerl the Archbishop's method of choosing candidates for promotion, a procedure court etiquette portrayed as progressing straight from his bosom or heart but which Leopold saw as a more complicated process: "From the bosom to the anus and therefrom discharged [*herausgelaxierte*] in the form of official promotions."

10 Three years earlier, in Weimar, Goethe had composed his *Iphigenia in Tauris,* in which an examination of conscience compels Thaos, king of a barbarian land, to restrain his anger and give his prisoners their freedom.

sensibilities of this kind, the work, exploring the individual's sense of moral responsibility, embodied the didactic social spirit the Emperor sought to bring to the Burgtheater.

The distinctive patterns of bourgeois thought and behavior—bookish, public-spirited, and with a pious, sentimental reverence for the family—had come to dominate Vienna, and prevailing opinion in its coffeehouses, salons, and the Hofburg itself now disparaged things foreign. Christian Gottlob Klemm, publisher of the weekly *Der österreichische Patriot*, thrust at Vienna's *grand monde*, which so consumed itself with the passion to speak French and Italian that it claimed to be no longer able to manage proper German.[11] (Marcellina in Mozart's *Figaro* would direct attention to her rising social position by permitting a bit of French to escape her lips.)

Klemm's criticism accorded with the Emperor's predilection for his native tongue. Like von Sonnenfels, however, he restricted himself to High German, rejecting that extraordinary Viennese linguistic idiosyncrasy, the *Wienerisch* home dialect, which his Imperial mother had often and without shame used to striking effect. He banished from his stage the crude and popular Hanswurst comedians, who, caricaturing south German peasants, gushed forth water-closet and sexual smut in Salzburg dialect.[12] (Ironic that one of Joseph's strongest critics, Georg Philipp Wucherer, compared him to a deceitful Hanswurst.) Joseph even heard demands that he instruct Vienna's priests to sing the Roman liturgy in German, and Kornelius von Ayrenhoff now defined the study of the national tongue as a duty, a goal root and branch Josephinian—at least for the moment.

Emperor Joseph came to function as his capital's leading dispenser of culture: in effect taking over direction of his German National theater, both its company of actors and its *singspiel* wing, he had made the Burgtheater Vienna's citadel of spoken and sung German, a composite called into being in answer to appeals of bourgeois savants like von Sonnenfels. Joseph felt at one with them in regarding drama and opera in German as vehicles to educate in Enlightened values and to make the Kaiserstadt the very center of

---

11 At the "Gluck festival" (see p. 593), along with Alxinger's sung German translation of *Iphigénie en Tauride*, the management felt obliged to provide Viennese society with a printed Italian version, too (see n. 18).

12 The century witnessed a parade of Hanswursts and their next of kin, the most significant among them: the coarse peasant Josef Anton Stranitzky put before the Viennese; the somewhat less vulgar figure created by his successor Gottfried Prehauser, a clown capable of stinging satire and very much of the city rather than a country lout visiting it; the German harlequin played by Bernadon (Felix von Kurz), who reclaimed some of the more subtle ways of the commedia dell'arte, the cradle of the Hanswurst; and the irresistible survivor of the line, Schikaneder and Mozart's Papageno. In the next century Johann Nepomuk Nestroy became heir to this tradition.

the German nation's literary and ethical development. Writers like Goethe, Lessing, Herder, Wieland, and Klopstock viewed Joseph's Vienna as the emerging center of German achievement—"Vienna," Wieland insisted, "should be to Germany what Paris is to France..."—yet "our German Joseph" (Goethe's phrase) had uphill work to counter the claims of critics like Friedrich Nicolai, who, identifying Berlin as the new cultural adornment of the German world, ridiculed Vienna as a dogmatic, repressive, anachronistic, indeed depraved stronghold of Catholic obscurantism, a city innocent, nay ignorant, of Europe's dominant intellectual tendencies. It would be difficult to deny that the spirit of southern Germany expressed itself more compellingly in the musical and plastic arts than in words: the glories of its Catholic traditions had exacted a toll in political and literary sophistication, costs Joseph now strove to remit. He saw his theater as a tool of the state: why, printed texts, when read along with the performances, might even help close the embarrassing cleft in his hereditary dominions between spoken and written German.

A heightened loyalty to German modes of expression became the fruitful ground upon which Joseph and Mozart first built together and brought *The Abduction* into being, the Emperor following his reason—the seemliness of the German Emperor exalting things German—the composer his heart, his fervor for the language and its mythical and mystical import. To the extent their stations in life permitted, the two had entered into a kind of friendship, Germanism its core, the kind of relationship Mozart had once attempted to foster with Karl Theodore of Mannheim.

Dedicating *La clemenza di Tito* to Emperor Charles VI, Metastasio had written: "My Lord, do not believe that I intended to portray you in Titus. Of course, I am assured that everyone will recognize you in him." Such obsequious flattery had passed from fashion at the Habsburg court by the time Mozart and Stephanie wrote *The Abduction*, yet they counted upon Joseph's seeing part of himself in Selim. Doubtless he did.

5

EVEN SO, HIS own and his capital's delight in the opera could not obscure its overripe didactic rhetoric. Reactive currents set in, taking exception to the reforming tone of Joseph's stage (a complaint also raised against other German national theaters). In time, only enthusiasm for its score and comic scenes continued to hold *The Abduction* on the boards, safe above these eddying critical waters. Pezzl inveighed against the concept of the theater as a religion of moral improvement and to the pretensions such a claim fostered, in particular among performers who looked upon themselves "as in utterly every respect indispensable to the state" (an abuse he laid first and foremost to the charge of Gotha's and Hamburg's literati). Besides, many feared that the open society advocated by such a work as *The Abduction* might encourage a cultural diversity of too high a price touching the diminution of tradition and hierarchy; and, to boot, such a text's often intolerable *Schwärmerei* (gush) masquerading as ethical instruction irritated many.

After attending *The Abduction* during its initial season, the critic Johann Friedrich Schink complained: "All in all, these eternal generosities are a repellent business. . . ." Though predisposed to the theater as a model of virtuous actions, he had become fed up with endless "magnanimities, bestowals, reconciliations, and pardons," all the more irksome because arrived at "in the most unnatural way." He wondered what inspiration for ethical improvement Germans might discover in outlandish adventures in remote places, situations powerless to "hold a mirror up to human nature," reveal moral truth, and make the beholder "wiser and better," since they appear "too unnatural for us to emulate." In Schink's opinion, dramas of this kind could but vitiate the German character.

This call for realistic theater put aside the fact that extravagant characters moving through preposterous plots and exotic settings, all alien to any experience of the spectators, can, even so, present temptations, tensions, and viscissitudes they may well recognize as part of the universal condition and thus as familiar and crucial. Such conventions constituted the baroque and rococo inheritance Diderot had renounced when his domestic theater substituted the palpable for the latent, the often clumsy dilemmas and earnest values of ordinary people for the fantastic, the legendary, and the marvelous. (Diderot could even pretend to have derived the plot of his *Fils naturel* from a contemporary incident, an assertion that also served to disarm the censor.) Yet Schink did concede that Mozart's music for *The Abduction* made amends for the offenses its libretto, in his eyes, perpetrated.

The usual singspiel offered no such compensation;[13] it held out little more than did an entertainment at a country fair and, in the context of a school of morals and manners, appeared very foolish: the stage as national altar, indeed! Demonstrators scoffing at such imposture and keen upon stamping out the singspiel attempted more than once to disrupt performances of the new work that threatened to give high standing to the genre—*The Abduction*—their hisses a symbolic call for the return of an Italian company to the Burgtheater. Mozart's success, they feared, might— and for a time did—put off that happy day.

---

13 The public did appreciate Umlauf's unassuming operas and Salieri's *Der Rauchfangkehrer* (see p. 616).

The most serious complaint against the Imperial singspiel bore upon its very essence: almost at once German hegemony at the Burgtheater had revealed itself an illusion; as already remarked, the repertory consisted in great measure of French and Italian works in translation; the schedule listed few original German pieces, and they evidenced little of quality. At the same time, Joseph's censors blocked the way of many superior German and foreign dramas in their eyes too subversive: plays by Klinger, Lenz, and Schiller would come under ban, Beaumarchais's *The Marriage of Figaro* being proscribed with particular emphasis. (At first approved, a projected production of it—at the Kärntnertortheater in Johann Rautenstrauch's German translation—would go down upon reconsideration.) Many Viennese wondered just what the Emperor's stage stood for: its only clear achievement remained negative, the unseating of the Italian opera, not the rise of a valid German counterpart; they beheld diminishment at the Burgtheater. Why, the offerings of the secondary Kärntnertortheater held more interest: not only the accustomed translated pieces but, from time to time, performances by visiting French and German companies.

Joseph II's building a German opera troupe could no more ensure it a worthy repertory than founding a printing house can call forth a literature. (Within the decade Goethe was to attempt to impose his powerful personality but dislocated aesthetic upon the Weimar stage and to fail no less miserably; see p. 152.) The tide of interest in German opera had receded: throughout the Reich the singspiel drew audiences only for the clownish Hanswurst; they hungrily awaited opportunities to howl at his *Lazzi*, those improvised and vulgar reactions to the stock turns of the plot—everything Joseph detested and, indeed, had proscribed at the Burgtheater.

Early in 1783, confronting his singspiel as a bad stumble, he dissolved its troupe.[14] Not even *The Abduction* could hold aloft a structure weakened by so many indifferent works dragged across the boards; Goethe observed that Mozart, in fact, undid the singspiel, in that *The Abduction*—which had nothing to do with the simplicities of the singspiel's watery style, but called for singers trained in the traditional Italian manner[15]—exposed the prevailing shabbiness of what had gone before and became the bridge to a grand da capo: making known his desire to gather Europe's strongest com-

14 Joseph retained his ensemble of German actors. In place at the Burgtheater to this day, the company continues as one of Vienna's glories. "How I wish you might see a tragedy enacted here [Vienna]," Mozart wrote his sister. For the first time he had found a "theater in which plays of every sort are *superbly* performed; here every role, even the least important and poorest, is well cast and well provided with understudies."

15 Although a singspiel composer like Umlauf did indulge in Italianate arias and vocal pyrotechnics, his musical world remained not that of the opera but of the play with songs.

pany of *buffa* singers, Joseph summoned Italian opera back to pre-eminence at the Burgtheater.

Even during the high days of the singspiel, the Burgtheater had given works in Italian; in like wise, with the theater's official return to enshrining Italian opera, singspiele did continue there as part of the general repertory. However, the conviction began to grow that this genre did not accord with the severe yet august surroundings of the Burgtheater, a wing of the Hofburg, and would be more appropriately accommodated in the Kärntnertortheater or in a private suburban playhouse such as Karl Marinelli's, which, with the Emperor's blessing, had opened (October 1781) in the Leopoldstadt.

Impressive resources stood at hand for Joseph's Italian enterprise: though Gluck's career had waned, within its walls Vienna numbered Salieri and Mozart (the pair a strong inducement to Joseph as he changed course); German vocalists like Aloisia and Adamberger, apt to the Italian style; and the Burgtheater's admirable orchestra and staff. News traveled that the court of the Holy Roman Emperor had begun to build a new Italian troupe, and through the city's gates passed singers, poets, including Giambattista Casti, and composers, among them Giuseppe Sarti and Giovanni Paisiello, the first en route from Italy to the court of Catherine the Great, which had engaged him to become her *maestro di capella* in place of the second, at the same moment making his way from St. Petersburg toward Naples. Converging upon Vienna—Mozart remarked the coincidence—they halted to discover in what way to profit by the Emperor's plans. Both received respectful audience. He sought advice near and far: his Ambassador to Venice, Count Durazzo (see p. 289), sent recommendations concerning Italian singers, and Salieri, while on an extended leave in Italy, as if ordained by providence, had taken stock of them. His prestige helped prepare the storm that swept away the singspiel's pretentions.

6

WHAT WITH UMLAUF in charge and relieving him of many duties, the heyday of the singspiel at the Burgtheater had provided Salieri an opportune time (spring 1778) to seek leave from the Emperor to fulfill a high Imperial commission: a work to inaugurate Milan's new opera house. From Vienna, Maria Theresa had decreed that it rise where the ruined church and appendages of Santa Maria alla Scala stood (see XV, n. 24), and the honor of composing for the first night as a matter of course went to a Habsburg favorite. Vienna helped sustain the exceptional luxuries of the court of Milan: replacing the burned-out theater in the palace, La Scala had the purpose of providing a sumptuous public background for Joseph's brother Archduke Ferdinand and his entourage. Joseph had continued his mother's support of the project, aware that he could not expect his Italian subjects to accommodate to the sobriety he extolled at home. Gluck, the Hofburg's first choice as composer for the premiere, his health declining and overwhelmed by work for Paris, had ceded the distinction to his disciple, Salieri, whose *L'Europa riconosciuta* opened the great auditorium on 3 August 1778. He remained in Italy two years, during which he also composed operas for Venice, Rome, and again Milan, returning there to turn his hand to *Il talismano* (August 1779; he wrote the first act, Salzburg's former kapellmeister, Giacomo Rust [see p. 362], the rest).

Vienna had welcomed Salieri back the following April. Within hours of his arrival, he was playing excerpts from his latest Italian triumphs before the Emperor, who, in his best schoolmaster manner, sent him on his way with a command: to attend the Burgtheater and acquaint himself with the latest singspiele. That soon thereafter he received the order to compose such a work (*Der Rauchfangkehrer* [*The Chimney Sweep*; 1781]), even in the face of his wretched German, evinced Joseph's desperate recognition of the need to inject a higher musical professionalism into the genre, no less his goal when he commissioned *The Abduction* from Mozart the next year.

He had arrived in Vienna some six weeks before the premiere of the well-crafted if unidiomatic *Rauchfangkehrer*, by which time currents counter to maintaining the privileges of the Imperial singspiel had begun their unremitting flow: no doubt Salieri had opened the sluices. Though in *The Abduction* Mozart created a monument to the Josephinian singspiel's highest ambitions, in less than a year Salieri's *La scuola de' gelosi* proclaimed their passing: first written for Venice, in revised form it opened the Emperor's reborn Italian opera at the Burgtheater (12 April 1783).

In setting Joseph on to reinstate Italian opera to primacy, Salieri shaped Mozart's course: in the end he had to follow in their steps. Even so, however unequal Mozart's and Salieri's talents, they did share much the same operatic goal, to reach an artistic terrain on which music not merely clothed a text but itself created the drama. And, in like spirit, the immediate impulses bending the operatic paths of both would flow from the same source—Paris. In Salieri's case the stately diction of Gluck's creations for the Opéra, in Mozart's the pithiness of Beaumarchais.

High aspirations also guided Emperor Joseph's pragmatic rearrangement of his musical establishment: with Italian opera again reigning at the Burgtheater, he made the decision to give the singspiel official status at the Kärntnertortheater, calling into being a new company and summoning Schikaneder from Pressburg to become its fellow director, along with Hubert Kumpf. (The first season opened on 5 November 1784 with Mozart's *The Abduction*.[16]) Thus Joseph found a way to play at the same time international connoisseur and patriotic German. Even before the Italian troupe made its debut, Mozart learned which direction the Hofburg wished him to take.

7

SEVENTEEN HUNDRED AND eighty-two had not ended when, in the course of a gathering at Prince Golicyn's, Count Rosenberg asked Mozart to consider writing an Italian opera. He heard the Emperor's voice in Rosenberg's, the request as an unwelcome command and, committed to the national cause, reacted with heavy heart to the "disgusting" spectacle of "Germans themselves killing German opera": "Is not German as easily singable as French or English?" He preferred German opera "although it costs me more bother [thanks to the scarcity of effective prototypes]. Every nation has its own opera; why should we Germans not have one?" Earlier, even without a commission in hand, he had resolved to follow *The Abduction* with another singspiel. He never composed without a specific purpose, and no doubt had an eye to the private theater in the Leopoldstadt. Considering the aesthetic vagaries of the moody, unpredictable Emperor, he had little faith "that the Italian opera [at the Burgtheater] will keep going for long." He settled upon Goldoni's *Il servitore di due padroni* (K. 416a/Anh. 28) turned into German by Freiherr Johann Nepomuk Binder von Kriegelstein and given the title *Der Diener zweier Herren*. The bass aria *"Männer suchen stets zu naschen"* (K. 433/416c) and an aria for tenor, *"Müsst ich auch durch tausend Drachen"* (K. 435/416b),[17] appear to be what survives of the unfinished score, probably of early 1783.

He must have broken off work on it not owing to any loss of fire but to the necessity of acting upon the royal behest and perhaps hoped for consolation in the pleasure of composing for the court's remarkable new

---

16 In this production by Schikaneder a substitute aria composed by Franz Teyber replaced *"Martern aller Arten,"* whose instrumental demands went beyond the capacity of any orchestra the directors could muster. (Franz Teyber was the brother of Therese and Anton Teyber [see pp. 632–33 and 635]. The "Herr Teyber" from whom Mozart borrowed the violin with which he entertained the Theatine fathers in Vienna on 7 August 1773 [see p. 312] was either Matthäus, the father of the above-mentioned Teybers or their eldest brother, Friedrich.) Margarethe Kaiser, with whom Mozart had once been infatuated (see XIX, n. 2), sang the role of Constanze. The Viennese continued to welcome new singspiele. With his *Doktor und Apotheker* of 1786, Dittersdorf began a wave of them that won the affection of Emperor and public. The greatest Viennese singspiel, Mozart and Schikaneder's *The Magic Flute*, remains outside any category.

17 Both arias derive from sources less than whole in detail but complete in concept.

collection of *buffa* singers. He forced himself to make a start, and in all likelihood the shipwreck of the ensuing pair of projects betrayed his inward resistance to having to alter course in the train of the Hofburg's changeableness. To his distress, he experienced—but not for the first time—an unsettling phenomenon: not even his powers could impel his pen to move; for months he seemed, in matters operatic, unable to subdue himself to the steady task. His hunt for *buffa* librettos led him to leaf over more than a hundred, but he "could hardly find a single one" adequate to his needs. Toward the end of 1783 he would attempt to make do with a text, *Lo sposo deluso*, which tradition ascribes to Lorenzo Da Ponte. He had established himself in Vienna in order to turn to account Italian opera's rebirth at the Burgtheater.

8

EN ROUTE FROM Gorizia to Dresden to visit Caterino Mazzolà, its court poet, Da Ponte had passed through a Vienna mourning Maria Theresa's death (29 November 1780). There had already entered his mind the idea of settling in the city of Metastasio and, in his footsteps, turning to the theater: he had to find a new career; much had been chaotic in the life of this baptized Jew, now a priest, a celebrant who raised the chalice untroubled by his lack of religious vocation. His true calling seemed to express itself in unrestrained sensuality; in Venice it had recently earned him a sentence in absentia to fifteen years' banishment on charges of libertinage, blasphemy, sacrilege, adultery, and public concubinage. A former professor of rhetoric at the seminary at Treviso, which had discharged him for radicalism, he had, in the wake of his latest imbroglio, fled to Austrian territory and, while tarrying in Gorizia, ventured his first commercial undertaking related to drama: cobbling a translation of a tragedy for the local stage.

With Vienna in mind, he had also worked to win the patronage of Gorizia's most distinguished inhabitant, Count Guido Cobenzl: his son, the Mozart family's admirer Johann Philipp, had just negotiated the Peace of Teschen on behalf of the House of Habsburg (see XXII, n. 4 and p. 567), and, to Count Guido's pleasure, Da Ponte composed an ode celebrating the younger Cobenzl's diplomatic genius; into the bargain, the verse had not missed the opportunity to throw bouquets at the Dowager Empress, whose death all at once turned this effort vain. Thus, while passing through Vienna, he had no reason to approach the Hofburg; he remained only long enough to gain audience with Johann Philipp and hand him letters from his father commending the ode and its author, an encounter laying the foundations of his Viennese connections. A generous gift from Johann Philipp in hand, he traveled on to Dresden.

Da Ponte's arrival at his threshold astonished Mazzolà: he had no knowledge of an invitation, supposedly bearing his signature, Da Ponte claimed to have received in Gorizia, its contents: the promise of a position at the court of Saxony. Expressing astonishment at having been fooled by a forgery, Da Ponte explained it away as probably the work of a rival in Gorizia eager to send him out of the city. But the letter must have been Da Ponte's invention—Mozart's and Beaumarchais's famous messages praising him have proved to be from his own pen—a device enabling the interloper to inflict himself upon Mazzolà as an apprentice. Straightway he took on the role of unofficial assistant, helping his doubtless bewildered host with adaptations of librettos and learning the ways of actors and singers.

It would appear that the thought took root in Mazzolà that his clever guest-helper might intend to topple him at court and take his place. He hit upon the idea of calling up a vision of yet greener pastures and began to expatiate upon Emperor Joseph's plan to restore Italian opera to the Burgtheater—Da Ponte already had this news from the Cobenzls—and the opportunities the impending death of the aged and failing Metastasio would open in Vienna. In any case, a talented mountebank senses when the game is over: by the close of 1781, Da Ponte, newly educated in matters of the theater, had returned to Vienna bearing a warm letter of recommendation from Mazzolà to Salieri.

Da Ponte hastened to call upon Metastasio, who, though close upon disintegration, read and praised the visitor's verse at one of those famous Sunday afternoon salons in the Michaelerhaus. The great relic's death on 12 April 1782 fulfilled the first of Da Ponte's expectations. However, the Hofburg put together its *opera-buffa* company in slow time, and for months he sustained himself with difficulty. When the turnabout at the Burgtheater at last came, Salieri and his close friend Count Rosenberg, the two charmed by the handsome, buoyant Da Ponte, recommended, and the Hofburg ratified, his appointment as librettist to the Italian troupe.[18] That

---

18 He had prepared the Italian version of Gluck's *Iphigénie en Tauride*, perhaps a trial of his qualifications (see n. 11). An unknown, Da Ponte somehow expected to receive the title of Caesarean Poet to the Roman Emperor, the distinction Metastasio had borne with such magnificence and the proudest literary dignity Europe could confer. Throughout his life, modesty remained foreign to Da Ponte; and veracity, too; excepting its broad outlines, his autobiography offers a fabric shot through with falsehood and evasion: depicting his every malpractice as an injury from the hand of an enemy, he paints himself as an eternal victim of misunderstanding, conspiracy, and ingratitude.

he succeeded in throwing dust in the eyes of this pair of veteran courtiers gives the measure of his talent for impersonation. He had plotted his course with cunning, and chance had lent support.

Though ever wary of Italians, Mozart understood the necessity of making proper approaches to Da Ponte. They met in a circle of converted and ennobled Jews, that of Karl Abraham Wetzlar von Plankenstern, probably in the house of his son, Raimund. Mozart summed up his impressions: "We have as our poet a certain Abbate Da Ponte. He has an excruciating amount of work to do on the theater repertory and at the moment has the *urgent charge* of writing an entirely new libretto for Salieri[19] [for whom he had already revised *La scuola de' gelosi*], which will take at least two months. He has [at Rosenberg's urging] promised next to write a new libretto for me, but who knows whether he will be able or want to keep his word? As you know, to one's face these Italian gentlemen are very charming. Enough! We know them! If he is going along with Salieri, I shall in my born days get nothing from him." Mozart had once again taken up the family practice of reading treachery in every Italian and conspiracy in every two—he found it difficult to concede that by administrative protocol Da Ponte functioned under Salieri—and this newcomer did seem to him, on the face of it, a villain.

Mozart's need of an Italian libretto became ever more acute; he had to respond to the Emperor's bidding. Those very few Italian texts in which he glimpsed promise required extensive revision, and it seemed wiser to secure an original work. Unwilling to bide his time waiting for Da Ponte and, in any case, unsure of his good faith, he asked Leopold to sound Varesco about putting together a book. Mozart planned a journey to Salzburg in order to introduce Constanze to his family. He suggested that Varesco send him a draft that he might study and rework in Vienna in preparation for consultations in Salzburg.

Varesco jumped at the idea, for in addition to his fee a poet received the box-office receipts of the third performance. By the end of June 1783 an outline of Varesco's *L'oca del Cairo* (The Goose of Cairo) and the verse of its first act lay on Mozart's worktable in Vienna, along with a request for an immediate payment. In strong, cynical tones learned from the likes of Stephanie, he let the Abbé know that he had only begun and would have to "alter and recast as much and as often as . . . required." He was to be an instrument of the composer and "not follow his own ideas." Mozart's voice had hardened: "Now that I know the plot, someone else can carry it through. . . ."

19 He delayed setting it, and *Il ricco d'un giorno* did not come to the Burgtheater until 6 December 1784, to prove an utter disaster.

The plot's absurdity strikes one dumb. It tells of a giant mechanical goose, its body sufficiently capacious to admit and conceal a lover bent upon gaining access to the tower in which his sweetheart's father has confined her; confederates get the mechanism through the fortress's gates by fobbing it off as an exotic toy with which to amuse the young lady. Without a model to lean upon, Varesco emerged altogether inept. That Mozart, even for a moment, judged this farrago worth dipping pen in ink seems out of all reckoning—even more his persistence in composing so much of the first act. When he awakened to the fact that his instincts had failed him and to the foolishness of his having "written such music to no purpose," in particular a lengthy and splendid finale, he blamed Leopold as well as Varesco: ". . . my only reason for not objecting to the whole of the goose business was that two men of greater insight and reflection than I [Leopold and Varesco] . . . did not take exception to it." He had regressed, blaming Papa for the dilemma even while encouraging him to hit upon a way, other than Varesco's, of smuggling the hero into the tower.

Early in 1784, Mozart faced the fact that the goose project had toppled; he brushed it aside with seeming indifference, his prospering career as soloist his extenuation: "At this time [10 February 1784], I have to write works that bring in money." In the course of the year he composed six splendid piano concertos, the cardinal lure at his concerts, which had begun to be of great moment in Vienna's musical life (see pp. 637 and 662–63); yet, as late as November, he still weighed the illusory prospect of again taking up *L'oca* once someone had put the libretto into workable condition. All along fearing that in the end he might have to disappoint Count Rosenberg, during the summer of 1783 he had turned to "an Italian poet here," within the bounds of possibility Da Ponte, whom the Hofburg may have induced to open his schedule. Adapted from the book Domenico Cimarosa had used for his *Le donne rivali* (1780)—in all likelihood by Petrosellini, the poet of *La finta giardiniera*—a new libretto came into Mozart's hands under the title of *Lo sposo deluso, ossia La rivalità di tre donne per un solo amante* (The Deluded Bridegroom, or The Rivalry of Three Women for the Same Lover, K. 430/424a.[20])

---

20 The woeful weakness of the changes worked upon *Le donne rivali* suggests ruling out Da Ponte's hand; yet, at Rosenberg's insistence, he may have conferred with Mozart, brought the text to his attention, and recommended a hack to do the job (see XXX, n. 9). To some commentators, Mozart's inclination to use the libretto given him by the "Italian poet" only "if he is willing to cut it to my liking," argues that the text could not have been that of *Lo sposo*, Mozart, quite the contrary, wishing not to cut but to expand it. However, the verb *zuschnizeln* can mean to tailor to the figure, a process involving letting out as well as taking in the seams. Composing the fragment of *Lo sposo* may have extended into 1785.

Among the five numbers, the overture included, he composed for it, a
marvelous trio reveals, as does the finale to Act I of *L'oca*, the hand that
would shape *The Marriage of Figaro*. A typical *buffa* affair of misunderstanding and reconciliation, *Lo sposo* might have had success. His abandoning it[21]
may have had roots in his continuing resentment of the powerful forces
driving him from German opera. On the other hand, Vienna still offered
him rich compensations strengthening his patriotism and also those Storm
and Stress perceptions and persuasions that would lead him to Beaumarchais's *Figaro*. Ideas he had long held emerged transformed anew: hatred of
oppressors, pity for their victims, and that overarching defiance of rank in-
carnating the Kantian query as to whether the Age of Enlightenment had
yet become an Enlightened age.

Even before taking up *Figaro*, Mozart could embrace the opportunity to
add heat to a warming social atmosphere by interpolating two ensembles
into an already premonitory work: Francesco Bianchi's *La villanella rapita*
(The Abducted Country Lass), its libretto by Giovanni Bertati. At the Viennese premiere of the Bianchi-Mozart composite in the Burgtheater (28
November 1785), Count Zinzendorf found the "words to a great degree
equivocal." *Pace* Zinzendorf; Mozart had, in fact, done his best to dispel
ambiguity, to elucidate and underline the grave implications of a plot pil-
lorying the arbitrary use of power: pressing into service expanded texts (no
doubt Da Ponte's) to replace sections Bianchi had composed as secco
recitative, he both inserted a trio (K. 480) depicting a young peasant who
interrupts his betrothed's seduction by a nobleman's plying her with gifts
and also introduced, as the climax of the opera, a quartet (K. 479) in
which the swain and the girl's father discover her with the count in a bedroom of the castle, their reproaches, her lamentations, and his threats mingling. (She, of course, proves innocent: he had drugged her.) With the
symphony K. 318 as overture, the opera must have been a strange concoc-
tion, Bianchi's pedestrian style contrasting with the ease and polish of
Mozart's, a disparity even the obtuse Zinzendorf grasped: "The quartetto
is admirable." Indeed, like the fragments of *L'oca* and *Lo sposo*, it already had
the sharp and intricate workmanship of *Figaro*.

Mozart's contribution to *La villanella* has a place in his sequence of Viennese masterpieces leading from *The Abduction* to *The Magic Flute*. However

---

21 Until the recent past, an incomplete trio, K. 434/480b, its text from Petrosellini's *Il regno delle
amazoni*, had been assigned to the period shortly after Mozart washed his hands of *Lo sposo*.
This dating identified the fragment as yet another attempt to settle upon an *opera-buffa* text before he pounced upon the idea of having Beaumarchais's *The Marriage of Figaro* made into an Italian libretto. Investigation now places the trio in the second half of 1786, that is, after the
premiere of *Figaro*.

varied their surfaces and structures, they all sprang from the same fixed purpose, for each harbored much the same aggressive intention: to attack society; to upset and change it. Cleansing works,[22] they lay open the depths beneath outward appearance and at times lead into and witness the abyss even while lighting the way to resolution; thus they manifest the Mozartean vision first glimpsed in *Idomeneo*: that of a virtuous community of ordered purpose. Questioning, searching, and challenging, Mozart the creator stood at a peculiar and at times exposed angle to Vienna; on the surface of its daily life, however, he followed and found assurance in familiar patterns.

---

22 Mozart's *The Impresario* (*Der Schauspieldirektor*), a slight entertainment contemporary with *Figaro*, does not figure in this series (see pp. 652–53).

CHAPTER XXX

Vienna:

Balancing Old Accounts

H E HAD PREPARED his new domestic arrangements with care. His
room chez Arnstein could not meet the needs of a couple, and a
week after the premiere of *The Abduction* he moved from the Graben to take
up residence on the Hohe Brücke, in the very building in which the
Mozarts had lodged upon their return from Brünn some fourteen and
a half years earlier. Here he led his betrothed, and they remained until
December 1782, when they settled into spacious and elegant quarters in
Baron Wetzlar's house a few doors farther along the same street. Alas, he
soon required the space for his own purposes and the following February
relocated the newlyweds in provisional rooms on the Kohlmarkt, paying
the costs of the removal and refusing rent for either flat. By the end of
April they had found a comfortable apartment on the Judenplatz.[1] Here a
son arrived on 17 June 1783. A prized anecdote, Constanze its alleged
source, tells of his entry into the world as his father, working on the string
quartet in D minor (K. 421), rose from his manuscript from time to time
to comfort his wife in her labor, the child presenting himself with the
Menuetto.

That Leopold refused a role in the christening bespoke towering difficulties yet to be confronted. True, by now he had to concede his son's good

---

1 From the beginning the Mozarts fell into a pattern of frequent changes of residence.

thinking in settling in Vienna: that the letters from Salzburg had lost their terrible sting may be deduced from Mozart's replies, which, no doubt in response to Polonius-like displays of rhetoric, too often turned to the saccharine endearments of his correspondence at its worst. But, if the father had ceased abusive censure, asperities continued to protrude from beneath his words, and he had not stayed his cries of poverty.

In a gesture symbolizing with clarity a closing of accounts, Mozart had sent him money above what he had laid out to scribes for copying the score of *The Abduction*.[2] Even while expressing confidence that he would put the gift to good use, Mozart had warned: "At the moment I cannot spare more, for I foresee many expenses in connection with my wife's confinement . . . ," a caution signaling that he wished never to hear another hint from Salzburg about money; that this "small amount" was the first and last requital from Vienna; that his earnings would be devoted to his own family. Perhaps this stand fueled Leopold's anger and led him to deny the baptism even his symbolic presence. Mozart had kept him informed of the dates projected for the birth of his first grandchild as they changed, and this observant Catholic's disengagement from the event presented his son with a tantalizing challenge.

Anticipating his father's and sister's arrival, Mozart awaited their word. None came, and in the end he abandoned his pride; if Leopold wanted to imagine him crushed by contrition, he himself would paint the picture: "falling to my knees, folding my hands together, and, fittingly submissive, entreating you, my beloved father, to be godfather; as perhaps there is still time, I am doing so now [7 June]." Although persisting "in the confident hope" that Leopold would attend, he did offer a graceful alternative: a proxy might present the child in Leopold's name; he had only to indicate his mind.

He delayed until circumstances decided the matter. At the church am Hof, Philipp Jakob Martin stood proxy for Baron Raimund Wetzlar, and with the first of the sacraments the child, in answer to the Baron's expectations,

2 Interested in mounting *The Abduction*, the Prussian court, through its ambassador, had applied for a score, not to the Burgtheater, but to the composer. He knew the procedure to be irregular—the Hofburg's scribes alone had the right to sell a manuscript copy of a Habsburg commission, and one of them, Wenzel Sukowaty, offered *The Abduction* at fifteen florins—yet Mozart called upon his father to pull the original from the archive and have local copyists fulfill the request. Although assuming that they would do the job with greater dispatch and less expense and setting his eyes upon the fee, Mozart, above all, wished to forestall any gossip in Vienna about the Hohenzollerns' interest in him: it would have been premature to set in march a rivalry involving the Habsburgs' antagonists. Prague had given *The Abduction* during the autumn of 1782; Leipzig would produce it a year later, Mainz and Mannheim in 1784, Munich in 1785 (despite Count Seeau's opposition; see XXVI, n. 44), but Berlin did not until 1788.

received his first name. At the last moment conciliatory tidings arrived—
Leopold dealt with the christening much as he had with the wedding—
and Mozart, refreshed in spirit, put a good face on the imbroglio. At least
Raimund had Leopold as a second name, and somehow matters might be
put to rights: Constanze and Mozart faced the disheartening idea so long
toyed with—a visit to Salzburg.

2

IF, IN THE eyes of the Salzburg Residenz, Mozart no longer existed—
officialdom avoided mention of his name—he did remain a presence to
many in the city (and, indeed, at court) who continued to perform his
music. In 1782 they had even received something new from his pen: to celebrate his elevation to the nobility, Siegmund Haffner the Younger had
commissioned a work from him. Even while laboring against the clock to
arrange *The Abduction* for winds—"otherwise someone will beat me to it
and have the profits instead of me"[3]—he made time, at Leopold's insistence, to write what would be refined into the second Haffner Symphony,
K. 385 (see XVIII, n. 21). It had been hard upon his wedding day when he
posted to Leopold the finale,[4] a Presto embodying a reference to Osmin's
aria in *The Abduction*: "How I will triumph!"

Such confidence sank as he confronted the reality of the Salzburg journey, which, one excuse after the other, had resolved itself into a series of
postponements. He fixed upon departing in high summer (when pupils
broke off their lessons) even though two dark patches hovered above the
plan: misgivings about the reception his bride might find in the Tanzmeisterhaus and his fear of arrest upon entering the archbishopric. ("A priest is
capable of anything.") He suggested a meeting in Munich rather than
Salzburg, but Leopold indicated that its officials had signaled indifference
to the visit. He recognized Mozart's prevarications as proceeding from a
divided spirit. But all at once Mozart determined to face the troublesome

---

3 Numbers from *The Abduction* as arranged for wind octet can be found in the Donaueschingen
archives; in the past attributed to an unknown, the transcription has been recognized as
Mozart's.
4 Leopold had dragooned him into fulfilling the request of a family that had supported his interests since his childhood. As he composed the new Haffner music, he sent it piecemeal to the
mail coach. When Leopold returned the entire composition to Vienna early the following year,
Mozart gazed in amazement at what he had conceived under pressure and scribbled as fast as
pen could travel: "The new Haffner Symphony has in truth surprised me, for I had forgotten
every note of it. Indeed, it must make a good effect." The march, K. 408, no. 2/385a, opened
and closed this original (Salzburg) version, which, it has been argued, also had two minuets and
thus the ramshackle layout—compared to a symphony—of a serenade.

issues and redefine himself in his family's eyes: to demonstrate his new commitments and demand respect for them. At the end of July 1783, he and Constanze left Raimund with a foster mother in the suburb of Ober-Neustift—they foresaw an absence of a month at most—and set out for Salzburg. Family letters wanting, little of importance concerning the visit has come down except passing words about the mass in C minor, K. 427/417a.

Its relationship to a vow Mozart had taken somewhat before his union with Constanze remains obscure, as does the nature of the promise itself. She had fallen ill, and he determined to make her his wife upon her recovery. His oath to compose a mass and perform it in Salzburg—"with all my heart and without condition I gave my word and in like manner I hope to keep it"—united concepts of love, thankfulness, reunion, reconciliation, repair, and, with Raimund's birth, took on the dimension of continuity (unless he committed himself after marrying and only with regard to her safe accouchement). The proof of his having undertaken the obligation, he assured a father ever suspicious of his high-flown assertions, resided in a "well-grounded hope" to complete "the score of half a mass lying here [Vienna]."

The performance of the mass was to take place in Salzburg's monastery church of St. Peter's, where he had old friends, among them Kajetan Hagenauer (Father Dominicus;[5] see pp. 226–27). Mozart's crossing the threshold of the cathedral where Colloredo presided remained out of the question. Yet, in diplomatic deference, St. Peter's, likewise, would have had to close its doors to the renegade had the Residenz remonstrated. It, however, looked away even as its own musicians joined the rehearsals in its Kapellhaus—the resources of St. Peter's alone would have been unequal to the score—which, without the Residenz's studied, in fact, beneficent aloofness, would also have been out of bounds.

Of the mass he brought to Salzburg only the Kyrie and Gloria stood complete, along with the substance of the Sanctus. The Credo existed only up to the Crucifixus, and nothing of the Agnus Dei had come to paper. (At the performance, plainchant or material adapted from his earlier masses may have filled the gaps.[6]) Sebastian Bach's and, in particular, Handel's spirit, breathed in at van Swieten's matinees (see VIII, n. 31 and pp. 634–35),

---

5 In 1784 he would become confessor at Salzburg's Nonnberg convent and two years later return to St. Peter's as its abbot.
6 Perhaps he formed an ad hoc Agnus Dei by putting to work music adapted from preceeding movements, the procedure in part followed in the posthumous completion of his Requiem. For a discussion of the components and structure of a mass, see pp. 752–53.

guides whole sections of the score; but, unlike so many period-style efforts by his contemporaries, these double choruses, fugues, and less formal contrapuntal passages never suggest a hand ruffling the shallows to give the impression of depth. Reinterpreted and given new dimension through Mozart's finely colored harmonies, ever fresh and scrupulous melodic detail, and volatility of humors, these units show forth as brilliant reinventions, as refinements of the pastiche of his Salzburg masses, the rhetorical grandeur of the Qui tollis for two four-part choirs the finest example. Moreover, in the tradition of the Salzburg works, he eggs and sugars the baroque pudding with *galant* touches: rococo and *empfindsam* enchantments from time to time take the lead, offering their tender beauties and with them textural contrast, as in the exquisite pathos of the Et incarnatus, the longest and most demanding of the three soprano solos shaped, so Constanze had it, for her voice.[7]

During the stay in Salzburg he would not or could not complete the mass: that the project fell through his fingers may well have been the effect of a change of heart wrought by his recent and intense labors in Vienna upon a set of string quartets (see pp. 635–36) arguing an aesthetic not of the evocative and reminiscent but, rather, of their assimilation within a new style fully his own. Yet the mass's incomplete state in no way compromises its distinction as a magnificent compendium juxtaposing the century's musical vocabularies. Its wanting sections somehow made good, K. 427 came to performance on 26 October 1783, the day before the Mozarts took their departure.

On the face of it, their stay had unfolded without strain, Leopold and Nannerl doing their best to stifle their preoccupations and snobbery, Mozart and Constanze trying no end to please,[8] rehearsals of the mass serving in a certain degree to bridge and assuage mutual feelings of broken faith. That the composition remained a fragment, something to be assembled and got through by making the best of what lay at hand, seems to have caught the spirit of the visit. At one ugly moment the mask fell: Leopold's deafness to Constanze's request to carry away some token of the

---

7 Commentators hostile to Constanze maintain that she sang only the Christe eleison of the Kyrie and the Laudamus of the Gloria, solos sharing traits of vocal exercises Mozart had written for her (K. 393/385b of August 1782). However, it seems reasonable to assume that the wife he praised for her performances of Ilia's "*Se il padre perdei*" (see XXVII, n. 26) also came off well in the Et incarnatus.

8 Leopold's pupil Margarethe Marchand (see XXVII, n. 2) must have provided Constanze an anchor at the Tanzmeisterhaus—they had known one another in Mannheim—and Hennerle no doubt offered his friendship. Constanze's early attempts to cultivate Leopold and Nannerl's sympathy through the post had foundered in awkwardness and bathos.

memorabilia her husband had garnered on his tours proclaimed her standing in the family's eyes: never could she be a Mozart.

The mass as a symbol admits some understanding of why a *séjour* in Salzburg planned to last no longer than three or four weeks extended beyond twelve: of course, Mozart required time to discuss *L'oca* with Varesco and to attend to social necessities, including a visit with the touring blind pianist Maria Theresia von Paradis (during which she commissioned a piano concerto, perhaps K. 456); but that St. Peter's scheduled the premiere of the mass for the eleventh hour suggests the particular purpose of giving him time to finish the score; this factor would have determined the Mozarts' schedule, even with the risk of losing impatient pupils in Vienna and leaving out of full account little Raimund with the nurse in Ober-Neustift (with whom they appear to have had no contact).

In Salzburg Mozart did compose,[9] but alas for posterity, not an Agnus Dei for the mass. A bizarre turn of events led him to write a pair of works for the Archbishop. An ailing Michael Haydn, helpless to complete a set of six duos (for violin and viola) impatiently awaited at the Residenz, turned to the visiting Mozart to furnish the final two. He emulated Haydn's style, and they passed as his.[10]

During his stay in Salzburg, Mozart increased by three piano sonatas his store of compositions for concerts and teaching.[11] K. 330/300h in C, a nostalgic excursion back to his *galant* days, to a world of passagework and simple accompaniment, sustains exquisitely detailed melodies that shade into Mannheim *Empfindsamkeit*. In a remarkable metamorphosis, they become their own self-sufficient ornamentation: like the sinuous sculptural

---

9 The theory that he had brought the book of *Lo sposo* with him to Salzburg and there began the score runs counter to probability. He arrived at the Tanzmeisterhaus but three weeks after his first allusion (5 July 1783) to the possibility of setting this text, were it redone to his specifications. His return to Vienna (the final days of November) with strong doubts as to the future of *L'oca* must have been the point at which he took up the libretto of *Lo sposo*, no doubt by this time revised for him.

10 Connoisseurs soon recognized these masterpieces of implied harmony (K. 423 and 424) as going beyond even Michael Haydn's considerable talent, and within the decade they appeared in print under Mozart's name. (Contrariwise, a symphony in G by Michael Haydn [1783; Perger no. 16] entered the Köchel listings because of an introduction, K. 444/425a, Mozart added to it in 1784 to create a work, K. Anh. A53, for his Viennese concerts.) That a sympathetic Colleredo, regardful of Haydn's declining health, had lightened his duties, suggests not illness but alcohol as the root of an indisposition exciting the court's impatience. In appreciation of Mozart's generous spirit, two of Haydn's students recorded the incident in their recollections of their master (1808), though without mention of his failing.

11 Somewhat before his visit to Salzburg he had begun the opening Allegro of a piano sonata (K. 400/372a, a fragment one day to be completed by Abbé Maximilian Stadler). In the development section, he wrote the names Constanze and Sophie above music of charming pathos.

plasterwork of south German rococo churches and palaces, they unfold organically, akin not to sculptured pink putti playing on stuccoed clouds, but, rather, to those mediating molded cartouches that reconcile the ambivalence between decoration and architecture by being both. From the point of view of style a loiterer, this ethereal sonata embodies a rococo both refined and serious, a design appropriate to the cultivated leisure of the Viennese drawing room.

If K. 331/300i in A lacks these aristocratic subtleties, it represents a popular Mozart at his most irresistible. An unorthodox, on the face of it arbitrary, sequence of movements begins with a theme and its inventive variations (Andante grazioso) and proceeds to a Menuetto anticipating in spirit the keyboard miniatures of the following century—those yearning, romantic creations of Schubert (the first movement also calls him to mind), Mendelssohn, and Schumann. The sonata closes with an Allegretto in the Turkish manner, an exhilarating Rondo with mercurial fluctuations of major and minor and conjuring up some kind of theatrical finale with a janissary band on stage. All three movements exclude the tonal and thematic dynamics associated with the sonata, and, in fact, unfold like a suite of dramatic actions. At all events, clearly K. 331 sought popular favor.

K. 332/300k in F completed the trio of Salzburg vacation sonatas (though they underwent recension before going to press in Vienna during 1784). With its opening Allegro's spacious lyricism broken by explosive turbulence and modulations of threatening power, its Adagio's grave and expressive detail, and its closing Allegro assai's impetuous and torrential drive, this hypnotic work of mysterious tensions rejoined the aesthetic mainstream flowing toward the late masterpieces.

3

THE JOURNEY BACK to Vienna led through Vöcklabruck and Lambach (entering its abbey church during mass, Mozart sat down at the organ and accompanied the Agnus Dei); then on to Ebelsberg on the edge of Linz, where he accepted an invitation to proceed to old Count Thun's palace, in the city, there to enjoy his hospitality and make music. With the Thun orchestra at his disposal, Mozart scheduled a concert for 4 November at the Linz Ballhaus and on 31 October wrote Leopold: "Inasmuch as I have not a single symphony with me, I am up to my ears composing a new one." Here he drew the long bow: not even Mozart could, in a matter of four or five days, conceive, compose, copy (or arranged to have copied), rehearse, and conduct the Linz Symphony (K. 425), a four-movement work on a grand scale and high level of inspiration, in particular a slow introduction of deep emotional urgency. Doubtless he had carried to Linz in his head, or even had earlier sketched, a new symphony to serve the coming season in Vienna.[12]

The Mozarts' stay in Linz must have been happy and profitable: they remained about a month. Returned home at the end of November, they found Raimund almost three and a half months in his grave, the victim of dysentery. Epidemics, parasites, and accidents wove a pattern of mortality permitting only about half the children of the time to survive infancy.[13] Parents for the most part brought into the world at least twice the number of offspring they hoped to raise: "Birth is halfway to death," observed Leopold Mozart, his two children the survivors of seven births. Mozart and Constanze mourned their "poor, round, fat, and darling little boy," who had looked so much like his father, "the face as if sculpted" after his. She would be pregnant early in 1784—toward the end of January they moved from the Judenplatz to the Trattnerhof (see p. 153) on the Graben—and their domestic world recovered its order and flourished, as did his career.

4

HE HAD ACHIEVED his immediate goals: a happy marriage; an operatic success; the Emperor's high opinion (he would now and then send to the Burgtheater for the score of *The Abduction* in order to peruse it); pupils; a cluster of staunch patrons; the interest of publishers; a flow of invitations to make music in the salons of the city's great families (who treated him with generosity and in the noblest manner); and a formidable schedule of public appearances. What would with the years become a plethora of Mozart concerts often took place in informal assembly rooms: the Mehlgrube, a casino on the Neuer Markt; the large hall (the Privatsaal) of the Trattnerhof; the commons of the Augarten, a Habsburg hunting preserve (in the Leopoldstadt) lately made into a public park; and, in times of good weather, the city's squares. The Augarten and open-air concerts represented a substantial business adventure for him: he entered into commercial association with the impresario Philipp Jakob Martin to found and

---

12 In Linz he also composed the piano sonata K. 333/315c, a postlude to the group just turned out in Salzburg. The opening phrase of the first movement reappears disguised in summary form as the beginning bar of the last. The melodic material forming this cyclical touch derives from Christian Bach and may well identify this tender and brilliant composition as a tribute to his old friend and colleague who had died in London on the first day of 1782. The piano concerto K. 414 had already offered a remembrance of this kind (see n. 20).

13 Widespread mistrust of the efficacy of breast-feeding had made Mozart at first insist that Raimund be given, as had he and Nannerl, not a wet nurse's milk but a pap concocted of various grains.

manage both and planned a like subscription series at the Trattnerhof with the pianist Georg Friedrich Richter.

He also stepped before the public as pianist and conductor in the formal surroundings of the Imperial theaters (available for private use when resident companies did not require them[14]). At his first independent appearance on an Imperial stage (3 March 1782), probably at the Burgtheater, he had introduced himself to Vienna as a composer of *opera seria* with excerpts from *Idomeneo*—a move to make capital out of the recent Gluck mania—and strengthened his reputation as a virtuoso pianist and instrumental composer with his concerto K. 175. Decked out with a new closing "*variazion Rondeau*" (see XVII, n. 16), it, he exulted, always "provokes a furor."

Viennese concert life gave him the opportunity to express an almost passionate altruism by his inviting colleagues to share the platform with him and by his contributing to their programs. A variety of performers, of course, stimulated the sale of tickets, yet Mozart prized such interaction for its own sake. In Vienna he had become part of a community of artists such as he had aspired to embrace since childhood. On 3 November 1782, at Josepha Auernhammer's concert in the Kärntnertortheater, he had joined her at the keyboard; and those attending Aloisia Lange's gala at the Burgtheater on 11 March 1783 heard the famous prima donna in the aria composed for her in Mannheim (K. 294, to which he now added coloratura), while he gave delight as conductor and pianist with his Paris Symphony and concerto K. 175. On this occasion Gluck, glowing with praise, invited the Mozarts and the Langes to dine at his home the following Sunday.

Within the same month (23 March), at Mozart's mammoth Burgtheater concert, he honored Gluck, again in attendance, by improvising piano variations (K. 455) on the aria "*Les hommes pieusement*" ("*Unser dummer Pöbel meint*") from his *La rencontre imprévue*. The event also included Mozart's extemporizing a set of variations upon a theme from Paisiello's *I filosofi immaginari* (K. 398/416e); further, he played two piano concertos, K. 175 and the recently composed K. 415/387b, and, as a gesture toward the Emperor, seated in the royal box, created a fugue on the spur of the moment. And three of the city's favorite vocalists participated in a sheaf of Mozart arias: Therese Teyber, the first Blondchen in *The Abduction*, sang "*Parto*" from *Lucio Silla*, Adamberger the solo written in Munich for Countess Paumgarten (K. 369, its protagonist's filial conflict overriding gender), while Aloisia Lange offered "*Se il padre*" from *Idomeneo* and a composition Mozart had only of late composed and dedicated to her—"*Mia speranza*

---

14 Thus many such concerts—so-called acadamies—took place during Lent.

adorata / Ah, non sai" (K. 416, which she had first performed on 11 January at a Mehlgrube concert). The overflowing crowd heard the sinfonia concertante movements of the Post Horn Serenade and the reworked second Haffner Symphony, its finale, as an isolated piece, bringing the Mozart marathon to a close. (The first three movements had opened the program.)[15] A critic reported with wonder to faraway Hamburg: ". . . our monarch, contrary to habit, honored the entire concert with his presence"; he sent Mozart twenty-five ducats.

A week later at the Burgtheater, Therese Teyber gave a concert (the Emperor again in the house) in which Mozart once more played K. 415, with pride reporting to Salzburg that the public had demanded that he "repeat the Rondeau."[16] The Viennese Society of Musicians would call upon him to perform a piano concerto at its charity Christmas concert in the Burgtheater (22 December 1783), and, indeed, the genre became the symbol of his ascending popularity, the very core of his extraordinary success in Vienna. Riding high, he seemed to be outstripping the wind, though good fortune could at times call forth less than his best qualities.

As he prospered, the family trait of perceiving enemies at every compass point revived with all its parts. On this issue he must have influenced Aloisia, for during the summer of 1783 he discussed with her "how to be more cunning than our enemies." At the moment she did feel threatened by the soprano Ann Selina (Nancy) Storace's arrival at the Burgtheater, while he had begun to imagine Salieri, now director of the *opera buffa*, as an adversary by dint of his powerful position. In many quarters Mozart's reputation for quirkiness and arrogance grew, the context in which to understand the imbroglio ensuing from his putting forward three substitute arias, K. 418, "*Vorrei spiegarvi,*" and 419, "*No, no, che non sei capace,*" for Aloisia and K. 420, "*Per pietà, non ricercate,*" for Adamberger, to be inserted into the work with which these popular singspiel singers were to make their debuts (30 June 1783) with the Italian company—Anfossi's *Il curioso indiscreto* in its Viennese premiere.

Mozart found himself forced to refute in print the charge that he intended these compositions to demonstrate his superiority to the Italian. Adamberger's politic decision not to use K. 420—the Hofburg had made known its discomfort with what had become an embarrassing wrangle—evoked Mozart's outcry of "a ploy on the part of Salieri," who opposed the interpolations, realizing that they would serve Mozart's interests, not the company's: in the midst of his futile search for a *buffa* libretto, he had

---

15 Fracturing a symphony in this manner in no way violated precedent (see p. 200).
16 K. 415 concludes with an Allegro in Rondo form.

felt the need to evince before the public his mastery of Italian opera, in which Vienna had heard him only haphazardly at concerts—never in dramatic context. (His ensembles for *La villanella rapita* lay in the future.) He sought to take advantage of the important debuts as an opportunity to shine, but, instead, brought a hornet's nest about his ears. (Even so, he maintained the stance of someone sinned against.) His strong ally, Aloisia, however, did have the power to insist upon embellishing *Il curioso* with her two new arias; the second, Mozart reported, had to be repeated, "thus confounding my enemies."

5

THIS EMBROILMENT APART, he managed his affairs with diplomacy. The first of the twelve subscription concerts he and Philipp Jakob Martin had presented in the Augarten pavilion (26 May 1782) included the double piano concerto K. 365 (with Mozart and Josepha Auernhammer) and two symphonies— one of Mozart's and another from the hand of an amateur composer whose vanity he felt it wise to gratify: Gottfried van Swieten (see XI, n. 1). His Bach-Handel afternoons, which Mozart called "our Sunday musical practice," provided him instruction and a welcome supplement to his income.

In 1770, after a *séjour* in England, van Swieten had become Vienna's Ambassador to Berlin, where he formed part of a circle (surrounding Princess Amalia; see VIII, n. 31) devoted to baroque music. Returning to Vienna in 1777 to serve the Imperial household, he founded that parallel group of connoisseurs in which Mozart took such pleasure: "Every Sunday at noon I go to Baron van Swieten's, where nothing but Handel and Bach is performed." In earlier days Mozart had used "Bach" to signify Christian, but in the course of the Vienna years Mozartean usage turned him into "the English Bach"; for Mozart the unadorned surname came to identify Sebastian Bach alone, a change begotten in the atmosphere of those workshops of baroque music.[17]

---

17 In time Van Swieten's band of enthusiasts sponsored full model performances of oratorios and cantatas, concerts over which Mozart presided (see pp. 682–83). A component of the organization would survive his death to promote the premieres of Joseph Haydn's *The Seven Last Words*, *The Creation*, and *The Seasons*, van Swieten having a hand in the texts of all three. He had commissioned from Emanuel Bach six string symphonies (1773) and received the dedication of his third collection of keyboard sonatas *"für Kenner und Liebhaber"* (for connoisseus and amateurs; 1781). The young Beethoven inscribed his first symphony to this arbiter of Vienna's musical world, who died in 1803.

Van Swieten had at first held them in his handsome private apartment in the Imperial library, which he headed (as had his father). The sessions attracted widening interest and in 1786 spawned a society of nobles that styled itself "The Associated." It met in more spacious chambers: the great hall of the library and then that of the Schwartzenberg palace, along with the Esterházy rooms of the Palais Pálffy, once Johann Nepomuk, Prince Schwartzenberg, and Johann Baptist, Count Esterházy—husband of Maria Anna, Countess Pálffy—had become enthusiasts. Van Swieten's position permitted him to call upon musicians in the Hofburg's service, among them Joseph Starzer, who presided over the gatherings. (When, during score-reading, the occasion demanded a vocal quartet, Swieten sang treble, Mozart alto [even as he played], Starzer tenor, and Anton Teyber [Therese's brother] bass.) Upon Starzer's death (1787), Mozart would take over as director, but from the beginning he had enjoyed van Swieten's particular favor and with it the run of the library and private access to the baroque scores in his possession.[18] They formed the matter of these investigative conclaves.

To give them a personal touch, Mozart asked his father (12 April 1783) to "search the attic" for some examples of his church music that van Swieten's group might read through as part of its consideration of modern accommodations to older styles. ". . . you and I," he assured Leopold, "recognize the continual changes taste undergoes and that, alas, they extend even as far as church music, which should not be the case. Thus true church music is to be discovered in worm-eaten state under the eaves." Here Mozart circles round the question of winnowing from old husks, in particular his own preoccupation with baroque pastiche. These very days he had the C-minor mass in hand, and it appears evident he put this case in order to convince himself of the aesthetic solidity of his own standpoint. At all events, an answer came to him, not from the Saxon past, but from contemporary Eszterháza.

If van Swieten's portfolios revealed to Mozart the riches of Bach's and Handel's contrapuntal art, Joseph Haydn's recent work taught him how to take personal possession of it. Just as Haydn's string quartets of 1771–1772 had inspired his own set of 1773, so now he found in Haydn's Russian quartets of 1781–1782 (Op. 33, dedicated to Grand Duke Paul) a yet stronger stimulus. In the past, he had most often restricted his use of counterpoint

---

18 In the spring of 1782 Mozart began to gather what he called his own "collection of Bach fugues: Sebastian's as well as Emanuel's and Friedemann's"; and, he added, "also [fugues by] Handel."

to injecting its texture and flavor into his compositions as a diversifying element, but now, putting himself into spiritual apprenticeship to Haydn, he strove to acquire a complete command of the polyphonic discipline: to become its easy master; to have in hand techniques strong and flexible enough to mold a venerable vocabulary and grammar into a language speaking in his authentic voice; to make baroque traditions serve the contemporary idiom of the sonata and thematic transformation.

The result of these labors, the so-called Haydn quartets—he would dedicate the six to the Esterháza master—betokens a remarkable synthesis absorbing high baroque polyphony within the tissue of Viennese musical classicism, itself woven of rococo, *empfindsam*, and *opera-buffa*-like melodic threads. Even in the quartets' promiscuous world of bold, lightning changes of idiom, the learned style remains a prominent strand in the varied tapestry, the polyphony commanding special admiration for being no longer an evocation of days of old but an element become both structure and substance. A new intellectual breadth and power had entered Mozart's work, Constanze's enthusiasm for fugues helping him stay the course in his passionate campaign to lay full claim to the German contrapuntal heritage. His arrangements for string quartet of clavier fugues by Bach (K. 405) confirm the recollection of Attwood (see p. 568) that *The Well-Tempered Clavier* had a permanent place near the master's piano.

Striking testimonials of the demanding curriculum he inflicted upon himself survive as contrapuntal exercises of a fierce determination, a few of them fragments suggesting desperation as the cause of their abandonment. However, this period of intense self-instruction, his so-called Bach crisis, did record a number of compelling victories on the polyphonic drill field: among them a fine prelude and fugue for piano in C major (K. 394/383a of spring 1782), close to Bach in its lineaments (much like the White Knight's taking pride in the "very clever pudding" he invented while partaking of the meat course, Mozart boasted to Nannerl that, having composed the fugue in his head, he put it to paper even as he simultaneously conceived the prelude); and the most cogent musical argument of these exertions: the fugue in C minor for two pianos, K. 426 of December 1783, which he would arrange for strings (K. 546) five years later, adding a trenchant Adagio as an introduction.

Although he had embarked upon the set of Haydn quartets (K. 387, 421/417b, 428/421b, 458, 464, 465) at the close of 1782, by the following June only the first two had reached completion. (The Finale of K. 387 in G put forth a brilliant hypothesis for reconciling fugal and sonata principles.) Looking upon the series as a program of study and reconciling himself to a slow gestation,[19] he interspersed the quartets' production with the composition of works for a wider public. The first of the Viennese piano concertos (K. 414/385p)[20] had preceded the inception of the quartets and in all likelihood came to paper in the autumn of 1782, the second concerto (K. 413/387a) before the year ran out, the third (K. 415/387b) by the spring of 1783, when he also composed a horn concerto (K. 417), for cheesemonger Leutgeb, for whom, some months earlier, he had written the horn quintet K. 407/386c, in effect a concerto with string accompaniment. By July the third quartet received its final touches, but more than a year passed before he hammered out the fourth (autumn 1784), the final two coming into being in January 1785. He took care to satisfy Vienna's varied musical tastes as he moved back and forth from the more popular bel canto of the concertos to the new speech of the quartets, though difficulties in coping with the intensifying complications he imposed upon his technique must also account for the cautious progress.

Not a few contemporary musicians of high quality and of goodwill toward Mozart found his new quartets closed to ready understanding. Attwood sent them as a gift to Paisiello in Naples with the caution that he withhold judgment until experiencing them several times. Paisiello attempted their performance with friends but discovered that they could negotiate only the slow movements. On the other hand, Attwood's former teacher, the venerable Gaetano Latilla, to whom Paisiello showed the quartets, without hesitation declared them masterly, as, in time, Paisiello did. As to Sarti, for all his attachment to Mozart, he declared them filled with "barbarisms," music to make the listener "stop his ears."

7

SEVENTEEN-EIGHTY-FOUR constituted an annus mirabilis of Mozartean activity. On 3 March he described just what kept him from posting more than the occasional letter to Salzburg: "Pupils consume my entire morning, almost every evening I perform," and "of necessity I must play new things." He had to ensure their steady flow. (On 9 February 1784 he had begun a catalogue of his works—each entry dated and with its incipit

---

19 The first edition of the quartets (brought out in 1785 by the firm of Artaria, which paid four hundred fifty gulden for them) bore the dedication to Joseph Haydn, the moving Italian prose describing them as "the fruit of long and laborious exertion."

20 Perhaps as a call to remembrance of Christian Bach (see n. 12), its Andante quotes the overture he had provided for the Galuppi-Goldoni *La calamità de' cuori*. The problematic K. 19d (see p. 197) also contains the citation.

or opening theme—maintaining it until five days before he took to his deathbed.) During March he produced the noble three-movement quintet for piano and winds (oboe, clarinet, bassoon, and horn), K. 452, which he ranked among his compositions as "the best I have yet written." (It would be Beethoven's inspiration for his opus 16.) On 1 April, the audience in the Burgtheater heard the first performance of the quintet along with the "completely new" piano concerto K. 451 and the Viennese premiere of the Linz Symphony.

This evening formed part of a schedule of Lenten concerts, whose number he had projected at twenty-two, to unfold between 26 February and 3 April: nine at Count Johann Baptist Esterházy's; five at Prince Golicyn's; three at the Trattnerhof, where he also had to appear in another three forming part of Richter's subscription series; and two at the Burgtheater. His list of subscribers to his own concerts at the Trattnerhof had become a matter of pride: "thirty more than Richter and Fisher[21] together" (one hundred seventy-six names and at six florins each) and embracing the summit of Vienna's nobility and high bourgeoisie.

He strained his every fiber to fulfill this calendar (a concert or two may have fallen by the way), details of which he dispatched to Salzburg: "Don't I have enough to do?" he asked Leopold (a glance at his old charge of indolence). "I believe this is a way of not falling out of practice." In the end he "confessed" to having "become tired of late from playing so much; but no small credit to me that my listeners *never* tired." These exertions helped prepare the sickness that overtook him on the first night of Paisiello's latest opera.

He and Mozart had met in Naples and Turin, and acquaintance ripened into friendship during the Italian's Viennese stay. On 12 June 1784, Mozart looked forward to a concert he and his pupil Barbara (Babette) Ployer would give the following day in Paisiello's presence at her family's country home in the suburb of Döbling.[22] Mozart very much wanted to impress

---

21 He referred to either the bass Fischer (the first Osmin) or the English violinist-composer John Abraham Fisher (who, on 21 March, married Nancy Storace; see p. 661).

22 "Miss Babette and I will play, she her new concerto in G," Mozart wrote in reference to K. 453 of April 1784, which he dedicated to her; he conceded that the piano concerto K. 449, composed for her two months earlier, might be performed *"a quattro"*—that is, to the accompaniment of a string quartet alone—but did not recommend such diminution with regard to K. 453: her father hired an orchestra for the occasion. Mozart not only conducted the concerto but also participated in both the quintet, K. 452, and, with Babette as partner, the sonata for two pianos (K. 448). He regretted that another famous Italian, who had also become part of his circle, could not attend: "If Maestro Sarti had not had to depart Vienna today [for St. Petersburg], he, too, would have come along with me. Sarti is an honest and fine fellow! I have played for him very often and even improvised variations on one of his arias, which

him: "I will fetch Paesello [*sic*] in my carriage, for I want him to hear my work and my pupil."

Paisiello remained in Vienna throughout the summer of 1784, for within days of his arrival (1 May), Emperor Joseph had commissioned him, at triple the usual fee, to compose an opera. He set *Il rè Teodoro in Venezia* (its libretto by Casti, based upon a narrative in Voltaire's *Candide*). In the course of its premiere at the Burgtheater on 23 August 1784, Mozart fell ill, "sweated through all his clothes," and decided to go home; however, "since an ordinance forbade retainers to enter the theater by the main portal," he first had to search through the cold night air for his servant, who had his overcoat. Mozart came down with what Doctor Sigmund Barisani identified as rheumatic fever (a broad diagnosis)[23] and suffered spells of violent vomiting. Barisani, son of Salzburg's Doctor Silvester Barisani and on the faculty of Vienna's famed General Hospital, felt it wise to make daily visits.

The household must have been put to the test, for Mozart's slow recovery coincided with the closing weeks of Constanze's pregnancy. She gave birth to her second child, Carl Thomas, on 21 September 1784,[24] by which time his father had regained his health: eight days later, the Mozarts moved from the Trattnerhof to elegant quarters in a house owned by the Camesina brothers[25] in the Grosse Schulerstrasse near the cathedral. Mozart required more space for his family and also for servants, visitors, pupils, and the assistants and copyists necessary to keep the torrent of concerts flowing. Moreover, he craved surroundings appropriate to his growing renown and furnished the rooms in fine style. The change of residence almost quadrupled his rent, to a sum thirty guldens higher than his Salzburg salary of former days.

---

pleased him ever so much." K. 460/454a (June 1784), eight variations on an air from Sarti's *Fra i due litiganti*, must reflect this performance. Two of the set come from Mozart's hand, the remaining six perhaps from Sarti's as he put his recollections of the improvisation to paper. Mozart used the same tune, "*Come un agnello*," in the supper scene of *Don Giovanni* (see p. 657).

23 Whatever the illness, Leopold learned that a number of Viennese had also taken to bed with it.

24 Johann Thomas von Trattner stood godfather at St. Peter's. As had his dead brother, the child seemed the image of Mozart.

25 A craftsman and designer of ornamental plasterwork, the father of Joseph and Alberto Camesina had embellished the ceiling of one of the front rooms in order to show prospective clients a model of his art. This rococo decoration, which survives, befits the chamber in which Mozart composed much of his *Figaro.* He displayed his new surroundings to his pupils with a name-day party for himself (31 October 1784) at which they performed. The imagination pictures Theresia von Trattner on this occasion seated beneath the stuccowork mythologies and playing the piano sonata in C minor, K. 457, completed for her some two weeks earlier. The following May he would furnish it with a prelude, the no less profound fantasy in C minor, K. 475.

Although Leopold reacted with sarcasm to descriptions of his son's new and comfortable way of life, for the moment they had balanced their accounts, an accommodation advanced on the father's side by the awe with which he viewed the latest compositions the post brought to the archive. He gave Salzburgers the opportunity to hear one of the finest examples when, on 15 September 1784, he conducted the Linz Symphony at either Doctor Silvester Barisani's city or country residence. And two days later Salzburg acclaimed its first production of *The Abduction*: "Even the Archbishop had the great graciousness to say: '*It really wasn't bad,*'" Leopold reported. He had come to terms with the work and seemed ready to resume his role of basking in his son's genius.

Over the months they had sought to preserve themselves from the externals of anger and begun to rediscover something of the profundity of their relationship. Their Salzburg reunion had been probative and fumbling; a second meeting might well come off better, and Leopold took the first step toward arranging it. But Nannerl could not participate: she had left Salzburg to wed.

Shortly before the departure of the Marchand children to rejoin their parents in Munich (the beginning of September 1784), they, or at least Margarethe, had accompanied Leopold to St. Gilgin to celebrate Nannerl's marriage²⁶ to its prefect, Johann Baptist Franz von Berchtold zu Sonnenburg on 23 August, the day Mozart fell ill at the Burgtheater.²⁷ Some fifteen years her senior, twice a widower (and with five children, in age from two to thirteen), prosperous, and a "von," he had doubtless been Leopold's choice. On 3 September, forlorn in a Tanzmeisterhaus bereft of his lively pensioners and Nannerl, he wrote her: "I am utterly alone in a true death-like stillness midst eight rooms. During the day I am unaffected, but at night, as I write this, it is rather painful. If only I could at least still hear the dog snore and bark. [Bimperl had died during the summer. "Did the canine shade (*Hundsseele*) of Bimpes appear to you?" he had asked her on 30 August.] But none of this matters: as long as I know that you two [Nannerl and Sonnenburg] are living in happiness, then I, too, am content."

No such all-embracing sympathy gave impulse to his plan to visit Vienna, but love did play its part—and loneliness, too. ("When the theater season ends, I don't know what I will do with my evenings. *Thinking* and

---

26 By this time Leopold had three pupils in his household: in 1783 Theobald Marchand's eight-year-old niece, Maria Johanna Brochard, had joined her two cousins at the Tanzmeisterhaus. She, too, went to the wedding.

27 Five days earlier he had sent Nannerl a letter wishing her joy and concluding with a humorous, well-turned poem on a wife's sexual responsibilities: "Soon familiarity will teach you / What even Eve once had to do."

vacant hours make me want to die.") Leopold created the occasion to make the journey "at no cost" to himself by asking Wolfgang to arrange concert appearances in the capital for Heinrich Marchand, whose father was to pay the expenses and provide a coach: the teacher would pick up pupil and coach in Munich and proceed to Vienna, where they would stay at the Camesina house. (Leopold had not lost his gift for manipulation.) The tour had to take place at the height of the concert season, for only during the whirlwind of Lenten concerts could Mozart find opportunities to wedge Heinrich into Vienna's musical life. The Archbishop conferred the leave, and Leopold departed for Munich on 28 January.[28]

---

28 Michael Haydn took over his duties in the cathedral, Anton Breymann, Leopold's pupil and a student at the university, those in the Kapellhaus.

CHAPTER XXXI

Vienna:

Diverse Production

H EAVY SNOWS AND freezing temperatures accompanied Leopold
and Heinrich to Vienna.[1] They arrived on 11 February 1785 to find
the apartment a hive of activity as Mozart oversaw the copying of a new
piano concerto (K. 466 in D minor)[2] he was to play that evening at his
first Mehlgrube concert of the season. During the performance, Leopold
marveled at the orchestra's ability to cope with the "superb" concerto it
had to play well nigh at sight. The next day, Joseph Haydn, visiting the
apartment for a celebration (see p. 645) that included a reading of Mozart's
last three quartets,[3] met Leopold and remarked to him: "Before God and

---

1 Nannerl did not want her father to make the journey in view of the icy weather of uncommon
  bite closing in upon Central Europe. And at this time she appears to have been indifferent, at
  best, to his move toward reconciliation, his estate no doubt among the factors; only upon its
  settlement did she look toward the healing of wounds (see pp. 672–73).
2 Lest copyists make duplicates to be hawked for their own profit, Mozart took the only possible
  precaution—keeping a sharp eye: "I myself have everything copied in my presence in my room."
  Yet, like all composers and writers, he remained defenseless against publishers who engraved copies
  over and above the count of the edition with intent to sell them at discount for private gain.
3 When their close friendship began cannot be documented. Over the years Haydn had from
  time to time made his way to Vienna from Esterháza and Eisenstadt, and their paths crossed
  (see XIV, n. 44). Haydn had already heard all six of the latest quartets on a visit to the
  Camesina house on 15 January.

as an honest man, I tell you that your son is the greatest composer known to me either in person or by name . . ."—gratifying praise from the master Europe now acknowledged as supreme. The following evening at the Burgtheater Leopold sat in a box near that of "the very beautiful" Princess of Württemberg. "Your brother," he reported to Nannerl, "played a glorious concerto [K. 456?], which he composed for Mlle. Paradis to perform in Paris. . . . Tears of sheer delight came to my eyes. . . . When your brother made his exit, the Emperor saluted him with his hat and called out: 'Bravo, Mozart!'"

Leopold continued the seeming unending round of concerts, plays, receptions, grand repasts at the homes of his son's colleagues, and family dinners given by Caecilia Weber and Aloisia Lange, whom only yesterday the Tanzmeisterhaus had so abhorred. Their hospitality laid the specters of the past: Caecilia, in her new apartment on the Kärntnerstasse, conquered him for good and all with her cooking. The demands of fast days had no hold upon such circles, and Leopold appears not at any time to have refused the pleasures of the Viennese table. He punctuated his letters to St. Gilgin with talk of wonderful meat dishes and pheasant in cabbage, of oysters and the most delicious preserves, and of flowing champagne.

Dazzled by the high rents Mozart and his friends paid, he nonetheless recognized such expenditures as justifiable in view of the abundant opportunities of making money the capital put forward. He could not get over the twenty-five hundred florins the oboist Ludwig August Lebrun and his wife, the soprano Franziska Dorothea Danzi, had taken in at three concerts in the Burgtheater during February and March, and hastened to inform Nannerl: "Your brother made 559 florins at his concert [10 March 1785 in the Burgtheater], which we did not expect because he is giving six subscription concerts at the Mehlgrube for more than 150 people, each of whom pays a sovereign for the series. [Thus two thousand twenty-five florins.] Moreover, just to be obliging, he has been playing very often at other concerts in the theater." There seemed to be no lessening of Vienna's clamor to hear him. Even so, Leopold believed he nosed decay in a structure to all appearances prospering.

Soon after the Mozarts' wedding, in the course of a letter (23 August 1782; see p. 610) thanking Countess Waldstätten for her "extraordinary graciousness" toward them, Leopold, aware that they confided in her, had embarked upon an elaborate self-justification, painting his son as someone "ruled by two opposing elements," at times indolence rendering him "inactive," at times impatience permitting "nothing to stand in his way": either "too much or too little, never the middle course." This analysis of what Leopold identified as a "major flaw" of personality bordered upon explicit and destructive mischief in that he had set this criticism before the eyes of a patron! Now, some two and a half years later,[4] his letters to Nannerl from the Camesina house took a similar path: he again observed a low degree of consistency in his son's attitudes and no leaning to set a balanced bearing; although, at the moment, he "without doubt" had "enough money to deposit 2,000 florins in the bank," yet this affluence glittered with high but false colors: he could start to build capital only "were he without debts."

At the beginning of 1783 he had borrowed to pay the cost of making manuscript copies of his piano concertos K. 413, 414, and 415, to be offered to the public by subscription. To his surprise, even the fact that all three could be performed as piano quintets (that is, with the orchestra reduced to a string quartet), and thus be appropriate to the salon, failed to excite a response sufficient to cover the short-term loan. An action impended, and by the middle of February he turned to Countess Waldstätten: "Here I am in a fine fix!" He appealed to her for funds to help him keep "honor and good name." Thus had begun his Peter-Paul practice of covering one loan with another.

Glimpsing the shadows beneath the high living, Leopold reserved his sharp and caustic observations to Nannerl. At the Camesina house there prevailed an exemplary truce, during which he applied his mind to pondering Viennese Freemasonry, then at its highest reputation.

Ignaz von Born, the renowned chemist and mineralogist, presided over Zur wahren Eintracht (True Concord), the most prominent of Vienna's eight Masonic lodges.[5] Its name, suggesting the harmony of the spheres, derived not from the mystical and hermetic but from Newtonian science, for the members eschewed any strain of the occult: they exalted ideals of personal and social ethics and, in search of the higher good, pursued a practical program of discussions, lectures, and publications, the main concerns being scientific, literary, and artistic. This intellectual circle dovetailed into Countess Thun's, and Mozart had become part of both. Yet when, on 14 December 1784, he made his formal entrance into the Masonic brotherhood—on 7 January 1785 he would become a Fellow, by the following spring a Master—he chose not von Born's lodge but the smaller Zur Wohltätigkeit (Beneficence).

---

4 The Countess had removed to the suburb of Klosterneuburg by the time Leopold visited her in 1785.
5 T. C. W. Blanning's claim that in 1780 Vienna had thirteen lodges suggests a process of amalgation under way before the Imperial directive of 1785 (see p. 655).

Its master, Baron Otto Heinrich von Gemmingen-Hornberg, known to Mozart since Mannheim days (see p. 393 and II, n. 12), had of late settled in Vienna. Not simply an old friendship but a shared devotion to Catholic tradition drew Mozart to this company. Though, with public virtue their goal, Masons made a point at their meetings of not championing any particular religious stance, Zur Wohltätigkeit nonetheless preserved a Roman sensibility colored by Muratorian compassion, an atmosphere with which Mozart felt at one. Moreover, he could have the best of two worlds: a sister lodge of von Born's, Zur Wohltätigkeit functioned within its corporate body, sharing its quarters and at times holding sessions in common. Mozart had found a place in an ethical commonwealth espousing a secular rule that did not impinge upon the substance and spirit of his traditional beliefs. The *Maurerische Trauermusik* (Masonic Funeral Music, K. 477/479a of November 1785), written for a memorial service, reveals the refinement with which he accommodated Catholicism and Masonry. This orchestral work puts to use as cantus firmus the tonus pelligrinus, the psalm tone for the chants of lamentation sung during Holy Week (a device Mozart had already employed in his *Betulia liberata*; see p. 292). The imagery of the liturgical text, unsung but implied, evokes the Masonic trials by earth and water.[6]

That Leopold followed his son into Freemasonry can be comprehended best in the light of Zur Wohltätigkeit's Catholic disposition; further, most of those important in Vienna's political, intellectual, and artistic life had some tie to the movement, and Haydn's recent entry into Zur wahren Eintracht set Leopold a personal example. (The concert of the three Mozart quartets at the Camesina house[7] had been the highlight of a party celebrating Haydn's initiation the previous evening, a ceremony Mozart's Mehlgrube concert had kept him from attending.) And no less compelling: in the midst of his son's social whirl in which mingled names such as Thun and Cobenzl, Sonnenfels and Swieten, Gemmingen and Born, Kaunitz and even Habsburg, Leopold felt at the very center of things and wished to do what he thought expected of him. On 6 April 1785, as proposed by Zur Wohltätigkeit, he became an Apprentice, on the sixteenth a Fellow—celebrated by Mozart's "A Journeyman on His Way" (K. 468 for voice and keyboard of 26 March 1785 to a text

---

6 K. 477 drew upon a Masonic *Meistermusik* with voices (K. Deest); he had composed it the previous July to mark a Brother's promotion to the rank of Master. For a later performance of K. 477 he deepened its colors by adding two basset horns and a double bassoon.

7 The performers: Leopold (violin), Mozart (viola), and the Tinti brothers, Anton and Bartholomäus, both barons and both Masons.

by Franz Joseph von Ratschky)—and on the twenty-second a Master. Two days later he and his son attended a meeting at which various lodges joined to honor Born, whose new smelting process had led the Emperor to create him a Knight of the Realm. Mozart conducted his new cantata, *Die Maurerfreude* (The Masons's Joy, K. 471, the text by Franz Petran). It called for an orchestra, a small male chorus, and a tenor soloist, at the premiere Adamberger, also a Mason. Father and son shared a golden evening.

Yet Leopold's *séjour* could not have been without moments of crippling guilt, chagrin, and jealousy as he contemplated a son, debonair and casual, living in comfort, and moving through an elegant world such as had been the father's vision for them both. At times the situation must have torn at his conscience: what he had worked to undercut and predicted would be, without his direction, only exorbitant hopes and dreams, had become a stunning reality once Mozart shed paternal control like a suit of old clothes. Further, it is easy to imagine Mozart not only making clear with ceremonial politeness his awareness of just how wrongheaded the Tanzmeisterhaus had been, but also now and then piling Pelion upon Ossa in order to demonstrate just how well he could manage his remorseless, self-punishing schedule. In the end, Leopold could not keep up with it.

In his sixty-sixth year and with accumulating infirmities, he found his energy ebbing. His rheumatism flared up, and the cold he had brought with him persisted. He found the apartment's heating insufficient and seemed relieved to have good reasons—perhaps unconscious ruses nursing inward hostility—to excuse himself from time to time and rest in a warm bed, drink tea, and perhaps enjoy a visit from the buoyant Sophie. By early March he confessed to Nannerl that the activities of the household had quite undone him: "We never get to bed before one in the morning and never get up before nine. We dine at two or half past the hour. The weather is horrible! Concerts every day and unending teaching, music-making, and composing. Where am I supposed to go? If only the concerts were over! It is impossible to describe the confusion and commotion. Since I have been here, your brother's pianoforte has been taken to the theater or to some house at least a dozen times. He has had a large pianoforte pedal constructed; it stands under the instrument . . . is astonishingly heavy,[8] and is

---

8 It would seem that here Leopold referred to a pedal-board connected to the instrument and, in the manner of the pedals on the modern piano, regulating a mechanism altering the timbre of the sound: that is, by lifting the dampers or shifting the keyboard action. Perhaps one of the

carried to the Mehlgrube every Friday and also to Count Zichy's and Prince Kaunitz's."

No less than this imposing instrument, the decorative appointments of the household impressed Leopold. Though he praised Constanze for regulating it with an eye to economy, the frugality of her kitchen left him of equivocal mind. The lavish dining he enjoyed in other establishments contrasted with her cook's spartan ideal of good and simple fare in those modest portions of which the always hungry serving maid from Salzburg complained in her letters home.9 The resident staff consisted of her and the cook; the hairdressers, launderers, scrubbers, and polishers worked by the day, as did Mozart's assistants and copyists. To Leopold the house seemed a whirlwind of admired disorder, and he held out in Vienna only for a particular end.

The date of his departure had come to depend upon the schedules of both the Wohltätigkeit and Eintracht lodges, and, though they loosened formalities, he had been obliged to wait until their officers put into place the painstaking arrangements even an abridged initiation entailed. Nannerl, to whom he gave no information about his Masonic adventure—doubtless he feared her husband's disapproval—required some explanation of the repeated postponements of his journey home. She and von Sonnenburg made visits to the Tanzmeisterhaus during his absence and learned that the Salzburg court, provoked by his overstaying, had decided to stop his salary did he not appear forthwith. For her benefit, and, indirectly, the Residenz's, he summoned up an old technique: exaggerating the harshness of the weather. True, the winter had been of an aberrant brutality, but his letters told of nature run wild: of the great capital paralyzed beneath towering snowdrifts, of an Easter of blustering winds more bitter than those of any Christmas, of both the secondary roads and the main highways become impassable, of the crop of winter grain obliterated and the peasants slaughtering their starving animals, of public prayer for an end to the chaos, and of the terrible cough that continued to shake his body. Some truth resided in every point, but at the same time his own prose described the city's uninterrupted concert life and the comings and goings of travelers.

On 25 April, Mozart and Constanze accompanied Leopold and Heinrich to nearby Purkersdorf, where the post road forked. They lunched, and

---

foot-levers also controlled a "Turkish" attachment that elevated a drumstick to strike against the bottom of the soundboard even while setting cymbals and triangles into motion.
9 A suspicious and then furious Mozart learned of this criticism by forcing one of them open.

then one coach turned toward Linz,[10] the other back toward Vienna. Father and son had taken their final farewell.

Their correspondence, through the years ever more widely spaced, now lost any semblance of an entity: with gaps of weeks intervening, letters made their way between Vienna and Salzburg, summaries of Mozart's being sent on to St. Gilgin. In contrast, Nannerl received paternal instruction in a steady flow: from afar he sought to direct the routine of her household, holding forth upon the rearing of her five stepchildren, the supervision of domestics, medical matters (in particular proper bowel movements and menstruation remedies), and even cookery. As her confinement approached, he fetched her back to Salzburg, the city's doctors no doubt his lure, and on 27 July 1785 Leopold Alois Pantaleon Berchtold von Sonnenburg arrived in the Tanzmeisterhaus.

Leopold used his best endeavor to persuade her and her husband to leave the infant in his care (that is, in the hands of his excellent servants) for several months and soon disclosed his hope to keep the boy for an indefinite time. Nannerl returned to St. Gilgin without him on 2 September. "We should not be overhasty," Leopold wrote his son-in-law. "You have five children in your charge and meanwhile, until you make a decision, the sixth is being well cared for here." Playing upon his loneliness, he confided that heaven would soon determine the matter: declining health gave evi-

---

10 Leopold tarried in Linz, enjoying the hospitality of the Thuns, for whom Heinrich performed. The pair went on to Munich. By the time Leopold returned to Salzburg c. 15 May, he had extended his leave of six weeks to fifteen. He had to have felt guilt at having taken ill advantage of Heinrich, of having, to selfish purpose, thrust before the Viennese a student who, as a virtuoso, skated on very thin ice. His immediate future lay as an orchestral musician, and Leopold, certainly painting his protégé's Viennese appearances in fine colors, did endeavor to have the court of Salzburg take him into service. Mozart's role in the Heinrich affair had shown him at his best: whatever his misgivings, he had smoothed the boy's way, with good grace making a place for him to play a violin concerto at a Mehlgrube concert of 18 February. The solo did not go well, and all at once Leopold took fright, voicing "worry about how things will turn out at Heinrich's academy" scheduled for 2 March in the Burgtheater. In the end, he did not disgrace himself but fiddled before an almost empty house. If nothing is known of his second concert (the fourteenth), it seems clear that Mozart strove to have the miserable adventure end with some dignity: he alone could have arranged Heinrich's performance of a violin concerto the next day at the Viennese Society of Musicians' charity concert, featuring a repeat performance of Mozart's *Davidde penitente* (see p. 651). Heinrich could not have been unaware of his limitations, and, on his way home, the easygoing music-making in the Thun palace provided a happy coda to his trials in Vienna. Even as he recommended Heinrich for a position in Salzburg, Leopold feared that his very advocacy would doom the plan. ("Heinrich would already be engaged . . . were he not my pupil.") For all that, in 1786 the Archbishop did select Heinrich as violinist and keyboard player. The Residenz's official and antipathetic view of the Mozarts had become less pronounced: Colloredo went as far as to ask Leopold to sound his son concerning the qualifications of candidates for Salzburg's musical staff.

dence of the little time remaining in which he might enjoy his grandson, whom he dubbed the Prince of Asturias.

This title, given the successor to the Spanish throne, now identified the true royal heir of the Mozarts. Little Leopold's entry upon the scene strengthened an earlier decision to disinherit Wolfgang. Heinrich had proved a failed double, but had God perhaps wrought a second Mozartean miracle in the infant? From the disposition and arch of its fingers Leopold conjured the vision of a keyboard master to be: indeed, the grandfather never tired of searching for signs that would argue the power of his heredity.[11]

2

SOMETIME NEAR THE joint of October and November, Leopold, for weeks without a word from his son, encountered Lorenz Hübner, editor of Salzburg's *Oberdeutsche Staatszeitung.* He expressed delight with the reports going round concerning Mozart's high reputation and spoke of the "new opera" he had in work. Of this Leopold knew nothing, but observed to Nannerl: "Basta! I daresay we shall hear about it!" Several days later, he received a letter in which Mozart attributed his long silence to the press of his labors upon *The Marriage of Figaro.* Leopold saw the undertaking as problematical; he knew Beaumarchais's play: "A tiresome affair, whose translation from the French will have to be free if it is to be effective as an opera. God grant that the libretto turn out well; about the music I have no doubts." On Mozart's desk in Vienna lay a transformed and tightened Italian version of the text.

In light of the Emperor's affectionate interest in him, commentators have wondered about his failure, *The Impresario* apart, to provide Vienna with a work for the stage between *The Abduction* and *Figaro.* They forget the wealth of music he created for the operatic torsos of an interim during which the Hofburg would have welcomed an Italian opera from his hand, had he been able to settle upon a libretto. His fastidiousness in coming to a decision appeared much like procrastination and had roots in his keen disappointment to observe the eclipse of German opera at court. As recently

---

11 Besides the von Sonnenburgs' desire to capture the full inheritance, other factors no doubt led to their participating in Leopold's obsessive fantasy of creating a second Wolfgang: Nannerl's historic and unquestioning obedience and the eagerness of her husband—late in middle age and with a stingy streak—to transfer the mess of an infant's early months to someone who, moreover, would assume all expenses. Von Sonnenburg's household had yet to emerge from the chaos that had overtaken it upon the death of his second wife in 1783. He found in Nannerl a woman capable of restoring order among the servants and the children, the reason for his marrying beneath his class.

as 21 May 1785, he had flared up into angry sarcasm in the course of acknowledging receipt of Anton Klein's German play about Rudolf von
Habsburg, sent for consideration as a libretto: "Were there but one patriot
with authority, things would show a different complexion; then, perhaps,
the German national theater, beautiful in the bud, would reach full bloom.
Of course, it would be an everlasting stain upon Germany were we Germans seriously to begin to think as Germans, to act as Germans, to speak
German, and even to sing in German!" In the matter of choosing an Italian text, in considerable measure he encumbered his own way, which, in the
end, Joseph II cleared as a result of his intoxication with Beaumarchais's famous pair of comedies.

The Emperor had attended the Viennese premiere (13 August 1783) of
Paisiello's *opera-buffa* version of *The Barber of Seville*—the work had, in fact,
first taken form in Beaumarchais's mind as an *opéra comique*—and desired a
musical setting of its sequel, *The Marriage of Figaro*. Count Rosenberg discussed this royal enthusiasm with Mozart, and only the assurance of a palpable commission could have led him to present the official court poet, Da
Ponte, with the problem of forging an acceptable libretto from Beaumarchais's text.[12]

Unlike the *Barber*'s, it included passages at odds with the Hofburg's
sense of propriety: even though much of *Figaro*'s ridicule of the nobility's
abuse of privilege met Joseph's own persuasions, he made clear that the
play's sharpest spurs of political satire had to be cut away. (One did not,
for example, discuss aristocratic birth in terms of chance.)[13] Da Ponte,
Mozart no doubt at his side, wielded the knife with finished craft: scenes,
characters, speeches, indeed, whole counterplots succumbed. Yet not a few
spiky points did remain embedded within the main action, its delicious intrigues versified in Italian with a rich variety of forms responding to the
composer's subtlest needs.

---

12 The Hofburg inclined to forget what a sorry figure Beaumarchais had cut in Vienna. Under the
pseudonym of Ronac he had presented himself at court (1774) with a tale of having inter-
cepted, not without personal injury, the only surviving copy of a pamphlet defaming Maria
Theresa and her daughter Marie Antoinette. As proof he showed the pamphlet and—a mis-
judgment—the wounds: superficial and, clear to the eye, self-inflicted. To crown all, in order
to demonstrate his trustworthiness, he also produced a document attesting to his membership
in Louis XVI's secret service. Even so, the Empress and Kaunitz treated him as an impostor and
adventurer; in fact, Kaunitz believed him the author of the libel as well as the wounds. He remained under house arrest for thirty-one days, until released at the request of Paris, an indulgent resolution, the Empress observed, for someone deserving severe punishment.
13 Joseph's sister Marie Antoinette had pressed for the public presentation of the play in Paris
even with some of the contentious passages intact.

The success of their collaboration lay in Da Ponte's readiness to be guided by Mozart in matters of meter, the placement of vowels, and the assignment of the poetic lines to the appropriate musical genre: recitativo secco, accompagnato, aria, and ensemble. The two had already worked together, perhaps on *Lo sposo* but for certain on a devotional cantata, *Davidde penitente*, K. 469, which the Viennese Society of Musicians had requested of Mozart (it approached Righini, too) for performance at its benefit Lenten concerts of 1785.[14] Cast aside by Salieri at the end of 1784 upon the failure of their *Il ricco d'un giorno* (see XXIX, n. 19), Da Ponte had turned a friendly face to Mozart and presented him with a text (drawn from the Psalms) to which he, pressed by overwork, adapted the Kyrie and Gloria of the C-minor mass;[15] composer and poet then added two new arias to the ingenius fabrication. It should not surprise that a cantata born under such stars evinced few traces of the refined matching of music and word that would characterize their *Figaro.*

They had its libretto in hand early in the autumn of 1785, for by November Mozart described himself to Leopold as "over neck and head" in composition. That at this moment Count Rosenberg felt it necessary to prod the effort along would indicate his at first contemplating *Figaro* as a Carnival presentation. But just as, some four years earlier, he and the Emperor, yielding to Gluck's faction, had put off the production of *The Abduction,* so now they turned to Valencia-born Vicente Martin y Soler: newly arrived and trailing the glory of a train of successful operas, he received the Carnival commission, a setting of *Il burbero di buon cuore* (whose

---

14 During the summer of 1784, he had spoken of composing a new setting of *La Betulia liberata* for the Society and looked forward to availing himself of ideas from his version of 1771: "Perhaps I can employ bits and pieces of it here and there." The project came to nothing.

15 A mass of its complications, scale, and weight would have received a sympathetic reception in few of Vienna's churches: Joseph II expected services to follow his reforms demanding a simple musical setting that left the text exposed. (Even had Colloredo and Mozart reconciled, the C-minor mass would have found no warmer welcome in Salzburg cathedral, with its similar musical aesthetic; a monastery church, Salzburg's St. Peter's, where the premiere of the mass took place, had direction of its own worship.) The desire to lighten his labors apart, in converting the mass into an oratorio, Mozart clutched at an opportunity to give what would otherwise become a silent score some kind of practical existence. (Only with the death in 1790 of Joseph and the accession of Leopold II, who made allowances for church music in the grand manner, did Mozart return to it in the Kyrie, K. 341/368a, and his Requiem; see p. 755.) Richness of style had also become suspect in the decoration of churches. A mandate of Elector Max Joseph of Bavaria (1770) had enjoined "a pure and regular architecture eliminating all superfluous stuccowork and other often nonsensical and ridiculous ornaments," the goal being Winckelmann's "noble simplicity": so much for the theatrical, often playful, but nonetheless sacred architectural rhetoric of such monuments as Die Wies and Vierzehnheiligen.

text Da Ponte took as plunder from Goldoni's French comedy *Le bourru bienfaisant*). As had been the case during the Gluck festival, some of the very musicians Mozart required became caught up in another composer's rehearsals. *Il burbero*, given its premiere on 4 January 1786, proved a hit, drawing full houses and quite consuming the energies of the Italian troupe. Though by this time much of *Figaro* stood complete, its postponement became an undisguised blessing, giving Mozart the gift of leisure in which to ponder and perfect his score.

A second Imperial behest also played a part in delaying *Figaro's* arrival at the Burgtheater: Mozart received a command to contribute a singspiel to a royal entertainment and answered with *The Impresario*, K. 486, to a text by the younger Stephanie. A banquet was to take place in the orangery of Schönbrunn in honor of visitors dear to Emperor Joseph: his sister Maria Christina and her husband, Albert, now rulers of the Austrian Lowlands (see XIV n. 23). On 7 February 1786, the reunited royals, along with the highest nobility of Vienna, dined to music from Salieri's *La grotta di Trofonio* as played by Joseph's *Harmonie*. The repast over, the entire company heard *The Impresario* performed on a stage set up at one end of the very long hall and then, once retainers had moved the chairs, settled down before a second stage at the opposite end to witness the premiere of Salieri's *Prima la musica e poi le parole* (First the Music, then the Text). This one-act *opera buffa* treated of the difficulties involved in the collaboration of composer and librettist (using *Prima la musica* as his point of departure, Richard Strauss would probe this aesthetic question in his last opera, *Capriccio)*, while Mozart's slender one-act singspiel concerned the egotism of performers. The Emperor had suggested both subjects, and their exploration offered the opportunity to show off to his sister the best of his Italian and German singers and, in particular, his German actors: they dominated *The Impresario.*

Its action revolves about a series of auditions given before an impresario forming a touring company. (That it has received a contract to open in Salzburg may have been Mozart's idea: references to the provincialism to be endured do not lack.)[16] Hopeful actors offer recitations from popular

---

16 Over and above the prescriptive Viennese denigration of Salzburg, the reference to the archbishopric reflected the Emperor's new scheme to shape its future. The impending bankruptcy of the House of Zweibrücken (see p. 392) had inspired him to return to his dream of exchanging the Austrian Lowlands for Bavaria (see p. 472), the wheels of the negotiations now to be oiled by the payment of three million florins to the ruined princes. Much of the bargaining seemed like a revival of his plan of 1778–1779, except that, in addition, he now called for the Habsburgs' annexation of Salzburg, for which they, in compensation, offered Archbishop Colloredo possession of Luxemburg, Limburg, and the bishopric of Lüttich (Liège). At Versailles, Marie

plays, two sopranos quarrel over precedence as a tenor seeks to mediate, and, in the end, under the impresario's threat to disband the company even before it sets out, all agree to put selfish ambitions aside. That in life the singers impersonating the prima donnas, Aloisia Lange and Caterina Cavalieri, enjoyed a fierce rivalry constituted the main fun of the piece, which, when translated to the Kärntnertortheater, would titillate the public no less than it did the palace.

If Giambattista Casti's delightful reverence for the absurd furnished *Prima la musica* with a witty situation and clever lines—the role of the librettist poked fun at Da Ponte, whose job Casti coveted—Stephanie's smaller talent had put together a blunt, disjointed affair wanting any intellectual purpose. The book's power to amuse depended upon coarse topical allusions laid on with a trowel—audiences loved them—the musical requirements demanding of Mozart only an overture, a dazzling aria apiece for the contentious ladies, and two ensembles. The quality of craftsmanship he invested in this clumsy trifle astounds, in particular the overture. Of a scale, indeed grandeur, suitable to a major work, it offers brilliant part-writing as does the trio for sopranos and tenor. The closing singspiel-style vaudeville apart, the score of *The Impresario* took nourishment from the contemporary *Figaro*.[17]

As his labors on it drew to a close, Mozart busied himself with *The Impresario* and also with a private operatic production: he revised *Idomeneo* for an amateur concert performance to be presented on 13 March 1786 in Prince Johann Adam Auersperg's private theater. The main changes concerned the castrato part of Idamante: Mozart adjusted its range and idiom to the tenor voice of a certain Pulini, for whom he composed a grand new aria with solo violin (*"Non più/ Non temer,"* K. 490; see n. 46)[18] to supersede the Idomeneo-Arbace scene in the second act; and he replaced the lovers' third-act duet with a new one (*"Spiegarti non poss'io"*; K. 489). These substitutions, for which Da Ponte provided the verse, have none of the air of alien intrusions: turning from the mordant world of *Figaro*, he picked up

---

Antoinette urged France's support of the grand barter, which the Mozarts favored for the pleasure of celebrating not only Colloredo's exit from Salzburg but Joseph's lordship over it. Karl Theodore of Bavaria showed himself open to discussions, which collapsed when a new league of German princes (1785) opposed their Emperor's second self-interested proposal to refashion the Reich.

17 Not only *The Impresario* but also *Prima la musica* stood in its way: so many members of the Emperor's theatrical establishment had become involved in the banquet entertainments that, until Maria Christina and Albert's visit belonged to the past, preparations for mounting *Figaro* could not begin in earnest.

18 Mozart would put the text of K. 490 to use again in K. 505; see p. 661.

the same enchanted brush with which he had first painted the fresh and luminous atmosphere encompassing Ilia and Idamante and at once found his way back, retaining the consistency of the whole.

The Auersperg *Idomeneo* had been well under way when, on 19 February 1786, Mozart made his remarkable appearance at a masked ball in the Hofburg's Redoutensaal. Dressed in the robes of an eastern philosopher, he paused to distribute to the public copies of a sheet containing riddles and proverbs.[19] Though from his pen, he put them forth as "Excerpts from the Fragments of Zoroaster." In the tradition of Shakespeare's riddles and of respectable literary artifice, Mozart's propound their enigmas in a nexus of images that at bottom speak of dislocation, self-censure, loss, and longing for catharsis, the still-unresolved conflict with the father their deep, underlying impulse: the return to *Idomeneo* had reawakened the oedipal theme and its pain. Mozart sent the broadside to Leopold, who made much of the sententious proverbs and passed it on to Nannerl and to Salzburg's *Oberdeutsche Staatszeitung.* (This newspaper published excerpts from it without the author's name.) Perhaps Leopold overpraised the proverbs to balance his refusal to face the disturbing undercurrents flowing through the riddles: "Your brother" wrote them, he assured Nannerl, ". . . only in fun."

The figure parading in exotic costume was also bound up with the disruptive changes that of late had overtaken Viennese Freemasonry. Almost overnight its standing had shifted in Habsburg eyes. Although the Emperor's aims coincided at many points with the Order's, he never—as had his father—became a member: he had long feared its secrecy and possible growth into an autonomous force strong enough to endanger the survival of his family's prerogatives. Late in 1785 he had taken protective measures, convinced that by this time the body of Freemasonry harbored diseased cells ready to spread the contagion of atheism and radicalism. Those of his subjects embracing variants of an extended Freemasonry gave him most cause for either contempt or alarm. In particular the Rosicrucians and the Illuminati: both had a presence in Viennese lodges.

The first, pursuing a poetical search for virtue through a mystical striving mixing Enlightened philosophy with excursions into the cabbala and alchemy, awakened Joseph's scorn of "mumbo jumbo"; but he developed a serious mistrust of the second, regarding as conspiratorial its grafting of

---

19 Mozart's obsession with games and puzzles informs the supper scene of *Don Giovanni,* where the unsung words of a series of popular operatic tunes probe the action in a commentary to be unriddled.

libertarian, egalitarian politics onto the aristocratic and high bourgeois rituals and ethos of traditional Freemasonry; this faction had become a refuge of the literate and affluent—men in the mold of von Born.

A master of satire—Pezzl described him as imbued with "the spirit of Lucian and Swift"—von Born shared the Emperor's sarcastic disdain of Rosicrucian doctrine, decrying its labyrinthian wanderings that had misled "many good Brothers from the straight path to the pool of folly, from which they believe themselves to be quaffing wisdom. . . ." At the same time, as Vienna's most famous Freemason—and a clandestine member of the Bavarian Illuminati—he opposed Joseph's sudden move to hem in every Masonic establishment: on 11 December 1785, the Emperor had decreed a drastic reorganization of all lodges under Habsburg dominion, those in Vienna being reduced to three at most, a consolidation serving both to break up cliques (thus encouraging resignations) and, most important, to facilitate governmental supervision.[20]

A significant number of members fell away—by the end of August 1786, von Born, himself, had withdrawn—but many, among them Mozart, for whom the lodge had become a reassuring, indeed, indispensable element in life (and who, perhaps, shared the Emperor's apprehensions), attempted to find their place in the amalgamated units. Mozart joined the Zur neugekrönten Hoffnung (New-crowned Hope) and to open and close its first session on 14 January 1786, provided a pair of songs to words by Augustin Veith: K. 483, "Zerfliesset" and K. 484, "Ihr unsre," both for tenor, chorus, and keyboard. Pervaded by Rosicrucian speculations, Zur neugekrönten Hoffnung saw itself as a temple of virtue enfolding the humanitarian goals of Enlightened morality; with no prejudice to his Catholic core, Mozart settled into the comfortable and comforting embrace of this Rosicrucian-tinged lodge.

Little more than a month had separated its inaugural meeting and his stepping forth in the Redoutensaal costumed as sage and lawgiver, a symbol bringing into notice the survival of the Order in Vienna with foundations intact, the Brothers their living stones. He did not survive to discover the error of this gesture: in the aftermath of the French Revolution, Viennese Freemasonry would become at all points suspect, and the Habsburgs would undo it.

---

20 Behind closed doors, Masons held free discussions, voted on issues according to their own laws, and selected or removed their leaders by ballot. These practices, in effect a school of constitutional governance, hardly recommended themselves to Joseph II, despite the fact that at the time a Mason swore allegiance to his lodge he received assurances of its abjuring anything hostile to "state, sovereign, religion, or public decency."

During April 1786, he put the last note to *Figaro,* already in production at the Burgtheater.[21] The dress rehearsal took place in the Emperor's presence on the twenty-ninth,[22] the premiere under Mozart's direction on 1 May. (After the first or second repetition the baton passed to the twenty-year-old Joseph Weigl, one of the regulars, along with his mentor, Salieri, at van Swieten's matinees.) Da Ponte and Mozart had hoped to give Vienna, in the former's words, "an, as it were, new kind of spectacle"—a connoisseur's work. They did not disappoint, although the opera's great length did evoke complaints along with the inevitable grumbling about the complicated orchestral writing. Finer ears, however, recognized an unsurpassed masterpiece.

In his Italian operas, Mozart, with scattered exceptions, had hitherto rendered the emotions of his characters by means of traditional juxtapositions of aria, recitative, and ensemble. The *Figaro* comedy had stirred him to turn from this seriate edifice to one made up of ongoing, animated, dovetailed sections, the ensemble becoming the most potent force in a new aesthetic of surging movement (see pp. 338–39). His contrapuntal studies had vouchsafed him the ability to weave together musical lines of individual character and tonal gesture, each strand with a life of its own and at the same time contributing to ensembles tersely fitted together and embracing every variety of combination. Bearing the action along, the musical current flows forward, only slowing to part around the arias, islands of stability that channel but do not dam the tonal stream. With the interchange between instrument and singer grown so intimate that one has no less part than the other in responding to the volatile ins and outs of the plot, the vocal and orchestral lines twine, separate, and reunite in confrontation, opposition, and accommodation—an ever-changing, effortless interlacing. The signature of the mature Mozartean style, to reach its apogee in the finale of the Jupiter Symphony, first shone forth with full brilliance and, above all, ease, in *The Marriage of Figaro.*

Da Ponte's witness that the Emperor thought the opera "divine" can be

---

21 Throughout much of March the company poured its strength into preparing the Viennese premiere of *La serva padrona,* not Pergolesi's, but the setting Paisiello had composed for the court of Catherine the Great (1781). His spirit hovers over Mozart's *Figaro,* many of its passages forming parallels, indeed, a series of musical homages to the score of Paisiello's *Barber:* Mozart wanted the Viennese to experience not only literary but also musical continuity between it and his *Figaro.* He had an enduring admiration of Paisiello.

22 Anecdotes describing Count Rosenberg's attempts to wreck the production derive from an elaborate invention in Da Ponte's memoirs, one from first to last at odds with the procedures and logistics of the Imperial theaters.

trusted, for in June Joseph summoned the cast to perform it on the intimate stage of Laxenburg castle. He had the pleasure of instructing the Burgtheater that at representations of *Figaro* the arias alone might be repeated at the audience's insistence; to answer calls also to reprise the ensembles would prolong the performances beyond reason.

For all such enthusiasm, the success remained of a special kind—one for cognoscenti. The general public made much more of Martín y Soler's *Una cosa rara* (to a book by Da Ponte): from the fall of the curtain at the premiere (17 November 1786), it proved so strong at the box office that *Figaro*, crowded out, dropped from the repertory for the next two seasons.[23] Mozart would acknowledge the reversal with delicious wit in the supper scene of *Don Giovanni*: "Bravi! [It's] *Cosa rara!*" Leporello cries as he hears Giovanni's *Harmonie*-musicians strike up a tune from its first finale.

Mozart preserved countenance and humor in the face of *Figaro*'s temporary eclipse. And the early months of the year had brought him particular joy as a teacher: by this time the eight-year-old Johann Nepomuk Hummel, bursting with talent, resided as a student in the Camesina House. Mozart refused payment for board or lessons, and Constanze fussed with the boy as if he were her own. The second half of 1786, however, saw two incidents painful for the Mozarts: their third son, Johann Thomas Leopold, born on 18 October,[24] suffered suffocating convulsions and lived only twenty-eight days; and at this very time they became tangled in an ugly contretemps with Leopold.

During his weeks in Vienna, he had learned of their plan for a tour. He feared that they would count upon his taking Carl Thomas into his charge during their absence, and, lest the residence of Nannerl's son in the Tanzmeisterhaus furnish a precedent, did his utmost to keep the fact from them. In time, the Mozarts' request that he perform the good office did arrive, and on 17 November he described to Nannerl "a most *emphatic letter*" he had just sent her brother "inasmuch as he puts to me the not inconsiderable proposition that I assume the care of *his two children*"[25] halfway through Carnival, when the parents "would like to start on a journey through Germany to England." He regretted that, through a certain Herr Miller, Wolfgang had learned "something about which I never wrote [to

---

23 Aristocrats hostile to Beaumarchais's play did not have the power to block the opera's way, their number balanced at the least by a public eager to experience some version of the notorious comedy: rather, *Una cosa rara* proved the immediate hindrance to *Figaro*'s walking over the course in Vienna.
24 Johann Thomas von Trattner stood godfather at the baptism in the cathedral.
25 Leopold could not yet know that Johann Thomas Leopold had died two days earlier.

him]: that the child [Nannerl's] is with me. As a result [of Miller's indiscretion], this capital idea occurred to him or perhaps to his wife. Not a bad arrangement! They set out, travel, perhaps even die, or remain in England [and require] me to run after them with the children etc." Moreover, he scoffed at the fee offered to cover board and the cost of extra servants.

That Leopold declined to give Mozart's progeny quarters in the Tanzmeisterhaus, even as Nannerl's resided there, betokened the end to whatever stirrings of reconciliation the stay in Vienna had awakened. Leopold, anticipating a resentful Wolfgang's long silence, wrote Nannerl on 29 November: "I have no letter from your brother . . . and don't expect to receive one soon, even though I explained everything to him in the most tender way."[26] Leopold saw no parity between the St. Gilgin and Vienna households: the first he regarded as loyal; not so the second, with which he had ventured a truce, not a permanent peace.

The failure of the London journey to occur cannot be ascribed to Leopold, however much his rebuff wounded and frustrated Mozart. Indeed, for a time, expectations of a triumphant tour had soared: the project had received support from his British friends in Vienna, who included two of the singers in *Figaro*, Ann Storace (Susanna) and Michael Kelly (Don Basilio and Don Curzio), as well as Ann's brother, the composer Stephen Storace,[27] and Thomas Attwood, Mozart's pupil (a protégé of the Prince of Wales). They all planned to return to England in the near future, and Constanze and Wolfgang had hoped to travel with them.[28] Although Attwood did make efforts to arrange matters in London, Mozart received no formal invitation, and without it the long journey would have been a financial hazard. For all that, consolation came at the end of the year.

3

MOZART'S NAME HAD been famous in Prague since the autumn of 1782, when its citizens applauded *The Abduction* as given by Karl Wahr's traveling troupe. Early in December 1786 they acclaimed *Figaro* to the skies in a pro-

---

26 Twelve days had sufficed to transform "most emphatic" (*nachdrücklich*, which also enfolds associations of insistence and warning) into "tender" (*liebreich*).

27 He had attended the conservatory of St. Onofrio in Naples. Prodded by his sister, the Burgtheater produced two of his operas (*Gli sposi malcontenti*, 1785, the libretto by Brunati; and *Gli equivoci*, 1786, its text a French translation of Shakespeare's *The Comedy of Errors* as put into Italian by Da Ponte). The orchestration of both owes a debt to Mozart, who no doubt became Stephen's mentor.

28 As late as 12 January 1787 Leopold wrote Nannerl: "The talk from Vienna, Prague, and Munich affirms that your brother will travel to England."

duction by Pasquale Bondini's company, now resident in the handsome new (1783) Nostitz theater.[29] Mozart received an invitation to visit the city on the part of its orchestra and "a society of *distinguished* connoisseurs and enthusiasts," over which hovered the figure of his patron and friend old Count Thun.

Even with his wide travels, Mozart had yet to set foot in this Habsburg provincial capital. It provided few opportunities for high patronage: many of its greatest families—the Lobkowitz, Hartig, Czernin, and Kinsky among them—preferred their country seats during summer, their Viennese palaces in winter, and dispensed their most bountiful largess not on the Moldau but on the Danube. Count Thun, on the other hand, figured among the handful of them who took up residence in Prague on a regular basis.[30]

Under the circumstances it should not surprise that a large number of Bohemia's finest musicians continued to make their way to centers such as Munich, Paris, and Vienna (see p. 99). They left behind a stolid musical life that stirred in fits and starts with stimuli from abroad: the widely spaced visits of the Imperial court, touring virtuosos, and wandering theatrical troupes. But *Figaro*, mounted by a company that not long before had sunk roots into the city, sent a new spirit sweeping through it: not only the opera's musical qualities but also its rebellious political tone delighted more than a few in a populace upon whom Vienna's hand at times weighed clumsily. Slavic nationalist aspirations hid not far beneath the surface: in the face of the German language's hegemony in Prague's cultural life, by 1786 a troupe of actors giving plays in Czech had begun to perform in their own theater. Close behind this development, the Germans of Prague hailed Mozart as "the German Apollo" to whom "the German fatherland extends its hand." The French-Italian libretto of *Figaro* notwithstanding, they viewed him in the light of *The Abduction*, that is, as a Teutonic champion opening the way for Germany's reconciliation with its own traditions (*mit Germaniens Musen*). More than one motive lay behind Prague's enthusiasm to behold the creator of *Figaro*—daring and needle-witted—whom both parties hoped might stay.

Early in the morning of 8 January 1787, the Mozarts left Vienna for Prague with a veritable entourage (see n. 57) divided between two coaches:

---

29 Before its construction, the troupe had used smaller houses, among them the private theater in the Thun palace. With his own money Franz Anton, Count Nostitz-Rieneck, had sponsored the construction of the splendid new opera house, the "National theater" his heirs would sell to the Bohemian Estates. The new Prague company also performed during the summer in Dresden and Leipzig.

30 He may well have persuaded Bondini to produce *Figaro*.

their servant Joseph, their dog Gaukerl, the violinists Franz de Paula Hofer and Kaspar Ramlo, the clarinet virtuoso Anton Paul Stadler, and the thirteen-year-old vocal, piano, and violin prodigy Maria Anna Crux, along with her aunt and chaperon, Elizabeth Barbara Qualenberg.[31] Word games helped pass the hours on the road, and each ended with a nonsense name, Mozart's, for example, Punkititi, Constanze's Schabla Pumfa, and the dog's Schamanuzky.[32] The party arrived in Prague on the eleventh and, after an evening at the Zu den drei goldenen Löwen, Mozart and Constanze, at Count Thun's insistence, moved into his palace, his orchestra welcoming the couple with music after lunch.

Prague beheld a composer's royal progress. At the ball given every Thursday (by Franz Joseph Anton, Freiherr von Bretfeld zu Cronenburg) Mozart beheld the beauties of the city dancing "to music from *Figaro* turned into plausible contredanses and German dances . . . ; here they talk of nothing but *Figaro*; play, blow, sing or whistle nothing but *Figaro*; go to no opera but *Figaro* and always *Figaro*:[33] a great compliment to me, to be sure."

On 17 January he attended *Figaro* at the Nostitz (Johann Joseph Strobach conducting, as he had the Prague premiere) and two days later answered a universal request by giving a concert during which his keyboard improvisations, in particular those upon Figaro's aria *"Non più andrai,"* made an overwhelming impression;[34] so did his most recent symphony (K. 504), completed in Vienna at the close of 1786 in all likelihood for a series of Advent concerts at the Trattnerhof.

It has been conjectured that K. 504 came into being in reverse: that, having made an attempt to travel a shortcut to a new symphony by fitting out the "Paris" with a fresh finale, he then went on to prefix two new movements to it. But K. 504 gives the impression of taking its rise from the opening Allegro's introduction, a monitory Adagio having the character of a herald to some solemn, mysterious ceremony; and though the Allegro manipulates the theme Clementi would claim as his own after it appeared in *The Magic Flute* (see XXVIII, n. 26), on the whole, the spirit coloring the work derives from *Figaro*, the Andante being an instrumental bel-canto aria

31 With characteristic generosity Mozart sought to open opportunities in Prague for the four musicians. Fräulein Crux, who with this journey began a northern tour, performed at the Thun palace.
32 His thoughts turning toward a pupil left behind in Vienna, Mozart sent him word of the new name the company had bestowed upon him: Franz Jakob Freystädtler became Gaulimauli.
33 Hyperbole, of course: he did attend—if not quite hear (see X, n. 7)—Paisiello's *Le gare generose.*
34 They vanished into the air of that Prague night: the fast tempo of the visit left him no time in which to reconstruct them after the concert, his usual procedure as to important extempore variations.

mixing joy and tragedy, the closing Presto returning echoes of motifs in the opera, references much appreciated by Prague's *"Figaro*-mad" public.

From the time Prague's connoisseurs first heard *The Abduction*, they marveled at its harmonic and instrumental richness,[35] qualities brought to an even higher level in *Figaro* and now no less in K. 504. The idea of the symphony as drama, as an affair of high purpose, as a tonal and moral universe, concepts Mozart affirmed as early as his Storm and Stress days and then put aside, had roused themselves in the Linz Symphony and then resurged with imaginative force: K. 504 vibrated with the transcendental overtones of the three final symphonies to come. The city burst into enthusiasm over a work that would become known as the Prague Symphony.

On the twenty-second, an audience, beside itself, heard him conduct *Figaro*. Singers, orchestra, and the cheers gave him pleasure, but, even so, he longed for Vienna and, indeed, had to be there in time for Nancy Storace's farewell. Before his departure (about 8 February)[36] he came to an understanding with Bondini and his former assistant and now partner, Domenico Guardasoni, to provide the Nostitz with a new opera for the coming season and made his exit with one thousand gulden in profit; so Leopold learned from his son's British friends.

They had left for England within hours of Storace's parting salutation to Vienna on 23 February 1787 in the Burgtheater, Mozart presiding. The program would seem to have included the imposing grand scena, among his finest, composed for her some two weeks before his journey to Prague: the recitative and aria *"Ch'io mi scordi di te? / Non temer, amato bene"*(That I will forget you? Do not fear it, beloved; K. 505; see n. 18), which enclosed piano obbligatos no doubt intended for his own fingers on the affecting occasion.

The comment he wrote when entering this heartfelt aria, its text from the revised *Idomeneo*, into his thematic catalogue—"for Mademoiselle Storace and myself"—has given rise to the supposition of a romance between them. K. 505, however, reflected the mutual regret of devoted colleagues to say good-bye, the concerto-like piano passages injected into the vocal-orchestral fabric a symbol of their professional collaboration. Though official word maintained that the Hofburg had banished her husband (see XXX, n. 21) for abusing her, the Viennese voiced the opinion that the Emperor had a quite different reason for sending him on his way; and rumor linked her not only to Joseph but also to the bass-baritone Francesco Benucci (the first Figaro) and, of late, to William Harry, Lord

---

35 Prague prided itself upon the excellence of its wind players, who reveled in Mozart's scores.
36 Some days earlier he had written, in all likelihood for a ball at the Pachta palace, a set of six German dances (K. 509), one linked to the other by modulating passages.

Barnard, one day to be Earl of Darlington and then Duke of Cleveland. This gossip traveled the streets, and, had the slightest thread of scandal linked her name to Mozart's, the Viennese would have spared neither their sarcasm.

Zinzendorf wrote of hearing a "rather boring bravura aria"—no doubt K. 505!—at the concert, which added three thousand florins to the fortune the prima donna had already gathered in Vienna. On the spot, she set out westward in the company of her mother and brother, along with Kelly, Attwood, and an unknown Englishman. They traveled in two stately coaches, each drawn by four horses and loaded down with a mass of baggage worthy of a royal retinue. (An attendant rode in advance to prepare for the next relays of fresh horses and proper accommodations.) This cavalcade appeared in Salzburg on 26 February 1787 before Leopold Mozart's astonished eyes.

Nancy stayed long enough to sing for the Archbishop and receive his handsome gift. Leopold showed the sights to the visitors and from them learned how high his son's hopes continued to soar for an English tour: once back home, Attwood, through his royal connections, was to arrange a contract. In a letter to his pupil and warm friend Emilian Gottfried von Jacquin, Mozart hinted that he and Constanze might well make London their home. (Leopold's fear had not been idle: that of having to deliver Carl across the Channel were the child to become his responsibility.) Laying the groundwork for engagements abroad[37] derived from Mozart's facing the fact of ebbing attendance at his concerts:[38] indeed, he appears to have had difficulty gathering subscribers to his Advent series of 1786. The pattern became unmistakable the following year, when he had need of not even a single new piano concerto. A passing but long view of his Viennese achievements in this genre—some of them already touched upon—reveals his dilemma in high relief.

4

THAT TRIO OF piano concertos he had written in 1782, K. 413, 414, and 415, had sounded but a modest prelude to his astounding sequence of no fewer than six composed in the course of 1784. They fell into two groups,

---

37 Through Attwood's efforts, the London concert manager Robert May O'Reilly would make a splendid offer in 1790 (see pp. 718–19).

38 *The Abduction* continued playing to full and enthusiastic houses, but they brought him not a florin (see XVII, n. 36). Teaching and the concert platform provided the basis of Mozart's living.

each of three: K. 449 (the "first Ployer"), 450, and 451 comprising one cluster; K. 453, (the "second Ployer"), 456 (the "Paradis"), and 459 (the "first Coronation") the other. The Viennese piano concertos continued with two more units of three: K. 466 (the D minor), 467, and 482, all in 1785, and, the next year, K. 488, 491 (the C minor), and 503. In 1788, K. 537 (the "second Coronation") appeared,[39] and early in 1791 he entered his final piano concerto, K. 595, in his catalogue.

Mozart poured the piano concertos of 1784 from similar molds, the varied charm and richness of their individual chasing notwithstanding. The D minor opened the sequence of crowning concertos, each of distinctive character and all with prodigious interchanges and collaborations between piano and orchestra, passages often taking on the attributes of lofty and powerful debate. In these works an emotional narrative unfolds: the opening movement of K. 466, in particular, offers a sense of surging, foreboding drama; midst their menacing rolls of thunder and flashes of lightning, soloist and instrumentalists lead the listener all but to expect the likes of Neptune's monster, Don Giovanni's stone guest, or the Queen of the Night to materialize. On pedestals no less lofty stand K. 491 and 503, not so theatrical and stormy but of a new spaciousness of design and with a marked richness of symphonic argument—of instrumentation, too, as respects the first, which includes clarinets as well as oboes.

At first the avidity of the Viennese to hear Mozart had required him to add to his repertory of concertos. The dramatic drop in production after 1786 reflected not only the extent to which other genres, in particular opera, consumed his creative energies but also the degree to which his novelty as a pianist had gone stale. (Toward the end of 1787, Franz Kratter remarked that "this splendid artist" did not take in enough at a concert "to meet costs.") In addition, political factors determined by Catherine of Russia would dictate that many of his subscribers absent themselves from the capital for a time. But before this remarkable turn of events, he provided Prague with the promised opera, a commission the Emperor bent to his own purposes.

5

EARLY IN FEBRUARY 1787, when Bondini and Guardasoni offered Mozart the *scrittura* for Prague's coming winter season, it must have been understood that the premiere would serve Habsburg policy. By the summer,

---

39 Mozart played K. 459 and 537 in Frankfurt during the days of festivity celebrating the coronation of Leopold of Austria as Holy Roman Emperor (October 1790; see p. 715).

Joseph had set into motion final plans for the pair of weddings long impending in the immediate family of his brother Leopold of Tuscany: the marriages of his eldest daughter, Maria Theresia (to the heir to the Saxon throne, Anton Clemens) and of his son Francis (to Elizabeth of Württemberg). To mark these events the Emperor commissioned two operas at the Burgtheater and also sanctioned a third proposed by the Bohemian Estates in Prague for performance in the Nostitz: Salieri had the task of reworking his recent Parisian success, *Tarare*, which, renamed *Axur rè d'Ormus*, was to salute the Habsburg-Württemberg union (soon put off until January 1788); Martin y Soler embarked upon *L'arbore di Diana* to celebrate the arrival in Vienna, early in October, of the Princess en route to Saxony; and, since the Hofburg's schedule required her to depart Vienna for Dresden in the company of her brother Francis, there to meet and wed Anton Clemens (to whom she had already been joined by proxy in Florence), the third opera was to be given during a break in their journey at Prague: sister and brother were to hear the first performance of Mozart's *Don Giovanni*. Da Ponte had charge of all three librettos.[40] The first two reflected traditional Imperial taste; the last, the tale of a mythical dissolute, would appear at first glance a strange affair to set before a princess-bride; the background of the decision to do so must be examined.

At the very time Mozart's visit to Prague drew to a close, Giuseppe Gazzaniga's *Don Giovanni*, to a text by Giovanni Bertati, had its successful premiere in Venice. Gazzaniga wrote the title role for the tenor Antonio Baglioni,[41] whose next engagement took him to Prague. No doubt he arrived during the summer with the score of this *Don Giovanni* and hopes of repeating his Venetian triumph. Bondini and Guardasoni took to the libretto but could not use Gazzaniga's music: they already had a commitment to Mozart and sent the book to him. Drawn to the text, he agreed to use it, but only as reworked and expanded—it had only one act—by Da Ponte. (One of the directors had to have gone to Vienna for consultations.) The Emperor, against expectation, did not take exception to the well-worn folktale, for it would embellish not the weighty *opera-seria* business of a coronation or marriage ceremony but a fleeting royal visit. Prague received the Imperial *placet*; to ensure it, the management of the Nostitz had Da Ponte prepare for the Hofburg a version of his new libretto shorn of the cries of "*Viva la libertà* (see p. 46). Although dropping the second half of Act I, indeed, showing it as ending midway through the quartet

---

40 His Italian adaptation of *Tarare* represented his second refashioning of a work by Beaumarchais.
41 He is not to be confused with Francesco Baglioni, the famous Bolognese tenor, to whom he may have been related.

"*Non ti fidar*," the misrepresentation appears not to have aroused the censors' suspicions: the act did not seem too short.

It has been suggested that at first Mozart saw *Don Giovanni* in terms of four acts: perhaps the first ending with Anna's "*Or sai chi l'onore*," the second with the ballroom scene, the third with the sextet in the courtyard, the fourth with the sextet in the ruins. At the last, he decided upon a twofold division; his purpose: to strengthen the forward, hard-driving flow of a libretto patched together out of a series of disparate episodes, some of them no more than vignettes, a structure the very antipode to that of Beaumarchais's *Figaro*, calibrated with precision. Da Ponte pilfered as much as possible from Bertati's short text and then, to account for a full evening, enlarged upon, indeed, padded this material not only with gleanings from Tirso, Molière, and Goldoni[42] but also with his own inventions.

They, as his *Il rico* for Salieri and the final act of *Figaro* had demonstrated, did not as yet show at his best this master of adaptation and adaptive translation.[43] Mozart's unified, fast-paced score disguises the spatchcocked nature of the libretto by covering its seams and propelling it hurtling toward Giovanni's downfall. Da Ponte's considerable artistic virtues resided in verse that kindled Mozart's imagination and provided him opportunities to seize the dramatic moment and draw his portraits in music. No doubt the literary architecture that brought into being the opera's extraordinary succession of ensembles—in particular, the exhilarating musical complexities of the ballroom scene—must be accounted Mozart's, although throughout the drama composer and poet worked as one in maintaining a balance of comedy and tragedy by fusing rather than alternating them.

Synthesis had become an ever stronger element in Mozart's aesthetic. No less than *Don Giovanni*, his instrumental works pursued a dialectic of, on the one hand, an incantatory lyricism and, on the other, an almost sacerdotal gravity at moments spilling into the tragic. These constituents—often touched with sardonic humor—merge into a process that opens, in particular to those at home in the realm of the Hegelian absolute, vast vistas of universal moral law and ultimate truth and assumes the quality of a summons through the Red Sea. Among composers, Mozart, in particular, awakens transcendent reactions of this kind.

---

42 Da Ponte's main sources comprised: Bertati's *Don Giovanni Tenorio ossia Il convitato di pietra* (1787); Goldoni's *Don Giovanni Tenorio ossia il dissoluto* (1736); Molière's *Dom Juan, ou Le festin de pierre* (1665); and Tirso de Molina's *El burlador de Sevilla y convidado de piedra* (c. 1618).
43 *L'arbore di Diana* (1787) was his first original libretto, *Così fan tutte* (1790) his second.

During the period of labor upon *Don Giovanni*—in terms of his short life, his autumn—he turned to the string quintet, a genre not much cultivated, perhaps because it presented problems of balance: Boccherini's solution lay in strengthening the deepest sounds by adding another cello to the instruments of the string quartet; Michael Haydn's in enhancing the mid-area of resonance by calling upon a second viola. This latter practice became Mozart's: in 1773 he had created the string quintet K. 174, an isolated example begun in the wake of his third and last Italian journey and then revised later in the year, close upon that stay in Vienna when the lively dialogue of Joseph Haydn's newest works had caught his ear.[44] In the spring of 1787 he revisited the string quintet, composing K. 515 in C (April) and K. 516 in G minor (May), a pair of four-movement masterpieces uniting symphonic dimension with the intimacy of the quartet,[45] the first expansive in mood and of sovereign ease and heroic proportion, the second, save its concluding Allegro, tragic in tone and of that poignant, desolate beauty already laid bare two months earlier in the Rondo for piano in A minor, K. 511. Its harmonies at moments suggest the coming century, which, indeed, soon knocked at Mozart's door.

On 7 April 1787, the sixteen-year-old Ludwig van Beethoven arrived in Vienna in order, it appears certain, to put himself under Mozart's tutelage. The lessons may very well have begun, but within two weeks the youth had to return to Bonn to attend his dying mother. In any case, he had appeared at an inopportune moment: Mozart felt unwell during April; furthermore, at this very time, preparations had begun for the family's departure from the Camesina house for quarters across the Wien River in the Landstrasse suburb.

Commentators have taken up Leopold's view of this move as an act of

---

44 Michael Haydn's string quintet in C of early 1773 provided the immediate inspiration for K. 174, its revision being influenced not only by Joseph Haydn's methods but also by Michael's string quintet in G written at the end of the year. Both quintets went under the name notturno.

45 Before winter's end, he created a third by recasting for the same five string instruments a composition already in existence, that remarkable example of canonic virtuosity, the serenade K. 388, which in its new guise became K. 406/516b (see p. 585): under the pressure of work on *Don Giovanni* and its impending production, he resorted to transcription in order to have in hand a marketable set of three quintets. By April 1788, he began to offer them for sale on subscription in manuscript copies, which were to be had through application to his Masonic brother Johann Michael Puchberg. This commercial arrangement bespoke a decline in Mozart's fortunes to which Puchberg bore particular witness. A poor response led Mozart to sell the first two quintets to Artaria & Co. The transformed serenade shows a certain quirkiness: the change did not bring new shades of meaning or raise the polyphonic mathematics to a higher power.

retrenchment brought on by extravagance. Yet Mozart had returned from Prague some two months before with a well-lined purse and looked forward to one filled even fuller by the premiere at the Nostitz of *Don Giovanni*, attendant public appearances, and its production, to follow as a matter of course, at the Burgtheater. The disintegration of his subscription concerts no longer made his residence in the center of the city an expedient: the dizzying goings and comings of his piano belonged to the past. A spacious house with a large garden and in a quiet district may have seemed a beckoning refuge to a composer, his health languishing and over his head in work, and to his wife, again pregnant and occupied with their son of two and a half years.

This same spring Leopold Mozart died in Salzburg (28 May). Accounts (in all likelihood communicated by Nannerl's former suitor, d'Yppold) of his slow but conspicuous decline had reached Vienna as early as February. Mozart had written to him from Prague and, under cover of discussing the death of Count August Clemens Ludwig Hatzfeld, a young friend,[46] called into play the vocabulary of Masonic-Rosicrucian teachings, as well as those of Moses Mendelssohn, to touch upon the consoling aspects of death. Learning that this letter had gone astray, Mozart again took up the subject on 4 April 1787 (see pp. 30–31), his final surviving words to his father.

Wrestling with the idea of arriving just as death stood before the door, he entreated his father, "by all that is sacred," not to hide the truth should there be an abrupt cause for alarm: word must be sent, Mozart implored, "so that I may come to your arms as fast as humanly possible." Yet, while to the Marchands Leopold had confided his certainty that he would not live beyond summer, neither he nor Nannerl, who had arrived in Salzburg to tend him, sent a like message to Mozart. He, in fact, learned of Leopold's death not from her but from d'Yppold. The news shook him to the core: "You can imagine my state," he wrote Gottfried von Jacquin, his most intimate acquaintance since the death of Hatzfeld.

---

46 The Hatzfeld family offers a picture of the era's high level of musical amateurism. During Count August Clemens's visit to Vienna early in 1786, his mastery of the bow so impressed Mozart that he composed a solo for him: a violin obbligato set within the accompaniment to the new tenor aria for the revised *Idomeneo* (see p. 653). Its production also put to use the talents of Countess Maria Anna Hortensia Hatzfeld, wife of August Clemens's half-brother. She enjoyed a role in the musical worlds of both Bonn—August Clemens's birthplace—and Vienna. (It must be recalled that the former city had become an appanage of the latter; see p. 348.) In Bonn a patron of the young Beethoven, in Vienna she became one of Mozart's subscribers and took on the arduous part of Elettra in the Auersperg *Idomeneo*. She appears to have belonged to the Jacquin circle.

6

OF THE FRIENDSHIPS Mozart formed during his Vienna years, few had
the intensity of his attachment to Hatzfeld. It had grown within a few
months and found immediate reciprocation: a canon of Eichstätt cathedral,
he had, in fact, begun plans to pull up roots and settle in Vienna. His unexpected death touched Mozart to the quick, his sense of disappointment and
loss, however, counterbalanced by a brotherly and older affection for Gottfried von Jacquin (son of the botanist Nikolaus Joseph von Jacquin), functionary in the Bohemian chancellery and both Mozart's companion and his
student of composition. Mozart produced a group of works associated with
him, perhaps the most delightful of them *"Liebes Mandel, wo is's Bandel?"*
("My dear little husband, where is the little ribbon?), K. 441, for certain of
1786. This private entertainment in the form of a string-accompanied trio
for soprano (Constanze), tenor (Wolfgang), and bass (Gottfried) reveals that
overflowing wild humor and a passion for the madcap proved foremost
among the many parallels between Mozart's and Gottfried's spirits: in one
another's company they often presented the spectacle of perpetual students
on perpetual holiday; each lay under the other's spell.

The trio's text, Mozart's in Viennese dialect, derived from an incident in
his household: about to set forth, Constanze discovered that his recent gift
to her, a ribbon with which she smartened her outfits, had gone astray.
Husband and wife searched in a fine frenzy until the tall Gottfried arrived,
found the band, and teased the tiny couple by holding it aloft, forcing
them to leap up after it, their dog joining the confusion that mounted until
Gottfried relented midst cries, laughter, and barks. This merrymaking in
the spirit of Jan Steen leads one to imagine Gottfried as setting Mozart on
to that marvelous and malicious prank *A Musical Joke*, K. 522; begun in
1785, put aside, and completed two years later, this sextet (a string quartet
and two horns) held inept composers up to ridicule through a series of
gross musical solecisms.[47]

Gottfried also appears as a stimulus to serious creation. Mozart tailored
the aria *"Mentre ti lascio"* (K. 513 of March 1787, the text from the Paisiello-
Morbilli *La disfatta di Dario*, 1776) to Gottfried's excellent voice and at times

---

47 Thus the expounding of *A Musical Joke* as a malicious burlesque, a parody of his father as composer written in the wake of his death, splits upon the rock of chronology; so does, as a matter of course, the suggestion that he composed that perfect and nostalgic essay on rococo
musical elegance, the serenade for strings in G, K. 525 (which he entered in his catalogue on 10
August 1787 as *"Eine kleine Nachtmusik,"* a short notturno), in expiation of the calculated musical barbarisms of the *Joke*. Attempts to link it with his charming poem to his dead starling (4
June 1787) appear no less misguided.

permitted him to play the master's assistant, an indulgence that has led to confusion. Constanze declared the bass aria *"Io ti lascio "*(K. Anh. 245/621a of c. 1788) a product of their collaboration, and in the past Gottfried received credit for two of Mozart's songs of 1787: *"Als Luise,"* K. 520 (text by Gabriele von Baumberg) and *"Das Traumbild,"* K. 530 (the poetry: Ludwig Heinrich Christopher Hölty); they were, in fact, written for Gottfried, not by him, an understandable mix-up, for Mozart not only oversaw his student-friend's compositions but also on occasion winked at his plagiarism: passing off something by his teacher as his own in order to impress a ladylove. Again, according to Constanze, the two joined to write the five vocal (two sopranos and a bass) notturnos of 1787: K. 436–439 and K. 346/439a, all calling upon the color of the basset horn in their wind-trio accompaniments, the texts of these short love songs coming for the most part from Metastasio. Constanze may have misremembered in ascribing the vocal lines to Jacquin: the notturnos maintain Mozart's standards at all points. The following year he completed the set of six with K. 549.

For Gottfried's sister, Franziska, who studied piano with Mozart, he wrote K. 498 of August 1786, the trio (clarinet, viola, and piano) called *The Kegelstatt* (Skittle Alley), thanks to a shaky tradition to the effect that he sketched it in the course of a game.[48] He admired the "enthusiasm and zeal" she brought to the keyboard and, upon completing the piano sonata in C major for four hands (K. 521, May 1787), dispatched it to Gottfried with the injunction that it be sent on to her: she was "to make a shot at it right away, for it is a bit difficult." In all likelihood Mozart wrote K. 521 as a vehicle for them both, and the four-hand sonata of the preceding August, K. 497 in F, a work of the highest quality, with a slow, introspective introduction, might also have been meant for the Jacquins' circle.

It, too, appears to have been associated with the five divertimentos for a trio of basset horns or a pair of them (or clarinets) with a bassoon (K. Anh. 229/439b),[49] as does the quartet in A major, K. 298 (it awaits renumbering) for flute, violin, viola, and cello. Here he put to use thematic material from three sources: a song by the composer-publisher Franz Anton Hoffmeister, French folk music, and Paisiello's *Le gare generose.* That

---

48 The idea of Mozart's composing between turns at bowling has some credibility in respect to the dozen horn duos (K. 487/496a; July 1786): "while playing at skittles" does appear on the manuscript—though not in his hand. Perhaps the anecdote about the duos in time became affiliated with the trio of the same period.

49 Tradition relates the dark timbres of two adagios for winds, apparently of 1782–1783— K. 410/484d (for two basset horns and bassoon) and K. 411/484a (for two clarinets and three basset horns)—to Masonic ritual. The five "Jacquin" divertimentos, perhaps of the same period, imply similar allusions.

Mozart had attended this opera during his first visit to Prague invites placing the flute quartet's origins in the days soon after his return.⁵⁰ In his instructions for the closing movement, the frolicsome idiom he shared with the Jacquins can be heard: "*Rondieaoux. Allegretto grazioso, ma non troppo presto, pero non troppo adagio. Così—così—con molto garbo, ed Expressione [sic]*." That is, "an allegretto-grazioso meow rondo, neither too fast nor too slow, but pretty much as it ought to be and with not a little charm and expression."

When seeking to envisage Mozart's last years, it profits no less to picture them in the light of such enlivening gatherings than in the shadows of his letters of distress (see pp. 687–88). He rejoiced in the Jacquins and their genial companions, in their conversation both bantering and serious, and in their musical discrimination. With prodigal hand he scattered works among these friends so close that they even savored singing his canons,⁵¹ whose moods did not shy from a Bäsle-like coarse mirth: this company can be pictured giving vent with rollicking animal spirits to K. 231/382c and 233/382d, both of c. 1782 and treating the faecal subject he had once suggested as the device on a target (see pp. 380–81).

He even attempted to furnish the Viennese salon with a musical species emerging of late in the capital: the piano quartet. It added a viola to the traditional piano trio (violin, violoncello, and piano). K. 478 in G minor (1785), the first of the pioneering piano quartets—conceived as a set of three—had such disappointing sales that the publisher, Franz Anton Hoffmeister, withdrew from the project. Artaria & Co. then picked it up and in 1787 issued the second, K. 493 in E flat (completed the year before), by using plates already engraved by Hoffmeister. The enterprise again foundered: the quartets, in particular the first, proved too serious and challenging in technique for the general public,⁵² and Mozart never composed

---

50 A year earlier, he did have the opportunity to attend a Viennese production of the opera.

51 Mozart inscribed a canon, K. 228/515b, in the album of Gottfried's elder brother, Joseph Franz, adding in English: "Don't never forget your true and faithfull friend [sic]." Joseph Franz would marry Maria Barbara Natorp, who, with her sister, Maria Anna Clara, mingled with the Jacquin circle. The sonata K. 521, first intended for Franziska Jacquin, ended with a dedication to the sisters.

52 Despite the less than satisfactory sales, one of the piano quartets circulated at once throughout Germany (perhaps also in manuscript copies) to become a symbol of high taste. "The cry made itself heard," Weimar's *Journal of Luxury and Fashion* of June 1788 reported, that Mozart had "written a new and very special quartet and that this or that princess or countess possesses and plays it." As a result, "a bizarre phenomenon": throughout the winter, at one musicale after another, "some young lady or pretentious middle-class demoiselle" came up with the quartet. "Very artfully set and demanding execution of the utmost precision in all voices," it, "in truth, can hardly be endured when it falls into mediocre and amateurish hands and is carelessly played." However, even though at most performances the "four instruments did not keep together four bars on end," the quartet won the praise of those who wanted to appear stylish.

the third. Indeed, his string quartet known as the "Hoffmeister" (K. 499 in D of 1786) would appear to have been a kind of reparation to Franz Anton for his losses on the piano-quartet affair.

Mozart's perception that he had embarked upon a commercial misadventure and had to right the helm, led him back to the piano trio,[53] which amateur musicians had taken up with enthusiasm: he helped supply their needs with K. 496 and 502 of 1786 and, two years later, K. 542, 548, and 564. Their community of discourse and mastery of invention, in particular the fluent handling of K. 502, astound.

Between the two groups of piano trios, Mozart returned to the violin-piano sonata (a genre to which he had last put his hand at the end of 1785 with K. 481 in E flat, its splendors residing in the harmonic depths of its Adagio and in closing variations speaking the theme in shifting voices of extraordinary address): in August 1787 he wrote the sonata for violin and piano in A, K. 526; a culminating work, its closing *Presto* has as model the finale of a sonata by Abel (Opus V, no. 5), a remembrance of this old friend who had died in London the previous June. Mozart's last violin sonata, K. 547 in F of 1788, falls into the category of "For Beginners" (as does the contemporary piano sonata in C, K. 545). Of all these heterogeneous and rich chamber compositions of the middle years in Vienna, posterity remains most in awe of the piano quartets, large in utterance, prodigal of ideas, the sublime intellectual tonal poetry of K. 478 placing it among the supreme masterworks.

If K. 478 could find an appreciative reception from connoisseurs like the Jacquins or the Thuns, their drawing rooms numbered among the few in which the Viennese digested with comfort all kinds of fine music: high and serious, simple and amiable. Mozart without embarrassment bent to this variety of taste even as he integrated work and pleasure to a remarkable degree. In a mood of relaxed and often playful creativity, he turned to completing his most ambitious work of this period of diverse production: *Il dissoluto punito ossia il Don Giovanni*, K. 527.

7

BEFORE SETTING OUT for its production in Prague, he strove to close the matter of Leopold's estate. Beyond doubt, all of the money still in his

---

53 "Back" in a special sense: he had written a piano trio in 1776, the timid K. 254, which went by the name divertimento. Lacking the animating principles of polyphonic chamber music, it is, in effect, a violin-accompanied piano sonata with a violoncello providing additional resonance to the bass.

name, some three thousand florins, went to Nannerl. His will—it has not come to light, but surviving papers permit extrapolation—divided between brother and sister their father's personal property except musical scores, which were to be hers. She laid claim to certain furnishings, musical instruments, and the family letters, and a public auction in the large room of the Tanzmeisterhaus was to dispose of the rest. In the end, Mozart resigned to her the entire contents of the house—and whatever money a public sale might bring—against a single payment of one thousand florins in Viennese coin. Although what survives of his contemporary letters to the Sonnenburgs breathes courtesy, that he did not claim a single memento betrays his unspoken anger toward the family: he had done with them; indeed, at one point he informed her—amiability enveloping the bitter message—that for his part he would wash his hands of the whole business did not his responsibilities as husband and father cry out that he assert his rights. Throughout the negotiations, again and again he returned to his main concern: the shipment of his archive—his life's work—to Vienna; by Christmas he had hold of it, and thus the ugliest chapter in his life came to a close. Even so, he could not have made an end of reflecting upon just where Leopold had relocated the bulk of his capital.

If important records of his estate have yet to be found, sufficient documentation of Nannerl's survives to offer a measure of the fortune he had passed on to her during his life. Her widow's right added nothing to her personal holdings: at her husband's death in 1803, his resources went to his children, she receiving the income of a modest sum set aside and earmarked to go to them upon her decease. This arrangement did not reflect a lack of concern for her welfare but, rather, a recognition of her independent means. She survived Leopold by forty-two years, through the decades no doubt now and then drawing upon capital. Yet she left behind assets of some fifteen times his annual salary. Although his business ventures—money-lending and dealing in musical instruments among them—had added to his substance, there can be no question that the heart of Nannerl's hoard represented the surviving profits, enhanced by accumulated interest and investment, from the prodigy's tours.[54]

Once Sonnenburg's and Mozart's signatures had put a period to a struggle that somehow avoided open confrontation, Nannerl attempted a reconciliation with him by taking on their father's old role of family correspondent. Flashes of sarcastic ill humor made clear her brother's opinion

[54] In her widowhood she continued to live well but, as a true daughter of Leopold, with the pretense of being on the edge of a plunge into poverty.

that the break between them gaped beyond repair: "Farewell (*lebe wohl* [words redolent of finality]), dear sister," he wrote on 19 December 1787 while awaiting the shipment of his manuscripts. She chose not to notice the implications of the nuance, or perhaps did not have the ear, or, indeed, the heart for it, and continued efforts to keep a path open. But the needs and condition of brother and sister had become incomprehensible, the one to the other: driven by their necessities, for years they had enacted the tragic and powerful drama Leopold had bequeathed them to perform, she at times sharing his role of scourge and minister of divine retribution. In calmer moments, did brother and sister contemplate the wreckage of their relationship and try to reach an understanding of what their father's suffocating attitudes had done to them? Nannerl did come to regret a deepening estrangement, but not Mozart. His last letter to her (2 August 1788), while icily reiterating willingness to read whatever lines she might have in mind to send, at the same time communicated the certainty that he would never find time to reply. Malice lurked beneath his final congratulations on her name day:[55] "With all my heart and soul I wish you everything you hold most profitable [*ersprieslichsten*: advantage its first connotation, pleasure its second] to yourself; and now an end to it [*Punktum*]"—a rapier thrust. In September 1790 on the return journey to Vienna from the coronation of Leopold II in Frankfurt, Mozart's carriage took him within an easy journey of Nannerl's door, but he traveled past the turn toward St. Gilgen. Her only link to him remained his Viennese piano concertos, which she fingered through, no doubt with wonder.[56]

As soon as he and Sonnenburg had concluded their settlement, Mozart directed him to forward the one thousand florins on a bill of exchange to "Herr Michael Puchberg in Count Walsegg's house on the Hohe Markt; he has authority to receive the money, for I depart for Prague early Monday morning."

---

55 Until he clapped hands on his archive, his letters to St. Gilgin had pursued a forced friendliness, which then dissipated to reveal a thin, hard shell of ironic politesse.

56 Outliving him by decades, she had the opportunity perhaps to recall those Grand Tour tokens denied Mozart and his bride during their only visit to Salzburg; perhaps to ponder his disclaiming any object from Leopold's estate, even the slightest memento—an angry repudiation of all the Tanzmeisterhaus had come to represent to him. Such reveries might have inspired a stipulation she insisted upon in her will: leaving to her son several objects, for the most part jewelry descending from the Mozart side of the family, she instructed that he, in turn, bequeath them to her brother's sons. Upon her death, he lost little time in presenting the articles to Constanze, a moving gesture on the part of the once little Leopold, in whom his grandfather had hoped to create a second Wolfgang. He entered Imperial service as a soldier, then joined the Salzburg army, and ended as a public administrator with a tour of duty in the Customs.

8

ON MONDAY, I October 1787, Mozart and Constanze once again set out for Prague.[57] Its "German Apollo" arrived three days later to find "so few arrangements and preparations in place that [the premiere of *Don Giovanni*] on the fourteenth . . . would have been nothing short of an impossibility." He sighed over "the theater's personnel, not as adroit as Vienna's at undertaking such an opera in so short a time" and struggled to bear with Bondini: presiding over a small troupe[58] and "in constant dread" of its members suffering "unanticipated indispositions that might throw him into the most serious of serious situations, that of not being able to put on any production whatsoever," he overindulged his singers: "Here everything is put off because, out of laziness, the vocalists do not wish to rehearse on days on which they perform, and the manager, worried and timid, will not press them." Accustomed to the discipline, efficiency, and resources of the opera houses of Milan, Munich, and Vienna, Mozart had to relearn the ways of a provincial company. The finished performances of his *Figaro* he had experienced in Prague had misled him; they had been the product of very many repetitions.

Over and above the vicissitudes of rehearsals, a diplomatic contretemps threatened: the premiere might be postponed but not the arrival of "the exalted Tuscan guests" (Archduke Francis and his sister) for whom it had been devised. Prague had to report to Vienna that the curtain could not rise on *Don Giovanni* according to plan and requested permission to substitute Mozart's *Figaro*, the composer conducting a gala performance. The Emperor consented. Their Highnesses appeared, and on the fourteenth,[59] midst special illuminations blazing in the Nostitz, gave every sign of appreciating the opera, though they had to slip away during the lengthy final

---

57 The three-year-old Carl Thomas, who during his parents' first *séjour* in Prague had remained behind, doubtless with his grandmother, this time stayed at the school run by Wenzel Bernhard Heeger in Perchtoldsdorf, on the edge of the Vienna Woods. The account of the Mozarts' journey in Eduard Mörike's famous and tender novella (1856) weaves together a series of artful fictions.

58 Its modest size did not of necessity require Mozart to cast Giuseppe Lolli as Masetto as well as the Commendatore: at the premiere of *Figaro*, with all the means of the Burgtheater at hand, he had assigned double roles to two singers, Kelly playing Basilio and Curzio, Francesco Bussani both Bartolo and Antonio. Audiences delighted in such virtuoso turns, as did the singers.

59 The previous day the Hofburg had answered Bondini's request for permission to produce Beaumarchais's original *Le mariage de Figaro* with the reminder that Prague, like Vienna, might hear it only in Mozart's *opera-buffa* version. A part of Prague society even felt that the radical play, in whatever guise, did not befit the visit of a Habsburg princess.

act: their state journey continued early the next morning.[60] Mozart returned to the business of *Don Giovanni.*

During the second week of October, Da Ponte had come to Prague. The puns enlivening the supper scene bear witness to the genial atmosphere in which he and Mozart brought their work on the opera to a close: the text exploits the last names of both Teresa Saporiti, the Donna Anna—*"Ah che piatto saporito!* (Oh, what a delicious dish)," Don Giovanni exclaims, repeating the adjective with relish—and of Jan Kritel Kuchar, a keyboard performer, the Czech *Kuchar* (cook) becoming the Italian *cuoco* in an exchange between Don Giovanni and Leporello![61] (This wordplay has Mozart's characteristic tone; as usual, he controlled the libretto to the last.) Within days, at Salieri's insistence, Da Ponte had to rush back to Vienna and address himself to *Axur.* His departure gave birth to the tale of Casanova's stepping into his place at Mozart's side.[62]

The ballroom scene with its multiple and overlapping dance bands and the many changes of décor tested the company, but, inspired by Mozart, its efforts ended in a triumphant premiere on 29 October 1787. (Little reliable has come down concerning the performances; it is assumed that Mozart conducted all of them.) The management urged him to stay on and write another opera, but after the third repetition (3 November), which provided his benefit, he took its proceeds and his fee of one hundred ducats and by the sixteenth had returned to Vienna.

As Mozart traveled home, Gluck, driving with his wife in the Vienna Woods, suffered an apoplectic stroke (14 November). The following day a

---

60 When they left Prague, Francis accompanied his sister only as far as Lobositz, where he and his Habsburg retinue turned back toward Vienna, a Saxon guard thenceforward forming her escort to Dresden.

61 A zealous supporter of Mozart, Kuchar had made a vocal score of *Figaro.*

62 The anecdote rests upon both the undocumented possibility of Casanova's having attended the premiere and the survival among his papers of a divergent text for a scene in *Don Gloranni* (see XXVIII, n. 14). Legends with even more brittle foundations cluster about its preparation: stories of love affairs on Mozart's part; of composer and librettist, since they lodged in hotel rooms on either side of a narrow street (Mozart in the Zu den drei goldenen Löwen, Da Ponte at the zum Platteis), shouting across to one another as they worked on the last act; of Constanze's telling her husband stories throughout the eve of the premiere so that he stay awake and have the overture—invariably the last number he composed—ready for the copyist. The tales of his passing happy days at the Villa Betramka, the home of his old friends Josepha and Franz Xaver Duschek have the ring of truth, although it is doubtful that she kept him locked in a garden pavilion until he provided her with a new concert scena (*"Bella mia fiamma / Resta, o cara,"* K. 528, its text [by D. M. Sarcone] from Jommelli's serenade *Cerere placata*). Mozart may have already sketched the aria with Gottfried Jacquin in mind and then adapted the draft to a soprano voice as a gift with which to return the Duscheks' hospitality.

second attack left him paralyzed and bereft of speech and sight; by evening he lay dead. Mozart arrived in a city shocked by the loss. Having followed the news from Prague, the Hofburg almost at once took up the question of a new relationship with the composer to whom Gluck's mantle had descended.

With his last breath, Gluck's yearly subvention of two thousand florins as honorary Imperial Court Composer became an unencumbered budget item, and Emperor Joseph let himself be persuaded to turn part of it into a benefice for Mozart. Gluck had first received the dignity as he entered upon his seventh decade; Mozart had just begun his fourth, and there can be no doubt of Joseph's intention that the emolument he now bestowed, generous if not munificent, be subject to increments through the years. On 7 December 1787, he named Mozart an Imperial Court Composer (*Kammermusicus* or *Kammer-Kompositeur*) at eight hundred florins per annum—"*only for the time being*," Mozart stressed—his sole and symbolic responsibility being to contribute minuets and German dances to the masked balls in the Redoutensaal.[63] A court communication would explain his title and salary in terms of freeing "so rare a genius of music from the necessity of seeking his reputation and income abroad." The Hofburg knew of his resolve to visit London and feared losing him.

Prince Kaunitz had observed to Archduke Maximilian that men of Mozart's quality "*come into the world but once a century and must not be driven from Germany, particularly when one is fortunate enough to have them in the capital.*"[64] (Joseph Haydn felt that nations should "vie to possess such a jewel [as Mozart] within their borders.") Affronted that a great German like Gluck had found it necessary to make his fortune and utmost fame in Paris, Kaunitz had doubtless been the force securing the two-thousand-florin sinecure for him in 1774.[65] Now, in all likelihood, he drove the same point home to the Emperor in respect to Mozart, who drew deep satisfaction from the title and the money.

In reply to a question concerning his position at court, a postscript to his last letter to Nannerl (2 August 1788) announced his new status in a most recondite manner: instead of spelling out the position of *Kammermusicus*, he wrote in vague terms of an Imperial appointment and then further muddled the matter by describing a Burgtheater placard identifying him as "duly appointed Kapellmeister to his Imperial and Royal Majesty."

---

63 In truth, two halls, one larger than the other.
64 Maximilian must have repeated to Mozart, here quoted, Kaunitz's flattering remarks.
65 Gluck acknowledged the "high protection and especial favor" Kaunitz "heaped" upon him.

Here the use of "Kapellmeister" represented an honorific, a courtesy to a very famous master in truth not a kapellmeister. What led him to this flimflam may have been a desire to underscore his good fortune in terms of the title the family had always hungered for: here he appears a mirror image of his father and, indeed, would seem, through the agency of his sister, to be reporting his achievement to Leopold's shade.

The benefice stood the Mozart family helpful stead, for soon the year-long political machinations of the Russian Empress would begin to have injurious repercussions upon Viennese economic and artistic life.

9

ON 18 JANUARY 1787, the day after Mozart first attended his *Figaro* in Prague, Empress Catherine of Russia had set out from her palace of Tsarskoye-Selo on a journey to her southern provinces. She moved in procession to Kiev. There she held state and waited for the ice on the Dnieper to break up; not until 1 May did it become navigable and permit her flotilla to travel down the broad stream toward the Crimea, which she, remembering Iphigenia, called by its classical name: Tauris. The mean villages and encampments she passed had been transformed by the theatrical magic of her minister and former lover Field Marshal Grigory Aleksandrovich Potemkin, now Prince of Tauris;[66] the flower-bedecked façades she beheld had been painted in trompe l'oeil on cardboard, canvas, and stucco; in the foreground stood soldiers dressed as prosperous peasants and under orders to cheer lustily as Her Majesty drifted by; she could not have been deceived by the changing décor or by the same supernumeraries reappearing from stop to stop in different costumes; no doubt she looked upon the extravaganza as an amusing homage picturing a Russia that might one day be.

Her purpose: to intimidate the Turks by a show of magnificence and power as prelude to her review of Potemkin's new Black Sea fleet. Her crowning touch had been to invite the Holy Roman Emperor to witness the spectacle, and Joseph, eager to strengthen their common alliance

---

66 In September 1791, a son-in-law of Countess Thun, Count Andrei Kyrillovich Rasumovsky (the Russian diplomat and future dedicatee of Beethoven's Quartets, Opus 59) would suggest to Potemkin that he take into service "the pre-eminent keyboard player of Germany and one of its most skillful composers, Mozart by name." Rasumovsky no doubt had discussed the idea beforehand with Mozart: at his death his library contained the *Geographical and Topographical Travel Book through all the States of the Austrian Monarchy together with the Travel Route to St. Petersburg by way of Poland* (Vienna, 1789).

against Constantinople, had agreed to join what in private he called her traveling circus. He overtook her just as the seven Imperial barges[67] and some seventy lighter vessels, all manned by crews totaling over three thousand, approached the first of the Dnieper cataracts. Catherine found him looking worn.

The Turks would have nothing to do with Potemkin's script: they refused to be awed by Catherine's luxurious progress or his naval pageant in the Bay of Sevastapol and, in fact, to underline their sense of outrage, had a squadron of ships show itself in the Dnieper lagoons. Although amazed by this defiance, Catherine spent idyllic days in the Crimea playing at being Queen of Tartary; a bored Joseph, appalled by the Asiatic pomp she affected, became eager to return to Vienna, especially upon receiving reports of troubles in Galicia and the Austrian Lowlands, where his governors-general, Marie Christine and Albert, had become encompassed with hostilities: Joseph had concentrated the best of his military forces on his Balkan frontiers with the Turks, and his Polish and Flemish provinces, sensing opportunity, had become restive. Catherine, too, had thoughts of home: reality invaded her fantasies as the oppressive heat mounted, forcing her to abandon plans to push on to Taganrog on the Sea of Azov. Empress and Emperor turned back toward their capitals.

With Joseph's compliance, she had sent menacing signals to Constantinople, and on 17 August 1787 it responded by committing the Russian Ambassador to the Castle of the Seven Towers: a declaration of war. Caught off guard, Catherine and Joseph, who had counted upon posturing as their chief weapon, required time to recover from surprise and to frame strategy. Even before he made his way to the new Turkish front during March of 1788, officialdom took pains to cajole the Viennese into a martial frame of mind. Mozart anticipated the Hofburg's tactics in his contredanse "La Bataille" (K. 535 of January), advertised as "The Siege of Belgrade," bows striking strings providing the noise of combat. Those attending the Leopoldstadt theater might hear the popular actor Friedrich Baumann the Younger sing Mozart's "German War Song" (K. 539, of 5 March, to a text by Johann Wilhelm Ludwig Gleim) decked out with the Turkish colors of piccolo, cymbals, and bass drum.

The campaign the Emperor waged, his health ever failing—he already bore the tubercle bacillus and would contract malaria in the pestilential

---

67 The dining barge could seat seventy at table, while the music galley accommodated an orchestra of one hundred and twenty under Giuseppi Sarti. The reader will recall his having to decline Mozart's invitation to the Ployer house in Döbling because of his impending departure for Russia (see XXX, n. 22).

bogs of the lower Dnieper[68]—but confirmed his lack of military competence. For a while, his armies did have the best of it in Croatia, Slavonia, Moldavia, and Wallachia, but even in inconclusive engagements, indeed in stalemate, what could go wrong for him did go wrong. Official Vienna strove to preserve a bold face: as disaster engulfed Joseph in the Banat, Mozart continued turning out patriotic works, his music-hall song "On Departing for the Front" (K. 552, its poet unknown, of 11 August 1788) coinciding with the Turkish devastation of Temesvar.

If Catherine at last gathered significant victories in December 1788, when Potemkin subdued the strategic Turkish fort at Ochakov and then took Akkerman (opposite the stockade that would become Odessa), Habsburg prestige continued at serious risk until General Ernst Gideon von Laudon emerged from retirement to assume supreme command of Joseph's army and capture Belgrade for him in October 1789, Bucharest falling the following month. Despite such successes, throughout its course the war discomposed the Viennese, and they charged the cost in lives, suffering—and inconvenience—to Joseph's account. Moreover, he came to ponder, and rather late, whether the Cossack or the Turk would be the more desirable neighbor on his eastern frontier, and, in the end, favored the turban! From the beginning Vienna sensed the absurdity of a bloody, pointless war fomented by Catherine of Russia, an ill-conceived, ill-managed, and ill-fated adventure no one, least of all the Emperor, could explain.

The capital, deep in distress, lost much of its power to enchant the privileged. The Emperor's reforms had already begun to sap their incomes when the outbreak of hostilities caused the economy to falter. From the field Joseph kept demanding more money; recession set in as supplementary war taxes, interest rates, and inflation mounted. The lower orders, desperate to observe the price of bread soar as the size of the loaf decreased, sacked the bakeries. While many nobles joined their military units, others shuttered their palaces to take up residence on their country estates in order to escape disorder and, moreover, to keep a sharp eye on the management of those farmholds and forests that represented a principal source of revenue. Universal discontent, hitherto rare in Vienna, moved toward crisis. Patronage of the arts dried up; Mozart found few salons functioning and in need of music and watched the base of his subscribers further erode. His last series of concerts took place late in 1788

---

68 He wrote of "every day waging a guerrilla war against mosquitoes . . . fever, and diarrhea." Between June 1788 and May 1789 illness felled more than one hundred seventy thousand of his soldiers, of whom at least thirty thousand died.

and in all probability included the piano concerto K. 537.[69] Though flaunting a *galanterie* bent upon courting popularity, it could not break the spell of Vienna's apathy. Before the end of the year he had begun a new piano concerto but did not go beyond sketches (see p. 717): he had no public for it.

It must be remembered that, injurious as the Turkish War proved to his subscription list, other factors had contributed to its decline: his overfrequent concerts and, no less damaging, the harmonic, contrapuntal, and instrumental richness of his compositions; an inner necessity he would not compromise—K. 537 an exception proving the rule—it perplexed much of the public. (As accomplished a musician as Dittersdorf found Mozart's superabundance of musical ideas and invention difficult to digest: to him it all seemed a series of marvelous offshoots sprouting from an infirm core; he could not grasp the whole.) The war might well have given some of his subscribers remaining in Vienna an excuse to hold back from signing on; and in addition, by the end of 1788, a new anxiety fed the flow of carriages leaving the city.

With its main armies engaged with either the Turks or revolutionaries in Poland and the Lowlands, Vienna had left itself shallow protection, a situation Berlin moved to profit by: Frederick the Great's nephew, who had succeeded him in 1786 as Frederick William II, gloated upon the spectacle of the Habsburgs sinking into the mire of the Balkans even as the Bourbons crumbled under the demand of political reformers that Versailles convoke the Estates-General (see n. 70); he contemplated taking European affairs into his own hands and began by stirring up the Hungarian separatists as prelude to descending upon Vienna itself, a danger every Imperial reversal in the east made more real.

Only in the autumn of 1789, when the success of Laudon at Belgrade and of Friedrich Josias, Prince of Coburg-Saalfeld, at Martinestie (the most impressive of the battles culminating in the fall of Bucharest) began to scatter the clouds of disaster overhanging the House of Habsburg,[70]

---

69 Mozart never completed on paper the piano part of K. 537: sections for the right hand appear only in outline and much for the left is lacking altogether. He intended this score, which appears to have had its premiere in February 1788 (see XXXII, n. 2), not for the eyes of others but to freshen his memory as he played and to provide a foundation for embellishment. Johann Anton André made good (composed!) the deficiencies when he published the concerto in 1794.

70 Even as Laudon's advance into Bosnia during the summer of 1789 began to lift Joseph's spirits, reports from France dashed them. During June, the third estate, having declared itself a national assembly, set about establishing a constitution for the nation; on 14 July the Bastille fell; and during the first week of October, a mob forced Joseph's sister and brother-in-law from their palace of Versailles and shut them up as virtual prisoners in the Tuileries.

could it attempt to rally the Viennese. Punctuated by postilion horns, the cries of couriers proclaimed the good news in the streets; Te Deums echoed in the churches; and artillery thundered in celebration. With the fall of Belgrade,[71] Anton Schmith, a physician and amateur violinist, united the siege with Mozart's name in a Latin chronogram-couplet: "Pallas reigns in Laudon, Apollo in Mozart / throughout his life, each will live illustrious in his art." The Emperor, who had crept back to Vienna on 5 December 1788, processed to St. Stephen's, and, though free wine and beer as well as money tossed to the crowds did help light up their enthusiasm, it did not go unnoticed that the tide had begun to turn only after he had relinquished the baton. The Hofburg lost no opportunity to glorify its turn of fortune. Written for the Imperial ballroom, Kammermusicus Wolfgang Mozart's contredanse K. 587, which he entitled "The Victory of Coburg the Hero," applauded the battle at Martinestie to the echo with calls to arms, military bustle, and a quotation from a popular war song.

His heart could not have been in such an effort. His German patriotism, founded in the Imperial ideal, love of Vienna, and Habsburg pension did not stay him from considering possibilities beyond the ramparts of the still-paralyzed capital. He fixed his eyes not only upon England and Frederick William's Prussia but upon Saxony, too: in Prague had not *Figaro* decidedly pleased Archduchess Maria Theresia, now playing a role in the cultural life of Dresden?

No doubt he already deliberated upon an exploratory trip to northern Germany; yet, opportunities remained in Vienna and helped sustain him there even as his career as a pianist continued its decline[72] and war gnawed at the capital's cultural life.

---

71 On 1 January 1791, London's Drury Lane theater offered an opera called *The Siege of Belgrade*, its "Music composed principally by Mr. Storace [Stephen], With a few Pieces selected from Martini, Salieri, and Paesiello [*sic*]." Stephen also should have made clear that the opening chorus of Turkish soldiers derived from Mozart's Rondo alla Turca of K. 331.

72 A decline, not the headlong plunge the usual reading of Mozart's letter of 12 July 1789 to Michael Puchberg implies. Its lament that only one supporter (van Swieten) had responded to his announcement of a series of concerts to be given at his home, provided a dramatic touch strengthening an appeal for a loan to pay Constanze's medical bills. Not until more than two weeks later (28 July) did Laudon take charge of the Imperial forces; only then did the tide begin to turn and Vienna dare hope for recovery: July 1789 found few potential subscribers in the city, which even in normal times would not have had many of them in residence during summer. This circulation of information about the concerts constituted advance notice to which patrons would respond upon their return in safer and cooler days. During these difficult months, Mozart doubtless performed in the salons of admirers—in particular members of the diplomatic corps—who had to remain in the capital.

CHAPTER XXXII

Vienna:
Plurality of Meanings; Moral Ambiguities

EARLY IN DECEMBER 1787, just before the public announcement of his appointment as court composer, he had moved his family back from its suburban garden apartment to the inner city, taking quarters not far from St. Peter's, in a house at the corner of Unter den Tuchlauben and Schultergasse. (There on the twenty-seventh, Constania gave birth to their first daughter, Theresia Constanzia.) He wanted once again to be at the center of things: the palace had ordered a production of *Don Giovanni*, but revised to meet the needs of the Burgtheater's singers,[1] and van Swieten drew him into ambitious plans for the Society of the Associated (see p. 635). The Emperor's Balkan campaign proper would not begin until the spring of 1789, and Vienna still bustled with musical activity.

At Count Esterházy's on 26 February 1788 and again on 4 and 11 March, the Society heard under Mozart's direction a much praised reading of Emanuel Bach's *The Resurrection and Ascension of Jesus*[2]—Mozart touched

---

1 Concentrating on preparing the Viennese *Don Giovanni*, he for the time being put aside the Nostitz theater's request for a new opera (see p. 675). He and Guardasoni would return to the idea in April 1789 (see p. 691).

2 Leipzig's *Germany's Musical Almanac for 1789* acclaimed the premiere performance, on which occasion Mozart may have used the intermission to unveil his piano concerto K. 537. The second performance of the cantata had its own added riches: Mozart had retrieved from his archive an aria sketched a decade earlier in Mannheim and finished it for Aloysia Lange—perhaps she had

up the instrumentation of one aria—with an orchestra of eighty-six, a chorus of thirty, and Aloysia and Adamberger among the soloists. The general public had access to a repetition of the cantata at the Burgtheater on the seventh.

These events preluded Mozart's major commission from van Swieten under the aegis of the Society, a project that would extend throughout the war (a court official, van Swieten had to remain in Vienna) and embrace the revision and presentation of four Handelian masterpieces. The series began with *Acis and Galatea* (K. 566, November 1788) and *Messiah* (K. 572, March 1789)[3] and ended with *Alexander's Feast* and the *Ode for St. Cecilia's Day* (K. 591 and 592, respectively, of summer 1790), by which time the Congress of Reichenbach had gathered to frame the protocols ending hostilities.

In the main, Mozart looked upon his task as that of filling out the orchestrations: they sounded lean without reinforcement by a continuo, which he chose not to use;[4] in recompense he added wind parts, dismaying to sticklers but nonetheless of particular enchantment when, in addition to strengthening and coloring, they strike out on their own and contribute independent melodic turns. If he answered only to himself in mending and arranging Handel's scores for contemporary ears,[5] this luxury did not sweeten for him his refashioning of *Don Giovanni*.

It required changes in what Prague had heard—two new arias (one a substitution, the other an interpolation) and an added scene: Francesco Morella, the Ottavio, could not manage the florid figuration of *"Il mio tesoro"* in act II, and Mozart gave him, instead, the lyrical *"Dalla sua pace"* to be sung in the first act after Anna's cries for vengeance upon Don Giovanni; Caterina Cavalieri agreed to apply herself to Elvira only if provided with a grand *opera-seria* aria on the scale of Anna's outpourings—Cavalieri's rival,

---

inspired the draft—in time for her to sing during the pause this exercise in vocal bravura (*"Ah se in ciel,"* K. 538, the verse from Metastasio's *L'eroe cinese*).

3 At the performance of *Messiah* chez Esterházy (6 March), Mozart had charge of the orchestra and soloists (again including Aloysia and Adamberger) while Umlauf conducted the chorus of twelve. Vienna heard German versions of these works Handel wrote to English words: Alxinger translated John Gay's (and others') *Acis*; Karl Wilhelm Ramler did the same service for John Dryden's *Alexander's Feast* and, it would appear, his *Ode*; and C. D. Ebeling turned his hand to Charles Jennens's compilation of biblical and prayer-book citations constituting the text of *Messiah*.

4 He did call upon a continuo in the Emanuel Bach cantata, Umlauf presiding at the keyboard. The possibility presents itself that in performances of his Handel arrangements, Mozart conducted the singers, the first violinist leading the orchestra.

5 In a letter (21 March 1789) to Mozart, van Swieten praised his capacity "to clothe" Handel's music in garments that "pleased those concerned with the latest fashions [*Modegecken*]" and at the same time preserved its "solemn grandeur." Though the authenticity of this letter has been questioned, its tone and aesthetic observations ring true.

Aloysia Lange, was to sing Anna—and to this purpose Mozart composed "*Mi tradi*"; it followed a freshly created Zerlina-Leporello *buffa* scene for those accomplished players Luisa Laschi-Mombelli and Benucci; tacked on to the end of the courtyard sextet, it occupied the place of the discarded "*Il mio tesoro.*" (The Don Giovanni, Francesco Albertarelli, a recent arrival at the Burgtheater, made no demands for changes in his part.[6]) The additions and the appertaining adjustments[7] brought Mozart two hundred twenty-five florins, half the fee for a complete opera.

Stemming from compromises with the realities of operatic life, the Viennese *Don Giovanni* has left posterity the choice of producing it, the Prague version, or a composite. On the whole, opera houses have followed the last path, but in a variety of accommodations. They prove happy in respect to including "*Mi tradi*"—growing out of the Prague Elvira's emotional struggles, it, in fact, clarifies them—but inopportune as to dramatic motivation when the tenor attempts both of Ottavio's arias. Assigning him a single, defining solo encapsulating his character, Mozart gave each city a different Ottavio: in Vienna an uncertain, uncommitted suitor; in Prague a deliberative, but in the end determined, indeed, at moments, heroic lover, ready to answer Anna's call to arms. Though including the two arias might picture a hitherto equivocal Ottavio of a sudden eager to cut a figure, Mozart did not intend them to be heard at the same performance. Perhaps he turned Morella's technical limitations into an opportunity to reconsider Ottavio's function in the drama and make a correction: the substance of the libretto does not admit of this cautious aristocrat's voicing so resolute an utterance as "*Il mio tesoro.*" The Ottavio at the Prague premiere had a reputation for mettlesome impersonations—he had sung the title role in the Bertati/Gazzaniga *Don Giovanni*—and it might have led Mozart astray.

The inserted Leporello-Zerlina scene resists adjustment and counts as the most extended lapse on the part of a master whose name has become a touchstone of refinement. The music has its rewards, but the tastelessness of both situation and text renders the episode unique in Mozart's operas: brandishing a razor, Zerlina threatens to carve up a bound and

---

6 The title role lacks a big aria—as does the part of Count Almaviva in Paisiello's *Barber*—and Mozart may have expected Albertarelli to request one. Perhaps Leporello's "*Ah, pietà*" fell victim to the cutting knife at Albertarelli's insistence that some measure of equality prevail between the length and musical weight of the master's and servant's parts. Mozart did provide Albertarelli with an aria, but for insertion into Anfossi's *Le gelosie fortunate*: "*Un bacio di mano*" (K. 541 of May 1788, the text in all probability Da Ponte's); some of its material would reappear in the opening movement of the Jupiter Symphony.

7 Mozart had in view eliminating the concluding sextet and having the final curtain fall upon the descent into hell; whether he carried out this intent remains unclear.

helpless Leporello, intimations of castration thick coming. It would seem that Mozart hoped the recitatives and duet would bend coarseness to his advantage by providing a picture of the ill-bred at their worst and thereby offer to those who spurned old-fashioned magic opera a naturalistic diversion to offset a walking and singing statue.

Even so, not a few showed marked impatience with what they viewed as the tattered business of yet another Don Giovanni receiving a commemorative monument as dinner companion.[8] "A shame it does not eat, too," the critic Schink scoffed, "only then would the fun be complete!" This meeting of the mortal and the supernatural appeared the tired stuff of the old court opera. Molière, the satirical scourge of excess, had, of course, treated the perambulating statue with wit, Goldoni, for his part, reducing it to a sculptured bust that kept its marble tongue (see XXXI, n. 42). The criticism attacking Mozart's stone guest derived not only from Wolff's view of the phenomenal world as distinguished by order but also from his disciple Gottsched's insistence upon the probable and reasonable as the material of art—the very spirit raising its voice against the stucco fantasies and playfulness of rococo churches. This cool, sober, in effect Josephinian aesthetic helps define the nature of the Emperor's absorbing interest in mounting *Don Giovanni* at the Burgtheater: for reason of the music alone. Yet the libretto's fabulous, mythical elements had inspired the score's most profound pages.

The fantasy and resounding passions of the story had attracted Mozart in Prague when his eyes fell upon the Bertati-Gazzaniga variant. Though speculation hedges what lay at the center of his imagination as he contemplated appropriating the tale's suggestive patterns and making them serve his own sensibilities, the case may be put that the Commendatore's return from the dead to exercise fearful judgment called to Mozart's mind the resurging monster in *Idomeneo*; that he saw the opportunity once again to represent a proud pair fighting the battle of authority and succession, but with a difference: now, above the very abyss of hell, filicide, unashamed, and with the game in its hands, unmasks and identifies itself to patricide before striking the decisive blow. A Frankfurt critic (1789) recognized an august spirit behind Giovanni's descent into the abyss, flames and demons—and Mozart's turbulent music—encompassing him: "A hollow and horrible sepulchral tone seemed to issue from the earth; one imagined seeing the shades of the departed rising from their coffins," a scene speaking a language "learned from Shakespeare."

---

8 In 1783 Vienna's Leopoldstadt theater had offered Marinelli's commedia del'arte versions of the tale.

Another Shakespearean element in the legend must have awakened Mozart's strong personal response: Giovanni dies like the poet's Coriolanus—"Tear him to pieces"—denying dependence, deaf to capitulation, and indifferent to all, a ferocious self-definition and self-sufficiency his only garment, the proud exit with which Mozart planned to end the Viennese production (see n. 7). In the coming century, Søren Kierkegaard and E. T. A. Hoffmann would help prepare *Don Giovanni's* fame as a stupendous, impassioned musical drama; few contemporary with the work viewed it in this light.

During Joseph's more than nine months in the field, Count Rosenberg kept him abreast of the opera's uphill rehearsals,[9] in particular the exertions of more than one singer to meet Mozart's vocal demands. Here he made matters "much too difficult," Joseph replied. (For certain he had a copy of the score in his tent.) That at last Rosenberg acknowledged a true admiration of Mozart pleased him—"your taste begins to grow reasonable"—but he did fear that the music of *Don Giovanni* might outstrip public taste and reap a fiasco.

Don Giovanni reached the boards on 7 May 1788 and proved the Emperor mistaken; it at once gained a reputation in Vienna, and then throughout Germany, as a work to be admired—but on musical grounds alone: Schink looked upon it as the victory of "excellent composition" over "poetic absurdity"; Frankfurt on Main's *Dramaturgische Blätter* found the "marvelous" score "about as well suited [to the libretto] as Raphael's manner to the ideas of a Teniers or a Callot"; and the *Chronik von Berlin,* while describing *Don Giovanni* as "wounding reason [and] offending modesty," acknowledged the music as "enchanting to the ear"—"never had the art . . . reached a higher state."[10] But, most surprising, from the outset the appeal of the opera extended even to the untutored in music: at the premiere Zinzendorf took pleasure in the "agreeable and varied" numbers and went back five more times. Not a Prague-like triumph but a conspicuous success, *Don Giovanni* had fourteen repetitions in Vienna before the premiere season came to an end.

The last of them, indeed the last in Vienna during Mozart's lifetime, took place on 15 December, ten days after Emperor Joseph, ill and

9 Elizabeth of Württemberg, now an archduchess of Austria, also sent news of *Don Giovanni* to the Turkish front: on 15 May she informed her husband, Archduke Franz, of "a new opera composed by Mozart." She seems not to have related it to Franz's journey with his sister to Prague and the postponed premiere of *Don Giovanni.*
10 The Frankfurt review referred to a performance of 1789, the comments from Berlin to one of 1791; Schink's observations, along with his criticism of the perambulating statue, concerned a Hamburg production of 1789. The opera moved across Germany with remarkable speed.

troubled, had come back to the capital from the Balkans. On the sixteenth, he wrote his sister Maria Christina that he had as yet to attend the theater: the tale of his dramatic appearance the previous evening at *Don Giovanni* belongs to myth. No doubt delighted to find his misgivings idle and the work in the repertory, this greatest and most consistent of Mozart's patrons, too sick to visit the Burgtheater, in all likelihood heard *Don Giovanni* from Mozart's throat and fingers in the privacy of the royal chambers.

2

THE EMPEROR'S PATRONAGE (the sinecure and the fee for the Burg-theater *Don Giovanni*); monies from van Swieten covering the Handel con-certs (which included a public performance of *Acis and Galatea* as Mozart's own benefit),[11] and income from students[12] and publishers—all should have enabled him for the while to clear a manageable path through the shambles of his concert career. Yet he could not free himself from what had become a tradition of grappling with money matters, first and fore-most because, after a gesture or two of retrenchment, he persisted in the struggle to keep up his high-living ways in imitation of colleagues like the Langes and Salieri, court retainers on generous and, above all, regular salaries. He had left the Landstrasse in debt to his landlord and lived on more and more slippery financial ground. Fearful to lose caste, he confided the full awkwardness of his situation only to Prince Karl Lichnowsky, Franz Hofdemel, a chancery clerk, and Johann Michael Puchberg, a busi-nessman,[13] all Freemasons and thus, if so requested, bound to secrecy. Of the three, only Puchberg became his close friend.

By the summer of 1788, he had begun to borrow from Puchberg, to whom he spelled out his long-standing difficulty of maintaining a steady flow of income: "... a nasty business; in truth, life becomes impossible when one must bide one's time between various odd bits of income." He requested a loan of "one or two thousand gulden for a year or two at a fit-ting rate of interest" so as to have sufficient capital "to meet necessary ex-penses *at the proper time*" instead of being obliged "to *postpone* payments and then, just at *the most awkward moment*, having to pay out one's *entire resources all at once*." Puchberg would respond to such pleas—Mozart's famous series

---

11 It took place during November 1788 in a hall adjoining Ignaz Jahn's catering establishment on the Himmelpfortgasse. Often put to use for performances, the chamber seated about four hundred.

12 Mozart, who had given up teaching, now asked that word be spread that he would return to it.

13 The head of the Salliet textile firm, he resided on the Hoher Markt in a house (belonging to Count Waldegg; see p. 673) that also accommodated his business.

of *Bittbriefe* or importuning letters—by sending gulden now and then and, as a rule, in small amounts; Mozart discharged the debts as best he could and often had to beg patience.[14]

His first step signaling a reining in of expenses had been to quit his rooms on Unter den Tuchlauben: on 17 June 1788, within some six and a half months of settling in, he uprooted his household to take quarters on the Währingerstrasse in the Alsergrund district (to the north of the center).[15] He had "not very much to do in town" once the premiere of *Don Giovanni* had passed, and for a few kreuzer a fiacre could take him wherever he had business. His new apartment proved not only "cheaper" but "more pleasant": for Puchberg's benefit he stressed frugality, but the stronger reason for the move may have been the agreeable garden. Here he completed his last three symphonies (all in four movements) for that series of concerts planned for late in the year (see pp. 679–80): K. 543 in E flat, 26 June; K. 550 in G minor, 25 July;[16] and K. 551 in C (the "Jupiter"), 10 August. If the Viennese held back from attending his concerts of piano concertos, perhaps new symphonies would draw them.

Joachim Daniel Preisler, an actor in Copenhagen's Royal theater visiting Vienna, paid a Sunday call on Mozart (24 August) during this summer of miraculous achievement and left an idyllic picture of the family at home on the Währingerstrasse: "This small man and great master *improvised* twice on a *pianoforte* with pedal [see XXXI, n. 8] and so wonderfully, so wonderfully, that it staggered belief! He interwove the most difficult passages with the loveliest *themes.* His wife cut quill pens for the copyist [working on the "Jupiter" or perhaps *Acis and Galatea*?], a pupil composed, and a little boy of four [Carl] walked about the garden singing recitatives. In short, everything surrounding this splendid man was musical!" Preisler and his companion, Michael Rosing, spoke of him with almost religious awe. He had become legend.

At the time of their visit, Vienna echoed to tales of the impending piecemeal dissolution of its Italian opera, a process to be completed, rumor ran, by Lent. The Emperor had found difficulty reconciling the

---

14 With interruptions, the *Bittbriefe* continued for three years: June 1788 to June 1791. They did not disturb a mutual and deep affection: as expressions of gratitude to this friend, Mozart wrote the piano trio K. 542 of June 1788 and the six-movement divertimento K. 563 of the following September (a string trio for violin, viola, and violoncello). At Mozart's death one thousand gulden remained outstanding to Puchberg, who, in a graceful gesture, made no claim upon the estate; once her affairs became settled, Constanze repaid him.

15 A dozen days after the move, the Mozarts lost their daughter of half a year to an intestinal disorder.

16 On 21 July he must have interrupted work on K. 550 to attend the marriage in the cathedral of his sister-in-law Josepha to the violinist and family friend Franz de Paula Hofer.

company's deficit of eighty thousand gulden with his importunities for funds to pursue the war. The order to suspend had gone out (29 July 1788), and the singers began to receive notice. The pall of uncertainty shadowing the capital's prime musical institution—in the end it survived[17]—fed Mozart's determination to investigate temporary opportunities elsewhere; but for the while he worked at leisure in his garden.

Adequate documentation of his life during the second half of 1788 is lacking, but even with the impediments imposed by the war, these months afforded him more than one gratification: the performances of *Acis*, the sheaf of six German dances (K. 567) along with twelve minuets (K. 568) for the balls in the Redoutensäle, and, above all, the concerts featuring the three new symphonies.[18]

Personal utterances with moments of the exalted and the tragic, they continue on the journey the Linz and Prague symphonies had opened. Like them, K. 543—which drops oboes in favor of clarinets[19]—begins with a weighty introductory Adagio. It stirs the depths with lacerating dissonances and mysterious scale passages. That these tragic tensions give way to an ethereal and at times joyful Allegro announces the spirit of what was to come: measures of high drama aside, the three symphonies indulge not only elegiac but also unclouded and downright jocular moods; indeed, does not the Allegro vivace of the Jupiter exploit the *opera-buffa* aria written for Albertarelli (see n. 6)? Bringing together the witty and ironic along with the monumental and pathetic, the symphonies achieve a complexity of musical humors and thought reaching an epitome in the finale of the Jupiter, a movement of unexcelled diversity and intellectual power. This Molto allegro stands as a tour de force whose accumulating contrapuntal intricacies call to mind the conclusion of Shakespeare's *Cymbeline*, in which

---

17 The company continued, Da Ponte maintained, thanks alone to a plan he set before the Emperor: it brought into being an auxiliary opera fund to which the nobles and diplomats subscribed. Zinzendorf's diary for 15 January 1789 refers to his overhearing Rosenberg and Da Ponte discussing the proposal; only with substantiation of this pedigree can such an assertion by Da Ponte be entertained. In an earlier move to economize (February 1788), the Emperor had moved productions in German back to the Burgtheater from the Kärntnertortheater, whose doors then closed until the end of 1791, though they might open on occasion for a special performance.

18 Mozart's undated letter to Puchberg referring to tickets presented to him for the series should be moved from its traditional but ungrounded position in June 1788 and placed some months ahead in the autumn. Also see n. 19.

19 Mozart created a second version of K. 550 by adding a pair of clarinets and adjusting the oboe parts to accommodate them. He also touched up the orchestration of two passages in the Andante of the first version. Such modifications could have followed only from the needs and results of specific performances: the popular idea that Mozart never heard his last three symphonies must be recognized as myth.

an astonishing variety of plot, counterplot, and subplot all converge and reach denouement within an overarching structure of universal pardon (Jupiter, in fact, presides over the reconciliations from on high).

The concerts featuring the three symphonies must have ended with a disappointing profit or even a deficit: soured on hiring halls and instrumentalists, Mozart contemplated selling tickets to musicales in his own home, the impulse behind his move back to the inner city early in 1789. He and Constanze took rooms on the Judenplatz in the house abutting the one they had lived in almost six years earlier.

By spring, having composed another set of German dances for the palace (K. 571) and reworked *Messiah*, he began to fix plans for a visit to the court of Berlin. They dovetailed tidily into those of Prince Lichnowsky, now making ready for a trip through Bohemia and Saxony to Prussia and Silesia. (Though born in Vienna, he descended, as did his title, from a family with holdings in Hohenzollern lands; he had always to take into account that its Silesian estates, once under Vienna's sovereignty, now lay under Berlin's; see p. 75.)[20] He invited Mozart along as companion.[21] It went for granted that Lichnowsky would assume the costs of coach, horses, and hotels, but Mozart still required more money than he had at hand: on 2 April he borrowed one hundred florins from Franz Hofdemel on a bill of exchange; it had not seemed good sense to seek them from the Prince, who, it appears certain, had already advanced a loan. Mozart and Constanze agreed that during this first separation since their marriage she and little Carl would take up residence with the Puchbergs. She had been pregnant since February and of late her step had become infirm.

3

THE TRAVELERS DEPARTED Vienna on 8 April 1789.[22] By way of Znaim, Mährisch-Budwitz (where they halted for the evening), Iglau, and

---

20 Born in 1761 and an enthusiastic amateur of music, Karl Alois von Lichnowsky in 1788 had married Maria Christiane, a daughter of Countess Thun. Mozart may have first met him in her salon; or perhaps van Swieten had been the link; it would be reinforced by the bonds of Freemasonry. Lichnowsky would become a patron of Beethoven.

21 The journey had precedent in Gluck's to London in the company of Prince Ferdinand Philipp Lobkowitz (1745). A commoner's close association with a high noble could give rise to stressful situations—such would be the case between Lichnowsky and Beethoven—but Mozart took pride in this privileged friendship and, at least at this stage, handled it with ease, luxuriating in a journey during which he "knew nothing of discomfort—of annoyance."

22 The preceding evening at Count Esterházy's, Mozart's arrangement of *Messiah* had received its second performance.

Caslau (their second overnight stop), they came to Prague early in the afternoon of the tenth, rested at the Zum goldenen Einhorn, and continued on their way at nine. During fewer than eight hours in the city, Mozart, having recovered from the buffeting of the roads through the ministrations of a barber and a hairdresser, proceeded both to seek out Franz Xaver Duschek—his wife, Josepha, had just left for concert engagements in Dresden—and to confer with Guardasoni about composing a new opera for the Prague autumn season. The travelers arrived in Dresden on the twelfth (Easter Sunday) and put up at the Hotel de Pologne.[23]

When Mozart identified himself, excitement spread. It would seem that at once the hotel (which had more than one concert room) became the scene of music-making; an impromptu ensemble materialized: the Elector of Saxony's Vienna-born organist, Anton Teyber (see XXIX, n. 16), took up a violin, Mozart a viola, and Anton Kraft, the visiting first cellist of the Esterházys, his own instrument. The next day (the afternoon?) they gave a concert featuring either the Puchberg divertimento, K. 563, or, with Mozart at the keyboard, K. 542 (see n. 14) and also arias from *Figaro* and *Don Giovanni* as sung by Josepha Duschek, Mozart no doubt accompanying her.

A guest at the home of Johann Leopold Neumann, a member of the Saxon council of war, she, along with her host, hovered over Mozart's stay, and doubtless they dispatched news of his presence to the palace posthaste: on the thirteenth, during mass in the court church[24] (an opportunity for him to observe Oberkapellmeister Johann Gottlieb Naumann [see p. 146] conduct a setting of the liturgy from his own hand[25]), a member of the Elector's household approached him to suggest that he petition to appear before Frederick Augustus III and his consort, Amalie von Pfalz-Zweibrücken. Mozart pointed out that, as Lichnowsky's traveling companion, he did not have latitude to hang about, heaven knew how long, awaiting the Electoral pleasure. Like a shot—a measure of his fame—the order came that he present himself in Electress Amalie's apartments the following day: there, at half past five in the afternoon of 14 April, he played his piano concerto K. 537 and in all likelihood conducted one of his

---

23 It remains unknown where they had paused during their journey of forty-five hours over deplorable roads. As regards this tour, at times the stopping places and even the route become a matter of conjecture.

24 Augustus the Strong had ordered the construction of this masterpiece designed by Gaetano Chiaveri.

25 Mozart found it "very mediocre." That he interchanged the spellings of Naumann and Neumann can render his narration of events in Dresden bewildering to the uninitiated.

three last symphonies.[26] In return he received "a very pretty snuffbox" filled with one hundred ducats—more than half his annual pension.[27]

On the fifteenth, Mozart lunched and gave a keyboard recital at the palace of the Russian Ambassador, Prince Alexander Michailovič Beloselsky. The company then repaired to the court church so that Mozart might confront Johann Wilhelm Hässler: an Erfurt-born clavier player of north-German reputation, he had but recently declared himself eager to go to Vienna to measure himself against Mozart at the keyboard. With his sudden appearance in Dresden, Hässler became less sure of himself, and, after Mozart exhibited unparalleled command of the church's Gottfried-Silbermann organ, had to be prodded to follow. His chief credentials, Mozart observed, lay not in his hands or feet but on paper as the pupil of a pupil of Sebastian Bach.[28] Hässler possessed, Mozart wrote Constanze, the ability of a talented student. The Ambassador and his guests returned from the church to his palace with both him and Mozart in tow so that they might continue the trial, this time at the piano. Mozart entered both "competitions" because the Ambassador doubtless rewarded him with a fee commensurate with a full day of performing.

That evening in the company of Lichnowsky, he had a most agreeable experience at the opera: not the performance of Domenico Cimarosa's *Le trame deluse*—"truly awful"—but discovering Rosa Manservisi in the cast; the original Sandrina in his *La finta giardiniera*, she had appeared in Vienna from 1783 to 1785. The happy reunion formed a prelude to the conviviality with which the stay in Dresden closed at the home of the literary connoisseur Christian Gottfried Körner.[29] During the reception, his sister-in-law, Doris (Johanna Dorothea) Stock, drew her famous sketch of Mozart.[30] It shows a serious, diminutive man in profile, deep shadow—perhaps fa-

---

26 Others took part in this concert: Josepha Duschek, the flutist Johann Friedrich Prinz, and the ten-year-old cellist Nikolaus Kraft (who had accompanied his father, Anton, on tour). The palace had scheduled them and the Electoral orchestra in the first place, Mozart being added to the list at the last moment.

27 Much has been made of his having written Constanze about the snuffbox without mention of the money inside. She, of course, knew that courts preserved the euphemistic tradition of stuffing fees into ornamental boxes in the pretense that money had no part in performances before the monarch: "very" intensifying "pretty," which Mozart threw into high relief by writing it in Saxon dialect (*schene*), without question indicated to her a box crammed full.

28 Hässler's uncle and teacher, Johann Christian Kittel, had worked under Bach during his last two years of life.

29 In 1791 he would become the father of Karl Theodor Körner, to be famous for his patriotic verse.

30 By the time she assembled her memoirs, Doris remembered a Mozart "making almost daily visits to the Körners'." His schedule permitted only a single visit, which took place on either 16 or 17 April.

tigue—underlining an eye bulging from its socket. She may have caught him unawares as he sat at the keyboard, for that evening he presented himself at his most airy, the company delighting in both his improvising and his "south-German vivacity," in particular that flow of *galant* compliments the Salzburger had perfected in Vienna. Though the Hohenzollern court at Berlin and Potsdam remained the object of the journey, the civility of Dresden's musical dilettantes, rulers, and public[31] could not have but awakened in him thoughts of closer ties; above all, the House of Wettin's renown for generosity had proved anything but myth.

Mozart and Lichnowsky quit Dresden on 18 April 1789 and two days later, by way of Meissen and Wurzen, entered Leipzig, in Mozart's eyes a place of pilgrimage, thanks to the church of St. Thomas, where Sebastian Bach had served as cantor and the city's music director. His second successor, Johann Friedrich Doles, and the organist, Karl Friedrich Görner, welcomed Mozart on the twenty-second, and he improvised upon the keyboard Bach's fingers had graced. According to an affecting anecdote, which must be approached with caution, Doles had found time to assemble the choir to honor Mozart with a performance of Bach's motet *Singet dem Herrn ein neues Lied*. Overwhelmed, he asked to see the manuscripts of the motets, works hitherto unknown to him, and in the church's library, the parts arranged about him, assembled the scores in his head.

The next day Mozart left Leipzig for Potsdam to arrive on the twenty-fifth. Frederick William II directed Mozart's request to perform before him to the court's supervisor of concerts, Jean-Pierre Duport (*l'aîné*). At the time he had met the almost eight-year-old Mozart in Paris, this cellist and composer, then in Prince Conti's orchestra, had already achieved success at the Concert spirituel. Summoned to Berlin by Frederick the Great in 1773, he became royal first cellist and also teacher of cello to the young Prince Frederick William, who soon excelled at it. While waiting to learn the date of his appearance,[32] Mozart took the practical step of composing a set of keyboard variations, K. 573, upon a minuet by Duport.

Information about Mozart's initial audience at the palace does not survive. Other appearances must have followed, for he remained in Potsdam

---

31 Ambassador Beloselsky indicated that part of this public preferred how Mozart played to what he played and gave the preference to Naumann as composer.

32 From the oboist Ramm, whom a tour had taken to Prussia, friends of Mozart in Prague had knowledge that the King had word (perhaps through Lichnowsky) of his impending visit. Written in a stiff, absurd style, the cabinet memorandum announcing Mozart's arrival to Frederick William—the contemptuous diction recalls that of Malvolio or the majordomo in Strauss's *Ariadne*—has puzzled and infuriated many. Yet every court had its stock of ignorant and snobbish retainers.

until 6 May, by which time there had come into his hands a commission to compose six string quartets for Frederick William's chamber group and six easy piano sonatas for Princess Friedericke Charlotte;[33] all augured well for a splendid fee.[34] He then broke his Prussian stay to make an excursion back to Leipzig, arriving on the eighth.

Four days later he gave a concert with Frau Duschek in Leipzig's handsome Gewandhaus (Cloth Hall).[35] Among other offerings, he performed two of his piano concertos (K. 456 and 503?) while she sang the scenas K. 505 and 528; and the public also heard two Mozart symphonies, perhaps chosen from among the last three. The cheers and applause turned out to be more striking than the size of the audience: the costs of hiring hall and orchestra had forced ticket prices beyond what the thrifty Leipzigers as a rule paid. In addition, Mozart discovered that he had entered into rivalry with himself: that very night the Leipzig opera house had his *Figaro* on the boards.

By this time he no longer had Lichnowsky's helping hand in the matter of living expenses:[36] during the first *séjour* in Leipzig the Prince had gone on alone to Berlin. And though he did return to Leipzig for the concert, having, in fact, been the spirit encouraging it, they again went their separate ways; but not before he seized the occasion to get back part of what he had lent Mozart. Aware of his receipt of one hundred ducats (four hundred fifty gulden) from the Elector of Saxony and of the impending reward from the King of Prussia, Lichnowsky claimed to be for the moment short of funds and "borrowed" one hundred gulden from his erstwhile fellow voyager. That he had as yet to come forward with any gesture toward squaring accounts may have disappointed Lichnowsky.

---

33 The King's daughter by his first wife, Elisabeth Christine Ulrike von Braunschweig, she would marry George III of England's second son, Frederick Augustus, since 1784 Duke of York, in two ceremonies: the first in Berlin, the second in London at Buckingham House (23 November 1791). During their honeymoon, they welcomed Haydn to the little castle of Oatlands (near Weybridge in Surrey) from which he took away the impression of an engaging new Duchess not without ability at the keyboard. Mozart had met the Dukes of York and Gloucester of the preceding generation in London (see p. 185) and encountered the latter Prince again in Milan in October 1771, during the days of *Ascanio in Alba*.

34 Mozart's surviving correspondence makes clear that he discussed the commission and fee with Constanze in one of his lost letters.

35 Built in 1781, it replaced an earlier Gewandhaus.

36 Once alone, Mozart avoided hotels and stayed with musicians: at Potsdam the horn player Karl Türrschmidt, who had been in service at Wallerstein; at Berlin the trumpeter Möser, father and teacher of violinist Karl Möser. Even so, the diplomat Karl August Varnhagen von Ense did hear of Mozart's having made a stop in Berlin at the inn Zur Stadt Paris.

Even so, there appears to have been no ill feeling between them: they parted as friends.[37]

Meanwhile, King Frederick William had returned from Potsdam to Berlin (some fifteen miles apart); there Mozart now betook himself, arriving on 19 May. That evening, anecdote would have it, he attended a performance of his *Abduction* (under the title *Belmonte and Constanze*[38]) at the Royal National theater, where the almost sixteen-year-old Johann Ludwig Tieck sought him out; a meeting no doubt took place: this poet-to-be and fiery admirer of Mozart would have made his acquaintance one way or another. On the twenty-third he may have gone to a concert by Hummel, now ten and on tour in the company of his father. Berlin's *Spenersche Zeitung* identified the *Wunderkind* as "a pupil of the famous Herr Mozart."[39]

Three days later he appeared before the King and Queen (his second wife, Friedericke von Hessen-Darmstadt[40]), in all probability the occasion upon which Frederick William gave him an auspicious token of Hohenzollern interest: one hundred friedrichs d'or, that is, eight hundred gulden. The sum must have represented not only a deposit on the quartets and sonatas but compensation for the concerts, whose confinement to the court—at royal insistence—had cost him the advantage of a public appearance[41]. Musicians knew of Frederick William's generosity to Boccherini, a resident of Spain who received a pension from Berlin in exchange for new compositions; did those friedrichs d'or raise Mozart's hopes that a parallel arrangement might be put into place for him? It seemed wise to make haste with the commission; and, more pressing, a revival of *Figaro* impended in Vienna and required revisions. He turned toward home.

On 28 May 1789 he quit Berlin for Dresden, stayed overnight, arrived on the thirty-first in Prague (where he remained until 2 June), and on the fourth passed through the gates of Vienna. He could not wait to embrace his Constanze. Without news of one another for long periods, both had suffered, she for his safety, he for her health. Blame, he insisted, lay with the postal relays and the vagaries of the poste restante: not a few of their

---

37 I have postulated Lichnowsky's reason for making the puzzling "loan," perhaps the turning point of a relationship that would soon sour and the root of the lawsuit he would bring against Mozart some two and a half years later (see pp. 742–43).

38 "A work that may be considered a model of the German style and does the German genius honor," Berlin's *Theater-Zeitung für Deutschland* reported.

39 The previous year he had ended the boy's lessons and declared him ready to tour.

40 Her sister, Louise, had married Duke Carl August von Sachsen-Weimar-Eisenach, the sovereign Goethe served.

41 "The King would not look upon it with pleasure," Mozart reported to Constanze.

letters had vanished, the reason for the holes punctuating what survives of the journey's narrative, gaps that have added to an air of mystery many find in it.[42]

Mozart had embarked upon the tour in order to take advantage of a princely invitation, though he may well have fished for it. The time and effort had been well spent: he had made new connections and returned with a heavy purse and reasonable expectations[43]—and this during the summer in which General Laudon took command of the Imperial forces and reversed their fortune. No doubt to his adjutants' relief, Emperor Joseph's continuing illness prevented his return to the front, and plans for the coming season at the Burgtheater took shape once again under his direct influence; they would as a matter of course include Mozart. He had surmounted the melting away of his Viennese career as a pianist, juggled his debts with no little guile, and, as his letters held out, seemed about to turn the corner.

4

THIS CORRESPONDENCE ALSO records his attempt to resolve a particular inner discord that had long resisted harmonizing: he suffered occasional jealous irritations troubling his relationship with Constanze. His prose has a playful, teasing quality persisting even as he confronts this issue as old as their courtship (see XXIX, n. 7): while protesting utter faith in her "honor," he nonetheless requests—though with caution—that she disport herself with more reserve at social gatherings, where "appearances" from time to time have spoken against her. He asks forgiveness for having raised the matter (not the first time, for certain), insisting that now she must love him even more since his having brought it up reveals the depth of his solicitude for the sanctity of their union. Throughout these letters, his need to play the fatherly husband comes to the fore, and accumulating diminutives leave the reader with thoughts of Ibsen's Torvald Helmer lecturing his wife, Nora. In Mozart's exercise, too, the "itsy-bitsy" locution envelopes a moral rebuke—a series of aggressive, preaching recommendations for self-improvement à la Leopold Mozart.

---

42 Nourished by the fact that little documentation other than his own words substantiates Mozart's account of his movements during this northern tour, the idea has grown that much of his tale borders upon fraud practiced to mask various amorous rendezvous with Madame Duschek. I find no grounds for this theory; see n. 49.

43 An advertisement that Rellstab's music shop placed in the *Berlinische Nachrichten von Staats—und gelehrten Sachen*, 9 May 1789, listed an item providing a measure of the interest Mozart's visit excited: "the complete works of Mozart," no doubt a miscellany bringing together printed scores and scribes' copies.

Constanze's free spirit[44] seems to have stood firm against this technique of putting her on the plane of a child as he burdened the air with accusations. Quite early she must have made out the pattern of this obsession of odd quirks and coped with it. On at least one occasion she had found it expedient to give ground, promising to resist her too easy ways (*zu nachgebend*), no doubt an olive branch held out to calm an excessive manifestation of his recurring anxiety. She could never have long played the role Ibsen's Nora assumes to please her husband, that of a foolish little squirrel's brain; rather, she had straightway become a partner from whose natural astuteness Mozart drew strength, and no doubt on his side an inner control applied a brake to infected fancy and stopped it from becoming insupportable delusion. If Constanze's reaction to the complex spirit of his latest lecture on proper demeanor can only be conjectured, she could not have but enjoyed those moments in his letters when he put the question aside to become a ruttish boy full of intimate erotic protestations and sexual passwords akin to those once exchanged with the Bäsle.

The Mozarts' love rested upon a rich sexuality. He professed his conjugal faithfulness by intimating to her that while on tour his only relief from the agonies of separation lay in masturbating with his eyes fixed upon her portrait: "My little wife . . . were I willing to tell you everything I do with your dear portrait, you would indeed laugh": midst sexual lispings of "Stru! Stru!, this word of such great significance and demanding a certain *emphasis*," he invoked the image of the portrait being "taken out of its case and bit by bit slipped back." The ground tone of his letters asserts the couple's joy in existing together and confidence in the future even if, though still a captive to her charms and certain of her devotion, he could not resist those sporadic attempts to reconstruct her according to his personal design.

He had always drawn upon his own nature and necessity to frame idealized images of the various women toward whom he felt powerful attraction: once he had projected these exalted qualities upon them, he became enamored of the resultant illusions, which, in turn, fed the need first evoking them. Such a self-referential cycle defining the Dulcinea in the lover's own terms remains self-sufficient and satisfying only while the idol stays intact; alas, the pressures of reality can at any moment turn it to dust, an experience Mozart suffered more than once. His Figaro, the scales fallen from his eyes—so he believes—denounces such "so-called goddesses" as "sirens who sing to make us [males] drown." The horns sound forth his supposed cuckoldry.

---

44 She had grown up in the world of actors and opera singers (see p. 558).

Mozart's criticism of Constanze's conviviality betrays the intricacies of his attitude toward women. It cannot be doubted that during the transformation of *Figaro* from play into opera, it was he who remade the Countess's "growing passion" (Beaumarchais's phrase) for the page into a not indifferent but aristocratic patience with his advances: by the final curtain Beaumarchais's hot-blooded Countess has become a Mozartean goddess presiding over an enchanted garden. At the root of Mozart's compulsion to raise up goddesses lay the mythical misogynistic belief in man's vulnerability before women's engulfing potential for fickleness and betrayal, covert ways that might well lead to venereal infection and thus threaten genital pleasures—solicitudes his next opera would transform into art. In *Così fan tutte* the maid of the women at the center of the plot would ask them: "Are you flesh and blood; just what are you?" And in like way, a friend would question their military lovers: "What species . . . do your beauties belong to . . . ; in short, are they goddesses or women?"

Mozart's own goddess remained intact excepting those flaws of irrepressible social exuberance that in a woman, he feared, invited misunderstanding. This thought, however, could in no way have taken the lead as he raced into Constanze's arms a moment after his coach pulled up to the post stage at Enzersdorf, just outside Vienna. He had asked that she drive out to meet him and bring along Carl, the Puchbergs, and Hofer (and also a factotum to deal with the luggage and the customs). From Berlin, Mozart had written to her like a bridegroom torn from his beloved and suddenly close upon reunion; he contemplated it in no other terms but of his penis, his diction calling to mind that of Lady Chatterley's lover: "Get your dear and lovely nest ready and most prettily, for my little fellow indeed deserves it. He has behaved very well and desires only to possess your beautiful [. . .].[45] Picture to yourself the rogue who, even as I write, creeps up onto the table and looks up at me questioningly. On guard, I give him a smart slap . . . but the rascal only burns yet more and can hardly be controlled." This exultation in the glory of an erected phallus would become a literary motif of *Così fan tutte*, in which a number of metaphors refer to the phenomenon (see n. 63).

The Mozarts settled into comfortable routine on the Judenplatz. He lost little time getting to work on the Prussian commission: by July he had completed both a quartet (K. 575) and a piano sonata (K. 576). The first took cognizance of Frederick William's talent, which eclipsed the usual limits of princely dilettantism: the violoncello has its share of handsome

---

45 In the original manuscript what must have been a coarse colloquialism has suffered obliteration.

melodic material;[46] in the second Mozart lost sight of its purpose as an easy vehicle for Princess Friedericke, its Bach-like contrapuntal devices and display-piece finale challenging the fingers.

5

ALL AT ONCE he lost the collected spirit necessary to composing; the Prussian commission lay dormant as crisis enveloped his household: Constanze had taken to bed with a menacing illness. His efforts to meet its mounting costs fed the crescendo rising in the *Bittbriefe*. If hyperbole and histrionism pervade the earlier letters to Puchberg,[47] unfeigned distress prevails when the matter concerns Constanze's needs, impassioned alarm often approaching hysteria. Death threatened, and he could not conceive of life without her. He remained too proud to apply for help to friends not part of the Masonic brotherhood; among others, Countess Thun would no doubt have stepped forward had he made a request. Giving subscription concerts at home again came to mind, but in the end he abstained from the idea. Constanze's malady had turned the household into a sick-chamber.

Delicate of frame, she had always been fragile. From the first days of their courtship her trim figure had bewitched him. He could, however, admire it only at rare intervals: at his death after nine years and four months of marriage, she had delivered six children, and the number of miscarriages can only be guessed; he kept her in an almost permanent state of pregnancy. Just when her perennial poor health turned toward the critical cannot be determined, but within weeks of his return from the tour, his laments concerned, not rent and merchants' bills, but how to cover the costs of medicines, treatments, and a possible long, expensive cure in the country.[48]

Even before his departure for Prussia, pain in one foot and the burden of carrying a child had made it difficult for her to go her rounds, and from Dresden he had warned of the risk of falling, cautioning her "not to go

---

46 The Andante of K. 575 has affinities to the most famous of Mozart's songs, *"Das Veilchen"* (K. 476; June, 1785), his only setting of a text by Goethe.

47 During the summer of 1788, for example, Mozart took items to the pawnshop and then asked Puchberg to raise money for him on the tickets; the request seems a ruse to stir pity and spur assistance.

48 His financial picture further darkened in August when, as the money brought from Prussia drained away, there fell due that bill of exchange arranged with Hofdemel (see p. 690), who, in turn, had endorsed it to a third party.

walking alone—and, still better—not to go out walking at all." Early in July 1789, Thomas Franz Closset, the Mozarts' physician (since Sigmund Barisani's death in 1787), informed him that a serious infection, indeed, ulceration, threatened the bone of the foot and could prove fatal. The danger lasted until late in the month even as she contracted bedsores and had no sleep. In despair Mozart watched her "await recovery or death with true philosophic composure."

Despite Dr. Closset's leeches, little by little her health and spirits began to repair, and by August he deemed her strong enough to leave for Baden, a spa some fifteen miles south of Vienna, to undergo its sulphur-spring cure. There Mozart rented ground-floor rooms for her—she still could not manage stairs with ease—and visited when he could escape the city. In his absence friends and pupils filled his place and, most important, took her to the baths: he feared she might fall on the paths or slip during the descent into the waters: "Never go out walking alone," he again cautioned; "the thought frightens me." These warnings and their purpose must be stressed because, wrenched from context, they have been misrepresented as reflecting his fears that, unescorted, she might have amatory encounters. If such distortion deserves contempt, so does his return, alas, to his old complaint.

At Baden she received an admiring letter and, as a matter of course, showed it to him. In turn he accused her of behavior that had "misled" a "well-behaved fellow very much respectful of women" into writing "the most coarse and disgusting sottise." Pointing to others with whom, in his view, she had been "too free," he mounted the pulpit to deliver his old tiring lesson: "A woman must always conduct herself with decorum lest people talk"; though delighted to observe her once again "happy," he returned to the same trampled ground, urging that she curb a manner sometimes giving the impression of her being "cheap" (*gemein*). "Be merry, cheerful, and obliging to me. Do not torment the two of us with unnecessary jealousy[!]. Trust in my love—surely you have proofs of it!—and you will see how happy we shall be."

He did not identify her supposed gallants but put to use the letters "N. N." indicating the Latin *nomen nescio* (I do not know the name) or *non nominato* (I do not name). For her part, Constanze appears to have conceived of her possible rivals in abstract terms: she had come to feel insecure when comparing herself to the glamorous women of society and the stage he knew. With humor he reassured her from Dresden that for the moment she need have no apprehension on this score inasmuch as the "large gathering" at the Neumanns' "for the most part consisted of ugly women, whose charm, however, made up for their lack of beauty." Whatever her anxieties, they seem to have been generic and of long standing.[49]

His sermons to a recuperating invalid in the sixth month of pregnancy touched the grotesque. Worry had undermined his self-possession, and apprehension of shortcomings not Constanze's but his own may well have been the undercurrent shaping this frame of mind. He resembled his Figaro spying as he scrambles through the gardens of Aguasfrescas at the close of the *folle journée*, tormenting himself with foolish imaginings: "Oh, Susanna, what pain you have cost me!" In the end this suffering proves a medicine for jealousy as Susanna teaches Figaro the meaning of trust.

During this summer of 1789, *Figaro* very much occupied Mozart: in fact, he made his way to Baden only by stealing time from work on its revival at the Burgtheater. There his immediate task consisted of coming to terms with Vienna's new prima donna: the soprano Adriana Ferrarese del Bene, called La Ferrarese. She had arrived with a reputation won at London's The King's Theater and at La Scala, and her Viennese debut (Burgtheater, 1788, in Martin y Soler's *L'abore di Diana*) had been a sensation. Now cast as Susanna in the *Figaro* revival, this imposing singer, who had become Da Ponte's mistress, found the part of the servant far from meeting her needs—she wanted to measure herself against Cavalieri, the new Countess—and Mozart had to replace two arias: the calm, heartfelt *"Deh vieni"* in the fourth act with the bigger, wider-ranging, bravura *"Al desio"* (K. 577) and *"Venite, inginocchiatevi"* in the second—in fact, less a true aria than a lovely vocal gloss set above the orchestra—with *"Un moto di gioia"* (K. 579), intended to demonstrate the soprano's ability to project a naïve simplicity and lightness. Mozart doubted she could: as yet, he did not have a high opinion of her art.

Cavalieri would not suffer the expansion of Susanna's role—from La Ferraresi's time to today well nigh every countess has resented it as far too important[50]—without seeking some enhancement of her own: Mozart tampered with her third-act aria, *"Dove sono,"* in the process weakening the

---

49 Would Mozart have dared dilate upon the subject of the N. N.s had he entangled himself in an affair with Madame Duschek (see n. 42), who by this time had, in fact, become quite plain? In light of the gossip and mistrust spawned as a matter of course by such a dalliance, would Constanze have availed herself of Madame Duschek's hospitality during the production of *La clemenza* in Prague (1791) or, after Mozart's death, extended a generous loan to her during a financial crisis? Through the years the two women preserved undiminished mutual good will.

50 Susanna forms the core of the opera: she sings in every ensemble.

finespun filaments. For the new Count, in all probability Albertarelli, he raised the tessitura of the grand aria in the same act.[51]

Constanze proved sufficiently restored in health[52] to attend the premiere of the acclaimed revival of *Figaro* (29 August) under the baton of the twenty-three-year-old Joseph Weigl. Mozart then continued to let the Prussian commission lie dormant as he turned to composing a four-movement quintet, K. 581 for clarinet and string quartet, to be performed by Anton Stadler at the Society of Musicians' Christmas concerts on 22 and 23 December. K. 581 has a minuet with two trios, the first for strings alone and thus permitting the soloist respite in the course of the demanding part. Mozart wrote this supreme achievement in the realm of chamber music for a variant instrument Stadler himself had developed by devising a downward extension of the clarinet's range.

The melody of a sketch (K. Anh. 88/581a) Mozart began for the quintet's finale and then discarded returns in *Così fan tutte* to open Ferrando's aria *"Ah! lo veggio."* The fragment[53] forms an evocative link between quintet and opera, as does their ravishing beauty, nourishing in the listener the Faustian hope that it abide.

6

SALIERI RECEIVED THE libretto of *Così*, made a start on the two opening trios, and then abandoned a text he found—so Constanze Mozart remembered—uncongenial. Yet, his desire to be done with it also may have arisen from his mounting antagonism toward Da Ponte, which mirrored the ever fiercer rivalry between their mistresses, Cavalieri and La Ferrarese. Salieri relinquished the libretto to Mozart, but the path that brought it to his desk may have had a yet earlier twist.

Mozart's influence upon the text appears pervasive, indeed determinative, and his direct contributions to it far and wide more than touches applied after Salieri's withdrawal. Thus the idea suggests itself that in the

51 As in the case of *Don Giovanni*, he must have received a substantial fee for such ad hoc changes, which today's productions for the most part ignore, holding fast to the first and superior version. He resisted any temptation to put his hand to the faulty structure of the final act with its unrelenting parade of five arias. To create the nimble flow of the earlier acts, he had postponed to the last the solos tradition demanded for Basilio, Marcellina, and even Barbarina: three arias had to be added to those of Figaro and Susanna. The matter remained beyond repair: indeed, he had made no attempt at it in Prague. Although *Così*'s second act has six arias, its better designed framework of ensembles accommodates them in graceful fashion.
52 On 16 November she would give birth to her fifth child, Anna Maria, who survived only one hour.
53 Some hold that it did not inspire but derived from the aria.

beginning Da Ponte put the book together for and with Mozart and then, whatever the compulsion, had to cede it to Salieri. He, once aware of his inability to come to terms with the idiosyncratic affair, turned it back to Mozart, who, in sequel, worked with Da Ponte on further refining the libretto.

Although his ill health continued to deepen, the Emperor could not have stayed aloof from the vagaries of the commission and its ultimate bestowal. In December 1789, Mozart told Puchberg that the opera would bring a double fee of two hundred ducats (nine hundred florins);[54] and here, perhaps, Joseph's hand may be glimpsed: he himself may have provided the supplement, having learned of Constanze's expensive illness. Or did he wish to neutralize rumors of renewed efforts to lure Mozart abroad? Indeed, the music publisher John Bland, who had arrived from England to persuade Joseph Haydn to visit London—they would confer at Esterháza early in November—extended a similar invitation to Mozart.

Whether or not Joseph had a voice in selecting the subject, its misogyny comported well with his own. Don Alfonso, *Così*'s master-manipulator, compares woman's constancy to a wonder often discussed but never beheld—"the phoenix of Araby." Da Ponte, who had employed the metaphor earlier in *Il ricco d'un giorno* and *Una cosa rara,* here has Alfonso adapt Metastasio's version of it (*Demetrio,* 1731), the verses also alluding to Shakespeare's "Arabian bird" (see p. 705). Later, Da Ponte puts into Alfonso's mouth Jacopo Sannazaro's simile likening trust in the female heart to "plowing the sea, sowing the sands, and gathering the wind in a net." Such references sent signals to a ruler, in his own estimate, "made neither to give nor receive love": Alfonso's capacity for disdain and brutality call to mind Joseph, who no doubt gave the book his blessing.

By August, when Mozart began work on the score of *Così,* he had entered upon the artistic courtship of Vienna's latest star, the soprano Louise Villeneuve, whom he provided with a trio of insert arias.[55] She was to play

---

54 That a theater ledger records Mozart's fee for *Così* at four hundred fifty florins does not exclude his having received an additional emolument from the throne: such had been the case in respect to the Munich *Idomeneo* (see p. 525). In the ingrown operatic world of Vienna, to exaggerate the payment for so important a premiere would have been an invitation to exposure.

55 *"Alma grande"* (K. 578, the words by Giuseppe Palomba) for Cimarosa's *I due baroni di Rocca Azzurra;* and then two arias (October) to be sung in Soler's *Il burbero:* "Chi sà" and *"Vado, ma dove?"* (K. 582 and 583, respectively, their texts attributed to Da Ponte). The month earlier, for performances of Paisiello's *Barber* in German proposed by the Freihaustheater (see pp. 720–21) and to feature Mozart's sister-in-law Josepha Hofer as Rosina, he started the aria *"Schon lacht der holde Frühling,"* K. 580, for the music-lesson scene. When the production fell through, he broke off the orchestration.

the role of Dorabella, La Ferrarese that of Fiordiligi,[56] the sisters about whom the intrigue of the new work turned.

At first Da Ponte had located the action in the Habsburg port of Trieste, in that Adriatic sphere he knew so well. It must have been Mozart who shifted the site to Naples: during his Grand Tour, the beauty of its environs had much impressed him and his father, as had the area's rich classical associations (see n. 64); they give a bizarre atmosphere to the precincts become residence to the sisters the libretto identifies as from Ferrara (Da Ponte's salute to his mistress). The Viennese, however, recognized the personages of the opera as their own.

When Mozart and Da Ponte sat down to *Così*, the Turkish War had months to run, and it provided the mainspring of the plot, the agents releasing the mechanism taking the form of Turks or all but Turks—Albanians. The Emperor's subjects could enter into the argument with ease: their cafés spilled over with swaggering young officers like Guglielmo and Ferrando (the first, Fiordiligi's lover; the second, Dorabella's)[57] awaiting posting, often peremptory, to the eastern front. In their own words, Guglielmo and Ferrando "do not lack women"[58] as they loll about.

Mozart gave the opera (K. 588) the name by which posterity would know it: adding a prefix to *La schuola degli amanti*, the title Da Ponte first chose, Mozart expanded it to *Così fan tutte ossia La schuola degli amanti* (*All Woman Act Like That or The School for Lovers*). He took the phrase from a remark in the opening act of his *Figaro*: Don Basilio, witnessing the discovery of the page, Cherubino, hiding in Susanna's room, observes of her and, indeed, of all beautiful women, "*Così fan tutte le belle.*" His chortling vocal line reappears in *Così*'s overture as part of a theme that seems to chase itself in mimicry of the circular route the main protagonists must travel,[59] a harsh course mapped by the officers' friend the philosophe Don Alfonso:

---

56 Mozart composed both roles for soprano. Today, mezzos most often sing the lower-lying part of Dorabella, perhaps because taste favors a contrast of timbres. As in the case of Wagnerian soprano roles now assumed by mezzos or even contraltos—Brangäne and Ortrud, for example—vocal strain often enough shows itself in the upper reaches of the voice.

57 Francesco Benucci sang the part of Guglielmo, Vincenzo Calvesi that of Ferrando. A lyric tenor admired for his sweet sound and finished technique, Calvesi had made his debut at the Burgtheater in 1785. For the role of the sisters' maid, Despina, Mozart chose his original Cherubino in *Figaro*, Dorotea Bussani; as Don Alfonso he cast the accomplished "doubler" who had first sung Bartolo and Antonio in *Figaro* and the Commendatore and Masetto at the Viennese premiere of *Don Giovanni*—Francesco Bussani, Dorotea's husband.

58 Despina urges the sisters to face the fact that "as to men and, in particular, soldiers, they labor in vain to put trust in fidelity."

59 The overture also presents the hortative phrase to which Don Alfonso, just before the finale to the last act, sings the lesson-motto, "*così fan tutte*," which the officers repeat after him like schoolboys. Whereas Basilio arraigned only beautiful women, Alfonso includes the ugly ("*e belle e brutte*").

he has received their wager that, under amatory assault, their women will not betray, and, to prove the point, each, taking on Albanian disguise, must woo the betrothed of the other in order to test her constancy.

Alfonso's calculated dissimulations, which guide their tactics, bring to mind the cunning valet Dubois, in Marivaux's *Les fausses confidences* (The Deceitful Disclosures, 1736). A man of few moral scruples, Dubois, too, sets schemes into motion through a series of *fausses confidences* that both ensnare and humiliate. His determination to make his social betters dance to his tune has given him a place in literary history as an ancestor of Beaumarchais's Figaro, a pedigree to be acknowledged only with the strong reminder that this personable rogue never explores the avenues of cruelty through which Dubois moves with ease. The bizarre ethics of *Les fausses confidences*—its hero, Dorante, for all his charm and gallantry, does not shun deceit—pervades the character of *Così*'s Don Alfonso: respectable birth offers no hindrance to his fastening upon devices worthy of Dubois, whom Mozart and Da Ponte had opportunities to observe on the stage of the Burgtheater in its revival of *Les fausses confidences* (translated by Gotter as *Die falschen Vertraulichkeiten*) in 1785. It returned to the repertory during 1790, the year of *Così*'s premiere.

At all events, even before experiencing the Burgtheater's production of *Die falschen Vertraulichkeiten*, Mozart had met with a well-born deceiver who would influence the evolution of *Così*: the cynic Iachimo, in Shakespeare's *Cymbeline*. He maintains that even if "you buy ladies' flesh at a million a dram, you cannot preserve it from tainting." Extending this bait for sheer mischief's sake, he draws the proud Posthumus into a gamble giving trial to the virtue of his wife, Imogen.[60] In Vienna, Mozart had no doubt seen the drama, first performed at the Burgtheater (under the title of *Imogen*[61]) on 16 December 1782. Moreover, his sister's diary records that during his visit to Salzburg the following year, he attended the theater on 10 October, on which date a touring company performed the tragicomedy.

Its motif of a wager on woman's fidelity along with odds and ends of the play's imagery can be discovered in the text of *Così*: Iachimo, first beholding the dazzling Imogen and wondering whether she "is alone the Arabian bird," cites the very marvel, "the phoenix of Araby," Don Alfonso would evoke in the second trio of *Così*; Posthumus, tricked by Iachimo into believing Imogen false, calls the ring she gave him "a basilisk unto mine eye,"

---

60 Although not a Shakespearean villain of Iago's or Edmund's stature, Iachimo has a place alongside Proteus among the scoundrels.

61 Friedrich Ludwig Wilhelm Meyer made this version.

an outburst echoed in the cry of Fiordiligi as she flees her first intimacy with Ferrando: "I have seen an asp, a hydra, a basilisk!"; and Posthumus, lamenting that the "vows of women / Of no more bondage be to where they are made / Than they are to their virtues, which is nothing. / O, above measure false!," enunciates the pithy substance of Don Alfonso's lesson as first interpreted, but in the wrong, by the officers.

Broader reflections of Shakespeare and Marivaux may be traced in the libretto of Così: symmetrical patterns, exploitation of disguise, and interchange of lovers. (Mozart and Da Ponte knew, indeed, very well, Shakespeare's *A Midsummer-Night's Dream*, with its errant couplings.[62]) Yet such devices have histories extending from the ancient era, and Da Ponte's wide reading had lodged in his memory a multitude of recollections to be absorbed into the new opera: incidents from other literary works—Ovid's *Metamorphoses* (the story of Cephalus and Procris in the seventh book), Boccaccio's *Decameron*, Ariosto's *Orlando Furioso*, Tasso's *Gerusalemme liberata*, Tirso de Molina's *El Amor medico* and *La celosa de sí misma*; and also ideas from operas—among them, the Gassmann-Goldoni *Le pescatrici* (1771; here, in particular, the motif of youths who assume disguise to test their sweethearts' fidelity), Salieri and Casti's *La Grotta di Trofonio* (1785) with its shuttling, realigning sex partners, and Martin y Soler and Da Ponte's own *L'arbore di Diana* (1787). Taking a leaf here and there, Da Ponte built an original scenario, its protagonists contemporary and wealthy bourgeois; proceeding with relentless logic, his elegant words sound a gamut ranging from elevated rhetoric to the most delicate shades of intimate emotion.[63] In company with Mozart he assembled his masterpiece.

---

62 After jarring discords, Shakespeare's four lovers fall asleep to awaken paired off as in the beginning. The two couples in *Così* experience no such magical and painless restoration: their Oberon and Puck appear in the mortal forms of the exacting Don Alfonso and his agent, Despina.

63 The libretto treats with polished style even the subject of raw sex. Mozart had Da Ponte replace Guglielmo's "*Rivolgete a lui*" with "*Non siate ritrosi*" (no. 15) not only because of the first aria's excessive length and very heavy accumulation of classical allusions (to Croesus, Narcissus, Mark Anthony, the Cyclops, and Aesop, to say nothing of those heroes of the legends of Charlemagne, Medor and Roland [Orlando]): "*Rivolgete*" concluded with a too pungent reference to the as yet hidden assets ("*qualch' altro capitale*") each soldier held ready for the conquest of his comrade's sweetheart, resources for which Fiordiligi found more inferential euphemisms. The substitute aria, too, sounded parallel images, but lyrical and less provocative: it, for example, celebrated the men's long mustaches as plumes of love (*pennachi d'amor*). (Even so, in the next act Mozart let stand Guglielmo's brusque extolling of his priapic superiority [*un poco di più merto*] over Ferrando.) Mozart entered the suppressed aria (K. 584) in his catalogue as an independent composition.

7

IN THEIR *DON GIOVANNI*, Vienna had experienced high pathos and low comedy, both fraught with a chilling and violent ruthlessness. It, however, dimmed but did not eclipse the colors of Christian chivalry and virtue; the opera had its origins in the miracle play: a crew of devils waited in the wings to haul the hero off to hell, and the listener, even while enjoying the spectacle of maleficence, had the certainty that the Divine would in the end assert Its will. *Così* offered no such assurances.

Deriving from the spirit of Enlightened science and system, it proceeds as a demonstration testing Alfonso's hypothesis that "all women act like that." He and Despina assemble the materials the trial requires—villagers, servants, caterers, musicians, soldiers, sailors (their boats, too!) along with two standard clowns of the commedia dell' arte tradition—the bogus doctor and the notary. Unfolding as a hoax played in a vacuum, *Così* gives God's dispensing power to the philosophe:[64] having established through brutal methods that the female's capacity for passion and change does not fall short of the male's, he advises the lovers to recognize the existence of this mutual potential and come to terms with it; the resolution, to be effected through Enlightened mediation and compromise, was to embrace that partial and reciprocal surrender called marriage, here the venerable comedic view of it as a social rather than a personal avowal.[65]

---

64 Throughout *Così*, its characters talk not of God but of the ancient gods (*dei* and *numi*): Giove, Palla, Citerea, Amore, and Bacco; Dorabella invokes the Eumenides, Fiordiligi starts at the thought of the hydra, and Alfonso and Guglielmo summon up the examples of goddesslike heroines, the first citing Penelope, the second bringing forward Artemesia. Although Fiordiligi makes mention of servants apart from Despina—Don Alfonso suborns and augments them with his own creatures—and there is talk of neighbors and the power of rumor, *Così*, its up-to-date setting apart, unfolds in a hermetic, self-contained pagan void, its remoteness intensified by classical references to the grotto of Vulcan, the gate to the underworld, and Charon's boat. They echo the sightseeing of Mozart and his father in the environs of Naples during their Grand Tour: Leopold Mozart's journal records their visits to "the underground grottos of the Cumaean Sybil" and "the Sea of the Dead on which Charon was ferryman." Mozart's direct contributions to the text, indeed his very personal touches, can be felt not only here—Da Ponte had never been to Naples—but also in the scene of Mesmeric "healing" (see p. 244), the thrust at Swabian dialect (see XXVI, n. 13), and the reference in Guglielmo's suppressed aria to Carlos de Picq, the famous dancer who had contributed to the premiere of Mozart's *Silla.*

65 I find in the pragmatic *Così* none of the pastoral spirit many ascribe to it, perhaps beguiled by its Neapolitan scenery, evocations of ancient names, paraphrases of Ariosto, and, above all, the heavenly wind-accompanied serenade (no. 21) for Guglielmo and Ferrando: the house and park on the bay represent anything but a bucolic haven in which to play at Virgilian shepherd and to seek security against the outer world, the suitors and their women anything but lovers yearning to repudiate its overcivilization, the strand and the dock anything but a port from which to embark for Cytherean isles.

The bitter and contradictory impulses at work in *Così* reveal a dark comedy in the Shakespearean sense and suggest links to that episode in Baden touching Constanze's liveliness and high temperament; Mozart's cruel and absurd observations at the time lead one to ponder what strange laws governed him during these hostile outbursts resembling paternal, Leopold-like reproofs: he may have taken an odd gratification in acting the stern father censuring his own kind of playfulness and delight in pleasure. Even more telling, *Così's* motif of two young men, each wooing one sister and then another, opens a view in dislocated perspective of his earlier days.

Although he had taken a virginal sweetheart to bed, his acquaintance with the story of a pregnant Aloisia kneeling before the marriage altar perhaps had intensified his qualms, emotional and practical, about Constanze's outgoing spirit and just how far it differed from Aloisia's. Horror of infection continued to occupy him: that each sister in *Così*, high attitudes notwithstanding, enjoys the sexual attentions of her soldier explains the men's violent reaction to Don Alfonso's raising the idea that their preserves stood vulnerable to poaching. The libretto, in fact, goes out of its way to make clear Fiordiligi's and Dorabella's free way of life: when not on duty, their officers live with them in the seaside house—to which Don Alfonso also has access—and maintain extensive wardrobes there (*molte uniformi*). In a remarkable scene, Fiordiligi, making ready to disguise herself as a soldier in order to rush to the front and join her Guglielmo, sends Despina to the press to fetch uniforms. Fiordiligi finds that not his attire but Ferrando's suits her and concludes that Dorabella must pull on Guglielmo's and make the journey with her. The voluptuous discovery presaging their infidelity (and not unrelated to Mozart's infatuation about dress) prepares Fiordiligi's great duet with the disguised Ferrando, "*Fra gli amplessi,*" in the course of which she sinks heart and soul under his spell.

Creating these unbuttoned characters helped Mozart lay to rest the strange specters of his mind concerning Constanze (many of them no doubt born of his sense of inadequacy when confronting the N. N.s of this world): Don Alfonso speaks through Mozart to Mozart as he instructs Guglielmo and Ferrando that "nature neither makes exceptions nor grants the favor of creating two women intrinsically unique." "Take them as they are," he advises. In the compliant, coquettish Dorabella, Mozart may have given play to aspects of Aloisia, in the tenacious, soul-searching Fiordiligi to those of his beloved Constanze. At all events, through *Così* he appears to have realized resolution: she would next materialize on stage as a protector and guide sharing her lover's struggle to the full. *Così* promised neither joy nor even simple happiness; *The Magic Flute* would guarantee both.

Although *Così* enfolds personal references, its deeper concerns touch the antagonisms between surface and substance, outward seeming and inner being (see p. 122). Like Choderlos de Laclos's *Les Liaisons dangereuses*, (1782), the opera calls upon the rich vocabulary of dissimulating seduction, here delineating, if not the *coups de maître* of Laclos's Vicomte de Valmont, at least the methods of lesser Don Giovannis; among its plurality of meanings and moral ambiguities, *Così* constitutes a *jeu de miroirs* reflecting the brutal sexual claims society can make: *Così* reveals a closed world in which strong and secure hunters play a game of pursuing, trapping, and torturing their vulnerable prey. Like Valmont and his former lover, the Marquise de Merteuil,[66] Mozart's Ferrando and Guglielmo follow a strategy of enticement and deception to undermine and demoralize their victims.[67] If, in the end, the young men find themselves little less undone than the women they have tormented, unlike Laclos's novel, in which disaster engulfs the principals, *Così* concludes with a kind of repair, intellectualism for the moment stabilizing a disintegrating world.

When a traditional comedy hinging upon disguise approaches its finale, the protagonists disclose their real identities. But in *Così* the officers drop their masks only to find that their sense of self has become clouded: astounded, they can no longer quite regain their distinctive voices; the disguise has become part of a new persona; what they and the women once had been to one another cannot be recovered, ambiguity penetrating the essence of all four. Does love still exist between any of them; has every attachment dissolved? There lingers in the Neapolitan air a disharmony such as Shakespeare might have resolved into divine verse. (The antagonisms of *The Two Gentlemen of Verona* yield to Valentine's proclamation of "One feast, one house, one mutual happiness.") Mozart, however, refuses to promise lasting renewal. Even though Don Alfonso's plot forced the couples into traditional vocal pairings—the tenor with the soprano of the higher range, the baritone with the soprano of the lower—Mozart returns the four principles to their original coupling—a state of musical casting out of the operatic ordinary and underscoring the uncommon problems they face.

The women bear the deeper scars: their amazement, chagrin, and guilt cannot be observed without compassion and discomfort. A cautious person would wish to keep a safe distance from the ultimate consequences of this tragicomic finale.

---

66 The reading public of Laclos's time perceived characteristics more male than female in the Marquise.

67 Even though Don Alfonso defines the officers and thus functions as a qualifier of their guilt, his good humor has precluded his receiving the harshness of censure posterity has reserved for them.

CHAPTER XXXIII

Vienna:
A Recipe for Exhaustion

I N THE COURSE of the autumn and winter of 1789, Mozart channeled his musical energies into the score of *Così*,[1] and on 26 January 1790 its premiere delighted a packed Burgtheater; but at a stroke this heartening success, with its promise of winging a triumphant way, toppled down, caught in the currents of dynastic accident.

On successive days of February 1790, death visited the Imperial family: Elizabeth of Württemberg died on the nineteenth, less than a week after giving birth to a daughter (who would die sixteen months later); the next morning Emperor Joseph succumbed. He had sent Elizabeth's husband, Archduke Francis, a jewel-studded dagger on his birthday (12 February) "in memory of an uncle who will soon be no more." The young widower became direct heir to the Habsburg crown, now the possession of his father, who quit his grand-ducal throne in Florence's Pitti palace and arrived in Vienna during March to attempt to heal his dynasty's afflictions even as he prepared for his election and coronation as Emperor Leopold II. To his sister Maria Christina, he described the spirit in the Hofburg as "sufficient to discourage

---

1 Those who decry his smaller musical output at this time overlook the sheer number of measures in *Così*, to say nothing of its quality and that of the clarinet quintet. Furthermore, the dances he composed for the palace in December, K. 585 and 586, have extraordinary depth of harmony and instrumentation.

anyone"; every constituent of his territories fermented with rage: "provinces, peasants, cities, nobles, merchants, bishops, clergy, monks, all demanding and attempting to recover—without considering justice or discretion—rights and privileges going as far back as Charlemagne; and they all want everything at once." Passing over artistic matters during the first months of his reign, Leopold plunged into the job of setting the realm to rights.

In truth, during his final weeks, Joseph, encompassed by the twin catastrophes of an Austrian Lowlands that had declared independence as "The United States of Belgium" and a Hungary in revolt, had begun dismantling those of his reforms most onerous to his subjects. But remedies lay beyond his powers: the Bavarian Ambassador reported the prevailing opinion that the House of Habsburg might retain its sway only through his death. Tradition reports that upon learning of it old Kaunitz remarked: "How very good of him."

For Mozart it came as a blow: his new year filled with tension as he attempted to assure himself of firm footing against the turbulent background of a court shedding officials and servants left and right. Even those on high levels felt the ground giving way: it became clear that van Swieten did not enjoy Leopold's favor; nor did Salieri, whom he would have replaced on the spot with Cimarosa had he not been in Catherine of Russia's service. Excepting those outright discharged, few at the Burgtheater knew where they stood, though they could guess the direction in which Leopold would turn it: after decades as lord of Florence, he admired *opera buffa* (in the manner of Cimarosa) but gave preference to *opera seria* (à la Paisiello); by drawing nourishment from elements of the first, the second, long abandoned by German courts, had managed to cling to life in Italy (see p. 148).

However unsettling Mozart found the atmosphere, the Hofburg did maintain his sinecure, and, with van Swieten's encouragement, by May he felt emboldened enough to explore new byways: he asked Archduke Francis to support his petition[2] calling upon Leopold to appoint him both second kapellmeister occupied with church music[3] (in which, he indicated, Salieri had limited experience) and also instructor in music to the

---

2 The draft survives. Here he took care to refer to Leopold not as emperor—he had yet to be elected and crowned—but as king: upon his brother's death he had inherited the titles of King of Hungary and King of Bohemia, but for the moment the Reich had not even an emperor elect, for Leopold had never become King of the Romans (see X, n. 34). Strict etiquette prevailed in these matters: only days before Leopold's election, the Regensburg *Diarium* described Mozart as "Royal Hungarian" Kapellmeister.

3 He may have written the magnificent Kyrie in D minor for large orchestra, K. 341/368a, to show the new court what he could do in a grand, pre-Josephinian style. In the past, the rich instrumentation misled scholars to place this composition in the period of *Idomeneo.*

royal family, a post he would have shunned in former days but now saw as a strategic perch from which to cultivate Leopold's trust. For the moment, Mozart remained in a strange limbo, his *Così* a mishap of the royal succession.

In terms of box-office receipts, the opera had promised to claim the lead for the season: Artaria scurried to publish a sheaf of excerpts. Had not the death of Emperor Joseph shut the Burgtheater's doors after the fifth presentation, a strong run matching that of *Cosa rara* might well have followed. But the mourning closure had flowed into the Lenten closure, and not until 6 June did *Così* return for another five performances, Mozart conducting the second on 12 June. When in January he had invited Puchberg and Haydn to a rehearsal of the premiere, Mozart could release a gossipy fillip: the latest chatter about "Salieri's cabals," which no doubt revolved about his dismay to observe the project he had let go evolving into an extraordinary hit. This prospect, alas, the long interruption by now had vitiated.

Even so, *Così's* fitful resurgence during the summer did brighten a time of anxious waiting during which Mozart strove to increase the number of his students but composed little. Joseph dead, the distant King of Prussia and van Swieten remained his only patrons: having completed the second Prussian quartet (K. 589)[4] in May, he turned out a third (K. 590), the most glittering of them, in June, and the next month reworked Handel's *Ode for St. Cecilia's Day* and *Alexander's Feast*.

Ever stronger pressures imperiled his financial position:[5] in May, Doctor Closset had ordered Constanze back to Baden; even another sixty baths, he cautioned, might not end the cure. The next month Mozart joined her, going into town only when necessary, for he himself had begun to feel unwell: since spring he had suffered rheumatic pains, headache, and toothache; now severe insomnia plagued him as he lingered with his Constanze in the country and Leopold moved toward ending the Turkish War[6] and restoring Vienna's tranquillity.

---

4 It and the "First Prussian," K. 575, formed part of a concert Mozart gave on 22 May in his home, perhaps part of a subscription series. Puchberg, who attended, had also been present at Count Johann Karl Hadik's on 9 April, when Mozart presided over an evening of music featuring the Puchberg divertimento and the clarinet quintet.

5 An accusatory tone colors his complaint to Puchberg about being "forced to give away" the three Prussian quartets "for a ridiculous sum" and the need to resort to usurers: he wanted to keep this friend's sympathy fresh and his purse open. (This sympathy could not have extended to the one hundred florins Mozart had run up at a fashionable haberdasher's.) At this time Mozart handed over the quartets, not to a publisher, but to scribes producing manuscript copies for special clients: he later sold the publication rights to Artaria.

6 It would reach conclusion with the Peace of Sistow (4 August 1791); by its terms the Habsburgs relinquished Belgrade and Wallachia.

The old days appeared to have returned in September, when Leopold's sister Queen Caroline of Naples and her husband, King Ferdinand—the couple who had found no time for the Mozarts during their Grand Tour—escorted their daughters, Maria Theresa and Louisa, to the Habsburg capital; they were to marry their first cousins, Leopold's sons, Archdukes Francis and Ferdinand. (As Habsburg heir, Francis could lose no time remarrying and begetting sons.) During the festivities surrounding the double wedding, Leopold attended Salieri's *Axur* at the Burgtheater (21 September), the inaugural royal visit since the accession. It seemed not the best of omens that the Hofburg did not summon Mozart to any of the princely apartments to perform for the visitors, though it invited Haydn to an audience with King Ferdinand (see XV, n. 43) and commanded Weigl and Da Ponte to prepare a new opera, *La caffettiera bizzarra* (15 September), as a mark of welcome. Nor did Mozart hear a call to join the musicians chosen to perform at Leopold's coronation in Frankfurt.

Mozart's perplexity mounted. Since his first visit to Vienna as a child, he had known Leopold and as an adolescent had appeared before him in Florence. That long ago, following his mother's advice, he had turned back Leopold Mozart's petition to take the boy into grand ducal service could hardly play any role in the Vienna of 1790; and if, in truth, Mozart's position at court remained that of an adjunct, did his fame count for so little? Or did Salieri, who still pulled the strings of the Hofburg's musical affairs, as yet harbor unmollified resentment over the matter of *Così*? At all events, above these questions hovered the reassuring fact of the sinecure, its quarterly payments continuing their flow from the exchequer into Mozart's pocket.

2

HE MADE THE sudden decision to travel on his own to the coronation and give a concert that would command the attention of the Imperial family and of the heads of state, aristocrats, and diplomats gathered in Frankfurt. He did not have sufficient money on hand and hesitated to approach Puchberg again: the family silver went to the pawnbroker, and on 23 September, in the company of Hofer and a servant, Mozart, who hated to travel alone, set out in a just-purchased carriage. (It delighted him: "I should like to give it a little kiss.") By way of Eferding (near Linz), Regensburg ("heavenly" food, drink, and "Tafelmusik" at the Zum weissen Lamm), Nürnberg (he denounced its gothic aspect as "ugly"), Würzburg ("magnificent" in its baroque-rococo grandeur), and Aschaffenburg (where a cheating innkeeper aroused his ire),[7] they reached Frankfurt early in the afternoon of the twenty-eighth. Visitors crowded every hotel and inn, even in the Sachsenhausen suburb across the Main. After two nights (at the Zu den drei Rindern and then the Zum weissen Schwan), the three set up at the house of Mozart's old friend the theater impresario Johann Böhm.

On this very day in Vienna, Constanze moved the family's possessions from the Judenplatz to an apartment in the little Kaiserhaus on the Rauhensteingasse (near the Neuer Markt). Well on the way to recovery, she had begun to emerge as a force in managing the household's financial affairs. In addition to having the relocation in hand, she applied herself to negotiating a loan with the merchant Heinrich Lackenbacher. It had to be large enough to settle Mozart's major debts and still leave him a reasonable reserve. An early plan involved repayment in installments deriving from new Mozartean scores; Hoffmeister was to publish them and in turn satisfy Lackenbacher out of the profits, an indulgent scheme permitting Mozart to think of his obligation in terms of composing. (He assured Constanze: "I want to work—to work—so that never again can unforeseen circumstances [her illness] place me in so embarrassing a position.") She pursued this enterprise as he occupied himself with the activities of the coronation days.

The Electors of the Holy Roman Empire chose Leopold of Austria as German Emperor on 30 September even as more than one hundred carriages (most of them drawn by six horses), a mounted escort of close to fifteen hundred, and more than thirteen hundred foot guards—a procession that a week earlier had issued from the gates of Vienna—moved toward the Main. Leopold made his Imperial entry into Frankfurt on 4 October and five days later received the crown of Charlemagne in the cathedral; Friedrich Karl Joseph von Erthal, the Elector-Archbishop of Mainz, administered the sacraments as his musical staff, augmented by fifteen musicians of the Viennese court under Salieri and Umlauf, performed a missa solemnis by Righini[8]—three years earlier he had become von Erthal's Kapellmeister— with Margarete Louise Schick as soprano soloist.

---

7 With moving effect the reader hears Leopold's voice sounding through these observations; did the son still hear it?

8 A literary society in Bonn, having commissioned Beethoven to set a text commemorating the death of Emperor Joseph II, turned a second time to the young composer, now for a work to honor the accession of Leopold. Whether either of these impressive cantatas achieved contemporary performance remains a question. Today it seems an irony that with Mozart and Beethoven in Habsburg service—the last at Archduke Maximilian's court in Bonn—Righini held center stage at Frankfurt (as did Paul Wranitzky; see n. 27). Nonetheless, Mozart did have an unofficial presence at the coronation rites: to enhance them, Salieri drew upon a repertory of

Mozart's schedule during the festivities had to have been haphazard at best. After two postponements, he did put his concert into place:[9] it could not have been easy to gather an orchestra, but at eleven in the morning of the fifteenth, dressed in navy-blue embroidered satin, he appeared in the large playhouse (Komödienhaus) to perform his concertos K. 459 and 537 on a piano built by Stein of Augsburg. The program opened with one of his earlier symphonies (K. 297, 319, or 385?). He may have planned to close with the Jupiter,[10] but the long waits between numbers[11] so prolonged matters that by two o'clock stomachs began to growl and he had to suppress the final offering. His audience made much of him, but what with two other events competing for the public's attention—a banquet and also a grand tattoo by the Hessian military—he had played to many empty seats.

Although he put himself on view—most often at the theater—and received the recognition and invitations due a master famous in particular for his operas,[12] the stay proved a disappointing gamble: he could not approach, much less make an impression upon, the Imperial family. At any rate, he did arrange an appearance at the neighboring archbishopric of Mainz (perhaps through Madame Schick, the wife of its Hofkapellmeister[13]).

The day after his concert, he journeyed there by market-boat and settled at the Arnsberger Hof. On the twentieth, he performed at the Elector-Archbishop's palace, in all likelihood repeating selections from the Frankfurt program.[14] Among the exalted guests sat the Archbishop of Salzburg's elder brother, Franz de Paula Gundakar Colloredo, now successor to their father as a prince of the Reich and its Vice-Chancellor. Almost twenty-four years had passed since he last heard Mozart at the keyboard (see p. 226).

He and his party quit Mainz on 21 October and two days later reached Mannheim. Its theater, in the thick of preparing *Figaro* in German, welcomed

---

Mozartean church music, which he again conducted at Leopold's coronation as king of Bohemia and that of his son, Francis, as the Last Holy Roman Emperor (see p. 731).

9 On 2 October he dined with Franz Maria Schweitzer, "the richest businessman in all of Frankfurt." He probably provided a subvention for the concert.

10 On the other hand, he might have had in mind splitting the first work and using its final movement as the last "symphony."

11 They also included an improvisation by Mozart at the keyboard and arias sung by Madame Schick. She also joined in a duet with his old friend from Salzburg the castrato Ceccarelli, who as his solo, very likely performed K. 374 (see p. 534).

12 Böhm's company offered *Lanassa* with music by Mozart (see p. 490) at the end of September and his *Abduction* on 12 October. The preceding year, Frankfurt's opera public had heard a trio of Mozart works: see n. 13.

13 In Frankfurt during 1789 she had sung in three of Mozart's operas: *Don Giovanni* (Zerlina), *The Abduction* (Blondchen), and *Figaro* (Susanna).

14 He received a fee of fifteen carolins, that is, one hundred sixty-five gulden, in his eyes "meager."

him to the dress rehearsal. The next day he made a sentimental excursion to
the gardens of Schwetzingen, returning in the evening for the performance
(see p. 103). On the twenty-fifth he proceeded eastward and within three
days, via Bruchsal, Cannstatt, Göppingen, Ulm, and Günzburg, had made
his way to Augsburg to take rooms at the Zum weissen Lamm. He could
not have had time to seek out the Bäsle—if, indeed, he wished to—for by
the next day the travelers had established themselves in the Zum schwarzen
Adler in Munich.

There followed reunions with the Cannabichs, Marchands, Brochards,
and Ramm. (Mozart had met Johann Baptist and Dorothea Wendling in
Frankfurt.) Elector Karl Theodore, whom Mozart had not seen since the
days of *Idomeneo*, summoned him to perform (4 or 5 November in the
Kaisersaal of the palace) before the visiting King and Queen of Naples, en
route back to Vienna from the coronation. Mozart found it peculiar that
the occasion for Germany's greatest pianist to entertain them had been created, not by Vienna's Hofburg, which he served, but by the Munich Residenz. The sarcasm of his words to Constanze on the subject reveals how
puzzling he found his relationship to an Emperor from whom he received
a generous stipend but to whom he had no access. At all events, doubtless
carrying splendid fees from the King and the Elector, by the Altötting
route he reached Vienna about 10 November.

He drove to his new home on the Rauhensteingasse, a corner apartment[15] on the second floor (American usage) of a three-story building, the
architectural detail of which included an impressive entablature atop a
wide portal. It led to a courtyard in which a coach might be stowed;
Mozart, it would seem, had no intention of giving up his handsome vehicle.[16] Constanze had fitted up their rooms in cozy style. His airy study
opened upon his private billiard room, it in turn connecting with a sitting
room and then a large living room.[17] She had decorated with fresh uphol-
stery and decorative wall panels, *gemütlich* furnishings intended to provide a
proper background for comfortable living, composing, lessons, and house
concerts.

In this apartment took place a legendary reading of Mozart's string
quintet in D, K. 593, of December 1790, with, tradition represents, Haydn
and Mozart on the violas. Johann Tost, once a violinist in the Esterházy

---

15 The house's façade jutted beyond the line of the houses to the left (south), and thus a side window in Mozart's study faced toward the Himmelpfortgasse.
16 At this time he also kept a horse, which he rode to local appointments and for exercise.
17 A vestibule opening upon the kitchen, and warmed by the stove, served as bedroom.

orchestra and, thanks to an inheritance, become a factory owner, commissioned the work, perhaps at Haydn's suggestion. A refined and intricate contrapuntal masterpiece, K. 593 reflects Haydn-like material and devices to the point of constituting a homage to him (no less the case with regard to Mozart's next string quintet, the superb K. 614 in E flat, to be completed the following April).

Early in the new year Mozart turned out a series of dances (K. 599–607), in his richest style. The Hofburg had come to expect these tokens confirming his sinecure and now his only link with the royal family; he in fact had become Vienna's most famous composer of ballroom music, and publishers and copiers competed for the privilege of issuing it. At the same time, he took steps to re-establish his reputation as a commanding figure in the city's concert life, which had made a recovery. A benefit in which he was to participate—for the clarinetist Joseph Beer at Jahn's Hall on the Himmelpfortgasse—provided the incentive to his return to ideas for a piano concerto put aside more than two years earlier (see p. 680).

Mozart's catalogue records the date of his last piano concerto, K. 595 in B flat, as 5 January 1791; yet sketches of its three movements had come into being during 1788, a genesis undermining the traditional view of it as a valedictory work of resignation and weariness, a parting in the twilight. An intimate composition—it lacks trumpets and drums—K. 595 has many passages speaking in that plainer tongue he would often use in his closing period, a restrained idiom of beautiful finish and with aesthetic links to the romantic neoclassicism overtaking European art, a voice also heard in, for example, the reposeful Andante of the string quintet K. 614. In a willful reduction of means, a purifying and refining that distilled the essential, Mozart created a simpler musical language of a new sensibility—at moments severe and with elements of the monumental. This ideal would culminate in the stoic poetic diction of the Ave verum corpus, the Requiem, and much of *The Magic Flute*, which, moreover, is replete with nursery rhymes, moral aphorisms, and an orientation toward folk music.[18]

K. 595, like its predecessor the second Coronation concerto, does not disguise its desire to attract at first encounter, and Mozart must have had

---

18 The guileless refrain of K. 595's closing rondo had already set forth in this direction, and Mozart indeed turned this folklike tune into his next composition, "*Sehnsucht nach dem Frühling*" (Longing for Spring), K. 596, a song of innocent and bucolic melancholy to a text by Christian Adolf Overbeck. Mozart's polished, aristocratic adaptation of such folk elements (in which the Viennese commercial theater abounded) shared the spirit of those eighteenth-century designers inspired with a passion for cottages, dovecotes, and farmhouses, for a preposterous vision of rustic life best exhibited in the *hameaux* at Chantilly (1775) and Versailles (1783–1787).

success with it at the concert in Jahn's Hall (Aloysia Lange also performed) on 4 March 1791.[19] The next month, with Salieri's nod, he returned to the Burgtheater itself and with a major work: on 16 and 17 April 1791, Salieri conducted an orchestra of more than one hundred eighty in a concert for the Society of Musicians. He included selections from Paisiello's *Fedra* with Madame Lange (who inserted either K. 418 or 419 into it; see p. 633) and "a grand symphony, an invention of Herr Mozart." Inasmuch as the brothers Stadler, Vienna's master clarinetists, figured among the instrumentalists, in all likelihood it was the G minor (K. 550) in the version with clarinets.

About a week later he took a resourceful step toward strengthening his financial position. Since the Hofburg of Leopold II continued to match willingness to support him with indifference to his art, he turned to Vienna's municipal authorities: that they, not the Hofburg, controlled the budget lines of the cathedral's musical staff opened a way to wedge himself into a venerable niche. Seizing, as pretext, upon the illness of St. Stephen's fading organist, Leopold Hofmann, he stepped forward to volunteer his services to assist him and act as his surrogate, the offer resting upon the understanding that with Hofmann's retirement or death, the position of organist would fall to him. It brought two thousand florins a year, along with perquisites in the form of candles and firewood. Moreover, such a position had a rich tradition of deputizing, and should, from time to time, cathedral Kapellmeister Mozart find himself too busy, a student could take his place.

Early in May the city council granted the request. Though the Emperor's operatic taste had worked to Mozart's disadvantage, the new Imperial tolerance of eloquent and weighty church music had reawakened his interest in the genre (see n. 3). If Hofmann confounded his plan by outliving him, in any case he had found his concerns about money soothed from the day of his return from Frankfurt.

Constanze had negotiated a substantial loan from Lackenbacher. Hoffmeister had withdrawn from any role in it, for, under a new arrangement, not Mozart's talent but his household goods served as security. Even so, the matter could not have been resolved had he not a clear potential of making good his borrowings: without such confidence, even warmhearted Puchberg would not have continued to advance funds.

Good omens had begun to multiply. Upon his arrival home, Mozart found a letter from the English impresario Robert May O'Reilly. It invited

---

19 Some two months earlier, at the Auersperg palace, his pupil Babette Ployer had played K. 595 at a concert before the King and Queen of Naples. Perhaps the Ployers commissioned the concerto.

him to London in December, there to remain half a year while he composed two operas for a fee of three hundred pounds sterling (at least twenty-four hundred florins); and all the while he would be free to give recitals. Moreover, the London concert manager Johann Peter Salomon, having heard of Prince Nikolaus Esterházy's death (28 September 1790) and the dissolution of most of his musical household,[20] had come to Vienna to persuade Haydn to close a contract for a season in England at five thousand florins. He approached Mozart with a no less advantageous offer.[21]

The idea of a triumphal reappearance in the great city he so loved captivated him. Yet he put the thought aside, choosing to let the matter stand until all doubt had vanished concerning the soundness of Constanze's recovery; he would not contemplate the journey without her: the correspondence of his recent excursions reveals the melancholy that engulfed him in the absence of his wife's reassuring ways. Separated from her, even for a short time, he felt incomplete. He had ended his letter of 30 September 1790 from Frankfurt in a melting mood revealing much: "I have a childlike pleasure at the thought of coming back to you; if people could look into my heart, I should almost feel embarrassed. To me everything is cold, as cold as ice; if you were only with me, perhaps I would take more pleasure in the courtesies extended to me; but everything is so empty. Adieu, beloved. I am ever your husband, who loves you with all his soul."[22] Now, in the face of the brilliant English offers, he prevaricated,[23] putting them aside to turn his energies to finding an immediate solution to a local and vexing quandary.

---

20 His son and successor, Prince Anton, retained only the wind band; Haydn became a titular kapellmeister: with a pension inherited from Nikolaus supplemented by Anton, he had the freedom either to remain at Esterháza without obligations or to travel.

21 For the fee, Salomon expected Haydn to compose an opera, a half dozen symphonies, and twenty other pieces, all of which he was to rehearse and conduct. He must have asked much the same of Mozart.

22 Commentators often rip "cold, as cold as ice" and "everything is so empty" from context to make the words into proofs of Mozart's apathy and despair; to the contrary, in context the quotations open up an opposite view: that of Constanze as a source of love shielding him from depressions.

23 His reply to O'Reilly does not survive. No doubt Salomon and Mozart conferred and looked upon his arrival in London as a matter of time. But Haydn's plans alarmed Mozart: he feared that a man of almost fifty-nine would find the journey to England overtaxing. At the conclusion of a dinner (14 December 1790) celebrating his departure the next day, an anxious, tearful Mozart bade him farewell with the famous and ironic "In all probability we are saying our last adieu in this life." A year later—almost to the day—Haydn, in England, learned of Mozart's death.

His works for the Burgtheater, he well knew, belonged to the Josephinian past; he had little hope of Leopold II's Hofburg proposing that he compose an opera: whatever the cost, the Emperor would bring Cimarosa to Vienna.[24] In a pragmatic shift, Mozart turned to the city's thriving commercial German theater. Here an old friend, Emanuel Schikaneder, held a commanding position: wandering byways had brought him to it, and they must now be followed.

4

SCHIKANEDER'S SINGSPIEL COMPANY at the Kärntnertortheater (see pp. 616–17) had stumbled on catastrophe and expired within a few months: by April 1785 he had found work at the Burgtheater as an actor, but the expanding waist of the tall and once lithe and handsome Hamlet,[25] Macbeth, Edgar, and Iago restricted him to secondary roles. Disheartened, he wanted once again to manage a troupe and appealed to his old patron, Joseph II, to grant him a royal license to establish a new suburban theater (that is, one situated beyond the glacis, the clearing around the fortifications) for the production of German plays: in short, to found a company not unlike Marinelli's in the Leopoldstadt (see p. 615). In 1786 the Emperor agreed, but Schikaneder found it necessary to hold his privilege in abeyance: he lacked capital.[26]

That same year he formed an enterprise within his resources: a troupe that took to the road, keeping to the provinces with forays into the larger towns (among them Salzburg). He did not return to Vienna until 1789, when his wife, the actress Eleonore (born Maria Magdalena) Arth summoned him. They had lived apart since the collapse of their Kärntnertor company. Laying the blame for their business and marital breakdown upon his infidelities, she in turn had taken his colleague the actor and playwright Johann Friedel as lover.

He and Eleonore had formed their own ensemble and, after seasons in such towns as Klagenfurt, Trieste, and Laibach, in 1788 became leaseholders of a suburban Viennese theater set within a remarkable enclosure also accommodating dwellings (for about eight hundred tenants), gardens, storerooms, ateliers, shops, an inn, an apothecary, and a chapel. Located

---

24 He became Leopold's Kapellmeister in 1791, and on 7 February 1792 the Burgtheater gave the premiere of his superb *Il matrimonio segreto* (to a text by Bertati).

25 In 1777 Count Seeau had hired him as a guest artist for Munich, where his Hamlet awakened a storm of admiration.

26 He would not be in a position to use the patent until 1801, when he built and opened the Theater an der Wien, which still stands.

less than a kilometer south of the Kärntnertor and just without the glacis, this village within itself stood upon a parcel called die Wieden (once part of an island in the river Wien). It and its complex of buildings belonged to the Starhembergs. In gratitude for services to the realm, the Habsburgs had exempted the family from land taxes on this real estate. Hence the name of the congeries of structures—the Starhemberg Freihaus (free house) auf der (on the) Wieden; hence the name of the theater tucked into one of the courtyards of the labyrinth—the Starhemberg Freihaus Theater auf der Wieden, since 1788 under Friedel's direction. His death in March of the following year led Eleonore to seek reconciliation with Schikaneder. They made peace, became business partners in the leasehold (of which Friedel had left her complete possession), and he took over management of the theater, rebuilding a troupe that, through Mozart, would live in history.

Schikaneder's actors addressed their public in German—often in dialect—their repertory consisting of light comedies and farces, singspiele, pantomimes, Hanswurst shows, and, at wider intervals, concerts, ballets, and serious spoken plays. On occasion he even produced a high drama like Schiller's *Don Carlos* as a gesture toward his past, but, as he proclaimed, the box office remained his central concern: presiding over a private business without subsidies (although Emperor Leopold and his heir visited the house[27]), he kept his eye on Karl Marinelli, his competitor, who leaned toward exotic productions. More and more Schikaneder's reputation, too, rested upon spectacle: elaborate costumes and décor, in particular, transformation scenes, embellished actions set in fantastic lands. He inserted fairy, magic, and chivalric tales into popular peasant farces abounding in outhouse humor, the unembarrassed mixture of romance and vulgarity composing the main traffic of the Freihaus theater's stage—its very specialty. (Not far beneath these entertainments could be glimpsed elements of their not too distant origins in mummery, the stuff of wandering fairground players, acrobats, and jugglers.) The theater had a well-equipped stage and a comfortable auditorium seating, after Schikaneder's renovations,

27 His many decades in Italy had not taken the edge off Emperor Leopold's taste for German popular theater. His coronation at Frankfurt had featured as one of its main entertainments Paul Wranitzky's *Oberon*, a singspiel commissioned by Schikaneder; its premiere had taken place at the Freihaus theater on 7 November 1789, its gala production in Frankfurt on 15 October 1790, the day of Mozart's concert. (The actor-singer Karl Ludwig Gieseke, one of Schikaneder's masters of properties and stage managers and, to boot, a writer and master filcher, feigned authorship of the Wieland-inspired text, in reality the work of the actress Sophie Friederike Seyler-Hensel [see p. 461].) After a year in operation, the Freihaus theater received Leopold's permission to use the prefix "Imperial and Royal."

about one thousand. Boxes accommodated those of the better class who drove or strolled out to the Wieden,[28] and a new drive permitted carriages to stop at the portals; he enriched the decoration of the public areas, and the atmosphere did not lack in elegance.

In the main he built his repertory around himself and undertook the task of putting together ever-new works for a public easily bored. He opened his first season (12 July 1789) with *Der dumme Gärtner aus dem Gebürge, oder Die zween Anton [sic]* (The Stupid Gardener from the Hills, or the Two Antons), a singspiel in which he functioned as writer, director, and star. (Mozart frequented the Freihaus theater and had kind words for what he called "The Antons."[29]) Two of the company's leading singers provided music for the premiere: the tenor Benedikt Schak[30] and the bass Franz Xaver Gerl. Both became close friends of Mozart, in particular Schak, with whom, so Constanze recalled, he stood "in closest intimacy . . . no one knew him better . . . to no one did he show more devotion." He orchestrated "*Nun, liebes Weibchen,*" K. 625/592a, a duet Schak contributed to Schikaneder's *Der Stein der Weisen, oder Die Zauberinsel* (The Wise Men's Stone or the Magic Isle;[31] 11 September 1790) and in March 1791 would create a set of piano variations, K. 613, upon "*Ein Weib ist das herrlichste Ding*" (A Woman Is the Most Wonderful Thing), a song in the Schak-Gerl score for *Die verdeckten Sachen* (Hidden Things; 26 September 1789, one of Schikaneder's six sequels to the "Anton" singspiel). That same March, Mozart wrote for Gerl "*Per questa bella mano,*" K. 612, an aria featuring an obbligato for Friedrich Pichelberger, Schikaneder's principal double-bass player. Mozart now made it his business to study and work with members of Schikaneder's troupe, for he had in mind a collaboration with them: a Singspiel that would exploit their strengths.

---

28 Friedel had erected lamps along the pavement connecting the Wieden and the Kärntnertor.

29 His involvement during the autumn of 1789 with Josepha Hofer's preparations to sing with the company in Paisiello's *Barber* (see XXXII, n. 55) helps date the rebirth of his interest in Schikaneder's activities and of the men's friendship.

30 As a member of Schikaneder's touring company, Schak had sung in Salzburg during 1786. His "beautiful voice" and "fine technique" made a strong impression upon Leopold Mozart.

31 Felix Joseph Lipowsky described (*Bairisches [sic] Musik-Lexicon,* 1811) how Mozart often waited for Schak in his dressing room at the Weiden theater—while he changed to street clothes to join in a promenade—and filled time by "sitting at his desk and composing pieces [for use] here and there in his operas, which explains why several sections from Mozart's hand and genius appear in Schak's operas." A quarter of a century after Mozart's death, Constanze, among other inquiries in a letter to Schak, asked for information about "a few Mozart compositions in your operas" and about Mozart autographs in his possession "over and above [those] in your scores." Her words seem in harmony with recent investigation pointing toward the likelihood of Mozart's having contributed more than hitherto suspected to Schikaneder's repertory of singspiele.

Little evidence survives—if much ever existed—concerning the writing and preparation of *The Magic Flute*: commissioned by Schikaneder, a private entrepreneur, it did not require official documentation, and Mozart's contemporary letters to his wife (since early June, again at Baden) yield only a few clues.

Constanze absent, he at once fell out of humor; it took his utmost to concentrate on composition. Averse to living without her company (in particular, to sleeping alone in their bed) and giving congé to the maid she had left to care for him, he spent a few nights with the Leutgebs. Upon returning home, he continued to enjoy their table and also that of both the Puchbergs and the Schikaneders, but often took meals at the nearby Zur goldenen Schlange, which, at his call, sent dinner to his worktable. As a distraction, on 11 June he visited the Leopoldstadt theater to satisfy his curiosity about Marinelli's latest hit, *Kaspar der Fagottist oder Die Zauberzither* (Kaspar the Bassoonist or the Magic Zither), its music by Wenzel Müller to a text by Joachim Perinet and starring Johann Laroche, Vienna's favorite Hanswurst comedian. This singspiel, Mozart assured Constanze, had "little to recommend it."

He seized every opportunity to slip away to Baden for a day or two, but, painful as he found separation from Constanze, could not remain long: he found it even more difficult to settle down to work there; his days of composing in hotel rooms had long passed; he had reached middle age and begun to reconcile himself to limitations it imposes; he required his own things within reach—his desk, his chair, his quills, his music paper, his clavier; and, of course, he had to be near Schikaneder and the cast.

Another distraction presented itself in François Blanchard's attempts to launch a balloon flight in Vienna. Turning to account the fame of his having crossed the English Channel in such a machine six years earlier, he had embarked upon tours demonstrating its latest model, which, in fact, could be viewed for a fee in the large hall of the Mehlgrube. In the Prater's open space reserved for fireworks, there had risen grandstands to accommodate those willing to pay for witnessing Monsieur Blanchard's latest flight. However, trials on 9 March and again 29 May had failed, and many declared him a charlatan. "At this very moment," Mozart wrote Constanze on 6 July, "Blanchard will either *ascend* or for the third time make fools of the Viennese." Yet, after Archduke Francis cut the restraining ropes, Blanchard, ensconced in his contraption, did rise into the sky to come to earth a few miles away at Gross-Enzersdorf. Mozart had not gone to the Prater because he "could picture" the scene should it occur and, more to the point, believed that "once more nothing will happen." But the shouts soon reached the center of the city, and he observed "the Viennese heaping upon Blanchard praise no less [intense] than their former abuse."[32]

On 11 June he had written Constanze that, though listless in her absence, he had succeeded in turning out an aria. He took most pleasure in composing when she sat at his side and, stressing his loneliness, made a humorous comment on the risk to his fidelity her absence incurred: he cited the second-act duet, *"Bewahret euch vor Weibertücken,"* in which the pair of priests warns against man's weakness in the face of the eternal temptations of women. The quotation suggests that all at once the score had moved forward with rapid strides: he must have taken up its composition at least by May; thus consultations on the libretto could not have begun later than March, he and Schikaneder "thinking the opera through," the latter recalled, "with much hard work."

They assembled the libretto by culling ideas from *Thamos*; the myth of Orpheus; *Sethos* in Matthias Claudius's German translation (1777–1778); *Dschinnistan*, a collection of fairy tales assembled and embellished by Wieland and his son-in-law, Jakob August Liebeskind (in three volumes: 1786, 1787, 1789); Wranitzsky's *Oberon*; Schikaneder's *Der Stein der Weisen* (itself inspired by *Dschinnistan*); Chrétien de Troyes's *Yvain*, a medieval romance made into German about 1200 by Hartmann von Aue (and available to Mozart in an edition by one of his lodge brothers); von Born's treatise "Concerning the Egyptian Mysteries" (with which he had ushered in the *Journal for Freemasons*, 1784); Shakespeare's *The Tempest*; and, above all, Mozart's own *The Abduction* and *Idomeneo*.

The Magic Flute's comic and farcical elements and its fantastic turns of plot—inspired by the Wieden theater's remarkable stage machinery—rotated about a solemn dramatic core: an allegory of a young prince's entry into a noble brotherhood. Mozart wished this compound of popular theater and a symbolic representation of Freemasonry's spiritual attributes to remind the Viennese of its contribution to the city's ethical life. Schikaneder had become a member of the Order during his days in Regensburg, a center of its Rosicrucian branch, and the scenario he and Mozart concocted evokes its symbols, in particular numerology: the action, text, music, and stage directions of more than one scene interlock with the elaborate protocols of the Lodge's system of degrees, the verses at times paraphrasing the very rubrics of the secret ritual. As to what Sarastro and his temple stood for, few in the Wieden theater could have been in doubt.

---

32 Vienna's Blanchard mania put a spoke into the wheels of a financial negotiation Mozart had begun with a businessman who, infected with balloon fever, spent his time in the Prater and neglected his appointments.

Of the sources detailed above, *The Abduction* weighs most; *The Magic Flute* follows the pattern of Stephanie's scenario: a hero journeys to a remote land to liberate a maiden held captive by an exotic potentate; at first believed an evil tyrant, he proves benevolent and, in the end, unites them. Papageno, Prince Tamino's farceur-companion, forms a counterpart to Pedrillo, as does the jailer, Monostatos, to Osmin. Clearly Mozart gave Schikaneder the task of both replicating the ground plan of his early German triumph at the Burgtheater[33] and at the same time dovetailing a Masonic allegory into the action, the new element transporting the lovers to a higher, indeed almost religious, moral level. (Tamino has none of Belmonte's blemishes.) Like their models, Pamina and Tamino face death together, but, by calling upon the power of music incapsulated in the magic flute, they emerge intact and strengthened, and, at the same time, cognizant of their survival as a passage of predestined purpose: they proceed to a final tableau built, in point of both situation and music, upon the closing scene of *Idomeneo*, here transformed by the mysteries of Rosicrucian Freemasonry: the young couple puts on sacerdotal royal robes, and a new era, universal and hallowed, begins.

Mozart may well have set much of the verse as it came from Schikaneder's pen: proceeding with the shorthand notation of the score, he sent it section by section to his student Franz Xaver Süssmayr, whom he had dispatched to Baden in June to be of service to Constanze. (One of the household's two maids, along with Carl, had accompanied her, but he wished a stronger arm to be of assistance on those sloping walks to the waters: her accouchement impended.) Süssmayr transliterated the stenography into a *particella*, or short score, which, packet by packet, he sent back to Vienna for his master to develop, refine, and orchestrate.

In mid-July Mozart fetched Constanze back to Vienna, and on the twenty-sixth she gave birth to their sixth child, Franz Xaver Wolfgang, baptized in St. Stephen's with the godfather, Johann Thomas von Trattner, represented by the bookseller Michael Klorf. About a month later, the Mozarts left for Bohemia, by which time most of *The Magic Flute* stood complete.[34]

---

33 To moving effect *The Magic Flute* reproduces the scene of Pasha Selim's distress to learn of Constanze's attempt to flee with her would-be rescuer, the new version emerging transformed—and not simply by the addition of lions to the ruler's entourage: the encounter gains the uncanny wonderment of a mythic vision as Pamina invokes "die Wahrheit" (the truth).

34 Although the opera appears in his catalogue under the heading "In July," an entry under "the 28th September" comprises: "for the opera, *The Magic Flute*—a march of the priests and the overture," numbers added to the score during the closing days of the month as he labored to fill the gaps in what had reached paper before the trip to Bohemia.

He had to leave its rehearsals in the hands of Johann Baptist Henneberg, since 1790 Schikaneder's kapellmeister.

Good fortune had given Mozart little choice: commissions now overwhelmed him; the Nostitz theater required his presence to complete and help prepare an *opera seria* Guardasoni had proposed and he had begun while at work on *The Magic Flute*; but whatever musical ideas came to him with respect to a recent anonymous order for a requiem would not reach paper until his return. He set out from Vienna carrying in his head elements of three major works in three different genres. A complicated series of political events had sown the seeds of this journey to Prague.

5

CEREMONIES SURROUNDING LEOPOLD of Austria's accession afforded him opportunities to appease two important provinces his brother had offended: Joseph had assumed the titles of King of Hungary and of Bohemia without deigning to go through a coronation in either realm; he feared the panoply might strengthen local pretensions to more than subordinate authority;[35] to take any oath before the Estates would have been, in his eyes, to acknowledge the importance of subalterns he looked upon as "children acting childishly." Leopold, in contrast, determined to hold both coronations, not only to resurrect Imperial splendors Joseph had let fade, but also to make a show of respect for regional traditions (even to the point of appearing before the Hungarians in their national costume, but recently the symbol of their resistance to Joseph). The Hungarian coronation (15 November 1790) had followed in the wake of the Imperial installation, but months would pass before Leopold's entry into Prague (29 August 1791) to assume the crown of St. Wenceslaus, a time during which the Bohemian Estates sat in protracted session to debate their relationship to the new sovereign. They made the decision to honor him with a coronation opera—and one to his taste: an *opera seria*. However, this step came rather late: not until 8 July did they contract with Guardasoni of the Nostitz theater.[36]

He traveled to Vienna, arriving on 14 July, and offered the commission to Salieri,[37] who pleaded that at the moment he had few hours in which to

35 He went as far as to have Hungary's crown of St. Stephen carried off to Vienna.
36 He had returned to Prague from Warsaw a month earlier. In 1788 exclusive direction of the theater's operatic wing had fallen to him.
37 By developing his plans in the Kaiserstadt, Guardasoni followed a politic path: he needed the resources of the Burgtheater to create or rework a libretto, which, whatever the choice, required Habsburg approval; in addition, approaching Imperial Kapellmeister Salieri, who had a high

compose: he found himself picking up extra tasks at the Burgtheater while his protégé and assistant, Deputy Kapellmeister Joseph Weigl, labored upon an important commission for the Esterházy;[38] and, into the bagain, to Salieri would fall the strenuous tasks of scheduling, arranging, rehearsing, and conducting much of the ceremonial music at the coronation. Guardasoni's repeated visits could not sway him to take up the new opera, and the impresario turned to Mozart.

Salieri's qualms had to have gone beyond the question of overwork: very little time remained before the premiere—less than two months and nothing yet in place. The agreement between Guardasoni and the Estates called for an imposing *opera seria* from the hand of a "distinguished maestro" and required Guardasoni to provide a strong cast: in fact, to go to Italy to engage a castrato and an *opera-seria* soprano, both of the first rank. Neither of the parties to the contract could have taken in earnest the clause proposing that, if possible, a new libretto be commissioned: all had to have recognized as reality the provision to the effect that, should the tight schedule exclude this idea, the text would be Metastasio's *La clemenza di Tito*; indeed, no libretto could have been more appropriate a vehicle to glorify Leopold, who wished to persuade all his subjects that he would exercise no less command over himself than over safeguarding their individual interests as well as those of the Reich.

Early in the year, Leopold had replaced Count Rosenberg with Count Johann Wenzel Ugarte as director of the court theaters, dismissed Da Ponte along with La Ferrarese, and, by the time of the Bohemian Estate's agreement with Guardasoni, begun to put into place a new *opera-seria* company at the Burgtheater. It cannot be ruled out that the idea of encouraging the Nostitz to produce yet another version of *La clemenza di Tito* came from Leopold, who, while Grand Duke of Tuscany, had more than once heard himself compared to that ancient Roman Emperor, tributes he had not discouraged and now, as Holy Roman Emperor, wished perpetuated in the public mind. He saw himself as personifying the Roman virtues: "Be it

---

reputation as a composer of *opera seria*, seemed statesmanlike. In this genre, Mozart, apart from the private presentation of *Idomeneo* in concert guise, had yet to show his ability in either Vienna or Prague.

38 With Haydn away in London, his godson, Joseph Weigl the Younger, received the commission to provide music for the fete (3–6 August) celebrating Esterházy lordship over Ödenburg (Sopron) and its district. Salieri had a cantata in work, *Venere ed Adone*, whose text (by Casti) he relinquished to Weigl as a vehicle in high degree suitable to the occasion at Esterháza; moreover, Salieri made Weigl's life easier by taking on, for the moment, several of his official duties. He also permitted a group of the Hofburg's finest singers to take part in the cantata's premiere: Dorotea Bussani, Calvesi, Adamberger, and the *opera-seria* soprano Cecilia Giuliani, just hired by Emperor Leopold at the request of the Empress.

known to Rome," Metastasio's and Mozart's Titus announces in a phrase drawn from Corneille's *Cinna, ou la clémence d'Auguste*, "that I remain the same; that I know, forgive, and forget all." (Leopold's coming pardon of the revolutionary Lowlanders, whom his armies would crush, reflected this self-image.) The libretto seemed ideal for his coronation, a flattering allegory that the German world might imagine as written just to extol this new ruler hard upon concluding the Turkish War by a course of relinquishing and giving over (see n. 6); a monarch whose personal qualities, in particular of conciliation, departed in so great a measure from those of his late elder brother, with whom few associated the word "clemenza."[39]

Mozart wanted to be part of the days of celebration in Prague even if undertaking the opera demanded his putting aside work on *The Magic Flute* and the first stages of the Requiem: before his eyes danced a fee (including a stipend for expenses) of more than one thousand florins—Salieri had lamented the necessity of declining it—and, more important, a heaven-born opportunity to demonstrate to the Hofburg his right to a place in plans for the Emperor's new opera troupe.[40]

With Da Ponte dismissed, Mazzolà, in all likelihood summoned by Salieri, took temporary leave of the court of Dresden and went to Vienna during May 1791 to fill for the moment the empty post. To him fell the

---

39 The harshness of which Joseph had proved so capable may be observed with appalling clarity in the matter of Franz Zaglauer von Zahlheim: a dissolute nobleman deep in debt, he stole money from his mistress, an older woman whom he had promised to marry but, instead, murdered; a deplorable crime but not unexampled. It so captured the Emperor's interest that, violating his theoretical insistence upon equality before the law, he interposed and commanded that Zahlheim meet death in medieval style. Three days before the premiere of Mozart's Auersperg *Idomeneo*, executioners dragged Zahlheim through the streets to the Hoher Markt. (The terrible process began not far from the windows of Mozart's music room in the Camesina house and on the day, 10 March 1786, he entered his new compositions for the opera in his catalogue.) They applied hot pincers to Zahlheim's body, broke his bones on the wheel "from the feet upward," the most lingering of tortures, and after hours of unimaginable horror, left the remains on public view. Enlightened Vienna's shock at this gaping view of the Emperor's obsessive cruelty left his reputation in ruins; it never recovered. In contrast, Leopold, while ruler of Tuscany, opened his mind to Beccaria's *On Crimes and Punishments* (1764) and reformed the duchy's penal system, capital punishment being abolished.

40 The court would have taken exception to Guardasoni's settling upon Mozart as coronation composer had he been either not a celebrated master or unacceptable to Leopold in terms of politics or morality. (Had he not dismissed Da Ponte and his mistress as arrogant profligates?) He had no objection to Mozart's Masonic outlook: had the new Hofburg taken exception to it, the sinecure would not have continued. In fact, the Emperor's sensibilities to a degree comported with the Muratorian- and Rosicrucian-tinged beliefs of those belonging to the Zur neugekrönten Hoffnung Lodge; not these romantic idealists, but the Illuminati aroused his fears of revolutionary plotting. His reservations with regard to Mozart had to do with his music, to which, according to the well-informed courtier Count Heinrich Franz Rottenhan, he had a "strong aversion."

task of working with Mozart to convert the venerable text of *Tito* into a drama answering his needs; they cut, tightened, and compressed to telling effect—under their scissors an entire major subplot fell away, the argument contracting from three acts to two—and made many an eloquent line Metastasio had conceived of in terms of recitative or aria into the building blocks of ensembles;[41] at points Mazzolà modified Metastasio's verse, adding lyric poetry of his own—the duet *"Deh prendi,"* for example—and even inserted material from one of his comic operas, *La dama soldato.* Nor did Mozart hesitate to avail himself of store from his own cupboard.

Some months earlier he had composed the type of extended aria called a vocal rondo[42] and sent it to Josepha Duschek for her Prague benefit concert of 26 April. He now inserted this Rondo's closing Allegro into *La clemenza di Tito* to form the peroration of *"Non più di fiori,"* Vitellia's aria (with basset-horn obbligato) preparing her confession to the Emperor. The expedient, which saved Mozart time in composition and, more important, worked to splendid theatrical and musical purpose, reveals the fullness of his partnership with Mazzolà: no awkward literary or musical joints betray themselves.[43]

The finale to the first act constitutes their master stroke of adaptation and reconstruction: a quintet with chorus forming a parallel to the storm scene in *Idomeneo* with its Opéra-inspired mise-en-scène. (The offstage voices decrying the revolution against Emperor Tito and its destructive path had to have awakened thoughts of Paris and Versailles in the audience—it included royalist émigrés from France—gathered about Marie Antoinette's brother in the Nostitz theater.)

---

41 Mozart did house sections of secco in the score—the interview between Tito and Sesto the prime example—and did not fail to provide magnificent accompagnati. However, excepting a few crucial measures of transition, a second hand—little question Süssmayr's—composed the secco; Mozart did not have time to write it, though doubtless he outlined its harmonic direction and most critical contours. Considering such close guidance and the fact that secco falls into patterns ordained by the flow of the Italian, the result could not have been so very different had Mozart taken up the entire job.

42 See p. 148. Ever more popular as the century aged, this variant could enjoy the best of two worlds as to its musical design: the overall binary structure's opening slow section often had a tripartite, that is, A B A design, the material of the first A returning embellished by the singer or varied in the accompaniment or with both elements modified.

43 If the poet of the Allegro taken over from Madame Duschek's rondo cannot be identified, there can be no doubt that Mazzolà created the words of the new aria's opening Larghetto, *"Non più di fiori."* Replacing the now lost slow section Madame Duschek had sung in April, it makes a handsome joint between an introductory accompagnato (its text indebted to Metastasio) and the appropriated Duschek finale. Why Mozart failed to enter the benefit-concert aria in his catalogue remains unknown.

The speed and energy the composition of *La clemenza di Tito* (K. 621) called for had sounded a no less penetrating alarm in Mozart than in Salieri,[44] who at least could have summoned into play shortcuts traditional when writing in the Italian manner: since it often availed itself of melodies set above patterns of notes repeated for many measures, the composer might write the figuration only once, an assistant then reproducing it until the text demanded a different accompanying design, perhaps along with an appropriate modulation; the composer then established the new course, the scribe pursuing it until the dramatic circumstances required a change or a double bar. Thus long stretches of such an opera could be set down in a terse musical stenography, which might also indicate a characteristic uncomplicated orchestration.

Such methods had limited usefulness in committing to paper Mozart's complex "German" scores: here the vocal and instrumental had become an indissoluble whole, and the subtlest nuances of color and contour imposed breaks upon whatever reiterated patterns might occur; his shorthand presented a code not to be cracked with mechanical ease. (He showed annoyance with the slow pace of even his own pupil Süssmayr in turning the stenographic sketches for *The Magic Flute* into a clean *particella*.) At times in *La clemenza* he did attempt to save time by resorting to Italian-style accompaniment and an orchestra of strings alone. Yet the opera's great moments emerged in high and involved Mozartean style.

By the time Mozart, Constanze, and Süssmayr departed for Prague on 25 August 1791,[45] the score of *La clemenza di Tito* had taken form to a substantial degree. Following his usual procedure, Mozart had first busied himself with the choruses and also the soloists' ensembles.[46] In respect to technique and range, they made no demands out of the ordinary, for, of the six principals, he knew only one: his first Don Ottavio, Antonio Baglioni, designated to perform the title role; Mozart hastened to work on his arias. As soon as Guardasoni had contracts with the other five singers, he must have described their musical capacities and idiosyncracies to Mozart, for, by the time of his arrival in Prague, every aria, at the least, had

---

44 Stories of an automatonlike Mozart composing with unparalleled celerity are myth: his detailed scores barred him from rivaling the Italians in this area; here they gathered the laurels, perhaps yet another reason why Guardasoni first turned to Salieri. The anecdotes about Mozart derive from a gift he himself alluded to: his ability to compose, revise, refine, and store works in his head. When he did summon up the material, the show of seeming to pour forth at will complex and finished inventions delighted him.

45 In all probability the Mozarts left Carl in boarding school at Perchtoldsdorf and Franz Xaver with his grandmother.

46 He carried to Prague the two magnificent finales, the quintet and sextet (both with chorus), the first in completed state, the second well on its way.

its foundations in place. Above all, the Estates expected brilliant moments from the pair of expensive Italians imported from Bologna: the soprano Maria Marchetti-Fantozzi (the wicked and then repentant Vitellia) and the castrato Domenico Bedini (the patrician rebel, Sesto).[47]

Mozart's associates gathered in Prague: Mazzolà to fulfill the librettist's traditional role of stage director at the premiere, Stadler to perform those obbligatos that were to embellish arias for the two Italian stars: Sesto's *"Parto"* with basset clarinet and Vitellia's *"Non più di fiori"* with basset horn.[48] Mozart appeared on the twenty-eighth, in all likelihood proceeding at once to the Duscheks' home, the Villa Bertramka. Two days earlier Salieri had arrived at the head of a contingent of Habsburg musicians, and when Emperor Leopold entered the city on the twenty-ninth, the festivities quickened: processions, illuminations, fireworks, street fairs, and daily entertainments—a circus, a magic theater, tumblers, the Sekunda company giving a selection of plays, and a local troupe offering Haydn's *Orlando paladino* in German (*Der Ritter Roland*). On the day of Leopold's arrival, the Nostitz flattered his taste by performing an *opera seria* by Paisiello (*Pirro*, 1787, to a text by de Gamerra), and, with the appearance of the Empress and her train on the thirtieth, began the suite of political-ecclesiastical ceremonies, at their center the two crownings: Leopold's and Maria Luisa's.

In the course of the rituals Mozart's music predominated, Salieri conducting three Salzburg masses (K. 258, 317, and 337), the offertory K. 222, and a chorus from *Thamos* as made into a Latin motet (see XXV, n. 24), the same group of works he had drawn upon at Frankfurt. What with this religious music, a performance of "Die Maurerfreude" (10 September?) to honor Mozart's visit to the Zur Wahrheit und Einigkeit (Truth and Unity) Lodge, the premiere of *La clemenza di Tito*, the Mozart dances played at balls throughout the city, and, at the Nostitz, a gala *Don Giovanni* (wind bands piped its tunes at Prague receptions), the coronation days, perhaps to the royal couple's amazement, offered Mozartean fare to banquet on—a Mozart feast.

The special performance of *Don Giovanni* (2 September, with most of the original cast) answered a "highest request"—in all probability that of Archduke Francis—and the royal family attended. Mozart, ill from the nervous fatigue of composing and rehearsing under extraordinary

---

47 Mozart had not expected Guardasoni to capture a castrato: the earliest sketches for the part of Sesto call for a tenor.

48 The basset clarinet is a soprano instrument with its range extended at the lower end; the basset horn is an alto clarinet.

stress,[49] relinquished the podium (to Strobach?) and took his place in the auditorium. Observing him and Emperor Leopold as the masterpiece unfolded, the writer Franz Alexander von Kleist pondered the immortality of a composer whose works would reach "to unborn generations when the bones of kings have long turned to rot." Von Kleist felt his fellow listeners' hearts beating to each "string's vibration, every lisp of the flute" as they drank in "the holy impressions" Mozart's "harmonies awoke." At the same time, the Imperial Couple, it would appear, did not share this Mozart intoxication, indeed, certainly not four days later when Leopold, having received the crown of Bohemia in St. Vitus's cathedral, attended the premiere of *La clemenza di Tito* in the evening, Mozart conducting.

The spectators included luminaries of the Hofburg, the Bohemian Estates, and the courts of the Reich. Zinzendorf found the opera "boring," as did the Empress. Until now full of admiration for Count Starhemberg's handling of the coronation ("*à merveille*"), she expressed her first dissatisfaction, the poverty of the spectacle[50] no doubt contributing to her dismissal of the music as "so bad that nearly all of us [the royal party] fell asleep."[51] "Nearly (*presque*)": Marchetti-Fantozzi's singing did keep the Emperor awake and earn his praise.

A bizarre situation: a score by Germany's greatest opera composer performed in a city that adored him met with indifference because the audience for the most part consisted of guests eager to follow the signals from the royal box. (The authorities had appealed "to the celebrated good na-

---

49 Even as he completed *La clemenza*, part of him remained occupied with *The Magic Flute*: he could be heard humming music from it.

50 Counseled by a group of committees, Starhemberg, Leopold's High Steward (and owner of the Wieden), had organized the coronation, arrangments ranging from transportation and accommodations for distinguished guests to the appropriate decoration of their rooms. In theory he had a voice concerning the mounting of *La clemenza*, but here Guardasoni had doubtless constitutued a committee unto himself. Whatever the case, the production proved a hasty and shoddy job even though, to save time, Guardasoni had divided responsibility for the scenery between Pietro Travaglia, in Esterházy service, and Johann Breysig of Coblenz; Cherubino Babbini of Mantua designed the costumes.

51 From this confidence to Maria Theresa de Bourbon, her daughter-in-law, may have grown the legend of Maria Luisa's having in open court proclaimed *La clemenza* a *porcheria tedesca* (a swinish German mess). Descended on her mother's side from the Houses of Wettin and Habsburg (see XV, n. 43), this great-granddaughter of the German Emperor Joseph I, sister of Ferdinand of the Two Sicilies, Infanta of Spain, Archduchess of Austria, former Grand Duchess of Tuscany, Queen of Hungary, Queen of Bohemia, and, since autumn 1791, German Empress, would not have disparaged things German in public, no matter her opinion. The acerbic phrase first appeared in a publication of 1871, eighty years after the premiere. Whatever private distress Mozart suffered from the court's coolness toward *La clemenza*, the royal enclosure harbored neither a nest of vipers nor a collection of imbeciles in high places: the matter had its center in questions of taste.

ture of the Prague public" to appreciate that, in respect to tickets, "foreign guests must be given preference.") Mozart placed *La clemenza* among his "very best" efforts; von Kleist judged it "at all points worthy of its master"; but such estimates did not become widespread until the visitors departed.[52] Then Prague celebrated *La clemenza*: on 30 September the final performance played before an audience of enthusiastic townspeople.

Perhaps Mozart attended the dinner at the Nostitz on 12 September, the Emperor and Empress present, during which Josepha Duschek sang a cantata of homage by Leopold Kozeluch. In any case, by the middle of the month the Mozarts and Süssmayr had started their journey back to Vienna. A prodigious schedule loomed ahead, a veritable recipe for exhaustion: the premiere of *The Magic Flute* was to take place on the thirtieth, and only two weeks remained in which to edit and polish whole sections of the score, compose more than one missing number (see n. 34), and supervise the final rehearsals. In addition, before the departure, Stadler had commissioned a clarinet concerto to be ready in October; there remained the matter of a two-movement horn concerto for Leutgeb (K. 412/386b/514 in D, already in hand);[53] Mozart's Masonic lodge had requested a composition for the opening of its new temple in November; and, most pressing, the Requiem awaited birth.

---

52 At the premiere, the theater distributed seats free according to the Estates' invitation list; for the second representation—on 7 or 8 September and thus still offered to the coronation crowds—the box office inflated the prices and found few buyers. Indeed, the *Krönungsjournal für Prag* observed sparse audiences at most of the celebration's dramatic performances: "Are [too many] other entertainments responsible for this, or do the high prices frighten away connoisseurs?"

53 He brought to conclusion only the first movement. The second, completed by Süssmayr the year after Mozart's death, long found acceptance as in all respects authentic. Overwhelmed by profitable commissions, he had put aside this gift to his old friend and did not survive to resume work on it.

CHAPTER XXXIV

Vienna:

A Normal Single Grave

T HAT THE *MAGIC FLUTE*'S production pleased Mozart on all
levels gives authoritative measure of its quality. Of course, the principal roles exploited their performers' special gifts: Schak's mellifluous
German tenor inspired Tamino's ardent phrases; Gerl's admired low
notes have given pause to many a subsequent Sarastro, while Josepha
Hofer's battery of coloratura missiles discharging her superb top F
has bequeathed a no less formidable challenge to her successors as
Queen of the Night (a predicament aggravated by rising pitch); the
Pamina, seventeen-year-old lyric soprano Anna Gottlieb (twelve when
she sang the first Barbarina in *Figaro*), commanded a finished legato;
and Papageno's vocal line gave Schikaneder's baritone—more accomplished than the usual Hanswurst's—not a few passages operatic in their
demands.

The premiere (30 September 1791), and, at least, the first repetition, unfolded under Mozart's direction; thereafter the task passed to Henneberg.
The opera carried Vienna by storm, no small part of the triumph owing
to the scenic designs of Herr Nesslthaler as painted by Joseph Gayl.
Schikaneder gave them, so the talk ran, five thousand gulden to lavish on
scenic wonders, which, in the sequel of Blanchard's flight to Gross-
Enzersdorf, included a flying basket cum balloon for the comings and go-

ings of the Three Boys.[1] Mozart's hand may be assumed in this inspired jest.

During autumn, Salieri, sensitive to the play of the political winds, had requested Emperor Leopold's permission to step down,[2] and, by the time of *The Magic Flute*'s premiere, the Viennese awaited "the arrival of the new Imperial Kapellmeister, *Cimarosa*," whose retinue included "some excellent singers from St. Petersburg." Those with eyes fixed upon the Hofburg and viewing the Burgtheater as alone capable of setting standards, could discern "on the horizon no very favorable epoch [in Vienna] for the German composer and musician." A commentator of this stripe found it necessary to denigrate "our Kapellmeister Mozart's new 'machine comedy' [a belittling phrase] produced at great expense and with much magnificence of decor" but "failing to receive the expected ovations because its content and language are far too inferior." Fact told a different story: *The Magic Flute* drew crowds so large that during October Schikaneder began to offer it on a daily basis, and there followed "an unbroken run of sixty-two performances. . . . Seats had to be secured by five o'clock, for at a later hour people were turned away by the hundreds."

The attack had to center upon the text: among critics, connoisseurs, and musicians, the quality of Mozart's music had become a matter beyond assessment. Perhaps the opera's lofty meditative scenes discomposed those organizing the Emperor's new Italian *seria* company. The printed libretto of *The Magic Flute* as well as the playbill called it, not a singspiel, but "a grand opera," while Mozart's catalog employed the phrase "a German opera"; that he continued to use this description suggests his sense of *The Magic Flute* as the edifice planned since the days when Karl Theodore and then Joseph II seemed to give promise of supporting his national vision. Now, instead of a German prince, a theatrical producer in a Viennese suburb had created the occasion engendering a supreme German masterpiece that would lead to Weber and Wagner.

Whatever the court's attitude toward Mozart's new singspiel and its coded, esoteric symbolism, the censor found no fault with it, nothing at odds with Habsburg policy or traditional Catholicism. In March, during

---

1 It appears that at first Mozart assigned their parts to two boys and a woman. (Anna, daughter of Schikaneder's elder brother Urban; he impersonated the priest to whom fell the grand accompagnati of the first finale.) No doubt Mozart wished to strengthen the ethereal but too often wayward trebles of choirboys by adding her steadier tone; at later performances he at times changed the mixture to two women and a boy.
2 The Hofburg responded with finesse, accepting his resignation even while asking him to continue to compose works for the repertory. He remained active as a Habsburg kapellmeister.

Mozart and Schikaneder's preliminary work on the opera, Pius VI, reacting in a Papal brief to the tumult in revolutionary France, had reminded the Faithful of the eternal verity of Original Sin, mankind's inheritance from Eve, with its unending potential for depravity and corruption against which the redeemed must wage diligent struggle. *The Magic Flute* seemed to underline this dogma, and until Emperor Leopold's death in March 1792 and the accession of Archduke Francis—crowned Francis II at Frankfurt—the metaphoric Masonic garment enfolding the opera's moral lessons gave no offense to the Hofburg or St. Stephen's. But when the excesses of the French Revolution shifted to the horrors of the Terror and there followed the guillotining of Emperor Francis's uncle, Louis XVI, in January 1793 and, nine months later, of Aunt Marie Antoinette, he embraced a repressive conservatism, at times extreme; he believed himself surrounded by radical conspiracies, Freemasonry among them. Taking fright to find themselves under suspicion of being haunts of treasonous activity, the lodges began to close, a proscriptive directive from Francis discharging the *coup de grâce* in June 1795.

Even as Viennese Freemasonry dissolved, *The Magic Flute* went on giving pleasure in Vienna, indeed, all over Germany, the opera now explained in terms not of Freemasonry but of contemporary politics, interpretations embracing both sides of the conflict in France: monarchists saw in Tamino a prince who, though at first in flight from a serpent dispatched by the Jacobins, in time would have them dancing to the melodies of his flute and then press on to free Pamina, to the royalist imagination a symbol of the immured Marie Antoinette; for their part, the Jacobins recognized in the Queen of the Night the spirit of despotism, in her daughter that of freedom; Sarastro, it seemed clear, presided over a kind of National Assembly in which Tamino sought membership, while Monostatos represented the aristocratic émigrés seeking to turn back the political clock.[3]

Even in Mozart's own days, very personal interpretations of the allegory flourished. (Staunch believers, for example, might view the action as incited by the serpent of Eden.) Yet Mozart did have the satisfaction of attending the opera ensconced among a number of listeners with clear clues to his intentions. They could make out an ecumenical message at its most moving in the scene of the Men in Armor on guard before the caverns of fire and water. Accompanied by an orchestral fugato, they sing the melody of the venerable Lutheran hymn *"Ach Gott von Himmel,"*[4] the

---

3 There have been few propagandist causes to which this opera has not been joined: not too long ago, Marxist and Nazi versions throve.
4 Mozart had heard and sung Protestant texts since childhood (see p. 32).

musical idiom and syntax evoking a chorale-prelude in the manner of Sebastian Bach. The pair of stern monitors, however, did not voice the Lutheran text, but, rather, words the audience could read on a backdrop depicting the wall of an ancient pyramid. The inscription tells of the difficulties of mounting the path toward a purification that will vanquish the fear of death and show the way to the heavenly rewards of virtue.[5] If only a handful of listeners inferred the devotional power of the biblical words hidden beneath this duet,[6] more than a few could discover in the compelling musico-dramatic situation a Muratorian Catholicism bordering upon Pietism—an exhilarating Christianity broad but individual, immediate, and resting upon a pursuit of brotherly love and good works, here capable of turning believers into priests. And somewhere beneath the multiple layers of this spacious and grand baroque picture—among the century's finest visions—can be sensed the moral force and gravity of Mozart and, indeed, of his father, the mentor of his youth, at their finest. Whatever the depth of the average spectator's comprehension, Mozart found at the Wieden theater a group of comprehending souls sufficient to provide him compensation for Constanze's being away.

Having remained in Vienna since the return from Prague, she had left for Baden with the infant, Franz Xaver, and her sister Sophie[7] soon after the premiere of *The Magic Flute*, that is, during the first days of October. She went at Mozart's insistence: though she felt well, he had taken it into his head that yet another series of baths would assure her a healthy winter. Delighting in *The Magic Flute's* triumph, he filled the days of her absence working on the Requiem and the clarinet concerto—the current of his genius flowed in full spate—"until it became time to go to the opera." Close to every night he attended the Wieden theater to sit entranced before his own creation. His letters to her draw the picture of a man purring with contentment and humor.

"I have just come from the opera. It was quite as full as usual. The duetto *Mann und Weib* etc. [*Bei Männer*] and the Glockenspiel in the first act [*Das klinget*] were repeated as always—likewise the trio in the second act with the boys [*Seid uns zum zweitenmal*]; but what pleases me most is the *silent applause* [that is, an apprehension on the part of the few of the work's spiritual and Masonic implications]; it becomes clear that interest in this opera soars day by day." Yet he did face the fact that some considered the message and the music altogether secondary to the spectacle.[8]

---

5 Mozart and Schikaneder took this text from *Sethos* (see pp. 316–17).
6 Such hymns derived from free German versifications of the Psalms.
7 Mozart assumed her expenses at Baden, and Süssmayr's, too, when they tended Constanze.
8 His mother-in-law, for example: ". . . she *sees* the opera but doesn't *hear* the opera."

Since he knew just when Constanze would return—the seventeenth—
he kept an easy heart and wrote of himself: "Right after you sailed away, I
played two games of billiards with Herr von Mozart, the one who wrote
the opera at Schikaneder's. Then I sold my nag (see XXXIII, n. 16) for
fourteen ducats, had Joseph [Preisinger] summon Primus [a neighborhood
factotem]⁹ to bring me a black coffee, puffed away at a marvelous pipe of
tobacco, and orchestrated almost the whole of the Rondo for Stadler [the
closing movement of K. 622]." At the same time, a letter from Stadler arrived, and Mozart learned that in Prague he and the Duscheks "all know
about the magnificent reception of my German opera." Stadler also sent
him an account of the final performance of *La clemenza* at the Nostitz (on
the very night of *The Magic Flute's* premiere); it had played to extraordinary
applause.

Constanze read the news amidst the comfortable surroundings of
Baden. At the same time, he had practical matters well under control on
the Rauhensteingasse. Primus fetched delectable meals—"What do I see?
What do I smell?" Mozart asked, looking up from a letter to Constanze:
"Don Primus with pork cutlets! *Che gusto!* I eat to your health."¹⁰ Primus
also did duty as a general domestic: he "came to light the fire at 5:30 and
to wake me at 5:45," Constanze learned from her husband, whose "hairdresser arrived precisely at 6."

Mozart had kept to the ways he had taken up a decade earlier upon establishing himself in Vienna and continued to accumulate formidable bills
due restaurant keepers, friseurs, haberdashers, tailors, and decorators. Yet
no one could pierce with more biting acuity the pretensions, self-delusions,
and trivialities of the fashionable life, with its foolish struggles for precedence and reputation and its drive to put others down: his gift for laughter, nonsense, the tart phrase, and sheer mischief remained intact.

One evening at *The Magic Flute*, under a sudden "impulse" to perform
on the glockenspiel himself, he went backstage, commandeered the instrument, and played it from the wings in the course of Papageno's aria "*Ein
Mädchen,*" Schikaneder all the while unaware of his collaborator's identity.
Later, "in jest," when Schikaneder had dialogue to speak, Mozart sounded
an arpeggio. "It startled him," Mozart continued in his recital to Constanze, and "he glanced behind the scenery and caught sight of me. When

---

9 Joseph Preisinger, the proprietor of the Zur goldenen Schlange, an inn on the Kärntnerstrasse,
  employed a waiter, another Joseph, who also did odd jobs for Mozart. He named him Joseph
  the First (in Latin, Josephus Primus), Preisinger no doubt being dubbed Josephus Secundus.
10 With Constanze, the strict manager, away, Mozart also indulged his expensive taste for Danube
  sturgeon.

his next lines came, I didn't play. This time he stopped, unwilling to keep going. I guessed his thoughts and again played a chord. He then struck the glockenspiel a blow and said, 'shut up,' whereupon everyone laughed. I believe that this joke for the first time taught many in the audience that he does not play the instrument."[11]

He had grown close to not only Schikaneder but also Salieri. They had never locked horns: at the height of their confrontations, both had known when to draw back; those few conflicts had centered upon Salieri's authority as head of the opera, a precedence Mozart had stuck at acknowledging whenever an official decision went against him; on such occasions—not out of character—he had cried out against conspiracy. Yet, on the whole, the two maintained an amicable understanding, which, all at once, became warmer: in the wake of Emperor Leopold's accession, they pulled together; both felt the chill of disfavor.

Talk of Salieri takes up a good part of Mozart's last letter (to Constanze in Baden; 14–15 October 1791). The preceding day, in his carriage, he and Hofer had gone to Carl's school at Perchtoldsdorf to bring him back to town, where Caecilia Weber awaited her grandson at the Hofers'. At six, Mozart picked up Salieri and Cavalieri, drove them to the Wieden theater, and escorted them to a box. As *The Magic Flute* progressed from the rocky landscape, through which the serpent slithers, to the triumph of virtue in the temple of the sun, they breathed in the work's enchantment. "You cannot imagine how gracious both were," Mozart wrote Constanze, "and how much pleasure they took not only in my music but also in the libretto and the whole representation. Both declared it a grand opera worthy of performance at the greatest festival before the greatest monarch and without doubt will return very often, never having experienced a more beautiful or delightful production. He [Salieri] listened and observed with the highest attention, and from the overture to the closing chorus not a number failed to entice from him either a 'bravo' or a 'bello.' They could not leave from thanking me for this favor."

Having settled his guests in their box, Mozart had dashed back to the Hofers to take his mother-in-law and Carl, as well, to the theater, the boy's first encounter with an opera. Right after the final curtain, Mozart drove Salieri and Cavalieri home and Carl and Mama back to the Hofers for supper. Then father and son went on to the Rauhensteingasse, where "both had a fine sleep."

Mozart found Carl happy and well, but for some time had been troubled by the low level of instruction at the academy in Perchtoldsdorf: "In

---

11 In contrast, the accomplished Schak performed Tamino's flute solos himself.

respect to health, he could not be in a better place. But, alas, everything else is miserable! About all they [the staff] can do is give another peasant to the world." On 9 October he had gone to the Josephstadt to attend mass in the church of the Piarist fathers with the purpose of discussing with the rector the possibility of enrolling Carl in their school, the groundwork of this visit having been laid some months before: though out of sympathy with public demonstrations of piety, nonetheless, on 26 June, "candle in hand," Mozart had joined a Corpus Christi procession[12] that set out from and returned to the Piarist church; his gesture, he hoped, might further Carl's candidacy; payment of fees sufficed to matriculate at Perchtoldsdorf.[13]

The day after father and son had attended *The Magic Flute*, Mozart began that last letter to Constanze. He had doubts about returning the boy to Perchtoldsdorf: "Since his serious studies—God have mercy!—do not begin until Monday, I have asked to keep Carl until after dinner on Sunday [the sixteenth]; I said that you would very much like to see him. . . . On Sunday I shall bring him out to you. You can continue to keep him, or I shall take him back to Heeger's [academy at Perchtoldsdorf] after dinner. Think it over: in my opinion, a month [away from school] can hardly harm him. In the meantime, the business with the Piarists, well under way, might be concluded."

His final letters reveal Mozart basking in praise; busying himself with creating two of the loftiest productions of the human mind; sending his wife almost daily messages overflowing with fun, love, and plans; and concerning himself with the welfare of their child. I search in vain for the guttering candle of Mozartean myth; to the end, he preserved Candide-like qualities: evergreen expectations, a passion to love, and muscle to survive.

Indeed, throughout 1791, he composed at a furious pace, and not only major works. He completed two commissions bearing upon Freemasonry: in July, what he called a "Little German Cantata" for tenor and piano (K. 619, to words by a member of a Regensburg Brotherhood, Franz Heinrich Ziegenhagen, who gave the commission); and four months later, a "Little Masonic Cantata" (K. 623, the words by Schikaneder) for two tenors, bass, and small orchestra. The final entry in his catalogue, this work was to solemnize the inauguration of his lodge's new hall. Having brought his family back from Baden to the Rauhensteingasse on 17 November, he conducted the premiere of K. 623 the following day. Both cantatas discourse in the sober, elevated language he favored during this period, a style reach-

12 It took place on the Sunday after the day of observance.
13 There the annual basic fee for tuition came to four hundred gulden (close to Mozart's former yearly salary at Salzburg); the Piarist fathers charged two hundred fifty. Economy, however, played no part in Mozart's plan.

ing an apotheosis in the Ave verum corpus (K. 618, for vocal quartet to the accompaniment of strings and organ continuo). He wrote it about the middle of June as a gift for Anton Stoll, organist and choirmaster of Baden's parish church.[14] This hymn for Corpus Christi seems to float down from the empyrean of the saints.

Less reverent pursuits also occupied him. His dalliance with music-making mechanisms demands notice, by dint of the quality of the resulting compositions, and also by their association with a nobleman who had become a kind of Viennese combination of E. T. A. Hoffmann's Coppelius and Madame Tussaud: Count Joseph Nepomuk Deym von Stržitež, who, close upon complications arising from a duel, had fled the capital for Holland to return around 1780 as Herr Müller (the equivalent in English of Mr. Jones, Smith—or, indeed, Miller), now an accomplished sculptor in wax. Five years later, on the Stock-im-Eisen Platz, he opened a gallery of plaster casts. It answered a growing popular interest in classical sculpture and accommodated quite different sensibilities by displays of wax portraits,[15] gypsum death masks—some of the heads and figures had a remarkable lifelike quality thanks to a colored paste of his invention—and mechanical curiosities including automatons and toys.

The death of Field Marshal Gideon von Laudon (14 July 1790) had suggested to him an unusual business opportunity: he created a so-called Mausoleum, which opened on the Himmelpfortgasse in March 1791; there, for one florin (the better seats) or thirty kreutzer, visitors might pay their respects to the national hero by contemplating an effigy of him in plaster and wax, the atmosphere of mourning intensified by artful lighting and, "on the stroke of the hour," special "Funeral Musique," for which Müller had turned to Mozart. It appears to have been "the Adagio [and Allegro] for the clockmaker" (K. 594) to which he made slurring reference in a letter to Constanze from Frankfurt (3 October 1790); not even the handsome fee could call up sufficient inspiration: he had to force himself to complete the composition as he stifled his contempt for Müller's catchpenny mechanical organs (called musical clocks) "made up only of high-pitched little pipes sounding too childish for me."

Müller did not realize his hope to provide his commemorative show with "a different composition each week, the name of the composer to be announced on posters." Mozart wrote two more pieces for musical

---

14 His chorus sang the Missa brevis, K. 275, the next month, having performed the Coronation Mass, K. 317, the preceding summer. Father Stoll held himself at Constanze's service and helped make the painstaking arrangements for her quarters.

15 He had in his employ Leonhard Posch, who made a well-known relief in wax of Mozart.

mechanisms (March and May 1791, respectively): K. 608 with its remarkable fugue, so admired by Beethoven, and K. 616, which has the disarming, immaterial quality of the trio of the Three Boys in *The Magic Flute*; the relationship of K. 608 and 616 to one or another of the museum's contrivances, perhaps the automatons, would appear a high probability.[16] Müller continued to value K. 594: at the end of July 1791, he closed the Mausoleum and by mid-August had installed the Laudon exhibit in his gallery, the announcement of the move promising the visitor that "as one contemplates the whole, exquisite funeral music by the famous Kapellmeister Mozart comes unawares."[17]

He stood at the high point of his fame: his operas now had a commanding presence in German theaters and even in companies beyond the boundaries of the Empire; and whenever he thought the time right, the tour to London could be set into motion; further, so Constanze remembered, "besides having but recently obtained the reversionary rights to the kapellmeister's position at St. Stephen's cathedral, he received . . . assurances of an annual subvention of one thousand florins from a group of Hungarian nobles; and from Amsterdam word came of a yet larger annual sum, which would require him to compose only a few works for the exclusive use of the subscribers."[18] With rising spirits she observed that "on all sides his prospects for the future had begun to brighten." Thus, while an unexpected lawsuit, brought against him by an old friend, might have proved awkward, it could not have threatened the basis of a financial position ameliorating at so many points.

In mid-November, the Provincial Tribunal of Lower Austria called the attention of the judicial authority in Vienna to a citation against Mozart for fourteen hundred thirty-five gulden and thirty-two kreutzer. Karl von Lichnowsky had moved to recover a debt that had proven uncollectible (see XXXII, n. 37), and a writ now ordered it to be made whole by attaching the defendant's personal property or one-half his salary (that is, his sinecure). Mozart must have let the matter slide in light of the Prince's enormous wealth, and he no doubt had been stirred up to institute the lit-

---

16 In connection with one of Müller's displays, Mozart may have rearranged for clockwork a composition written in the first place for glass harmonica: K. 617 (see p. 127).

17 By the turn of the century, Müller had moved his gallery via the Kohlmarkt to a Palladian-style mansion at the Rotenturmtor on the Danube canal. He married Countess Josephine von Brunsvik, with whom Beethoven would become infatuated after Müller's death in 1804.

18 Although Constanze's recollections suggest that the Hungarian and Dutch admirers had first been in touch during October or November, I believe them to have been the source of a sum—otherwise unaccounted for—Mozart made known to Michael Puchberg during the summer: two thousand florins expected at the Rauhensteingasse at the end of June or early in July and to be sent on to him.

igation by reports of Mozart's increasing good fortune: the big commissions, fees, and grants. But the action never finished its course; Lichnowsky retreated, no doubt in shock and embarrassment: within the month, Mozart lay dead.[19]

2

ON 20 NOVEMBER, two days after he had conducted K. 623 in his lodge's new quarters, an indisposition forced him to take to his bed; for certain he believed that rest, along with Doctor Closset's ministrations, would, as in the past, restore him in little time. Day followed day in a cycle of seeming recovery, relapse, and then, again, repair. (A pattern not unusual when treatment had its essence in emetics, enemas, and bloodletting; the era's classical cure, it kept the funeral wagons in full swing.) At the most reassuring points of this round, he may have given thought to the Requiem, whose completion had been in abeyance while he worked on the Masonic cantata; however, though he remained in command of his brain, it must be doubted that after the twentieth he possessed the strength or particular intellectual focus to put notes to paper.

His body swelled: he found lying on his back the only comfortable position and soon could not turn or even raise himself. His mother-in-law and Sophie, who, along with his pupils Süssmayr and Joseph Leopold Eybler, helped Constanze tend him, "made him a nightshirt that could be pulled on frontways," and, in anticipation of his relaxing during recuperation, "a quilted dressing gown." He looked forward to wearing it but remained bedridden. Yet his fate did not become clear to him until 4 December, when Constanze, too, beheld the ultimate crisis at hand and made the decision to summon a priest.

In an attempt to spare him alarm at the sight and sounds of the last rites in full form—sextons ringing bells as they escorted a cleric in vestments—she wished a priest to arrive alone, as if on a passing, spontaneous sick call. She asked Sophie to run with this request to St. Peter's, where the Mozarts and the Webers had old and close ties. But Sophie failed to make the stratagem clear, even to impart the urgency of the situation: only at his own tempo did a father make his way from the Auge Gottes to Mozart's bedside, and late in the afternoon.[20] He received the sacred oil of extreme

---

19 Lichnowsky made no claim against Mozart's estate.

20 She mistook the priests' misunderstanding of her errand for a truculent disregard of their vows, a view that gave birth to the myth of the clergy's refusal to attend Mozart (see n. 22). This misconception, in turn, strengthened a second myth: that of the incompatibility of Roman Catholicism and Freemasonry in eighteenth-century Vienna.

unction, but apparently a period of unconsciousness foreclosed the administering of the viaticum.

Constanze had sent a message of emergency to Doctor Closset: located at the theater after much searching, he waited until the final curtain to make his way to the Rauhensteingasse.[21] Evening had fallen, and he found Mozart awake and capable of coherent speech but with his body "inflamed and much swollen." Closset ordered Sophie to apply "cold compresses" [of vinegar and water] to the patient's "burning brow"; she protested, resisted, but had to obey. The sudden chill "threw him into convulsions." Torpor followed, and then final coma. Attended by Constanze, Sophie, and Closset, Mozart died at "one hour past midnight, between the fourth and fifth of December."[22]

Doctor Eduard Guldener von Lobes, a colleague of Closset and of his associate and consultant, Doctor Matthias von Sallaba, remembered "nothing at all unusual [alcuna cosa d'insolito] in the examination of the corpse" (required by law) and attributed the death to "a rheumatic and inflammatory fever" (una febbre reumatico-infiammatoria[23]), altogether in line with the description on the death certificate: "acute miliary fever." These medical phrases embraced so wide a variety of illnesses that they cannot be narrowed to any of today's diagnostic terms. Perhaps Mozart died of renal failure, perhaps of a rheumatic malady; whatever the case, the illness invaded a system weakened by overwork.[24] The doctor did the rest.

Beside herself, Constanze had to be pulled from the body. She later wrote in his album: "For eight years [in fact, more than nine] we were united by the tenderest bonds never to be severed here below! Oh! Soon may I join you forever." Through the night, news of the "irreplaceable" loss—so the Wiener Zeitung would describe it on the seventh—traveled the

---

21 Perhaps he functioned as house physician and felt in duty bound to remain until the end of the performance. In conversation with the Novellos (see II, n. 14), Sophie recalled Closset's having been at the opera.

22 Concerning Mozart's last hours, Sophie has left the fullest and most reliable information: in 1824 she sent these reminiscences to Nissen (the Mozart biographer and Constanze's second husband), and later discussed them with the Novellos, who took notes. The honesty of her moving accounts shines through the occasional and understandable confusion and embellishment of thoughts gathered more than three decades after the event.

23 When, on 10 June 1824, Guldener put to paper his recollections of the circumstances surrounding Mozart's death, he wrote in Italian for the benefit of Giuseppe Carpani. This distinguished poet and critic had begun to gather information countering the absurd and fashionable rumor charging Salieri with having poisoned Mozart (see n. 24).

24 Theories based upon no reasonable evidence continue to evolve with regard to Mozart's death, a sport often pursued with an irrational fervor. Such endeavors include a most popular subspecies picturing Mozart as the victim of assassination, the quality of argument well summed up by the once widespread idea that the Jews did away with him.

city: by morning a crowd had gathered before the house to give evidence of sympathy and grief. Once Müller had taken a death mask,[25] mourners could mount the stairs to view the master, "in a black suit, lying in a coffin, over his forehead a cowl hiding his blond hair, his hands folded over his breast. . . ." In the unseasonably mild weather the remains had begun to give way to putrefaction and required quick burial.

The following afternoon, led by a crucifer flanked by four hooded choirboys with lamps, pallbearers muffled in cloaks carried the body to St. Stephen's, the procession following in their train no doubt made up of Constanze and her family, van Swieten (who had arranged the funeral[26]), Albrechtsberger, students, friends, colleagues, and members of the Imperial musical household, including—so he affirmed to his pupil Anselm Hüttenbrenner—Salieri.

Constanze and van Swieten had ordered a third-class funeral, the category most Viennese chose. In respect to the cathedral, it did not include use of the nave or chancel but admitted a service—as a rule a low mass—in one of the chapels. But in light of an elaborate high mass to be sung in Mozart's memory at St. Michael's on the tenth, the order of the day followed a modified course: his cortege progressed straight to the Crucifix Chapel, a porchlike structure built over the stairs descending to the long-closed catacombs and attached to the cathedral's north wall. There Mozart received a final blessing on his passage to eternity, and, with this ceremony's prayers and benediction, the Church, as to obsequies, completed its work; his soul in God's hands, only the mechanics of disposal remained, an outright secular matter. That he made his final journey alone was in no way unusual: the gathering dispersed, and at the hour set by the health code,[27] a rented private hearse pulled by a pair of horses arrived for the coffin and bore it to one of the cemeteries serving St. Stephen's, that of the suburban village of St. Marx.

Gravediggers deposited him in a "normal simple grave" (*allgemeines einfaches Grab*), not a communal (*gemeinschaftlich*) pit, a point to be stressed since myth perpetuates the idea of his having been laid to rest among others (perhaps because multiple interments did take place as a matter of course). Excepting the mausoleums of the aristocratic and wealthy, all burial sites

25 He kept it for exhibition in his gallery but sent Constanze a copy. Neither example has survived.
26 On the day of Mozart's death, van Swieten suffered dismissal from his position at court: having linked him to the Bavarian Illuminati, the Emperor's advisers now mistrusted his loyalty. Heedless of shock, he at once took in hand the matter of Mozart's burial.
27 The pertinent regulations forbade the carting of corpses through the streets during the warmest and busiest hours.

constituted, not personal property, but leaseholds of ten years: every decade the authorities plowed them, sowing back into the soil whatever stray bones turned up and thus preparing for new occupants. Such a furrowing dispersed whatever remained of Mozart and demolished a memorial marking his grave. Within a month of his death, a notice in the *Wiener Zeitung* (31 December 1791) had alluded to this stone tablet, the contributor suggesting an epitaph in Latin for it: "As a child, he who lies here, through his harmonies, added to the wonders of the world; as a man, he surpassed Orpheus. Go your way and pray earnestly for his soul."

Since the reforms of Joseph II, graves in outlying districts accommodated the overwhelming number of Viennese: only those with family tombs could, by law, find their final rest within the walls of the city. Although most went to burial in linen sacks, Mozart probably wore the black suit in which visitors to the Rauhensteingasse had viewed him, for Constanze and van Swieten had purchased the coffin. (Often families rented one for use only during the service and the trip to the cemetery, the gravediggers returning it to the sexton once they had slipped the shroud-encased body through a trapdoor in the casket and into the ground.)

Four days after the burial, so the *Auszug aller europäischen Zeitungen* (*European Press Digest*) of 13 December reported, the Viennese "celebrated solemn obsequies for the great composer Mozart" in St. Michael's. (Across from the Hofburg and the Burgtheater, it functioned as both parish church to the court and chapel to its musicians' special society, the Congregation of St. Cecilia, to which Mozart had belonged.) On the sixteenth, the Viennese journal *Der heimliche Botschafter* (*The Secret Messenger*), which circulated in scribes' copies, identified the music at this service as "the requiem he composed during his final illness. . . ." With remarkable speed, disciples had extracted from the score those parts that had reached performable state as, with no less urgency, singers and instrumentalists learned them. In view of the manuscript's unfinished condition, only the first movement, and perhaps the second with some instrumental touches added, could have been performed with orchestra; the other sections very likely took the form of Mozart's choruses sung by a quartet[28] and supported by organ continuo; plainchant might have filled the missing sections. Schikaneder hovered over this labor of devotion.[29]

---

28 Such a circumstance might have given birth to one of the most romantic of Mozart myths: that of the dying composer (propped up by pillows) and three friends at his bedside, all rehearsing the vocal lines of the Requiem.

29 Prague marked Mozart's death four days later with a requiem (a setting by Franz Anton Rössler, also known as Antonio Rosetti) in St. Nicholas's, packed by a throng of more than four thousand overflowing into the surrounding streets.

The commissioning and completion of the Requiem (K. 626) constituted a bizarre adventure entangling the client, the composer, and then his widow and disciples. To follow in full its course dictates a countermarch of some nine months, back to 14 February 1791, when the twenty-year-old Countess Anna von Walsegg died at Stuppach castle on the superb Alpine pass called the Semmering.

CHAPTER XXXV

Lux Perpetua

H ER WIDOWER, FRANZ Paola Joseph Anton von Walsegg-Stuppach,
an amateur composer, wished to write a new setting of the requiem,
to be performed each year on the anniversary of her death. At the same
time, facing the fact of his limited talent, he decided to commission the
work and pass it off as his own. (Not his first resort to this kind of deception: Hoffmeister provided him with the quartets his retainers found it
wise to applaud as his own creations.) Through intermediaries bound in
duty to shield his identity, he turned to Mozart, who, though he knew of
the Count, did not recognize him as the author of the commission.[1] His
attorney in Vienna, Johann Nepomuk Sortschan, had charge of the negotiations, he, too, by indirection: his clerk approached Mozart,[2] who lent
himself to the misrepresentation, and in July they reached an agreement
centering about a handsome fee of two hundred twenty-five florins.[3] Before

---

1 It suggests itself that Michael Puchberg, who worked and had quarters in a house owned by the
Count (see p. 673), recommended Mozart to him. Yet, it seems hard to believe that Puchberg
would not have apprised his close friend of such a discussion.
2 The clerk entered legend as a gaunt, grey-clad messenger arrived from the Stygian shore to incite Mozart to compose his own requiem, a fantasy in the manner of E. T. A. Hoffmann.
3 Half the Burgtheater's standard payment for a complete opera, the fee, under these circumstances, was high, for, in the case of an opera, remuneration required not only the score but also
revisions, rehearsals, and conducting the premiere.

his departure for Prague to produce *La clemenza*, Mozart received a substantial deposit.

There can be no doubt that he saw limits to his co-operation with the feint and intended in time to enter the Requiem into his catalogue and assert his authorship. The client would be able to do little more than ruffle his borrowed plumes: to protest in public or take legal action would be to reveal his fraud in glaring light. Indeed, as early as the performance at St. Michael's, Constanze and van Swieten took the first step toward putting the matter on a course of indifference to his rights. Vienna knew the Requiem before Walsegg received and paid the balance outstanding on the score (perhaps as early as February 1792), made a copy of it in his own hand, and thus transformed—free from exposure, he somehow believed—the Mozart into the Walsegg Requiem. It has been supposed that on the distant Semmering he heard nothing of the memorial service at St. Michael's or of a later presentation of the Requiem in Vienna at caterer Jahn's establishment: a benefit for Constanze and her sons arranged by van Swieten, which took place on 2 January 1793,[4] almost a year before Walsegg conducted the premiere of "his" requiem in the Cistercian Neuklosterkirche of Wiener Neustadt, the largest town near Stuppach castle.

Of what did the Walsegg Requiem consist and how did it differ, if at all, from what the Viennese heard at Jahn's? The answer will be found in the course of following Constanze's tactics (as deployed under van Swieten's tutelage) straightway after Mozart's death.

In a petition that reached the Emperor six days later (11 December 1791), she acknowledged that, inasmuch as her husband had not completed the mandatory decade of Imperial service, her legal right to a pension from the Hofburg did not exist; nor, she continued, had he enrolled in the Society of Musicians (see XXVIII, n. 28), and thus his family had no claim to draw upon its fund for widows and orphans. Constanze declared herself on the edge of penury, on the surface the case in that she had no income.

---

4 An entry of this date in Zinzendorf's diary tells of an evening visit "to Princess Schwarzenberg [Maria Eleonora, widow of Johann Nepomuk] and from there to old Princess Colloredo [Marie Gabriele, widow of Prince Rudolph], which resulted in my missing Mozart's Requiem." One way or another, Walsegg had succeeded in stopping his eyes and ears to news of the Viennese performances and to the stories about the Requiem in circulation from the day of Mozart's funeral. On 18 January 1792, Graz's *Zeitung für Damen and andere Frauenzimmer* recounted a fabricated version of the commission's origin and announced that, once the work, "completed a few days before his death," had "been copied," the Viennese would give it "in his memory at St. Michael's church" (the performance of some six weeks earlier). Readers further learned that the unknown who had ordered the composition paid the balance of the fee but "did not ask for" the score: "and since then there has been no further request for it." Had it been true, the incident would have put Constanze at ease.

Underlining Mozart's achievement, fame, concern for the well-being of his dependents, and loyalty to the House of Habsburg, she identified her trust in its favor and generosity as her only shield. She stressed the bitterness of a tragedy that had struck at a moment of soaring expectations. Death had taken him by surprise.[5]

Even so, he had left a house in order, having paid back Lackenbacher in full (see p. 718); and, as luck had it, neither Lichnowsky nor Puchberg made a claim upon the legacy.[6] Medical bills run up during the final illness had drained but not emptied the household's coffers. Further, the transfer of five hundred florins representing Constanze's dowry to the estate's column of liabilities[7]—at its heart nine hundred eighteen florins and sixteen kreuzer owed tradesmen—along with an obliging assessor's low estimate of the household's movables, helped ease the matter of probate duty. And here a technicality opened a passage to stability and, in time, prosperity: royal statutes exempted manuscripts from taxation; heirs did not even have to list them in inventory. In this case they formed the family's major property and one capable of generating substantial revenue. With the reassurances this circumstance provided, Constanze could borrow; she paid the estate's debt and with generous heart committed herself to settling two hundred florins apiece upon her sons in their father's name.[8]

Within three months of his death, Constanze handed over to the Prussian embassy in Vienna a copy of the Requiem[9] and with it a number of Mozart's scores in manuscript to be reproduced and then returned to her; they included *La Betulia liberata* and the litanies K. 125 and 243.[10] King

5 Her years with Mozart had polished her German prose (and knowledge of foreign languages), but, without doubt, van Swieten helped compose this well-turned appeal.

6 On 7 March 1792, a public notice (from Vienna's City Council) appearing in the *Wiener Zeitung* called upon anyone with such an assertion to step forward.

7 Mozart appears to have forgiven a debt of five hundred gulden owed him by Anton Stadler; not the case in respect to an obligation for three hundred gulden on the part of Franz Gilowsky recorded in 1786 and listed as "presumed lost" in the papers of the estate.

8 Since Mozart died intestate, the magistracy, as a matter of course, appointed a temporary guardian, Doctor Niklas Ramor, to watch over the children's interests. He and Constanze cooperated in complete harmony.

9 As completed by his disciples (see pp. 752–54). She claimed not to be riding over the unknown client's rights when insisting upon her own authority to "give facsimiles to princes who, in the nature of things, would not make them public." At the time she gave Johann Anton André (the son of Johann André; see XXVIII, n. 39) the privilege of bringing her Mozart archive to print, Constanze did not include the completed Requiem in the sale (1799; for thirty-one hundred fifty gulden); although no one had raised objections to performances of the work, she did fear a legal challenge to publication.

10 Archduke Maximilian, since 1784 Elector-Archbishop of Cologne, who sent Constanze a gift of twenty-four ducats to help tide her over, also had inquiries made about buying copies of Mozart scores, but it appears that the high prices she asked turned him away.

Frederick William made these purchases for eight hundred ducats (including four hundred fifty for the Requiem), which translated into thirty-six hundred florins or well over four times Mozart's annual sinecure. The sum put the family on an even keel, and Constanze could hold back from selling items from the archive itself; she had time to ponder the best way of profiting from this heritage while at the same time preserving its integrity. In the meantime, organizing her own benefit concerts opened a way of gathering florins under the banner of Mozart's name.[11]

Her success to a considerable degree depended upon sustaining the public image of a widow plunged into poverty. This pose helped form the false picture still surviving: a Mozart family short of the necessities, indeed, sitting on straw. Mozart's colleagues contributed their musical services to her concerts and, in time, so did she: the appearance on stage of the great man's wife singing his music had the power to fill a theater. Most often she took part in ensembles from *La clemenza di Tito* and *Idomeneo*, a work she wished to make better known. (As late as the Advent and Lenten seasons of 1794–1795, the Hofburg would sponsor for her benefit two concert performances of *La clemenza*, in which Aloisia sang Sesto; during a pause in the second, Beethoven played a Mozart piano concerto, in all likelihood K. 466.)

While Constanze's transaction with the court of Prussia proceeded, the Hofburg, responding to her plea for a subvention, began hammering out a

---

11 Accompanied by Aloisia, in the autumn of 1795 Constanze set out on a tour, during which King Frederick William put the Berlin opera house with its singers and instrumentalists at her disposal for a concert (28 February 1796) that included "the most important selections" from *La clemenza*. A royal and public encomium insinuated that had her husband made his career in Prussia, he would have had the better of it, His Majesty's phrase, "unfortunate circumstances," a slap at the court of Leopold II. Berlin extended the hand of sympathy to Constanze and her sons, who, it would appear, received at least part of their inheritance before their mother's death (1842). In 1809 she married Georg Nikolaus Nissen, the Danish chargé d'affaires in Vienna, and a letter he wrote to Carl on 13 June of the following year seems a response to his having petitioned the estate for a loan. (Carl was approaching twenty-six.) Nissen underplayed his wife's assets, reminding Carl that "through tours as well as the sale of your father's manuscript scores . . . your mother had the good fortune not only to pay the debts [to the tradesmen and to Puchberg] but also to gather a *small* capital. With God's help, this will not decline, and you may expect half of it [and his brother his share] at a time both you and I desire to be in the most distant future. She will continue to draw interest [to provide] income." Carl pursued the matter, for on 29 December Constanze wrote him, insisting that in the light of the very low rate of exchange current in Vienna, where the funds had been invested, "it would be unpardonable, foolish, and detrimental to disturb this capital. In other circumstances I would make over—not lend—your half to you as your own property." She had good reason to postpone the matter: by 1810 Austrian currency has depreciated to a point of crisis only to be resolved the following year by the introduction of new currency. The relationship between Mozart's sons and their mother and stepfather remained affectionate.

solution by gathering depositions and warrants verifying her statements and on 13 March implemented a "special favor" that, above all, was "not to establish a precedent" (*ohne Konsequenz*): an annual pension for Constanze amounting to one third of Mozart's. Recognizing that it had created his sinecure only to keep him in Vienna, and that the idiosyncratic post had died with him, the court moved the eight hundred florins allotted him to the credit side of the treasury's ledger; and, inasmuch as the smaller payment to Constanze would come from "general funds"—perhaps the Emperor's—the change could be pronounced a double savings! Francis II's signature validated the gesture, his father, Emperor Leopold, having died twelve days earlier.[12]

2

DURING THE FRAMING of the pension, she formed a small and secret council of Mozart's closest students and colleagues to fix upon a way to deliver a finished requiem and collect the balance of the fee. (She also wanted to liberate the score, in her opinion among Mozart's finest, from the limbo of the stillborn.) Should the effort fail, the legal clerk in grey might reappear and demand the return of the deposit; at the moment the Mozarts had stepped into their carriage for that last journey to Prague, he, in fact, had presented himself to ask how long the matter of *La clemenza* would delay delivery of the Requiem. (Mozart pledged that it would receive his full attention upon his return to Vienna, but matters did not fall out to this end.)

Now, striving to cope with questions buzzing about the point the Requiem had reached at Mozart's death, she had no recourse but subterfuge: perhaps assurances that little remained to do but add some touches he, in any case, had outlined. His *particella*, or short score, survives and reveals the sober truth: the completed Requiem did not come into being without mystification, indeed, substantial misrepresentation on her part. The atmosphere of suspicion still hanging over that sheaf of manuscript pages Mozart left behind must be considered against the background of the all-embracing religious structure from which they derived: the Holy Sacrifice of the Altar.

The mass comprises two comprehensive categories: texts forming the Or-

---

12 Two days after enacting the symbolic end of the long struggle with Constantinople by receiving a Turkish ambassador (26 February), Emperor Leopold suffered a serious indisposition. His doctors bled him four times within forty-eight hours, and he expired in the arms of his wife on 1 March. Suspicion of poisoning fell upon Freemasons, Jesuits, and disaffected Turks, but many insisted that his doctors, with best intentions, had dispatched him. They, in fact, found themselves under strong attack: bleeding had begun to fall into disrepute.

dinary, which remain unmodifiable, whatever the liturgical occasion, and those of the Proper, which vary in accordance with the church calendar. The Ordinary most often consists of Kyrie, Gloria, Credo, Sanctus (the Benedictus its second part), and Agnus Dei, but a requiem mass omits both Gloria and Credo. The Proper of Mozart's Requiem comprises an Introit ("*Requiem aeternam*"); Sequence (a trope or literary embellishment, in this case beginning with the words "*Dies irae*"); Offertory ("*Domine Jesu Christe*"); and Communion ("*Lux aeterna*"). The Sequence, here painting the Last Judgment, takes pride of place in Mozart's Mass for the Dead: he lavished his genius upon this dramatic medieval poem, most of it attributed to Thomas of Celano and consisting of nineteen stanzas, the opening couplet of the eighteenth being "*Lacrimosa dies illa / Qua resurget ex favilla*" (That day of tears, when [man rises] from the dust). Having composed the Sequence up to and including these words, written two measures for the following line ("*Judicandus homo reus*"), and sketched a fugue on the terminal "*Amen*" of the concluding stanza, Mozart broke off work on the Sequence, leaving four lines to be set in full, and jumped to the Offertory: it seems clear that he had not yet decided upon how to relate the "*Dona eis requiem*" in the Sequence's nineteenth stanza to corresponding phrases in both the Introit, already completed, and the Agnus, yet to be composed. He must have intended to give final shape to the Sequence's closing lines once he had forged his way through the entire text of the mass: delicate aesthetic decisions had arisen, questions of cross-connections and proportion.

The essence of Mozart's *particella* resides in a four-part chorus supported by figured bass, this composite being complete in the Introit, Kyrie, Offertory, Communion (in that Mozart intended it to be a recapitulation of music drawn from the Introit and Kyrie), and, as observed, almost all of the Sequence. The Introit alone had its complete instrumentation. With the help of sporadic and fragmentary indications, which Mozart had set down in the score as an *aide-mémoire*, the orchestral parts of the Kyrie, Sequence, and Offertory could be worked out; but there remained serious shortcomings next to which the missing tail of the Sequence offered but a trifling challenge: Mozart had entered into his *particella* not a note of the Sanctus or Agnus; they existed only as sketches on separate leaves (most of them now lost). To complete the Requiem required filling in the orchestration, composing the end of the Sequence, and fabricating a convincing Sanctus and Agnus from the implications of the sketches.[13] Constanze's

---

13 Sketches of this kind doubtless formed the roots of the *particella*, which, at the point Mozart's death interrupted work on it, represented his penultimate stage of composition; by additions, he would have turned these very leaves into the finished score.

advisory council—Freystädtler (alias Gaulimauli; see XXXI, n. 32), Eybler, and Süssmayr—all had a hand in the job, which, in the end, Süssmayr took over and, incorporating contributions of his associates,[14] brought to a close. To characterize the Sanctus and Agnus, he enlisted the evocative and exculpatory phrase *"ganz neu von mir verfertigt,"* which might be rendered as "a new entity put together by my hand," a description not at variance with Abbé Stadler's defense of the entire salvage project: "All the essentials come from Moz[art]. . . ."[15]

Within less than three months of Mozart's death, the grey messenger could collect the Requiem: with great speed, Süssmayr had succeeded to a remarkable degree in patching together an integrated score.[16] (Unlike the C-minor mass, which exploited contrasts of style, the Requiem emerged of a piece.) If, at moments, solecisms mar its instrumentation or musical grammar,[17] the burden sustained by a mediocre talent attempting to intuit the processes of genius provides pardon: that scholars still debate assigning certain passages to either Mozart or Süssmayr enshrines the laurels of a devoted student and friend.

Legend alone furnishes the picture of a Mozart in relentless decline and rounding his life with a swan song taking the shape of a requiem. Indeed, its musical impulse appears to have come not from thoughts of the Lethe,[18] but, rather, the Thames: before him lay, so he thought, the happy inevitability of a tour to London, and the opening movements of the Re-

14 If the "premiere" of the Requiem at St. Michael's included an orchestra, it put to use Freystädtler's additions to the Kyrie's instrumentation.
15 Abbé Maximilian (Johann Karl Dominik) Stadler, a priest, theologian, and musician, studied under the Benedictines of Melk (where he heard Mozart, almost twelve, play the organ). He became prior of Melk in 1784 and, five years later, Abbot of Kremsmünster. In 1796 he settled in Vienna, where Constanze Mozart adopted him as friend and adviser. With Nissen, he put her archive of Mozart manuscripts into order. Beethoven praised his defense of the Mozart Requiem's intrinsic authenticity (1826), under attack by Jacob Gottfried Weber.
16 Walsegg received a manuscript combining Mozart's and Süssmayr's writing. Like many a pupil, Süssmayr could mimic his teacher's hand with extraordinary accuracy: here the Count had small chance to detect inconsistencies. The score conveyed to him—it came to light in 1838 by way of his estate—bears Süssmayr's splendid forgery of Mozart's signature and the date of 1792. (It would not have been exceptional for a composer to put his name to a composition alongside its projected date of completion.) Süssmayr had to have been done with the Requiem by 4 March 1792, when Constanze delivered a copy to the Prussian Ambassador.
17 Mozart did not have the opportunity given Benjamin Disraeli, who, stretched out on his deathbed, insisted upon correcting the proofs of his final speech: "I will not go down to posterity talking bad grammar."
18 Johann Friedrich Rochlitz made a false analogy when declaring that a foreknowledge of impending death linked Mozart's labors on the Requiem and Raphael's on the *Transfiguration*. Yet a valid comparison can be made: each work stood within sight of completion at its creator's death, and, in

quiem encase an extended tribute to a composer born a German but by the time of his death no less English than the House of Hanover.

Beneath the Introit lies not only melodic, harmonic, and textural material from the opening chorus of Handel's *Funeral Anthem for Queen Caroline* (1737), but also a Lutheran funeral hymn Handel used in it. In addition, Mozart put to work the ninth psalm tone or Gregorian tonus peregrinus as he had so long ago in *La Betulia liberata* (see p. 292). Further, the Requiem's Kyrie fugue dips into the closing chorus of Handel's *Dettingen Te Deum*, that aural symbol of British prestige. Mozart reshaped these Handelian elements, engrafting new subtleties, the elder master's example generating the oxygen of the younger's creative imagination.

This long look toward the past on Mozart's part had nothing of what would become the romantic century's fearful flight back to the security of earlier ages: Mozart did not take up a venerable tongue to provide atmosphere for the fossilized retelling of an old tale; rather, once again he gave play to an appreciative appraisal of what might yet be done to gain fresh insights through the recovery and renewal of that bulwark against chaos, the learned, elevated style. Mozart's last manner has about it much of a search for the sober and monumental; the rich contrapuntal textures of the Requiem call to mind the fruits of an archaeological quest: a polyphony not of applied flourishes but of organic structures built deep into the rock of the work. The completed Requiem—it follows Mozart's ground plan—contains seven fugal sections (including repetitions), a tribute to the baroque masters he revered and to the wife who had encouraged his studies of their work, their fugues in particular.[19]

The fugal texture of the overture to *The Magic Flute* as well as its armed guards' chorale-prelude had pointed the way toward the powerful counterpoint of the Requiem. Both works breathe a spiritual transformation of Mozart's idiom; had he lived longer, it might have resolved itself by degrees into a tonal aesthetic paralleling the transition in German architecture from the stark elegance of Michel d'Ixnard to the elemental geometry of Karl Langhans. The works of Mozart's closing months betray a ripening judgment strengthened by tradition and cutting a passage to the new.

---

both cases, disciples had at hand studies from the master as guides toward practical posthumous solutions. (Süssmayr's contributions remain less obtrusive than Giulio Romano's.)

19 The taut fugues of the Requiem renounce the length of Mozart's earlier examples with their spacious and at times exhibitionistic strettos (passages in which the imitative phrases pile up and dovetail in close succession).

3

WITH THE SUPPORT of Rosicrucian Freemasonry and, above all, a Catholicism with which he never ceased to associate the glories of the Imperial idea—a concept he had never let go, even during the exuberance of his Storm and Stress adolescence—he did not suffer the painful disillusionment felt by so many Enlightened reformers and firebrands: almost in disbelief, they learned the terrible lessons the French Revolution had begun to teach as it opened fissures unexampled in Europe's historical continuity. The year of Mozart's death, Goethe began a group of minor and affected works, their current flowing opposite to the teachings of the Revolution. He had grown to fear very much the unruliness of the human horde, in whose eyes, it became clear to him, liberty, envy, and avarice now merged into one. He recast *Der Gross-Cophta* as a drama (see XXVIII, n. 12) and undertook two new plays: *Der Bürgergeneral* (The Civilian General), which advised the exclusion of the peasantry from public affairs lest it lose its happy simplicity, and *Die Aufgeregten* (The Insurgents; 1793), an unfinished work and no less foolish, irrespective of its call for the reconciliation of German aristocrats and democrats.[20]

In a more aloof spirit, Schiller would found a magazine, *Die Horen* (*horae*, or hours), excluding the transient and frivolous, here signifying the political, from pages devoted to matters of high culture, which he saw as alone fit to unite intellectual Germans on a level above questions of authority and government. After an initial burst of enthusiasm on the part of close admirers, *Die Horen* collapsed.

As Goethe turned to trifling scribbling and Schiller toward aesthetic reclusion, Mozart, who in life and art had clung to the well-defined and time-honored, answered the aspirations of his countrymen with a *Seelendrama* (an action of internal conflict) in which all Germans—prince, princess, priest, and peasant—find reassuring places in a compassionate society; and there followed a sacred composition of ineffable beauty drawing inspiration from a holy text and the German spirit and soil. With Goethe, he viewed their national heritage as an ancient domain to be transformed, a concept with links to Schiller's view of history as an ideal selection of facts to be shaped into new and transcendent configurations. Yet, for the time, Mozart alone of the three, provided humanizing works of noble measure and hymnic cadence and speaking the fortifying, redeeming

---

20 Goethe's passing season of political confusion would find finer literary expression in *Die natürliche Tochter* (1803), it, too, a fragment (of what he hoped to develop into a trilogy). More shard than fragment, *Das Mädchen von Oberkirch* also formed part of this series. In time Goethe did rouse himself and show alarm at Jacobinism's growing strength in Germany.

word the moment required: the new if, alas, transient paradigm took form, not in Goethe's and Schiller's Weimar, but in Mozart's Vienna;[21] within three years of his death, Weimar's *Journal of Luxury and Fashion*, contemplating the unexampled success of *The Magic Flute*, opined that "something with this effect upon an entire nation must of a certainty be one of the most potent agents of fermentation. . . ." Mozart had bestowed his gifts of all-renewing pardon and restoration.

With the years, the degradations and mutilations life can inflict had provided him profound sources of strength helping form a toughness of mind and with it a career of never-failing self-confidence and pride. Adept at scrambling out of shipwreck and at once pressing forward to new scenes of action, there once again to fight the fight, he had learned that the done cannot be undone and eschewed indulging remorse in nostalgic and sterile attempts to recover and repair his own past, a restraint deepening the roots of his astonishing ability to concentrate and thus produce. A moralist in the Catholic tradition of intense self-examination, he nonetheless continued young and bright in spirit and preserved an idealism that, though time altered it, remained nourished by faith in God's grace and never withered. He tendered the world a message—to echo Carlyle's praise of Goethe— like that of the Evangelists, for he, too, had the power to ransom the soul. Beloved of youth with its infinite longings and no less of age with its failed aspirations, he confronted his time and confronts posterity as a universal touchstone. Like all geniuses of his rank, he stands as a law to himself: incommensurable, incalculable, sublime.

---

21 To provide music for his singspiel texts and, on occasion, for his lyric poems, Goethe encouraged mediocre composers. (Philipp Christoph Kayser, Johann Friedrich Reichhardt, and Carl Friedrich Zelter, for example), too late perceiving as a gross blunder his failure to cultivate Mozart: after a performance of *Don Giovanni* in 1797, he lamented to Schiller that Mozart's death had deprived *Faust* of such music. The hypothesis suggests itself that Goethe's fragment of a libretto continuing the story of *The Magic Flute* (*Der Zauberflöte zweiter Theil*, 1794) fulfilled the poet's fantasy of working with the departed master.

SELECTED BIBLIOGRAPHY

Abbreviations

AM = *Allgemeine Musikalische Zeitung.* Leipzig, 1798–1849

BA = *Mozart: Briefe und Aufzeichnungen* (see *Letters* . . . below)

D = *Mozart: Die Dokumente seines Lebens* (see *Letters* . . . below)

EB = *The Encyclopaedia Britannica* (see *Catalogues* . . . below)

G = *The New Grove Dictionary* (see *Catalogues* . . . below)

GB = *Der Grosse Brockhaus* (see *Catalogues* . . . below)

K = Köchel. *Chronologisch-thematisches Verzeichnis* (see *Catalogues* . . . below)

MJ = *Mozart–Jahrbuch des Zentralinstituts für Mozartforschung der Internationalen Stiftung Mozarteum.* Géza Rech, 1951–; Rudolph Angemüller and others, eds. 1976–. Salzburg: 1951–

MM = *Mitteilungen der Internationalen Stiftung Mozarteum.* Géza Rech and Rudolph Angemüller, eds. Salzburg: 1952–

NMA = Mozart. *Neue Ausgabe sämtlicher Werke (Neue Mozart-Ausgabe)* (see *Letters* . . . below)

O = *The Shorter Oxford English Dictionary* (2 vols., 1980)

Letters, Related Correspondence, Documents, Sources

Wolfgang Amadeus Mozart: Neue Ausgabe sämtlicher Werke. Various eds. Kassel: 1955–1991.

Mozart, Wolfgang Amadeus. "Die neugeborne Ros' entzückt." (Facsimile Edition) Salzburg: 1996.

Mozart: Briefe und Aufzeichnungen. Gesamtausgabe. Wilhelm A. Bauer, Otto Erich

Deutsch, Joseph Heinz Eibl, eds. 7 vols. Kassel: 1962–1975. (A selection of the letters in English translation may be found in *Books and Articles* below, under Sadie, Stanley, ed.)

Mozart: Die Dokumente seines Lebens (NMA, X, 34). Otto Erich Deutsch, ed. Kassel: 1961. *Addenda und Corrigenda* in NMA, X, 31, 1. (Both appear in English as *Mozart: A Documentary Biography.* Stanford, CA: 1966; a supplement may be found in *Books and Articles* below, under Eisen.)

Mozart, Constanze. *Konstanze Mozart: Briefe, Aufzeichnungen, Dokumente 1782–1842.* Arthur Schurig, ed. Dresden: 1922.

Mozart, Maria Anna. *Nannerl Mozarts Tagebuchblätter mit Eintragungen ihres Bruders Wolfgang Amadeus.* Walter Hummel, ed. Salzburg and Stuttgart: 1958.

Catalogues and Reference Works

Cappelli, A. *Cronologia, Cronografia, e Calendario Perpetuo dal Principio dell' Era Cristiana ai nostri Giorni.* Milan: 1969.

Encyclopaedia Britannica. 24 vols. Chicago, London, Toronto: 1945.

Der Grosse Brockhaus: Handbuch des Wissens in zwanzig Bänden (and *Ergänzungsband*). Leipzig: 1928–1935.

Köchel, Ludwig, Ritter von. *Chronologisch-thematisches Verzeichnis sämtlicher Tonwerke Wolfgang Amadé Mozarts.* 6th ed. Franz Giegling, Alexander Weinmann, Gerd Sievers, eds. Wiesbaden: 1964.

Mozart, Wolfgang Amadé. *Verzeichnüss aller meiner Werke.* (Mozart's Thematic Catalogue: A Facsimile; British Library, Stefan Zweig MS 63.) Albi Rosenthal and Alan Tyson, eds. Ithaca, NY: 1990.

Mozart in the British Museum. London: 1975.

Mueller von Asow, Erich H., ed. *Wolfgang Amadeus Mozart: Verzeichnis aller meiner Werke und Leopold Mozart: Verzeichnis der Jugendwerke W. A. Mozarts.* Vienna–Wiesbaden: 1956.

Die Musik in Geschichte und Gegenwart. Friedrich Blume, ed. 17 vols. Kassel: 1949–1986.

The New Grove Dictionary of Music and Musicians. Stanley Sadie, ed. 20 vols. London: 1980. Also: *Grove's Dictionary of Music and Musicians,* 6 vols. New York: 1944.

Offizieller Führer durch Hellbrunn. Salzburg: 1964.

Riemann Musik Lexicon. Wilibald Gurlitt, ed. 3 vols. Mainz: 1959–1967.

Salzburg zur Zeit Mozarts: Führer durch die Gedächtnis-Ausstellung (Residenzgalerie, Salzburg) *zum 200 Geburstjahr W. A. Mozarts.* Salzburg: 1956.

Wien Zur Zeit Joseph Haydns: Sonderausstellung des Historischen Museums der Stadt Wien. Vienna: 1982.

Books and Articles of particular influence in shaping the text

Abert, Hermann. *W. A. Mozart: neu bearbeitete und erweiterte Ausgabe* von Otto Jahns 'Mozart.' 2d ed. 2 vols. Leipzig: 1955.

Acton, Harold. *The Bourbons of Naples.* London: 1956.

Allanbrook, Wye Jamison. *Rhythmic Gesture in Mozart: Le nozze di Figaro and Don Giovanni.* Chicago: 1983.

Anchor, Robert. *The Enlightenment Tradition.* Berkeley, CA: 1967.

Andrieux, Maurice. *Daily Life in Papal Rome in the Eighteenth Century.* Trans. Mary Fitton. London: 1968.

Angermüller, Rudolph. *Antonio Salieri: Sein Leben und seine weltlichen Werke unter besonderer Berücksichtigung seiner grossen Opern.* 3 vols. Munich: 1971–1974.

————. "Leopold Mozarts Verlassenschaft." MM 41, 1993.

————. *Mozart und seine Welt.* Kassel: 1979.

————. *Mozart's Operas.* Trans. Stewart Spencer. New York: 1988.

————. "Testament, Kodizill, Nachtrag und Sperrelation der Freifrau Maria Anna von Berchtold zu Sonnenburg, geb. Mozart (1751–1829)." MJ 1986.

Aretin, Karl Otmar Freiherr von. *Heiliges römisches Reich: Reichs-verfassung und Staatssouveränität.* 2 vols. Wiesbaden: 1967.

Bach, Carl Philipp Emanuel. *Essay on the True Art of Playing Keyboard Instruments.* Trans. and ed. William J. Mitchell. New York: 1949.

Bach, Johann Sebastian. *Werke: Bach-Gesellschaft.* 47 vols. Leipzig: 1851–1899.

Badura-Skoda, Eva and Paul. *Interpreting Mozart on the Keyboard.* Trans. Leo Black. London: 1962.

Bahr, Hermann. *Salzburg.* Vienna: [1947].

Banks, C. A. and J. Rigbie Turner. *Mozart: Prodigy of Nature.* New York and London: 1991.

Bär, Carl. *Mozart: Krankheit, Tod, Begräbnis.* Salzburg: 1966.

Barraclough, Geoffrey. *The Origins of Modern Germany.* New York: 1963.

Bauer, Wilhelm A. "Amadeus?" *Festschrift Otto Erick Deutsch zum Achtzigsten Geburtstag.* Kassel: 1963.

Bauman, Thomas. *North German Opera in the Age of Goethe.* Cambridge: 1985.

————. *W. A. Mozart: Die Entführung aus dem Serail.* Cambridge: 1987.

Beales, Derek. *Joseph II.* Vol. 1: *In the Shadow of Maria Theresa, 1741–1780.* Cambridge: 1987.

Beaumarchais, Pierre-Augustin, Caron de. *Le Mariage de Figaro ou La Folle Journée.* Jean Meyer, ed. Paris: 1953.

Berlin, Isaiah. *Vico and Herder, Two Studies in the History of Ideas.* New York: 1976.

Bernard, Paul P. *Jesuits and Jacobins: Enlightenment and Enlightened Despotism in Austria.* Urbana, IL, Chicago, London: 1971.

————. *Joseph II and Bavaria: Two Eighteenth Century Attempts at German Unification.* The Hague: 1965.

Bernis, François-Joachim de Pierre, Cardinal de. *Mémoires et Lettres,* 2 vols. Paris: 1878.

Besterman, Theodore. *Voltaire.* New York: 1969.

Bibl, Viktor. *Kaiser Joseph II: Ein Vorkämpfer der grossdeutschen Idee.* Vienna and Leipzig: 1943.

Blanning, T. C. W. *Joseph II.* London and New York: 1994.

————. *Joseph II and Enlightened Despotism.* London: 1970.

Blom, Eric. *Mozart.* New York: 1966.

Blümml, Emil Karl. *Aus Mozarts Freundes—und Familienkreis.* Vienna, Prague, Leipzig: 1923.

Boyden, David D. *The History of Violin Playing from its Origins to 1761: and its Relationship to the Violin and Violin Music.* London: 1967.

Boyer, Noel. *La Guerre Des Bouffons Et La Musique Française (1752–1754).* Paris: 1945.

Brandes, Georg. *Voltaire.* Trans. Otto Kruger and Pierce Butler. 2 vols. New York: 1930.

————. *Wolfgang Goethe.* Trans. Allen W. Porterfield. 2 vols. New York: 1925.

Branscombe, Peter. *W. A. Mozart: Die Zauberflöte.* Cambridge: 1991.

Braunbehrens, Volkmar. *Mozart in Vienna 1781–1791.* Trans. Timothy Bell. New York: 1990.

Brauneis, Walther, "Exequien für Mozart." *Singende Kirche* 37, 1991.

————. "Unveröffentlichte Nachrichten zum December 1991 aus einer Wiener Lokalzeitung." MM, 1991.

————. "'... wegen schuldigen 1435 32 xr': Neuer Archivfund zur Finanzmisere Mozarts im November 1791," MM 39, 1991.

Brion, Marcel. *Daily Life in the Vienna of Mozart and Schubert.* Trans. Jean Stewart. New York: 1962.

Bronson, Bertrand Harris. *Facets of the Enlightenment.* Berkeley, CA: 1968.

Brophy, Brigid. *Mozart the Dramatist: A New View of Mozart, his Operas, and his Age.* New York: 1964.

Brosses, Le Président de. *Lettres Familières Ecrites d'Italie en 1739 et 1740.* Paris: 1858.

Brown, Bruce Alan. *Gluck and the French Theatre in Vienna.* Oxford: 1991.

————. *W. A. Mozart: Così fan tutte.* Cambridge: 1995.

Brown, Howard Mayer and Stanley Sadie, eds. *Performance Practice, Music After 1600.* New York: 1989.

Brown, P. Hume. *Life of Goethe.* 2 vols. New York: 1971.

Bruford, W. H. *Germany in the Eighteenth Century: The Social Background of the Literary Revival.* Cambridge: 1971.

Bryce, James, *The Holy Roman Empire.* New York: 1961.

Bukofzer, Manfred F. *Music in the Baroque Era.* New York: 1947.

Burk, John N. *Mozart and his Music.* New York: 1959.

Burney, Charles. *Dr. Charles Burney's Continental Travels 1770–1772.* Cedric Howard Glover, ed. London: 1927.

————. *A General History of Music: From the Earliest Ages to the Present Period (1789).* 2 vols. Frank Mercer, ed. New York: 1957.

————. *Music, Men, and Manners in France and Italy, 1770. Being the Journal Written by Charles Burney, Mus. D., during a Tour through those Countries. ...* H. E. Poole, ed. London: 1969.

————. *The Present State of Music in Germany, the Netherlands, and United Provinces.* 2 vols. London: 1773.

Burney, Fanny. *The Famous Miss Burney: The Diaries and Letters of Fanny Burney.* Barbara G. Schrank and David J. Supino, eds. New York: 1976.

Butler, E. M. *The Tyranny of Greece over Germany: A study of the influence exercised by Greek art and poetry over the great German writers of the eighteenth, nineteenth and twentieth centuries.* Boston: 1958.

Byrd, Max. *London Transformed: Images of the City in the Eighteenth Century.* New Haven, CT and London: 1978.

Campbell-Everden, William Preston. *Freemasonry and Its Etiquette.* New York: 1978.

Carter, Tim. *W. A. Mozart: Le nozze di Figaro.* Cambridge: 1987.

Casanova de Seingalt, Jacques. *The Memoires of Jacques Casanova de Seingalt.* Trans. Arthur Machen. Frederick A. Blossom, ed. 2 vols. New York: 1938.

Chailley, Jacques. *The Magic Flute, Masonic Opera: An Interpretation of the Libretto and the Music.* Trans. Herbert Weinstock. New York: 1971.

Chambers, Frank P. *The History of Taste: An Account of the Revolutions of Art Criticism and Theory in Europe.* Westport, CT: 1971.

Cheke, Marcus. *The Cardinal de Bernis.* New York: 1959.

Clifford, James L. *Hester Lynch Piozzi (Mrs. Thrale).* New York: 1987.

Clive, Peter. *Mozart and His Circle: A Biographical Dictionary.* New Haven, CT and London: 1993.

Coleman, Francis X. J. *The Aesthetic Thought of the French Enlightenment.* Pittsburgh: 1971.

Cook, E. Thornton. *The Royal Line of France.* Freeport, NY: 1967.

Cooper Clarke, B. "Albert von Mölk: Mozart Myth-Maker?" MJ 1995.

Cormican, Brendan. *Mozart's Death—Mozart's Requiem: An Investigation.* Belfast: 1991.

Cox, Cynthia. *The Real Figaro: The Extraordinary Career of Caron de Beaumarchais.* New York: 1963.

Crankshaw, Edward. *Maria Theresa.* New York: 1970.

Crocker, Lester G. *Diderot: The Embattled Philosopher.* New York: 1954.

Dalchow, Johannes. *W. A. Mozarts Krankheiten, 1756–1763.* Bergisch Gladbach: 1955.

Dalchow, Johannes, Gunther Duda, and Dieter Kerner. *Mozarts Tod 1791–1971.* Pähl: 1971.

Da Ponte, Lorenzo. *Memorie.* G. Gambarin and F. Nicolini, eds. 2 vols. Bari: 1918.
————. *Memoirs.* Trans. Elisabeth Abbott. Arthur Livingston, ed. New York: 1929.

Darnton, Robert. *Mesmerism and the End of the Enlightenment in France.* Cambridge, MA and London: 1968.

Darnton, Robert, Bernhard Fabian, and Roy McKeen Wiles. *The Widening Circle.* Paul J. Korshin, ed. Philadelphia: 1976.

David, Hans T., and Arthur Mendel, eds. *The Bach Reader: A Life of Johann Sebastian Bach in Letters and Documents.* New York: 1945.

Davies, Peter J. *Mozart in Person: His Character and Health.* New York: 1989.

Davis, James Herbert, Jr. *Fénelon.* Boston: 1979.

Dean, Winton. *Handel and the Opera Seria.* Berkeley, CA: 1969.

Dean, Winton, and John Merrill Knapp. *Handel's Operas, 1704–1726.* Oxford, 1987.

Dearling, Robert. *The Music of Wolfgang Amadeus Mozart: The Symphonies.* London: 1982.

Demetz, Peter. *Prague in Black and Gold: Scenes from the Life of a European City.* New York: 1997.

Dennerlein, Hanns. *Der unbekannte Mozart. Die Welt seiner Klavierwerke.* Leipzig: 1951.

Dent, Edward J. *Mozart's Operas: A Critical Study.* London and New York: 1947.

Dent, Edward J., and Erich Valentin. *The Earliest Compositions of Wolfgang Amadeus Mozart.* Munich: 1956.

Deutsch, Otto Erich. *Das Freihaustheater auf der Wieden.* Vienna: 1937.

———. *Mozart und die Wiener Logen: Zur Geschichte seiner Freimaurer-Kompositionen.* Vienna: 1932.

———. *Mozart und seine Welt in zeitgenössischen Bildern.* Kassel: 1961.

Diderot, Denis. *Correspondance.* Georges Roth and Jean Varloot, eds. 16 vols. Paris: 1955–1970.

———. *Le Neveu de Rameau.* Paris: 1925.

———. *Oeuvres Complètes.* 20 vols. Paris: 1875–1879.

———. *Oeuvres romanesques.* Paris, 1962.

———. *This is Not a Story and Other Stories.* Trans. P. N. Furbank. Columbia, MO and London: 1991.

Dietrich, Margret. "'Wiener Fassungen' des *Idomeneo.*" MJ 1973–1974.

Dimond, Peter. *A Mozart Diary.* Westport, CT and London: 1997.

Dittersdorf, Karl Ditters von. *Lebensbeschreibung: Seinem Sohne in die Feder diktiert.* Munich: 1967.

Donadoni, Eugenio. *A History of Italian Literature.* 2 vols. New York and London: 1969.

Dorian, Frederick. *The History of Music in Performance.* New York: 1942.

Dorn, Walter L. *Competition for Empire: 1740–1763.* New York: 1940.

Eggebrecht, Hans Heinrich. *Versuch über die Wiener Klassik: Die Tanzszene in Mozarts "Don Giovanni."* Wiesbaden: 1972.

Eibl, Joseph Heinz. *Wolfgang Amadeus Mozart: Chronik eines Lebens.* Kassel: 1965.

Eibl, Joseph Heinz, and Walter Senn. *Mozarts Bäsle–Briefe.* Kassel: 1978.

Einaudi, Mario. *The Early Rousseau.* Ithaca, NY: 1967.

Einstein, Alfred. *Gluck.* Trans. Eric Blom. London and New York: 1954.

———. *Mozart: His Character, His Work.* Trans. Arthur Mendel and Nathan Broder. New York: 1965.

Eisen, Cliff. "Leopold Mozart Discoveries." MM 35, July 1987.

———. *New Mozart Documents: A Supplement to O. E. Deutsch's Documentary Biography.* Stanford, CA: 1991.

Eisen, Cliff, ed. *Mozart Studies.* Oxford: 1991.

Eissler, K. R. *Goethe: A Psychoanalytic Study, 1775–1786.* 2 vols. Detroit: 1963.

Ellis, Madeleine B. *Rousseau's Venetian Story: An Essay Upon Art and Truth in "Les Confessions."* Baltimore: 1966.

Engerth, Ruediger. *Hier hat Mozart gespielt.* Salzburg: 1968.

Etheridge, David. *Mozart's Clarinet Concerto: The Clarinetist's View.* Gretna, LA: 1983.

Evans, R. J. W. *The Making of the Habsburg Monarchy 1550–1700: An Interpretation.* Oxford: 1970.

Falck, Martin. *Wilhelm Friedemann Bach.* Leipzig: 1919.

Farga, Franz. *Die Wiener Oper: Von ihren Anfängen bis 1938.* Vienna: 1947.

Fauchier-Magnan, A. *The Small German Courts of the Eighteenth Century.* London: 1958.

FitzLyon, April. *Lorenzo Da Ponte: A Biography of Mozart's Librettist.* London and New York: 1982.

Foss, Michael. *The Age of Patronage: The Arts in England, 1660–1750.* Ithaca. NY: 1971.

Friedenthal, Richard. *Goethe: His Life and Times.* Cleveland and New York: 1965.

Friedrich, Carl J. *The Age of the Baroque.* New York: 1962.

Gage, John. *Goethe on Art.* Berkeley, CA: 1980.

Gagliardo, John G. *Enlightened Despotism.* New York: 1967.

––––––. *From Pariah to Patriot: The Changing Image of the German Peasant, 1770–1840.* Lexington, KY: 1969.

Gallaway, Francis. *Reason, Rule, and Revolt in English Classicism.* Lexington, KY: 1966.

Gärtner, Heinz. *Johann Christian Bach, Mozarts Freund und Lehrmeister.* Munich: 1989.

––––––. *Mozarts Requiem und die Geschäfte der Constanze Mozart.* Munich: 1986.

Gaudefroy-Demombynes, J. *Les Jugements Allemands sur la Musique Française au XVIIIᵉ Siècle.* Paris: 1941.

Gay, Peter. *The Enlightenment, an Interpretation,* vol 1: *The Rise of Modern Paganism.* New York: 1967; vol. 2: *The Science of Freedom.* New York: 1969.

Geiringer, Karl. *Haydn: A Creative Life in Music.* Berkeley, CA: 1968.

Ghéon, Henri. *Promenades avec Mozart.* Paris: 1932.

Girdlestone, Cuthbert. *Mozart and his Piano Concertos.* New York: 1964.

Gluck, Christoph Willibald. *The Collected Correspondence and Papers of Christoph Willibald Gluck.* Trans. Stewart Thomson. Hedwig and E. H. Mueller von Asow, eds. New York: 1962.

Gnau, Hermann. *Die Zensur unter Joseph II.* Strassburg: 1911.

Goethe, Johann Wolfgang von. *Goethes Werke (Sophienausgabe).* 133 vols. in IV sections. Weimar: 1887–1918.

––––––. *Goethes Sämtliche Werke (Jubiläums-Ausgabe).* 40 vols. Eduard von der Hellen, et al., eds. Stuttgart and Berlin: 1902–1907.

––––––. *Gespräche mit Goethe in den letzten Jahren seines Lebens / Johann Peter Eckermann.* Fritz Bergemann, ed. Wiesbaden: 1955.

Goldoni, Carlo. *Mémoires de M. Goldoni pour servir à l'histoire de sa vie et à celle de son théâtre.* Paul de Roux, ed. Paris: 1965.

––––––. *Tutte le opere di Carlo Goldoni.* Giuseppe Ortolani, ed. 14 vols. Milan: 1952.

Gooch, G. P. *Louis XV, The Monarchy in Decline.* London: 1962.

Grimm, Friedrich Melchior von. *Correspondance littéraire, philosophique et critique par Grimm, Diderot, Raynal, Meister et al.* M. Tourneux, ed. 16 vols. Paris: 1877–1882.

Grossegger, Elisabeth. *Freimaurerei und Theater 1770–1800: Freimaurerdramen an den K. K. privilegierten Theatern in Wien.* Vienna and Graz: 1981.

Grout, Donald Jay. *A Short History of Opera.* New York and London: 1965.

Gruber, Gernot. *Mozart und die Nachwelt.* Salzburg and Vienna: 1985.

Gugitz, Gustav. "Mozarts Finanzen und Freund Puchberg: Ein Beitrag zur Mozart-Biographie," *Österreichische Musikzeitschrift* 7, 1952.

Gutwirth, Madelyn. *Madame de Staël, Novelist: The Emergence of the Artist as Woman.* Urbana, IL, Chicago, and London: 1978.

Haas, Robert. *Wolfgang Amadeus Mozart.* Potsdam: 1950.

Hadamowsky, Franz. *Die Wiener Hoftheater (Staatstheater) 1776–1966. Teil 1: 1776–1810.* Vienna: 1966.

Halliwell, Ruth. *The Mozart Family: Four Lives in a Social Context.* Oxford: 1998.

Hammer, Carl, Jr. *Goethe and Rousseau: Resonances of the Mind.* Lexington, KY: 1973.

Harries, Karsten, *The Bavarian Rococo Church: Between Faith and Aestheticism.* New Haven, CT and London: 1983.

Haslip, Joan, *Catherine the Great.* New York: 1977.

Hauser, Arnold. *The Social History of Art.* Trans. Arnold Hauser and Stanley Godman. 2 vols. New York: 1951.

Heartz, Daniel. *Haydn, Mozart and the Viennese School: 1740–1780.* New York and London: 1995.

———. *Mozart's Operas.* Ed., with contributing essays, Thomas Bauman. Berkeley, CA: 1990.

Helm, Ernest Eugene. *Music at the Court of Frederick the Great.* Norman, OK: 1960.

Heriot, Angus. *The Castrati in Opera.* London: 1956.

Hertzberg, Arthur. *The French Enlightenment and the Jews.* New York and London: 1968.

Hess, Ernst. "Zur Ergänzung des Requiems von Mozart durch F. X. Süssmayr." MJ, 1959.

Hildesheimer, Wolfgang. *Mozart.* Frankfurt am Main: 1977.

Hiller, Johann Adam, ed. *Wöchentliche Nachrichten und Anmerkungen die Musik Betreffend.* Leipzig: 1766–1770.

Hodges, Sheila. *Lorenzo Da Ponte: The Life and Times of Mozart's Librettist.* New York: 1985.

Holmes, Edward. *The Life of Mozart.* London and New York: 1944.

Honolka, Kurt. *Papageno: Emanuel Schikaneder, der grosse Theatermann der Mozart-Zeit.* Salzburg and Vienna: 1984.

Howard, Patricia. *C. W. von Gluck: Orfeo.* Cambridge: 1981.

Hubatsch, Walther. *Frederick the Great of Prussia: Absolutism and Administration.* Trans. Patrick Doran. London: 1975.

Hummel, Walter. *Nannerl: Wolfgang Amadeus Mozarts Schwester.* Zurich: 1952.

————. *W. A. Mozarts Söhne.* Kassel and Basel: 1956.

Hunter, Mary, and James Webster, eds. *Opera Buffa in Mozart's Vienna.* Cambridge: 1997.

Hutchings, Arthur. *A Companion to Mozart's Piano Concertos.* Oxford and New York: 1989.

Iacuzzi, Alfred. *The European Vogue of Favart: The Diffusion of the Opéra-Comique.* New York: 1932.

Irving, John. *Mozart: The 'Haydn' Quartets.* Cambridge: 1998.

Jacob, Heinrich Eduard. *Mozart: Geist-Musik-Schicksal.* Munich: 1977.

Jacob, Margaret C. *Living the Enlightenment: Freemasonry and Politics in Eighteenth-Century Europe.* New York and Oxford: 1991.

Jahn, Otto. See Abert, Hermann.

Jarrett, Derek. *England in the Age of Hogarth.* Frogmore, St. Albans, Herts: 1976.

Kelly, Michael. *Reminiscences of Michael Kelly, of the King's Theatre, and Theatre Royal, During Lane.* London: 1826. Reprint. Roger Fiske, ed. London: 1975.

Kennett, Lee. *The French Armies in the Seven Years' War.* Durham, NC: 1967.

Kerman, Joseph. *Opera as Drama.* Berkeley, CA: 1988.

Ketton-Cremer, R. W. *Horace Walpole.* Ithaca, NY: 1964.

Keys, Ivor. *Mozart: His Music in His Life.* New York: 1980.

King, Alec Hyatt. *Mozart Chamber Music.* London: 1968.

————. *Mozart in Retrospect: Studies in Criticism and Bibliography.* London: 1970.

————. *A Mozart Legacy: Aspects of the British Library Collections.* Seattle: 1984.

————. *Mozart Wind and String Concertos.* Seattle: 1978.

Kivy, Peter. *Osmin's Rage: Philosophical Reflections on Opera, Drama, and Text.* Princeton: 1988.

Knepler, Georg. *Wolfgang Amadé Mozart.* Trans. J. Bradford Robinson. Cambridge: 1994.

Komorzynski, Egon. *Emanuel Schikaneder: Ein Beitrag zur Geschichte des deutschen Theaters.* Vienna: 1951.

Kraemer, Uwe. "Wer hate Mozart verhungern laseen?" *Musica* 30, 1976.

Küster, Konrad. *Mozart.* Stuttgart: 1990.

Lanapoppi, Aleramo. *Un certain Da Ponte.* Trans. Denis Authier. Paris: 1991.

Landon, H. C. Robbins. *Essays on the Viennesse Classical Style: Gluck, Haydn, Mozart, Beethoven.* New York: 1970.

————. *Haydn: Chronicle and Works.* 5 vols. Bloomington, IN: 1976–1980.

————. *Haydn: A Documentary Study.* New York: 1981.

————. *Mozart and the Masons: New Light on the Lodge "Crowned Hope."* New York: 1991.

————. *Mozart and Vienna.* New York: 1991.

————. *The Mozart Essays.* New York: 1995.

————. *Mozart: The Golden Years: 1781–1791.* New York: 1989.

————. *Mozart's Last Year.* New York: 1988.

Landon, H. C. Robbins, ed. *The Mozart Compendium.* New York: 1990.

Landon, H. C. Robbins, and Donald Mitchell, eds. *The Mozart Companion: A Symposium by Leading Mozart Scholars.* New York: 1969.

Lang, Paul Henry. *George Frideric Handel.* New York: 1966.

————. *Music in Western Civilization.* New York: 1941.

Lang, Paul Henry, ed. *The Creative World of Mozart.* New York: 1963.

Langegger, Florian. *Mozart, Vater und Sohn: Eine psychologische Untersuchung.* Zurich and Freiburg i. Br.: 1978.

Laurencie, Lionel de la. *Les Créateurs de l'Opéra Français.* Paris: 1930.

Layer, Adolf. *Eine Jugend in Augsburg: Leopold Mozart 1719–1737.* Augsburg: n.d.

Leibniz Gottfried Wilhelm. *Philosophical Essays.* Trans. and ed. Roger Ariew and Daniel Garber. Indianapolis and Cambridge: 1989.

Lert, Ernst. *Mozart Auf Dem Theater.* Berlin: 1921.

Lessing, Gotthold Ephraim. *Laocoön: An Essay on the Limits of Painting and Poetry.* Trans. Edward Allen McCormick. Baltimore and London: 1984.

Levarie, Siegmund. *Mozart's Le Nozze di Figaro: A Critical Analysis.* Chicago: 1952.

Levey, Michael. *The Life and Death of Mozart.* New York: 1972.

Levin, Robert D. *Who Wrote the Mozart Four-Wind Concertante?* Stuyvesant, NY: 1988.

Lewes, George Henry. *The Life of Goethe.* New York: 1965.

Lichtenberg, Georg Christoph. *Lichtenberg's Commentaries on Hogarth's Engravings.* Trans. Innes and Gustav Herdan. London: 1966.

Liebner, János. *Mozart on the Stage.* New York: 1972.

Lindsay, Jack. *Hogarth: His Art and His World.* New York: 1979.

Lowinsky, Edward E. "Taste, Style, and Ideology in Eighteenth-Century Music." See Wasserman.

Ludendorff, Mathilde. *Mozarts Leben und Gewaltsamer Tod.* Munich: 1936.

MacIntyre, Bruce C. *The Viennese Concerted Mass of the Early Classic Period.* Ann Arbor, MI: 1986.

Madariaga, Isabel de. *Russia in the Age of Catherine the Great.* London: 1981.

Mančal, Josef. "Vom 'Orden der geflicten Hosen': Leopold Mozarts Heirat und Bürgerrecht." *Leopold Mozart und Augsburg.* Ottmar F. W. Beck, ed. Augsburg: 1987.

Mann, Alfred. "Leopold Mozart als Lehrer seines Sohnes." MJ 1989–1990.

Mann, William. *The Operas of Mozart.* New York: 1977.

Marshall, Robert L. *Mozart Speaks: Views on Music, Musicians, and the World.* New York: 1991.

Martin, Franz. *Kleine Landesgeschichte von Salzburg.* Salzburg: 1949.

————. *Salzburgs Fürsten in der Barockzeit: 1587 bis 1771.* Salzburg and Stuttgart: 1949.

Marty, Jean-Pierre. *The Tempo Indications of Mozart.* New Haven, CT and London: 1988.

Massin, Jean and Brigitte. *Wolfgang Amadeus Mozart.* Paris: 1970.

Maunder, Richard. *Mozart's Requiem: On Preparing a New Edition.* Oxford: 1988.

Maurois, André. *Disraeli: A Picture of the Victorian Age.* Trans. Hamish Miles. New York: 1942.

———. *A History of France.* Trans. Henry L. Binsse. New York: 1960.

McCarthy, John A. *Chistoph Martin Wieland.* Boston: 1979.

McGrew, Roderick E. *Paul I of Russia, 1754–1801.* Oxford: 1992.

McVeigh, Simon. *Concert Life in London from Mozart to Haydn.* Cambridge: 1993.

Meinecke, Friedrich. *The Age of German Liberation, 1795–1815.* Peter Paret, ed. Berkeley, CA: 1977.

Mercado, Mario R. *The Evolution of Mozart's Pianistic Style.* Carbondale and Edwardsville, IL: 1992.

Metastasio, Pietro. *Tutte le opere di Pietro Metastasio.* Bruno Brunelli, ed. 5 vols. Milan: 1943–1954.

Michtner, Otto. *Das alte Burgtheater als Opernbühne: Von der Einführung des deutschen Singspiels (1778) bis zum Tode Kaiser Leopolds II (1792).* Vienna: 1970.

Miller, Jonathan. "Mesmerism." *The Listener,* vol. 90, no. 2330, 22 Nov. 1973.

Miller, Jonathan, ed. *Don Giovanni: Myths of Seduction and Betrayal.* Baltimore: 1991.

Mitford, Nancy. *Frederick the Great.* New York: 1970.

———. *Madame de Pompadour.* London: 1955.

Moberly, R. B. *Three Mozart Operas: Figaro, Don Giovanni, The Magic Flute.* New York: 1968.

Montesquieu, Charles Louis de Secondat, *Lettres Persanes.* Paris: 1964.

Mozart, Leopold, *Versuch einer gründlichen Violinschule.* Augsburg: 1756. Facsimile of 1789 edition: Hans Joachim Moser, ed. Leipzig: 1956. English trans. (of first edition) Editha Knocker, as *A Treatise on the Fundamental Principles of Violin Playing.* London: 1951.

Mutton, Alice F. *Central Europe: A Regional and Human Geography.* New York: 1968.

Nagel, Ivan. *Autonomy and Mercy: Reflections on Mozart's Operas.* Trans. Marion Faber and Ivan Nagel. Cambridge, MA and London: 1991.

Nettl, Paul. *Mozart and Masonry.* New York: 1957.

———. *Mozart in Böhmen.* Prague: 1938.

Neumann, Frederick. *Ornamentation and Improvisation in Mozart.* Princeton: 1986.

Newman, William S. *The Sonata in the Baroque Era.* New York: 1972.

———. *The Sonata in the Classic Era.* New York: 1972.

Niemetschek, Franz Xaver. *Leben des K. K. Kapellmeisters Wolfgang Gottlieb Mozart, nach Originalquellen beschrieben.* Prague, 1798. Enlarged in 1808 and trans. Helen Mautner, as *Life of Mozart.* London: 1956.

Nissen, Georg Nikolaus von. *Biographie W. A. Mozarts nach Originalbriefen.* Leipzig: 1828. Facsimile edition: Hildesheim: 1972.

Nohl, Ludwig. *Mozarts Leben.* Paul Sakolowski, ed. Berlin: n.d.

Noske, Frits. *The Signifier and the Signified: Studies in the Operas of Mozart and Verdi.* Oxford: 1990.

Novello, Vincent and Mary. *A Mozart Pilgrimage; Being the Travel Diaries of Vincent and*

Mary Novello in the Year 1829. Nerina Marignano and Rosemary Hughes, eds. London: 1955.

Noverre, Jean-Georges. *Lettres sur La Danse et sur Les Ballets.* André Levinson, ed. Paris: n.d.

O'Flaherty, James C. *Johann Georg Hamann.* Boston: 1979.

Ogg, David. *Europe of the Ancien Régime, 1715–1783.* New York: 1965.

Oliver, Alfred Richard. *The Encyclopedists as Critics of Music.* New York: 1947.

Osborne, Charles. *The Complete Operas of Mozart: A Critical Guide.* New York: 1986.

Ostwald, Peter, and Leonard S. Zegans, eds. *The Pleasures and Perils of Genius: Mostly Mozart.* Madison, CT: 1993.

Ottaway, Hugh. *Mozart.* Detroit: 1980.

Pahlen, Kurt, ed. *Das Mozart-Buch: Chronik von Leben und Werk.* Stuttgart: 1969.

Paldi, Cesare and Ida. *Le Grandi Opere Liriche di Mozart.* Rome: 1985.

Paret, Peter, ed. *Frederick the Great: A Profile.* New York: 1972.

Patterson, Annabel, ed. *Roman Images: Selected Papers from the English Institute, 1982.* Baltimore and London: 1984.

Paumgartner, Bernhard. *Mozart.* Zurich and Freiburg i. BR.: 1967.

Pezzl, Johann. *Skizze von Wien: Ein Kultur–und Sittenbild aus der Josefinischen Zeit.* Gustav Gugitz and Anton Schlossar, eds. Graz: 1923.

Piozzi, Hester Lynch. *Observations and Reflections: Made in the Course of a Journey Through France, Italy, and Germany.* Herbert Barrows, ed. Ann Arbor: 1967.

Pirro, André. *J. S. Bach.* Trans. Mervyn Savill. New York: 1957.

Plantinga, Leon. *Clementi: His Life and Music.* London: 1977.

Plath, Wolfgang. "Leopold Mozarts Notenbuch für Wolfgang (1762)—eine Fälschung?" MJ 1971–1972.

———. "Zur Echtheitsfrage bei Mozart." MJ 1971–1972.

Pretzell, Lothar. *Fischer von Erlach in Salzburg.* Berlin: 1944.

Radant, Friedhelm. *From Baroque to Storm and Stress, 1720–1775.* New York: 1977.

Radcliffe, Philip. *Mozart Piano Concertos.* Seattle: 1978.

Ratner, Leonard G. *Classic Music: Expression, Form, and Style.* New York: 1980.

Raugel, Félix. "Note sur les rapports de Léopold et Wolfgang Mozart avec les Établissements religieux d'Augsbourg." *La Revue Musicale,* No. 198, 1946.

Reddaway, W. F. *Frederick The Great and The Rise of Prussia.* New York: 1969.

Reill, Peter Hanns. *The German Enlightenment and the Rise of Historicism.* Berkeley, CA: 1975.

Rice, John A. *W. A. Mozart: La clemenza di Tito.* Cambridge: 1991.

Richardson, Samuel. *Pamela; Or, Virtue Rewarded.* Peter Sabor, ed. New York: 1980.

Rieger, E. *Nannerl Mozart: Leben einer Künstlerin im 18. Jahrhundert.* Frankfurt am Main: 1991.

Ripin, Edwin M., ed. *Keyboard Instruments: Studies in Keyboard Organology.* Edinburgh: 1971.

Ritschel, Karl Heinz. *Salzburg: Anmut und Macht.* Vienna and Hamburg: 1970.

Ritter, Gerhard. *Frederick the Great: A Historical Profile.* Trans. Peter Paret. Berkeley, CA: 1970.

Robinson, Michael F. *Naples and Neapolitan Opera.* Oxford: 1972.

———. *Opera Before Mozart.* New York: 1967.

Roider, Karl A., Jr. *The Reluctant Ally: Austria's Policy in the Austro-Turkish War, 1737–1739.* Baton Rouge: 1972.

Rosbottom, Ronald C. *Choderlos de Laclos.* Boston: 1978.

Rosen, Charles. *The Classical Style: Haydn, Mozart, Beethoven.* New York: 1972.

———. *Sonata Forms.* New York and London: 1988.

Rosenberg, Alfons. *Don Giovanni: Mozarts Oper und Don Juans Gestalt.* Munich: 1968.

———. *Die Zauberflöte: Geschichte und Deutung von Mozarts Oper.* Munich: 1964.

Rosenberg, Pierre. *Fragonard.* New York: 1988.

Rousseau, Jean-Jacques. *The Confessions.* Trans J. M. Cohen. Harmondsworth: 1975.

———. *Oeuvres complètes.* Bernard Gagnebin and Marcel Raymond, eds. 3 vols. Paris: 1959–1964.

Rushton, Julian. *W. A. Mozart: Don Giovanni.* Cambridge: 1981.

———. *W. A. Mozart: Idomeneo.* Cambridge: 1993.

Sachs, Curt. *The Commonwealth of Art: Style in the Fine Arts, Music and the Dance.* New York: 1946.

———. *The History of Musical Instruments.* New York: 1940.

———. *World History of the Dance.* Trans. Bessie Schönberg. New York: 1937.

Sadie, Stanley. *Mozart.* London: 1982.

Sadie, Stanley, ed. *Wolfgang Amadè Mozart: Essays on his Life and his Music.* Oxford: 1996.

Sadie, Stanley, and Fiona Smart, eds. *The Letters of Mozart and his Family.* Trans. Emily Anderson. New York: 1985.

St Cyres, Viscount. *François de Fénelon.* Port Washington, NY and London: 1970.

Saint-Evremond, Charles de. *Oeuvres.* 7 vols. London: 1725.

Saint-Foix, Georges de. *Les Symphonies de Mozart.* Paris: 1932.

Saint-Simon. Louis, Duc de. *Memoirs of the Duc de Saint-Simon.* Trans. and ed. Katherine Prescott Wormely. 4 vols. London: 1899.

Sainte-Beuve, Charles-Augustin. *Portraits of the Eighteenth Century: Historic and Literary.* Trans. Katherine Prescott Wormeley. New York: 1964.

Schenk, Erich. *Wolfgang Amadeus Mozart: Eine Biographie.* Zurich, Leipzig, and Vienna: 1955.

Schiedermair, Ludwig. *Mozart: Sein Leben und Seine Werke.* Munich: 1922.

Schlichtegroll, Friedrich. *Mozarts Leben.* Graz: 1794. Facsimile. Joseph Heinz Eibl, ed. Kassel, Basel, Tours, and London: 1974.

Schmid, Manfred Hermann. *Mozart und die Salzburger Tradition.* Tutzing, 1976.

Schneider, Otto, and Anton Algatzy. *Mozart-Handbuch: Chronik-Werk-Bibliographie.* Vienna: 1962.

Schubart, Christian Friedrich Daniel. *Schubarts Werke in einem Band.* Ursula Wertheim and Hans Böhm, eds. Weimar: 1962.

Schuler, Heinz. *Mozart und die Freimaurerei: Daten, Fakten, Biographien.* Wilhelmshaven: 1992.

Schurig, Arthur. *Wolfgang Amadeus Mozart: Sein Leben und sein Werk.* 2 vols. Leipzig: 1913.

Schweitzer, Albert. *J. S. Bach.* Trans. Ernest Newman. 2 vols. New York: 1949.

Schwerin, Erna. *Constanze Mozart: Woman and Wife of a Genius.* New York: 1981.

———. *Leopold Mozart: Profile of a Personality.* New York: 1987.

———. Monographs on Anna Maria Mozart, Maria Anna Mozart, and Prince Lichnowsky in *Newsletter of the Friends of Mozart.* New York: 1984, 1985–1986, and 1991, respectively.

Selfridge-Field, Eleanor. *Venetian Instrumental Music from Gabrieli to Vivaldi.* New York: 1975.

Senn, Walter. "Zur Erbteilung nach Leopold Mozart," *Zeitschrift des historischen Vereins für Schwaben,* 1962.

Seznec, Jean. "Diderot and the Pictures in Edinburgh." *Scottish Art Review,* VIII, no. 4, 1962. Also see Wasserman.

Shakespeare, William. *The Norton Shakespeare.* Stephen Greenblatt, ed. New York and London: 1997.

Sharp, Samuel. *Letters from Italy, Describing the Customs and Manners of that Country, in the Years 1765, and 1766.* London: 1766.

Simons, George E. *Standard Masonic Monitor of the Degrees of Entered Apprentice, Fellow Craft and Master Mason.* New York: 1920.

Singer, Irving. *Mozart & Beethoven: The Concept of Love in Their Operas.* Baltimore and London: 1977.

Sisman, Elaine R. *Haydn and the Classical Variation.* Cambridge, MA: 1993.

———. *Mozart: The "Jupiter" Symphony.* Cambridge: 1993.

Smith, Patrick J. *The Tenth Muse: A Historical Study of the Opera Libretto.* London: 1971.

Smith, Winifred. *The Commedia Dell'arte.* New York and London: 1964.

Solomon, Maynard. *Mozart: A Life.* New York: 1995.

———. "The Rochlitz Anecdotes." See Eisen, *Mozart Studies.*

Sonnenfels, Joseph von. *Briefe über die Wienerische Schaubühne.* Hilde Haider-Pregler, ed. Graz: [1988].

Spiel, Hilde. *Fanny von Arnstein oder Die Emanzipation: Ein Fravenleben an der Zeitenwende 1758–1818.* Frankfurt: 1962.

Spitta, Philipp. *Johann Sebastian Bach: His Work and Influence on the Music of Germany, 1685–1750.* Trans. Clara Bell and J. A. Fuller Maitland. 3 vols. London and New York: 1899.

Stafford, William. *The Mozart Myths: A Critical Reassessment.* Stanford, CA: 1991.

Steblin, Rita. *A History of Key Characteristics in the Eighteenth and Early Nineteenth Centuries.* Ann Arbor: 1983.

Steegmuller, Francis. *A Woman, a Man, and Two Kingdoms: The Story of Madame d'Épinay and the Abbé Galiani.* New York: 1991.

Stendhal (Marie Henri Beyle). *Lives of Haydn, Mozart, & Metastasio.* Trans. and ed. Richard N. Coe. London: 1972.

Steptoe, Andrew. *The Mozart–Da Ponte Operas.* Oxford: 1988.

Stewart, K. J. *The Freemason's Manual: A Companion for the Initiated through all the Degrees of Freemasonry.* . . . Philadelphia: 1855.

Strachey, Lytton. *Biographical Essays.* New York: n.d.

Sturgill, Claude C. *Marshal Villars and the War of the Spanish Succession.* Lexington, KY: 1965.

Sutton, John L. *The King's Honor & the King's Cardinal: The War of the Polish Succession.* Lexington, KY: 1980.

Tagliacozzo, Georgio, and Hayden V. White, eds. *Giambattista Vico: An International Symposium.* Baltimore: 1969.

Tenschert, Roland. *Wolfgang Amadeus Mozart.* Salzburg: 1951.

Terry, Charles Sanford. *Johann Christian Bach.* London: 1967.

Thayer, Alexander Wheelock. *Salieri: Rival of Mozart.* Theodore Albrecht, ed. Kansas City, MO: 1989.

Till, Nicholas. *Mozart and the Enlightenment: Truth, Virtue and Beauty in Mozart's Operas.* London and Boston: 1992.

Todd, R. Larry, and Peter Williams, eds. *Perspectives on Mozart Performance.* Cambridge and New York: 1991.

Troyat, Henri. *Catherine the Great.* Trans. Joan Pinkham. New York: 1994.

Turner, W. J. *Mozart: The Man & His Works.* Christopher Raeburn, ed. London: 1965.

Tyson, Alan. *Mozart: Studies of the Autograph Scores.* Cambridge, MA and London: 1987.

Ulibischeff, Alexander. *Mozart's Leben und Werke.* 2 vols. Stuttgart: 1859–1864.

Ulrich, Homer. *Chamber Music.* New York and London: 1966.

Vaillat, Léandre. *Histoire de la danse.* Paris: 1942.

Valentin, Erich. *Zeitgenosse Mozart: Vier Vorträge.* Augsburg: n.d.

Van Doren, Carl. *Benjamin Franklin.* New York: 1938.

Vann, James Allen. *The Making of a State: Württemberg, 1593–1793.* Ithaca, NY and London: 1984.

Venturi, Franco. *Italy and the Enlightenment: Studies in a Cosmopolitan Century.* Trans. Susan Corsi. Stuart Woolf, ed. New York: 1972.

Voltaire. *The Complete Romances, including "Candide".* . . . New York: 1940.

Walker, Mack. *German Home Towns: Community, State, and General Estate, 1648–1871.* Ithaca, NY and London: 1971.

Wangermann, Ernst. *The Austrian Achievement, 1700–1800.* London: 1973.

———. *From Joseph II to the Jacobin Trials.* Oxford: 1969.

Wasserman, Earl R., ed. *Aspects of the Eighteenth Century.* Baltimore: 1965.

Wegele, Ludwig. *Der Augsburger Maler Anton Mozart.* Augsburg: 1969.

———. *Der Lebenslauf der Marianne Thekla Mozart.* Augsburg: 1967.

———. *Das Mozarthaus in Augsburg.* Augsburg: 1962.

Weinstein, Leo. *The Metamorphoses of Don Juan.* Stanford, CA: 1959.

Wheatcroft, Andrew. *The Habsburgs: Embodying Empire.* New York: 1995.

White, Jon Manchip. *Marshal of France: The Life and Times of Maurice, Comte De Saxe, 1696–1750.* Chicago, New York, and San Francisco: 1962.

White, Newman Ivey. *Portrait of Shelley.* New York: 1945.

Widmann, Hans. *Geschichte Salzburgs.* 3 vols. Gotha: 1907–1914.

Wignall, Harrison James. *In Mozart's Footsteps.* New York: 1991.

Wilson, Arthur M. *Diderot.* New York: 1972.

Winckelmann, Johann Joachim. *Winckelmann: Writings on Art.* David Irwin, ed. London and New York: 1972.

Winters, Stanley B., and Joseph Held, eds. *Intellectual and Social Developments in the Habsburg Empire from Maria Theresa to World War I.* New York and London: 1975.

Wolff, Christoph. *Mozart's Requiem: Historical and Analytical Studies, Documents, Score.* Trans. Mary Whittall. Berkeley, CA: 1994.

Wyzewa, Théodore de, and Georges de Saint-Foix. *W.-A. Mozart: sa vie musicale et son oeuvre. . . .* 5 vols. Paris: 1936–1946.

Yates, Frances A. *The Rosicrucian Enlightenment.* London and Boston: 1972.

Yorke-Long, Alan. *Music at Court: Four Eighteenth Century Studies.* London: 1954.

Young, G. F. *The Medici.* New York: 1930.

Zaslaw, Neal. *Mozart's Symphonies: Context, Performance Practice, Reception.* Oxford: 1989.

Zaslaw, Neal, ed. *Man and His Music: The Classical Era: From the 1740s to the End of the 18th Century.* Englewood Cliffs, NJ: 1989.

———. *Mozart's Piano Concertos: Text, Context, Interpretation.* Ann Arbor: 1996.

Zaslaw, Neal, and Fiona Morgan Fein. *The Mozart Repertory: A Guide for Musicians, Programmers and Researchers.* Ithaca, NY and London: 1991.

Zaslaw Neal, ed., with William Cowdery. *The Compleat Mozart: A Guide to the Musical Works of Wolfgang Amadeus Mozart.* New York and London: 1990.

SOURCE NOTES

Chapter IX

163 "all in gold   BA I, 126
163 "*la bonne reine*   Gooch, 114
164 "The comparison   Rousseau, *The Confessions*, 357
164 "perpetual   BA I, 126
164 "Have I not   Gooch, 124
164 "Nothing interested   Gooch, 124
165 "Sieur   D, 30
165 "A kapellmeister   D, 27
166 "if he would   D, 28
166 "They are said   Wilson, 557
167 "*maître*   Steegmuller, 69
167 "the most German   Crocker, 114
167 "What is this   Crocker, 131
168 "*Hic*   Wilson, 179
168 "the French   Oliver, 96
168 "It is a pity   D, 28
169 "composite   Grimm, XI, 465
169 "a mixed   Sachs, *Commonwealth*, 174
170 "to paint   Oliver, 64
170 "Music   Oliver, 62
170 "divine   Diderot, *Correspondance*, VIII, 93
170 "fad   Oliver, 65
171 "play   D, 428
171 "were taking   BA I, 126
171 "honest   BA I, 126
171 ". . . not at all   BA I, 127
171 "My little girl   BA I, 126
172 "light   Newman, *Classical*, 630
172 "spirit   Burney, *A History*, II, 956
172 "within ten   BA I, 126
172 "completely   BA I, 126
172 "took   BA V, 99
173 "Prince   BA I, 117
173 "a monthly   BA II, 334
174 "I only   BA I, 134
174 "disgust   BA I, 134
174 "poisonous   Steegmuller, 66–67
174 "One must   BA I, 130
175 "general   BA I, 130
175 "whether He   BA I, 131
175 "our servant   D, 426
175 "Amateurs   BA I, 137
175 "Dearest   BA III, 590
175 "four rascals   BA I, 452
176 "I cannot   Terry, 94
176 "You will not   BA I, 125

176 "from the ugly   BA I, 125
176 "I will tell   Piozzi, 11
177 "very few   BA I, 135
177 "large number   BA I, 135–36
177 "On both   BA I, 136
177 "astounding   BA I, 125
177 "Whether Parisian   BA I, 121
177 "idiotic mode   BA I, 125
178 "bound   BA I, 125
178 "for the French   BA I, 124–25
178 "as dark   BA I, 138
178 "The sun   Mitford, *Pompadour*, 254
178 "one of us   Brandes, *Voltaire*, II, 80
178 "possessed   BA I, 140
179 "Wolfgang plays   BA I, 142
179 "well-arranged   D, 520

Chapter XII

180 "Whoever   BA I, 145
180 "how the ocean   BA I, 145
181 "Perhaps even   BA I, 147
181 "It will do   BA I, 158
181 "balance   BA I, 178
181 "*Aut*   BA I, 169
182 "Born   EB X, George III, 186
183 "not doubting   D, 35
183 "played quite   Terry, 74
185 "London   D, 34
185 "I didn't   BA I, 157
186 "If such   BA I, 151
186 "What he knew   BA I, 151–52
186 "You yourself   BA I, 154
186 "from the clavier   BA I, 152
186 "nobody who   BA I, 155
186 "shock   BA I, 153
187 "nothing but   BA I, 146
187 "No woman   BA I, 148
187 "Bugger   BA I, 148
187 "Once out   BA I, 169
187 "an act   BA I, 159
187 "Brave   Brandes, *Voltaire*, I, 164
188 "impossible   BA I, 159
188 "Imagine   BA I, 159
188 "Here each   BA I, 159–60
188 "Here everyone   BA I, 158
188 "This is   BA I, 160
188 "a mixture   Terry, 96

189 "rather middle   BA I, 173
189 "to distinguish   BA I, 166
189 "They have another   BA I, 173
189 "One prefers   BA I, 157
189 "most beautiful   BA I, 171
189 "When one stands   BA I, 171
190 "How good   BA I, 188
190 "in the main   BA I, 167
191 "I am a   BA III, 239
191 "an hour   BA I, 161
191 "I must tell   BA I, 162
191 "To cut   BA I, 163
191 "How could you   Montesquieu, 252
191 "most beautiful   BA I, 150
192 "*des*   BA I, 164
192 "missionary   BA I, 165
192 "One must   BA I, 165
192 "a place   Besterman, 119
192 ". . . nothing   BA I, 181
192 "do not wear   Hertzberg, 291
193 "Wasn't it   BA I, 181
193 "a good   BA I, 181
193 "Good morrow   BA I, 169
193 "galloping   BA I, 169
193 ". . . my children   BA I, 190
193 "led to   BA I, 190
193 "If the   BA I, 169
194 "Although they   D, 38
194 "a common   G (1944), I, 727
194 "masculine   Terry, 91
195 "tea   Terry, 95
195 "took him   D, 55
195 "frequent   D, 448
195 "played   Eisen, *New,* 5
196 "vent   BA I, 179
196 "As soon   BA I, 156
196 "several sleepless   BA I, 180
197 "Not as   BA I, 180
197 "curiosities   BA I, 184
197 "the little   D, 44
197 ". . . the decrease   D, 47
197 "his extraordinary   D, 47
198 "the Benefit   D, 43
198 "by taking   D, 43
198 "find the family   D, 44–45
198 "the Great   D, 45
199 "a German   Eisen, *New,* 6
199 "irrefragable   D, 88
199 "that the scale   D, 100

200 "our father   D, 426
200 "Oh   BA I, 180
200 "Doctor   BA I, 194
201 "and worked   D, 90
201 "5 or 6   BA I, 179
201 "About all   BA I, 179
201 "continual   BA I, 152
201 "No one   BA I, 178–79
201 "his manner   Terry, 82
201 "Having heard   D, 55
202 "Time   BA I, 186
202 "one servant   BA I, 224

Chapter XIII

203 "from the Hague   BA I, 200
203 "We are not   BA I, 147
203 "a bit   BA I, 147
204 "What horses   BA I, 149
204 "the celebrated   Eisen, *New,* 8
204 "I had to come   BA I, 205
205 "the present   BA I, 220
205 "I should have   BA I, 203
205 "excessive   BA I, 203
206 "several   Eisen, *New,* 9
206 "principal   Eisen, *New,* 9
206 "a priest   BA I, 206
206 "Had anyone   BA I, 206
207 "good calves   BA I, 207
207 "be long   Eisen, *New,* 10
207 "completely   BA I, 211
207 "across   BA I, 211
207 "risen   BA I, 214
207 "Your generosity   Eisen, *New,* 11
207 "At all   BA I, 213
208 "To propagate   BA I, 218
208 "overtures   D, 50
208 "Wolfgang's   BA I, 218
209 "*Poesie*   BA I, 213
209 "Where   BA I, 213
209 "our little   BA I, 219
210 "Of great   BA I, 267
210 "Herr   BA I, 204
211 "Kingdom   Wilson, 222
211 "held in   Wilson, 223
212 "The nearer   BA I, 236
212 "There will be   BA I, 223
212 ". . . many a   D, 55
213 "how my   BA I, 221
213 "against   D, 55

252 "*elegantissima* D, 85
253 "about fifty D, 86
253 "the remuneration D, 86
254 *Maestro* D, 117
254 "obliged David, 67
254 "no longer BA II, 473
254 "Formerly BA II, 485
254 "would preside BA II, 465
255 "a little science Landon, *Golden,*
181
256 "as warm BA I, 293
256 "the sight Piozzi, 357
256 "a fine BA I, 292
256 "astonishingly BA I, 292
257 "Several strong BA I, 298–99
257 "Greek Piozzi, 353
258 "Such a mob BA I, 300
258 "But you know BA I, 304
258 "present *maestro* D, 95
259 "a most beautiful D, 95–96
259 "What fun BA I, 302
261 "Nothing but BA I, 304
261 "unspeakable D, 100
261 "Prima BA I, 310
262 "as if he BA I, 303
263 "the finest BA V, 222
266 "from some misfortune Burney,
Fanny, 54
268 "eating BA I, 331
268 "I wish BA I, 331
268 "a miracle D, 98
269 "not as boys BA I, 338
269 "Oh BA I, 336
272 "the so-called BA I, 343
272 "prodigious D, 107
272 "bourgeoise D, 110
272 "*a stupore* BA V, 253
272 "where he BA V, 253; Eisen,
New, 19
272 "You cannot BA I, 335
273 "Though it Gay II, 230–31
274 "the principal Acton, 33
276 "As beautiful BA I, 350
276 "Merditeranischen BA I, 361
276 "Ay *The Merchant of Venice* I, 2
276 "... at least Acton, 138
276 "In your heart Acton, 132
278 "save death Acton, 160
278 "the little D, 113
278 "*Il* Steegmuller, 124

279 "coarse BA I, 358
279 "certain people BA I, 352
279 "What kind BA I, 366
280 "You realize BA I, 366
280 "excelled D, 112
280 "deign D, 118
280 "Chevalier BA I, 369
280 "Bruder BA I, 361
281 "Shit BA I, 369
281 "Little bells BA I, 371
281 "You can BA I, 374
282 "celebrated D, 113
283 "measure BA I, 405
283 "Beautiful BA I, 395
284 "His endeavor D, 114
284 "I cannot BA I, 397
284 "concerned BA I, 402
284 "shit BA I, 400
284 "inevitable BA I, 401
285 "completely BA I, 406
285 "nibble BA I, 401
285 "too partisan BA I, 410
285 "A good BA I, 409
285 "*Viva* BA I, 411
286 "If about BA I, 414
286 "fail BA I, 408
287 "barbarous BA I, 412
287 "Il Sigr: BA I, 412
287 "Trogermariandl BA I, 414
288 "a true BA I, 420
288 "As for Rousseau, *Confessions,*
296
288 "What can BA I, 426
288 "I do not D, 119
289 "a beautiful BA I, 425
289 "big concert BA I, 421–22
289 "magnificent D, 121
290 "incomparable BA I, 425

Chapter XVI

293 "genius G, VIII, 287
293 "great master D, 166
294 "if well D, 166
294 "Subject to BA III, 44–45
295 "like two BA I, 429
295 "three hundred Eisen, *New,* 20
295 "Above us BA I, 432
295 "Since Papa BA I, 448–49
297 "*Bravissimo* BA I, 445

298 "all those mishaps   G, VIII, 285
298 "I regret   BA I, 444
298 "Perhaps   BA I, 442
298 "*le jeune*   D, 124
298 "If it   D, 124
299 "I am   Massin, 115
299 "The matter   BA I, 452
301 "very serious   D, 447
301 "extremely yellow   D, 447
301 "will write   BA I, 456
302 "...she is now   D, 132
303 "pigsty   BA I, 458
303 "*Di farle*   BA I, 459
303 "You know   BA I, 462
303 "favorite   BA II, 38
304 "I still have   BA I, 465
304 "Though the prima   BA I, 472
305 "the proud   *Mithridate*, I, 4
307 "the terrifying   BA II, 227
308 "So far   BA I, 479
308 "being overwhelmed   BA I, 482
309 "As to   BA I, 483
309 "I find   BA I, 483
311 "fools   BA I, 496
311 "Her Majesty   BA I, 485
312 "the impudence   BA I, 486
312 "Now it is   BA I, 494
313 "By the sixteenth   BA I, 494
313 "that the Jesuits   BA I, 494
313 "To extort   Crankshaw, 284
313 "a set   Reddaway, 325
313 "fishing   Crankshaw, 284
313 "She is always   Reddaway, 328
313 "known to all   BA I, 502
314 "The reason   BA I, 497
314 "of his patron   BA I, 497
314 "Things will   BA I, 491
315 "nothing to do   BA I, 497
316 "Wolfgang is   BA I, 503
317 "Kings exist   EB IX, "Fénelon," 159

Chapter XVII

320 "Were the ghosts'   BA III, 35
320 "a bardic   BA III, 246
320 "fine ears   BA III, 246
321 "Tomorrow   *Don Giovanni*, no. 11
321 "the lion   Brandes, *Goethe*, I, 185

322 "The young   Brandes, *Goethe*, I, 186
322 "shadow   Brandes, *Goethe*, I, 178
322 "the most sedentary   Einaudi, 205
322 "*der Magus*   GB VIII, 83
323 "unhappy peoples   Rousseau, *Oeuvres*, III, 609–10
324 "...I can write   BA II, 164
325 "He dances   Brandes, *Goethe*, I, 78
325 "...you [Wolfgang]   BA II, 274
325 "original   Newman, *Classic*, 383
325 "...since Goethe's   Newman, *Classic*, 42
325 "humanitarian   Landon, *Documentary*, 86
326 "strange mixture   Hiller, 1768, 107
326 "next to   Landon, *Documentary*, 176
326 "Long live   Brandes, *Goethe*, I, 145
326 "Have you alone   Brandes, *Goethe*, I, 154, 192
326 "What do you know   Brandes, *Goethe*, I, 259
326 "Feeling   Brandes, *Goethe*, I, 201
327 "Not a   Winckelmann, 49
329 "discrimination   BA II, 485
329 "I have released   BA II, 485
330 "If necessary   BA II, 164
332 "first compositions   BA IV, 311
335 "suitable   BA I, 504
335 "especially   BA I, 507
335 "*geschopfte*   BA II, 351, 396
336 "I beseech   BA I, 511
339 "an orchestral   Heartz, *Operas*, 155
339 "a kind of   Da Ponte, *Memoirs*, 59
339 "noise   Da Ponte, *Memoirs*, 59
341 "Flames   D, 138
341 "A motley   D, 298–99
341 "majestic   D, 293
342 "every hope   BA I, 516
342 "general applause   D,135
343 "He became   BA I, 517
343 "another one   BA I, 522
344 "read anything   D, 138

377 "When one   BA II, 68
377 "balanced   BA II, 68
377 "incomparable   BA II, 69
377 "I wanted   BA II, 152
377 "I really   BA II, 66
377 "I actually   BA II, 66
377 "By no means   BA II, 66
377 "The orchestra   BA II, 65
377 "went like oil   BA II, 82
378 "Chevalier   D, 150
378 "a splendid   BA II, 84
378 "Nanette   BA VI, 606
378 "All the   BA II, 59
379 "The truly   BA IV, 269
379 "Whom love   Eissler, II, 1269
379 "Ah   BA II, 105
379 "*Je vous*   BA II, 122–23
379 "Why should   BA II, 105
379 "spuni   BA II, 104
380 "sad farewell   BA II, 99
380 "company   BA II, 94
380 "Accursed   BA II, 128
380 "capital   BA II, 139
380 "A small   BA II, 103
380 "Apropos   BA II, 164
381 "the young   BA II, 65
381 "A miserable   BA II, 93
381 "with much courtesy   BA II, 118
382 "He [von   BA II, 110
382 "To Paris?   BA II, 131–32
382 "... since   BA II, 289
382 "rays   BA II, 117

Chapter XX

383 "set all   BA I, 79
383 "They seem   BA II, 94
383 "Your pride   BA II, 296
384 "I believe it   BA II, 109–10
384 "... *on ne peut*   BA II, 109–10
384 "a miserable   BA II, 102
384 "hear nothing   BA II, 406
384 "right next to   BA II, 109
385 "through surpassing   BA II, 107
385 "a clever   BA II, 107
385 "conquer   BA II, 227
385 "I believe   BA II, 228
386 "I have heard   BA II, 110
386 "Yes, your Highness   BA II, 110

386 "I ask   BA II, 110
386 "Thank and praise   BA II, 110
386 "very beautiful   BA II, 125
386 "That might   BA II, 110
386 "*Ich bin*   BA II, 170
387 "The most   BA II, 143
387 "I am at   BA II, 171
387 "I am in   BA II, 119
387 "I never   BA II, 195
388 "for fun   BA II, 120
388 "I, Johannes   BA II, 123–24
388 "You must not   BA II, 75
388 "You must have   BA II, 144
389 "Good God!   BA II, 167
389 "mishmash   BA II, 144
389 "Of course   BA II, 142
389 "in the end   BA II, 144
389 "What?   BA II, 173
389 "Carelessness   BA II, 153
389 "undeserved   BA II, 152
389 "nothing can   BA II, 174
390 "I often   BA II, 163
390 "in greatest   BA II, 255
390 "In a word   BA II, 255
390 "three modest   BA II, 178
391 "Here one hears   BA II, 237
392 "just too   BA II, 280
392 "would be fought   BA II, 231
392 "The Duke   BA II, 336
393 "God   BA II, 214
393 "My journey   BA II, 226
393 "sad   BA II, 252
393 "a libertine   BA II, 252
393 "never liked   BA II, 255, 263
393 "Bavaria   BA II, 266
394 "bosom friend   BA II, 178
394 "a certain   BA II, 226–27
394 "oracularly   BA II, 138
394 "a girl   BA II, 327
395 "When Wolfgang   BA II, 255
395 "incomparable   BA II, 255
395 "... everyone   BA II, 512
395 "five   BA II, 227
395 "I think   BA II, 254
396 "As you   BA II, 256
396 "the *bitter*   BA II, 257
396 "I do not wish   BA II, 258
396 "Afflict   BA II, 279
396 "Amazement   BA II, 272
396 "intoxication   BA II, 286

439 "Concerning Mlle.   BA II, 465
439 "I will certainly   BA II, 465
439 "to give her   BA II, 407
440 "solace   BA II, 406
440 "Most of them   BA II, 406
440 "most young men   BA II, 410
440 "In my view   BA II, 411
440 "a position   BA II, 452
440 "building   BA II, 452
440 "It is inexplicably   BA II, 404
441 "Were it not for   BA II, 474
441 "M. Grimm   BA II, 474
441 "commission   BA II, 478
441 "very elaborate   D, 166
442 "absolutely not   BA II, 464
442 "a dangerous   BA II, 479
442 "empty hopes   BA II, 464
442 "credit   BA II, 479
443 "to remain   BA II, 479
443 "I might have   BA II, 479
443 "Like the Archbishop   BA II, 485
444 "possessed   BA II, 474
444 "Bach   BA II, 458
444 "so long   Terry, 134
444 "Just because   BA II, 442
444 "requested   Terry, 134
445 "warmth   Terry, 134
445 "a labor   BA II, 397
445 "half   BA II, 397
445 "as well as   BA II, 473
445 "new ballet   BA II, 358
446 "too many modulations   BA II, 398
446 "from the fact   BA II, 398
447 "Each is   BA II, 398
449 "truly to commit   BA II, 495
449 "honor   BA II, 495
449 "Of course   BA II, 495
450 "I might   BA II, 477
450 "I would not   BA II, 487–88
450 "You should do   BA II, 489
450 "a noted   BA II, 489
451 "Were I with   BA II, 488
451 "At the moment   BA II, 489
451 "One must know   BA II, 489
451 "depart within   BA II, 476
451 "Since I   BA II, 476–77
451 "pretty cabriolet   BA II, 484
452 "We Germans   BA II, 476

452 "six trios   BA II, 476
452 "It goes   BA II, 490
452 "the French   BA II, 491
452 "stylish   BA II, 504
453 "handsome   BA II, 491
453 "One thunderclap   BA II, 495
453 "the step   BA II, 460
453 "should we   BA II, 481
454 "many thousands   BA II, 482

Chapter XXIV

455 "*bravo*   BA II, 501
455 "which is   BA II, 501
456 "Nothing is   BA II, 502
456 "In foreign   BA II, 503
456 "that throughout   BA II, 503
456 "dear Mannheim   BA II, 505
457 "best and   BA II, 521
457 "One would scarcely   Lewes, 432
457 "What a language   BA II, 506
457 "You cannot believe   BA II, 536
458 "with the greatest   BA II, 505–06
459 "excluded all   BA V, 433
459 "miserable   BA II, 125
459 "The Seyler   BA II, 505
460 "... as with all   BA II, 417
460 "Just imagine   BA III, 153
462 "very beautiful   BA II, 137–38
463 "the declaimed   BA II, 516
463 "final conditions   BA II, 515
463 "I have called   BA II, 515
463 "I really don't   BA II, 508–09
464 "in fourteen   BA II, 510
464 "Were I to   BA II, 510
465 "so extravagantly   BA II, 507
465 "Truly   BA II, 516
465 "not wicked   BA II, 515
465 "thinking things   BA II, 512
466 "I was not   BA II, 512
466 "a great admirer   BA II, 51
466 "We believed   BA II, 521
466 "fierce   BA II, 522
466 "to what   BA II, 522
466 "*eine der*   BA II, 520
467 "Let the devil   BA II, 528
467 "If you remain   BA II, 469
468 "Perhaps you   BA II, 524

534 "I had to   BA III, 101
535 "five ducats   BA III, 101
535 "grand   BA III, 105
535 "had been invited   BA III, 105
535 "Vienna's greatest   BA III, 98
535 "stealing   BA III, 109
535 "the size   BA II, 159
536 "endure   BA III, 184
536 "I'll go   BA III, 101
536 "main objective   BA III, 99
536 "in some becoming   BA III, 99
536 "I am *absolument*   BA III, 99
536 "short oratorio   BA III, 99
536 "all the [Viennese]   BA III, 99
537 "I did not know   BA III, 113
537 "The Emperor   BA III, 111
538 "As yet   BA III, 102
538 "A glorious   BA III, 102
538 "Be assured   BA III, 103
538 "Think no more   BA III, 103
538 "When Bonno   BA III, 106
538 "How sad   BA III, 104
538 "You must   BA III, 120
538 "friendly   BA III, 104
538 "*Mon très*   BA III, 93
539 "Oh, if he   BA III, 108
539 "If you   BA III, 112
539 "At this   BA III, 107
539 "I cannot   BA III, 109
540 "to move   BA III, 110
540 "Surely   BA III, 110
540 "Well   BA III, 111
541 "He did not   BA III, 111
541 "Unable   BA III, 111
541 "blood began   BA III, 111
541 "I banish   *The Tragedy of Coriolanus*, III, 3
541 "our Archboor   BA III, 101
541 "I hate   BA III, 112
542 "Be in no way   BA III, 111
542 "no longer   BA III, 110
542 "snakes   BA III, 115
542 "The Count   BA III, 113
542 "You must   BA III, 113
542 "To please   BA III, 119
542 "obligation   BA III, 121–22
543 "By the next   BA III, 111–12
543 "If he   BA III, 113
543 "A pretty   BA III, 113
543 "... in the middle   BA III, 113

543 "this fine   BA III, 113
543 "I am nothing   BA III, 113
544 "Were I offered   BA III, 113–14
544 "I could only   BA III, 116
544 "... I have yet   BA III, 117–18
544 "You cannot possibly   BA III, 118
544 "I beg you   BA III, 116
544 "I know and   BA III, 120
544 "Have undoubted   BA III, 121
544 "Never in all   D, 451
544 "A sin   BA III, 129
545 "Meanwhile   BA III, 102
545 "What about   BA III, 100
545 "And where   BA III, 121
545 "I cannot send   BA III, 125
545 "I shall remit   BA III, 130
545 "Be assured   BA III, 131
545 "You must never   BA III, 131
545 "... should I   BA III, 130
545 "took hold   BA III, 137
546 "Am I   BA III, 118–19
546 "What deters   BA III, 136
547 "The Archbishop   BA III, 123
547 "with all possible   BA III, 122–23
547 "What purpose   BA III, 123
547 "Believe me   BA III, 124
547 "specialty   BA III, 124
547 "this is the   BA III, 125
547 "You are right   BA III, 124
547 "But do you   BA III, 124
547 "That this affair   BA III, 124
547 "Well, the Archbishop   BA III, 124
547 "I know it   BA III, 124
548 "he, too   BA III, 124
548 "You have   BA III, 124
548 "I could not   BA III, 126
548 "snapped   BA III, 126
549 "clown" and "knave"   BA III, 127
549 "by order   BA III, 127
549 "to avoid   BA III, 126
549 "The affair   BA III, 126
549 "To hoof   BA III, 127
549 "I am so   BA III, 127
550 "Let him   BA III, 127
550 "The Emperor   BA III, 127
550 "Were you   BA III, 127

550 "He hurls   BA III, 129
550 "the Tyrolese   BA III, 145
550 "I had nothing   BA III, 155
550 "The clothes   BA III, 155
551 "for in Innsbruck   BA III, 146
551 "the lashes   BA III, 146
551 "Were I   BA III, 146–47
552 "I can assure   BA III, 116
552 "That you set   BA III, 127
553 "[You write   BA III, 118
553 "For the moment   BA III, 118
554 "born   BA III, 182
554 "in two   BA III, 181
556 "believe and trust   BA III, 142
556 "take another   BA III, 140
556 "God   BA III, 140
556 "no other   BA III, 141
556 "though, in truth   BA III, 141
556 "malicious tongues   BA III, 140
556 "comfort   BA III, 141
557 "young [Joseph   BA III, 139
558 ". . . as a rule   BA III, 144
558 "Whenever   BA III, 144
558 "without being   BA III, 144
558 "did not go   BA III, 144
558 "as early as   BA III, 144
558 "waste   BA III, 144
558 "hold back   BA III, 151
558 "this *meuble*   BA III, 151
558 "the most   BA III, 150–51
558 "the finest   BA III, 150
558 "a holy fright   BA II, 135
559 "As to   BA III, 151
559 "*ich unglücklicher*   BA III, 16
559 "The young   BA III, 135
560 "everyone who   BA III, 151
560 "She is not   BA III, 151–52
560 "The good   BA III, 150
560 "for rats   BA III, 150
561 "Ah   BA III, 150
561 "bargaining   BA III, 150

Chapter XXVIII

562 "a Mlle. Weber   Braunbehrens, 69
563 "But let   Landon, *Vienna*, 71–72
564 "I despise   Casanova, I, 529
565 "a sensible   Landon, *Vienna*, 77
566 "a peculiar   BA III, 99

566 "On such   Niemetschek, 88
566 "that grace   Jahn/Townsend II, 353
566 "She would   BA III, 174
567 "in the most   BA III, 43
567 "The little house   BA III, 139
567 ". . . when everything   BA III, 128
568 "splendid   BA III, 139
568 "English poems   Braunbehrens, 156
568 "the Viennese dandy   Landon, *Vienna*, 77
568 "young or   Landon, *Vienna*, 159
568 "my thoughts   Brown, P. Hume, I, 138
569 "My father   Braunbehrens, 160
569 "Every morning   BA III, 187
569 "a handsome   BA III, 232
569 "mother-of-pearl   BA III, 233
569 "crimson pelisse   D, 457
570 "You have to be   Casanova, I, 527
570 "opened up   Goethe, *Sophienausgabe*, I, 35:11
571 "city in Spain   NMA II, 5; 17, [2]
571 "Go look for   *Don Giovanni*, no. 11
572 "betrayal   *Don Giovanni*, II, 2
573 "*in un ritiro   Don Giovanni*, final scene
576 "Both parts   O, I, 414
576 "No one ever   Casanova, I, 529
577 "You ought not   BA III, 166
577 "as if he had   BA III, 166
578 "from youth on   BA II, 521
578 "If I could   BA III, 194–95
578 "one cannot deal   BA III, 238
580 "the Messalina   Haslip, 284
580 "*die schwere*   Haslip, 285
580 "bought Clementi   G, IV, 485
581 "*talent décidé*   BA III, 188
581 "clavier player   BA III, 188
581 "had hardly   D, 464
581 "After we   BA III, 193
581 "The composer   Einstein, *Mozart*, 137
581 "Such was   BA III, 193
581 "Of no   BA III, 193

582 "he had so   Casanova, I, 529
582 "great execution   D, 454
582 "Clementi   BA III, 191
582 "He worked   BA III, 272
582 "valueless   BA III, 272
582 "delight   G, IV, 485
583 "endlessly   D, 184
583 "He delighted   Casanova, I, 529
584 "had to have been   BA III, 302
584 "I had written   BA III, 171–72
586 "had the front   BA III, 172
586 "poor devils   BA III, 171
587 "Unique   D, 190
588 "to look   BA III, 177
588 "charming   BA III, 175
588 "an eighteen   BA III, 175
588 "Prince   BA VI, 173
589 "As yet   BA III, 173
589 "No lover   BA III, 178
589 "All the while   BA III, 178
590 "It hangs   BA III, 178–79
590 "To spare himself   BA III, 177–78
590 "created   Gluck, 193
590 "*Grosthier*   BA III, 177
591 "paid me   Gluck, 193
591 "I shall be   BA III, 132
592 "Well, the day   BA III, 143
592 "The time   BA III, 143
592 "at the moment   BA III, 144
592 "with greater   BA III, 153
592 "fresh turn   BA III, 163–64
592 "He may write   BA III, 132
592 "One cannot   G, I, 403
593 "with great effort   BA III, 153
593 "permitted himself   BA III, 153
593 "squandered   Einstein, *Gluck*, 182
593 "bardic   Einstein, *Gluck*, 124
593 "All in all   BA III, 157
594 "supernumeraries   BA III, 157
594 "sorry remnants   BA III, 157
594 "they haven't moved   BA III, 157
594 "In an opera   BA III, 167
594 "had earned   BA III, 158
594 "no less   BA III, 158
594 "all [of   BA III, 165
594 "flexible   BA III, 163
594 "beautiful deep   BA III, 162

598 "precious winners   *The Winter's Tale*, V, 3
598 "most ridiculous   *The Tempest*, II, 2

Chapter XXIX

600 "as if I   BA III, 154
600 "trust   BA III, 154
600 "A slut   BA III, 188
600 "worst enemy   BA III, 187
600 "shabby prank   BA III, 386
600 "Gilowsky   BA III, 252
601 "slanderous tongue   BA III, 139
601 "at court   BA III, 187–88
601 "How can   BA III, 184
601 "a comfortable   BA III, 154
601 "The foolishness   BA III, 154
601 "People may   BA III, 154–55
601 "From all   BA III, 155
602 "going straight   BA III, 155
602 "fit   BA III, 160
602 "In all   BA III, 158
602 "I feel   BA III, 158–59
602 "But my father   BA III, 159
602 "take axle   BA III, 166
603 "Against the will   D, 405
604 "the stronger   BA IV, 259
604 "... I credit   BA III, 145
604 "I am well   BA III, 167
604 "I shall send   BA III, 135
604 "With your   BA III, 196
604 "Voltaire reads   BA II, 354
605 "Beyond question   BA III, 173
605 "as to sleeping   BA III, 174
605 "to fulfill   BA III, 179
605 "You require   BA III, 180
605 "Nature speaks   BA III, 180
605 "fear of   BA III, 180
605 "I would not   BA III, 180
605 "from youth   BA III, 180–81
606 "Now, who is   BA III, 181
606 "Without my   BA III, 190
606 "as yet   BA III, 181
606 "the martyr   BA III, 181
606 "lazy   BA III, 181
606 "perfidious   BA III, 181
606 "must have shouted   BA III, 185
607 "Can anyone   BA III, 186

643 "ruled by   BA III, 222–23
643 "too much   BA III, 223
644 "major flaw   BA III, 222
644 "without doubt   BA III, 380
644 "if he has   BA III, 380
644 "Here I am   BA III, 257
644 "honor   BA III, 258
646 "We never   BA III, 379
648 "We should not   BA III, 405
648 "You have five   BA III, 405
648 "worry about   BA III, 376
648 "Heinrich would   BA III, 435
649 "new opera   BA III, 439
649 "Basta   BA III, 439
649 "A tiresome   BA III, 443
650 "Were there but   BA III, 393
651 "over neck   BA III, 443
651 "Perhaps I   BA III, 319
651 "a pure   Harries, 196
654 "Excerpts   D, 234
654 "Your brother   BA III, 524
654 "mumbo   Blanning, *Joseph II*, 165
655 "the spirit   Knepler (Robinson), 129
655 "state, sovereign   Braunbehrens, 228
656 "an, as it   Heartz, *Operas*, 121; D, 239
657 "divine   Da Ponte, *Memoirs*, 76
657 "Bravi!   *Don Giovanni*, no. 24, Finale, scene 13
657 "a most   BA III, 606
657 "something about   BA III, 606
658 "I have no   BA III, 613
658 "The talk   BA IV, 7
659 "a society   BA IV, 7
659 "the German   D, 249
660 "to music   D, 10
661 "for Mademoiselle   Mozart, W. A., *Verzeichnüss*, 38; F. 9.
662 "rather boring   Landon, *Golden*, 187, 244
663 "this splendid   D, 272
667 "by all   BA IV, 41–42
667 "You can   BA IV, 48
669 "enthusiasm   BA IV, 11
669 "to make a stab   BA IV, 48
669 "while playing   K, 552
670 "*Rondieaoux*   K, 310
670 "Don't never   K, 576

670 "The cry   D, 279
671 "For Beginners   K, 619
673 "Farewell   BA IV, 60
673 "With all   BA IV, 72
673 "Herr Michael   BA IV, 54
674 "It's German   D, 249
674 "so few   BA IV, 55
674 "the theater   BA IV, 54–55
674 "in constant   BA IV, 55
675 "*Ah che piatto*   *Don Giovanni*, no. 24, Finale, scene 13
676 "*only for*   BA IV, 72
676 "so rare   D, 378
676 "*come into*   BA III, 221
676 "vie to   Landon, *Golden*, 138
676 "duly appointed   BA IV, 72
676 "high protection   Gluck, 25
677 "the pre-eminent   D, 355
679 "every day   Blanning, *Joseph II*, 178
681 "Pallas   D, 313
681 "Music composed   Eisen, *New*, 152

Chapter XXXII

683 "to clothe   D, 296
685 "A shame   D, 311
685 "A hollow   D, 299
686 "Tear him   *The Tragedy of Coriolanus*, V, 6
686 "much too   D, 277
686 "your taste   Landon, *Golden*, 173
686 "excellent   D, 310–11
686 "marvelous   D, 299
686 "wounding   D, 343
686 "agreeable   D, 276
686 "a new opera   D, 276
687 "… a nasty   BA IV, 66
687 "one or   BA IV, 65
688 "not very   BA IV, 66
688 "cheaper   BA IV, 66
688 "This small   BA IV, 285
690 "knew nothing   BA IV, 79
691 "very mediocre   BA IV, 82
692 "a very pretty   BA IV, 83
692 "truly awful   BA IV, 83
692 "making almost   D, 481
693 "south-German   D, 481
695 "a pupil   D, 304

695 "A work Eisen, *New,* 58
695 "The King BA IV, 90
696 "honor BA IV, 84
696 "the complete Eisen, *New,* 59
697 "My little BA IV, 81
697 "so-called *The Marriage of Figaro,* no. 26
698 "growing Carter, 46
698 "Are you *Così fan tutte,* II, 1
698 "What species *Così fan tutte,* I, 1
698 "Get your BA IV, 90
699 "not to go BA IV, 84
700 "await recovery BA IV, 95
700 "Never go BA IV, 97
700 "misled BA IV, 96–97
700 "large gathering BA IV, 81
701 "Oh, Susanna *The Marriage of Figaro,* between nos. 25 and 26
703 "The phoenix *Così fan tutte,* no. 2
703 "Arabian *Cymbeline,* I, 6, 17
703 "plowing Brown, Bruce Alan, *Così,* 69–70
703 "made neither Blanning, *Joseph II,* 63
704 "do not lack *Così fan tutte,* between nos. 29 and 30
704 "*Così fan tutte le belle* *The Marriage of Figaro,* between nos. 7 and 8
704 "as to men *Così fan tutte,* no. 12
704 "*e belle e* *Così fan tutte,* no. 30
705 "you buy *Cymbeline,* I, 4, 118–19
705 "is alone *Cymbeline,* I, 6, 17
705 "the phoenix *Così fan tutte,* no. 2
705 "a basilisk *Cymbeline,* II, 4, 107
706 "I have seen *Così fan tutte,* between nos. 23 and 24
706 "vows of *Cymbeline,* II, 4, 110–13
707 "the underground BA I, 360–61
708 "nature neither *Così fan tutte,* between nos. 29 and 30
709 "One feast *The Two Gentlemen of Verona,* V, 4, 170

Chapter XXXIII

710 "in memory Wheatcroft, 236
710 "sufficient Wheatcroft, 237
711 "How very Blanning. *Joseph II,* 198

711 "Royal D, 326
712 "Salieri's BA IV, 100
712 "forced to BA IV, 110
713 "I should like BA IV, 113
713 "heavenly BA IV, 113
713 "ugly BA IV, 113
713 "magnificent BA IV, 113
714 "I want to BA IV, 113
715 "the richest BA IV, 116
715 "meager BA IV, 119
718 "a grand D, 344
719 "I have a BA IV, 114
719 "In all probability Landon, *Documentary,* 93
722 "in closest BA IV, 476
722 "beautiful voice BA III, 549
722 "sitting at D, 532
722 "a few Mozart BA IV, 477
723 "little to BA IV, 137
723 "At this BA IV, 148
723 "could picture BA IV, 149–50
724 "thinking the Branscombe, 89
725 "die Wahrheit *The Magic Flute,* I, 18
725 "In July Mozart, W. A., *Verzeichnüss,* 57, F. 28
726 "children acting Blanning. *Joseph II,* 65
727 "distinguished Landon, *Last,* 88
727 "Be it Rice, 101
728 "from the feet Braunbehrens, 273
728 "a strong D (*Documentary*), 411
731 "highest request D, 353
732 "to unborn D, 381
732 "string's D, 381
732 "boring D, 355
732 "*a merveille* [*sic*] Rice, 165
732 "so bad Rice, 165
732 "to the celebrated Landon, *Golden,* 262
733 "at all points D, 381
733 "Are [too D (*Documentary*), 406

Chapter XXXIV

735 "the arrival D, 358
735 "on the horizon D, 358
735 "our Kapellmeister D, 358

735 "an unbroken Landon, *Golden*,
    260
735 "a grand D, 356
735 "a German Mozart, W. A.,
    Verzeichnüss, 57, F. 28
737 "until it D, 160
737 "I have just BA IV, 157
737 ". . . she *sees* BA IV, 160
738 "Right BA IV, 157
738 "all know BA IV, 157
738 "What do I BA IV, 158
738 "came to BA IV, 158
738 "impulse BA IV, 160
738 "in jest BA IV, 160
739 "You cannot BA IV, 161–62
739 "both had BA IV, 162
739 "In respect BA IV, 162
740 "candle in BA IV, 142
740 "Since his BA IV, 162
741 "on the stroke D, 341
741 "the Adagio BA IV, 115
741 "made up BA IV, 116
741 "a different D, 345
742 "as one contemplates D, 352
742 "besides having D, 371–72
742 "on all sides D, 371
743 "made him D, 450
744 "cold compresses BA IV, 464

744 "one hour D, 367
744 "nothing at all D, 449
744 "acute miliary D, 449
744 "For eight D, 367
744 "irreplaceable D, 369
745 "in a black Landon, *Last*, 168
745 "normal simple Brauneis,
    "*Exequien*," 8–11
746 "As a child D, 379
746 "celebrated Wolff, 120–21
746 "the requiem D, 374

Chapter XXXV

749 "to Princess D, 409
749 "completed D (*Documentary*),
    439
750 "presumed D, 494
750 "give facsimiles BA IV, 246
751 "the most important D, 417
751 "unfortunate D, 416
751 "through tours D, 441
751 "it would be D, 442
752 "special favor D, 391
752 "general funds D, 391
754 "*ganz neu* Wolff, 42
754 "I will not go Maurois, 361
757 "something with Nagel, 22

GENERAL INDEX

Heufeld, Franz Reinhard von, 316, 419*n*; *Die Haushaltung nach der Mode*, 334
Heymans, Levie, 205
Hickel, Joseph von, 585
Hildburghausen, Prince, 254
Hildebrant, Johann Lukas von, 9
Hiller, Johann Adam, 50*n*, 242, 326, 488
Hilverding, Franz, 121*n*, 538*n*
Hobbes, Thomas, 576
Hochstetter, Baron Gottfried Adam von, 562
Hochwanger, Johann Michael, 303*n*
Hofdemel, Franz, 687, 690, 699
Hofer, Franz de Paula, 660, 688*n*, 698, 739
Hofer, Josepha (*née* Weber), 540, 554, 606, 688*n*, 703*n*, 713, 722*n*, 734, 737, 739, 743, 744
Hoffmann, E. T. A., 686, 741, 748*n*
Hoffmeister, Franz Anton, 669–71, 718, 748
"Hoffmeister" Quartet (K. 499), 671
Hofmann, Leopold, 249, 718
Hofmannsthal, Hugo von, 565*n*
Hogarth, William, 196
Hohenzollern, 45*n*, 75, 111, 148, 625*n*
Holbach, Baron Paul Heinrich Dietrich d', 157, 167, 168
Holl, Elias, 93
Hölty, Ludwig Heinrich Christopher, 669
"Holy Trinity" Mass (K. 167), 310, 331
Holzbauer, Ignaz Jakob, 102, 249, 383, 384, 388, 410, 443, 460; *Günther von Schwarzburg*, 386
Homer, 320
Honauer, Leontzi, 171
Hopfgarten, Georg Wilhelm von, 32, 92, 93, 95, 178
Houdart de la Motte, Antoine, 404*n*
Howe, Adm. Richard, 320*n*
Hubertusburg, Peace of, 85
Hübner, Beda, 48*n*, 54, 58, 213*n*, 221, 222, 223; *Diarium*, 57
Hübner, Lorenz, 45, 649
Hume, David, 19, 28, 157, 273
Hummel, Johann Nepomuk, 569, 657, 695
Hüttenbrenner, Anselm, 745

Ibsen, Henrik, 696, 697
"Ich würd' auf meinen Pfad" (K. 390/340c), 153
Ickstatt, Adam, 27, 36

Idomeneo (K. 366), 21, 28, 29, 78, 79, 89, 108*n*, 154, 320, 340, 484, 492–530, 549, 554*n*, 584, 623, 661, 685, 711*n*, 716, 724, 725, 729, 751; Auersperg concert performance version of, 653, 654, 728*n*; conducted by Cannabich, 101, 499; Gluck's influence on, 273, 445, 497, 516, 518–19, 594; Leopold Mozart and, 501–7, 509, 544, 522–24, 526, 528–30, 544, 604*n*; libretto for, 492–94, 511–12, 595; Munich premiere of, 477, 500*n*, 505–6, 522–28, 703*n*; and opera seria, 132, 134, 135, 137, 140, 141, 143, 148, 495, 498–500, 511, 513, 515, 516, 727*n*; Schachtner as translator of, 51, 593; Storm and Stress in, 513, 518; Winckelmann and, 519–21
arias, duets and chorus: "*Ah il gioir,*" 155; "*Idol mio,*" 515; "*Non più / Non temer,*" 653, 667*n*; "*Padre, germani,*" 515; *Pietà Numi*, 515; "*Se il padre,*" 632; "*S'io non moro,*" 155; "*Soavi Zeffiri,*" 516; "*Su conca d'oro,*" 155; "*Tutte nel cor,*" 515
Iffland, August Wilhelm, 460
Ihr unsre neuen Leiter (K. 484), 655
Illuminati, 36*n*, 654, 655, 728*n*, 745*n*
Imbachhausen, Edler von, 10
Imperial Diet, 6
Impresario, The (K. 486), 623*n*, 649, 652–53
Innocent XII, Pope, 271
Introduction to symphony by Michael Haydn (K. 444/425a), 629*n*
"Io ti lascio" (K. Anh. 245/621a), 669
Ippold, Franz Armand d', 503*n*, 602, 667
Isabella of Parma, 66, 67, 86, 146, 162, 264*n*
Iselin, Isaak, 26*n*
Ixnard, Michel, 755

Jackson, William, 62, 195*n*
Jacobins, 736, 756*n*
Jacquin, Emilian Gottfried von, 662, 667–70, 675*n*
Jacquin, Franziska von, 669, 670*n*
Jacquin, Joseph Franz, 670*n*
Jacquin, Nikolaus Joseph von, 668
Jahn, Ignaz, 687*n*
Jahn, Otto, 242*n*, 487
James I, King of England, 182
James II, King of England, 268*n*

700–701, 724, 738–41; courtship of,
553–57, 559, 587, 596, 599, 605–6;
deaths of children of, 631, 657, 688n;
household management by, 647, 714;
illnesses of, 681n, 699–702, 712, 719;
marriage contract of Wolfgang and,
606–8; Nannerl's hostility toward,
30n, 603; Prague trips of, 659–60,
674, 730; and proposed English tour,
657, 658, 662; Salzburg visit of, 620,
626–29; singing of, 563–64, 628,
629n, 668; wedding of, 585, 598,
609–10; widowhood of, 30n, 58n,
688n, 749–54; von Mölk's
defamation of, 603n; Winter's
defamation of, 600, 606; and
Wolfgang's death, 743–46
Mozart, David (great-great-grandfather), 15
Mozart, Franz Alois (uncle), 14, 375, 450
Mozart, Franz Xaver Wolfgang (son), 30n,
725, 730n, 737, 749
Mozart, Johann Georg (grandfather), 12
Mozart, Johann Thomas Leopold (son),
657
Mozart, Joseph Ignaz (uncle), 14
Mozart, Leopold (father), 11–18, 37, 83,
222, 274, 333, 355–57, 358n, 412, 463,
486n, 527n, 535n, 537, 567, 584n, 596,
639n, 651, 654, 661, 666, 677, 696,
708, 714n, 722n; attitude toward
aristocracy of, 8, 10; background of,
11–12; in Brabant, 161, 205, 210–11;
birth of, 11, 12; births of children of,
44, 52–53; Caecilia Weber denounced
by, 552–53, 606–8; and Catholic
Church, 13–14, 22, 32–35, 41–42,
312–13, 575; code devised for letter-
writing by, 11; Colloredo and, 16,
302–3, 343, 361–65, 435, 475, 506,
542–44, 549–50; Constanze and,
553–57, 600–602, 605–6, 610, 620,
626, 628; correspondence of
Wolfgang and, 45, 141, 156, 294, 325,
350, 370, 373–74, 377, 380–82, 383n,
385, 389, 400–402, 411, 417, 418,
427, 434–35, 441, 449, 455, 464–6,
471, 477–78, 526, 538, 539n, 542,
556–57, 561, 600, 630, 635, 638; and
courtship of Aloisia, 394–98, 431,
432, 438–40, 466, 469, 470, 474;

courtship of Anna Maria by, 43, 77;
death of, 667; education of, 12, 15; in
England, 183, 185–204, 347, 578n; and
Enlightenment thought, 18, 25–28,
31–33; estate of, 671–73; estrangement
of Wolfgang and, 470–78, 501–2,
528–29, 544–46, 602–5, 625–26,
643–44; final visit of Wolfgang and,
640–48; in France, xix–xxi, 81, 86,
121, 162–67, 170n, 171–80, 204,
211–15; Freemasonry and, 645–46; on
German concert tours with children,
63–64, 90–95, 97, 98, 100–10;
Grand Tour planned by, 72;
grandchildren and, 624–26, 631,
648–49, 657–58, 662; in Holland,
46n, 203, 205–10, 213; and *Idomeneo*,
494n, 496, 498, 499, 502–5, 507,
509, 511, 522–24, 530; in Italy, 17,
253–72, 274, 275, 277–83, 285n,
286–90, 292, 295, 298, 299, 301,
304, 307–9, 534, 707n; and Joseph II,
40n; Linz Symphony conducted by,
640; and Lisbon earthquake, 24;
literary tastes of, 152–53, 519n; at
masked ball, 155; Mesmer and, 241,
242, 244–46; mother's relationship
with, 14–15; and Munich court,
335–36, 340, 342, 467–68, 492;
musical career of, 16, 47–49, 70–71,
111, 226, 251, 310–11; musical tastes of,
112, 100–101, 115–17, 120, 123, 127;
and Nannerl's marriage, 640; and *opera
seria*, 147–50, 156; political
observations of, 84, 89, 158, 182, 314,
391–92, 425–26, 472–73, 510n;
pupils of, 349, 353, 531–32, 640, 641;
role in Wolfgang's childhood
compositions of, 49, 55–56, 224–25,
237–41, 273n; Schachtner and, 51, 55,
56, 60; and singspiel, 460n; social
aspirations of, 16–18, 47, 51; Storm
and Stress disliked by, 329; in
Switzerland, 215–19; theater
companies and, 485; Varesco secured
as librettist by, 620, 621; in Vienna
during Wolfgang's childhood and
adolescence, 64–70, 84, 228–32,
234–41, 247–51, 311–12, 316; wedding
of, 43–44; and wife's death, 428, 429,

Villeneuve, Louise, 703–4

Vinciguerra Collalto, Count Thomas, 65

viola: concerto for flute, violin, violoncello and, 402; duos for violin and, 629*n*; sinfonia concertante for violin and, 482; sinfonia concertante for violin, violoncello, and, 482

violin: adagio for orchestra and, 352*n*; concerto for flute, viola, violoncello and, 402; concertos, 310, 350–52; duets for continuo and, 249*n*; duos for viola and, 629*n*; rondo for orchestra and, 534–35; sinfonia concertante for, 482–84; sonatas, 161, 195, 196, 199, 209, 345*n*, 354*n*, 403, 447, 448, 526–27, 535, 587, 671; trio for clarinet, piano, and, 669; variations for keyboard and, 567*n*

violoncello: concerto for flute, violin, viola, and, 402; lost pieces for, 219; sinfonia concertante for violin, viola, and, 482; sonata for bassoon and, 333*n*

Visme, Louis de, 302

Vivaldi, Antonio, 145*n*, 287, 289, 351

Vogler, Abbé, 384–86, 390, 600

Volland, Sophie, 88

Voltaire, 21, 25–26, 28, 37, 176, 178, 214*n*, 216–17, 488, 512*n*, 578*n*; advice to actors from, 124–25; death of, 407–9, 427–28, 604*n*; and England, 20, 181*n*, 187*n*, 189*n*, 190, 192; Frederick the Great and, 82–83; Grimm and, 167, 431; Jesuit education of, 35; Rousseau's antipathy to, 323, 359

works: *Brutus*, 124; *Candide*, 24–25, 98; *Century of Louis XIV*, 36; *Droit du seigneur*, 38*n*; *Irène*, 409; *L'orphelin de la Chine*, 129; *Poeme sur le désastre de Lisbonne*, 24; *Traité sur la tolérance*, 88; *Zaire*, 352*n*, 486–87

"Vorrei spiegarvi" (K. 418), 633, 718

Wagenseil, Georg Christoph, 54, 61, 65, 73, 116, 119, 169, 171, 186, 187*n*, 197, 235, 249, 292*n*, 302

Wagner, Richard, 137, 142, 246*n*, 704*n*, 735

Wahler, Johann Georg, 165

Wahr, Karl, 316, 658

Waldburg zu Wolfegg und Waaldsee, Canon Anton Willibald, Count, 94

Waldburg-Zeil, Ferdinand Christoph, Count, Bishop of Chiemsee, 7, 47, 48, 340, 369, 370, 387

Waldegg, Count, 687*n*

Walderdorff, Archbishop Johann Philipp, Reichsgraf von, 107

Waldstätten, Baroness Martha Elizabeth von, 586*n*, 608, 609*n*, 610, 643, 644

Waldstein, Count, 572*n*

Wallis, Countess Maria Franziska, 423, 435*n*

Walpole, Horace, 26, 85

Walpurgis, Maria Antonia, 79, 290*n*

Walsegg, Countess Anna von, 747, 748

Walsegg-Stuppach, Count Franz Paola Joseph Anton von, 673, 748–49, 754*n*

Waltz, Gustavus, 118*n*

Watteau, Jean-Antoine, 154

Weber, Aloisia, *see* Lange, Aloisia

Weber, Caecilia, 540, 552–58, 561–63, 601, 606–9, 643, 739, 743

Weber, Carl Maria von, 385*n*, 395, 735

Weber, Constanze, *see* Mozart, Constanze

Weber, Franz Fridolin, 394–97, 406, 420, 421, 433, 436, 437, 455, 460, 469, 535, 540

Weber, Jacob Gottfried, 754*n*

Weber, Josepha, *see* Hofer, Josepha

Weigl, Joseph, 656, 702, 727; *La caffettiera bizzara*, 713

Weinlig, Christian Traugott, 271

Weiser, Ignaz Anton, 10, 44, 93, 224, 356, 367*n*; *Die Schuldigkeit des ersten Gebots*, 209

Weiskern, Friedrich Wilhelm, 239

Weldeeren, Count Jan Walraad van, 204

Wendling, Dorothea, 404, 492, 499, 716

Wendling, Elizabeth Augusta (Gustl), 102, 141*n*, 394, 404, 492, 499

Wendling, Johann Baptist, 101–2, 169*n*, 389, 390, 393, 394, 398, 399*n*, 405, 409, 411, 451, 716

Wendling family, 101–2, 384, 387, 395, 402, 405, 436

Werthes, Friedrich August, *Peter der Grausame, oder Die zwey schlaflosen Nächte*, 526*n*

Westminster, Convention of, 81

Westphalia, Peace of (1648), 41, 42*n*, 205, 427*n*

INDEX BY KÖCHEL LISTING
OF WORKS DISCUSSED